Date Due

ill 10/29/91			
JUN - 3 1994			
JUN 2 8 1996			

THE DISTRIBUTION HANDBOOK

Editor-in-Chief

JAMES F. ROBESON, Ph.D.
Professor of Marketing
The Ohio State University

Associate Editor

ROBERT G. HOUSE, D.B.A.
Manager, Material Logistics Systems
General Electric Company

THE FREE PRESS
A Division of Macmillan, Inc.
NEW YORK

Collier Macmillan Publishers
LONDON

HF
5415.7
.D55
1985

The Free Press
A Division of Macmillan, Inc.
866 Third Avenue, New York, N. Y. 10022

Collier Macmillan Canada, Inc.

Printed in the United States of America

printing number   # 10998599   3.9.87 Ac

  2 3 4 5 6 7 8 9 10

Library of Congress Cataloging in Publication Data

Main entry under title:

The Distribution handbook.

  Bibliography: p.
  Includes index.
  1. Physical distribution of goods—Management.
I. Robeson, James F.   II. House, Robert G.   III. National
Council of Physical Distribution Management.
HF5415.7.D55   1985   658.7'88   83-49340
ISBN 0-02-922700-3

CONTENTS

SECTION FOURTEEN   Distribution Personnel

Appendices

KENNETH B. ACKERMAN is President of The Ackerman Company, a management consulting firm in Columbus, Ohio. He earned his bachelor's degree from Princeton University and an M.B.A. degree from Harvard University. Before establishing his own consulting business, he worked in the public warehousing industry for over twenty years, the last of which he served as Chairman of Distribution Centers, Inc. After restructuring the ownership of DCI, he joined the Management Consulting Division of Coopers & Lybrand in 1980. In 1981, he established The Ackerman Company. Mr. Ackerman is the author of *Practical Handbook of Warehousing* (Traffic Service Corporation, 1983) and co-author (with Bernard J. La Londe) of "Making Warehousing More Efficient," an article published by Harvard Business Review in 1980. He is also editor of *Warehousing and Physical Distribution Productivity Report*, a monthly newsletter published by Marketing Publications, Inc. A former president of NCPDM, he was awarded its John Drury Sheahan Award in 1977.

WILLIAM W. ALLPORT is Chief Labor Counsel for Leaseway Transportation Corp., headquartered in Cleveland, Ohio. Leaseway Transportation grosses $1.3 billion in revenues and is a leading company in the transportation industry. He received a B.A. from Gettysburg College and a J.D. from the Case Western Reserve University School of Law, where he was an editor of the Law Review. Prior to joining the Leaseway Transportation staff, he practiced law with the firm of Baker, Hostetler, & Patterson (now Baker & Hostetler) in Cleveland. Admitted to practice in the states of Ohio and New York, Mr. Allport is also licensed to practice before the Supreme Court of the United States. He is a member of the labor sections of the American, Ohio, and Cleveland Bar Associations.

Ronald H. Ballou is Professor of Operations and Logistics Management at Case Western Reserve University and Head of the Division of Operations Management in the Weatherhead School of Management. He received a Bachelor's Degree in Engineering and Masters and Ph.D. Degrees in Business Administration from The Ohio State University. Dr. Ballou has published widely in the field of business logistics in the form of professional articles, monographs, and books. He is the author of two textbooks, *Business Logistics Management* (2d edition, 1985) and *Basic Business Logistics* (1978) both published by Prentice-Hall, Inc. Dr. Ballou has been a consultant to many of the country's leading firms. He serves on the editorial board of the *Journal of Physical Distribution and Materials Management*.

Paul S. Bender is President of BENDER Management Consultants in New York. He is a Certified Management Consultant and a Founding Member of the Institute of Management Consultants. Mr. Bender has degrees in Mathematics, Engineering, Operations Research, and Information Science. He has studied at the Massachusetts Institute of Technology, the Polytechnic School in Paris, the Swiss Federal Institute of Technology, and the University of Chile. Mr. Bender is the author of *Principles of Physicial Distribution Systems Configuration Design* (Marketing Publications, 1971), *Design and Operation of Customer Service Systems* (AMA, 1976), *Resource Management: An Alternative View of the Management Process* (Wiley, 1983). He is a co-author of *The Economics of Information Processing* (Wiley, 1982), and *Using Logical Techniques for Making Better Decisions* (Wiley, 1983). He is currently working on a new book *Physical Resource Management: Beyond Physical Distribution and Logistics* (Wiley, 1986). Mr. Bender has been active in NCPDM since 1965, and is a past member of NCPDM's Executive Committee.

Donald J. Bowersox is President of Technology Venture Management and Professor of Marketing and Logistics, Michigan State University. He has served in various management capacities including Vice President and General Manager of the E. F. MacDonald Company. He has served as a consultant to numerous corporations and government agencies. Dr. Bowersox has written over one hundred articles on marketing, transportation, and logistics. He is the author of *Logistical Management*, co-author of *A Managerial Introduction to Marketing, Introduction to Transportation, Dynamic Simulation of Physical Distribution Systems, Management in Marketing Channels, Simulated Product Sales Forecasting*, and co-editor of *Readings in Physical Distribution Management*. He was a founder and the second president of NCPDM.

James A. Constantin is David Ross Boyd Professor of Business Administration at The University of Oklahoma. He received the B.B.A., M.B.A., and Ph.D. degrees from The University of Texas. He is the author or co-author of four books and over 80 logistics-related monographs and articles in both scholarly and professional journals. His business experience includes a sojourn with Delta Airlines, a wide range of consulting assignments, and the ownership and management of both a small trucking company and a distribution center.

Martha C. Cooper is Assistant Professor of marketing and logistics at The Ohio State University. She received her bachelor's and master's degrees from Purdue University and her doctorate (Ph.D.) from Ohio State. She received the 1981 A. T. Kearney, Inc., Award from the NCPDM for her dissertation on freight consolidation and warehousing. She has published in *Industrial Marketing Management*, the *Journal of Marketing Research*, and the *Journal of Business Logistics*.

RALPH M. COX is Vice President–Engineering of Industrial Handling Engineers, Inc., of Houston. He and his staff serve the petroleum, chemical, and foods industries as consultants in packaging, materials handling, warehousing, and shipping. He is thoroughly experienced in the analysis, planning, and construction of effective bulk handling, packaging, unit handling, and warehousing systems. Mr. Cox holds a B.S. in mechanical engineering from the University of Texas in Arlington and an M.S. in industrial engineering from the University of Houston. He is a member of the Association of Professional Materials Handling Consultants, Warehousing Education and Research Council, and The Packaging Institute. Also, he currently serves on the joint ASME–IMMS editorial committee for the *Materials Handling Handbook* (Wiley, 1984).

LAWRENCE F. CUNNINGHAM is Associate Professor of Transportation and Marketing at the University of Colorado. Dr. Cunningham received his B.S. degree from Niagara University, his M.S. from the Transportation Center at Northwestern University, and his M.B.A. (marketing) and D.B.A. (transportation and logistics) from the University of Tennessee. Prior to obtaining his doctorate, Dr. Cunningham spent six years in industry, as a senior analyst with Eastern Airlines, and subsequently as a Vice President overseas with the Chase Manhattan Bank. He has published numerous scholarly and professional journal articles in the transportation and logistics fields.

JOHN R. DOWDLE is a Senior Vice President of Booz, Allen & Hamilton, Inc., and managing officer of the firm's Middle Eastern Region. In addition, he serves on its Board of Directors and was formerly Director of Distribution Services and President of the Transportation Consulting Division. Mr. Dowdle received his bachelor's degree in mathematics with highest honors from the New Mexico Institute of Mining and Technology and a Master's degree in economics from the Graduate School of Industrial Administration at Carnegie-Mellon University. He has written numerous articles, including "Designing and Implementing an Improved Distribution System," which appeared in the *Presidential Issue of Handling and Shipping* magazine; "Changing Patterns of Distribution" in *Tomorrow's Marketing*, published by the Conference Board; and "Management Information for Improved Control of Budgets, Costs and Schedules in Capital Projects," which was published in the *Engineering News Record*. He belongs to the Institute of Management Consultants, is a member of the Business Advisory Committee of the Transportation Center at Northwestern University, and has served on the Executive Committee of NCPDM.

PAUL E. FULCHINO is Vice President of the Transportation & Logistics Group at Temple, Barker & Sloane, Inc., a management consulting firm in Lexington, Massachusetts. Mr. Fulchino has directed more than 250 studies for the nation's major shippers and leading carriers. Before he became a consultant, Mr. Fulchino worked in financial analysis and industrial engineering for Raytheon Co. and for Lockwood Greene engineers. He holds a bachelor's degree in mathematics from Boston College and a master's degree, with concentration in finance and operations research, from the Columbia University Graduate School of Business.

MICHAEL S. GALARDI is a partner in Temple, Barker & Sloane, Inc., Lexington, Massachusetts. He is responsible for the firm's motor carrier, railroad, truck leasing, and shipper transportation practices. His particular areas of specialization include marketing and market research, financial planning, transportation economics and costing, and corporate strategy development. A frequent speaker at industry meetings, Mr. Galardi has published a wide range of articles on various for-hire and private trucking issues. Moreover, he is the author of *A Carrier's Handbook for Costing Individual Less-Than-Truckload Shipments* and a co-author of NCPDM's book *Transportation Strategies for the Eighties*. Prior to joining TBS, Mr. Galardi was a Wall Street investment analyst focusing on transportation. He received a B.S. in industrial engineering (cum laude) from Lehigh University and an M.B.A. with concentration in finance from Columbia University.

R. WILLIAM GARDNER is Chairman and Chief Executive Officer of Distek, a public warehousing and direct distribution firm based in Columbus, Ohio. Mr. Gardner joined a subsidiary, Distribution Centers, Inc., in 1963 and served in a number of capacities until becoming President of DCI in 1976. He became Chairman and Chief Executive Officer of the parent company, Distek, in 1980. A Registered Professional Engineer, he received a B.S. in Industrial Engineering and an M.B.A. from The Ohio State University. He has been active with NCPDM, IIE, and AWA in educational roles and recently served as President of WERC. In addition, he has authored several articles in the field of distribution and warehousing and is co-author of *Understanding Today's Distribution Center* (Traffic Service Corporation, 1972).

GEORGE A. GECOWETS is the Vice President and Chief Operating Officer of NCPDM. He received a B.S. in business administration from Tri-State College and an M.B.A. from Michigan State University. During the Korean War he served as an officer in the Army Corps of Engineers. He has held positions as director of order processing for the Kroger Company, as transportation editor of *Handling & Shipping*, as editor of *Transportation & Distribution Management*, and as general manager of ComTrac. He has served on NCPDM's executive committee in various capacities since 1967. In 1970, he was retained as NCPDM's first full-time executive director.

LYNN E. GILL is Associate Professor of Marketing and Logistics at the Unviersity of Southern California. Dr. Gill received a Ph.D. in business logistics from The Ohio State University, an M.B.A. in marketing from University of Southern California, and a B.A. in engineering from Michigan State University. He is past president of the Southern California Roundtable of NCPDM, and is active in other physical distribution and transportation organizations. Dr. Gill has published extensively in the field of physical distribution management. Dr. Gill's industrial experience includes prior positions as Senior Logistics Specialist for McDonnell Douglas Corporation and as Packaging and Transportation Engineer for North American Aviation. He also has extensive consulting background and has directed a transportation planning study in Taiwan for the National Science Council of the Republic of China.

JOHN R. GRABNER is Associate Professor of Marketing at The Ohio State University. Dr. Grabner received his bachelor's degree from Wichita University and his M.B.A. and D.B.A. from Indiana University. He has written numerous articles in the areas of logistics and marketing and has served as a consultant to several firms and trade associations. He is the co-author of several books, including *Managerial Analysis in Marketing* (Scott Foresman, 1970) and *Competition in the Marketplace* (Scott Foresman, 1970).

BERNARD J. HALE has served as a Corporate Officer and Vice President, Distribution Services, of Bergen Brunswig Corporation since February, 1973. Prior to joining Bergen Brunswig Corporation, he held numerous executive positions with Mattel, Inc. over a nine-year period. Dr. Hale received a B.S. in business administration from the University of Utah, an M.B.A. from Utah State University, and a Ph.D. in business administration from Pacific Western University. He is a graduate of the Executive Management Program of the UCLA Graduate School of Business in Los Angeles, California. He is a Registered Interstate Commerce Commission Practitioner and a Certified Member of the American Society of Traffic and Transportation, having served as a member of the National Board of Directors of that organization for many years. He served for nine years as a member of the Executive Committee of NCPDM, completing a term as its Chairman in 1980. He received the NCPDM Distinguished Service Award in 1983.

DAVID P. HERRON is a Senior Management Consultant at SRI International. He holds a B.S. and M.S. from M.I.T. in engineering and an M.B.A. from Harvard. He has published over thirty articles in the fields of physical distribution, inventory management, transportation, and energy economics. Recently he has been specializing in assisting companies to determine the most profitable balance between distribution costs and the level of customer service they provide. For the 1983 volume of the annual publication *Applications of Management Science*, Mr. Herron prepared the chapter on "Management Science in Industrial Logistics."

JAMES L. HESKETT is senior Associate Dean and 1907 Professor of Business Logistics at the Harvard University Graduate School of Business Administration. Dr. Heskett received his bachelor's degree from Iowa State Teachers College and his master's and Ph.D. degrees from Stanford University. He is consultant to a number of major firms and is a member of the Board of Editors of the *Transportation Journal* and the *Journal of Business Logistics*. Dr. Heskett has published numerous articles and monographs. In addition, he is author of *Marketing* (Macmillan, 1976) and co-author of *Business Logistics* (Ronald, 1973) and *Case Problems in Business Logistics* (Ronald, 1973).

ROBERT G. HOUSE is Manager, Material Logistics Systems, in the Corporate Purchasing department of the General Electric Company. He is responsible for the design and implementation of systems to support consolidated contracting across the various business units of the Company. Prior to joining General Electric in 1979 he was on the faculty of The Ohio State University and prior to that with the University of Maine. He holds his master and doctorate in business from Indiana University and did his undergraduate work at Michigan State University. He is the author of numerous papers and articles in the area of distribution planning which have appeared in *The Logistics and Transportation Review*, *Journal of Business Logistics*, *Transportation Research*, and the *International Journal of Physical Distribution Management*.

GEORGE ISOMA has been associated with Southern California Consultants as a principal for over ten years. In the early 1970s he was an assistant professor of finance at the University of Southern California, and he has also taught finance and production management at California State University at Dominguez Hills. After graduating from Case-Western Reserve University with a B.S. in mechanical engineering, Mr. Isoma studied at The Ohio State University, where he earned an M.B.A. and completed course work for a Ph.D. in physical distribution. He is currently working toward a B.S. in mathematics and statistics at CSU–Dominguez Hills.

JEFFREY KARRENBAUER is Vice President of INSIGHT, Inc., a consulting firm specializing in management support systems in the areas of manufacturing and logistics. He earned his B.B.A. in marketing from the University of Notre Dame and his Ph.D. in business logistics from The Ohio State University. He has conducted extensive research in the area of shipment planning policies and their impact on transportation costs, inventory costs, and customer service. Dr. Karrenbauer has published in physical distribution journals, has made numerous presentations to conferences for logisticians and management scientists, and for several years was a regular speaker for the IBM Customer Executive Education Program on physical distribution management. His areas of special interest include the development and application of optimization and simulation models to the analysis of complex distribution systems, and the development of efficient techniques for constructing data bases to support such analyses.

C. CHARLES KIMM is Manager of Transportation Economics and Planning Research at Battelle Memorial Institute Columbus Laboratories. He holds an M.B.A. degree from Michigan State University and worked on the Ph.D. program from the same institution. He has planned, participated in, and directed more than one hundred research programs worldwide covering economic analysis, commodity flow modeling and forecasting, policy analysis, intermodal transportation planning, and logistics system design and analysis. He has presented a number of seminars on transportation operations and logistics management to professional societies and industrial organizations in Japan, New Zealand, and Venezuela as well as in the United States. He is author of "Application of Demographic and Econometric Models to Regional Transportation Planning," *Proceedings of the World Conference of Transport Research*, and co-author, with S. L. Fawcett, of "Frontiers in Physical Distribution Development," *Handling and Shipping Management Presidential Issue*. He is a member of the Hazardous Material Transportation Committee, Transportation Research Board, and National Academy of Sciences.

DAVID T. KOLLAT is Executive Vice President of The Limited, Inc., and serves as Director of The Limited, Mast Industries, and Decor Corporation. Dr. Kollat received his Doctor of Business Administration degree from Indiana University. He has co-authored six books and numerous articles dealing with various dimensions of consumer behavior and corporate and marketing strategy.

JOHN KREITNER is Manager–Transportation Management Services, Corporate Purchasing, at General Electric. His specialty is the application of management information to transportation and logistics. In 1979, Mr. Kreitner developed GE's corporate formats for transportation productivity measurement and cost reporting. The resulting standardization of transportation information across GE divisions became a key building block in a collective buying program he launched in 1980 in response to transportation price deregulation. Mr. Kreitner earned a B.A. and M.B.A. from the State University of New York at Buffalo, where he was elected to Phi Beta Kappa.

BERNARD J. LA LONDE is Riley Professor of Marketing and Logistics at The Ohio State University. Dr. La Londe earned his bachelor's degree from the University of Notre Dame, his master's degree from the Univeristy of Detroit, and his Ph.D. degree from Michigan State University. He is author or co-author of a number of books and monographs and is a frequent contributor of articles to professional journals and the trade press. He is co-author, with Paul H. Zinszer, of *Customer Service: Meaning and Measurement* (NCPDM, 1976). Dr. La Londe serves on the Editorial Advisory Boards of *Distribution* and the *Journal of Marketing*. He is Editor of the *Journal of Business Logistics*.

DOUGLAS M. LAMBERT is a Professor of Marketing in the Graduate School of Business Administration at Michigan State University. He holds an honors B.A. and M.B.A. from the Univeristy of Western Ontario and a Ph.D. from The Ohio State University. Dr. Lambert is author of *The Development of an Inventory Costing Methodology* (NCPDM, 1976), *The Distribution Channels Decision* (NAA/SMA, 1978), and co-author of *Management in Marketing Channels* (McGraw-Hill, 1980) and *Strategic Physical Distribution Management* (Richard D. Irwin, 1982). He received the NCPDM's 1975 A. T. Kearney Award for his Ph.D. dissertation on inventory carrying costs. In 1982, Dr. Lambert was appointed the North America Editor of the *International Jouranl of Physical Distribution and Materials Management*. Dr. Lambert is a frequent speaker on such topics as accounting systems for marketing management, customer service, financial control of distribution performance, inventory management, least total cost physical distribution systems, physical distribution management, and strategic planning.

NORMAN E. LANDES provides consulting services in the area of distribution and warehousing. He is also president of Slidemasters Inc., a computer graphics firm making slides for business presentations. Formerly, he was with Distribution Centers Incorporated, where his responsibilities included productivity management and labor relations in eight cities. In addition, he was responsible for two subsidiaries engaged in product fulfillment and computer software programming. Mr. Landes has a bachelor's degree in industrial engineering and an M.B.A. in logistics from The Ohio State University. He is the author of articles which have appeared in *Handling and Shipping Management Magazine* and the *Warehousing and Physical Distribution Productivity Report*. In addition, he has presented numerous sessions on warehouse productivity for WERC, NCPDM, IMMS, and Distribution Education.

DAVID E. LLOYD is an Assistant Professor of Logistics Management at the Air Force Institute of Technology (AFIT), Wright-Patterson Air Force Base, Fairborn, Ohio. Lt. Col. Lloyd earned his bachelor's degree from San Diego State University and his master's degree from the Air Force Institute of Technology. He is completing his Ph.D. degree at The Ohio State University. He has co-authored two articles on distribution career patterns. His background includes seventeen years of military logistics experience in the United States Air Force. For his efforts in logistics he has been awarded the Bronze Star and four Meritorious Service Medals.

WILLIAM J. MARKHAM is a Principal in the Logistics Group of Kearney: Management Consultants (A. T. Kearney, Inc.). During his eleven years with Kearney, he has participated in a variety of logistics consulting assignments in the United States, Canada, and Europe. Mr. Markham holds an honors B.S. in business administration from the University of Illinois and has completed the Management Program in Logistics at Northwestern University. He played a key research role in the 1978 study for NCPDM, *Productivity*

Measurement in Physical Distribution, and directed similar research studies in Canada (1979) and Western Europe (1981). He played a lead role in the 1981 research study entitled *Organizing Physical Distribution to Improve Bottom Line Results*, jointly sponsored by Kearney and *Traffic Management* magazine. He was project director and primary author of the 1983 update study for NCPDM, *Productivity Measurement and Improvement in Physical Distribution*.

ROBERT M. MONCZKA is Professor of Materials Management in the Graduate School of Business Administration at Michigan State University, where he earned a Ph.D. Dr. Monczka is an Associate Editor of the *Journal of Purchasing and Materials Management* and Contributing Editor to the *Purchasing Handbook*. He is the author and co-author of numerous publications in purchasing and materials management, including the book *Purchasing Performance: Measurement and Control*. Dr. Monczka has also consulted with a variety of firms and has conducted purchasing/materials management research on computer applications and international purchasing.

ROBERT D. PASHEK is Professor of Business Logistics and Associate Dean of the College of Business Administration of The Pensylvania State University. Dr. Pashek received his bachelor's degree at Central Washington College, master's degree from the University of Iowa, and his doctorate from the University of Illinois. He is past President of the Council of University Transportation Centers, American Society of Traffic and Transportation, and the Transportation and Public Utilities Group of the American Economic Association. He is the author of research monographs and articles in the fields of transport economics and logistics systems. He serves as a consultant on transportation matters with the Commonwealth of Pennsylvania and for various agencies of the federal government.

JAMES F. ROBESON is Professor of Marketing at The Ohio State University and served as Editor-in-Chief of *The Distribution Handbook*. Dr. Robeson received his bachelor's and master's degrees from the University of Cincinnati and his Ph.D. degree from Penn State University. He is the author of numerous research monographs and scholarly and professional journal articles in the fields of physical distribution management and marketing and serves as a consultant to a number of major firms. In addition, he is co-author of *Strategic Marketing* (Holt, Rinehart and Winston, 1972), *Selling* (Richard D. Irwin, 1978), *Managerial Marketing: A Strategic Perspective* (Dryden Press, in process), and *Market Share Trends in Wholesale Distribution* (National Association of Wholesalers/Distributors, 1983).

LEWIS M. SCHNEIDER is Senior Vice President at Temple, Barker & Sloane, Inc. He received his A.B. in economics, magna cum laude, his M.B.A., with high distinction, and his D.B.A. from Harvard University. He is a member of Phi Beta Kappa, the NCPDM, and the Transportation Research Forum. At TBS, he is responsible for general direction of five of the consulting firm's divisions—Transportation & Logistics, Maritime and International Commerce, Public Policy and Management, Energy, and Information Management and Systems. He is the author of *Marketing Urban Mass Transit: A Comparative Study of Management Strategies* (Harvard Business School, 1964) and *The Future of the U.S. Domestic Air Freight Industry* (Harvard Business School, 1973). He is also co-author of *Transportation and Logistics Education in Graduate Schools of Business Administration* (Harvard Business School, 1967), *Case Problems in Business Logistics* (Ronald, 1973), and *Transportation Strategies for the Eighties* (NCPDM, 1982).

JEREMY F. SHAPIRO is Professor of Operations Research and Management at the Alfred P. Sloan School of Management and Co-Director of MIT's Operations Research Center. Dr. Shapiro received his bachelor's and master's degrees in mechanical engineering and industrial engineering, respectively, from Cornell University. He received a Ph.D. in operations research from Stanford University. He has also served as a senior research associate at the National Bureau of Economic Research and as a consultant to more than two dozen companies. Dr. Shapiro is the author of numerous publications in operations research, especially in the area of mathematical programming, and a book, *Mathematical Programming: Structures and Algorithms* (Wiley, 1979). His current professional interests are in the application of operations research models and methodologies to a variety of business planning problems.

E. RALPH SIMS, JR., is President of The Sims Consulting Group, Inc., a management and engineering consulting firm with headquarters in Lancaster, Ohio, and an affiliate office in London, England. He received his Bachelor of Administrative Engineering degree from New York University and Master of Business Administration from Ohio University. Mr. Sims is a registered Professional Engineer whose professional background includes positions held with consulting, manufacturing, distribution, and research organizations. In addition, he regularly lectures throughout the United States, Canada, and Europe on general management techniques, physical distribution, warehousing, materials management, cost control, and data processing. He was Consulting Engineering Editor to *Material Handling Engineering Magazine* and is the author of numerous articles published in professional and trade magazines.

THOMAS W. SPEH is Professor of Marketing and Logistics at Miami University (Ohio). Dr. Speh earned his bachelor's and master's degree from Miami University and his Ph.D. from Michigan State University. He is co-author of *Industrial Marketing Management* (Dryden Press, 1981) and is a frequent contributor of articles to professional journals and the trade press. Dr. Speh is a consultant to a number of firms and is a participant in numerous executive development programs. He is President-elect (1984–85) of the Warehousing Education and Research Council and a member of the executive committee of NCPDM (1984). Dr. Speh is the book review editor of the *Journal of Business Logistics*.

WENDELL M. STEWART was Corporate Vice President, Logistics, of A. T. Kearney, Inc., for twenty-eight years until his retirement from the firm in 1983. Mr. Stewart holds a B.S./B.A. and an M.B.A. from Northwestern University as well as a Certificate from the College of Advanced Traffic. In 1979 he was selected John Drury Sheahan Distribution Professional "Man of the Year" by NCPDM. A substantial contributor to the science of logistics management, Mr. Stewart organized the landmark study entitled *Productivity Measurement in Physical Distribution* (NCPDM, 1978). He was also responsible for the major study *Organizing Distribution to Improve Bottom Line Results* (NCPDM, 1980). More recently, he has conducted major research into the problems of increasing administrative white-collar and distribution productivity in the food industry.

JOEL SUTHERLAND is the Senior Manager of Production for Nippondenso of Los Angeles, a subsidiary of one of the world's largest automotive parts suppliers. Mr. Sutherland received his bachelor's degree from the University of Southern California (with his area of concentration in physical distribution management), and his M.B.A. from Pepperdine University. He is past president of the Southern California NCPDM Roundtable and is currently the president of the Southern California WER Council. He is a frequent guest speaker at local universities and professional groups covering various topics within the field of physical distribution management and has written a number of articles for professional magazines. In addition, he serves as a consultant specializing in the area of materials management.

KENNETH G. VAN TASSEL is an Area Manager with Mobil Chemical Company. He received his Bachelor of Science degree in industrial technology from Texas A and M University in 1953. Since that time he has held a variety of positions in the packaging, materials handling, and distribution fields. Mr. Van Tassel has had industrial experience in distribution operations, engineering, and purchasing. He has also spent several years as a consultant in distribution areas.

JOHN A. WHITE, JR., is Regents' Professor, Industrial and Systems Engineering, and Director of the Material Handling Research Center at Georgia Institute of Technology. He is also Chairman of SysteCon, Inc., and Past President of Institute of Industrial Engineers. Dr. White received his B.S.I.E. from the University of Arkansas, his M.S.I.E. from Virginia Polytechnic Institute, and his Ph.D. from The Ohio State University. Dr. White is co-author of *Facility Layout and Location: An Analytical Approach* (Prentice-Hall, 1974), *Analysis of Queueing Systems* (Academic, 1975), *Capital Investment Decision Analysis for Management and Engineering* (Prentice-Hall, 1980), *Facilities Planning* (Wiley, 1984), and *Principles of Engineering Economic Analysis*, Second Edition (Wiley, 1984). He is author of numerous papers in magazines and journals, a contributor to several handbooks, and is a frequent speaker on the subjects of material handling, facilities planning, warehousing, productivity, and economic justification.

PAUL H. ZINSZER is Associate Professor of Marketing and Logistics at Syracuse University, having previously taught at The University of Oklahoma and at The Ohio State University. While a student at Ohio State, he earned the following degrees: B.S.C.E., M.S., M.B.A., and Ph.D. with a major in physical distribution. Dr. Zinszer's previous business experience includes consulting as a Project Manager with Systems Research, Incorporated. He has published in both the professional and trade press and co-authored the books, *Customer Service: Meaning and Measurement*, *Contemporary Issues in Marketing Channels*, and *Distribution Consultants: A Managerial Guide to their Identification, Selection and Use*. Dr. Zinszer is an active lecturer to professional groups, addressing both issues of practice and the application of theory to business.

The Distribution Handbook was developed to serve as a single source to which those interested in distribution could turn for sufficiently complete, authoritative information. Readers can look up almost any distribution or distribution-related topic and find a conceptual explanation followed by practical, "how-to" information.

The *Handbook* has been designed primarily as a reference book. It may be used as a text, however, especially when the student is interested in tracing how a particular thread or functional activity is woven into the total fabric of distribution.

While the contents are applicable at all levels of the channel of distribution—producer, wholesaler, and retailer—much of the material is treated from the total-channel or producer's perspective.

The experienced distribution executive should find the structure of the book, and of most chapters, predictable. However, since most of the materials are original efforts by the most respected members of the profession, there are fresh, helpful insights in every section. The distribution neophyte should find the structure comforting and the chapter content both informative and useful. Both groups of distribution executives should find the book a valuable resource that often contains exhaustive checklists and an extensive bibliography where an expanded, more in-depth treatment of many important subjects can be found.

The Distribution Handbook is the result of the combined efforts of many people. What distinguishes it from books with similar titles is the number and qualifications of those who developed, wrote, and edited it. The authors and editors of this book are, by any standards, the finest educators, practitioners, and consultants in the field of distribution.

The book has been divided into fourteen major sections, which contain a total of thirty-two chapters. The authors of Section One, "Perspectives on Distribution Management," focus on the history, current status, and future of the field of physical distribution. The "Distribution Planning" section (Section Two) contains material on basic as well as advanced planning concepts at both the operational and strategic levels. A chapter on how to develop a contingency plan is also included.

Section Three, "The Distribution System: Components and Design," begins with material describing how distribution or logistic systems should be designed, then examines channels of distribution and concludes with a treatment of one of the most critical measurements of distribution system effectiveness, customer service.

"Financial Analysis and Productivity Measurement" (Section Four) includes ideas on how to translate the physical distribution strategy into a financial plan and procedures for analyzing distribution cost, productivity, and performance, as well as the reprint of a piece dealing specifically with distribution productivity.

Section Five, "The Computer and Quantitative Analysis," covers each of these topics in appropriate depth as they apply to distribution. Sections Six and Seven, "Demand Forecasting" and "Purchasing," are single-chapter sections that deal with their particular subjects in a comprehensive manner.

Sections Eight, Nine, Ten, and Eleven each deal with one of the functional or operational aspects of distribution. Specifically, those aspects are "Transportation," "Facilities," "Inventory Management," and "Packaging."

Sections Twelve and Thirteen contain one-chapter, comprehensive units covering the issues of "International Distribution" and "Distribution Organization" respectively. The final section, Section Fourteen, "Distribution Personnel," contains chapters treating the subjects of career patterns in distribution, the educational needs of physical distribution managers, and labor relations.

The appendices should prove quite helpful to those seeking a list of associations and organizations in distribution as well as publications that specialize, for the most part, in the field of distribution. Depositor–warehouseman agreements are also included.

"Publications and Other Sources of Information" contains suggestions for additional reading that should prove helpful to the reader with a specialized interest or a particular problem. The bibliographic entries are arranged in the same sequence as the chapters.

Working with the author and editors has been an interesting experience. It has been exciting and informative. I am confident you will experience these same feelings as you read, reread, and use the book.

This *Handbook* was published with the assistance of the National Council of Physical Distribution Management, whose staff and executive committee members recommended many of the articles and authors whose works are included. The authors and editors took the book from the idea stage through to the complete manuscript. There were, however, a number of other people whose vision in recognizing the need for the book and patience in waiting for the finished product proved extremely valuable. These included the Vice President and Executive Director of NCPDM, George Gecowets, as well as the current President and recent Past Presidents of NCPDM, Roger Kallock, Gene Sailer, Ron Seger, Vern Goodwin, Mort Yeomans, Bernie Hale, and Cliff Lynch. Bob Delaney and Frank McMillan offered valuable suggestions at various stages of the project. Bob Wallace, Megan Keller, and Celia Knight of The Free Press were supportive, hopeful, and, above all, patient. To all of these people, a sincere thank you.

J.F.R.

Perspectives on Distribution Management

CHAPTER 1

Distribution: A Historical Perspective

Jeffrey Karrenbauer

A Background Perspective

Only two decades ago, the notion of integrated physical distribution management was so foreign to the corporate boardroom that it was variously described as "The Frontier of Modern Management"[1] and "The Economy's Dark Continent."[2] During the intervening years since these melancholy observations were made, the concept has enjoyed a remarkable development of both theory and application, as evidenced by the development of new educational material and curricula, and by practitioner acceptance. Each is briefly reviewed below.

Educational Materials and Curricula

The field of business logistics was devoid of even a basic text until 1962;[3] recently, the discipline offered several current texts,[4] two journals,[5] and a number of trade publications.[6] In addition, representatives of the academic, government, and private enterprise communities have contributed with increasing frequency to other respected publications, whose proper domain has included, yet extended far beyond, the primary interests of the logistician.[7] Finally, the limited and typically uncoordinated academic offerings of earlier days have given way to a number of sophisticated curricula, where training has been extended through the doctoral and continuing education levels.[8]

Practitioner Acceptance

Practitioner interest, acceptance, and status have grown concurrently with the academic surge, a trend noted by a number of authors and documented by a survey conducted annually since 1972 by faculty members of the Ohio State University. In particular, twelve years of canvassing and subsequent data analysis have established certain apparent trends. While the survey's authors pleaded caution against overgeneralization of the results, the data have tentatively indicated that the senior distribution executive (1) has increasingly selected a pure line or combination line and staff organization form as opposed to a purely staff model; (2) has more frequently been given the title of a director or functional vice-president rather than one applicable to a lower level manager; (3) has spent a greater proportion of time dealing with expanded responsibilities that have carried him far beyond the traditional functional boundaries of distribution; (4) has been granted compensation increases in excess of the inflation rate; (5) has frequently received formal academic training in the discipline; (6) has displayed a growing interest in management science-based techniques; (7) has increasingly attempted to integrate the full material flow process of the firm, from raw material sourcing, through production, to finished goods distribution; and (8) has more frequently experienced pressure from top management to expand and clarify the role of physical distribution management ("top down") rather than having to convince top management of the importance of the role of the logistician ("bottom up").[9]

Finally, it should be noted that no formal organization of logisticians existed prior to 1963. During that year, representatives of both industry and academia established the National Council of Physical Distribution Management (NCPDM), an organization that now numbers within its ranks several thousand individuals.

A sister organization, the Society of Logistics Engineers, founded in 1966, has pursued objectives similar to those of NCPDM, and has established the first certification program for the profession.[10]

Business Logistics: Assessment of Current Status

No attempt will be made here to trace the development of logistics concepts and theories from the origins of the Industrial Revolution to contemporary thought. Other writers have already mapped that territory with considerable skill.[11] This exercise will demonstrate that the concerns of logisticians have necessarily become sharply focused in recent years, yet have remained consistent with traditional interests.

Overview

The passing of a decade has often been marked by retrospective examinations of the status of a profession by leaders in the field. The business logistics community proved to be no exception around 1970, although scarcely a decade had passed since organized, serious inquiry into the nature and scope of the discipline had begun. Representative works by La Londe et al.,[12] Bowersox,[13] Schneider,[14] and Heskett et al.[15] revealed a remarkable similarity of thought. A synthesis of their positions yielded the following principal factors responsible for the development of the field: (1) severe economic pressures, (2) development of quantitative tools and the means to apply them, (3) adoption of the total system perspective, (4) increased competitive pressures in the channels of distribution, and (5) increased competitive pressures in the marketplace.

The Contemporary Business Environment

From its earliest days, the logistics literature has been dominated by the theme of cost pressure alleviation. Two antagonists have traditionally been identified, the prevailing economic climate and government intervention. It was not difficult to establish that concerns about each have only intensified in recent years. However, contemporary analysts have portrayed a substantially more complex environment. In a mid-1970s work, La Londe pointed out that businessmen in the United States traditionally adopted a core management philosophy predicated on three basic assumptions: (1) that the firm will enjoy a constant increment of growth, regardless of operating policies; (2) that low-cost and abundant energy supplies will be available; and (3) that demand is the principal determinant of sales and profit levels. He went on to suggest that "these three traditional assumptions have been seriously eroded during the past two years"[16] and suggested several "key factors" that were primarily responsible for this erosion, among which were the availability and cost of energy, the availability and cost of other resources, and the "capital gap" faced by the United States economy.[17]

In a related work, La Londe and Zinszer identified seven economic factors which would "cause continued upheaval in the business climate": (1) continued world-wide inflation; (2) relatively high levels of unemployment; (3) high interest rates; (4) shortages of selected raw materials and components; (5) uncertainty about pricing and availability of energy resources; (6) substantial fluctuations in international rates of exchange; and (7) synchronization of world economies.[18]

The National Economy

The rapidly changing state of the national economy makes it difficult to assess its current strength, much less its longer-term direction. Published analyses often reflect the political viewpoints and objectives of the authors.[19] But this is precisely the point advanced in the works by La Londe cited above: beyond all other considerations, the contemporary business environment is plagued by uncertainty. The Congressional Budget Office offered a typical observation late in 1982:

> Most economic forecasters project a moderate upswing in output and employment during the next two to three years, along with further progress in reducing inflation. Underlying this outlook, however, is much more uncertainty than the similarity of forecasts might suggest. The major question is the outlook for credit conditions, which is affected by monetary policy, and by expectations about future inflation and credit demands.[20]

Earlier in the year, the Bureau of Labor Statistics, in releasing its economic forecasts for the decade, felt compelled to offer both multiple scenarios and an extended discussion of why the assumptions underlying each, however carefully formulated, rendered the projections uncertain at best.[21]

Resource Availability

While discussions of resource scarcity have generally focused on energy shortages, in recent years several authors have suggested that the problem was substantially more pervasive. As La Londe pointed out:

> The U.S. is critically dependent on offshore resources for a wide range of basic minerals in addition to energy. This dependence is further complicated by the fact that there are major resource cartels in every one of the resources . . . where there exist concentrations of those resources in a limited number of countries. This could in turn lead to an occurrence of an OPEC-type boycott in other resources and/or rapidly escalating raw material input costs.[22]

Other authors have also focused on the impacts of resource shortages on a logistics system. In the most recent edition of *Logistical Management*, Bowersox contended that the problem has significantly altered the priorities of the corporate distribution professional:

> The impact of the eight year period [1970–1978] upon the development and implementation of logistical concepts was significant. Almost overnight, enterprise priorities and related programs to cope with the ever changing situation shifted from servicing demand to maintaining supply. Top management attention was forced to procurement by the sheer consequences of failure. The result was the rapid advancement of the materials management professional. Whereas the physical distribution profession grew from the potential of the marketing concept, the materials management profession matured from the impact of supply discontinuity. In response to an immediate need, traditional methods of material procurement changed overnight. In replacement, a new systems orientation based upon time-phased movement and long-term commitment emerged. Emphasis began to focus on pre-action control rather than reaction. In other words, rather than planning operations to react to marketing needs, management began to formulate plans around the maintenance of continuous manufacturing and processing given a high probability of material shortages.[23]

Logistics Costs

It is axiomatic that inflation, energy shortages, and resource constraints would necessarily impact various categories of logistics costs. For example, such economic pressures have been directly linked by numerous authors to the rapidly escalating costs of carrying inventory.[24] With regard to transportation costs, a study prepared for the U.S. Department of Defense in 1976 developed annual rate increase forecasts through 1985 as follows:[25]

Less-than-truckload (LTL)	5.0%
Truckload	2.7%
Carload	5.2%
Domestic air	8.3%
International air	8.5%

Six years later, the consulting firm of Temple, Barker & Sloane, Inc., under contract to NCPDM, developed the following "most likely" projections for the period 1980–1990:[26]

Producers Price Index	8.5%
Small shipments	
Motor carrier—LTL	7.5%

Surface small parcel	8.3%
Air—Small parcel	9.2%
Air—Combination carrier	9.0%
Air—All cargo	9.1%
Volume shipments	
Intermodal	8.4%
General truckload	8.6%
Private truck	8.4%
Rail carload	8.7%
Bulk truckload	9.2%
Barge tow	9.8%
Mass volume shipments	
Rail unit train	9.2%
Large barge tow	9.7%
Oil pipeline	5.7%

It is sobering to observe that in all instances the anticipated compound growth rates were significantly higher than those developed earlier.

During the past decade or so, an enhanced awareness of the problems attendant to inflation, energy availability, and materials shortages has evidenced itself via a blizzard of technical reports and popular press analyses. However, it is not the intent of this chapter to comprehensively review the applicable literature. Rather, the objective has been to demonstrate the ongoing validity of concerns voiced by logisticians in light of the prevailing economic climate. The available data have left little doubt that the economy will continue to serve as a primary motivational force underlying the growth of the business logistics profession.

Computer Technology

According to La Londe et al., the second facilitating factor that contributed to the development of business logistics was sophisticated computer technology. During the past two decades, numerous references in the literature have established that the computer has been used with increasing regularity in the design and operation of distribution systems. However, few data were gathered which documented the scope and depth of application. The first detailed information was obtained by means of two surveys of members of the NCPDM conducted in 1972 and again in 1975 by faculty members of the Ohio State University.

Analysis of the 1975 data, both alone and in conjunction with the 1972 results, yielded a number of findings which are summarized here:

1. The major "trend" was simply that many projects begun in 1972 had been completed by 1975.

2. Principal application areas that could be regarded as fully operational were limited largely to inventory control and distribution accounting, especially freight bill analysis.

3. Control of corporate computer resources has migrated from data processing experts to a major corporate administrative office such as the controller. The trend

has magnified internal communication and coordination problems for the distribution manager but has not significantly impaired the computerization of various distribution activities.

4. Likely future applications were said to include automated freight rating and general distribution cost/budget analysis.

5. Corporate data bases have typically been unable to support expanded applications. In particular, historical records of freight rates, inventory carrying costs, stockout costs, and warehouse operations costs were rarely maintained, thereby rendering cost analyses virtually impossible.

6. While hardware-to-hardware communication has become possible even across vendors, the lack of uniform data base structure and coding standards has tended to nullify such capability.[27]

Composite results of the Ohio State University surveys demonstrated that the computer has increasingly become a routine part of corporate logistics life. On the other hand, serious questions remain about the degree of sophistication with which the machine has been employed. These questions were addressed in a survey commissioned by *Traffic Management* and conducted by Cleveland Consulting Associates in 1982–83. The principal findings are summarized below:

1. Many firms have yet to computerize certain critical logistics functions, especially transportation, forecasting, and procurement. Even traditionally computer-oriented tasks, such as order processing/customer service, production planning, and inventory control are still performed manually by some firms.

2. Existing computer-based systems are perceived as inadequate by many executives. Reasons advanced for this dissatisfaction include: (a) lack of multi-function integration; (b) failure to employ formal data base management systems; (c) inability of management to properly conduct a systems development project; and (d) inadequacy of packaged software without significant modification.

3. Distribution departments expect to invest heavily in both hardware and software in the next five years. With respect to the former, distribution executives will increasingly develop or purchase micro computer-based systems so as to free themselves as much as possible from large, unresponsive central data processing organizations. Software investment will be concentrated in the areas of customer service, production planning, inventory control, and logistics modeling. In each category applications will be split between mainframes and micros, with the latter accounting for a steadily increasing share of the tasks.[28]

Examination of the results from all three surveys cited above leads one to conclude that, while the potential of the computer to assist the distribution executive may be limited only by the imagination, realization of that potential has left much to be desired. To the extent that implementation has been deficient, a major facilitating force in the development and application of sophisticated business logistics practices has been stymied. The conclusion is of special concern in light of the severe adverse external environmental forces described above.

Quantitative Analysis Capability

The final facilitating factor cited by La Londe which contributed to the rapid evolution of business logistics was the advent of quantitative analysis capability. Since 1970, the discipline has witnessed a rapid development of highly sophisticated quantitative tools of sufficient power to supply penetrating analyses of even the most complex logistics systems. Bowersox offered a succinct confirmation:

> From a technological perspective, the early 1970s was one of the most prolific periods of research and development in computer models for logistical system design and control. Logistical models of all types with substantial capability became a reality.[29]

A number of authors have documented this trend in detail, including Geoffrion,[30] Schuster and La Londe,[31] House and Jackson,[32] Bowersox,[33] Ballou,[34] and Mossman et al.[35] Their analyses convincingly demonstrated that, if anything, such developments were even more dramatic in the latter half of the 1970s. A consistent rationale for the trend was evident across these works as typified by the following observation of Geoffrion:

> Every firm that ships a variety of products from several plants (or other supply sources) through a number of warehouses (or distribution centers) to a widely dispersed clientele has a continuing need to monitor and readjust its distribution system in response to changing conditions. Changes in plant capacity, addition and deletion of product lines, changes in the economics of warehousing and transportation, shifting markets and competitors' actions all impact the effectiveness of a physical distribution system in complex ways. Many firms have found that a comprehensive computerized model of a distribution system can be an effective tool for dealing with such complexities, and that it is able to disclose important opportunities for improvement that are likely to escape conventional analysis based on traditional tools.[36]

Ballou adopted a similar perspective as a central theme of his text:

> In this text, quantitative approaches to problem solution are encouraged. This is not naively to imply that all logistics problems yield to quantitative analysis or that any logistics problem yields completely to a quantitative approach. Rather, quantitative techniques amplify managerial analysis beyond what can often be achieved by intuitive approaches alone. Specifically, scientific analysis helps to uncover alternative courses of action that may not have been obvious or to evaluate more effectively and efficiently alternatives that could not be considered without the aid of quantitative tools. More generally, quantitative analysis works best for the manager if the goals of problem solution can be expressed in economic terms and if the manager believes that scientific analysis can be beneficial.[37]

These observations constitute but a fraction of the literature devoted to the application of quantitative tools to logistics system design and management. The methods often seem threatening to managers not previously exposed to the seemingly arcane worlds of computer technology and mathematical modeling. However, experience has demonstrated that when properly explained and applied, quantitative analysis tools become the powerful ally of the manager struggling to deal with the uncertainties and complexities of the contemporary business environment.

ᵖerspective

ᵤmphasis

The preceding sections have demonstrated that the forces responsible for the development of the logistics discipline have not abated. One might reasonably have concluded, therefore, that the concerns and goals of the logistician had concurrently stabilized. However, further analysis has revealed that a somewhat different result obtained. A clear illustration was supplied by again examining the discipline status assessment literature. It was observed earlier that authors typically devoted substantial portions of their work to a projection of likely trends and concerns. By way of example, in 1969 Bowersox advanced a series of research concerns for which reliable data were unavailable:

1. The true aggregate costs of physical distribution in the United States had never been accurately assessed; moreover, little was known about likely future trends.

2. Traditional accounting methods within the typical firm were unable to either accurately measure current distribution costs or adequately support analyses designed to improve system structure or operations.

3. Knowledge of channel costs, operations, and relationships was inadequate in light of serious questions that had been raised regarding leadership, power, integration, and efficiencies; moreover, the necessity for the existence of intermediaries was questioned with increasing regularity.

4. Little or nothing was known about the magnitude and operating characteristics of the firms and agencies engaged in international distribution activities.

5. Existing mathematical planning models failed to integrate properly both spatial and temporal considerations.

6. The logistics discipline suffered from a lack of standardized definitions and vocabulary.

7. The proper placement of the logistics function within the corporate organizational structure had not been satisfactorily resolved.

8. The development of corporate data coding and information storage/retrieval systems within the firm had not been satisfactorily influenced by the data requirements of the discipline.

9. There existed a widening gap between the recent contributions of academic research and existing corporate logistical practice, a situation attributed to the failure of academicians to disseminate properly the results of their work.[38]

On the other hand, the historical review of the discipline offered in the 1978 edition of *Logistical Management* did not cite a single research issue advanced in the 1969 article, although Bowersox specifically acknowledged the latter as a primary source for the material presented.[39] Instead, he substituted an extended discussion of the concerns of the 1970s, labeling the decade "a period of changing priorities." Topic areas discussed included: (1) energy shortages and costs, (2) raw materials shortages, (3) ecological con-

cerns, (4) the faltering United States economy, (5) the necessity f(
materials management and physical distribution in light of materials
velopment of sophisticated quantitative tools, (7) the organizationa
pects of logistics problems, and (8) the spread of logistics concepts a
ety of private and public enterprises.[40]

La Londe and Zinszer also underscored the concerns of a ne'
increased emphasis on strategic planning in light of extant economic anu
pressures. In particular, the authors pointed out that reductions in inventory levels would
require a greater degree of cross-functional coordination:

> These pressures could in turn lead to a more comprehensive view of the functions of all
> materials flow within many companies. That is, these pressures could force a functional
> and organizational integration of purchasing, production planning and finished goods
> distribution. Without the buffer of abundant inventory, closer functional integration is
> required. The pressure of high long-term interest rates directly influences inventory hold-
> ing costs. This concern has already forced some companies in the direction of coordinat-
> ing inventory flows prior to the unstable economic conditions of today.[41]

In establishing the case for planning, La Londe and Zinszer were calling for a renewed emphasis on integrated system analysis in light of marketplace realities. They later
suggested how that might be accomplished in terms of nine specific "distribution strategies": (1) improved intrachannel cooperation, (2) reassessment of customer service levels,
(3) evaluation of inventory positioning, (4) evaluation of inventory level, (5) evaluation of
product mix, (6) increased order size, (7) increased shipment size, (8) improved vehicle
scheduling, and (9) shipment consolidation.[42]

By the early 1980s the revised perspectives suggested above had become even more
firmly established. While the influence of the OPEC boycott and double digit inflation
had waned somewhat, logisticians were confronted with the worst recession since the
Great Depression. In response, many authors were again moved to prescribe non-tradi-
tional strategies for coping with the attendant severe disruptions and uncertainties in the
marketplace. For example, La Londe again stressed the weaknesses of the assumptions
upon which management has traditionally based planning and policy; he prescribed five
key elements of logistics system reconfiguration: (1) redefine sourcing/procurement strategy; (2) tailor customer service strategies; (3) realign physical facilities networks; (4) integrate the material flow process; and (5) utilize information flow trade-offs.[43] Heskett
offered similar recommendations in light of the uncertain external environment, the Japanese experience, and challenges posed by senior management: (1) postponement of inventory commitment; (2) customization of distribution strategy by product category; (3)
elimination—not just reduction—of certain costs in light of information technology advances; and (4) the substitution of information/communications in the marketplace.[44] Finally, citing uncertainties with respect to capital, energy, inflation, government regulation, and multinational operations, all exacerbated by the 1980–82 recession, Bowersox
advocated: (1) an integrated organizational structure for materials logistics management,
encompassing the traditionally separate areas of purchasing, manufacturing, and physical distribution; (2) more vigorous management of inventory assets; (3) revised performance measurement systems; (4) increased emphasis on form, identity, and inventory location postponement strategies; (5) improved communication systems, especially those
that trade assets for information; and (6) a fresh analysis of shipment planning strategies.[45]

Final Perspective

It is clear that the common threads that have run through this discussion are cost and competitive pressures in a highly uncertain environment. While it is readily acknowledged that such matters have always rested comfortably within the domain of the logistician, a sense of greater urgency has been evident in recent writings. In addition, some of the prescribed management responses are anything but traditional: fully integrated logistics organizations, harsh reevaluations of customer service standards and the aggressive utilization of information as a substitute for asset deployment are doubtless foreign concepts to many within the logistics community. The economic and technological forces that helped to establish the discipline of business logistics have markedly intensified in recent years. Because of the harsh realities imposed by the resulting uncertain external environment, the concerns expressed by logisticians have become sharply focused. In particular, transportation, inventory, and customer service policies have been more critically evaluated in light of a realistic assessment of potential benefits against required dollar and asset expenditures.

Notes

1. Peter F. Drucker, "Physical Distribution: The Frontier of Modern Management," speech reprinted in Donald J. Bowersox, Bernard J. La Londe, and Edward W. Smykay, eds., *Readings in Physical Distribution Management: The Logistics of Marketing* (London: Macmillan, 1969), pp. 3–8.
2. Peter F. Drucker, "The Economy's Dark Continent," *Fortune* (April 1962), pp. 103–104.
3. The initial text in the field of business logistics was Edward W. Smykay, Donald J. Bowersox, and Frank H. Mossman, *Physical Distribution Management* (New York: Macmillan, 1961).
4. Representative examples include Donald J. Bowersox, *Logistical Management: A Systems Integration of Physical Distribution Management and Materials Management*, 2d ed. (New York: Macmillan, 1978); Ronald H. Ballou, *Business Logistics Management* (Englewood Cliffs, N.J.: Prentice-Hall, 1973); and James L. Heskett, Nicholas A. Glaskowsky, Jr., and Robert M. Ivie, *Business Logistics*, 2d ed. (New York: Ronald Press, 1973).
5. The two journals are the *International Journal of Physical Distribution* and the *Journal of Business Logistics*.
6. Representative examples include *Handling and Shipping Management*, *Traffic World*, *Distribution*, and *Traffic Management*.
7. Representative examples include *Harvard Business Review*, *Sloan Management Review*, *Journal of Marketing*, *Business Horizons*, *Management Science*, and *Interfaces*.
8. A number of examples are provided in James F. Robeson, ed., *Logistics Education: Curriculum Design and Teaching Technology*, Proceedings from a Symposium for Educators in Logistics, Distribution and Related Areas, Transportation Research Foundation and the National Council of Physical Distribution Management (Columbus, Ohio: The Ohio State University, 1971). Also see Joseph V. Barks, "Definitely Not Old School," *Distribution* (August 1983), pp. 52–56.
9. Bernard J. La Londe and David E. Lloyd, "Distribution Careers 1983," *Distribution* (November 1983), pp. 44–47.
10. Upon satisfaction of the necessary requirements, a candidate is designated "Certified Professional Logistician, Society of Logistics Engineers."

11. See, for example, Bernard J. La Londe and Leslie M. Dawson, "Early Development of Physical Distribution Thought," in Bowersox et al., *Readings*, pp. 9–18; Bowersox, *Logistical Management*, pp. 3–12; Heskett et al., *Business Logistics Management*, pp. 14–26.

12. Bernard J. La Londe, John R. Grabner, and James F. Robeson, "Integrated Distribution Systems: A Management Perspective," *The International Journal of Physical Distribution*, 1 (October 1970), pp. 133–139.

13. Donald J. Bowersox, "Physical Distribution Development, Current Status, and Potential," *Journal of Marketing*, 33 (January 1969), pp. 63–70.

14. Lewis M. Schneider, "Milestones on the Road of Physical Distribution," in David Mc-Conaughy, ed., *Readings in Business Logistics* (Homewood, Ill.: Richard D. Irwin, 1969), pp. 51–63.

15. Heskett et al., *Business Logistics*, p. 39.

16. Bernard J. La Londe, "Some Thoughts on Corporate Strategy in Changing Times," *Warehousing Review*, (March–April 1976), pp. 4–7.

17. Ibid., pp. 2–5.

18. Bernard J. La Londe and Paul H. Zinszer, "Managing in Uncertain Times: The Case For Planning," *Long Range Planning* (October 1975), pp. 18–19.

19. See, for example, *Economic Report of the President*, Transmitted to the Congress, January, 1978 (Washington, D.C.: U.S. Government Printing Office, 1978), and *Economic Report of the President*, Transmitted to the Congress, January, 1982 (Washington, D.C.: U.S. Government Printing Office, 1982).

20. *The Economic and Budget Outlook: An Update*, A Report to the Senate and House Committees on the Budget, Congressional Budget Office, Congress of the United States (Washington, D.C.: U.S. Government Printing Office, September 1982).

21. *Economic Projections to 1990*, Bulletin 2121, Bureau of Labor Statistics, U.S. Department of Labor (Washington, D.C.: U.S. Government Printing Office, March 1982).

22. La Londe, "Some Thoughts on Corporate Strategy," pp. 4–5.

23. Bowersox, *Logistical Management*, p. 10.

24. La Londe and Zinszer, "Managing in Uncertain Times," p. 20. Also see Heskett et al., *Business Logistics*, pp. 19–20; and Bowersox, *Logistical Management*, pp. 157–159. The most extensive study of inventory carrying costs known is Douglas M. Lambert, *The Development of an Inventory Costing Methodology: A Study of the Costs Associated with Holding Inventory* (Chicago: NCPDM, 1975).

25. *Commercial Transportation Rate Forecast*, report prepared for the U.S. Department of Defense Material Distribution System (DODMDS) Study (Washington, D.C.: Department of Defense, 1976).

26. *Transportation Strategies for the Eighties*, report prepared by Temple, Barker & Sloane, Inc. (Chicago: NCPDM, 1982), p. xv.

27. Robert G. House and George C. Jackson, "Trends in Computer Applications in Transportation and Distribution Management," *International Journal of Physical Distribution*, 7 (1977), p. 176. Also see Robert G. House and George C. Jackson, "Trends in Computer Applications: A Survey," *Handling and Shipping* (June 1977), pp. 52–57.

28. Jack W. Farrell, "Computers in Distribution: A State-of-the-Art Report," *Traffic Management* (September 1983), pp. 32–38.

29. Bowersox, *Logistical Management*, p. 10.

30. Arthur M. Geoffrion, "A Guide to Computer-Assisted Methods for Distribution Systems Planning," *Sloan Management Review*, 16 (Winter 1975), pp. 17–41.

31. Allan D. Schuster and Bernard J. La Londe, "Distribution Modeling," in Ken Elliot, ed., *Management Bibliographies and Reviews*, vol. 1 (Bradford, England: MCB Books, 1975).

32. House and Jackson, "Trends in Computer Applications," p. 177.

33. Bowersox, *Logistical Management*, pp. 367–414.

34. Ballou, *Business Logistics Management*, pp. 222–421.

35. Frank H. Mossman, Paul Bankit, and Omar Keith Halferich, *Logistics System Analyses*, rev. ed. (Washington, D.C.: University Press of America, 1977), pp. 233–351.

36. Geoffrion, "A Guide," p. 17. Also see Arthur M. Geoffrion, "The Purpose of Mathematical Programming is Insight, Not Numbers," *Interfaces*, **7** (November 1976), pp. 81–82; and Arthur M. Geoffrion and Richard F. Powers, "Facility Location Analysis is Just the Beginning (If You Do It Right)," *Interfaces*, **10** (April 1980), pp. 22–30.

37. Ballou, *Business Logistics Management*, p. 51.

38. Bowersox, "Physical Distribution Development," pp. 67–70.

39. Bowersox, *Logistical Management*, n. 4, p. 5.

40. Ibid., pp. 9–10.

41. La Londe and Zinszer, "Managing in Uncertain Times," p. 20.

42. Ibid., pp. 19–22.

43. Bernard J. La Londe, "A Reconfiguration of Logistics Systems in the 80s: Strategies and Challenges," *Journal of Business Logistics*, **4**, No. 1 (1983), pp. 1–11.

44. James L. Heskett, "Challenges and Opportunities for Logistics Executives in the 80s," *Journal of Business Logistics*, **4**, No. 1 (1983), pp. 13–19.

45. Donald J. Bowersox, "Emerging From the Recession: The Role of Logistical Management," *Journal of Business Logistics*, **4**, No. 1 (1983), pp. 21–33.

Integrated Distribution Systems
Past, Present, and Future

BERNARD J. LA LONDE, JOHN R. GRABNER, JR., *and* JAMES F. ROBESON

Introduction

In less than twenty years a significant change has occurred in management's attitude toward the role and importance of the distribution function in business firms. The concept of integrated distribution management has progressed from the conceptual stage to a central part of forward looking firms' strategic plans during that short span of time. This change has not been confined by international boundaries or concentrated in any one narrow segment of industry. Since 1960, a new management philosophy toward physical distribution as well as an extensive body of literature have emerged supported by vigorous efforts by the trade associations, the trade press, government, and the academic community.

Prior to 1960, management did not view the distribution mission of the firm as an integrated task. Instead, distribution was carried out in a series of fragmented, uncoordinated movements of goods and information. For example, customer order processing was frequently the responsibility of the accounting function; traffic or transportation management might be the responsibility of marketing, while warehousing of raw materials and in-process goods was typically the responsibility of manufacturing. Similar fragmentation existed with respect to other activities which affected the flow of goods into, through, and out of a business to its customers.

It was virtually impossible to integrate the various activities involved in the total distribution task, either conceptually or operationally, with this state of functional fragmentation. The suboptimization that resulted from poor coordination not only led to poor distribution performance as viewed by the customers, but also frequently led to inefficiency, aste, and morale problems within individual firms. The traffic manager, evaluated on the size of his freight bill, would try to ship in large quantities, frequently car loads or truck loads, and by the most economical transport load. The salesman, evaluated on the basis of total sales, expected reliable and rapid customer order service but was not concerned with the cost of providing that service. The manufacturing manager, evaluated on the basis of unit production cost, typically wanted to maximize the length of production runs of individual items to minimize his set-up and change over costs. These types of conflicts within the organization were frequently resolved on the basis of departmental power struggles with resulting adverse effects upon morale, efficiency, and service.

A number of progressive firms began to consider the potential of integrating distribution members into a unified organizational whole for the purpose of planning operations and control during the 1960s. This trend accelerated during the 1970s, when the movement rapidly progressed from considering integration to actually implementing an integration of fragmented distribution activities into a systemic whole. The distribution function has risen to organizational importance in firms of all sizes not only in the United States, but throughout the world. The distribution manager is perceived to be a key member of the management team on a par with executives in the conventional business functions of manufacturing, marketing, accounting, and the like in a large number of companies throughout the world.

Three questions are of current interest:

1. What are the alternative management approaches most commonly utilized in the corporate development of integrated distribution systems?

2. What forces led to the development of a management focus on integrated distribution systems during the 1960s and 1970s?

3. What forces will shape the scope, influence, and concern of management thinking during the 1980s?

What Is Integrated Distribution Management?

One of the initial problems encountered when the concept of integrated distribution is discussed is that of definition. No single "model" distribution system exists that is applicable for all firms. The distribution function, like other functions within a firm, has evolved within the framework of the management philosophy and available resources of individual firms. However, three general approaches to integrated distribution management have emerged. They are: (1) physical distribution management, (2) materials management, and (3) business logistics. These distinctions are not necessarily accepted by all distribution managers or firms. A sizable, although steadily diminishing, segment of business has not implemented and/or is not aware of the advantages of an integrated distribution system even today.

The distinctions between these three approaches are illustrated in Figure 2–1. *Physical distribution* is basically concerned with the integration of finished goods distribution. The National Council of Physical Distribution Management (NCPDM), an association of well over 2000 distribution executives, defines physical distribution management as

the term describing the integration of two or more activities for the purpose of planning, implementing, and controlling the efficient flow of raw materials, in-process inventory, and finished goods from point of origin to point of consumption. These activities may include, but are not limited to, customer service, demand forecasting, distribution communication, inventory control, material handling, order processing, parts and service support, plant and warehouse site selection, procurement, packaging, return goods handling, salvage and scrap disposal, traffic and transportation, and warehousing and storage.[1]

Many of the firms that have taken this approach are in high-volume consumer packaged goods businesses where the sales or marketing department has traditionally been functionally responsible for the distribution task. It should be noted, however, that physical distribution management organizations were widely adopted by industrial goods firms during the 1970s.

In some cases, implementation of the physical distribution concept has led to the establishment of a separate distribution division within the firm. While specific applications of divisional organization cover a wide spectrum, a common form is to establish a division that distributes either a majority or all of a firm's products. It is generally independently organized as either a profit center or a cost center with budget responsibility. Such firms as Westinghouse and General Foods use this type of organization form as their basic distribution organization.

The *materials management* approach, on the other hand, easily evolves from a traditional purchasing orientation to materials flow. As noted in Figure 2–1, this approach focuses on the acquisition of raw materials, supplies, and goods-in-process inventory. One expert has defined materials management as

> that aspect of industrial management concerned with the activities involved in the acquisition and use of all materials employed in the production of the finished product. These activities may include production and inventory control, purchasing, traffic, materials handling and receiving.[2]

Many of the firms that take this type of approach are involved in industrial markets where the range of potential customers is limited and the value added by manufacturers is relatively high.

The third area, and the most comprehensive approach to integrated distribution systems, is *business logistics*. Business logistics may be defined as

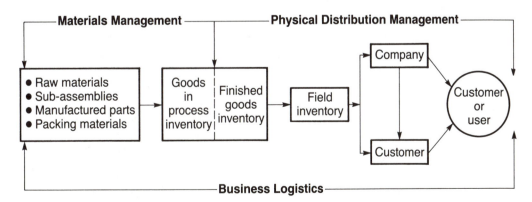

Figure 2-1   Alternative Orientation to Integrated Distribution Management

Source: Professor Bernard J. La Londe, The Ohio State University.

> a total approach to the management of all activities involved in physically acquiring, moving, and storing raw materials, in-process inventory, and finished goods inventory from point of origin to point of use or consumption.[3]

The business logistics concept has its roots in the science of military logistics and, as such, it can be expanded to include people as well as goods. However, to date, most business applications of this approach have been limited to the movement of goods rather than people.

Total logistics systems were first utilized by commercial business firms with multiple production points, wide product lines, and a wide range of potential customers or users. This application has been particularly appropriate where the business firm has multinational operations with raw material, assembly, distribution, and export networks reaching into different countries.

The terminology of distribution or logistics typically becomes identified with specific companies or specific authors. What is more important than semantics is an understanding of the concept of tying together two or more distribution-related activities and viewing the result as a system. In a general sense, the concept of integrated distribution may be defined as

> an approach to the distribution mission of the firm whereby two or more of the functions involved in moving goods from source to user are integrated and viewed as an interrelated system or subsystem for purposes of managerial planning, implementation, and control.[4]

The task of implementing an integrated distribution system in a traditionally organized business is not a simple one. The distribution function cuts across almost every function of the firm including production, marketing, accounting, data processing, finance, and purchasing. Attempts to change the flow of information and the exercise of control within an operating organization are almost certain to meet with strong resistance. However, the cost reduction opportunities available from such a move and the resulting service improvement have encouraged this type of change in many business firms.

The scope of the alternative approaches to integrated distribution management has not been clearly established both because the concept is new and because the individual business firm tailors the concept to an ongoing business organizational environment. In a general sense, the concept as applied encompasses two or more of the activities listed below.

1. Facilities location
2. Purchasing
3. Packaging
4. Production planning
5. Materials handling
6. Warehousing and storage
7. Inventory control
8. Traffic and transportation
9. Order processing
10. Distribution communications
11. Parts and service support
12. Personnel movement
13. Returned goods
14. Salvage and scrap disposal
15. Customer distribution programs
16. Vendor distribution programs

Obviously, each of the activities can be further subdivided. For example, "facilities location" could be subdivided into plant, warehouse, and retail location. Warehouse location could be further subdivided into company owned, customer owned, and public warehouse facilities.

Several of the functions should probably be clarified. Functions in the preceding list 11 through 16 have been selectively added to the distribution responsibility by a number of firms during the past few years. For durable goods manufacturers, parts and service support subsystems can represent a significant cost and also represent a major source of achieving market advantage. Lack of coordination and effective communication regarding this element of corporate responsibility can lead to high costs or dissatisfied customers or both. The personnel movement function usually includes household movement, corporate non-scheduled movement (for example, corporate aircraft), and scheduled commercial transportaion. By centralizing these corporate personnel movement functions, economies of scale, functional specialization, coordinated scheduling, and concentration of purchasing power can lead to cost reductions and/or service improvements. The problem of returned goods increases geometrically as the ultimate customer and the manufacturer become further separated in the national and international market. For example, one company in the United States recently discovered that the cost of a shipment returned for any reason was eight times as much as the cost of shipping it to the customer. Most distribution systems are designed for outbound one-way movement and returned goods can result in a serious profit drain. Centralizing this function allows for a more effective analysis of the cost of trade-offs involved in improved packaging and improved order processing to reduce errors and damage in shipment.

The problems of salvage and waste disposal have been intensified by the developing broad-based interest in environmental control. It is no longer legal to burn scrap or dump waste in most parts of the United States. The problem of effective disposal, either through salvage or disposal, is rapidly becoming a key issue in distribution planning and is likely to become more critical during the 1980s.

The functions of customer and vendor distribution programs have grown in importance as more business firms have realized the potential for joint cost savings by working closely with suppliers and customers on improving intra-channel distribution efficiency. A number of companies have instituted internal distribution consulting teams to work with vendors and suppliers on distribution efficiency. In a broader concept, the growth of interest in the entire area of channel relationships has paralleled the growth of interest in integrated distribution systems.

The functions positioned within the distribution organization depend upon a number of factors. The attitude of top management and the type of products processed or manufactured are probably among the most important variables. However, other factors such as geographic scope of operations, size of enterprise, and multinational orientation of the individual firm can also be important variables in explaining the distribution orientation of the firm.

Why Integrated Distribution Developed

A recognition of the importance of the distribution task is not particularly new. As early as 1915, the two functions of marketing were identified as (1) demand creation and (2) physical supply.[5] The problem of distribution in a commercial sense probably first occurred during prehistoric times when a caveman caught more fish than he could eat or manufactured more arrowheads or axe-heads than he needed for his immediate use. In a military sense, the importance of logistics was also well recognized by military leaders down through history.[6] The familiar cliché that "an army travels on its stomach" is not a 20th innovation—and certainly all students of military history recognize that one of ᴄne reasons for Napoleon's difficulties in Russia was the lack of logistical support caused by extended supply lines. In any case, the concern with effective distribution is not particularly new. What does appear to be a phenomenon of the 1960s and 1970s is the emphasis upon developing integrated distribution systems.

It might be worthwhile to speculate at this point on the causes for the growing interest by businessmen in integrated distribution systems developed during the 1950s and 1960s. There are probably four primary factors which shaped the development of distribution thinking during this period. First, there was a renewed interest in scientific management of the business enterprise. By the end of World War II, large gains had been made in the technology of production. During the post-World War II periods, particularly during the late 1950s and 1960s, there was increasing emphasis upon the marketing function. The amount spent on advertising in the American economy quadrupled during this period. The number of new products launched increased almost geometrically. Thus, by the mid-1950s, the businessman found himself in a situation where production technology was well advanced and marketing costs were steadily increasing. In order to reduce costs and remain competitive in the market place, it was necessary to look to one of the few areas that was relatively untouched—the *distribution* of the product.

In most firms the cost of distribution represents from 18 to 45 percent of total costs. These costs, however, are diffused throughout the company. Some of the costs are incurred in inventory, some in materials handling, some in transportation, others in warehousing and storage, and so on. It would seem, therefore, that the new focus upon efficiency in distribution was a logical outgrowth of the American business environment. That is, the distribution area was one of the last remaining frontiers for significant cost savings in the business firm. The principal method of securing such cost reduction opportunity was to view distribution as an integrated task rather than as the traditional fragmented task taking place in many parts of the firm. Aggregate distribution costs and costs in selected industries are discussed in more detail below.

A second major cause of the "distribution revolution" was the advent of new technology in data processing. As computer technology became increasingly powerful, less costly, and more accessible, the possibility of automated inventory control procedures was increasingly realized. Distribution data are generally classified as a high-input, low-calculation, and high-output form of processing. The new technology contributed to the technical capability of handling large amounts of distribution data in a rapid and efficient manner. One side effect of the computer has been its impact upon total integration of management within the firm. This has caused a breakdown in some of the traditional departmentalization within the firm and paved the way for integrated distribution management, which, of course, must cut across departmental lines. Undoubtedly, increasing levels of computer technology will continue to contribute to expanding data-processing applications in distribution problem-solving and distribution systems development.

A third reason for the increased management attention to distribution was management's recognition of its importance in providing customer satisfaction. In other words, management finally began to realize that selling a product is really only one-half of the job. Getting the product to the customer at the right time in the right quantity and with the right logistical support (parts and service) is the other half—and it is a very important half. There was increased recognition that marketing management could not have a successful sales promotion program unless the distribution system provided logistical support for the promotion. This factor was of particular importance for those companies selling

relatively homogeneous products (e.g., chemical companies). Such companies often co
pete on the basis of efficiency in distribution, and their profits in large measure are determined by their success in effecting sound distribution.

The fourth major influence upon management thinking about distribution was the
profit leverage available from reduced logistics cost. As markets constantly expanded during the 1950s and 1960s, emphasis was upon increased sales. As the tempo of domestic and
international competition increased, a "profit squeeze" was reflected in many American
firms' financial statements. This prompted many firms to look for cost reduction opportunities along with market expansion opportunity. For example, if a firm makes a 4 percent
net profit from $1 sales, then a saving of 4 cents in logistics is equivalent to a $1 expansion
in sales (Table 2–1), assuming that all fixed costs remain constant. A $4 distribution cost
saving is equivalent to $100 in sales expansion; a $4000 saving in distribution cost is equivalent to $100,000 in additional sales. The profit leverage argument made a persuasive ar-
gument for reviewing cost reduction opportunities available from integrated distribution
management.

Finally, the world was rudely jolted by the Arab oil embargo of 1973–74 and the subsequent rise of the Organization of Petroleum Exporting Countries (OPEC) as the controlling force in world petroleum supplies. The rapid escalation of petroleum prices since
1974, coupled with the rapid rate of inflation in prices and labor costs of the last half of
the 1970s, has brought transportation and distribution costs to a sharp focus and has
forced management attention towards distribution system costs and efficiency simply as a
means of insuring that firms can remain competitive and profitable in an uncertain and
volatile economy.

The extent to which American business had adopted the integrated distribution concept was explored in 1976 in a study of the 1000 largest manufacturing firms in the United
States.[7] It was found that 78 percent of the firms responding had recognized and adopted
an integrated approach to the management of distribution activities although only 50 percent of the respondents felt it had been successfully implemented.[8] A similar study in 1971
had found that only 62 percent of responding firms had recognized and adopted the concept, with 42 percent reporting successful implementation.[9] These figures provide an indication of the rapidity with which the concept has spread in recent years.

The firms that responded to the 1976 study indicated that the most common form of
organization (60 percent of respondents) was a combination of a central corporate staff
with line operating responsibilities handled on a divisional basis. A significant minority
(22 percent) of firms reported that all distribution responsibilities were handled on a divisional basis with no corporate staff for coordination among divisions.[10]

Table 2–1   Profit Leverage Provided by
Physical Distribution Cost Reduction

If Net Profit on the Sales Dollar Is 4 %, Then . . .	
A Saving of	*Is Equivalent to a Sales Increase of*
$ .04	$ 1.00
4.00	100.00
400.00	10,000.00
4,000.00	100,000.00
40,000.00	1,000,000.00

In summary then, the principal causes of increased management attention to integrated distribution during the 1950s, '60s, and '70s were:

1. A more scientific approach to business management

2. Advances in computer technology

3. Recognition of the role of distribution in providing increased levels of customer satisfaction

4. A "profit squeeze" and the consequent potential "profit leverage" from increased efficiency in distribution

5. The rapid increase in energy and labor costs associated with the dramatic upheaval in world petroleum markets

A Perspective for the 1980s

If we take the spirit of the so-called "marketing concept" literally, it means that for successful implementation of the concept a firm must generate satisfied customers at a profit. One way of looking at customer satisfaction is in terms of the utilities provided by the business enterprise in the product-service mix. In a classical or traditional context, these utilities are generally identified as form, possession, time, and place utility. It is generally conceded that most of the form utility of a product is generated in the manufacturing process. This is where the automobile company takes an ingot of steel and ends up with an automobile or where a breakfast food manufacturer takes the grain cereal and ends up with a product that "snaps, crackles, and pops." Likewise, it is generally conceded that the marketing function creates possession utility in the product by informing the potential consumer about the product's availability and arranging the transaction phase of the marketing process.

Many marketing authors include time and possession utility as a basic responsibility of the marketing function. However, perhaps a more enlightened approach is to regard these functions as part of the firm's distribution function. Traditionally, this has not been the case because the distribution function within most business enterprises was diffused and fragmented throughout the organization. However, the new concern with integrating the distribution function under the new names of materials management, physical distribution, business logistics (and probably a few titles yet to be invented) has identified the distribution mission of the firm as an integrated function. A perspective for this type of thinking is provided in Figure 2–2. The figure indicates that distribution is the third largest expense of doing business and is responsible for the creation of both time and place utility in the product.

What we are suggesting is that in order to have a satisfied customer, the product must have time and place utility as well as form and possession utility. A well-conceived product with an optimum packaging and promotional mix that is in the wrong place geographically and not available at the time the consumer needs it results in a "short circuit" in the successful implementation of the marketing concept.

It is a truism to state that the marketplace is dynamic. Examples of the dynamism of a high-level economy abound in the literature. For example, many company presidents and marketing executives have stated that over 50 percent of the sales volume is derived

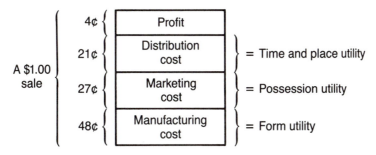

Figure 2-2 One Way of Viewing the Major Costs of Doing Business

SOURCE: Professor Bernard J. La Londe, The Ohio State University.

from products that were unknown to the company ten years ago. These changes exert continuing pressure on the business firm to maintain an effective and efficient system for providing time and place utility to potential customers or users.

Forces Affecting Distribution Management in the 1980s

Individual companies face a variety of factors—both external and internal—that will affect the nature of integrated distribution management during the 1980s. We will touch only on the most important of those factors here.

External Pressures on Distribution in the 1980s

There are five major factors which will affect the distribution missions of most firms in the next decade. Briefly stated, these are energy availability, capital availability, the maturation of domestic markets with subsequent pressures to develop international markets, deregulation of logistics activities—especially transportation—within the United States, and customer pressures for changes in customer service levels. Let's examine each of these in turn.

Energy availability and cost will be a primary concern of distribution managers during the 1980s. While projections of energy costs and usage are obsolete almost before they are prepared, it is still a reasonably safe assumption that energy costs will continue to escalate. Even though there now appear to be adequate supplies of energy, assuming the willingness and ability to pay the price, the rapid escalation of energy costs will increasingly call into question traditional approaches to the distribution of products both within the United States and in international markets. Additionally, energy costs affect logistics operations in a variety of hidden ways, such as the costs of heating and cooling warehouse space and costs of operating handling equipment. Either escalating costs must be passed on to customers or profit margins must be reduced. The solution to these problems is outside the hands of any one individual firm; however, all firms will be affected by the way in which our government does or does not develop energy policies and the way in which the American public responds in its own consumption habits to the dramatically different "rules of the game" that will obtain in the future.

A second major influence on distribution in the years ahead will be the cost and availability of capital. Since 1974 interest costs have risen to heretofore unheard of levels.

While current interest costs may well be higher than the expected long-run equilibrium, it is safe to say that the interest costs that American business will face in the years ahead will be substantially higher than those they faced in the past. Once again, individual firms can do little to affect the overall level of interest; rather they will be forced to alter their patterns of internal distribution and operations to accommodate these high levels of costs and better control them.

An even more disturbing possibility is that unless savings and investment patterns are dramatically changed within the United States, there may well be an inadequate supply of capital at almost any price to enable U.S. industry to rebuild its capital base and to provide for needed inventory investment.

A third factor external to most companies is the maturation of domestic markets throughout the so-called developed world. As domestic markets mature, companies are increasingly forced to seek international markets as a means of maintaining efficient production rates in existing facilities as well as to maintain levels of profitability.

European and Japanese firms have long been faced with this problem. As a consequence they have developed considerable expertise in developing export markets from domestic plants. United States firms have traditionally moved in the direction of investing in foreign subsidiaries rather than developing export markets for their U.S. plants. The reasons for this have been many and varied but basically boil down to the fact that historically it has been cheaper for U.S. firms to manufacture in offshore locations because of higher labor costs in this country. Changes in the relative level of labor costs in the United States and in other developed economies have occurred during the past few years. Today we see many foreign firms making direct investments in the United States as a means of entering our maturing markets. U.S. companies are increasingly being forced to develop export expertise—a skill that has been traditionally lacking in many concerns—as a means of preserving growth rates and maintaining efficient production volumes.

We can expect to see smaller U.S. companies increasingly turn to developing export markets for their products as a means for maintaining their economies of scale in the future. However, pressures from Third World countries for direct investment in plants in those countries will probably result in an increasingly complex distribution task facing large multinational companies. Increasingly, the distribution function of these companies can be expected to have to deal with omnidirectional moves among the plants producing subassemblies in various countries moving toward a final assembly operation in other countries with the finished products being exported to yet other countries. The development of international logistics expertise and the planning, implementing, and controlling of omnidirectional movements through the maze of international tariffs and other trade regulations will become critical for many companies during the 1980s as they seek to maintain historic growth rates.

A fourth external factor affecting distribution management will be increased customer service demands. This factor is difficult to define precisely because it tends to be situational with individual businesses. Generally speaking, it refers to the tendency of customers to "push back" inventory in the distribution channel and to expect the manufacturer to provide highly responsive distribution systems. In addition, customers are more closely monitoring vendor performance and can be expected to make increasing demands on vendors for specialized routing, packing, billing arrangements, and other nontraditional changes in the customer-vendor relationship.

This pattern of higher-level response requirements by customers will increase during the 1980s. The development of sophisticated information systems makes it easier for customers to track vendor performance and take steps to insure vendor adherence to agreed upon service levels. The high cost of carrying inventory for all participants in the distribution channel will continue to make attempts to shift inventory burdens back on vendors an attractive option.

It is important that firms recognize the service options and costs associated with each service option in order to design distribution systems that will be responsive to the needs of the core market. Failure to do so will lead to excessive costs of service which ultimately must be passed on to the consumer or end user of the product. This in turn may have a negative impact upon market share as other vendors find ways of doing the job effectively.

The fifth external factor that will affect distribution during the 1980s is government regulation. As this is written, in late 1983, the United States seems to be moving in the direction of lessening rather than increasing the amount of regulation that applies to distribution activities. The recent deregulation of airlines, railroads, and motor carriers is forcing companies to re-examine traditional transportation practices. In the years ahead we may expect to see radical changes both in the structure of the transportation industry and in the nature of services and the way in which they are provided by for-hire carriers. It is still too early to tell whether transportation deregulation efforts will in the end enhance or harm the market share enjoyed by for-hire carriers. Suffice it to say, many companies' private transportation fleets will be looked at very carefully during the coming years to determine whether they should be expanded into for-hire fleets offering their services to other companies or whether it would be more profitable for operators of private fleets to pull out of the transportation business entirely and rely upon new services tailored to their needs by for-hire transportation specialists.

Regulations governing the distribution of hazardous materials and the manufacture and distribution of so-called "critical" items that may cause dangerous failures of products such as automobiles and necessitate recall will also be open to close scrutiny. Distribution managers in the coming decade can expect to see continual dynamism in the nature and scope of the regulations with which they must contend in dealing with their primary task of moving products to final users.

Internal Pressures

Two major types of internal pressures will tend to dominate distribution decision making during the 1980s.

The first of these, rapid increase in physical distribution costs, is due in large part to the high labor component in physical distribution operations. Distribution operations tend to be very labor-intensive and hence are highly susceptible to labor cost increases. We can expect to see increased use of mechanization and automation in certain types of logistics operations. But many other operations have limited potential for the substitution of capital for labor. The result will be an increased attention to labor productivity as a means of controlling cost increases in the distribution function. American industry has exhibited a rather poor productivity pattern over the past two decades. During the 1980s distribution managers will increasingly find themselves concerned with such issues as

- Recruiting and training of a quality work force

- Developing and maintaining work climates that are conducive to employee productivity

- Searching for new techniques of organizing work to enable employees to make full use of their potential

- Learning to utilize new technology or utilizing old technology more effectively as a means of improving employee productivity

- Increased attention to monitoring productivity levels in the distribution function and taking steps to remedy declines in productivity as they occur

The second major type of internal cost pressure will be that stemming from the cost and availability of capital. Asset management will become a crucial concern as companies seek to keep capacity requirements as low as possible and to enhance the efficiency with which existing assets are utilized. The sorts of concerns that can be expected to materialize in this area are

- The effective utilization of inventory

- The substitution of rapid communication for inventory in the system

- The pruning of marginal product lines and marginal customers to assure that inventory investment is focused on those products and customers which will yield the greatest return to the company

- Careful attention to increasing the effectiveness and efficiency of utilization of fixed assets such as warehouses, handling equipment, and transportation equipment

The last item identified above suggests that distribution management during the next decade will become increasingly concerned not only with the strategic planning of the distribution system but also with the careful and effective planning of internal distribution operations. We can expect to see increased "joint ventures" in the use of distribution equipment and facilities such as transportation equipment and warehouses. This will enable firms to utilize peak capacity and minimize empty backhauls for transportation equipment among other innovative approaches to enhancing asset utilization.

The effective use of information technology will become very important for distribution management, allowing firms to substitute information for inventory in both storage and transportation portions of the system. Information systems will also be crucial to the effective planning and control of productivity systems within distribution operation.

The increased cost of capital will place continuing pressures upon the design and implementation of effective customer service systems. A principal focus of management information systems will be the monitoring of customer service levels as well as the cost associated with those service levels. We may expect to see companies refining their service levels in ways that may slow overall response to customer demands slightly, but will substantially enhance the reliability with which those demands are met. The overall result should be lower costs not only to the company providing the service but also lower costs to the customers of those companies. The implication of this, of course, is that companies will need to become increasingly sophisticated in their ability to identify and measure distribution costs and the causes of the cost levels that are observed. Product profitability, customer profitability, and the profitability of market areas will increasingly become factors of major concern as companies attempt to focus increasingly expensive capital resources upon those products, customers, and markets which have the greatest potential yield to them.

Notes

1. National Council of Physical Distribution Management, *1983 Membership Roster*, back cover.
2. Dean S. Ammer, "Materials Management as a Profit Center," *Harvard Business Review*, 47, No. 1 (January–February 1969), pp. 39–47.
3. Bernard J. LaLonde, John R. Grabner, and James F. Robeson, "Integrated Distribution Management: A Management Perspective," *International Journal of Physical Distribution*, 1, No. 1 (October 1970), p. 44.
4. Ibid.
5. Arch W. Shaw, *Some Problems in Market Distribution*, (Cambridge: Harvard University Press, 1915).
6. See James A. Huston, *The Sinews of War: Army Logistics 1775–1953*, (Washington: U.S. Government Printing Office, 1966) and H. Liddell Hart, *Strategy*, New York: Praeger Publishers, 1967.
7. D. M. Lambert, J. F. Robeson, and J. R. Stock, "An Appraisal of the Integrated Physical Distribution Management Concept," *International Journal of Physical Distribution and Materials Management*, 9, No. 1 (1978), pp. 74–88.
8. Ibid., p. 84.
9. M. L. Densmore and J. F. Robeson, "Integrated Distribution Management in Multi-Division Corporations," in J. R. Grabner, ed., *Perspectives in Logistics Research*, Proceedings of the Third Annual Transportation and Logistics Educators Conference, (Columbus, Ohio: The Ohio State University, 1973), pp. 273–82.
10. Lambert, Robeson, and Stock, "An Appraisal," p. 76.

CHAPTER 3

The Role of the Physical Distribution Manager

Wendell M. Stewart *and* William J. Markham

The Physical Distribution Process

To define the role of the physical distribution (PD) manager, it is first necessary to understand the physical distribution process that must be managed: What is it? How does it operate? What is required to manage it effectively?

Figure 3–1 depicts the total distribution process from sources of raw material through manufacturing/conversion, to primary and secondary distribution to customers. Each step in the process influences each successive step; thus the process is a continuum from start to finish.

In the logistics continuum depicted in Figure 3–1—whether a company participates at the manufacturing, wholesaling, or retailing level—there are eight functional areas to be addressed in providing a balanced, effective approach to management of the distribution process. These are discussed below.

Customer Service

This function is responsible for handling the key interfaces between the company and its customers. It involves servicing customer inquiries, handling order changes, and dealing with many other situations that arise in the typical customer–supplier relationship. Customer service may also include the order processing activity. In addition, it is responsible for monitoring the levels of service provided to customers against the service goals estab-

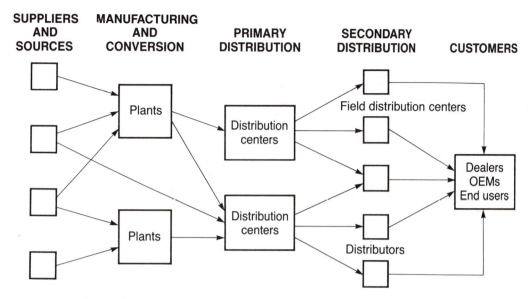

Figure 3-1   The Total Distribution Process

lished by management for each product or market segment. In this respect, customer service provides a form of quality control over distribution operations, much like quality control in manufacturing. Customer service goals are the performance criteria to which the entire demand satisfaction process must respond; these goals act like a magnetic force pulling inventory through the distribution process.

Strategic, Tactical, and Operations Planning

Three important aspects of distribution planning are strategic planning, tactical planning, and operations planning, which will be discussed in turn.

Strategic Planning

With a projected timeframe of two to five years or more, strategic planning aims to establish general direction and long-range plans for achieving basic PD structural changes and strategic goals. Types of strategic planning include:

Organizational structure

Allocation of resources

New sourcing patterns

Channels of distribution

Realignment of capacities

Network optimization

Economic feasibility studies

Impact of environmental factors (e.g., deregulation, energy)

The primary thrust of strategic planning is toward definition of the network of procurement/production/distribution facilities capable of satisfying customer service goals at the maximum return on investment.

Tactical Planning

Tactical planning has a timeframe of about one to two years. Its goals are to preplan specific policies, plans, and programs required to implement agreed-upon strategies within the framework of the anticipated PD workload. Types of tactical planning include:

Inventory policies

Freight (sales) terms

Near-term capacity utilization

Freight rate negotiation targets

Cost reduction and productivity improvement programs

Information system enhancements and additions

Organizational development (near term)

Equipment and procedures evaluation

Operations Planning

The timeframe of the third type of planning—operations—can vary from daily to weekly or monthly, up to one year. Its purpose is to implement selected tactical policies, plans, and programs within the framework of current actual PD workload. Types of operations planning include:

Distribution center scheduling   Productivity improvement/cost reduction
Vehicle scheduling   Inventory budgeting
Shipment consolidation   Operations expense budgeting

Materials Planning and Control

This functional area generally includes the activities of sales forecasting, inventory management, production planning, and distribution scheduling. It sometimes includes purchasing, at least the sourcing and scheduling of purchases if not actual supplier negotiation.

Usually, the daily and weekly scheduling of production is done by manufacturing management within the overall monthly production plan established by the materials planning activity.

The primary purpose of materials planning and control is to minimize the amounts of procurement inventory, production inventory, and distribution inventory flowing through the logistics facility network to satisfy customer service requirements.

Distribution Operations

Physical distribution operations normally include those work elements that act to move inventories through the procurement/production/distribution facility network in a manner that satisfies customers' service requirements. These distribution operating activities include: (1) order processing and preparation of related shipping documents, etc.; (2) warehousing and materials handling; (3) inbound, interplant, and plant-to-warehouse transportation (both private and for-hire); (4) outbound transportation and distribution to customers.

Distribution Engineering

Distribution operations require the services of skilled engineers in a number of areas, including (1) the designing and selection of material handling storage and transportation equipment; (2) the development of improved workplace layout and flow procedures; (3) conducting economic and operational feasibility studies; (4) the establishment of productivity measurement systems and improvement programs; and (5) the establishment of performance standards for manpower, and for capacity and equipment utilization.

In general, it is the role of distribution engineering to contribute to improved operating efficiency, increased return on investment, and more effective managerial control.

Information Systems Development

Information transmission, processing, storage, and retrieval technology has outstripped management's ability to capitalize on new management information system (MIS) technology developments. In the 1980s—dubbed the "information era" by some—the emphasis will be on using computers to provide much more complete and timely support for planning and operations decision making. Many PD departments now have full-time information systems design personnel whose basic mission is to understand the physical distribution process and the key management decisions required to operate the process in the most cost-effective manner. This involves identification of the basic information required to make key decisions and the data sources from which such information can be derived. It may also include the design or purchase of software programs to record, analyze, report, and summarize required information. Systems designers must interface those PD programs with other corporate information systems and maintain valid documentation of the various programs.

Cost Measurement Control

It is generally acknowledged that distribution costs have escalated more rapidly than other cost elements. Consequently, increased attention is now being directed toward understanding and controlling PD costs. Cost analysis and controllers are showing up in increasing numbers on PD organization charts. Their twofold purpose is to establish improved control over PD costs and tie those costs more closely into corporate accounting systems. The results of these efforts are a noticeable increase in the available number of standard cost/flexible budgeting systems and a sharp increase in the number of companies developing customer profitability analysis systems.

Organization Planning

Because distribution costs are escalating rapidly, physical distribution is gaining top management visibility and stature. This has led to a significant amount of organizational change in its reporting relationship and its internal alignment. The A. T. Kearney, Inc. study of organizational trends and factors influencing those trends[1] discovered that PD organizations generally evolve through three distinct stages of development. The most successful companies have made it a practice to devote special effort to planning the organizational changes and human resource development needs associated with each stage:

- *Stage I*—An operational orientation directed toward day-to-day control of individual activities (e.g., transportation, warehousing)

- *Stage II*—A managerial orientation directed at integrating finished goods physical distribution activities

- *Stage III*—A strategic orientation directed at integrating both physical distribution and materials management into an overall logistics system

Fundamental Issues Facing PD Managers

The overall physical distribution process operates to satisfy the sales demand generated by marketing and sales, and PD management must resolve a number of fundamental, largely strategic issues. Some of these are discussed below.

Establishing Distribution Performance Goals

The PD manager is responsible for setting performance goals in the areas of customer service, operating costs, and return on investment.

Customer service goals can include ensuring that inventory is available (i.e., order-, line-item–, and case-fill rates), that delivery is prompt and dependable, and that invoices, and shipments are accurate.

Depending on an individual company's situation, these goals may vary by type of customers and by type of order (e.g., normal, emergency, back-order or promotional fill-in).

In addition to customer service, the PD manager must set operating cost goals for all PD-related operating functions, and return on investment goals for all capitalized leases or investments in PD-related facilities or services.

Setting Distribution Policy

The PD manager must set policy in the following areas:

Deployment of Capacities

The PD manager must determine, by geographic location, the nature and amount of capacity required to procure, produce, convert, store, assemble, transport, and distribute the company's goods.

Staging of Inventories

The question to be resolved here is: How much inventory should be held at each stage— raw, work-in-process, partly-completed, or finished goods—in order to minimize the total value of inventories in the logistics "pipeline" within acceptable operating constraints? In this regard, there appears to be an increasing tendency to hold more inventory in the earlier stages in order to delay product, brand-labeling, pack-sizing (i.e., dozens, gross), or geographic differentiation as long as possible in the inventory conversion cycle.

Geographic Deployment of Inventories

This issue tends to relate more to finished goods than to raw material or work-in-process inventories. The basic question to be resolved is: How should inventory be deployed in order to minimize the investment required to produce acceptable levels of customer service? Other, related questions involve the number, size, and location of each distribution center in the network and the amount of each item to be stocked at each center.

Transportation Mode Mix

Between each node (supplier, plant, distribution center, warehouse, customer) in the total distribution network is an origin-destination transportation link. The service required on each type of shipment (i.e., regular order, back-order fill-in, emergency), as well as other factors such as shipment size, cost sensitivity, and customer's receiving facilities, combine to determine the mix of transportation modes (truck, rail, intermodal) suitable for each link.

Considerations Influencing Resolution of Issues

To resolve the foregoing issues, the PD manager needs to consider a number of factors for each family or class of items to be distributed.

1. *Volume.* High-volume items have more storage, transportation, and distribution options than low-volume items.

2. *Form.* Bulk products, either dry or liquid, have different distribution requirements than packaged goods.

3. *Value/Weight/Cube Ratios.* Low value-per-pound products are faced with certain economic restrictions that high value-to-weight products are not. Similarly, bulky products encounter certain restraints that dense products can avoid.

4. *Seasonality.* Whenever the volume of seasonal sales or raw material supplies varies more than 20 percent from off-season to high season there are unique storage and transportation requirements that must be accommodated by the distribution system.

Other considerations include how the goods are distributed (as whole goods or as piece parts, components, and subassemblies, and what channels of distribution are involved (i.e., manufacturer to wholesaler, or manufacturer direct to retailer or original equipment manufacturer). Distribution operations will vary depending on whether products have a raw material source orientation (e.g., primary metals) or a market orientation (e.g., consumer goods). Finally, the PD manager must review all of these considerations in light of the company's current tactics—are they aimed at cost reduction and retrenchment or expansion?

Up to this point, the nature and composition of the modern PD process has been described, as have some of the key issues requiring resolution by PD management. The next section discusses how objectives and goals are set for the PD manager and his team.

Physical Distribution Management's Objectives

Physical distribution or, in its broader context, logistics is a very complex process operating in an increasingly volatile environment. Successful PD managers establish objectives to guide them through these difficult waters and, at the same time, to give top management something against which to measure PD performance. These objectives typically include several or all of the following: (1) cost minimization, (2) service maximization, (3) profit optimization, (4) business mix improvement, and (5) improved return on investment.

The original objective of early physical distribution practitioners was *cost minimization*. The minimization of all distribution-related costs remains one of contemporary PD management's primary objectives.

Some PD managers, especially those in companies whose sales volumes are very sensitive to the levels of service provided to customers, place the *maximization* of *service* even above cost minimization. This may be justifiable in situations where the market will pay a premium for superior service and the company has the opportunity to recover the extra costs of providing premium service. It may also be warranted in situations where the market will not pay a premium price for superior service but management recognizes service as an integral part of the marketing mix and realigns (reduces) marketing and sales budgets to be able to accommodate extra distribution costs without jeopardizing basic profitability.

As companies become (1) more aware of the cost, service, and sales trade-offs and (2) more sophisticated in evaluating these trade-offs, they invariably move away from unilateral approaches to either cost minimization or service maximization and toward *profit optimization*. The profit equation is optimized when all relevant distribution costs are minimized *within* acceptable, economical, and competitive service goals.

Business mix improvement has become increasingly practicable, since management is getting more sophisticated and profit-oriented. Contemporary management realizes that total operating profit is nothing more than the sum of the individual profits earned losses incurred) on each customer order. The order is the ultimate profit center. The of all the operating profits and losses on individual orders for a given customer is the measure of that customer's total profitability. The profitability of all customers of a given type, size, or location can be the measure of total profitability of specific classes of customers, sales territories, or channels of distribution. Distribution costs are the key to measuring customer profitability, and it is the range of these costs per transaction that is important, not the average cost per dollar of sales. To improve the business mix requires, first of all, measuring the net operating profit contribution of individual market segments and then adjusting distribution policies and programs to increase the profitability of desirable segments while systematically de-emphasizing undesirable segments.

Physical distribution managers also seek to achieve an improved return on investment. In some businesses, inventories and accounts receivable represent over 50 percent of the asset base. In that type of situation, the *reduction of inventories*—to maintain them at the lowest level consistent with service requirements—can be one of PD management's major objectives. Speeding up cash flow—converting inventories more rapidly into accounts receivable (through faster, more accurate order processing) and then into cash—is frequently a corollary objective.

The Role of the PD Manager

To understand the current as well as the future roles of the PD Manager in optimizing corporate profits and return on investment, it is desirable to look at the evolution of this role over the recent past. To do this, A. T. Kearney, Inc. undertook a mail survey of 500 manufacturing, wholesaling, and retailing companies, augmented by 100 in-depth personal interviews with a selected group of respondents. The findings from this survey are very descriptive of the evolving role of PD management in the emerging logistics environment. Some of the key survey findings include those discussed in the paragraphs that follow.

Scope of Responsibilities Is Broadening

To identify the present position and measure change in PD management's role, the survey identified PD management's scope of responsibilities since 1970. Survey findings indicated there was little change in this scope during the 1970–73 period but that the oil embargo and the so-called "inventory recession" of 1974 triggered significant change.

Figure 3–2 shows the responsibilities typically assigned to the PD organizations in 1973. Some of these responsibilities were managed on a direct line-control basis, but most were managed on a staff or functional/dotted-line basis.

In 1973 only 13 percent of the companies surveyed assigned line control responsibilities for inbound transportation to their distribution organizations. Responsibility for the control and placement of finished goods inventory was assigned to only 8 percent of the distribution organizations. Similarly, few organizations in 1973 had responsibility for:

Finished goods plant warehousing (12%)

Customer service (11%)

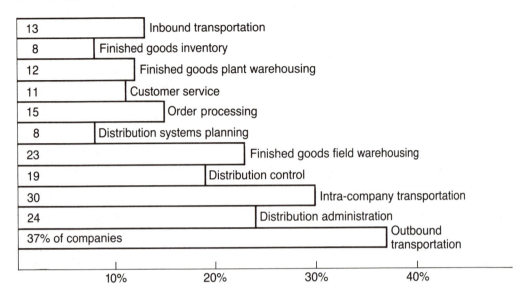

Figure 3-2   Responsibilities Assigned PD Organizations in 1973

Order processing (15%)

Distribution information systems planning (8%)

A greater portion of respondents had line-control responsibility for the five activities on the bottom of Figure 3-2.

Finished goods field warehousing (23%)

Distribution cost and financial control (19%)

Intracompany transportation (30%)

Distribution administration (24%)

Outbound transportation of finished goods to customers (37%)

In looking at the overall pattern of line responsibilities in 1973, it can be seen that only one area—outbound transportation—was included in the "world of distribution" in more than a third of the companies. Most of the companies assigned line-control responsibility for distribution activities to other departments such as marketing or manufacturing.

By 1980, however, the picture had changed dramatically and distribution's responsibilities for the 11 activities listed in Figure 3-2 had expanded significantly.

Figure 3-3 describes the same group of companies and shows the expansion that took place in these 11 responsibilities between 1973 and 1980.

For example, the top bar on the chart shows that in 1980, 47 percent of the companies assigned responsibility for inbound transportation to the distribution organization. The left-hand part of the bar shows the 13 percent that assigned this activity to distribution in 1973. The right-hand part of the bar shows the increase between 1973 and 1980. For inbound transportation, the increase was two and a half times the 1973 level.

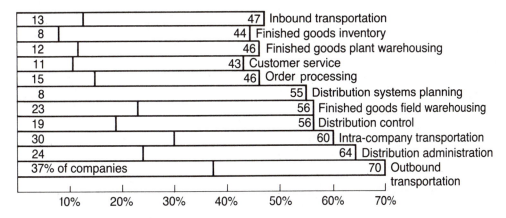

Figure 3-3   Expansion of Responsibilities Assigned to PD Organizations by 1980

In addition to this dramatic expansion of responsibility for these 11 activities, Figure 3–4 shows that a second type of growth took place between 1973 and 1980. Five new activities were added to the "world of distribution." They are:

Sales forecasting (in 8% of the companies)

Responsibility for the placement and control of raw material and work-in-process inventory (13%)

Sourcing and purchasing (18%)

Production planning, or development of master production schedules (22%)

Distribution engineering—the engineering of productivity standards as well as of facilities and equipment to support distribution operations (30%)

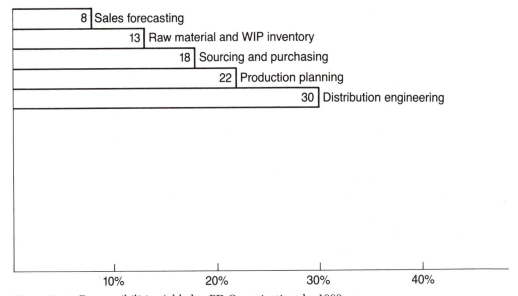

Figure 3-4   Responsibilities Added to PD Organizations by 1980

It is interesting to note that none of the distribution organizations surveyed had responsibility for any of these five new functions in 1973. Yet by 1980, one in five distribution organizations in the survey was scheduling production, and almost one-third had their own engineering groups.

Thus, it can be seen that distribution responsibilities have expanded in two significant ways: (1) the number of companies assigning the 11 most common activities to distribution has tripled, and (2) distribution's span of control has broadened to include five new activities.

What does this mean for the individual company and its distribution organization? Figure 3–5 provides some insights which are discussed below.

Centralization Is Increasing

In 1973, the average distribution organization was responsible for centralized line control of only 2.6 activities—out of a possible 11. Now, the same central organization has line responsibility for 8.9 activities from the expanded list of 16. This is a tripling of line responsibilities in only seven years. Most significantly, this strong trend toward centralization was taking place during the time when corporate management was *decentralizing* many companies into multiple strategic business units (profit centers).

The Rate of Change Has Been Accelerating

To measure the rate of change the survey identified the year in which the first new responsibility was added to the PD department. Figure 3–6 shows the results. Note that the top part of each of the bars represents the percentage of companies in the survey which *first* added new responsibility to distribution management in that year. The bottom part shows the cumulative percent of companies adding responsibilities during the surveyed time frame.

In 1973, for example, fewer than 3 percent of the respondents had begun adding re-

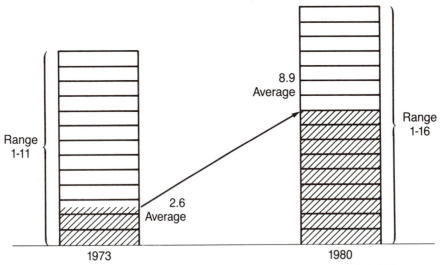

Figure 3–5   Increase in Average Number of Line Control Activities, 1973-1980

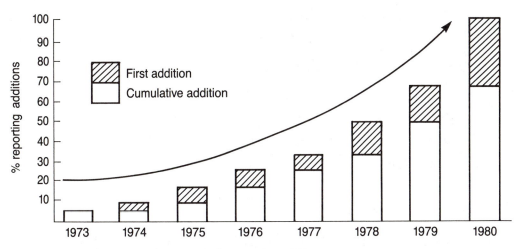

Figure 3-6   Acceleration in the Rate of Change, 1973-1980

sponsibilities. In 1976, this nearly tripled to about 10 percent; however, the cumulative number of companies was still less than one-third of the respondents.

During 1978–80, more than two-thirds of the companies had begun the process of adding responsibility to distribution. In fact, almost one-fourth of the respondents took their first expanding step in 1980.

Clearly, in more recent years, change has been rapidly accelerating, suggesting that the process is both strong and dynamic.

Evolution Occurs in Three Stages

A major conclusion of the foregoing organization survey was that the role of the PD manager evolves as the mission of the PD organization changes. This evolution takes place in three distinct stages. At each stage there is a broadening in scope and in management approach.

Scope of Responsibilities

A profile of the Stage I organizations shows that the "world" of a Stage I distribution organization consists of the following six activities, although the typical organization has *line-control* responsibility for only two to three of them. The activities are:

Distribution systems planning (23%)   Intracompany transportation (51%)
Finished goods field warehousing (32%)   Distribution administration (44%)
Distribution control (28%)   Outbound Transportation (58%)

Twenty-six percent of companies in the survey fell into Stage I.
Stage II organizations typically include 11 activities; all the Stage I activities plus:

Inbound transportation   Customer service
Finished goods inventory   Order processing
Finished goods plant warehousing

The typical Stage II organization is responsible for about eight activities, or three times the scope of responsibility of a Stage I organization. Fifty-eight percent of surveyed companies fell into Stage II.

The profile of Stage III organizations show 16 activities: the II already mentioned and the following:

Sales forecasting

Raw materials and work-in-process inventory management

Sourcing and purchasing

Production planning

Distribution engineering

The average Stage III logistics organization has responsibility for about 13 activities—or nearly six times the span of control of a Stage I organization. Sixteen percent of surveyed companies fell into Stage III.

Management Approach

The management approach of the Stage I organization can be described as being *operational* in nature, with a focus on current operating events. In this sense, the perspective is that of a caretaking responsibility typified by a "mind the store" attitude.

The primary activities in this environment center on expediting the day's work load, such as making sure that the day's orders are filled or that the day's shipments are made. Operating improvements tend to be made on a piecemeal basis, for example, the reprofiling of a warehouse for greater order-picking efficiency, or the rerouting of traffic between two points for improved transit time or cost.

The overall stimulus, therefore, is a reaction to current events with short-term objectives and performance measurement. For example, one Stage I company studied could only track individual monthly freight costs at aggregate levels. It had no way of tracking or budgeting shipping volumes, mode utilization, or variances from planned costs per hundredweight.

The approach to administering these responsibilities in a Stage II organization can be described as being *managerial*. This suggests, first, that Stage II organizations manage distribution as a total system. In addition to keeping up with the daily activities, the Stage II distribution management team is concerned with the impacts that different but related operating activities have on one another.

Second, this perspective enables management to capitalize on the trade-offs inherent in the full scope of its responsibilities, including customer service versus inventory, warehousing versus transportation, and so on. As a result, planning systems and operational controls are established to manage the function as an integrated operating entity.

Third, through its planning activities, management is able to recognize the potential impacts of the changing environment in order to determine in advance how best to cope, instead of reacting after the fact. Advance awareness of the impact of potential changes permits the rebalancing of operations in an orderly, planned manner that capitalizes on the new trade-off opportunities.

Stage II management typically teams with other functions to identify areas of shared responsibility and develop common approaches to their administration. One very large Stage II retailing company indicated that it went so far as to develop shared performance measures for distribution and procurement managers as a way of recognizing their shared responsibilities and unifying their objectives. Other examples of teaming that surfaced in the survey included many instances of joint development of customer service policies and goals with marketing, and raw material load consolidation programs with manufacturing and purchasing.

Important changes occur in a Stage III management approach and orientation. Management develops new interests that are essentially strategic in nature. The logistics process is now regarded and managed as an integral part of the total corporate endeavor. Logistics management recognizes that part of the function's role is to increase support to other company functions and business units. As the need to support other units becomes recognized, logistics management begins to evaluate basic changes in logistics and operations strategy that are required to best meet those needs. In addition, it actively pursues opportunities in the changing environment that could create unique competitive advantages. This is a far cry from the reactive Stage I organization.

Logistics Is Emerging as a Top Management Function

The result of these evolutionary trends is the emergence of logistics as a senior management function (Figure 3–7). The management orientation evolves from an operational focus at Stage I, through a managerial approach at Stage II, to the strategic top management level at Stage III. Simultaneously, the financial orientation evolves from that of cost reduction at Stage I, to profit maximization in Stage II, to the optimization of return on investment in Stage III—the orientation of senior corporate executives.

As logistics organizations take on the appearance of a senior management function, they assume senior-level positions within the company. Fifty-nine percent of the Stage I organizations report to general management, 14 percent report to marketing and sales, and 27 percent report to manufacturing. By Stage III, a dramatic shift has occurred: 73

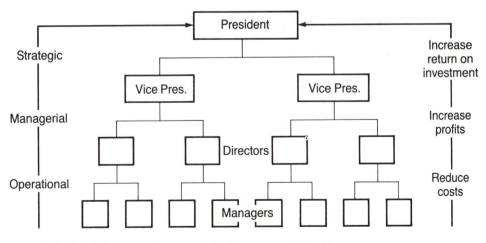

Figure 3-7   Logistics Emerging as a Senior Management Function

percent of logistics organizations report to general management. Thus, it is at Stage III that logistics organizations assume a truly top management position in the general management structure.

Figure 3–8 shows that, concurrent with the trend toward positioning of the function at the general management level, the stature of the top distribution/logistics executive increases within the company.

Impact on the Bottom-Line Is Substantial

The survey identified the benefits of PD management's expanding role and indicated that the trauma and effort required to effect the change are worth it—the opportunity is great!

To document this point, survey respondents provided information on the magnitude of their logistics costs as a percent of sales. Figure 3–9 presents an index of total logistics costs as a percent of sales. Included in these costs are:

- Inbound, intracompany, and outbound transportation

- Plant and field warehousing

- Inventory carrying costs

- Customer service and other administrative costs

The average has been set with Stage I logistics costs as an index of 100. Note that in Stage II the index has dropped to 85.1, and at Stage III, the index has dropped again to 80.6. Thus, the improvement between Stage I and Stage III represents a 19.4 percent reduction in these costs. The impact of this reduction on the bottom line is impressive.

In addition to these improvements, respondents reported added benefits. Compared to Stage I respondents, *twice* as many Stage III respondents reported customer service levels higher than their competitors, and nearly *three times* as many reported greater cost effectiveness than their competitors. Benefits also accrue to other organizational units. One

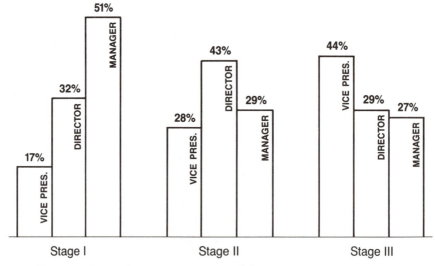

Figure 3-8   Executive Stature Increasing as Responsibility Increases

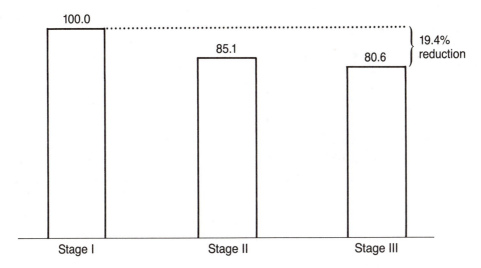

Figure 3-9   Index of Total Logistics Costs as a Percentage of Sales

Stage III organization reported that integrated logistics planning had increased manufacturing labor and equipment productivity by 40 percent. Benefits were also reported in terms of enhanced balance sheet performance: Fixed asset utilization increased, and current assets (inventory and receivables) were reduced and turnover improved.

In summary, this chapter has focused on the role of PD management by describing:

1. The PD process and fundamental issues to be resolved by management

2. External environmental changes acting to shape that process and influence the emerging role of PD management

3. PD management objectives in managing the process within the changing environment

4. The basic role of PD management within the corporate organization structure, how that role is evolving, and the benefits being achieved at each stage

Note

1. A. T. Kearney, Inc., *Organizing Physical Distribution to Improve Bottom Line Results*, (A. T. Kearney, Inc., 1981; cosponsored by *Traffic Management* magazine).

CHAPTER 4

A Look to the Future

Wendell M. Stewart (Subsection 1)
Bernard J. La Londe (Subsection 2)
James L. Heskett (Subsection 3)
Donald J. Bowersox (Subsection 4)

The previous chapter discussed the role of the physical distribution (PD) manager as it is generally understood and accepted today. However, a number of forces are now impacting the business world for the first time. The need for skilled managers who recognize, understand, and can effectively deal with these forces will increasingly cast a spotlight on the PD manager's role in the decade to come. The trend toward a senior management role for the PD executive should be all the more pronounced in the future.

1. Forces Influencing the Emerging Role of the Physical Distribution Manager

The role of today's physical distribution manager is being reshaped by the following forces:

1. Geographic shifts in production and consumption

2. Increasing market segmentation

3. Low capital supply and high cost of borrowing

4. Revolution in manufacturing technology

5. New supply sources and constraints

6. Energy cost and availability

7. New regulatory freedoms and constraints

8. New labor–management and socioeconomic considerations

9. Internationalization of sources and markets

In the discussion that follows, each of these nine forces will be described first in terms of the evidence of its occurrence and then in terms of its impact on PD.

Geographic Shifts in Production and Consumption

Evidence of Change

Among the most important forces are the geographic shifts that have already taken place and are continuing to take place. The U.S. population (consumption) base is shifting and the industrial (production) base is following. The most notable shifts have been to the Sunbelt from the Northeast and Midwest. The magnitude of this migration is tremendous. For example:

- The center of U.S. population gravity has marched south and west over the past 20 years, from Indiana to Illinois to a point now in eastern Missouri.

- 74 percent of all new housing starts in 1980 were in the South and West, even though those areas have only 52 percent of the existing housing units.

- Production jobs in the South and West increased 32 percent during the 1970s, while declining 9 percent in the Midwest and East.

Impact of Change

The impact of these shifts has been significant. First of all, geographic shifts have created *plant/market misalignments.* Plants that were positioned years ago to serve the midwestern and eastern markets now find the sales volumes in their traditional markets declining. As a result, plant capacity utilization is often below acceptable levels. In addition, *increased distribution costs* are being incurred to offset plant/market misalignments. For example, it is commonplace to find companies with out-of-date plant locations being forced to ship products on average an extra 200, 300, or even 400 miles. The extra transportation can amount to a substantial premium cost per unit.

As markets move away from plants, companies have used various means of positioning finished goods inventories closer to customers, especially in specific geographic areas to which transportation service is unreliable. One approach, an increase in the number of inventory stocking locations, means more total inventory. More inventory pushes up the total value of current assets and dilutes the return on assets dedicated to the distribution process. More inventory can also require *more warehouses* in which to store and from which to distribute the inventory. Surveys show that the average number of field warehouses per manufacturer increased from six to ten over the past decade. If these additional warehouses are owned, all other things being equal, the company's asset base has increased and its return on assets has declined.

Increasing Market Segmentation

Evidence of Change

Another force to be reckoned with is the increasing differentiation of product/market segments taking place in both consumer and industrial goods. This increasing differentiation is taking the form of:

- *More market segments*, each with its own unique service requirements.

- *Shifts in channel leverage*, for example, food retailers striving for more influence on and control over manufacturing and wholesaling activities. Another example would be wood products manufacturers who acquire retail do-it-yourself home improvement chains to assure distribution outlets for their products.

- *New service requirements* by customers, designed to reduce their inventories and distribution work load by pushing more work back on their suppliers.

- *More precise measurement*—frequently computerized—by customers of suppliers' service performance. Many suppliers of commodity-type products are using service as a sharp-edged competitive tool.

Impact of Change

The increase in differentiated product/market segments can result in the following:

1. *Fragmented production focus.* This can mean more specialized setups, more frequent changeovers, and other situations which are contrary to traditional economy-of-scale concepts and production economics.

2. *Increasing inventory differentiation.* This creates more stockkeeping units, which tends to increase inventory levels and reduce turnover. Unfortunately, it is all too frequently the high-sales-volume items that tend to be out of stock.

3. *Service program proliferation.* As service needs for individual product/market segments become more differentiated, many companies are tailoring manufacturing and logistics response capabilities to the unique requirements of individual market segments.

4. *Varying segment profitability.* This is the not-surprising result of segment differentiation. Today, a key measure of profitability—net operating contribution—can vary by as much as 700 percent from the least profitable segment to the most profitable. In view of this, it is necessary to balance the levels of profitability with the amount of sales volume available at each level in arriving at the overall mix of high-volume–low-margin business and low-volume–high-margin business which will maximize the company's long-term profits and return on investment.

Capital Supply and the Cost of Borrowing

Evidence of Change

The operating environment is also shaped by the short capital supply and the high cost of borrowing money. This important factor diminishes opportunities for financing new machinery and techniques.

Inadequate corporate profits have limited the amount of capital for reinvestment. In 1977, for example, total corporate profits were less than the underlying inflation rate. Some industries, like steel, have been literally decapitalizing for years while their capital needs for nonproduction purposes such as pollution control have been growing, thus compounding their capital shortage problems.

Capital formation is declining as a result of reduced profits and declining personal savings. The United States has the lowest rate of savings and capital growth in the free world, about 6 percent, and that rate has been declining in recent years.

The structure and emphasis of capital markets has led to more money being channeled into short-term instruments, because they offer investors higher interest rates, and less money channeled into long-term instruments. All this happens at a time when the government is trying to finance the National Debt and is competing heavily with private borrowers for an increasing share of the declining volume of long-term capital. The cost of financing that debt is now nearly twice the annual budget deficit.

The economy is also contending with *rising borrowing costs*. The prime rate topped out in this last run-up at 21.5 percent. Certainly few expect to see a 6 percent interest rate ever again; the new "norm" may well be around 12 percent.

Impact of Change

Low capital supply and high borrowing cost result in *aging plants and equipment*. The average age of today's plants is 17.5 years. Businesses are finding it increasingly difficult to keep up-to-date in manufacturing and logistics technology, and inadequate earnings and depreciation rules do not provide sufficient cash flow to fund plant replacement.

Changing make-versus-buy economics are encouraging many companies that had previously been moving toward greater vertical integration to reverse that trend and buy more on the outside. *Higher inventory carrying costs* have brought inventory into a new position of prominence in strategic operations planning. There is a tendency for inventory to be pushed back upstream as the costs of carrying it rise. In consumer goods, for example, retailers have pushed the responsibility for carrying inventory back to wholesalers and manufacturers. Wholesalers are also pushing responsibility back to manufacturers who, in turn, are pushing responsibility for raw materials and manufacturing supplies back onto their suppliers through stockless purchasing and just-in-time delivery programs (such as the *kanban* system used in Japan).

Interestingly, some manufacturers have recognized the inevitability of these trends and have set up inventory deployment and scheduled ordering and delivery systems capable of providing highly reliable service at a lower total cost. The key to their success has been the elimination of random demand patterns by finding ways of motivating customers to give up the relative freedom of ordering any quantity of any item on any day of any week no matter where the customers are located. Random ordering is a luxury few industries can continue to afford.

Revolution in Manufacturing Technology

Evidence of Change

A revolution in manufacturing technology is taking place in the United States. It has been long overdue but is now coming on with a rush. The characteristics of this revolution include the following:

- *Technological sophistication*, with heavy emphasis on machine flexibility and quick, low-cost changeover. Unfortunately, while the United States was concentrating on developing production equipment capable of handling high volumes in long runs, the Japanese were concentrating on manufacturing flexibility, numerical control, and robots. Now, the United States is also implementing these concepts.

- *Computer assisted design* (CAD) and *computer assisted manufacturing* (CAM) to improve quality and productivity.

- *Manufacturing operations integration* to improve coordination between activities comprising the total manufacturing process, thus minimizing bottle-necks and inventory or work-load imbalances.

- *Increased planning and control* to provide more effective capacity management and control over both manufacturing activities and costs.

Impact of Change

The revolution in manufacturing technology has led to *higher levels of investment in equipment*. Fortunately, the new tax laws will permit faster equipment depreciation, thus generating additional cash flow needed to finance new equipment purchases.

U.S. manufacturers have traditionally been preoccupied with economies of scale, which often led to problems such as an inability to "turn around" quickly in manufacturing, along with excess inventories, and poor response time. Now management is beginning to consider "economy of scope" together with economy of scale in manufacturing operations in order to facilitate interchangeability between operations and equipment. Management has discovered that more numerous small, dispersed plant facilities can result in lower transportation costs, more defined operational focus, and operations of a more manageable size.

The advantages are as follows:

- Less emphasis upon *shifting scale economies* with volume of throughput

- *Higher productivity* or output from the same level of resource inputs

- *Improved quality and cost* due to the improved control stemming from the marriage of more sophisticated technology to the integrated organization with improved information support

- *Shorter lead times* resulting from the increased flexibility and faster changeover of the newer types of equipment

- *Reduced work-in-process inventories* and, in all probability, reduced finished goods inventories as a result of being able to produce items more frequently and in smaller quantities without significant cost penalties

The revolution in manufacturing technology will also have its drawbacks. One will be a serious shortage of people with the necessary skills to operate new machinery. Extensive retraining programs will be necessary. The mentality required for operating a numerically controlled machine tool is different from that required for running a hand-operated lathe.

New Supply Sources and Constraints

Evidence of Change

New supply sources and constraints are manifesting themselves in the form of:

- *Diminishing U.S. resources*

- *Greater reliance* on offshore producers

- *More OPEC-type cartels,* whose avowed purpose is to control supply and thereby increase price

- *Longer inbound supply lines,* as sources become more distant from the United States

Consider these facts. We import half of our oil requirements. Moreover, 94 percent of our bauxite for aluminum comes from unsettled, less developed countries; 91 percent of our chromium is imported from South Africa and the Soviet Union, and 97 percent of our manganese comes from Africa. In fact, there are ten critical minerals for which we depend on supply sources that cannot be regarded as staunchly pro-American.

Impact of Change

All of these factors will pose significant problems for the U.S. economy as a whole, and for individual businesses, which will be faced with:

- Higher material costs

- A loss of control over both the quality and availability of materials

- Greater vulnerability to unanticipated supply disruptions

- Potential plant/source misalignments (much like the plant/market misalignments noted previously)

- The need for a *longer-term* approach to sourcing

- Increasing substitutions of materials, sources, and processes

- Increasing emphasis on backward integration to obtain greater control over supply and thus ensure more stability

Energy Cost and Availability

Evidence of Change

Energy costs have increased at a disproportionate rate. For example, the energy inflator in the cost index for the period 1973 to 1979 went up 20.3 percent per year on average, which was three times as fast as the concurrent increase in labor costs. By the mid 1980s, half of the United States will be receiving several hundred billion dollars for the production and sale of petroleum-based energy; the other half of the United States will consume that energy. This will cause a further shift in the job base.

The outlook for the future is uncertain. At the present time we have a world-wide glut of oil, but with the historic instability of the Middle East who knows what may happen tomorrow?

Impact of Change

The long-term effects of the energy situation are significant:

- Products and processes must be redesigned to make them less energy-intensive.

- Reduced location options due to limitations on energy availability will become a very important consideration in future site selection.

- Operations disruptions from brownouts and energy shortages will become more commonplace.

- Increased costs of diesel fuel up to $3 a gallon near term and possibly $5 a gallon by 1990 or sooner.

Customers will try to shift the responsibility for transportation back onto their suppliers. For example, a major retail chain has developed contingency plans to reverse a two-decade trend toward fewer distribution centers. It is now defining where it will re-establish distribution centers so that suppliers will have to deliver products, on average, closer to its stores. Thus, when fuel supplies are allocated, the chain will conserve fuel used by its private fleet.

New Regulatory Freedoms and Constraints

Evidence of Change

The mixture of new legislative initiatives affecting distribution consists of such elements as:

- New research and development designed to re-energize our lagging creative skills, develop new products and processes, and regain our position of technological leadership.

- Investment incentives that encourage the infusion of new capital into blighted areas and declining industries.

- Liberalized tax rules such as the 15-5-3 depreciation plan contained in the 1981 tax law.

- New cost-effective criteria for all future pollution-control laws to force a more realistic relationship between efforts to protect the environment and the cost of that protection.

- Deregulation of transportation in particular, along with a movement toward less government regulation in general. Deregulation may well be the single most important development in distribution in the last 30 years.

Impact of Change

Over the next ten to twenty years this new legislation will result in significant changes.

- Upgrading of our manufacturing and distribution technology will be substantial.

- The modernizing of outdated facilities will be greatly aided by more liberal depreciation rules.

- Less investment in nonproductive plant and equipment should result from proper application of the new cost-effective criteria.

- The reconfiguration of facility networks made possible by the revolution in manufacturing technology and encouraged by the new faster depreciation laws will be greatly facilitated by deregulation.

- Product design control will be returned, at least partially, to the design engineers.

- Cost-based transport rates will eliminate the extensive cross-subsidization that existed prior to deregulation, when the larger shipments of denser products moving longer distances subsidized smaller shipments of light and bulky products moving shorter distances. This development could be a benefit or a disadvantage, depending upon the nature of one's product shipment profiles.

Many new distribution services and service/price packages are cropping up under deregulation. For example, for one of its major shippers an innovative midwestern railroad has put together a three-tiered service/price package that makes more money for both shipper and carrier. The lowest rate is charged for the longest turnaround time on cars leased by the shipper. For a faster turnaround, the carrier charges a higher rate. For a still faster turnaround, the highest tier of the three-tiered rate structure applies. The carrier is motivated to move the cars faster because it is able to charge higher rates when it does so. The shipper is willing to pay higher rates because the potential sales volume is higher, service is better, and inventory investment is reduced, thus creating a significant profit advantage.

New assembly and distribution services are also beginning to appear in profusion. There are now about 600 pool distributors in operation, many offering special services such as billing, labeling, and even contract packaging.

New Labor–Management and Socioeconomic Considerations

Evidence of Change

In the last few years we have seen a trend toward better cooperation between labor and management, especially in those industries most threatened by foreign competition. Another trend has been an increasing use of foreign industrial relations approaches, such as those employed by the Japanese to help employees identify more closely with their employers. In Ezra F. Vogel's remarkable book, *Japan as Number One* (Harvard University Press, 1979), there is a most interesting description of how the Japanese worker has merged his goals with those of his employer and, as a result, turns out more products of better quality at lower cost that his U.S. counterpart. But this is not something that only

Japanese workers can accomplish. The president of Honda claims that the most productive factory Honda has is the one located in the United States, employing primarily U.S. workers, but using Japanese management techniques.

Evolving work force attitudes and increasing concerns for the quality of work life are also becoming a more important factor with which management must deal. While much as been written about loss the the American work ethic, there appears to be a growing body of opinion to support the idea that people still like to work hard *if* they feel involved in the process *and* get proper recognition for their efforts and ideas.

On the other hand, the geographic shift of production and consumption has led to severe socioeconomic problems in the key industrial centers and markets of earlier eras. Fear of further loss of their *industrial revenue base* is causing many northeastern and midwestern states to take a more obstructionist stand against companies planning to relocate their plants to the south and west.

Impact of Change

The changing labor–management relationship and socioeconomic climate has already brought about more shared decision making as labor gains increased representation on boards of directors, and as management and employees form joint councils to address common problems.

Changes in the socioeconomic climate will include:

- An increasing amount of relocation inflexibility as union locals are joined by state and city governments in efforts to delay plant closings that will further erode the employment and revenue base of already hard-hit areas.

- Skyrocketing implementation costs for one-time plant relocations as companies are forced to spend more to buy their way out of bad locations.

- Plant and distribution-facility site selection based on existing labor concentrations, which will become increasingly important as special tax incentives and worker-retraining subsidies attract new business to the midwest and east and slow the migration south and west.

Internationalization of Sources and Markets

In many industries, the internationalization of both resources and markets is developing rapidly. This internationalization is the result of the following factors:

- The long-term decline in the value of the U.S. dollar that has made many of our products more attractive in foreign markets.

- The decline in U.S. technological leadership that has led many manufacturers to look overseas for their sourcing requirements.

- The drive to increase U.S. exports in order to attain a better balance of payments.

- Heavy U.S. investment in overseas raw material sources and manufacturing capabilities.

- The tremendous thrust into the U.S. market of foreign competition in every conceivable product, including the venerable barber chair, a product now 100 percent imported from Japan.

- The increasingly heavy *foreign investment* in the United States.

Implications

Internationalization will have a tremendous effect on distribution. Some of the implications are already discernible.

Companies operating internationally will have to forge effective, responsive, worldwide operating control systems that take into account not only the physical supply and demand volumes required to operate the business, but the comparative costs and availability of alternative sources, the comparative profitability of alternative markets, the dynamics of the exchange value of the dollar, and political stability of each trading partner, all on a globalized basis.

Inefficient producers will be forced out of the picture. No longer will there be three or four industry leaders and five or six followers with white fingernails hanging on to the competitive window ledge. Only the top three or four will survive and then only if they are among the most efficient producers world-wide.

Market share-maintenance expenditures will go up for those staying in the game. For example, a major supplier of brake and transmission parts to the automotive industry has discovered that it must spend $20 million on new production facilities just to maintain its share of a specific market in which foreign competition has come on strongly. The big question is: Should it invest and thereby further reduce the profitability and ROI of that segment of its business or should it abandon the segment and invest in more promising opportunities, if it can find them?

Non-tailored marketers that try to offer too many different products to too many different market segments will also lose out. The key to survival will be to find specific niches either here or abroad and then go all out to capture leading positions in them.

Pressure on margins will increase, especially for those trying to serve international markets from disadvantageous operating locations. Mattel recognized this fact of life early on and has maintained its competitive advantage, in part, by aggressively pursuing lower labor and material costs, first in Japan and then, as costs went up there, moving its sources successively to Hong Kong, Taiwan, Singapore, Saigon, and Manila.

Nevertheless, there are still reasons to anticipate new business. Export opportunities should increase as we regain our technological advantage, increase our product quality, and learn how to market more effectively in offshore markets.

Summary

From the foregoing it can be seen that PD management must prepare and position itself for an increasingly dynamic, uncertain, computerized, globalized future. This preparation should focus on (1) further identification of how these factors will influence specific companies, (2) development of management teams and support systems to deal with the complexities presented, and (3) contingency planning, that is, development of alternative strategies and plans to deal with the uncertainties posed. — *W. M. S.*

2.   A Reconfiguration of Logistics Systems in the 1980s: Strategies and Challenges

Introduction

There have been few periods in recent economic history that have both frustrated and challenged the U.S. business manager as much as the period of the past ten years. During this time the businessman experienced soaring prices, recession, and prime interest rates of twenty percent (the highest in history).

Historically, a majority of U.S. businessmen have managed their businesses with three basic assumptions. These assumptions have usually been implicit rather than explicit, but have nonetheless formed a core management philosophy for planning and policy. The first assumption is that there will be a constant opportunity for future growth even if the business only shares in an expanding economy. The corporate forecast (up until the past few years) assumed a 5 to 10 percent-plus growth as a matter of course. The loyalty, attitude, and competency of the executive responsible for the forecast would be suspect if his forecast indicated a declining or even static sales volume.

A second assumption of the businessman has been that energy resources will be low-cost and abundant. Plants were located, production processes selected, and end products designed assuming low-cost and abundant energy resources.

A third traditional assumption is that demand is the engine that pulls the business system. This assumption implies that the only limitation on increased sales and profits is the amount of demand that can be generated. Energy and other raw material resources are assumed to be inexhaustible.

During the past ten years all of those traditional assumptions have been swept away by the spectre of economic uncertainty, OPEC price actions, or political instability in some areas of the world. Growth is no longer a given in the five-year plan of many companies. The price of energy has increased tenfold, and political uncertainty threatens the assured, traditional sources of offshore raw material necessary to fuel the industrial machine.

It is often noted that "hindsight is always 20/20," but even so, what crystal ball gazer in 1970 would have believed that by 1980 the prime rate would triple, oil would cost 1400% more, the inflation rate would double, and the U.S. auto industry would lose more than 25% of its market share?

The objective of this paper is threefold:

1. To explore in a general way the current environment for planning and decision making in U.S. business.

2. To identify some of the important trends in distribution logistics that are occurring in the United States.

3. To evaluate the impact of these trends on technology application and the practice of management in the distribution logistics area.

How Did We Get Where We Are?

It is probably somewhat oversimplified to state that somehow in the last ten years or so the rules have been changed. Several generations of managers in U.S. firms have been carefully nurtured on a base of conventional wisdom with conventional solutions to traditional problems.

In this same period there have been some dramatic and unprecedented changes in the external environment. These changes in growth prospects, resources, pace of technological change, competition, and inflationary impact have changed the ground rules for business planning and execution.

The conventional wisdom developed during the post-World War II period was essentially related to market share and volume in the marketing area, and to profit center and short-run return on investment (ROI) in the financial area. These strategies worked well for 30 years and became embedded in the actions and attitudes of contemporary management. They have also led to an almost conditioned response on the part of management to the typical problems of day-to-day operations. However, when the ground rules change—when time-tested solutions no longer work in an efficient way—conventional organiza-tion, reporting, and control systems also may fall short of the mark.

Conventional wisdom suggests an objective of building a large market share. This in turn leads to a high-volume orientation which often results in locked-in technology. Rapid growth expectations frequently moved a company outside of its areas of competitive advantage and declining margins were a likely result. High service levels typically lead to increased inventories and low asset productivity. A multiple profit center philosophy leads to more divisionalization and ultimately can result in suboptimization. The pressure of a constant increase in earnings per share and dividends forces a short-term orientation and leaves the firm vulnerable to long-run development lapses. The time appears opportune for some new conventional wisdom.

What's Going to Be Different in the Future?

It is not our purpose here to add to the long list of forecasts by management fururologists, but rather to examine some of the structural assumptions. These assumptions are often not an explicit part of management philosophy, but they provide a set of guidelines for management planning and action. A colleague who deals regularly with high-powered operations research and modeling types offers the advice, "Go for the assumptions, not the conclusions."

One of the important characteristics of the management environment of recent years has been a general reduction in available response time. During most of the post–World War II period, change occurred gradually, often spanning a generation or more of managers. In the 1970s, the tempo of change accelerated. In terms of management style this has meant that decision makers no longer have the luxury of sitting back and waiting for a trend to unfold. If the decision maker waits too long the opportunity is lost and the firm finds itself riding the downward slope of the power curve.

The days of the single scenario plan have passed. As the costs of being wrong in a business decision have increased exponentially, the validity of the assumptions that form the foundation for a business strategy have come under more careful scrutiny.

Management decision making is affected by traditional management reactions to a set of issues *and* by pressures from the external environment. A corporate plan has embedded in it some important assumptions about the external environment. For example, as noted earlier, most firms have used an assumption of strong growth rates in their planning. Our recent experience suggests that growth has been spotty at best. Future forecasts suggest a selective pattern of growth for the U.S. industrial base.

Similarly, assumptions regarding resources, rate of technological change, competition, and inflation all require an objective and explicit scrutiny by top management. We have seen rapid changes occur in these areas in the past five years and can expect continuing change in the future.

The management challenge for the 1980s requires an ability to anticipate on the part of management in a very dynamic external setting. While this is neither a new nor particularly profound piece of news, it requires a new style of management. A combination of a rapidly changing external environment, limited response time, and the increased downside risk have created one of the most challenging business environments since the late 1940s. A demonstrated ability to grow—or even to cope—does not mean that all management teams will demonstrate equal skill in anticipating change.

Reconfiguration of Logistics Systems

An underlying thesis of this discussion is that there are major changes taking place in how management views the planning and development of logistics systems for the 1980s. For purposes of this discussion the term "business logistics" is defined as "the design, implementation, and management of total material flow systems to meet target customer service goals at lowest total systems cost."

The traditional structure for manufacturing firms is to have three separate segments within the material flow system. The first segment is the procurement loop and extends from source of raw material to production site. The second segment extends from production site to the end of the production line. The third segment or loop extends from the end of the production line to the consumer or user of the finished product. Traditionally, these three segments have been treated separately in both the managerial and the organizational design sense. However, many firms are now restructuring their materials flow systems in order to coordinate these three segments.

There are a number of objectives of the reconfiguration process. Perhaps the most important objective is to improve asset utilization. The primary focus of improved asset utilization appears to be on inventory assets, but it also includes utilization of fixed investment in the firm. A second objective is to improve the firm's flexibility and efficiency in the competitive process. With rapidly changing end user markets and some uncertainty in the price and availability in supply markets, increased flexibility is required in order to meet competitive domestic and international pressures in the marketplace. A third important objective is to align corporate resources with current and future market opportunity. While this appears to be an obvious objective of business management, the cost of misallocation of resources has increased enormously during the past several years and is very likely to remain high during the decade of the 1980s. If this projection is true, it suggests that strategic planning related to corporate resource allocation has become a paramount issue with many firms and will remain a key management focus in the years ahead. Again, the downside risk of being wrong has increased. Firms who do not deploy assets against market opportunity may well find that the marketplace of the 1980s is unforgiving and does not offer them a second chance for recovery.

A New Management Style for the 1980s

Five basic strategy elements can be tied directly to a reconfiguration strategy:

1. Redefining a sourcing and procurement strategy

2. Tailoring customer service strategy

3. Realigning the physical facilities network

4. Integrating the material flow process

5. Utilizing the information trade-off

The first of these strategies, that is, redefining the sourcing and procurement strategy, involves a number of different activities. As an initial step it requires an evaluation of current vendor location and capability. There is some strong evidence that the traditional buyer-seller relationship between vendor and customers is beginning to change. Instead of regarding a seller as an adversary, many firms are developing strategies to enhance cooperation between buyer and seller in order to ensure long-run stability of supply markets. Some of these strategies involve financial commitments to vendors and, in some cases, actual investment in vendor facilities. A second important element of this new procurement strategy is the development of an asset-based information system. For most firms, 20 to 40 percent of their inventory investment is in raw materials, and an investment of this magnitude has a profound effect on the overall asset performance of the firm. However, even in light of this obvious conclusion there has been little effort expended to control raw material in an asset-based accountability system similar to those used in finished goods. The third element of the procurement strategy is to integrate the purchasing function into the corporate strategic planning process. This, of course, is based on the premise that in the 1980s resource-based corporate strategies will become more important than market share–based strategies.

A second major element of the reconfiguration strategy is the tailoring of customer service strategy. Recent empirical evidence suggests that less than a quarter of large U.S. manufacturing firms have developed management information systems to define and measure customer service standards. This suggests that one key task in the area of customer service is evaluating current service levels as they relate to both asset investment and marketing strategy. A second element of this strategy following from this type of analysis is to develop differential rates of customer service by customer, product, and geographic area. The idea of having a 95 percent in-stock level with four-day delivery for all customers is losing some appeal in the face of rapidly escalating costs. Having rediscovered Pareto's Law, business management is beginning to recognize that the top 20 percent of their customers and the top 20 percent of their product line account for 80 percent of sales. This requires a redefining of customer service levels and leads naturally to a third major point, which is matching customer service investment. Corporate management in the 1980s is more agreeable to taking risks with stock availability and delivery times in the marketplace. However, management does not want to take risks with key customers and key products. What appears to be developing is a philosophy of "selective risk": management is prepared to take risks, but only in those areas where possible service failures will affect only non-critical parts of the product line or marketplace.

The third major element of the reconfiguration strategy is to realign the physical facilities network. Essentially, this involves rethinking the relationship between raw materials manufacturing, marketing channels, and the distribution process. It may well involve a closer integration of international manufacturing and distribution capability. It could involve selection of new channels of distribution for the product with channel ownership or control. It could include a redefinition of manufacturing relationships including the make-or-buy decision, joint manufacturing and distribution facilities, or some hybrid manufacturing system.

The fourth element of the reconfiguration strategy is identified as integrating the material flow process. Important to this integration are improvement of both forecasting capability and accuracy, and the linking of various elements of the process together with some higher degree of certainty in outcomes. This, of course, addresses the frequently encountered problem where sales forecast, production schedules, and distribution requirements are not directly synchronized within the firm. The predictable result is poor asset utilization. A second major element of integrating the material flow process is found in the area of organizational requirements. In an organizational design and behavior sense, integrating the three segments of the total material flow process is a "boundary spanning" function. This has a direct impact on the traditional organizational patterns found in a business and requires some careful planning in evolving an organizational framework for accomplishing this transition. Decisions in this area involve all of the behavior and political problems that surface in periods of organizational change. Firms have reacted to these pressures by setting up separate distribution divisions, by developing matrix organizations, and with various other strategies to mitigate the impact of severe strain in organizational relationships.

The fifth major element of the reconfiguration strategy focuses on the utilization of the information trade-off. This major element is based on the fact that the cost of information is the only major resource available to the manager that has decreased in price over the past 10 years. All of the other major resources such as raw materials, labor, and capital have all increased in cost. Thus, the manager must find a way to affect a resource transformation between information resources and the other basic resources used in managing the firm. This indeed suggests that the manager of the 1980s and beyond will utilize information in the same manner that his or her counterpart in the 1960s and 1970s utilized capital as a major driving element of the production and distribution process of the firm.

An important resource transformation in the 1980s will be the substitution of information for inventory. Traditionally, the manager has buffered uncertainty in the marketplace with inventory. The manager has deployed inventory in the field by building warehouses and filling these warehouses with inventory. In this process, finished goods inventory investment increases and asset productivity declines. In the 1980s it is likely that information instead of inventory will be used to buffer uncertainty in the marketplace. New technology allows on-line and off-line communication with customers and vendors, and a whole range of technology associated with on-line integrated order processing systems provides the technological base for this transition. A number of experiments are currently underway in the United States. The largest test is being conducted in the food industry, where preliminary results suggest that over one-third of a billion dollars a year can be saved in paperwork alone.

A second part of the resource transformation process is the substitution of information for transportation. Until recently, manufacturers and middlemen freely used transportation to buffer uncertainty. Small shipments and premium transportation were used to level peaks in demand or unexpected demand from customers. In the 1980s this solution is proving very expensive and new ways are being sought to solve the problem in a cost effective way. For example, an increasing number of shippers are adapting a "scheduled transportation" system. With this system customers in a specific geographic area must order on a Monday to get delivery on Friday. The shipper schedules transportation so that all of the orders for a given geographic area are clustered on a specific day within a specific timeframe. This lowers the cost of transportation and may actually increase service levels to the customers. The key trigger point in the system is early recognition and transmission of demand requirements (information) by the customer.

A third element of the transformation process for many firms will be the substitution of capital for labor. The marginal costs of both capital and labor have increased dramatically in the past decade. However, the productivity impact of a more capital-intensive logistics system appears to be a better choice than a more labor-intensive logistics system. In short, the marginal productivity of capital is likely to be higher than the marginal productivity of labor. This, of course, suggests more mechanized warehousing, order processing systems, delivery systems, and so on.

The fourth resource transformation is the substitution of computer assisted decision making for human decision making. On first impression one might construe this comment to be a bit Orwellian. It is not intended that way, but rather to emphasize the importance of improving decision making by selectively supporting the decision making process with computer technology. This support might range all the way from an order picking vehicle equipped with a computer input/output device to a cathode-ray tube on the desk of the chairman of the board. As an example, 80 percent of the errors in a warehouse are human errors. Evidence has suggested that the application of technology such as computer input/output devices, high speed electronic weighing equipment, and the like can substantially offset human errors in the warehouse. These are the types of changes that will have high yield during the 1980s.

It should be noted that all of these information trade-offs apply to the front end of the materials flow process as well as the back end. That is, information systems can be used to buffer uncertainty with vendors as well as with customers. It is possible by careful planning and communications to reduce transportation costs of inbound materials and work-in-process materials as well as outbound materials.

Key Managerial Components

There are a number of management challenges presented in the implementation of integrated logistics systems. On the technical side, it requires an understanding of both the available technology and the application of the technology in a business setting. On the economic side, it may require large investment in development, training, and acquisition of equipment. The problem of cost justification for better systems or better information frequently is an issue in the planning process. A third and critical area is the management of change in the organization. Integrated logistics management prompts a new management style for the firm. It is an information-based system rather than an activity-based system. Traditional managers sometimes experience difficulty in adjusting to new tools and new rules. The entire range of behavior influences may surface as impediments to change.

All of these management issues can be solved by effective planning. Careful consideration of both external and internal factors is important to the planning process. However, an acceptance of the planning process as an important managerial priority may be even more important. This is particularly true for managers in the distribution and transportation areas. The very nature of the traditional tasks in these areas promotes a "crisis management" type of management style. These managers are applied, hands-on problem solvers with a typical planning horizon of days or weeks. From this, one might conclude that the key priority in implementing integrated logistics systems for the 1980s is not capital or technology but management skills.

A Concluding Note

In the decade of the 1980s, significant change is occurring in the management of material flow in the business firm both in the United States and in other industrialized countries of the world.

These changes focus on three key issues. First, a comprehensive view of total material flow systems is beginning to replace a fragmented view of raw materials, work-in-process, and finished goods inventories. Second, the information-driven logistics systems are being developed to replace activity-driven systems. The implementation of these systems will require the substitution of information for human resource input, inventory investment, and transportation activity. Third, there is an increased concern with asset productivity as a key objective and performance criterion to measure systems performance. —*B. J. L.*

3.   Challenges and Opportunities for Logistics Executives in the 1980s

This subsection addresses four challenges and opportunities for today's logistics executives: (1) the opportunity to reconfigure our logistics systems; (2) the unprecedented opportunity to anticipate the interests and needs of senior managers; (3) the challenge to managers to think the unthinkable; and (4) the unique opportunity to work our way out of our respective jobs.

Reconfiguring the Logistics System

In the previous subsection Professor La Londe provided an excellent background concerning the changing nature of logistics-oriented costs and their relationships. He observed that costs associated with carrying inventory have risen dramatically in recent years, and that transportation costs and costs associated with product movement have fluctuated widely. Our experiences during energy crises of the recent past have determined our responses to such issues, and will continue to do so, even in times of plentiful supplies.

On the other hand, the costs of movement have also been affected by such factors as deregulation, which has contributed to cost increases for some movements and cost reductions for others. All this suggests that in recent years there has been more change than ever before in the basic cost structures that we have been responsible for as logistics managers.

This is not to say that we should discard our carefully developed concepts of the past. Indeed, the future will provide even greater opportunity to apply some of these concepts.

This era of one crisis after another has had the benefit of calling the importance of distribution to the attention of top management. We will need to examine our distribution systems in terms of the principle of postponing our commitment of inventories to a particular form and place as long as possible. An example of this is the practice of holding canned goods in "bright" form and labeling them at a late stage in the distribution process. He suggested that there were other ways in which we could postpone our commitment of particular stockkeeping units to specific locations as long as possible. This suggests that we may engage in a greater amount of very light manufacturing activity quite close to the point of sale, manufacturing activity that is not asset intensive but that enables us to conserve assets, including inventories, in a variety of ways.

All of these opportunities will become apparent to the senior managements of our organizations and will give rise to a variety of questions that might be asked of us as logistics managers, questions to which we ought to be prepared to respond. They will provide opportunities for us to display our wares as managers and to display the strategic importance of the field of logistics management.

Anticipating the Needs and Interests of Senior Management

What is top management interested in these days? Based on the frequency with which I see books written by my colleagues on the bookshelves of senior managers, we can predict one area of interest. At some point in time these executives are going to ask their respective logistics groups what they are doing in the area of competitive strategies. How does their strategy stack up against company B's, what they are doing differently, and do they understand what company B is doing? There will be an opportunity for us as logistics managers to make major strides if we carefully study what our two or three major competitors are doing. It doesn't require espionage. What it requires is a knowledge of where their plants are, what their approximate capacities are, where their warehouses are located, and what forms of warehousing and methods of transportation they are using. All this can be readily obvious to any observant manager today. Given that set of information, we can construct a reasonably accurate logistics cost profile of our competition.

We are going to be asked often by our senior managers why we aren't doing what the Japanese are doing. We have heard about and witnessed some of the remarkable ways in which the Japanese accomplish distribution. They are remarkable for a variety of reasons, and we cannot expect to emulate all of these practices. But certainly one practice that is intriguing is *kanban*, which I am told means "signboard" in Japanese and refers to the little signs that appear on the carts that bring in small amounts of material to the plant. The signboards contain instructions to the supplier as to the month, day, hour, and sometimes the minute at which that cart is to be refilled and delivered back to the plant once the contents of the cart are exhausted. It is a fascinating concept. Essentially, it has allowed the manufacturing process to be carried out with dramatic reductions in raw material and in-process inventories, something that has significant implications for manufacturing and procurement activities.

The Japanese have concluded that a clean, well-kept manufacturing facility communicates an important message to the labor force about work habits, punctuality, and a variety of things related to that process. Furthermore, it reduces the time spent looking for materials. In many of those systems materials and parts are almost handed from one work station to the next as needed. It has led—so Japanese managers tell us—to a significant improvement in the quantity of the work performed and the quality of the product produced.

We are unlikely to have a wholesale adoption of *kanban* in this country in our procurement and manufacturing processes. The first person who tries it will probably be confronted with undependable delivery schedules. But it certainly is a customer-driven system of the sort that senior management is going to become curious about. And we had better have a good answer for their questions, an answer that has to do with either how we can implement that kind of system or the reasons why it may take a considerable period of time to achieve an environment in which it can be implemented.

Another senior management interest that we are going to have to respond to relates to the area of multinational logistics activity. To a greater and greater extent we are going to be asked about opportunities for supporting manufacturing and sales efforts on a worldwide basis. The competitive environment today demands it in many of our businesses, and it would be important for us to think about ways of organizing and managing that kind of activity.

Research performed in a number of companies suggests that companies that are successful in the management of multinational activities, both marketing and manufacturing logistics, have gone through a cycle of various organizational designs. They have started out typically by exporting, have continued to grow into multinational business activities by assigning certain sales resources abroad, and, at some point in time, have decided to manufacture abroad. It is typically at the latter point that they begin to decentralize their management, setting up what has come to be known as area-oriented organizations.

Companies that produce consumer goods somewhat idiosyncratically for a particular culture may continue to use a centralized organization for a considerable period of time. Other companies may manufacture products in stages at points throughout the world in the most cost-effective manner, and market these products in many areas of the world. Sooner or later these companies tend to evolve into product-oriented organizations. It is in these organizations that logistics management comes front and center in the form of product managers who essentially are worldwide logistics managers dealing with production on a multinational basis. These people will have some of the most challenging jobs in the field, jobs that will be created as American firms become global in their outlook, planning, and execution.

Thinking the Unthinkable

Think the unthinkable. Maybe that sounds too dramatic, but there are a number of things we haven't thought much about. For example, it may be that for some portions of our business, small is beautiful.

Think about what happens in our organizations. We start a business, we're small, we're flexible, and we ship within a relatively small region. Over a period of time we expand our markets; we increase our facilities; we build our volume to the extent that we can support our own efficient, larger manufacturing plants. Perhaps we build our own warehouses in order to achieve the efficiencies associated with handling at least a base load of product through our own facilities. Some of us even acquire private transportation fleets. We build a tremendous operation intended to serve a high-volume, very successful business.

Then we introduce a new product, or we sell a product that may have a relatively small volume to a specialized market on a continuing basis. This product may be quite closely related to our other products, but it doesn't carry the volume or the opportunities for economies of scale that some of our other products do. What do we do? We force it into the monolithic system because it is there and we need as much volume as possible moving through that system in order to help pay for it. This may not be the right way to handle those items at all. In fact, the most effective way to market those products may be to go back to the way we started the business in the first place—to maintain our flexibility by using contracted services. We will need to think more effectively about how to manage those sometimes peripheral items in the product line that consume great quantities of management time. Small indeed may be beautiful for a part of our business.

We may place greater emphasis in the future on the elimination of costs, rather than balancing costs as we have been taught to do through total cost analysis. For example, what if we set out to eliminate reorder costs in the inventory formula, rather than continuing to manage our inventories according to the economic order quantity (EOQ) formula that so many of us have been taught in our courses? You'll remember that EOQ calculations trade off inventory holding costs against inventory ordering costs. What if we eliminate order costs? Or what if order costs fell to such a small figure that they suggested that we carry almost no inventory? Given the dramatic changes in computing and communications technology, we may have an opportunity to move rapidly toward this kind of objective.

While thinking the unthinkable, we ought to at least entertain the idea that the field of logistics, as we define it currently, is in a period of decline. This is occurring as a result of dramatic reductions in the costs of computing and communications. At the same time we see rising costs of transportation and inventory holding. If we're only associated with the asset-based side of operations, we are going to be associated with an activity of declining importance. The most dramatic examples in which communication today eliminates many asset-based logistics activities is in the trading activities that go on among chemical producers and petroleum refineries. Through a worldwide network of information I can, as a manager, trade commodity of like quality that I have in excess at point A with a competitor who needs the same product at point B. If the trading process can be handled in ways that better align raw materials with markets, the need for much asset-based logistics activity can be eliminated. It will be carried out more and more frequently by means of improved communications systems. Forward-looking logistics management must concern itself with the communications-network associated with logistics activities. We may want to give serious thought to recognition of these trends in formulating new definitions of the field in the future.

Working Our Way Out of a Job

One additional unthinkable has to do with the fourth challenge or opportunity that we face as managers in the 1980s. That is the opportunity to lose our jobs. Some logistics managers have been particularly effective at losing their jobs. They've done it through the best of means, by building bridges between logistics and marketing, production, finance, and ultimately general management. They've built these bridges by thinking ahead, by trying to anticipate the needs of top management, by taking a "world view" of the corporation. They have been rewarded by being promoted to positions in general management. The logistics managers who have succeeded over the last decade in losing their jobs in this way have insured that logistics will have a high profile in the activities of their firms. Through this process we will develop cadres of senior managers who are tremendously sensitive to the opportunities that exist to gain strategic competitive advantages through logistics. This is the best way I can think of to insure that logistics managers as individuals will be able to assemble in the 1990s to discuss even more interesting challenges and opportunities.—*J. L. H.*

4.   Emerging from the Recession: The Role of Logistical Management

Introduction

The role logistical managers must play in emerging from the current recession may well represent the greatest challenge they have ever confronted. There are signs that the recession of the early 1980s is at an end. Recovery is well under way. It is clear that business operations will never again be quite the same as prior to the global recession. Many major firms have failed and the survivors have been forced to make major modifications in almost every aspect of their operations.

To gain an appreciation of the far reaching ramifications of this recession upon future management practice, it is useful to trace briefly the development of the logistical concept. The development of business logistics from 1950 to 1983 can be divided into three time periods. From 1950 to 1964 the physical distribution concept emerged and gained widespread recognition around the world. The second, or maturity period, spanned the fifteen years from 1965 to 1979. It was during this period that the concept of materials management joined the arena of physical distribution operations. A careful assessment of the characteristics of the past four years, from 1980 through 1983 provides the foundation for speculation regarding what is ahead for logistics as the world emerges from recession. Each of the three periods is reviewed briefly. In conclusion, six features that appear likely to characterize the future logistical environment will be identified and discussed.

Origination and a New Direction, 1950–1964

The science of Physical Distribution dates back to the early 1950s. Let's reflect back upon the world economy of that period. The dominant feature was growth. Business operations were characterized by certainty and general market affluence. Production capacities were being expanded. The pent-up demand of World War II provided a growth stimulant.

Among industrialized nations the capacity to mass manufacture and mass market during those early years far outstripped our capacity to mass distribute. Most firms could make products rapidly and sell them regularly, but they had difficulty with timely and efficient delivery. Product proliferation, the expansion of product lines, was a way of business life. A good example of the impact of product proliferation is toilet tissue. At one time you could buy two types of toilet tissue, super soft and military rough. By the late 1950s we had two packs, four packs, six packs, and family packs. Product assortment featured colors ranging across the rainbow. Some firms even introduced psychedelics, birds, bees, flowers, and other assorted decorative patterns. The impact on physical distribution operations was awesome. It appeared that only physical distribution managers knew that each item introduced by marketers constituted a separate stockkeeping unit which had to be cared for, warehoused, handled, and transported through the entire distribution channel.

In addition to product proliferation, the marketing people developed a strategy called scrambled merchandising. Scrambled merchandise means the marketing system will sell any product in any place and at any time that is legal, providing consumers are willing to make a purchase. No longer did the long-standing or conventional channels of distribution prevail. At one time if a person wanted to purchase a garden tool such as a rake or a hoe they would go to a specialty store that traditionally offered that category of products. But by the mid-1950s firms were selling garden tools in almost every kind of retail outlet ranging from department stores to supermarkets to discount stores to gasoline stations to hardware stores to garden specialty stores. In short, whatever a consumer was willing to purchase, marketers were willing to sell. Scrambled merchandising does horrible things to the physical distribution process because it diffuses volume. It hinders the capability to consolidate transportation tonnage. The aggregate impact of scrambled merchandising is a proliferation of small shipments here and there and the need for more and more field inventories at more and more warehouses.

These two basic marketing trends, product proliferation and scrambled merchandising, forced the need for a new management logic to help control distribution cost. Physical distribution management was born in a *reactive* posture. The original concepts of physical distribution involved reacting to marketing. Physical distribution management provided the logic to control and contain the costs associated with modern marketing practices.

The costs of physical distribution's support of marketing were enormous. The total cost of physical distribution in the United States consumes approximately 20 percent of our gross national product. For individual firms total cost ranged from 10 to 30 percent of every sales dollar. It became clear that the efficiency of physical distribution was directly related to corporate profitability. To obtain approval to revamp physical distribution systems required top management commitment.

In retrospect, the challenge of effective communication with top management became the physical distribution manager's most difficult task. Accounting systems were not designed to hold the people responsible who were creating most of the physical distribution costs. Many of the costs involved in physical distribution could not be readily identified from traditional profit and loss statements. The initial challenge was to gain top management's awareness of the total cost of physical distribution.

The organization structure that evolved to help contain cost was basically concerned with the control of finished goods. Very little attention was given to work in process inventories or procurement. The main concern was to measure cost-to-cost trade-offs. The challenge was to contain cost in one area, for example warehousing, by spending more or less in another area, perhaps transportation, in an effort to minimize total cost.

Physical distribution began to have an organizational identity in some corporations. But typically the unit created to manage physical distribution was not positioned at a high organizational level. It was not headed by an officer. What developed is classified as a Stage One organization. Under such limited organizational arrangements a manager is given broader responsibility, but not complete authority over all facets of the logistical operation. The notable deficiency of Stage One organizations is the lack of direct responsibility for inventory control. Such early physical distribution organizations typically had control over warehousing, transportation, and to some degree order processing. Few such early organizations were able to directly manage trade-offs between transportation and inventory.

Physical Distribution and Materials Management Maturity, 1965-1979

During the period from 1965 to 1979 physical distribution matured and was joined by materials management. To a large degree maturity resulted from the fact that the customer service requirements became more demanding. Throughout the world, business began to experience a series of economic ups and downs. While a true depression was not experienced until the 1980s, some time periods and geographic areas represented serious declines and prolonged recessions. As operations became more demanding, top management began to ask penetrating questions concerning alternative marketing strategies. The natural evolution was that trade-off analysis moved from a purely cost-to-cost orientation to one that included revenue analysis. Physical distribution managers began to examine marketing programs and ask questions concerning the quantity and quality of planned customer service. This focus on customer service as representing a significant part of physical distribution management did a great deal to create maturity. Physical distribution managers began to participate in inventory management strategy decisions. For example, a critical system design issue involved how much inventory a firm should have, where it should be located, and who should be serviced from each location.

With the focus on inventory, distribution executives began to be concerned with the balance sheet and operating statement impact of their decisions. They began to realize that reduced inventory and accounts receivable would have a positive impact on cash flow. Such an understanding created the realization that well-planned physical distribution operations could significantly improve corporate profitability. Perhaps the most significant feature of this maturing period was that physical distribution executives began to gain respectability among their financial and marketing counterparts. Financial and marketing officers began to look to physical distribution as more than purely a reactive effort aimed at cost reduction or containment. It became common for physical distribution executives to become *proactive* in planning strategies as contrasted to reacting to strategies.

A significant development of the late 1960s was the emergence of the materials management concept. The physical distribution concept evolved from a marketing orientation wherein customer satisfaction dominated. In contrast, the materials management concept matured from the forces of shortages and supply disruptions. In many ways the central thrust of materials management was similar to physical distribution. Both concepts were concerned with the achievement of a predetermined support level at the lowest total cost. Each concept used systems technology as its primary integrative logic. Similar to physical distribution, materials management was quick to embrace a proactive posture to support strategic manufacturing operations. The development of materials management was observable throughout industrialized nations.

A significant factor in the development of both physical distribution and materials management was the rapid expansion of computer technology. The development of strategic and operational computer programs, strategic in the sense of planning, and operational in the sense of management, were vital to the maturity of both concepts. New systems providing order processing and procurement on a real time basis became common.

The significant point is that during the maturity period the development of a customer service perspective, the increased sensitivity to inventories, and the capability to manage effectively through computer technologies began to shift physical distribution and materials management from a reactive to a proactive posture. Within this change came a significant shift in organization to what is referred to as a Stage II structure. An increasing number of organizations were structured to expand control over all components of physical distribution or materials management. The typical span of control in physical distribution included order processing, customer service, finished goods inventory, transportation, and warehousing. The most significant aspect of this organizational shift was the common assignment of an officer such as a vice-president to head the Stage II physical distribution organization. Similar developments in materials management often placed a top level executive in charge of the procurement process. The important point is that the establishment of vice-presidents created a voice in top management circles. These vice-presidents did not talk exclusively about cost reduction or containment. They talked about profit contribution. They communicated with top management in financial terms such as return on investment (ROI). They focused their attention on the challenges of asset deployment and management.

The Recession, 1980-1982

Thus, physical distribution and materials management arrived at the 1980s. Some felt these fields had achieved utopia. The problem was that the 1980s were ushered in by massive uncertainty and the most extensive economic decline since the early 1930s. To adjust to the ever present uncertainty, contingency planning became a major concern. For example, the prime rate varied as much as four points during a single month during 1981. Capital availability became almost as crucial as capital cost. Capital shortage was critical because physical distribution and materials management are capital intensive processes. If you can't get adequate capital you can't put trucks on the highway. You can't build new warehouses. You can't finance inventory. Long-term capital availability and cost remain a significant issue in the post-recession period.

A second area of uncertainty was energy. Logistics represents an energy intense process. For example, in the United States we consume approximately eight million barrel equivalents of petroleum products each and every day to run our distribution procurement system. Much of the petroleum supply of industrialized nations is dependent upon offshore sources. While the post-recession outlook is for adequate petroleum at moderated cost, such stability is directly dependent upon world politics.

Inflation was a third dimension of uncertainty. Most industrialized nations have confronted double digit inflation for a substantial period of time. While some relief is currently in sight, inflation and its counterpart—productivity lag—remain critical problems for the post-recession period. In the United States most industries encountered labor negotiations during 1982. These negotiations were the most critical since the dock workers and the automobile workers first organized and gained the right to collective bargaining. In an unprecedented move, the automobile workers and management reopened and settled contracts in advance of scheduled negotiations in an effort to work out solutions to inflationary and productivity pressures. Trucking contracts were negotiated and settled ahead of schedule for the first time in the history of the Teamsters Union.

A fourth area of uncertainty was and is the future of transportation regulation and its impact upon supply. In many ways deregulation is a limited concern of the United States. In a short period of time, the Motor Carrier Act and the Staggers Rail Act of 1980 were passed. For all effective purposes transportation is now totally deregulated in the United States and it appears that the ground work is being laid to "sunset" the Interstate Commerce Commission. For the first time since 1938 our commercial carriers are not guided by government in the establishment and control of prices. For-hire carriers now compete in the open marketplace with private carriage for the right to haul freight. In the railroad industry, deregulation has helped develop a stronger market posture. For motor carriers, deregulation has resulted in a sorting out period. A number of common motor carriers have gone bankrupt. A reasonable question exists regarding the adequacy of future transportation supply given today's low rate of capital reinvestment by carriers.

A final concern for the future is the impact of increased multinational operations upon business operations. Multinational operations mean a greater commitment to international operations than merely importing and exporting. Progressive firms recognize they must produce and distribute products world-wide to achieve substantial long-term success in growth markets. To gain and maintain competitive superiority and achieve maximum manufacturing economies of scale, it is necessary to capitalize on the inherent advantages of all nations within which a firm operates. Thus, multinational corporations are distinguished by their capability to integrate and control international operations using global manufacturing and marketing strategies. Such "globalism" requires the capability to coordinate complex activities so that purchasing, production, and financing are accomplished in least-cost countries. Such a global perspective has created a need for the development of a logic to guide world-wide logistical management. Specifically, this new logistical logic must be capable of controlling the complex process of asset deployment within and between a large number of countries which have different laws, cultures, levels of economic development, and national aspirations.

A Statement of Strategic Logistical Requirements, 1983 and Beyond

All of these uncertainties—the cost and availability of capital, energy, inflation and productivity, transportation deregulation, and multinational requirements—form the prerequisites for operations during the post-recession period. The critical question is: What should we expect from logistical managers as the world emerges from the current recession? The anser is productivity leadership as the result of innovative solutions to the logistical requirements during the 1980s and 1990s. While it is always difficult to look ahead with any degree of certainty, a few solid trends appear to reflect the emerging nature of future strategic logistics.

Organizational Structure

It now appears clear that a new philosophy and associated organization structure is developing to guide the post-recession period. An appropriate term for what is required is materials logistics management. It is essential to realize that the concepts of physical distribution and materials management were useful when they developed. Both management approaches were necessary to satisfy operational requirements at a specific point in time. However, in terms of future requirements they are obsolete because they offer at best partial solutions to the opportunities of the future.

The materials logistics management notion offers a single logic to guide the efficient application of financial and human assets from material sourcing and procurement into a multi-facility manufacturing and assembly operation and then to direct finished products through multiple channels of distribution to customers. Materials logistics management embraces a single system to manage trade-offs between purchasing, manufacturing, and physical distribution. An example is purchasing in a manner that will provide a balanced two-way transportation haul. The key to materials logistics management is that it offers a way to coordinate multinational operations. In a global perspective logistics becomes the activity that links individual national distribution operations into a multinational system.

It is clear that the business environment of the 1980s will require a different style of management. Organizational patterns in the United States are being modified to meet the new requirements. A Stage III type organization is emerging that is structuring procurement, manufacturing operations, and physical distribution under single management guidance. This organizational logic permits maximum coordination of all trade-offs under a single top level executive.

System Reconfiguration

Concerns regarding network structure could appropriately be labeled system reconfiguration. In the future, much more so than in the past, where and how a firm plans to conduct business will be essential to gaining negotiation leverage. To achieve meaningful changes in performance capability and cost it is necessary to redesign materials logistics systems to minimize assets committed to inventory and to maximize long haul transportation movements.

The result of reducing inventories is typically a greater probability of stockouts as well as a greater magnitude to the stockouts when they occur. When a stockout develops, chances are that it will be longer and impact more orders than might have been the case in a more abundant inventory era. Inventory management is the art of balancing shortages and excessive stocks. Strategies must be developed to avoid situations where 80 percent of the products do 20 percent of the business. Product burials are very expensive, their funerals are long, and there's always somebody who thinks those products are worth having or they wouldn't be in the line. Nevertheless, slow movers must be purged from the product line.

The final characteristics of inventory are far more subjective than the financial characteristics of transportation. The main categories of cost are capital, obsolescence, insurance, taxes, theft, shrinkage, space, handling, and utilities.

The key is that assets committed to inventory, just like any other asset committed to any other aspect of a business, must earn an adequate return. In today's operating environment, the total cost of inventory is 35 to 40 percent of the average value per year. That means, in financial terms, that $1.00 worth of inventory held for one year must be sold for between $1.35 and $1.45 a year later in order to recover costs. A $5 million average inventory carried one year at 40 percent costs $2 million to maintain. Inventories are expensive. The way inventory pressures impact a business depends on the number of stockkeeping units, the geographical dispersion of market areas, product values, uncertainty of supply and order cycle times. These factors vary from one business situation to another.

A key to productivity gains is to reconfigure the system design to maximize inventory asset deployment. From a strategic perspective it is necessary to design logistical systems to improve productivity in coordination with vendor and customer systems. An integrated system performance requires coordination between carriers, warehouse service organizations, and other third party suppliers. This need to develop systems in a way that enables all parties to enjoy synergistic benefits is the hallmark reason why reconfiguration is an essential part of the strategic game plan for the post-recession era.

Reevaluation of Performance Measurement Systems

To improve future productivity it appears essential that profit center boundaries be reevaluated to assure that substantial trade-offs are not neglected between the timing, location, and economy of manufacturing scale and procurement and distribution operations. What is required is the capability to group functions as necessary to capture improvements. The basic notion that the lowest total cost of conducting business may result from short, less than fully optimal manufacturing runs is foreign to a great many managers. The integration of manufacturing, procurement, and distribution economies is beginning to substantiate the existence of a new form of optimality that traditional practices of management have not been able to capture. *Kanban*, the popular logic of Japanese "just in time" procurement is just one approach to the realization of such trade-offs. Without doubt countless other integrative logics capable of realizing cross-functional economies are waiting to be innovated. One of the primary tasks for logistical managers in the 1980s is to develop improved total cost measurement systems. Total cost analysis is an easy concept to articulate, but it's a tough concept to implement. To improve productivity more exacting functional costing techniques and procedures are essential. Future operating strategies will stress selectivity. The key to establishing and maintaining a selective strategy is accurate measurement.

Increased Postponement

A powerful concept for improving productivity is postponement. The logic of postponement has been around for a long time. However, we are just starting to develop systems capable of reaping the benefits of strategic postponement. The concept of postponement is one dimension of the sequence, timing, and scale of operation necessary to support differentiated marketing. At the root of postponement is the economic principle of substitutability. In brief, the two notions of postponement are (1) postpone changes in form and identity to the latest possible point in the distribution system, and (2) postpone changes in inventory location to the latest possible point in time.

The reality of business in the 1980s is that more and more examples of all types of postponement are becoming commonplace. Some often quoted examples are: (1) Sunoco's process of mixing gasoline at retail pumps; (2) the mixing of paint at retail stores to the demand specification of customers; (3) Hiram Walker's process of bottling liquors within the distribution system at field warehouses; (4) the packaging of frozen foods at warehouses; (5) the labeling of silver cans of graded food products at warehouses; and (6) customizing appliances by adding timers, color panels, or ice makers at dealerships.

Such postponement of final manufacturing requires that products be held within the distributor's system, as homogeneous or nondifferentiated items for as long as possible. The cost of final conversion or assembly at or near the point of sale is expensive in contrast to traditional manufacturing economies of scale. However, when all uncertainties and their associated costs are examined, the lowest total cost may favor postponement as contrasted to anticipatory manufacturing and distribution. Given available technology, the future potential for customized light manufacturing operations embedded within the logistics system is unlimited. The decades of the 1980s and 1990s will experience a basic shift from a complex manufacturing to a complex materials-logistics environment.

The timing dimension of postponement also offers new potential given today's available telecommunication capabilities. The application of "real time" features has created a new range of opportunities to postpone the physical transfer of inventories throughout the channel of distribution. These are discussed next.

More Sophisticated Communication

An important opportunity for productivity improvement is to integrate more sophisticated communications into logistical operations. Communication trade-offs are more subtle and difficult to operationalize than more visible trade-offs such as transportation for inventory. A communication trade-off requires full exploitation of data processing technology. The cost of computerized information has been getting cheaper. However, a firm could afford to pay a premium for communication in order to enjoy the benefits that are attainable from high quality and timely information. If a firm could implement trade-offs that reduce assets committed to inventory and transportation any reasonable cost of communication would be a bargain. The key to improved productivity is to provide selective customer service. To achieve this goal it has become necessary to manage customer orders as contrasted to allowing them to impact a distribution system at random. What is needed is the capability to re-work and re-configure customer orders to gain economical logistical performance while meeting customer specifications. In part, such control can be realized by rapid customer feedback.

One large U.S. food processor is constantly ranked in their segment of the industry as being among the tops in customer service. You may be shocked to learn that in terms of satisfying a customer's original order they are very poor. Where they rank very high is that they are the best communicators in their industry. There are no surprises when customers do business with them. They take the order as submitted, evaluate it in terms of what they can and can't do, and then they talk to the customers and work out the differences. Customers are being told every day, "We can't do that for you," "We can't give you that when you want it; would you accept this?" and on and on. The customers love it! What this processor is doing is eliminating surprise while at the same time formulating and configuring an economic flow of products to the market. Customers cannot afford surprises. Customers *can* adapt to almost anything. The power of communication applied in a logistical operating context has the potential to render traditional measures of customer service as textbook relics.

Shipment Reconfiguration

An additional opportunity for improved productivity is shipment reconfiguration. The basic idea of shipment reconfiguration is to expand our traditional theories concerning scheduled distribution and transportation consolidation. Orders need not always be processed in the sequence they are received from customers. The traditional notion of consolidation is to process orders, and drop them on a consolidator who then tries to combine small shipments into larger loads. The potential of improved shipment configuration is to stage orders by computer for release in a manner that maximizes transportation economies. To achieve maximum shipment configuration, computer technology must be exploited to plan aggregate loading, to sequence loads, for scheduling, for priority ordering, and for mortgaging inventories. The essence of shipment reconfiguration is to manage product flow to customers in the most economical manner.

The combination of forces that have resulted from the recession have lead to "an era of transportation negotiation." If a firm has the necessary leverage, a positive impact can be made upon transportation cost. What does leverage mean? It means that a firm has cost effective tonnage that will favorably impact transportation costs. The result is the potential for shippers to negotiate a share of the benefits. Some firms are enjoying as much as a 10 to 20 percent reduction in total transportation cost since passage of the deregulatory acts of 1980. The primary source of increased transportation productivity has been increased negotiation leverage by virtue of shipment reconfiguration.

A Concluding Note

While the years from 1950 to 1983 are rich with accomplishment, it is clear that the post-recession period will demand greater levels of performance. The traditional notions of physical distribution and materials management are giving way to a new logic called materials logistics management. Despite the ever present uncertainties characteristic of today's world, significant productivity improvements appear obtainable providing logistical managers are willing to seek new and innovative solutions to the problems and opportunities of tommorow. Perhaps the single most different feature of the post-recession period is that top management has been conditioned to expect increasingly better performance from materials logistics managers.—D. J. B.

Distribution Planning

Introduction

Planning at two levels in the managerial hierarchy is a competence that differentiates the *good* distribution manager from the distribution manager. The first hierarchical level involves the critical role of distribution in strategic planning for the firm and for its strategic management. The second level involves planning not only for the strategic management of the distribution function, but also planning for the management of the day-to-day distribution operations and tasks. The purpose of this section of the *Handbook* is to help sharpen the planning competence at both hierarchical levels of those who either hold or aspire to positions as distribution executives. To this end, the "general" concepts of planning are transferred from their overall managerial context to create a planning framework in a distribution context.

Three premises have been influential in determining the character and content of the discussions and analyses of the elements of the planning framework. First, most readers have or are developing a strong competence in distribution and probably have been engaged in planning in one way or another, but they are not necessarily knowledgeable in the field of planning. Second, readers need an introduction to planning concepts and their application to a framework for distribution planning. Third, readers want neither a complete treatise on planning nor a cookbook approach, but a melding of those extremes into a how-to-do-it discussion with sufficient philosophical and conceptual content to explain "why" and to make "how" transferable to all situations.

Few, if any, distribution managers would claim to be experts in all of the elements of the function they manage. Most are experts in some of those elements but are knowledgeable in all. This chapter is designed to provide managers with some new information on planning, to improve understanding of the concepts, processes, and usefulness of planning, and to help fit both the new information and the already considerable bits and pieces of planning knowledge and experience into an orderly framework. Accordingly, this section contains three chapters.

Chapter 5 provides a foundation for planning by placing in a modern context an explanation of what planning is and what it does; strategic perspectives of planning are examined in the context of modern functionalism. Chapter 6 introduces certain planning concepts, and then develops three dimensions of the planning process: the development of a conceptual framework for planning; an analysis of the strategic aspects of planning; and the managerial aspects of planning. These two chapters flow into Chapter 7, which is concerned with the implementation and use of plans, especially operating plans.

CHAPTER 5

Planning Perceptions and Concepts

JAMES A. CONSTANTIN

The Planning Imperative

Territorial imperative is a term applied to the instinctive process by which certain members of the wild kingdom sort out their territorial claims, their problems of living together, and their approach to the future of the species. Planning is a consciously arrived at managerial counterpart to the territorial imperative, and it accomplishes similar but perhaps loftier ends with considerably more finesse and considerably less violence: the design of a future for the organization; the coordination and integration of functional activities; but with a view that subordinates functional territorialism to the well-being of the firm.

The effectiveness of the planning imperative for distribution managers depends upon more than just superficial and intuitive knowledge of planning. It depends upon the strategic perspectives managers have on management, planning, distribution as a concept, and logistics management; on an understanding of various concepts of planning; and upon a logical framework for planning. We are headed toward a discussion of these perspectives, concepts, and a framework. First, however, it is desirable to look at the meaning of planning and to examine certain types of planning.

The Meaning of Planning

Four common-sense implications of the word planning point to its meaning. The first is that planning has to do with the future, for few would see any merit in planning for the past. The second indicates a desire to have some sort of influence on that future or there would be no reason for the exercise. A third implication is that planning pertains to change, even if the thrust of the plan is resistance to change. Fourth, planning supposes that a current decision about the future is imminent even if that decision is to do nothing now.

In the context of a managerial function, the act of planning means that managers are going to make a decision today that will help make happen in the future what they want to have happen. Or, it will help them cope with those features of the anticipated future that they can do nothing about. The plan itself is a statement by the managers who make it that they intend to be activists in designing the destiny of their firm, instead of passively accepting whatever destiny has in store. In this sense, a plan is a guide to managerial action, a means of making less uncertain an uncertain future, and a method of taking steps today to position the firm in that uncertain future. While this shows that planning is a process of making decisions about either a desired future or an expected future, it says little about the nature of future desired events to be planned for or the decisions to be made to bring them about.

Types of Planning

Events seem to fall into a natural hierarchical arrangement, depending upon their ramifications. For example, events and their related decisions which affect distribution managers include: (1) those which relate to the objectives and resources of the firm as a whole; (2) those which relate to the objectives of the distribution division and the resources used by it to attain the objectives of the firm; and (3) the day-to-day tasks performed or operations carried on under the jurisdiction of the distribution manager. These three types of events are, respectively, strategic, managerial, and operational in nature.

Planning for those desired future events involves, or should involve, distribution managers in different ways. *First*, they should be involved in the planning at the top managerial level for those *strategic* events which relate to the firm as a whole. One reason is that certain types of plans affecting marketing objectives and processes which relate to customer service are inextricably intertwined with the work of distribution managers. The same can be said for the interrelationships of production and finance with distribution. It is at this level that policies for coordination of objectives of different functional areas should be worked out. The resolution of the conflict of objectives is the managerial counterpart to the territorial imperative of the wild kingdom. Policies to sort out problems of "managerial turf" are developed, and trade-offs for the good of the firm are designed. Another reason for involvement of distribution managers in top level planning is that significant amounts of resources are assigned to the distribution function. These resources may be either in the form of fixed capital (for acquisition of warehouses and trucks) or in the form of working capital (for the payment of public warehouse and for-hire transportation rates) or both.

Second, the corporate plan typically merely establishes parameters for planning for the distribution function; it does not devise distribution plans. Accordingly, distribution managers are responsible for managerial planning within those corporate parameters. While the corporate plan, for example, may establish minimum levels of reliability in delivery, it is left to distribution managers to develop distribution strategies, plans, and policies to meet or beat the minimum standards. *Third*, those managerial plans, strategies, and policies in turn may set parameters for the day-to-day performance of the distribution tasks required to carry on operations. For example, the parameters of performance may require that operations be carried on in such a manner that third-morning delivery to customers in Region A will be made. Those parameters will not tell the warehouse manager where in the building to locate the goods or what time the truck should be dispatched. It is that manager's responsibility to develop operating plans and policies.

The hierarchy of events leads to a hierarchy of plans and a hierarchy of planners. When these three hierarchical structures are melded into one structure, we have a rational and coherent planning framework. The three elements of that framework are strategic planning, managerial control, and operational control. Examples of events that each of the three elements of the framework is designed to cope with will help fix the differences and distinctions among the elements.

The Strategic Element

Assume that the firm recognizes a potential for growth by increased market penetration in the Sun Belt. Only a few of the many questions involving distribution are raised, and they are designed to show the interrelationships with other functional areas. Should a new private warehouse be built in the region to assure timely service? Or should a public warehouseman in the region be used? Or should the area be served from existing facilities at the expense of timely service? The first alternative places a demand on scarce fixed capital for the new facility as well as on working capital for staffing and stocking it. The second alternative only demands working capital for stocking the facility and paying warehouse charges. The third alternative impinges upon marketing plans if longer delivery times are required and may require less capital for inventory.

Without digging below the surface of the questions raised, it is clear that the decision touches the jurisdictions of managers other than just the distribution manager: finance, controller, personnel, marketing. While the decision is a distribution decision involving distribution planning, it is not a decision to be made by the distribution manager. It is a corporate decision affecting distribution but involving corporate strategy and resources and requiring corporate level planning, and probably resulting in trade-offs among functional areas which may in turn result in suboptimizing certain functions in order to optimize corporate effectiveness. The strategic element of the planning hierarchy deals with overall objectives, resources, and policies related to them.

The Managerial Control Element

The second element in the planning hierarchy relates to the management and control activities associated with the ongoing administration of the firm within the parameters established in the strategic planning process. This element is primarily concerned with implementation of policy. The strategic plan may have allocated sufficient resources for the use of one or more public distribution centers in the region to provide a defined level of timely service to customers in the region.

It is now the function of the distribution manager and staff to develop plans and policies for the implementation of the strategic objectives. This involves a series of questions. Where will the new distribution point be located? What distribution center will be used in the location chosen? What performance criteria will be used to assure quality service by warehousemen and carriers?

These decisions also touch the jurisdiction of other functional managers, but if the strategic planning process has been properly managed, the internal conflicts have already been resolved. Accordingly, decisions of these types are distribution decisions and are to be planned for and made by the distribution manager.

The management control element of the planning hierarchy deals with planning for the effective and efficient use of distribution resources to attain the objectives of the firm as a whole. It is at this level of the planning hierarchy that decision rules for operational control are formulated.

The Operational Control Element

The third element of the planning hierarchy is concerned with the performance of tasks within the parameters of plans and policies of the distribution manager. For example, the distribution manager may have established certain policies for *management* of inventory at the new distribution point. The inventory management policies should identify the amount of goods to be on hand to assure the attainment of customer service standards demanded by the strategic plan. While inventory management is a complex function, inventory *control* is a simple task that requires little or no judgment. For example, as a part of the inventory management function, plans should have been made for economic order quantities and vendors to be used, and trigger points should have been established for reordering. Therefore, when inventory falls to the reorder point the simple task of reordering needs to be performed.

Similarly, decision rules for other distribution tasks should have been formulated. Accordingly no judgment is required in what form of transportation to use; the task is to call the proper carrier. Routes for private trucks have been determined; the task is to load trailers on time. Performance standards for public warehousemen and carriers have been determined; the task is to monitor performance and report.

The operational control element of the planning hierarchy deals with the effectiveness and efficiency with which specific tasks are carried out.

Framework and Definitions of Planning

The conceptual aspects of the three elements of the planning framework were developed before precise definitions were given. This was done to provide a "feeling" for the hierarchical nature of the framework, an understanding of the distinctions between its three elements, and to show the role of the distribution manager in each of those elements. Many distinguished planning experts have developed useful frameworks for planning and definitions of their elements. All have certain characteristics in common. The framework and definitions used here were developed by Robert N. Anthony.[1] Later discussions will enlarge upon and complete this barebones framework.

- *Strategic planning* is the process of deciding on objectives of the organization, on changes in these objectives, on the resources used to attain these objectives, and on the policies that are to govern the acquisition, use, and disposition of these resources.

- *Management control* is the process by which managers assure that resources are obtained and used effectively and efficiently in the accomplishment of the organization's objectives.

- *Operational control* is the process of assuring that specific tasks are carried out effectively and efficiently.

Exhibit 5–1 shows some examples of activities included in the framework headings. Professor Anthony's more complete exhibit is shortened and adapted to reflect some specific activities of distribution managers. Those adaptations are marked with asterisks on the exhibit.

These examples, when combined with prior discussions, should make the three elements of the framework more meaningful. It should be noted that the strategic planning activities are oriented toward planning which includes policy making. Those listed under management control involve both planning and control activities. For example, when planning for the management of inventory to meet the corporate marketing objective, the policies of distribution managers necessarily provide bases for control of such things as re-order points, economic order quantities, vendors to be used, and the like. Those activities listed under operational control are almost exclusively control activities which require no judgment. Decision rules formulated as a part of the management control process determine the way the tasks are to be performed.

It should also be noted that while all of the three elements of the framework are discrete processes, they are also a part of a planning continuum. Strategic matters blend into

Exhibit 5–1   Examples of Activities in a Business Organization Included in Major Framework Headings

Strategic Planning	*Management Control*	*Operational Control*
Choosing objectives *Expand the Sun Belt market	Formulating budgets	—
	*Establish budget	—
Planning the organization	Planning staff levels	Controlling hiring
Setting financial policies	Working capital planning	Controlling credit extension
Setting marketing policies	Formulating advertising programs	Controlling placement of advertisements
*Setting distribution policies	Formulating distribution programs	Controlling tasks below
*Use public warehouses	*Selection of warehouseman	*Report performance
*Use private fleet	*Establish transport policies	*Dispatch trucks
*Use for-hire carriers	*Carrier selection policies	*Call carrier
*Product delivery service levels (marketing policy)	*Inventory management policies (order quantities, re-order points)	*Control inventory
Deciding on non-routine capital expenditures *Acquisition of trucks	Deciding on routine capital expenditures *Replacement of trucks	— *Order parts

SOURCE: From Robert N. Anthony, *Planning and Control Systems: A Framework for Analysis* (Boston: Division of Research, Harvard University, Graduate School of Business Administration, 1965), p. 19. Professor Anthony's table does not include those items marked with an asterisk and contains several other examples of activities which are omitted here. This version is reprinted with permission.

management control matters which blend into operational control matters. This could cause some debate on whether certain "gray area" subjects fall into one or the other of the categories; whether something is "strategic" or "management control"; and whether "management control" includes any elements of strategic planning. Such a debate could be as fruitful, conclusive, and entertaining as one on how many multivariates can dance on the head of a non-parametric (to use the statistical era's counterpart to angels and heads of pins).

These definitions of the three elements of the planning framework lead to some significant observations about planners, planning, and plans. *First*, the planners are the top managers of the organization headed by the chief executive officer. In those organizations with formal planning departments, the planners do not make plans—or if they do they shouldn't. Their function is to assist the actual planners. Planning departments do a lot of things to assist the actual planners. They analyze the worlds of today and the future seeking clues to those things which could affect the firm. In doing so they study all relevant aspects of the firm's environment that could affect its future: technology, competition, politics, law, opportunities, pitfalls, whatever. They provide the basic information needed by management to develop or change objectives. They analyze alternative courses for the firm. They respond to specific requests by the planners for analyses. And, they may even actually draft the plans outlined by the planners. But they do not, or should not, plan. One of the best ways to assure a slow death for a corporate plan is for executives to find it on their desks Monday morning.

Second, the definitions clearly indicate that the purpose of planning is to facilitate the practice of strategic management. It is a part of the functional continuum of management: function of the firm—strategic planning—strategic management—management of operations. The function of the firm is determined by the proper response to the classic question of planners, "What business are we in?" In a simplified sort of way, the work of managers can be said to consist of two steps: they decide to do something; they do it. Change underlies the first step, and it is implied that something needs to be done. Here is where objectives are set, policies made, and resources allocated—all to the end of identifying a desired destiny. The second step, "doing it," implies that resources will be used both effectively and efficiently in carrying out the necessary tasks leading to attainment of objectives.

Third, the definitions imply that policy coordination will take place before the fact and that obvious potential conflicts will be resolved at the policy formulation stage. This in turn implies that the hierarchy of managerial roles requires functional area managers also to be managers of the organization in setting objectives, making policies, resolving conflicts, and allocating resources. The policies will seek to assure that all functional area managers act as if they work for the same firm. (A fine objective, often not attained!)

Finally, the definitions reflect the real world of management and planning in both a hierarchical sense and in the sense of a managerial continuum. As pointed out above:

1. There is a hierarchy of plans which constitute a planning continuum—strategic, managerial, operational.

2. There is a hierarchy of managerial roles that constitute a managerial continuum—manager of the organization helping to plan for the organization, manager of the functional area who plans for that area, and manager of the functional area who implements both sets of plans.

It is no longer enough for distribution managers to be qualified just in distribution matters. *Good* distribution managers will also be qualified in planning at both levels, and they should cultivate appropriate perspectives of certain strategic matters.

Managerial Perceptions as Bases for Planning

The quality of a plan depends upon many things, including the quality of input to it. Managerial premises (or assumptions) concerning all those things related to the development of the plan are likely to be the major influences on both the planning process and the plan itself. As will be discussed later, premises cover a wide range of subjects ranging from the state of the technological art through economic, social, legal, political, and competitive relations. Also they are often shaped by the perceptions managers have of various concepts. For example, if managers saw no difference between traffic management and distribution management, a distribution plan would be devoted to transportation strategies designed to reduce transportation costs. Also, in the past managers equated selling with marketing, and production with turning out goods regardless of market design factors.

This section is devoted to a brief examination of four subjects—management, planning, distribution, and logistics—all of which are bases for managerial premises because they deal with concepts and different perceptions managers may have of them. These discussions will enable the reader to see where the author is "coming from" and thus establish a context for later discussions. They will also show the changes that are taking place in thinking about the subjects. In the first three concepts, the traditional line of thinking is discussed under the heading "The Old Orthodoxy" while the changes are discussed under the heading "Modern Functionalism." Naturally, very little space can be devoted to a complete analysis of the points covered, much less to a complete coverage of all points. Some may level charges of "word games" or "hair splitting". Neither is intended, and neither is practiced. Others may charge "dogmatic" or "a pronouncement." Both are intended and both are practiced. There is no room for a scholarly appraisal of "on the one hand, this; on the other hand, that." People have often criticized the professoriate—especially the economics sector—by saying, "I would like to see a one-handed professor." While this professor has two hands, he is writing with one. On the other hand. . . .

Oxbows and Mainstream Management

Anyone who has flown over a river of almost any size knows of the "oxbows" created when the main stream changed its course. Almost everything about the region of the oxbow changes: habitation, topography, vegetation, wildlife. The process usually starts gradually as the river begins to erode its bank or as silting fills the channel. Then a major rain, cave-in, or something causes the stream to change its course. As a result almost all of the natural patterns in the vicinity and even downstream undergo radical changes.

Business history has many illustrations of the impact on firms when entrepreneurial managers chipped away at mainstream management thought, created a new channel of thinking, and left behind managerial oxbows. For example, vertical integration of manufacturing, wholesaling, and retailing was a departure in thinking. Some of those left behind created their own voluntary chains. The creation of the supermarket was another radical departure from traditional thinking. When that movement became the mainstream way of thinking about grocery retailing, it stimulated a new industry, the convenience store. The discount store as a new concept in retailing grew out of the reluctance of mainstream managements to change their way of thinking.

While technological changes have had similar results, our concern here is with the more abstract changes in strategy and other aspects of managerial thinking that can be related to planning because that is our subject. For example our concern is for new ways of doing old things, new ways of adapting the firm to its present environment, and new ways of adapting the environment to the needs of the firm.

Planning is at the heart of management of change. It is through a portion of the planning process that mainstream thought, wisdom, and action are examined; that managers discover potential hazards in the environment that may dictate shoring up of weakness in the banks of the mainstream; and that managers discover potential opportunities by a conscious creation of a new channel of mainstream thought. There are signs in the working environment of distribution managers that indicate that mainstream thinking about distribution *should* change and that it *is* in process of changing. Accordingly, it is very important to their planning that distribution managers become aware of some of the subtle forces that are eroding the mainstream of distribution thought.

Some Perceptions of Management

The Old Orthodoxy

It should be of passing interest to distribution managers that the term "scientific management" was popularized by a lawyer (Louis D. Brandeis, later to become a Supreme Court Justice) in a railroad rate case in 1910. Frederick W. Taylor used it in 1903, but it did not come into widespread use until Brandeis used it.[2] While that term became acceptable in 1910, management scholars and practitioners failed to reach a consensus on some other terminology as late as 1962 at a conference centering on "Toward a Unified Theory of Management." In 1973 they still were having troubles with the subject.[3]

The purpose of this brief historical note is to emphasize that management experts have not been able to come to terms with each other in terminology to the extent of casting it in bronze or even in strong clay. Accordingly, if the acknowledged management theory experts can't agree with one another, perhaps an acknowledged non-expert (this author) can be forgiven for his selective agreement and disagreement.

In a summary of the conference mentioned above Professor Harold Koontz provided a useful conceptual framework for management. The activities that managers do were divided into the familiar functions of planning, organizing, staffing, direction, and control. The subsets of planning were identified as the choosing of goals, policies, procedures, and programs from among available alternatives.

Modern Functionalism

In the July–August 1960 issue of the *Harvard Business Review*, Theodore Levitt wrote of "Marketing Myopia." In that article he took railroad managements (among others) to task for their failure to meaningfully identify what business they were in. He insisted they should have originally identified the business they were in as the transportation business rather than the railroad business. (He was myopically wrong, as will be explained later.)

This would have been more of a *functional* identification of their business rather than a *commodity* or *activity* identification.

The activity identification of a business has a tendency to make managers think rather narrowly about opportunities and threats. On the other hand a functional identification broadens managerial horizons. There are many illustrations of the implications of these broader horizons starting with the field of distribution management. When managers quit thinking narrowly of traffic management, they broadened the field to distribution management which includes the concern for rates and routes. Similarly oil companies began to view themselves as being in the energy business which opened new opportunities. Likewise cosmetics companies now look upon themselves as being in the image enhancement business; McDonald's is in the fast food business, not the restaurant business.

One purpose of the foregoing is to introduce the notion of functionalism in determining what business a firm is in. A second purpose is to use some well understood situations to show that we are not playing word games and splitting hairs about managerial perceptions of managerial activities.

In 1968 the Association of Consulting Management Engineers (ACME) concluded that management comprises three steps: establishing objectives, directing the attainment of them, and measuring results.[4] This is more nearly consistent with a broad functional approach; it would be even more consistent if ACME had used establishing "plans" instead of "objectives." Planning, organizing, staffing, direction, and control are subsets of the broader functions in the same sense that traffic, warehouse, inventory, and other management activities are subsets of distribution management. Also, the set of functions is consistent with our earlier stated view that management basically does three things. It decides to do something (sets objectives), does it (directs attainment of objectives), and does it well (measures results).

Some Perceptions of Planning

The Old Orthodoxy

Since the days of Eve, who was the first mortal planner, people have both planned and have been planned on. When the good guys do it, it is planning; when those in the black hats do it, it is plotting; and when the con artists do it, it is scheming.

Planning and physical distribution came on the scene as modern management functions at about the same time—in the late 1950s and early 1960s. Each grew out of a relatively narrow activity and blossomed into a full function with a broad responsibility. Physical distribution grew from traffic management and similar activities; planning grew from budgeting and the extension of past performance into the future. For the most part, those companies that did corporate planning apparently did it in a rather simple way with the primary tools being forecasting and budgeting, and the plans apparently were based upon a passive view of the future. Markets were forecast for several years ahead, often by extending past rates of change into the future, budgets were prepared based upon the anticipated change, and the results were called long-range planning. Basically this was planning for what was projected to happen at some future time. The result was that instead of managing change, many companies reacted to it and thus were managed by change.

Modern Functionalism

While planning is an ancient art, its use as a tool for managing change and creating a corporate destiny dates from about 1960. For example, eight companies which participated in one study said they initiated corporate-wide formal planning as follows:[5]

Company	Year of First Plan
General Mills	1955
Time Inc.	1961
American Airlines	1961
Raytheon	1963
J.C. Penney	1963
Caterpillar	1964
Norton	1966
Cities Service	1966

David Ewing, in commenting on the newness of the formal planning process, cited other studies made in 1967.[6] A National Planning Association study showed that 85 percent of the respondents were then preparing long-term plans and that well over half of them started work about 1960. Also, Ewing reported, a 1967 *Business Week* study showed that 71 percent of the respondents did long-range planning, many having established their programs during the preceding few years.

Modern planning is based upon the premise that the organization should manage change when possible and seek to make its own destiny. It involves an active and creative approach to analysis of the environment. Either the firm adjusts to the expected environment or it attempts to change the environment to one more hospitable to the objectives of the firm. The assumption is that the firm will first identify those things it wants to have happen and then set out to make them happen. Accordingly, the new functional view of planning is that it is the foundation for strategic management—it helps position the firm in relation to all aspects of its environment.

Strategic distribution planning is primarily an outside thing, for the responsibilities of distribution managers mostly involve coping with matters outside the firm or outside the functional area. For example, delivery times are often established for marketing reasons. Distribution points are located, transportation systems designed, and inventory levels established to cope with those delivery times at the "best" cost to the firm. In short, the framework of a distribution system is established to meet requirements external to the firm. Internal considerations come into play primarily in matters concerning the improvement of efficiency in operation.

Some Perceptions of Distribution

Vertical Integration in the Channel

Only two aspects of distribution perceptions are considered in this section: (1) the traditional concept and role of the channels of distribution, and (2) the apparent orientation of the channel members toward task performance in their relationships with each other.

These represent major areas of mainstream thought which offer opportunities for distribution managers in planning for and managing an integrated distribution system.

The concept of channels held by vertically integrated companies, while substantially different from that of non-integrated companies, serves as a useful device to contrast an integrated system with practices of non-integrated channel members. Also, it is useful to compare "what could be" and "what should be" for non-integrated firms with "what is" for integrated companies. For the latter, manufacturing, transporting, wholesaling-warehousing, and retailing are each considered as integrated elements of a total system. While each element may be considered a profit center for management and control purposes, each has a definite role to perform in implementing the strategy of the firm to attain its objectives. Resources of each element are allocated and deployed and policies written to that end. Certainly, conflicts can arise *which* cause one of the elements to act as if it doesn't work for the same firm the others do. When those all-too-common situations exist, it is not the fault of the system but the fault of managers who allow them to exist. When a firm in effect operates its own channel for the bulk of its business, it plans for the effectiveness and efficiency of the *system*.

At least three characteristics or features of the channel system are important to the integrated firm in planning its destiny. *First*, each of the elements is a part of a continuum starting with raw material sources and going through all of the intermediate steps to the ultimate satisfaction of the user. *Second*, because each intermediary has the same objective—effectiveness and efficiency in attaining marketing objectives of the firm—efficiency of one element is likely to be suboptimized and a trade-off worked out in favor of greater long term effectiveness and efficiency of the system. For example, more efficient use of transportation resources in favor of less frequent deliveries may contribute more to the marketing effort as a whole. *Third*, to enable these trade-offs to work, there is a well-established two-way flow of information on wants and needs of each intermediary. That is, the several channel components apply the marketing concept to each other as both buyers and sellers.

These three features of the channel system of the integrated firm point to the fact the individual components and the whole system that comprises them have one overall function: to support the marketing effort of the firm. That function serves as the basis for the design of an overall strategy set for the system. It also serves as the basic design for acquisition, production, transportation, warehousing, and inventory strategies for the manufacturing, wholesaling, and retailing components. Finally, because of their functional approach, integrated firms view the channel system as a *marketing* channel rather than as a channel of *distribution*.

The Old Orthodoxy

The many firms who have integrated their channel activities in whole or in part have done so with the objective of improving the effectiveness and efficiency of their marketing effort. The characteristics of the non-integrated members of the channel system are almost the antithesis of those of the integrated system.

First, instead of a continuum from raw material to ultimate user, the several elements consider themselves, and are considered to be, discrete units in the channel. Any application of the marketing concept is toward the ultimate user of the product and the channel member that the goods are being sold to. *Second*, each independent intermediary attempts to attain its own marketing objectives by optimizing for itself the efficiency and effectiveness of the transaction with the channel component from which it acquires goods and services and the component to which it provides them. Any trade-offs worked out in the channel are likely to be between immediate trading partners, and the trade-off is likely to favor the short-term interests of the partner with the power. For example, if the retailer has the power, it may dictate more frequent deliveries of smaller sized shipments in order to serve its short-term interests. The impact on manufacturers, wholesalers, warehousemen, and transportation companies and their marketing objectives is of no concern to the retailer. *Third*, the flow of communication about wants and needs of channel members is likely to be limited to immediate trading partners. The marketing concept is likely to be applied only in the buyer-seller relationship if at all.

These three features of the channel system of non-integrated firms point to a number of facts. *First*, there is no integrated view of the *function* of the channel as a whole other than organizations exist out there that produce, buy, sort, break bulk, transport, warehouse, and otherwise engage in activities that cause raw materials to reach a user in the form desired. *Second*, the several intermediaries in the channel have a transactional or operational view of their own function and confuse activities with functions or confuse means with ends. For example, the activities of wholesalers include breaking large lots into small lots, sorting them, creating assortments, and shipping them to the retailer. But bulk breaking, sorting, assorting, and shipping are neither the function of wholesalers nor the ends to be attained. They are means to the end of providing a smooth flow and satisfying wants and needs of themselves, their customers, and their customers' customers. Their function is to support the marketing effort of their customers—at a profit to themselves.

Similarly, the carriers engage in transportation related activities including moving goods. But transportation is a means to an end, not an end in itself. The function of the carrier is to support the marketing effort of its customers. Earlier, reference was made to Professor Levitt's comment that the railroads were in the transportation business and not in the railroad business. In fact that is not their business at all. They are in the marketing support business; transportation is merely a generic activity; and rail transportation is one subset of that transportation activity.

Third, channel strategy, as it is typically viewed, seems to be concerned primarily with the number, type, and location of agencies to be used in moving goods through the channel. Once those strategic determinations are made, emphasis shifts to an operational orientation that bypasses a second set of strategic determinations which relate to the function of the channel. The missing strategic link involves the way the channel as a whole and its individual members can best serve their function of market support. When those functional strategies are devised, plans for efficient management of the activities can be developed. One possible explanation for this missing strategic link may be the narrow interpretation of the channel function as one of *distribution* instead of *marketing*.

Modern Functionalism

The modern functional approach to distribution planning, management, and operation is very easy to identify. It is nothing more—and nothing less—than the application of the *conceptual* approach used by the integrated organizations. Its strategic characteristic is the recognition that the function of the channel is to support the marketing efforts of its members. Its requirements are (1) a channel system orientation and (2) consideration of the marketing environments of the several members of the channel. Exhibit 5–2 summarizes prior discussions of characteristic perceptions of the channels of both vertically integrated and non-integrated firms.

Exhibit 5–2   Some Characteristics of Channel Perceptions

Characteristics	Integrated Firms (Modern Functionalism)	Non-Integrated Firms (The Old Orthodoxy)

1. Perception of channel components
  Application of marketing concept
	1. Each component a part of a continuum
	  Multidirectional among all components
		1. Each component a discrete entity
		  By seller to buyer, if at all

2. Objectives of the firm
 	
  Trade-off beneficiaries
 	
  Time horizon
	2. Effectiveness and efficiency of channel system
	  The system
	
	  Long term
		2. Effectiveness and efficiency of each component
		  The channel member with power
		  Short term

3. Communication flow	3. Multidirectional among components	3. One-way from powerful member

4. Function of channel
  Strategic orientation
 	
  Nature of the channel
	4. Support marketing effort
	  Design a system and component strategies
	  A *marketing* channel
		4. Perform activities
		  Design transactions for efficiency
		  A *distribution* channel

The concept of the channel held by integrated firms is what is called here "modern functionalism" even though it is an age-old concept that was used in whole or in part by the operators of merchant ships who had their own buying agents abroad, sent their own ships after the goods, brought them to their own warehouses, and sold them through their own facilities. Somehow, the concept of a total system got lost in the move toward division of labor and specialization of activities. While integrated companies have regained the concept, non-integrated components of the channel have not.

Certainly, non-integrated firms cannot function completely in the way integrated firms can. Earlier an example was given of a trade-off which involved improving transportation efficiency at the cost of less frequent deliveries to improve long-term effectiveness and efficiency of the integrated firm. Few if any expect an independent transportation company to operate inefficiently voluntarily merely to create greater efficiency and effectiveness for others. Nor would any reasonable person expect any other independent component of the channel to act in that manner for that reason. (They may do such things but only for such competitive and marketing reasons as to attract or retain customers—not for altruistic reasons for the good of the channel.)

Functionalism in Distribution Planning

In 1976, the National Council of Physical Distribution Management (NCPDM) took a major step away from the old orthodoxy and toward modern functionalism. In that year it made important changes when it redefined the field as follows:

> Physical distribution management is the term describing the integration of two or more activities for the purpose of planning, implementing and controlling the efficient flow of raw materials, in-process inventory and finished goods from point of origin to point of consumption. These activities may include, but are not limited to, customer service, demand forecasting, distribution communications, inventory control, material handling, order processing, parts and service support, plant and warehouse site selection, procure-

ment, packaging, return goods handling, salvage and scrap disposal, traffic and transportation, and warehousing and storage.

The earlier definition read:

A term employed in manufacturing and commerce to describe the broad range of activities concerned with the efficient movement of finished products from the end of the production line to the consumer, and in some cases includes the movement of raw materials from the source of supply to the beginning of the production line. These activities include freight transportation, warehousing, material handling, protective packaging, inventory control, plant and warehouse selection, order processing, market forecasting and customer service.

The revised definition adopts a functional posture for the field and expresses concern for all elements of the channel when it refers to integration of activities for planning the flow of goods from origin to consumption and even mentions return of goods and scrap disposal. Note how this differs from the earlier more orthodox approach which emphasized efficient *movement of finished products* outward from the end of the production line. Also, note that only in some unidentified situations was supply to be included. Third, note how the activities were merely listed with no reference to integration. The professional people writing and adopting the revised definition were not playing word games or splitting hairs in making these changes. There are still two flaws remaining in the revised definition. First, it would have been desirable to have abandoned the words *physical distribution* with its outbound connotation in favor of the more inclusive world *logistics*. Second, the addition of the word *effective* to the phrase *efficient flow* would have tied the subject clearly to the real function of the flow. It may be desirable to trade off a certain amount of efficiency in order to be effective (or vice versa).

Even earlier, in 1961 Lazo and Corbin were addressing the subject of a "truly customer-oriented channels policy." They said:

The essence of the marketing concept is of course *customer orientation* at all levels of distribution. It is particularly important that customer orientation motivate all relations between a manufacturer and his customers—both immediate and ultimate. It must permeate his entire channels-of-distribution policy.

. . . Their very *mutuality of interest* demands that the manufacturer base his distribution program not only on what he would like from distributors, but perhaps more importantly, on what they would like from him.[7]

Without specifically using our term *marketing support*, Professors Lazo and Corbin were referring to that concept in their emphasis on two-way communication.

There are several impediments that stand in the way of introducing a functional concept of channels into distribution planning.

1. The failure to recognize the true function of the channel narrows managerial options in relationship with other components. Recognition that the function of the channel is to support the marketing effort of its members will help remove this impediment.

2. Similarly, the traditional concept of the marketing channel encourages managers to think of other channel members as discrete components. Recognition that the components constitute a continuum as visualized by the revised NCPDM defini-

tions reference to the flow from raw material stage onward will remove this impediment.

3. The failure of transportation and warehousing companies to define properly the business they are in inhibits their marketing oriented thinking. This problem will be overcome when they realize that each is in the marketing support business and that their activities are means to an end, not ends unto themselves.

4. There is an apparent assumption that only integrated companies can integrate distribution activities among the components of the channel. Multidirectional application of the marketing concept among components will make it possible to circumvent many of the conflicts—certainly not all.

Some Perceptions of Logistics Management

A Note on Terminology

Until now the terms *distribution, distribution manager, physical distribution*, and *channels of distribution* have been used. Distribution is a narrow and very precise word that does not embrace all of the things implied by its usage. From this point the more inclusive word *logistics* will be used in place of physical distribution. Logistics has a dictionary definition of "having to do with moving, supplying, and quartering troops." Business has adapted the term also by widespread use, so that business logistics has to do with all those things covered in the NCPDM definition of physical distribution. For similar reasons, *marketing* channels will be used in place of *distribution* channels. The broader—and more accurate—terms will make it possible for the logistics manager to consider more options in logistics planning. The modern functional approach is important to logistics planning at the strategic, managerial, and operational levels.

Strategic, Managerial, and Operational Perception

At the strategic level it is important to recognize the marketing support function of the channel and its independent components. This leads to a greater awareness of the application of the marketing concept throughout the channel. The full value of that concept can be realized if the total marketing and logistics needs and wants of customers and their customers are recognized and taken into account in the development of strategic plans.

Marketing patterns and processes are the outward manifestation of marketing objectives and strategy. It is in the logistics aspects of marketing processes that conflicts of objectives among components of the marketing channel arise. If logistics planners understand both the marketing plans and operations of their customers, some of the conflicts can be coped with to the advantage of all concerned. Otherwise, the component with the power will optimize its operation; the less powerful will suboptimize.

At the managerial level, transportation and warehousing are major elements involved in logistics planning. Many manufacturers and wholesalers especially, but also retailers, have the option of providing their own transportation and warehouse services or using for-hire carriers and public warehouses. As users, they do not have to be fully integrated firms, nor do they have to be very large to bypass the for-hire groups. Many firms with sales of under $5,000,000 use private trucks and warehouses for much of their business. Their reasons for performing these services for themselves center almost exclusively on the inability or unwillingness of the for-hire segment to meet the marketing wants and needs of their customers as those customers see their wants and needs.

Logistics planning for managerial control by carriers and warehousemen should center on three basic points, all consistent with the business they are in—the marketing support business. *First*, they should consider themselves to be, in effect, extensions of the arms of their customers' firms and determine how they can fit into the users' logistics systems. *Second*, they should anticipate users' needs and wants and attempt to design transportation and/or warehousing packages to meet them. It is noted in passing that this is exactly what users do when (1) they set out to market their product, and (2) they determine to provide their own transport and warehousing service. *Third*, they should integrate users' marketing and logistics needs and wants with each other and with their own service capability.

At the operational level, transportation and warehousing companies are at the crucial stages. Here they get down to the nitty-gritty, or they look at the bottom line—or whatever expressive term is in vogue. This is where strategic and managerial planning levels are translated into operational plans and find their payoff. Again three basic elements are involved: (1) cost management with its implications for cost and service trade-offs; (2) effectiveness of customer service; and (3) efficiency of operations. The term cost management poses another problem with words and word meanings. Too often *cost reduction* and *cost control* are the terms used when *cost management* is better. Cost management is both an art and a science. It includes cost reduction, cost control, and even cost increase. It becomes an art when the logistics planner and manager is able to increase certain costs selectively and at the same time increase profits either by attracting or retaining customers through better service or by reducing higher costs elsewhere in the organization. It is a science when costs can be accurately determined and when adequate control systems are established for monitoring and controlling them.

Any half-baked idiot with authority can reduce costs with the order, "Cut costs six percent across the board." The *first* step in developing the operational segment of logistics planning by carriers and warehousemen is the abandonment of cost reduction as a basic concept and the adoption of the operating concept of cost management with its three subsets of cost reduction, cost increase, and cost control. More options are open to the logistics planner and manager for cost and service trade-offs. This step is directed toward blending the ideal of what the customer wants with the reality of what the carrier can provide. The *second* phase of operational planning is to use the cost and service trade-offs as a handle to assure that customer service objectives are effectively attained. This step is outwardly oriented toward keeping customers happy by fulfilling promises made to them and meeting their expectations. The *third* step is to perform the service efficiently. It has an inward thrust and its effects are felt directly in profits.

While perceptions of planning at the strategic level were generalized to all channel components in the above discussion, those at the managerial and operational levels were applied specifically to transportation and warehousing firms. This does not imply that the several factors considered are in the exclusive province of transport and warehouse planners. Logistics planners of user firms are actively concerned with exactly the same matters when they plan for private carriage and warehousing. Also, they are passively involved if the for-hire firms are doing their planning properly. Their involvement includes (1) furnishing information to the planners of the for-hire firms on marketing wants and needs, marketing processes and patterns, and on appropriate logistics matters; and (2) helping develop ways of circumventing as many as possible of the problems arising from conflicts in objectives of user firms and supplier firms.

Conclusion

Several points emerge from the preceding discussion.

1. Proper planning is the only way we now have of attempting to provide a basis for managing change and to some extent determining the destiny of the firm.

2. Planning is the making of decisions today that will affect the firm in the future.

3. There is a planning hierarchy with three levels, each of which deals with different subjects on a functional, strategic, managerial, and operational continuum.

4. The managers are the planners and thus constitute a managerial continuum in that they help make the plans for the organization and implement them through their functional areas.

5. Their perceptions of certain concepts are important tools managers bring to the planning process, and it is nearly vital that those perceptions be functionally rather than operationally based.

6. Changes in mainstream management thinking are creating a series of managerial oxbows in the stream of management thought.

   a. In management, the primary functions relate to setting objectives, attaining them, and measuring results. Organizing, directing, staffing, and the like are subsets.

   b. In planning, the objective is to plan to make happen those things managers want to have happen. Extending the past into the future is no longer desirable.

   c. In distribution, the term *distribution* inadequately describes what logistics managers do, and the term *channels of distribution* describes half a bird with half a wing. *Marketing channels* provides a better description of what goes on in the channel.

   d. In logistics management, independent members of the channel can be treated in a fashion similar to the way vertically integrated firms treat their "channel" components.

7. The function of the marketing channel is to support the marketing effort of members of the channel.

8. Members of the channel should consider themselves as interdependent parts of a channel continuum, not as discrete activities.

9. Transportation and warehousing companies are in the marketing support business, not the transportation business.

10. Recognition of the functional aspects of logistics management and the institutions it deals with broadens the opportunity horizon for logistics planners and managers.

Notes

1. Robert N. Anthony, *Planning and Control Systems: A Framework for Analysis*, (Boston: Division of Research, Harvard University, Graduate School of Business Administration, 1965), pp. 16–18.

2. Marian V. Sears, "Management," in Anthony, *Planning and Control*, pp. 118–120, Appendix A, Notes on Terminology. These notes summarize divergent points of view that appear in the literature regarding the field of management. Unless otherwise stated these "notes" are the basis for references to historical aspects of management thought.

3. Fred Luthans, "The Contingency Theory of Management: A Path Out of the Jungle," *Business Horizons* (June 1973), pp. 67–72.

4. Dale D. McConkey, "MBO—Twenty Years Later, Where Do We Stand?" *Business Horizons* (August 1973), p. 27.

5. A. Chapman Dix, Will E. Kaffenberger, and John L. Withers, "Start-up and Evolution of Formal Planning Systems," in David W. Ewing, ed., *Long-Range Planning for Management*, 3d ed., (New York: Harper and Row, 1972), p. 69.

6. David W. Ewing, *The Human Side of Planning* (London: Macmillan, 1969), p. 5.

7. Hector Lazo and Arnold Corbin, *Management in Marketing*, (New York: McGraw-Hill, 1961), p. 379.

CHAPTER 6

A Framework for Logistics Planning

JAMES A. CONSTANTIN

Introduction and Plan of Work

The shortest of the good books on planning takes 130 to 160 pages to cover the subject; others range up to 795 pages. One of the objectives of the planning section of this *Distribution Handbook* is to put in the perspective of distribution planning certain environmental elements of the channel with which distribution people must cope, and therefore must plan for. One of the premises underlying the objectives of this section is that readers need an introduction to planning concepts and elements of the environment which impinge upon distribution planning and functioning. To attain the objective it is necessary to do two things: (1) deal with the appropriate "environmental elements of the channel" which impinge upon logistics planning and functioning; and (2) relate them both to the framework of the plan and to the steps in developing a plan. Both of these things have to be done in about 10 percent of the space even the shortest books allocate just to planning; so both of them are necessarily incomplete. Here is the plan for coping with the situation.

1. Recognize that the basic elements of the framework have already been presented in Chapter 5.

2. List and annotate the steps in planning to enable readers to become more familiar with the general nature of the process.

3. List some objectives of strategic planning for the logistics function to enable readers to develop a preliminary understanding of some of the substance of the subjects to be covered.

4. Comment briefly on previous observations about the need to adopt a functional concept of the firm and of logistics in order to plan properly.

These steps are to be handled by either listing or by making very brief comments. They will serve as points of departure for the other steps.

5. Present a framework for the development of information concerning the relation of logistics channel institutions and the total environment in the context of overall corporate planning.

6. Present a micro model for a logistics planning framework by relating the structural elements of the environment to the structural elements of the planning framework and the types of subjects which are candidates for inclusion in the logistics plan.

7. Conclude and briefly summarize.

There is a reasonable parallel between building a working plan and erecting a working building. Both start with subsets of a basic framework. The steps above allude to the subsets of the planning framework. The subsets of the building framework are the building plans, foundation, walls, and roof. No framework exists for either until the subsets are tied together; and the framework for each has to be fleshed out before either is a useful finished product.

Before developing these steps, it is appropriate to consider a few important concepts that underlie planning. These have been stated or implied in various places in Chapter 5, but mentioning them in a plan-making context will help underscore their importance.

1. *Effectiveness* in attaining goals and *efficiency* in resource use are assumed to be desirable aspects of the systems approach.

2. The *systems approach* is a technique for bringing together diverse activities to perform a specific function effectively and efficiently.

3. *Function* is a broad term that refers to the normal or characteristic action of something, such as a special duty or performance required of something in the course of work or activity. For example, the function of the digestive system is to facilitate the digestive process. The function of logistics is to support a marketing effort.

4. An *activity* is one of several specific actions which, as a group, perform a function. For example the activities of the stomach, liver, and other organs work together to perform the function of the digestive system. Order processing, transportation, and other activities of the logistics manager work together to perform the logistics function.

5. *Functionalism* is a theory or practice emphasizing the necessity of adapting the structure or design of anything to its function. For example, in planning functionalism is the adaptation of the structure or design of the firm and/or its environment to accomplish its objectives.

6. The *function of management* is to acquire and manage resources effectively and efficiently in attaining its objectives.

7. The *function of planning* is to develop a product which will help management make decisions that will influence the future and the destiny of the firm.

Elements of the Planning Framework

The Basic Framework

The skeletal framework for planning consists of several subsets. The first subset concerns the hierarchy of plans. This hierarchy was introduced in Chapter 5 and was shown to consist of *strategic planning, managerial control,* and *operational control.* The second subset concerns the external environment in which the firm exists. Because perceptions of elements of the environment influence managerial interpretation of the results of environmental analysis, these perceptions are a third subset of the overall planning framework. The fourth subset is concerned with the elements of both the external and internal environment and their role in logistics planning. These are the four interdependent subsets of the overall planning framework. In the following pages each will be discussed separately, tied together into a coherent framework, and "specifications" for fleshing it out will be identified.

Steps In The Planning Process

Functional Steps

The first five steps in the planning process are labeled functional because they establish the function of the organization and because they help set the functional tone of the entire plan.

Step 1. Establish the concept of the organization. This is a statement of the *purpose* of the organization which establishes its philosophy. Some refer to it as the "grand design."

Step 2. Determine the *mission* of the organization. The mission statement establishes the central thrust of the organization both by defining the market and by indicating what the firm is going to do for whom. Charles H. Granger cited the philosophy attributed to Theodore Vail when he set out to create AT&T: "We will build a telephone system so that anybody, anywhere, can talk with anyone else, any place in the world, quickly, cheaply, and satisfactorily."[1]

While the statement of purpose of the organization is at the top of the hierarchy of aims, it often blends into the mission in such a way that the two are indistinguishable. In fact many planning experts make no distinction between purpose and mission. One distribution center made the distinction. It stated its purpose and mission:

Purpose: To support the marketing effort of our customers everywhere through innovative strategic, managerial, and operational leadership in all facets of our industry; to improve the effectiveness of the distribution system and the efficiency of the several distribution processes.

Mission: To be in all facets of the industry necessary to fulfill our purpose and meet market requirements.

Statements of this type—the motherhood type—by their nature are abstract because they deal with abstract concepts. They are as abstract as "good service at low cost," "reliable performance," and "ample stock on hand." However, by further refinements through policy statements and quantification of objectives they become concrete.

These are statements which position the firm strategically. Logistics managers may not be involved directly in their preparation. However, mission statements should be prepared for the logistics division in order to identify its central thrust. It is very important that the logistics mission be stated in terms that reflect the stated or implied objectives of the firm. Each of the following logistics mission statements may be in line with stated objectives of the firm, even though as a generalization each is faulty: "To assure the lowest costs of acquisition, holding, and distribution of the company's inbound and outbound products." "To assure the highest quality of service to the company and its customers in acquiring, holding and distribution of . . . products." A more fitting generalization in the form of a *purpose* covers both cost and customer service: "To support the marketing effort of the firm in a manner consistent with financial and other objectives of the firm." This purpose can be followed with a mission statement which picks up on the support notion as well as relates it to the several logistics activities. "To provide logistical support through. . . ." Here the logistics activities can be fed into the statements as can the logistics relationships with vendors, customers, and customers' customers.

Step 3. Develop planning premises. These are critical in developing not only the plan itself but also the plan for planning. Basically premises are nothing more than guidelines (or standards or assumptions) for writing the plan. These guidelines are derived from information developed about all relevant aspects of the environment as a result of what is often called a *situation audit*. George Steiner put premises in four major categories:[2]

1. Expectations of outsiders including customers, suppliers, stockholders, and society, among others.

2. Expectations of insiders including top managers and hourly workers.

3. The data base reflecting past and current performance of the firm and forecasts of the economy, the industry, the firm, and any other relevant aspects of the environment.

4. Evaluations of the perceived threats and opportunities in the environment and of the company's strengths and weaknesses as they pertain to threats and opportunities.

While premises derived from information of all these types are important, only managerial expectations are singled out for further comment here. These expectations are derived from the value systems of the top management group, sometimes from the top manager. These are the people who make the rules. A horror story—selected because it is extreme—dramatically illustrates the point. In the World War II period, the chairman of Montgomery Ward became enamored with economic forecasts that predicted a major depression following the war. He decided to hold cash until the expected depression was well underway, and then begin a major expansion program. Year after year he waited for costs to fall to a sensible level. Cash accumulated, the depression didn't come, competitors expanded, building costs rose, and Ward's expansion was delayed.

That he was so wrong is not the point; many have been wrong before. (Besides, he was in distinguished company.) The point is that *he* made the rules. This brings up another point previously made and which will be made again: Managerial perceptions are major factors which absolutely must be given major attention in planning. In fact, as the horror story illustrates, regardless of what facts show, if the top people say there is to be a depression, there will be one as far as the plan is concerned.

In this connection, David Ewing wrote:[3]

> One of the most tragic illusions in planning is that "hard facts" alone can determine what goals and courses of action should be taken. Again and again we hear statements such as "The company's peculiar strengths and weaknesses determine its optimum strategy." This is nonsense.

Ewing's reason for calling the notion nonsense is that the analysis does not determine strategy. Managers do, and their values, attitudes, and perceptions of matters determine their interpretation of data and thus their strategy.

The logistics field is an excellent case in point. As an integrated discipline it is only about two decades old. It moved from almost sole concern for rail rates and routes to transportation considerations, to physical distribution as a cost reduction technique, to a profit-oriented concept, to a customer service-based marketing tool. There are positive signs that it is now moving into a functionally based logistics concept oriented toward marketing support.

Step 4. Set objectives for the firm and for functional areas. The corporate objectives establish parameters and guidelines for logistics objectives. There are two broad types of objectives: standard operating objectives and what Merritt L. Kastens calls developmental objectives.[4] The operating objectives usually relate to sales, earnings, and profitability for the firm as a whole. These are easily quantified. Logistics managers have their counterpart objectives, also easily quantifiable. They include such things as a desired level of performance and reliability standards, cost-volume relationships, and return on logistics assets.

The developmental objectives deal with the long-term structure and development of the company. These are the objectives stated when the company decides to design its destiny—to make happen those things it wants to have happen. Logistics managers also have their own developmental objectives. These may include such things as developing better communications systems and techniques with public warehousemen in order to improve the quality of inventory reporting and to improve their order processing and delivery time. One firm installed a computer in the office of at least one of its public distribution centers. Orders were entered in the distribution center computer as soon as they were received at the regional office, making possible same day delivery in many cases. Other steps may involve increasing mechanization in company-owned warehouses, and reducing or increasing reliance on for-hire carriers and warehousemen.

Step 5. Plan the planning effort. Like other managerial activities, the effectiveness of the planning effort depends upon how well planned it is. Here are the basic requirements, some of the characteristics, and the fundamental steps involved in planning for planning.

1. The chief executive *must* be totally committed to the value of planning. In the case of logistics planning, this means the logistics manager.

2. Other involved managers must have a strong commitment to the value of planning, a strong desire to keep their jobs, or a strong sense of responsibility to doing a job well that they may not want to do at all.

3. Everyone involved should recognize that planning is designed to manage change as well as to control the firm's destiny.

4. The process of selecting objectives is an interactive one. It starts at the top, goes through the ranks to the bottom, and back up again. This ensures the participation of everyone who should be involved, and the development of new ideas from others. Of course, not everyone will be involved in every item being planned for.

5. While it is important to have projections of markets, the economy, and the like as finely tuned as possible, it is equally important to recognize that a lot can happen in three years or five years to make the projections way off. Accordingly planners should not allow projections to become their masters.

6. Specific tasks should be assigned to specific people with deadline dates for completion. Otherwise, the process will go on and on from one extension to another.

7. Everything should be in writing.

8. A contingency plan to cope with unforeseen developments should be prepared.

Operational Steps

The functional steps provide the foundation and philosophical framework for the plan. In a real sense they establish the strategies and policies underlying planning. Operational steps involve the process and are designed to show the activities the planners engage in.

Step 6. Develop plans, strategies, and policies to attain objectives. These will, of course, be tied to both the primary operating objectives of earnings, sales, and profitability and the several development objectives. It is possible that in certain instances the three primary objectives will not be directly related to each other, but except for a brief illustration, we are going to assume that they are interdependent, not only with each other but also with at least some of the development objectives.

An objective to increase earnings can be attained in several ways: increase advertising, decrease costs by improving efficiency, develop a new product, buy another company, sell a part of the company, enter a new territory, and on and on. Similar listings of alternative ways to increase sales and profitability can be made. This gives an idea of the almost unlimited number of alternatives available for the one objective. Some of those alternatives can be disposed of or selected easily. For example, if management has been doing its job well, the first three alternatives—increase advertising, decrease costs, develop new products—should be under control. If the remaining objectives appear to be consistent with the purpose, the process of analysis can begin. This process will relate objectives to each other, to any of the development objectives that are appropriate, and to the purpose and mission. They will then be tested against the planning premises discussed in Step 3. Then the alternatives will be checked to see if they are in conflict with existing objectives of the company, and conflicts can be worked out.

Remember, the mission, purpose, objectives, and plans establish the central thrust and a route for the company. But neither the thrust nor the route should be considered immutable. The plan should be flexible—it could be thought of as, in effect, an interstate highway with many "on" and "off" ramps that can accommodate changes in direction as new opportunities or threats are uncovered. Once more, emphasis is given to the importance of having a contingency plan ready to cope with unforeseen emergencies.

The selection of objectives is itself a strategy for change. After this strategy has been decided on, a strategy for implementation has to be devised. In a very real way, when a particular objective is selected the strategy for implementation is already built into the objective. For example, suppose that the objective selected for increase in earnings was to enter a new territory. Before that objective could be analyzed meaningfully, the planning staff would have prepared a study of the cost, effect, and method of implementation. In those cases, the selection would be of an "objective package" consisting of the objective, strategy for implementation, study of feasibility, and so on.

Among the analyses required to consider the new territory would be a series of logistics alternatives discussed earlier: service levels in new territory, the use of private or public warehousing and transportation, and so on. The results of these logistics analyses and the most desirable logistics alternatives would have been a part of the objective-selection decision. Accordingly, when that decision was made, at least a part of the logistics, marketing, financial, and other strategies would have been a part of the strategy to attain the objective.

Policies then have to be developed that will assure coordination among the several functional areas involved. Finally, all of these have to be put in writing.

Step 7. Develop systems for evaluation and control. To keep the plan from becoming "cast in bronze" a system to provide for periodic review should be established. This system will do several things. It will see if the company is progressing according to plan, and if not, it will provide a means for both determining the causes and setting in motion corrective procedures. In addition, contingency plans should be worked out, either as a part of this step or as an independent step.

Step 8. Develop systems for the periodic review of the purpose, mission, objectives, plans, and policies. While Step 7 is concerned with review and evaluation of a particular plan, this step is concerned with everything about the company and its direction. Should the purpose of the company be changed? Its mission?

Step 9. Develop implementation plans for the logistics function. Planning experts differ on their interpretation of functional area planning. Some say that functional managers should plan for their function at the strategic, managerial, and operational levels; some say they should only be responsible for implementation planning. The three-level approach is used here because logistics managers, within corporate parameters, do decide on logistics objectives and on resource deployment to attain them; they do go through the process of seeing that logistics resources are acquired and used effectively and efficiently; and they do set up procedures to assure that tasks are performed efficiently and effectively.

The logistics planning process involves the same steps as the corporate planning process, even to the point of developing contingency plans; so there is no reason to go further than we have gone. We shift direction to consider some logistics objectives.

Objectives of Strategic Planning for Logistics

Even though these objectives have been previously mentioned in another context and will be referred to again in still another context, they are brought together here in a convenient form. Peter R. Attwood said that fundamentally there are five objectives of strategic planning for logistics.[5] They are:

1. To provide the service required by customers

2. To minimize system costs while providing the desired service level

3. To comply with overall policies of the company

4. To deploy resources effectively and efficiently

5. To control the system and plan for future developments

The Functional Hierarchy

For distribution planning to be effective, much more is required than going through the steps of planning and having objectives for logistics planning. Because of the significance of logistics relations in the marketing channel, at the risk of some repetition, the notion of what business a firm is in will be enlarged upon here.

What Business Are They In?[6]

Providing transportation, selling cosmetics, providing foods, and storing money are all means to ends for the industries mentioned, not ends themselves. They represent the transactions engaged in, or the tasks performed, to fulfill a larger function. The overall function of business is to create and retain profitable customers. Within the overall framework specific firms in specific industries establish a basic philosophy of their function which identifies the business they are in and which in turn provides a basis for their strategic marketing planning. Finally, they sell their products.

For example, the *function* of the cosmetics industry is to enhance the image women (and men) have of themselves. Thus they are in the *business* of providing beauty or the illusion of beauty; they *market* a line of beauty-enhancing products; they *sell* lipstick, eye shadow, and perfume. Each of the several segments of the restaurant business has a different function. One segment sees its *function* as reducing time and dollar costs of eating; its *business* is fast foods; it *markets* time and dollar savings; and it *sells* hamburgers, fish, or whatever. As for banks, their *function* is to assist in individual, commercial, and industrial financial planning; their *business* is financial commitments; they *market* a sense of financial well being; and they *sell* consumer and business loans, money storage, check-cashing services, and interest income.

These and other industries have one thing in common: each has developed a philosophy of its *functional identity*. From that philosophy, each has decided what its *real business* is, as distinct from its apparent business. Also, all have developed *marketing strategies* to serve as guides to *selling* their output as means to their ends of fulfilling their function and to create and retain profitable customers.

What Difference Does It Make?

When those involved in logistics and with the channel reach the philosophical stage where their primary concern is the marketing channel, they will have joined the cosmetics, restaurant, and banking industries, among others, in (1) establishing an appropriate functional identity, (2) deciding what their real business is, and (3) providing themselves foundations for strategic marketing. Also, they will have joined others in differentiating among (1) the function and tasks of industry, (2) strategic and operational matters, and (3) marketing and selling.

What Planning Is Not

What planning is and does has been examined at some length. Here is a list of things David Ewing says planning is not.[7]

1. Planning and budgeting are not the same.

2. Planning and forecasting are not the same.

3. Planning and report writing are not the same.

4. Planning is not designed to avoid risk.

5. Planning is not the maintenance of a formal planning organization.

6. Planning is not necessarily an attempt to improve efficiency.

7. Planning is not words, communication, and public relations.

Our discussion of the several elements of the planning framework, including the steps in the planning process, is complete. We turn now to a two-dimensional discussion of ways in which the framework can be used for either overall planning or logistics planning. The first dimension involves an approach to the analysis of the overall environment.[8] The second more closely ties logistics planning to marketing channel orientation.

Environmental Analyses for Logistics Planning

Step 3 of the planning process is concerned with the development of planning premises. Reference was made to a situation audit as a means of developing information about the environment. This section presents a model that shows the research necessary to develop information that pertains to certain environmental characteristics. It provides an approach to environmental analysis that relates significant and relevant aspects of the environment to the logistics and other institutions in the marketing channel.

Bert C. McCammon, Jr. holds that "strategists continuously search for inflection points, undertow problems, and performance gaps."[9] Inflection points reflect a dramatic change in the way of doing business. Undertow problems are those with potential to undermine the base business. A performance gap is the difference between the forecast of where the firm's momentum will take it and where the firm wants to be. This is sometimes referred to as the planning gap.

Some of the logistics inflection points that have dramatically changed the way of doing business for both carriers and users are (1) the shift in emphasis to the integrated concept of distribution management from the older method; (2) the rapid growth of piggyback; (3) the various interpretations of law which affect private carriers and intra-corporate hauling; and (4) the great move toward vertical integration in the marketing channel. Some of the undertow problems relate to the substantial changes in regulation of transportation companies and the changes that place private carriers in a new competitive position with for-hire carriers. The relaxation of entry rules and rate regulation has created new problems for motor carriers and thus for their users because new competitors, whether private or for-hire, do not have to take much traffic from established carriers. Considering operating ratios of large Class I general commodity motor carriers (96.5 in 1979), a small loss in tonnage to competitors can create serious problems. Also, a small loss in revenue from rate erosion can have serious consequences—all of which tend to undermine the base business of carriers.

Elements of Environmental Analysis

Central Thrust and Nuclear Subject

The first element an environmental analysis should have combines a central thrust to provide direction for the analysis and a nuclear subject to serve as an integrating factor. In this case, logistics is the central thrust of the environmental analysis. In keeping with the functional approach, the factor chosen to serve as a means of keeping the analysis "on track" has a common ground with all members of the channel. It relates to the basic function both of the channel as a whole and of the individual members. Because the channel system exists and functions in order to support the marketing effort of the several firms (industries) in the channel, the marketing support system becomes the nuclear subject because of the function of the channel system.

The concept of the marketing support system serves well as a nuclear subject for logistics planning for several reasons:

1. It recognizes the strategic, managerial, and operational roles of all manufacturing, buying, selling, and handling institutions in the channel.

2. It recognizes, but is neither constrained by nor confined to, the task of performing activities of institutions.

3. It recognizes the multidirectional application of the marketing concept.

4. It views the channel and its institutions as a continuum stretching from the mine to the garbage dump or recycling center.

5. It considers the channel to be a means to an end instead of a series of individual ends.

The Institutions Involved

The second element of an environmental analysis identifies the institutions involved. They are:

1. *Physical handlers*: transporters, warehousemen, and freight forwarders

2. *Producers*: manufacturers, miners, farmers, foresters, and fishermen

3. *Middlemen*: brokers, wholesalers, and retailers

4. *Consumers*: intermediate users of parts and supplies and ultimate users

5. *Disposers of waste*: recyclers and others

All are considered as suppliers and customers. All expect the traditional satisfactions of being suppliers and of being customers and users. All have their own objectives, some of which can be meshed with those of their suppliers and customers and some of which are in conflict. All have strategies to develop, managerial decisions to make, and operating tasks to perform. All have a variety of problems and opportunities arising from the pressure points inherent in the changing environment.

The Changing Environment

The third element of an environmental analysis is, of course, the environment itself. Characteristics and trends in the environment provide the straws in the wind of those factors strategists search for: inflection points and undertow problems. They also provide clues for the discovery of opportunities to help planners decide upon those things they want to make happen. Several environmental characteristics represent pressure points that have substantial impact on the future of both logistics and marketing channels. The pressure points discussed here are actually "branch points" for many alternative environmental factors, and have been chosen for their general applicability. Naturally, they can be changed to meet the needs of a specific logistics manager.

Structure and Use of a Model for Environmental Analysis

A model for use in environmental analysis is shown in Table 6–1. It embraces the three elements just discussed. The matrix makes it possible for the analyst to examine the relationship between nine major marketing institutions and eight pressure points or environmental factors. The central thrust of the analysis is in the context of logistics, and the nuclear subject is the marketing support function of the channel. Every cell in the matrix represents an area of importance, to both logistics planning in particular and marketing channel planning in general. Seventy-two cells are shown, but even that number grossly underestimates the number of potential subjects for analysis because of the broadness of each cell. Each cell may be subdivided depending upon whether the objectives are strategic, managerial, or operational in nature.

This model is more than an interesting exercise—it points out at least four separate environmental research approaches. First, one could study a single cell—for example, the impact of turbulence on carriers (Cell 7). Second, one could study the logistics impact of a single pressure point on the channel system. In such a case one would be researching an entire vertical dimension of the matrix. For example an in-depth study of the impact of regional shifts to the Sunbelt on the entire channel system would encompass an entire column of the matrix. Third, an entire horizontal dimension of the matrix could be studied. As an example consider a study on strategic planning for warehousemen. Central to such a study would be an investigation of emerging pressure points as portrayed in the matrix, and their implications for strategic planning. Fourth, there exists the possibility of studying the entire matrix in one large research endeavor. Consider for example a broad study on the future of either logistics or the marketing channel. A realistic study of this type would theoretically need to examine all of the potential pressure points and their interactions with channel institutions.

A Micro Model for Logistics Planning

Structural Elements of the Model

Table 6–1 provides a framework for the design of an orderly logistics research *program* designed to investigate the environment. This section suggests a framework for the orderly design of *projects* to become elements of the program. As with the framework for the

Table 6–1   A Model for Environmental Analysis

Channel Institution	PRESSURE POINTS							
	Capital Shortages	Inflation	Power Shifts	Regional Shifts	Other Resource Shortages	Technology	Turbulence	Legal and Political
Carriers	1	2	3	4	5	6	7	8
Warehousemen	9	10	11	12	13	14	15	16
Freight forwarders	17	18	19	20	21	22	23	24
Miners, mfrs., others	25	26	27	28	29	30	31	32
Brokers	33	34	35	36	37	38	39	40
Wholesalers	41	42	43	44	45	46	47	48
Retailers	49	50	51	52	53	54	55	56
Consumers	57	58	59	60	61	62	63	64
Recyclers	65	66	67	68	69	70	71	72

overall, or macro research program, the thrust is logistics, and the market support system (MSS) is the nuclear subject. The strategic, managerial, and operational elements of the planning framework constitute one axis of the logistics planning model of Table 6–2, a micro logistics research model. The other axis consists of three sets of environmental conditions.

The first set consists of those conditions external to the firm that cannot be controlled. The firm must either adapt to them or attempt to adapt them to the needs of the firm. In a logistics context related to the MSS concept, these conditions may consist of marketing or purchasing processes that are economically or operationally incompatible with those of the planner's company.

The second group includes conditions internal to the firm but which affect logistics relations with other departments. For example if the marketing department wants to make certain delivery promises to customers, the logistics manager must cope with the impact on logistics. Or, vice versa, that manager may want to make certain changes that would have an impact on marketing, finance, or some other department, and which may require a reaction by those departments.

The third set of conditions are those which are internal to the logistics department. Dealing with them has no impact on other departments to which they have to react. Examples include such things as reorganization of the logistics department or devising a more efficient method of making deliveries.

Using the Model

The planning and environmental legs of the framework are combined to make the model shown in Table 6–2. The analysis is presumed to be made in a logistics context against the backdrop of the concept of the marketing support system. Again, the purpose of this table is to provide a framework for the selection of specific research *projects* to meet the needs of the logistics plan. There are several ways the model may be used.

First, if immediate needs center on a complete strategic planning program through all environmental conditions, then Cells 1, 4, and 7 are the relevant ones. Appropriate projects in Cell 1 involve research into environmental trends to serve as a basis for further research designed to determine the most critical of the pressure points. This ties directly to the research program contemplated by the macro model of Table 6–1. The findings will suggest some of the objectives of the firm which in turn will serve to identify the appropriate policies for resource acquisition and use, including resolution of conflicts in objectives and coordination among departments (or firms).

The projects planned from Cell 1 (and decisions reached) serve as the input to Cell 4. The emphasis in Cell 4 has shifted from the external to the internal where additional objectives applicable to functional areas—including logistics—are identified. Finally, in Cell 7, the research, while still strategically oriented, focuses on intradepartmental logistics issues.

A *second* way of using the model is a horizontal approach, if the motive is to develop background for a complete planning program as distinct from just a strategic planning program. In this case Cells 1, 2, and 3 are relevant for research concerned with the external environment. Or, if primary concern is with the other environmental conditions, Cells 4, 5, and 6 and Cells 7, 8, and 9 are appropriate. For present purposes discussions are centered on Cells 1, 2, and 3. The types of projects for Cell 1 are, of course, the same as discussed above. The research for planning for management control in the external environment will center on customer marketing policies and practices to serve as a basis for design of the planning firm's logistics system to make it mesh with customer needs, if possible. Conversely, a motive for the research may be to suggest changes in the customer's program based upon the supplier's system which would benefit both supplier and customer.

The obvious follow-on research then centers on the efficient performance of tasks. These purely operational-applied projects center on determining parameters for operation, derivation of decision rules for performing tasks, operating procedures, and control systems.

A *third* way of using the model for orderly selection of projects is based upon the need of the logistics manager at a given time. The research program may call for systematic projects from any one or series of cells such as Cells 1, 5, and 9. Or, needs may dictate research for decisions related to strategies for use of resources for the logistics area (Cell 5, Project 3).

Obviously, if the researcher breaks in at any of the points other than Cell 1, Project 1, certain assumptions must be made about all that has gone before. Depending upon circumstances, this is an entirely legitimate thing to do and the assumptions may be equally legitimate. Again, using the example of Cell 5, Project 3, the logistics planner may be concerned with the strategies for the use of logistics resources. The manager may undertake the project in the normal course of events within the framework of established corporate objectives and policies. The purpose may be to find a strategy to improve effectiveness and efficiency in resources devoted to a local pickup and delivery activity. On the other hand, the purpose may be to find a new way of accomplishing the same end. For example, the project may be to test a hypothesis that receivers would prefer to do their own pickup and delivery. Other purposes may be to study feasibility of a consolidated service for all suppliers and customers; to examine the economics of alternative types of vehicles to use; to study the technology and its application to improve functioning of existing vehicles.

Implications of the Model

There are two sets of implications that the model suggests other than that of providing an orderly framework for selection of projects to fit a research program. First, it suggests the following strategic, managerial, and operating implications:

1. Better integration of the channel because functional needs are met

2. Reduction of motives for a firm to integrate backward and forward because many objectives are compatible

3. Two-way communication of wants and needs because of mutual benefits

4. Mutual recognition and consideration of customer and supplier objectives because of broader application of the marketing concept

5. Congruence of customer expectations and supplier promises because it is profitable.

Table 6–2 A Logistics Planning Model

Types of Planning Environmental Conditions	Strategic Planning	Managerial Control	Operational Control
External	**Cell 1** *Internal-External:* 1. Environmental analyses 2. Premises on pressure points 3. Corporate objectives 4. Resource use policies	**Cell 2** *Interfirm:* 1. Marketing systems 2. Resource use strategies 3. Marketing relationships 4. Customer expectations and supplier promises	**Cell 3** *Interfirm:* 1. Operating parameters 2. Decision rules 3. Operating procedures 4. Control system
Logistics—Other Functional Areas (Interdepartmental)	**Cell 4** *Intrafirm:* 1. Objectives 2. Resource use policies 3. Policy and conflict coordination 4. Control system	**Cell 5** *Intrafirm:* 1. Systems analysis 2. Trade-offs 3. Functional resource use strategies 4. Functional policies	**Cell 6** *Intrafirm:* 1. Operating parameters 2. Decision rules 3. Operating procedures 4. Information system
Logistics—Intradepartmental	**Cell 7** *Intradepartmental:* 1. Objectives 2. Organization structure 3. Resource deployment	**Cell 8** *Intradepartmental:* 1. Systems analysis 2. Rationalization process 3. Operations plan	**Cell 9** *Intradepartmental:* 1. Operating parameters 2. Decision rules 3. Operating procedures 4. Control system

Second, some conceptual implications are also apparent from the structure of the model.

1. *Functional*: The marketing concept can serve as a basis for application of the principle of comparative advantage.

2. *Strategic*: Inter-firm application of the marketing concept.

3. *Managerial*: Each channel member may tend to operate to support the marketing efforts of all rather than act as a task performer.

4. *Operational*: Wiser use of resources.

5. *General*: Each of the several channel institutions becomes a marketing support system. Central to the concept of the marketing support system are the adoption of the marketing concept: the development of a marketing-oriented firm and the evaluation of a marketing-oriented industry. Self-interest, conflicts of objectives, and involuntary suboptimizing continue to exist, but on a smaller scale and in fewer instances.

Conclusions

As the art and science of logistics management become more sophisticated, as the discipline moves to higher levels of performance, as logistics managers accept more responsibility, improvements at the margin become more difficult. An orderly research program is an essential ingredient for logistics planning and for continued advancement of the art and science of logistics management.

The mission of this paper was to develop a framework for logistics planning. One objective was to outline the elements of the framework. This was done in several phases. After a very brief restatement of the basic framework the several steps in the process of planning were traced. Then, the objectives of strategic logistics planning were listed. Also, some of the managerial perceptions about functions were revisited by examining the functional hierarchy. To close this section, a negative approach was taken which summarized some of the earlier points made about what planning is *not*.

The second objective was to "flesh out" the planning framework. This was done by developing a different kind of framework to assist the logistics planner. This model was to help the planner design a research *program* which would explore several facets of the environment. The two major elements of that model are the channel institutions and the environmental pressure points logistics managers will have to cope with in the future. The concept of a marketing support system was stated as the nuclear subject around which the environmental research model was developed. This concept fits into an underlying thesis of all logistics systems we know of: a systems approach. The dimensions of the systems approach were extended from the firm to the entire marketing channel.

The third objective was also to "flesh out" the planning framework. Another model was developed to meet this objective by focusing on the logistics plan. The elements of this model were planning and the environmental conditions in which the several levels of planning take place. We continued the use of the concept of the marketing support system as a nuclear subject in designing the micro model because of its significance to an inter-firm relationship.

Notes

1. Charles H. Granger, "The Hierarchy of Objectives," *Harvard Business Review* (May–June 1964), p. 66.
2. George A. Steiner, *Strategic Planning* (New York: Free Press, 1979), pp. 17–20.
3. David W. Ewing, *The Practice of Planning* (New York: Harper and Row, 1968), p. 81.
4. Merritt L. Kastens, *Long-Range Planning for Your Business* (New York: Amacom, 1976), pp. 65 and 79.
5. Peter R. Attwood, *Planning a Distribution System* (London: Gower Press, 1971), p. 24.
6. Several background papers have been prepared by Professors James A. Constantin and Robert F. Lusch for work they are doing on the concept of the market support system. This section is taken from one of those unpublished working papers, "Motor Carriers Face an Identity Crisis," 1979.
7. Ewing, *Practice of Planning*, pp. 14–17.
8. Parts of this section are adapted from an unpublished background paper by James A. Constantin and Robert F. Lusch entitled "Applied Distribution Research," 1977.
9. Bert C. McCammon, Jr., "Developing High Performance Strategies for the 1980s: A Managerial Analysis" (Norman, Okla.: Distribution Research Program, 1979), p. 1. (Prepared for "The State of the Arts Conference," College of Business Administration, The University of Oklahoma.)

CHAPTER 7

Operational Planning

PAUL H. ZINSZER

Introduction

Muhammad Ali was once asked on his way to the ring what his fight strategy was. His response was, "It's too late to plan a strategy as you step into the ring. You meet each punch as they come!" Unfortunately, all too often this describes the operating style of many executives.

In most firms, the skills required of the distribution executive are as demanding as in any other area within the firm. In the area of labor management the executive is frequently responsible for a large number of decentralized and often militant employees. In the area of responsibility for corporate assets, distribution is generally second only to production in terms of asset intensity. Finally, because technology is changing so rapidly within the distribution field, the distribution executive must apply new concepts not only to today's issues, but to those of tomorrow. Under these conditions the unexpected becomes the expected, the nonroutine becomes routine, and operating flexibility becomes the prerequisite management style.

It is the purpose of this chapter to discuss operational planning from a general perspective, examining issues such as how operational planning complements managerial and strategic planning, the key steps in operational planning, and how a manager controls and measures the operational planning process.

For an extended discussion of these and other issues relating to operational planning, the reader should consult the bibliography for this chapter, which includes separated sections for distribution and corporate operational planning.

Development of the Operational Plan

The operational plan is a marriage between the managerial plan and daily operations. (Recall that the development of the managerial plan was based upon the strategies identified during the strategic planning process.) It is at this interface that the planning process often fails. This failure occurs primarily because the operational plan too often consists of 98 percent operations and 2 percent implementation. The managerial and strategic plans by their very nature presumed operating conditions while looking forward up to ten years. At the same time, at the operations level it is difficult to perceive the benefit of planning when 98 percent or more of the daily operational activities are not affected by the existence of a plan.

Therefore the goal of the successful planner is not the development of the most exhaustive plan, but rather the development of a satisfactory plan that can in fact be implemented. Too often top management fails to recognize this major prerequisite for successful planning. Many businesses do, however, tend to grow by external rather than internal expansion. That is, management buys business instead of growing its own. The major advantage of growth by acquisition is that the operational component of the strategic plan has generally been implemented.

One philosophy of growth is "growth for growth's sake." In fact, some components of growth are detrimental to the efficient operation of the firm. Communication and coordination are factors that can seem to deteriorate as firms expand. Therefore, firms should have a more compelling goal than growth for its own sake to justify continued expansion.

What Is the Operational Plan?

The operational plan incorporates the daily routine of the business with the specific thrusts developed in the managerial plan. Recall that the strategic plan determined the key objectives towards which the firm should be striving. Strategic objectives can include the identification of advantageous markets, considerations of synergy of the firm's business, and economics of scale. Both synergy and economy of scale imply that output will be greater than input. An economy of scale that most firms aim for is to increase market share and at the same time lower the per unit cost associated with purchasing, production, advertising, and particularly distribution. An example of synergism would be developing a new market for a product, but keeping the existing distribution system, thereby reducing overall per unit distribution costs. The Anheuser–Busch Company's move into snack foods and the merger creating Nabisco–Brands Inc. may prove to be examples of distribution synergy.

The managerial plan is a temporal spanning tool linking day-to-day operations with the key elements developed in the strategic plan. Its primary purpose is to set targets, both in terms of actions to be taken and their timing, that will move the firm to the accomplishment of its long-term strategic objectives. Timing is a significant variable—in most firms the primary scarce resources are capable management and adequate capital which must be developed over time. The actions defined in the managerial plan are the deployment of these resources towards the achievement of the goals of the strategic plan. For example, if the firm wished to modify radically its present distribution system, consideration must necessarily be given to issues such as changes in operating procedures, managerial training, and capital availability. The resolution of these issues would satisfy the goals of the managerial plan.

The operational plan is different from "operations." It incorporates the philosophies of the strategic plan—e.g., to improve customer service through order cycle time improvement—with the general timing of events outlined in the managerial plan—e.g., to open two new distribution centers and add five additional tractors to the delivery fleet. However, because operations may well be 98 percent routine and 2 percent plan, on a daily basis one can easily lose sight of the goal to improve customer response time.

Components of the Operational Plan

The three basic components of operational planning are:

1. *Implementation* of operational changes to meet managerial and strategic objectives

2. *Management* of resources (primarily labor and fixed assets)

3. *Evaluation* of performance and replanning if necessary

The first component includes all changes undertaken to achieve the strategic opportunities identified for the firm. This includes changes in operating procedures, and in labor management and asset management. The implementation of projects can be, and often is, slighted in terms of managerial efforts. Unfortunately, as managers, we too often view our objectives as of minor consequence—at best transitory or easily mandated by demanding compliance. However, that is seldom the case. Many new operating systems have required postponement or substantial modification as a result of inadequate preparation and implementation of a new system. Implementation is a critical step in successful operational planning.

Resource management constitutes the major efforts of most distribution executives. This is the management of the labor and assets that are under the supervision of the distribution department. In most firms the asset base over which distribution has managerial control is very large. In addition, the labor component of the distribution budget is usually substantial. Control of these major cost components of the firm receives extended treatment in subsequent sections of this *Handbook*.

The management of resources involves (1) measuring performance and establishing "performance standards," (2) comparing the actual performance to the standard, and (3) considering alternatives. If in the long run actual performance does not meet planned goals, the gap between them must be explained in terms of operating procedures or the plan must be adjusted. It is this cycle of information that allows management to evaluate the achievement of operational, managerial, and strategic goals.

Change Implementation: Tactical Planning

The implementation of change is referred to as tactical planning, particularly when the change being implemented is viewed as a discrete activity. Tactical planning generally consists of identifying key steps or stages, allocating resources, and timing the specific resources or decisions required for successful completion of the plan.

For example, some of the steps necessary in relocating a warehouse might include the following:

1. Locate new facility

2. Modify new facility to meet needs

3. Begin transfer of personnel

4. Stock new facility

5. Start shipping from new facility

6. Deplete inventory at old facility—transfer remaining stock to new facility

7. Complete transfer of personnel

8. Close old facility ·

The tactical plan first would attempt to provide timing for each event. Second, consideration would be given to major issues such as identifying specific skills required to accomplish the plan, and the quantity and duration of time they will be needed at each step of the plan. Third, specific capital requirements would be identified at each step of the plan. A fourth component often formally included in the tactical plan is the coordination of outside services. In a warehouse relocation this might include renting trailers to move inventory between facilities or hiring a construction crew to prepare the new facility to receive stock.

Experience has generally indicated that over-preparation is not only necessary but well worth the additional costs. Generally this takes the form of contingency planning, a subject developed in some detail in Chapter 8.

Resource Management

Resource management has two major goals. The first involves the need to meet the service requirements of the marketplace. The second is the efficient management of resources. The following list outlines a number of facets of the distribution process that involve consideration of both of these major goals.

1. Customer service

    a. Inventory management
    b. Order entry
    c. Setting service standards

2. Transportation

    a. Shipment routing
    b. Vehicle scheduling
    c. Freight consolidation

3. Warehousing and inventory control

  a. Warehouse location
  b. Warehouse layout
  c. Inventory control
  d. Productivity—short interval scheduling

4. Monitoring changing technology

  a. Software
  b. Hardware

5. Corporate policy management

  a. Liability avoidance
  b. Creation and maintenance of corporate image

While most firms continually push for increased operating efficiency and productivity, operating managers do not always understand how their decisions affect overall corporate financial performance. The following example demonstrates how the resource variables just listed can affect corporate performance.

Figure 7–1 depicts a strategic profit model showing the relationship between operating decisions and their overall effect on the firm. The financial performance of a hypothetical firm is presented in the bottom portions of the boxes, and the changes in operations are reflected in the top portions.

1. *Customer Service*. By better meeting customers' needs, sales for this hypothetical firm increased 10 percent (cost of goods sold also increased 10 percent). The increase in distribution cost required to improve service is only $5 million to operate two additional public warehouses on a variable cost basis. Therefore the improvement in customer service results in an improvement of the net profit margin from 4.0 to 6.9 percent.

2. *Transportation*. An increase in fleet utilization through improved routing and scheduling results directly in either fleet reduction or nonreplacement, resulting in a reduction in fixed assets. In this example, a $1 million savings in assets is realized. (A reduction in personnel might also result but in this example no financial saving is taken.)

3. *Warehousing*. Improvements in warehousing might occur by increasing throughput by utilizing greater materials-handling capability. An alternate improvement might involve increasing warehouse labor productivity, thereby reducing labor costs. Either step would result in a reduction of the cost of goods sold. In this case, labor productivity increases result in a savings of $1 million.

4. *Inventory*. An increase in inventory turnover can improve financial performance in two ways. First, total assets are reduced, increasing asset turnover. Second, the cost of carrying inventory is reduced. In this example, if inventory is reduced 10 percent, turns go from 6.7 to 7.4 times per year, which results in a $1.5 million reduction in inventory.

All these changes combine to produce a net profit margin of 6.9 percent (formerly 4.0 percent), and the asset turnover rate becomes 2.2 times (formerly 2.0). This produces a return on assets of 15 percent (formerly 8 percent), almost doubling the previous financial performance.

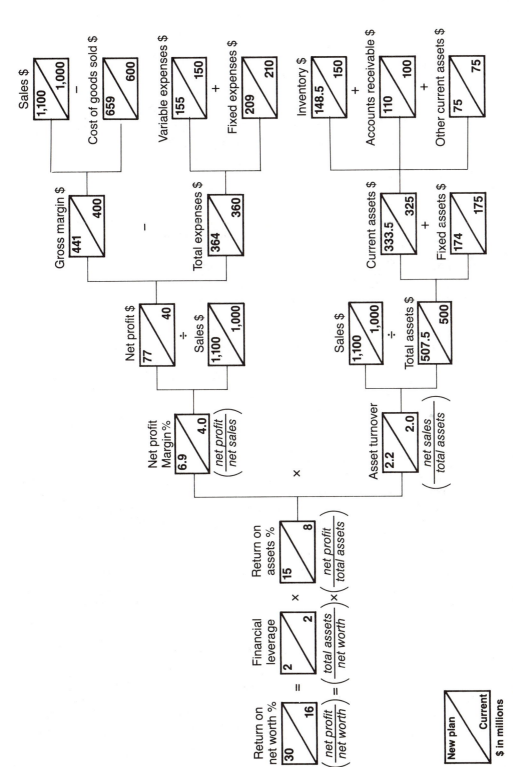

Figure 7-1 The Strategic Profit Model

115

The purpose of this example is to demonstrate the effects of improved distribution resource management on overall corporate financial performance. The strategic profit model provides a framework for comparing financially complex modifications to operating systems in terms of their overall effect on the corporation. In this manner the model can assist management in determining the relative financial rewards for changes to the present operating system. Other considerations being equal, modifications to the system would be undertaken relative to their respective financial contribution to overall corporate performance. That is, those projects which realize the greatest financial return would be undertaken first.

Performance Measurement and Control

A critical component of operational planning is the measurement and control of performance. The information system provides management with feedback on the operation of the various components of the distribution system.

For purposes of interpretation and analysis, information is generally arranged in a manner that reflects the contributory manner of each performance measure. The strategic profit model presented in Figure 7–1 is arranged in such a hierarchical manner. Hierarchical forms of data presentation aid the manager not only in comprehending the interaction of the system, but also in better isolating those areas requiring attention.

Data measurement generally starts at the lowest level of discrete activity. For example, labor can be measured as a function of the activity (case units picked per man hour) or the person (three hours picking, four hours receiving). These data can then be combined to reflect the overall operation of the distribution function being managed. A great many measurements may have to be taken in order to determine the status of the system. For example, Xerox measures forty different labor functions in order to provide continual monitoring of their warehouse operations.

With the generation of all these numbers, new methods of data reduction must be employed to assist management in focusing on areas that require their attention. The two general methods currently in use are the flagging of exceptional performance and presentation of data in a graphic form which allows the manager to synthesize greater quantities of data.

Procedures for flagging exceptional performance generally consist of establishing norms or standards around which performance latitude is granted (e.g., ± 10 percent, or one standard deviation around norm). When operating within this range of tolerance, no particular note is made of the variance. However, once performance exceeds the allowable parameters, it is flagged and brought to the manager's attention. When all the flagged performance data are assembled they are referred to as an exception report. This report summarizes those areas that require management attention because performance has exceeded the limits of acceptable variance.

The major steps to be followed in data management and control are (1) data collection, by all the activities to be managed; (2) data reduction, by comparing each data set with performance standards and tolerance limits; and (3) data summary, presenting the major data measures of overall performance and those items where performance exceeds the tolerance limits. The manager who follows these steps will be able to collect and analyze considerable amounts of data that will assist him in the management of the distribution function.

Conclusions

The operational plan is the key to realizing the goals of the strategic plan. However, since the term is similar to "operations," managers easily confuse the two. They often assume that operational planning is occurring just because they are managing operations satisfactorily. The major components of operational planning involve:

1. Implementing the operational plan, developed in the managerial plan

2. Managing resources, including labor and assets

3. Measuring performance, both with regard to aiding operating efficiency and anticipating future operating issues

Through their reasoned use of these three components strategic objectives are ultimately attainable.

CHAPTER 8

Contingency Planning for Distribution Managers

BERNARD J. HALE

A Basic Look at Contingency Planning

The profession of logistics has become a relatively complicated and demanding field for its practitioners. The successful manager in this profession will need to call upon a wide range of managerial tools to achieve his or her objectives.

One of the often overlooked managerial tools that has a particularly meaningful application to sound logistics management is the area of contingency planning. The wide range of activities that fall under the official definition of physical distribution management—now synonymous with logistics management—are often directly affected by a wide range of calamitous events that are both man-made and natural in origin. The wise logistics manager should make use of sound contingency planning to assist in countering the potentially devastating impact of the many emergency situations that may directly involve areas of physical distribution. This portion of *The Distribution Handbook* addresses contingency planning for such specific situations as labor strikes, energy shortages, natural disasters, and product recalls.

An Introduction to Contingency Planning

Contingency plans are advanced preparations for dealing with emergencies not considered in the regular planning process. The regular planning process is based upon the most probable events. But even events considered most probable, if they take place without warning, can bring disastrous consequences upon any organization. Such events will demand swift and sure management action.

It is suggested that the best approach to contingency planning is to ask the very simple question, "What if?": What if our major suppliers are on strike? What if we are unable to obtain sufficient gasoline to run our truck fleets? What if an earthquake or a tornado hit at our biggest distribution center? What if we simply cannot find enough secretaries, order pickers, or industrial engineers to man our distribution facilities' staffs? What if we have to recall one of our major products?

Contingency planning should identify possible emergency situations that management can and should do something about. Feasible, defensive strategies should be determined. The most desirable strategies should then be identified and any desired tactical plans should be made.

There is no uniform content to contingency plans. In one of the best books on the subject, George A. Steiner defines the fundamental purpose of contingency planning as a way to place managers in a better position to deal with unexpected developments than if they had not made such preparations.[1] He points out that by failing to anticipate certain events managers may not act as quickly as they should in critical situations and the event may create more damage than it otherwise would have. Contingency planning should eliminate fumbling, uncertainty, and time delays in making the needed response to an emergency. Contingency planning also should make such responses more rational.

An additional advantage to contingency planning is that it forces managers to look at dimensions in the environment other than probable events. This endeavor, together with their experience in strategic planning, should make managers more adept at dealing with unexpected turns of events. Keep in mind that events dealt with in a contingency plan are not likely to take place precisely as expected in the plan; hence, even with contingency plans, a manager will likely be forced to improvise further.

Steiner makes a point that contingency plans also have certain disadvantages. One problem with them is that they may stimulate negative attitudes in the minds of managers. For example, many contingency plans deal with pessimistic possibilities such as disasters, strikes, lower market share, and the like. Dwelling on such potentialities can certainly create negative thinking, pessimism, and fear, and those attitudes may be in conflict with the desired enthusiasm and optimism that effective managers should have.

Another disadvantage is that contingency plans may generate fear and uncertainty in an organization if they are revealed. For example, a contingency plan to reduce employment in the event of a sales decline may cause morale problems among employees. Managers also may tend to be overly optimistic in their strategic plans because they know what to do if the planned objectives and goals are not met, through the use of contingency plans.

Dealing with "What If?" Questions

An important step in contingency planning is to develop strategies and tactical plans to deal with the possible occurrence of each event selected for planning. The objective here is to neutralize or offset as much as possible the effects of the event when and if it occurs.

Alternative strategies should be identified and evaluated in light of the anticipated nature of the event and the company's capabilities and strengths in dealing with it. The result may be a decision to take advance action as well as to set forth strategies to be followed at the time of the event. For instance, in the case of a key distribution center, the company may decide to stockpile inventory in other distribution centers within a geographic range of the market now served by that distribution center. It may decide to set up additional centers as a second choice, or it may make arrangements with another company, such as a public warehouse, to perform the services in the event its own distribution center is lost. Such strategies may not completely offset the damages of the loss of this distribution center, and additional strategies may be formulated to be implemented at the time of such a loss.

Strategies in contingency plans should be as specific as possible. For instance, an organization may develop a contingency plan to be implemented in the event of a drop in sales below a certain level. Strategies such as reduced employment, reduced advertising expenses, or delayed construction are simply too broad. They really must be more specific. An example would be, "If sales drop by 10 percent below expectations our net income will decline by X million dollars. In order to reduce this loss by a specific goal—say 75 percent—it will be necessary to defer the program of expansion of plant X, to reduce the number of employees by 500, and to cut variable production costs in proportion to the sales decline."

Steiner spoke of "trigger points"[2] in connection with contingency plans. By this he meant that contingency plans may specify trigger points, or warning signals, of the imminence of the event for which the plan was developed. For example, if a plan is prepared to deal with a 10 percent decline in sales below estimate, there will be warning signals. Sales may fluctuate daily, weekly, or monthly. What will trigger the implementation of the plan? Such plans really need to address that situation. In some cases, such as in the case of a fire, the trigger point is the event itself, but in others the point at which the plan should be implemented is not so clear. In those cases a trigger point should be specified. The contingency plan should, thus, indicate the type of information to be collected and the action to be taken at the trigger point. Also, it is a good idea to assign specific responsibilities to someone to collect relevant information and to keep informed the person who makes the decision to implement the plan.

The Contingency Plan in Detail

Steiner also offered an interesting insight regarding the volume of contingency plans.[3] He noted that O'Connor[4] had interviewed 58 executives whose companies did contingency planning and she concluded "most companies emphasized that no more than a half-dozen critical events—those that would have a significant impact on the financial or strategic goals of the company—should be selected for contingency planning."[5] This is probably a wise guide. Too many contingency plans can take too much staff and executive time to prepare. Contingency plans, according to O'Connor, should be made for really critical events, not merely troublesome ones.

A review of existing contingency plans in various organizations indicates that such plans relate directly to short-range operating plans and not long-range strategies. If, however, the short-range actions contemplated in the contingency plan have long-range strategic implications of importance, the reformulation of long-range strategies should be made at the time the contingency plans are formulated and become part of them. When a contingency plan then becomes reality, top management may decide to redo its entire strategic plan. It is probably a good idea to consider the long-range, strategic implications of immediate actions spelled out in contingency plans. Otherwise, managers in their desire to deal aggressively with an emergency may lay the basis for a future crisis.

Logistics, or physical distribution, deals with a broad range of activities. With such a range of activities so very dependent upon outside forces, the likelihood of potential disruption from any number of serious events is obvious. In organizations that have developed formal contingency plans, it is commonplace to include a high-level logistics manager in the formulation and implementation management stages, simply because of the direct impact that disrupted logistics activities might have on the well-being of the organization. In organizations that haven't set up formal contingency plans—the significant majority according to most experts—the logistics manager is likely to be in an excellent strategic position to seize the opportunity to do so.

Planning to Deal with Energy Shortages

Energy shortages now seem universal, inevitable, and apparently inescapable. Any organization that has not yet felt an energy problem pinch in terms of availability, usage, or cost has indeed been most fortunate. Needless to say, however, the age of low cost and abundant power is past.

Logistics managers are likely to be confronted with all types of potential energy crises over the next decade. It is particularly important that they devote some thought to contingency planning so that their organizations can continue to achieve their physical distribution missions in spite of setbacks caused by more expensive or less plentiful energy.

Energy-related problems seem to proliferate throughout a wide range of physical distribution activities, including warehousing, transportation, packaging, and inventory management.

In warehousing, the way you process your orders, handle your inbound supplies and raw materials, and receive, store, and ship your finished goods has a direct impact on energy consumption. The physical operation of the warehouse or distribution center itself has a major impact on an organization's energy costs. Lighting, heating, the actual design of the building shell, and the operation of material-handling equipment all are directly related to energy consumption. "What if" questions can abound here. What if your warehousing facilities are gas heated and you find your supply allocated or actually cut off for short periods of time?

Transportation management is the most talked about segment of logistics management that is affected by energy shortages. The movement of materials between facilities, whether they be raw materials or finished goods, may require alternative means of energy conservation in a crisis situation. "What if" questions also abound in the area of potential shortages of petroleum products. For instance, what if fuel supplies for your delivery equipment are allocated on a level of 50 percent of the amount you are currently using? How do you maintain your customer service levels under such circumstances? This is a particularly important area for consideration in contingency planning.

Fuel costs have a direct effect on how an organization packages its goods and assembles its shipments for distribution. These areas should not be neglected in the contingency planning process.

Managing inventory offers a great potential for energy conservation when energy shortages occur. The deployment of inventories throughout a distribution system obviously will consume large amounts of energy. Are there ways in which this energy consumption can be reduced? Obviously, the answer is "yes." Maybe it means better inventory management systems. Perhaps it means narrowing the product lines offered and lowering safety stock levels. A contingency plan should focus on these potential steps in case such policy changes must be implemented.

There are several considerations to keep in mind when setting up an energy management program as a basis for further contingency planning. You must decide what portions of such a program require long-range planning and where contingency plans for coping with the possible emergency situation should be devised. Here are some recommendations:

1. Evaluations of your future needs for all forms of energy should be updated periodically. Keep in mind not only such obvious areas as fuel for your operation and for your suppliers, but also electricity supplies for lighting, heating, and material-handling equipment.

2. Keep in close and frequent contact with your fuel suppliers. If formal requests for allocations have been made, make sure that you keep them updated. Make sure that your fuel suppliers know your organization's energy needs and your priority status. If allocations haven't been granted, you still should try to obtain an agreement, preferably in writing, on amounts of fuel to be provided, the schedule of such supplies and service, and the costs of same.

3. Address areas where specific contingency plans for possible fuel shortages should be made. Try to develop plans of action for various levels of shortages. This becomes particularly important for your transportation fleets.

4. Consider having an alternate fuel system capacity.

5. Have on paper and in effect a fuel conservation program, especially for gasoline. If you are already a priority user of gasoline, such a plan is already required by allocation regulations.

6. Have at least one person in each company location responsible for keeping up with all energy-related matters and, especially, conservation.

7. Because each state will play an expanded role in energy allocation—especially emergency allocations—and in enforcing conservation, learn which state office and which officials are responsible, and make sure they know your company's needs.

8. Carefully consider various types of energy savings techniques available for warehouses and transportation systems. Your contingency program should include the specific identification of those techniques that you would employ at various stages of an emergency.

One of the most difficult tasks in any company is to define and set specific goals for both the base energy plan and the contingency plan. Essentially, your goals will fall into three major categories: (1) securing energy sources, (2) controlling energy costs, and (3) minimizing energy costs. Perhaps the most important of these is to secure energy sources. The first line of attack is to make sure that your company will have sufficient quantities of energy available during periods of energy shortage. That may simply mean renegotiating contracts with energy suppliers. It may, however, be far more complex and necessitate buying and installing fuel tanks for additional supplies of fuel oil or gas reserves, as well as providing alternate methods of heating your offices and operating your transportation systems. It could also be necessary to consider subcontracting parts or processes that require significant amounts of energy in order to be less dependent upon your own energy sources in case of severe shortages.

Conservation methods can start with very simple acts, such as turning off lights in areas that aren't being used. They can also involve highly technical programs, such as the implementation of computerized energy conservation systems. Energy conservation should be looked at from both the short-range and the long-range viewpoints. Immediate actions must be balanced against long-term predictions of energy costs and availability.

Minimizing energy costs should be viewed in terms of the long run. Switching fuels or installing heat exchangers can be very costly. Amortization and other tax benefits, however, must be figured into any analysis of your energy problems. You must be prepared to revise additional goals since state and federal regulations do change from time to time.

Basic Procedures

The initial task in contingency planning is to outline basic plans and procedures for achieving energy conservation goals. A suggested course of action is presented here.

The first step is to set general goals in terms of overall availability, conservation efforts, and energy costs.

Next, an energy survey should be conducted. This should include an energy audit as well as a survey of current and predictable availability of fuel supplies or energy sources and likely rate changes.

The third step is to set *specific* goals for each department or system. These goals must be quantified—the more detailed and quantified your goals are, the better chance you have of achieving your energy conservation objectives.

Fourth, develop feedback systems. You'll need to do this in such a way that you'll have controls without excessive paperwork. This may require the purchase of special monitoring equipment. Or it may simply mean using records of fuel expenditures or meter readings that are already available.

At this point, the development of contingency plans for energy shortages becomes important. The most sophisticated contingency plans pinpoint alternative methods of staying in business while undergoing an energy crisis.[6] Incidentally, this means designating someone who is able to assess the company's situation and see that the appropriate policies are implemented at the right time. Some useful guidelines for such a policy follow:

1. First, determine what your company's energy requirements are by major function or department. If your company is involved in manufacturing, then it is best to determine energy requirements by product line or manufacturing process.

2. Next, determine the relative importance of each department's functions or process to your business. Then determine if emergency backup equipment might be justified. As an example, you might determine that your data-processing operation is of very high priority to the continued functioning of the organization. You might want to install an uninterruptable power supply system such as a generator as a backup energy source. Remember to consider the interdependency that many departments and processes have when

doing the prioritizing. A manufacturing process may be a high priority but it may also be dependent upon other functions such as engineering and raw materials supply.

3. Don't overlook the possible use of outside resources as a means of backup to your own organization's high priority functions. As an example, you could make arrangements for a remote computer operation compatible with your own systems during a crisis.

4. Develop a formal list of specific action plans to be used during any energy crisis. Include instructions on how to handle communication with your customers, employees, unions, suppliers, and common carriers. Advanced communication with your unions regarding potential layoff risks should take place.

5. Finally, become familiar with your industrial neighbors. Discuss your plans with them. Perhaps you can share ideas or even energy sources during a crisis.

Federal regulations allow companies whose natural gas allocations are being curtailed by their suppliers to buy it at unregulated prices from another interstate supplier. There are gas brokers around to help you find one. You should be familiar with how to contact such brokers. In Ohio, for example, there is also a self-help program where companies can pool their capital resources and drill for gas themselves through a subcontractor company. These steps all require careful advance planning.

The Research Institute of America (RIA) makes another point about make-or-buy decisions and their impact on energy consumption.[7] A cut-off in your supply of energy may dictate relocation of production facilities, redesign of products to substitute low energy consumption parts or processes, or purchases of parts from suppliers. All of these, of course, can have a direct bearing on logistics.

Energy management must develop specific criteria for such make-or-buy decisions within the contingency plan. Remember to heed your own production department's input regarding the need for special processes in such relocations.

Backup Measures

Your energy conservation contingency plan should include a study of general backup measures to prevent electricity blackouts and brownouts as well as short-term shortages of fuel oil and gas. Blackouts and brownouts are usually caused by heavy use of air conditioners, but can also result from utility blowouts and severe storm damage. Examples of backup measures might include:

1. *Installation of fuel tanks on site.* It is also wise to make advance arrangements with fuel suppliers to contract for delivery of fuel for the tanks during an energy crisis. Remember . . . there will likely be a scramble for service from such suppliers after a crisis begins, and tank trucks may simply not be in sufficient supply to handle the demand. You must also provide adequate security for your full tanks to be sure you aren't victimized by theft—but you should be doing this with or without a fuel crisis.

2. *Installation of auxiliary generators for backup power for all high priority functions.* Care must be taken in connection with the use of such alternative power supplies for many data-processing systems since such systems can not only lose the information being processed during a power failure, but also be damaged by sudden complete power losses. Backup systems are available that sense power failures within microseconds of total power loss, and switch on automatically to take over the load so that data-processing equipment

doesn't lose the power source. This equipment is not inexpensive, but then neither is a complete loss of your data processing for an extended period of time.

Remember that it isn't just the computers themselves that may need emergency backup power. Your switchboard and some strategic lighting should also be given consideration.

3. *Provisions for dealing with cold weather.* If your facilities are in areas where they are subject to severe cold, you must also consider the need to institute backup measures to prevent heat systems from failing. This will be necessary in order to keep water lines from freezing and bursting.[8]

Planning to Cope with Strikes

One of the most commonplace crisis situations facing logistics managers is the impact of strikes. As a result, this is a primary consideration in contingency planning. If your own firm is not unionized, that alone will not provide you with immunity from the potentially devastating impact of strikes. Your firm certainly will be dependent in some measure on other suppliers, on customers, on common carriers, or on public services that will, indeed, be affected by strikes. These strikes could have serious implications for your firm.

Strike Preparations for Your Own Firm

If your organization is of significant size you will probably have an industrial relations department, or perhaps even a labor relations department. You should certainly avail yourself of the expertise that that department can offer in connection with the suggestions presented here. The first step in establishing contingency plans for potential strike situations is to understand the key factors involved. Such factors should include the following:

Contract Deadlines

All labor organizations within your operational responsibility have contract deadlines that may have a bearing on your operational capabilities. Many labor relations departments within organizations publish these deadlines in order to keep operations management informed. You should begin to make contingency plans as far in advance as possible. It is unlikely that this can be done very many months in advance because it is difficult to evaluate all the factors that can lead to strikes very far in advance. (There are certainly exceptions to this rule.) You'll probably want to be kept posted by your labor relations internal experts in order that you will have a good understanding about the likelihood of a potential strike as far in advance as possible. Experience indicates that most organizations have from six to eight weeks of long-term planning capability, but it may take as little as several hours.

Key Issues that Lead to Strikes

An understanding of the key issues in labor disputes will give you a better idea of the likelihood of a strike against your firm and will also give you a better understanding about your company's philosophies with regard to key issues. Again, one of the best sources for this information would be your own labor relations department. There are, however, outside sources that can also help. The Research Institute of America, for example, issues a yearly labor outlook.

Management Alternatives

You should understand your alternatives in the event that your firm is subjected to a strike. As logistics manager, for example, will you be able to service market areas within the territory of strike-bound centers from other company distribution centers outside the stricken area? Could you use public warehouses, non-union truck lines? This is a crucial area because it begins to focus on detailed planning necessary to combat the effects of a strike.

Rights of Parties

You should understand the rights of all parties involved, whether they be management, the employees, or the union. This is important because a lack of understanding in this area can create unwarranted crises when one party inappropriately oversteps its limits.

Once you have a good understanding of the key factors involved in any labor disagreement, it will be appropriate to consider your firm's main objectives in any preparation for a strike. Paul W. Bockley, director of labor relations for Honeywell, Inc., has proposed some general objectives of a strike preparation plan:[9]

1. To protect personnel, property, and maintain essential maintenance, production and service, thereby to minimize financial losses to the company and personal losses to employees

2. To maintain the good will of customers, the public, and employees to the maximum extent practical

3. To enable the company to deal fairly in terms of its personnel policy with both striking and non-striking employees

4. To enable the company to resume normal operations within the shortest possible time after the strike ends

5. To demonstrate to the union that the company will accept a strike if necessary in order to continue to manage the business effectively

A contingency plan for strike preparation should focus on the fact that a number of critical decisions should be made before the strike begins. All of them and any other policy decisions should be reviewed with the company's spokesperson before they are implemented. Those decisions include: (1) whether to build up inventory and/or make advance shipments; (2) whether to contract out or to divert work to other plants; (3) whether to attempt to get an agreement from the union that certain essential employees (maintenance persons, for example) will be given union passes permitting them to cross picket lines and work; (4) whether to lay off certain non-striking employees; (5) whether to continue to operate non-struck portions of the business; (6) whether to attempt to operate struck areas of the business with non-striking employees and/or temporary hires; (7) whether, and if so, when, to replace the strikers with new hires; (8) whether to receive or ship material during a strike and, if so, how.

Planning to Cope with Other People's Strikes

There are many options available to you in order to help cope with strikes that occur in connection with your suppliers and customers.[10]

It is wise to assess such risks by first determining where your organization might be most vulnerable. For example, who are your biggest suppliers or customers? Are there certain suppliers that provide special parts that are of special importance to your operations?

You should also become aware of the various labor union issues that might have a direct bearing on the suppliers or customers that you have now determined are of special importance to your organization. As an example, what unions are involved? When are the contracts due to expire?

Determine what alternatives you might have regarding service from or to the key suppliers or customers. It is important that you communicate with such suppliers and customers in order to determine what, if any, contingency plans they may have set up. Keep in mind, however, that such communications will be very sensitive and you might well want to hold them at relatively high levels in order to insure adequate confidentiality.

You have a number of potential alternative resources to call upon when you need to consider service from or to struck suppliers or customers. Your own labor experts are a good start. So may be your own unions, trade associations, governmental agencies, outside labor law experts, and motor carriers who often are confronted with such problems in connection with their customers.

If a strike appears likely in connection with a key supplier, you can stockpile in advance of the strike date. You can often turn to new sources, such as imports, jobbers, or even your competitors. Your own labor unions may be able to help you get emergency orders cleared even though a strike is in effect.

Once you know the potential impact of a strike and have concluded that it could be serious, you might want to plan to provide special accommodations, such as accelerated deliveries, or storage of your customer's stockpiles of your products within your facilities or in public warehouses. You also might want to attract new customers to take the place of the stricken customers. Other alternatives would include tightening production schedules, deferring hiring plans, or accelerating vacations of your staff members. If you're involved in making large, capital items, under a contractual delivery date, and such a date might fall within a potential strike period, you would want to arrange for accelerated production of that item and for delivery of that item before the contract expiration date.

Transportion Tie-ups

Logistics managers probably already have some experience in this area. In any event, one of the best solutions is to have a good traffic manager, equipped with a good contingency plan. A qualified expert in traffic can certainly ease the crises involved in freight carrier tie-ups.

You also should consider such alternatives as discussing possible solutions with your suppliers, who certainly have something at stake as well and may be willing to use their own equipment to deliver the merchandise to you.

There are a number of steps that you might consider to offset the squeeze of a truck strike. You might consider the use of non-union truck lines. You should be forewarned, however, that in some areas of the country, violence can erupt when a non-union truck crosses a picket line. Non-union truckers may not be willing to risk serious injury to their employees or destruction of their equipment. In other geographic areas, however, this is a viable alternative. Another alternative may be owner-operators who are sometimes willing to risk running picket lines.

During truck strikes customers are often permitted to pick up small packages in private cars, station wagons, or even non-struck trucks. If the volume of such pickups is significant, however, there is little likelihood that this would be permitted for any length of time.

If a strike by carriers offers an extreme threat to the vitality of your organization, you might well decide to agree in advance to the settlement terms demanded by the union. The signing of such an agreement would insure operations even if the union declares a major strike on a wide-range basis. This is becoming commonplace in certain parts of the country. It should be considered only as a last ditch effort, however, because once you commit yourself to such an agreement, you must live with it. Firms that do this also are now generally expected to agree to pay the accelerated terms of the settlement during the negotiation process. This could mean paying higher rates for days, weeks, or even months, before the actual contract is settled.

Longshoremen's strikes are another area that requires careful contingency planning. Some of the steps you can consider are early shipments from your in-port sources, or diversion of ships to alternate ports that might not be affected by the strikes. You could then trans-ship the merchandise from the ships, via rail or truck, to your destination. An increasing use of air freight, even in big-volume charters, has been commonplace during major longshoremen's strikes.

Postal service strikes also can create havoc unless your contingency plans address alternatives. You could plan to use United Parcel Service or one of the increasingly wide range of other small package service carriers. If the strike is local, another option open to you would be bulk shipping of your mail to open cities for redistribution through the Post Office. You could also consider using bus services that pick up mail at locations on their routes by prearrangement. Don't overlook the use of telephones or facsimile machines.

In a related area, don't overlook the impact that a commuter rail or bus strike might have on your work force if a significant number of your employees depend upon such commuter systems. Some firms have blocked space in local motels or formed car pools with rented vans in order to cope with this sort of problem.

Making Advance Plans to Cope with Natural Disasters

In the past few years hardly a section of our country has gone unscathed by such natural disasters as forest fires, tornadoes, floods, or hurricanes. Stricken companies have faced difficult questions, as have their suppliers and customers. It is unlikely very many such organizations ever took the time to make up a disaster guide for management.

One of the most thorough looks at this type of contingency planning was recently completed by the Research Institute of America.[11] They claim it is the first disaster guide for management ever prepared. The RIA disaster guide is an excellent starting point for the preparation of a contingency plan for the operation of your logistics facilities in the event of natural disasters. It includes the following recommendations.

1. Assign someone to keep in contact with the local disaster central authorities.

2. If your own facilities are not useable, establish temporary headquarters as easily accessible as possible to your employees and carriers or suppliers. Make the address and phone number widely known to your key employees, suppliers, and the common carriers generally serving you.

3. Notify the Post Office of your temporary address and arrange for mail service. Also make a master list of phone numbers for key employees who may have been displaced during the disaster. Keep a copy updated and at a designated location as the centralized source of information.

4. If your company records are salvageable, start this process as soon as possible: Have photos of the damage taken and include them along with newspaper accounts of the disaster in a file that will be invaluable for insurance and tax claims.

5. Security of your property and records must also be provided. If any valuable merchandise or items such as controlled drugs are involved, a round-the-clock guard service not only would be wise, but may be required by governmental regulations.

Tackling the Clean-up

The experience of companies caught in such natural disasters as floods, or hurricanes, underscores the importance of organizing the staff for quick action in digging out and salvaging corporate property. Unless machinery is cleaned promptly it may be damaged beyond repair. Also, you'll want to rescue undamaged materials, parts, and inventory, and remove them to a safe place before clean-up operations begin. The steps required will obviously vary according to the nature and extent of the disaster, but in almost all cases there are basic rules to follow in organizing the salvage effort, according to the Research Institute of America.

First of all, before any employees enter the plant, have an experienced construction engineer determine the extent of the damage and the hazards. Needless to say, power, gas and water lines should be turned off at the main source. Any apparent structural weaknesses in the foundation, floors, walls, etc., should be clearly marked for early attention. Obvious hazards like broken fuel lines or live wires should be repaired or removed immediately. This initial inspection will also show which part of the facility, if any, might be most quickly restored for resumption of operations on a limited basis.

The RIA warns that if there has been water damage spontaneous combustion hazards can exist.[12] Certain materials heat up when they are water-soaked and can burst into flame in confined spaces. Dangerous materials include hay and grain, sawdust, burlap bags, jute, and bituminous coal. Chemicals in the danger class include unslaked lime, sodium, potassium, and magnesium. Finely powdered metals and metallic sulphides may also become combustible when wet. Your local fire department can advise you about the combustibility of materials.

Skilled maintenance people should supervise salvage and repair work. In emergency situations they can be more valuable in directing unskilled clean-up squads than in doing the work themselves. Salvage of maintenance tools and equipment should get high priority. If the disaster has hit other plants in the area, there will be a run on supplies available locally. Include names, addresses, and telephone numbers of such skilled people in your contingency plan.

Resuming Operations

Your purchasing people can go into action as soon as they have desk space and a telephone, even if it's in someone's home. They can act quickly to round up materials and supplies needed to begin repairs or reconstruction, including tools, transportation equipment, drying equipment for salvaged records, cleaning compounds, paints, etc. Machinery manufacturers should be consulted for technical help in salvaging and repairing damaged equipment. Your contingency plan should include such sources as a special section. In recent disasters many manufacturers have sent sales engineers into stricken areas to give any technical help that was needed.

Find out about repair shops outside the disaster area to overhaul motors, transformers, and the like. In any major disaster local repair shops are so swamped with work that it may be weeks before companies can get their equipment back. Order replacement parts for equipment that doesn't need an outside overhaul. Remember to remind your purchasing people to specify "emergency" on all orders for repair parts and replacement materials in order to ensure that priority treatment will be given to the orders by suppliers. Purchasing agents should never automatically assume that suppliers will give special help and should always request it. Someone should be responsible for tagging all items sent in for repair with durable, waterproof identification tags. A record of each item should be kept in your files. In one disaster a manufacturer lost several pieces of equipment because the company's name was hastily chalked or greased on the housings and the marking rubbed off.

Decentralize Authority to Make Decisions

One of the major problems in an emergency is the breakdown of normal communication channels at a time when on-the-spot decisions often mean the difference between life or death, big loss or small loss. Department heads or supervisors should be given as much authority as possible on matters regarding safety, salvage decisions, purchase requisitions for replacement materials and parts, etc. In a large facility authority may also have to be given to foremen to avoid serious delays in returning to normal operations.

Establish a Temporary Record-keeping System

For tax, insurance, and legal purposes it is very important that records be kept of all steps taken and decisions made during the emergency period. Failure to do so can result in misunderstandings later on concerning purchase orders, customer orders, location of equipment, etc. These records are especially important when decisions are made by someone other than the usual supervisor. Someone should be designated with responsibility for taking care of salvaged records, such as engineering drawings, blueprints, or production records. These documents will obviously be vital in restructuring your business. Even fragments might be helpful. They should be protected against deterioration and filed in a safe place.

Restoring Order

After the damage has been surveyed and initial steps have been taken to restore a semblance of order, management must face a number of urgent operating problems. Many of them must be dealt with spontaneously because there are no company precedents for handling them. The following suggestions may be helpful.

Assistance from Suppliers

Ask your suppliers for help. They are often most willing to provide assistance in a number of ways including price concessions on replacement inventory, waiving payment terms, rushing shipments, providing technical advice, and suggesting the names of subcontractors that you can use to finish orders using undamaged parts you already have.[13]

Legal Obligations

Keep in mind that your organization does have contractual obligations too. The best bet here is to get your legal department involved promptly. Contract law generally assumes that contracts that are impossible to complete are automatically invalidated without damages. From a logistics standpoint, however, there are other implications that you must consider for your contingency plan. For instance, if you have entered a contract with specified delivery dates and you find it absolutely impossible to deliver goods on time, your customer has the option of cancelling the contract or of accepting later delivery, wherein your obligation is merely postponed. What will your policy be? If the goods contracted for sale cannot be duplicated then the contract may be invalidated. The destruction of a seller's factory, warehouse, or store does not in and of itself relieve him of the obligation to deliver goods according to contract. What does your plan provide for in this situation?

Relations with Customers

You will have already sent wires and cards to customers, informing them of your predicament. Keep in mind that while they may be sympathetic, some of them may have been placed in a very tough spot by your inability to deliver your merchandise. You will want to keep them informed about the exact extent of the damage, how long before normal operations will resume, details of the merchandise available, and when shipments can be made and by what means.

Remember that salesmen, distributors, and agents may need particularly clear instructions in certain areas, such as the status of orders on the books at the time of the damage. You may have to work from salesmen's or distributors' notes if you have lost your records. This should be a priority job since salesmen may be able to handle many customers who would otherwise want to deal with you directly.

Plans for emergency allocations of whatever stocks are available should be outlined as quickly as possible to forestall time-consuming inquiries. These should be clearly outlined in your contingency plan. If you sell and ship to distributors and dealers they will obviously have to be consulted on allocation plans. It may be wise for a key man to make flying trips to some of the top distributors to sell them on the advantages of full cooperation.

Assignment of capable personnel to handle incoming phone calls can take many burdens off busy executives. Where possible, they can refer inquiries to the salesmen in the territories, or directly to distributors or dealers. The quickest, most effective way to pass along information may be to arrange a telephone conference hook-up with key field staff, distributors, or dealers. Even if local phones aren't operating yet, it may be possible to set up calls from nearby cities where such service is available.

When Customers Suffer Disasters

When a customer's firm is struck by a disaster that leaves your own business unharmed, you may be in a position to offer assistance. It is suggested that you make a *specific* offer that can be answered by a quick "yes" or "no." Don't just ask, "What can we do to help?" The customer may be just too harassed to figure that out for you. It's probably better to make your offer by mail, unless you have some urgent aid in mind. Keep in mind the telephone service is usually going to be disrupted. In any case, the customer may not be in a position to handle a flood of incoming calls.

Salesmen should call to serve, not to sell. If salesmen are to offer assistance, make sure they understand the limits of what your organization is willing to do. Otherwise, they may promise aid that you may not be able to deliver. Teams of key sales and service personnel may be able to visit the damaged areas to determine where your help will be most useful. You may be able to lend equipment to the damaged customers. Your credit department may be able to assist customers in situations that affect credit policies. At the same time consideration should be given to such questions as "Will concessions be made beyond normal credit policies, and, if so, how far?" "What paper will be accepted?" and "Can short-term loans be offered?"

Don't forget long-range problems. Sometimes it takes months before sales conditions in disaster areas are back to normal. In the meantime, you will want to keep your area sales force at work. If immediate service opportunities decreased, you may want to put your salesmen to work on market surveys, technical and promotional work, etc. You may have to make temporary reassignments to open territories, to training squads, or to refresher courses. Your contingency plan should list such alternative work opportunities or reassignments.

Employee Relations in a Disaster

A shutdown of any period longer than a few days will raise important questions about employer's obligations to employees, whether unionized or not. Most firms will naturally want to do as much for their people as they can, but in shaping plans several points should be carefully considered.

Wages and Salaries

Should you pay workers for time lost? The history of past disasters really doesn't show any uniform practice. It seems to depend mainly on the size of the company and what it can afford. Some firms have continued to pay workers who were laid off during short shutdowns. Others pay them and let them make up the work later. One ingenious solution was to let the people make up lost time by working overtime. Thus they reduced their debit at time-and-one-half rates.

If hourly workers do jobs other than their regular work should you make special pay arrangements? Immediately following a disaster most of the work involves debris removal, searching for records, salvaging materials and equipment, reconstructing business records, etc. Firms that want to pay their people on a scale roughly equivalent to what they normally make face a problem with skilled workers because the basic hourly rate for clean-up work may be far below their normal level. In such cases you may want to use the solution adopted in recent years by many companies that have been hit by disasters: (1) Set an arbitrary, minimum wage for clean-up work. (2) Pay hourly people their usual basic rate, or the special minimum, whichever is greater.

In many cases skilled people have probably netted less than their regular pay; nevertheless the arrangement has been considered a fair compromise. The Research Institute of America cautions, however, that companies must not set an arbitrary minimum wage that is beneath the legal floor set by federal or state law. It was noted that firms practicing this policy generally continued to pay salaried employees at their regular rates, although many of them did not do their regular work. Maintenance people and others who worked overtime were paid accordingly.

Layoffs

How can you handle layoffs so as to minimize their impact both on the employees and on your company costs? This is an important question if your operations are to be curtailed substantially. The fact that a business is shut down by an act of God doesn't alter the normal relationship between an employer and its employees. Unless the firm announces that it won't reopen, the workers are laid off permanently or indefinitely. Although you don't have any obligation to pay them when they're not working, they will be drawing unemployment compensation and your experience rate will be affected. Some pointers to be considered in dealing with this situation follow.[14]

1. An attempt should be made to effectively use as many employees as possible for the clean-up phase. If some must be let go, you will have to decide between permanent separation and indefinite layoff.

2. Should permanent separation be necessary, aim to minimize your unemployment tax liabilities and other related liabilities such as pay in lieu of notice by releasing employees with the least seniority.

3. If you provide fringe benefits such as group life and medical insurance, check with your insurance carriers regarding the effect of a shutdown. Employees may not have premiums deducted or paid on time since paychecks might be delayed, and thus coverage might be risked. The company might decide to pay the entire premium themselves or remind the employees to make their contributions even though they may not be working. You should notify the insurance carrier of the names of the employees laid off in order to discontinue their coverage.

In this area of employee relations you must remember that when a disaster strikes, fear of losing income will be uppermost in people's minds after they have coped with the immediate, personal crises. In disaster situations it is recommended that employers tell their employees exactly what they intend to do. When employees must draw unemployment compensation, employers should advise them on how and where to obtain it.

Summary

Disasters can strike anywhere at any time. You should recognize that it is only good sense to prepare for the unexpected. The following steps involve little trouble or expense, and could pay off many times over if a disaster should strike:

1. Keep duplicate copies of essential records in a safe place, off premises. Your plan should determine in advance just which documents are "essential."

2. Consider appointing a disaster coordinator to set up activities as part of the contingency plan.

3. Give your supervisors and/or foremen some training in the responsibilities they would have to undertake in the case of a disaster.

4. Have flashlights and simple tools located in spots where they would be needed most.

5. Set up a priority for the evacuation of equipment and inventory. List possible hazards that might arise from emergencies, such as the handling of flammable materials.

6. Consider participating in community or industry disaster plans.

7. Periodically review insurance coverage.

Planning to Handle Product Recalls

What steps must be taken if a product is found to be hazardous and subject to recall? Warren Blanding suggests that the response to this question would cover the following five points:[15]

1. *Lot identification.* It must be possible to trace the lot through the distribution system.

2. *Communication and lot segregation on return procedures.* The plan must identify individuals to be notified and the manner in which distribution is to be frozen or reversed.

3. *Legal obligations.* Agencies to be notified, manner of notification, and timetables for doing so must be set forth.

4. *Production contingencies.* Criteria and authority for a production freeze must be defined.

5. *Marketing and public relations aspects.* The plan must identify individuals responsible for setting policy on handling of press and customers, as well as policy on replacements, allowances, etc.

The points mentioned above are, of course, just the bare outlines of a contingency plan for product recalls. The plan must go into considerable detail. Fine points, such as the order of notification, may seem relatively unimportant, but if federal officials or customers learn of a product recall plan before all contact personnel in the firm are notified, the public relations consequences could be disastrous.

Do you know the difference between "imminent danger" and "inherent danger"? How about the difference between product recall, market withdrawal, and stock recovery? Who must be notified when a recall program is initiated and whose responsibility is it to initiate such a program?

The establishment of the Consumer Product Safety Commission placed general products under regulations comparable to what already existed for food and drug products. As a result, a growing number of traffic and distribution executives are now required to know the definitions of the above terms. Except for tobacco, food, drugs, cosmetics, and transportation equipment, which are already covered by other agencies, the Consumer Product Safety Commission is essentially responsible for any product or substance, or component thereof, normally found in any home, school, or recreational facility. It is clear from that definition that very few firms are *not* subject to the agency's jurisdiction.

Even if your organization does not sell to consumers, don't be fooled into thinking that products that are not bought by consumers are not subject to the Commission's jurisdiction. That is simply not so—the agency now also covers components of consumer goods, regardless of their source.

Another area that is often overlooked is the packaging of consumer products. Packages, packaging material, closures, and the like that constitute a hazard have the same status as a hazardous product or substance. Technically, then, the responsibility to report a product hazard and initiate remedial action can occur anywhere in the manufacturing, marketing, and distribution cycle. As a practical matter, the manufacturer often has to assume the principal burden of a recall program if his customers choose not to cooperate.

Categories of Recall

There are different categories of product recall according to the seriousness of the hazard, and there are some instances where the product is not actually recalled but retrofitted on site. When automobiles are recalled they are actually called back to dealer service departments rather than to the manufacturing site. In some situations, products will be destroyed where they are found rather than risk further hazard and exposure. Your contingency plan must show who has the authority to make such decisions.

As indicated earlier, there is also a distinction between *imminent* and *inherent* danger. An imminent danger or hazard would be one that is almost certain to bring injury or death unless remedial action is taken. An inherent danger or hazard is often a design defect. One example would be a dishwasher that was recalled when it was discovered that the door could come in contact with electrical wiring and possibly cause a lethal shock.

The Food and Drug Administration has three principal categories of recall urgency—Class One, emergency or life-threatening; Class Two, priority or possibly life-threatening; and Class Three, routine or remote hazard. A Class One recall—for example, botulism in food or a labeling error on a dangerous drug—would require recall from all holders of the product, including ultimate consumers, and a public warning through the press. Class Two recalls include products that might be misused by consumers and also those which have been misrepresented or deliberately adulterated. Although there is some hazard to consumers, it is not considered immediate, and usually recall extends only to the retail level. Class Three recalls cover products where there is little, if any, hazard but where the product violates some specific regulation—sub-potent vitamins, for example— and thus must be removed from marketing channels. In this category the product must be recalled down to the wholesale distribution level but retailers are permitted to sell out their inventories.

A company may also choose to recall for purposes of market withdrawal, that is, to remove from the market a product of inferior quality. Although such products are not in violation of any particular law, they may be considered to be a threat to the corporate image or trademark. The term "stock recovery" is used when the product being recalled is still within the direct control of the firm, that is, at its own manufacturing sites or warehouses.

Organizing for Product Recall

What types of firms should organize contingency programs for product recall? It is assumed that food and drug firms and transportation equipment manufacturers are already organized in this respect. For firms outside of those fields the basic determinant is whether or not their products are under the jurisdiction of the Consumer Product Safety Commission. Since to some extent that Commission decides its own jurisdiction, the only way to find out about this is to ask the Commission. Companies that make what they term "strictly industrial products" also fall under the jurisdiction of the Commission because a small percentage of those products would normally be sold in due course to consumers.

Contingency Planning Steps for Product Recall

Establishing a Product Recall Committee

The basic purpose of a product recall committee is to facilitate communication between all affected departments and insure that recall procedures are carried out in an orderly fashion. The committee functions first to identify the defect or hazard requiring recall, and second, to carry out the recall procedures.

The committee should include representatives of affected departments such as sales, distribution, customer service, law, manufacturing, engineering, and public relations. Quite frequently firms assign a distribution executive as chairman because so much of the committee's duties will be concerned with pulling the product back through channels of distribution.

How does the Committee determine when a product is in non-compliance or when a safety defect is sufficient to require product recall? Since existing federal standards cover relatively few products, the firm's own control group may have to apply its own standards for other than obvious defects or hazards. In any event, the decision rules should be fully spelled out, including the specific responsibility and authority to: (1) freeze production, (2) initiate recall, and (3) carry out required compliance steps, including notification of appropriate agencies.

Defining the Responsibilities of the Product Recall Committee

As mentioned above, the committee must have clearly specified responsibilities. The next step would be to determine if the controls within the organization would facilitate identification and location of the affected product lots. That may require the upgrading of the order-processing system or the development of subroutines to permit the tracing of specific lots through the firm's distribution system.

Next, individuals who will be expected to participate in the recall program at different levels of the distribution process must be identified and the scope of their responsibilities defined. Keep in mind that recall could happen at any time, so night and weekend telephone numbers for Committee members should be available.

Provision should also be made for products that move outside of normal distribution channels, such as private label products or products that have special characteristics, such as foreign language labels. Consumers or distributors who have these recalled products in their possession might not realize that such products were in fact the ones being described in news reports. For that reason, every exception should be anticipated and some sort of plan of action defined.

Implementing the Recall Program

When it becomes known that there is indeed a product defect or hazard, the recall committee should be ready to swing into action. Blanding suggests the following course of action:[16]

A. Stop production and freeze distribution at all levels.

B. Identify lots affected and their location.

C. Identify all individuals in the firm involved in customer contact.

D. Notify customers. Note that it is important that all personnel in the firm be notified first so that they won't be caught off base by customers who have heard about the problem and are calling them for additional information.

E. Notify appropriate Federal agencies.

F. Develop recall plan.

The nature of the product defect or hazard and the extent of that product's distribution are obviously major factors in determining the extent and urgency of the recall program. Sometimes such products will not have identifying marks or numbers on them. Furthermore, it might be difficult to determine just where in the channels of distribution such products might still be on hand. In such cases, the only practical procedure is to identify as many lots as possible that are still out of reach of consumers and freeze distribution on those. Next, a massive publicity campaign should be mounted to warn buyers who have already purchased such products. The Consumer Product Safety Commission will allow a firm to conduct its own publicity as long as it spells out the hazards explicitly and as long as such publicity is picked up by the media.

Keep in mind that an actual recall may not be necessary. If only a part is defective, a replacement part can be mailed to consumers. Automobile manufacturers have done this with gasoline caps and defective ash trays in the past. Whatever procedure is followed, you should remember that a least-cost program can generally be defined that will do the job. Cost is a major factor in any product recall program.

Costs of Recall Programs

Finding the consumers who have purchased items will be a major cost in any recall program. Much care must be given to this aspect of your contingency plan. As an added impetus, you should be aware that the Consumer Product Safety Commission has *reopened* recall cases and has done its own random sampling of consumers to verify that retrofitting that was claimed by the manufacturers had actually been done. It is recommended that a special accounting be made of all costs assignable to a recall program. Among other things, the opportunity to review those costs at a later time can enable management to determine just how much it can reasonably invest in improved quality control and preventive measures.

You should not overlook the possible use of a third party to carry out the mechanics of a product recall program. Blanding suggests that there are many advantages in using a third party, such as a public warehouse, for such a program. Those advantages include keeping affected products out of normal distribution channels and thus preventing them from being reshipped as nondefective products.[17] If the public warehouse handles no other like products for your firm, so much the better. The use of a third party also helps separate recall costs for both transportation and warehousing, including accessorial charges unique to recalls charged by warehousemen experienced in handling such programs. Many public warehouses specialize in this area and are experienced in handling such programs.

The disposition of the recalled product is naturally an important consideration. In some cases it may be necessary to provide an environmental impact statement—if, for example, a substantial amount of product has to be burned or buried. This might require providing the regulatory agency with a certification document ascertaining that the items were indeed destroyed.

The recall process is not essentially different from the movement of existing distribution channels, except in the matter of disposition of the product itself. Even that may not be unfamiliar to most firms—many already have ways to process regular returns, and some already have salvage operations for repairing damaged shipments.

We all hope our firm will never be involved in a product recall, but the chances of this happening have certainly grown in the past few years. A well-planned recall program, even if it never has to be implemented, is an important area of focus for logistics managers.

Notes

1. George A. Steiner, *Strategic Planning* (New York: Free Press, 1979), p. 229.
2. Ibid., p. 233.
3. Ibid., p. 234.
4. Ibid., p. 234. See Rochelle O'Connor, "Planning Under Uncertainty: Multiple Scenarios and Contingency Planning" (New York: Conference Board, 1978), p. 17.
5. Steiner, p. 234.

6. The Research Institute of America (RIA) has compiled a report, "Coping with Energy Shortages and Higher Costs" (1977), that includes detailed recommendations on contingency planning. For further information, write to the Research Institute of America, 589 Fifth Avenue, New York, NY 10017.

7. Ibid.

8. Ibid.

9. Lester Bittel, ed., *Encyclopedia of Professional Management* (New York: McGraw-Hill, 1978), pp. 602, 603.

10. Step-by-step instructions on this kind of contingency planning are given in a report by the Research Institute of America, "How to Survive the Squeeze of Other People's Strikes" (New York: RIA, 1979).

11. Research Institute of America, "Selectron Special Report For Research Institute Executive Members: Disaster Guide For Management" (New York: RIA, n.d.).

12. Ibid.

13. Ibid.

14. Ibid.

15. Warren Blanding, *Blanding's Practical Physical Distribution* (Washington, D.C.: The Traffic Service Corporation, 1978), Chapter 9, pp. 156–167.

16. Ibid., Chapter 9, pp. 166–167.

17. Ibid., Chapter 9, p. 168.

The Distribution System: Components and Design

Logistic System Design

PAUL S. BENDER

Introduction

The economic system has traditionally been described in terms of three types of re-sources—labor, capital, and land. It is useful to look at logistics from the perspective of the economic system, because it becomes apparent that logistics deals with the *management* of the three traditional resources:

> *Labor*, reflected in the human resources needed to plan, operate, and control the lo-gistic system

> *Capital*, reflected in the money, facilities, equipment, and materials involved in the logistic process

> *Land*, reflected in the physical sites upon which most logistic activities take place: transportation, production, warehousing

The optimal allocation and administration of those economic resources is the overall aim of logistics.

The Structure of a Logistic System

From a logistic point of view, an organization can be conceptually described as an entity that *procures* goods and services from supply markets, *converts* them by production and logistic processes at production and logistic facilities, and *distributes* them to demand markets. The physical means for accomplishing these three steps constitute the organization's logistic system. Thus, a company's logistic system can be viewed as the bridge between its supply markets and its demand markets.

Analyzing the structure of this bridge, we find that the logistic system can be described as a network whose nodes are stationary inventories with variable levels such as plants and warehouses, and whose links are transportation operations, or flowing inventories with constant, intermittent levels. The physical functioning of the network can in turn be viewed as a cascade of material movements between inventory systems that replenish each other in sequence, triggered by demand markets.

Figure 9-1 illustrates the material flows between markets, through facilities. The behavior of the logistic system can be briefly described as follows:

1. When the inventory systems at the demand markets need replenishment, they trigger reorder signals: purchase or replenishment orders.

2. The reorder signals are received at one or more of the other inventories in the system: logistic facilities (distribution centers, warehouses, branches), plants, or supply markets.

3. The reorder signals trigger material movements that replenish the demand market inventory systems, while at the same time, facility inventories are reduced until depletion.

4. The material movement from one inventory to another takes place through a transportation system that constitutes a series of in-transit or flowing inventories.

5. The depleted inventories at production and logistic facilities in turn trigger peri-

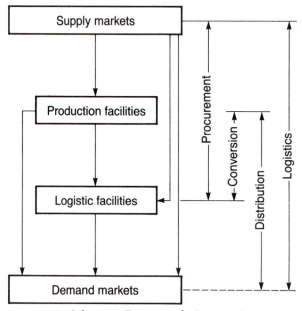

Figure 9-1   Schematic Diagram of a Logistic System

odic reorder signals on the higher-level inventories, which generate in-transit inventories to replenish them, and so on.

It is helpful to describe the logistic system in terms of a concatenation of inventory systems, because this highlights the need to consider the impact of stationary as well as flowing inventories in evaluating the configuration of a logistic system. It also highlights the need to relate closely the company's logistic system with its customer's and supplier's inventory systems, to ensure its maximum effectiveness.

We can illustrate the material flow in a logistic system around its major functions. Figure 9–2 shows that the logistic system constitutes the physical interface between supply and demand markets. There are two points worth noting in this figure.

1. Material flow between the logistic system and the markets it connects takes place in both directions, because of returns and replacements. The replacement backflow is becoming increasingly important because of the need to recycle materials. Furthermore, in some industries—such as book publishing—returns may constitute a very high proportion of original shipments.

2. Because of the close interaction between the logistic and the production systems, it is necessary to clearly define their interface. This is normally accomplished by assigning the responsibility for production planning to the logistic function; this function consists of translating sales forecasts into shipping forecasts which in turn are used to calculate the inventory levels required at different points of the logistic system. On that basis, the production system can then be assigned the responsibility for scheduling production, to produce the required inventories when and where they are needed.

The physical components involved in the logistic system described above are markets, facilities, and equipment. *Markets* are terminal nodes of the system that can only originate or receive freight. *Supply markets* originate freight; they are sources only. *Demand markets* receive freight; they are sinks only.

Facilities are intermediate nodes of the system that originate and receive freight; they are both sources and sinks, and can be of two types: *production* or *logistic*. For both types of facilities, it is useful to define the following attributes:

Throughput capacity is the maximum amount of freight that a facility is capable of receiving or of shipping in a given time period, whichever is larger. Receiving and shipping installed capacities are usually equal by design, since any facility has a limited capacity to hold inventory.

Throughput is the smaller of outbound or inbound freight shipped or received by a facility in a given time period.

Inventory variation is the amount of outbound minus inbound freight shipped and received by a facility in a given time period.

The usual time period considered for logistic system design is one year.

The principal types of facilities are production facilities, logistic facilities, and equipment. *Production facilities* include plants for basic manufacturing subassembly, assem-

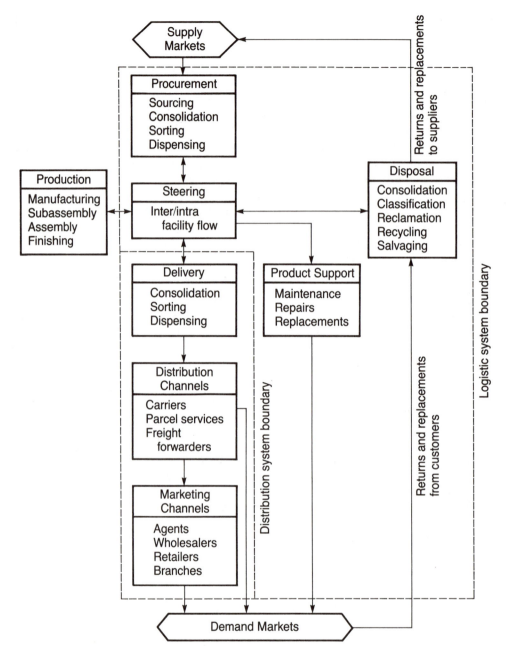

Figure 9-2   Material Flow and Major Functions in the Logistic System

bly, and finishing. These facilities receive raw materials and components and convert them into finished products by physical, chemical, or biological processes. The second category, *logistic facilities*, includes consolidation and distribution centers, warehouses, branches, terminals, and salvaging, re-cycling, and maintenance centers. These facilities receive and ship finished products. They transform them through physical operations such as repacking and order assembly, and add value to them by making them available at strategically located points. Furthermore, they allow the consolidation of freight, thus producing savings in transportation costs and improvements in delivery times.

The materials handling and transportation *equipment* establishes the links between facilities and markets in the logistic system, and can be described, as we saw before, as a set of flowing inventories with constant, intermittent levels.

In addition to these physical components, which constitute the configuration or network of a logistic system, two other components complete the logistic system:

The organization needed to operate the system

The management system, represented by the information management techniques, and the hardware and software for data collection, transmission, storage, retrieval, processing, and display, needed to support the organization and the physical configuration

These three components constitute the equivalent of the three legs of a logistic tripod—they support each other and the total system.

Important Trends to Consider

In analyzing and designing a logistic system it is important to view it in the context of several long-term trends that continuously modify the requirements the system has to meet. Major trends to consider involve:

1. Unit costs
2. Service requirements
3. Supranational dependency
4. Environmental controls
5. Population movements
6. Product life
7. Resource scarcity

Unit Costs

A fact of major importance is that while the unit costs of raw materials, energy, labor, equipment, facilities, surface transportation, and warehousing are steadily increasing, the unit costs of information gathering, transmission, processing, storage, and display are steadily decreasing, and sea and air transportation costs seem to be stable. As a consequence, the optimal cost trade-offs in a logistic system are continuously shifting.

Service Requirements

Increasingly sophisticated business management techniques, used by a growing number of companies, result in a continuous upgrading of their demands for better, more reliable customer service. As a consequence, the structure of the logistic system must be updated periodically to provide the required service in the most profitable way: that which provides the optimal trade-off between costs and service.

Supranational Dependency

The industrialized countries of the world are becoming progressively more dependent on imports of raw materials and energy. At the same time, improved means of world-wide communications and transportation are narrowing product differentiation on a geographic basis. This provides increasing opportunities for companies to export the products they originally developed for their traditional markets. As a consequence of this simultaneous convergence of worldwide supply and demand markets, there is increasing need to look at logistic systems on a global basis rather than a national or continental basis to arrive at the most profitable system configuration. Moreover, this means that the distinction between domestic and international logistic systems is becoming less and less meaningful.

Environmental Controls

Increasing concern over environmental protection, reflected in an increasing number of laws and regulations being established throughout the world, is having a significant impact on the location of economic activity, and its associated costs. As a consequence, it is becoming increasingly important in the evaluation of potential sites for production and logistic facilities to consider the possibility of future environmental legislation, which can change in a short time the costs associated with any facility at a given site.

Population Movements

In the United States as well as in many other countries important migration movements are significantly shifting the geographic dispersion of markets and labor pools. These movements are producing significant changes in land costs, labor costs, and taxes, which in turn are continuously changing the optimal cost tradeoff in a logistic system.

Product Life

Over the past few decades there has been a marked trend towards shorter product life. As a consequence, companies are changing their product mix with increasing frequency to support a given level of sales, and this in turn is translated into increasingly frequent adjustments to the logistic system to keep it working at near optimal levels.

Resource Scarcity

The increasing scarcity of traditional natural resources—especially raw materials and fuels—will place increasing pressure on private and public organizations to make more efficient use of the resources available. This trend is likely to produce significant changes in the way business is organized and run, and therefore, in the scope, structure, and characteristics of logistic systems.

In this author's judgement, it seems highly probable that in the coming years we will see business organizations structure their operations around the need to maximize the use of all resources available. Thus, instead of the traditional functions found in most organizations today—marketing, production, and finance—we may find that it will be more effective to structure operations as shown in Figure 9–3. Details on how such an organization would work will be discussed later in this chapter. The most important point at this stage of this discussion is that it is likely that the area of logistics will become part of a physical resources function that will be integrated with other functions through advanced information systems.

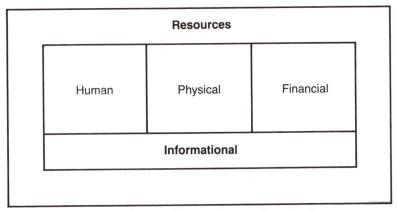

Figure 9-3   Possible Structure of Future Business Organizations

Such a development would be a natural progression from past trends. Although logistic activities are as old as human economic activity, they were not generally recognized as such in business until after World War II. At that time transportation and warehousing of finished goods started to converge in most manufacturing companies; the process culminated in the early 1960s with the concept of physical distribution, encompassing the control, movement, and storage of finished goods from the end of the production line to demand markets. By the late 1960s it was apparent that additional efficiencies were available by integrating all material flows—from suppliers of raw materials all the way to customers for finished goods. This idea crystallized in the logistic system concept discussed above. As the logistic concept is implemented in more companies, it will also reach a point where additional efficiencies can only be gained by expanding the scope of analysis. That step, likely to happen in the 1980s, will probably be in the direction of expanding logistic operations to encompass the management of all physical resources in the organization—not only materials, but also facilities, equipment, and land.

For all the reasons given above, it is important to build enough flexibility into the structure of logistic systems to enable them to adapt to changing requirements. It is also important to review the structure of the logistic system every few years, to keep it working at maximum efficiency by ensuring the optimal trade-offs between costs, and between cost and performance. Periodic reviews also ensure that the scope of the system under analysis is adequate, and that it will continue to work with maximum effectiveness.

Statement of the Problem

The structure of a logistic system, as previously described, can be depicted as in Figure 9–4. The design of a logistic system should clearly specify (1) the structure and characteristics of each of its three components, (2) the fashion in which each component ties in with the other two, and (3) the relationship between the logistic system and the other major functions with which it is directly related: marketing, production, and finance.

The first two points can be accomplished simultaneously by designing the three components sequentially as in Figure 9–5. The third point is accomplished by including in the logistic system requirements the major policies established by the marketing, production, and finance functions. In this regard, the main objective is to design the logistic system in

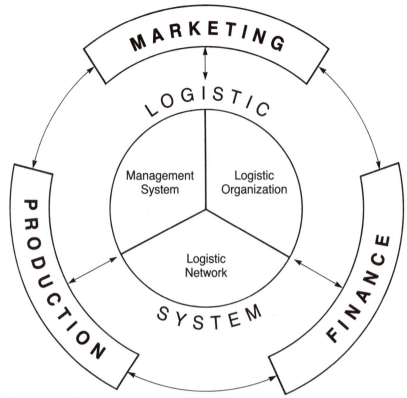

Figure 9-4 The Components of the Logistic System

such a way that it serves as a mechanism to reconcile the needs of all functions in an optimal fashion.

The logistic needs of marketing, production, and finance are usually translated in terms of three factors: (1) number and extent of product lines, (2) number and location of inventory points such as warehouses and branches, and (3) level of inventory investment. Generally, these needs are reflected as shown in Table 9-1. In the usual management process, marketing, production, and finance executives tend to consider each other's requirements. However, it is necessary for them to have a mechanism to ensure the optimal trade-offs between their conflicting interests.

The logistic function is in the best position to draw together all the above requirements, add to them the pertinent logistic costs, and arrive at the optimum compromise: the solution that maximizes the company's total profit. To this effect, it is necessary to specify the main features of each component of the logistic system.

The Logistic Network

The specification of the logistic network configuration must include market allocation, facility determination, and equipment description.

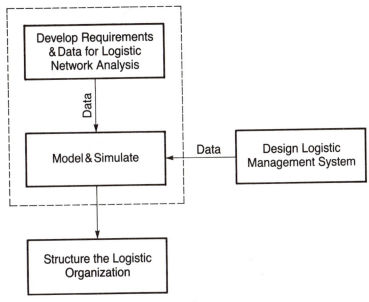

Figure 9-5 Logistic System Design Sequence

1. *Market allocation* includes the assignment of each *demand market* to one or more facilities from which it must be served; and the assignment of *supply markets* to the production or logistic facilities they must serve, and the quantities they must supply.

2. *Facility determination* includes the *number and location* of production and logistic facilities; the *mission* of each facility (the functions to be performed, and the products to be processed at each one); and the throughput capacity of each facility, and the maximum inventory it must be capable of holding.

3. *Equipment description* includes the type of materials handling equipment needed in all facilities, to move, store and retrieve materials; and the type of transportation equipment and arrangements needed to move freight throughout the system.

Table 9-1   Logistic Needs of Major Business Functions

| | *Factors* | | |
Functions	*Number of Products*	*Number of Inventory Points*	*Inventory Investment Level*
Marketing	HIGH To maximize sales volume	HIGH To increase proximity to customers	HIGH To minimize back orders
Production	Low To minimize set up costs	Low To simplify transfers to distribution	HIGH To obtain economies of scale through long runs
Finance	Low To minimize promotion costs and risks	Low To reduce fixed costs and obtain economies of scale	Low To conserve cash and credit and minimize inventory carrying costs

The Logistic Management System

A management system is needed to plan, execute, and control the operation of the logistic network. This includes specifications for information requirements, management techniques, hardware, and software.

Information

The first step in this process is to determine what information is needed to support the logistic management process. The information enables the allocation and administration of all resources involved in the network.

Management Techniques

The main directions and guidelines for running the logistic system, as well as the specific techniques to be used, will be the responsibility of management. The most important management techniques to be defined are:

> *Policies*, covering such matters as inventory carrying costs, depreciation, replacement, customer service objectives, and attitudes towards competition.

> *Procedures*, covering such areas as forecasting responsibilities and reporting requirements.

> *Formulas*, to be used in decision making, such as economic order quantities.

An important trend in logistics management is the increasing use of quantitative techniques—such as management sciences and econometrics—and of normative techniques—such as behavioral sciences—in the development of management techniques. The main consequence of this trend is to continuously lower the organizational level at which decisions are made. For example, a few years ago virtually all decisions concerning inventory management were the responsibility of top management. Now, with the introduction of quantitative techniques and efficient computers, most decisions affecting inventory management have been effectively delegated to middle management.

Hardware

Hardware includes all the devices needed to handle data for such operations as data capturing and recording, data communications, information storage and retrieval, data processing, and information display. The hardware needed to support management systems is currently undergoing major transformations that are very likely to continue for many years; these transformations can be summarized as follows:

- There is a clear trend away from centralized data processing, towards communications-oriented distributed processing. This trend is likely to accelerate as better and cheaper microcomputers and communications systems become available.

- The size and speed of hardware are increasing rapidly while at the same time their costs are decreasing.

- As a consequence of these two trends there is a clear trend towards designing systems that integrate the hardware needed for data processing and communications with word-processing and process control hardware.

As a result of these trends, management systems increasingly rely on interaction between management personnel and information processing machines.

Furthermore, the integration of traditional data-processing hardware with communications, word-processing, and process control equipment makes it possible to design systems that can be managed and operated by a single system. For example, process control techniques used to operate automated warehouses can be directly linked to the order-processing and inventory management systems so that when an order is processed, inventory records are updated, reorder decisions are made, and orders are picked simultaneously. When those operations are also linked to word-processing hardware, it becomes possible to generate all documentation needed for shipping and invoicing concurrently with the warehousing and inventory management activities.

Software

It is necessary to provide software for operating the hardware that supports the management system. There are three types of software that must be specified in designing a system:

Operating systems, that manage the use of all hardware linked in the system

Application programs, that constitute the vehicles through which the management techniques are applied in the system

Data management systems, that allow the efficient manipulation of data by users with limited data-processing training

The most important trend in this area is the increasing use of data base–oriented systems instead of traditional data files. There are two main advantages of a data base–oriented system. First, all data needed throughout the system are entered only once. This eliminates the need to reconcile information and ensures that all decisions and operations are based on the same information. Second, because of the ease with which data can be handled (sorted, merged, etc.) it is possible to replace fixed format reports and displays by variable format outputs; thus, the user is presented with a menu of options from which to choose what information to display, and in what form.

The Logistic Organization

An organization is needed to support the operation of the logistic network and its management system. It is necessary to specify:

Job descriptions for all positions in the organization, outlining job content, reporting relationships, qualifications and experience needed, levels of authority and responsibility

Organization charts showing formal and informal reporting relationships, and personnel filling each position

Training requirements for all individuals to ensure that their background and experience is enhanced in the best possible way to meet the needs of their positions

Design Methodology

The design methodology proposed here is structured around a basic idea that provides the direction for this effort, and unifies the results of the individual steps proposed below. The basic idea underlying logistic system design is that the system should be built in such a way that it maximizes its profit contribution, while providing the optimum level of customer service. In this regard, the evaluation of alternative logistic systems should be treated like any other investment: each alternative should be characterized by its cash flow—including depreciation of design and implementation costs, and salvage value—so that its return on investment (ROI) can be calculated. By the same token, the decision to replace an existing system should be evaluated in a form analogous to that used for the replacement of any piece of equipment or asset.

Since the design of the logistic management system, and of the logistic organization, is covered in detail elsewhere in this book, we will concentrate here on the design of the logistic network. The methodology recommended here can be graphically described in flow chart form as shown in Figure 9–6.

The first step in the design process is to describe the current system, including its logistic network, management system, and organization. This provides a basis for all the subsequent analysis. Once the description of the current system is completed, and a "base year" is established, the next step is to establish the requirements that an alternative system should meet, to solve current problems and profit from current and projected opportunities. These requirements cover all three components of the logistic system.

After the requirements have been determined, two phases can start simultaneously: (1) the development of the logistic management system, and (2) the development of all pertinent costs, constraints, and conditions needed to design the logistic network. These two phases are related, because both provide inputs to the next step, which is to build a model of the logistic network and, through successive simulations, arrive at a recommended configuration that will operate under the management system, run by the logistic organization.

After the characteristics of the logistic network and the management system have been established, it is possible to develop the logistic organization needed to support both. At this point, all the necessary information is available to perform the financial analysis that relates investment requirements and anticipated savings, and summarizes the financial characteristics of the project as a return on investment.

The next step in the process is to develop an implementation plan, indicating how to manage the transition from the existing system—or lack of system—to the proposed system. At this point, the design process should be carefully documented, to facilitate subsequent reviews and to support the periodic auditing of operations that should take place after implementation.

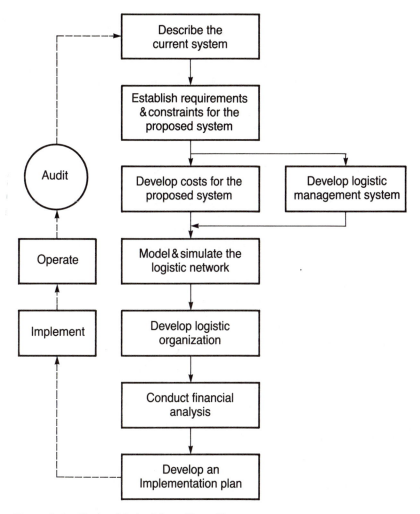

Figure 9-6   Design Methodology Flow Chart

The design process is almost—but not entirely—completed at this point. Further design refinements will be needed during the implementation and operation of the proposed system, to "fine tune" the components of the logistic system and their interaction.

In addition to the ongoing process of "fine tuning," the performance and cost of the logistic system should be audited periodically, to ensure that further needed modifications take place, and to maintain the efficiency of the system. Normally these audits should take place every two to three years. A basic objective of the audits should be to evaluate the need to replace or overhaul the current system, and thus trigger a new design phase.

Two important conclusions can be drawn from the methodology outlined above. *First*, logistic system design is mainly a sequential process, in which each step provides the foundation for the next one. As a consequence, if the information resulting from any step is already available, that step can be omitted. *Second*, logistic system design is a continuous, cyclical process. As we have discussed earlier, trends in costs and services are continuously changing the optimal trade-off between them; thus it is important to update the characteristics of the system to maintain it at or near a maximum efficiency level. This process is accomplished through periodic audits of the system; the audits may follow all or some of the steps outlined in the methodology.

Let us now examine in greater detail each one of the steps in the design methodology.

Describe the Current System

If there is no system in existence, this step should be skipped. When there is already a logistic system in existence, it is advisable to start the design process by studying the characteristics of the existing system. Beginning the design procedure with a description of existing conditions can help to:

1. Gain a good understanding of the current system, its products, markets, facilities, and other resources available, and of how the overall business mission and goals relate to the logistic system.

2. Identify problems that must be corrected, and potential improvement areas. At this stage problems are often uncovered that were not known to management.

3. Identify existing features that are worth preserving, thus simplifying system design and implementation.

4. Identify existing features that must be preserved for legal, policy, or other reasons.

5. Gather the data needed to describe the characteristics of the system at a "base year." This is then used as a basis to "grow" data for the "design year." A frequent by-product of this process is the identification of important data that have never been available before.

The information describing the current system can be most effectively displayed using flow charts and tables. These charts and tables should:

1. Provide data at different levels of aggregation. This facilitates the understanding of the system by allowing analysis of data from the most general to the most detailed levels of aggregation.

2. Provide meaningful comparisons between performance and associated costs. This helps spot problems and opportunities.

3. Use the same formats that will be needed later on for design year input data. This will make possible direct comparisons between base year and design year data, and will facilitate data projections.

The most important types of information that must be included in a display of the logistic system are:

1. A *description of the logistic network* to cover the following areas:

   a. *Performance*, including order completeness, response times, throughput volume, and inventory levels

b. *Costs*, including purchasing, production, warehousing, inventorying, and transportation costs

c. *Characteristics*, including products (descriptions and classification), markets (supply and demand statistics), demand characteristics, capacity constraints, policy constraints, facilities (location, layout, methods), and equipment (inventory and age)

2. A *description of the management system*, best explained through the use of system documentation that includes logic flow charts, tabulations of volumes and costs, and narratives of policies, methods, and procedures

3. A *description of the organization*, best presented through the use of organization charts, job descriptions, and tabulations of manning levels

A major point that is often overlooked is that all information used to describe the current system should be carefully checked by means of visits and inspections, to ensure that it reflects what *actually* happens, and not what *should* happen. This is particularly important with regard to system documentation, organization charts, and job descriptions.

Since management systems and organization are discussed elsewhere in this *Handbook*, we will concentrate here on the logistic network design phase. The most critical step in the analysis and design process is to determine the right level of data aggregation: the more aggregated the data, the greater the potential errors in analysis, but the simpler it is to analyze, and the cheaper it is to assemble. Most data can be readily aggregated in a simple way; for example if several plants producing the same products are located in the same city, they may be considered as a single production facility.

Generally, the most difficult decisions on level of aggregation deal with products, and with demand markets. In this regard, it is sometimes difficult to establish their levels of aggregation *before* surveying the current system. When possible, however, it is advisable to do so, to avoid having to reformat base year data later on.

To aggregate products and demand markets, it is necessary to consider a variety of factors. To aggregate products, there are four types of factors to consider: marketing, logistic, production, and organizational. In all cases, it is important to account for trends in these factors.

1. *Marketing Factors*

a. *Sales volume.* Analysis by contribution of sales volume for all products or logical groupings of them can identify the main products that account for the bulk of volume shipped (for example, the products that account for 85% or more of the total volume). The rest of the products can be added to similar products identified within that percentage, or combined into additional groups.

b. *Sales mix.* If similar products are sold in significantly different ratios in different markets, they may have to be considered separately to account for their different geographic dispersion.

c. *Service requirements.* Similar products being sold to different market segments, or through different marketing channels within an area, may have to be separated to account for differences in service requirements.

2. *Logistic Factors*

   a. *Transportation rates.* Try to aggregate all products moving at similar transportation rates.

   b. *Warehousing costs.* Try to aggregate all products that can be handled and stored at similar unit costs.

   c. *Inventory costs.* Try to aggregate all products that have a similar unit inventory carrying cost.

   d. *Shipment characteristics.* Try to aggregate all products that have a similar frequency distribution of shipment sizes or a similar average shipment size in all markets.

3. *Production Factors*

   a. *Eligible plants.* If certain products can only be made at certain plants, they may have to be identified separately.

   b. *Production costs.* Try to aggregate all products that have similar unit production costs.

   c. *Production mix.* Try to aggregate all products that are made together at the same plants, in the same ratios.

4. **Organizational Factors** When it is necessary to display inputs or outputs by organizational unit, similar products from different units may have to be kept separate.

To aggregate demand markets, to establish market area boundaries, use a well-balanced number of areas (as explained below), take trends into account, and try to develop common market areas for all organizational units involved. In this regard, there are marketing, logistic, and organizational factors to consider, as follows:

1. *Marketing Factors*

   a. *Sales volume.* Analysis by contribution of total sales volume by city can identify those cities that account for the bulk of the volume shipped. These major cities can then be used as base points, around which boundaries can be drawn to include the rest of the cities.

   b. *Sales concentration.* Boundaries around base points should be drawn in such a way that the base point contains the bulk of the demand within the area. The rest of the demand should be spread as uniformly as possible throughout the area.

   c. *Sales territories.* Try to follow sales territory lines as much as possible, or at least use consistent criteria for geographic agglomeration (such as standard point location code, ZIP Code, and standard marketing statistical areas).

   d. *Marketing channels.* If different marketing areas are served through different marketing channels, it is advisable to draw the boundaries according to demarcation lines established by those marketing channels.

   e. *Competition.* When competition is unusually strong (or weak) in certain areas, it may be advisable to define those areas separately to facilitate analysis.

   f. *Special conditions.* Other marketing factors that may guide the drawing of boundaries are major customer locations, test market areas, advertising arrangements, and duty-free areas.

2. *Logistic Factors*

    a. *Transportation rates.* Avoid having, in a single area, points that constitute destinations with significantly different transportation rates or local charges.

    b. *Selectivity.* Avoid having very few, but large, demand areas, because that constrains logistic analysis by forcing major areas to be considered as units that must be entirely assigned to given facilities, for example. On the other hand, having far too many market areas does not increase the accuracy of transportation cost projections enough to justify the additional efforts in data collection and processing, and increases demand-forecasting errors. The number of market areas needed for accurate demand representation depends on the type of business—consumer or industrial goods—and on the overall market characteristics. Table 9–2 gives a summary of typical numbers of market areas that provide a good balance between accuracy needs, and simplicity of analysis.

    c. *Distribution channels.* If different marketing areas are served through different distribution channels (such as parcel post, or freight forwarders), it is advisable to try to draw the boundaries respecting the demarcation lines established by those distribution channels.

    d. *Port areas.* When exports are a significant part of the volume processed in the system, export demands may be represented as being at the ports of loading, ignoring the logistic systems overseas. If port selection is part of the logistic network design problem, this cannot be done, and demand areas overseas must be defined, and included in the analysis.

3. *Organizational Factors.* Even if it is necessary to display inputs or outputs by organizational unit, it is advisable to try to use a common set of boundaries for all units in order to simplify file structures, data collection and processing, and analysis.

The factors outlined above should give a good idea of the considerations involved in aggregating data for products and demand markets. Similar considerations apply to other types of data aggregation, including suppliers, plants, warehouses, and transportation modes.

Again, the objective of data aggregation is to simplify its analysis, without hiding any characteristics that may be influential in determining the features of the final design. With regard to precision, in most practical applications it is enough to express all data with four significant digits.

Once data aggregation levels have been established, they can be documented in a data dictionary that defines the components of each data element to be used in the analysis. Table 9–3 shows typical contents of a definition of supply markets. The *designation* is the label to be used throughout the analysis; the *location* is the point at which the supply market will be considered situated; *includes* lists the names and locations of all the actual

Table 9–2 Typical Number of Demand Market Areas

Region	Consumer Products	Industrial Products
United States	80–150	30–50
Canada	20–40	10–20
Western Europe	60–120	20–40

Table 9–3   Example of Data Dictionary Showing a Definition of Suppliers

	Definition of Supply Markets		
Designation	*Location*	*Includes*	*Products*
Supplier 01	Los Angeles, CA	Ajax Corp. Bakersfield, CA	01, 02
		XYZ Corp. Los Angeles, CA	01, 02
		A & B Inc. Long Beach, CA	01, 02
Supplier 02	Chicago, IL	Lake Shore Corp. Chicago, IL	03
		Bears Inc. Schaumberg, IL	03

companies that are grouped as one supplier; the *products* are the product groups that the supplier can offer. Table 9–4 shows typical contents of a definition of products. The *designation* is the label to be used throughout the analysis; the *type* identifies whether the product group is a raw material, in process, or finished goods; *includes* defines the actual products to be agglomerated under each designation. Table 9–5 shows typical contents of a definition of demand markets. The *designation* is the label to be used throughout the analysis; the *location* is the point at which the demand will be considered situated; *includes* lists the ranges of ZIP codes that constitute each demand area. Demands may be aggregated using ZIP codes, counties, or census tracts, for example. It is also useful to draw a map showing the boundaries of each demand, and its central point or location.

After the levels of data aggregation have been defined, it is possible to develop the necessary information to describe the current system. There are no "standard" ways of displaying the information, but the following typical examples should serve as a guide:

Figure 9–7 shows a typical base year summary flow chart. In it, the major levels in the logistic network are consolidated each in one block: suppliers, plants, warehouses, wholesalers, and retailers.

Table 9–4   Example of Data Dictionary Showing a Definition of Products

	Definition of Products	
Designation	*Type*	*Includes*
Product 01	Raw material	Caustic soda, 83% Caustic soda, 95%
Product 02	Raw material	PVC in drums PVC in sacks
Product 03	Raw material	PVC in bulk
Product 04	Finished good	Detergents Cat. #A-100 to A-108, B-115 to B-128

Table 9-5   Example of Data Dictionary Showing a Definition of Demand Markets

	Definition of Demand Markets	
Designation	*Location*	*Includes (ZIP nos. starting with)*
Demand 001	Philadelphia, PA	190 to 199
Demand 002	Tampa, FL	327 to 329 335 to 339
Demand 003	Omaha, NB	510 to 519 680 to 699
Demand 004	San Antonio, TX	780 to 782 786 to 789

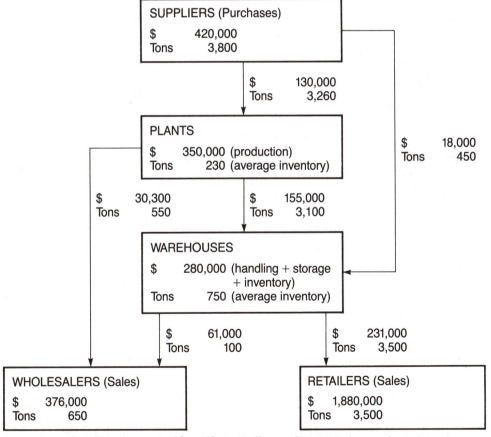

Figure 9-7   Base Year Summary Flow Chart (Dollars and Tons in Thousands). Inbound tonnages may not equal outbound tonnages due to inventory variations, tonnages added locally, purchases or sales not yet shipped, or shipped in anticipation.

Table 9-6 Base Year Operations Summary (Dollars and Tons in Thousands)

Facility	Through-put (Tons)	Average Inventory (Tons)	Average Inventory (Dollars)	Fixed Cost (Dollars)	Operating Cost (Dollars)	Transportation Inbound No. of Shipments	Inbound Tons	Inbound Dollars	Outbound No. of Shipments	Outbound Tons	Outbound Dollars	Inbound-to-Outbound Ratio Tons per Shipment	Dollars per Ton
Plants													
1	880	64	13,100	23,100	75,200	28,000	880	41,000	31,000	980	56,000	31:32	47:57
2	1,120	78	18,500	26,500	92,400	33,000	1,120	44,800	40,000	1,240	63,000	34:31	40:51
3	1,260	88	16,300	28,400	104,400	34,000	1,260	44,200	47,000	1,430	66,300	37:30	35:46
Total	3,260	230	47,900	78,000	272,000	95,000	3,260	130,000	118,000	3,650	185,300	34:31	40:51
Warehouses													
A	280	60	19,300	4,500	10,900	9,900	240	18,600	21,800	350	34,600	24:16	78:99
B	460	99	31,600	6,800	17,800	16,100	400	24,800	35,500	500	46,700	25:14	62:93
C	745	158	50,500	11,000	27,600	26,000	650	31,000	57,300	700	58,400	25:12	48:83
D	960	201	64,800	13,700	34,900	33,450	843	37,200	73,700	910	70,000	25:12	44:77
E	1,105	232	73,800	15,000	37,800	38,550	967	43,400	84,700	1,140	82,300	25:13	45:72
Total	3,550	750	240,000	51,000	129,000	124,000	3,100	155,000	273,000	3,600	292,000	25:13	50:81
Total for System	6,810	980	287,900	129,000	401,000	219,000	6,360	285,000	391,000	7,250	477,300		

The *suppliers* block shows the volume of purchases from all suppliers, in dollars and in physical units; the *wholesalers* and *retailers* blocks show the volume of sales to each group; *plants* and *warehouses* show the total average inventories carried at each type of facility along with their operating costs; the arrows indicate the volumes transported between all entities, expressed in physical units and their associated transportation costs.

Table 9–6 is a base year operations summary, showing for each facility in the system, as well as for the system as a whole,

- Actual throughput in physical units or dollars

- Average value of inventories maintained, both in dollars and physical units

- Fixed cost

- Variable operating cost

- Transportation characteristics, including:

  Number of inbound shipments received
  Number of inbound tons received
  Inbound transportation costs
  Number of outbound shipments originated
  Number of outbound tons originated
  Outbound transportation costs
  Tons per shipment inbound, and outbound
  Dollars per ton inbound and outbound

Table 9–7, a base year market summary, shows for every market the volume supplied or demanded (in dollars and physical units), the location of the market, and the main products supplied or demanded.

Table 9–7   Base Year Market Summary   (Dollars and Tons in Thousands)

	Volume		*Location (SPLC)**			
Markets	*(Tons)*	*($)*	*(State)*	*(County)*	*(City)*	*Main Products*
Supply						
1	610	67,400	17	03	02	01
2	1,420	160,000	31	01	08	01,02
3	1,630	180,100	15	11	14	01,02
Other	140	12,500				
Total	3,800	420,000				
Demand						
1	250	112,000	17	07	12	03,04,05
2	400	178,900	08	08	07	03,04,05
3	420	187,800	31	22	18	03,04,05
4	630	281,700	12	04	05	03,04,05
5	1,080	483,000	15	09	11	03,04,05
6	1,250	559,000	21	13	01	03,04,05
Other	120	53,600				03,04
Total	4,150	1,856,000				

*SPLC = Standard point location system.

Table 9–8, base year demand characteristics, shows for every demand market, by product group, the number of physical units shipped at various weight breaks, and the fraction represented by each weight break. The same information is summarized at the end for the entire system.

Table 9–9, base year cash flow summary, shows for each product included, its volume purchased or sold in Physical Units, and the variable costs associated with each one, including purchasing or manufacturing, warehousing, inventory carrying, and transportation. In addition it is useful to show the sales income generated by each finished product

Table 9–8   Base Year Demand Characteristics for Each Demand Market

| Shipment Size (Lbs) | Service Cycle (Days) | Annual Tonnage Demanded | | | |
| | | Product 11 | | Product 12 | |
		Tons	Fraction	Tons	Fraction
Under 150	2	.24	.0020	0.00	.0000
	5	.38	.0031	0.00	.0000
	10	.56	.0046	0.00	.0000
		1.18	.0097	0.00	.0000
150–500	5	.61	.0050	0.00	.0000
	10	.48	.0039	0.00	.0000
		1.09	.0089	0.00	.0000
500–1,000	5	2.52	.0206	0.00	.0000
	10	.57	.0047	0.00	.0000
		3.09	.0253	0.00	.0000
1,000–2,000	5	3.14	.0257	2.17	.0240
	10	.93	.0076	3.94	.0435
		4.07	.0333	6.11	.0675
2,000–5,000	5	6.54	.0536	8.37	.0924
	10	2.57	.0210	4.51	.0498
		9.11	.0746	12.88	.1422
5,000–10,000	5	3.31	.0271	3.61	.0399
	10	6.84	.0560	7.49	.0827
	15	5.96	.0488	10.83	.1196
		16.11	.1319	21.93	.2422
10,000–20,000	5	8.68	.0711	0.00	.0000
	10	14.72	.1204	7.15	.0790
	15	23.34	.1911	12.92	.1427
		46.74	.3826	20.07	.2217
20,000–40,000	10	7.58	.0621	8.56	.0945
	15	16.41	.1343	14.32	.1582
		23.99	.1964	22.88	.2527
Over 40,000	15	14.38	.1177	6.67	.0737
CPU		1.06	.0087	0.00	.0000
PP		1.33	.0109	0.00	.0000
Total		122.15	1.0000	90.54	1.0000

NOTE: CPU = Customer pick up; PP = Parcel post.

Table 9-9 Base Year Cash Flow Summary   (Dollars and Tons in Thousands)

Product	Volume (Tons)	Variable Costs (Dollars)						Sales Income (Dollars)
		Purch.	Mfg.	Whsing.	Inv.	Transp.	Total	
Raw Materials								
01	850	103,500	0	0	0	36,300	139,800	0
02	1,380	178,300	0	0	0	53,600	231,900	0
03	1,030	98,200	0	0	0	40,100	138,300	0
Total	3,260	380,000	0	0	0	130,000	510,000	0
Finished Goods								
11	450	40,000	0	0	0	36,100	76,100	143,600
12	780	0	66,500	58,200	34,600	82,100	241,400	424,020
13	1,620	0	173,100	136,500	89,200	227,500	626,300	874,020
14	930	0	89,300	74,900	18,300	118,200	300,700	508,200
15	370	0	21,100	10,400	11,700	31,400	74,600	305,380
Total	4,150	40,000	350,000	280,000	153,800	495,300	1,319,100	2,256,000
Total for System	7,410	420,000	350,000	280,000	153,800	625,300	1,829,100	2,256,000

to compare it with the total variable cost. At the end of the report, all figures are summarized for the entire system.

Table 9–10, a base year service performance summary, shows for each demand market, and for each product shipped there, the mean response time, order completeness, and associated standard deviations (SD).

In addition to these charts, other documents can complete the description of the current system, including maps showing facility locations, maps showing demand market boundaries, and facility layouts and methods descriptions. The analysis of all the information described here permits the identification of problem areas and opportunities for improvement. Furthermore, it establishes the level of data breakdown to be used in analysis.

Establish Requirements and Constraints for an Alternative System

The description of the current system provides a definition of current and potential problems that require attention; it also identifies opportunities for improving costs and performance. These elements are a first statement of requirements and constraints that should be met by the system.

In addition, several other types of requirements and constraints must be identified. These can be classified as follows:

- *Service requirements* (response time, order completeness, shipping accuracy, shipment condition)

- *Capacity constraints* (supplier and facility constraints)

- *Handling and storage* (established by characteristics of packaging, and unitization methods and equipment used)

- *Facility location requirements*

Table 9–10   Base Year Service Performance Summary

Demand Market	Product	Response Time (Days)		Order Completeness ($ Fraction)	
		Mean	*SD*	*Mean*	*SD*
001	01	2.83	.23	.92	.08
	02	4.61	.51	.96	.03
	03	3.84	.43	.93	.02
002	01	1.98	.17	.98	.01
	02	3.51	.31	.97	.02
003	01	2.03	.28	.89	.09
	02	4.16	.61	.91	.11
System	01	2.54	.27	.88	.07
	02	4.01	.43	.93	.04
	03	3.48	.36	.97	.05
	04	5.17	.48	.95	.03
	05	2.11	.24	.96	.04

NOTE: SD = Standard deviation; $ fraction = fraction of dollar value ordered that was shipped on time.

- *Transportation arrangements*

- *Demand characteristics*

- *Management systems requirements*

Other planning factors and constraints may also be involved, including financial, legal, organizational, and other requirements that must be met by the logistic system. Because by their nature these are unique to each situation, we will not discuss them here.

It is important to establish, for each type of requirement or constraint, whether it is different for each product or applies overall, to all products. Let us now examine in more detail each of the groups of requirements.

Service Requirements

Response time or service cycle is the time elapsed from receipt of a customer order until the goods are delivered to the customer. As response time varies, so do the corresponding sales and logistic costs. These relationships are shown graphically in Figure 9–8. The sales income curve can be developed using market research techniques. The logistic cost curve can be developed by simulation, as described later in this chapter; this curve represents

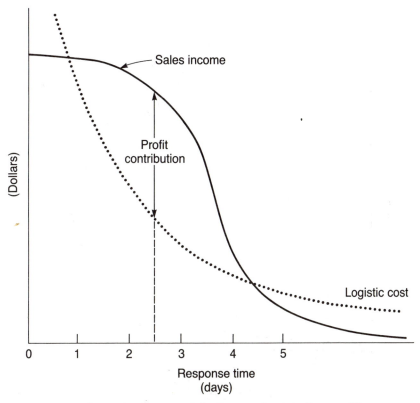

Figure 9-8   Relationship between Sales Income, Logistic Cost, and Response Time

the optimal costs for varying response times. The difference between the two curves is the profit contribution of the logistic system. The example in Figure 9–8 shows an optimum response time of 2.5 days.

Order completeness is the fraction of customer demand that is shipped within the optimal—or agreed upon—response time. As order completeness varies, so do the corresponding sales and inventory costs. These relationships are shown graphically in Figure 9–9. The sales income curve can be developed using market research techniques. The inventory cost can be developed as a result of the inventory control system rules that relate order completeness levels to the inventory-carrying costs needed to ensure them.

Shipping accuracy is the ratio between the number of shipments that have the right items, correct count, and correct address, and the total number of shipments in a given time period. Accuracy is determined by the control procedures used in the system. The more intensive the control procedures, the higher the accuracy obtained and the higher the cost of controlling; on the other hand, the higher the accuracy, the lower the cost of correcting mistakes—including paying for and processing returns, reshipping orders, cancelling orders, etc.

The costs of controlling and correcting for different levels of shipping accuracy are usually developed empirically by trying different levels of control and measuring their impact on costs and accuracy. The analysis to determine the optimum accuracy level is shown graphically in Figure 9–10. The lowest total cost point determines the optimum

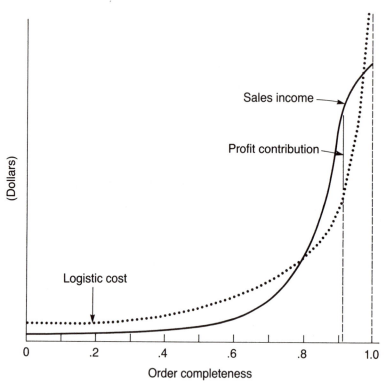

Figure 9-9   Relationship between Sales Income, Inventory Cost, and Order Completeness

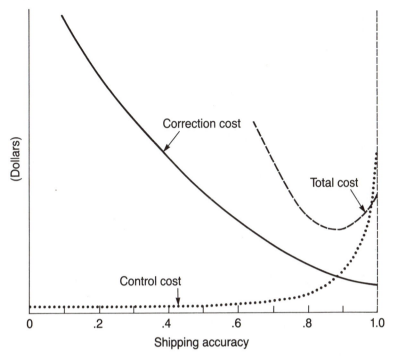

Figure 9-10 Relationship between Shipping Accuracy Control and
Correction Costs

level of accuracy. It is advisable to structure the control system to get near the optimum
level of accuracy. In some cases, however, marketing considerations may dictate the need
for higher than optimum levels of accuracy; in those cases, the penalty of higher accuracy
can be determined, and compared with the additional profits stemming from higher accuracy, to determine whether higher accuracy is worthwhile.

Shipment condition is the ratio between the number of shipments delivered in good
condition and the total number of shipments dispatched. Shipment condition is determined mainly by the quality of protective packaging used, and to a certain extent by the
transportation mode. To select the best packaging design, it is advisable to trade packaging costs against claims costs and related expenses. This analysis is illustrated in Figure
9-11. The lowest total cost point determines the best packaging design: the actual package
design should have a cost close to the lowest total cost, to justify the protection it provides.

Capacity Constraints

These constraints refer to facility throughputs and, by extension, to supply capacity. For
each facility and each supplier considered in the analysis it is necessary to determine
which, if any, constraints apply. *Maximum constraints* establish the maximum throughput capacity or supply capacity acceptable. These constraints may be applied to the facility or supplier, and to products that flow through the facility or are provided by the supplier. *Minimum constraints* can be of two types. *Conditional* constraints apply only if the
facility or supplier is included in the optimum solution as a desirable entity; in that case,

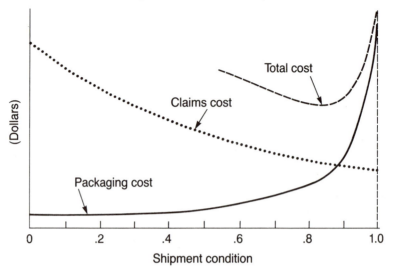

Figure 9-11   Relationship between Shipment Condition, Packaging Cost, and Claims Cost

the entity must have a specified minimum throughput or supply volume either overall or by product, or both. *Unconditional* constraints force the entity into the solution by demanding that it provide a specified minimum throughput or supply volume overall and/or by product.

Handling and Storage Requirements

These requirements are the basis for developing warehousing and transportation costs. The two major characteristics of the material handling system to be established concern (1) packaging and unitization, and (2) handling systems and equipment.

PACKAGING AND UNITIZATION

In this regard it is necessary to establish a relationship between the quantity of goods moved and the type of packaging and unitization devices used, for groups of items with similar handling characteristics. This implies the selection of cases for packaging units, pallets to unitize cases, and containers to unitize pallets for transportation. The dimensions, materials, and construction of each type of packaging or unitization device must be specified.

The materials and construction used have a direct impact on the extent of damaged goods in handling and transportation operations. The problem here is to minimize the total cost of packaging plus damage losses, as shown in Figure 9-11. The dimensions of unitization devices have a direct impact on handling costs and also on transportation costs. This impact can be quite substantial; for example, the cost of handling a given weight in two 20 ft containers is typically about 60 percent higher than the cost of handling the same weight in one 40 ft container.

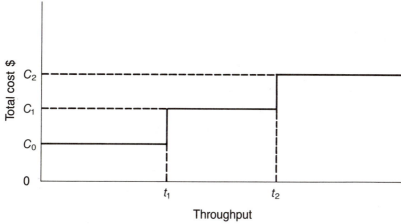

Figure 9-12   Discontinuous Costs

HANDLING SYSTEMS AND EQUIPMENT

These must be specified as a function of annual throughput to be handled in, through, and out of a warehouse. The major operations covered in these specifications are

Receiving	Assembling
Storing	Packaging
Retrieving	Shipping

Given the handling characteristics of products—physical state, packaging types and dimensions, density—as well as important allied characteristics such as flammability and fragility, it is possible to define the handling systems and equipment to be used, and the throughput ranges over which they are valid.

Facility Location Requirements

All active facilities in existence in the current system should be considered in the design of a logistic system. In addition, potential sites for production and logistic facilities should be identified. If any important markets do not have nearby facilities, potential sites near them may be worth evaluating in the search for greater profitability. Usually *production* facilities will tend to be located close to supply markets when the production process involves important loss of weight (e.g., chemical processes) and will tend to be close to demand markets when the production process involves important gain of weight (e.g., beverage manufacturing). *Logistic* facilities tend to be close to production facilities when their primary role is to mix products from many plants, and tend to be close to demand markets when their primary role is to minimize freight costs. All these considerations are tempered by other factors, such as local availability of labor, taxes, and wages.

When the current system has many dispersed facilities, it is worth considering *central* facilities that can consolidate them. If the current system has only a few regional facilities, it may be worthwhile to replace them with a number of dispersed facilities.

Transportation Arrangements

Some of the most important transportation arrangements to consider are

Pool cars	Shippers' associations
Consolidators	In-transit arrangements
Freight forwarders	Stop-offs and routes

Of these, the freight forwarding concept is of great interest because it provides opportunities for by-passing intermediate locations, thus eliminating the need for logistic facilities with their associated rehandling and trans-shipping costs, while reducing total field inventory.

Demand Characteristics

For each product shipped, and at each market area, it is necessary to develop detailed sales forecasts. Included in the forecasts is information relating to certain characteristics of demand.

1. *Annual volume* (in physical units) to be shipped each year is indicated. These figures show the varying patterns of geographic dispersion of sales, resulting from factors such as population shifts, changes in market penetration, relative changes in disposable income, new customers gained, and old customers lost.

2. The forecasts also cover *monthly volumes* by market area, groups of areas, or for the system, depending on the geographic differences expected. If the monthly patterns are such that any one month differs by more than 50 percent from the monthly average over the year, this is an indication that a variable logistic network should be considered instead of a fixed one. In this type of network some facilities may operate only at certain times of the year, re-allocating material flows accordingly. A variable logistic network may be appropriate for highly seasonal products such as antifreeze, agricultural chemicals, or air conditioners.

3. Information on *shipment characteristics*, by market area, by product, for annual volumes, is also provided. This can be displayed in the format shown in the base year demand characteristic report (Table 9–8). This information is used to calculate the transportation rates for each product into each market area.

Management System Requirements

Factors that should be considered when planning for an efficient system of management include:

1. *System outputs*, including definitions of information that must be displayed for management, and documents that must be generated to support operations

2. *System integration* with the other functions in the organization, including especially the finance, marketing, and production functions

3. *Information files* that must be retained for legal or operational purposes

4. *Control* procedures for

   a. *data entry and processing*, to ensure data integrity, result accuracy, and timely turnaround;
   b. *authorizations* to retrieve and enter data and to change files; and
   c. *security*, including data protection and backup procedures

5. *Data characteristics*, including types of data to be handled, and volumes of each type of data

Projected Planning Factors and Constraints

There are certain assumptions that provide the groundwork for each analysis. These basic assumptions include:

1. *Base year and design year* volumes and characteristics

2. *Financial limitations* such as maximum allowable investment in new facilities

3. *Legal and political constraints* determining, for example, the need to avoid certain areas in evaluating potential sites

4. *Manpower limitations*, such as the number and quality of personnel available to support new strategies

5. *Deadlines* to be met

6. *Facilities* that must be kept operating

7. *Contractual conditions*, both existing and anticipated

Develop Costs for the Proposed System

Cost development is the critical part of the logistic system design process. It is also the most difficult, in part because of the lack of definition or understanding about the structure of costs that affect the behavior of the logistic system.

Costs fall into two main categories—operational and transportation. Operational costs are those relating to markets or facilities, and can be of two types: (1) *discontinuous* costs that vary stepwise with throughput; and (2) *continuous* costs, which vary in linear or nonlinear fashion with throughput. Transportation costs are determined by origin and destination points, commodity, mode, and weight carried.

Operational Costs

Market and facilities costs have two components, *discontinuous* and *continuous* costs.

Discontinuous costs are a stepwise function of throughput (see Figure 9–12, p. 171). These costs have constant values within prescribed ranges of throughput. Figure 9–12 shows that for throughputs between 0 and t_1 there is a constant cost C_0; between t_1 and t_2 the constant cost becomes C_1, and so on. Cost C_0—the cost incurred when throughput is zero—is a fixed cost, by definition. It may represent either start-up and operating condi-

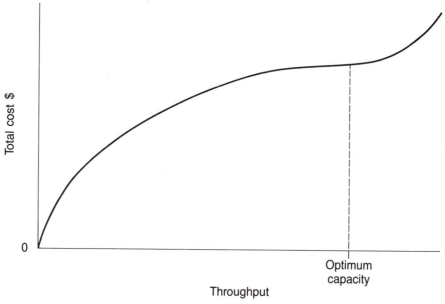

Figure 9-13   Continuous Costs

tions, or closing-down conditions. Discontinuous costs can be originated by many differ-ent cost factors, including annual depreciation, property taxes, minimum management and maintenance, shutting down a facility, and so on.

   Continuous costs are a continuous function of throughput, as shown in Figure 9–13. They are generally nonlinear, although in many instances they can be adequately repre-sented as linear costs. Continuous costs are nonlinear in nature for a number of reasons, including (1) the learning curve effect, (2) economies of scale, and (3) diseconomies of scale. Let us take them in order.

   1. *The learning curve effect* is described graphically in Figure 9–14. As the number of units made increases, the time needed to make one unit decreases exponentially; there-

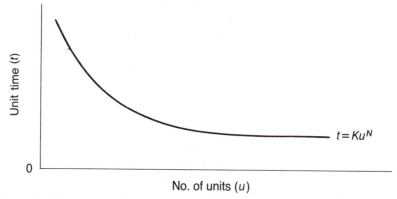

Figure 9-14   Learning Curve

fore, the labor cost associated with the manufacturing process decreases accordingly. The relationship is of the type

$$t = Ku^N$$

where K and N are constants developed statistically after a number of observations. Typically, in manufacturing operations, a doubling in the number of units produced brings about a reduction in unit time of the order of .15 to .20. The main reasons for the reduction in unit time are:

Practice—as an operation is repeated the time needed to perform it decreases because of growing familiarity.

Simplification—as the volume to be processed increases, specialization increases; thus, each worker performs fewer operations on a larger volume of units. This compounds the effect of practice, by allowing each worker to repeat each task more frequently.

2. *Economies of scale* can result from volume discounts on purchased items, from more efficient processing due to fewer change-overs per unit processed, and from thinner spread of overhead expenses and better materials utilization. Figure 9–15 shows that in the case of purchased materials, the unit costs decrease in stepwise fashion. In the case of in-house data processing, unit costs decrease continuously.

3. *Diseconomies of scale* can result because all facilities have an optimum throughput capacity that is close to but not equal to the maximum capacity. As costs approach the optimum capacity, their rate of increase decreases; beyond the optimum rate, they increase at an increasing rate, as shown in Figure 9–13. This effect is usually much more pronounced in production facilities than in logistic facilities, but is always present.

Transportation Costs

Let us now look at transportation costs. These are a function of origin, destination, commodity, mode, and weight. For a given combination of origin and destination, commod-

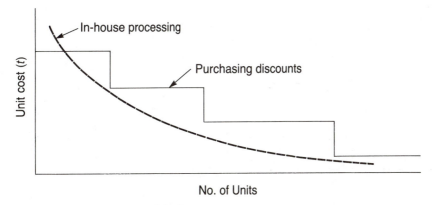

Figure 9-15 Economies of Scale

ity and mode, the transportation rate—or unit cost—is a discontinuous step function of weight, as shown in Figure 9–16.

The reason for the discontinuities between w_1' and w_1, between w_2' and w_2, and so on, is that rates may be defined, for example, as r_0 \$/cwt up to w_1 cwt, r_1 \$/cwt between w_1 and w_2 cwt, etc., but when the weight shipped exceeds a value such as w_1' it is cheaper to pay for w_1 cwt and get a lower rate than to pay for w_1' cwt at a higher rate. Thus, freight rates are never calculated for weights between w_1' and w_1; the same applies between w_2' and w_2, and so on.

As a consequence of rate structures, the relationship between total transportation cost and weight transported assumes the structure shown in Figure 9–17. We can see that a transportation cost has a complex relationship with volume transported; it is a continuous step function.

It is important to define one more general concept before continuing with this discussion: that of *relevant range*. This is the range of throughput or volume defined by the minimum and maximum values that are acceptable from a practical point of view. For example, a plant may not be allowed to operate at less than .8 of its design capacity—for contractual or engineering reasons— or at more than 1.1 times its design capacity—for economic reasons. Thus, those two points constitute the relevant range for which accurate costs are important, and within which the recommended solution must operate.

In the preceding paragraphs we have outlined the basic characteristics of the costs involved in logistic system design. We will now examine the main considerations to take into account when developing each type of cost.

Purchasing Costs

The following factors must be considered in a discussion of purchasing costs:

Minimum quantities that must be purchased

Quantity discounts offered by vendors

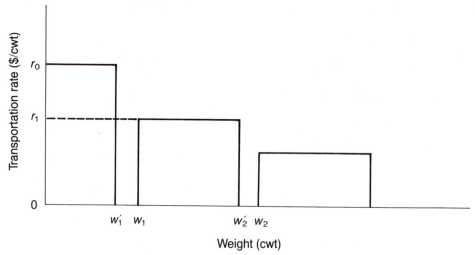

Figure 9-16   Transportation Rate Structure

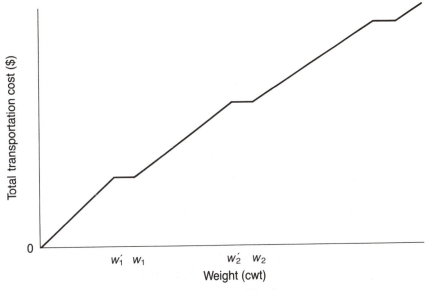

Figure 9-17 Total Transportation Cost versus Weight

Ratios between different products that are sold together, as is the case with some chemicals

Transportation cost to deliver the materials where needed

When modeling purchasing costs, it is advisable to separate the actual purchasing cost from the transportation cost involved, to compare vendors on a realistic basis; in doing so, the transportation cost to be added separately should reflect freight equalization agreements. Under these conditions, purchasing costs typically take the form illustrated in Figure 9–18.

Purchasing costs must be developed for each raw material or group of raw materials considered in the analysis, at every supply market. Supply markets may be defined as individual suppliers, or groups of suppliers that ship from nearby locations.

Production Costs

These costs include the following factors:

- *Discontinuous costs*—on an annual basis—accounting for depreciation, taxes, insurance, basic maintenance, administration, etc. These should also identify potential change-over costs from products currently manufactured, to other products, and potential closing-down costs for each facility.

- *Continuous costs*—as a function of volume manufactured—including labor, energy, pollution control, and raw material costs. Raw material costs should always be identified separately so that they can be accounted for as purchasing costs without double-counting them in the manufacturing costs.

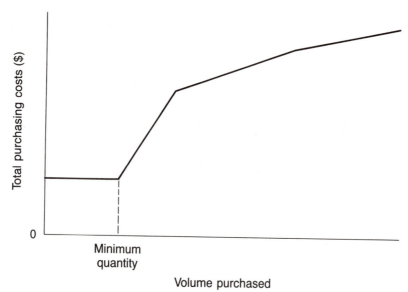

Figure 9-18   Purchasing Cost Structure

   In developing continuous manufacturing costs, it is necessary to identify some important points, including the minimum and maximum volumes that can be manufactured, and the optimum or design volume for each product and facility. This is important because when several of these points must be considered simultaneously, they can originate a convex cost function, as shown in Figure 9–19.

   We can see that even if the manufacturing cost follows a linear relationship to volume as in line *AF* on the figure, the "real" relationship that must be considered in the analysis, when minimum and design volumes are present is a relationship as *BCEG*. The reason is that since *M* is the minimum volume that can be manufactured, *OB* is the minimum cost that can be incurred; and since *D* is the design (or optimum) volume, larger volumes will be manufactured at a penalty, as illustrated by *EG*, rather than at the normal cost, as illustrated by *EF*. The fact that the "real" cost relationship is convex (as shown in Figure 9–19) has important consequences in selecting an optimization technique, as will be seen later on. Furthermore, the effect of convex costs in the structure of the solution network is very often reflected in "counterintuitive" solutions.

   Production costs can be developed by regression analysis of historical data, engineering standards, or extrapolation of pilot plant data.

Warehousing Costs

These should be developed through the design of prototype warehouses, and by relating materials handling systems and equipment to warehouse throughput. Given the handling characteristics of products—physical state, packaging types and dimensions, density—as well as important allied characteristics such as flammability and fragility, it is possible to define unitization and handling systems and equipment to be used, and the throughput ranges over which they are valid. Thus, for different ranges of throughput, different sys-

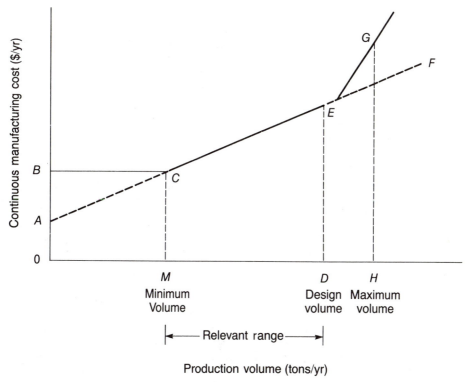

Figure 9-19 Continuous Production Cost as a Function of Volume

tems and equipment are specified, and their resulting costs are then related to throughput usually by a nonlinear function. The most important factors to consider here are:

- *Discontinuous costs* for different throughput ranges, by warehouse; these include factors similar to those considered for production facilities.

- *Continuous costs*, usually nonlinear, to account for economics of scale. These costs are developed by product within a warehouse, in cases where warehousing systems and equipment differ from each other according to product differences. When the product mix to be handled at a warehouse is homogeneous, these costs are developed for each warehouse, for the product mix to be handled there.

In the development of warehousing costs, it is advisable to break down these costs into:

Processing costs, including receiving, storing, retrieving, assemblying, packing and shipping operations costs. These are a function of throughput only. These costs can be developed by regression of historic data or by engineering standards.

Storage costs, which are a function of throughput and of time. These costs are better handled together with inventory costs, as explained next.

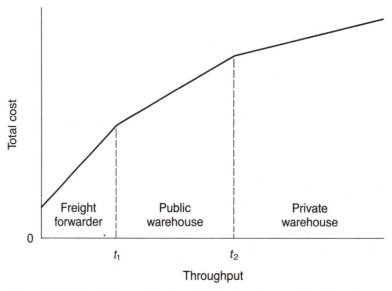

Figure 9-20   Total Composite Cost of Warehousing as a Function of
Throughput

When public warehouses are to be used, costs should be based on the actual or proposed figures for each facility to be considered. Public warehousing costs vary significantly from city to city, and even within a city; therefore, it is not realistic to adopt a single cost relationship for all public warehouses considered in the system. When a mix of public and private warehousing and other distribution channels (such as freight forwarders) is contemplated, it is necessary to develop a composite cost structure reflecting the different cost structures and their associated break-even points. This principle is illustrated in Figure 9-20.

The type of cost relationship illustrated in Figure 9-20 can be developed for each location considered as a warehouse point. For a given location, a throughput t_1 can be identified, such that below that value a freight forwarder should be used because warehousing is not economical. Between t_1 and t_2, it is advantageous to use public warehouses, and beyond t_2, it is best to use private warehouses.

The cost analysis outlined above must be tempered by other considerations, such as long-term trends and risks. For example, in a given location private warehousing may look attractive from a cost point of view, but projected demand dispersion could indicate that in a short time that location might become uneconomical. It might be better to use a public warehouse and pay a premium for that short time than commit funds to a private facility. Conversely, it may be found that certain customer service requirements cannot be handled adequately at any of the public warehouses available in the locality. In that case, it might be advantageous to use a private warehouse for the long run even at a premium cost or it might be more economical to avoid that location altogether and use facilities in other locations at an additional transportation cost.

Inventory Costs

These are a function of the inventory management system used, and of the number of regional warehouses used. For a given inventory management system, as the number of warehouses increases, the regional inventory needed to support 🖋 given sales volume with a given service level increases. The relationship between the number of regional warehouses and total system inventory can be approximated by an expression of the form

$$I_N = I_1 N^a \tag{9.1}$$

where I_i = total inventory for i warehouses, N = number of regional warehouses, and a = coefficient. The value of I_1 and a can be determined from the inventory control system or by correlating different numbers of warehouses with their associated inventories.

An increase in the number of regional warehouses may produce a measurable increase in sales; this happens when the initial service cycle is too long, and is shortened by establishing additional warehouses closer to demands. In graphical terms, looking at the sales curve in Figure 9–8, the system is displaced from a point in the inclined part of the curve, toward the upper, horizontal part of the curve. When the system is already in the upper horizontal part of the curve, the additional sales produced by additional warehouses are negligible. The relationship between sales and number of regional warehouses can be calculated from the sales curve in Figure 9–8 by relating the number of warehouses with their service cycles, or response times, and then relating service cycle to sales. It is usually found that this type of relationship can be approximated by an expression of the form

$$V_N = V_1 N^b \tag{9.2}$$

where V_i = total sales volume with i warehouses, N = number of regional warehouses, and b = coefficient.

To express the combined effect on sales and inventories of a varying number of warehouses as a function of the throughput per warehouse, we can proceed as follows: Defining v_i = average sales volume through one of i warehouses, and i_i = average inventory at one of i warehouses, we have

$$N = \frac{V_N}{v_N}$$

therefore

$$I_N = I_1 \left(\frac{V_N}{v_N} \right)^a \tag{9.3}$$

From Eq. (9.2):

$$V_N = V_1 \left(\frac{V_N}{v_N} \right)^b .$$

Replacing this value in Eq. (9.3):

$$I_N = I_1 \left(\frac{V_1}{v_N} \right)^{\frac{a}{1-b}}$$

and since

$$i_N = \frac{I_N}{N} = I_N \frac{v_N}{V_N}$$

we have

$$i_N = I_1 \left(\frac{v_N}{V_1} \right)^{\frac{1-a}{1-b}} \tag{9.4}$$

which is a relationship between inventory and sales volume through a warehouse given the values of a, b, I_1, and V_1. By multiplying i_N by the inventory-carrying cost, we can obtain a relationship between the throughput v_N through a regional warehouse and the associated inventory-carrying cost.

If sales are independent of the number of regional warehouses, $b = 0$, and $V_1 = V$, therefore

$$i_N = I_1 \left(\frac{v_N}{V} \right)^{1-a}$$

which can be used instead of Eq (9.4). From the last expression we can see that when all regional inventory is concentrated at one warehouse, $v_N = V$, and $i_N = I_1$.

Our experience with this approach indicates that in most practical situations

$$.4 \le a \le .6$$
$$0 < b \le .4$$

These values can be used to estimate a relationship between inventory-carrying cost and throughput, given a known point or system state.

Transportation Costs

To facilitate the discussion of transportation cost determination, we will define the following concepts:

> *Lane*—a combination of an origin and a destination. It is important to note that the lane from A to B is different from the lane from B to A.

> *Arc*—a combination of a lane and a commodity.

> *Link*—a combination of an arc and a mode.

These definitions are graphically represented as follows:

Origin - Destination - Commodity - Mode

Lane

Arc

Link

The transportation cost used in logistic system design will be a product of several cost elements, including transportation *rate*, and costs for packaging, insurance, inventory carrying (at destination and in transit), and documentation. Each of these costs will be determined by several transportation parameters, including:

1. *Lane*—the origin and destination considered

2. *Product*—transportation commodity, weight shipped, and special requirements, such as refrigeration, flammability, handling equipment, etc.

3. *Arrangements*—the transportation modes to be used and the manner in which they are used. They may be of several types:

   a. *Point-to-point*, where freight moves and is costed from origin to destination. These arrangements may include:
      Direct, with one carrier involved, even though freight may be processed at a break-bulk facility
      Interline, with more than one carrier of the same mode participating in the move
      Intermodal, with more than one mode participating in the move, represented by one or more carriers
   b. *Routes*, where freight moves and is costed as part of a multistop route. To facilitate the analysis of logistic systems, route costs are transformed into equivalent point-to-point costs. These arrangements may include:
      Delivery routes, where a set of destinations are served by one vehicle out of a single origin, on a periodic basis
      Stop-offs, which are similar to delivery routes, except that they are not necessarily periodic
      Consolidators, or freight forwarders, who pick up or receive small shipments and transport them as a group, before breaking them for final delivery
   c. *Other arrangements*, such as Shippers Associations, truck pools, etc., give rise to similar considerations as in point to point, or route arrangements.

To determine the transportation costs to be used in the design of the logistic network the following procedure is recommended.

DEFINE POTENTIAL ORIGINS FOR EACH DESTINATION

All entities receiving freight—markets and facilities—should be evaluated to determine, for each product received at each entity, what origins are of interest to consider as potential supply points. Typical potential origins for demand markets are warehouses, distribution centers, branches, and plants. For warehouses, origins can be distribution centers, plants, and supply markets. In defining potential origins for a destination, it is important to include in the analysis all origins that could ship the product considered to the given destination. In this regard, many potential origins are usually eliminated because of unacceptable response times involved.

DEFINE ALTERNATIVE TRANSPORTATION MODES FOR EACH ARC

After all potential arcs have been defined, each arc must be analyzed to define what transportation modes should be considered to move freight along the arc. Again, response time is the main criterion, at this stage of the evaluation, to define the modes to be considered.

CALCULATE TRANSPORTATION RATES FOR EACH LINK

Since transportation rates are discussed at length in Section VIII of this *Handbook*, we will not enter into further details here. However a short discussion is necessary to highlight some basic points. First, all rates should be expressed on a point to point basis. When common carriers are considered, their published rates are in the desired format. When using private carriage for point to point moves, an equivalent rate can be established on a cost plus profit basis for each link. When private carriage is used to deliver in routes the route costs must be allocated to each stop, to transform the route cost into a series of point to point rates. Another method is to consolidate all points served in a route as one destination; the route cost can then be used as the rate.

Second, projected rates should be used. Normally, logistic system design is conducted for a "design year" several years in the future. Thus, it is important to project the rates used to reflect cost increases as well as potential cost reductions stemming from rate negotiations.

CALCULATE PACKAGING AND INSURANCE COSTS

Different modes of transportation have different packaging and insurance costs that must be added to the rate. As a rule of thumb, the slower the mode used, the more expensive the packaging and insurance costs; on the other hand, the lower the rate. If packaging and insurance do not vary significantly, as may be the case in domestic or regional systems using surface transportation exclusively, these items may be disregarded. However, in international systems or systems comparing surface with air transportation, for example, these factors become significant.

CALCULATE INVENTORY CARRYING COSTS

The transportation system influences the levels of two types of inventories, *safety stocks* (at destination) and *in-transit* inventories. Thus, it is important to assess the impact on those inventories of the different modes considered for each.

Safety stocks are necessary to compensate for variations in expected demand, in expected replenishment lead times, and shrinkage. Since lead times and their variations are mainly determined by the transportation time—which, in turn, depends on the mode—we can relate the impact of different modes on safety stock investment, through the inventory management system rules. Thus we can calculate the safety stock inventory-carrying cost associated with each transportation mode, for each destination.

In-transit inventory-carrying costs can be calculated for a given lane as follows:

$$C_i = \frac{t_i}{365} \times c \times V$$

where: C_i = total annual inventory-carrying cost ($/yr); t_i = transit time for mode i (days); c = unit inventory-carrying cost ($/ton/yr), and V = annual volume shipped in the arc (tons/yr).

CALCULATE THE DOCUMENTATION COSTS

Transportation documentation costs are affected by the mode used in two different ways. First, different modes require different types of documents. Second, different modes impose different turnaround times on document preparation: the faster the mode used, the shorter the time available to prepare documentation, therefore, the higher the document preparation cost. Given the informational and turnaround requirements of different modes, the cost of preparing all necessary documents for each can be established. These costs may include some or all order entry and processing costs, plus the costs needed to prepare shipping orders, manifests, and labels.

In this regard, significant improvements are being realized from the standardization of documentation, data formats, and systems work currently being done by the Transportation Data Coordinating Committee (TDCC) in Washington, D.C., by the National Committee for International Trade Documentation (NCITD) in New York, and by similar organizations in Europe, Canada, and Japan.

CALCULATE TRANSPORTATION COSTS

The obvious next step is to select that link with the lowest total transportation cost, and adopt it for the analysis of the logistic network. This procedure is followed in most cases; however, in many instances it is desirable to select a combination of modes for a given arc, because that way response time requirements may be met at lower total cost. This is accomplished by segmenting the total volume to be shipped in the arc by response time requirement, and evaluating every segment on its own in the same fashion outlined above. This analysis may indicate that a mix of modes is most appropriate. Mode mixes are usually very practical to consider in international systems and in evaluating very different modes such as air and surface, or air and ocean carrier.

A useful way to relate the costs involved in mode selection is to establish the break-even relationship between transportation costs and inventory-carrying costs. If we define:

$$T_i = \text{transportation unit cost for mode } i \text{ (\$/ton)}$$
$$V = \text{annual volume shipped in the arc (tons/yr)}$$
$$I_i = \text{average inventory carried at destination when using mode } i \text{ (tons/yr)}$$
$$U = \text{unit cost of product inventoried (\$/ton)}$$
$$c = \text{unit inventory carrying cost (fraction)}$$

then, for two modes, fast (F) and slow (S), we can establish the break-even relationship:

$$(T_F - T_S)V = (I_S - I_F)Uc$$

or

$$I_S - I_F = \frac{V}{Uc}(T_F - T_S)$$

which can be represented graphically as shown in Figure 9–21.

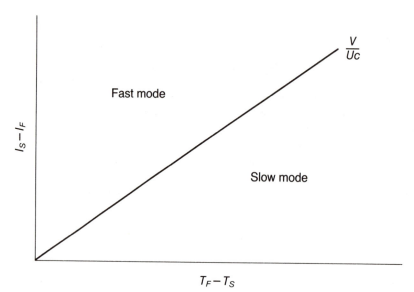

Figure 9-21   Break-even Relationship between Transportation and
Inventorying Costs

Since for a given arc the values of V, U, and c are constant, the slope of the dividing line is fixed. Thus, the effect of variations in inventories and transportation costs differentials can be assessed graphically. If the transportation cost differential is expanded to include the net effect of adding packaging, insurance, and documentation costs, then all cost elements can be represented in the diagram above.

Another type of graph that is useful in describing the effect of mode mix on total transportation cost is shown in Figure 9–22. When the total transportation cost for alter-

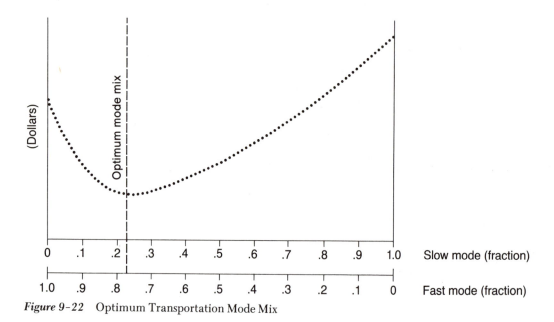

Figure 9-22   Optimum Transportation Mode Mix

native mode mixes is plotted against the mix, a curve as shown in Figure 9–22 is obtained. The lowest point in the curve represents the optimal cost; by examining the curvature of the function around the optimum it is easy to establish the sensitivity of transportation cost with changes in mode mix.

In modeling a logistic network it is usually most convenient to calculate a weighted average rate for each link. The rate represents the demand characteristics at destination in regard to both shipment size distribution and service cycle requirements. (See Table 9–11.) To illustrate this calculation, we will refer to Product 11 in Market 1, from a given origin, as shown in Table 9–11. To model the demand characteristics at Market 1 for Product 11, we would use a transportation rate of $167.55 from the origin considered. In

Table 9–11   Weighted Average Rates for Transportation Links

Shipment Size (Lbs)	Service Cycle (Days)	Demand		Rate Used		Weighted Rate
		Tons	Fraction	Mode	$/Ton	($/Ton × Fraction)
Under 150	2	.24	.0020	A	1,897	3.7940
	5	.38	.0031	T	362	1.1222
	10	.56	.0046	T	351	1.6146
		1.18	.0097			
150–500	5	.61	.0050	T	315	1.5750
	10	.48	.0039	T	302	1.1778
		1.09	.0089			
500–1,000	5	2.52	.0206	T	275	5.6650
	10	.57	.0047	T	263	1.2361
		3.09	.0253			
1,000–2,000	5	3.14	.0257	T	258	6.6306
		.93	.0076	T	241	1.8316
		4.07	.0333			
2,000–5,000	5	6.54	.0536	T	235	12.5960
	10	2.57	.0210		227	4.7670
		9.11	.0746			
5,000–10,000	5	3.31	.0271	T	200	5.4200
	10	6.84	.0560	T	190	10.6400
	15	5.96	.0488	T	178	8.6864
		16.11	.1319			
10,000–20,000	5	8.68	.0711	T	175	12.4425
	10	14.72	.1204	T	165	19.8660
	15	23.34	.1911	T	151	28.8561
		46.74	.3826			
20,000–40,000	10	7.58	.0621	T	149	9.2529
	15	16.41	.1343	R	103	13.8329
		23.99	.1964			
Over 40,000	15	14.38	.1177	R	87	10.2399
CPU		1.06	.0087	—	0.00	0.0000
PP		1.33	.0109	PP	578	6.3002
Total		122.15	1.0000			167.5468

Notes: CPU = Customer pick-up; PP = Parcel post; A = Air; T = Truck; R = Rail.

the calculation illustrated above, it is important to consider two points. First, in many cases, for a given shipment size, the same transportation mode may have different rates for different service cycles. The reason is usually that the longer the service cycle, the greater the possibility of consolidation, therefore the lower the transportation cost. Second, in calculating the transportation cost for a given shipment size and service cycle combination, it is important to consider limitations on vehicle utilization that are due to product density. If we define payload density (D) for a vehicle as

$$D = \frac{\text{Maximum weight}}{\text{Maximum volume}}$$

that the vehicle can carry, then for a given product with density d, we have

If $d > D$:   there is a weight limitation that will force the vehicle to move with empty volume

If $d < D$:   there is a volume limitation that will force the vehicle to move less weight than it is capable of carrying

The two conditions stated above influence the transportation cost to be used.

Income Function

To develop a solution that maximizes profit instead of minimizing cost, it is necessary to establish an income function for every product, at every demand market at which it is delivered. An income function can be derived by combining a market research study to gather data with some basic economic analysis. The data gathered should enable the designer to establish relationships between price, demand, and supply; these usually take the forms illustrated in Figure 9–23. The supply and demand curves are usually developed for the total market considered, to assess the likely total demand and to establish the expected equilibrium price.

Further data from the market research study allow the designer to focus on the company's market share, by refining the demand curve and expressing it as a function of price and service, as illustrated in Figure 9–24. From these relationships, we can calculate income functions by extending price times demand for each curve; thus we obtain the curves shown in Figure 9–25. The income curves are used as input into a logistic model to find the demand level to be satisfied for each product at each demand market.

When the data outlined above are not available, or are impractical to develop on account of time or cost constraints, then current prices, demands, and response times can be used as an initial point, to estimate income functions.

Model and Simulate

The data needed for the design of a logistic network are virtually the same regardless of the method of analysis; it is always necessary to know the costs, constraints, and conditions involved in order to find the best solution. Whether this solution is developed manually or with the aid of computers, the design process always consists of building a model of

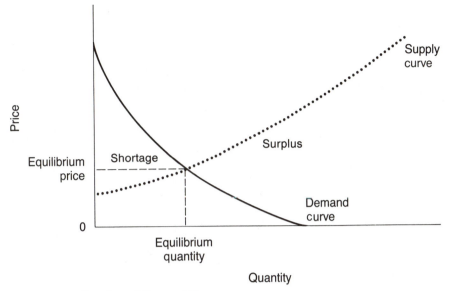

Figure 9-23 Supply and Demand Curves

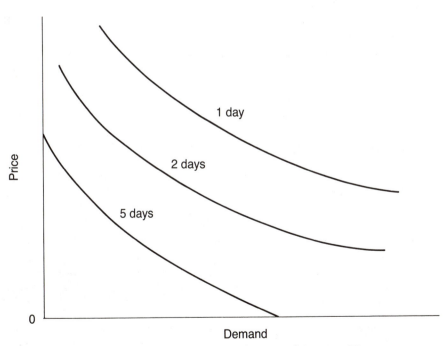

Figure 9-24 Demand Curves as a Function of Price and Response Time

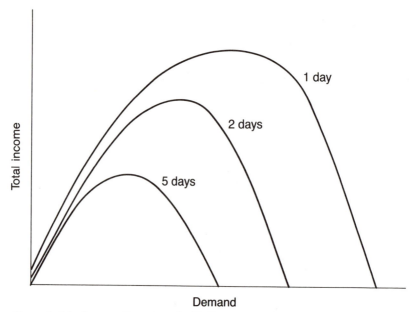

Figure 9-25   Income Functions for Different Response Times

the logistic network that will represent its characteristics and options. From such a model a series of alternatives can be examined to establish the most profitable one that meets all practical requirements. This is accomplished by simulating the behavior of the system under different conditions.

With regard to modeling and simulation, it is not unusual to find a tendency to structure logistic networks on a more or less empirical basis, with whatever data are available; in those cases the reasoning is that it would be impractical to collect all the data needed for a model that would properly solve the problem. That kind of approach not only increases significantly the risks of ending up with the wrong solution, but it also ignores a basic principle of sound management:

"What cannot be modeled cannot be managed."

Computer Simulation

The design of a logistic system is best accomplished through computerized modeling and simulation for several reasons:

The size and complexity of the problem. Even a small logistic system is a large, complex problem to handle if all pertinent characteristics are accounted for. Furthermore, any changes in one part of the system reverberate throughout the entire system, sometimes in unexpected ways. Usually it is physically impossible to calculate manually all the implications resulting from a few simultaneous changes in system parameters.

The availability of efficient hardware. The large size, high speed, and low cost of computers currently available make it impractical to attempt manual solutions in any but the most trivial problems. Furthermore, when fast reaction to changes is important, the computer represents the best means of providing it.

The availability of efficient optimization programs. There are currently many general purpose optimization programs available from computer manufacturers, and other companies, that make it relatively simple and inexpensive to build and solve very large-scale optimization models.

The possibility of conducting sensitivity analysis. In any problem of the complexity of a logistic system, it is necessary to conduct sensitivity analysis. This allows the designer to evaluate the importance of data accuracy on the solution, and to identify those constraints and conditions that have major impact on the solution structure.

The possibility of incorporating the model into the operating system. This not only improves the quality of short-term decision making, but also ensures that the data and method used to design the system are also reflected in the operating system.

General Principles

In developing a model for logistic system design, there are a few principles that are worth following:

1. *Have a definite purpose.* Don't build models that can answer any and all questions for all time. The time and effort needed to build the model and the data base needed to run it can easily get out of hand and can complicate unnecessarily the analysis of the solution. The best approach is to keep the model as simple as possible to solve the problem at hand, while encompassing enough features to ensure that the model faithfully represents the problem, and that the answers are practical.

2. *Use optimization techniques.* The design of the logistic system should be based on the use of optimization techniques. They ensure the best possible solution for a given set of conditions, and make possible the calculation of penalties associated with alternative solutions. In addition, they provide sensitivity analysis, which is an indispensable technique to ensure the quality of the solution of any large-scale, complex problem.

3. *Use consistent precision and accuracy.* Precision is the number of significant digits with which a magnitude is measured. Accuracy is the potential error with which a magnitude is measured, for a given level of confidence. If some of the data are accurate within .20, there is little to be gained by developing other data within .02; if some data are precise to four significant digits there is no need to develop other data to six significant digits. Usually a small fraction of the system's parameters have great impact on the solution; these can be identified through sensitivity analysis, and their accuracy refined subsequently, if needed.

4. *Maximize profit contribution.* Operations personnel have a tendency to try to minimize cost as a basic objective; sales personnel tend to try to maximize sales volume. Logistic system analysis is the best approach to balance those two objectives to find the best compromise between them: the solution that maximizes profit contribution by trading off sales income against the operating costs needed to generate it, subject to practical constraints.

5. *Establish the data base as part of the information system.* To maximize the usefulness of the approach outlined here, it is important to look at system design as a continuous process and not as a one-time study. Since data development is the most resource-intensive part of this effort, it pays to build the necessary data as part of the company's information system to be able to retrieve or generate on demand. With this approach, up-to-date data are always available to react to external changes promptly; furthermore, this makes it possible to use models as operational tools.

6. *Beware of accounting figures.* Accounting figures contain, of necessity, arbitrary definitions and allocations of costs; thus, in arriving at realistic conclusions it is often necessary to develop operational costs on a different basis from those used in the accounting system—using engineering standards, or ignoring sunk costs, for example. The important consideration is to ensure that the total operating costs used in logistic analysis correspond to the total operating costs used in accounting, even though their breakdown may be different. This is especially important in the definition of fixed costs: in modeling, the fixed cost is simply the intercept of the total cost function with the cost axis; in accounting, the fixed cost is the result of adding specific cost elements. The two values can be substantially different although they may both be correct for the purposes they are developed.

7. *Ensure that all magnitudes are expressed in common units.* The basic units used in logistic system modeling are of two types:

> *Physical units* measure three main magnitudes:
>
>> *Space* (e.g., feet, square feet, meters, cubic meters, miles, kilometers)
>> *Weight* (e.g., pounds, kilograms, tons)
>> *Time* (e.g., days, months, years)
>
> *Monetary units* are always expressed in terms of one single currency, such as dollars or francs, even in the analysis of international systems

Once the unit of measure for each of the four basic magnitudes—space, weight, time, money—have been chosen, all other magnitudes can be expressed in terms of them, to facilitate calculations.

Types of Models

The historical evolution of modeling methods available for logistic system design has been dramatically shaped by the capabilities available in computers and their software. Three major types of models have been used in logistic system design. In chronological sequence, they are:

- Center of gravity models

- Costing/heuristic models

- Mathematical programming models

CENTER OF GRAVITY MODELS

In this type of model, given all sources and sinks in the system, and the volumes they originate or receive, the approach is to calculate the center of gravity of all volumes, and locate a trans-shipment facility there.

Given the coordinates (X_i, Y_i) of all sources and sinks with respect to an arbitrary pair of axes, and the volumes w_i attached to each, the coordinates $\overline{X}$, and $\overline{Y}$ of the center of gravity can be calculated as follows:

$$\overline{X} = \frac{\Sigma\, wi\, xi}{\Sigma\, wi}$$

$$\overline{Y} = \frac{\Sigma\, wi\, yi}{\Sigma\, wi}$$

This approach presents numerous problems.

1. It assumes that the solution includes only one trans-shipment location, or it assumes arbitrary boundaries to produce multiple trans-shipment–location solutions, with one trans-shipment location within each arbitrary boundary. This approach ignores the interactions between the arbitrary zones.

2. It assumes that transportation costs are directly proportional to distance, and that the same proportionality constant applies in all directions. In practice, these assumptions are unrealistic even with private carriage: there are fixed costs, and nonlinear relationships between costs and distances.

3. It assumes that the straight-line distance between two points is representative of actual distance. In practice, U.S. highway mileages, for example, are between 1.05 and 1.4 times higher than straight line distances measured on a map.

4. It ignores processing cost differentials at different facilities.

5. It ignores capacity constraints, service requirements, and multilevel logistic systems.

6. It yields answers that are often impractical locations: the middle of a lake or desert, or a point far from transportation services.

7. It assumes given shipment volumes out of each plant.

8. It does not provide the means to estimate how far from the optimum is the calculated cost.

9. It does not provide sensitivity analysis.

10. It assumes one product, or a uniform mix of products throughout.

Under these conditions, it is obvious that this technique should not be used for facility location—its results are guaranteed to be wrong unless none of the problems cited above holds true. This technique was popular before the advent of computers. It was rendered obsolete in the late 1950s when the use of costing and heuristic techniques became practical through the use of computers.

Costing/Heuristic Models

Given a solution, completely defined by its market allocations, facilities, links, and their associated volumes, and a data base containing all costs, rates, demands, and constraints, a *costing* model will calculate the cost of the solution input and display the cost elements.

A *heuristic* model is a costing model with the capability to generate automatically—following pre-established rules—alternative solutions that are in turn costed, so that the model can pick the lowest cost alternative among those evaluated. An example of the logic followed in a typical heuristic model is presented in Figure 9–26. This approach has severe limitations:

1. It does not guarantee that the best possible solution available has been identified; it only selects a "good" solution from a limited set of alternatives.

2. It does not provide an estimate of the penalty to be paid with respect to the best possible solution.

3. It does not handle capacity constraints, or it does so in an arbitrary way.

4. It does not provide sensitivity analysis, to determine the impact on the solution of data accuracy and constraints.

This approach is a significant improvement over the center of gravity approach. However, because of its limitations it is not practical for solving facility location problems and structuring logistic networks.

From the late 1950s to the mid 1960s this approach made it possible to model larger models at a lower cost than models using a mathematical programming approach. The most popular heuristic models were based on the Kuehn-Hamburger algorithm, or variations of it. Around the mid-1960s, the size, speed, and cost of computers and the optimization packages that came with them reached a break-even point with heuristic techniques. Since then, the mathematical programming approach has rendered costing/heuristic models obsolete for logistic system design.

Mathematical Programming Models

The availability of large-scale, high-speed, low-cost computers since the mid-1960s has made it practical to use mathematical programming techniques to model, simulate, and optimize the configuration of logistic networks. More specifically, the use of mixed integer programming affords the analyst the tools needed to model faithfully the behavior of logistic systems, and to calculate optimal strategies considering the effects of fixed costs, nonlinear costs, and a variety of real life constraints. As a consequence, the problems encountered with center of gravity and costing/heuristic programs can be eliminated.

Furthermore, the use of mathematical programming techniques for logistic system simulation provides three unique advantages of great value:

- *Guaranteed optimality.* For a given set of conditions that allow a feasible solution, the optimal solution or solutions can be calculated. If a different solution is desirable, then the penalty with respect to the optimal solution can be calculated.

- *Sensitivity analysis.* Given a solution, it is possible to calculate for input parameters how much they can vary without changing the optimal solution—that is, the sensitivity of the solution to changes in system conditions. This feature makes it possible

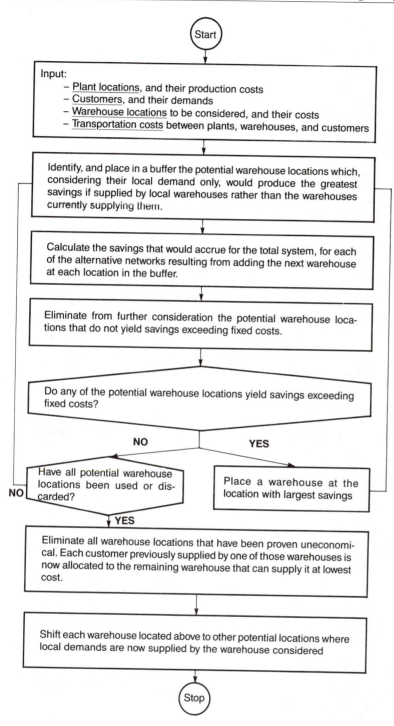

Figure 9-26   Heuristic Model for Logistic System Design

to identify the few parameters that determine the structure of the solution, so that their accuracy may be refined if necessary.

- *Marginal analysis.* Given a solution, it is possible to calculate the marginal cost or profit for any flow in the solution—that is, the penalty or gain that would be incurred if the flow considered were changed by one unit, with everything else in the system remaining constant. A very important use of marginal costs is to establish transfer prices in the system.

To structure the solution to a distribution problem, it is useful to think in terms of a logistic network built with two types of elements:

Nodes: Stationary inventories of variable level, such as markets and facilities

Links: Flowing inventories of intermittent constant level, such as transportation links

Both elements may have associated costs and capacity constraints. In addition, nodes may have material balance equations relating quantities of incoming and outgoing products, and links may have response times associated with them. Using nodes and links, the structure of a logistic network can be defined as shown in Figure 9–27.

The use of mathematical programming in the design of logistic networks makes it possible to state the problem in economic terms, as a resource allocation problem. From an economic point of view, there is a resource allocation problem when there exists a set of requirements that must be satisfied through the use of available resources when (1) *requirements* are multiple, and can be ranked in order of preference or priority, and (2) *resources* are scarce and can be used optionally to meet several requirements.

In a logistic system, the basic requirements are market demands that are usually represented by a large number of customers or demand areas, and that can be ranked according to their profit contribution. The resources available—facilities, equipment, and materials—are scarce in the sense that they impose capacity or supply constraints, and they can be used optionally to produce or distribute a variety of products. Thus, the design of a logistic network meets all the necessary and sufficient conditions that define a resource allocation problem. Therefore, we can use mathematical programming to find the optimal solution to the problem.

The problem can be stated mathematically as follows: Given a set k_i of cost or profit contributions associated to each relevant material flow or activity X_i in the system, we can construct an objective function Z, such that:

$$Z = \Sigma \, k_i \, X_i$$

We want to determine the value of each element X_i in such a way that the value of Z is optimized—that is, maximized if Z is a profit function or minimized if it is a cost function. This must be done subject to a set of constraints of the form:

$$\Sigma \, C_{ij} X_i \leq r_i$$

These constraints represent maximum capacities, demands, material balances, and so on.

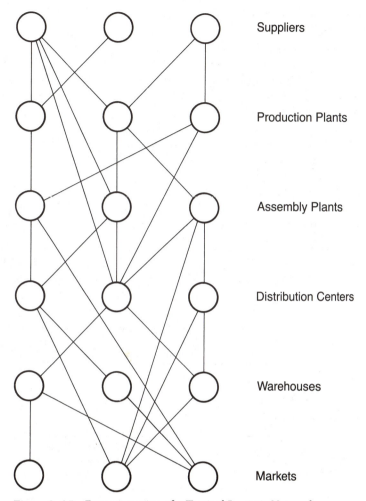

Suppliers

Production Plants

Assembly Plants

Distribution Centers

Warehouses

Markets

Figure 9-27   Representation of a Typical Logistic Network

It is customary to represent the problem in matrix form in a so-called detached coefficient matrix as follows:

$$
\begin{array}{llll}
k_1 \quad k_2 \quad k_3 \quad \ldots k_n & = Z \\
C_{11} \ C_{12} \ C_{13} \ldots C_{1n} & \leq r_1 \\
C_{21} \ C_{22} \ C_{23} \ldots C_{2n} & \leq r_2 \\
\ \bullet \quad\ \ \bullet \quad\ \ \bullet \ \ldots \ \bullet & \quad\ \bullet \\
C_{m1} \ C_{m2} \ C_{m3} \ldots C_{mn} & \leq r_m
\end{array}
$$

In the matrix above, the first row represents the coefficients of the objective function; the other rows represent the coefficients of all the constraints in the problem. Columns 1 through n represent the coefficients of the variables contained in the objective function and the constraints. The last column, known as the right-hand side, contains the coefficients representing the limits of the model's variables.

All the values in the detached coefficient matrix are set by the inputs to the model, including demands, capacities, operational costs, and transportation costs. The structuring of the input values in a detached coefficient matrix that represents all the characteristics of the problem is known as "matrix generation." Once the matrix is generated, the calculation of the values of X_i that optimize Z subject to the row constraints is known as the optimization. Once the optimal solution has been found, it is possible to conduct sensitivity analysis of the problem, which can take several forms:

- *Ranging analysis*, or static sensitivity analysis, is a calculation of the upper and lower values that a matrix coefficient can take without changing the solution. This procedure is extremely useful in assessing the impact of potential error in the value of a variable: if the range is wide, a large error in the value assumed for the variable will not affect the solution. Conversely, if the range is narrow, a small error in the value assumed for the variable may affect the solution.

- *Parametric analysis*, or dynamic sensitivity analysis, is a method to assess the impact on the solution of simultaneous changes in many coefficients. Its value goes beyond that of ranging because it identifies not only the specific values where signifi-

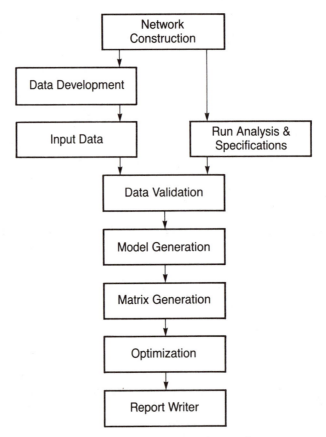

Figure 9-28   Flow Chart of the Modeling and Simulation Process

cant errors may or may not be tolerable, but in addition serves to identify those parts of the solution that are likely to remain in it in spite of substantial changes in system characteristics.

- *Recursive analysis* is a form of parametric analysis. The difference is that whereas a parametric analysis program conducts a set of changes in a pre-established way, a recursive analysis program conducts each change on the basis of the results obtained in each run, given pre-established rules to do so.

The Simulation Process

A typical modeling and simulation process is illustrated in Figure 9–28. The process starts with a network analysis phase, in which the network structure to be considered is identified. This includes the definition of market areas, product groups, facilities, and transportation arrangements to be considered, constraints and conditions in the system, and the costs involved.

The next step is the development of all the data needed in the model; concurrently, the modeling process starts with the analysis of the model runs that will be necessary to analyze the behavior of the logistic network, and to identify the optimal solution and any alternatives of interest. The result of the run analysis phase is a run strategy that outlines the sequence and structure of model runs that are planned. The structures of alternatives to be modeled are defined by run specifications, identifying for each planned run the facilities to be considered, demand levels, cost levels, and similar parameters. It is very common to find that after a few model runs, the initial run strategy is modified to take advantage of the additional knowledge acquired.

Once the data have been developed they are usually stored in files with standard data formats that simplify subsequent accessing and processing of the data. The most common formats used are unit record and tabular formats. Input for transportation rates from warehouse WO1 to demand markets DO1, DO2, and DO3, for product AA can be represented as follows:

In unit record format:	*In tabular format:*
T WO1 DO1 AA 3.75	T WO1 AA
T WO1 DO2 AA 5.83	DO1 3.75
T WO1 DO3 AA 1.92	DO2 5.83
	DO3 1.92

In this example, "T" identifies the record or table as containing transportation rates, and the all-numeric data reflect the transportation rates.

The selection of one input format or another depends on several factors, including the programming language to be used, the mode of file updating (manual or computerized), and the repetitiveness of the data fields (the more repetitive the data, the more efficient the tabular format).

Once the input data and the run specifications have been input and stored in a computer file, they can be automatically inspected to verify their validity and the correctness of their format. This is done with a data validation program, which examines the data to identify possible format errors or logical errors. *Format* validation programs include checks for data fields that should be blank, or all numeric, or contain special symbols, or should be right-justified, for example. *Logic* validation programs include checks to verify that there is a feasible solution to the problem. An example of this type of check is the scanning of transportation rates to ensure that every demand area has at least one inbound rate for each product demanded. It is advisable to provide data validation programs as part of any logistic model, to be used before any run containing a significant portion of new data is made.

After all data have been validated and corrected as needed, the next step is to run a model generator program. This type of program specifies for a given run the characteristics of the network to be evaluated, and can include the nodes to be considered, their constraints and costs, the characteristics of each cost function (linear or nonlinear), or whether or not it contains a fixed cost element.

The next step is matrix generation. This program reads the input data and model characteristics, and formats them in a detached coefficient matrix that is then fed into the optimization program. The optimization program, in turn, reads in the matrix, and finds the values that optimize the objective function. In addition, it performs all the calculations needed for sensitivity analysis, calculates marginal costs, and creates an output file that can be used by a report writer. Optimization programs are available from most computer manufacturers, and from software companies. To facilitate the analysis of the optimization run, it is desirable to provide some standard report formats that display the structure of the solution in a meaningful, edited fashion. A report writer fulfills this function.

Usually the reports generated by a logistic model are of six types:

1. *Link-oriented* reports show material flows and associated costs for each link in the system. Table 9–12 shows an Outbound Freight Report of this type. From that report we can see that the optimal solution includes a warehouse in Hartford that serves Boston, Providence, and Hartford customers. For each destination the report shows the type of

Table 9–12   Outbound Freight Report
From: Warehouses
To: Customers

Origin	Destination	Product	Volume (Tons)	Variable Cost (Dollars) Warehousing	Inventory	Transportation	Total
Hartford	Boston	Wheat	12.73	253	280	483	1,016
		Corn	8.59	141	147	294	582
		TOTAL	21.32	394	427	777	1,598
	Providence	Wheat	3.46	59	68	143	270
		Corn	1.38	18	23	33	74
		TOTAL	4.84	77	91	176	344
	Hartford	Wheat	5.26	108	117	146	371
		Corn	7.11	128	131	188	447
		TOTAL	12.37	236	248	334	818
	Total	Wheat	21.45	420	465	772	1,657
		Corn	17.08	287	301	515	1,103
		TOTAL	38.53	707	766	1,287	2,760
	Fixed cost						23,185
	Grand total						25,945

product considered, the volume shipped, and the associated warehousing, inventory, transportation, and total variable cost for each link. At the bottom of each "origin" entry the fixed cost for the facility is added to the total variable cost.

2. *Node-oriented* reports show material flows and associated costs for each node in the system. Table 9–13 shows a Facility Utilization Report of this type. This report contains all facilities included in the solution. They are shown grouped by type of facility; within each type, facilities are displayed in decreasing order of throughput. In addition, the report shows for each facility the fraction it represents of total system throughput for that type of facility; fractions are usually shown in direct and cumulative fashion to help the analysis. This report also shows for each facility the maximum capacity modeled, and the fraction of it that the solution has used.

3. *Product* reports show the material flows and associated costs for each product in the system. Table 9–14 shows a Product Flow Report of this type. The report shows, for each product in the system, the facilities through which it flows in the optimum solution. Facilities are grouped by type, and for each type the report shows the quantity of product processed; the facilities are displayed in decreasing sequence of throughput quantity, and the direct and cumulative fractions of throughput are shown for analysis. The report also shows the average cost per ton to process the product at each facility and type of facility, as well as the corresponding marginal costs.

4. *Financial* reports show marginal costs, income, and cost breakdowns for the different products involved in the system. Table 9–15 shows a Logistic Profit and Loss Statement report of this type. It shows, for every product in the system, the quantity flowing and the different variable costs incurred by each. In addition, the report shows the income generated by each product delivered to a demand market. It also shows the fixed

Table 9–13   Facility Utilization Report

Facility	Throughput (Tons/Yr)	Fraction Direct	Fraction Cumulative	Capacity (Tons/Yr)	Throughput Capacity
Production system					
Brooklyn	43,610	.4189	.4189	43,610	1.0000
Baltimore	25,530	.2453	.6642	25,530	1.0000
Reno	13,740	.1320	.7962	14,000	.9814
Denver	10,100	.0970	.8932	12,000	.8417
Champaign	6,830	.0656	.9588	7,600	.8987
El Paso	4,290	.0412	1.0000	5,200	.8250
Total	104,100	1.0000		107,940	.9644
Warehousing system					
Whippany	18,210	.2519	.2519	20,000	.9105
Tallman	15,340	.2122	.4641	16,500	.9297
New Orleans	11,650	.1612	.6253	12,000	.9708
Dallas	8,720	.1206	.7459	12,500	.6976
Chicago	6,630	.0917	.8376	7,500	.8840
Minneapolis	4,180	.0578	.8954	6,000	.6967
Brunswick	2,970	.0411	.9365	5,000	.5940
Framingham	2,180	.0302	.9667	5,500	.3964
Atlanta	1,540	.0213	.9880	3,200	.4813
Bakersfield	870	.0120	1.0000	2,100	.4143
Total	72,290	1.0000		90,300	.8006

Table 9-14 Product Flow Report

Product	Facility	Quantity (Units)	Fraction Direct	Fraction Cumulative	Average $/Unit	Marginal Cost ($)
Rear axles	Champaign, IL	28,375	0.6542	0.6542	115.44	10.03
	Baltimore, MD	15,000	0.3458	1.0000	120.35	6.61
	Production system	43,375	1.0000		117.14	
	San Leandro, CA	27,211	0.6273	0.6273	22.12	18.80
	Billings, MT	10,974	0.2530	0.8803	24.15	20.01
	Jersey City, NJ	5,190	0.1197	1.0000	31.17	3.91
	Warehousing system	43,375	1.0000		23.72	
Transmissions	Dallas, TX	5,380	.9027	.9027	128.57	1.75
	Denver, CO	580	.0972	1.0000	131.46	103.17
	Production system	5,960	1.0000		129.13	
	Baltimore, MD	3,170	.7101	.7107	25.03	3.45
	St. Louis, MO	1,294	.2899	1.0000	24.41	10.72
	Warehousing system	4,464	1.0000		24.77	

costs incurred in the optimal solution, the grand total cost for the optimal system, and the profit contribution of the system—calculated as the difference between the grand total cost and the total income.

5. *Service* reports show the expected transit times, response times, or service cycles in the system. Table 9–16 shows a Response Time Summary of this type. This report shows, for each product in the system, the tons shipped within various time intervals (1 to 2 days, 3 to 6 days, etc.). For each time interval, the report shows the tons delivered within that time and the fraction of total tons for that product that were delivered within that time interval. In addition, the report shows the weighted average time that it took to deliver each product to all demand markets in the system.

6. *Sensitivity* reports show the impact of different parameters on the solution's structure. Table 9–17 shows a Ranging Report of this type. This report shows for every facility in the solution the throughput required in the optimal solution, and the maximum and minimum values between which the throughput can vary without changing the structure of the answer. When the solution is very insensitive to changes in certain parameters, the maximum value may be very high, as in the case of Boston in the example, or the minimum may be a negative value, as in the case of Philadelphia.

In developing and using a logistic system model it is advisable to observe certain rules.

General Rules

1. *Keep modeling costs in the right perspective.* Typically, the cost of development and use of an optimization model for logistic system design can be broken down as follows:

Project Phase	Fraction of Total Cost
Input data development and validation	.65 to .75
Running matrix generator, report writer, and analysis	.20 to .35
Running optimization program	.05 to .10

From these figures it is clear that the bulk of the cost is in data development; therefore, that is where most attention should be paid to control costs and schedules. However, it is very common to find that technical personnel are far more inclined to look for ways to reduce the running time for optimization, matrix generators, or report writers instead. While these efforts are commendable, they may reflect lack of understanding of the true priorities. Another major consideration is the relation of savings to modeling costs. The optimal solution of a logistic network usually shows cost reductions or profit improvements in the range of 5 to 20 percent of existing annual costs, with the mode usually at about 10 percent. Another way of stating this fact is that in practice, savings from this type of study are usually about 100 times the cost of the study.

2. *Beware of relative magnitudes.* Computers have physical limitations that determine the largest and smallest numbers that can be used in them. In addition, calculation times can be significantly affected by the relative magnitudes of the figures used in a model. To avoid accuracy problems, and expedite calculations, it is desirable to choose

Table 9-15 Logistic Profit and Loss Statement

Product	Quantity (Tons)	Variable Costs (Dollars)						Income (Dollars)
		Purchasing	Production	Whsing.	Inventory	Transport.	Total	
Steel plate	3,817	723,800				85,160	808,960	
Aluminum	3,492	681,400				72,380	753,780	
Brass	261	45,700				5,296	50,996	
Transmissions	4,958		103,200	98,750	87,510	185,600	475,060	2,950,000
Rear axles	1,273		27,690	23,440	22,640	48,230	122,000	813,600
Gear boxes	741		14,330	11,980	14,580	29,100	69,990	495,200
Total	14,542	1,450,900	145,220	134,170	124,730	425,766	2,280,786	4,258,800
Fixed costs							1,076,000	
Total							3,356,786	
Profit contribution							902,014	
Grand total							4,258,800	

Table 9-16 Response Time Summary

Product	Response Time (Days)												Weighted Average (Days)
	1–2		3–6		7–10		11–14		15–21		Total		
	Tons	Frac.	Tons	Frac.	Tons	Frac.	Tons	Frac.	Tons	Frac.	Tons	Frac.	
Transmissions	0	0.000	5,000	0.073	6,000	0.087	3,000	0.043	55,000	0.797	69,000	1.000	15.90
Rear axles	0	0.000	1,000	0.018	5,000	0.086	5,000	0.086	47,000	0.810	58,000	1.000	16.50
Gear boxes	0	0.000	2,000	0.026	6,000	0.079	8,000	0.106	60,000	0.789	76,000	1.000	16.30
Carburetors	150	0.300	150	0.300	200	0.400	0	0.000	0	0.000	500	1.000	5.25
Total	150	0.001	8,150	0.040	17,200	0.085	16,000	0.078	162,000	0.796	203,500	1.000	16.20

Table 9–17 Ranging Report

Facility	Solution Throughput	Range	
		Maximum	Minimum
Chicago	117.00	117.00	111.00
New York	82.75	88.95	82.75
Boston	135.00	74999904.00	135.00
Philadelphia	62.75	62.75	− 135.00
Baltimore	30.00	30.00	20.00
Denver	60.00	70.00	60.00
Salt Lake City	150.00	99999840.00	150.00
St. Louis	45.00	70.00	35.00
Atlanta	25.00	50.00	0.00
Dallas	25.00	25.00	25.00
Houston	25.00	35.00	25.00
Seattle	75.00	75.00	75.00
San Jose	20.00	30.00	− 40.00
Los Angeles	10.00	30.00	− 15.00
Harrisburg	50.00	99999744.00	50.00
Ames	100.00	99999792.00	100.00
Montreal	60.00	70.00	40.00
Toronto	50.00	50.00	− 25.00
Vancouver	20.00	45.00	20.00
Portland	25.00	50.00	0.00
Reno	25.00	25.00	25.00
High Point	75.00	100.00	25.00

units in such a way that the ratio between the largest and the smallest numbers used in the model does not exceed 1,000,000; if possible, it should be closer to 1,000.

3. *Use as many constraints as practical.* The more constraints used in the formulation of the problem, the faster it is to arrive at the optimal answer, and vice versa. On the other hand, the more constraints used, the narrower the field of possible solutions and therefore of opportunities to maximize profit.

4. *Remember that common sense is the least common of all senses.* Because of their complexity, logistic system structures are extremely hard to visualize. For this reason, very frequently, the optimal answer contains counterintuitive features—that is, features that go against "common sense"—although further analysis of the detailed structure of the answer provides logical explanations for such features. This is also a very important reason for avoiding the use of non-optimization models, which depend too much on common sense to structure the alternatives to be evaluated and to select the answer, and thus miss original solutions.

MATRIX GENERATION RULES

1. *Use a revise feature.* When generating the initial matrix, it is advisable to include in it all possible elements that may be included in the analysis; in this way, the matrix can be easily changed by revising some of its values, or parts of the matrix, instead of regenerating the whole matrix every time there are changes in it. The use of the revise feature makes it possible to run large-scale models at processing times and costs that are competitive with those of heuristic and other simpler models.

2. *Use inequalities for demands.* Although demands are usually expressed as fixed quantities that must be delivered, models can be solved faster when demands are not expressed as equalities, but as inequalities. To this effect, if a model is *maximizing profit,* demands are expressed as values not to be exceeded (less than or equal to). If a model is *minimizing cost,* demands are expressed as values to be met or exceeded (greater than or equal to).

3. *Consider using a multi–time-period model.* This can be done by generating a matrix representing successive time periods with an objective function representing the present value of all the cash flows at all time periods considered. Another approach is to use dynamic programming for the multi-period problem. It is important to note that the size of the problems that can be solved with commercially available hardware and software is limited. Also, the data needed to state the problem are usually very hard to obtain (see the discussion of financial analysis, pages 218–222). When these limitations preclude the use of multi–time-period models, the next best approach is to use successive single period models and develop a set of optimal answers from which the final solution can be selected. Multi–time-period analysis is indispensable to arrive at a solution that will be stable over a period of years accounting for diverse trends in inputs.

OPTIMIZATION RULES

1. *Use mixed integer programming to model costs.* This feature makes it possible to model fixed costs in such a way that they are accounted for if a facility is in the solution, and they are ignored if the facility is not in the solution. It can also efficiently represent nonlinear variable costs, either concave or convex. The use of separable programming to model nonlinear costs is not recommended because it does not guarantee a global optimum solution. This can become an important limitation when cost structures used contain both convex and concave relationships, of the types discussed earlier.

2. *Use re-start procedures.* When a matrix is revised, the new matrix can be solved quickly by using the previous solution as an initial solution rather than starting from scratch; this can be accomplished through re-start procedures. The use of revise and re-start procedures together makes it possible to use optimization models at costs that are competitive with those of simpler formulations, such as costing or heuristic models.

3. *Use sensitivity analysis.* As explained before on page 194, this feature of optimization models is one of their biggest advantages over other kinds of models. Although the cost of performing sensitivity analysis can be significant, it is usually well worth it because of the valuable insights that can be gained about the system's behavior.

POST-OPTIMAL ANALYSIS

After the optimal answer has been calculated, it is always necessary to conduct a series of additional runs to test the behavior of the system for quasi-optimal conditions. The purposes of these post-optimal runs are:

- To establish the sensitivity of the solution to changes in different input parameters

- To identify quasi-optimal solutions—non-optimal solutions having an acceptable penalty—that may offer intangible advantages

• To identify the "anchors" or features of the system that are unlikely to change in spite of important changes in the conditions imposed on the system, or system parameters

Post-optimal analysis is usually conducted as follows:

1. *Evaluate the sensitivity of the optimal solution.* This is accomplished through the use of ranging, parametric, and recursive analysis, as mentioned before. With the information derived from those types of analyses, it is possible to determine how the optimum solution would change if input parameters change. This type of analysis is important because it allows the designer to evaluate the impact on the answer of errors in input estimates, and also to identify the types of exogenous changes that could seriously affect the solution, and how they would affect it.

2. *Identify the structure of quasi-optimal systems.* The logistic network profit contribution is usually rather insensitive to minor changes to the optimal solution. Thus, it is generally possible to modify somewhat the optimal answer without incurring excessive penalties. Using an optimization model, it is possible to determine not only the optimal configuration, but also to force the model to arrive at solutions containing more than or less than optimal numbers of facilities. Thus, a series of forced "optimal" answers can be arrived at describing how the total logistic cost or profit varies with a varying number of facilities. For example, if we were to plot a varying number of plants and warehouses against the highest profit solution for different combinations of facilities, we would obtain a cost surface such as shown in Figure 9–29. This type of surface is rather flat around the optimum, and in practical problems it tends to be steeper in the direction of plants than warehouses, indicating that solutions are usually more sensitive to changes in the number of plants than in the number of warehouses. The usual reasons are that manufacturing costs tend to be much higher than warehousing costs, and that the number of plants is usually much smaller than the number of warehouses.

If we were to cut that cost surface by a plane representing a given number of plants, we would then obtain a curve such as that shown in Figure 9–30, describing how logistic profit contribution varies with varying numbers of warehouses for the given number of plants. The curve is rather flat around the optimum (highest point). Thus, there is only a very slight penalty associated with the quasi-optimal systems when the number of warehouses is only a few more or less than optimum. However, as the number of warehouses diverges from the optimum the penalty increases at an increasing rate. This point illustrates the dangers of choosing an answer without knowing the value of the optimum solution: if the answer chosen is far from the optimum, the penalty associated to it can be substantial.

Quasi-optimal systems thus identified provide valuable information about the system's behavior, which can be useful when selecting a solution for several reasons:

• Some of the input data contain forecasting or other types of errors; thus quasi-optimal solutions may be as good as the optimal one.

• Conditions in and around the logistic system change continuously, sometimes in ways not foreseen during the analysis; therefore, the structure of the optimal solution tends to change in time.

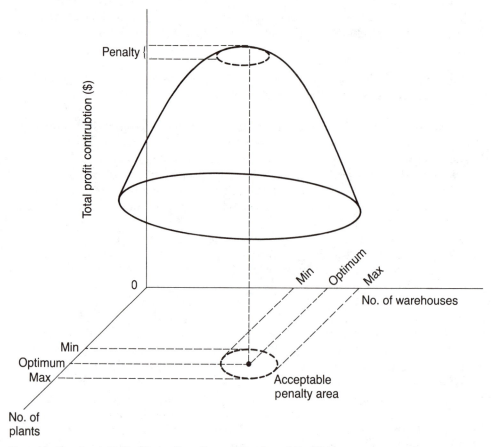

Figure 9-29   Logistic Profit as a Function of Number of Facilities

- Sometimes a suboptimal solution may have important operational advantages at a slight penalty. Being able to measure the penalty enables the designer to quantify the value of the intangibles.

- Intangibles are ignored in the models because of their non-quantitative nature. Thus it is important to bring them into the analysis during the post-optimal analysis phase.

For these reasons, it is important not to consider the optimal solution as a final answer, but to use it as a guide to structure the final solution and, as a benchmark, to calculate the potential penalties resulting from a non-optimal strategy.

3. *Identify the "anchors" in the solution.* Sensitivity and quasi-optimal analysis will usually identify certain features in the preferred solution—facilities, or flow paths—that remain in the solution in spite of important changes in forecasts, costs, income, or constraints. Those features can be considered the "anchors" of the system, in the sense that they constitute the essential, unchanging parts of the system around which all other features must be built and modified. In establishing the final characteristics of the solution it is necessary to provide built-in flexibility around the system's anchors. Examples of how

this can be accomplished include the use of public warehouses instead of private warehouses, for locations other than anchors, or common carriers instead of private carriage, for flows outside the anchors, even at a premium.

   The end result of the post-optimal analysis described here is the selection of a preferred solution, or in some instances of a small group of solutions with similar profit contributions but different network structures and therefore different intangible advantages. The best solution is then chosen on the basis of cash flow analysis and analysis of intangibles. These types of analysis should be performed after the specifications for the logistic management system and for the logistic organization have been developed. Thus, the final evaluation contains the cash flows derived from the implementation of the logistic network, as well as those derived from the development and implementation of the management system and organization.

   At this point in our discussion we need to review briefly the scope of the specifications for the management system and the organization, to describe their characteristics and the way they relate to the logistic network. Since those two topics are covered at length in other chapters, we will confine our discussion here to the major points to be considered in their development. This discussion will provide the context for a later description of the final analysis process recommended to arrive at the selection of the proposed logistic system.

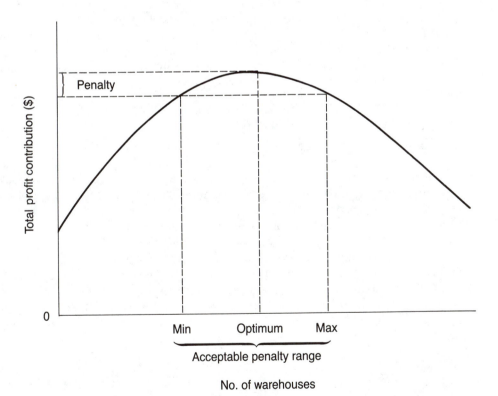

Figure 9-30   Logistic Profit as a Function of Number of Warehouses

Develop Management System Specifications

General Considerations

To provide effective support for the design and management of the logistic network, it is necessary to provide a logistic management system that will meet the following criteria.

RELATION TO CORPORATE STRATEGY

A successful management system is an informational representation of the company's strategy, its mission, goals, and objectives. The design of a management system starts from the premise that information is one of the company's main resources and must be managed accordingly to support the company's strategy. The best way to ensure this, in organizational terms, is to design the system from the top down, and to implement it from the bottom up.

INDEPENDENCE FROM ORGANIZATION STRUCTURE

The management system must be structured around the business functions it has to support, regardless of the way in which they are organized at any one time. As long as the company's mission and strategy remain unchanged, a management system can be expected to undergo minor revisions and updatings, reflecting developing experience and the need to profit from new technology as it becomes available. However, the characteristics of a well-designed management system would not change significantly simply because the organizational structure had changed. The well-designed system will interface with the organization by establishing the responsibility for inputting and maintaining data, and by distributing and displaying outputs among users.

INTEGRATION WITH COMPANY SYSTEMS AND DATA

The logistic management information system should be related to the rest of the company's systems, and especially with the marketing, financial, and production systems. Most logistic data must be used by these other systems; therefore it is important to ensure that all company operations are managed with common data, and that each data element be entered into the system only once.

Furthermore, as the logistic system is reevaluated, updated, or modified, all the data needed for analysis can be obtained directly from operating systems by compiling actual operating data or standard data. An example of this type of application is presented in Figure 9–31. Each point in the figure represents one existing warehouse, characterized by its annual throughput and total cost. Given all points in the system, a curve can be fitted as shown, by using standard regression techniques. In our example, the best fitting equation is

$$y = 383,000 + 7.83X^{.61}$$

Under these conditions, the constant term f_0 showing the intercept of the cost function with the cost axis is \$383,000. This value can be used as the fixed cost, and the term

$7.83X^{.61}$ can be used to calculate the variable cost, for any throughput. On the other hand, if there is a condition that imposes a minimum size warehouse, such as t_1, the corresponding fixed cost f_1 can be calculated from the equation.

In addition, an examination of the cost function allows the determination of operating ranges for which the nonlinear function may be considered linear to simplify subsequent modeling. The capabilities needed to retrieve the data and fit the curves should be part of the company's operating systems.

TAKING ADVANTAGE OF CURRENT TECHNOLOGICAL TRENDS

One of the worst mistakes that is commonly made by management is simply to computerize existing manual systems. A computer has significant advantages over human beings—it can perform with great accuracy and at very high speeds operations such as:

- Reading data

- Storing and retrieving data

- Typing or displaying data

- Performing arithmetical and logical operations

In addition, it can store vast amounts of information for long periods of time, and perform repetitive operations for any length of time without loss of efficiency.

On the other hand, human beings have significant advantages over computers. For example, they can perform creative thinking, they can improvise solutions to unexpected problems, they can interpret data that are not clearly written or are written in different scripts. Because of these substantial differences, a well designed system takes advantage of the strong points of both computers and human beings. Thus, it relies on computers to manipulate data repetitively, and on human beings to interpret information and trigger actions.

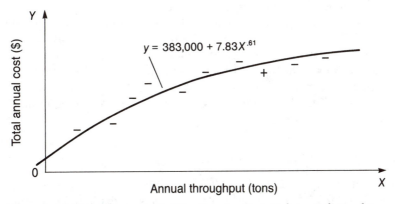

Figure 9-31 Development of a Warehousing Cost–Volume Relationship from Actual Operating Data

Computerizing a manual system means simply that the computer is used to simulate clerical operations, which is an inefficient, wasteful use of its capabilities. The design of a computerized system should address in detail the question of man-machine interface, to ensure that both people and machines are used in the most effective way, from a total system point of view.

TAKING ADVANTAGE OF STANDARDIZATION WORK

A number of organizations, both in the United States and abroad, are currently developing ways to standardize data formats, coding structures, and documentation. Two U.S. organizations are spearheading this work: the Transportation Data Coordinating Committee (TDCC) in Washington, D.C., and the National Committee on International Trade Documentation (NCITD), in New York.

USER COMMITMENT

The most common problems found with the design and operation of management systems are almost always the consequence of lack of user commitment and direct participation in the development of the system's specifications. To ensure the success of a management system it is imperative that the ultimate users be directly involved in the development of the system, and that they give final approval of specifications as well as of the operating system after its installation.

MANAGEMENT BY EXCEPTION

The operating and control subsystems should be designed to report only deviations from plans or standards, not to display all transactions in the system. This enables management to focus on situations that require attention, and saves searching time that can be better used in analysis and problem solving. Management by exception is especially important in cases where the volume of data is substantial. In the case of transportation costs, for example, the only practical way to identify situations that require corrective actions is by flagging only the cases where actual performance differs from a pre-established standard by more than a pre-established value.

The most useful technique for management by exception is *analysis by contribution*, also known as ABC analysis, or the 20/80 rule; briefly stated, this principle says that in any set of items with different values or contributions, a small fraction of the items contributes a large fraction of the total value of the set. Management by exception consists of identifying the few important items in the set, to establish strict limits for their control, while setting broader limits for the majority of the items representing a small fraction of the total value.

AUTOMATIC DATA PROCESSING AS A SKILL-TRANSFERRING TOOL

One of the most important features of automated data-processing techniques is that they make possible the efficient transfer of skills which results in upgraded management quality. Thus, very complex techniques developed by specialists can be put at a manager's fingertips with a minimum of technical training.

THE LEARNING CURVE EFFECT

A successful management system must account for the fact that users will become increasingly proficient in its use as they learn its characteristics. For this reason, the design should include redundancy, backup, and error control features that can be used initially, but discarded as user familiarity increases.

Logistic Management System Content

A complete logistic management system should include three categories of interrelated subsystems, defined by their direction in time:

Future: Forecasting, planning, and budgeting systems

Present: Operations support, performance, documentation, and costs accounting systems

Past: Control and analysis systems

The common thread of all these subsystems is that they all deal with planning, operating, and controlling the movement, storage, and processing of materials, and the facilities, equipment, information, money, and personnel needed to do so.

A complete logistic management system should include the following subsystems:

1. *Forecasting.* This subsystem must translate the company's sales forecasts into a forecast of shipping requirements, including the quantities that must be shipped on a daily or weekly basis from each shipping location to all destinations served.

2. *Planning.* This subsystem must translate long-term corporate plans into long-term logistic plans, including planned levels of operation, and facilities, equipment, and personnel needed to support them. Its horizon is usually five years, covered in yearly increments:

3. *Budgeting.* This subsystem must take the plans for the next year and transform them into cash flow and operational performance targets. Its horizon is usually one year, covered in monthly increments.

4. *Inventory management.* This subsystem must provide the capabilities for:

   - Inventory record keeping for raw materials, in-process, and finished products by inventory location
   - Safety stock calculation procedures to ensure that required service levels are maintained
   - Inventory replenishment procedures to ensure that shipping forecasts can be met
   - Auditing procedures to ensure that physical and book inventories are in acceptable correspondence
   - Make or buy analysis procedures to determine what items must be produced or purchased
   - Control procedures to ensure that inventory levels are appropriately related to forecast usage

5. *Production planning and control.* This subsystem must take into account inventory replenishment and other requirements that must be manufactured or purchased. The system must be capable of:

- Allocating forecast demands and available raw materials to available machines, to maximize profit; this calculation must include all relevant costs such as transportation, production, and purchasing, and all relevant constraints such as minimum purchase quantities and maximum manufacturing capacities
- Establishing production deadlines that account for production and transfer times to ensure timeliness of inventory replenishment and of direct shipments to customers
- Establishing raw material and component needs to meet production plans
- Controlling production progress to ensure timely replenishment of inventories, or re-assessment of the situation

6. *Procurement.* This subsystem must take the inventory replenishment requirements that must be purchased—including finished products, raw materials, maintenance, repair, and operating items, equipment, and energy—and support:

- Vendor selection
- Vendor control
- Purchasing procedures, including types of purchase orders and quantities to buy for different requirements
- Open order contract control
- Quality control and acceptance procedures
- Status inquiry capability

7. *Order processing and invoicing.* This subsystem must provide for customer order procedures:

- Receipt and logging
- Editing and validation
- Entry
- Processing, including picking, packaging, and shipping
- Status inquiry
- Invoicing

8. *Customer service.* This subsystem must provide the informational support for customer service operations, including:

- Inside sales
- Information exchange, including price quotations, sales terms, etc.
- Claims handling
- Customer service planning and control

9. *Transportation management.* This subsystem must provide information to support:

- Traffic analysis including, for example, tonnages shipped by lane by month
- Use of special services, such as freight forwarders, and pools
- All documentation needed to move freight
- Private fleet accounting, including asset ledger, depreciation, operating costs, and maintenance and repair costs

- Fleet routing, scheduling dispatching, and control
- Fleet maintenance scheduling
- Transportation planning, including equipment requirements, mode mix, etc.

10. *Facilities management*. This subsystem must provide information to support:

- Facility work scheduling and control
- Documentation needed, including picking lists, packaging instructions and labels, etc.
- Facility accounting including depreciation, operating costs, overtime, etc.
- Inventory accounting, including quantities on hand, on order, and reserved; stock location; reorder points and quantities; safety stocks to be carried

Logistic Management System Specifications

For each subsystem outlined above, it is necessary to define six types of specifications:

- *Inputs:* Their source, content, use, frequency, and volume

- *Outputs*: Their distribution, format, content, use, frequency, and display mode

- *Files*: Their content, size, use, and updating responsibility and procedures

- *Algorithms*: Transformation of inputs and files into outputs

- *Support*: Manual procedures to gather, control, and distribute information

- *Service*: Turnaround performance to generate outputs and update files

Develop the Logistic System Organizational Structure

We have seen that organization is one of the legs of the logistic tripod; we have also examined the major resources that the other two legs or components of the logistic system encompass: (1) the *logistic network*, including facilities, equipment, and materials; and (2) the *management system*, including information, techniques, hardware, software, and documents. We can define the logistic system's third leg, *organization*, as encompassing one major resource: *people*.

From the discussion on logistic network design we could see that the configuration of the logistic system network is arrived at independently from the organization structure. In the discussion on management system design we saw that its characteristics should be developed independently from the organization structure, and around business functions. For these reasons, it is advisable to develop the system's organization structure after both the logistic network and the management system have been specified. This approach ensures the effectiveness of the organization by structuring it around the system it has to manage.

Organizational Principles

The design of the logistic system organization, discussed in detail in Chapter 29, should be guided by the application of some basic principles that are common to any organizational structuring effort. These principles can be applied sequentially as follows.

DIVISION OF WORK

The first step in the process is to classify all the work that must be performed to manage the logistic system into logical units that follow a hierarchy. Typically, this is done by identifying:

1. *Functions* that characterize the logistic system, such as transportation, warehousing, inventory control, and order processing.

2. *Tasks* that characterize each function. For example, within the transportation function we may identify transportation planning, fleet management, rate negotiations, and so on.

3. *Activities* that constitute each task. For example, within the fleet management task, we may identify routing, scheduling, dispatching, control, preventive maintenance, and other activities.

The division of work along these lines accomplishes two purposes: (1) It identifies the elemental building blocks—the activities—to be used in constructing the organizational structure; and (2) it enables the subsequent analysis to group similar activities, and to introduce the element of work specialization, both of which result in increased operational efficiency.

UNITY OF OBJECTIVES

Each activity must have clearly defined objectives that are explicitly related to and support the overall mission, goals, and objectives of the total organization. Once the objectives of each activity have been identified, they can be detailed through the development of work content statements, methods, and procedures, outlining how each activity is to be performed in relation to the logistic network and the management system.

For example, the *preventive maintenance* activity can be characterized as having one major objective: to minimize maintenance costs for the company, as part of an overall objective to control and reduce costs. By relating the procedures to be followed in performing preventive maintenance, more specific objectives can be identified for this activity. For example, when the costs of operating inefficiency resulting from need for maintenance are traded off against the cost of performing more frequent maintenance, optimal preventive maintenance schedules can be determined.

BALANCE OF AUTHORITY AND RESPONSIBILITY

Given the work content statements prepared for each activity, the scope of responsibility for their performance can be established. To ensure effective performance the appropriate authority must accompany each activity, to balance the responsibility for its performance. Failure to do so is one of the most common causes of organizational problems. Another major cause of organizational problems is failure to realize that although authority can be delegated, responsibility cannot.

Continuing with our preventive maintenance example, it is necessary to identify the activity that will be assigned the responsibility for establishing maintenance schedules, and the scope of the authority needed to fulfill this responsibility.

DEFINITION OF POSITIONS

Once the levels of authority and responsibility have been established by activity, it is possible to group similar activities into positions. The procedure to follow can be summarized as follows:

1. *Establish manning levels.* Given the activity definitions, and the projected work volumes for each one, it is possible to estimate the manning levels for each activity. This is done either on the basis of similar experiences, or by using industrial engineering techniques. Manning levels are usually expressed in man-days per year.

2. *Establish manpower levels.* Once manning levels are determined, the number of people needed for each activity is calculated by dividing the number of man-days per year by the number of working days per year.

3. *Reevaluate activity definitions.* The next step is to reevaluate and redefine activity definitions so that the resulting activities require roughly integer numbers of people for their performance; this will determine the number of positions needed for each activity.

SPAN OF CONTROL

The number of people that one individual can effectively manage is limited. The higher the level in the organization, the lower the number of people that can be managed effectively, and vice versa. There used to be a rule of thumb that put the number of direct reports to any manager at about five, and certainly at less than seven. With the availability of powerful information systems at reasonable cost, it is becoming feasible to increase the number of people reporting to an individual. Today's manager can command a vast array of information that he can retrieve on-line, with flexible formats; thus, a manager can supervise more people with less effort and time, because he has better knowledge of what his people are doing.

In any case, there are physical limits on the number of direct reports that an individual manager can handle with proper attention. For this reason, it is necessary to structure activities, tasks, and functions in successive levels of supervision so that span of control is limited. This is accomplished by grouping similar activities within tasks, and similar tasks within functions.

The principle of span of control guides the structuring of functions into an organization. This can be accomplished by creating a classical pyramidal structure with a chain of command, or by creating an organizational matrix in which each position may report to more than one other position within a network of command. The matrix form of organization is becoming increasingly popular, especially in support functions such as logistics. Essentially what a matrix organization does is formalize the "dotted line" relationships usually found in pyramidal organizations, recognizing that an individual may have to report to several supervisors.

Organizational Documentation

After the positions and the organizational structure have been developed, it is necessary to document the results. This is usually done by developing (1) *organization charts*, showing the chain or network of command, and (2) *job descriptions*. A thorough job description will contain the following information:

Job title	Knowledge and skills required
Reporting relationships	Education and experience required
Position objectives	Measures of performance
General functions	Position grade and compensation ranges
Specific responsibilities	

Based on the job descriptions and the personnel that may be available to fill the positions, it is necessary to identify which individuals should be assigned to what positions. As a part of that process, each individual's skills should be reviewed to identify training requirements to ensure appropriate performance. Positions that cannot be filled with available personnel—assuming reasonable training—can then be identified, so that a recruiting and selection campaign can be started. The basic tool to guide that effort is the job description.

The procedure outlined here is seldom implemented in practice in a sequential manner. It is common to find that some steps may be taken concurrently and very often successive steps may be repeated several times, until the final organization structure emerges.

Organizational Trends

We pointed out in the introduction to this chapter that there is a trend toward expanding the scope of logistics to encompass all physical resources in the company: materials, equipment, facilities, and land. Projecting this trend, we can conceive of a company organization structure along the lines shown in Figure 9–32.

In a resource-oriented organization structure based on the principles of matrix organization, we would find that the current functions of marketing, production, and logistics would be redefined into *human resources*-oriented functions such as sales and customer service, and *physical resources*-oriented functions such as production, transportation, purchasing, and warehousing. In such a scheme, financial resources would remain essentially unchanged from current practices, while informational resources would be substantially upgraded as one of the basic resources of a company. This type of organization would change the problem of logistic system design into a problem of optimal deployment and use of physical resources. The design process would be substantially the same outlined in this chapter. The difference would be that the objective function would increase in value, and the complexity of the network to be optimized would be greater.

Conduct Financial Analysis

Following the analyses of the logistic network, management system, and organization structure, it is necessary to reduce these analyses to a series of conclusions and recommendations outlining the specific course of action to be taken to install a new logistic system or modify an existing one. This process must weld together the three components of the logistic system in a manner that meets customer service requirements while maximizing profit.

In the design process outlined above, we have seen the sequence in which the three components of the logistic system were structured. There was major interaction between the management system rules and the structuring of the logistic system network. This in-

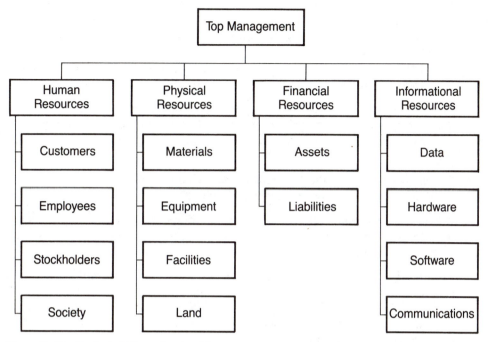

Figure 9-32   Projected Organization Chart

teraction was reflected in the cost relationships developed in the management system and used in modeling the logistic network. Both the logistic network and the management system have been developed to account for their costs and their profit impact. In this step of the design process we concern ourselves with further analysis to account for the additional requirements and costs deriving from the implementation of the solutions. In this regard, a major consideration is to minimize the changes needed in the existing network, systems, and organization, in order to make implementation as simple and inexpensive as possible.

Cash Flow Analysis

The design of the logistic network, management system, and organization yield the projected costs to implement and operate each component, as well as the income or savings that will be generated. With that information, the annual net cash flow for the system or alternative systems can be projected for each year considered.

The number of years to consider in cash flow analysis is a fundamental question. The proper answer—from an economic analysis point of view—is that the cash flow analysis should cover the entire life of the project, so that the calculation includes complete life-cycle costing. In practice, this approach presents serious problems because the life of facilities and equipment is very long. As tax depreciation schedules will show, buildings are usually depreciated over a 40-year life, and equipment over an 8- to 15-year life depending on its kind. Under these conditions, cash flow analysis would have to be performed over a 40-year horizon in order to account fully for the life of private facilities to be built. The problems with this requirement are numerous:

1. *Different growth rates for different cost elements.* As pointed out earlier in this chapter, some cost elements are growing faster than others, while other costs are

declining. This makes it difficult—if not impossible—to forecast very far into the future such parameters as operational costs, transportation costs, demands by product by market, and supply conditions. Forecasting errors normally increase exponentially with time; thus, given historical data, even a ten-year forecast of any of the parameters mentioned would have expected errors large enough to make them meaningless.

2. *Shifting geographical dispersion of demand.* Population migrations, customer shifts when new facilities are opened and old ones closed down, varying market penetration rates, and changes in marketing channel mix can all affect long-range analysis.

3. *Product life cycle.* Product demand varies at changing rates over a long period of time; thus product mix is continuously evolving.

4. *Competitive environment changes.* Lateral competition from new products or from foreign competition are examples of changes that are hard to assess over a long period of time.

5. *Planning horizon.* Corporate long-range plans are usually formulated for up to five years in the future; some companies prepare more general assessments up to ten years ahead, and a few companies speculate about business conditions twenty years in the future. However, planning information is seldom available in detail beyond about five years in the future.

Under these conditions, no hard general rules can be developed to perform financial evaluations of alternative logistic systems. Each company follows a different procedure based on its own policies and accounting methods. However, we can recommend some general guidelines that have proven effective in most practical situations. These can be modified to comply with each company's financial principles and risk-taking philosophy.

1. *Annualize all costs* to be incurred during the life cycle of the alternative considered. This is to be done using the expected or "tax" life of assets, i.e., buildings are depreciated over 40 years.

2. *Select a "base year"* that has the latest annual information available, and a "design year" that is three to five years beyond the "base year." Do *not* attempt to go far beyond five years because the speed of environmental changes will make further projections of dubious value.

3. *Assume that cost trends for the previous five years, ending with the base year, will continue through the design year.* An alternative is to develop probability distributions for each parameter, at each year, and input them to a Monte Carlo simulator, as described in Chapter 15. The output from the simulator can then be input to an optimizing model.

4. *Calculate the expected cash flows for each year up to the design year.* For the remainder of the project life use the same cash flow as for the design year, unless reliable information about events further in the future is available to modify them.

5. *Calculate the return on investment (ROI) for each alternative considered.*

6. *Evaluate the impact of risks,* using sensitivity analysis or Monte Carlo simulation, and Decision Tree techniques.

7. *Select the most desirable alternative* on the basis of expected ROI and risk analysis.

The procedure recommended above has proven effective in most practical situations, and it usually blends in well with different corporate rules and policies.

Monte Carlo simulation and Decision Tree analysis will be covered in Chapter 15. However, there is a simple technique that can be used to perform overall cost sensitivity analysis. The technique can be used to calculate the probability distribution of total logistic cost (or profit) given the probability distributions of each cost element. In this analysis we will assume that all probability distributions are normal, which is a valid assumption in most practical situations. To describe the probability distributions of each cost element, we can take three points representing probabilities of .10, .50, and .90 that the cost will not exceed a given value.

For example, consider the following values:

| Cost Element | Squares of the Deviations | | |
	.10	.50	.90
Purchasing	18.5	0	23.0
Production	42.3	0	19.4
Warehousing	31.4	0	24.0
Transportation	41.0	0	57.8
Total	133.2	0	124.2
$\sqrt{\text{Total}}$	11.5	0	11.1

We can see that there is a .10 probability that purchasing costs will not exceed $8.5 million, and a .50 probability that transportation costs will not exceed $28.7 million.

Given these data, we could simply add the numbers in each column to obtain the totals of 73.3, 96.1 and 117.8. That procedure, however, would be statistically incorrect, because it ignores the effects the various cost elements have on one another. The correct calculation would be to take the values for the mean of the distribution (.50 probability) and add them to obtain the mean of the total distribution; then calculate the square root of the sum of the squares of the deviations of each value with respect to the mean value; the results of the .10 and .90 columns are subtracted and added, respectively, to the total of the .50 column.

In our example, when we calculate the squares of the deviations, we obtain:

| Cost Element | Total Costs (10^6 Dollars) Probability | | |
	.10	.50	.90
Purchasing	8.5	12.8	17.6
Production	32.8	39.3	43.7
Warehousing	9.7	15.3	20.2
Transportation	22.3	28.7	36.3
Total	73.3	96.1	117.8

To calculate the values of the total cost at .10 and .90 probabilities, we now subtract 11.5 from 96.1 and we add 11.1 to 96.1 thus, we obtain:

$$\text{Total system cost} = \frac{.10}{84.6} \quad \frac{.50}{96.1} \quad \frac{.90}{107.2}$$

If the distribution cannot be assumed normal, then using Monte Carlo simulation is the best approach to determine the probability distribution of the total cost.

Project Financing

The final step in the financial analysis is the preparation of a project financing recommendation. In this area there is no standard procedure; each company develops its own policies and rules, and changes them as the situation warrants. However, in each case all of the following information must be provided.

- *Investment needed*—amount, timing, and proposed use

- *Investment sources*—internal, external, and at what interest rates

- *Repayment procedure*—amounts to be repaid, timing, payees, and the source of funds

- *Tax implications* for the corporation

Certain rules should be followed when preparing this information:

1. *Base all figures on the DCF calculation.* The discounted cash flow (DCF) calculation should be used as the source of all the data needed to evaluate project financing.

2. *Base audits on project financing figures.* Once the project financing strategy has been developed, the information contained in it should be the standard against which subsequent audits are performed.

3. *Separate depreciation from other sources.* To facilitate financial analysis and subsequent control it is advisable to identify Depreciation separately from all other internal sources of funds.

Develop an Implementation Plan

The final product of the system design effort must be an implementation plan outlining the actions that must be taken to manage the transition from existing to recommended conditions. A good implementation plan usually provides several benefits:

- It defines the actions that must be taken to implement the system and the sequence, resources, and timing needed to execute the actions.

- It identifies potential problems far in advance so that good solutions to them can be developed on time.

- It provides a tool to track progress during implementation.

- It identifies critical activities so that resources available can be applied in the most effective manner.

- It ensures the feasibility of the project by assemblying a complete strategy to implement the desired system.

- It provides documentation supporting the recommended course of action.

Implementation Plan Contents

The specific contents of an implementation plan will vary depending on each situation. However, certain types of information should be considered for inclusion in every case.

To begin with, there should be a *definition of elements*, including projects, tasks, and activities needed to manage the transition to the proposed system. For each project, for each task within each project, and for each activity within each task, it is necessary to state its *objective* (what that planning element is supposed to accomplish, in measurable terms), and its *scope* (indicating the content of the planning element).

For example, a project may be "Closing down the Tuscon Warehouse"; its objective being to eliminate that warehouse from the system, and its scope being all tasks and activities of a legal, financial and logistic nature, to accomplish the objective. Within that project there can be several tasks, such as "negotiating lease termination," or "transfer all remaining inventories." Within the last task there could be several activities, such as "determine destination of remaining inventory," or "take a physical inventory."

Other information useful to the plan includes the following:

- *Characteristics of activities*. For each activity defined, it is necessary to define three characteristics: (1) the *resources* needed to accomplish it, including manpower and cost; (2) the *duration* expected for the activity; and (3) the *responsibility* for its performance.

- *Activity sequence*. All activities must then be placed in their relative sequence. The best way to accomplish this is to create a logic network, showing each activity as an arrow, as in any standard Critical Path Method or program evaluation and review technique (PERT) system.

- *Identification of milestones*, including expected dates for the completion of each project, and major tasks, as well as deadlines and check points throughout the plan.

- *Identification of constraints*, such as financial, human, or legal constraints that must be observed in the implementation plan.

- *Calculation of dates and slacks*, for each activity in the plan. This includes calculating the earliest and latest dates at which each activity can start and finish, as well as the slack, or difference between earliest and latest dates, indicating how long the activity can be delayed without delaying the project.

- *Financial statement*, identifying the magnitude and timing of the necessary investments and expected savings. There should be a summary of the ROI calculation.

- *Identification of risks*, associated with the plan, broken down at the lowest level of detail possible.

- *Audit plan*, showing when and how auditing will take place after the implementation phase, to determine whether performance, costs, and savings are close to the estimates.

Project Documentation

The final step in the logistic system design process should be the preparation of complete documentation describing what was done, how, and why. This documentation should contain at least the following information:

1. The objectives of the project

2. The details of the recommendations

3. A description of the methodology used

4. A statement about the current system, including

    — A description of its main features
    — An analysis of the system, its problems and opportunities, and important constraints imposed by it

5. A description of the alternative solutions considered

6. The details of input data development, including

    — The sources of data
    — The age and accuracy of data
    — The methods used to compile the final inputs

7. The details of the analysis and the conclusions stemming from it

8. The implementation plan

9. The audit plan

10. The support data used

11. References and bibliography

Channels of Distribution: Structure and Change

JAMES F. ROBESON *and* DAVID T. KOLLAT

Channels of distribution are quietly but perceptibly undergoing a series of important changes. The distribution executive, if he is to develop viable distribution systems in the decade of the 1980s, must understand the rationale of channel design and the nature of changing channel structures as well as the factors in the marketplace giving rise to the need for such change.

Channel Structure

The traditional marketing channels in which most distribution executives are involved are loosely structured networks of vertically aligned firms. The structuring of these networks depends largely upon the nature of the product being distributed and its target market. A few of the numerous channel structures that might be relied upon to effectively distribute goods to ultimate consumers and industrial end users are illustrated in Figure 10–1.

The various configurations illustrated in the figure may help us visualize some of the many ways in which channels might be structured. However, the diagram is deceiving in two respects. First, it does not accurately indicate the many existing forms of each of the various middlemen. For example, as illustrated in Figure 10–2, there are numerous variations in the type and number of organizations at the wholesale level. The complexity of channel design is further magnified when the vast number of various types of retail orga-

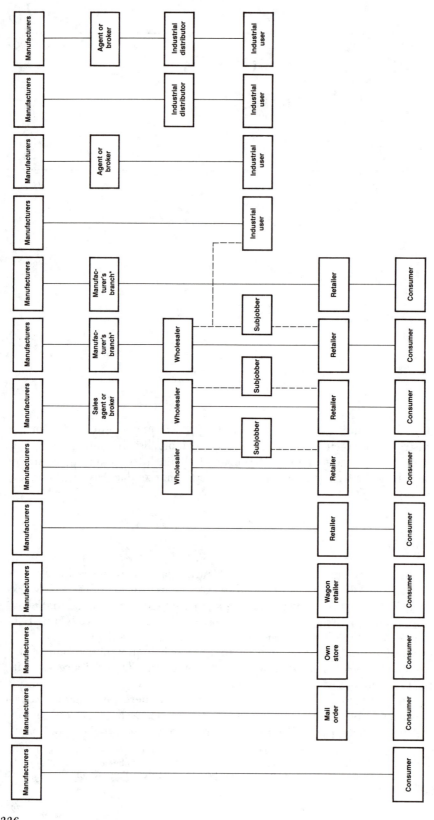

*A manufacturer's branch is owned by the manufacturer

Figure 10-1   Alternative Channels of Distribution

Source: Adapted from John R. Bromell, *Primary Channels of Distribution for Manufacturers*, Business Information Source, U.S. Department of Commerce (July 1950), p. 3.

nizations are also taken into consideration. The ways in which all these middlemen might be combined to form channels are almost innumerable.

The second area of possible misunderstanding also concerns the number and type of various middlemen. However, in this instance it involves the recognition that not all classes of middlemen are available in every geographic area or line of trade. That is, all classes of wholesalers are not usually available in every trading area to distribute each product line. Thus, "in a product line such as fashion apparel, a garment maker may have an extremely limited choice of types of middlemen: the selling agent, the broker, the direct-buying retailer, or the chain store buying office."[1] There is no one "best" channel configuration for all companies involved in distributing similar classes of products, even though they may be serving the same end users.

Figure 10-2 is, however, extremely helpful in one respect. It permits us to visualize the overall structure of distribution.

Channel Geometry

The reason alternative channels are essential can perhaps best be seen from a geometric perspective. Figure 10-3 shows two alternative approaches to structuring product flow from the point of production to the point of consumption. The diagram on the left represents a "direct" form of distribution from producer to retailer. The diagram on the right demonstrates how a wholesaler might be positioned in the channel, thereby effecting a more "indirect" form of distribution.

The geometry of these diagrams clearly illustrates two important structural factors that otherwise might be difficult to describe: the principle of minimum total transactions and the concept of sorting. Direct distribution requires 16 transactions to complete the exchange activity between four producers and four retailers. However, by employing an intermediary—a wholesaler—the total number of transactions is reduced to eight. In addition, since distribution costs are relatively fixed per transaction, the use of middlemen also tends to reduce distribution costs for the channel as a whole.[2]

The concept of sorting was singled out by Wroe Alderson as the most essential role of marketing intermediaries.[3] He pointed out that middlemen serve to reconcile relatively narrow product offerings from each of several sources of supply into a wide assortment at the point of final sale. That is, consumer demand or industrial need is usually for a much broader assortment of goods than can be made available by any one producer. In addition, the customer typically wishes to buy this broader assortment of products in small quantities. Thus, the wholesaler seeks to (1) develop an assortment of merchandise that satisfies the diverse needs of the customers he serves, and (2) sell it in the quantities they demand.

Major Trends in Distribution

Developing an Historical Perspective[4]

The role of the middleman has been misunderstood by many for decades. As early as 1913 a publication of the American Academy of Political and Social Science entitled "Reducing the Cost of Food Distribution" focused largely on ways of getting around middlemen—

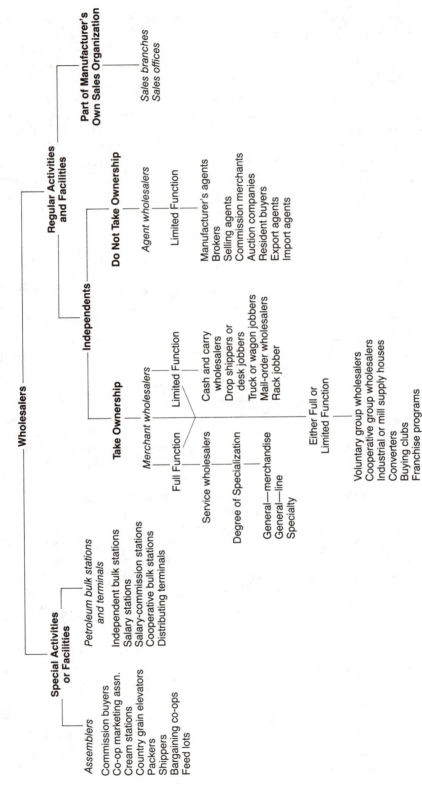

Figure 10-2 The Structure of Wholesaling

From *Strategic Marketing* by David T. Kollat, Roger D. Blackwell, and James F. Robeson. Copyright © 1972 by Holt, Rinehart and Winston, Inc. Reprinted by permission of Holt, Rinehart and Winston, CBS College Publishing.

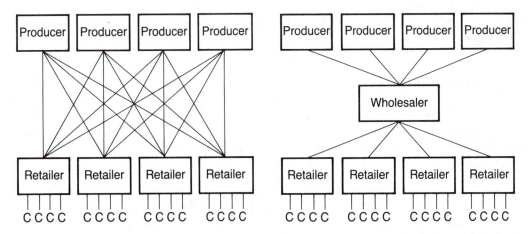

Figure 10-3   Channel Geometry

From *Strategic Marketing* by David T. Kollat, Roger D. Blackwell, and James F. Robeson. Copyright © 1972 by Holt, Rinehart and Winston, Inc. Reprinted by permission of Holt, Rinehart and Winston, CBS College Publishing.

wholesalers in particular—as a major means of reducing the cost of grocery distribution. More specifically, the publication stated, "The first move has been toward the elimination as far as possible of the wholesaler as a distributive factor." The publication went on to say that the attack upon the wholesaler had come from four sources:

1. From the chain stores. "The chain stores also organized as wholesale houses and claimed the same right as other wholesalers to buy direct from the manufacturer."

2. From associations of independent retail dealers, some of whom made arrangements to purchase direct from manufacturers and some of whom formed separate wholesale organizations for direct buying.

3. From some manufacturers who sold direct to retailers at the same price charged to wholesalers.

4. From an attack on quantity prices which were advantageous to wholesalers and other large buyers but allegedly served as handicaps to the smaller dealer.

This analysis is most interesting and enlightening because it clearly identifies a series of false notions about the wholesaler's position in the distributive process that have persisted for well over a half-century.

This same source describes how "goods pass from the manufacturer through the hands of the wholesaler who adds 10 per cent to the price, and then to the retailer who adds an additional 20 per cent before they reach the consumer." The 20 percent added by the retailers was referred to as a "profit . . . for those who are hopelessly incompetent." This statement by a presumed marketing authority clearly establishes the notion that middlemen—wholesalers and retailers—merely add to the price of products without giving value in terms of services and utilities wanted and needed by the consumer. The 20 percent *gross profit* of the retailer is erroneously or carelessly taken as the *net profit*. In fact, net profits in food retailing—then and now—approximate 10 percent or less of the gross profit.

These erroneous statements and analyses are apparently as commonplace today as they were years ago.

Conventional Channels

At the end of World War II, the structure of distribution in the American economy was highly stable and relatively atomistic. Small and medium-sized firms dominated most lines of trade, and traditional channel linkages were the dominant means of distribution. They were expected to perform a conventionally defined set of marketing functions. Small retailers, for example, typically price-marked merchandise, maintained unit control records, reordered goods, and initiated local promotional campaigns.

While these linkages seemed appropriate when established, many were actually or potentially sources of diseconomies. The need for each member of the channel to establish and maintain a field sales force that repeatedly called on the same accounts resulted in high selling costs. The persistence of many small-scale units resulted in the sacrifice of scale economies. In addition, the autonomy of the operating units frequently resulted in duplicative programming, as when manufacturers, wholesalers, and retailers each price-marked merchandise. Finally, and perhaps most importantly, the rigidity characteristic of such channels did not permit economies to be effected even when the need for them was recognized.

Vertical Marketing Systems[5]

In contrast to conventional channels of distribution, vertical marketing systems consist of networks of horizontally coordinated and vertically aligned establishments managed as a total system.[6] They no longer require each channel member to perform an "expected" set of marketing functions, but rely instead upon the concept of functional shiftability to improve total system performance. That is, establishments at each level are reprogrammed so that marketing functions within the system are performed at the most advantageous level or position.[7] The salient characteristics of each form of distribution network are shown in Figure 10–4, and summarized in Table 10–1.

Three major types of vertically aligned networks have evolved—corporate, contractual, and administered systems.

Corporate Systems

The vertically integrated corporate distribution system has an extended history. Singer, for example, operated company-owned warehouses and stores in the 1870s. However, vertically integrated corporations did not become a clearly discernible factor in distribution until the mid-1950s. Manufacturers' sales branches and offices are clearly a part of this phenomenon. But, while extremely important, this phenomenon presents a somewhat misleading perspective in that it only shows movement forward in the channel. Indeed, some of the more exciting developments in the formation of vertical marketing systems involve movement backward in the channel by wholesalers or retailers.

Large food chains now obtain 15 to 20 percent of their requirements from company-owned manufacturing and processing facilities. Sears reportedly obtains 50 percent of its

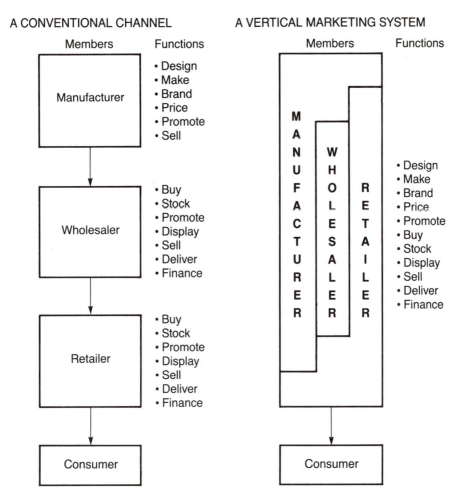

Figure 10-4   The Concept of Functional Shiftability

throughput from manufacturing facilities in which it has an equity interest, and Holiday Inns is rapidly evolving into a self-supply network that includes a carpet mill, a furniture manufacturing plant, and numerous captive redistribution facilities. Among manufacturers, Sherwin-Williams now operates over 1,400 retail outlets, while Hart Schaffner & Marx owns more than 270 stores. In short, these and similar organizations are massive, vertically integrated corporate systems.

Contractual Systems

The three principal versions of contractual systems are wholesaler-sponsored voluntary groups, retailer-owned cooperatives, and franchised store programs. Firms operating in these configurations "pool" their resources to achieve operating economies and market impact that are difficult, if not impossible, to achieve through independent action. More

Table 10–1   Salient Characteristics of Competing Networks

Network Characteristics	Conventional Marketing Channel	Vertical Marketing System
Composition of network	Network composed of isolated and autonomous units, each of which performs a conventionally defined set of marketing functions. Coordination primarily achieved through bargaining and negotiation.	Network composed of interconnected units each of which performs the most desirable combination of marketing functions. Coordination achieved through the use of detailed plans and comprehensive programs.
Economic capabilities of member units	Operating units frequently unable to achieve systemic economies.	Operating units *programmed* to achieve systemic economies.
Organizational stability	Open network with low index of member loyalty and relative ease of entry. Network therefore tends to be unstable.	Open network but entry rigorously controlled by the system's requirements and by market conditions. Membership loyalty assured through the use of ownership or contractual agreements. As a result, network tends to be relatively stable.
Number and composition of decision makers	Large number of strategists supported by a slightly larger number of operating executives.	Limited number of strategists supported by a significantly larger number of staff and operating executives.
Analytical focus of strategic decision makers	Strategists preoccupied with cost, volume, and investment relationships at a *single* stage of the marketing process.	Strategists preoccupied with cost, volume, and investment relationships at *all* stages of the marketing process. Corresponding emphasis on the "total cost" concept accompanied by a continuous search for favorable economic trade-offs.
Underlying decision-making process	Heavy reliance on judgmental decisions made by generalists.	Heavy reliance on "scientific" decisions made by specialists or committees of specialists.
Institutional loyalties of decision makers	Decision makers committed to traditional forms of distribution.	Decision makers committed to marketing concept and viable institutions.

From *Strategic Marketing* by David T. Kollat, Roger D. Blackwell, and James F. Robeson, p. 290. Copyright © 1972 by Holt, Rinehart and Winston, Inc. Reprinted by permission of Holt, Rinehart and Winston, CBS College Publishing.

specifically, such vertically aligned enterprises contribute to a common advertising fund, adhere to compatible merchandising programs, share computer and warehouse facilities, and combine their purchases to achieve effective buying power.

Voluntary, cooperative, and franchise networks are more formidable today than they were a decade ago. Consider a few dramatic examples:

- *Wholesaler-sponsored voluntary groups*—In the hardware field, wholesalers affiliated with the Pro, Liberty, and Sentry merchandising group networks now supply over 10,000 "independent" stores with supporting services that are comparable to, or in some cases superior to, those enjoyed by chain outlets.

- *Retailer-owned cooperatives*—Of the approximately 207,000 retail food stores in the United States, 47 percent are member-stores of cooperative or voluntary groups. Super-Value is the largest of these and generates over $2.6 billion in sales annually. In appliances, MARTA (Metropolitan Appliance Radio Television Association) has a total membership of over 250 stores.

- *Franchises*—Franchises are particularly popular in the fast food market with companies such as McDonald's, Burger King, and Kentucky Fried Chicken. Franchising is also growing in other sectors of retailing—Midas in automotive repair; Century 21 and Red Carpet in real estate; and Adia in employment services.

Administered Systems

Administered programs affect a particular line of merchandise in a store rather than the store's entire operation. Such programs go beyond traditional store-vendor compacts into joint ventures that involve the development of comprehensive programs for a specified line of merchandise.

Programs of this type have been developed by both manufacturing and wholesaling organizations. Common manufacturer examples are the programs developed and administered by the O.M. Scott & Sons Company in lawn products, by Magnavox in the home entertainment field, and by Kraft Foods in supermarkets. Within wholesaling, administered systems are found in drug, hardware, sporting goods, phonograph records, and many other merchandise classifications.

Significance

How important are these systems in the American economy at the present time? The market share held by companies operating 11 or more units increased from 18 percent in 1951 to an estimated 35 percent in 1980. In addition, stores affiliated with voluntary, cooperative, and franchise networks captured about 45 percent of retail sales in 1980. When these figures are combined, it is apparent that approximately 80 percent of total retail sales are generated by outlets affiliated with some type of vertical marketing system.[8] Moreover, these statistics do not take into direct account the impact of administered systems, about which very little is known statistically.

Notes

1. Phillip McVey, "Are Channels of Distribution What the Textbooks Say?" *Journal of Marketing*, 24 (January 1960), p. 62.

2. While it is commonly accepted that direct distribution is the most costly form of distribution, this should not be construed as meaning that distribution costs will automatically decline in relation to the number of intermediaries or even that the use of an intermediary will *always* result in lower total distribution costs. A detailed cost/benefit analysis should always be conducted in the course of developing and choosing among alternative channel structures.

3. Wroe Alderson, *Marketing Behavior and Executive Action* (Homewood, Ill.: Richard D. Irwin, 1957), pp. 195–227.

4. Materials in this section were adapted from Theodore N. Beckman, *The True Facts About Wholesaler-Distributors* (Washington, D.C.: The National Association of Wholesaler-Distributors, 1970).

5. This discussion of vertical marketing systems is based in large part on material developed by Alton F. Doody of The Doody Company, William R. Davidson, Chairman, Management Horizons, Inc., and Bert C. McCammon, Jr., of The University of Oklahoma.

6. Bert C. McCammon, Jr., Albert D. Bates, and Joseph P. Guiltinan, "Alternative Models for Programming Vertical Marketing Networks," a paper presented at the 1968 Fall Conference of the American Marketing Association, Denver, August 30, 1968, p. 25.

7. William R. Davidson, "Changes in Distributive Institutions," *Journal of Marketing*, 34 (January 1970), p. 7.

8. U.S. Department of Commerce, Bureau of the Census, and author's estimates.

Customer Service

BERNARD J. LA LONDE

Overview

During the past several years the U.S. economy has been beset by inflation, high interest rates, recession, and a variety of other ills which have taxed the skills of the most effective business manager. This period of very rapid change has produced a number of important shifts in management philosophy. First, business managers have become much more sensitive to the effective use of inventory assets. They have been under constant pressure to improve inventory turn, reduce inventory, eliminate slow turn items, and use other measures designed to improve inventory utilization. At the same time, other distribution channel members such as wholesalers and retailers have attempted to reduce their inventory investment and speed their inventory turns. This, of course, results in a back-up pressure in the channel of distribution and forces management at all levels to become more acutely aware of the product and service requirements of their customers.

This drive to more efficient management of inventory assets has had a direct impact on customer service. Improvement in inventory turn has been accomplished by most firms through some combination of: (1) a reduction in the number of warehouses and field stocking locations for specific products; (2) reevaluations of appropriate customer mix and product mix; and (3) a reduction of the total number of stock keeping units (SKUs) stocked in the system. All of these measures require a closer monitoring of service levels on the part of most firms if an erosion of market position is to be avoided.

The Management Environment

The Concept of Customer Service

By definition, all firms have a customer service system or perhaps several different customer service systems. Any firm that adds value to a product or service must interface with the customer at the transaction phase of the service or delivery phase of the product. On the basis of the research to date it would seem that a majority of the firms do not explicitly separate the sales interface from the other customer service interfaces involved in the transaction and post-transaction phases of a customer relationship. To be sure, the product must be delivered, invoices completed, claims handled, and so on, but these functions are not managed as part of the customer interface. Furthermore, they are often not explicitly costed so that trade-off analysis or profitability analysis may be determined in providing an optimum mix of product and service to the marketplace.

Of the firms which do explicitly recognize a customer service activity or function, there appear to be three levels of involvement or awareness on the part of management. Obviously these three levels are not mutually exclusive and they are presented here as primary orientations to customer service rather than three alternative models.

Customer Service as an Activity

In a relatively large number of firms the term *customer service* appears in a job title to describe an activity. The most common use of the term is to describe an order-processing related activity. However, the term is also used to describe activity centers ranging from a new name for the old customer complaint department to specially organized trouble-shooting sections.

When order-processing related matters are the principal emphasis, customer service is usually treated as an activity to be managed. The problem is that the activity is often treated as a specific goal to be accomplished (e.g., process orders) rather than as an integral part of achieving the total mission of the firm.

Customer Service as Performance Levels

In some firms customer service is regarded as synonymous with performance levels. Questions regarding the firm's customer service are responded to in terms of specific numbers (e.g., 95% in stock, or four-day delivery).

While these are often good measures of how the distribution system performs, they frequently represent incomplete, proxy measures from the firm's point of view rather than the customers' point of view. A situation may evolve where specific performance standards become an end objective rather than a reflection of the true level and range of service provided to the customer.

Customer Service as a Management Philosophy

In the early 1950s, the *marketing concept* was introduced and discussed in the management literature. The underlying rationale of the marketing concept was that the total mission of the firm was conditioned by how well management was able to understand customer needs and meet these needs at a profit to the firm. The marketing concept was usually framed in terms of a product, although there were some attempts to broaden the concept to product-in-use (e.g., convenience goods). The marketing concept seemed to assume away the problems of physical movement of the product to the consumer or user. Further, an orientation to the end user or consumer often shifted the primary marketing orientation to the end user and away from the problems of channel management.

In one respect, the emerging concept of customer service might be termed "the other half of the marketing concept." Like the *marketing concept*, the concept of *customer service* pervades the entire corporation and is not the exclusive responsibility of any one functional department. However, just as implementation of the marketing concept is the responsibility of the sales and marketing function, implementation of the customer service concept is the responsibility of the distribution function.

Firms that adopt this approach to customer service treat it as an element of total corporate philosophy rather than as an activity or a set of performance measures. In this context, *customer service* may be defined as "a customer-oriented corporate philosophy which integrates and manages all of the elements of the customer interface within a predetermined optimum cost-service mix."

This definition offers a rationale for the existence of the distribution function as a major corporate function. It also provides an "integrating" bottom line for measuring performance of the distribution function and points a more visible direction for improvement in performance of the customer interface. The definition does not include—other than in a coordinating sense—the specific sales contact with the customer.

Acceptance of this definition has some important implications for top management involvement in the organization and measurement of the customer service function, and for the use of data processing as an information resource.

A Research Perspective

The majority of customer service research is done by individual firms to solve specific problems. Hence, there is not a rich literature or long research tradition in the customer service area. However, a number of non-proprietary studies have been done since 1965. These studies are summarized in Table 11–1.

Management Focus

In many firms the level and performance dimensions of customer service are not considered to be a responsibility or concern of top management. In these firms customer service is usually considered to be an activity (i.e., order processing, claims, complaints) rather than a policy issue. The question remains, "Why should top management be concerned with customer service?" There are at least two persuasive reasons. The first and perhaps the most persuasive is the impact of customer service on the operating cost of the firm. Statistically speaking, it requires twice as much inventory to operate at 99.8 percent product availability levels as to operate at a 95 percent level of inventory availability. Further, transportation and warehousing costs are a substantial part of the operating cost structure of most firms. As indicated in Table 11–2, these costs range from a high of 11.6 percent of sales in food industry to a low of 2.6 percent in the pharmaceutical industry, with a man-

Table 11–1   Summary of Major Customer Service Studies*

	Channel Studied	Emphasis of Study	Comparison of Opinions at Different Channel Levels		Customer Services	
			Are There Any?	If Yes Which?	How Many?	How Derived?
Simon (1965)	Chemicals, electronic data processing, and electrical equipment	Index of technical services	No	(NA)†	31	Interview
Hutchinson and Stolle (1968)	Not specified	Management of customer service to achieve cost reductions	No	(NA)	7	Not stated
Willett and Stephenson (1969)	Drugs and drug sundries (manufacturers and retailers)	Buyers' perceptions of changes in service levels	No	(NA)	2	Literature
Hopkins and Bailey (1970)	Survey of many industries	State of the art in customer service research	No	(NA)	65	Literature
Gilmour (1973)	Scientific instruments	Use of customer service for market segmentation	Yes	Suppliers and customers	17	Interview
Perreault (1973)	Various	Physical distribution customer service	No	(NA)	9	Literature

*This research summary was developed by Professor Fran Tucker of Syracuse University and reproduced with her permission.

†Not applicable.

SOURCES: Leonard S. Simon, "Measuring the Market Impact of Technical Services," *Journal of Marketing Research* **2** (February 1965): 32–39; William M. Hutchinson and John F. Stolle, "How to Manage Customer Service," *Harvard Business Review* **46** (November–December 1968): 85–96; Ronald P. Willett and P. Ronald Stephenson, "Determinants of Buyer Response to Physical Distribution Service," *Journal of Marketing Research* **6** (August 1969): 279–83; David S. Hopkins and Earl L. Bailey, *Customer Service: A Progress Report* (New York: Conference Board, 1970); Peter Gilmour, "Customer Service: Differentiating by Market Segment," *International Journal of Physical Distribution* **7**, No. 3 (1973): 141–48; William D. Perreault, Jr., "The Role of Physical Distribution Customer Services in Industrial

Dimensions		Types of Measures of Customer Service (Level of Measurement)	Market Segmentation	Conclusions
How Many?	*How Derived?*			
14	Intuition	Importance (interval) Satisfaction (interval)	None	An index of satisfaction can be constructed to optimize service levels and expenditures
None derived	(NA)	Service level	*A priori*—by class of buyer: retail vs. institutional	Customer service affects profits
(NA)	(NA)	Satisfaction (interval)	No	Satisfaction is a linear function of service time
6	Unknown	None	None	Customer service has many definitions
None	(NA)	Similarity (interval) Importance (nominal)	Yes, using similarity and importance measures	Perceptions of similarity among services is the same between suppliers and buyers; however, the importance of services within similarity groups is not
Attempted: 2 found by factor analysis but were not consistent across industries	Literature	Satisfaction (interval) Preference (paired comparison)	None found based on operating characteristics	Customer service is important to purchasing managers, but the importance of its elements varies in different situations. Purchasing managers do not evaluate customer service as they should. Constant sum method of trade-off analysis is superior to other methods

Purchasing Decisions" (Ph.D. dissertation, Chapel Hill: University of North Carolina, 1973); William Wagner, "Formalisation of the Customer Service Function in Distribution," *International Journal of Physical Distribution* 7, No. 3 (1973): 159–75; M. T. Cunningham and D. A. Roberts, "The Role of Customer Service in Industrial Marketing," *European Journal of Marketing* 8, No. 1 (Spring 1974): 15–29; M. K. Wilson, "A Multidimensional Scaling Analysis of Customer Service: An Evaluation of Manufacturers by Their Distributors" (Ph.D. dissertation, Bloomington: Indiana University, 1974); Bernard J. La Londe and Michael Levy, "Customer Service: A Distributor-Packer/Processor Perspective," *Frozen Food Factbook* (1977); 27–47; Bernard J. La Londe and Paul H. Zinszer, *Customer Service: Meaning and Measurement* (Chicago: NCPDM, 1976); and Michael Levy, "Methodology for Improving Marketing Productivity Through Efficient Utilization of Customer Service Requirements" (Ph.D. dissertation, Columbus: The Ohio State University, 1978).

Table 11-1 *Cont.*

	Channel Studied	Emphasis of Study	Comparison of Opinions at Different Channel Levels		Customer Services	
			Are There Any?	If Yes Which?	How Many?	How Derived?
Wagner (1973)	None	How to formalize customer service in physical distribution	No	(NA)	55 (implied)	Empirically
Cunningham and Roberts (1974); Banting (1976)	Valve and pump industries	Role of customer service in industrial marketing	No	(NA)	9	Interview
Wilson (1974)	Plumbing fixtures	Application of multidimensional scaling in customer service research	No	(NA)	16	Literature
La Londe and Levy (1977)	Frozen foods	Differences of opinion about customer services	Yes	Distributor-packers, distributor-processors	29	Interview, literature
La Londe and Zinszer (1976)	Several industries	Definition of customer service	No	(NA)	21	Literature, interview
Levy (1978)	Over-the-counter drugs	Economic trade-offs among customer services	Yes	Manufacturers and wholesalers	71	Interview

ufacturing industry average of 9.8 percent. Any customer service decisions that force changes in the number and location of warehouses, inventory availability, and deployment or type and speed of transportation significantly affect the cost structure and profitability of the firm.

A second reason for top management's attention to customer service is that customer service is a key element of the firm's product offer to the marketplace. Table 11–3 illus-

Dimensions		Types of Measures of Customer Service (Level of Measurement)	Market Segmentation	Conclusions
How Many?	*How Derived?*			
4	Unknown	Frequency of occurrence (nominal)	None	Customer service needs to improve methods for acting and reacting to customers. Organizational changes needed
2 (convenience and reliability)	Literature	Importance (nominal) Performance (interval)	By industry Within industry by operating characteristics	There is probably a threshold of minimally satisfactory service
2	Indirectly by naming axes for multidimensional scaling	Similarity (ordinal) Preference (ordinal) Performance (internal)	Yes, by clustering distributors on their opinions of individual suppliers	Respondents were unable to provide consistent answers when evaluating alternative suppliers on many customer service offerings. Aspects not related to customer service such as price and product quality interfered
7	Literature, empirical	Importance (interval)	Yes, by dollar volume	Differences of opinions do exist
6, 3 (depending on classification)	Literature and interview	Importance (ordinal) Importance (nominal) Importance (ratio) Service level	None found by industry or operating characteristics	Definitions of customer service vary by function within the company, by company, and by industry.
7	Factor analysis	Importance (interval) Performance (interval) Utility (through conjoint analysis) Service level	Attempted without success using operating and geographic characteristics to identify groups found by clustering on importance scores	Different service packages can be assigned costs

trates the relative importance of customer service compared to product, price, and advertising and sales effort by manufacturing segment. The findings indicate that customer service is a key element of the marketing mix and that there is some substantial variation among industry groups in their perception of the relative importance of the elements of the marketing mix. In most firms a major share of human and financial resources is devoted to research and to developing and implementing product price and promotional

Table 11-2 Costs as a Percentage of Sales by Selected Manufacturing Industry Segment

	All Manufacturing (%)	*Manufacturing*						
		Chemicals & Plastics (%)	Food (%)	Pharmaceuticals (%)	Electronics (%)	Paper (%)	Machine Tools (%)	Other (%)
Inbound transportation	2.3	3.0	2.5	0.2	1.8	0.0*	1.0	2.6
Outbound transportation	3.9	3.3	5.6	1.2	1.4	5.8	3.5	4.2
Warehousing	3.6	3.3	3.5	1.2	3.2	4.6	2.0	2.9
Total	9.8	9.6	11.6	2.6	6.4	10.4	6.5	9.7

*No inbound transportation costs reported.

SOURCE: Bernard J. La Londe and Paul H. Zinszer, *Customer Service: Meaning and Measurement* (Chicago: NCPDM, 1976), p. 116. Reprinted by permission.

strategies. Yet one of the key conclusions to be drawn from these findings was that a majority of the firms studied do not have specific policies or means for operationally defining and measuring customer service performance.

Table 11-4 shows the relative importance of the key elements of the marketing mix by functional area or group. The findings indicate—and further research has confirmed—that there are substantial variations in how different elements of the marketing mix are weighted. As might be expected, purchasing executives tend to attach much more importance to product and less to advetising and sales efforts than their marketing counterparts. It is interesting that top management's view most closely parallels that of the physical distribution function and customer segment. As noted above, it should be recognized that these are perceptions of the relative important of these elements, and probably do not reflect proportionate managerial or financial resource commitments of the firm.

The Customer Service Mix

One of the most important yet most consistently frustrating tasks of customer service research is to arrive at an operational definition of customer service. This frustration stems

Table 11-3 Relative Importance of Elements of the Marketing Mix by Selected Manufacturing Industry Segments

	Product	Price	Customer Service	Advertising & Sales Effort	Total Points
All manufacturing	38	24	20	18	100
Chemicals and plastics	38	26	18	18	100
Food	36	27	15	22	100
Pharmaceuticals	47	20	12	21	100
Electronics	48	14	22	16	100
Paper	29	26	24	21	100
Machine tools	43	30	20	7	100
All other	38	25	22	15	100

SOURCE: Bernard J. La Londe and Paul H. Zinszer, *Customer Service: Meaning and Measurement* (Chicago: NCPDM, 1976), p. 117. Reprinted by permission.

Table 11–4   Relative Importance of Elements of the Marketing Mix by Selected Respondent Groups

	Sup-pliers	Pur-chasing	Top Manage-ment	Produc-tion	Mar-keting	Physical Distri-bution	Cus-tomer
Product	30	42	37	42	27	36	34
Customer service	23	20	22	18	24	23	28
Price	31	28	21	23	27	23	20
Advertising, sales effort	16	10	20	17	22	18	18
Total points	100	100	100	100	100	100	100

SOURCE: Bernard J. La Londe and Paul H. Zinszer, *Customer Service: Meaning and Measurement* (Chicago: NCPDM, 1976), p. 122. Reprinted by permission.

from the fact that most companies use the phrase "customer service" somewhere in their policies, procedures, or organization, but there is no consensus about the operational definition of the term. To some companies "customer service" is a euphemism for "complaint department." Others think of it as an order-processing activity. To still others it represents an individual designated as a quasi-ombudsman at a regional sales office.

Out of this research, six elements of customer service were identified. These elements are outlined in Table 11–5. It should be noted that each of the individual elements of customer service is in itself a complex concept. That is, what appears to be a relatively simple concept such as "product availability" can indeed present some formidable problems of measurement. For example, product availability can be measured in order lines, specific product lines, dollars, units of product. It can also have a geographic, temporal, and organizational dimension. From a control and customer point of view, these different measurement bases could yield different results and have significantly different cost patterns.

In Table 11–6, survey respondents were asked to distribute 100 points among the six elements of customer service based on relative importance. Several important conclusions may be drawn from the table.

- "Product availability" is the single most important element of the customer service mix, with "order cycle" being second most important for most manufacturing sectors.

- Almost 40 percent of the points were allocated to customer service elements other than "product availability" and "order cycle."

- "Post-sale product support" is an especially important element of customer service in the electronics and machine tool industries.

- There are significant differences in the relative importance of the customer service elements by industry sector.

A Customer Service Model

Introduction

The objective of this section of the chapter is to outline a general model of customer service. The model is general in the sense that it applies to those companies that use middle-

Table 11-5   Key Elements of Customer Service

Element	Brief Description	Typical Measurement Unit(s)
Product availability	The most common measure of customer service. Usually defined as percent in stock (target performance level) in some base unit (i.e., order, product, dollars).	% availability in base units
Order cycle time	Elapsed time from order placement to order receipt. Usually measured in time units and variation from standard or target order cycle. Note: Frequently, product availability and order cycle time combined into one standard. For example, "95% of orders delivered within 10 days."	Speed and consistency measurement base
Distribution system flexibility	Ability of system to respond to special and/or unexpected needs of customer. Includes expedite and substitute capability.	Response time to special requests
Distribution system information	Ability of information system of firm to respond in timely and accurate manner to customers' requests for information.	Speed, accuracy, and message detail of response
Distribution system malfunction	Efficiency of procedures and time required to recover from distribution system malfunction (i.e., errors in billing, shipping, damage, claims).	Response and recovery time requirements
Post-sale product support	Efficiency in providing product support after delivery, including technical information, spare parts, equipment modification, etc. as appropriate.	Response-time quality of response

men in the distribution of their product as well as those companies that market their product direct to the end user. Further, it has equal applicability to the "distribution service" sector and to the manufacturing and merchandising sectors of United States industry. It is critical that those firms engaged in distribution services such as transportation and public warehousing companies have their service objectives in synchronization with their target market if the total system is to work effectively. In Figure 11–1 a schematic or overview of the total customer service model is presented. The reader will note that there are six steps in the development of an effective customer service program. Each of the steps is discussed in turn and the findings of the field work integrated into both the overall design and the operation or implementation of each individual step in the process.

Step One—The Customer Service Audit

It is fashionable in business today to talk of various types of management audits. There are financial audits, social audits, marketing audits, as well as a variety of other audits. The basic objective of the audit is to determine the parameters of behavior and measurement of a specific functional area. To a large extent, it is easier to do an audit within the firm than outside of the firm. Unfortunately this is not possible in the customer service audit since both the customer—perhaps several customers in the channel (for example, wholesaler, retailer)—and the competition have a significant impact on the customer service

Table 11–6   Relative Importance of Elements of the Customer Service Mix by Selected Manufacturing Industry Groups

	Manufacturing							
	All Manufac-turing	*Chem-icals & Plastics*	*Food*	*Pharma-ceuticals*	*Elec-tronics*	*Paper*	*Machine Tools*	*Other*
Product availability	42.7	44.5	37.1	39.7	32.7	41.3	56.3	50.5
Order cycle	19.4	17.4	21.4	28.0	17.4	12.3	10.7	18.0
Distribution system flexibility	11.6	10.6	12.9	10.6	12.9	18.5	17.3	12.4
Distribution system information	12.4	11.7	14.8	9.0	16.7	20.1	1.0	9.5
Distribution system malfunction	8.0	9.1	10.3	7.8	7.9	4.5	4.0	5.4
Post-sale product support	5.1	6.2	2.3	2.9	11.7	1.8	10.0	4.1
Other	0.8	0.5	1.2	2.0	0.7	1.5	0.7	0.1
Total points	100.0	100.0	100.0	100.0	100.0	100.0	100.0	100.0

Source: Bernard J. La Londe and Paul H. Zinszer, *Customer Service: Meaning and Measurement* (Chicago: NCPDM, 1976), p. 171. Reprinted by permission.

program. This problem is compounded by the fact that the distribution function in most cases is insulated from direct contact with the customer except in the case of a service malfunction. The levels of customer service expected by the customer and provided by the firm's competitors are estimated from feedback from the sales and marketing organization. The fidelity of this feedback is frankly questioned in many firms. In most cases, firms that have conducted surveys of customer expectations of services have found that the firm was attempting to provide higher levels of service than the customers required. Furthermore, customers' interests have shifted from a focus on speed of delivery to a focus on consistency of delivery. In some industries, primarily in the food industry, it is considered as bad a practice for a shipment to arrive early as for it to arrive late because of unloading or warehouse constraints.

There are essentially three elements to the customer service audit. The first element is the customer segment of the survey, and this involves determining the reasonable expectations of customers relative to the full range of service provided by the firm. It is important to note that most firms consider the customer audit as a broad inquiry into the company-customer interface rather than a study of expectations regarding speed and consistency of delivery.

The customer segment of the audit should focus on determining those factors on which a customer or potential customer evaluates the supplier firm. It should be noted that customer service is measured differently by various functional managers of the customer's firm. The dock foreman has one measurement, the controller has another measurement, and the marketing manager may have a third. For a true picture of service perceptions, all of these elements must be integrated into an overall view of the customer service process.

The simplest way to collect data on the customer segment of the service audit is to go directly to the customer, either with a mail questionnaire or by personal interview. Cau-

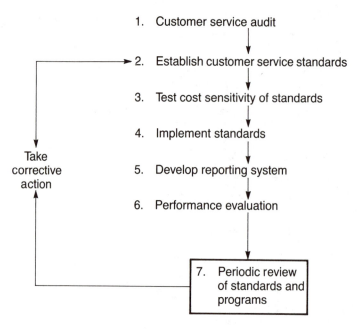

Figure 11-1   A Customer Service Model

SOURCE: Bernard J. La Londe and Paul H. Zinszer, *Customer Service: Meaning and Measurement* (Chicago, Ill.: National Council of Physical Distribution Management, 1976).

tion should be used to assure that the data collected are the objective response of the customer and that the information received can be analyzed by customer characteristics and geographical segment of the market.

The second part of the customer service audit should be focused on competitive service levels. While the results of one study[1] indicate that competition is not as strong an influence on customer service levels as most distribution executives seem to think, competitive activity is nonetheless important. Of key importance in measuring competitive customer service levels is to first determine what will be measured. That is, if a firm is developing a customer service program, it must decide on the important elements on which it will attempt to compete. These elements in turn should be integrated into the competitive audit.

The easiest way of obtaining competitive information is through the firm's own sales force. However, care must be taken to make sure that the data collected do indeed reflect competitive service levels as stated by the firm's customers rather than as perceived by the firm's salesmen. Some firms establish a feedback mechanism for salesmen to report changes in the customer service programs of competitors. For example, such information as new warehouse location, special pallet programs, changes in billing terms, etc., can all be collected on a routine basis through the firm's sales force once the information feedback mechanism is established as part of the company's operating procedure.

The third—and often most difficult—element of the program focuses on the management information system support requirements. The objectives of this part of the audit are to determine: (1) current levels of customer service within the firm, (2) the type and frequency of reports dealing with customer service performance, and (3) who in the firm receives the reports. While this might seem like a very obvious step, it is important because it establishes the baseline level and format of the current system. Any changes to that system will require changes in the way information is captured and the way it flows within the system, and also may change the method of corrective action to be taken by the firm.

In summary then, the customer service audit is a comprehensive look at the current state of the firm's customer service program. The activity is viewed both internally as a management control and reporting process, and externally as a study of competitive policies and competitive requirements. It is a vital first step in outlining the firm's current approach to providing service to its customers.

Step Two—Establish Customer Service Standards

The second step in the process of developing an effective customer service program is to establish customer service standards. These standards should (1) reflect the customer's point of view, (2) provide an operational and objective measure of service performance, and (3) provide management cues for corrective action.

The specific customer service standards established by any firm are situational to that firm. A company may have different service standards in urban areas and rural areas or in the far western and eastern parts of the United States for cost or competitive reasons. Standards may well reflect an overall importance of product or class of customer to the firm.

Distribution performance standards or customer service standards are an integral part of total corporate strategy. They must be consistent with the way a firm desires to manage its business and must be internally consistent with all other standards of the organization both inside and outside the distribution function. For example, if a firm is using a materials requirement planning (MRP) type of system for production scheduling and procurement, it must tie directly to customer lead times. Any alteration in vendor lead times in a job shop environment could substantially affect customer service lead times.

Service standards which are established as goals of the system should be flexible enough to allow overriding of standards for appropriate reasons. If the system is too rigid, frequently either a shadow performance system evolves which provides the right number by "adjusting the data," or the system disintegrates when extreme pressures are brought to bear. This, of course, argues that any customer service standards should be capable of change under the right circumstances, either on a temporary or a permanent basis, to accommodate shifting market conditions. Many firms will have special service standards when new products are introduced to facilitate product availability in the marketplace. Other firms will maintain high product availability during certain periods of the year to meet peak demand requirements. In Table 11–7 a selected list of the most common service level measurements used by manufacturing and merchandising firms is presented. The list is not intended to be comprehensive, nor does it suggest that all firms should use all the measurement devices. For example, firms in durable goods manufacturing typically have a whole range of standards relative to parts availability, repair manuals, etc. Similarly, in recent years companies in the food and drug and other industries have developed standards for recall procedures.

There remain a number of philosophical questions relative to setting customer service standards. Perhaps the most important question is "Who should set customer service standards?" If a product availability target of 92 percent delivery within one week is a goal of

Table 11–7   Selected Service Level Measurements used by Manufacturing and Merchandising Firms

Major Category	Sub-Category
Prodct availability	Line item availability Product group availability Invoice fill Cases/Units
Order cycle time	Order entry Order processing Total cycle time
Consistency	In order cycle time In shipment dispatch In transit time In arrival time In warehouse handling
Response time	Order status Order tracing Back order status Order confirmation Product substitution Order shortages Product information requests
Error rates	Shipment delays Order errors Picking & packing errors Shipping & labeling errors Paperwork errors
Product/shipment related malfunction	Damaged merchandise Merchandise refusals Claims Returned goods Customer complaints
Special handling	Transshipment Expedited orders Expedited transportation Special packaging Customer backhauls

the firm, should it be set by top management, marketing management, or the distribution function? The consensus appears to be that customer service standards should be set by all three of these functions, with the predominant role being played by the top management of the firm. On the other hand, implementation of the standards is perceived as primarily a distribution function with strong support from marketing.

A second question is "What type of standards should be used?" The available research findings suggest that the most appropriate answer to this question rests with the individual firm. Customer service standards indeed reflect the management style of the company and the goals of the company in the marketplace. It would appear that there can and should be substantial variations in the service level measurement of two firms in the same industry. Normally, there will be a clustering of specific target service measurements such as in-stock percentage and total order cycle time, but this is frequently where the similarity in performance measurements ends. The reasons for these variations are probably: 1) management style of the top management of the firm; 2) positioning of the physical distribution function within the firm; 3) the nature, sophistication, and positioning of the order-processing function; and 4) willingness to trade off advertising for customer service dollars.

Step Three—Test Cost Sensitivity of Standards

If variants in standards are to be appreciated fully, some cost figure must be attached to alternative levels of performance. One of the biggest weaknesses in the entire area of customer service is a lack of recognition of the cost implications of varying levels of customer service. It is difficult, if not impossible, to develop an effective customer service program without the capability of attaching costs to its various levels. From a conceptual point of view it can be argued that the higher and more rigid the service levels, the higher will be the price attached to maintaining those service levels. For example, assuming a normal bell-shaped distribution of orders around an average order, it will take three times as much inventory to operate at a 95 percent stock availability level as it will to operate at an 80 percent stock availability level. However, the inventory investment required to move from a 95 percent stock level to a 99 percent stock level will again double the amount of inventory investment. Similarly, transit time consistency which is programmed plus or minus two hours on a specific target date will cost several times the consistency of plus or minus one day. This, of course, argues that service levels that are set very high with little tolerance for variation tend to be very expensive.

While this argument would probably be accepted by most distribution managers in concept, it must be demonstrated statistically as the foundation for developing effective service levels. The questions is, how may this be done?

There are essentially two ways in which the cost sensitivity of service levels can be determined. The first method is somewhat similar to "destructive testing" used in certain types of manufacturing operations. It is possible to experiment with different levels of customer service in either different geographic segments of the market or different end user segments of the market. If service levels are programmed to vary in the marketplace and the cost implications of these service variations are carefully measured, then management insights into cost sensitivity of standards can be developed. During the customer audit some customer cost sensitivity to changes in service should be determined prior to experimentation.

A second method of testing standards is what might be termed "laboratory" testing. Firms utilizing this technique build computer models which contain a probabilistic dimension of customer demand. Order levels and order types are simulated through a computer-based distribution model and the impact of changes on service levels are analyzed. These models range from relatively simple warehouse location models to very large-scale total system simulation. They may be static in the sense that they look at orders at one point in time or dynamic in that they reflect a total flow of orders on a day-by-day processing cycle. The major advantage of this type of testing is that it allows greater flexibility in testing standards without disturbing the firm's position in the marketplace. The major disadvantages of this approach are that it requires a good data base and, depending upon the complexity of the model, can be relatively expensive.

There are several other factors in cost sensitivity which should be discussed at this point. It is important to face squarely the issue of inventory holding costs. That is, what does it cost to hold an average dollar of inventory in stock for a given time period. Many firms use some perceived cost of money as the value of inventory. The research evidence suggests that the cost of holding inventory is indeed higher than the cost of money alone.[2] It is possible to cost-justify almost any strategic or operational decision in the distribution area if inventory holding costs are flexible. For example, if inventory holding costs are set very low, many firms will typically have a large number of warehouses, high in-stock availability, and short order cycle times. On the other hand, if a firm in the same industry uses a high inventory carrying cost they will have few warehouses, lower in-stock availability, and longer lead times to customers. Thus, it might be concluded that the cost of holding inventory is a critical determinant of the total customer service mix. If a firm does not develop a realistic inventory carrying cost for its particular operating environment and use it consistently across functional areas, then the customer service program of the firm will be distorted by this important cost. It should be carefully noted at this point that inventory carrying cost is specific to a firm, since the determinants of inventory carrying cost flow from the operating environment and market position of the firm. Two firms in the same industry might have substantially different costs of money due to differences in debt and equity financing. Thus, each of these firms in the same industry would probably use a different inventory carrying cost figure.

There are a number of other problems in costing which seem to occur frequently over a wide range of business firms. First, there is a general problem of the availability of reliable cost information. Firms that are organized by profit center frequently do not have cost information in a form that reflects flow characteristics. A related problem is that the profit center concept in evaluating different segments of the business frequently leads to distorted cost patterns—particularly those relative to customer service. For example, depending upon how a firm internally accounts for inventory a division or section of the business operation might either be encouraged to accumulate inventory or to resist the accumulation of inventory. Since the location of inventory has a direct impact upon customer service, it follows that profit center accounting can impact an effective customer service program in a negative way.

A third problem noted earlier in the report is the "lost sale/lost customer" syndrome. Firms that are sales- and marketing-oriented often want to focus on the lost sale side of the equation as opposed to the service cost side of the equation. This frequently results in extended and sometimes heated discussions regarding the cost of being out of stock rather than the cost of product availability. While this may appear to be a subtle difference, it is a critical kind of issue to many firms that are attempting to analyze the cost of target levels of customer service rather than the cost of being out of stock. This is not to suggest that being out of stock is an event to be taken lightly, but rather that in a cost context it is easier to measure the cost of being in stock at different levels and in different parts of the country.

Step Four—Implement Customer Service Standards

By this point in the procedure the customer-competitor-management information dimension of customer service has been analyzed, available service standards have been reviewed, and the service standards most appropriate to the firm have been selected. Moreover, the cost sensitivity of the standards has been analyzed and service levels have been determined. The major steps remaining—to make the standards operational—are to implement standards and develop a realistic reporting system.

The question of implementation, while it may seem a relatively obvious step in the process, is nonetheless important. The first question that occurs is "implement the standards with whom?" Since customers are presumably the object of customer service standards, the question arises early in the process whether customers should be informed of systems standards or whether standards should be kept confidential to the originating firm. A second question is "Who in the organization should be aware of the explicit service levels of the firm?" Certainly top managment must be since they should have a hand in setting service standards, and the sales and marketing function should be since they have a direct contact point with the customer.

An explicit and operational customer service policy statement must be developed. The statement should contain target levels of customer service as they are to be measured by the firm (and presumably desired by the customer), as well as whatever qualitative or special procedures may be offered as part of the overall customer service policy of the firm. Without a specific written statement, other functional areas, as well as different sections of the distribution function, are free to interpret standards as they see fit. This may result in conflicting or contradictory customer service standards in the organization. Each firm must decide for itself whether to make its service policy public. Previous research findings indicate that approximately one-third of the firms surveyed have written customer service statements and less than 10 percent of the firms provide their customers with a copy of their service statements.

Implementing customer service standards, particularly in those organizations where explicit service standards did not exist prior to time of implementation, is essentially an educational task. As such, it should be approached from the basis of what the individual needs to know. In other words, what should a salesman, or an individual working the order-processing desk, know about his role in providing customer service? Solutions to this educational objective range all the way from customer cocktail parties to comprehensive program instructions for order-processing personnel. One company with centralized order processing developed a very successful tape cassette learning program text that was made available to all order-processing personnel. The employees completed this course on company time and although the program costs were in the range of $20,000 to $30,000 it was deemed a most successful effort on the part of the firm. On the other hand, another firm that implemented a new on-line order-processing system with distributors provided education to the distributor principals with a series of dealer meetings around the country. When the system came on-line it was discovered that the distributors did not know how to use the system because order clerks—not the distributor principals—were at the communication interfaces. In this case, the sponsoring firm had to conduct another round of education and meetings for those individuals who actually operated the hardware that accessed the central computer.

Step Five—Develop Reporting System

In Step One it was suggested that a management information audit be conducted for the purpose of determining current information flows within the organization relative to customer service measurement and accountability. The general objective of Step Five is to develop a sound reporting system that provides timely information to those individuals accountable for various elements of the customer service objectives of the firm.

The first step in designing a reporting system is to determine the alternative sources for the information required. In the area of customer service, the sources of information can lie both inside and outside the firm. In the case of outside information, if common carriers and public warehouses are used in the distribution network, then information feedback from these sources is critical in determining certain performance measures of the system (e.g., order cycle time). Needless to say, the capability of providing information feedback to principals and to customers is an important aspect of the customer service program for the transportation and public warehousing industries. When the data source is outside the firm, frequently a firm will use a sampling procedure rather than attempt to collect all of the transactions data. For example, a firm may sample transit time on 5 percent of the shipments during a given time period. Other firms may send a postcard with the shipment requesting the consignee to fill it out—noting time and date of arrival and, in some cases, condition of shipment—and return it to the shipper. This procedure does not result in 100 percent return, but firms that utilize this method generally report a return in the range of 30 to 40 percent. Further, they state that after the system has been in use for a period of six to nine months, it is possible to get good generalizations on transit times by carrier and by traffic lane. Those shippers that are rail-oriented have typically developed railcar management programs for assigned cars or are actively working with the railroads to develop car reporting systems.

A similar type of information-gathering problem can occur for data that is generated internally. The assumption that internally generated data are readily available for a customer service reporting system appears to be at best optimistic. Because of the functional specialization that occurs in many firms, data may be more readily available from carriers and public warehousemen used by the firm than from internal data-processing operations. For example, because of increasing freight rates, a number of firms that ship small to medium-sized lots have been investigating the possibility of outbound shipment consolidation. The best place to do order consolidation is at order entry point since at that point, production schedules can be arranged so that all completed orders feed into the appropriate consolidation. However, many firms find it impossible to provide this capability at order entry point and are forced to wait until the shipping documents are generated in order to search for consolidation opportunities. Firms that have reasonably sophisticated customer service reporting systems almost always place a high priority on the data-processing capability of the firm.

There are several other important issues relating to customer service reporting systems. High speed computers provide the capability of printing massive amounts of information. Since the distribution function is a large generator of data, it is possible for the distribution function to drown in its own paperwork. Care should be taken to determine the pattern of report dissemination. That is, "Who should get the report?" A second and related question is, "How frequently should the report be generated?" It is possible to generate listings of shipments each day. While it might be comforting to the manager to know that products have actually been shipped, it can also take a substantial part of his time to read those reports.

In order to develop a reporting system that provides for the efficient flow of timely and actionable data, two strategies are used. First, the concept of exception reporting is becoming more common in logistics information systems. Exception reports are possible only after a firm has set objective, measurable standards for the customer service function. Information flow can then be monitored and a format developed to report those cases that fall outside the target standards. For example, a report might be generated listing all shipments having a variance of more than plus or minus one day from target delivery time. In some cases the exception reporting is tied to the information dissemination function. That is, a report which lists all shipments plus or minus five days (a serious service failure) is routed to the distribution manager. A report on the plus or minus one day target delivery is sent to the traffic manager for action by an expediter. In order to function efficiently, such a system obviously needs clear and objective standards that reflect the service goals and desired performance characteristics of the distribution function.

User demand–oriented reporting is another means of coping with the potential flood of paperwork within the distribution function. New technology on integrated data-base management and simplified programming languages have made it possible to develop a system that generates reports on demand by the user. An increasing number of firms have the capability of generating special purpose reports by using a readily available CRT (cathode ray tube) to request that the computer display sales and shipment data for specific customers or for other segments of the business. If a hard copy report of the data is required, it can be obtained with a simple instruction to the data center. These systems have been used in conjunction with a standard exception reporting system to provide tailored information needs.

This user demand–oriented reporting format also facilitates another requirement of the customer service reporting system. As noted earlier in this chapter, implementation of the customer service goals of the firm is shared primarily by the marketing and distribution functions. The reporting format should provide usable information to the sales manager or marketing manager as well as to the distribution manager.

In the past few years there has been an increasing interest in the possibility of communicating on-line with customers, carriers, vendors, and public warehousemen. The literature is full of reports on experimental programs utilizing the latest technology and new levels of interchannel cooperation. As the technology of on-line communications improves, and if normal postal service deteriorates further, the question of reporting format to individuals outside the firm will become more important. This point will be amplified later in the chapter. Here it is necessary to note that there must be a high level of compatibility in reporting systems among the partners in the distribution process if efficient on-line communication is to become a cost-effective reality.

Step Six—Performance Evaluation

In the performance evaluation phase of the firm's customer service program, actual performance is compared to target performance levels. A key objective of this step is to provide the capability of taking timely and appropriate corrective action. This requires efficient and timely information flow as well as a well-defined organizational accountability. At points where actual performance is not achieving target levels, some action must be taken to bring the actual performance in line with objectives. If there is no accountability within the system for these actions, then there is a tendency for any overall objective standards to become lost in "knee jerk" reactions to problems. The system must be flexible enough to accommodate change, to provide for expedited shipments, or to incur additional costs in meeting standards where appropriate. However, these actions cannot be taken randomly but must be made within some decision logic and accountability framework. For example, in one company's order-processing system, a customer calls in to order a specific product. The order is accepted on the basis of inventory availability, and the customer service representative prepares the shipping order. If he discovers that the product is not available at the prime shipping location he has the option of using a secondary location. The CRT displays to the representative the additional incremental cost of shipping from the secondary location. At this point he can authorize a shipment, but he must provide a reason (numbered for convenience of entry) and initial the authorized action. A monthly computer printout shows all shipments shipped from secondary locations, who authorized the shipments, and the cost of this action. This information is reviewed by management, and necessary corrective action is taken where necessary.

Some Future Perspectives

There are present in the economy, in technology, and in the added involvement of government in the marketing and distribution process a number of factors which will undoubtedly enhance the importance of effective customer service to the business firm. While the factors noted below will impact a great range of business activities, customer service will be the area most directly affected.

Economic Change

A majority of the economic forecasts predict a relatively high level of interest rates in the U.S. economy; and some recent economic studies have presented persuasive evidence that there will be a "capital crunch" during the next ten years. If indeed these events come to pass, it will make the management of inventory a critical element of overall corporate strategy. Since the level and positioning of inventory stock have a direct relation to customer service, any change in availability and/or cost of capital will tend to place greater emphasis on the management of inventory assets in the future.

The availability of money and the level of interest rates coupled with economic uncertainty and problems of labor productivity in some sectors of the economy will continue to put pressure on the business firm for more effective management of assets. With labor contracts containing clauses on guaranteed annual wages and minimum number of weeks' employment per year, labor costs have become a fixed cost for many businesses. This leaves the inventory asset as the single most important "flexible" resource over which management policy and direction can be exercised. In an effort to cope with wide swings in economic conditions and the uncertain future, a great deal of attention has been devoted to improving forecasting accuracy in U.S. business enterprises. To the extent that this effort yields results in terms of improved forecasting procedures, customer service management will become a more predictable type of management activity. On the other hand, if the nature of the uncertainties is external to the company (e.g., petroleum cost and supply and uncertain world markets), the customer service function will assume in the future a more strategic role in assuring the firm's position in the marketplace than it has in the past.

Role of the Government

The government at the federal, state, and local levels has shown increasing evidence of involvement in both the distribution of goods and the protection of consumers and the environment. The impact of government involvement has already been felt by a number of industries, such as those in the areas of hazardous materials, food products, and drugs. Added government involvement in the area of assuring product availability as advertised in the retail market and parts availability for products already purchased will place pressures on the channel of distribution to perform with a high level of responsiveness and integrity. This will add cost to the channel, of course, and will place a premium on effective communication within the channel. In the past few years the advent of "recall" procedures has made it necessary for many firms to design distribution systems and service levels as a two-way flow process in the marketplace. This has changed the character and control requirements for both the customer service function and for the operating policies of many U.S. firms' distribution departments.

Integrated Order Processing

During the past few years the availability of computer technology, along with the demand for a higher performance level in communications, has focused a good deal of interest on the potential of integrated order processing. In this context, the term *integrated order processing* does not simply mean the processing of customer orders, but rather refers to a process by which communication flows between customers and the firm are organized. In this sense, the integrated order-processing system represents a management tool which provides data input into both the operating and planning environments of the firm. In both of those environments it provides a vital input into planning and managing the customer service function of the firm.

Advances in computer technology and the importance of better use of information will force increased management attention into this area. It seems obvious to say that you cannot have good customer service without good information. The goal of most integrated order-processing systems is to speed information flow and improve the fidelity and accessibility of information provided to management for decision making. Thus, it could be argued that in the future there will be a direct connection between the availability of high performance order-processing systems and the capability of providing effective customer service.

On-Line Communication

Along with the development of integrated order-processing systems has come an interest in on-line communication both internal and external to the firm. Internally, most firms have linked together plants, warehouses, and in some cases sales offices or branches for more rapid data communication. This is relatively easier to accomplish than external communication networks because the internal environment is controlled by top management of the firm. As noted earlier, there has been a good deal of experimentation devoted to linking external elements of the channel to the firm's information system. This includes vendor-to-customer communications and customer-to-carrier or public warehouse communications. Much of this experimentation is still in the embryo stage and is fraught with difficulties. The primary difficulties appear to be in developing standardized coding, standardized hardware, and acceptable arrangements for sharing the cost of such a system. From a technological point of view, on-line data communication does not appear to present a major problem for most firms.

The on-line (or off-line) external communication network raises a whole array of important questions for the partners in the process. For example, in designing communications systems the firm must take into account what types of questions its customers might ask. If automated communication responses are to be programmed, these questions must be anticipated. Another area of concern is the quantity and type of information to which a customer should have access. Should the customer know the amount of inventory the vendor has on hand before he places an order? These questions will undoubtedly be resolved over the next few years, since the potential benefits both in economic terms and in improved customer service will probably force the development of much more sophisticated channel communication networks.

A Concluding Note

This report has focused on the concept of customer service as it is defined and implemented by a broad base of firms in the United States. The findings suggest that many firms have not fully developed an integrated corporate philosophy of customer service. However, the evidence also suggests a real interest on the part of a significant number of firms to more fully explore the profit potential and market potential of an improved customer service policy. This concern appears to be broad-based, extending from top management through functional executives in distribution, marketing, and production, and outside the firm to its wholesalers, brokers, and ultimately to the consumer.

Both the economic and managerial environment seem receptive to a new management perspective on customer service. It is incumbent upon the distribution function to encourage this new management thinking and to implement the results of the thinking in cooperation with the other functional executives of the firm. In the considered view of the researchers, effective implementation of the customer service program represents the "bottom line" for the corporate distribution function.

Notes

1. See Bernard J. La Londe and Paul H. Zinzser, *Customer Service: Meaning and Measurement* (Chicago: NCPDM, 1976).
2. Douglas M. Lambert, *The Development of an Inventory Costing Methodology: A Study of the Costs Associated with Holding Inventory*, doctoral dissertation (1975) published by the National Council of Physical Distribution Management.

Financial Analysis and Productivity Measurement

Translating the Physical Distribution Strategy into a Financial Plan

JOHN R. DOWDLE

Introduction

This article presents a proposed framework within which physical distribution executives can logically and systematically develop financial plans together with the operating and capital budgets necessary to implement a new physical distribution strategy. The development of this framework proceeds from the point of acceptance of a new distribution strategy through preparation and submission of a physical distribution budget and financial plan for corporate approval.

The approach emphasizes the requirement for careful structuring of the budgeting process and encourages utilization of all levels of physical distribution personnel. It also emphasizes the need for coordination of financial planning activities within the physical distribution function as well as between distribution and other corporate entities. Some of the key benefits of the recommended approach are that it allows management to: (1) consider the distribution strategy as a whole when translating it into a financial plan, so that suggested changes from the budgeting and financial process can be weighed in terms of the impact on comprehensive distribution strategy; (2) make adjustments in the total strategy with an appropriate recognition of offsets; and (3) maintain the "integrity" of the distribution strategy throughout the process. From the distribution executive's perspective, however, the most important aspect of the approach is that it maintains the integrity of the distribution strategy throughout the financial planning process and balances financial constraints and distribution objectives.

Background

Changes in the regulatory environment and increasing energy costs have severely affected two fundamental distribution variables—cost and availability of service. These two factors form the basis upon which most corporate distribution strategies have traditionally been developed. In addition, these changes have caused many firms to reevaluate and restructure their distribution strategies to reflect current and anticipated changes in the economic environment. Development of a new physical distribution strategy is, however, only the first step in accomplishing change. Before implementation can begin, the business strategy must be translated into a meaningful financial plan.

The accuracy and completeness of financial planning at this stage are critical for two reasons. First, from the corporate perspective, it is imperative that the total corporate budget reflect the potential financial impact associated with a new distribution strategy. Second, at the distribution activity level, the financial planning process is the first step in implementation of a plan. It is during this time that a myriad of complex decisions are required to translate strategy into action plans. It is traditionally at this point—translation of the distribution plan into a financial plan—that distribution managers have encountered difficulties. Problems arise basically because of deficiencies in the approach to financial planning that firms have used when faced with the task of implementing a new distribution strategy. Historically, firms have employed one of two basic approaches in developing these financial plans:

- *Micro approach*, which builds a financial plan from individual requests for facilities, equipment, and staff from the bottom up

- *Macro approach*, which generates the distribution budget from the top down

Problems with Traditional Approaches

Neither the micro nor the macro approach is satisfactory. In a totally micro approach, the lack of adequate integration of micro-level plans makes it difficult to assess the ability of the distribution system to meet customer service objectives. The specific question "Do we really get to where we want to be with this hodge-podge of requests for buildings, trucks, and people?" may go unanswered. It is quite difficult to determine whether plans prepared in this way come together at all. It is even more difficult to assess how effective the aggregate result of such planning will be. The totally macro approach suffers from a similar fault—however, the problems come from the other direction. The key question now becomes "How can corporate level planners assess the impact of budgetary decisions on distribution service objectives given the complexity of the linkages that exist between dollars and performance in distribution?"

Each of the traditional approaches misses the mark on two counts. First, both approaches fail to recognize the complexity of distribution and the synergistic nature of its components. The addition or deletion of funds from any element of the distribution system—transportation, warehousing, inventory, personnel, or equipment—can have far-reaching impacts on other areas. For example, deletion of capital funds for the purchase of trucks could require relocation of warehouses if transport connections are inadequate. Also, additional inventory might be required to meet constraints of contracted carrier service, or order-processing times might have to be reduced to meet customer service requirements. The second shortcoming of the traditional approach is that it loses sight of the original purpose for the whole planning exercise—adoption of a new distribution strategy that best balances the cost and service considerations that will be crucial in the future business environment.

Financial planning must begin with the original distribution cost and service objectives. It must balance the financial requirements of the distribution activity against the performance objectives the strategy was developed to achieve.

What Is Needed

For the financial planning exercise to be meaningful to corporate level financial planners as well as physical distribution managers, the process must include several critical components that will facilitate weighing financial considerations against distribution performance. First, and probably foremost, the end result must permit meaningful corporate level evaluation. In this regard, financial plans should link distribution funding requirements with performance parameters. This linkage permits corporate planners to balance thoughtfully the financial requirements of the competitive programs in the funding arena in a manner that is consistent with overall corporate strategy. Next, the final planning process used must facilitate analysis of trade-offs. Corporate financial planning is not static. Changes in the fiscal policy of the organization are almost certain to occur after submission of a financial plan, if not during its preparation. Thus, if the distribution function is to attain and maintain its "fair share" of corporate resources, physical distribution managers must quickly translate changes in dollars into changes in performance. Simply stated, the financial planning process must facilitate micro-level financial trade-off analyses.

Another characteristic of the planning approach must be that it is an integrated approach. The distribution function itself is a set of integrated activities, bringing together the diverse resources of its component parts—warehousing, transportation, inventory, personnel, communications, and systems—to achieve specific levels of cost and service performance. Financial planning for distribution strategy implementation must be capable of reflecting these interdependencies in physical distribution activities.

Further, the process must be comprehensive. Financial planning for distribution strategy implementation must accurately reflect estimated financial requirements of *all* aspects of distribution activities. Old rules of thumb such as ratios, freight costs per ton-mile, cost of personnel to square feet of warehouse space, are only valid when conditions remain relatively constant. Implementation of a new distribution strategy presupposes change, and the impact of change on old financial planning assumptions may not be felt for some time. Thus, each activity must be viewed independently in light of the new strategy. Then financial requirements can be developed accordingly.

Finally, whatever approach to financial planning activity is selected, when it is completed, the distribution plan should remain intact. It may not be the plan management started with, but an integrated, workable plan should be on hand after the financial review is completed.

Fundamental Aspects of an Integrated Approach to Financial Policy for Distribution Strategy Implementation

Figure 12.1 provides an overview of the decision stream between corporate strategy and the financial plan during development and implementation of a new distribution strategy. Although it is clearly an oversimplification of the flow of decisions, the figure does give an indication of the complexity of the process. Now the question is: "How do we make all these decisions come together?" The answer is through an integrated approach to planning the implementation of the distribution strategy. An integrated approach is needed to bring forth a financial plan that maintains the distribution strategy's integrity throughout the process.

An Integrated Approach Should Be Developed by the Distribution Function

The distribution function should be maintained as the focal point for distribution financial planning and decision making. A plethora of complex, interactive distribution-specific issues must be resolved before a physical distribution strategy can be translated into a

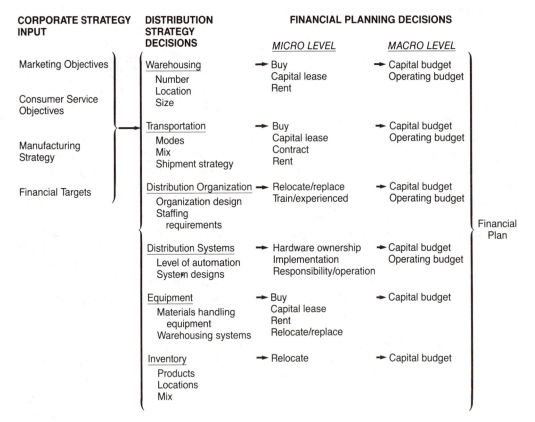

Figure 12-1   Strategy to Financial Plan

meaningful financial plan. (See Figure 12–1.) This complexity makes it crucial that decision-making authority be maintained within the distribution activity. It would be difficult, if not impossible, for corporate-level financial planners to assess the impacts on distribution cost and service objectives of a shift in capital between warehousing and transportation. On the other hand, it should be emphasized that saying "distribution should be the focal point for *distribution* planning and decision making" does not advocate that distribution managers operate in a vacuum, independent of other corporate functions. Instead, it suggests that distribution management should be given responsibility and authority for decision making as long as that decision making affects the distribution function and the results are within the corporate strategic and financial constraints dictated at the beginning of the financial planning process.

An Integrated Approach Should Incorporate Functional Analyses

Again referring to Figure 12–1, it is apparent that the types of financial decisions that must be made in translating a distribution strategy into a financial plan boil down to a series of options such as "buy, lease, or rent." These decisions must be made, however, for a diverse group of activities: transportation, warehousing organization, systems, and equipment. Although the decisions are similar, the analytic processes undertaken to arrive at the decisions are quite different. The diversity of knowledge required to perform these backup analyses requires application of specialized talents, experience, and expertise.

An Integrated Approach Consists of Two Levels of Analysis

Development of a financial plan for implementing a distribution strategy clearly calls for two levels of analysis. First, as pointed out earlier, there is a requirement for micro-level analysis of each of the functional components of the distribution activity. These analyses require specialized expertise and familiarity with the activity. If we stopped here, however, the plan would suffer from the shortcomings of traditional micro approaches. What is also needed is a macro-level analysis of the micro-level functional plans. By stepping back and reviewing the structural and financial compatibility of the functional plans from a total distribution management perspective, we maintain the focus on the overall strategy that is essential during the financial planning process.

An Integrated Approach Calls for Both Horizontal and Vertical Integration

The requirement for horizontal integration—that is, between the functional components of distribution activities—is clear both from the structural and financial perspectives. Equally important is vertical integration within the corporation during the financial-planning process. The requirement for vertical integration arises from the fact that distribution is viewed as a service activity and, as such, is driven largely by the strategies of other elements of the firm, mainly marketing and production. Each of these activities can set up tactical plans that impose a set of conflicting constraints on the distribution activity which may prove impossible or unfeasible to satisfy. Thus, it is imperative that distribution management coordinate with other corporate elements to assure that the impact of other corporate planning activities on the distribution strategy is assessed quickly and that conflicts are resolved satisfactorily.

An Integrated Approach Requires Consistency in Analysis and Assumptions

As pointed out earlier, an integrated approach calls for two levels of analysis—micro and macro. Overlaying the macro analysis on the micro or functional financial analyses imposes a requirement for consistency in analysis among the functional business plans. Without such consistency, comparison, integration, and restructuring of plans will be impossible. Such an approach requires consistency in methodology and consistency of assumptions. For example, if an accepted corporate measure of financial attractiveness is return on investment (ROI), the ROI measure should be used as often as possible in all financial planning activities. Similarly, financial analyses should be based on assumptions that are consistent. In addition, similar costs of capital, depreciation schedules, tax assumptions, and the like should also be used whenever possible.

An Integrated Approach Calls for Maintenance of an Audit Trail

Recall that an integrated approach to financial planning for distribution strategy implementation has as its fundamental objective the development of a financial plan which retains a distribution strategy perspective. Accomplishing this objective requires establishment of cause-effect relationships between distribution performance parameters and financial constraints. Given the complexity of these linkages, it is imperative that the decision-making process that establishes the corrections be maintained through a structured audit trail of documentation. It is only when this audit trail is presented that effective horizontal integration can occur and that meaningful macro analyses can be undertaken.

How the Integrated Approach Works

The Key to the Integrated Approach Is the Physical Distribution Executive

The physical distribution executive is of paramount importance in the financial planning process for three reasons. First, he is the focal point in achieving coordination with other corporate functions during the financial planning cycle. Second, he must actively coordinate and control the planning and budgeting activities of his subordinates. In this coordination and control role, the physical distribution manager must delegate responsibility for the preparation of elemental budgets. He must also provide guidance to each of the elemental managers by acting as a filter for and translator of corporate level strategies, physical distribution objectives, and tactical decisions. Finally, the physical distribution executive must also play the role of analyst. He must assemble the elemental plans and validate them. After assimilating these plans into an overall physical distribution budget, he must analyze the budget for structural compatability with physical distribution and corporate objectives, and for financial viability and risks. He then institutes the "feedback" process to refine the budget as required.

Where Does the Physical Distribution Executive Start?

The starting point for the physical distribution executive in the integrated approach is assimilation⌐ of input information as depicted in Figure 12–2. In fact, the requirement for strong vertical and horizontal integration defines the inputs required. The three key sets of inputs required in the formation of the financial plan can be termed:

- Corporate strategic
- Physical distribution strategic
- Corporate tactical

Corporate strategic inputs come primarily from the major corporate functions—marketing and production. The marketing function basically drives the overall development of physical distribution strategies and tactics and, hence, its budgeting process. The principal inputs required from marketing include specification of products, product packaging, sales forecasts, designation of geographic markets, methods and channels of sale (wholesale, retail, etc.), customer service requirements, and price sensitivity of products. These factors clearly have a broad and direct impact on the distribution budget. The impacts range from number, size, and location of warehouses to the number and types of personnel required. Marketing, probably more than any other corporate function, directly influences the capital and operating budgets of physical distribution.

Production is also driven, to a large degree, by marketing considerations and constraints. Production, however, translates marketing strategy requirements into manufacturing plans that, in turn, further prescribe opportunities and constraints on physical

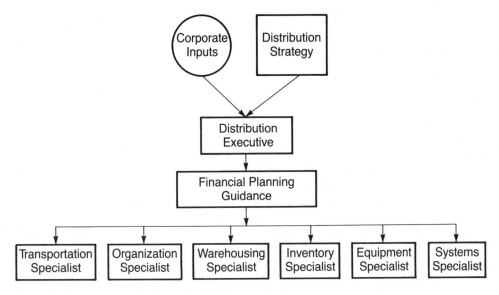

Figure 12-2   Integrated Approach: The Starting Point

distribution activities, operations, and budgets. Decisions such as production facility location and product mix, make-or-buy, and length of production runs all affect distribution activities. These factors must be included when making decisions on size and location of warehouse space, transportation modes and mix, and so forth. While these two areas, to a large degree, provide the framework within which the physical distribution executive must plan and budget his operations, finance personnel and other functions also impact distribution decision making and budgeting.

After marketing and production, the finance function probably has the most important impact on distribution budgeting. Finance will generally provide the distribution manager with capital-funding policy and guidelines on cost of capital consideration and required ROI. In addition, the physical distribution executive must be aware of how strategies of other departments, such as personnel, will affect availability of resources or provide constraints or opportunities in the development of strategy, tactics, and financial plans.

The physical distribution strategy data make up the second set of inputs required in the process. These consist of specific data on the basic elements of distributing the finished product, including warehousing (number, size, location, and markets served); transportation (modes, mix of modes, shipment size and frequency); equipment (material handling, warehousing, transportation, communications and data processing); personnel (organization, level and numbers of personnel); and supporting distribution systems (order processing, inventory, management). To budget effectively, the physical distribution executive must understand how each of these elements relates to his firm, how the application or removal of capital or operating funds will affect the performance of any element, and how the performance of any element is related to the overall performance of physical distribution with respect to costs and service.

The final set of data required in the budget process is corporate tactical information. The term *corporate tactical* has wide application; here we are primarily concerned with near-term production or marketing considerations. These include (1) introduction of a new product; (2) expansion of a geographic market; and (3) financial considerations such as capital decisions, methods of financial analysis, and documentation.

Each set of inputs must be provided to the physical distribution executive who will screen information and translate it into meaningful guidelines to be used by his subordinates in preparation of elemental budget submissions.

What Happens Next?

The financial plan is a dual purpose tool. First, the budget must be a planning tool to be used by both distribution and corporate management during the initial financial planning cycle. Equally important, however, is the use of the budget as a measurement tool which can be used by the distribution manager to gauge his performance throughout the year *and* which will support continuing management of the activity. Acceptance of the budget concept requires the development of a budget detailed enough to support both planning and the measurement of performance. To satisfy this dual purpose, the financial plan must be relatively "fine grained" and should be disaggregated (or built up) according to three major components:

- Distribution element (transportation, warehousing, inventory, systems, personnel)

- Service region or customer group

- Product

Individual plans must be prepared for transportation, warehousing systems, personnel, equipment, and inventory. These plans themselves should be further disaggregated by product and by service region or site. The goal here is to develop individual pro forma plans for transportation, warehousing, equipment, personnel, and systems. These individual plans should be developed by specialists in their respective areas under the guidance of the physical distribution manager.

In addition to the financial aspects, functional plans also should include an assessment of the risk involved in each project, an analysis of the sensitivity of output measures to input parameters, and schedules for implementation.

Application of specialized expertise at the functional level will enhance the possibility that funds will be spent more productively within each functional area. Problems of suboptimization and structural incompatibility can be minimized by coordinating all financial planning activities at the executive level and by encouraging strong communications among functional areas.

These functional financial plans are interim products that will be incorporated by the distribution executive into the final physical distribution budget and plan. After consolidating and analyzing the final budget, the physical distribution executive is then responsible for instituting and monitoring the "feedback" process. Feedback during this step is required to refine the overall physical distribution budget by making interactive adjustments in the functional budgets and—at the same time—assuring coordination with other corporate financial and budgeting activities.

Finally, the physical distribution executive is responsible for providing an overall assessment of project risk. He should be prepared to furnish a time-phased schedule of costs and events and a capital allocation plan that meets distribution requirements. The capital plan must be developed in cooperation with corporate level financial personnel. Figure 12–3 illustrates the high degree of interaction required in the financial planning process.

What Is the Role of the Functional Specialist?

Functional area managers are responsible for developing individual budgets for each of the distribution elements (transportation, warehousing, systems). These functional specialists will perform micro-level site- and product-specific analyses of the operating and capital requirements imposed by the overall strategy. They will be responsible for assessing risk, measuring the sensitivity of key input parameters, and developing an overall schedule. Finally, they will be responsible for maintaining the documentation that supports their plans, and performing the interactive analyses required before the overall physical distribution budget can be made final.

Development of the Elemental Plans

The Sequence of Events

We have emphasized the interdependence of each of the distribution functions and the attendant requirement for coordination. Not all of the functional plans should be initiated

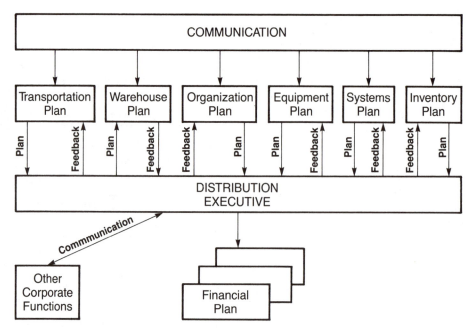

Figure 12-3   Integrated Approach: The Process

simultaneously, however, since this course is both impractical and inefficient. There is an order of precedence which expedites the planning process and minimizes redundant effort. The order we propose begins with the warehousing analysis. Identification of specific sites is not required, but general locational parameters are required *before* the transportation analysis can begin, since the latter requires a basic knowledge of the availability of service into and out of areas where storage facilities are located.

After a preliminary feasibility analysis of potential warehouse locations has been completed, the transportation analysis can begin. The first step should be to review such transportation-related aspects of the potential warehouse locations as availability and adequacy of service between the origin/destination pairs to be served by the facility. Significant give and take should be expected in these deliberations before the final set of sites that meet transportation criteria is agreed on. Financial planning relating to equipment systems, personnel, and inventory can be initiated after the major transportation and warehousing decisions have been made. Since site specification has a relatively insignificant impact on these elements, it seems logical to begin preliminary planning by doing the warehousing analysis.

The Process of Developing Functional-Level Plans

Each of the financial analyses that must be undertaken is distinctly different, but the process that should be used in each case is basically the same. As Figure 12-4 illustrates, the first step in the process is to assimilate financial planning guidelines and to review the distribution strategy. The synthesis of these data will define the functional specialist's marching orders *and* any constraints in acting on those orders. The specialist is expected to utilize his or her expertise in developing cost-effective distribution solutions that are sensitive to financial planning constraints and to the interplay between financial strategy and the plans in other functional areas. At this stage, the functional specialist must obtain an overview of the entire strategy; an understanding of the "big picture" that will permit efficient movement toward mutually acceptable solutions. This perspective is at the heart of the integrated approach we propose.

The actual financial planning process at the micro level consists of the five major steps shown in Figure 12–4.

Identification of Requirements

The first task for each functional specialist is identification and specification of the requirements placed on his functional area by the distribution strategy. The degree of detail included in the strategy will determine the starting point of the analysis, and will vary according to functional area. The basic information needed will include:

- Number, location, and size of warehouses

- Modes and mix of transportation elements

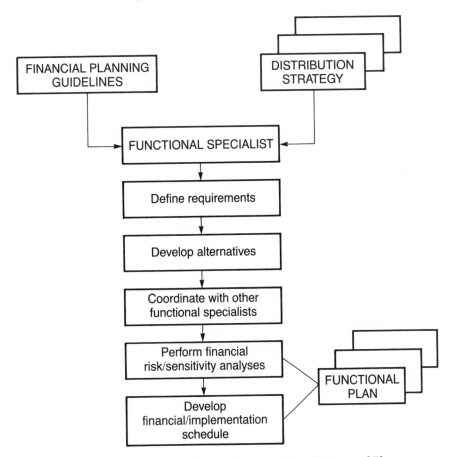

Figure 12-4   The Process of Developing Functional Level Financial Plans

- Level of automation of warehousing
- Systems (order processing, inventory, etc.)
- Service policy

These basic elements must be translated into detailed specifications that will be used to develop specific cost projections. For example, in the case of warehousing, the level of specificity must be sufficient to support actual site selection. For each facility in the network, the warehousing specialist must specify requirements in terms of:

- Number of square feet of warehouse space
- Number of square feet of office space
- Building construction specifications (material, ceiling height, floor thickness, etc.)
- Number of loading docks, docks with levelers, weather shelters, etc.
- Requirements for climate control, security, etc.
- Utility requirements
- Transportation connection requirements (rail siding, interstate access, etc.)

In developing these specifications, the functional specialist will utilize his or her experience and expertise to define a model of that functional area's requirements to meet the overall strategic objectives.

The requirements for each functional area should be developed on a location-specific and product-specific basis to facilitate the almost inevitable trade-off analysis which will occur later.

Development of Alternatives

After requirements have been specified, the next step in the planning process involves the development of alternatives to satisfy these requirements. In the case of transportation, some alternatives that might arise are whether to buy, lease, or contract motor carrier services, or to use a combination of these options. The buy-or-lease decision should not be made at this point—only the feasibility of the options should be examined.

This phase of the planning process calls for the creative development of realistic alternatives; it also demands some specific information—especially in terms of availability and cost of the space, personnel, and services required by each of the distribution functions in each area. This also is the appropriate time for analysis of the labor market, equipment suppliers, taxes, rent, construction costs, and other detailed information. These data should be collected both for preliminary screening purposes and to expedite later detailed analyses.

Coordination with Other Elements

When specific alternatives have been developed fully and screened by the functional specialist, they should be disseminated to other members of the financial planning team for review and comment. Piecemeal evaluation of functional alternatives becomes a protracted, inefficient process. Thus, each functional manager should review all other functional alternatives simultaneously to provide consistency and compatibility.

This coordination process will yield a variety of what we will call distribution scenarios. Optimally, these scenarios will be mutually compatible sets of functional alternatives which together represent one approach to satisfying distribution strategy objectives. (In practice, of course, this will not often be the case.) These distribution scenarios will be evaluated by the distribution executive later in the planning process. Figure 12–5 illustrates how these scenarios are constructed. The distribution scenario is simply a macro representation of *distribution* alternatives consisting of mutually compatible *functional* alternatives.

Financial Analysis of Alternatives

Each functional specialist must rank the alternatives that he has to work with in order of financial preference. This involves preparing analyses that should include relatively detailed but straightforward financial summaries of the capital and operating funds required to support each alternative. The methods and measures to be used in the financial analysis are those specified by the physical distribution manager to provide both internal and external (corporate) consistency. The financial analysis should be conducted on a site-specific basis, reflecting actual costs of goods and services for each geographic location. To the extent possible, costing should be further disaggregated within each site on a product-specific basis. Thus, for example, the warehousing specialist should determine by product type the actual capital and operating fund streams for each specific site. The financial analysis must also include a sensitivity analysis and a risk assessment. The sensitivity analysis is critical in performing trade-offs at the macro level since even relatively minor changes in the cost of fuel tax rates, utility rates, and the like can alter the financial attractiveness of any alternative. Finally, the functional specialist must use his experience and

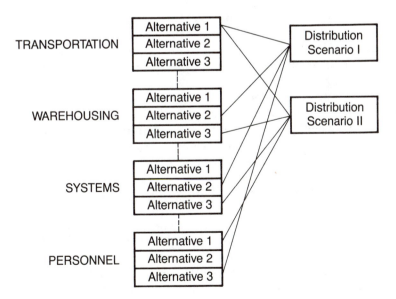

Figure 12-5   Elements in the Construction of a Distribution Scenario

professional judgment together with the information he has collected in the performance of micro-level analyses to assess the risk associated with each alternative. To the extent possible, risk should be quantified. For example, in the warehousing analyses, if a decision is made to buy space, it is necessary to estimate the expected ease and financial return should liquidation of the asset be required. Quantitative analyses are possible for transportation and warehousing and material-handling equipment but become more difficult in softer areas such as personnel and systems.

Scheduling

The final step in the micro-level planning process is development of an implementation schedule that specifies not only major implementation milestones, but also timing of commitments for capital and operating dollars. Again, development of a project schedule must be performed jointly by all functional specialists for each distribution scenario. Using this approach, the end product of the micro-level analyses will be a set of detailed, time-phased financial plans for each distribution scenario. These plans should be structurally compatible and have the requisite backup to permit meaningful evaluation at the macro level by the physical distribution executive.

One-Time Decisions

Adoption of a new distribution strategy will require a number of one-time decisions. These decisions are basically transition related: should current personnel be relocated; should current equipment be sold or relocated; should inventory stocks be depleted at obsolete warehouse locations or should stocks be transferred? Each of these decisions must be considered from a financial as well as an operational perspective when developing the financial plan and schedule. In most instances, these implementation decisions are clearly within the purview of one of the functional specialists involved in the financial planning process. It is the responsibility of the physical distribution executive to see that each of these decisions is addressed by some member of the team. In event of ambiguity, decision-making authority should be delegated to the most appropriate member of the team. In many cases, these implementation decisions will become the driving force in development of functional alternatives, such as whether to replace or relocate equipment. To the extent possible then, implementation approach-related costs and other one-time costs associated with adoption of the new distribution strategy should be broken out from costs which are implementation independent. This separation will permit analysis of the effectiveness of the implementation approach apart from the longer-term distribution strategy costs.

Testing the Physical Distribution Financial Plan

The physical distribution executive also plays a major role in testing the financial plan schedules. To evaluate the distribution scenarios, the financial plans must be tested at two levels—the distribution level and the corporate level. At the distribution activity level, the physician distribution executive will review the distribution scenario's financial requirements and evaluate its ability to support the strategic objectives of the distribution function in a cost-effective manner. Modifications of both the scenario and the financial plan may be necessary before the plan can be submitted for corporate-level financial analysis and possible further modification.

Review of Distribution Scenarios

The physical distribution executive must review each of the elemental financial plans comprising the final distribution scenario first individually, and then as an entity to validate the decisions made in terms of financial performance, risk, and sensitivity. When all plans have been reviewed, their structural compatibility can be ascertained and a decision made as to whether the aggregate (the scenario) will achieve the agreed-on distribution objectives within general budget guidelines. Capital and operating funds streams can be combined at this point to obtain an activity-level picture of funding requirements for the scenario.

Financial Evaluation and Refinement of Distribution Plan

The surviving distribution scenarios can now be subjected to the more rigorous financial analyses required at the corporate level. These analyses may require further refinement of the budget. In that case, the physical distribution executive must make further decisions based on his understanding of the elemental plans concerning where, at what level, and when action must be taken. The feedback process should involve all elemental managers because of the interrelationship of the elemental plans. Given the disaggregate nature of budget submission, the impact of prospective changes in elemental budgets can be traced readily to their effect on cost and service for specific products and in individual regions. If basic customer service priorities or cost/service balances have been altered as a result of the revision process, it will be necessary to involve marketing, production, finance, or other functions for additional guidance. This interactive process should continue until a satisfactory compromise is achieved. The final selection of a distribution scenario and financial plans of course will require balancing of subjective and quantitative assessment of risk with the financial performance and service capacity.

Benefits of an Integrated Approach

There are a number of benefits inherent in an integrated approach for developing financial plans for distribution strategy implementation.

1. *The approach permits meaningful corporate evaluation.* Maintenance of an overall distribution strategy perspective throughout the planning process, involving evaluation of trade-offs between cost and service performance, will assure the firm's ability to balance the requirements of distribution and other departments in light of overall corporate strategy and financial constraints. Although this approach does not assure that distribution will be funded at the levels requested, it is probable that distribution performance will be judged against the levels of performance that can be provided for the resources (dollars and people) that are committed.

2. *It provides an accurate assessment of distribution requirements.* Because the plan is built from the bottom up, the strong coordination and involvement of the distribution executive assure adequate analysis of micro-level issues while maintaining an overall strategic perspective.

3. *Most importantly, it retains the integrity of the distribution strategy through the total process.* Maintenance of the macro-level overview by the distribution executive throughout the financial planning process insures that the distribution strategy remains intact. Financial constraints or opportunities presented during the financial planning exercise are filtered through the distribution executive to functional managers for coordinated analysis. Following this approach, the distribution executive can balance priorities and make rational decisions regarding the impact of strategic distribution objectives and the projected capability of the distribution function to meet these corporate objectives.

CHAPTER 1

Distribution Cost, Productivity, and Performance Analysis

DOUGLAS M. LAMBERT

The Importance of Accounting in Distribution

In the 1970s, economic uncertainty and inflation combined to cause serious erosion of the profitability of most firms. The impact of higher-cost energy on transportation costs and of record high interest rates on corporate cash flow directed the attention of top management to the physical distribution function. This increased interest on the part of corporate management represents both an opportunity and a challenge for the distribution professional. With the recognition that distribution costs are a major component of the total cost of doing business and that distribution assets represent a major portion of a firm's total assets comes the responsibility to improve corporate profits by improving distribution productivity.

Total cost analysis is the key to the successful management of the physical distribution function. Rather than attempt to minimize the costs of individual components such as transportation, warehousing, inventory, order processing, production, or customer service, the goal should be to select the level of expenditure for each of these components that leads to the greatest profit for the firm. Obviously accounting information plays a significant role in this process. Without accurate cost data it is impossible to design or control the distribution system.

Portions of this material are from *Strategic Physical Distribution Management* by Douglas M. Lambert and James R. Stock, published by Richard D. Irwin, Inc., Homewood, Illinois, 1982. No part of this material may be reproduced in any form without the written permission of the publisher. For expanded treatment of these and other distribution related issues the interested reader is referred to *Strategic Physical Distribution Management*.

The Need for Accounting Information

Most of the early obstacles confronting implementation of the integrated physical distribution management concept have been eliminated. However, the lack of adequate cost data has prevented its full implementation in many firms. In general, accountants have not kept pace with developments in physical distribution and, in fact, have shown relatively little interest in the area. Consequently, much of the necessary cost analysis has not been carried out.[1]

Accurate cost data are required for the successful implementation of the integrated physical distribution management concept using total cost analysis, for the management and control of physical distribution operations, and to aid in setting selling prices and in justifying price differentials.

As the cost of physical distribution increases, the need for accurate accounting for the costs becomes increasingly critical. Since the physical distribution function is relatively more energy intensive and labor intensive than other areas of the firm, its ratio of costs to total company costs has been steadily increasing. Efficient and effective distribution policies cannot be determined until the costs related to separate functional areas and their interaction are made available to distribution decision makers.

The quality of the accounting data will influence management's ability to exploit new markets, take advantage of innovative transportation systems, make changes in packaging, choose between common carriers and private trucking, increase deliveries or increase inventories, and determine to what extent the order-processing system should be automated.

The accounting system must be capable of providing information to answer the following questions:

1. What are the impacts of physical distribution costs on contribution by product, by territory, by customer, and by salesperson?

2. What are the costs associated with providing additional levels of customer service? What trade-offs are necessary and what are the incremental benefits or losses?

3. What is the optimal amount of inventory? How sensitive is the inventory level to changes in warehousing patterns or to changes in customer service levels? How much does it cost to hold inventory?

4. What mix of transportation modes and carriers should be used?

5. How many field warehouses should be used and where should they be located?

6. How many production set-ups are required? Which plants will be used to produce each product?

7. To what extent should the order-processing system be automated?

To answer these and other questions requires knowledge of the costs and revenues that will change if the physical distribution system changes. That is, determination of a product's contribution should be based on how corporate revenues, expenses, and hence profitability would change if the product line were dropped. Any costs or revenues that are unaffected by this decision are irrelevant to the problem. For example, a relevant cost would be public warehouse handling charges associated with a product's sales; a non-relevant cost would be the overhead costs associated with the firm's private trucking fleet.

Implementation of this approach to decision making is severely hampered by the lack of availability of the right accounting data or the inability to use the data when they are available. The best and most sophisticated of our models are only as good as the accounting input, and a number of recent studies attest to the gross inadequacies of distribution cost data.[2]

Key Accounting Concepts

The accounting concepts necessary for distribution are the same as those used in manufacturing cost analysis. In both cases, functional cost analysis is a prerequisite to the identification of costs and their behavior. Although distribution activities are organized along functional lines such as warehousing, transportation, order processing, and inventory, in many firms costs are not captured on a functional basis but rather in broad natural account categories such as salaries, depreciation, and general and administrative expenses. Natural accounts are used to group costs for financial reporting on the firm's income statement and balance sheet. For example, all payments for salaries might be grouped into a salaries account, whether they be for production, marketing, physical distribution or finance, and the total shown on the financial statements at the end of the reporting period.[3] Other examples of natural accounts might include rent, depreciation, selling expenses, general and administrative expenses, and interest expense. It is entirely possible that in a firm with a strong financial accounting orientation, physical distribution costs such as warehousing and transportation may not be given separate headings in the natural accounts. Instead they are lumped into such diverse catch-alls as overhead, selling, or general expense. Further there has been a tendency, particularly in the case of freight, to abandon the accrual accounting concept and match costs of one period with revenues of another period. These conditions make it difficult to determine distribution expenditures, control costs, or perform trade-off analysis.

Each firm must analyze its own distribution activities in order to determine meaningful functional account categories. The next step is to code the accounting data in such a manner as to make identification of the costs possible.

A number of key accounting concepts are applicable to the distribution function, including:

- Controllable and noncontrollable costs

- Direct and indirect costs

- Fixed and variable costs

- Standards and standard costs

- Actual (or historic) and opportunity costs

- Relevant costs and sunk costs

- Full costing and marginal or incremental costing

- Break-even analysis

- Cost of capital

Controllable and Noncontrollable Costs

It is necessary to separate the more controllable costs from the less controllable so that individual managers are held responsible only for the incurrence of those costs over which they exercise control. Generally, costs that vary with the volume of effort expended in an activity tend to be more controllable. These costs should be related to an appropriate unit of service, and separately identified to assist in cost control. Those costs that are fixed or budgeted for the fiscal period should be considered when distribution effort and capacity is subject to change.

Direct and Indirect Costs

In manufacturing, "direct costs" refer to costs that are readily traceable to products—for example, direct material and direct labor. The term is also used to identify costs that are traced as incurred to specific functions, to distinguish them from allocated or transferred costs. In distribution the classification of costs as direct or indirect depends on the segment. The more general the segment (sales division or sales territory), the greater the portion of costs directly traceable to it; the more specific the segment (products, customers), the greater the proportion of indirect costs. Direct costs are those costs that can be traced to a business segment. If that segment were eliminated, the costs no longer would be incurred.

Indirect costs, costs such as general administrative expenses, are often allocated to segments, but this process is arbitrary at best and should be avoided.

Fixed and Variable Costs

The study of cost behavior in physical distribution is quite similar to that in manufacturing because most of the activities are repetitive in nature. Under such conditions physical measurements such as man-hours, units handled, and orders processed can be used to measure the activity. Changes in the level of cost incurred usually are caused by changes in the level of activity experienced.

The first step in understanding the cost behavior of physical distribution activities is to establish the relationship between the amount of each cost and an appropriate measurement of the level of activity. Variable costs are those costs that change in proportion to changes in volume and fixed costs (see Figure 13–1). Examples of variable costs include the handling charge in a public warehouse and the cost of packing material used in a shipping department. Fixed costs include depreciation, security costs and taxes on company-owned warehouses, and the salary of the transportation manager.

Some costs are mixed, that is, they contain both a fixed and a variable component. An example might be warehouse labor. A basic crew of three may be required to cover the normal range of activity. However, if the volume of activity exceeds a certain amount, overtime or part-time employees may be necessary.

In some cases costs may be fixed over a relevant range but may increase in steps. These costs may be referred to as step variable costs or step fixed costs. The major distinction is the size of the steps. For example, in an order-processing department of twenty people labor may be considered a variable cost without making a serious error. This is because a relatively small percentage change in the number of orders could result in a change in the number of employees. However, in a department of three people the cost should be considered a step fixed cost since a large percentage change in the number of orders processed usually would be required in order to eliminate an employee. Other examples of step fixed costs include the costs of management salaries, depreciation, and taxes associated with each warehouse that the company owns and operates.

Effective planning and control require that the total costs be separated into the fixed and variable components.

Standards and Standard Costs

The application of performance standards to the efficient control of manufacturing costs is widespread, but relatively few firms have developed standards for distribution activities.

A decision to use standard costs requires a systematic review of physical distribution operations in order to determine the most efficient means of achieving the desired output. Accounting, physical distribution, and engineering personnel must work together using regression analysis, time and motion studies, and efficiency studies so that a series of flexible budgets can be drawn up for various operating levels in different physical distribution cost centers. Standards can and have been set for such warehouse operations as stock pick-

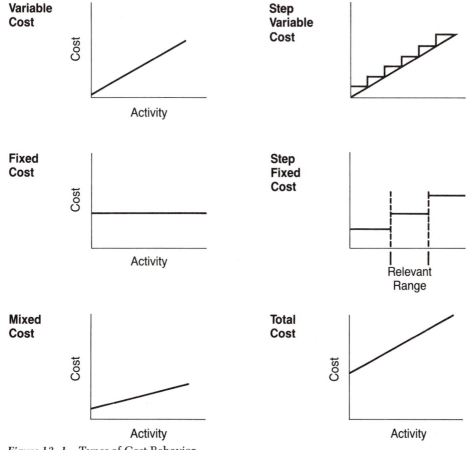

Figure 13-1 Types of Cost Behavior

ing, loading, receiving, replenishing, storing, and packing merchandise. In addition, they have been successfully utilized in order processing, transportation, and even clerical functions.

It may not be necessary to have standards for all distribution costs. Management should be selective about the activities to which standards are applied, so that they are used only where the costs involved and the possibilities of inefficiency suggest the need for continued attention to cost control.

Actual (Historic) and Opportunity Costs

The conservative nature of accounting requires the use of current actual costs or allocations of historic costs in the case of such costs as depreciation. However, for management decision making, actual costs and opportunity costs must be considered. An opportunity cost is the sacrifice associated with the choice of a specific alternative. Examples of opportunity costs include the rate of return that could be earned on dollars if they were not invested in inventory and the income that could be earned by leasing or selling a company-owned warehouse.

Relevant Costs and Sunk Costs

Relevant costs are costs that will change with a decision management is about to make. Any costs that are unaffected by the decision should not be included in the evaluation of the alternatives. The costs that will not change are referred to as sunk costs. An example of a sunk cost is the price of a forklift truck after it has been purchased. When making the decision to keep or sell the forklift truck, the relevant costs are the cash flows experienced by keeping the piece of equipment, its current market value, and any income tax implications associated with the decision to sell it.

Full Costing and Marginal or Incremental Costing

Full costing or absorption costing is a system of product costing in which the product is charged with both variable and fixed manufacturing costs. Marginal or incremental costing (also called direct or variable costing) is a system of product costing in which variable costs are associated with products and fixed costs are treated as period costs. In addition to the direct costing versus absorption costing distinction, companies may value inventories based upon actual costs or standard costs. The following represent four distinct costing alternatives:

- *Actual absorption costing.* Includes actual costs for direct material and direct labor plus predetermined variable and fixed manufacturing overhead.

- *Standard absorption costing.* Includes predetermined direct material and direct labor costs plus predetermined variable and fixed overhead.

- *Actual direct costing.* Includes actual costs for direct material and direct labor plus predetermined variable manufacturing overhead; excludes fixed manufacturing overhead.

• *Standard direct costing.* Includes predetermined costs for direct material and direct labor plus predetermined variable manufacturing overhead; excludes fixed manufacturing overhead.

The distinction between full costing and direct costing is particularly meaningful for the calculation of inventory carrying costs since only the direct costs are converted to cash by reducing inventory levels.

Break-even Analysis

Break-even analysis is also a useful tool for distribution analysis. The break-even is the level of sales required to cover variable costs plus fixed costs (see Figure 13–2). For example, management may wish to determine if customer service levels should be increased from 90 percent to 95 percent. When making this decision it is important to know how much sales would have to increase to break even on the service improvement. If such an increase is not likely to be realized, the service level should not be increased to 95 percent.

Cost of Capital

A precise definition of the cost of capital is elusive; however, Goodman has defined it as follows:

The cost of capital refers to that amount of money which a company, as a result of accepting a proposal, is expected to pay to and/or reinvest for the suppliers of funds during

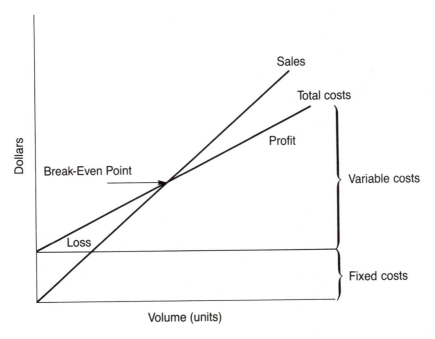

Figure 13-2   Break-even Analysis

the life of the proposal, over and above the amount of funds required to initially finance the proposal.[4]

He made the point that it is a fallacy to think of the cost of capital as the interest rate plus financing charges since such a position assumes that the owner's investment, including retained earnings, is cost free.

The measurement of cost of capital is a complex process, and can be confusing to academicians and businessmen alike. Basic financial management texts often employ a device commonly referred to as "weighted-average cost of capital." The principal deficiency of this device is the assumption that it is possible to raise capital at the same cost as in the past. Also, the "weighted-average cost of capital" will be dependent upon the firm's debt-equity mix, the firm's dividend policy, and the type of financing selected.

Some authors maintain that any project that yields more than the cost of money should be accepted. Horngren cautioned against the use of a short-run approach:

> The principal objection to the short-run approach is the insidious effect of low-cost debt financing on projects over a series of years. To illustrate, the cost of 100 percent financing by 6 percent bonds is only 3 percent after applying a tax rate of 50 percent. If unlimited debt could be arranged in a given year, any project with an after-tax return of over 3 percent would be accepted. Next year, the debt limit for an optimum capital structure may already be reached, and equity financing may show a high cost of 20 percent after taxes. This would mean that any project that could not produce such a high return would be automatically rejected.[5]

What is required is a straightforward method of calculating the cost of capital that can be easily understood and applied by businesspeople. Mao examined the concept of hurdle rate—the rate over which projects will be accepted—as it pertained to a perfect capital market and to capital rationing. Although the real world is probably far removed from a perfect capital market, the concept deserves explanation.

> Under perfect capital market conditions the supply of funds to a firm is completely elastic, meaning that there is no limit to the amount of funds that the firm can raise at the prevailing rate of interest. It is reasonable to assume that the firm has already taken advantage of all existing opportunities for profitable investments, so the market rate of interest accurately measures the return on the firm's marginal investments.
>
> In a perfect capital market, firms and security buyers know precisely what present and future cash flows may be expected from any project. So security buyers need not distinguish between stocks and bonds, and there is only one yield on securities, designated here as the rate of interest. Because there is no uncertainty, the firm may justly regard the market rate of interest as the hurdle rate that the IRR [internal rate of return] of any investment must exceed if the project is to be judged worthwhile.[6]

However, when a firm's capital is rationed, Mao defined the hurdle rate as the rate of return on marginal investments, due to the principle of opportunity cost.

> Consider, for example, a firm which pays 10 percent for the funds that it acquires and that, because of capital rationing, is currently turning down marginal investments promising annual returns of 15 percent. For this company the hurdle rate in investment decisions is 15 percent, although the cost of capital is only 10 percent. This means that the relevant time value of money is measured by the return on the most lucrative investments foregone by the firm, rather than by the price at which the funds were originally ac-

quired. Of course, the 15 percent hurdle rate could also be designated as the cost of capital to the firm, if this term is interpreted generically.[7]

Goodman supported Mao's view concerning opportunity cost. For most pragmatic business decisions, he stated that "capital rationing" was a more meaningful concept than "capital budgeting" and that a weighted-average cost of capital was inferior to the concept of opportunity cost. "For most decision-making situations, it is the opportunity calculated cost of capital which is far more important for a given decision than an actual calculated cost of capital based upon something which happened yesterday."[8]

Distribution Cost Trade-off Analysis*

Profitable business development requires that management allocate scarce resources to physical distribution and the other elements of the marketing mix—product, price, and promotion. This is because the total dollars spent on the various components of the marketing mix influence the company's market share and profitability. The more dollars that a company invests in the marketing mix relative to its competitors, the larger the market share achieved, assuming that all competitors spend their dollars equally effectively. However, this is rarely the case. Significant advantage can be achieved by allocating dollars to the marketing mix more efficiently and effectively than one's competitors. The objective is to allocate resources to the price, product, promotion, and place components of the marketing mix in a manner that will lead to the greatest long-run profits.

The place component represents the manufacturer's expenditure for customer service, which is the output of the physical distribution system. The area of customer service represents physical distribution's interface with the demand creation portion of marketing. Physical distribution represents the demand supply part of marketing. Customer service not only impacts the *place* component of the marketing mix, but also influences the *price* of the product. Product availability and order cycle time can be used to differentiate the product and may influence the market price if customers are willing to pay more for better service. In addition, physical distribution costs are added to product costs and as such may affect the market price set by the company. Figure 13–3 illustrates the cost trade-offs that are required to successfully implement the integrated physical distribution management concept. It will be used throughout this section as the financial model for making physical distribution decisions.

Importance of Total Cost Analysis

Total cost analysis is the key to managing the physical distribution function. Management should strive to minimize the total costs of physical distribution rather than attempt to minimize the cost of each component. Attempts to reduce the cost of individual physical distribution activities may be suboptimal and lead to increased total costs.[9] For example,

*This section draws heavily from Douglas M. Lambert, *The Development of An Inventory Costing Methodology: A Study of the Costs Associated with Holding Inventory* (Chicago, Illinois: National Council of Physical Distribution Management, 1976), pp. 5–15 and pp. 59–67.

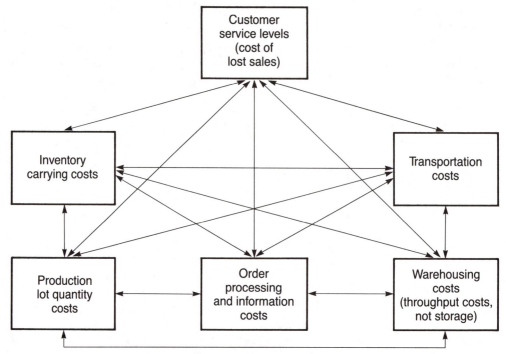

Figure 13-3   Cost Trade-offs Required to Minimize Total Costs in Physical Distribution

Total Costs = Transportation Costs + Warehousing Costs
+ Order Processing and Information Costs
+ Production Lot Quantity Costs + Inventory Carrying Costs + Cost of Lost Sales

Adapted from Douglas M. Lambert, *The Development of an Inventory Costing Methodology: A Study of the Costs Associated with Holding Inventory* (Chicago: NCPDM, 1976), p. 7. Copyright © 1975 by Douglas M. Lambert.

consolidating finished goods inventory in a small number of distribution centers will re-duce inventory carrying costs and warehousing costs but may lead to a substantial in-crease in freight expense or lower sales volume as a result of reduced levels of customer ser-vice. Similarly, the savings associated with large volume purchases may be less than the increased inventory carrying costs.

It is important that management consider the total of all of the costs of physical dis-tribution. Reductions in the cost of one physical distribution activity invariably lead to in-creased costs of other cost components. Effective management and real cost savings can be accomplished only by viewing physical distribution as an integrated system and minimiz-ing its total cost. The cost categories introduced in Figure 13–3 are customer service levels (the cost of lost sales), transportation costs, warehousing costs, order-processing and infor-mation costs, production lot quantity costs, and inventory carrying costs. Each category will be discussed in turn.

Customer Service Levels

The cost associated with customer service levels is the cost of lost sales—not only the mar-gin lost by not meeting the current sales demand, but the present value of all future contributions to profit forfeited when a customer is lost because of poor product availability. This cost is difficult, if not impossible, for most businesspeople to measure. For this reason, it is recommended that only the measurable costs associated with back ordering or expediting be included in this category. The objective then becomes one of minimizing the total of the other physical distribution costs, given a level of customer service. With this type of information, it is possible for management to make a knowledgeable judgment concerning the likelihood of recovering, through increased sales, the increase in total system costs brought about by an increase in customer service levels. Another possibility, of course, would be to reduce spending in some other component of the marketing mix, promotion for example, in order to maintain profits with a similar sales volume. Likewise, with decreases in customer service levels, profitability can be improved or other components of the marketing mix may enjoy increased levels of expenditure in an effort to maintain or improve market position.

It becomes apparent that even though the costs of lost sales associated with customer service are elusive, if management determines customer service levels based on customer needs and on an understanding of the interaction between customer service and the other marketing mix elements, better decisions are possible. The goal is to determine the least total cost method of physical distribution given the customer service objectives, which requires that good cost data are available for the other five cost categories shown in Figure 13–3.

Transportation Costs

The next category of costs are those associated with the transportation function. These costs can be dealt with in total or on an incremental basis. Transportation costs, if not currently available in any other form, can be determined by a statistical audit of freight bills for common carriers or from corporate accounting records for private fleets. Also, standard costs can be established for the transportation activity. One example of a successful application of standard costs in transportation was given by Schiff.[10] The firm used a computerized system with standard charges and routes for 25,000 routes and eight different methods of transportation. Up to 300,000 combinations were possible and the system was updated regularly. Clerks at any location could obtain from the computer the optimum method of shipment. A monthly computer printout listed the following information by customer:

Destination

Standard freight cost to customer

Actual freight paid for shipments to customer

Standard freight to warehouse cost

Total freight cost

Origin of shipment

Sales district office

Method of shipment

Container used

Weight of shipment

Variance in excess of a given amount per hundredweight

Also, another monthly report listed the deviation from standard freight cost for each customer and the amount of the variance. This system obviously provided the firm with a measure of freight performance. Equally important, the standards provided the means for determining individual customer profitability and for identifying opportunities for physical distribution cost trade-offs. Because this firm used standards as an integral part of its management information system it would be relatively straightforward to determine the impact of a system change such as an improved, automated order-processing system on transportation costs.

Warehousing Costs

Warehousing costs comprise all of the expenses that can be eliminated or must be increased as the result of a change in the number of warehousing facilities. There has been a great deal of confusion in the literature about these costs. Many authors have included warehousing costs in inventory carrying costs. This is a misconception since most of these costs will not change with the level of inventory stocked, but rather with the number of stocking locations. In addition, the costs of leased or owned facilities are primarily fixed and would not change with a change in the amount of inventory. However, additional labor costs may be incurred if the throughput increases. Therefore the most straightforward method is to separate the warehousing costs into two distinct categories—those related to throughput and those related to storage. Throughput costs are the costs associated with selling a product in a given market by moving it into and out of a warehouse in that market. Examples of throughput costs are the charges that public warehousemen assess for product handlings into and out of their facilities. These charges are related to how much of a product is sold in that market and are distinct from storage space costs which public warehousemen assign to their customers based on the amount of inventory stored in the facility. The former group of costs should be included in warehousing costs so that the increments can be added or subtracted easily with changes in distribution system configuration. The difficulty experienced in isolating warehousing costs will be different for public warehouses and privately owned or leased facilities.

Public Warehouses

Generally, the determination of the behavior of public warehousing costs presents no problem. Most public warehousemen charge on a per hundredweight or per case basis for both handling and storage. Consequently, these costs are totally variable. In some instances, however, a "one-shot" billing system is used whereby the handling charge implicitly includes a storage component. With this type of billing it is usually necessary to guarantee a specified number of inventory turns, and a penalty is charged for recurring storage if turns do not meet or exceed the standard.

Privately Owned or Leased Facilities

As discussed previously, most of the costs associated with company-owned or leased facilities are fixed and will not change over the course of the year. Those costs that are variable will vary with throughput. Care must be exercised when allocating these costs to users. For example, a multi-division corporation that manufactured and sold high margin pharmaceuticals as well as a number of lower margin packaged goods products maintained a number of field warehouse locations managed by the corporate physical distribution group. These climate-controlled facilities were designed for the pharmaceutical business and required security and housekeeping practices which far exceeded those necessary for packaged goods. In order to utilize the facilities fully, however, the corporation encouraged non-pharmaceutical divisions to store their products in these distribution centers. The costs of operating the warehouses were primarily fixed, although additional warehouse employees or overtime payments were necessary if the volume of product handled (throughput) increased. The corporate policy was to allocate costs to user divisions based on the percentage of the total number of square feet used by each division in the warehouses. The high cost associated with facilities used for warehousing pharmaceuticals made the corporate allocations significantly higher than they would have been for public warehousing rates for general merchandise. Furthermore, the corporate divisions were managed on a decentralized profit center basis. The vice president of physical distribution in one of the divisions realized that similar services could be obtained at lower cost to his division by using public warehouses. For this reason, he withdrew the division's products from the corporate facilities and put them in public warehouses in the same cities. Although the volume of product handled and stored in the corporate distribution centers decreased substantially, the cost savings were minimal in terms of the total costs incurred by these facilities. This was due to the high proportion of fixed costs. Consequently, approximately the same cost was allocated to fewer users which made it even more attractive for the other divisions to change to public warehouses in order to obtain lower rates. The end result was higher, not lower, total company warehousing costs. The corporate warehousing costs were primarily fixed and would not be altered significantly if the space was totally occupied or a major portion of it was left unused. When the non-pharmaceutical divisions moved to public warehouses, the company continued to incur approximately the same total expense for the corporate owned and operated warehouses, and also incurred additional public warehousing charges. In effect, the distribution costing system motivated the divisional distribution managers to act in a manner which was not in the best interests of the company and total costs escalated. The importance of understanding cost behavior cannot be over-emphasized.

Order-Processing and Information Costs

Order-processing and information costs include the cost of issuing and closing orders, the related handling costs, and associated communication costs. The important thing to remember when establishing these costs is to include in the analysis only those costs that will change with the decision that is being made. Many managers make the mistake of arriving at estimates of these costs by dividing the total cost of the order-processing department by the number of orders processed. This is incorrect because of the large portion of fixed costs that are included. Such a procedure overstates the savings associated with a reduction in the number of orders processed. A more correct estimate could be obtained by dividing the change in order-processing department costs over the previous two years (adjusted for inflation) by the change in the number of orders processed. Other methods include engineering-type time and motion studies and regression analysis, which will be discussed later in the section on inventory-related damage.

Production Lot Quantity Costs

Production lot quantity costs are those costs that will change as a result of a change in the distribution system and usually will include some or all of the following:

- Production preparation costs (set-up time, inspection, set-up scrap, inefficiency of beginning operation)
- Lost capacity due to changeover
- Materials handling, scheduling, and expediting.

The production preparation costs and lost capacity costs are usually available since they are used as inputs to production planning. The other costs can be approximated by taking the incremental total costs incurred for two different levels of activity and dividing by the increment in volume. Regression analysis is another technique that can be used to isolate fixed and variable cost components. The numbers obtained can be used as an input to the design of a physical distribution system.

Inventory Carrying Costs

Conceptually, inventory carrying costs have been one of the most difficult costs to determine, and next to the cost of lost sales probably the most difficult. Inventory carrying costs should include only those costs that vary with the level of inventory stored. They can be categorized into the following groups: (1) capital costs, (2) inventory service costs, (3) storage space costs, and (4) inventory risk costs.

Capital Costs on Inventory Investment

Holding inventory ties up money that could be used for other types of investments. This applies to internally generated funds as well as capital obtained from sources external to the firm such as debt from banks and insurance companies or from the sale of common stock. Consequently, the company's opportunity cost of capital, the rate of return that could be realized from some other use of the money, should be used in order to reflect accurately the true cost involved. In companies experiencing capital rationing, which is the rule rather than the exception, the hurdle rate—the minimum rate of return on new investments—should be used as the cost of capital. Where capital rationing does not exist, the capital invested in inventory should reflect the alternative use of the money. That is, if the inventory investment was reduced, where would the capital be invested? If the money were placed in a bank account or used to reduce some form of debt, then the appropriate interest rate applies.

Some companies may differentiate among projects by categorizing them according to risk and looking for rates of return that reflect the perceived level of risk. For example, management could group projects into high, medium, and low categories of risk. High-risk projects might include investments in new products, since market acceptance is difficult to predict, or new equipment for the plant, if technology is changing so rapidly that the equipment could be obsolete within a short period of time. The desired rate of return on high-risk projects might be 25 percent after taxes. Medium-risk projects, on the other hand, may be required to obtain an 18 percent tax return. Low-risk projects, which may include such investments as warehouses, private trucking, and inventory, might be expected to achieve an after-tax return of 10 percent. In the company just described, corporate aversion to risk would require that cash made available by a reduction in inventory be used for another low-risk category investment. Consequently, the cost of money for inventory carrying costs would be 10 percent after taxes which equals 20 percent before taxes. It should be emphasized that all inventory carrying cost components must be stated in before-tax numbers because all of the other costs in the trade-off analysis, such as transportation and warehousing, are reported in before-tax dollars. In some very special circumstances, such as the fruit-canning industry, short-term financing may be used to finance the seasonal build-up of inventories. The seasonal build-up of inventory is in contrast to the inventories determined by the strategic deployment of product to achieve least total cost physical distribution. In the latter case, any change in the quantity of inventory will cause other cost components of physical distribution to change. In the former situation, the actual cost of borrowing is the acceptable cost of money.

Once the cost of money has been established, it is necessary to determine the value of the inventory on which the inventory carrying cost is to be based. At this point, it is necessary to know which of the costing alternatives is being used. For example, is the company using direct costs in determining the inventory value or is it using some form of absorption costing?

Direct costing is that method of cost accounting which is based upon the segregation of costs into fixed and variable components. For management planning and control purposes, the fixed–variable cost breakdown yields more information than that obtained from current financial statements designed for external reporting. Under direct costing, the fixed costs of production are excluded from inventory values. With absorption costing—also known as full costing or full absorption costing—which is the traditional approach used by most companies, fixed manufacturing overhead is inventoried. These differences support the conclusion that using industry averages for inventory carrying costs is not a good policy. The reason is that the various component percentages may not be calculated using comparable inventory valuation systems.

The situation may seem to be complicated even further if one considers the various methods of accounting for inventory. The American Institute of Certified Public Accountants made the following statement concerning inventory valuation:

> Cost for inventory purposes may be determined under any one of several assumptions as to the flow of cost factors (such as first-in first-out, and last-in first-out), the major objective in selecting a method should be to choose the one which under the circumstances most clearly reflects periodic income. . . .
>
> Although selection of the method should be made on the basis of individual circumstances it is obvious that financial statements will be more useful if uniform methods of inventory pricing are adopted by all companies within a given industry.[11]

Most accounting companies use one of the following three methods of accounting for inventory:

- *First-in, first out (FIFO)*—Stock acquired earliest is assumed to be sold first leaving stock acquired more recently in inventory.

- *Last-in, first out (LIFO)*—Sales are made from the most recently acquired stock leaving items acquired in the earliest time period in inventory. This method attempts to match the most recent costs of acquiring inventory with sales. LIFO will result in lower inventory valuation and lower profits than the FIFO method in periods of rising prices. The converse is true when prices are declining.

- *Average cost*—This method could use either a moving average in which *each* new purchase is averaged with the remaining inventory to obtain a new average price, or a weighted average in which the total cost of the opening inventory plus all purchases is divided by the total number of units.

Neither FIFO nor LIFO isolates and measures the effects of cost fluctuations as special managerial problems. However, when standard costing is used, the currently attainable standards automatically provide a measure of cost variance, "gains" or "losses," that can be reported separately.[12]

For the purposes of calculating inventory carrying costs, it is immaterial whether the company uses LIFO, FIFO, or average cost for inventory valuation. The value of the inventory for calculating carrying costs is determined by multiplying the number of units of each product in inventory by the standard or actual variable costs associated with manufacturing the product and moving it to the storage location. A manufacturer decreases its inventory investment by selling a unit from inventory and not producing a replacement. Similarly, inventories are increased by manufacturing more product units than are currently demanded. Consequently, in either case, it is the current manufacturing costs that are relevant for decision making, since these are the costs that will be saved if inventories are reduced and they are the costs that will be incurred if inventories are increased. Likewise, if products are held in field locations, the transportation cost incurred to move them there plus the variable costs associated with moving them into storage are costs that are inventoried just as are direct labor costs, direct material costs, and the variable manufacturing overhead.

The implicit assumption is that a reduction in finished goods inventory will lead to a corresponding reduction in inventory throughout the system (see Figure 13–4). That is, a one-time reduction in finished goods inventory results in a one-time reduction in raw materials purchases as inventory is pushed back through the system. Similarly, a planned increase in finished goods inventory results in a one-time increase in the quantity of raw materials purchased and subsequently pushed through the system. When this one-time change in inventory value, a balance sheet account, is multiplied by the opportunity cost of money it becomes an annual cost, a profit and loss statement account. This is important because all other components of the inventory carrying annual cost are annual costs and affect the profit and loss statement, as do the other cost categories such as transportation, warehousing, production lot quantity, and order processing.

In summary, many business people think that inventory is a relatively liquid and riskless investment. For this reason, they feel that a somewhat lower return can be justified on inventory investments. However, inventory requires capital that could be used for other corporate investments, and by having funds invested in inventory a company foregoes the rate of return that could be obtained from such investments. Therefore, the company's opportunity cost of capital should be applied to the investment in inventory. The cost of capital should be applied to the out-of-pocket investment in inventory. Although most manufacturers use some form of absorption costing for inventory, only variable manufacturing costs are relevant. That is, the cost of capital—the company's minimum acceptable rate of return or the appropriate opportunity cost of money—should be applied to only the variable costs directly associated with the inventory.

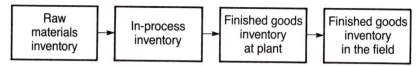

Figure 13-4   Inventory Positions in the Physical Distribution System.
Assumption: A one-time increase (decrease) in finished goods inventory results is
a one-time increase (decrease) in raw materials purchased.

Adapted from Douglas M. Lambert, *The Development of an Inventory Costing Methodology: A Study
of the Costs Associated with Holding Inventory* (Chicago: NCPDM, 1976), p. 14. Copyright © 1975 by
Douglas M. Lambert.

Inventory Service Costs

Inventory service costs are comprised of taxes and insurance paid as a result of holding the
inventory. Taxes vary depending on the state in which inventories are held. The tax rates
range from zero in states where inventories are exempt to 19.8 percent of the assessed
value (in Indiana).[13] In general, taxes vary directly with inventory levels. Insurance rates
are not strictly proportional to inventory levels, since insurance is usually purchased to
cover a certain value of product for a specified time period. However, the policy will be
revised periodically based on expected inventory policy changes. In some instances, policies can be issued where premiums are based on the monthly amounts insured. Insurance
rates vary depending on the materials used in the construction of the building, its age, and
considerations such as the type of fire prevention equipment installed.

For both insurance and taxes, the actual dollars spent on each of these expenses during the past year can be calculated as a percentage of that year's inventory value and
added to the cost of money component of the carrying cost. If budgeted figures are available for the coming year, they can be used as a percentage of the inventory value based on
the inventory plan, the forecasted inventory level, in order to provide a future-oriented
carrying cost. In most cases, there will be few, if any, significant changes from year to
year in the taxes and insurance components of the inventory carrying cost.

Storage Space Costs

In general, there are four types of facilities that should be considered: (1) plant warehouses, (2) public warehouses, (3) rented (leased) warehouses, and (4) privately owned
warehouses.

PLANT WAREHOUSES

The costs associated with plant warehouses are primarily fixed in nature. If any costs
are variable, they are usually variable with the amount of product that moves through the
facility—the throughput—and not with the quantity of inventory stored. If there are any
variable costs—such as the cost of taking an inventory or any other expense that would
change with the level of inventory—they should be included in inventory carrying costs.
Fixed charges and allocated costs are not relevant for inventory policy decisions. If the
warehouse space could be rented or used for some other productive purpose when not
used for storing inventory, and the associated opportunity costs are not readily available
to the manager, then it may make sense to substitute the appropriate fixed or allocated
costs as surrogate measures.

PUBLIC WAREHOUSES

Charges for public warehouse facilities usually are based on the amount of product that is handled and the amount of inventory held in storage. In some cases, the first month's storage must be paid when the products are moved into the facility. In effect, this makes the first month's storage a handling charge since it must be paid on every case of product regardless of how long it is held in storage.

The use of public warehouses is a policy decision made because it is the most economical way to provide the desired level of customer service without incurring excessive transportation costs. For this reason, the majority of costs incurred from the use of public warehouses, the related handling charges, should be considered as throughput costs, and only charges for recurring storage that are explicitly included in the warehouse rates should be considered in inventory carrying costs.

In situations where a throughput rate is given based on the number of inventory turns, it will be necessary to estimate the storage cost component by considering how the throughput cost per case would change if the number of inventory turns changed. Of course, the public warehouse charges paid at the time that inventory is placed into field storage should be included when calculating the value of the inventory investment.

RENTED (LEASED) WAREHOUSES

Space in rented or leased facilities is normally contracted for a specified period of time. The amount of space rented is based on the maximum storage required during the period covered by the contract. Thus, the rate of warehouse rental charges does not fluctuate from day to day with changes in the inventory level, although the rental rates can vary from month to month or year to year when a new contract is negotiated. Most costs, such as rent payment, the manager's salary, security costs, and maintenance expenses, are fixed when related to time. However, some expenses, such as warehouse labor and equipment-operating costs, vary with throughput. During the contract very few, if any, costs will vary with the amount of inventory stored.

All of the costs could be eliminated by not renewing the contract and are therefore a relevant input for decision making. However, operating costs that are not variable with the quantity of inventory held should not be included in the carrying costs, but rather in the warehousing cost category of the cost trade-off analysis. Fixed costs and costs that are variable with throughput should not be included in inventory carrying costs. Such a practice is simply incorrect and will result in erroneous decisions.

COMPANY-OWNED WAREHOUSES

The costs associated with company-owned warehouses are primarily fixed, although some may be variable with throughput. All operating costs that could be eliminated by closing a company-owned warehouse or the net savings resulting from a change to public warehouses should be included in the warehousing costs and not in inventory carrying costs. Only those costs that are variable with the quantity of inventory belong in inventory carrying costs.

Inventory Risk Costs

Inventory risk costs vary from company to company, but typically will include charges for: (1) obsolescence, (2) damage, (3) pilferage, and (4) relocation of inventory.

OBSOLESCENCE

The cost of obsolescence is the aggregate cost of each unit that must be disposed of at a loss because it is no longer possible to sell it at regular price. It is the difference between the original cost of the unit and its salvage value, or the original selling price and the reduced selling price if the price has been lowered to move the product to avoid obsolescence. This figure may or may not show up on the profit and loss statement as a separate item. Usually, obsolescence results in an over-statement of the cost of goods manufactured account or the cost of goods sold account. Consequently, some difficulty may be experienced in arriving at this figure.

DAMAGE

This cost should include only the portion of damage that is variable with the amount of inventory held. Damage incurred during shipping should be considered a throughput cost since this damage will be incurred regardless of inventory levels. Damage attributed to a public warehouse operation is usually charged to the warehouse operator if it is above some specified maximum amount. Often damage is identified as the net amount after claims.

Since it is not always known just what portions of damage, shrinkage, and relocation costs are related to the amount of inventory held, it may be necessary to determine mathematically if a relationship does exist. Damage can be a function of such factors as throughput, general housekeeping, the quality and training of management and labor, the type of product, the protective packaging used, the materials handling system, the number of times that the product is handled, and how it is handled. To say which of these factors is most important and how much damage each one accounts for is extremely difficult. Even an elaborate reporting system may not yield the desired results because employees may try to shift the blame. The quality of inspection during the receiving function and the fact that higher inventories may hide damaged product until inventories are reduced may contribute to the level of damage reported, regardless of the cause.

The portion of a cost that is variable with inventory can be determined by the use of regression analysis, or plotting the data graphically.[14] Simple linear regression can be used as a tool for segregating the portion of a cost component that is related to the level of inventory held. The principal objective in simple linear regression analysis is to establish a quantitative relationship between two related variables.

In order to establish the relationship between two variables, X and Y, a number of paired observations similar to those in Table 13–1 must be obtained. Suppose we are able to obtain the total damage figure in dollars for a number of time periods, but we do not know how much of this damage is directly related to the level of inventory. The first pair of observations ($Y = 8$, $X = 11$) indicates that $80,000 worth of damage occurred in the period when inventory was worth $11 million.

Table 13-1   Damage and Corresponding Inventory Levels at Various Points in Time

Time Periods	1	2	3	4	5	6	7
Y, damage in thousands of dollars	80	100	70	60	50	70	100
X, inventory in millions of dollars	11	15	13	10	7	9	13

SOURCE: Douglas M. Lambert and James R. Stock, *Strategic Physical Distribution Management* (Homewood, Ill.: Richard D. Irwin, Inc., 1982), p. 248.

Now the data can be plotted on graph paper with each pair of observations represented by a point on the chart (see Figure 13–5). A point is obtained by plotting the independent variable, X, along the horizontal axis and the dependent variable, Y, along the vertical axis. When all the pairs of observations have been plotted, a straight line is drawn that attempts to minimize the distance of all the points from the line (the statistical technique is referred to as least-squares regression).

Once this has been done, any two points, A and B, should be selected on the estimated regression line (see Figure 13–5). The increment in the damage from A to B and the change in the inventory from A to B should be expressed as a percentage:

$$(\triangle D / \triangle I) \times 100\% = \frac{\$10,000}{\$2,000,000} \times 100\% = 0.5\%$$

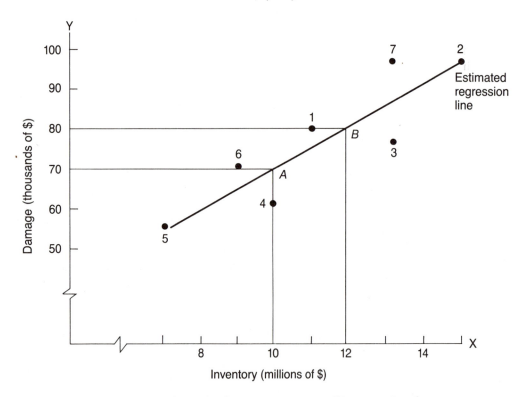

Figure 13-5   Graphing the Relationship between Damage and Inventory Levels

SOURCE: Douglas M. Lambert and James R. Stock, *Strategic Physical Distribution Management* (Homewood, Ill.: Richard D. Irwin, Inc., 1982), p. 248.

The 0.5 percent can be interpreted as the percentage of the inventory investment that is damaged because product is being held in inventory. This percentage can be added to the other cost components to determine the total carrying cost percentage. It should be noted that if damage does in fact increase with increased levels of inventory, then the estimated regression line must move upward to the right. A line that is vertical, horizontal, or sloping upward to the left would indicate that such a relationship does not exist.

The ability to fit a line through the plotted points successfully will depend upon the strength of the relationship present—the degree of correlation. Figure 13–6 depicts three possibilities:

1. *No correlation.* Points are scattered, indicating that no relationship exists.

2. *Moderate correlation.* Points are all situated relatively close to the estimated regression line, indicating a moderate relationship.

3. *Perfect correlation.* All of the points fall on the line. This would be a correlation of 1.0. The closer the correlation is to 1.0, the stronger the relationship.

SHRINKAGE

In the opinion of many authorities, inventory theft is a more serious problem than cash embezzlement. It is far more common, involves far more employees, and is difficult to control. However, this cost may be more closely related to company security measures than to inventory levels, even though it will definitely vary with the number of warehouse locations. Consequently, in many companies it may be appropriate to assign some or all of the shrinkage costs to the warehousing cost category.

RELOCATION

Relocation costs are incurred when inventory is trans-shipped from one warehouse location to another to avoid obsolescence. For example, products that are selling well in the Midwest may not be selling on the West Coast. By shipping the products to the location where they will sell, the company avoids the obsolescence cost but incurs additional

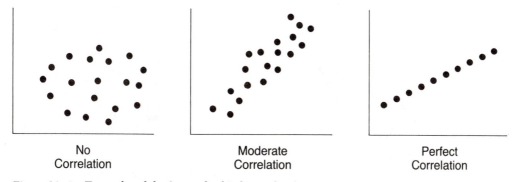

| No Correlation | Moderate Correlation | Perfect Correlation |

Figure 13–6   Examples of the Strength of Relationship between Two Variables

SOURCE: Douglas M. Lambert and James R. Stock, *Strategic Physical Distribution Management* (Homewood, Ill.: Richard D. Irwin, Inc., 1982), p. 249.

transportation costs. Often, these costs are not reported separately, but are simply included in transportation costs. In such cases, a managerial estimate or a statistical audit of freight bills can be used to isolate the trans-shipment costs. The frequency of these shipments will determine which approach is most practical in any given situation. That is, if such shipments are rare, the percentage component of the carrying cost will be very small and a managerial estimate should suffice.

In some cases, trans-shipment costs may be incurred as a result of inventory stocking policies. For example, if inventories are set too low in field locations, stockouts may occur and may be rectified by shipping products from the nearest warehouse that has the items in stock. Consequently, the costs are a result of decisions that involve trade-offs between or among transportation costs, warehousing costs, inventory carrying costs, and/or stockout costs. These are transportation costs and should not be classified as inventory carrying costs.

Summary

The methodology that should be used to calculate inventory carrying costs is summarized in Figure 13–7. The model shown there is referred to as "normative" because its use will result in a carrying cost figure that accurately reflects a firm's costs.

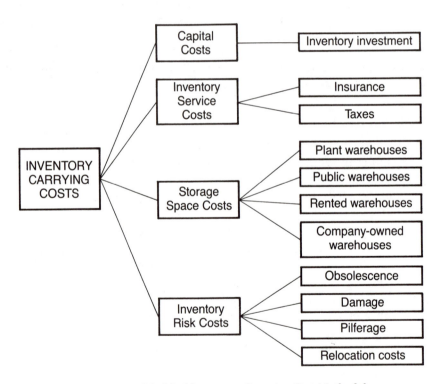

Figure 13-7   Normative Model of Inventory Carrying Cost Methodology

SOURCE: Douglas M. Lambert, *The Development of an Inventory Costing Methodology: A Study of the Costs Associated with Holding Inventory* (Chicago: NCPDM, 1976), p. 68. Copyright © 1975 by Douglas M. Lambert.

Controlling Physical Distribution Activities

One of the major reasons for improving the availability of distribution cost data is to control and monitor physical distribution performance. Without accurate cost data, performance analysis is next to impossible. How, for example, can a firm expect to control the cost of shipping a product to a customer if it does not know what the cost should be? How can management determine if distribution center costs are high or low in the absence of performance measurements? Are inventory levels satisfactory, too high or, too low? The list is not all-inclusive, but it serves to illustrate the need for accurate cost data.

The importance of a good measurement program for the management and control of distribution performance was addressed by the NCPDM in a 1978 study:

> If no measurement program exists, the "natural" forces shaping the behavior of busy managers tend to place the emphasis on the negative. Issues only attract management attention when something is "wrong." In this type of situation, there is often little reinforcement of positive results. A *formal* measurement program helps improve employee morale. . . . Once a plan has been established, actual results can be measured and compared with the plan to identify variances requiring management attention. . . .[15]

The challenge is not so much to create new data, since much of it already exists in one form or another, but to tailor the existing data in the accounting system to meet the needs of the physical distribution function.* By improving the availability of physical distribution cost data, management will be in a better position to make both operational and strategic decisions. It stands to reason that abnormal levels of costs can be detected and controlled only if normal cost ranges have been determined for various levels of activity. As shown in Figure 13–8, physical distribution performance can be monitored by using standard costs, budgets, and productivity standards.

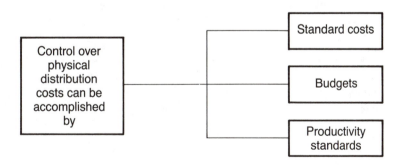

---

*A system for recording accounting data in the necessary format is discussed in this chapter on pp. 311–315.

Standard Costs and Flexible Budgets †

Control of costs through predetermined standards and flexible budgets is the most comprehensive type of control system available. The use of standard costs represents a frontal assault on the physical distribution costing problem because it attempts to determine what the costs *should* be rather than basing future cost predictions on past cost behavior. Nevertheless, the use of standards has not been widespread. In part, this is due to the belief that physical distribution costs are, by nature, quite different from those in other areas of the business. While there may be some merit to this argument, physical distribution activities are, by nature, repetitive operations, and such operations lend themselves to control by standards. A more compelling reason why standard costs have not achieved widespread acceptance is that few attempts have been made to install such systems. In fact, it is only recently that the importance of physical distribution cost control has been recognized. The lack of standard costs for physical distribution is unfortunate because management accountants and industrial engineers of most firms have developed a wealth of experience in installing standard costs in the production area, which, with some effort, could be expanded into physical distribution. However, developing standards for physical distribution may be more complex because the output measures are often more diverse than they are in the case of production. For example, in developing a standard for the picking function, it is possible that the eventual control measure could be stated as a standard cost per order, a standard cost per order line, a standard cost per unit shipped, or a standard cost per shipment. Despite these complexities, work measurement does appear to be increasing in physical distribution activities.

The use of standards as a management control system is illustrated in Figure 13–9, which shows how standards may result from formal investigation, from philosophy or intuition, or from both. The following explains the various steps in the system.[16]

> Once standards have been set the firm must compare actual performance with the particular standard to see if it is acceptable. If performance is acceptable the system is deemed to be under control and that is the end of the control process. Inherent in this notion is that management operates under the principle of exception, exerting no changes in the system so long as it operates satisfactorily; and the measure of "satisfactory" is found in the standard.
>
> It is highly unlikely that performance will exactly equal standard. Where there is a departure, the procedure is to break the variance down into its component parts to try to ascertain its sources. For example, the standard may be a budgeted amount for transportation in a territory. If the actual exceeds the budget, management would like to see the variance analyzed into separate measures of volume and efficiency. It is impossible to know how to proceed unless the variance is analyzed into meaningful sources.
>
> The next question is whether the observed variance is great enough to be deemed significant. It is possible to handle such a question in strictly statistical terms, setting quality control limits about the standard. This may be done in terms of standard deviations and an acceptable limit established on the down side only or the limit may be on either side of the standard. Thus, in the latter case, if performance exceeds standard, man-

---

†The following sections on standard costs, budgets and productivity standards are adapted from Douglas M. Lambert and Howard M. Armitage, "Managing Distribution Costs for Better Profit Performance," *Business* (September–October 1980), pp. 50–51.

THE CONTROL SYSTEM

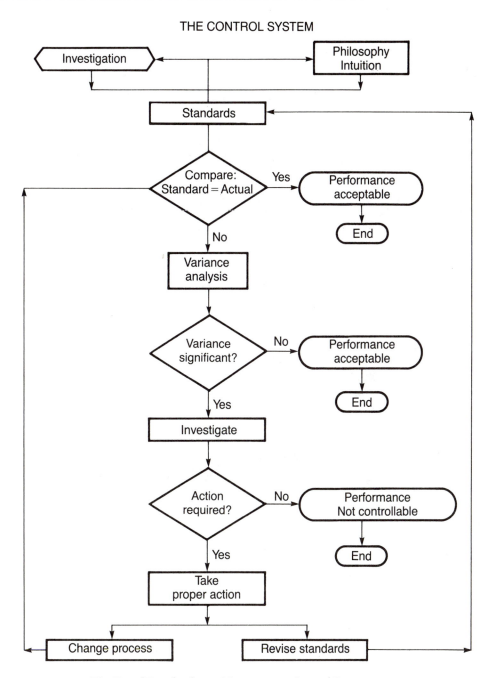

Figure 13-9   The Use of Standards as a Management Control System

Source: Richard J. Lewis and Leo G. Erickson, "Distribution System Costing: An Overview," in John R. Grabner and William S. Sargent, Eds., *Distribution System Costing: Concepts and Procedures* (Columbus, Ohio: Transportation and Logistics Research Foundation, 1972), p. 17A.

agement may decide to raise the standard or reward the performer accordingly. Probably of greater concern are those departures in which performance is below standard.

Much of physical distribution lends itself to measures of statistical significance in departures from standard. However, as with demand obtaining activities, it is probably more meaningful to judge departures from standards in terms of their *practical* significance. A form of sensitivity analysis goes on here in which the question is raised of how critical is the departure in its effects on bottom line performance, net profit.

Regardless of how the assessment is made, the variance will be termed either significant or not significant. If it is not significant, performance is judged acceptable and the control process is ended. If significant, the next question is whether action is required.

The variance may be significant but, in analyzing it and explaining it, the departure from standard is not judged controllable. If so, no action may be indicated and the control process terminated. If action is indicated, it will be one of two broad kinds. Either the standard is held to be wrong and must be changed, or the process itself is not producing the results it should and thus must be changed. The feedbacks go up to the appropriate levels. If the process is changed and the standard is held, comparisons are again made. If the standard is changed and the process remains unchanged, the feedback is to the standard. It is possible they both would be changed. Thus, both feedbacks may result from the action phase and the system cycles through again.

A standard tells management the expected cost of performing selected activities and allows comparisons to be made to determine whether operating inefficiencies have occurred. For example, Table 13–2 shows a sample report that can be useful at the operating level. It shows why warehouse labor for the picking activity was $320 over budget for a one-week period. Actual costs of physical distribution activities can be aggregated by department, division, function, or total, and then compared to their standard. The results can be included as part of a regular weekly or monthly performance report. One such level of aggregation which would be of interest to a company president is shown in Table 13–3. This report allows the president to see why targeted net income has not been reached. On the one hand, there is a $3 million difference due to ineffectiveness, which simply indicates the net income that the company has foregone because of its inability to meet its budgeted level of sales. On the other hand, there is also an inefficiency factor of $1.4 million. This factor indicates that at the level of sales actually achieved, the segment controllable margin should have been $18 million. The difference between $18 million

Table 13–2   Summary of Warehouse Picking Operation—Week of _____

Items picked during week	14,500
Hours accumulated on picking activities	330
Standard hours allowed for picks performed (based on 50 items per hour)	290
Difference between hours allowed and hours accumulated	(40)
Standard cost per labor hour	$8.00
Variation in cost due to inefficiency	$320.00

*The cost was $320.00 over budget because of 40 picking hours in excess of the standard number of hours allowed for efficient operation.

SOURCE: Douglas M. Lambert and James R. Stock, *Strategic Physical Distribution Management* (Homewood, Ill.: Richard D. Irwin, Inc., 1982), p. 381.

Table 13-3 Segmental Analysis Using a Contribution Approach Explanation of Variation from Budget*

	Budget	Variance Due To Ineffectiveness	Standard Allowed for Output Level Achieved	Variance Due to Inefficiency	Actual Results
			(in thousands)		
Net sales	$90,000	$10,000	$80,000	—	$80,000
Cost of goods sold (Variable Manufacturing Cost)	40,500	4,500	36,000	—	36,000
Manufacturing Contribution	$49,500	$5,500	$44,000	—	$44,000
Variable marketing and physical distribution costs† (out-of-pocket costs that vary directly with sales to the segment)	$22,500	2,500	20,000	$1,400	21,400
Segment contribution margin	$27,000	$3,000	$24,000	$1,400	$22,600
Assignable nonvariable costs‡ (costs incurred specifically for the segment during the period)	6,000	—	6,000	—	6,000
Segment controllable margin	$21,000	$3,000	$18,000	$1,400	$16,600

Difference in income = $21,000 − 16,600 = $4,400

Explained by:
a. Ineffectiveness—inability to reach target sales objective $3,000
b. Inefficiency at operating level achieved at $80,000 1,400
$4,400

ASSUMPTION: Actual sales revenue decreased as result of lower volume. The average price paid per unit sold remained the same. (If the average price per unit changes then an additional variance—the marketing variance—can be computed.)

---

*Segments could be products, customers, geographic areas, or divisions.

†Costs might include sales commissions, transportation costs, warehouse handling costs, order-processing costs, and inventory carrying costs.

‡Costs might include salaries, segment-related advertising, and bad debts. The fixed costs associated with corporate owned and operated facilities would be included if, and only if, the warehouse was solely for this segment of the business.

SOURCE: Douglas M. Lambert and James R. Stock, *Strategic Physical Distribution Management* (Homewood, Ill.: Richard D. Irwin, Inc., 1982). p. 381.

and the actual outcome of $16.6 million is the variation due to inefficiencies within the marketing and physical distribution functions.

Standard Costs and Flexible Budgets for Warehousing*

The first step in the development of standard costs and flexible budgets is to define operating characteristics and the possible units of measure such as: order, case, shipment, stock-keeping unit, line item, arrival, and/or overpacked carton. In this example, the basic operating elements consist of receiving (unloading and clerical), shipping (clerical and order consolidation), stock put away, stock replenishment, order picking, and overpacking. A description of the process is shown in Figure 13–10.

Next, a 45-day sample was obtained and data were accumulated for the various important functions of the operation. The results of the sample are shown in Table 13–4. Also included are the average number of occurrences observed and the standard deviation (SD), which is measure of central tendency or variation around the average. The larger the standard deviation, the more variation there is in day-to-day activity. Because receiving activities tend to fluctuate more than the shipping activities, the receiving function has higher standard deviations than the shipping function.

Now that the process has been described, and its operating characteristics and activity levels are known, the next step is to develop activity standards. These have been developed using empirical standards. They could have been developed based upon industry standards, engineering studies, or historical data, but the empirical method of observing the operation and using judgment to develop estimates is thought to be the most appropriate in the example being described (see Table 13–5). With the daily activities, the approxi-

Table 13–4   Activity Levels (45-Day Sample)

Function	Unit of Measure	Average (Per Day)	Standard Deviation (Per Day)
Receiving Functions			
Arrivals	Arrivals	18	14
Unloaded	Pieces	735	731
Stock put away	Pieces	735	731
Replenishment Functions			
Volume	SKUs	200	0
Shipping Functions			
Order picking	Line items	279	72
Overpacking	Pieces	85	37
Orders	Orders	113	31
Freight shipments	Bill of lading	61	41
Small shipments	Pieces	83	24
Load	Pieces	863	198

SOURCE: Howard M. Armitage and James F. Dickow, "Controlling Distribution with Standard Cost and Flexible Budgets," *1979 Annual Conference Proceedings* of the National Council of Physical Distribution Management (Chicago: NCPDM, 1979), p. 117. Reprinted by permission.

*This material is adapted from Howard M. Armitage and James F. Dickow, "Controlling Distribution with Standard Costs and Flexible Budgets," *1979 Annual Conference Proceedings* of the National Council of Physical Distribution Management (Chicago, Ill.: NCPDM, 1979), pp. 116–120. Adapted by permission.

OPERATING CHARACTERISTICS

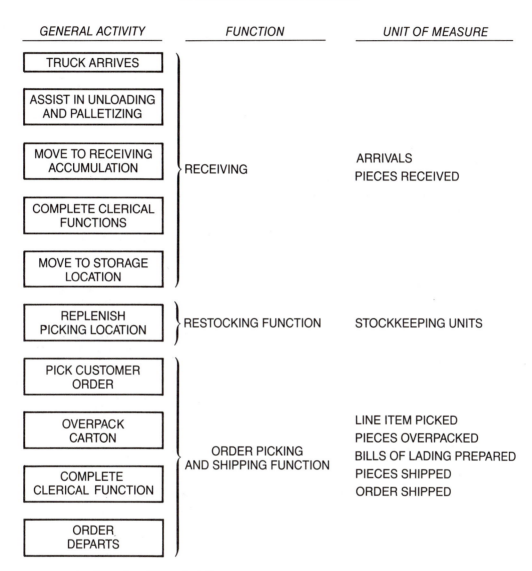

GENERAL ACTIVITY	FUNCTION	UNIT OF MEASURE

TRUCK ARRIVES

ASSIST IN UNLOADING AND PALLETIZING

MOVE TO RECEIVING ACCUMULATION — RECEIVING — ARRIVALS / PIECES RECEIVED

COMPLETE CLERICAL FUNCTIONS

MOVE TO STORAGE LOCATION

REPLENISH PICKING LOCATION — RESTOCKING FUNCTION — STOCKKEEPING UNITS

PICK CUSTOMER ORDER

OVERPACK CARTON — ORDER PICKING AND SHIPPING FUNCTION — LINE ITEM PICKED / PIECES OVERPACKED / BILLS OF LADING PREPARED / PIECES SHIPPED / ORDER SHIPPED

COMPLETE CLERICAL FUNCTION

ORDER DEPARTS

Figure 13-10   Operating Characteristics

From Howard M. Armitage and James F. Dickow, "Controlling Distribution with Standard Cost and Flexible Budgets," *1979 Annual Conference Proceedings* of the National Council of Physical Distribution Management (NCPDM, 1979), p. 117. Reproduced by permission.

mate levels of activity, and knowledge of the process determined, this information is used to develop standard costs.

The information in Table 13–6, which includes the standard times and hourly wage rates, allows an incremental cost per unit of measure to be calculated. The unit of measure for each one of the activities might be different—and in this case they are different, that is, piece, SKU, line item, and freight shipment. In some cases it is possible to lump

Table 13–5   Activity Standards Developed Empirically

Operating Function	Unit of Measure	Time Standard
Warehouse Receiving		
Unload truck	Pieces/man-hour	250
Check receipts	Pieces/man-hour	167
Clerical function	Pieces/man-hour	500
Putaway stock	Pieces/man-hour	150
Warehouse Shipping		
Order picking	Line items/man-hour	30
Order packing	Pieces/man-hour	22.7
UPS/small shipment	Pieces/man-hour	100
Freight shipping	Bills of lading/man-hour	15
Warehouse Stockkeeping		
Bulk items	Skill/man-hour	70
QA and shelf items	Skill/man-hour	50

SOURCE: Howard M. Armitage and James F. Dickow, "Controlling Distribution with Standard Cost and Flexible Budgets," *1979 Annual Conference Proceedings* of the National Council of Physicai Distribution Management (Chicago: NCPDM, 1979), p. 118. Reprinted by permission.

activities together as they are in the receiving function, but this is not possible in every situation. The standard cost per unit of measure is obtained by dividing the labor costs per manhour by the estimated standard time.

If this warehousing operation were using flexible budgeting, the standard costs would be used to develop the flexible budget. An example is contained in Table 13–7. In this week 4200 cases were received, 1000 stockkeeping units were replenished, and so on. These activity levels, when multiplied by the standard costs per unit, gave the total standard costs for each activity. The actual costs incurred during the week also are shown, and variances—favorable or unfavorable—are calculated. For the activity levels achieved

Table 13–6   Standard Costs

Function	Unit of Meas.: u/m	Daily Activity	Time Standard (u/m per Min.)	Hourly Rate ($ per Min.)	Standard Cost (¢ per u/m)
Receiving					
Unload truck	Pieces	735	250	7.50	3.0
Check receipts	Pieces	735	167	7.50	4.5
Clerical	Pieces	735	500	7.50	1.5
Putaway stock	Pieces	735	150	7.50	5.0
					14.0
Replenishment					
Replenish	SKUs	200	50	7.50	5.0
Shipping					
Order picking	Line item	279	30	8.00	27.0
Overpacking	Pieces	86	23	7.50	33.0
Small shipping	Pieces	83	100	8.00	8.0
Freight shipping	Shipments	61	15	8.25	55.0

SOURCE: Howard M. Armitage and James F. Dickow, "Controlling Distribution with Standard Cost and Flexible Budgets," *1979 Annual Conference Proceedings* of the National Council of Physical Distribution Management (Chicago: NCPDM, 1979), p. 119. Reprinted by permission.

Table 13–7 Application to a Flexible Budget

Function	Unit of Meas.: u/m	Standard Cost ($ per u/m)	Weekly Summary			
			Activity (u/m)	Std. Cost ($)	Actual Cost ($)	Variance ($)
Receiving	Piece	0.14	4200	588	800	212 U
Replenishment	SKU	0.15	1000	150	100	50 F
Shipping						
Order picking	Line item	0.27	1430	386	450	64 U
Order packing	Piece	0.33	350	116	100	16 F
Small shipping	Piece	0.03	500	40	25	15 F
Freight shipping	Shipments	0.55	400	220	150	70 F
				1500	1625	125 U

*U, F stand for units of measure.

Source: Howard M. Armitage and James F. Dickow, "Controlling Distribution with Standard Cost and Flexible Budgets," *1979 Annual Conference Proceedings* of the National Council of Physical Distribution Management (Chicago: NCPDM, 1979), p. 120. Reprinted by permission.

during the week, a net unfavorable variance of $125 was calculated. Since this activity level was significantly higher than the average level of activity, the unfavorable variance would have been larger had a fixed budget approach been used. Developing standard costs and using them to develop a flexible budget gives management a tool to *measure* the *performance* of individuals. The minimization of unfavorable variances is a goal that, when achieved, will yield increased profits.

Budgets

Conceptually, there is little doubt regarding the general superiority of standard costs for control. However, there will be times when the use of standards is inappropriate. This is particularly true in situations that involve essentially nonrepetitive tasks and for which work unit measurements are difficult to establish. In these situations, control still can be achieved through budgetary practices. However, the extent to which the budget is successful depends on whether individual cost behavior patterns can be predicted and whether the budget can be "flexed" to reflect changes in operating conditions.

Most physical distribution budgets are static. That is, they are plans developed for a budgeted level of output. If actual activity happens to be the same as the budgeted level, a realistic comparison of costs can be made and control will be effective. However, this is seldom the case. Seasonality and internal factors invariably will lead to different levels of activity, the efficiency of which can be determined only if the reporting system can compare the actual costs with what they should have been at the operating level actually achieved. In a warehousing example, for instance, the estimated or budgeted level of activity may be 1000 line items per week. The actual level of activity, however, may be only 750.

Comparing the budgeted costs at 1000 line items against the actual costs at 750 leads to the erroneous conclusion that the operation has been efficient since items such as overtime, temporary help, packing, postage and order processing are less than the budgeted figures. A flexible budget, on the other hand, indicates what the costs should have been at the 750 line items level of activity and a true dollar measure of efficiency results.

The key to successful implementation of a flexible budget lies in the analysis of cost behavior patterns. To date, little of this analysis has been carried out in the physical distribution function. The expertise of the management accountant and industrial engineer can be invaluable in applying tools such as scatter diagram techniques and regression analysis to determine the fixed and variable components of costs. These techniques utilize previous cost data to determine a variable rate per unit of activity and a total fixed cost component. However, unlike engineered standards, the techniques are based on past cost behavior patterns which undoubtedly contain inefficiencies. The predicted measure of cost, therefore, may not be a measure of what the activity should cost but an estimate of what it will cost based on the results of previous periods. Once fixed and variable costs have been determined, flexible budget for control becomes a reality.

Productivity Ratios

Physical distribution costs also can be controlled by the use of productivity ratios. These ratios take the form of:

$$\text{Productivity} = \frac{\text{Measure of output}}{\text{Measure of input}}$$

For example, a warehouse operation might make use of such productivity ratios as:

$$\frac{\text{Number of orders shipped this period}}{\text{Number of orders received this period}}$$

$$\frac{\text{Number of orders shipped this period}}{\text{Average number of orders shipped per period}}$$

$$\frac{\text{Number of orders shipped this period}}{\text{Number of direct labor hours worked this period}}$$

Productivity ratios for transportation might include:

$$\frac{\text{Ton-miles transported}}{\text{Total actual transportation cost}}$$

$$\frac{\text{Stops served}}{\text{Total actual transportation cost}}$$

$$\frac{\text{Shipments transportated to destination}}{\text{Total actual transportation cost}}$$

The transportation resource inputs for which productivity ratios can be generated include: labor, equipment, energy, and cost. The specific relationships between these inputs and transportation activities are illustrated in Table 13–8. An "X" in a cell of the matrix denotes an activity/input combination which could be measured. Similar activity/input matrices are shown for warehousing (Table 13–9); purchasing, inventory management, and production management (Table 13–10); and customer service (Table 13–11).

Productivity measures of this type can and have been developed for most physical distribution activities. They are particularly useful in the absence of a standard costing system with flexible budgeting since they do provide some guidelines on operating efficiencies. Furthermore, they are measures that are easily understood by management and employees. However, productivity measures are not without their shortcomings:

1. Productivity measures are expressed in terms of physical units; therefore, actual dollar losses due to inefficiencies, and predictions of future physical distribution costs cannot be made. This makes it extremely difficult to cost-justify any system changes that will result in improved productivity.

2. The actual productivity measure calculated is seldom compared to a productivity standard. For example, a productivity measure may compare the number of orders shipped during a period to the number of direct labor hours worked during that period but it does not indicate what the relationship ought to be. Without work measurement or some form of cost estimation it is impossible to know what the productivity standard should be at efficient operations.

3. Finally, changes in output levels may in some cases distort measures of productivity. Distortion occurs because the fixed and variable elements are seldom delineated. Con-

Table 13–8   Transportation Activity/Input Matrix

Activities	Labor	Facilities	Equipment	Energy	Financial Investment	Overall (cost)
Company-Operated						
Over-the-Road Trucking						
Loading	X					X
Line-haul	X			X		X
Unloading	X					X
Overall	X		X	X		X
Company-Operated						
Pickup/Delivery Trucking						
Pre-trip	X					X
Stem driving	X			X		X
On-route driving	X			X		X
At-stop	X					X
End-of-trip	X					X
Overall	X		X	X		X
Outside Transportation						
—All Modes						
Loading						X
Line-haul						X
Unloading						X
Transportation/Traffic						
Management						
Company-Operated						X
Outside transportation						X

SOURCE: Reprinted from the research report, *Measuring Productivity in Distribution*, National Council of Physical Distribution Management, Chicago, 1978, p. 51.

Table 13–9   Warehouse Activity/Input Matrix

Activities	Labor	Facilities	Equipment	Energy	Financial	Overall
Company-Operated Warehousing						
Receiving	X	X	X			X
Put-away	X		X			X
Storage		X		X		X
Replenishment	X		X			X
Order selection	X		X			X
Checking	X		X			X
Packing and marking	X	X	X			X
Staging and order consolidation	X	X	X			X
Shipping	X	X	X			X
Clerical and administration	X		X			X
Overall	X	X	X	X	X	X
Purchased-Outside Warehousing						
Storage						X
Handling						X
Consolidation						X
Administration						X
Overall						X

Source: Reprinted from the research report, *Measuring Productivity in Distribution*, National Council of Physical Distribution Management, Chicago, 1978, p. 101.

Table 13–10   Purchasing, Inventory Management, and Production Management Activity/Input Matrix

Functions/Activities	Inputs			
	Labor	*Equipment*	*Financial*	*Overall*
Purchasing				
Sourcing	X			X
Procurement	X	X		X
Cost control	X			X
Overall				X
Inventory Management				
Forecasting	X	X		X
Planning & budgeting	X	X		X
Execution & control	X	X		X
Overall			X	X
Production Management				
Production planning	X			X
Production control	X			X
Scheduling & dispatching	X	X		X
Shop floor data collection	X	X		X
Overall				X

SOURCE: Reprinted from the research report, *Measuring Productivity in Distribution*, National Council of Physical Distribution Management, Chicago, 1978, p. 152.

sequently, the productivity measure computes utilization, not efficiency. For example, if 100 orders shipped represents full labor utilization and 100 orders were received this period, then productivity as measured by

$$\frac{\text{Number of orders shipped this period}}{\text{Number of orders received this period}} \times 100\,\%$$

is 100 percent. However, if 150 orders had been received, and 100 orders shipped, productivity would have been 66.67 percent, even though there was no real drop in either efficiency or productivity.

Performance Measurement

For performance measurement systems to be truly effective the data must be captured on formal reports. Reporting practices for transportation and warehousing will be covered in this subsection.

Transportation Performance Measurement

Successful administration of the traffic function requires that day-to-day performance of for-hire carriers and private carriage be measured and controlled. Operating standards in terms of speed of service, size of order shipped, on-time delivery, transit time variability, and damage must be established and individual carrier performance must be measured. In cases where performance standards are not being met, corrective action must be taken.

Table 13–11 Customer Service (Order Processing/Customer Communication) Activity/Input Matrix

Activity	Labor	Facilities/ Equipment	Working Capital	Overall
Order Processing				
Order entry/editing	X	X	X	X
Scheduling	X			X
Order/shipping set preparation	X	X		X
Invoicing	X	X		X
Customer Communication				
Order modification	X	X		X
Order status inquiries	X	X		X
Tracing and expediting	X	X		X
Error correction	X			X
Product information requests	X			X
Credit and Collection				
Credit checking	X	X		X
Accounts receivable processing & collecting	X	X	X	X

SOURCE: Reprinted from the research report, *Measuring Productivity in Distribution*, National Council of Physical Distribution Management, Chicago, 1978, p. 191.

In a survey of members of the National Council of Physical Distribution Management, Lambert and Stock asked senior physical distribution executives to report on mode usage by their firms and how carrier performance was measured. The largest single group of firms were in the packaged goods industry. Ninety-three percent of the firms used common or contract motor carriage. The next most commonly used modes were United Parcel Service or Parcel Post (69 percent), common carrier rail (67 percent) and private carrier (63 percent).

The criteria that were used to measure transportation performance are summarized in Table 13–12, along with data that appeared on a formal report. By comparing the two columns in Table 13–12, it becomes apparent that most carrier performance measurement is accomplished on an informal basis and not by using data that appear on formal reports.

Warehousing Performance Measurement

It is important, irrespective of the method used, that some measures of warehousing performance be determined by a firm. In the same survey mentioned above, senior physical distribution executives were asked to report the data that were used by their firms to evaluate warehousing performance, and the performance data that appeared on a formal report. The results of the survey are summarized in Table 13–13. Although total costs were the most often-mentioned method of evaluating both public and private warehousing and were considered to be the most useful performance measure, only 33 percent of the firms reported having such data on a formal report for judging public warehouses. The corresponding figure for private warehouses was 45 percent. Similar discrepancies between data used and the data appearing on a formal report were found to varying degrees for all of the measures of performance used. This would support the conclusion that performance evaluation of warehousing takes place primarily on an informal basis.

Table 13–12   Data Used to Evaluate Transportation Performance—Percentage Response
($n = 363$)

Data	Presently Using	Data Appearing on a Formal Report
Common Contract Carriers:		
Damage/claims	65.0	43.0
Transit time	59.8	30.9
Customer complaints	59.5	27.8
Shipment tracing	60.1	28.1
On-time delivery performance	55.6	29.5
Shipment expediting	50.7	19.0
Billing accuracy	48.8	25.1
Equipment availability	46.0	19.6
On-time pickup performance	44.6	19.3
Data from freight payment system	47.4	33.6
Equipment condition	37.5	13.5
Assigned rail cars	26.2	17.1
Sanitation	23.7	8.8
Post card survey of customers	22.6	14.6
Cost per ton mile	19.8	11.8
Form letter to customers regarding performance	11.3	7.2
Private Carriers:		
Utilization	38.6	25.1
On-time delivery performance	33.6	18.2
Transit time	34.7	19.3
Damage	33.6	19.6
Customer complaints	30.6	15.4
Cost per ton mile	30.9	21.2
On-time pickup performance	25.1	13.5

SOURCE: Douglas M. Lambert and James R. Stock, *Strategic Physical Distribution Management* (Homewood, Ill.: Richard D. Irwin, Inc., 1982), pp. 168 and 170.

The multitude of warehouse performance measures used by various firms suggests that performance data are available. However, it is not sufficient simply to identify problem areas—appropriate action must be taken by the firm to improve poor performance whenever possible. A company should develop decision strategies to handle problem areas *before* the problems develop. This is the essence of contingency planning.

There is no single best approach. Management action is determined by combinations of many factors, including customer service levels, competition, and product mix. There is, however, universal acceptance of the principle that problems should be pinpointed and corrective actions taken to improve warehouse performance.

A Distribution Data Base for Decision Making

One of the most promising data-base systems for generating distribution cost information and profit contribution performance reports is the modular data base concept (see Figure 13–11).[18] This is a central storage system where source documents such as invoices, transportation bills, and other expenses and revenue items are fed into a data base in coded form.

Table 13–13   Data Used to Evaluate Warehousing Performance—Percentage Response ($n = 363$)

Data	Presently Using	Data Appearing on a Formal Report
Public Warehouses		
Total cost	48.5	33.1
Handling costs/unit	44.6	30.6
Storage costs/unit	43.5	28.9
Accuracy and promptness of inventory reports	39.9	23.7
Annual warehouse inspection	40.2	23.4
Damage/claims	38.0	20.4
On-site audits	36.9	18.7
Sanitation/housekeeping	36.6	17.6
Warehouse operations performance	36.4	20.9
Customer complaints	33.3	14.6
Billing accuracy	31.1	14.6
Consolidation of outbound freight	30.9	15.2
Salesmen's comments	27.5	8.9
Safety & environmental factors	24.5	13.2
Cost measured against standard	22.3	16.5
Company-Owned (Leased) Distribution Centers		
Total cost	60.1	44.7
In-stock availability	52.1	36.9
Inventory turns	50.1	35.8
Damage/claims	39.7	24.2
Order cycle availability	38.6	27.3
Cost by product	28.4	21.5

SOURCE: Douglas M. Lambert and James R. Stock, *Strategic Physical Distribution Management* (Homewood, Ill.: Richard D. Irwin, Inc., 1982), pp. 218 and 220.

Inputs are coded at the lowest possible level of aggregation according to function, subfunction, territory, product, salesperson, channel of distribution, revenue, or expense, to name just a few categories. For example, the following information may be recorded by customer order:

Customer number	Territory
Customer name	Region
Order number	Partial shipment backorder number
Previous order number	Credit limit
Customer order number	Credit outstanding
Customer billing address	Prepaid/collect freight
Customer shipping address	Terms
Customer order date	Instruction, shipping, product substitution
Requested shipping date	Quantity, product number, price
Ship date	Packing and shipping instructions
Date, time, and operator	Carrier
Priority code	Bill of lading number
Salesperson number	

The system is capable of filing large amounts of data and allows rapid aggregation and retrieval of various modules of information for decision making or external reporting. When combined with standard costs, the modular data base is capable of generating both cost reports for functions such as warehousing and transportation, and segment contribution reports. The system works by charging functions, such as warehousing and transportation, with actual costs which are then compared to predetermined standards. Individual segments such as customers or products are credited with segment revenues and charged the standard cost plus controllable variances.

A channels of distribution example will illustrate this approach.* In order to monitor the contribution from selling to department stores, grocery chains, drug stores, and discount stores, the accounting system must be able to provide revenue data by channel (which requires summing the revenues of all products sold per channel type) as well as the manufacturing, distribution, and marketing costs associated with the sales to each channel.

The first step is to determine the variable costs of goods manufactured. Firms using a direct costing system for internal reporting already have this information available. Firms that include all overhead costs (fixed and variable) as product costs must remove the fixed costs. The marketing and physical distribution costs associated with warehousing, transportation, order processing, inventory, accounts receivable, and sales commissions must

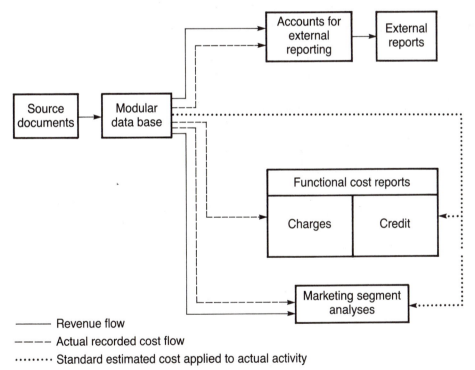

——— Revenue flow

————— Actual recorded cost flow

·········· Standard estimated cost applied to actual activity

Figure 13-11 A Modular Data Base System for Reporting Cost and Revenue Flows

Source: Frank H. Mossman, Paul M. Fischer, and W. J. E. Crissy, "New Approaches to Analyzing Marketing Profitability," *Journal of Marketing*, 38 (April 1974): p. 45. Reproduced by permission.

*Douglas M. Lambert and Howard M. Armitage, "An Information System for Effective Channel Management." Reprinted from *Business Topics* (Autumn 1979), pp. 13–22, by permission of the Graduate School of Business Administration, Michigan State University, East Lansing, Mich.

be attached to each channel of distribution. Finally assignable nonvariable costs such as sales promotion, advertising, and bad debts should be identified by the specific channel in which they were incurred. It should be emphasized that only those assignable nonvariable costs that would be incurred or eliminated by adding or dropping a channel should be included.

Referring to the example illustrated in Table 13–14, traditional accounting data might reveal that a profit of $2 million has been earned on sales of $43.5 million. Management knows that this profit is not adequate, but traditional accounting leaves few, if any, clues with regard to the specific problem. However, profitability analysis by type of account using a contribution approach will enable management to diagnose areas where performance is inadequate. In this example, sales to drugstores constituted the largest of the four channels used by the manufacturer, but the segment controllable margin-to-sales ratio there was the lowest. The segment controllable margin-to-sales ratio was almost one-half that of the third most profitable segment and less than one-half that of the cost profitable segment. Nevertheless, the segment controllable margin of $3.5 million is still substantial and it is doubtful that elimination of sales to drugstores would be a wise decision. A product–channel matrix might be generated to determine the impact of product mix on channel profitability. If this analysis showed that product mix was not the source of the problem, then a customer–channel matrix might reveal that small drugstore accounts are the least profitable, medium-sized drug accounts are moderately profitable, and drug chains have a segment controllable margin-to-sales ratio almost as large as that of department stores.

Using this information and cost trade-off analysis, management could determine potential channel profitability if small and medium drugstore accounts were served either by drug wholesalers or by strategically located field warehouses. The alternative that would lead to the greatest improvement in corporate profitability would be selected, resulting in the addition of a new channel of distribution. A framework for performing this analysis that incorporates marketing cost trade-offs is illustrated in Form 13–1.

Poor performance by a channel does not necessarily mean the channel should be eliminated. Factors such as the percentage of potential market being reached by the channel, the stage of the product life cycle of the products involved, and the stage in the life cycle of the institutions involved also deserve consideration. In addition, elimination of an unprofitable channel may not be the only viable solution for the firm striving to improve corporate profitability. Changing the logistical system or shifting some of the business to another channel, as in the previous example, may be the most desirable solution. Also, a customer–product contribution matrix may be used *within* a channel to isolate customers or products as candidates for elimination or revitalization.

In addition to being able to evaluate the profitability of individual customers, product lines, territories, and channels of distribution, the data-base system permits the user to simulate trade-off decisions and determine the effect of proposed system changes on total cost. The report generating capabilities of the modular data base are summarized in Figure 13–12. In order to implement the modular data-base approach, it is necessary to collect the raw distribution cost data and break them down into fixed variable and direct-indirect components. In other words, the data must be sufficiently refined to permit the formulation of meaningful modules. Full implementation of the integrated physical distribution management concept and knowledgeable decision making in the areas of strategic and operational planning require a sophisticated management information system.

Table 13–14 Profitability by Type of Account—A Contribution Approach (in Millions)

	Total Company	Type of Account			
		Department Stores	Grocery Chains	Drug Stores	Discount Stores
Sales	$43,500	$6,500	$11,000	$20,000	$6,000
Less discounts, returns and allowances	3,500	500	1,000	2,000	—
Net sales	40,000	6,000	10,000	18,000	6,000
Cost of goods sold*	20,000	3,000	5,000	9,000	3,000
Manufacturing contribution	20,000	3,000	5,000	9,000	3,000
Variable selling and distribution costs:					
Sales commissions	800	120	200	360	120
Transportation costs	2,000	250	150	1,500	100
Warehouse handling	300	50	—	250	—
Order-processing costs	400	60	25	280	35
Inventory carrying costs	1,000	100	75	695	130
Charge for investment in accounts receivable	500	20	50	415	15
Contribution margin	15,000	2,400	4,500	5,500	2,600
Assignable nonvariable costs (costs incurred specifically for the segment during the period)					
Sales promotion	1,000	100	300	200	400
Advertising	1,500	200	—	1,300	—
Bad debts	300	—	—	300	—
Display racks	200	—	—	200	—
Other	200	—	—	200	—
Segment controllable margin	12,000	2,100	4,200	3,500	2,200
Segment controllable margin-to-sales ratio	27.6%	32.3%	38.2%	17.5%	36.7%

*Variable manufacturing costs

NOTE: This approach could be modified to include a charge for the assets employed by each of the segments as well as a deduction for the change in market value of these assets. The result would be referred to as the net segment margin (residual income).

SOURCE: Douglas M. Lambert and Howard M. Armitage, "An Information System for Effective Channel Management." Reprinted from *Business Topics* (Autumn 1979), pp. 13–22, by permission of the Graduate School of Business Administration, Michigan State University, East Lansing, Mich.

Form 13–1   How Manufacturers Can Calculate the Impact of Using a Wholesaler

Costs Associated with Manufacturer Selling Direct To Retailers

Costs of Direct Selling versus Using an Intermediary		$_____
Additional Promotional Expenses Associated with Direct Sales		_____
Customer Service Costs		
Cost of sales lost at retail level due to stockouts resulting from long and/or erratic lead time	$_____	
Return foregone on capital invested in accounts receivable	_____	
Credit losses associated with accounts receivable	_____	_____
Order Filling Costs		
Cost of dealing with many customers	$_____	
Cost of filling small orders	_____	
Cost of filling frequent orders	_____	_____
Inventory Carrying Costs		
Return foregone on capital invested in inventory	$_____	
Insurance paid on inventory	_____	
Taxes paid on inventory	_____	
Storage costs	_____	
Cost of obsolescence	_____	
Cost of damaged product	_____	
Cost of pilferage	_____	
Trans-shipment costs	_____	_____
Warehousing Costs		
Return foregone on capital invested in field warehouses (if owned)	$_____	
Operating expenses associated with such warehouses	_____	_____
Transportation Costs		
Cost of processing shipping documents (for many LTL shipments)	$_____	
Cost of processing freight claims	_____	
Excessive freight costs (associated with LTL shipments)	_____	_____
General and Administrative		
Reduction in management costs associated with holding and supervising inventory		$_____
Annual Cost of Direct Selling Total		$_____
Less volume discounts to wholesaler		_____
Total Amount Saved by Using a Wholesaler		$_____

Adapted from Douglas M. Lambert and Bernard J. La Londe, "The Economics of Using A Frozen Food Distributor," *Frozen Food Factbook and Directory* (Hershey, Pa.: National Frozen Food Association, Inc., 1975), p. 60. Reprinted by permission.

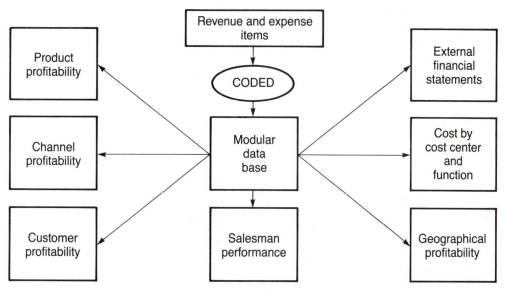

Figure 13-12   Report Generating Capabilities of the Modular Data Base

Source: Douglas M. Lambert and James R. Stock, *Strategic Physical Distribution Management* (Homewood, Ill.: Richard D. Irwin, Inc., 1982), p. 332.

Notes

1. Douglas M. Lambert and Howard M. Armitage, "Distribution Costs: The Challenge," *Management Accounting* (May 1979), p. 33.

2. For example, David Ray, "Distribution Costing and The Current State of the Art," *International Journal of Physical Distribution*, 6, No. 2 (1975), pp. 75–107 at p. 88; Michael Schiff, *Accounting and Control in Physical Distribution Management* (Chicago: NCPDM, 1971), pp. 4–21; R. E. Bream and R. Galer, *A National Survey of Physical Distribution Management*, (Whitehead and Partners, 1974); Douglas M. Lambert and John T. Mentzer, "Is Integrated Physical Distribution Management A Reality?", *Journal of Business Logistics*, 2, No. 1 (1980), pp. 18–34; and Douglas M. Lambert, *The Distribution Channels Decision* (New York: The National Association of Accountants, and Hamilton, Ontario: The Society of Management Accountants of Canada, 1978).

3. Wilbur S. Wayman, "Harnessing the Corporate Accounting System for Physical Distribution Cost Information," *Distribution System Costing: Concepts And Procedures*, Proceedings of the Fourth Annual James R. Riley Symposium on Business Logistics (Columbus, Ohio: Transportation and Logistics Research Foundation, 1972), p. 35.

4. Sam R. Goodman, *Financial Manager's Manual and Guide* (Englewood Cliffs, N.J.: Prentice-Hall, 1973), p. 219.

5. Charles T. Horngren, *Cost Accounting: A Managerial Emphasis*, 3d ed. (Englewood Cliffs, N.J.: Prentice-Hall, 1972), pp. 516–517.

6. James C. T. Mao, *Quantitative Analysis of Financial Decisions* (Toronto, Canada: Collier-Macmillan Canada, 1969), p. 373.

7. Mao, *Quantitative Analysis*, p. 373.

8. Goodman, *Financial Manager's Manual*, p. 220.

9. See Marvin Flaks, "Total Cost Approach To Physical Distribution," *Business Management*, **24** (August 1963), pp. 55–61; and Raymond LeKashman and John F. Stolle, "The Total Cost Approach to Distribution," *Business Horizons*, 8 (Winter, 1965), pp. 33–46.

10. Michael Schiff, *Accounting and Control in Physical Distribution Management* (Chicago: NCPDM, 1972), pp. 4–63 to 4–70.

11. American Institute of Certified Public Accountants, *Accounting Research Bulletin No. 43* (New York: AICPA, 1959), Statement 4.

12. Horngren, *Cost Accounting*, p. 558.

13. "Inventory Taxes," *Transportation & Distribution Management* (July/August 1975), pp. 31–36.

14. The interested reader may find the following sources informative: Morris Hamburg, *Statistical Analysis for Decision Making* (New York: Harcourt, Brace & World, 1970), pp. 459–507; William Mendenhall and Lyman Ott, *Understanding Statistics* (Belmont, Calif.: Duxbury Press, 1972), pp. 173–197; and John E. Freund and Frank J. Williams, *Elementary Business Statistics: The Modern Approach*, 2d ed. (Englewood Cliffs, N.J.: Prentice-Hall, 1972), pp. 344–376.

15. A. T. Kearney, *Measuring Productivity in Physical Distribution* (Chicago: NCPDM, 1978), pp. 18–19.

16. Richard J. Lewis and Leo G. Erickson, "Distribution System Costing: An Overview," in John R. Grabner and William S. Sargent, eds., *Distribution System Costing: Concepts and Procedures* (Columbus, Ohio: Transportation and Logistics Research Foundation, 1972), pp. 18–20.

17. A. T. Kearney, Inc., *Measuring Productivity in Physical Distribution* (Chicago: NCPDM, 1978), p. 76.

18. See Frank H. Mossman, Paul M. Fischer, and W. J. E. Crissy, "New Approaches to Analyzing Marketing Profitability," *Journal of Marketing*, 38 (April 1974), pp. 43–48.

CHAPTER 14

Management Guide to Productivity

John A. White, Jr.

Introduction

The decade of the 70s saw an increased awareness among U.S. business leaders of the need for productivity improvement. The term, productivity, became a part of their daily vocabulary—to be used and abused. Today the relationship between inflation and productivity is better understood; and America's productivity position relative to her international competitors' is a source of national concern.

As Figure 14–1 shows, for several years the U.S. rate of productivity increase has been lower than that of any other major industrial nation. If the situation is going to change, it will have to be done by management—by improving the productivity of their respective firms. For how they perform in productivity improvement determines how the nation performs.

What Is Productivity?

The simplest definition of productivity is the ratio of output to input. The output might be goods and/or services; the input might be labor, capital, technology, materials, and/or energy. An order-picking example of productivity is the number of cases picked per labor hour.

Reprinted with permission of Eaton Corporation, Industrial Truck Division, maker of Yale industrial lift trucks.

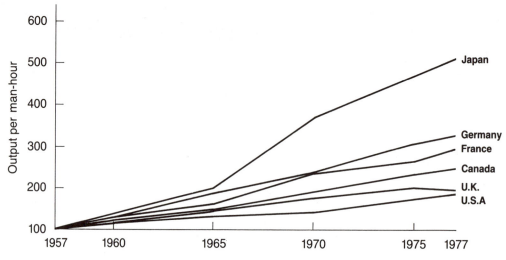

Figure 14-1   Increase in Output per Man-hour, 1957–1977

SOURCE: Bureau of Labor Statistics

On a national basis, productivity improvement is needed to prevent inflation. Without improvements in productivity to counteract increases in wages, costs, and prices, such increases lead to inflationary conditions. As William F. May, chairman of American Can Co. stated, "Productivity gains remain this nation's best defense against inflation."

To the individual businessman, improved productivity means increased profits. In addition to increased profits, productivity improvement means:

Using scarce resources wisely

Working smarter

Investing in labor saving technology

Doing the right things and doing them right

Improved management control

Increased operating efficiency

Caring about the performance of people

Management authority Peter Drucker states that "productivity is the first test of management." A study by the Hardware Institute for Research and Development concluded that "once you begin measuring productivity you begin improving it." In its special report on productivity, *Hardware Retailing* emphasized the need to "begin measuring productivity and let your employees know you are doing it. You will achieve some productivity gains by that simple action."

Measurement is a key ingredient toward productivity improvement. As Lord Kelvin put it, "When you can measure what you are speaking about, and express it in numbers, you know something about it; but when you cannot measure it, when you cannot express it in numbers, your knowledge is of a meager and unsatisfactory kind."

The National-American Wholesale Grocers Association (NAWGA) has developed a productivity program that measures 23 different productivity ratios for each department in a warehouse. As Gerald E. Peck of NAWGA observed, "Cost ratios tell us that we are in a position to compete today. Productivity ratios tell whether we will be in a position to compete tomorrow."

Productivity Programs

The fact that productivity tends to increase when management shows an interest in it is not surprising. The famous Hawthorne experiment performed at Western Electric established the relationship between productivity and management attention. However, if increased productivity levels are to be maintained, then more than management interest is required—a productivity program must be established.

One approach is the Productivity Improvement for Profit (PIP) program developed for the American Institute of Industrial Engineers by James M. Apple. The PIP program provides a structured approach for an organization by focusing on 12 major areas:

Receiving	Work standards
Stores	Plant layout
Product and processes	Production control
Material flow	Warehousing
Material handling	Shipping
Work methods	Maintenance

In 1978 the National Council of Physical Distribution Management published a report titled *Measuring Productivity in Physical Distribution*. The report presents the findings of a study on productivity performed by A. T. Kearney, Inc. It includes an extensive discussion of productivity measurement in warehousing.

How to Use the Productivity Measures

Productivity measures should be used as tracking signals to monitor the performances over time for an individual operating unit. To a limited extent, they can be used for comparative purposes—however, the comparisons must be valid.

Just as statistical quality control charts are used to track the quality performance of a manufacturing process, productivity charts should be used to track the productivity performance of individual operating units. Where standards exist *absolute* performance comparisons can be made; otherwise only *relative* comparisons can be made. Used consistently, periodically, and as yardsticks, productivity measures will enable you to gauge the movement of materials handling costs—to see if they are increasing or decreasing.

Depending upon the particular performance measure, daily, weekly, monthly, or quarterly observations should be made. Inefficiencies and/or declines in productivity generally do not suddenly occur. Rather, creeping inefficiencies or gradual deteriorations in productivity tend to be more common. Hence, it is essential that you periodically monitor the productivity pulse of your operation.

In subsequent sections a number of productivity ratios are presented. It should be noted that there are no "magic numbers" that can be applied to any of the ratios. The ratios provide a quantitative measurement of some aspect of productivity. In short, they can be used as controls to guide short- and long-range profit improvement.

In developing a productivity improvement program, *keep the systems approach in mind*. Since productivity measures tend to focus attention on an individual department or worker, there is a natural tendency to suboptimize. Suboptimization occurs when you optimize a component of the system, at the expense of the overall system. As an example, if one of our productivity measures is pallets delivered per operator then it could be maximized by providing only one operator and letting material pile up awaiting delivery.

To avoid suboptimization, a comprehensive productivity improvement program is needed. If the measurement program is comprehensive then the effect on the total system can be measured when a change is made in one part of the system.

In addition to the systems approach, it is also important "to do first things first." The 80–20 rule indicates that 80 percent of the productivity improvement will come from 20 percent of the operations. It is important to focus first on the right 20 percent of the operations.

Management Guide

This guide is organized into four parts.

In the first part you will learn: Why the effective management of people continues to be the key to productivity; when management action may be necessary to convert materials handling functions to the use of indirect labor, automated systems, modular work stations and other alternatives; how and when capital equipment acquisition allows for materials to be moved faster, more accurately and with less loss; how to achieve optimum space utilization; and how to control energy.

Part two is devoted to the management control of: materials—providing ratios on monitoring and controlling raw material, work-in-process, and finished goods; movement—assessing and controlling the manner in which materials are moved so that only the right amount of material arrives at the right place at the right time; and loss—accidents, damage and inventory shrinkage.

Part three focuses on operating efficiency in: receiving and shipping—where the greatest productivity improvements often can be achieved; storage and retrieval—employing an orderpicking productivity ratio and throughput performance index to determine productivity improvement; and manufacturing—analyzing process and product layouts using manufacturing cycle efficiency and job lateness ratios.

The fourth part introduces several concepts associated with economic justification of systems alternatives and ways to improve the productivity of the investment dollar.

A glossary of terms and abbreviations used in this guide can be found at the end of the chapter (pages 366–369).

Our concern will be with the analysis and measurement of productivity of individual operations. A very pragmatic approach will be taken. This guide is intended to provide positive steps in improving productivity.

Resource Utilization

People

The most popular definition of productivity is output per man-hour. With suc.. an approach to productivity measurement, the focus is on a single resource—people.

The two traditional methods used to increase productivity have been the substitution of capital or technology for labor and the development of more efficient work methods. While the emphasis on technology and methods improvement has produced dramatic productivity improvements in manufacturing, considerable opportunity exists for both in the areas of materials handling and warehousing.

Few organizations have developed engineered work methods and standards for materials handling and warehousing. Additionally, both areas are usually labor intensive.

In addition to improving productivity through technology and methods improvement, significant gains in productivity can occur through improved *management*. The key to productivity improvement continues to be the effective management of people. Being *busy* is not necessarily being *productive*; good management is needed to insure that people are being productive.

Utilization Measures

Two measures that you can use to track the utilization of people in performing materials handling are the *materials handling labor* (MHL) ratio and the *direct labor materials handling* (DLMH) ratio. They are defined as follows:

$$\text{MHL ratio} = \frac{\text{Personnel assigned to materials handling duties}}{\text{Total operating workforce}}$$

$$\text{DLMH ratio} = \frac{\text{Materials handling time spent by direct labor}}{\text{Total direct labor time}}$$

Work sampling studies* are effective in providing feedback about the utilization of personnel. Both ratios require inputs that can be obtained via work sampling.

MATERIALS HANDLING LABOR RATIO

The MHL ratio measures the proportion of your labor force assigned to materials handling duties. The ratio can be based on either the number of personnel or the direct cost of the personnel involved.

The ratio is to be used as a tracking signal. The values of the ratio should be charted monthly to detect changes that occur; when changes occur, follow up to determine why

---

*Work sampling studies consist of randomly spaced observations of a work situation.

the change occurred. It is best to consider the MHL ratio as a bench mark to be used in evaluating alternative manufacturing plans.

Example: Computation of Materials Handling Labor Ratio. A survey was made of a manufacturing plant in the southeast with the following results:

Materials Handling Equipment Operators

Type Equipment	No. of People	Payroll Cost/Year
Walkie pallet jacks	2	$ 20,500
Counterbalanced lift truck	4	44,800
Narrow aisle reach truck	4	42,500
Sideloader truck	1	11,200
Bridge crane	4	50,400
Manual labor	6	54,000
Total	21	$223,400

Materials Handling Related Activities

Activity	No. of People	Payroll Cost/Year
Receiving dock	3	$ 37,200
Shipping dock	3	36,500
Raw materials storage	2	22,200
WIP materials storage	2	21,800
Finished goods storage	6	68,500
Waste material removal	2	17,500
Total	18	$203,700

Supporting Activities

Activity	No. of People	Annual Payroll	% Charge- able to MH	Net Annual MH Cost
Tool room & supplies issue	2	$20,200	40%	$ 8,080
Maintenance of MH equipt.	2	26,500	100%	26,500
Production control	3	44,200	80%	35,360
Packaging/packing operations	5	52,500	40%	21,000
Inventory control records	4	48,100	60%	28,860
In-bound/ out-bound QC	4	54,300	30%	16,290
Traffic	1	13,200	40%	5,280
Training	2	29,500	20%	5,900
Total	23			$147,270

Annual Materials Handling Labor Cost

MH equipment labor	$223,400
MH activities labor	203,700
Supporting activities labor	147,270
Total MH labor	$574,370
Total annual payroll	$5,887,300

$$\text{MHL ratio} = \frac{\$574,370}{\$5,887,300} = 9.76\%$$

Figure 14–1 shows a sample worksheet to facilitate the computation of the MHL ratio.

DIRECT LABOR MATERIALS HANDLING RATIO

The DLMH ratio measures the proportion of your direct labor time spent in performing materials handling. It is generally desirable to maintain a low value for the DLMH ratio.

The alternatives available to you in reducing the value of the DLMH ratio include using indirect labor to perform the materials handling and eliminating or reducing the amount of materials handling required. The latter can be achieved by mechanizing or automating the handling activities.

Target levels should be established and monthly observation made to evaluate performance. As noted, work sampling studies can be used to obtain estimates of the DLMH ratio.

Example: Direct Labor Materials Handling Ratio.   Assume that a work sampling study has been performed of 5 departments. Of the 1,000 random observations made, 140 times the direct laborers being observed were performing materials handling duties. The results are summarized below.

(1) Dept.	(2) # DL	(3) # OBS	(4) # MH	(5) % MH	(6) Annual Payroll	(7) (5×6) $ DLMH
A	25	200	20	10.00	$ 500,000	$ 50,000
B	35	280	34	12.14	725,000	88,036
C	10	80	6	7.50	180,000	13,500
D	40	320	65	20.31	850,000	172,656
E	15	120	15	12.50	265,000	33,125
	125	1,000	140	14.00*	$2,520,000	$357,317

*Average % MH

Note: 1,000 observations are not sufficient to make strong statements concerning individual departments' % MH. The example is intended for illustrative purposes only.

$$\text{DLMH ratio} = \frac{\$357,317}{\$2,520,000} = 14.18\%$$

For each department, the DLMH ratio is, of course, the % MH given in Column 5.

Based on the results of the study, it appears that Department D should be studied further and attempts made to reduce the materials handling cost.

Productivity Improvement

Tracking personnel utilization is an important step in achieving productivity improvement. However, this is not sufficient. Management action is needed to bring about improved personnel utilization.

Some possible areas for productivity improvement include:

1. Indirect labor to perform materials handling

2. Industrial robots to perform routine handling tasks

3. Moving material, tooling, and supplies to the person's work station, rather than having the person travel to obtain such items

4. Modular work stations to facilitate materials handling and storage

5. Pre-kitting materials to minimize the handling required at the work station

6. Automated storage and retrieval systems

7. Automatic loading and unloading of trailers at shipping and receiving

8. Automatic identification systems with optical or magnetic sensors for automatic data entry

9. Ball transfer tables, gravity chutes and hoppers, pneumatic feeding of materials, magnetic and vacuum lifting devices, air film handling, and turntables equipped with special jigs and fixtures to reduce materials handling at the work station

10. Containers for unitizing materials and reducing the number of moves required.

Equipment

In an issue of *Purchasing*, John T. Burns, president, Sperry Vickers, observed, "Capital equipment acquisition is looked on as the key to increasing productivity." This viewpoint is shared by many business leaders. Consequently, as both the cost of labor and the availability of reliable equipment alternatives increase, a greater portion of the capital acquisition budget is allocated to materials handling equipment. Such equipment allows material to be moved faster, more accurately, and with less loss; material can be stored higher and deeper using aisles that are longer and narrower; and both material and the equipment can be tracked using real time computer controls.

Despite the availability of automated storage and retrieval systems, driverless carts and tractors, laser beam scanners, and computer controlled industrial trucks, opportunities continue to exist for significant productivity improvement using less sophisticated equipment. Simple solutions can yield quick productivity payoffs.

The appropriate blend of people and equipment and the level of sophistication that is right for you depend on your needs. Your material characteristics and flow requirements, coupled with your personnel capabilities, will indicate the equipment combination to be used.

Among the factors to be considered in selecting materials handling and warehousing equipment are the following:

Material characteristics	Expandability
Move (flow) requirements	Contractability
Storage requirements	Mobility
Costs and savings	Capability (capacity)
"Bilities":	Modularity
Reliability	Safety
Maintainability	Control requirements
Operability	Layout
Salvageability	Facilities limitations
Flexibility	Management and labor attitude
Adaptability	Delivery times
Compatibility	

A related, but separate, issue in equipment selection is vendor or supplier selection. Vendor selection is based on a number of the same factors as equipment selection, plus a consideration of vendor reputation, service or maintenance capability, proximity, and the coverage of the field provided by other lines of equipment.

Utilization Measures

Two measures are suggested to assist you in monitoring the utilization of your equipment investment. The measures, *production equipment* (PE) *utilization*, and *handling equipment* (HE) *utilization*, are defined as follows:

$$\text{Production equipment utilization} = \frac{\text{Actual output}}{\text{Theoretical output}}$$

$$\text{Handling equipment utilization} = \frac{\text{Weight moved/hour}}{\text{Theoretical capacity}}$$

PRODUCTION EQUIPMENT UTILIZATION

PE utilization provides an indication of the extent to which production equipment is being utilized to its fullest potential. Knowing the utilization provided currently, decisions can be made concerning the need for developing better handling systems to increase the PE utilization.

In most cases, the appropriate objective is to increase PE utilization until it is at least 90 percent. However, in those cases where the production capacity of an individual machine far exceeds the production requirements for any individual production order, short production runs and frequent setups might be preferred to carrying large inventories of finished parts.

The PE utilization can be determined from production records (if available and accurate) and work sampling or time studies. It should be used as an indicator for determining if further efforts to increase equipment utilization are justified.

Example: Computation of Production Equipment Utilization Ratio. A key stamping press forming the chassis for a piece of electronic gear is capable of 20 cycles per minute.

A study of production records over the previous 4 weeks shows that the press produced 124,800 pieces in 9,600 running minutes (4 weeks × 40 hours per week × 60 min. per hr.). In 9,600 minutes, the press is capable of producing 192,000 pieces (20 pieces per minute × 9,600 minutes).

Therefore, the production equipment utilization is:

$$\text{PE utilization} = \frac{\text{Actual output}}{\text{Theoretical capacity}} = \frac{124,800}{192,000} = 65\,\%$$

HANDLING EQUIPMENT UTILIZATION

One of the most difficult evaluations to perform is the determination of the utilization of materials handling equipment. In general, handling equipment is in one of the following states:

1. Moving with a full load

2. Moving, with less than a full load

3. Moving, but empty

4. Being loaded/unloaded

5. Available, but idle due to no operator available

6. Available, but idle due to no material available for movement

7. Unavailable due to maintenance

Some consider handling equipment to be 100 percent utilized if it is either *moving or being loaded/unloaded*. Others contend the equipment is being utilized when it is *moving*, but not *empty*. Yet another definition of utilization is when the equipment is moving *with a full load*. The latter definition will be used in this discussion of handling equipment utilization.

Different definitions of utilization might be used for different types of equipment. Industrial trucks, conveyors, and cranes and hoists, for example, are used for different purposes; hence, different utilization measures might be appropriate.

Not only might handling equipment utilization be defined differently, but also the definition of a full load can vary. In some cases the weight of the load might dictate; in others, the size of the load will determine the load capacity.

The utilization of industrial trucks and storage and retrieval machines is very much dependent upon the effectiveness of the dispatching system. For example, if only single command cycles are performed, then a maximum utilization of 50 percent can be expected from the handling equipment even if it is loaded to capacity. (Note: a *single command cycle* occurs when the equipment either moves a load to a specified destination and returns empty or travels empty to a specified location and returns with a load. A *dual command cycle* occurs when the equipment moves a load to a specified destination, deposits the load, travels empty to another specified location, retrieves a load, and travels loaded to the originating point.)

HE utilization is determined by considering the weight of the loads, the number of loads moved, and the time spent in moving material. It should be noted that the calculation of HE utilization does not distinguish between an industrial truck that travels excessively long distances fully loaded 50 percent of the time and empty 50 percent of the time and one that travels 50 percent loaded all of the time. Additionally, the theoretical capacity is not easily computed for some classes of equipment.

HE utilization can be approximated by using work sampling. By making random observations of the equipment a determination can be made concerning not only the busy versus idle state of the equipment, but also the percent utilization of its carrying capacity at the time of the observation. The carrying capacity is a function of both weight and speed.

The handling equipment utilization measure will provide an indication of both under- and over-utilization. Handling equipment will be defined to be busy if it is either being loaded/unloaded or moving (with or without a load). The percentage of time handling equipment is busy will be called the *busy percentage*.

Whereas it is usually desirable to maximize the utilization of production equipment, for some classes of handling equipment (e.g. industrial trucks and cranes) it is generally not desirable to have very large values of busy percentage. The reason for the difference in philosophies is that materials handling equipment is typically used to provide a service. Demands for handling equipment normally occur at random and the times required to perform the handling service are also often random. In such a random environment, as the busy percentage increases, the number of loads waiting to be moved increases exponentially. A busy percentage from 65 to 75 percent is a reasonable upper limit for such conditions.

If the random environment does not exist then it is likely that either tractor/trailers or fixed path equipment such as conveyors and driverless tractors should be used, rather than lift trucks.

Example: Computation of Handling Equipment Utilization. A work sampling study is performed of a 3000 lb. industrial truck. Of the 25 observations made, 4 found the truck to be idle. The truck was traveling empty 5 times. The following tabulation resulted:

Busy Observation	Speed Rating	Load Rating	Product
1	75 %	100 %	75 %
2	80	80	64
3	50	60	30
4	100	80	80
5	100	80	80

Busy Observation	Speed Rating	Load Rating	Product
6	90	0	0
7	100	0	0
8	80	90	72
9	100	75	75
10	80	100	80
11	100	80	80
12	90	0	0
13	80	90	72
14	100	80	80
15	80	80	64
16	90	0	0
17	100	60	60
18	100	0	0
19	80	60	48
20	100	80	80
21	75	80	60
Total	1850	1275	1100

$$\text{HE utilization} = \frac{1100 \; \text{(total product)}}{25 \; \text{total observations}} = 44\%$$

$$\text{Busy percentage} = \frac{21 \; \text{busy observations}}{25 \; \text{total observations}} = 84\%$$

Note: The low value of HE utilization is due to both a low average speed rating of 74% (1850 ÷ 25) and a low average load rating of 51% (1275 ÷ 25). The speed rating could be due to a number of short hauls with considerable maneuvering required. The low load rating is due to 4 idle and 5 empty observations. Depending upon the particular application, an HE utilization value of 50% would be very good. In this case, the situation should be examined to determine if "deadheading" can be reduced, speed can be increased, and the size of the unit load can be increased.

Productivity Improvement

Some areas for productivity improvement that relate to equipment utilization include the following:

1. Special lift truck attachments, such as side shifters, clamp attachments, and load, push-pull attachments, to reduce pick-up and deposit times and to increase space utilization

2. Computer controlled equipment

3. Real time dispatching systems to reduce the number of "deadhead" trips by lift trucks

4. "Point-of-use" storage of tooling and supplies at the machining center to reduce the travel time required for set-ups

5. Larger unit loads

6. Stretchwrap and shrinkwrap for unitizing loads

7. Automatic palletizers and depalletizers

8. Size the load and match the equipment to the job

9. Fixed path equipment, such as conveyors and driverless tractors and carts, for repetitive moves between well-defined points

10. Batching work orders and using short interval scheduling to increase the number of dual command cycles

Space

Among the four resources—people, equipment, space, and energy—the one that is generally the most difficult to increase or decrease is space. Typically, you can hire or lay off people, and acquire or sell equipment much more quickly than you can increase or decrease space. Hence, it is essential that well-informed decisions be made concerning space acquisition and its subsequent utilization.

Space utilization is literally and figuratively a multi-dimensional issue. On the one hand, both two- and three-dimensional measurements are needed, while on the other hand, you can have both too low and too high a utilization of your space.

In both manufacturing and warehousing, some functions do not lend themselves to efficient utilization of overhead or vertical space. Some examples include receiving, shipping, inspection, parts preparation, packaging and packing, assembly, and administration/management. Conversely, materials storage and retrieval can utilize high-bay space effectively. For this reason, space utilization should be carefully evaluated.

In general, manufacturing space is quite expensive. The relative differences in the costs of manufacturing and warehousing space will depend upon the specific location and requirements of a particular organization. Due to the special construction and service requirements, manufacturing facilities might, for example, cost from $70 to $200 per square foot; whereas, warehouse space might cost from $20 to $80 per square foot.

Due to the high cost of manufacturing space, it is essential that it be planned and that efficient layouts be developed. Work-in-process (WIP) storage and handling systems are needed to insure that WIP is controlled. Overhead space can be utilized by moving and storing materials on conveyors and by installing mezzanines for low-bay activities. Handling and storage systems are needed not only for raw material, WIP, and finished goods, but also for maintenance supplies, tooling, and scrap and waste removal. Equipment installation, maintenance, and removal, as well as personnel flow, must be planned for in the layout.

To achieve optimum space utilization, space standards are needed. With space standards one can determine objectively whether or not space is over-utilized or under-utilized. Standards are needed for *all* areas, including receiving, inspection, storage, manufacturing, maintenance, administration, and shipping. Standards for aisles, bin storage, block stacking, rack storage, battery charging, equipment storage, rest rooms, offices, etc. are required if a comprehensive program is planned.

Recognizing that few companies are in a position to immediately install a space standards program, several different utilization measures are suggested. They should provide management with insights concerning space utilization, as well as an indication of the potential benefits to be gained from installing a space standards program.

Utilization Measures

A number of measures can be developed to provide management with feedback concerning the effective use of their storage space. The following are suggested for the initiation of a space utilization program for storage areas in a warehouse.

$$\text{Storage space utilization} = \frac{\text{Storage space occupied by material}}{\text{Total storage space}}$$

$$\text{Aisle space percentage} = \frac{\text{Space occupied by aisles}}{\text{Total space}}$$

Two additional measures of storage space utilization are the *storage slot occupancy ratio* and the *storage turnover ratio*. The storage slot occupancy ratio measures the percentage of the storage slots (pallet slots or bin slots) that are occupied; occupancy occurs if there is something in the slot, whether the slot is full or not. The annual storage turnover ratio is the ratio of the number of loads retrieved to the average number of loads in storage during the year; it measures the movement or turnover of the materials in storage. Both measures provide additional information concerning the effectiveness of the storage space utilization program.

Other measures can be defined to determine the utilization of space in other areas of the company. For example, space utilization in receiving, inspection, manufacturing, packing, shipping, and office areas needs to be measured.

STORAGE SPACE UTILIZATION

The *storage space utilization* (SSU) ratio measures the effectiveness of cube space utilization. SSU values need to be computed for the storage of items, cases, pallets, bags, drums, and containers. Also, separate calculations are needed for each method of storage, e.g., block stacking, selective pallet rack, drive-in rack, and deep lane storage.

The SSU can be computed in different ways. One approach is to evaluate the utilization of the storage space for each storage slot. Another approach is to divide the material cube stored by the overall cube space required to store the material. The latter approach is used here.

If you are not already aware of it, you will find that the storage space lost due to the placement of building columns can be quite large. Ideally, the column placement should be determined after the layout is developed. However, it is often the case that either a building already exists or the building is designed before layout decisions are made.

Example: Computation of Storage Space Utilization for a Pallet Storage Area in a Warehouse. Materials are stored on 48″ × 40″ pallets in selective pallet rack (one-deep). The pallet has a height of 6″. A 48″ load is stored on the pallet. Two pallets are stored (side-by-side) in each rack opening. A 4″ clearance is used between loads in an opening and between a load and a vertical rack member (upright truss). Each vertical rack member is 3″ wide. Pallets are placed on 4″ load beams; the bottom load is stored on a beam. There is a clearance of 4″ between the floor and the bottom load beam and between the top of each load and the load beam above it. A 72″ aisle (load-to-load) and a back-to-back (flue) spacing of 9″ between loads is used. The rack has 5 tiers or levels of storage. The load does not overhang the pallet.

The vertical dimensions of the storage space (floor to top of the load on the fifth tier) are equal to 5 × (4″ clearance + 4″ load beam + 6″ pallet + 48″ load) or 310″ (25′ 10″).

The width of a storage opening (centerline of upright truss to centerline of upright truss) is equal to:

1 upright truss	3″
3 clearances of 4″	12″
2 loads of 40″ width	80″
Total	95″

The dimension of storage from centerline of a flue to centerline of a flue is equal to:

1 flue spacing	9″
1 aisle	72″
2 loads of 48″ depth	96″
Total	177″

A storage cube (310″ × 95″ × 177″) has a volume of 3,016.58 cubic feet. However, the volume of the 20 loads of material stored (5 tiers, 2 loads per opening, and 2 sides of an aisle) equals 20 × (48″ × 40″ × 48″) or 1,066.67 cubic feet. Hence, the storage space utilization equals:

$$\text{SSU} = \frac{1,066.67}{3,016.58} = 35.36\%$$

If the loads, on the average, are half-full with a vertical dimension of 24″ then the SSU reduces to one-half the value obtained above for full-loads.

Note: Claims of 90% storage space utilization should be examined closely. The above calculation for a narrow aisle application indicates such claims must be based on a different definition of storage space utilization than used above.

AISLE SPACE PERCENTAGE

The amount of space devoted to aisles in both warehousing and manufacturing can be sizeable. For example, percentages of floor space for main and service aisles as high as 60 to 75 percent for storage areas and 30 to 40 percent for manufacturing areas can occur if careful planning is not performed in developing the layouts. In well-planned facilities the space required for main aisles alone can still be as great as 15 to 25 percent of the floor space.

Different philosophies exist in the types of aisles that should be considered in the aisle space percentage calculation. Some include *all* aisles; others only include main or traffic aisles. The latter do not include service or access aisles, which are used for access to storage faces, production equipment, and service equipment.

It is recommended that all aisles, main and service, be included in the calculation of the aisle space percentage. Also, depending upon the application, the percentage should be based on the cube space required.

In storage areas, cross aisles can be bridged and slow moving materials stored above the cross aisles. In orderpicking areas, the picking aisles can be bridged for either multiple pick levels on mezzanines or picking tunnels.

Both the length and the width of a service aisle in storage areas influence the aisle space percentage. Additionally, the storage depth served by the service aisle affects the percentage of space devoted to aisles.

Care must be taken in applying the aisle space percentage. Just as it's undesirable to have too high a value, it is also possible to have too low a value. Aisle space must be provided for people and equipment to maneuver and have the required access to material. Throughput can suffer and damage can occur when there is insufficient aisle space. A proper balance in space utilization and operating efficiency is required.

In computing the aisle space percentage, measurements should be made in the working area, rather than depending upon prints and drawings. Aisles have a way of shrinking and disappearing over time, due to material being placed in the aisles. Well marked aisles can serve to minimize the shrinkage effect, but management attention will still be needed.

> *Example.* In the previous example, let the service aisle be 30 openings long. (Recall each opening had a width of 95".) A 15' main aisle intersects each end of the service aisle. For one aisle of storage the "footprint" for both storage, flue space, and aisles would be 177" wide and 3,210" long; the length is equal to the sum of two 15' main aisle widths and 30 openings 95" wide. The vertical dimension is 310" for both aisle and non-aisle space.
>
> The aisle space percentage is obtained as follows:

Floor space for aisles:

Main aisles 177" × 2 aisles × 15' × 12" per ft. =	63,720 in.²
Service aisles 30 open. × 95"/open. × 72" aisle =	205,200 in.²
Total	268,920 in.²

Cube space for aisles:

268,920 in.² × 310 in. (vertical dim.) =	83,365,200 in.³
	or 48,243.75 ft.³

Total space:

177" wide × 3,210" long × 310" height ÷ 1,728 in.³/ft.³ =	101,928.64 ft.³

$$\text{Aisle space percentage} = \frac{48{,}243.75}{101{,}928.64} = 47.33\%$$

Note: If counterbalanced trucks were used, a 12-foot service aisle would be required and the aisle space percentage would be 62.56%.

Productivity Improvement

To achieve increased productivity through improved space utilization, consider the following:

1. Narrow aisles (8.5') and very narrow aisles (6.0')

2. Medium-rise (20' to 40'), high-rise (40' to 60'), and very high-rise (60' to 100') storage systems

3. Mezzanines and second-floor operations for low-bay activities

4. Multiple sized (vertical dimension) storage rack openings for matching multiple sized loads with openings

5. Longer working aisles and fewer cross aisles in storage

6. Bridging cross aisles and storing slow moving material above cross aisles

7. Use modular work stations in manufacturing

8. Randomized storage versus dedicated storage

9. Hand stacking cases on decked cantilever or pallet rack to eliminate the space required for the pallet

10. Block stacking and deep lane storage

11. Eliminating obsolete materials

12. Meet peak demand for space with rented or leased space

13. Provide storage racks in staging areas to eliminate floor stacking

14. Paint aisle boundaries on the floor

15. Use a combination of storage methods (hybrid storage system)

Energy

The need for improved utilization of energy has become much more acute in recent years. Facilities planning and materials handling systems design decisions are being influenced by energy considerations. Materials handling equipment design changes are occurring, due to the impact of energy costs. Although materials handling equipment is not a major consumer of energy, decisions concerning materials handling equipment can have a dramatic impact on the energy consumption for a facility.

To illustrate the issues that are raised because of the concern for energy, consider the design of a warehouse. An important question concerns the need for heating, ventilation, air conditioning (HVAC) and lighting throughout the warehouse. If an automatic storage and retrieval system is self-enclosed, the environmental requirements are dictated by the material requirements, not by the personnel requirements.

Similar energy gains can be made by enclosing the materials storage area of a conventional warehouse and providing task lighting and an environmentally equipped cab on the handling equipment. If the idea sounds far-fetched, then observe a nearby farm. The fields are not lighted, heated, and air-conditioned for the farmer; if anything is, it's the tractor!

The utilization of space in a warehouse also has an impact on energy consumption. A full warehouse is much more energy efficient than an empty one!

The use of dock enclosures, battery powered trucks, solar heating and cooling, and recirculation of heated waste water from chemical processes to heat other areas in the plant are examples of attempts to deal with the energy issue. Additionally, computer controlled energy systems are being installed to reduce peak loads and achieve energy savings.

The energy efficiency of battery powered (BP) industrial trucks compared to internal combustion engine (ICE) powered industrial trucks for indoor operation is due not to mo-

iency, but to the ventilation requirements. The only ventilation requirement for
s is in the battery charging area and it can be contained. For ICE trucks ventila-
_ _,_ems are needed throughout the operating area and they exhaust not just fumes,
but also heated or cooled air. The load placed on the overall HVAC system due to the
fume exhaust requirements can be significant—and costly!

In addition to the conservation measures directed at heating, ventilation, air conditioning, and lighting, other energy related actions have occurred. Power conductor bars,
installed in aisles, provide the power for specially designed industrial trucks operating in
the aisle; when the truck leaves the aisle it switches over to its own battery power. Programmable controllers used on conveyors turn on and turn off drives, as needed, to move
materials. Alternative methods of powering roller conveyors have been developed, to
minimize the number of drives required.

Dr. Wayne C. Turner of Oklahoma State University and the Oklahoma Industrial
Energy Management Program observed that actions taken to improve productivity tend
also to improve energy management. He noted that narrow aisle and high rise storage and
the unit load philosophy not only yield materials handling efficiencies, but also yield energy savings.

Utilization Measures

Due to the relatively recent emphasis given to energy and the lack of a well-developed experience base, very few utilization measures have been developed for energy as it relates
to materials handling. *Energy utilization indices* (EUIs) have been developed for some areas, but much work remains to be performed in order to track energy performance effectively and to make both relative and absolute comparisons.

The objective of this chapter is to stimulate an increased awareness of the effect of
materials handling decisions on energy consumption, rather than to provide proven utilization measures for your operation. Three alternative indices related to energy consumption are Btu/ft^3, Btu/ft^2, and Btu/unit of production. For office activities Btu/ft^2 is a satisfactory index; however, for warehousing operations Btu/ft^3 is preferred due to the varying
building heights. The Btu/unit of production index would be meaningful for manufacturing areas; however, there will be extreme variations depending upon the production process involved, e.g. aluminum production versus electronic assembly.

The energy utilization index (EUI) to be used here is Btu/ft^3 and is computed as follows:

$$EUI = \frac{\text{Btus consumed/day}}{\text{Cubic space}}$$

Cubic space, rather than square footage, is used in order to provide a basis for comparing
low rise, medium rise, and high rise construction. Also, the energy impact of conventional
storage aisles, narrow aisles, and very narrow aisles can be better compared using cubic
footage.

ENERGY UTILIZATION INDEX

The EUI calculation is based on Btu consumption, rather than energy costs, due to
the rapidly changing cost per Btu. In order to have an index that can be used to make

valid comparisons over time it must be deinflated. The objective is to monitor energy consumption, rather than the cost of energy.

To convert various energy sources to Btu equivalents, the following approximate conversion factors can be used:

Energy Source	Units	Btus/Unit
Natural gas	Cubic feet	1,000
Propane	Pounds	21,500
Gasoline	Gallons	120,000
Diesel oil	Gallons	136,000
No. 2 fuel oil	Gallons	140,000
No. 4 fuel oil	Gallons	146,000
No. 6 fuel oil	Gallons	150,000
Bituminous coal	Pounds	12,500
Purchased steam	Pounds	1,000
Electric current	Kilowatt hours	3,413

Example: Computation of the Energy Utilization Index.   Located in Dallas, Texas is a 50,000 ft² warehouse that is 24 feet high. It uses electricity and natural gas. In October, 65,000 kwh of electricity and 11,500 cubic feet of natural gas were consumed. The warehouse operated 22 days during the month.

Btu equivalent
Electrical

$$65,000 \text{ kwh}$$
$$\times 3,413 \text{ Btus/kwh}$$
$$\overline{\hspace{2cm}}$$
$$221,845,000 \text{ Btus}$$

Natural gas

$$11,500 \text{ ft}^3$$
$$\times 1,000 \text{ Btus/ft}^3$$
$$\overline{\hspace{2cm}}$$
$$11,500,000 \text{ Btus}$$

Total   233,345,000 Btus

$$\text{EUI} = \frac{233,345,000 \text{ Btu/mo.} \div 22 \text{ days/mo.}}{50,000 \text{ ft}^2 \times 24 \text{ ft of space}}$$

$$\text{EUI} = 8.84 \text{ Btu/ft}^3\text{-day}$$

Productivity Improvement

Some possible areas for improvement in the utilization of energy include:

1. Replacing incandescent and mercury vapor lights with high performance sodium bulbs

2. Task lighting, rather than area lighting

3. Placing lights above aisles, rather than above the racks

4. Placing unit heaters and fans properly

5. Installing automatic energy control for lighting systems

6. Designing facilities to allow the use of natural light in warehouses

7. Using low-pressure lighting in parking lots

8. Using dock enclosures

9. Reducing the heating and air conditioning levels to that required for *materials* storage

10. Enclosing and installing separate ventilation systems for battery charging areas

11. Insulating walls and roof, as well as bare steam pipes

12. Partitioning heated/air conditioned areas in the warehouse

13. Monitoring utility bills to determine when peak loads occur and scheduling work accordingly

14. Installing microprocessor based energy control system to regulate electrical energy consumption

15. Considering alternative energy sources, such as solar energy

16. Evaluating energy requirements in the comparison of shrinkwrap versus stretch-wrap

17. Providing "plastic strip" doors between areas having different HVAC requirements

18. Cleaning floors regularly to maximize their reflectance

19. Using energy efficient tires on lift trucks and energy efficient belts on motor drives

20. Performing battery charging only when needed and during non-peak load periods

21. Using drop-in DC generators on industrial trucks

22. Improving pick-up and deposit procedures to reduce idling time of equipment

23. Sizing conveyor and hoist motors to meet the actual handling requirements

24. Installing automatic start/stop controls on conveyors so that they run only when needed

25. Performing maintenance on a scheduled basis

Management Control

Materials

Materials or inventory control is an important ingredient in the overall productivity of a company. Doing a better job of getting the right amount of material to the right place at the right time means productivity improvement. The materials management function is concerned with purchasing, inventory control, quality control, materials handling, and distribution; and each sub-function of materials management should be included in the overall productivity program.

In recent years, considerable emphasis has been placed on increased real time control of materials from receiving through shipping. The need for increased control of materials is especially great in the area of work-in-process. Many firms fail to maintain good visibility of the status of material once it has been released to manufacturing.

Raw material, work-in-process, and finished goods inventories need to be monitored and controlled. Turnover ratios, shortage or fill ratios, stock replenishment ratios, error ratios, and obsolete material ratios can be used to improve materials control and increase productivity.

Control Measures

As with the other areas for productivity improvement, a number of different measures can be used to monitor the effectiveness of the materials control function. Some control measures to consider are the *inventory turnover ratio* and the *inventory fill ratio.*

$$\text{Inventory turnover ratio} = \frac{\text{Annual sales}}{\text{Average annual inventory investment}}$$

$$\text{Inventory fill ratio} = \frac{\dfrac{\text{Line item demands}}{\text{Filled per day}}}{\text{Line item demands per day}}$$

Other useful ratios include the *inventory replenishment ratio* for comparing actual stock replenishment lead times against desired lead times; the *perpetual inventory error ratio* for measuring the accuracy of the inventory transaction reporting system; the *inventory location error ratio* for monitoring the accuracy of the stock locator system; and the *obsolete inventory ratio* for measuring the percentage of storage space consumed by obsolete materials.

If accountability is to be maintained in the area of materials control, management feedback is required. It is important not only to manage materials *efficiently*, but also to *effectively* manage the materials management function. The accuracy of the record-keeping function, as well as the productivity of the office staff supporting materials management, must be monitored closely.

INVENTORY TURNOVER RATIO

The *inventory turnover* (IT) *ratio* provides a measure of the return obtained from inventory investments; it also provides an indication of the movement of materials. Just as it's important to "handle different things differently" and "store different things differently," it's also important to "control different things differently." The inventory turnover ratio provides a means of discovering the differences in materials and developing material classifications for control purposes.

Pareto's law applied to materials control, indicates a high percentage of sales is derived from a low percentage of the products. Likewise, a high percentage of the products contribute a low percentage of the annual sales. The ABC inventory control system is based on the notion of controlling different things differently. The A items are those few items (such as 10 percent) that account for perhaps 50 percent of the annual sales; C items are the many items (such as 50 percent) that account for very little (maybe 1 percent) of the annual sales; and B items are the remaining items (such as 40 percent) that represent perhaps 49 percent of the annual sales.

Management must pay particular attention to the A items and attempt to maintain a high turnover of the items, since they represent the highest invenment materials. C items justify only very simple control procedures. B items merit sound control systems, but should require minimal management attention.

Typically, inventory turnover ratios are not calculated for all classes of material: raw materials and supplies, purchased parts, work-in-process, and finished goods. However, they should be! The investment in work-in-process, for some firms, is far greater than that in finished goods and equals or exceeds the investment in raw materials.

Example: Computation of Inventory Turnover Ratio. A distribution center has adopted an ABC inventory classification system. There are 20,000 stockkeeping units, in inventory. Monthly calculations of the inventory turnover ratio are made as follows:

Month: October, 19____
Number of Working Days: 23

Inventory Class	Number of Items	End of Month Inventory ($)	Monthly Sales ($)
A	1,900	76,000	52,000
B	6,850	105,000	46,000
C	11,250	19,000	2,000
Total	20,000	200,000	100,000

$$\text{Inventory turnover ratio} = \frac{\text{Monthly sales}}{\text{End of month inventory}} \times \frac{\text{Number of annual working days}}{\text{Number of monthly working days}}$$

$$\text{A items: IT ratio} = \frac{52,000 \times 250}{76,000 \times 23} = 7.437$$

$$\text{B items: IT ratio} = \frac{46,000 \times 250}{105,000 \times 23} = 4.762$$

$$\text{C items: IT ratio} = \frac{2,000 \times 250}{19,000 \times 23} = 1.144$$

$$\text{All items: IT ratio} = \frac{100,000 \times 250}{200,000 \times 23} = 5.435$$

Note: A 10% increase in the IT ratio for A items caused by reducing its inventory level by $6,900 would increase the overall IT ratio by approximately 3.6%.

INVENTORY FILL RATIO

The inventory fill ratio provides a measure of the out-of-stock condition. It, too, should be computed for all classes of material from raw materials through finished goods. As with the other ratios, a proper balance must be maintained. If no shortages occur then excess inventory is probably being maintained; if shortages frequently occur then poor service is being provided.

Some people compute fill ratios for orders rather than line items or SKUs (stockkeeping units) ordered. The appropriate measure to use depends on the particular set of circumstances. For example, if partial orders cannot be shipped to a customer then a ratio based on orders filled is appropriate. However, if an order is received for 10 line items, a shortage exists for one line item, the remaining nine are filled, and the partial order is shipped, then a fill ratio based on line items would be used. A third condition arises if orders for nine of the line items can be completely filled and the order for the remaining line item can be only partially filled.

Example: Computation of Inventory Fill Ratio. A warehouse receives orders for multiple line items. Fill ratios are calculated daily on both orders and line items. If a demand for a line item is only partially filled, it is counted as a "no fill" condition.

Date: September _____, 19_____

Orders processed:	200
Orders completely filled:	162
Line items processed:	2,150
Line items completely filled	2,040

Inventory fill ratio

$$\text{Orders: IF ratio} = \frac{162}{200} = 81\%$$

$$\text{Lines: IF ratio} = \frac{2,040}{2,150} = 94.9\%$$

Note: If a particular SKU is out-of-stock and it is ordered on multiple orders then multiple "no fill" conditions occur.

Productivity Improvement

A number of possibilities exist for improving the control of materials. Some suggested areas for you to explore include the following:

1. Standardized design specifications on both purchased parts and manufactured parts to reduce the number of different SKUs in inventory

2. Value analysis program to achieve cost reduction in product design

3. ABC inventory classification and different control systems for each class

4. MRP (material requirements planning) system

5. Automatic identification system using bar codes for tracking material

6. Cycle counting for physical inventory

7. Monthly or quarterly purges of obsolete materials

8. Computerized inventory locator system

9. Stock status reports, including inventory and activity levels, for identification of non-moving or inactive material

10. Random sampling (audit) of material to measure accuracy of locator system, age of material, and accuracy of labeling on material.

Movement

Introduction

Movement control, flow control, and throughput control all refer to the control of the movement of materials, people, and equipment. The primary function of materials handling is to *move* material, but to do so in a controlled manner. Movement by itself is not productive; for other functions to be productive, materials must be moved to the right place at the right time.

In controlling the movement of material our concern will be with the accuracy, timeliness, speed, distance, size, and number of moves performed. A move is accurate if the right amount of material is delivered to the right place; it is timely if it arrives at the right time. The efficency of the operation is a function of the rate of speed of movement, the distance moved, the size of the load, and the number of moves required to provide the required service.

From a productivity measurement point of view, it is necessary for the control measures to be meaningful, easily understood, and simple to compute and use. Additionally, they must require data inputs that are readily available. In terms of movement control there often exist record-keeping systems that generate move tickets, trip records, etc. and provide feedback concerning the move performance. For such inputs to be used in a productivity measurement program, the records must also be accurate.

The wide variety of materials handling equipment currently available provides a number of alternative ways to move material. In order picking, the person can move to the storage location or the stored materials can be moved to the person; in one case people move and in the other case materials move. Examples of person-to-material moves are order-picker trucks, walking, and aisle-captive, man-aboard storage/retrieval (S/R) machines. Examples of material-to-person moves are mini load S/R systems and S/R carousel conveyors.

Control Measures

Measures for controlling the movement of material are included elsewhere in this chapter. In particular, the handling equipment utilization measure (p. 329) and the throughput performance index (p. 354) are concerned with the movement of materials. However, both focus on the movement of the handling equipment.

Two additional measures for controlling the movement of material are the *movement/operation* ratio and the *average distance/move* ratio, defined as follows:

$$\text{Movement/operation ratio} = \frac{\text{Total number of moves}}{\text{Total number of productive operations}}$$

and

$$\text{Average distance/move ratio} = \frac{\text{Total distance traveled/day}}{\text{Total number of moves/day}}$$

Both ratios are based on the flow of material as it moves through the entire system.

Movement/Operation Ratio

The M/O ratio measures the relative efficiency of the overall handling *plan*. It focuses on the number of moves, rather than how the moves are performed. Material is followed from the time it arrives at the receiving dock until it leaves the shipping dock. The number of times the material is picked up and put down is recorded and compared with the number of times a productive operation is performed on the material. Particular attention is paid to the number of times material is handled at work stations and machines in manufacturing.

Moves are expensive; not only do they consume time and energy and require people, equipment, and space, but also they increase the likelihood of loss. By eliminating operations, simplifying operations, and changing the sequence of operations, the number of moves possibly can be reduced.

The interfaces between functions typically are not well-planned. In particular, the interfaces between (a) receiving and inspection, (b) inspection and storage, (c) storage and manufacturing, (d) manufacturing stages, (e) manufacturing and assembly, (f) assembly and packaging, (g) packaging and warehousing, (h) warehousing and packing, and (i) packing and shipping must be examined closely to determine the number of times material is handled.

A procedure that is commonly used in methods improvement studies is to develop a *flow process chart* of an operation. The flow process chart portrays the operations, inspections, delays, storages, and moves or transportations required to process material through a production process. Hence, if flow process charts have been prepared previously, they should facilitate the computation of the M/O ratio.

An example of the computation of the M/O ratio is given in Figure 14–2.

Average Distance/Move Ratio

The AD/M ratio is used with the M/O ratio to measure the relative efficiency of the overall handling plan. Whereas the M/O ratio focuses on the production *system*, the AD/M ratio focuses on the *layout*. The *length* of the moves required is addressed, rather than the number of moves.

The AD/M ratio is computed using the data provided on the M/O ratio data sheets (Figure 14.2). Additionally, flow process charts provide the distance for each move.

In determining the distances traveled *the data must be collected on the shop floor, not in the office!* Actual travel paths should be observed and measured, rather than assuming moves will be equal to the shortest distance between the originating location and destination.

Example: Computation of the Average Distance/Move Ratio.   For the previous example of the M/O ratio there were 17 moves recorded in getting the purchased component onto the assembly operator's bench. The total distance traveled was 224 feet (assuming an average distance of 4 feet for moves 8 and 9 and 30 feet for move 15). Hence,

$$\text{Average distance/move ratio} = \frac{224 \text{ feet}}{17 \text{ moves}} = 13.18 \text{ ft/move}$$

For such a small value of the AD/M ratio there are obviously several very short moves. The longest move was 60 feet; most moves were performed manually.

Worksheet No. 2 — Sheet 1

FOR COMPUTATION OF YOUR MOVEMENT/OPERATION RATIO

NOTE: There are two ways to obtain these data. *One.* For a quick impression of your handling plan, just walk through the shop, tallying moves and operations. Then compute the ratio.

Two. For a more detailed job and information for corrective action, use the form below. Fill in data on "moves" and "operations" in sequence, and add explanatory detail as desired. Totals of Columns 1 and 2 will give data for the M/O ratio. Remaining columns provide guidance for corrective action. Add comments, queries and suggestions as needed.

$$\frac{\text{Movement/}}{\text{Operation Ratio}} = \frac{\text{No. of moves}}{\text{No. of production operations}}$$

Product _Components for lawn mowers_ Observer _Jones_

Location _Receiving_   To _Finished Goods Storage_ Date _January 10th_

1	2	3	4	5		6		
Productive operation	Moves or delays (x) distance		Description, or reason for activity	Handling technique used		Needs further investigating		
	No.	Ft.		Manual (✓)	Mechanized (✓)	Methods (✓)	Layout (✓)	Equipment (✓)
Receiving	1	2	Cartons from R.R. car to pallet	✓		✓		✓
	2	20	to rec dock		✓			
	X	—	await checking					
	3	30	to storage (incoming goods)		✓			
	X	—	Identify. Prepare storage plan					
	4	5	Unpacked-moved to storage table	✓		✓	✓	✓
Inspect	5	2	Set clear of inspect. table	✓		✓	✓	
	6	3	Place on pallet after full load completed	✓		✓		
	7	10	moved to storage location		✓	✓		
	8	2-6	Put on shelves	✓		✓		
Issue	9	2-6	Put on handcart	✓				
	10	40	to assembly line pick-up area	✓		✓		✓

Figure 14-2 Computation of Movement/Operations Ratio. The analysis should be carried out similarly through the balance of the operations. Note that it has required 17 moves and five delays to get the purchased component onto the assembly operator's bench! Even if "inspection" is counted as a "productive operation," the Movement/Operation ratio will be 17/2 = 8½ to 1.

Worksheet No. 2 — Sheet 2

FOR COMPUTATION OF YOUR
MOVEMENT/OPERATION RATIO *(cont'd)*

1	2	3	4	5		6		
	Moves or delays (x) distance			Handling technique used		Needs further investigating		
Productive operation	No.	Ft.	Description, or reason for activity	Manual (✓)	Mechanized (✓)	Methods (✓)	Layout (✓)	Equipment (✓)
	11	2	Put on floor	✓		✓	✓	✓
	x	—	await consolidation with other parts					
	12	2	Put on pallet	✓		✓		
	13	60	Fork truck to assembly location		✓	✓		
	x	—	await distribution			✓		
	14	2	Put on hand truck	✓				
	15	10-50	Move to work station	✓		✓	Can't this be mechanized?	
	16		Place on floor	✓				
	x	—	await need					
	17	8	operator moves to bench	✓		✓	✓	✓
Assembly								

Productivity Improvement

Some activities that have potential for significant productivity improvement in the area of movement control are given below.

1. Plot the flow lines for material, equipment, and personnel and develop alternative layouts to eliminate backtracking, reduce travel distances, and provide straight flow lines.

2. Develop a flow process chart for manufacturing and warehousing flows; eliminate moves, change operation sequences, and consider applying group technology concepts.

3. Investigate the use of real time dispatching systems for equipment and generate computerized performance reports on moves performed.

4. Investigate the use of a modular materials handling system to meet the changing requirements for movement.

5. Install automatic identification systems for not only data entry on materials movement, but equipment movement as well.

6. Develop larger unit loads to reduce the number of moves; investigate containerization.

7. Batch process orders so that they can be sequenced to obtain minimum deadheading of equipment.

8. Evaluate the impact of one-way aisles on material, equipment, and personnel flow.

9. Provide a primary handling system for routine handling requirements and a secondary handling system for handling exceptions and meeting peak demand requirements.

10. Handle different things differently, store different things differently, and control different things differently.

11. Use computer controlled equipment not only for storing and retrieving materials, but also for material delivery.

12. Develop standard containers for use throughout the system to eliminate double handling of material.

13. De-trash inbound materials at receiving to minimize the amount of waste material that has to be removed from manufacturing.

14. For inbound material having a single manufacturing user, consider point of use storage and dispatching the material directly to the manufacturing user for storage.

15. Consider installing incentive systems for materials handling labor.

16. Evaluate the order-picking alternatives of material-to-person and person-to-material.

17. Investigate the use of driverless tractors and driverless carts.

18. Consider the use of transporters and other conveyor based material dispatching systems.

19. Use fixed path equipment (conveyors and automated guided vehicles) for fixed path moves and use variable path equipment (industrial trucks) for variable path moves.

20. Evaluate the flexibility of the material flow system; if a "change" environment exists, determine how easily the system can be expanded or modified.

Loss

Losses due to accidents, fires, damage, misplaced material, and pilferage can be costly to your company. In fact, such losses can easily wipe out productivity gains in other areas of the organization.

One of the greatest difficulties in controlling loss is a lack of knowledge concerning its magnitude. For example, few companies have a good understanding of how much product damage occurs due to poor materials handling and at what cost. As another example, the cost of industrial accidents is not one you can readily obtain by consulting your accountant.

A major weakness of the typical treatment of loss is that it tends to be addressed after the facility and materials handling system have been planned. Additionally, the emphasis on loss control is relatively new; hence, most existing facilities probably were not planned with a view toward loss control. For these reasons, the emphasis here will be on loss measurement to focus management attention on areas that are having an adverse effect on overall productivity.

The following U.S. statistics serve to motivate a consideration of loss control:

1. As much as 3 to 5% of all products handled are damaged
2. The costs of property damage range from 5 to 50 times the cost of personnel injuries
3. Product theft and pilferage costs have been estimated at over $160 billion per year
4. Vandalism and arson lead to losses in excess of $600 million per year
5. Over 40% of businesses having fires do not resume operation; of those that do, 60% permanently go out of business within one year of reopening.

If loss control programs are to be effective, formal audits must be performed on a regular basis to ascertain if current procedures and operations are conducive to loss control. Banks perform such audits with a similar objective, to minimize losses. Hence, it is recommended that an audit team be appointed and given the responsibility of developing a hard-nosed audit program.

Control Measures

Due to the large number of areas for which loss control is needed, several control measures can be used to facilitate productivity improvement. The following are examples of the control measures that might be used:

$$\text{Damaged loads ratio} = \frac{\text{Number of damaged loads}}{\text{Number of loads}}$$

$$\text{Inventory shrinkage ratio} = \frac{\text{Inventory investment verified}}{\text{Inventory investment expected}}$$

Note: *Time between accidents* is not a productivity ratio; however, it is a worthwhile statistic to compile and publicize. Other statistics that can be used are *percentage of accident-free operators*, and *number of accidents per industrial truck—operating hours*.

DAMAGED LOADS RATIO

The *damaged loads* ratio provides a measure of the loss due to poor handling. The ratio should be computed at each stage of flow throughout the system, beginning with receiving and ending with shipping. A load is defined to be damaged if there are *any* damages to the load.

It is not likely that individual equipment operators will maintain accurate damage reports, even if they are not at fault. The time required to prepare the reports and a lack of interest in the task combine to create an atmosphere that is not conducive to reliable reporting of damaged loads.

Random samples should be performed on a periodic basis to ascertain the damage percentage on loads being staged in receiving, in-bound inspection, packing, and shipping. Additionally, when perpetual inventory audits are performed, a damage report can also be prepared.

Example: Computation of Damaged Loads Ratio.   In a receiving department pallet loads are staged awaiting movement to storage. An audit of the loads is performed with the following results:

Number of loads   =   64
Number of damaged loads   =   4
Number of cases   = 670
Number of damaged cases   =   12

$$\text{Damaged loads ratio} = \frac{4 \text{ damaged loads}}{64 \text{ total loads}} = 6.25\%$$

Also, the following calculation can be performed:

$$\text{Damaged cases ratio} = \frac{12 \text{ damaged cases}}{670 \text{ total cases}} = 1.79\%$$

INVENTORY SHRINKAGE RATIO

The *inventory shrinkage* ratio provides a measure of the loss of material due to pilferage, errors in recordkeeping, errors in material shipments to customers, and misplacement of inventory in storage. The ratio compares what was found from a physical inventory of the material in storage with what was believed to be there, based on inventory records.

Unfortunately, one does not always know why differences exist, if there are differences. In fact, even if there are no differences in the physical inventory and the inventory records, there is no guarantee that losses have not occurred. Furthermore, offsetting errors can cause the verified value of overall inventory investment to equal the expected value.

Example: Computation of Inventory Shrinkage Ratio. A physical audit yielded an inventory investment of \$2,500,000. Inventory records indicate the investment in inventory was \$2,550,000.

$$\text{Inventory shrinkage ratio} = \frac{\$2,500,000}{\$2,550,000} = 98\%$$

Therefore, there was a 2 percent "shrinkage" due to losses, errors, or both.

Productivity Improvement

The primary method of measuring loss control performance is by conducting audits. As such audits are performed, determine if any of the following opportunities for improvement exist:

1. Aisles are clear, well-marked, and sufficiently wide to allow equipment to maneuver

2. Special guards are used to protect racks and columns and guided aisles have guide rail entries

3. Block stacking is not leading to load crushing or leaning stacks and loads do not overhang the pallet

4. Floor loading, rack loading, and structural loads have not been exceeded by recent changes in material or equipment

5. Equipment is not being overloaded or operated at excessive speeds

6. Front-to-back members are installed in selective pallet racks to prevent loads falling through rack openings

7. Masts on industrial trucks fit through doorways and passageways and there are no overhead obstructions to the use of the trucks

8. Safety screens are located beneath overhead conveyors

9. Sprinklers and smoke detectors are installed

10. Hazardous and flammable materials are well-marked and are stored, handled, and transported according to regulations

11. Proper ventilation is provided in battery charging area and in other areas generating hazardous fumes

12. Entrances and exits to buildings and plant property are secured

13. Waste and trash containers are not located near receiving and shipping

14. Insurance audits have been performed and recommended changes have been made

15. Fire extinguishers are marked and in good operating condition

16. Exterior and interior lighting is used to illuminate where security problems might occur

17. A contingency plan exists in the case of a major fire loss; purchasing has available suppliers that can deliver materials on an emergency basis

8. No sagging load beams and no bent upright trusses are present in the storage rack

.9. Materials handlers have undergone formal training in the use of handling equipment

20. Preventive maintenance programs are used for all handling equipment

Operating Efficiency

Receiving and Shipping

Of all the functions encountered in a manufacturing plant, the ones that present the greatest challenges in terms of developing integrated control and efficient operating systems are receiving and shipping. In terms of equipment technology and distributed computer processing the emphasis has been on storage and retrieval, not receiving and shipping. Yet, the opportunities for productivity improvements appear to be far greater in receiving and shipping than in storage and retrieval.

System design responsibilities begin prior to receiving and extend beyond shipping. Your purchasing agents need to influence your vendors and suppliers to ship materials in a manner that facilitates receiving. In a like manner, your customers will influence the manner in which you ship goods to them. Additionally, post-shipping responsibilities can include consideration for returnable containers/pallets, returning trucks (deadheading), and returned goods (due to shipping errors or unacceptable product).

Productivity Measures

The difficulty in obtaining productivity measures for receiving and shipping is one of determining which ones to use from among the many measures that come to mind. For example, consider the following possibilities:

1. Pounds, pallets, cubic feet, dollar value, trailer loads, lines, cases, and/or units received and shipped per day

2. Receiving and shipping employees per pallet load moved daily

3. Daily pallet turnover in receiving and shipping

4. Daily cube utilization of inbound and outbound carriers

5. Daily payload utilization of inbound and outbound carriers

6. Daily freight cost per pallet received

7. Total receiving (shipping) cycle time/receipt (shipment)

8. Hours dock doors used/available hours

9. Receiving (shipping) labor cost/total warehousing costs

10. Total receiving (shipping) cost/total warehousing costs

11. Demurrage costs/total receiving (shipping) costs

12. Orders (lines, items, or pounds) unpacked and verified/labor hours

13. Orders (lines, items, or pounds) packed and marked/labor hours

14. Orders (lines, items, or pounds) staged and consolidated/labor hours

15. Orders (lines, items, or pounds) staged and consolidated/square feet of floor space

16. Orders (lines, items, or pounds) staged and consolidated/equipment hour

17. Orders (lines, items, or pounds) actually staged and consolidated/standard time

18. Percent of orders (lines, items, or pounds) processed in error

19. Pounds shipped/pounds received

20. Cubic volume shipped/cubic volume received

Each measure contributes to our understanding of the productivity of the receiving and shipping functions.

The two ratios that will be used to illustrate receiving and shipping productivity computations are the *receiving productivity* ratio (RPR) and the *shipping productivity* ratio (SPR).

$$\text{RP ratio} = \frac{\text{Pounds received/day}}{\text{Labor hours/day}}$$

$$\text{SP ratio} = \frac{\text{Pounds shipped/day}}{\text{Labor hours/day}}$$

RECEIVING AND SHIPPING PRODUCTIVITY RATIOS

The RPR and SPR values provide a measure of the daily output of the receiving and shipping functions.

It should be noted that "pounds" is not necessarily the best measure. In some cases the number of loads or cubic feet of material will be a better output measure; likewise, inputs other than labor will sometimes be preferred.

Example: Computation of Receiving Productivity Ratio. A warehouse has four receiving doors. A crew of two people is assigned to unload each trailer. There are three crews available. When no trailers are present, the people assist in moving material to QC and storage. When there are four trailers present, the senior crew splits up and one person works on a trailer. The following results were obtained for one day's operation:

Number of hours/shift:	8
Number of trailers unloaded:	30
Labor hours spent in unloading:	28
Pounds unloaded:	875,500

$$\text{Receiving productivity ratio} = \frac{875,500 \text{ pounds received}}{28 \text{ labor hours required}}$$

$$\text{RP ratio} = 31,268 \text{ pounds/labor hour}$$

Note: Since the calculation for the shipping productivity ratio is identical to that for the RP ratio, no example is given.

Productivity Improvement

To improve productivity in receiving and shipping, review the following areas and topics for feasible application in your operation:

1. Automatic loading and unloading trailers

2. Automatic identification systems, label printers, and scanner/readers to facilitate data entry in both receiving and shipping

3. Automatic palletizers and depalletizers, shrinkwrap/stretchwrap/strapping for unitizing/stabilizing loads

4. Special attachments on industrial trucks, e.g. slipsheet, clamp, barrel, and appliance attachments

5. Extendable conveyors that go into trailers to facilitate loading/unloading trailers

6. Dock levelers or sturdy dock boards

7. Scheduled arrival of both outbound and inbound carriers and preassigned spots for loading/unloading

8. Centralize receiving and shipping; receive and ship at different times of the day or different days of the week

9. Require inbound shipments to be unitized and, possibly, palletized

10. Provide ample number of dock doors

11. Eliminate floor stacking materials and provide racks for staging materials

12. For in-bound shipments requiring inspection, pull samples for quality control (QC), dispatch remainder to storage, and "lock" material in storage until released by QC

13. Preassign receiving numbers and provide computer terminals at the dock area for expediting receiving

14. Evaluate side-loading and top-loading trailers to facilitate automated loading

15. Consider unpacking small parts at receiving and placing in standard containers for movement throughout the system; compact and bale waste packing materials.

Storage and Retrieval

Storage and retrieval of material has already received considerable coverage here. It is difficult not to dwell on the subject, since it has been the focus of attention within the materials handling field for at least the past decade.

Despite the attention it has received, there continues to exist a significant gap between the state-of-the-art and warehousing practice. Additionally, a number of very progressive companies have installed very sophisticated storage/retrieval systems and assumed that the problem had been solved, once and for all. Productivity programs are needed to help *upgrade* the weak operations and to help *sustain* the strong operations. Conditions change too rapidly for a company to rest on its laurels.

The primary concern here is the productivity of the system for storing and retrieving (putting in and taking out) of materials. The equipment, space, and movement aspects of materials storage have been previously addressed.

Throughput is a term that is defined in many different ways. Literally, throughput implies the rate of movement of material through the system. In the context of storage and retrieval, throughput can be defined as the storage and retrieval rate in terms of storages per hour and retrievals per hour.

Two types of storage that should be defined are randomized and dedicated storage. With randomized storage a particular pallet load of material can be stored anywhere in the system; whereas, with dedicated storage, each SKU has an address or location assigned to it.

One form of dedicated storage is to store material in part number sequence. Such a procedure is very inefficient from a throughput point of view. The preferred method of performing dedicated storage is to rank SKUs on the basis of the ratio of their activity to the number of openings or slots assigned to the SKU. The highest ranking SKU is assigned to the closest slots and so forth, until the lowest ranking SKU, which is assigned to the worst slots.

Productivity Measures

The productivity measures to be used in measuring the performance of the storage and retrieval activity are the *orderpicking productivity* ratio (OPR) and the *throughput performance* index (TPI) defined as follows:

$$\text{OP ratio} = \frac{\text{Equivalent lines or orders picked/day}}{\text{Labor hours required/day}}$$

and

$$\text{TPI} = \frac{\text{Throughput achieved/day}}{\text{Throughput capacity/day}}$$

ORDER-PICKING PRODUCTIVITY RATIO

The order-picking productivity ratio measures the productivity of an order-picking activity. The scope of the ratio begins with the removal of an individual item and includes the accumulation of the various line items that constitute an order, as well as the replenishment activity for the system.

Since orders have a different number of line items and different pick quantities can be required for each line item, it is necessary to define an equivalent order. For example, you might wish to define an order to be the equivalent of 10 line items or you might argue that the differences in the size of an order will "average out" over the long run and simply count the number of different orders received.

A further complication arises when an order is split and zone or aisle-captive picking is performed. In such a case, team productivity rather than individual productivity is measured if orders are counted.

As can be seen there can arise difficulties in defining the productivity measure. Also, measuring the inputs and outputs required is not a simple task.

Example: Computation of Order-picking Productivity Ratio. A service parts distribution center for an electronics firm received orders for parts from 210 different customers. Even though several customers order the same line item, each time one is ordered it is counted as a separate line item, since the order-picker has to bag and label the part for each customer. A total of 1820 line items were ordered (including duplicates). Three individuals perform the actual order-picking on aisle-captive, man-aboard machines. The order-pickers travel to the end of the aisle and place tote boxes of parts on conveyors that go to order accumulation and pack stations. The labor requirements for the activities are given below:

Number of orders: 210
Number of lines: 1820
Number of hours to order-pick: 11
Number of hours to replenish: 13
Number of hours to accumulate: 20
Number of hours to pack: 18
Total number of hours: 62

Orders:

$$\text{OP ratio} = \frac{210 \text{ orders/day}}{62 \text{ hours/day}}$$

$$\text{OP ratio} = 3.387 \text{ orders/hour}$$

Lines:

$$\text{OP ratio} = \frac{1820 \text{ lines/day}}{62 \text{ hours/day}}$$

$$\text{OP ratio} = 29.35 \text{ lines/hour}$$

Note: Claims of 250 picks per hour for one type storage and retrieval system versus "only" 50 picks per hour for another system must be closely examined to insure that both are addressing the same set of activities.

THROUGHOUT PERFORMANCE INDEX

The throughput performance index compares the actual throughput with the theoretical throughput capacity for the storage and retrieval system. Depending upon the particular application the theoretical throughput capacity could be based on 100 percent single command cycles, 100 percent dual command cycles, or some combination of single and dual command cycles (see page 329).

The theoretical throughput capacity establishes a standard against which actual performance is compared. For the case of randomized storage and aisle-captive storage/retrieval equipment the theoretical throughput capacity can be determined easily.

In the case of an AS/RS (unit load or mini load) where horizontal and vertical travel occur simultaneously and the P/D station is at floor level, the travel time for a single command cycle is obtained as follows. Let t_H equal the horizontal travel time required to go to the furthest location from the P/D station and let t_v equal the "worst case" vertical travel time. Let the largest worst case time equal T. Divide the smaller worst case time by T and let the quotient equal Q. The travel time for a single command cycle (SC) is given by

$$\text{SC} = T \times (Q^2 + 3) \div 3$$

The travel time for a dual command cycle (DC) is given by

$$DC = T \times (40 + 15Q^2 - Q^3) \div 30$$

In the case of an aisle-captive industrial truck that performs sequential horizontal and vertical travel, rather than simultaneous, the travel time for a single command cycle is obtained as follows:

$$SC = t_H + t_V$$

and the travel time for a dual command cycle is given by

$$DC = \frac{4\,SC}{3}$$

Example: Computation of Throughput Performance Index. An AS/RS consists of 6 aisles, with an S/R machine in each aisle. Randomized storage is used. The S/R travels horizontally and vertically at speeds of 450 fpm and 80 fpm, an aisle is 360 feet long and 70 feet high. The time required to pick up or put down a load is 0.25 min. Over an 8-hour period the total system performed 500 single command cycles and 750 dual command cycles.

The theoretical time required to perform a single command cycle is obtained as follows:

$$t_H = 360 \text{ feet} \div 450 \text{ fpm} = 0.800 \text{ min.}$$
$$t_V = 70 \text{ feet} \div 80 \text{ fpm} = 0.875 \text{ min.}$$

or

$$T = 0.875 \text{ min.}$$

and

$$Q = \frac{0.800}{0.875} = 0.9143$$

Therefore,

$$SC = 0.875 \times [(0.9143)^2 + 3] \div 3$$
$$= 1.12 \text{ min.}$$

and

$$DC = 0.875 \times [40 + 15(0.9143)^2 - (0.9143)^3] \div 30$$
$$= 1.51 \text{ min.}$$

Considering the P/D times, the following theoretical cycle times are obtained:

$$\text{Single command cycle time} = 1.12 + 0.50$$
$$= 1.62 \text{ min.}$$
$$\text{Dual command cycle time} = 1.51 + 1.00$$
$$= 2.51 \text{ min.}$$

The theoretical time required to do 500 single command cycles is 500×1.62 min. or 13.50 hours; to do 750 dual command cycles requires 750×2.51 min. or 31.375 hours.

An equivalent representation of the throughput productivity index is

$$TPI = \frac{\text{Theoretical time required/day}}{\text{Actual time required/day}}$$

Hence,

$$\text{TPI} = \frac{13.50 + 31.375}{48} = 93.5\%$$

Example: Computation of Throughput Performance Index.   An aisle-captive industrial truck is used in an aisle that is 400 feet long and 25 feet high. Randomized storage is used. The truck travels horizontally at a speed of 350 fpm and vertically at a speed of 60 fpm. The P/D time is 0.35 min. Over an 8-hour period the truck performed 50 single command cycles and 100 dual command cycles.

$$t_H = 400 \text{ feet} \div 350 \text{ fpm} = 1.143 \text{ min.}$$
$$t_V = 25 \text{ feet} \div 60 \text{ fpm} = 0.417 \text{ min.}$$
$$\text{SC} = 1.143 + 0.417 = 1.56 \text{ min.}$$
$$\text{DC} = 4 \times \frac{1.56}{3} = 2.08 \text{ min.}$$

Adding the P/D times gives

$$\text{Single command cycle time} = 1.56 + 0.70$$
$$= 2.26 \text{ min.}$$
$$\text{Dual command cycle time} = 2.08 + 1.40$$
$$= 3.48 \text{ min.}$$

To do 50 single commands requires 50×2.26, or 113 minutes;
To do 100 dual commands requires 100×3.48, or 348 minutes.

Hence, over an 8-hour period a total of $113 + 348$, or 461 minutes of work are performed for a throughput performance index of

$$\text{TPI} = \frac{461 \text{ min.}}{480 \text{ min.}} = 96\%$$

Productivity Improvement

In attempting to improve productivity in storage and retrieval, consider the following:

1. Arrange items by popularity, material characteristics, and space requirements

2. Use dedicated storage to maximize throughput and use randomized storage to minimize space

3. Use dedicated picking faces and randomized reserve storage

4. Batch process storages and retrievals to increase the dual command percentage

5. Use multiple-sized (vertical dimension) openings in palletized storage

6. Use narrow aisle and very narrow aisle storage

7. Evaluate medium rise, high rise, and very high rise storage

8. Automate the input/output of materials for storage/retrieval

9. Provide for real time dispatching, with interrupt capability, for emergency retrieval requirements

10. Pre-process retrievals and sequence for optimum picking

11. Evaluate mini loads, carousels, man-aboards, and walking for picking small parts

12. Evaluate "picker-to-picking face" and "picking face-to-picker" alternatives for unit loads

13. Arrange picking lists in picking sequences

14. Evaluate single order picking vs. batch picking vs. zone picking

15. Install a computerized locator system

16. Locate a minicomputer in the warehouse, dedicated to receiving, storage, retrieval, and shipping functions

17. Periodically reclassify materials as fast, medium, slow, and non-movers and appropriately relocate stock

18. Consider retrieval rates, storage and replenishment rates, and perpetual inventory or cycle counting rates in establishing throughput requirements for the system

19. Establish aisle lengths based on throughput and order-picking requirements

20. Consider honeycombing effects in establishing storage requirements for the system

21. Consider storing different things differently by using hybrid systems

22. Use slave pallets when precision storage and retrieval are required

23. Eliminate obsolete material or at least move it to a separate area

24. Eliminate storage in part number sequence

25. Plan for sprinklers (ceiling, in-rack, or both)

26. Block stack material if possible and feasible

27. Provide mezzanines to utilize overhead space in item picking areas

28. Consider gravity flow racks for case picking

29. Evaluate high speed sortation systems for packages

30. Investigate the use of deep lane storage systems, pallet flow rack, and drive-in storage rack

31. Base aisle widths on load-to-load dimensions, rather than rack-to-rack dimensions

32. Automatically size loads before storing to insure the load is compatible with the opening

33. Check for load overhangs before placing in storage

34. Consider dedicating an industrial type truck to an aisle and providing input/output for the truck similar to that used for an AS/RS

35. Remember that it's easy to develop complex solutions to problems, but it's difficult to develop simple solutions to problems; keep it simple!

Manufacturing

Introduction

During the decade of the 1970s, the emphasis was on materials handling in warehousing. It is anticipated that during the 1980s the emphasis will be on materials handling in manufacturing.

Approximately 75 percent of U.S. metal working is performed in job shops. Additionally, approximately 40 percent of the total manufacturing labor force is employed in job shops. Hence, the focus of this chapter is on job shop processes.

Currently, a subject of considerable interest in designing materials handling systems and layouts for job shops is *group technology*. The use of group technology, coupled with greater application of robots and flexible manufacturing systems, is credited with placing European and Japanese manufacturers in a strong competitive position relative to the United States. Only recently has group technology (GT) become popular in the United States. However, it has been used abroad for several decades. GT is "an approach to finding common solutions to similar problems."

Traditional manufacturing layouts are either *process* or *product* layouts. The process layout, also referred to as the functional layout, groups like functions or processing equipment together; as an example, milling machines would be located in one department, lathes would be placed together in another department, and drilling machines would be grouped together in another department. The product layout, also referred to as the assembly line layout, arranges equipment according to the processing sequence required to manufacture a product; hence, if four distinct products are made, then four distinct lines of equipment would be provided.

In a job shop environment, where literally hundreds of different parts are made in small quantities, the process layout results in flow lines that resemble a "spaghetti bowl." A tremendous amount of backtracking and intersecting flow lines results.

Group technology is based on the premise that dissimilar parts and/or products can be grouped into parts families. Manufacturing cells can be formed for processing individual families. The cellular layout structure minimizes the intercell flow, since material that enters a cell is completely processed within the cell. By grouping parts, the production quantity within a cell is sufficient to achieve many of the economies of a product layout.

Computer-aided design (CAD) and computer-aided manufacturing (CAM) emphasis has tended to be on manufacturing and assembly methods. Little emphasis has been placed on materials handling. As a result, a "hurry up and wait" situation exists—parts are manufactured faster than ever, but then wait for the next operation.

In a typical job shop environment a workpiece spends only 5 percent of its time on a machine once it reaches the production department; 95 percent of the time it is either staged, awaiting processing, or being moved. Of the time the workpiece is on the machine, it is actually being machined only 30 percent of the time; the remaining 70 percent of the time it is being positioned, loaded, gauged, idle, etc. The "95 percent problem" of materials waiting and handling provides an opportunity for significant productivity improvement.

Manufacturing performance is multidimensional. Some of the performance measures used are cost, quality, and on-time delivery. Interestingly, top management might rank the performance measures as listed (cost, quality, and delivery). However, because of the control systems actually used to evaluate the performance of the manufacturing manager, the system operates using a reverse ordering of priorities, on-time delivery, quality, and cost.

As mentioned at the beginning of the chapter, suboptimization can occur when one measure (on-time delivery) becomes the "tail that wags the dog." Care must be taken to ensure that productivity measures suggested here do not become "ends in themselves."

Productivity Measures

In measuring manufacturing productivity a number of ratios can be used. Of those that relate to materials handling the following two are offered for your consideration: *manufacturing cycle efficiency* (MCE) and the *job lateness* ratio, (JLR).

$$MCE = \frac{\text{Total time spent on machines}}{\text{Total time spent in production system}}$$

and

$$JL\ ratio = \frac{\text{Number of jobs completed or in process that are late/week}}{\text{Number of jobs completed/week}}$$

Manufacturing Cycle Efficiency

The MCE ratio compares the time materials spend being processed to the total time they spend in the manufacturing department. In terms of the previous discussion, the focus is on the "95 percent problem." The utilization of the machine during the "5 percent" period of time is addressed by the production equipment utilization ratio (see page 327).

The total time spent in the production system is measured from the time materials arrive at the department until they leave the department. Hence, a log-in and log-out procedure is required; either a manual system or a computerized data entry system can be used. To facilitate data entry, bar code readers are used in some firms.

In our opinion, one of the greatest needs in manufacturing is improved control over work-in-process. For many firms, material loses visibility once it is dispatched from the storage facility to manufacturing. It becomes visible again when it completes manufacturing. The time it is in manufacturing, from a materials control viewpoint, is like being in a dark tunnel with no knowledge of its status.

The MCE ratio provides a measure of the lack of planning and control concerning the flow of materials through manufacturing. It can range from a maximum value of 1.0 for automated, continuous processing to as low as a fraction of a percent. Improved planning, layout, production control, materials handling, materials control, and information flow can increase the MCE ratio.

Example: Computation of Manufacturing Cycle Efficiency.   Part 10876, pinion gear, is processed from a blank to a polished gear with groove broached in the hub for spline fit to a shaft.

Sum of all production operations times:

Machining (8 operations)	4 hr. 10 min.
Heat treatment	1 hr. 24 min.
Inspection	10 min.
Rust inhibition treatment and packaging	4 min.
Total required production time	5 hr. 48 min.
	(or 5.80 hr.)

Elapsed time in production system—(1 shift operation)

Part entered system	June 4, 8:00 am
Part delivered to finished goods storage	June 20, 2:30 pm

Therefore, elapsed time = (12 work days × 8 hr.) + 5½ hr. = 101½ hr.

$$\text{MCE} = \frac{5.8}{101.5} = 5.7\%$$

JOB LATENESS RATIO

The job lateness ratio (JLR) is simply a measure of the due-date performance of manufacturing. Care must be taken to ensure that due-date performance does not become the only concern of manufacturing management. While job lateness should be avoided, it is not to be avoided at any cost!

We are familiar with a number of companies that have over-emphasized the avoidance of job lateness. One West Coast firm discovered their manufacturing managers were subcontracting on the East Coast relatively simple machining operations in order to avoid late delivery on orders. The bottom line was that the company was losing money on the job due to the subcontracting arrangement, but they weren't late in meeting the delivery dates.

A variation of the emphasis on "job lateness avoidance" was observed in another company that evaluated managers on the basis of monthly billings. An order was counted and "billed" if it was shipped during the month. As a result of the emphasis on monthly billings, 40 to 50 percent of the monthly billings were made in the last week of the month. Additionally, the overtime incurred during the last week of the month was enormous.

To compute values of JLR, due dates and *actual* completion dates must be known. The validity of the measures are dependent upon accurate inputs.

Example: Computation of the Job Lateness Ratio. At the end of the 45th week of a work year the following job status was observed in Department 386 of a metalworking company located in the South:

Job Number	Due Date (Week)	Status
80-100-80	44	Completed (late)
80-100-81	44	In process (late)
80-100-82	44	In process (late)
80-101-20	45	In process (late)
80-101-21	45	Completed
80-101-22	45	In process (late)
80-101-23	45	Completed
80-101-24	45	Completed
80-101-25	45	Completed

Job Number	Due Date (Week)	Status
80-102-01	46	Completed
80-102-03	46	In process
80-102-06	46	In process
80-102-10	46	Waiting to start
80-103-01	47	Waiting to start
80-103-02	47	Waiting to start
80-104-01	48	Waiting to start

Summary:

Number of jobs in Department 386 at beginning of Week 45:	16
Number of jobs in process during Week 45:	12
Number of late jobs in process at the end of Week 45:	4
Number of jobs completed during Week 45:	6
Number of jobs completed late during Week 45:	1

$$\text{Job lateness ratio} = \frac{1 \text{ job completed late} + 4 \text{ late jobs in process}}{6 \text{ jobs completed}}$$

$$\text{JL ratio} \quad = \frac{5}{6} = 83.3\%$$

Note: The JLR appears to be very high; management attention is needed to determine if the lateness condition is justified and, if not, the changes needing to be made.

Productivity Improvement

To improve manufacturing productivity a number of areas can be considered, including materials selection, tool and die design, product design, and equipment selection. Our focus is on the improvement of manufacturing productivity via materials handling and related approaches. The following should be considered:

1. Delivering materials, tooling, and supplies to the manufacturing center

2. Planning the manufacturing work station and developing workplace layouts via methods improvement programs

3. Considering group technology and cellular layout in manufacturing

4. Installing a real time WIP control system for controlling materials

5. Designing job shop scheduling systems based on controlled storage of WIP and delivery to manufacturing

6. Minimizing walking by operators

7. Performing parts preparation operations prior to dispatching material to manufacturing

8. Using automatic identification systems for improved materials control data entry

9. Standardizing materials handling methods and using standardized material containers

10. Automating scrap removal

Economic Justification

Introduction

Whether you are contemplating a $50,000 investment or a $5 million investment in materials handling equipment, the investment must be justified. Consider the following observations concerning production equipment justification made in an issue of *Automation*,

> "That machine is worn, and . . . you want to replace it. Can you justify the necessary capital expenditure? You know that it is outdated, obsolete, and plain worn out. Perhaps it goes pocketa-queep, pocketa-queep like a Walter Mitty fantasy; it represents the highest extension of prewar thinking, and it is woefully inadequate for today's production."

Sounds familiar, doesn't it? The article goes on to state,

> ". . . you know that your request for replacement will bring down the shrill cries of 'Justification! Justification!' from the front-office boo-birds. How can you justify the purchase? How can you keep the flinty-eyed accountants happy, who speak only dollars, and are totally unable to appreciate and understand the basic demands of modern production?"

The objective of this subunit is to introduce a number of concepts associated with economic justification. A number of texts are available on the subject for those interested in pursuing the subject further. (See pages 933–934.)

Three texts that come immediately to mind are *Principles of Engineering Economics* (Grant, Ireson, and Levenworth); *Engineering Economics* (Thuesen, Fabrycky, and Thuesen); and *Principles of Engineering Economic Analysis* (White, Agee, and Case).

Systematic Economic Analysis Technique

In conducting an economic comparison of materials handling alternatives, an eight-step procedure, referred to as the Systematic Economic Analysis Technique (SEAT), should be used. SEAT involves the following steps:

1. *Identify the set of mutually exclusive alternatives to be compared.* In the context of materials handling, the alternatives might include one or more industrial truck alternatives. A warehouse layout design problem might produce layout alternatives involving aisle widths, ceiling heights, and types of storage racks. Regardless of the type of materials handling problem, a number of alternatives will be generated; otherwise, no problem exists! By mutually exclusive is meant either-or, but not both.

2. *Specify the planning horizon to be used in the comparison.* The planning horizon defines the width of a window through which the cash flows will be viewed for each alternative. A planning horizon that is too short can eliminate profitable alternatives whose primary benefits are realized downstream rather than immediately. Highly automated materials handling systems typically require a number of years for design, installation, and de-bugging; as a result, tangible savings might not be realized until two or three years following installation. Too short a planning horizon would eliminate such an alternative.

Just as a planning horizon that is too short can be detrimental to your long run success, too long a planning horizon can also jeopardize your performance. In particular, if a sizeable investment is made in a materials handling system and no benefits are realized for several years, your economic condition can deteriorate to a point that its very existence is threatened. Likewise, investments in an alternative that can only be justified over a prolonged period of time might preclude the possibility of investing in other, more profitable, alternatives which arise in the interim.

3. *Estimate the cash flows on a year-by-year basis for each alternative.* Given the alternatives to be analyzed and the planning horizon to be used, the cash flows that result should be estimated for each alternative. It is important that the estimates reflect future anticipations. Likewise, all benefits that can be quantified in economic terms should be included in the estimates. After-tax cash flows should be provided, rather than before-tax cash flows. Likewise, consideration should be given to inflationary effects.

4. *Select the discount rate, interest rate, or minimum attractive rate of return to be used.* The discount rate or minimum attractive rate of return used in the analysis should reflect your opportunity for investment elsewhere. If the cash flow estimates have incorporated components for inflation, then the discount rate should also incorporate an inflation component.

5. *Choose the measure of economic performance to employ.* A host of measures of economic performance are available, including present worth, annual worth, future worth, payback period, benefit-cost ratio, and rate of return. With the exception of the payback period method, all of the other measures of economic performance are equivalent methods for comparing investment alternatives. Although quite popular, the payback period is a dangerous measure to use; it ignores both the timing of cash flows and any cash flows that occur after the payback period. Due to its simplicity, we recommend you use the present worth method. However, if you are more familiar with the rate of return method, then it should be used.

6. *Compare the investment alternatives using the measure of economic performance.* Using the present worth method, the cash flows for the alternatives are converted into equivalent present worth, using the specific interest rate.

7. *Perform supplementary analyses.* The comparison of the investment alternatives using the appropriate measure of economic performance is normally quite straightforward and the alternative having the greatest present worth is normally recommended. However, estimates are provided for the cash flows, the planning horizon is probably specified somewhat arbitrarily, and it is likely that the discount rate is determined in a manner not entirely objective and precise. Consequently, supplementary analyses are used to determine the effects of the estimating process on the economic desirability of the alternatives. "What if" questions are answered using break-even and sensitivity analyses.

8. *Specify the preferred alternative.* The final step in conducting an economic comparison involves the selection of the preferred alternative. The choice of the alternative to be pursued is normally influenced by both monetary and non-monetary considerations. Management's reaction to risk and uncertainty plays an important part in the final decision, as does the availability of capital for investment.

Income Taxes

Income taxes can have a significant effect on the profitability of investments in materials handling equipment. If, for example, the corporate tax rate is 46 percent, every $1 spent on *expense* items has an after-tax cost of 54¢. Whereas, every $1 spent on equipment that must be capitalized or depreciated over an eight-year period has an after-tax cost of approximately 60¢, based on a 15 percent required return on investment (ROI), and sum-of-years digits depreciation method. On large investments the 6¢ difference can become significant!

A number of firms have received favorable tax treatments on rack-supported warehouses. Since it is a special structure, a significant portion of the investment in a rack-supported warehouse qualifies for tax treatment as equipment, rather than structure. Hence, an 8 to 10 year writeoff is allowed, rather than the 40 to 50 year period for conventional warehouses. Additionally, as equipment, the rack-supported warehouse qualifies for the 10 percent investment tax credit.

For the portion of the rack-supported warehouse that qualifies as equipment, each $1 spent can cost as little as 60¢ after taxes. A conventional warehouse, on the other hand, can cost as much as 88¢ after taxes for each $1 spent. Additionally, construction costs for the rack-supported warehouse typically are significantly less than those for conventional construction; savings in excess of $6 per square foot have been reported!

FASB 13 *

The Financial Accounting Standards Board (FASB) establishes the accounting principles generally accepted and adopted by most companies. FASB's statement of Financial Accounting Standards No. 13, "Accounting for Leases," is having a dramatic impact on leasing.

Although it became effective January 1977, the full impact of "FASB 13" has yet to be felt on materials handling. Leasing, in general, is big business—over $15 billion in 1978. In materials handling, more than 25 percent of all industrial trucks procured in 1978 were leased.

FASB 13 categorizes leases as either operating leases or capital leases. Operating leases are recorded as expenses; capital leases are treated as assets and are depreciated over the lease term. Leasing data, so categorized, are to be placed on the balance sheet for the benefit of the stockholders.

A lease is classified as a capital lease if it meets any of the following paraphrased criteria; otherwise, it is classified as an operating lease.

The lease transfers ownership of the property (equipment) to the leasee by the end of the lease term.

The lease contains a bargain purchase option.

The lease term is equal to 75 percent or more of the estimated economic life of the leased property.

The present value, at the beginning of the lease term, of the minimum lease payments, is not less than 90 percent of the excess of the leased property to the lessor at the inception of the lease, over any related investment tax credit retained by and expected to be realized by the lessor.

---

*The following discussion is drawn from White, J. A., "Facilities Planning Forum," *Modern Materials Handling* (November 1978), p. 23

The Financial Accounting Standards Board establishes the accounting principles used by your accountants and auditors. While FASB's standards are not legal restrictions, for many firms FASB 13 is de facto tax law. Controllers for a number of U.S. firms indicate they will not maintain different books of account for tax purposes and stockholders. They compute their tax liability following the guidelines of FASB 13.

Prior to FASB 13, one of the attractions of leases, from a tax viewpoint, was that lease payments could be expensed. Hence, with a 46 percent tax rate, each $1 spent on a lease would cost 54¢ after taxes. If the lease is treated as a capital lease, then each $1 spent on a lease might cost as much as 65¢ to 70¢ after taxes, depending on the depreciation method, write-off period, and time value of money. Hence, FASB 13 can have a significantly negative impact on the profitability of a lease arrangement.

Productivity Improvement

Just as we are interested in improving the productivity of people, equipment, space, and energy, it is essential that we improve the productivity of the investment dollar. Some suggestions for you to consider in improving your economic justifications are as follows:

1. Adopt a formalized approach in performing economic justifications

2. Incorporate time value of money concepts, income tax considerations, and inflationary effects in your analyses

3. Perform supplementary analyses on all expenditures in excess of $50,000

4. Use accelerated depreciation methods

5. Quantify as many of the benefits and costs as possible

6. Obtain IRS approval to "expense" all investments having unit costs less than $500

7. Develop a formalized equipment replacement program

8. Develop cost control systems for materials handling; measure the cost of materials handling

9. Consider leasing, as well as other alternative financing plans

10. Develop a formal post-audit program to insure that promised benefits are delivered

Summary

Throughout this chapter a number of measures have been provided to facilitate the development of a productivity improvement program. The measures represent only the beginning point for a program; additional measures will need to be developed to capture the unique aspects of any particular business.

Any approach to the productivity improvement program should follow certain logical steps:

1. Recognize the need for productivity improvement

2. Set objectives for quantifying expected results

3. Perform audits of current systems to identify improvement opportunities

4. Select specific areas for their greatest potential for improvement and involve relevant personnel in the corrective action

5. Develop productivity measures to be used in establishing base lines from which improvements may be confirmed or denied

6. Monitor the performance of the revised system

7. Assess the overall effect of the change on the system

8. Apprise management of the results obtained

9. Recognize and reward participating individuals for their performance

To be effective, a productivity improvement program must have top management commitment. Management discipline is required to ensure that (a) productivity measures are developed, (b) accurate reports are generated on a regular basis (at least monthly), (c) follow-up actions are taken, and (d) proper recognition is given to those that are successful in improving productivity. A formal productivity audit program should be developed.

In designing new materials handling systems, as well as improving existing systems, it is important to first establish the objectives to be realized. After establishing the objectives, the Principles of Material Handling should be applied.*

In conclusion, the need for productivity improvement is real and the opportunity for significant improvements are plentiful. This chapter was prepared with the objective of providing positive and logical steps for improving productivity together with the basic "tools" for their implementation. It remains for each individual concerned to take the initiative and accept the challenge if a national commitment to increase productivity is to become a reality.

Glossary

Aisle space percentage (ASP)   proportion of space devoted to aisles.

$$ASP = \frac{\text{Cube space occupied by aisles}}{\text{Total cube space}}$$

AS/RS   Automated Storage and Retrieval System.

Average distance/move ratio (AD/M ratio)   measures the ratio of the length of moves required to the total number of moves made.

$$AD/M \text{ ratio} = \frac{\text{Total distance traveled/day}}{\text{Total number of moves/day}}$$

BP   battery powered

Busy percentage (BP)   the percentage of time handling equipment is busy.

$$BP = \frac{\text{Busy observations}}{\text{Total observations}}$$

*See Tompkins, J. A., and White, J. A., *Facilities Planning* (New York: Wiley, 1984).

Damaged loads ratio (DLR)   measures loss due to poor handling.

$$\text{DL Ratio} = \frac{\text{Number of damaged loads}}{\text{Number of loads}}$$

Direct labor materials handling (DLMH) ratio   measures the proportion of the direct labor time spent in performing materials handling.

$$\text{DLMH ratio} = \frac{\text{Materials handling time spent by direct labor}}{\text{Total direct labor time}}$$

Dual command cycle   occurs when equipment moves a load to a specified destination, departs to another specified location, retrieves a load, and travels loaded to the originating point.

Energy utilization index (EUI)   compares the Btus consumed per day with the total cube space.

$$\text{EUI} = \frac{\text{Btus consumed/day}}{\text{Cubic space}}$$

Financial Accounting Standards Board (FASB)   an independent organization that establishes the accounting principles used by accountants and auditors. Although their standards are not legal restrictions, for many firms they are de facto tax law.

Flow process chart   portrays the operations, inspection, delays, storages, and moves or transportations required to process material through a productive process.

Group technology (GT)   forming parts families by grouping parts according to one or more characteristics.

Handling equipment utilization (HEU)   determined by considering the weight of a load, the number of loads moved and the time spent in moving the load.

$$\text{HEU} = \frac{\text{Weight moved/hour}}{\text{Theoretical capacity}}$$

HVAC   heating, ventilation, and air conditioning

ICE   internal combustion engine

Inventory fill ratio   provides a measure of out-of-stock conditions.

$$\text{IF ratio} = \frac{\text{Line item demands filled/day}}{\text{Line items demands/day}}$$

Inventory location error ratio   monitors the accuracy of the stock location system.

Inventory shrinkage ratio (ISR)   measures loss of material due to pilferage, error in record keeping, error in material shipments to customer, and misplacement of inventory in storage.

$$\text{IS ratio} = \frac{\text{Inventory investment verified}}{\text{Inventory investment expected}}$$

Inventory replenishment ratio   compares actual stock replenishment lead times against desired lead times.

Inventory turnover ratio   measures the return obtained from inventory investments and provides an indication of the movement of materials.

$$\text{IT ratio} = \frac{\text{Annual labor}}{\text{Average annual inventory investment}}$$

Job lateness ratio (JLR)   measures the due date performance of manufacturing.

$$\text{JL ratio} = \frac{\text{Jobs that are late/week}}{\text{Number of jobs completed/week}}$$

Manufacturing cell   a collection of machines, grouped together for processing a family of parts.

Manufacturing cycle efficiency (MCE)   compares the time materials spend being processed to the total time spent in the manufacturing department.

$$\text{MCE} = \frac{\text{Total time spent on machining}}{\text{Total time spent in production system}}$$

MH   materials handling

Materials handling labor ratio (MHL ratio)   measures the proportion of the total labor force devoted to materials handling duties.

$$\text{MHL ratio} = \frac{\begin{array}{c}\text{Personnel assigned to}\\\text{materials handling duties}\end{array}}{\text{Total operating workforce}}$$

MRP   materials requirement planning

Microprocessor   an integrated circuit that provides arithmetic, logic, and program control between input and output circuitry.

Movement/operation ratio (M/O ratio)   measures the relative efficiency of the overall materials handling plan

$$\text{M/O ratio} = \frac{\text{Total number of moves}}{\text{Total number of productive operations}}$$

OBS   observations

Obsolete inventory ratio   measures the percentage of storage space consumed by obsolete materials.

Order-picking productivity ratio (OPR)   measures the productivity of an order-picking activity.

$$\text{OP ratio} = \frac{\text{Equivalent lines or orders picked/day}}{\text{Labor hours required/day}}$$

Pareto's Law   a common phenomenon also known as the "80/20 Rule" in which a 20% cause produces an 80% effect and/or an 80% cause produces a 20% effect.

Perpetual inventory error ratio   measures the accuracy of the inventory transactions reporting system.

P/D   pick-up and deposit

Process layout or functional layout   the grouping of like processing or function equipment.

Product layout or assembly line layout   an arrangement of equipment according to the processing sequence required to manufacture a product.

Production equipment utilization (PEU)   provides an indication of the extent to which production equipment is being utilized to its fullest potential.

$$\text{PEU} = \frac{\text{Actual output}}{\text{Theoretical output}}$$

Productivity   the ratio of output to input; popularly defined as output per man-hour.

Productivity improvement for profit (PIP)   provides a structured approach for productivity improvement focusing on twelve major areas.

QC   quality control

Receiving productivity ratio (RPR)   measures daily output of receiving functions.

$$\text{RP ratio} = \frac{\text{Pounds received/day}}{\text{Labor hours/day}}$$

Single command cycle   occurs when equipment moves a load to a specific destination and returns empty, or travels empty to a specified location and returns with a load.

Shipping productivity ratio (SPR)   measures daily output of shipping functions.

$$\text{SP ratio} = \frac{\text{Pounds shipped/day}}{\text{Labor hours/day}}$$

SKU   stockkeeping units

Storage slot occupancy ratio   measures the percentage of storage slots or bin slots that are occupied.

$$\text{SSO ratio} = \frac{\text{Storage slots occupied}}{\text{Total storage slots}}$$

Storage space utilization ratio (SSU ratio)   proportion of storage space occupied by materials.

$$\text{SSU ratio} = \frac{\text{Materials cube stored}}{\text{Total cube space required}}$$

Storage turnover ratio   measures the movement or turnover of materials in storage. It is the ratio of loads retrieved to loads stored.

Suboptimize   optimizing a component of a system at the expense of the overall system.

Systematic economic analysis technique (SEAT)   an eight-step procedure for conducting an economic comparison of materials handling alternatives.

The Financial Accounting Standards Board Statement of Financial Accounting Number 13 (FASB 13)   the statement on "Accounting for Leases" effective January, 1977.

Throughput   the rate of movement of material through a system.

Throughput performance index (TPI)   compares the actual throughput with the theoretical throughput capacity for the storage and retrieval system.

$$\text{TPI} = \frac{\text{Throughput achieved/day}}{\text{Throughput capacity/day}}$$

WIP   work in process

The Computer and Quantitative Analysis

Quantitative Methods in Distribution

JEREMY F. SHAPIRO

Introduction and Overview

The major goal of this chapter is to survey the successful applications of quantitative methods in the analysis and solution of practical distribution management problems. In the process, the reader will be provided with a conceptual framework for understanding the various methods, their strengths and weaknesses, and how they are interrelated. The cited references document important applications or provide background information about specific methods. Included in the latter category are a number of recent surveys. An extensive survey of software for physical distribution is given by Searcy and Miller.[1]

In the past few years, quantitative methods have made significant new contributions to distribution management. There are several reasons for this development. First, the increasing power of computer hardware and software systems, and their decreasing costs, have made computer-based quantitative methods much more economical to use for planning purposes. At the same time, the scope of distribution management has expanded, and along with it the analytic methods needed to assist management decision making. Education is a third factor contributing to the increased use of quantitative methods. A significant percentage of middle- and upper-level distribution managers have now had at least an exposure to these methods and, as a result, are more open to trying them out. It is hoped this chapter will assist the reader in furthering his or her education in the use of quantitative methods.

Models and Techniques

Quantitative methods consist of models and techniques. A *model* is an abstract mathematical system that is devised to serve as a surrogate for reality. A *technique*, sometimes referred to as an algorithm, is used to optimize, or more generally, analyze a model. This distinction is not completely clear-cut because a model and a technique often are, or at least appear to be, inseparable. This is the case, for example, with linear programming models which have traditionally been optimized by the simplex algorithm. In the subsection below on transportation planning (see pages 386–390), we will discuss why even this well-known and traditional identification of a technique with a model is open to scrutiny for certain applications.

For the vast majority of applications, the effective use of quantitative methods requires that our efforts be directed first at model construction from the relevant data bases followed by its analysis using an appropriate technique. The current state of the science, technology, and art of quantitative methods is such that computer techniques for analyzing models after they have been constructed are better understood and implemented than computer systems for model description. This point is discussed in more detail throughout the chapter, especially in the final subsection on integrated planning systems.

Benefits of Quantitative Methods

The first and foremost benefit to be derived from using quantitative models and techniques is that they permit large quantities of data to be compared and integrated on a computer according to rational rules. The bottom line is an overall reduction in cost or an increase in profits. There are, however, significant secondary benefits to be gained. The creation and use of a model can facilitate and encourage communication among managers with differing responsibilities and viewpoints about common business problems. For example, an on-line transportation scheduling system available to both warehouse dispatchers and the operations planning manager at corporate headquarters can be used to reach agreement about the capabilities of the company's transportation network and to resolve controversies arising from emergency rescheduling. Similarly, the existence and use of a model can focus data collection efforts. Finally, the exercise of designing a model can be instructive to the manager in pinpointing his or her goals, decision options, and the constraints under which he or she must operate.

Model Taxonomies

Quantitative models can be differentiated along a number of dimensions. One distinction is between *normative* and *descriptive* models. A normative model is explicitly optimized to reflect an underlying objective criterion such as cost or profit. Linear programming and EOQ (economic order quantity) models are examples of normative models. By contrast, a descriptive model attempts only to describe the outputs of a physical system, given the inputs, without concern for the value of the outputs with respect to objective measures. An exponentially smoothed forecasting model is an example of a descriptive model.

Models can also be categorized as *deterministic* or *probabilistic*. A deterministic model assumes that data describing the past, current, and future decision environments are known with certainty. As a result, the solutions produced by the model are unequivocal prescriptions about the actions to be taken; for example, locate new facilities with storage capacities equal to one million tons in Detroit and Los Angeles next year. By contrast, a probabilistic model explicitly accepts the notion that some of its data are uncertain and produces strategies that hedge against these uncertainties. For example, a probabilistic model might yield the following strategy: If actual demand in December for home heating oil is 175,000 barrels or less, ship 200,000 barrels to our storage tanks on January 10; if actual demand in December exceeds 175,000 barrels, ship an amount equal to the demand on January 2.

In some areas of physical distribution management, such as inventory control, uncertainties in demand and delivery lead times are important factors which must be explicitly addressed. In other areas, such as transportation planning or facilities location, deterministic models are usually the only practical approach possible. The importance of uncertainties in these latter problems can be tested by evaluating the deterministic models according to a number of different data scenarios. *Sensitivity analysis* of solutions to data inputs plays a central role in such calculations.

A third view of models is derived from the nature of the decision problems they address: *operational, tactical,* or *strategic*. The differences in models addressing these different decisions are shown in Table 15–1.[2] The family of models that are appropriate to a particular distribution planning environment will naturally range from the operational to the strategic. Specific models should not be viewed separately, but rather as representing a continuum of management concerns. Thus, for example, a strategic planning model of facilities location must contain an aggregation description of the firm's operations given various location configurations. This is not to say that strategic models can be effectively constructed simply by piecing together a number of operational models. It is better for integrated planning to construct and use models from the top down, starting with aggregate models and filling in detail where necessary.

Table 15–1   Taxonomy of Decision Making

	Strategic Planning	*Tactical Planning*	*Operational Planning*
Objective	Resource acquisition	Resource utilization	Execution
Time horizon	Long	Middle	Short
Level of management involvement	Top	Medium	Low
Sources of information	External and internal	External and internal	Internal
Level of detail of information	Highly aggregated	Moderately aggregated	Detailed
Degree of uncertainty about data	High	Medium	Low
Degree of risk	High	Moderate	Low

The desire for better integrated planning has created a need for systematic methods to aggregate and disaggregate forecasting and decision models. This is an area of current research and development which could have important pay-offs in the next five years. For example, in many circumstances it is desirable for reasons of accuracy and efficiency to forecast demand by product families and then disaggregate to arrive at the forecasts for individual items. Similarly, some companies have developed monthly allocation models that assign forecast demand by product families to production at specific plants so as to minimize aggregate production and distribution costs. The monthly plans are then disaggregated to develop specific production runs and distribution schedules. In short, there is a hierarchy of management decisions and associated models ranging from the strategic to the operational which should be addressed in an integrated fashion.[3] Integrated planning systems are discussed in more detail in the final subsection of this chapter.

Techniques

The quantitative techniques relevant to physical distribution management are:

- Applied statistics

- Optimization—by mathematical programming or heuristics

- Monte Carlo simulation

- Queueing theory

The first two techniques, statistics and optimization, are the most widely used in distribution management. Statistical techniques will be discussed in detail in the context of methods for forecasting and inventory management in the next two subsections. Optimization techniques will be discussed in greatest detail in the context of methods for inventory management, transportation planning, facilities location, vehicle routing, and integrated planning (see pages 380–385, 386–402, and 402–405). Monte Carlo simulation will be discussed in the context of models of customer service (see pages 396–397). Queueing theory will be discussed in the context of facilities layout (see page 1399).

The balance between exact optimization techniques, that is, mathematical programming, and approximation or heuristic techniques has been shifting through the years. For example, heuristic techniques for facilities location models (see pages 390–393) were developed and used in the 1960s because mixed integer programming codes for efficiently optimizing these problems were not available. These models can now be optimized with much greater confidence and efficiency by commercially available mixed integer programming codes, thereby reducing the need to resort to heuristics.

In general, exact optimization is preferred to heuristics not only because it provides better answers. Heuristics tend to be defined for narrow classes of models, and time and money can be wasted in modifying them to fit constantly changing model features. To be sure, there remain classes of optimization models, such as the vehicle routing problems discussed below (pages 400–402), whose complexity precludes exact optimization.

A related point is that regardless of the optimization technique used, exact or heuristic, slavish pursuit of an optimal solution can be counterproductive in many circumstances. This is because data are never known with complete accuracy, nor is reality completely described by a model. It is more important to be able to use an optimization technique flexibly on a variety of models than to optimize quickly a given model.

The discussion in the previous paragraphs illustrates an important point about quantitative methods for distribution planning. The nature and use of these methods have changed drastically over the past thirty years, and we can expect this trend to continue. The evolution is dictated in large part by complementary changes in computer hardware and software.

Role of the Specialist

A key responsibility of the specialist in quantitative methods is to cut through the masses of data and ambiguities associated with a complex decision problem to construct a model that will successfully enhance the manager's understanding of the problem and his or her ability to make rational and effective decisions. The selection of a particular model from among all relevant models requires a careful balancing of the expected costs of quantitative analysis against the expected benefits to be realized from it. After the fact, an implemented model may seem quite simple and obvious, but it usually takes considerable expertise and talent to achieve this simplicity. The implication for the discussion here is that it is impossible to provide a foolproof, cookbook approach to the effective use of quantitative methods. Instead, the intention in this chapter is to provide a framework permitting physical distribution managers to better understand what is possible in practice, and how to begin applying quantitative methods to specific problems.

A final word about models. There will always be ways in which a model fails to mirror reality. Nevertheless, the usefulness of a model should be judged primarily by the accuracy and precision of the numbers it provides relative to what would be available without a model. In short, one should judge a model on the extent to which it provides valid and insightful answers rather than on those aspects of the real problem that it may fail to capture.

Forecasting and Statistical Analysis

Probably the oldest quantitative methods in business are forecasting and other methods of statistical analysis. Many of the forecasting models and techniques used today, including their advantages and limitations, were known ten and even twenty years ago.[4] Nevertheless, the traditional methods and their current realizations as computer systems are still not perceived as totally satisfactory. A widespread view is that currently available forecasting packages are efficient at data handling but do not permit the user sufficient choice or flexibility in model selection and manipulation.

There are several reasons that possibly explain this situation. Forecasting of complex business phenomena will always be difficult, regardless of any theories that are ultimately developed and implemented. Moreover, there is greater immediate concern today about simply managing the huge quantities of data generated by the latest computer and informational technologies. This problem has received the greatest attention in recent years and much progress has been made in badly needed data-base management techniques. Less progress has been made on how to apply statistical methods efficiently to analyze the data bases so that managers can extract the greatest usefulness from them.

Naive versus Causal Models

Forecasting models can be compared and contrasted along a number of dimensions. A traditional approach is to contrast *naive* versus *causal* models. Naive models forecast the future by extrapolation of historical data. Causal models attempt to capture at least part of the underlying structure of the data-generating process by the statistical estimation of functional relationships among variables.

Naive models include moving average, exponential smoothing, and more sophisticated time series models. As an example, suppose that we wish to predict the sales demand d_{t+1} in tons of a particular product in period $t+1$. We have observed the sales quantities $d_1, \ldots, d_t$. Suppose further that we believe the underlying data-generating process in any period k is

$$d_k = \overline{d} + \varepsilon$$

where $\overline{d}$ is the average sales for any period and ε is an error term which we assume to have zero mean and constant variance. A *moving average* forecast of sales in period $t+1$, say d_{t+1}, is given by

$$\hat{d}_{t+1} = \overline{d}_t$$

where

$$\overline{d}_t = \frac{1}{N}(a_1 d_t + a_2 d_{t-1} + \ldots + a_N d_{t-N+1}) \tag{15.1}$$

and

$$\sum_{i=1}^{N} a_i = 1, \ a_i > 0 \text{ for all } i.$$

In this model, the data are the quantities $d_{t-N+1}, \ldots, d_t$, and the model is specified by selecting the parameters N and the a_i. The usual rule is to choose $a_i > a_{i+1}$ in order to give greater weight to more recent data. More generally, there are no hard and fast rules for selecting these parameters. Large values of N tend to produce more stable predictions, but at the expense of slower response to changes in the average sales $\overline{d}$.

The major drawback of the moving average model (15.1) is that there are $N+1$ bits of information ($N, d_t, \ldots, d_{t-N+1}$) that need to be stored and retrieved in each period. This can be expensive computationally if sales forecasts for several thousand products are required each week. An alternative is the exponential smoothing model with forecast $\hat{d}_{t+1} = \overline{d}_t$ where

$$\begin{aligned}
\overline{d}_t &= a d_t + (1-a)\overline{d}_{t-1} \\
&= \overline{d}_{t-1} + a(d_t - \overline{d}_{t-1}) \\
&= a d_t + a(1-a)d_{t-1} + a(1-a)^2 d_{t-2} + a(1-a)^{t-1}d_1 + (1-a)^t \overline{d}_0
\end{aligned} \tag{15.2}$$

Thus, the only data needed to make the forecast $\hat{d}_{t+1}$ are the smoothing constant a, which typically lies between 0.01 and 0.3, and the last forecast which equalled $\overline{d}_{t-1}$. Note also that the forecast depends on the initial estimate $\overline{d}_0$, as well as the choice of the smoothing constant.

The choice of the parameter a depends on a number of factors, including the stability of the data-generating process and whether the demand being forecast is slow- or fast-moving. Stable demand patterns and slow-moving items should be modeled with a small smoothing constant $(0.01 \leq a \leq 0.05)$, whereas unstable demand and fast-moving items take larger values $(0.1 \leq a \leq 0.3)$. A more flexible approach is to adaptively change the smoothing constant to permit, for example, the constant to be increased when forecasting errors have increased.[5] This has the effect of giving greater weight to the most recent observations.

The forecasting models just described assume a simple structure for the data generation process. The exponential smoothing model can be readily extended to account for trends and seasonality effects. Such models are inexpensive to implement and are typically used to forecast inventories, sales, and other high volume data that need to be forecast on a day-to-day basis. The ad hoc nature of the rules for selecting the models' parameters and the associated lack of statistical analysis of forecasting errors make these models inadequate for some purposes.

A number of computer software companies sell statistical forecasting packages based on exponential smoothing models. These packages are either integrated with, or can be combined with, inventory management systems that use the forecasts to determine safety stocks, order quantities, and other relevant information. The packages vary in style from complete "black boxes" that are easy to use but permit little model experimentation to those that are more difficult to learn how to use but permit experimentation and model development.

Sophisticated time series models, which generalize exponential smoothing, are based more securely on statistical principles. The models can estimate the autoregressive nature of time-series data and certain types of nonstationarities. Autoregression refers to the time dependent behavior of the variances of the variables in the time series. The ARIMA (autoregressive integrated moving average) models developed and popularized by Box and Jenkins can be used to capture many patterns of autoregressive and non-stationary behavior.[6]

The family of models just described makes forecasts by manipulating the time stream of sales demand data. By contrast, a causal model forecasts sales as a function of independent variables which affect it; for example, advertising budget b and selling price p. The exact nature of the functional relationship is almost always unknown and needs to be selected by judgment, perhaps after considerable statistical experimentation. Often, the relationship is assumed to be linear, namely

$$d = \alpha_0 + \alpha_1 b + \alpha_2 p + \varepsilon$$

where ε is an error term with zero mean, and known or unknown variance. The parameters α_0, α_1, α_2 that specify the model are usually estimated from previously observed values of the variables b_k, p_k, d_k by solving the problem

$$\min \sum_{k=1}^{t} (d_k - \alpha_0 - \alpha_1 b_k - \alpha_2 p_k)^2$$

This is the so-called least squares regression technique. The values $\hat{\alpha}_0$, $\hat{\alpha}_1$ and $\hat{\alpha}_2$ that minimize this sum of squares are the estimates of $\hat{\alpha}_0$, $\hat{\alpha}_1$, $\hat{\alpha}_2$ used to specify the model. Least squares estimation is a traditional approach which has the advantage of permitting $\hat{\alpha}_0$, $\hat{\alpha}_1$, $\hat{\alpha}_2$ and their variances to be computed by matrix inversions.[7] A drawback of least squares estimation, however, is the heavy weight given to outliers. Recent research has been devoted to studying statistical properties of alternatives to least squares which do not have this drawback; for example, minimizing the sum of the least absolute deviations, or some other function of the deviations.[8] Although these methods, called *robust estimation* procedures, have found wide application in the physical and social sciences, they have yet to make an impact on business forecasting.

An *econometric model* consists of a system of equations describing relationships between economic variables based on economic theory and accounting equations. The distinction between dependent and independent variables is blurred, but regression techniques such as least squares are still used to estimate the parameters. The system of equations is intended to give better insight about underlying structure than simple regression, thereby justifying the greater time and expense of an econometric model.[9]

A number of companies sell computer packages, or services through a time-sharing network, for developing econometric models. These companies also provide extensive data bases of historical and projected economic information for use in the models. This makes it easier, for example, to develop models relating forecasted sales for a particular product to relevant economic indicators as well as industry and company data.

Forecasting Techniques and Product Life Cycle

Sales forecasting techniques can be usefully related to the particular phase of a product's life cycle. When a product is under development and little is known about its market and potential market responses, forecasting techniques that rely heavily on expert judgment are indicated. Examples are the Delphi method for systematically soliciting and consolidating experts' opinions, panels, and historical analysis of comparable products.[10] During market testing and early product introduction, tracking and warning methods for estimating and checking growth rates are indicated. These statistical methods will hopefully signal when turning points in market demand can be expected to occur. The rapid growth phase of the product can be analyzed and forecasted by the more sophisticated time series models discussed above. Although the data is not stationary, first or second order differences may be. New models must be tested regularly, to forecast the flattening out of demand. When the product reaches steady state, the time-series analysis can be continued, or more causal models can be developed if sufficient insight into market mechanisms has been achieved.

Inventory Management*

The two basic problems of inventory management are *how much* to order, and *when* to order. The problems are typically resolved by balancing holding and replenishment costs against stock-out costs. The cost of an inventory control system should also be included in the analysis. Quantitative methods for answering these questions have a long history. Indeed, a version of the EOQ (economic order quantity) formula in wide use today dates back to 1915.

*Also see Chapter 26, "Inventory and Physical Distribution Management."

The gap between theory and practice in inventory management research is probably greater than in the other areas of quantitative methods discussed in this chapter. Gross and Schrady[11] and Silver[12] discuss the nature and causes of the gap and make suggestions for bridging it. The aim in this chapter, is, of course, to emphasize the practical side. Nevertheless, there is value in discussing certain methods falling in the gray area between theory and practice which have potential and should be given greater attention.

Inventory management problems exist at all stages of a business and can involve raw materials, work-in-process, and finished goods. The specific qualitative approach taken for a particular inventory problem depends on the nature of demand and costs. When demand is continuous, as for example when we are considering finished goods, the inventory policies for each item can often be derived optimally by considering each item independently. When demand is discrete and interrelated, as for example when we are considering items used in the manufacture of assemblies, then the determination of optimal or efficient inventory policies is more complicated. *Materials requirement planning* (MRP), which we discuss below, was invented in part to handle inventory management of dependent demand items.

A number of surveys of the state-of-the-art in inventory management have been published through the years; several recent publications indicate that the field is still changing quickly.[13]

How Much to Order

This basic question of inventory management is often answered by the application of deterministic cost minimization models. One such model gave rise to the economic order quantity (EOQ) formula

$$x^* = \sqrt{\frac{2 \cdot d \cdot K}{h}} \tag{15.3}$$

where d = demand per period (units)
  K = cost per order ($)
  h = carrying cost per unit per period ($/unit)
  x^* = economic order quantity (units)

Many variations of the basic EOQ model and formula can be derived by adjusting some of the assumptions. Nevertheless, all these formulas rely heavily on the assumption that the relevant data is known and remains unchanged with time.

Conceptually, the simplistic EOQ model is but one of a family of richer normative models that could be used to derive order quantities. To be sure, the simplicity of the EOQ formula is an important reason for its widespread use in managing inventory systems with thousands of items. Nevertheless, richer models have had some impact on the practice of inventory management and are not necessarily so complicated that they should be summarily dismissed, especially when we take into account the improvements in computer technology.

The formalism best suited to describe the richer models is *dynamic programming*. Let T denote the number of periods we wish to consider in our planning horizon. These periods are indexed by t. Let d_t denote the demand in period t, which we assume to be forecast with certainty. The decision variables are the order quantities x_t for all t. The values of these variables determine the ending inventory variables y_t by the equations

$$y_{t+1} = y_t + x_t - d_t$$

Let $c_t(x,y)$ denote the immediate cost incurred in period t when x is the quantity ordered and y is the ending inventory. An example of such a cost function is

$$c_t(x,y) = \begin{cases} K + h \cdot \left(y + \dfrac{1}{2}(d_t - x) \right) & \text{if } x > 0 \\[2ex] h \cdot \left(y + \dfrac{1}{2}d_t \right) & \text{if } x = 0. \end{cases} \qquad (15.4)$$

The parameter K is the fixed cost of an order. The parameter h is the unit holding cost which we have chosen to attribute to average inventory which equals $y + \frac{1}{2}(d_t - x)$. This function coincides with the cost function used in the EOQ derivation. The objective is to minimize the sum of costs

$$\sum_{t=1}^{T} c_t(x_t, y_t)$$

over the planning horizon while meeting demands in each period. For simplicity, we assume there is a target inventory level y_T which we wish to achieve at the end of the planning horizon.

An optimal order policy for the inventory problem just described is computed recursively. For $t = 1, \ldots, T$, we let $F^t(y)$ equal the minimal cost of meeting demand in each of the first t periods and having y units of inventory at the end of period t. The functions F^t satisfy the recursions

$$F^t(y) = \underset{x_t \geq 0}{\text{minimum}} \ \{c_t(x_t,y) + F^{t-1}(y - x_t + d_t)\} \qquad (15.5)$$

subject to $y - x_t + d_t \geq 0 \qquad$ for $t = 1, \ldots, T$

$F^0(y) = 0 \qquad\qquad\qquad$ for all y.

An initial inventory state y_0 is assumed to be given. For fixed t, the function $F^t(y)$ is solved in principle for all ending inventory states y of potential interest. Then t is indexed to $t + 1$ and the process repeated. An optimal solution to the inventory problem has been found when we have computed $F^T(y_T)$, which is the cost of an optimal policy. The computations naturally produce as well an optimal policy $x_1^*, \ldots, x_t^*, \ldots, x_T^*$, where x_t^* is an optimal order quantity or lot size for the item in period t.

The relationship of the dynamic programming model just presented to the EOQ formula (15.3) is the following. Suppose demand $d_t = d$ in all periods t and that the immediate cost function $c_t(x,y)$ is the one given in (15.4). Suppose further that we let the planning horizon grow very large. Then, in the limit, an optimal policy would be $x_t^* = x^* = \sqrt{[(2 \cdot d \cdot K)/h]}$ for all t sufficiently large; that is, use the EOQ formula (15.3) in every period to compute the order quantity. Clearly, these assumptions leading to an optimal EOQ policy are very restrictive.

Aspects of the dynamic programming approach just discussed can be found in the dynamic lot size research of Wagner and Whitin[14] and Zangwill.[15] The basic single item models have been embedded in multi-item models that integrate production and inventory planning under shared resource constraints.[16] A model for lot sizing of the components in multi-stage assemblies that anticipated MRP was studied by Crowston, Wagner and Williams.[17] The textbook by Wagner[18] contains several chapters on dynamic programming and inventory management.

The deterministic models for computing optimal lot sizes can be conceptually extended to the probabilistic case if probabilities p_{tk} associated with demands d_{tk} are known and backlogging is permitted. The objective function is to minimize expected inventory costs over the planning horizon. With these assumptions, the recursion (15.5) becomes

$$F^t(y) = \text{minimum}_{x_t \geq 0} \left\{ c_t(x_t, y) + \sum_{k=1}^{K} p_{tk} F^{t-1}(y - x_t + d_t) \right\} \qquad \text{for } t = 1, \ldots, T$$

$$F^0(y) = 0 \qquad \qquad \text{for all } y.$$

The practical difficulty with this model is the determination of the probabilities associated with demands in each period. Currently, it is difficult enough to forecast accurate and consistent single point estimates of demand in each period. As the computer systems supporting quantitative methods improve, however, it may eventually be possible to implement probablistic models such as this one efficiently.

DYNAMO is a software package, based on systems dynamics, to model and analyze inventory systems.[19] The idea is that the states of an inventory system can be described by differential or difference equations. These equations can be solved using well established mathematical methods and graphically displayed on a terminal.

Dynamic programming models which are richer than the one producing the EOQ formula have not found widespread use in inventory management. However, computation is now sufficiently fast and inexpensive to permit the more realistic models to be used in the appropriate circumstances—for example, to analyze inventory policies for product classes. The more accurate descriptions of demand patterns and costs in these models would surely lead in many cases to lower inventory costs.

Aggregation in tactical or medium-term inventory management is a factor deserving greater study and attention. Although very simple models will still be needed for the operational control of components in a large inventory system, richer aggregate models would provide greater realism for longer-term planning. The issue is how to aggregate and disaggregate between short- and medium-term inventory management problems. This and other questions have been studied under the general heading of hierarchical planning.[20] Peterson and Silver[21] have discussed how aggregate regression relationships for families of items can be used to forecast demands for individual inventory items.

When to Order

The question of when to order inventory for items with continuous, independent demand is typically answered by the statistical analysis of demand patterns for the item. These analyses are based on the results of the forecasting models discussed in the previous section. Estimates of variances as well as mean values of demand are required, and the usual assumption is that demand is normally distributed. The situation is depicted in Figure

15-1. The heavy lines represent a deterministic expectation of the inventory pattern. An order is placed at the reorder point leaving sufficient lead time for the order to be received. The uneven line shows the actual random demand pattern that may cause demand to be backlogged if the safety stock is expanded. Uncertainty is due to randomness in the order delivery time and in demand during that time. An optimal calculation of the safety stock level and the reorder point is based on a balancing of holding costs against stock-out costs.

If stock-out costs are not known, then the analysis can be performed in terms of service level, which may be defined as the percentage of time a customer's order is met. Figure 15-2 shows the trade-off between service level and safety stock costs—the manager's decision about service level is then based on service level standards in the industry and his or her judgment about the best place to be on the curve.

Material Requirements Planning

As previously indicated, different methods from those just discussed are needed to determine inventory management policies when demand for various items is dependent and not continuous, as is the case of demand for components in assembly departments. If dependent demand items were treated as independent using the methods outlined above, massive excessive inventories with high safety stocks would result. MRP systems are designed to eliminate such inefficiencies by coordinating decisions involving production plans for finished products, purchase of raw materials, control of component part inventories, and the scheduling of assembly fabrication.[22]

In MRP, demand for the components depends on demand for the end items as determined by forecasts and customer orders. These demands can be treated as independent and continuous. The implied requirements for components and their timing are then derived from a master production schedule by the MRP system. Systematic methods have not yet been derived for the determination of safety stocks and lead times for the components. Recent research has indicated that these control variables can be determined for

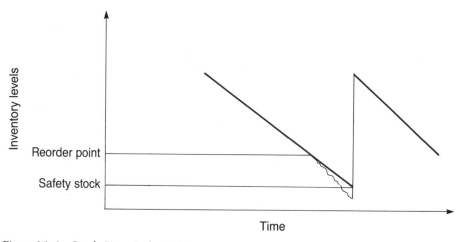

Figure 15-1   Single Item Order Policy

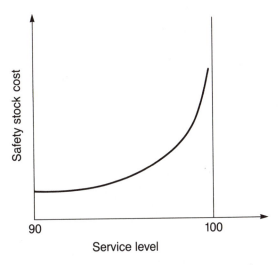

Figure 15-2   Safety Stock versus Service Level

MRP systems,[23] but the uncertainties can be complex and non-stationary, suggesting the need for adaptive methods.[24]

Current Developments

Despite the long and successful history of quantitative methods in inventory management, recent articles by several experts[25] suggest there is considerable room for improved models and analysis. For example, the costs used in optimizing many inventory systems often do not reflect the true marginal benefits or losses to be expected from variations around normal operating levels. Often accounting costs are used that include prorated overhead costs which are unavoidable and should therefore be ignored for the purpose of system improvement. Similarly, forecasting inaccuracies still plague inventory management policies. Although forecasts of aggregate, annual demand might be quite accurate, detailed forecasts for individual items tend to be more volatile. In addition, forecasts based on historical data can be systematically inaccurate if a company changes its planning processes. Thus, efforts at cost data and forecasting improvements are still needed.

Methods for diagnosing the potential for improvement of an inventory management system are another important area of research and development. The need for diagnosis arises when a system is exhibiting symptoms of poor control. For example, there may be high inventories at some locations and too frequent stockouts at others, or there may be large numbers of changes in scheduled production run sizes. The idea underlying the diagnostic methods is to use statistical sampling techniques to uncover the potential cost savings. The results of the sampling analysis are then extrapolated to provide estimates of overall potential cost improvement for the system.

A common viewpoint shared by many experts and practitioners is that inventory management decisions need to be better integrated with distribution, production, and marketing decisions. This point will be taken up again in the final subsection of this chapter when we discuss recent developments in integrated business planning systems.

Transportation Planning and Facilities Location

The classical *transportation* problem is to minimize the sum of freight and inventory carrying costs over short- and medium-term planning horizons given a distribution network with fixed facilities and capacities. The problem is a tactical one concerned with aggregate flows between plants and distribution centers and between distribution centers and markets. The more detailed operational problem of routing vehicles carrying products to individual customers is discussed below (see pages 400–402). Over a long-term planning horizon, the *facilities location* problem is to design the configuration of the distribution network and its capacities, so as to minimize the sum of investment, yearly production, transportation, and inventory carrying costs to meet anticipated demand, or so as to maximize yearly net profit if product mix is allowed to vary. Customer service constraints are often imposed on the facilities location problem.

In this section, network methods are discussed that have been used in transportation planning and facilities location. In addition, it is shown how mixed integer programming modeling techniques can be combined with network concepts to produce richer models that capture nonlinear costs and policy constraints of a logical, non-quantitative nature. With this background, several models are presented that have been used successfully to assist in transportation planning and facilities location. The section concludes with a brief discussion of current modeling and analysis developments.

Network Optimization

A typical network optimization model is illustrated in Figure 15–3. The network consists of nodes and directed arcs connecting pairs of nodes. The nodes correspond to facilities, namely, a plant, two warehouses, and four markets. The plant produces two products (A, B) which can be shipped directly to the markets in the case of product A, or via the warehouses. There is an arc connecting a pair of nodes for a given product if it is physically possible or reasonable for the product to flow directly between the nodes in the indicated direction. Associated with each arc is a constant freight cost per unit flow and a capacity limitation on total flow. The objective is to minimize the sum of freight costs to meet fixed demands at the markets.

An algebraic statement of the network optimization model just described is a linear programming model, but one with a simple structure that can be exploited.[26] Special purpose network optimization algorithms can solve large models much more rapidly than a standard linear programming algorithm based on the simplex method. Further details are discussed later in the section.

It is possible to incorporate additional features of a transportation planning problem into a optimization model, but sometimes at the expense of complicating its underlying mathematical structure. For example, inventory carrying costs at the warehouses can be computed and added to the transportation costs based on total throughput of the products. Multiple modes of transportation are easily modeled by the creation of arcs for each product-mode combination with associated unit freight costs and capacities. Conversion or production processes can be added by specifying recipes; for example, two units of A and three units of B can be converted at each of the warehouses to produce one unit of C and one unit of D to be sold to the markets. Modeling nonlinear costs and logical policy constraints requires the use of mixed integer programming as described below.

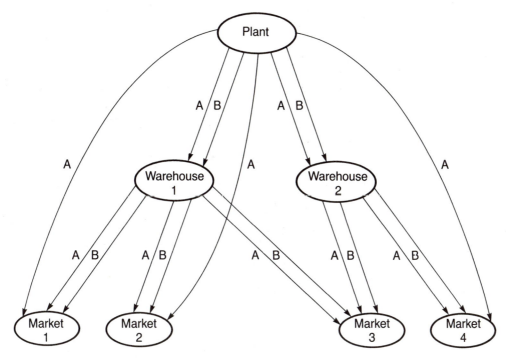

Figure 15-3   Network Optimization Model

Mixed Integer Programming

Mixed integer programming refers to optimization problems that contain variables constrained to integer values, usually zero or one, as well as variables taking on continuous values. Integer variables are used to describe certain cost functions and constraints that cannot be modeled by continuous variables alone. For example, we need not be confined to constant unit freight costs associated with product flows in the transportation network shown in Figure 15–3.

Consider first the cost curve shown in Figure 15–4, where the decision variable is x representing the flow of product k from facility i to facility (or market) j. We have suppressed subscripts for expositional simplicity. The curve with continuously changing slope is approximated by the piecewise linear curve. In this case, the total freight cost is modeled by introducing two new decision variables, x_1 and x_2, which we substitute for x wherever it occurs in the model by the equation $x = x_1 + x_2$. The cost term in the objective function is $c_1 x_1 + c_1 x_2$. In addition, the variables are constrained to satisfy $0 \leq x_1 \leq M_1$ and $0 \leq x_2 \leq M_2$.

In the example of Figure 15–4, since $c_1 < c_2$, any optimization procedure will ship as much of the product at the lower rate before shipping any at the higher rate. By contrast, additional modeling is required to capture the cost curve shown in Figure 15–5 where $c_1 > c_2$. The same substitution and modifications made above need to be made for this case. However, an additional variable and additional constraints are needed to enforce the condition that $x_2 > 0$ always implies $x_1 = M_1$. Specifically, we introduce the zero–one variable δ and the constraints

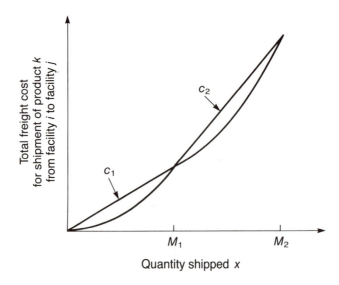

Figure 15-4   Increasing Marginal Freight Cost Curve

$$x_1 - \delta M_1 \geq 0$$
$$x_2 - \delta M_2 \leq 0$$

$$(15.6)$$

When $\delta = 0$, these constraints give us the conditions $x_1 \geq 0$ and $x_2 \leq 0$ which, along with the other constraints, imply $0 \leq x_1 \leq M_1$ and $x_2 = 0$. In words, $\delta = 0$ corresponds to operating along the left-hand linear segment in Figure 15–5. When $\delta = 1$, the constraints (15.6) give us $x_1 \geq M_1$ and $x_2 \leq M_2$ which, along with the other constraints, imply $x_1 = M_1$ and $0 \leq x_2 \leq M_2$. In words, $\delta = 1$ corresponds to operating along the right-hand linear segment in Figure 15–5. In a similar fashion, integer variables can be used to model more general cost curves such as the one shown in Figure 15–6.

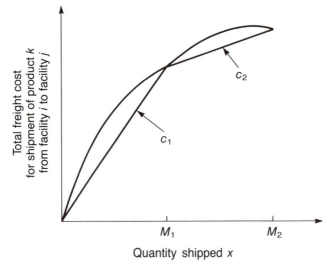

Figure 15-5   Decreasing Marginal Freight Cost Curve

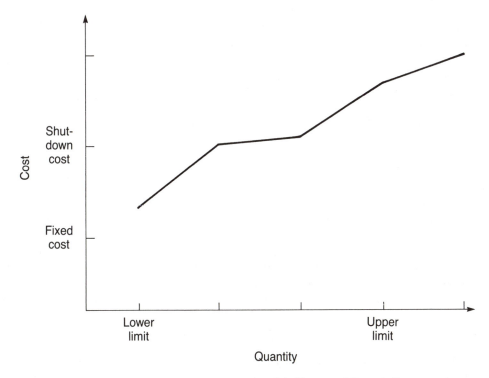

Figure 15-6   General Nonlinear Cost Curve Modeled by Mixed-Integer Programming

Integer variables can also be used to model logical constraints. For example, suppose there is a management policy that Market 3 in Figure 15–3 can be served by only one warehouse. Let x_{1A3}, x_{1B3}, x_{2A3}, x_{2B3} be the variable quantities of A and B shipped from warehouses 1 and 2 to market 3. To model this constraint, we introduce the zero–one variable δ and the constraints

$$x_{1A3} - M_A\delta \leq 0$$

$$x_{1B3} - M_B\delta \leq 0$$

$$x_{2A3} - M_A(1 - \delta) \leq 0$$

$$x_{2B3} - M_B(1 - \delta) \leq 0$$

where M_A and M_B are upper bounds on the amount to be shipped into market 3. It is easy to see that when $\delta = 1$, x_{1A3} and x_{1B3} can take on any positive values up to their upper bounds, whereas x_{2A3} and x_{2B3} must take on non-positive and therefore zero values. Thus, $\delta = 1$ corresponds to assigning market 3 to warehouse 1. Similarly, $\delta = 0$ can be shown to correspond to assigning market 3 to warehouse 2.

A variety of other modeling tricks are possible using zero–one decision variables.[27] The resulting mixed integer programming models are more difficult to solve than pure linear programming or network optimization models that have only continuous variables.

For this reason, mixed integer programming models were considered undesirable in the past. The situation, however, has improved significantly in the last few years with the development of commercial mixed integer programming codes on faster computers which combine efficient linear programming subroutines and branch-and-bound.[28] Most problems with 2000 rows and several hundred zero–one variables can be optimized, or at least optimized to a reasonable degree of objective function error, with a high degree of confidence.[29] For this reason, it is generally unnecessary to resort to the heuristic methods developed in the 1960s to solve the mixed integer programming models of facilities location problems discussed below.

Transportation Planning

The network optimization models discussed above have found extensive use in transportation planning. Models as large as 10,000 nodes (facilities) and 50,000 arcs (physical links) have been successfuly optimized in times as small as a minute or less on large computers.[30] Larger models can also be optimized efficiently. Thus, the most difficult aspect of applying network optimization to distribution problems is often the preparation of vast quantities of freight rate data. At a minimum, a unit freight rate cost figure is needed for each arc in the network. The preparation, validation, and updating on a timely basis of 100,000, or more, bits of information requires a well designed and operating management information system.

Figure 15–7 gives a schematic representation of a typical distribution planning system based on optimization models. Note the central role played by the program that generates the model from the appropriate demand, freight rate and supply data. The least cost distribution zone maps show the markets that can be supplied at least cost from each distribution center.

The formalism of network optimization has been applied to a wide range of decision problems beyond the transportation problems just discussed. Included are cash management problems, project scheduling, communications routing and water resources management.[31]

Facilities Location

The location of facilities for a physical distribution system is a strategic planning problem involving investment and long-term contract decisions that are difficult or impossible to change. In making these decisions, top management balances investment costs, including inventory carrying costs, against the costs of transportation and providing satisfactory customer service. Thus, facilities location models must implicitly incorporate aggregate descriptions of the transportation systems that are determined by any set of locational decisions. The network models of the previous section are used for this purpose, and decision variables and model structure have been added that describe the locational decisions that constitute, in effect, the network design options.

The facilities location models discussed in this section assume that the locations are geographical points where production, storage, and sales activities take place. The more detailed problems of facilities layout, where the facilities take up a positive area in which equipment is placed and people work, are discussed in the subsection on facilities layout and design, below.

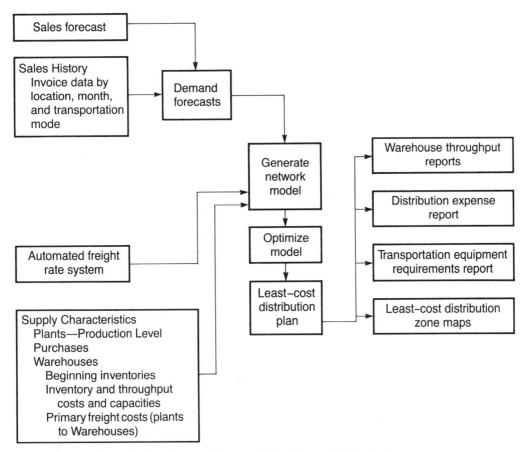

Figure 15-7   Scheme for Distribution Planning Using Network Optimization

For expositional purposes, we discuss in some detail a specific facilities location model. The model is representative of the general class of models that are being increasingly used to study a wide range of problems. Such models play an important conceptual and practical role in helping to integrate distribution planning with purchasing, production, and sales activities. For this reason, a relatively large portion of this chapter is devoted to their study.

A typical facilities location problem is as follows. A company wishes to establish regional distribution centers (DCs) from which to service its customers. The distribution centers are to be stocked with many products that are received from several plants with known production capacities operated by the company. The products can be aggregated into a small number of product classes, say 25 or less. Customer demands for each product are also assumed to be known, and the individual customers can be aggregated into a smaller number of geographical markets. Associated with each DC are lower and upper bounds on the allowable total annual throughput. The possible locations for the DCs are given, but the actual sites to be used are to be optimally selected. The questions to be answered simultaneously by the model are

• Which DC sites should be used?

• What size DC should be constructed at each site selected?

- What markets should be served by each DC?

- Which products should be produced by each plant, and in what quantities?

- What pattern of transportation flows from the plants to the DCs, and from the DCs to the markets, should be selected for each product class?

The objective is to minimize the annualized sum of investment, production, transportation, inventory, and handling costs for meeting the known demands, subject to plant capacity and DC throughput constraints.

A mixed integer programming model of this facility location problem is constructed as follows. Let i be the index for plants, j the index for possible DC sites, k the index for markets and l the index for products (product classes). The input parameters for the model are the following:

a_i = annual production capacity of plant i

a_{il} = production capacity used per unit of output for product l at plant i

P_{il} = production cost per unit of output of product l at plant i

f_j = annualized fixed cost associated with establishing a DC at site j

b_{jl} = DC capacity used per unit of product l shipped through DC at site j

$\underline{b}_j, \overline{b}_j$ = minimal and maximal allowed total annual throughput for a DC at site j

v_j = variable unit cost of throughput for a DC at site j

c_{ijl} = unit cost of shipping product l from plant i to a DC at site j

h_{jkl} = unit cost of shipping product l from a DC at site j to market k

d_{kl} = annual demand for product l in market k

Define the variables x_{ijl} as the non-negative amount of product l produced at i and shipped to a DC at site j. Similarly, define the variables y_{jkl} as the non-negative amount of product l shipped to market k from a DC at site j. Let the zero–one variables z_j determine whether ($z_j = 1$) or not ($z_j = 0$) a DC is located at site j. Of course, only those combinations that are feasible or reasonable from a cost viewpoint are permitted as x_{kjl} and y_{jkl} variables.

The model is: minimize

$$\sum_{i,j,l} p_{il} x_{ijl} + \sum_j \{f_j z_j + v_j \sum_{k,l} b_{jl} y_{jkl}\}$$

$$+ \sum_{i,j,l} c_{ijl} x_{ijl} + \sum_{j,k,l} h_{jkl} y_{jkl} \qquad (15.6\text{a})$$

subject to

$$\sum_{j,l} a_{il} x_{ijl} \le a_i \qquad \text{for all } i \qquad (15.6\text{b})$$

$$\sum_i x_{ijl} = \sum_k y_{jkl} \qquad \text{for all } j,l \qquad (15.6\text{c})$$

$$\sum_j y_{jkl} = d_{kl} \qquad \text{for all } k,l \qquad (15.6\text{d})$$

$$\underline{b}_j z_j \le \sum_{k,l} b_{jl} y_{jkl} \le \overline{b}_j z_j \qquad \text{for all } j \qquad (15.6\text{e})$$

$$x_{ijk} \ge 0, y_{jkl} \ge 0, z_j = 0 \text{ or } 1 \qquad \text{for all } i,j,k,l \qquad (15.6\text{f})$$

The four terms in the objective function (15.6a) are the annualized values of, respectively, production costs, DC fixed investment and variable costs, transportation costs from plants to DCs, and transportation costs from DCs to markets. The costs reflect different production costs for each product in various plants, different DC costs in different regions, and transportation by different modes, with different unit costs, between the plants, the DCs, and the markets. The constraints (15.6b) limit total production at each plant i to its total capacity a_i. The equations (15.6c) balance the material flow of each product into each DC against the flows out. The constraints (15.6d) require that demand d_{kl} be met for each product l in each market k. The constraints (15.6e) relate throughput at DC site j to the decision whether or not to locate a DC there. In particular, if the model selects $z_j = 0$ (a DC is not located at site j) then (15.6e) becomes $\Sigma_{k,l} b_{jl} y_{jkl} = 0$ which implies $y_{jkl} = 0$ for that j and all markets and products k, l; on the other hand, if $z_j = 1$ (a DC is located at site j), then (15.6e) limits the throughput $\Sigma_{k,l} b_{jl} y_{jkl}$ to lie between the specified limits b_j and $\overline{b}_j$.

Commercial mixed integer programming codes currently available can easily handle models of the form (15.6) with 100 to 200 DC sites, 100 markets for 20 products, and 20 plants. The advent of these codes in the early 1970s made the solution of such facilities location models a practical matter. Before that time, practitioners often had to resort to heuristic methods for selecting reasonable site locations based on ad hoc rules for evaluating the desirability of individual sites.[32] The heuristics have the drawback that they may fail to find an optimal or near optimal solution, and they are problem specific. A small change in the model may destroy the effectiveness of a given heuristic, but it usually does not affect the effectiveness of a general purpose mixed integer programming code.

The model (15.6) possesses embedded network structures which can sometimes be exploited by special purpose optimization codes. The networks are the smaller one connecting the plants to the DC sites, and the larger one (because there are usually many more markets than plants) connecting the DC sites to the markets. Under the additional assumptions that each market is serviced by a unique DC for all products, and that production constraints are on individual products at plants, Geoffrion and Graves[33] developed an efficient solution technique for (15.6). The technique, based on Bender's decomposition method,[34] consists of separating or decomposing (15.6) into a master problem involving the locational variables z_j, which is linked to a number of network subproblems, one for the distribution of each product from the plants through the DCs to the markets. Glover et al.[35] also extended the network analysis discussed above to a study of facilities location problems.

The generation and optimization of a large scale facilities location model naturally involves a number of developmental stages. Eight types of runs with the model can be identified:[36]

Validation exercises—to expose shortcomings of the model, data, or solution techniques

Regional optimizations—to focus on natural geographical regions and serve as bridges between validation and global optimization

Global optimizations—to optimize the entire DC location production/distribution problem

"What if . . .?"—to test questions raised by global optimizations

Sensitivity analyses—to measure the sensitivity of optimal solutions to the data

Continuity analyses—to test for large changes in optimal objective function values due to small changes in the data that cause additional DCs to be opened

Trade-off analyses—to generate the trade-off curves between optimal costs and secondary criteria such as average delivery delay

Priority analyses—to identify which aspects of the optimal solution to implement immediately and which can be postponed

In effect, the model (15.6) can be manipulated to provide a continuum of related models for analyzing overlapping planning problems.

Thus far, we have not discussed how customer service constraints are represented in the facilities location model (15.6). One approach is the addition of constraints of the form

$$\left(\sum_{j,k} t_{jkl} d_{kl} y_{jkl} \right) / \sum_{k} d_{kl} \leq T_l$$

where t_{jkl} is the average time to make a delivery of product l to market k from DC j, and T_l is a bound on the average delivery delay for product l. Methods for incorporating more detail about customer service into the model are given in the following subsection.

There are obviously a large number of other extensions and changes possible for the model. For example, the location and customer assignment decisions can be studied under variable rather than fixed demand by incorporating sales revenue functions and maximizing net profit. Similarly, the single-period model can be replicated in time to investigate the phasing of DC investment decisions. Another possibility is an extension of the model to treat production in greater detail by including supply decisions and nonlinear production costs. Space does not permit further discussion of these points.[37]

Current Developments

In developing the facilities location problem (15.6), it was necessary for computational efficiency to aggregate products into product classes and customers into customer zones. Although there are often some natural rules suggesting the spirit of the aggregations (e.g., consumer products aggregated by type of retailer, customers aggregated by geographical proximity), some arbitrariness is inevitable. A focus for selection of the aggregation methods is an integration with optimization techniques that produces bounds on the objective function errors due to the approximations inherent in aggregation.[38] The goal of this line of research is to permit the user of transportation planning and facilities location optimization techniques to specify the product and customer data in disaggregated form. The optimization model generators would deal directly with these data and automatically make aggregation, possibly ensuring that approximation errors do not exceed those specified by the user.

The efficiency of network optimization codes suggests that it is worthwhile to try to transform other optimization problems into that form. Considerable research and experimentation has been devoted to such transformations.[39] The results thus far have been mixed. The danger with the approach is that it tends to put too great a focus on the techniques of network optimization at the expense of deriving an accurate model.

Another promising current development in the analysis of facilities location models and other distribution models is the use of *Lagrange multiplier* techniques to optimize a given model,[40] and to perform parametric analyses on a family of models.[41] Lagrange multiplier techniques permit specific structures of mixed integer programming models to be exploited by special purpose algorithms which provide better solutions than ordinary linear programming approximations. These solutions are also obtained more quickly than solutions produced by the simplex method, with fewer demands made on computer storage space. In effect, Lagrange multiplier techniques are an attractive alternative to the simplex method for solving linear programming problems when these problems are only approximations to the optimization problem we really wish to solve. In addition to facilities location problems, Lagrangean techniques have proven very effective for a variety of mixed integer programming and other combinatorial optimization problems.[42]

A final important current development is the increasing interest in *multi-objective* techniques for the facilities location and other optimization models.[43] These techniques are designed to measure and account for the trade-offs between conflicting objectives, such as cost versus customer service. A variety of techniques are available, many of them based on parametric methods of linear programming.[44] Commercial mixed integer programming codes can be programmed to search for alternative solutions within a given percentage of the best known or optimal solution. The solutions can then be evaluated with respect to secondary objectives to select one that is most attractive from the multi-objective viewpoint.

Customer Service

It was discussed above in the subsection on inventory management how customer service requirements are a key factor in inventory management. In this section, the discussion focuses on how customer service characteristics of a distribution system can be measured in the aggregate using results from the models discussed in the previous section. There are two distinct approaches: parametric analysis of facilities location and distribution optimization models; and Monte Carlo simulation.

Parametric Analysis

One type of parametric analysis of facilities location problems of the type (15.6) is to develop the system cost versus number curve.[45] This curve gives the minimal objective function cost as a function of the number of open facilities. Customer service response time improves when more than the optimal number of facilities are opened. A typical measure of customer service to be extracted from each optimal solution is the percentage of demand that can be filled within one-day, two-day, and three-day delivery. Management can use this information to assess the trade-offs between increased cost and increased customer service by opening more than the optimal number of facilities. It is worth noting that there are other cost categories not captured directly by models such as (15.6) that *increase* with increasing numbers of facilities; included are central administrative costs, cycle and safety stock carrying costs, customer order size effects, and interwarehouse transfer costs.

Another type of parametric analysis of the model (15.6) is to vary the maximal allowable distance between each market or customer zone and the distribution center which serves it. The analysis produces another curve showing the trade-off between minimal system cost and customer distance. The parametric mixed integer programming analysis should begin with the minimal allowable distance for markets and proceed by increasing this distance. In so doing, an optimal facilities location and distribution solution for a given distance becomes a starting feasible solution for the next larger distance. Good starting feasible solutions can greatly facilitate mixed integer programming calculations. Tailor-made parametric procedures such as the one just described are needed because, unlike linear programming, mixed integer programming parametric analysis cannot be achieved by standardized subroutines.

Monte Carlo Simulation

Monte Carlo simulation models attempt to capture the behavior of probabilistic, dynamic systems as a series of time staged formulas or subroutines. The models are descriptive and usually considered as tools for analyzing systems with uncertainties, dynamic interactions, and complex interdependencies that are difficult to capture by optimization models. A widespread feeling is that simulation is a method of last resort to be used after other quantitative methods have failed. This is because the statistical nature of a simulation's output makes it difficult to draw conclusions about the relative merits of different policies. Moreover, if a system is so complex that other quantitative methods fail, the simulation itself will be complex and costly to implement. The pros and cons of simulation models versus optimization models are discussed by Wagner,[46] who also discusses computer simulation languages.

A simulation begins with the system at a specific starting state. The state changes with time as the result of decisions and the outcome of controllable and uncontrollable events, some of which are random. Time is often divided into small intervals and extended over a long horizon. A vast number of calculations are rapidly performed by a computer to compress the time span of the horizon into a few minutes of running time. Each simulation produces a scenario describing the system which may be different from all other scenarios. Statistical methods are required to analyze and validate the outputs of a simulation model.[47]

Clearly, Monte Carlo simulation models can be developed for a wide variety of distribution planning problems. The purpose in this section is to discuss their use in analyzing customer service. Bowersox et al.[48] report on a general purpose system, called LREPS (Long-Range Environmental Planning Simulator), which integrates descriptions of physical facilities, order processing, inventory, material throughput, and transportation to analyze total cost and customer delivery performance measures.

A simulation begins with a fixed configuration of facility locations, distribution networks, and associated costs. This configuration could be supplied by an optimization model such as (15.6). In performing the simulation, however, individual customers rather than markets would be represented in the network. Inventory management policies are also inputs to the simulation. To this structure, information is added about key random events such as the inter-arrival times and sizes of customer orders, and deliver times. Statistical analysis of historical data is needed to specify the distributions of these random variables. With this information, a simulation run produces scenarios of actual customer deliveries which can be compared with promised delivery dates and order quantities.

Modifications to the distribution configuration determined by an optimization model can be tested by varying the appropriate parameters in the simulation model. It is possible, for example, to change the assignments of a few customers with deficient customer service characteristics to different distribution centers to see if service is improved. Radical changes in a configuration, however, can be counterproductive since simulation models do not have the capability to reoptimize decision variables in the new configuration.

The integration of optimization and simulation models, despite its obvious importance, has not been widely studied and tried. Currently available commercial linear and mixed integer programming codes permit the optimization of a distribution model to be interrupted. Thus, it is possible, at least in principle, to exit from such an optimization code to use a simulation model to test candidate distribution network configurations for feasibility with respect to customer service criteria.[49] The optimization would be resumed after the test was completed. The combined optimization/simulation analysis would produce a minimal cost distribution network configuration that satisfies, according to a simulation analysis, a variety of customer service constraints.

Facilities Layout and Design

In the subsection on transportation planning and facilities location above, distribution facilities were treated as points to be optimally located. Once the facilities locations have been established, the facilities assume positive areas into which equipment is to be placed and arranged. Layout design problems are not easily analyzed by quantitative methods because it is difficult to quantify fully the relative merit of one layout over another. In addition, the spatial complexity of layout design is difficult to capture by analytic models.

Nevertheless, useful quantitative methods for layout design have been developed, sometimes in an interactive, man-machine mode. Francis and White[50] describe a broad survey of facilities location methods.

Materials handling equipment such as conveyor systems and forklift trucks link work stations, storage areas, and loading bays. Quantitative methods for analyzing materials handling systems and related operational planning problems are also discussed in this section.

Quadratic Assignment Model for Facilities Layout

A well-defined mathematical programming model that incorporates many of the costs of layout design can be derived by viewing the design problem as optimally assigning n centers to n discrete locations. The centers can be storage areas, service areas, machines, departments, or offices. The costs captured by the model are of two types. There is the linear or absolute cost a_{ij} associated with assigning center i to location j. In addition, there is the relative cost c_{ijkl} associated with assigning center i to location j *and* center k to location l. The cost c_{ijkl} is often derived by the equation

$$c_{ijkl} = K \cdot f_{ik} d_{jl}$$

where

$K =$ conversion factor to dollars

$f_{ik} =$ a measure of the desirability of locating centers i and k close together. This could be the traffic in tons that move between the centers, or some subjective composite measure

$d_{jl} =$ distance between locations j and l

The *quadratic assignment problem* is to assign centers to locations so as to minimize the sum of absolute and relative costs; namely

$$\min \sum_{i=1}^{n} \sum_{j=1}^{n} a_{ij} x_{ij} + \frac{1}{2} \sum_{i=1}^{n} \sum_{j=1}^{n} \sum_{k=1}^{n} \sum_{l=1}^{n} c_{ijkl} x_{ij} x_{kl}$$

subject to

$$\sum_{j=1}^{n} x_{ij} = 1 \qquad \text{for } i = 1, \ldots, n$$

$$\sum_{i=1}^{n} x_{ij} = 1 \qquad \text{for } j = 1, \ldots, n \qquad (15.7)$$

$$x_{ij} = 0 \text{ or } 1$$

The quadratic assignment problem is a difficult one to optimize. Exact mathematical programming techniques, such as branch-and-bound combined with ordinary (linear) integer programming, could be used to solve it. At least until 1972, however, the time requirements of exact methods were found to be excessive for most problems of real interest with $n \geq 15$.[51] For this reason, heuristic algorithms have been developed for extracting useful answers from the model.[52] Ritzman[53] compared experimentally four promising heuristic algorithms for problems with n as large as 40. Scriabin and Vergin[54] compared the performances of three heuristic algorithms with the performances of human subjects using manual and visual methods to locate centers. They found that the human subjects did better on larger problems ($n = 20$) due to their superior ability to recognize and visualize complex patterns.

Unfortunately, the quadratic assignment model (15.7) does not allow for accurate modeling of the materials handling costs on flows between centers. The linear dependence of the relative cost term c_{ijkl} on distance is unrealistic when there are economies of scale in conveyor installation costs. Moreover, some equipment such as forklift trucks can be bought only in discrete units. The development of models that integrate facilities location and materials handling is an important area of future study.

Conveyor Models

Muth and White[55] give an extensive survey of quantitative methods used to model conveyor systems. They review conveyor models intended to expose fundamental relationships among key parameters such as conveyor speed, length of forward and return paths, spacing of carriers, number and spacing of work stations, amounts of in process storage, service disciplines, and material flow rates. Included are optimization, heuristic, queueing theory and other probabilistic models. In some cases, the objective is simply to determine conveyor design parameters that will ensure the compatability of loading and unloading patterns. In other cases, there is some minimization of dollar costs such as the total expected conveyor costs per shift. Despite the successful implementation of a number of such models, there remains a place for larger scale models, either optimization or Monte Carlo simulation, that can cope with the complexity of actual conveyor systems to assist in the design and operational control of the systems.

Bender[56] reports on the successful use of Monte Carlo simulation to design a conveyorized warehouse. The key design parameters were the placement of the inventory items in the storage racks, according to their classification (A, B, or C), and the speeds and lengths of the conveyor. The simulation model was also used to check unusual operating conditions.

Bender also reports on the application of queueing theory to determine the optimal number of loading bays in a distribution warehouse.[57] Waiting time distributions were derived for vehicles arriving at the bays—the queueing discipline was first-come-first-served. This implementation was used to compute the expected cost of vehicle delay for each configuration of the warehouse. The optimal design was the one that minimized the annualized sum of waiting and construction costs.

Trim and Packaging Problems

Quantitative methods have been used to analyze some of the many trim and packaging problems widely prevalent in materials handling. The general abstract problem is to cut up or fit together two- and three-dimensional shapes so as to minimize waste or occupy the smallest area or volume. The paper trim problem successfully analyzed and solved by Gilmore and Gomory[58] is a classic application of quantitative methods to this type of problem. Specifically, the paper trim problem is to cut rolls of paper of large width into rolls of narrower width. The objective is to minimize the total number of rolls that must be trimmed to meet a given profile of customer orders for the rolls with the narrower width.

The same type of quantitative method has been applied by Smith and DeCani[59] to optimizing the layout of boxes in pallets. Their paper contains a number of references to other materials handling problems that have been analyzed by similar methods. The pallet layout problem can be posed as a two-dimensional trim problem which is difficult to optimize exactly. Smith and DeCani report on a heuristic method that performed well when compared with exact methods.

Vehicle Scheduling and Routing

Vehicle routing problems exist in many varieties ranging from the dispatching of delivery trucks of consumer goods to the scheduling of oil tankers. The basic problem is an operational one in which a fleet of vehicles with fixed capabilities (number, capacity, speed, etc.) is to be used to transport goods between specified pickup and delivery points to meet given demands. The problem is to determine which demands will be satisfied by each vehicle and what route each vehicle will follow in servicing its assigned demand. The usual objective is to minimize the total cost of operating the fleet including fuel, personnel, and vehicle depreciation costs. The selected routes must often satisfy a variety of constraints due to fixed vehicle capacity, time windows for delivery, and union regulations on driver work schedules. Magnanti[60] gives an extensive survey of models and approaches to vehicle routing and fleet scheduling.

Single Depot Delivery Problem

For the purpose of discussion, the focus in this subsection is on an important and common special case of the vehicle routing problem.[61] A vehicle fleet delivers products stored at a central depot to satisfy daily customer orders. The customers specify their orders prior to the start of each day and the vehicles must then be scheduled to deliver the day's orders. Each vehicle has a fixed capacity. Each order uses a fixed portion of vehicle capacity and must be delivered within a specified time window. This is the vehicle routing problem faced, for example, by a large department store or a processed food distributor. This problem is called the *single depot delivery problem*.

The single depot delivery problem has an exact formulation as a mixed integer programming model.[62] The objective function is to minimize the total costs of travel to the customers. The constraints partition into three types. The first type assigns customers to vehicles. For each vehicle, there are two types of constraints. One set ensures that the vehicle makes a complete tour of the customers assigned to it. These are the constraints of a *traveling salesman problem* which is a well known combinatorial optimization problem for which efficient, exact, and approximate algorithms are known.[63] The second type of constraint set for each vehicle contains precedence and timing constraints on deliveries to the customers assigned to it.

This mixed integer programming formulation is enormous for single depot vehicle delivery problems of reasonable size—say, those involving 10 to 30 vehicles and 100 to 1000 customers. The difficulty is reduced somewhat if Bender's decomposition method is used (see also page 394) because it breaks the problem down into manageable components which have special structures (i.e., traveling salesman, generalized assignment) that can be exploited. Thus far, however, the decomposition approach has not been perfected and heuristic solution methods have been the most viable and universally applicable.

The heuristic methods that have been developed for the single depot delivery problem can be categorized into five types:

1. Tour building heuristics[64]

2. Tour improvement heuristics[65]

3. Two-phase methods[66]

4. Incomplete optimization methods[67]

5. Generalized assignment heuristic[68]

The first three types are modified traveling salesman problem heuristics. In the first type, a link between two customers is added sequentially until all customers have been assigned to some route. Every time a link is added, the vehicle capacity constraints are checked for violation. The choice of a link is motivated by some measure of cost savings.

Tour improvement heuristics begin with a feasible vehicle routing schedule. At every iteration some combination of links are exchanged for another and a check is made to see if the exchange is both feasible and reduces cost. In the two-phase method, customers are first assigned to vehicles without specifying the sequence in which they are to be visited. Subsequently, routes are obtained for each vehicle using a traveling salesman problem heuristic. Incomplete optimization methods apply some implicitly exhaustive algorithm, such as branch-and-bound, and simply terminate prior to optimality.

The approach of Fisher and Jaikumar[69] is a heuristic in which an assignment of customers to vehicles is obtained by solving optimally a generalized assignment problem with an objective function that approximates delivery cost. The approximation is derived from traveling salesman calculations which also produce feasible solutions to the problem. The initial guess at an assignment of customers to vehicles is important to the efficiency of the method. Fisher and Jaikumar provide heuristic rules for doing this. This approach has a number of attractive features. It will always find a feasible solution if one exists, something no other existing heuristic can guarantee. It can be easily adapted to accommodate many additional problem complexities. For example, by parametrically varying the number of vehicles in the fleet, the method can be used to optimally solve the problem of finding the minimum size fleet that can feasibly service the specified demand. Fisher and Jaikumar[70] report on favorable computational experience with their method as compared to several other methods for problems with 5 to 19 vehicles and 50 to 200 customers. Solution times were on the order of six seconds to two minutes on a DEC-10 computer.

The generalized assignment heuristic just discussed has been used to plan routes for a national delivery operation involving about five depots, 1200 customers, and 12 trucks. The approach was generalized to incorporate a number of additional constraints on the problem, including multiple depots, a constraint on total route time, and the possibility for each order of alternative delivery by common carrier. The delivery routes for this operation are reorganized every six months. The new system was first used in the June 1980 reorganization of routes and produced a reduction of 15 percent in annual delivery costs.

Other Vehicle Routing Problems

The single depot vehicle delivery problem is clearly one of a large number of related vehicle routing problems encountered in practice. The approaches just discussed are the ones to consider using on most variations. More generally, vehicle routing problems must sometimes be integrated into tactical and strategic decision making involving, for example, driver manpower scheduling, depot location, and vehicular fleet selection. At the moment, hierarchical integration of vehicle routing models with longer term planning models can best be described as an important but not well developed research area.

Two other specific approaches to vehicle routing are worth mentioning. One is a model and solution technique developed by Agin and Cullen,[71] applied to large size military vehicle routing problems with multiple stops, commodities, modes of transportation, and time periods. The model structure resembles a multi-commodity network flow problem with variable arc capacities. The objective function can include operating costs and penalties on early or late arrivals at destinations. A heuristic decomposition approach, similar in spirit to the one of Fisher and Jaikumar,[72] is used to break the model up into subproblems, one for each vehicle to be scheduled.

Brown and Graves[73] report on a real-time system for dispatching petroleum tank trucks. Their system is designed to assist the dispatcher who still controls the dispatching decisions by specifying certain vehicle routes, customer assignments, and tank truck loads. The system uses heuristics based on optimizing network models that reflect only part of the overall dispatching problem. Brown and Graves quote the following figures to support the assertion that the dispatching system has improved operations. Individual dispatchers using the system have the capacity to deal with up to 400 loads per day, compared with an industry average performance of 80 to 150 loads per day. In addition, transportation costs were reduced by about 3 percent.

Integrated Planning Systems

Several times in previous subsections, we have alluded to the trend towards planning systems in which distribution models are integrated with models of purchasing, production, inventory management, and sales. We see two major reasons for this trend. First, the business planning today is increasingly concerned with scarcities and uncertainties. Companies can no longer plan along the linear sequence in which demand determines desired production and distribution which in turn determines investment. Instead, most companies are trying to adapt to changing constraints and costs by selecting the combination of products and services, geographical markets, and production and distribution strategies which will yield the best overall return on its resources. These points are discussed in detail in *Resource Management* by P. S. Bender.[74]

A second major reason for the trend toward the use of integrated business planning systems is the improvement in computer hardware and software. The speed, flexibility, and low cost of today's computer systems are sufficient to provide managers with timely and reliable analyses of a wide variety of overlapping planning problems. Increased productivity can be expected as computational facilities are used to manage resources more effectively.

These reasons nothwithstanding, the design, implementation, and use of integrated planning systems is still a difficult and not well-established activity. There have been some notable failures in the past, as well as successes. It is worthwhile, therefore, to review briefly the history of planning models and systems that have influenced the state-of-the-art, and to draw some conclusions about the most effective approaches.

History

An early attempt at a system for integrated distribution planning was the Distribution Systems Simulator (DSS) described in the paper by Connors et al.[75] DSS was developed by IBM as a general purpose tool to be used by its customers. LREPS (Long Range Environmental Planning System), developed by Bowersox et al.[76] (see page 397), was a simulation program similar in concept to DSS.

The purpose of DSS was to assist a distribution manager in producing a mathematical model of the firm's distribution system from which good or optimal strategies could be determined. The user of DSS developed a model by responding to a questionnaire which contained options describing his or her problem. The options included the characteristics of customers' demand for products, buying patterns of customers, order filling policies, replenishment policies, transportation policies, distribution channels, factory locations, production capabilities, and others. The model produced by DSS was a simulation model. However, the user had the capability to apply vehicle scheduling algorithms, forecasting techniques, and pricing mechanisms to specific parts of the model. DSS was not a notable success, perhaps because of its generality, but also because of the diffuse nature of its programs which did not always fit the specific problems to be addressed. LREPS has fared better, however, and has been used in a number of applications.[77]

The advent of commercial linear and mixed integer programming systems in the early 1970s made it possible and practical for models such as (15.6) to be used in integrating certain production, locational, and distribution decisions. Geoffrion and Graves[78] demonstrated further that large models could be successfully optimized. Similarly, Glover et al.[79] demonstrated the effectiveness of network optimization models for analyzing a variety of integrated production, distribution and inventory management problems. There have been several other models of this general type developed in the past five years. The analysis of Harrison[80] has the interesting feature that the probabilistic nature of demand is treated explicitly by a stochastic programming with recourse model.[81] Brown, Northup, and Shapiro[82] report on an integrated planning system, called LOGS, that automatically generates mathematical programming models for a wide range of planning problems. LOGS has been used successfully in a number of applications in a large paper manufacturer.[83]

Design Philosophies

A major conclusion that we can draw from the experience to date is that mathematical programming models, such as the facilities location model discussed above (see pages 390–394), offer the most favorable structure on which to base integrated planning systems. By its very nature, such a model consists of an explicit mathematical system in which thousands of decision variables are linked together in a rigorous manner by means of resource and logical constraints. Moreover, it can be explicitly optimized. A final point is that these models encourage the decision maker to develop global views of the planning problems they represent.

Once it is posited that mathematical programming models are the preferred method for the design and implementation of integrated planning systems, serious questions remain about the most effective way to proceed. One should dismiss immediately the approach in which smaller models are stitched together to form an integrated system. Stitching submodels together is generally ineffective because the submodels are not designed to be combined. As a result, the linkages are invariably arbitrary, computationally inefficient, and difficult to change. Moreover, the decision maker is often stuck with submodel details that may not be important or relevant for a particular study. By contrast, a top-down approach to modeling is preferred because it permits the form and details of a model to evolve naturally as the result of its application to a coherent set of planning problems.

The basic algorithmic techniques of mathematical programming, although not totally perfected, can now be expected in most applications to yield optimal or near optimal solutions with sufficient speed and reliability. Today, the focus has shifted to methods for model generation. In fact, generating large-scale mathematical programming models, from the top down or in any other manner, is almost always much more difficult to accomplish than the model's optimization.

Three distinct approaches to model generation can be identified. The first is to use commercial matrix generators which are capable of describing any linear or mixed integer programming problem. Unfortunately, these generators have several deficiencies. They require the analyst to be skilled in mathematical programming modeling techniques, and to be sensitive to the importance of alternative formulations to optimization efficiency. Moreover, minor conceptual changes in a model may require extensive, time-consuming revisions to the matrix generation program.

A second approach to modeling integrated planning problems is to develop a fixed model for all problems of interest. This permits the streamlining of the data inputs, model construction, optimization, and report writing. The approach has the clear disadvantage, however, that it produces inaccurate models of planning problems that do not fit the preconceived structure.

The system LOGS[84] embodies an approach which avoids the pitfalls on the two others just mentioned. The idea is to design and implement a modeling language for the family of planning problems of interest to a specific company or industry. Such a language consists of a set of primitive decision elements which permit the decision maker to describe his or her decision problem in natural terms. For the types of problems faced by distribution managers, these primitive decision elements are derived from network formalisms, although the resulting mathematical programming problems are usually not pure network optimization problems.

Referring to the network in Figure 15–1, the facilities where products are stored or transformed correspond to nodes, and product flows correspond to arcs. The modeling language expands on this idea by permitting the analyst to specify material balance and individual product conservation constraints at the nodes, as well as recipes for transforming products. Costs at a node can be based on any number of node activities. Thus, for example, costs at a plant can be incurred at three levels, namely, overhead costs on total throughput, indirect costs associated with specific machines, and direct costs of producing specific products. Cost functions can be nonlinear with fixed and shutdown costs.

LOGS has been used successfully at a large paper company for a number of diverse applications including vendor selection analysis, production allocation and distribution, facilities location, and acquisition evaluation. These applications have all used models fed by overlapping data bases. For example, quarterly and yearly production and distribution models used for setting budgeting standards are aggregate versions drawn of the monthly models used to allocate production to mills. The system has subsequently been used to analyze logistics problems in several other industries including consumer products, agribusiness, household products, computer manufacture, and food distribution.[85]

Notes

1. T. Searcy and J. A. Miller, *A Survey of Software for Physical Distribution* (Chicago: Arthur Andersen & Co., 1981).

2. This taxonomy of decision making is discussed in A. C. Hax, "The Design of Large Scale Logistics Systems: A Survey and an Approach," Chapter 6 in W. H. Marlow (ed.), *Modern Trends in Logistics* (Boston: MIT Press, 1974); see also R. N. Anthony, *Planning and Control Systems: A Framework for Analysis* (Cambridge, Mass.: Harvard University Graduate School of Business Administration, Studies in Management Control, 1965).

3. For an extensive discussion of issues involved in hierarchical planning see A. C. Hax and H. C. Meal, "Hierarchical Integration of Production Planning and Scheduling," in M. A. Geisler (ed.), *Logistics, Studies in Management Sciences*, Vol. 1 (Amsterdam and New York: North-Holland-American Elsevier (1975). See also G. R. Bitran and A. C. Hax, "On the Design of Hierarchical Production Planning Systems," *Decision Science*, 8 (1977), pp. 28–55.

4. For useful introductions to the subject, see G. E. P. Box and G. M. Jenkins, *Time Series Analysis, Forecasting and Control* (San Francisco: Holden-Day, 1970); R. G. Brown, *Smoothing, Forecasting and Prediction of Discrete Time Series* (Englewood Cliffs, N.J.: Prentice-Hall, 1963); or J. C. Chambers, S. K. Mullick, and D. D. Smith, "How to Choose the Right Forecasting Technique," *Harvard Business Review*, 48 (1971), pp. 45–74. More recent references are D. C. Montgomery and L. A. Johnson, *Forecasting and Time Series Analysis* (New York: McGraw-Hill, 1976); C. R. Nelson, *Applied Time Series Analysis for Managerial Forecasting* (San Francisco: Holden-Day, 1973); and S. Makridakis and S. C. Wheelwright, *The Handbook of Forecasting: A Manager's Guide* (New York: Wiley, 1982).

5. D. W. Trigg and A. G. Leach, "Exponential Smoothing with an Adaptive Response Rate," *Operations Research Quarterly*, 13 (1967), pp. 53–59.

6. See Box and Jenkins, *Time Series Analysis*; and Nelson, *Applied Time Series Analysis*.

7. J. T. Helwig, *SAS Introductory Guide* (Raleigh, N.C.: SAS Institute, Inc., 1978).

8. J. Tukey, *Exploratory Data Analysis* (Reading, Massachusetts: Addison-Wesley, 1977).

9. R. J. Wonnacott and T. H. Wonnacott, *Econometrics* (New York: Wiley, 1977); see also L. R. Klein and R. M. Young, *An Introduction to Econometric Forecasting and Forecasting Models* (Lexington, Mass.: Lexington Books, 1980); R. S. Pindyck and D. L. Rubinfeld, *Econometric Models and Economic Forecasts* (New York: McGraw-Hill, 1976).

10. N. C. Dalkey and O. Helmen, "An Experimental Application of the Delphi Method to the Use of Experts," *Management Science*, 9 (1963), p. 458; see also, G. L. Urban and J. R. Hauser, *Design and Marketing of New Products* (Englewood Cliffs, N.J.: Prentice-Hall, 1980).

11. D. Gross and D. A. Schrady, "A Survey of Inventory Theory and Practice," in W. H. Marlow (ed.), *Modern Trends in Logistics Research* (Cambridge, Mass.: MIT Press, 1974), Chapter 11.

12. E. A. Silver, "Inventory Management: A Review and Critique," Working Paper No. 131, Department of Management Sciences, University of Waterloo, Ontario, Canada, 1979.

13. S. C. Aggarwal, "A Review of Current Inventory Theory and Its Applications," *International Journal of Product Research*, 12 (1974), pp. 443–482; A. C. Hax and D. I. Candea, "Inventory Management," Tech. Report No. 168 (Cambridge, Mass: Operations Research Center, MIT,

1979); S. Nahmias, "Inventory Models," in J. Belzer, A. Holzman, and A. Kent (eds.), *The Encyclopedia of Computer Science and Technology*, Vol. 9 (New York: Marcel Dekker, 1978); Silver, "Inventory Management"; and H. M. Wagner, "Research Portfolio for Inventory Management and Production Planning Systems," *Operations Research*, **28** (1980), pp. 445–475. For a representative selection of textbooks, see Brown, *Smoothing, Forecasting and Prediction*; G. Hadley and T. M. Whitin, *Analysis of Inventory Systems* (Englewood Cliffs, N.J.: Prentice-Hall, 1963); E. Naddor, *Inventory Systems* (New York: Wiley, 1966); and R. Peterson and E. A. Silver, *Decision Systems for Inventory Management and Production Planning* (New York: Wiley, 1979).

14. H. M. Wagner and T. M. Whitin, "Dynamic Version of the Economic Lot Size Model," *Management Science*, **5** (1958), pp. 89–96.

15. W. I. Zangwill, "A Deterministic Multi-product, Multi-facility Production and Inventory Model," *Operations Research*, **14** (1966), pp. 486–507.

16. B. Dzielinski and R. Gomory, "Optimal Programming of Lot Sizes, Inventory and Labor Allocations," *Management Science*, **11** (1965), pp. 874–890; see also L. Lasdon and R. Terjung, "An Efficient Algorithm for Multi-Item Scheduling," *Operations Research*, **19** (1971), pp. 946–969.

17. W. B. Crowston, M. H. Wagner, and J. F. Williams, "Economic Lot Size Determination in Multi-Stage Assembly Systems," *Management Science*, **19** (1973), pp. 517–527.

18. H. M. Wagner, *Principles of Operations Research*, 2d ed. (Englewood Cliffs, N.J.: Prentice-Hall, 1975).

19. J. W. Forrester, *Industrial Dynamics* (Cambridge, Mass.: MIT Press, 1961).

20. Hax and Meal, "Hierarchical Integration."

21. Peterson and Silver, *Decision Systems*.

22. J. Orlicky, *Materials Requirements Planning* (New York: McGraw-Hill, 1975); R. Tersine, *Production/Operations Management: Concepts, Structure, Analysis* (Amsterdam and New York: Elsevier North Holland, 1980); E. Steinberg and H. A. Napier, "Multi-level Lot Sizing for Requirements Planning Systems," *Management Science*, **26** (1980), pp. 1258–1271; P. J. Billington, J. O. McClain and L. J. Thomas "Mathematical Programming Approaches to Capacity Constrained MRP Systems: Review, Formulation and Problem Reduction," *Management Science*, **29** (1983), pp. 1126–1141.

23. C. C. New, "Lot Sizing in Multi-level Requirements Planning," *Production and Inventory Management*, **15** (1975), pp. 57–71; D. C. Whybark and J. G. Williams, "Materials Requirements Planning under Uncertainty," *Decision Science*, **7** (1976), pp. 595–606.

24. H. C. Meal, "Safety Stocks in MRP Systems," Tech. Report No. 166 (Cambridge, Mass.: Operations Research Center, MIT, 1979).

25. Gross and Schrady, "A Survey of Inventory Theory"; Silver, "Inventory Management"; Wagner, "Research Portfolio for Inventory Management."

26. J. F. Shapiro, *Mathematical Programming: Structures and Algorithms* (New York: Wiley, 1979).

27. For further discussion see H. P. Williams, *Model Building in Mathematical Programming* (New York: Wiley, 1978).

28. For discussions of mixed integer programming algorithms, see A. M. Geoffrion and R. E. Marsten, "Integer Programming: A Framework and State-of-the-Art Survey," *Management Science*, **18** (1972), pp. 465–491; A. Land and S. Powell, "Computer Codes for Problems of Integer Programming," in P. L. Hammer, E. L. Johnson, and B. H. Korte (eds.), *Discrete Optimization II* (Amsterdam: North Holland, 1979), pp. 221–270; and Shapiro, *Mathematical Programming*.

29. For example, see T. G. Mairs, G. W. Wakefield, E. L. Johnson, and K. Spielberg, "On a Production Allocation and Distribution Problem," *Management Science*, **16** (1978), pp. 1622–

1630; or C. B. Krabek, "Experiments in Mixed Integer Matrix Reduction," paper presented at the Institute of Management Science 24th International Meeting (Honolulu, Hawaii, 1979).

30. G. H. Bradley, G. G. Brown, and G. W. Graves, "Design and Implementation of Large Scale Primal Transshipment Algorithms," *Management Science*, **24** (1977), pp. 1–34; and F. Glover, G. Jones, D. Karney, D. Klingman, and J. Mote, "An Integrated Production, Distribution and Inventory Planning System," *Interfaces*, **9** (1979), pp. 21–35.

31. For more information, see F. Glover and D. Klingman, "Models and Methods for Network-related Problems," Proceedings of NATO Advanced Study Institute on Computer Methods in Practical Applications (Sogesta, Urbino, Italy, 1977); and B. Golden and T. L. Magnanti, "Transportation Planning: Network Models and Their Implementation," in A. C. Hax (ed.), *Studies in Operations Management* (Amsterdam: North Holland; New York: American Elsevier, 1978).

32. A. A. Kuehn and M. J. Hamburger, "A Heuristic Program for Locating Warehouses," *Management Science*, **9** (1963), pp. 643–666.

33. A. M. Geoffrion and G. W. Graves, "Multicommodity Distribution System Design by Bender's Decomposition," *Management Science*, **20** (1974), pp. 822–844.

34. Shapiro, *Mathematical Programming.*

35. Glover et al., "An Integrated Production . . . System."

36. P. S. Bender, *Principles of Physical Distribution Systems Configuration Design* (Washington, D.C.: Marketing Publications, Inc., 1971); Geoffrion and Graves, "Multicommodity Distribution System Design."

37. For additional information and references, see J. Krarup and P. Pruzan, "Selected Families of Location Problems," in P. L. Hammer, E. L. Johnson, and B. H. Korte (eds.), *Discrete Optimization II* (Amsterdam: North Holland, 1979); and L. F. McGinnis, "A Survey of Recent Results for a Class of Facilities Location Problems," *AIEE Transactions*, **9** (1977), pp. 1–18.

38. A. M. Geoffrion, "A Priori Error Bounds for Procurement Commodity Aggregates in Logistics Planning Models," *Naval Research Logistics Quarterly*, **24** (1977), pp. 201–212; R. W. Brown, W. D. Northup and J. F. Shapiro, "LOGS: An Optimization System for Logistics Planning," Working Paper OR 107–82 (Cambridge, Mass.: Operations Research Center, MIT, 1982); and P. H. Zipkin, "Bounds for Row-Aggregation in Linear Programming," *Operations Research*, **28** (1980), pp. 903–916.

39. See, for example, R. E. Bixby and W. H. Cunningham, "Converting Linear Programs to Network Problems," *Mathematics of Operations Research*, **5** (1980), pp. 321–357; and F. Glover and J. M. Mulvey, "Equivalence of the 0–1 Integer Programming Problem to Discrete Generalized and Pure Networks," *Operations Research*, **28** (1980), pp. 829–835.

40. A. M. Geoffrion and R. D. McBride, "Lagrangean Relaxation Applied to Capacitated Facility Location Problems," *AIIE Transactions*, **10** (1978), pp. 40–47; and J. F. Shapiro, "A Survey of Lagrangean Techniques for Discrete Optimization," in P. L. Hammer, E. L. Johnson, and B. H. Korte (eds.), *Annals of Discrete Mathematics 5: Discrete Optimization* (Amsterdam: North Holland, 1979), pp. 113–138.

41. G. R. Bitran, V. Chandru, D. E. Sempolinski, and J. F. Shapiro, "Inverse Optimization: An Application to the Capacitated Plant Location Problem," *Management Science*, **27** (1981), pp. 1120–1141.

42. Shapiro, "A Survey of Lagrangean Techniques."

43. R. G. House, "An Interactive Facilities Location Model," mimeo report (1979).

44. M. K. Starr and M. Zeleny, eds., *Multiple Criteria Decision Making*, TIMS Studies in the Management Sciences, Vol. 6 (Amsterdam: North Holland, 1977).

45. Bender, *Principles of Physical Distribution Systems*; A. M. Geoffrion, "Making Better Use of Optimization Capability in Distribution System Planning," *AIEE Transactions*, **11** (1979), pp. 96–108.

46. Wagner, *Principles of Operations Research*, Chapter 21.

47. See G. D. Eppen and F. J. Gould, *Quantitative Concepts for Management* (Englewood Cliffs, N.J.: Prentice-Hall, 1979); G. S. Fishman, *Concepts and Methods in Discrete Event Digital Simulation* (New York: Wiley, 1973); G. Gordon, *System Simulation* (Englewood Cliffs, N.J.: Prentice-Hall, 1978).

48. D. J. Bowersox et al., *Dynamic Simulation of Physical Distribution Systems* (East Lansing, Mich.: Michigan State University Business Studies, 1972).

49. See L. Slate and R. Spielberg, "The Extended Control Language of MPSX/370 and Possible Applications," *IBM Systems Journal*, 17 (1978), pp. 64–81.

50. R. L. Francis and J. A. White, *Facility Layout and Location: An Analytical Approach* (Englewood Cliffs, N.J.: Prentice-Hall, 1974).

51. L. P. Ritzman, "The Efficiency of Computer Algorithms for Plant Layout," *Management Science*, 19 (1972), pp. 240–248.

52. See R. G. Armour and E. S. Buffa, "A Heuristic Algorithm and Simulation Approach to the Relative Allocation of Facilities," *Management Science*, 9 (1963), pp. 294–309; and F. S. Hillier and M. M. Connors, "Quadratic Assignment Problem Algorithms and the Location of Individual Facilities," *Management Science*, 13 (1966), pp. 42–57.

53. Ritzman, "The Efficiency of Computer Algorithms."

54. M. Scriabin and R. C. Vergin, "Comparison of Computer Algorithms and Visual Based Methods for Plant Layout," *Management Science*, 22 (1975), pp. 172–181.

55. E. J. Muth and J. A. White, "Conveyor Theory: A Survey," *AIIE Transactions*, 11 (1979), pp. 270–277.

56. P. S. Bender, personal communication (1980).

57. Ibid.

58. P. Gilmore and R. E. Gomory, "A Linear Programming Approach to the Cutting Stock Problem, part II," *Operations Research*, 11 (1963), pp. 863–888.

59. A. Smith and P. DeCani, "An Algorithm to Optimize the Layout of Boxes in Pallets," *Journal of Operations Research Society*, 31 (1980), pp. 573–578.

60. T. L. Magnanti, "Combinatorial Optimization and Vehicle Fleet Planning: Perspectives and Prospects," *Networks*, 11 (1981), pp. 179–213.

61. See M. L. Fisher and R. Jaikumar, "A Decomposition Algorithm for Large-scale Vehicle Routing," Working Paper No. 78-11-05 (Philadelphia: Decision Sciences Department, The Wharton School, University of Pennsylvania, 1978); and M. L. Fisher and R. Jaikumar, "A Generalized Assignment Heuristic for Vehicle Routing," *Networks*, 11 (1981), pp. 109–124.

62. Fisher and Jaikumar, "A Decomposition Algorithm."

63. M. Held and R. M. Karp, "The Traveling Salesman Problem and Minimum Spanning Trees," *Operations Research*, 18 (1970), pp. 1138–1162; N. Christofedes, *Graph Theory: An Algorithmic Approach* (New York: Academic, 1975).

64. G. Clarke and J. Wright, "Scheduling of Vehicles from a Central Depot to a Number of Delivery Points," *Operations Research*, 12 (1964), pp. 568–581.

65. S. Lin and B. Kernighian, "An Effective Heuristic Algorithm for the Traveling Salesman Problem," *Operations Research*, 21 (1973), p. 498.

66. M. Tyagi, "A Practical Method for the Truck Dispatching Problem," *Journal of the Operations Research Society of Japan*, 10 (1968), pp. 76–92.

67. N. Christofedes, A. Mingozzi, and P. Toth, "State Space Relaxation Procedures for the Computation of Bounds to Routing Problems," *Networks*, 11 (1981), pp. 145–164.

68. Fisher and Jaikumar, "A Generalized Assignment Heuristic."

69. Ibid.

70. Ibid.

71. N. I. Agin and D. E. Cullen, "An Algorithm for Transportation Routing and Vehicle Loading," in M. A. Geisler (ed.), *Logistics*, Studies in Management Sciences, Vol. 1 (Amsterdam: North Holland; New York: American Elsevier, 1975), pp. 1–20.

72. Fisher and Jaikumar, "A Decomposition Algorithm."

73. G. G. Brown and G. W. Graves, "Real-time Dispatch of Petroleum Tank Trucks," Working Paper No. 306 (Los Angeles: Western Management Science Institute, U.C.L.A., 1980).

74. P. S. Bender, *Resource Management: An Alternative View of the Management Process* (New York: Wiley, 1983.)

75. M. M. Connors, C. Coray, D. J. Cuccaro, W. K. Green, D. W. Low, and H. M. Markowitz, "The Distribution System Simulator," *Management Science*, 18 (1972), pp. B425–B453.

76. Bowersox et al., *Dynamic Simulation*.

77. R. G. House, personal communication (1980).

78. Geoffrion and Graves, "Multicommodity Distribution System Design."

79. Glover et al., "An Integrated Production. . . ."

80. H. Harrison, "A Planning System for Facilities and Resources in Distribution Networks," *Interfaces*, 9 (1979), pp. 6–22.

81. See Wagner, *Principles of Operations Research*; or Shapiro, *Mathematical Programming*.

82. Brown, Northup and Shapiro, "LOGS: An Optimization System."

83. See P. S. Bender, W. D. Northup, and J. F. Shapiro, "Practical Modeling for Resource Management," *Harvard Business Review*, 59, No. 2 (1981), pp. 163–173; also appeared as Chapter 29 in *Using Logical Techniques for Making Better Decisions*, ed. by D. N. Dickson (New York: Wiley, 1983).

84. Brown, Northup and Shapiro, "LOGS: An Optimization System."

85. Some of these applications are discussed in J. F. Shapiro, "Practical Experience with Optimization Models," to appear in *The Future of Optimization Models for Strategic Planning*, forthcoming from North Holland.

Computer Methods in Physical Distribution Management

RONALD H. BALLOU *and* ROBERT G. HOUSE

The inherently vital nature of distribution activities—transportation, inventory management, order processing, warehousing, materials handling, procurement, and protective packaging—is evidenced by the high percentage of the sales dollar represented by these activities. Without the cost of purchased goods, physical distribution costs have been estimated to average 24 to 26 percent of the sales dollar.[1] Since on the average about 50 percent of the sales dollar represents purchased goods and services,[2] it is not uncommon for a manager with broadly defined distribution responsibilities to have some impact on as much as 75 percent or more of his or her firm's controllable costs. However, costs are not the sole determinant of the importance of distribution; the quality of service can be an even more important consideration. As one company producing and distributing life science products found in the delivery of rats, mice, and hampsters to medical research laboratories, service can be more of a consideration than cost or price. Any method of delivery—regardless of cost—that left the animals in a hypertensive condition or that resulted in the death of a portion of them because of the failure to adequately control the trip environment was unsatisfactory. Animals in poor condition meant substantial future lost sales and additional costs for their replacement.

Managing logistics activities so as to maintain the proper balance between costs and desired levels of customer service has become more difficult with the passing years. Product variety has proliferated, putting upward pressure on inventory costs; the cost of capital has fluctuated over the years, making inventory-level planning difficult; increasing energy costs and decreasing regulation have distorted past transportation modal relationships; and the rapidly expanding availability of electronic equipment for order transmission and processing has sent the minds of businessmen spinning from too much

choice and change. With the added pressures of alternating economic recession and inflation, and incessant competition both domestic and foreign, computer-assisted decision-
making methodology represents an area of hope for the manager that he will be able to
cope with the complex distribution problems facing him.

To many businessmen, physical distribution is a new area of managerial focus. It represents more complex organizational relationships than were needed in the past. Distribution requires the coordination of transportation with inventories, purchasing, and production scheduling, warehousing with packaging, and materials with traffic. It is through
better coordination that businessmen often seek to lower costs and improve service. The
computer and the associated methodology have developed along with distribution management theory and practice, and to a substantial extent the methodology has been applied to distribution planning and control problems.

The key question then is: What computer methods are proving to be of particular
value to distribution managers? Selected examples of both strategic planning and operational methods and models will be discussed.

Computer Methods Overview

Computer methods can be conveniently divided into two classes, those for long-range or
strategic planning and those for short-term or operational control. Strategic planning typically involves setting policies, structuring the distribution system, or committing resources for a planning horizon longer than one year. On the other hand, operational control problems are those encountered repeatedly in the monitoring of orders processed,
inventory levels, or shipment routing and scheduling that result from the execution of the
strategic plan. While some methods and models can be used in both of these applications
(vehicle scheduling models, for example), most are designed with a particular planning
horizon in mind. Therefore, this chapter will deal with these two methods and model
types separately.

The Strategic Planning Problem

The desired scope of the strategic planning problem may be thought of as three key decision areas: (1) facility location, (2) inventory planning, and (3) transport selection and
routing. Although there are many more problem areas such as warehouse layout or materials handling system design, the first three typically have the greatest economic impact
on the firm. The major questions that define these key decision areas are shown in Figure
16–1.

The Facility Location Problem

The keystone planning problem is that of locating facilities: deciding on the proper number, location, and sizing of stocking points, which vendors or plants should serve these
stocking points, and which stocking points should serve the various customers. The geographical placement of facilities creates an outline for the overall logistics strategy by
specifying the paths over which products flow to the marketplace.

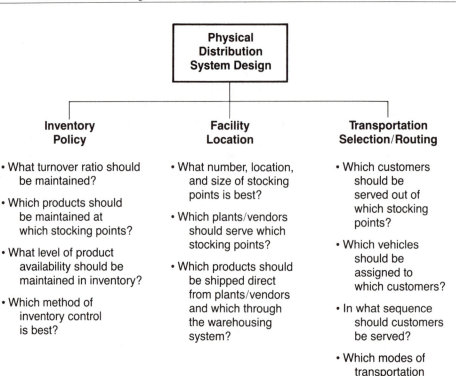

Figure 16-1   The Three Key Decision Areas in Logistics System Design with Typical Decisions Questions

SOURCE: R. H. Ballou, "Reformulating a Logistics Strategy," *International Journal of Physical Distribution and Materials Management*, 11, No. 8 (1981), pp. 71–83.

The Inventory Planning Problem

Since the level of inventory in the distribution system depends on the number of stocking points and the demand assigned to them, and the inventory policy that is used influences the number of stocking points and their placement in the distribution network, inventory policy and facility location are interrelated problems. Therefore, inventory policy—the methods by which inventory levels are controlled—must be described at an aggregate level of analysis so as to be compatible with the facility location analysis. The goal of strategic planning involving inventory policy is to answer such questions as: Which method of inventory control is best, taking into account both inventory and transportation cost considerations? Should a push or pull inventory strategy be used? Which products should be maintained at which stocking points?

The Transport Selection/Routing Problem

The planning of transport modes and routes also has an important impact on facility location decisions, and vice versa. Shipment consolidation is the key economic force that links these three major planning problems. The use of additional distribution points (either warehouses or cross dock break bulk operations) will tend to lower total transportation costs. However, facility location planning involves assigning customer demand to distribution points, and increasing the number of points will decrease the opportunity for shipment consolidation and efficient routing so that transportation costs will increase. Decisions about the types of carrier to use and the customers to be served out of each warehouse are issues to be resolved jointly using both facility location and transportation planning.

The interrelationship of the three problem areas described above defines the proper scope for strategic distribution planning in most firms. But what role does the computer play in the planning process? When a strategic planning problem is national in scope and involves multiple products, plants, warehouses, and customers, the difficulty of manipulating such costs as purchase/production, inventory, warehouse, order processing, and transportation while searching for the best distribution system design can be impractical when manual methods are used. As computers have become more powerful in terms of speed and memory capacity, computer models and the methods to support them have been developed to deal effectively with such problems. However, no one model seems to handle the entire range of problems effectively at this time. Models that deal effectively with transport selection and routing are clumsy and inefficient in handling facility location issues. Thus, computer approaches to planning have tended to use separate models for each of the three problem areas, working them in concert to achieve the desired overall results. More will be said about these models later in this chapter.

The Operational Control Problem

The operational control of a logistics system to keep its performance within the guidelines established by the strategic planning process is a critical area for the application of computer technology in distribution management. Computer-assisted planning methods, as discussed above, have led to the development of a comprehensive set of actions which is referred to as strategic distribution planning. Strategy implementation through a myriad set of individual decisions and actions must be monitored in order to ensure that each individual action is consistent with the overall strategy. Without effective monitoring of system performance, distribution strategies are realized only by accident.

A schema of the role of planning and performance monitoring in the distribution environment is shown in Figure 16–2. Strategic and tactical planning techniques influence the set of distribution facilities and the transportation decisions made during the order processing function.

The degree to which the planning activities will cause changes in the order processing system's behavior is related to the nature of the integration of the planning system output and the data base employed by the order processing system. The output of an effective planning system is a file of instructions which can be incorporated directly into the order processing system. This linking closes the gap between strategic planning and operations.

The overall performance of the distribution system is documented through the reporting system which is driven by the activities of the transportation function. In the performance of the transportation activity the individual order is dispatched from the firm and the satisfaction of the customer's request is completed. The reporting system can then use the documentation generated by the transportation function (usually a bill of lading or manifest) to update inventory status and provide historical records of information. The data gathered by the reporting system can then be fed back to management.

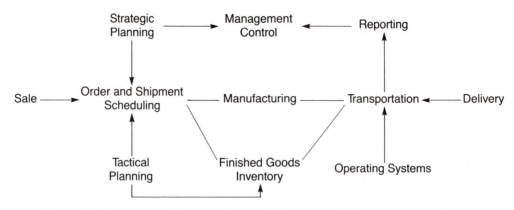

Figure 16-2   The Integration of Computer-assisted Planning and Measurement

The information reported to management must be consistent with the data provided by the planning function. That is, it must be organized in the same manner and reported at the same level of aggregation. If it is not, then management is faced with two irreconcilable reports. The successful integration of the planning system and the reporting system is a must in effective control of the distribution system.

The integration of planning and reporting resolves into a problem of data base organization. The two key elements of organization are the schema for aggregation and the items to be stored in the data base. Unfortunately, no single schema has been found which will serve all distribution systems equally well. It may be that the enhancement of the ZIP code from five to nine digits will provide the necessary level of detail for all types of distribution systems. However, current practice, as discussed later, indicates that even the nine-digit ZIP code will not be the universal organization schema.

The data elements captured in a reporting system are more standardized than is the organization technique. Basic descriptive information on products, customers, shipments, and inventories is maintained in almost all systems, as discussed below. However, the way in which these data enter the system varies widely; the currency of the data can also vary. In the following section the issues of data base organization, data base elements, and use of information are explored in detail.

Computerized Distribution Information

This subsection will explore the ways computers can be used as management information tools in distribution. The material presented in this section has been drawn from two articles by House and Jackson.[3] A somewhat more specialized analysis of the use of computers in transportation management can be found in Farrell.[4] House and Jackson[5] conducted a survey of 90 major firms who were known to possess a degree of sophistication in their application of computer technology to the solution of logistics problems. The survey results provide a relatively accurate representation of the degree of computerization of logistics information systems in the late 1970s.

A measure of the degree of the sophistication in computer use is shown in Table 16–1. The primary links in the computerized information system are between company plants and warehouses. A major thrust in modifying current computer systems to provide on-line

Table 16–1   Computer Communication Capabilities

Form of Communication	Computer Capability (%)			
	Currently Using	Developing	Planning to Develop	Not Using or Developing
Computer communications with customers				
On-line	9.4	4.7	9.4	76.5
Off-line	16.7	2.4	11.9	69.0
Computer communications with public warehousemen				
On-line	15.9	1.2	12.2	70.7
Off-line	23.2	1.2	6.1	69.5
Computer communications with carriers				
On-line	4.7	0.0	7.1	88.2
Off-line	9.6	0.0	7.2	83.1
Computer communication with international affiliates	38.4	2.3	9.3	50.0
Computer communication between plants and company-owned warehouses	70.9	4.7	8.1	16.3
On-line data entry	51.2	19.8	14.0	15.1

SOURCE: R. G. House and G. J. Jackson, "Trends in Computer Applications: A Survey." Reprinted with permission of *Handling & Shipping Management*, 18, No. 6 (1977), Penton/IPC, Cleveland, OH, pp. 176–187.

data entry capabilities is underway in many firms. The survey data indicated that 34.8 percent of the firms were developing or planning to develop this on-line capability. The survey also revealed a low degree of development of either on-line or off-line communication capabilities with customers, public warehousemen, or carriers.

The effective use of the computer as a management tool is dependent upon the availability of timely and accurate data. Computerized data bases are seen as one method of providing distribution managers with data that meet their needs. However, the amount and type of data usually found in a computerized data base, as shown in Table 16–2, may not be sufficient for all of the decisions which distribution managers must make.

The information available in most computerized data bases is primarily inventory status data: inventory level, back orders, and forecasted sales. Other types of data typically found in the data bases are shipping, open-order files, customer names, and product descriptions.

The omissions from the typical data base are interesting in light of the data that are maintained. For example, the omission of customer credit limits makes the establishment of an effective integrated order entry system difficult. In general, the survey indicated that computerized data bases for distribution maintained quantity data but not cost data. It can be seen that warehousing costs, inventory carrying costs, stock-out costs, and packaging costs are not part of the typical data base.

The typical data base is organized by either geographic point code (Standard Point Location Code) or by ZIP code. The geographic grid codes (PICADAD, REA grid) do not

Table 16-2   Data Elements in the Typical Computerized Data Base

Data Item	Contained in Computerized Data Base (%)	
	Yes	No
Transportation data		
Carrier file	56.5	43.5
Freight rates	44.6	55.4
Transit times	34.5	65.5
Shipment schedules	33.7	66.3
Shipping open order files	84.3	15.7
Shipping manifest or bill of lading	49.4	50.6
Freight bill payment	51.2	48.8
Warehouse data		
Warehousing costs per unit:		
Storage	29.4	70.6
Handling	29.8	70.2
Inventory data		
Inventory levels	83.7	16.3
Back orders	73.8	26.2
Inventory carrying costs	28.6	71.4
Stock-out costs	7.1	92.9
Purchasing open order files	51.2	48.8
Deleted order files	41.0	59.0
Forecasted sales	64.7	35.3
Customer data		
Customer names and locations	91.8	8.2
Customer financial limits	60.0	40.0
Product data		
Product description	83.1	16.9
Master model file	23.7	76.3
Production costs	60.2	39.8
Packaging costs	34.1	65.9
External market data	28.4	71.6

SOURCE: R. G. House and G. J. Jackson, "Trends in Computer Applications: A Survey." Reprinted with permission of *Handling & Shipping Management*, 18, No. 6 (1977), Penton/IPC, Cleveland, OH, pp. 176–187.

appear to be as popular as one might expect. Product data are usually organized by company codes, which creates problems in interorganizational communications.

Distribution managers employ the computer primarily in order processing, inventory control, and freight accounting (Table 16–3). These traditional areas of application for the computer represent the state-of-the-art in computerized distribution management. The data in Table 16–3 indicate for the functional areas of transportation, inventory, warehousing, and customer service how the computer is used or is planned to be used.

The use of the computer as an operations control tool appears to be limited to inventory and accounting. Relatively little work is done in warehouse operations management (product locator systems) despite the development of the minicomputer. The complex tasks of freight rating and vehicle routing are also not highly computerized. However, approximately 35 percent of the responding firms report programs underway to develop computerized freight rating and auditing.

When one looks to the future, the direction of computerization in distribution is not clear. Freight rating and distribution costing and budgeting appear to be the only distribution activities that have major program development efforts planned for the future. These efforts will require a substantial improvement in the data base that most firms maintain. Freight rates, inventory carrying costs, stock-out costs, and warehouse operations costs will have to be added to the data base of most firms before work on these programs can begin. It would appear that the data base the firm maintains may be the most seriously limiting factor for further computerization of distribution activity.

The quality of data is also the primary limitation on the development of more sophisticated interfirm communication systems. There are several computer hardware systems that are capable of transmitting and receiving information from each other; however, the data that are generated by one data base will not readily fit another. The lack of standardized product codes and standardized data organization techniques prohibits data interchange. The gradual adoption of the ZIP code as a data-base organization technique by the distribution industry may help solve the problem of report comparability. However, data interchange from computer to computer requires standardized product codes. The development of a uniform distribution code may well provide the standardization of product data that is needed to facilitate data interchange.

Until such uniform codes are developed, computer applications in distribution management will remain limited. All management problems require data for intelligent solu-

Table 16-3   Use of Computer in Control of Operations

Operating System Function	Degree of Use of Computer (%)			
	Presently Used	Development Stage	Planning Stage	Do Not Use
Control over transportation activities				
Freight rating and auditing	27.9	14.0	20.9	37.2
Bill of lading preparation	63.2	6.9	11.5	18.4
Order consolidation	39.5	7.0	11.6	41.9
Shipment routing	58.1	5.8	7.0	29.1
Vehicle routing	12.9	5.9	5.9	75.3
Shipment tracing	22.6	2.4	9.5	65.5
Rail car fleet control	24.4	0.0	2.3	73.3
Carrier payments	45.9	9.4	11.8	32.9
Freight accounting	64.0	9.3	5.8	20.9
Carrier evaluations	20.9	7.0	9.3	62.8
Control over inventory activities				
Order processing	92.1	1.1	2.2	4.5
Inventory control	90.9	4.5	2.3	2.3
Production scheduling	58.3	11.9	10.7	17.9
Control over warehousing activities				
Warehousing product locator systems	44.7	8.2	9.4	37.6
Warehouse storage & handling payments	29.9	0.0	9.2	60.9
Warehouse accounting	58.1	4.1	5.8	31.4
Customer service performance measurement	49.4	4.7	15.3	30.6

Source: R. G. House and G. J. Jackson, "Trends in Computer Applications: A Survey." Reprinted with permission of *Handling & Shipping Management*, 18, No. 6 (1977), Penton/IPC, Cleveland, OH, pp. 176–187.

tion. The lack of ready access to timely and reliable data is the key limitation to using computers in controlling distribution activities.

Strategic Planning Models

The three key areas of strategic distribution planning have already been identified as facility location, inventory planning, and transport mode selection and routing. A brief description of the models used in each type will be identified along with their major characteristics. Then a discussion of the important methods that support these models will be presented. Since facility location is the key planning problem, it will be emphasized within the limited space available in this chapter.

Facility Location Models

The problem of locating stocking points in a distribution network has intrigued management scientists for many years. As a result, a number of effective models have been developed. They range from computer simulation and sampling approaches[6] through heuristic approaches[7] to exact solution approaches.[8] These approaches represent different degrees of modeling accuracy and rigor used in the solution procedure. For example, simulation models have the advantage of permitting cost relationships to be described in great detail and the problem scope to be as broad as needed. The solution procedure is one that costs out specified numbers and locations of warehouses. Many computer runs are required to evaluate different warehousing configurations in order to be assured of a low-cost solution. In contrast, the so-called "exact" solution approaches compromise in favor of the solution procedure that guarantees the mathematical optimum number, size, and location of warehouses. The demands of the optimization procedure often result in the sacrifice of some degree of problem description and detail. Heuristic approaches usually provide good problem detail and often provide optimal solutions, although optimal solutions cannot be guaranteed. The choice of procedure should be made on the basis of the compromise that is most important in the particular problem situation.

Problems of significant size are now being handled by these computer models, which are able to deal with warehouse location problems on a nationwide-scale. Multiple product groups, plants and vendors, warehouses, and demand clusters are possible. Among the cost factors included in these models are:

- Production and purchase costs
- Warehouse storage and handling costs
- Capital costs on inventory
- Stock order and customer order processing costs
- Warehouse inbound and outbound transportation costs
- Insurance and taxes on inventory

The potential savings from the application of such computer models typically range between 5 and 15 percent of current distribution costs.

Inventory Planning Models

Computer models for inventory planning purposes are typically of the simulation type. The objective of the models is to replicate the action of the product as it moves through one or more stocking levels in the distribution channel. Actual order patterns are replicated under different inventory policy, transportation, and order processing policy selections. Costs are summarized, as are operating results. Several such models have been identified.[9]

Vehicle Selection and Routing Models

Rapidly rising fuel costs have heightened interest in computer programs that assist in selecting and routing vehicles, especially trucks. Trucking represents one-fourth of all intercity freight movement[10] and on the average absorbs nearly 60 percent of the distribution dollar for private firms.[11] Some practical programs have been developed to assist in such problem areas as shipment consolidation[12] and routing.[13] However, the bulk of the modeling effort has been directed toward the problem of scheduling of vehicles on routes where the vehicles can make multiple stops before returning to their starting points.[14] Newer versions of these models now include mode selection along with the scheduling features.[15]

Methods for Analysis

Now that we have briefly discussed the nature of the strategic distribution planning problem and some of the models that assist in the planning process, let us consider some of the methods that are used to support these efforts. These methods are oriented toward the requirements of large-scale problem analysis and toward the computer as the computational medium.

Demand Clusters

The large-scale planning problem typically involves multiple product groups distributed to thousands of individual customer locations. If this degree of detail were carried into the problem, the number of links between stocking points and customers and the associated data requirements would be enormous. Fortunately, aggregating the demand geographically reduces this part of the problem to manageable proportions with little loss in accuracy. The key is selecting the proper number and configuration of the clusters.

Grouping demand into a fixed number of territories assumes that all of the demand is concentrated at a point within the territory. The smaller the territory, the better the center of demand approximates the true demand location center. However, increasing the territory size and thereby reducing the number of demand clusters does not necessarily reduce the accuracy of portraying demand at a location. In practice, demand is naturally concentrated at city locations, centers of production, or groupings of service activity. These form natural geographic locations around which a demand cluster can be constructed. The number of clusters that will be formed depends on the level of error acceptable in approximating transportation costs to the demand center. Research has shown that the error in costs can be controlled to within 2 to 3 percent if 150 to 200 demand clusters are used nationwide. The error increases rapidly when less than about 120 clusters are used (see Figure 16–3).

Configuration plays an important role in controlling the error due to approximation. A circular territory with the demand assumed to be concentrated at the territory center is ideal. However, unequal demand distribution and geographical barriers such as lakes, mountains, or political boundaries can force territories of noncircular shapes. The size and number of territories can often be used to assure the more desirable circular shape with the weighted average demand concentrated at the center of the circle.

From a practical standpoint, territory configuration and to some extent the number of demand clusters are usually predetermined by the way sales data are typically collected. Common clustering methods are product sales territories, ZIP codes, and counties. Combining territories can effectively control the number of clusters. Regions of little sales can be grouped into fewer but larger clusters without significantly distorting the demand profile. One leading consulting firm developed the demand clusters shown in Figure 16–4. Note that cluster size and placement are oriented toward consumer goods with na-

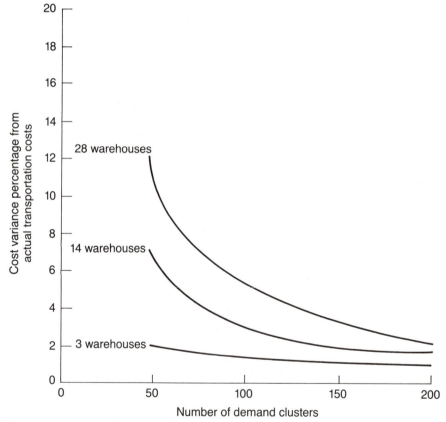

Figure 16–3   Generalized Error in Transportation Cost Estimation Due to Demand Clustering

SOURCE: R. G. House and Kenneth D. Jamie, "Measuring the Impact of Alternative Market Classification Systems in Distribution Planning," *Journal of Business Logistics*, 2 No. 2 (1981), pp. 1–31.

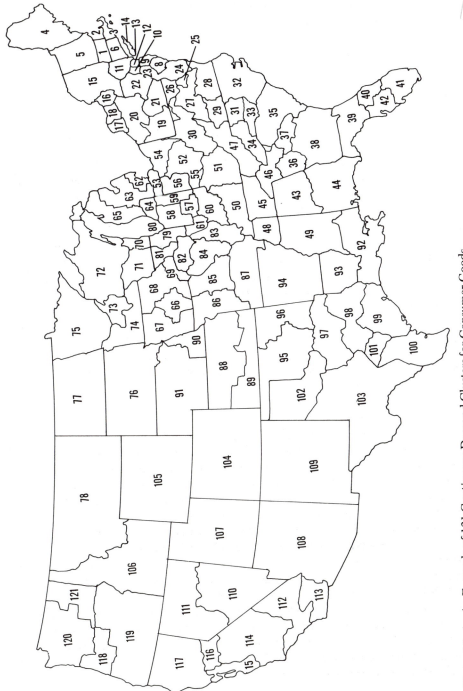

Figure 16–4 An Example of 121 Contiguous Demand Clusters for Consumer Goods

Source: Drake Sheahan/Stewart Dougall, Inc., used by permission.

tional distribution. The clusters are chosen to be groups of three-digit ZIP codes for easy data collection. The number of clusters reflects the relative amount of demand in a cluster. Therefore, smaller clusters are used in the more populated sections of the country; fewer in the less populated sections.

Location Coordinates

Once centers of demand have been established, locating them arithmetically instead of by city, county, or state facilitates computer handling of the information. Geographical coding of demand centers as well as warehouse and plant locations allows distances to be computed between points. These distances are needed for estimating transportation rates between pairs of points, determining plant and warehouse territories, and controlling customer service distances. The important question is: What geographical location coding scheme is best to use?

In a government-sponsored study,[16] 33 separate national geocoding systems were identified. These range from the familiar ZIP code used by the U.S. Postal Service to the little-known GEO code developed for the purposes of describing the location of plant and animal species. Many of these are not particularly suitable for distribution planning purposes although they may be quite useful for operational purposes. The Standard Point Location Code is a case in point. This has been a popular coding scheme used in computerized freight rating systems where origin and destination points must be specified in great detail so that the proper transportation rate can be found between them. The problem with such coding systems is that a given location number is a build-up of numbers for locations nested within larger locations. As such, there is little mathematical relation between location code pairs. However, it is this property that is desired in a location code for strategic planning purposes.

The second feature should be as little distortion as possible due to the map projection technique inherent in the coding system. Grid lines on a plane laid against a globe will show distance distortions at points away from the region of contact. Geopolitical and area codes, such as the census code, ZIP code, and Standard Point Location Code are examples of those coding schemes that avoid the map distortion problem. The linear grid (lines on a map), the Railway Express Agency coordinate system, and the vertical–horizontal coordinate system of American Telephone and Telegraph are subject to this problem.

The choice of a geocoding system will be greatly influenced by practical considerations. One researcher favors longitude–latitude as the best all around geocoding system.[15] The difficulty or expense of obtaining longitudes and latitudes for selected points sometimes precludes their use, and sales data are not referenced to these coordinates. Therefore, demand data are usually first collected in terms of ZIP code, geopolitical reference scheme, or company-generated scheme (e.g., sales territories). Then some form of simple linear grid is used. Distances are then computed as the hypotenuse of a right triangle where the sides of the triangle are given as V_1-V_2 and H_1-H_2, and V and H are the respective vertical and horizontal coordinate values for each point.

Transport Rate Estimation

Once distances can be computer generated, one step remains to estimate the transportation rates between origin and destination point pairs. This step is to find a workable relationship between actual transportation rates charged as a function of distance as shown by the equation $R = 4.45 + 0.0042D$ in Figure 16–5. By substituting the distance D between two points into the rate equation, we can approximate the transportation rate R. Although transportation rates are a result of many factors, volume and distance seem to be the primary determinants of the rate level. Fortunately, within each major weight break category, rates and distance show a very high degree of linear correlation. An example is shown in Figure 16–5.

When using this basic concept for distribution planning, it is necessary to construct a set of curves that capture major differences in how these curves are generated. First, there are significant differences in the rate levels depending on where shipments originate. There remain substantial differences in rates for shipments originating in the South versus the North. The rate level often is 10 percent lower in the South within a given weight break as shown in Figure 16–6. To the extent that other regions of the country may show higher or lower rate levels than these two, additional rate curves should be prepared.

Second, different degrees of regulation may be a reason for more rate curves. Local delivery, intrastate shipments, and interstate shipments are three primary categories that can show substantial cost differences. Local delivery costs result from local cartage rates that are in effect roughly within 30 miles of a city center. Since these rates are peculiar to each origin point, they should be defined for each point of interest such as a potential warehouse location. On the other hand, where shipments move beyond the local cartage

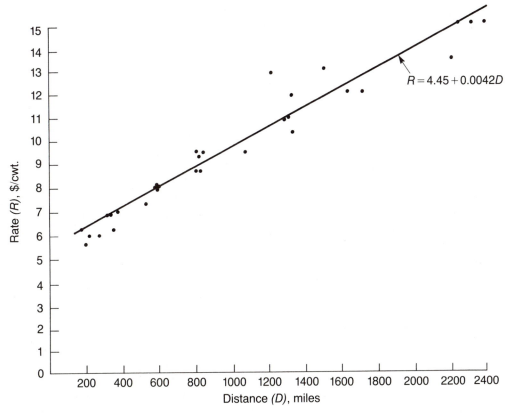

Figure 16-5   Common Carrier Truck Transportation Rates for Selected Distances out of Detroit, Michigan

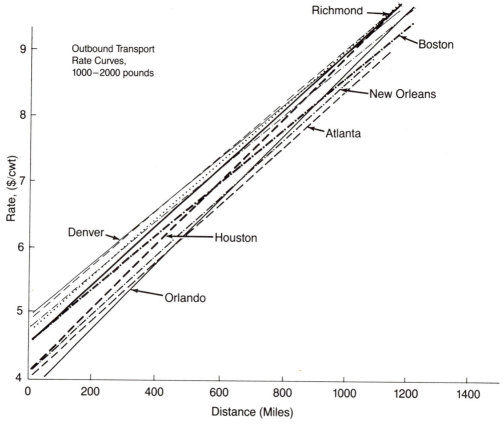

Figure 16-6   Transport Rate Curves with Different Origin Cities

range but remain within the origin state, intrastate rates will apply. For most strategic planning purposes, intrastate and interstate rate curves may be combined without substantial error. However, in very large states such as Texas and California separate rate curves should be developed to preserve estimating accuracy.

The procedure for generating these curves is based on statistical techniques. That is, take 30 to 50 points at varying distances from the origin point and radiating in all directions. Then, by graphical means or by simple linear regression analysis, determine the line that best fits the sample data. A straight-line fit usually will be quite good for both intrastate and interstate rates.

An Inventory-Demand Relationship

Strategic planning as well as the operational control of inventory levels can benefit from methods that allow inventory levels to be analyzed overall rather than on an item-by-item basis. Warehouse location computer models in particular require such an aggregate inventory-to-demand relationship. This allows inventory levels to be estimated from the demand assigned to a warehouse. Such a graphical relationship is illustrated in Figure 16–7.

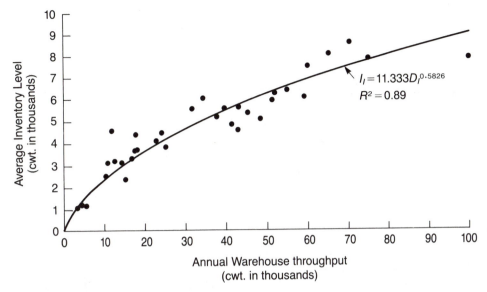

Figure 16-7 An Inventory-to-Warehouse Throughput Relationship for a Pull Inventory Strategy for 34 Field Warehouses

To determine the inventory–demand curve, find the average inventory level and the annual throughput for each stocking point in the distribution network. Purge the data of unrepresentative observations. With the remaining data pairs, either by manual means or by the use of multiple regression techniques, determine the curve that best fits the data points. This curve then shows the execution of the firm's inventory policy. Since the curve is expressed mathematically, it can be easily incorporated into strategic planning models for warehouse location to estimate warehouse inventory levels when the number and therefore the warehouse throughput is changed.

The curve is also useful in an operational sense by serving as a tool for auditing and controlling overall inventory levels. Deviations from the curve by individual warehouses may indicate departures from desired inventory policy and the need for corrective action. In addition, the curve generated from actual data may be compared with the curve that the company's inventory policy would suggest, to determine if it is being executed properly. More detailed information on the inventory–demand relationship can be found in a recently published article.[18]

Summary

This chapter has discussed the use of the computer for both strategic planning and operational control of physical distribution systems. User surveys show that in these areas, computers are used primarily for inventory control and accounting. Further use, especially for operational control purposes, seems limited by the quality of the data in the data base. This may explain the slow progress made in such areas as freight rating and routing, and warehouse operations.

The slow progress of computerization in the operations control areas may raise questions about the availability of models to deal effectively with distribution problems. This is generally not the case either at the control or the strategic planning level. We have attempted to identify a number of model types that are useful in the practice of physical distribution management. Of particular utility for strategic planning are the computer models that assist in warehouse location, inventory planning, and vehicle routing and scheduling. For operational control, the computer models dealing with order consolidation, shipment scheduling, and freight rate retrieval and auditing are likely to have much greater use in the future.

Finally, this chapter has discussed several specific methods that facilitate transportation rate estimation, inventory level approximation in warehouses, and demand clustering. These methods are some of the techniques that make distribution computer models practical in dealing with actual problems.

Notes

1. B. J. La Londe and P. H. Zinszer. *Customer Service: Meaning and Measurement* (Chicago: NCPDM, 1976).

2. *1964 Census of Manufacturers General Summary, December 1970* (U.S. Department of Commerce, Bureau of the Census, March 1971, Reader Microprint No. 4248), p. 28.

3. R. G. House and G. C. Jackson, "Trends in Computer Applications in Transportation and Distribution Management," *International Journal of Physical Distribution*, 7, No. 3 (1977), pp. 176–187; R. G. House and G. J. Jackson, "Trends in Computer Applications: A Survey," *Handling & Shipping*, 18, No. 6 (1977), pp. 52–56.

4. J. W. Farrell, "Computerization," *Traffic Management*, 14, No. 9 (1975), pp. 35–44.

5. House and Jackson, "Trends in Computer Applications: A Survey."

6. H. N. Shycon and R. B. Maffei, "Simulation—Tool for Better Distribution," *Harvard Business Review*, 39 (November–December 1960), pp. 65–75; V. A. Mabert and D. C. Whybark, "Sampling as a Solution Methodology," *Decision Sciences*, 8, No. 1 (January 1977), pp. 167–179.

7. R. H. Ballou, "DISPLAN—A Multiproduct Facility Location Model with Nonlinear Inventory Costs," in Proceedings of the 12th Annual Transportation and Logistics Educator's Conference, San Francisco, October 10, 1982; A. A. Kuehn and M. J. Hamburger, "A Heuristic Program for Locating Warehouses," *Management Science*, 9 (1963), pp. 643–666.

8. M. A. Efroymson and T. L. Roy, "A Branch-bound Algorithm for Planning Location," *Operations Research*, 14 (May–June 1966); A. M. Geoffrion and G. W. Graves, "Multicommodity Distribution System Design by Benders Decomposition," *Management Science*, 20 (January 1974), pp. 822–844; B. M. Khumawala, "An Efficient Branch and Bound Algorithm for the Warehouse Location Problem," *Management Science*, 18 (August 1972).

9. D. J. Bowersox, "Planning Physical Distribution Operations with Dynamic Simulation," *Journal of Marketing* (January 1972), pp. 17–25; M. M. Conners, C. Coray, C. J. Cuccaro, W. K. Green, D. W. Low, and H. M. Markowitz, "The Distribution System Simulator," *Management Science*, 18 (1972), pp. B425–B453; R. H. Ballou, *Business Logistics Management* (Englewood Cliffs, N.J.: Prentice-Hall, 1973), pp. 494–506.

10. *Yearbook of Railroad Facts*, 1980 ed. (Washington D.C.: Association of American Railroads, 1980), p. 36.

11. J. L. Heskett, N. A. Glaskowsky, Jr., and R. M. Ivie, *Business Logistics*, 2d ed. (New York: Ronald Press, 1973), p. 19.

12. A. W. Lai and B. J. La Londe, "Cost Reduction Opportunity in Shipment Consolidation: A Computer Simulation Approach," *Proceedings of the Ninth Annual Meeting, American Institute of Decision Sciences* (1977), pp. 378–380.

13. COMPU.MAP, a product of Logistics Systems, Inc., Wellesley, Mass.

14. See, for example, G. Clarke and J. W. Wright, "Scheduling of Vehicles from a Central Depot to a Number of Delivery Points," *Operations Research*, 11 (1963), pp. 568–581; and B. L. Golden, T. L. Magnanti, and H. Q. Nguyen, "Implementing Vehicle Routing Algorithms," *Networks*, 7 (1977), pp. 113–148.

15. R. H. Ballou and M. Chowdhury, MSVS: "An Extended Computer Model for Transport Mode Selection and Vehicle Scheduling," *The Transportation and Logistics Review*, forthcoming.

16. P. A. Werner, *A Survey of National Geocoding Systems*, Report No. DOT-TSC-OST-74-26 (Washington, D.C.: U.S. Department of Transportation, 1974).

17. R. J. Lewis, "A Business Logistics Information and Accounting System for Marketing Analysis," Ph.D. dissertation, Michigan State University, 1964.

18. R. H. Ballou, "Estimating and Auditing Aggregate Inventory Levels at Multiple Stocking Points," *Journal of Operations Management*, 1, No. 3 (February 1981), pp. 143–153.

Computer-Assisted Freight Bill Rating

Robert G. House *and* C. Charles Kimm

The general goal of traffic management is to control and monitor the flows of inbound and outbound product movement. Firms need to monitor product movements to obtain reports on the cost of doing business in selective markets, and transportation costs are an important portion of the cost of serving a market. Another reason for a firm's interest in product movement data is the need for a current and accurate picture of the way in which product moves through the firm. Product flow data can be used to diagnose distribution system deficiencies and to detect changes in consumption patterns associated with changes in the firm's marketing strategy.

Although product flow data may be obtained from sales reports in marketing, a more reliable source of product movement information is the freight bill. The data on the freight bill accurately characterize product flow without distortions introduced by rising prices. Thus it is important to capture and manage the information on freight bills efficiently.

Recognizing the importance of the freight bill as a source of traffic flow information, several studies have been made which explore the feasibility of computerized freight bill processing. The initial study was conducted by Battelle Laboratories in 1970. Significant progress has been made since that time. In the summer of 1978 the authors interviewed numerous shippers, carriers, and traffic service bureaus in an attempt to document the changes that had taken place since the initial work in the area. The information gathered in those interviews formed the basis for the comments below.

A total traffic information system includes provisions for data encoding (capturing freight bill information), data verification (verifying rates charged on the freight bill), and data summarization (reporting). Data verification (rating) represents the heart of the problem in traffic information systems. The problem facing the shipper is to examine the freight bill presented by the carrier and verify the charges. To verify the charges the shipper must "rate" the bill. While conceptually a simple task, actual freight bill rating is a highly complex task involving both extensive data bases and complex logic to arrive at the lowest applicable rate. Accurate rating is essential—traffic service bureaus can demonstrate an average recovery (rating error) of $1.01 for every bill rated. For a typical high-volume shipper, the savings level is around $100,000 annually. However, many large-scale traffic information systems like International Paper's TIMS system characterize rating as an operational detail and give it relatively little consideration in the overall system, preferring to concentrate on data capture and summarization.

Typically, corporate traffic information systems introduce the rating module late in system development because of the cost of initializing the data bases and the complexity of the rating logic. The situation facing the shipper is that he cannot justify the acceleration of the rating-module schedule because of the cost/benefit ratio in comparison to other priorities within the traffic management area and within the firm in general. At the same time, traffic managers are aware of the magnitude of savings available and, thus, turn to traffic service bureaus to check the accuracy of their freight bills. The traffic service bureau is asked to rate a large number of bills and to come up with the "lowest applicable rate" for each bill. Thus the need to check the bill has not disappeared; rather it has been placed with an outside agency.

Process of Rating a Freight Bill

The paper flow associated with the payment of freight bills starts when the shipper generates a bill of lading. The bill of lading serves as the shipper's request to the carrier to perform transportation service between a point of origin and a point of destination. The bill of lading is a standard document which designates the shipper (consignor), the origin, the destination, and the consignee. Individual lines in the bill of lading describe the number of units of each article, the article description, and the classification of the article (optional information). The bill of lading serves as the basic contract between origin and destination.

When the carrier receives the bill of lading, he transfers the information on it to a freight bill, "rates" the movement of the products between the origin and destination, and places those charges on the freight bill. The freight bill is then delivered to the shipper for payment.

The freight bill serves as the official documentation of charges for the movement of the goods described on the bill of lading. The determination of the charges placed on the freight bill follows a fixed sequence of steps:

1. Determination of basing points

2. Determination of rate base number (RBN)

3. Determination of classification and class rate applicable

4. Determination of rate from class rate table

5. Search for alternative applicable rates such as commodity rates

6. Placement of lowest applicable rate on freight bill

The rating process begins with the determination of the basing points for the origin and the destination. For example, Worthington, Ohio, a Columbus suburb, takes Columbus, Ohio, as its basing point. Basing points are found in a tariff usually called the rate group tariff which is also known as the grouping tariff. A typical rate group tariff is Tariff 151 of the Eastern Central Motor Carriers Association (ECMCA).

Once the basing points have been determined, the rate base number (RBN) can be found through a table look-up process. The rate base table is usually found in the class rate tariff (for example Tariff 531 of the ECMCA). The table consists of pairs of points and their associated RBN. The rate base number is rough approximation for the highway miles between the two points. The use of the RBN in finding a rate in the tariff is discussed below.

Computerized rating systems maintain both the grouping tariff and the rate base numbers as individual files if the rate extraction process is table driven. If the system stores only point-to-point rates, then the entire grouping tariff and rate base number files do not have to be maintained.

After the origin, destination, and rate base number have been identified, the product must be identified. Every product shipped in the United States has been classified in the National Motor Freight Classification (NMFC). The NMFC consists of item numbers, item descriptions, and the less-than-truckload (LTL) class rating and the truckload (TL) class rating. The item is said to "take" the class rating specified in the NMFC. Classification of items is a complex problem which may dramatically affect the class rating; therefore, many shippers are putting the NMFC item number and class rating on the bill of lading. Computerization of the NMFC would be neither feasible nor desirable given the direction of the shippers vis-à-vis their bills of lading.

The origin, destination, rate base number, NMFC item number, class rating, and shipment size in hundredweight (cwt) are all the items needed to rate a shipment. One first determines the governing tariff by examining the origin and the destination. For example, a shipment from Columbus, Ohio, to Detroit, Michigan, would be governed by ECMCA Tariff 531.

If the class rating for the item were 100 (LTL) and 70 (TL), and the rate base number between the origin and the destination were 219, then the appropriate section of the tariff would be that shown in Table 17–1. The data shown in the table indicate that the shipper must pay at a minimum $16.87. A shipment of 300 pounds would move at a rate of $9.36 per cwt for a total charge of $28.08. A truckload shipment would move under Class 70 at a rate of $2.69 per cwt. The volume necessary to qualify for a truckload rating is also given in the NMFC. The rating process demonstrated here is known as class rating and is the simplest form of rating. All computerized rating systems are capable of class rating in the manner described above.

Sophisticated rating (either manual or computerized) does not stop once the class rate has been determined. The class rate may not be the lowest applicable rate. Thus a search for an alternative rate is begun. A common alternative rate is a commodity rate. Commodity rates are either point-to-point rates (rates between A and B for a given commodity at a stated shipment size) or column commodity rates (rates for a given commodity at a stated shipment size where the distance the commodity moves is determined from the RBN). Commodity rates are usually applied for and published by individual carriers in conjunction with individual shippers to that the carrier may obtain the shipper's business. Commodity rates represent alternative rates which must be checked and which are, in general, idiosyncratic to every shipper and to every origin and destination.

A second type of alternative rate which must be checked when the freight bill is rated is the exception rate. An exception rate is one filed independently by carriers who by filing

Table 17–1 Section from Tariff 531-3, Published by Eastern Central Motor Carriers
Association

Rate Basis	Minimum Charge	Weight Group	Classes	
			100	*70*
211	1687	L 5C	936	629
to		M 5C	820•	546
220		M 1M	715	475
		M 2M	636	423
		M 5M	490	313
		M10M	464	297
		M15M	440	282
		T	419	269

Data taken from Supplement 49 to Tariff 531-3, published by ECMCA.

the rate indicate that they will or will not participate in a given rate for movement of a commodity from Point A to Point B. When a carrier does not participate in a rate he is said to "flag out." If a carrier has flagged out of a rate and that carrier performs the movement, then the commodity rate would not apply. Exception rates are merely the beginning of the problem of dealing with commodity rates. For example, some commodity rates only apply over certain routes. The difficulties in dealing with commodity rates is that all computerized rating systems treat these rates as point-to-point rates loaded into the client's special use files. No computerized rating system maintains all the commodity rates published.

Additional complexity in rating is found in conjunction with freight moving under pool distribution, stop-offs, mixed truckload, mixed carload, trailer on flatcar, accessorial, exclusive use, in-transit, and intermodal service rates to name a few. Rating is further complicated by use of irregular route, exempt, and specialized carriers. No existing fully computerized rating system is able to handle all the complexities associated with freight movement.

The rating of the freight bill is not the end of the paper flow associated with the movement of product from Point A to Point B. Once the freight bill has been captured and rated either manually or on the computer, the bill must be paid within seven days* from presentation of the bill by the carrier. To avoid paying the same freight bill twice, control for duplicate payment must be instituted in either manual or computerized systems. These duplicate payment controls are usually based on bill of lading control or on the freight bill (pro number). Sophisticated duplicate payment control procedures usually result in substantial cost savings.

The pressure on the carrier to present the bill within seven days and upon the shipper to pay within seven days from presentation leads to errors in rating and in duplicate billings. Thus both rating accuracy and duplicate payment control are key issues in controlling transportation cost. Data collected by the Interstate Commerce Commission (ICC) (Table 17–2) indicate the magnitude of bills outstanding at a given time. These data may explain why the control of the paper flow in traffic information management systems is so difficult.

---

*Interstate Commerce Commission regulations in effect at time of writing.

Table 17-2   Results of ICC Survey of Freight Bills

	Average	Standard Error
RAILROADS		
Workdays		
From delivery to payment	12.8 days	1.1 days
From delivery to presentation of bill	2.5 days	0.7 days
From presentation of bill, on delivery to payment	8.7 days	1.4 days
Calendar days		
From delivery to payment	18.6 days	1.1 days
From delivery to presentation of bill	3.8 days	1.8 days
From presentation of bill, on delivery to payment	12.7 days	1.3 days
Average value of bills	$1,428	$428
Average dollar-days (calendar) from delivery to payment	23,225	3,949
Total dollar-days (calendar) (for all railroads)	647,000,000,000	110,000,000,000
MOTOR CARRIERS		
Workdays		
From delivery to payment	12.6 days	1.9 days
From delivery to billing	0.8 days	1.3 days
From billing to payment or delivery to payment	10.8 days	3.3 days
Calendar days		
From delivery to payment	17.7 days	2.8 days
From delivery to billing	1.3 days	3.1 days
From billing to payment or delivery to payment	14.5 days	2.0 days
Average value of bills	$108	$138
Average dollar-days (calendar) from delivery to payment	2341	2601
Total dollar-days (calendar) (for all motor carriers)	766,000,000,000	851,000,000,000

SOURCE: Bureau of Operations and Accounts, Interstate Commerce Commission, 1978.

Reporting in a Traffic Information System

Once the freight bills have been paid, the third phase of the traffic information system—reporting—begins. Traffic data are usually summarized by the lane, by carrier, by region, and by shipment size. The data are then used to support rate negotiations, to obtain better service from the carrier, to plan for future distribution activities, and to assess the impact of changes in distribution practices.

Corporate traffic information systems tend to visualize summarized traffic data as the starting point for further analysis of freight flows. The typical traffic service bureau prepares these data for its clients but does not become involved in interpreting the data. The more computerized traffic service bureaus tend to emphasize computerized rating rather than reporting and consultation. More progressive traffic service bureaus recognize the value of the reports and attempt to educate their clients in the need for careful review of this information.

Problems Facing the Shipper

Shippers can be categorized as those likely to use rating services and those that are not. Firms unlikely to be active users of externally provided rating services possess one or more of the following characteristics:

1. *F.O.B. origin shippers.* Shippers who deal with outbound freight under F.O.B. origin conditions have no traffic problems. This type of shipper transfers freight problems to its customers. The shipper will receive no freight bill and, thus, will not have to rate or process these bills in a traffic information system.

2. *Small shippers.* A small shipper, defined in terms of number of shipments, is most likely to use a guidebook like Leonard's *Guide* to rate shipments. If the small shipper has a small total annual transportation bill, there will be little impetus to exercise control of transportation costs.

3. *Shippers under corporate constraints.* Some corporations have corporate policies prohibiting release of corporate information, such as freight bills, to outside agencies. When this type of policy exists, the corporation usually is involved in evaluating or installing an internal tariff information management system.

Firms using outside or internal computerized tariff information systems tended to share three characteristics:

1. *Large volume of shipments.* Shippers who generate in excess of 300 freight bills per month tend to use some form of computer-assisted rating and reporting. The typical shipper who uses an outside rating agency generates approximately 6000 shipments per month. Firms that generate over 10,000 shipments tend to consider and can justify the internal computerized rating of freight bills. The large volume of shipments tends to create significant clerical problems and costs which need to be solved and controlled.

2. *Need for cost control.* As the volume of shipments increases, the shipper needs to control the cost associated with each shipment. Small savings—even a dollar per bill—become significant when the number of annual shipments is over 50,000. Several shippers interviewed reported saving $100,000 annually, on an average per bill savings of around $1.

3. *Need for accurate information for distribution planning.* As firms become more concerned with distribution system planning, their need for detailed data on product movement increases. The source of this information is the traffic information system and the freight bill in particular. Since this document must be captured, and the freight rates need to be maintained for planning purposes, these firms often complete the system by acquiring some form of rating capability. Often a relationship with a traffic service bureau can be justified because its reports provide better information to management, thereby facilitating the recognition of transportation opportunities. Savings from more accurate freight bill rating are an added benefit to the report generation process.

In general, the firms that are most likely to employ a traffic service bureau are those firms that are high-volume shippers of less-than-truckload quantities. The movement patterns or transportation requirements involve a large number of destinations in a relatively sporadic fashion. In contrast, it is unlikely that a firm with highly regular movements of truckload or carload volumes would be a prime customer of a traffic service bureau.

Shippers' Needs from a Traffic Service Bureau

The composite picture that can be drawn is that shippers want a freight payment information system that is complete. A complete system would encompass rate maintenance, pre-audit, payment, and reporting. The shippers interviewed, in general, described the essential elements of a total traffic information system. One element of such a system, freight rating, was characterized as fitting into an integrated transportation information system through its reporting capacity. Currently only one traffic service bureau, Distribution Sciences, Inc. (DSI), appears to have developed its product offering in line with this concept of fitting into an overall information system. However, as Table 17–3 indicates, the system offered by DSI is not complete.

Shippers expressed a need for computerized traffic service bureaus that could rate accurately 90 percent or more of the shipments. From an internal operating viewpoint, such a service should have no more than 5 to 6 percent kickouts. This means that the system should be able to rate 94 to 95 percent of the bills submitted to it and at least 90 percent of those bills should be rated accurately. The system must also operate and pay the freight bills within the seven-day constraint imposed by the ICC.

Shippers would also like the system to check for duplicate payments on either the bill-of-lading or pro-number control system. The general consensus among those interviewed was that nine months to a year of historical information would have to be maintained in order to provide for close control over duplicate payments.

Shippers also indicated that the system would have to provide informative and readable reports at a regular interval (monthly). While recognizing the difficulty in producing customized reports, shippers believed that this would be a primary attribute of a successful package.

Finally, shippers wanted a system that they could grow with. For example, a shipper might begin by using an external service bureau and later introduce that system into its own operations when volume warranted.

Evaluation of Current Offerings of Traffic Service Bureaus

Four major forms of traffic service bureaus were identified in this study: 1) manual operations, 2) semi-automated operations, 3) totally automated operations, and 4) internal software systems. In this section, each of these categories of traffic service bureaus is evaluated in light of the shippers' desires. Typical firms in each type of operation are identified and the market's view of this type of operation is described.

Manual traffic service bureaus usually operate only on a post-audit basis. The post-auditing field is large and competitive. While the normal split in recovery from the post-audit is 50–50, the competitive environment allows the shipper to bid this down to a return of 40 percent to the auditor. The post-audit field is dominated by a few large firms like Atlas, Climax, and Nationwide. However, most of the work is done by moonlighting rate analysts from various corporations. The bulk of the firms in this business are one- and two-man operations. Post-auditing is under no time pressure because the shipper is allowed one year to file a recovery claim against the carrier. Post-auditors usually do not produce reports based on the bills that they have reviewed.

Table 17-3 Characteristics of Traffic Service Bureaus Included in Study—As of July, 1978

Traffic Service Bureau	Services Offered					Degree of Computerization	Package for Sale
	Rate Maintenance	Pre-Audit	Payment	Post-Audit	Reporting		
Ball Corporation*	X	X	X		X	High	Yes
Bank of America			X		X	Moderate	No
Cass Bank			X		X	Moderate	No
Chase Manhattan Bank*			X		X	Moderate	No
Comtrac	X	X	X	X	X	High	No
Distribution Sciences	X	X				High	Yes†
Goodyear	X	X	X		X	Low	Yes
Industrial Traffic*	X	X	X	X	X	High	No
InTra Con	X	X	X	X	X	Moderate	Yes
McAuto	X		X	X		Moderate	No
Numerax	X	X			X	Moderate	Yes†
Phillips Petroleum*	X	X	X		X	High	Yes
TCS	X	X	X		X	Moderate	No
TDS	X	X	X	X	X	Moderate	Yes
Union Carbide	X	X	X		X	High	Yes

*Data obtained from secondary sources.

†Cannot be accurately determined at time of report.

Although there are significant dollars found in post-auditing, this area is of little importance to the traffic service bureau because post-auditors cannot meet ICC initial payment time frames or produce the reports that management requires. These two qualifications exist for all manual systems.

A semi-automated traffic service bureau operation does some computer-assisted rating (usually class rates) and perform extensive computerization of the reporting function. The semi-automated traffic service bureau is characterized by operations like TDS, InTraCon, Numerax, and Comtrac. Operations in this category employ around 100 employees. Approximately 80 percent of the firm's employees are engaged in purely clerical functions. The other employees perform the rating, run the computer system, and sell the product. A semi-automated traffic service bureau can be expected to generate sales of around $2 million annually, although some may reach sales volumes around $5 million.

Shippers tend to view semi-automated traffic service bureaus as valuable adjuncts to their businesses. However, shippers have questions about the bureau's financial stability, their longevity, and the quality of non-rating services provided.

A special variety of traffic service bureau is the bank payment plan. The bank payment plan usually involves a bank paying the firm's freight bills are they are presented (without an audit) and then summarizing the paid bills in various management reports. Bank payment plans like those offered by Cass Bank, Chase Manhattan, and Bank of America offer duplicate payment control and management reporting. Bank payment plans offer financial stability and longevity; however, they do little to reduce the firm's transportation bill. The market seems to be moving away from bank payment plans because of their inability to pre-audit or to provide transportation consultation. In response to this, the banks have developed arrangements with small traffic service bureaus to provide pre-audit services and initial data capture. This places the bank in a more competitive position with the traffic service bureau.

A totally automated operation, like that found at DSI, is the third major type of traffic service bureau. The DSI operation is unique among traffic service bureaus in that it is totally automated and performs only pre-auditing. The firm using DSI must be capable of transmitting and receiving an electronic message which represents the bill of lading. This requires a sophistication on the part of the client firm not found in many organizations. DSI offers the advantage of an externally maintained rate base, external rating, and internal management report generation.

An internal software system brings rate maintenance, pre-auditing, payment and reporting into the shippers' own computer system. Typical packages offered include the Goodyear system, the Ball system, the TCS system, the Phillips Petroleum system, the McAuto system, and the Union Carbide system. All of these systems rate freight bills as part of a total freight management information system. A minimum of 100,000 bills of lading per year is required to justify the typical internal system. Relatively few firms have chosen to implement the internal system despite considerable discussion of these systems in the trade press. The shippers interviewed indicated that the computer resources required for these sytems could not be justified. The survey also revealed that those firms that purchased the systems often had to make extensive modifications to the code to make it run in their particular problem environment. Various degrees of success in implementing these systems have been reported by Champion International, St. Regis Paper, Owens Illinois, Johns Mansville, Corning Glass, Borden Chemical, and Anchor Hocking. In general, currently available internal traffic software packages have not been well received by the shippers.

A summary evaluation of current traffic service bureau offerings reveals that they are not fulfilling the shippers' needs. Current traffic service bureau offerings do not offer the shipper a complete package backed up by a financially sound, stable organization that can handle all of the shipper's requests within a reasonable time frame.

One important criterion in evaluating traffic service bureaus is the ability of the bureau to rate the shipper's bills within the required time frame. The ability to rate the individual shipment is the greatest as one moves towards totally automated internal and external systems. Internal systems are usually customized to deal with selected modes and selected movements within the firm. This in turn limits the coverage of the internal system across modes and types of shipments. Thus speed of rating sacrifices coverage. The manual system tends to be able to rate any type of shipment because it relies on published rate files which are more complete than computerized rate files. However, manual systems have difficulty coping with large volumes of bills without extensive manpower.

Computer-assisted rating tends to have difficulties with complex shipping patterns such as pooling, stop-offs, and in-transit privileges. This is an important limitation because the more complex the type of the shipment the greater is the potential for freight savings. Traffic managers recognize the potential of these types of shipments and thus use them with increasing frequency. This then leads to an increasing number of kickouts by the computerized rating system. This problem can be solved only by attempting to computerize the rules tariff.

The ability of the traffic service bureau to handle duplicate payments is also of great concern to the shipper. In general, the greater the degree of computerization, the greater the degree of control over duplicate payments. In our study, the most sophisticated duplicate payments control routine was that offered by InTraCon. They used a total of ten different tests on an 18-month history base of pro numbers. This system emphasized identification of suspect duplicate payments as well as actual duplicate payment checking. Manual systems rarely incorporate this form of control.

A third major concern of the shipper is the ability to receive transportation reports from the traffic service bureau. Manual systems are incapable of providing transportation information summarized in a meaningful way, while even the most rudimentary computerized system provides information of significant value to the shipper.

The reports generated by the various traffic service bureaus are almost identical. The report set offered as standard output usually includes: 1) a disbursements journal organized by carrier and by date, 2) a traffic journal which shows the amount of traffic placed with each carrier, and 3) a lane analysis which shows the tonnage moved over specific origin destination pairs.

In summary, all forms of computerized traffic service bureaus provide about the same level of skills in rating, the same coverage in rates, and the same types of reports. The major differentiation among the various bureaus is in their ability to rate complex shipments on the computer. A greater ability to rate complex shipments can be found in those organizations that have invested more heavily in computerized rating logic and in rate data base.

Traffic service bureaus represent a viable option for the traffic manager who wishes to control his costs and receive timely and accurate traffic information. The bureaus cited in this paper all appear to be capable of removing a burden from the traffic manager and returning to him valuable information. In providing a rating and reporting service, these bureaus offer a cost effective service that should be considered seriously as a key ingredient in the establishment of an effective traffic information system.

Demand Forecasting

CHAPTER 18

Demand Forecasting: *A Vital Tool in Logistics Management*

Lynn E. Gill

Introduction

Forecasting, a familiar term in business, is basically concerned with projecting past occurrences into the future. Forecasting involves (1) the identification of variables which influence demand, and (2) the development of equations which state the relationship among the variables in mathematical terms. A multitude of forecasting techniques are available to business management, ranging from surveys and simple trend projections to complex and sophisticated econometric models.

The importance of demand forecasting to business decision making has been recognized for decades. There are volumes of information available on the role of forecasting in setting sales quotas, scheduling production, inventory control, and in financial planning and budgeting. However, there is a shortage of reference material on the role of forecasting in logistics management, a management area which has been developing rapidly in recent years. Logistics includes many of the functions previously controlled by manufacturing, marketing, and finance, such as inventory management, production scheduling, purchasing and procurement, and order processing. Typically, most logistics textbooks and other reference sources brush forecasting aside as the responsibility of another corporate department, although the data it provides about the future is admittedly useful to logistics management. However, forecasting future demand is more than just useful—it is *vital* in effective logistics management. A prime responsibility of logistics managers is to make decisions today about an uncertain tomorrow. Demand forecasting, because it reduces uncertainty, is of tremendous value in carrying out this responsibility.

The purpose of this chapter is to explore the role that demand forecasting plays in logistics management, examine forecast variables and considerations, and discuss the useful techniques (both subjective and statistical) available for preparing a forecast. Two additional areas of significance, forecast responsibility and control, follow at the conclusion.

The Role of Forecasting in Logistics

Demand forecasting is an important consideration in logistics decision making. Almost all areas of logistics management (except routine clerical and operational duties) require some degree of forecasting and planning. Two broad aspects of logistics planning are: (1) planning for physical stocks of inventories for raw materials and finished goods, and (2) design of the system through which the goods move. In the first case, the present and projected intensity of market demand is of great importance. In the second case, both the intensity of demand and its present and projected spatial aspects are significant.

The role of demand forecasting in logistics is currently taking on added importance. Many large corporations are establishing logistics planning staffs which devote their time exclusively to medium and long-range logistics planning. Forecasting, of course, is the basis for any kind of planning, particularly medium- and long-range which extends several years into the future. Typical projects of logistics planning staffs include selecting plant and warehouse site locations, studying the feasibility of utilizing private trucks or leased rail equipment in lieu of common carriers, and determining future sources of raw materials. Also important is analyzing new technologies in transportation and materials handling which could alter the firm's logistics system in future years by making its present one obsolete. Examples of logistics functional areas where forecast considerations aid heavily management's decision making are illustrated below.

Purchasing and Procurement

In a manufacturing company there can be no interruption of the production line while the purchasing department is out scouting up more raw materials or parts for assembly. The fact that demand for the product has doubled over the past two weeks, for example, is no excuse. Accurate demand forecasting is essential in planning future procurement needs well in advance of their actual usage.

The forest products industry is an example of long-range procurement planning. Demand must be forecasted 20, 30, and even 50 years in advance so that the correct species of timber can be planted and grown to maturity for harvest. This example may be an extreme one, but it points out the importance of long-range procurement forecasts.

Production Control

The role of forecasting is crucial to provide a basis for proper production control. In a company with multi-product lines, sizes, flavors, and colors, decisions of which items to produce, on what production line, at what time, and in which plant are challenging, to say the least. A great deal of information is required about the distribution of demand among products, customers, time periods, and geographical areas to make these complex decisions correctly.

Inventory Control

Again, the need for accurate forecasts is of utmost importance. A company with many plants and warehouses must determine how much of each product to stock at each warehouse or distribution center. Forecasting future demand in each market area is essential in making these decisions. The objective is to stock only enough inventory to cover a reasonable percentage of expected demand. Carrying inventory to assure that no stock-outs will occur is technically possible, of course, but economically unsound. Complicating factors are new products, upcoming price changes, and competitors' actions.

Materials Handling

Demand forecasting is important in planning next month's (or next quarter's) manpower needs in the warehouse or plant. This is particularly true of such personnel as forklift truck drivers or order pickers, who require some training to become proficient. Another consideration involves planning future materials handling systems. For example, should a company build an automated (and expensive) system in anticipation of heavy future demand, or rely on manual methods which are more flexible if unexpected changes occur? An adequate forecast of future demand is an important input to such a decision.

Warehousing

Future warehouse needs, that is, floor space and facilities, must be determined well in advance. Planning for construction of warehouses or distribution centers must take place, in many cases, years before the actual need date. Also, in day-to-day operation one of the most important responsibilities of warehouse management is adequate product turnover. The oldest product in the warehouse should be moved out first, if at all possible. Demand forecasts assist in planning the location of products in the warehouse to assure proper stock rotation. Although it is generally not available, daily demand forecasting would be of great help in scheduling both inbound and outbound shipments at the warehouse.

Transportation

Planning for future transportation needs is generally an important part of logistics. This is particularly true in those manufacturing companies where transportation costs are a high percentage of selling price. Examples are the food, forest products, and steel industries, which all ship huge quantities of products. Among the important considerations in transportation are rail car supply needs next week and next month, whether leased rail cars should be used, whether private trucks should be used to offer better customer service, planning for private truck dispatching, and so forth. Demand forecasting is needed as a yardstick in all these areas.

Fixed Facilities

The logistics manager is often heavily involved in selecting plant and distribution center locations. Not the least important of the factors considered is future demand. A company doesn't want to construct a $100 million new plant complex if demand for that product decreases or switches to another area of the country. For example, it is estimated that by the year 2000, 50 percent of the U.S. population will reside in three megalopolises located in the Boston–Washington D.C., Chicago–Pittsburgh, and San Francisco–San Diego areas. What effect will this have on plant location? A company may not want to build a chemical plant in rural New Jersey in 1980 and find it in the middle of suburbia in 30 years. In addition to demand forecasting, there are a host of other variables that should be considered prior to locating a fixed facility such as a manufacturing plant. Examples are projections of labor conditions, utilities service, transportation service, freight rates, raw materials supplies, and weather. Planning a fixed facility is almost entirely dependent on correct forecasting of the future.

Forecast Lead Time and Interval

An important consideration in forecasting future demand is lead time. That is, how far into the future should demand be forecasted? Depending on the type of logistics decision, the lead time could be one week or ten years, or even longer. Forecast lead time can be divided into three basic time horizons: short-term (less than six months), medium-term (six month to three years), and long-term (more than three years). This is a realistic breakdown in most manufacturing companies. Some of the types of logistics decisions that would typically fall into each category are as follows:

- Short-term (less than six months)

    Production scheduling
    Inventory control
    Procurement and purchasing
    Plant and warehouse manpower
    Number of forklift trucks necessary
    Car supply requirements
    Warehouse floor layout, turnover
    Private carriage dispatching

- Medium-term (six months to three years)

    Warehouse and distribution center capacity
    Management needs
    Material handling systems
    Budgeting—logistics gross income statement
    Computerized ordering systems
    Freight rate adjustments
    Contract production
    Leased or contract carriers

- Long-term (more than three years)

    Fixed facilities locations—plant and distribution centers
    Long lead time procurement contracts
    Future sources of ingredients or raw materials
    Private carriage requirements and considerations
    Technologies in transport, warehousing, materials handling, etc.

An additional consideration is forecast interval, which can be defined as the actual time period covered by the forecast. For example, forecasts might be for periods of weeks, months, years, or even longer. Forecast interval is closely related to lead time, but it is not the same. For example, a short-term forecast would typically have a rather short forecast interval, that is, demand might be forecast by the week, but six months in advance. Similarly, a long-term forecast would be more concerned with a forecast interval of a year or more, and might be forecast (have a lead time) of several years in advance. Lead time and interval may be related in that generally the longer the forecast lead time, the longer the forecast time interval.

Logistics decisions involving daily scheduling of shipments and planning warehouse work load require lead time in days, while inventory control and production scheduling utilize demand data by the week or month. Locating a manufacturing plant calls for forecasts covering demand five to ten years in advance, since this is normally a large-scale capital investment that will become a sunk cost once completed.

Patterns of Demand

A complicating factor in forecasting is the fluctuating patterns in demand activity with time. There is rarely a situation where demand remains constant over time, at least on a daily, weekly, or monthly basis. Demand consists of four basic patterns or components—trend, seasonal, cyclical, and irregular (Figure 18–1). Each of these must be separated from the demand function and analyzed separately to assure forecast accuracy.

Trend

The trend is the overall growth or decline in demand over a relatively long period of time. An example of a product with constantly rising demand is frozen food items, while a de-

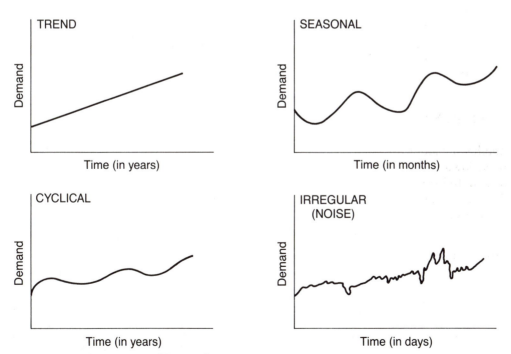

Figure 18-1   Components of Demand

clining one is railroad passenger service. Trend is the most obvious of the four demand components, since almost all products or services exhibit some form of trend over the years.

Seasonal Variation

The seasonal is a fluctuation that completes its entire cycle of change within the span of one year and is repetitive year after year. Seasonal patterns are also widespread; for example, toys, heating oil in winter climates, antifreeze, and bathing suits exhibit seasonal patterns.

Cyclical Variation

The cyclical pertains to a series of repeated sequences of no specific time period that may range from a few months to many years. Cyclical patterns are often closely aligned with the business cycles, that is, the cycling of the economy between periods of prosperity and recessionary periods. The business cycle is a phenomenon that seemed to disappear during the 1960s and 1970s, but it seems to have reappeared in the early 1980s. Examples of products that tend to be affected by the business cycle are automobiles, major appliances, and new home construction.

Irregular Movements (Noise)

Noise refers to the apparent random or unexplained movement in the demand function with time. In many cases, demand may be forecasted fairly accurately from a determination of the trend, seasonal, and cyclical. However, there will always be a residual difference between forecasted and actual demand due to the inability to anticipate all factors that may cause demand to vary.

Forecast Detail

Another major consideration in forecasting concerns the degree of demand detail or breakdown required. Again, this varies with the logistics decision. For example, inventory control and production-scheduling decisions require more forecast detail—i.e., by individual product item—than forecasts for purchasing or planning a new distribution center. Forecasts, therefore, must be broken down in various ways.

Product Item Breakdown

Individual forecasts are often prepared for each product item in a company's product line. Many firms have found that often a large percentage of demand is made up by relatively few products in the product line. In fact, this distribution is so widespread that it has come to be known as the "80–20 Rule." That is, 80 percent of demand derives from 20 percent of the items in the product line. The word "rule," of course, is not meant literally.

The implication of the "rule" is that one frequently encounters situations in which a small percentage of one variable accounts for a large percentage of a second variable, and that relative bivariate distributions approximating 80–20 are not uncommon. For example, in Figure 18–2, Point A indicates that 20 percent of the product line contributes 85 percent of total sales. This also means, of course, that the remaining 15 percent of sales is contributed by the other 80 percent of the product line. Similarly, Point B shows that 50 percent of the product line accounts for 95 percent of total sales; the remaining 5 percent of sales must come from the other 50 percent of products. This illustrates quite clearly that a relatively small percent of the product line may account for a rather large percent of total sales.

Geographic Area Breakdown

Demand forecasts are prepared for various areas within the company's total market area. In many firms the sales force is grouped into regions which often correspond to regional distribution centers or manufacturing plants. It is therefore useful to break down demand by region. Also, population concentrations in certain parts of the country or regional differences in preference for certain types of goods make geographical breakdowns necessary.

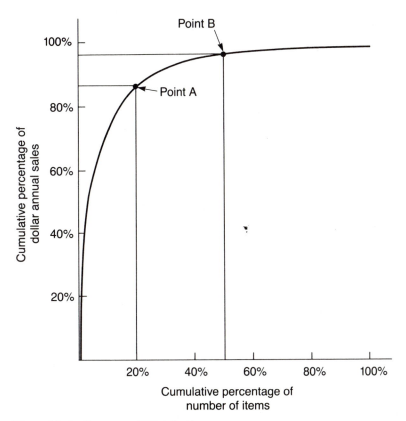

Figure 18-2   Lognormal Distribution

Market Breakdown

Most companies sell their products or services in more than one type of market. For example, a manufacturer of processed potatoes sells instant mashed potatoes to wholesalers, retailers, restaurants, and other manufacturers of food products. Since there may be private labeling, bulk packaging, and different channels of distribution involved, it is helpful to forecast future demand in each of these markets.

Customer Breakdown

In industries and companies dominated by a few major customers it is essential to forecast demand for these large buyers since they may have different customer service standards, prices, and so forth. A good example would be a tire manufacturer supplying tires to Sears. The 80–20 rule is also often applicable to customer distribution; that is, 80 percent of the business may be often done with 20 percent of the customers.

Demand Over Time

It is also helpful to forecast the timing of demand. When will the orders be placed? Typically there will be a "bunching" of orders at some time during the year, particularly in firms engaged in producing highly seasonal items, such as toys. This is a very basic breakdown, and one that was discussed more completely in the previous subsection.

Forecasting Techniques

Numerous techniques or methods of demand forecasting are available to logistics managers. They range from simple assumptions that there will be no change in demand, to sophisticated mathematical models. Forecast techniques fall into four basic groups: subjective methods, time-series analysis, barometric techniques, and econometric models.

Time-series analysis is the most prevalent method in business forecasting. The other three methods, therefore, are discussed in lesser detail, particularly econometric models which are generally used only by very large firms and the federal and state governments.

The usefulness of the forecast to logistics management has a great deal to do with selecting the proper techniques. For example, short-term forecasts, that is, forecasts of less than six months, are generally handled best by survey methods, time-series analysis (particularly exponential smoothing and moving averages), and barometric techniques. Long-term forecasting (more than three years in advance) tends more heavily toward determining trend and cyclical patterns, and econometric models.

Subjective Methods

Mathematical models and forecast projections have not been completely perfected. Despite the advent of sophisticated data-processing systems and equipment, they will probably never be one hundred percent accurate in forecasting demand. They often cannot predict short-run changes in demand patterns such as sudden and unexpected impulses in buying by major customers. For the judgmental aspects of forecasting, therefore, business firms need the experienced manager, the marketing specialist, and other staff people who can be aided but never entirely replaced by quantitative computations. Subjective methods of forecasting demand can be broken down into four subgroups: the "naive" approach, intuition, surveys, and "loaded dice" techniques.

The "Naive" (No Change) Approach

An all too common approach to forecasting in small businesses is simply to assume that the previous level of demand will continue unchanged into the future. For example, a concession stand at the county fair may have sold 10,000 hotdogs on opening day last year. This figure is then used as a forecast for this year's demand. The naive approach has little merit, however, in more sizable companies where the stakes are measurably higher. There are too many outside factors that affect demand.

Intuition

The old idea of intuition, or having a feeling about some future happening, is very much alive in forecasting. Many business managers have developed a fairly accurate sense of coming events. Clues are available from many sources, including the stock market, economy, general business conditions, government attitudes, and trends in society. For example, a diet fruit canner had a hunch that the Federal Drug Administration's routine testing of cyclamates would lead to a ban on products containing the artificial sweetener. This was not indicated by official information. He therefore reduced the size of his cyclamate-sweetened production, using saccharin instead. Many of his competitors suffered heavily when the cyclamate ban was announced. It can be safely stated that every big business decision contains some intuitive judgment.

Survey Methods

Survey methods are probably the most useful of the subjective techniques in forecasting. Although there are many different types, executive opinion, field sales force estimates, and customer opinion polling are typical.

Jury of Executive Opinion

A cross-section of opinion among mature, responsible executives about future demand is solicited. In a way, this is really a survey of executive intuition. The implicit assumption is made that those in top management positions should be the best sources of information on future happenings. The chief disadvantage of this method, of course, is the lack of factual data. Another problem is the possibility of the executive's bias toward his own company. He may hesitate to "tell it like it is," or he might not see it as it actually is. However, the jury of executive opinion is quick and inexpensive, and does provide some basis for insight into the future. It is certainly better than no forecast at all.

Field Sales Force Estimates

Sales force estimates are often the starting point of demand forecasting. The idea is to go where the action is—the "firing line"—where contact with the customers is made.

Generally the field sales people have a definite feel for future demand, particularly if no big product or price changes are planned. An added advantage of using field sales estimates is the rapid feedback mechanism which provides current information on a routine basis. Forecast errors from the previous period can be quickly identified when the orders start coming in, and adjustments can be made in present and future forecasts, if necessary. One disadvantage in this method is that the demand may tend to be purposely underestimated so that sales quotas might more easily be attained and possibly exceeded, thereby making the sales force look good.

CUSTOMER OPINION POLLING

Who can better forecast demand than a firm's customers? There are two basic problems with this method, however. Do customers know what they will be buying ahead of time, and if so, will they tell you? Nevertheless, sophisticated methods of customer opinion polling are used, for example, by McGraw-Hill Publishing Co. Their findings are published in *Business Week* as a forecast of industrial buying expectations. In most firms, however, opinion polling consists of more casual encounters with major customers and discussions about what their needs might be next month, three months hence, and so forth. Becoming increasingly popular is the non-quantitative approach, whereby customers are asked if they anticipate buying more, less, or the same as they did previously.

"Loaded Dice" Techniques

There are numerous other non-quantitative ways of looking into the future, some of which are more ethical than others. "Loaded dice" techniques are based on getting information not generally available or securing it sooner than other people. For example, the Rothchilds in England got advance word on the outcome of the Battle of Waterloo in 1815

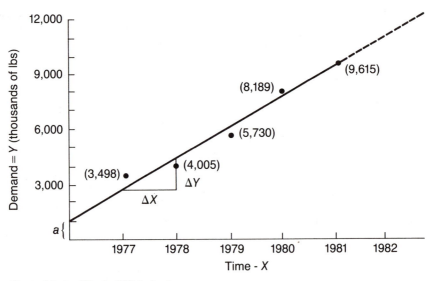

WILSON CHEMICAL COMPANY

Figure 18-3 "Eyeball" Method

through their own information service, and consequently made a fortune on the London Stock Exchange. Loaded dice techniques include tip-offs from inside sources, undercover work, wiretapping, bugging devices, and so forth, all designed to find out future plans of customers, suppliers, or competitors. Most are unethical—and often illegal—and are certainly not recommended. It is important, however, to know that they exist.

Time-Series Analysis

The most widely used method of forecasting utilizes patterns of past demand related to time, and projects them into the future. A time series may be defined as a collection of readings of some economic variable, or composite of variables, that vary over time, taken at different time periods. In time-series analysis, it is implicitly assumed that there will be no drastic changes in the conditions that determined past demand. An example of a "drastic" change would be the passage of a new federal law prohibiting the ownership or possession of more than one motor vehicle per family. Needless to say, past trends in auto sales when projected into the future would not account for this development. As indicated previously, demand consists of four parts, that is, the trend, seasonal, cyclical, and irregular components, each of which must be analyzed separately (Figure 18–1).

Trend Extension

The trend has been defined as the overall growth or decline in demand over time. This growth or decline may take many different mathematical forms and patterns, ranging from simple straight-line relationships to the more complicated curvilinear functions. Regardless of the complexity of the mathematical form, it is important that the pattern be identified and, if possible, described mathematically. The purpose of the mathematical description is to facilitate the extrapolation of these functions for forecasting considerations. Otherwise it becomes difficult, if not impossible, to forecast accurately future demand, except in the case of very simple linear relationships.

Five common methods of forecasting the trend are described and illustrated in this section. They are the "eyeball" or free-hand technique, the method of semi-averages, the least squares methods, moving averages, and exponential smoothing. The examples used to illustrate the first three methods have linear demand functions, which can be described by the familiar equation $y = a + bX$, where a equals the y intercept and b represents the slope of the line (Figure 18–3).

THE "EYEBALL" METHOD

It is often possible to obtain a fairly accurate estimate of future demand simply by plotting past results on graph paper, visually drawing with a straight edge a trend line through the data, and projecting it out to future time periods. This method is particularly useful where past demand patterns approximate a straight line, where demand variability is not great, or when complete accuracy is not needed.

For example, consider the data on the Wilson Chemical Company presented in Table 18–1. Using the "eyeball" method, a trend line is drawn through the 1977–81 data in Figure 18–3 and extended out to the year 1982. Based on this free-hand projection, 1982 demand is expected to be approximately 11.2 million pounds.

Table 18–1   Total Shipments of Chemicals from Wilson Chemical Company by Year

Year	Total (thousands of pounds)
1977	3498
1978	4005
1979	5730
1980	8189
1981	9615

METHOD OF SEMI-AVERAGES

The shortcomings of the eyeball technique are apparent. It is generally not possible accurately to fit a trend line to a group of points by trial and error unless they lie in almost a perfect straight line. This is not true for Wilson Chemical Company or, for that matter, very many demand situations. A slight error in drawing the trend line could mean a forecast error of thousands of pounds. If it were possible to establish two "mean" points through which to draw the line, the necessity for judgement would be eliminated. The method of semi-averages provides a way of establishing two points by dividing a given series into two equal parts (hence, the name *semi-averages*). The line of semi-averages then passes through the mean of each half of the time series. The trend therefore represents a more accurate fit than the eyeball method, since it is derived mathematically.

For an example of the semi-averages method of forecasting, again consider the Wilson Chemical Company. The data for the years 1979–81 have now been tabulated by quarters (2), as indicated in Table 18–2. The data have been separated into two equal parts:

$$\text{The mean of component A:} \quad X_a = \frac{55}{10} = 5.5 \qquad Y_a = \frac{10{,}331}{10} = 1033$$

$$\text{The mean of component B:} \quad X_b = \frac{155}{10} = 15.5 \qquad Y_b = \frac{20{,}706}{10} = 2071$$

The trend line, or slope of the demand function, may be determined mathematically by:

$$\text{Slope} = b = \frac{Y_b - Y_a}{n} + \frac{2071 - 1033}{10} = 103.8 \text{ thousand pounds per quarter}$$

The variable n denotes the number of periods between the two means, which in this case is 10 quarters.

The mean of component A (Y_a) falls between Q1 and Q2 of 1978, that is, at $X_a = 5.5$. The mean of B (Y_b) falls between Q3 and Q4 of 1980, that is, at $X_b = 15.5$. Since $Y = 1033$ at $X = 5.5$, the equation of the trend line $Y = a + bX$ may be solved for the intercept a, that is, $1033 = a + 103.8 (5.5)$, thus $a = 462$. Therefore, $Y = 462 + 103.8X$.

As an example, a forecast of the demand for the fourth quarter would be determined using the above equation. Since the origin would be at the fourth quarter in 1976, the value of X, or the time span from Q4 1976 to Q4 1982, is 24 periods. Therefore, $Y = 462 + 103.8 (24) = 295.3$ thousand pounds, the forecasted demand for the fourth quarter of 1982.

Table 18–2   Total Shipments from Wilson Chemical Company by Quarters
(In Thousands of Pounds)

	Component A				*Component B*		
	Quarter	*(X)*	*Amount (Y)*		*Quarter*	*(X)*	*Amount (Y)*
1977	Q1	1	972	1979	Q3	11	1,747
	Q2	2	925		Q4	12	1,155
	Q3	3	772	1980	Q1	13	1,654
	Q4	4	829		Q2	14	2,190
1978	Q1	5	904		Q3	15	2,315
	Q2	6	1,039		Q4	16	2,030
	Q3	7	1,269	1981	Q1	17	2,086
	Q4	8	793		Q2	18	2,629
1979	Q1	9	1,081		Q3	19	2,400
	Q2	10	1,747		Q4	20	2,500
Total		55	10,331	Total		155	20,706

METHOD OF LEAST SQUARES

The least squares method allows a trend line to be mathematically fitted to the data points such that the vertical distances of each point to the line, when squared, will be at a minimum (Figure 18–4). Since the squared differences are minimized, the total distances of the points from the line are also minimized. The resulting line is called the line of least squares, or the line of best fit. The mathematical method used is called *linear regression.*

Finding the general expression for the straight line with the least squares method requires the solution of two simultaneous equations, called normal equations:

$$\Sigma Y = na + b\Sigma X \tag{18.1}$$

$$\Sigma XY = a\Sigma X + b\Sigma X^2 \tag{18.2}$$

where Y is the sum of the historical series, n is the number of time units, X is the value of the time unit, a is the value of Y at the origin, and b is the slope of the straight line. The values a and b thus can be found by solving the normal equations simultaneously, using

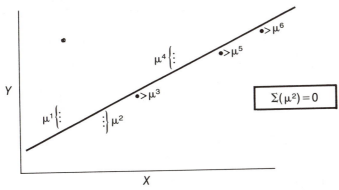

Figure 18–4   Line of Least Squares

values from the historical data themselves. Many inexpensive hand-held calculators have the least squares program as a built-in feature. Typically, parts of the data are entered (i.e., period and sales) and a and b are calculated by the program.

Using the Wilson Chemical Company data from Table 18–1 once more, but tabulating values for X, X^2, and XY also, Table 18–3 is constructed. Substituting these values into the two simultaneous equations, they become:

$$31,037 = 5a + 15b$$

$$109,529 = 15a + 55b$$

Solving for a, $a = 1282$. If this value of a is substituted into either equation 18.1 or 18.2, then $b = 1642$. Thus a and b have both been determined and the equation of the straight line (of the form $y = a + bX$) becomes:

$$Y = 1282 + 1642X$$

Using this equation, forecasted 1982 demand is:

$$Y = 1282 + 1642\ (6) = 11,134 \text{ thousand pounds}$$

In this case, $X = 6$, because the origin of the series is 1976. It is interesting to note that the above forecast varied from the one derived by the eyeball approach (11.2 million pounds) by only a small amount. The eyeball method may be sufficient in situations where demand is needed only in broad terms, or only approximately. It can provide a close approximation of demand in many cases.

MOVING AVERAGES

A useful method for determining the trend of a series in certain cases is that of moving averages. The moving average can be used to determine the trend of a series if the series is basically linear and is regular in duration and amplitude. For example, if a product were seasonal on a yearly basis, a moving average taken over the period of a year would remove the seasonal, leaving a good approximation of the trend. That is, when demand is averaged together for four quarters or twelve months, the periods with demand below the trend will "cancel out" the months with demand above the trend in the averaging process. For the same reason, noise is also averaged out.

Table 18–3 Total Shipments from Wilson Chemical Company (Thousands of Pounds)

Year	X (Period)	Y (Period)	X²	XY
1977	3,498	1	1	3,498
1978	4,005	2	4	8,010
1979	5,730	3	9	17,190
1980	8,189	4	16	32,756
1981	9,615	5	25	48,075
Totals $n = 5$	$\Sigma Y = 31,037$	$\Sigma X = 15$	$\Sigma X^2 = 55$	$\Sigma XY = 109,529$

The moving average forecast is a short-range forecasting technique, where the present data are used to forecast the demand for the next period only. It develops no mathematical description of the line that can be used for extrapolation. It is useful, however, for evaluating current results and for detection of abrupt changes in the expected pattern.

A moving average computation is shown in Table 18–4. The moving average is based on four periods; that is, the first four quarters are totaled and then averaged to provide a forecast for the fifth period. The next average is obtained by eliminating the first quarter when actual experience for the fifth quarter becomes available. Then, the second through fifth quarters are averaged to forecast the next (sixth) period, and the process continues. For example, to compute the forecast for quarter one of 1982, the actual demand for quarters one through four of 1981 are averaged. The four-period moving average of 2404 units then becomes the estimated demand for the next quarter, or 1982 Q1.

Exponential Smoothing

The moving average method of computing demand forecasts requires a firm to keep on file historical information for as many periods back as are necessary to compute the average. This does not pose any great problem for forecasting demand for a few products. However, it is not at all uncommon for a firm to manufacture thousands of items, and when variations such as sizes, colors, and styles are added in, there may be as many as half a million stockkeeping units (SKUs) to be forecast. A saving of even a tenth of a second in forecasting each SKU could result in saving several hours of computer time.

Table 18–4   Computation of a Four-Period Moving Average Forecast   (Data in Thousands of Pounds)

Year	Quarter	Realized Demand	Four-Period Moving Total	Four-Period Moving Average	Forecast for Period	
1977	Q1	972	—	—		
	Q2	925	—	—		
	Q3	772	3498	875	1978	Q1
	Q4	829	3430	858		Q2
1978	Q1	904	3544	886		Q3
	Q2	1039	4041	1010		Q4
	Q3	1269	4005	1001	1979	Q1
	Q4	793	4182	1046		Q2
1979	Q1	1081	4890	1223		Q3
	Q2	1747	5368	1342		Q4
	Q3	1747	5730	1433	1980	Q1
	Q4	1155	6303	1475		Q2
1980	Q1	1654	6746	1562		Q3
	Q2	2190	7314	1829		Q4
	Q3	2315	8189	2047	1981	Q1
	Q4	2030	8621	2155		Q2
1981	Q1	2086	9060	2265		Q3
	Q2	2629	9145	2286		Q4
	Q3	2400	9615	2404	1982	Q1
	Q4	2500				

Exponential smoothing is a special type of "moving average" which reduces the amount of data which must be stored by providing a heavier weighting of the most recent demand data. It is designed to "track" short-run changes in the overall trend and adjust future forecasts accordingly. The main feature of exponential smoothing is that it updates the forecast on a period-by-period basis by applying a correction to the prior forecast that is determined by the difference between the last forecast and actual demand for that period. Therefore only one piece of information—the prior forecast—must be stored to compute the new forecast.

The proportion of the difference between the prior period forecast and actual realized demand, or forecast error, which is added to the prior forecast to get a new updated forecast is called the smoothing constant. It is designated α, the Greek letter alpha, and its size determines how influential the forecast errors are to be in adjusting future forecasts. The value of α can range from 0 to 1.0 with typical values between 0.1 and 0.5. A large smoothing constant gives large and almost immediate correction, while small constants provide a small and longer-term correction. In effect, then, a large smoothing constant has the same effect as computing a moving average with a small number of periods included. A large change in any one period would therefore have an immediate effect on the next period forecast. Similarly, a small smoothing constant has the effect of averaging a large number of periods, and the effect of a large change in any one period would be reduced by the averaging process. Table 18-5 indicates the effect of various values for the smoothing constant. For other values of α, the number of periods included in an equivalent moving average may be computed by the formula:

$$\alpha = \frac{2}{n+1}$$

For example, a smoothing constant of 0.01 is equivalent to a 199-period moving average. The advantage of exponential smoothing to reduce data storage is especially clear in this case.

The use of the smoothing constant to weight most recent information is based upon the following reasoning. A forecast is made for a given period, and eventually the realized or actual demand for that period becomes known. It seems logical that if a wrong prediction had been made and demand is actually higher than the forecast, then in predicting next period's demand, we should increase our estimate. Similarly, if the demand turns out to be less than our forecast, the new estimate should be lower. Furthermore, if the difference between realized demand and the forecast is small, the adjustment should be small,

Table 18-5   Relationship Between Smoothing Constant and Periods in a Moving Average

Smoothing Constant	Periods in Moving Average
0.01	199
0.1	19
0.2	9
0.3	5
0.4	4
0.5	3

but if the difference is great, then the correction should be rather large. This rationale can be summarized by a formula:

New forecast = old forecast + α (realized demand – old forecast)

If, for example, a large value is selected for α, then a large portion of the difference (forecast error) between the forecast and what actually happened will be added to the old forecast to determine a new forecast. The question of what value should be selected for α is deferred until later.

The terms in the exponential smoothing formula can be rearranged slightly to facilitate mathematical calculations. The resulting formula, then, is the basic rule of exponential smoothing,

New forecast = α (realized demand) + $(1 - \alpha)$ (prior forecast)

The exponential smoothing formula works well so long as demand is relatively constant (no trend). If demand follows a steadily rising or falling trend, the magnitude of the trend must be estimated to make the necessary correction to arrive at a correct estimate of demand. The correction is necessary because with a trend, the forecasted value tends to lag behind actual demand due to the process of averaging.

An estimate of the trend is the difference between the new forecast and the prior forecast. This also must be weighted, similar to the exponential smoothing calculation.

New trend = α (new forecast – prior forecast) + $(1 - \alpha)$ (old trend)

Finally, the demand that is expected for next period may be determined by correcting the new forecast for the lag by utilizing the computed new trend.

$$\text{Expected demand} = \text{new forecast} + \frac{(1 - \alpha)}{\alpha} \text{ (new trend)}$$

To illustrate the use of exponential smoothing for short-term forecasting, let us again utilize the data from Table 18–4. Assume that the exponential smoothing procedure is already in progress, and that 2000 units were forecasted for Q1 in 1981. Further, the trend was calculated as 76 units and a smoothing constant $\alpha = 0.3$ is being used. Therefore, in forecasting demand for Q2 1971,

New forecast = 0.3 (2086) + (1 – 0.3) (2000) = 2026 units

New trend = 0.3 (2026 – 2000) + (1 – 0.3) (76) = 61 units

$$\text{Expected demand} = 2026 + \frac{(1 - 0.3)}{0.3}(61) = 2168$$

Since there appears to be a seasonal effect present in the data of Table 18–4, the accuracy of the estimate could be improved by adjusting for the seasonal, which is the topic of the next section.

The inevitable question has been saved until last: How is the value for the smoothing constant selected? A more meaningful way of asking this question is: How much weight should be given to previous periods in computing the new forecast? Table 18–5 will again be useful at this point. A smoothing constant of 0.1 is equivalent to a moving average of 19 periods, while one of 0.5 is equivalent to only 3 periods. A low value, therefore, gives less weight to current information than does a large weight. When a low value is used, then, the response to changes will be slow and gradual; that is, the system is very stable. Conversely, when a high value is used, the estimates respond very quickly to change, not only real changes in demand but to random variations (noise).

In practice, the trick is to find a value for α which is a compromise between a very stable system that fails to track real changes and a wildly fluctuating system that moves rapidly with changes in demand. Many firms have found that 0.1 is likely to be the most effective smoothing constant. Quite often, when a firm is beginning to use exponential smoothing, $\alpha = 0.3$ is used for several months until the inevitable ups and downs of beginning have begun to damp out, and then the constant is adjusted downward until the relative magnitude of forecast errors assumes a reasonable level.

Seasonal Adjustments

Extension of the trend provides the user with a forecast of the overall growth or decline in demand. It is relatively efficient for forecasting demand on an aggregate basis, but is not specifically designed to break this demand into shorter time periods of unequal intensity. For example, if demand for four quarters were 60, 100, 60, and 100 respectively, trend extension methods would forecast a demand of 80 for each period (no trend), which overstates the first and third quarters and understates the second and fourth quarters.

With *seasonal* fluctuation the entire cycle of change is completed within the span of one year and is repetitive year after year. In order to compensate for the tendency of trend extension methods to smooth out seasonal variations, adjustments to account for the seasonal variation must be made. Therefore, seasonal indexes are usually computed and used to correct for the over- and understatement resulting from averaging by trend. Of the several mathematical methods of computing seasonal adjustment, three of the most useful methods are discussed here—the simple average method, the ratio of actual to predicted value method, and the ratio-to-moving-average method.

THE SIMPLE AVERAGE METHOD

The simple average method of calculating seasonal indices compares a representative value for each period to a common denominator or "average" period. The representative value for each period is generally determined by finding the mean or median value of all first periods, all second periods, and so forth. In Table 18–6, the data from Wilson Chemical Corporation have been arranged by quarters. With the data arranged in this manner, computation of the seasonal values is as follows:

1. Find the representative value for each period (quarter) by calculating the arithmetic average of all such periods included in the data. In some cases, the median provides a more appropriate value, especially if the data have a great degree of skewness.

Table 18-6   Simple Average Method (Thousands of Pounds)

Year	Q1	Q2	Q3	Q4
1977	972	925	772	829
1978	904	1039	1269	793
1979	1081	1747	1747	1155
1980	1654	2190	2315	2030
1981	2086	2629	2400	2500
Total	6797	8530	8503	7307

Step 1.   Average   1339   1706   1701   1461

Step 2.   Adjustment
for trend $-1(100)$ $-2(100)$ $-3(100)$ $-4(100)$
Adjusted   1239   1506   1401   1061 $= 5207$

Step 3.

$$\text{Hypothetical quarter} = \frac{1239 + 1506 + 1401 + 1061}{4} = \frac{5207}{4} = 1302$$

Step 4.   Seasonal index for each quarter

Q1 $1239/1302 = 0.95$ Q3 $1401/1302 = 1.08$
Q2 $1506/1302 = 1.16$ Q4 $1061/1302 = 0.81$

2. If the trend value of the data is substantial, the seasonal must be corrected to remove the trend. The trend is represented by the slope b of the trend equation $(Y = a + bX)$. Using the method of least squares, the trend equation for quarterly data of Wilson Chemical Corporation is $Y = 501.3 + 100.0X$.

3. Calculate the common denominator or average period. The mean of the adjusted averages for the four quarters is used for this average value.

4. Calculate the seasonal index for each period by dividing the representative value for each period by the common denominator period.

The season indices computed in Table 18–6 can be applied to adjust the values forecasted by the trend equation. The trend equation averages out all values falling above and below the trend line. The seasonal index adjusts the value which is forecasted on the trend line to its proper relation above or below the trend.

For example, the forecast for the third quarter of 1982 using the method of least squares is $Y = 501.3 + 100.1(23) = 2803.6$. This value on the trend line must be adjusted by the seasonal index for the third quarter, since the actual value is expected to be above the trend line. The forecast for the third quarter of 1982, adjusted by the seasonal index, is therefore $2803.6(1.08)$, or 3028 thousand pounds.

The seasonal indices may also be used to break down data forecasted on a yearly basis into forecasts for quarters or months. For example, the method of least squares was used above to forecast yearly data for Wilson Chemical Company. Demand for 1982 was forecasted at 11,133 thousand pounds, or 2,783,250 pounds per average quarter. Using the seasonal indices, 1982 demand can be adjusted to a quarterly forecast:

Q1   2,783,250 (0.95) = 2,644,088 pounds
Q2   2,783,250 (1.16) = 3,228,570 pounds
Q3   2,783,250 (1.08) = 3,005,910 pounds
Q4   2,783,250 (0.81) = 2,254,433 pounds

RATIO OF ACTUAL TO PREDICTED VALUES

The simple average method described above has the advantage of being simple to calculate and easy to understand. However, since it depends on a gross averaging process, the method is not as accurate as alternative methods. One method that involves slightly more calculation, since the trend value for each quarter must be determined, is shown in Table 18–7. The least squares equation is determined; then the equation is used to calculate the value the equation would have forecasted for each quarter. This predicted value is then compared to the actual value to calculate the ratio between what the trend line would forecast and the actual value. The averages for each first period, second period, and so on are then determined to calculate the seasonal indices.

RATIO-TO-MOVING-AVERAGE METHOD

A basic characteristic of the moving average method makes it also useful for determining seasonal adjustment. That is, if the period over which the moving average is taken corresponds to the period of the seasonal, the moving average will remove that seasonal. In the averaging process, the periods with demand above the trend cancel out the periods below the trend. Therefore, the seasonal, which is a cycle of twelve months or four quarters duration, lends itself to the use of the moving average to calculate seasonal indices. To compute the specific seasonal index for each quarter the following procedure is used:

1. Compute a four-period moving average, and properly center.

2. Express each value of the original series as a ratio of the corresponding centered moving average value.

3. Arrange the data so that the same quarterly figures can be averaged, that is, all of Q1, all of Q2, etc.

4. Compute the most representative value for each quarter, using either the arithmetic mean or median value.

5. Compute a hypothetical quarter by computing the average of the representative values.

6. Express each representative quarter as a percentage of the hypothetical quarter. This is the *seasonal index* for that quarter.

This procedure is applied to the data from Wilson Chemical Company. In Table 18–8, Column B, the four-period centered moving average is determined from the data in Table 18–4. The data must be centered, that is, adjusted so that the value falls squarely on a spe-

Table 18-7 Ratio of Actual to Predicted Value Method [$Y = 501.3 + 100.1(X)$; Data in Thousands of Pounds]

		Actual Sales (A)	*Predicted Sales (B)*	*Ratio of Actual to Predicted*
1977	Q1	972	601	1.61
	Q2	925	701	1.32
	Q3	772	801	.97
	Q4	829	902	.91
1978	Q1	904	1002	.90
	Q2	1039	1102	.91
	Q3	1269	1202	1.05
	Q4	793	1302	.60
1979	Q1	1081	1402	.77
	Q2	1747	1502	1.16
	Q3	1747	1602	1.09
	Q4	1155	1702	.68
1980	Q1	1654	1802	.92
	Q2	2190	1902	1.15
	Q3	2315	2002	1.15
	Q4	2030	2102	.97
1981	Q1	2086	2202	.95
	Q2	2629	2303	1.10
	Q3	2400	2403	1.00
	Q4	2500	2503	1.00

	Q1		*Q2*	*Q3*	*Q4*
1977	1.61	*	1.32	.97	.91
1978	.90	(.90)	.91	1.05	.60
1979	.77	(.77)	1.16	1.09	.68
1980	.92	(.92)	1.15	1.15	.97
1981	.95	(.95)	1.10	1.00	1.00
Total	5.15	(3.54)	5.64	5.26	4.16
Average (Seasonal indices)	1.03	(0.89)	1.13	1.05	0.83

*Judgment was made to throw out the first quarter as unrepresentative, because of a large random variation. Analysis indicated that a special sale of merchandise biased the data for that period. The value 0.89 is used, therefore, rather than 1.03 for the seasonal index for Q1. This illustrates the use of logic to refine forecast results.

cific quarter. The four-period moving average calculated by averaging the first four quarters in Table 18–4 falls between Q2 and Q3. When the first quarter is dropped and Q1 of 1978 is added to calculate the second four-quarter moving average, the moving average falls between Q3 and Q4. To center the data specifically on a quarter rather than between two quarters, two succeeding four-period moving averages are averaged. For example, the first two four-period moving averages in Table 18–4, 875 and 858, are averaged to center the first datum (867) on Q3 in Table 18–8.

Cyclical Variations

Cyclical variations are defined as a series of repeated sequences of time periods that may range from a few months to many years. The best example is the business cycle, which at

Table 18–8   Ratio-to-Moving-Average Method (Data in Thousands of Pounds)

		Sales (A)	Four-Period Moving Average	Four-Period Centered Moving Average (B) (Step 1)	Ratio of Actual Value to Moving Average [Step 2 ÷ (A/B)]
1977	Q1	972			
	Q2	925			
	Q3	772	875	867	.89
	Q4	829	858	872	.95
1978	Q1	904	886	948	.95
	Q2	1039	1010	1005	1.04
	Q3	1269	1001	1024	1.23
	Q4	793	1046	1135	.70
1979	Q1	1081	1223	1282	.85
	Q2	1747	1342	1388	1.26
	Q3	1747	1433	1454	1.20
	Q4	1155	1475	1519	.77
1980	Q1	1654	1562	1696	.98
	Q2	2190	1829	1938	1.13
	Q3	2315	2047	2101	1.10
	Q4	2030	2155	2210	.92
1981	Q1	2086	2265	2276	.92
	Q2	2629	2286	2345	1.12
	Q3	2400	2404		
	Q4	2500			

Rearrangement of data (*Step 3*)

	Q1	Q2	Q3	Q4	Total
1977	—	—	.89	.95	
1978	.95	1.04	1.23	.70	
1979	.85	1.26	1.20	.77	
1980	.98	1.13	1.10	.92	
1981	.92	1.12	—	—	
Total	3.70	4.55	4.42	3.34	
Average for quarter (*Step 4*)	0.925	1.14	1.11	0.84	4.015

Calculation of hypothetical quarter (*Step 5*)

$$\frac{0.925 + 1.14 + 1.11 + 0.84}{4} = \frac{4.015}{4} = 1.004$$

Seasonal index (*Step 6*)

$$Q1 = \frac{.925}{1.004} = 0.92 \qquad Q3 = \frac{1.14}{1.004} = 1.11$$

$$Q2 = \frac{1.14}{1.004} = 1.13 \qquad Q4 = \frac{.84}{1.004} = 0.84$$

present has not been adequately isolated or mathematically described. However, if a cyclical pattern of some type can be established, for example, one occurring every five years, then a ratio-to-moving-average method similar to that used for determining the seasonal could be utilized to adjust the forecast for long-term cyclical considerations. Unfortunately, very few cyclical patterns have been isolated to this degree.

Perhaps the best means of coping with cyclical variations of no specific time period is a combination of trend extensions (particularly exponential smoothing) and barometric techniques, which are discussed in the next subsection. Econometric models are designed to predict changes in the whole economy, and are useful in forecasting cycles. Economic indicators that have in the past corresponded closely with demand are probably the best source of data on upcoming cyclical developments. For example, a drop in new housing starts is viewed as an indicator of economic down turn.

Irregular Movement or "Noise"

Noise is defined as an apparent random or chance movement in demand. Factors causing such irregular movements are not likely to be repeated with any regularity. Forecasting, therefore, cannot allow specifically for "noise" in mathematical terms, other than to make certain assumptions about the error term, μ. The straight-line demand equation which includes the error term is $y = a + bx + \mu$.

The mathematical basis for calculating the least squares estimate of the demand equation depends upon an assumption that the values of the error term μ at different points on the curve are randomly distributed. Often, however, they are not random. For example, in forecasting inventory levels, if a chance shift in demand causes a build-up in inventory in one period, there may be a corresponding slackening in the following period. This would indicate a non-random error pattern, which must be taken account of mathematically. Techniques may be found in most forecasting texts under "autocorrelated errors."

It should be emphasized that large irregularities (or noise) in demand should be deleted when analyzing a time series for trend and seasonal. If this is not done, the entire series could be distorted, because chances of the irregularity happening again (at least on the same scale) are almost nil. For example, in the fall of 1967, Ford Motor Company was hit hard by a strike of several weeks' duration, and lost over a billion dollars in revenue. The forecasts for 1968 and other future years would have been distorted downward if 1967 had been taken at face value.

Errors in forecasts are typically provided for in inventory systems by the carrying of safety stock inventories. Safety stocks allow an acceptable percentage of sales to be filled from stock. Safety stock quantities are calculated from a statistical measurement of forecast errors, either the standard deviation of forecast errors or, frequently, the mean absolute deviation (MAD).

Mean absolute deviation is the average (mean) of the absolute differences (deviations) between what is forecasted to occur and what actually does occur. Table 18–9 shows how MAD may be calculated. Forecasted sales were determined by the method of least squares trend extension, seasonally adjusted using the seasonal indices calculated in Table 18–7. Use of MAD to calculate safety stock is discussed completely in Chapter 27 of this handbook.

Mean absolute deviation may also be updated easily in a forecasting system utilizing exponential smoothing. Once the MAD has been determined as shown in Table 18–9, it can be determined on a period-by-period basis using this formula:

$$\text{New MAD} = \alpha \, (\text{actual sales} - \text{old forecast}) + (1 - \alpha) \, \text{old MAD}$$

The updated MAD can then be used to calculate safety stock requirements on a period-by-period basis.

Table 18–9   Calculation of Mean Absolute Deviation $[Y = 501.3 + 100.1(X)]$

		Forecasted Sales	Actual Sales	Absolute Deviation of Forecast Error
1977	Q1	535	972	| 437|
	Q2	792	925	| 133|
	Q3	841	772	| 69|
	Q4	749	829	| 80|
1978	Q1	892	904	| 12|
	Q2	1245	1039	| 206|
	Q3	1262	1269	| 7|
	Q4	1081	793	| 288|
1979	Q1	1248	1081	| 167|
	Q2	1697	1747	| 50|
	Q3	1682	1747	| 65|
	Q4	1412	1155	| 257|
1980	Q1	1604	1654	| 53|
	Q2	2149	2190	| 41|
	Q3	2102	2315	| 213|
	Q4	1744	2030	| 286|
1981	Q1	1960	2086	| 126|
	Q2	2602	2629	| 27|
	Q3	2523	2400	| 123|
	Q4	2077	2500	| 423|
				3063

$n = 20$

$$\text{MAD} = \sum_{i=1}^{n} \frac{Xi - \overline{X1}}{n} = \frac{3063}{20} = 153$$

Barometric Techniques

As has been suggested, the main shortcoming of time-series analysis as a forecasting technique is its inability to encompass the vital demand fluctuations, both upward and downward, in the series under consideration. It is these unforeseen changes that cause panic in many logistics decision-making areas such as purchasing, inventory policy, production scheduling, and transportation needs, which are all highly responsive to sudden changes in demand.

Barometric techniques are based on the idea that the future can be predicted from certain happenings in the *present*, whereas time-series analysis (including exponential smoothing) implies that the future may be forecast by extension of *past* data. Barometric methods usually involve the use of "statistical indicators," which are selected external time series that provide an indication of the direction of the economy and particular industries. For example, the sales of roofing materials in a given period would be indicated by the number of new houses started in previous periods. In the history of forecasting, no method has been given more attention that the leading indicator approach. Forecasters have long sought leading indicators for predicting the future course of business, and hence demand for business services. The most extensive periodic reports on business cycle indicators have appeared, since October 1961, in a monthly magazine entitled *Business Cycle Development*, published by the Census Bureau of the U.S. Department of Commerce. It is closely related to the work of the National Bureau of Economic Research (NBER), a private organization in New York, which has been the world's leader in business cycle research and analysis for decades.

Examples of NBER "leading" indicators are: new private nonfarm dwelling units started, number of new business incorporations, corporate profits after taxes, Standard & Poor's Index of 500 Common Stock Prices, and contracts and orders for plants and equipment. With the exception of "corporate profits after taxes," all are available monthly.

The technique for determining the equation describing the relation between two variables is called regression analysis. The closeness of the relationship may be measured by correlation. Some companies have found a high correlation of demand in their industry or company with economic indicators such as those listed above. Where an index can be found to which company sales are highly correlated, but with a lag, regression and correlation techniques may be highly useful. If the lag is long enough, the company can use the reported index figures as a basis for forecasting future demand. Various suppliers of building materials, for example, have found their sales tend to lag behind indices of construction contracts awarded by a few months.

The two basic types of regression and correlation analysis are single and multiple. Single correlation analysis involves a relationship between demand and one other variable. The regression equation determined is of the form $y = a + bx$. Since only two variables are involved, the regression line can be plotted (Figure 18–5).

Multiple correlation analysis involves more than two variables. The regression equation is of the form $Y = a + b_1x_1 + b_2x_2 + \ldots + b_nx_n$. There can be any number of variables, but of course the compilations become burdensome, unless a computer is used.

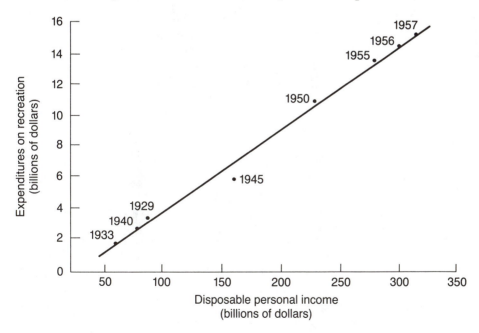

Figure 18-5   Expenditures on Recreation Follow Disposable Personal Income

Econometric Models

Econometric models are based on the idea that changes in economic activity can be explained by a complex set of relationships between economic variables. They are the most elegant (and sometimes best) methods of forecasting. Although their chief use is by various federal government agencies, e.g., Federal Reserve, Treasury, Budget, and Department of Commerce, several large firms such as IBM and General Electric use them for general demand forecasting and corporate planning. Their primary use in logistics management would be in facilities location, to forecast the long-term business outlook and decide whether or not a new manufacturing plant should be built. Econometric models may include many hundreds of equations and thousands of variables.

Adjusting the Forecast Mix

It is not the purpose of this chapter to select the one best method, or combination of methods, to use in demand forecasting. However, a brief discussion of the forecast mix in general terms may be helpful. How much emphasis should the logistics manager put on survey methods, on time-series analysis, and so forth?

Subjective versus Quantitative Techniques

Several subjective methods of forecasting demand as well as several quantitative or mathematical techniques available for forecasting demand have been discussed. The forecast system has room for both subjective and quantitative methods of demand forecasting. Subjective methods are most valuable as "benchmarks" in the forecast system. If mathematical methods result in forecasts that are radically different from those derived from subjective methods (naive, intuition, surveys, etc.), the forecast system should be reevaluated. This provides a system of checks and balances. The proper mix between subjective and quantitative techniques will differ with the industry, company, and management, depending on which has worked in the past. The idea is to provide forecasters with programs based on historical data which can then be modified to incorporate known factors that will affect the forecast. An example would be adding a big new account.

Extrinsic versus Intrinsic Techniques

Extrinsic forecasting relies heavily on external factors, or those outside the control of the firm, such as business conditions, the economy, and government attitudes. Intrinsic forecasting is involved with internal factors at the firm, or those under its control, such as pricing, quality control, customer service, and advertising. The logistics manager is often more concerned with intrinsic forecasting, since many of these internal factors are under his control. Among them are inventory policy and customer service levels, which directly affect demand. Therefore, logistics managers are actually managers of some of their own forecast variables. The real forecasting challenge is in coping with the extrinsic variables, however. In summary, a demand forecast should rely on several techniques. The forecast opinion should be a majority rule. Pure mathematical models have not been entirely perfected. There is no better evidence than the forecasts of 1969 gross national product (GNP) by several sophisticated econometric models by the federal government and various universities. Almost every model understated GNP by billions of dollars, whereas in 1967 and 1968 their predictions were very close to correct.

Cost Trade-offs in Forecasting

Another way of treating forecasting is to reduce the need for it, particularly the sophisticated and expensive types. Demand forecasting costs money—often lots of money—for staff salaries and computer systems. Perhaps some of this money could be better used to improve the firm's information system and speed up feedback response. This technique is known as a "maximum response" information system. The need for elaborate and long-term forecasting could be cut down if the order system's lead time were reduced almost to a "real-time" basis. Changes in demand patterns would be known almost instantaneously, and inventory and production schedules could be adjusted at once to allow for these changes. A "real-time" order-processing and inventory system requires a massive computer complex, however, and many firms have been reluctant to move this way. Examples of other cost trade-offs in forecasting are as follows:

1. Increased safety stocks versus a better (and more expensive) forecast system

2. Excess warehouse capacity versus a better forecast system

3. Use of more flexible common carrier transportation in lieu of private trucks versus a better forecast system (particularly for long-term demand)

Responsibility and Control

Much forecast data originate outside the logistics department. The responsibility for data preparation is thus external to logistics. Therefore, there has to be a spirit of cooperation among corporate departments. The logistics manager often has no direct authority to order data to be collected and delivered to him on a specified date. On the other hand, proper demand forecasting is an important input to the logistics function, and has far-reaching effects on company operations.

Not all forecast data required by logistics come from secondary sources. The logistics department generates quite a bit of its own original data. Control is strictly a matter of authority in this case. The importance of accuracy in collecting forecast data should be emphasized to the people assigned this task.

Controlling Errors

A forecast without an estimate of possible error is incomplete and misleading. Exponential smoothing is a method of forecasting which continually adjust itself for errors. Most of the others covered in this chapter do not do this. In such cases, it is important that forecast errors be measured when comparing prior forecasts with realized demand. Adjustments can then be made in present and future forecasts. Feedback is the most important key to error adjustments. The shorter the feedback mechanism, the quicker errors (the differences between forecast and actual demand) can be identified and handled.

Purchasing

CHAPTER 19

Managing the Purchasing Function

ROBERT M. MONCZKA

Introduction

Purchasing includes the basic activities of purchasing research and planning, buying, negotiation, expediting, cost management, and administration and control. In many firms it may also include many other material-related activities. A narrower focus is taken here since many of these activities—transportation, inventory, etc.—will be discussed in other sections of this *Handbook*.

Purchasing efforts and actions exert a key influence on American business. On average, over 50 percent of the sales dollar in manufacturing firms is accounted for by payments to external suppliers. A cost saving in purchasing affects profits directly and in full. Purchasing considerations also impact decisions in other functional areas. These include engineering, manufacturing, quality, and all material-related activities such as production scheduling, inventory management, and physical distribution.

Because the environment is becoming one of scarcity and uncertainty, and because purchasing can have a significant impact on the firm, it is increasingly important that materials and distribution managers have an understanding of purchasing. The following topics were chosen to provide this understanding in this section of the *Physical Distribution Handbook*.

- Purchasing responsibilities and processes

- Purchasing decisions

- Purchasing research and planning

- Purchasing cost management and reduction

- Organization

- Purchasing information and control

These topics impact all aspects of the purchasing function. Furthermore, the approach taken here has been to discuss purchasing generically, but with a production-oriented focus, instead of discussing specific types of purchasing individually, such as capital equipment purchasing, construction purchasing, purchasing for service industries, and so forth.

Purchasing Responsibilities and Processes

A knowledge of what purchasers should be doing is necessary to manage the function and understand major purchasing decision areas and their impact on total cost. Key sequential activities which must be carefully performed by purchasers include:

- Determination and evaluation of purchase requirements

- Identification of possible suppliers

- Development of the request for quotation (RFQ)

- Choice of suppliers to be quoted

- Review, summarization, and analysis of quotations

- Application of appropriate analytic techniques to price and cost

- Negotiation

- Supplier selection and order/contract completion

- Monitoring and improving supplier performance

- Closing out the purchase

In addition, other non-sequential activities are required for purchasing effectiveness:

- Supplier development

- Enhancement of supplier relations

- Cost reduction and price change management

- Working with other departments to provide accurate and timely lead-time and price/cost information

These responsibilities will be discussed along with the key purchasing decisions, alternatives, and information requirements identified for each responsibility.

Furthermore, sufficient authority and time is required for purchasers to carry out these functions adequately. General and functional management must clearly establish purchasing authority for each activity. Effective and efficient performance in each of these areas contributes to purchasing's primary objectives of profit contribution, continuity of supply, maintenance of quality, maintenance of appropriate stocking levels, fostering interdepartmental cooperation, and reporting supply market trends to top management.

Purchasing Decisions

Purchasers make decisions and take action on a regular basis in each of the responsibility areas. Those decisions have an impact on the total costs for purchased items, levels of supplier competition, and buyer-seller cooperation. These decisions, information needs, and economic and other trade-offs will be discussed using the purchasing process responsibility framework. Recommendations are included in each decision area.

Determination and Evaluation of Requirements

Purchasers should question current and future requirements including quality and specifications, quantity, and timing based on their expert knowledge of the supply market. Appropriate questioning of specifications and quality levels may result in cost reduction through material substitution, standardization, and improved manufacturing methods.

An understanding of quantity, capacity, and timing requirements may also facilitate identification of current and future requirements which can be used as leverage for the firm's buying power. User requirements must be reviewed by purchasers with superior information about price, availability, and technology so that specifications, grades, purchase quantities, and so on will be of benefit to the firm.

Choice of Suppliers to Quote and Development of Requests for Quotation

Which suppliers should be given the opportunity to quote? How should the request for quotation be structured? These are important decisions that influence the degree of supplier competition and the form of the supplier's proposal. Purchasers need to establish carefully the criteria to be used in determining which suppliers to quote and to whom to award the business.

Selected supplier selection criteria minimally include:

- Prior experience in the industry

- Prior experience in providing type of item needed

- Required capacity, facilities, equipment, finances, manufacturing capabilities, logistical support, material supply, energy, quality control, research, and warranty

- Past and potential performance including quality, delivery, price, terms, contribution to design, reaction to problems, overall reliability, flexibility, responsiveness, and cost improvement

The request for quotation should also be used to increase the perceived value of the buying firm's business and to stimulate supplier competition. The RFQ can be used to indicate a range of requirements, including items to be purchased, quality, receiving locations, and timing. Various types of information from the supplier may be also required, such as price, tool cost, transportation methods and cost, terms and conditions, and special services provided. As data become more inclusive and detailed, the purchaser gains useful information on which to evaluate prospective suppliers' quotations.

For example, the RFQ could require a price quotation for a given quantity by a certain date at a specified quality level. Depending on the purchase situation (for example, for a combination of maintenance, repair, and operating supply items such as pipes, valves, and fittings), the RFQ could also request that prospective suppliers provide a delivery performance plan, special service features, inventory stocking program capabilities, special capabilities, quality control methods, product line coverage, financial data, management data, price, shipping methods, and suggestions for cost reduction. An RFQ requesting such comprehensive information can be better used to make the optimum total cost purchase decisions because the purchaser is better able to evaluate supplier proposals, make comparisons, and negotiate.

Review, Summarization, and Analysis of Quotations

When reviewing quotations, the purchaser must ask a series of questions, which at minimum will include:

- Have all bids been received and are they adequate in number?

- What is the total cost associated with each bid?

- How does the quality of the low bidder's quote compare with the others—have any exceptions been taken and what is their impact?

- Are these buy-in prices?

- Have bidders misinterpreted requirements?

Summarization and application of various analytic techniques can also be used where appropriate. These techniques may include price, cost, supplier financial, learning curve, price discount, and terms analyses. Complete description of these techniques are included in selected references.[1]

Form 19–1 shows a typical Quotation Analysis form which can be used to evaluate supplier bids on a total cost basis. This quotation analysis emphasizes a number of key cost elements which are easily quantifiable and which impact making a total cost decision when selecting a supplier. Other factors could be added.

Negotiation

Key negotiation decisions made by the purchaser are when to negotiate and what strategy to use. This discussion will provide information about both these topics. Fuller discussions of negotiation processes and strategy development can be found in more specialized references.[2]

Form 19–1   Quotation Analysis

Part Number _____   RFQ No. _____
Part Name _____   RFQ Date _____
Where Used _____   RFQ Rec'd. _____

Quantity Used

Daily _____   Monthly _____
Weekly _____   Annually _____

Vendor	Unit Price	Discount	Annual Cost	Tool Cost	Lead Time	Freight Unit	Current Price
_____	_____	_____	_____	_____	_____	_____	_____
_____	_____	_____	_____	_____	_____	_____	_____
_____	_____	_____	_____	_____	_____	_____	_____
_____	_____	_____	_____	_____	_____	_____	_____
_____	_____	_____	_____	_____	_____	_____	_____
_____	_____	_____	_____	_____	_____	_____	_____

Negotiation should be considered when:

• There is high dollar value (unit and volume)

• The purchase is extended over time

• The item purchased is produced to unique buyer's specification

• There is a lack of adequate price competition

• Many design or specification changes are expected

Application of these criteria will ensure that negotiation efforts will be well-spent based on possible financial return. If the negotiation process is to be successful, a considerable amount of time will have to be devoted to the product, supplier, and market research effort. Therefore if the competitive bidding process leads to "reasonable" prices with little opportunity for improvement, then negotiation, in its fullest sense, may not be appropriate.

Effective negotiation usually requires that the purchaser to be able to:

• Develop product knowledge

• Develop market knowledge

• Develop supplier knowledge

• Establish a target price

• Estimate supplier costs

- Identify alternative sources and products
- Develop competition (where possible)
- Determine supplier motivations
- Determine cost trade-offs
- Classify own and suppliers' musts, wants, and give positions
- Determine time available to negotiate
- Arrange the negotiation (who, where, when)
- Manage the actual negotiation
- Establish the order or contract

Supplier Selection and Monitoring Supplier Performance

Supplier selection should be done on a total cost, rather than a lowest unit price basis. All easily quantifiable costs should be included in the supplier evaluation. The following material-related costs are needed for a complete analysis:

1. Unit price and price breaks
2. Payment terms and discounts
3. Transportation
4. Tooling
5. Incremental inventory required related to lead times
6. Late delivery
7. Quality-related costs (claims for rejects, non-recoverable rework, inspection)
8. Expediting

The first four costs are easily obtained from supplier quotations. The others need to be imputed or calculated through analysis and based on supplier performance history. For example, as the shipping lead time increases because of the distance of the supplier shipping location from the using location, the amount of inventory held may be increased at a real cost to the firm. The incremental cost of carrying the additional inventory should be calculated and included as a total cost of doing business with a particular supplier. This is easily visualized when considering offshore sources.

Source selection decisions require that economic and other data (based on criteria established above) be used in making the award. For example, should a supplier with a lower price but with a history of less reliable delivery—resulting in higher inventory and expediting costs—be selected over one with a high unit price but an on-time delivery history? The purchaser must evaluate the imputed cost trade-off of the price benefits to be gained versus the inefficiencies and other costs incurred.

Monitoring supplier performance for quality and delivery over time provides buying firms further "benchmarks" to use when evaluating competing supplier's capabilities and selecting suppliers. Various approaches to monitoring supplier performance through quantifiable measurements are in use and include:

Quality performance

— Number counts and percentages of units, lots, and dollars accepted or rejected
— Quality cost index indicating the total cost of purchasing one dollar's worth of acceptable product from a supplier
— Number of quality problems of various types associated with particular suppliers
— Supplier quality index which can be based on both frequency and severity of quality defect

Quantity performance

— On-time, early, or late delivery percentages (number of pieces, orders, shipments, dollar value early/on-time/late divided by total pieces, orders, shipments, dollar value received per time period)

Such supplier performance information is useful when selecting suppliers. These indicators can also be used to improve supplier performance by identifying quality and delivery problems and unfavorable trends and communications to those suppliers and taking appropriate actions. Budgeted or target performance levels can also be established.

Purchase Close Out

This step of the purchasing process, although procedural in nature, usually requires that a series of checks be performed to ensure that the order or contract is fully completed and all obligations discharged. With few exceptions, the purchaser is not, and should not be, directly involved in the activities resulting in purchase close.

Typical activities that must be fully completed before an order can be closed are:

• Receiving

• Quantity check

• Quality inspection and approval

• Invoice review

• Cash discounts

Purchasing should become involved only when specific problems in the normal process of completing the order are encountered. These may include rework costs for quality problems, billings for unauthorized overtime by the supplier, and so forth.

Conclusions

Purchasers can make important contributions to a firm's profitability in at least three major ways during the purchasing process. These include:

1. Thoroughly reviewing and questioning all aspects of the firm's requirements in order to take advantage of opportunities for standardization, tolerance changes, material substitution, quantity grouping, and other value techniques to reduce cost and improve value.

2. Carefully developing a quotation and sourcing plan to ensure competition and supplier capability and the opportunity to be able to review and compare numerous elements of supplier proposals by asking for detailed information in the request for quotation.

3. Taking adequate time to prepare for negotiation, when appropriate; doing the necessary research, and applying analytic techniques. Conducting the negotiation with a thoroughly developed plan.

Management should ensure that purchasing personnel recognize these as key ingredients of successful purchasing. The final source selection should be the result of careful planning and strategy development, and the use of available market forces, resulting in the best total cost decision to the buying firm.

Purchasing Research and Planning

Purchase decisions for key items are becoming more complex and effects of these decisions more long lasting because of the increasing uncertainty and volatility of the external environment. Important environmental considerations include:

- Supply uncertainty and dependence on foreign sources (where volatile political influences are often at work) for key commodities

- Inflationary and rapidly changing prices

- Extended and variable lead times

- Energy shortages and price increases

- Increasing world-wide competition

Because of the changing environment, purchasing must be able to do a more effective job of research (supply market) and planning. Information about supply conditions (changes in process, lead times, technology, etc.) needs to be provided by purchasing—often considered the "window" to the outside world—to different groups within the firm including top management, engineering and design, and manufacturing. This information can play an important role in long-term strategy and short-term decisions.

Research and Planning Techniques

Improved purchasing research and strategy development is needed in many organizations. Key purchased items for which availability, pricing, and quality problems may develop need to be highlighted to develop action plans before the problem becomes critical and costly to the buying firm. The techniques described here provide an outline for a firm to follow in establishing improved research and planning capability.

Strategic materials planning involves a number of systematic activities including:

- Materials screening

- Risk assessment

- Strategy development

- Implementation

The strategic materials planning process should be used to determine if materials bottlenecks will jeopardize current or future operations, if new products should be introduced, and whether future quality may be expected to change. Other important considerations are the direction and magnitude of material price changes and whether financial resources should be used for supply protection. Specific actions to increase the likelihood that the material supply chain will operate uninterrupted should also be developed as a result of the planning process.

Materials screening can be done for both internal and external purposes to develop a critical purchased item list. Typical criteria to be used for internal and external criticality are:

Internal	*External.*
• Percentage of product cost	• Number of suppliers
• Percentage of total purchase expenditure	• Availability of raw materials to suppliers
• End item commonality	• Supplier cost and profitability needs
• Use on high margin end items	• Supply capacity and technological trends

Risk assessment requires that the purchaser or team determine the likelihood of best or worst conditions developing. The impact of potential situations on the business should be determined. This can also be labeled "scenario development."

Supply strategies should then be developed against the best predictions of possible events and their impact on the business. Monczka and Fearon have identified a number of potential purchasing strategies including:[3]

- Evaluation of supplier relations

- Buying out supplier (i.e., vertical integration)

- World-wide source development

- Supplier development with long-term supplier

- Long-term contracts

- Customer provision of materials supply

- Joint venture and purchasing

- Trading

- Multiple sourcing

- Centralized coordination of purchasing

- Reduction of scrap rate

Implementation of particular supply strategies requires top management involvement and often integration into the overall business plans. Time schedules and responsibilities must also be determined and a follow-up program established.

Purchasing Cost Management and Reduction

Purchasing departments, like other functional areas, are required to manage and reduce costs. A number of key purchasing approaches and techniques should be considered for use by most purchasing departments to reduce administrative costs, purchase prices, and inventory carrying costs. The most prevalent approaches and techniques in use include:

1. Purchase cost reduction programs

2. Price change management programs

3. Volume contracts (time and/or quantity)

4. Systems contracts and stockless purchasing

Cost Reduction Program

An effective purchase cost reduction program requires:

1. Top management support

2. Definition of cost reduction or avoidance

3. Effective goal setting

4. Review and approval of cost reductions or avoidances

5. Measurement to goal

6. Reporting

7. Individual cost reduction or avoidance achievement made part of the performance appraisal process

Top management must continually communicate the need for cost saving accomplishments to provide credibility to any functional cost saving program, in both good and bad economic times. Cost reductions or avoidances must also be adequately defined so accomplishments can be reasonably measured and compared to goals. For example, many firms define a cost reduction as a reduction from prior purchase price and cost avoidance as the amount that would have been paid minus the amount actually paid. Furthermore reductions and avoidances are often required to be the result of a planned and deliberate action or change made by purchasing.

Goals need to be set with buyers based on opportunities for cost reduction and stretch. Establishment of cost reduction programs, goals, measurement, and reporting, and appraising individual performance on the basis of cost reduction achievements focuses attention on a key area of purchasing performance.

Techniques and cost reduction approaches should at least include:

- Development of competition

- Requirement of supplier cost reduction

- Substitution of materials

- Standardization

- Make or buy analysis

- Value analysis

- Reduction of scrap

- Change in tolerances

- Improvement of payment terms and conditions

- Volume buying

- Process changes

Price Change Management

Managing the purchasing function requires the development of an attitude on the part of managers and buyers that requests for price increases be challenged and not just treated as pass-through costs. Buyers should be innovative in working with suppliers to restrict the rate of price increases to a reasonable and equitable level, and to offset inflation to the maximum extent possible.

Furthermore, purchasing should establish a systematic method of handling all price increase requests from suppliers. The system should at least require that:

1. The reason for the price change (up or down) request be determined (e.g., material increase, changes in labor content, quality, tolerance, quantity, etc.)

2. The total dollar value impact on the firm be established

3. Suppliers be required to justify the request

4. Exposure be given to the request for price change at the management level

5. Strategies be developed, when appropriate, to deal with the price increase request.

Other tactics to restrict price increases may include:

- Price protection clauses over a specified time period

- Requirement of a 30, 60, or 90-day notification of price increases

Furthermore, as part of a price change management effort, purchasing could determine the economic impact on product costs of engineering changes. This information could be useful in determining whether the engineering change should be made.

Volume Contracts

Volume contracts consolidate requirements for purchase over time or combine different line item requirements into purchase families. They can also have a significant impact on leverage of purchase requirements and reduction of purchase prices and administrative costs. A review of spot buys for a particular purchased item often reveals the opportunity to have suppliers quote the business on a semi-annual or annual contract basis. An increase in the potential buy quantity often enables suppliers to reduce their costs through economics of production or materials purchases so that they can quote a lower price to the purchaser. The supplier may also be willing to take lower margins on higher volume business.

Information about historical purchase patterns should be available from buy-history cards, computer-generated requirements plans, copies of historical purchase requisitions and orders, and from suppliers. Even though the use of volume contracts is a basic purchasing technique, firms need to review their purchase history regularly and systematically for new opportunities to take advantage of volume contracting.

Systems Contracts and Stockless Purchasing

Like volume contracts, systems contracts and stockless purchasing are material cost reduction techniques that can affect productivity. Systems contracts are a means to reduce various materials-related costs, including unit purchase price, transportation, inventory, and administration. Stockless purchasing implies that the buying firm does not carry inventory for particular items. A systems contract may or may not operate with a "zero" level of inventory, but the underlying principles of systems contracting are necessary for stockless purchasing.

The primary purposes of these systems are to:

1. Lower inventory levels

2. Reduce the number of suppliers

3. Reduce administrative cost and paperwork

4. Reduce the number of small dollar value purchases and requisitions purchasers have to handle (and thereby increase the amount of time available for other key activities)

5. Provide the opportunity for larger dollar volumes of business to suppliers

6. Provide for timely delivery of material directly to the user

7. Standardize purchase items where possible

Systems contracts and stockless purchasing systems are best suited for repetitive type items of low dollar value with relatively high administrative processing costs compared to the unit prices. Often the combined administrative processing and inventory carrying costs may be higher than the cost of the item. Through systems contracting, supplier discounts may be increased, processing costs between buyer and supplier reduced, and supply availability enhanced. Both systems require:

1. Identification of the items to be included

2. Request for quotation development, identification of appropriate supplies, and supplier selection

3. Use of a standard item catalog for availability and ordering

4. Establishment of order communication methods

5. Identification of acceptable receipt areas (docks, warehouses, etc.)

6. Monitoring of supplier delivery performance within established delivery parameters (e.g., 4, 8, 24, or 48 hours)

7. Established payment methods to accumulate receipts and pay for all items received over a given time period (e.g., 30 days)

Length of life of the contract may vary from one to three years with appropriate price protection clauses. The buying organization should have the right to market test the items to ensure that current suppliers' unit prices are meeting the "reasonableness" test when compared to the market.

Purchasing Organization

Effective purchasing is based on the ability of the managers responsible for organizing the function to consider corporate strategy, internal needs, and the external market when structuring the department. This section discusses the basic forms of purchasing organizations and functional activities, issues of centralization and decentralization, and basic principles underlying purchasing organizations.

Types of Purchasing Organizations

The typical organizational approaches are by (1) commodity or function, (2) project or product, and (3) matrix. The commodity approach recognizes the need to specialize buying of purchased items into manageable activities. The buying function is normally split into areas of responsibility such as (1) production, (2) maintenance, repair, and operating (MRO) or supplies and services, and (3) capital and construction. In addition, specialized non-direct buying responsibilities are also established as organizational units. These usually include systems development, purchasing research, administrative support, and technical liaison depending on the firm.

Buying is specialized by commodity groups and specific purchasers buy for needs of all users. The advantage is development of specialized knowledge about the supply market and commodity which often allows economic use of highly paid personnel. Figure 19–1 shows a typical example of this organizational form.

Project purchasing is sometimes developed around major products and programs to ensure that purchasing will provide all requirements within budget, time, and quality constraints. This form of structure provides careful attention to the specific project but may involve duplication of efforts. For example, three different buyers may be purchasing the same semiconductors from the same suppliers for three different projects.

A matrix type of purchasing organization can be used to provide the opportunity for specialized activities to be performed without duplication of effort. Figure 19–2 shows a basic form of the matrix organization.

In the matrix form, the functional purchasing manager, buyers, and others would play key roles as members of a project team or teams. For example, a semiconductor buyer could be a member of three project teams so as to ensure that needs for each project were being met. However, duplication of buying efforts would be eliminated and coordination enhanced when working with suppliers providing items for multiple projects.

Centralization or Decentralization

In multi-location purchasing environments with headquarter and plant facilities, three major questions generally surface. These include:

1. How should responsibilities be split between headquarters and operating units?

2. Where in the organization should buying decisions be made?

3. How can the firm better coordinate its buying functions?

Unpublished research findings about these questions seem to indicate the following:[4]

- Purchasing activities usually conducted by a corporate purchasing staff include establishing policy and procedure, conducting functional reviews, developing systems, developing and conducting education and training programs, and improving coordination between operating unit purchasing operations.

- Most purchasing has been done at the decentralized operating unit level because of historical management philosophy.

- Purchasing authority has been found to be centralized only to the level where specific economic benefits can accrue.

- There is an identifiable trend toward improving purchasing coordination between purchasing units through better information flow, purchasing councils, lead buyer assignments, and corporate planning staffs.

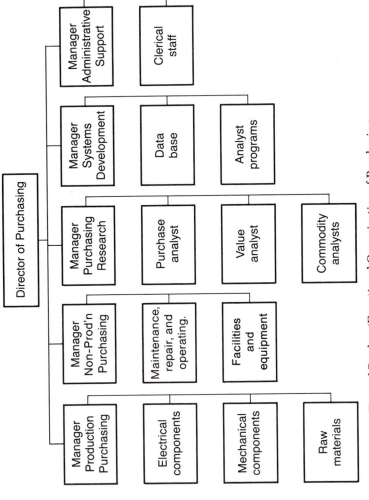

Figure 19-1 Typical Product/Functional Organization of Purchasing

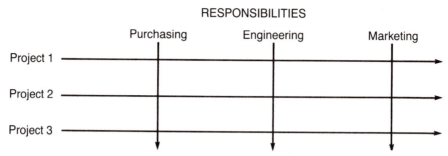

RESPONSIBILITIES

Figure 19-2   Matrix Organization

Basic Principles

A number of important guidelines can be used when organizing for purchasing (and materials management). They are:

- Centralization or decentralization of buying responsibility and authority should be analyzed separately for production and non-production items.

- Purchasing authority should be located at the level in the organization where purchases for production and non-production items can be optimally grouped to obtain maximum economic leverage.

- Purchasing structures will (and should) differ between plants that produce the same or similar items and plants that manufacture dissimilar items.

- Management of the physical flow of materials (scheduling, receiving, stores inventory control, etc.) is often best accomplished at the decentralized operating locations.

Purchasing Information and Control

Purchasing should play an important role in enabling the firm to identify the information that is necessary to perform purchasing activities and to measure and evaluate overall purchasing performance. This section describes basic purchasing information requirements and how purchasing performance can be measured and evaluated.

Purchasing Information

Basic data that should be systematically collected include:

- Purchase item number and description

- Quantity required

- Date item required

- Date purchase requisition received or authorized

- Purchase requisition or authorization number

- Supplier(s) quoted

- Date supplier(s) quoted

- Date quotes required from supplier(s)

- Supplier quote(s)

- Supplier price discount schedule

- Purchase order number

- Date purchase order placed

- Purchase price per unit

- Quantity or percent of annual requirements purchased

- Planned purchase price per unit

- Supplier name

- Supplier address

- Supplier promise ship date

- Supplier lead time (days or weeks for purchase item)

- Date purchase item received

- Quantity received

- Purchase item accepted or rejected (unit/lot)

- Storage location

- Buyer

- Work unit

- Requested price change

- Effective date of requested price change

- Date price change approved

- Ship to location

These basic transaction data are needed for purchasing decisions and management control systems, especially if these are computerized.

Purchasing Measurement and Control

Management of the purchasing function requires control, often using the transaction data above. Control requires measurement and evaluation against performance standards.

Figure 19–3 illustrates the typical management control process. The impact of internal and external environment on performance expectations for the many purchasing responsibilities can be stated both quantitatively and qualitatively. Situational analysis should then be conducted based on audits, functional reviews, or regularly collected measures. Based on the difference between the current situation and goals or standards, corrective action may have to be taken to modify department activities and behavior.

Key questions associated with this process include:

1. What types of purchasing evaluation may be performed?
2. What performance measures are being used in purchasing?

Types of Evaluation

Purchasing measurement and evaluation can be categorized based on who is using the results and the type of information required. Four general users include:

1. Top-level non-functional management
2. Top-level corporate functional managers
3. Operating unit top level functional managers
4. Middle managers at plant and operating unit sites

Each user will have different needs. For example, top management wants to know how their purchasing department compares with others and how effective it is. To answer these questions may require an *overall functional review* where a team collects information through use of historical data and records, review of purchasing objectives and organization and personnel data, and through interviews with purchasers, personnel from other departments, and suppliers. Data may be collected about

- Purchasing acceptance by various groups
- Organization
- Policy and procedures
- Supplier selection methods
- Use of data processing systems
- Control methods
- Research and planning
- Personnel training and development

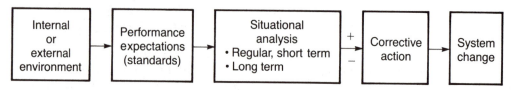

Figure 19-3   Basic Control Process

- Cost management

- Expediting methods and systems

- Problem identification

Evaluation for corporate top-level functional managers, such as a corporate vice-president of purchasing, may include complete functional reviews, policy and procedure audits, and review of a few key quantitative indicators regularly provided such as inventory, minority purchases, and administrative budget measures. Evaluation at the operating unit purchasing department location is likely to be operational and continuing in nature and based on a series of regularly reported indicators. These measures will be used to monitor and correct performance, usually on a weekly and monthly basis.

Purchasing Measures

A study by Monczka et al.[5] found that purchasing organizations systematically use a number of key performance measures for purchasing control which include:

1. Price effectiveness

2. Cost savings

3. Workload

4. Administration and control

5. Efficiency

6. Vendor quality and delivery

7. Material flow control

8. Regulatory, societal, and environmental factors

9. Procurement planning and research

10. Competition

11. Inventory

12. Transportation

Price Effectiveness

Price effectiveness measures are used to determine: (1) actual purchasing price performance against plan, (2) actual purchasing price performance against market, and (3) actual purchasing price performance among buying groups and locations. Purchase price variances from plan can be calculated on an individual line item and on a total purchasing budget basis. Typical indicators are price variances measured in terms of: (1) actual unit cost minus planned cost; (2) a price variance percentage—actual unit cost over planned cost; or (3) an extended price variance—actual unit cost minus planned cost multiplied by an estimated annual quantity (or the needed quantity for the remainder of a planning period).

Cost Savings

Cost savings measures include indicators of both cost reduction and cost avoidance. Cost reduction requires that the new unit cost be lower than the old unit cost on a line-item basis. Cost avoidance is more loosely defined and can be obtained, for example, by buying at a price lower than the average price being quoted, even though the new unit price would be an increase over the old price.

Cost reduction and avoidance are measured on the basis of an absolute unit or an annual cost reduction or avoidance, or by comparing actual cost reduction and avoidance to the budgeted or targeted goals.

Workload

Workload can be broken down into three categories: (1) workload-in: a measure of the new work coming into the purchasing department; (2) workload-current: a measure of the backlog of work; and (3) workload-completed: a measure of the work accomplished. Workload-in measures are usually counts of work received, including purchase requisitions received, purchase information requests received, and number of pricing requests received.

Measures of the workload-current category are, typically, counts of the backlog of work in the purchasing department. The two most common counts are purchase requisitions on hand, and line items on hand.

Measures in the workload-completed category include purchase orders placed, line items placed, dollars placed, contracts written, and price proposals written.

Administration and Control

These measures are used to help plan the annual administrative budget for the purchasing function and help control administrative expenses during the budget period. The most common method for establishing a budget is to start with the current budget and adjust it up or down, depending on the business forecast. The adjustment reflects management views on both the projected purchasing workload and the projected profit margins, based on economic conditions.

Efficiency

Efficiency measures relate the purchasing outputs, such as line items placed, to purchasing inputs, such as buyers. These measures range from two-factor measures that have one input and one output, to multi-factor measures that relate several outputs to several inputs.

Among the more common two-factor measures are the following: purchase orders per buyer, line items per buyer, dollars committed per buyer, change notices per buyer, contracts written per buyer, average open order commitment, worker hours per line item, worker hours per purchase order, worker hours per contract, administrative dollars per purchase order, administrative dollars per contract, and administrative dollars per purchase dollar.

Vendor Quality and Delivery

Both vendor quality and delivery measures are used. Characteristics such as dollars by vendors are also measured. Vendor quality and delivery measures were discussed above (see pages 476–477).

Material Flow Control

Many organizations have reports and measures concerned with the flow of material from vendors to the buying organizations. These reports can be classified into four functions: (1) identification of all open purchase orders and their due dates; (2) identification of past-due open orders; (3) identification of material or orders that are needed immediately by manufacturing, that is, a hot list; and (4) measurement of how well purchasing buyers and vendors are doing in meeting due dates.

In many organizations, the first two functions are combined in the same reports. For example, a buyer might get a weekly listing of all open purchase orders, with overdue orders as a percentage of the total orders. The hot list in an organization is often a separate report generated by manufacturing.

The most sophisticated material flow control reports show projected manufacturing requirements by part number by time period (usually weekly or monthly). The promised delivery time is shown in the same report. As manufacturing requirements and vendor delivery dates are updated, the report should reflect these changes.

Regulatory, Societal, and Environmental Measures

Some measures provide information about a purchasing department's achievement of regulatory, societal, and environmental goals. Examples include: (1) purchase dollars and percentage of purchase dollars placed with small and minority businesses; (2) purchase dollars and percentage of purchase dollars placed in labor surplus areas; and (3) number and percentage of minority employees in purchasing.

Procurement Planning and Research

Various indicators can be categorized into the broadly defined area of procurement planning and research. The measures are generally used to monitor the planning and research activity and its accuracy. These measures include the number of procurement plans established per year (including availability and price forecasting), price forecasting accuracy (actual to forecast), lead-time forecasting accuracy (actual to forecast), and number of make-buy studies completed.

Competition

These measures provide information about the extent to which the buying organization is developing competition in the supply marketplace and improving purchase prices and terms. Measures may include annual purchase dollars and percentage of annual purchases on annual contracts (thereby leveraging volume over time) and with sole source suppliers (thereby limiting competition).

Inventory

Inventory measures are used in many purchasing departments to monitor turnover, tracked consignments, and projected inventory levels. Purchasing departments only use such measures when inventory management is their responsibility.

Transportation

Transportation measures are used to determine how much was being spent on premium transportation to obtain needed materials or products. Premium transportation costs are incurred when other than normal transportation is used, e.g., air freight instead of truck.

General Conclusions

The *key* measures in purchasing appear to be price effectiveness, work load, cost savings, administration and control, vendor quality and delivery, and material flow control. However, important differences can be found in how the various organizations measure performance in each of these areas.

Several important systems-related and people-related principles for measurement of purchasing performance have been suggested.[6] Important systems principles include the following:

1. A few narrowly defined measures are apparently more effective than several loosely defined and partially understood measures.

2. Every measure must be based on a valid and comprehensive data base used by all individuals in the purchasing organization.

3. There is no one best way of measuring purchasing performance. Each organization must tailor the measures to its own situation. However, some approaches are better than others.

4. Standards for purchasing performance cannot be fixed once and for all but must be adapted to changing situations.

5. One overall measure of purchasing performance is not feasible or desirable.

6. The performance measures and data base must be reviewed periodically to weed out unnecessary measures and to add new measures.

7. Purchasing performance measurement is not free! Its costs must be weighed against the benefits.

Important people-related principles include the following:

1. Purchasing measurement is not a substitute for good management. However, good managers have and use good performance measures.

2. Communication is of paramount importance in creating an effective measurement system. Expected performance levels and the use of the measures in personnel evaluation must be clearly understood by all.

3. The measures should be used to motivate and direct behavior, and not primarily as a basis for punishing individuals.

Notes

1. George W. Aljian, ed., *Purchasing Handbook*, 4th ed. (New York: McGraw-Hill, 1982); John M. Browning and M. A. Andrews, "Target Purchasing: The Price–Volume Distinction," *Journal of Purchasing and Materials Management*, Summer 1978; National Association of Purchasing Management, Inc., Guide to Purchasing, 1–3 (New York: NAPM, 1965, 1968, 1973).
2. H. H. Calero, *Winning the Negotiation* (New York: Hawthorne Books); H. H. Calero and G. I. Nierenberg, *How to Read a Person Like a Book* (New York: Hawthorne Books, 1971); Chester L. Karrass, *Give and Take* (New York: Thomas Y. Crowell, 1974); Chester L. Karrass, *The Negotiating Game* (New York: Thomas Y. Crowell, 1970).
3. R. M. Monczka and H. F. Fearon, "Coping with Material Shortages," *Journal of Purchasing and Materials Management*, May 1974, pp. 5–19.
4. R. M. Monczka, unpublished research on purchasing organization.
5. R. M. Monczka, P. L. Carter, and J. H. Hoagland, *Purchasing Performance: Measurement and Control* (East Lansing, Mich.: Michigan State University, Graduate School of Business Administration, Division of Research, 1979).
6. Ibid.

Transportation

CHAPTER 20

Transportation and Distribution Management: *The New Options*

LAWRENCE F. CUNNINGHAM

Understanding the New Transportation Environment

Traditionally the transportation cost component of the logistical system was relatively easy to plan, and costs were relatively predictable. Major cost savings were usually dependent upon the skill and experience of traffic managers who could obtain the best possible freight rates for their companies' products. However, the recent institution of regulatory reform in the transportation industry has encouraged greater carrier innovation in pricing and services and has created more opportunities for cost savings than at any previous time in the last hundred years.

The distribution manager who wishes to exploit fully all possible cost savings during the latter half of the 1980s requires a comprehensive knowledge of the regulatory tradition and its impacts, regulatory reform and its consequences for carriers and shippers, and the new options for traffic management in the deregulated environment.

The Regulatory Tradition

Transportation costs and services provided by carriers had been traditionally regulated by government agencies such as the Interstate Commerce Commission, for domestic water carriers and railroad and trucking companies, and the Civil Aeronautics Board, which had authority over air cargo.

The government bodies granted fare increases on industry-wide or regional bases to carriers within each mode of transportation. Increases in rates were granted to carriers to enable them to reap sufficient returns on investments so they could replace equipment. Carrier rates and services were identified in tariffs that were distributed to shippers and placed on file with the respective regulatory commission.

In the trucking, domestic water carrier, and air cargo industries, several different types of carriers were granted authorities to operate by the regulatory commissions. The most frequent form of carrier operation was that of the "common carrier," which was granted a certificate of public convenience and necessity.

A common carrier was basically required to serve all shippers requesting services listed in its tariffs. Under the authority vested in its certificate, such a carrier typically enjoyed either a monopoly or limited competition within the geographical area in which its services were provided. In return, the common carrier was obliged to assume extreme care in fulfilling its duties and to provide reasonable and non-discriminatory rates to as many individual shippers as possible.

The concept of common carriage originated in British common law. It was first used in U.S. business regulation at the federal level in 1887 when Congress enacted the Act to Regulate Commerce, which called for the creation of the Interstate Commerce Commission (ICC).

The act was directed specifically toward correcting the public abuses and destructive competition rampant among railroads. Enjoying virtual monopolies, railroads had practiced extreme forms of price discrimination, charging low tariffs at competitive points and "what the market would bear" at others.

The creation of the Interstate Commerce Commission was an attempt to control the railroads. Designating the railroads as public utilities, the ICC conferred legal status upon their monopolies, but in exchange for such recognition, the ICC asserted its authority over their pricing, financial, and service policies.

The same basic regulatory model was extended, with some slight differences, to the trucking, airline, and freight-forwarding industries. The extension of the model to the trucking industry was particularly interesting because, unlike the case of the railroad industry, there were no monopolistic abuses occurring when the Motor Carrier Act of 1935 was passed. This legislation sought to resolve the problems caused by destructive competition taking place during the Great Depression. In many instances, such competition had resulted in safety problems.

Some individuals were troubled by the fact that pricing, entry and exit, and many other aspects of the trucking industry were controlled by the same public utility form of regulation applied to railroads, even though the trucking industry possessed few characteristics of a natural monopoly.

The ICC was nearly granted regulatory authority over the airline industry, but important political forces decided instead to support a variant of the public utility model. The authority to control pricing, entry, exit, and route certification was conferred upon a regulatory forerunner of the present-day Civil Aeronautics Board. The safety function was placed ultimately under the purview of the Federal Aviation Administration, which was created in 1958. Again, the fundamental regulation of the airline industry as a public utility was suspect at best.

The railroad industry and regulators at the ICC encouraged Congressional efforts to extend the same regulatory model to inland waterway operators. Although the public utility concept was extended to these carriers in the 1940 Transportation Act, there were numerous exemptions from economic regulation. The 6 to 10 percent of inland waterway carriers that were brought under ICC jurisdiction faced many of the same restrictions that applied to the railroad and trucking industries.

The regulatory mechanism was extended to freight forwarders in 1942, when Congress subjected them to the Interstate Commerce Act and established controls over entry and exit and rates and services. Forwarders were designated as common carriers in 1950. Again, the concept of a public utility was applied to another form of transportation that was, in reality, a competitive industry.

Impacts of Regulation

The common carrier concept and the overall regulatory structure of transportation were based on the regulatory commission's ability to balance properly the forces of supply and demand in the marketplace and to limit competition.

Unfortunately, regulated carriers experienced gradually worsening financial situations as population and industrial shifts occurred in the post–World War II period. Since carriers had either made massive investments in rights of way or acquired operating rights for specific geographic areas, it was difficult for them to redeploy their assets in more profitable markets under the regulatory model. The poor performance of these regulated carriers was also aggravated by the growth of carriage that was exempt from regulation, such as truck fleets owned by corporations that hauled their own goods.

George Eads, a noted transportation economist, suggested that in such an environment regulatory authorities were confronted by three options. They could (1) subsidize unprofitable sources of common carrier business; (2) allow abandonment of such businesses; or (3) allow the carriers to go bankrupt.[1] Eads has suggested that, in many cases, the carriers deprived the regulatory authorities of the third option by their diversification of their business operations.[2]

While many shippers enjoyed stability in transportation rates and services, the cost to the public of the regulatory structure was enormous. Some public interest groups have suggested that the cost was approximately $6 to $12 billion annually. The Office of Management and Budget in various studies has suggested a total of $6 to $13 billion annually.

Regulatory Reform

With this background, the Ford Administration in the mid-1970s called for regulatory reform in the transportation industries. The basic philosophical premise of this policy was to remove the cost of regulation by allowing market forces to prevail. The Administration recognized that the treatment of the transportation industries as public utilities had been a valid concept many years ago. However, with the passage of time, it was evident that government faced the choice of functioning as the provider of last resort or of forcing the subsidized elements of the shipping public to pay the true cost of transportation services.

Regulatory reform in the transportation industries occurred largely because a coalition of very diverse political forces viewed such reform as beneficial to their constituencies. Conservative Republicans supported reform because of its reliance on marketplace forces. To liberal Democrats, regulatory reform promised less rapidly increasing prices in the distribution system of the country during an era of high inflation. Many academics and economists had been debating the merits and demerits of regulatory reform for 40 years, and several of these individuals assumed positions of authority and/or influence in the Ford and Carter Administrations.

Airline Regulatory Reform

The first meaningful step in regulatory reform occurred with the appointment of Alfred Kahn as Chairman of the Civil Aeronautics Board (CAB) in 1976. Kahn strongly encouraged the airlines to introduce experimental and discount fares. In addition, he encouraged the CAB to award routes, without regard to the impact on existing competitors, to carriers that would offer low prices. These changes in policy, as well as others, were later codified in the 1978 Airline Deregulation Act.

The first significant piece of regulatory reform legislation passed by Congress was the Air Cargo Deregulation Act, enacted in November 1977. Basically, the act gave carriers the right to establish any rates they wanted as long as the rates were not unjustly discriminatory. The all-cargo carriers with grandfather rights (i.e., certified before November 1977) were allowed to enter new routes or withdraw from existing routes according to their own discretion. After a brief one-year transitional period, new all-cargo entrants could initiate service in any markets they wanted. In addition, all-cargo carriers could use any size aircraft they so desired.

Trucking and Railroad Regulatory Reform

In 1980, regulatory reform was extended to the trucking and railroad industries. The 1980 Motor Carrier Act (MCA) and the Staggers Rail Act of 1980 were the Congressional instruments of regulatory reform.

Trucking Reform

The 1980 Motor Carrier Act included the following major provisions:

- Established a "zone of reasonableness" in pricing motor carrier services. Motor carriers were allowed to increase or decrease rates by 10 percent without challenge being filed with the ICC by other carriers or shippers. The legislation also provided for increases in rates to occur automatically with changes in the Producer Price Index.

- Created new entry provisions regarding common carriers. Under the Motor Carrier Act of 1935, applicants had been required only to demonstrate that they were "fit, willing, and able to provide service" and that their services were required by present or future public convenience and necessity. The 1980 act provided for certification unless the applicant's proposed service was inconsistent with the public convenience and necessity.

- Limited protests to carriers that were directly affected by the new entry. In addition, the legislation shifted the burden of proof of harm to competitors from the applicants to the protestors.

- Increased exemptions from federal regulation. Traditionally, some agricu
products were exempt from federal regulation. The MCA increased the exemp
to include (1) additional agricultural food products, (2) owner-operators engage
transportation of food products, (3) carriers whose service was a direct substitute
for abandoned rail service, and (4) carriers of small shipments of less than 100
pounds.

- Directed the ICC to process applications for broader geographic, route, and commodity authority for common and contract carriers. In addition, it forced the ICC
to virtually eliminate one-way provisions and other restrictions.

- Removed restrictions on the number of shippers a contract carrier could serve. Previously such carriers could have contracts with a maximum of eight shippers.

- Limited the power of common carrier rate bureaus by reducing the circumstances
in which they could establish rates for carriers.

- Provided complete freedom for pickup and delivery services of trucking operations
owned and operated by domestic airlines.

- Created significant opportunities for privately owned carriers to engage in intercorporate hauling. Intercorporate hauling basically allows the private trucking fleet of
a parent or related subsidiary to provide trucking services to another related subsidiary for a fee. The original requirement of the legislation was that the subsidiaries
be 100 percent owned by the parent or holding companies.

Such liberalizations facilitate better utilization of private trucking fleets. In addition,
the legislation offered other advantages that have been equally beneficial. For example, it
is permissible for a private trucking fleet to apply for common carrier authority in backhaul operations. As a result, the private trucking fleet can offer its services to all shippers
at low rates on a routing from which it had previously been barred from carrying traffic.

Railroad Reform

The Staggers Rail Act of 1980 was enacted in an attempt to introduce competitive forces
into an industry that had suffered a regulatory burden for many years. In essence, the legislation recognized the fact that the railroad industry was no longer a natural monopoly
but was, in fact, subject in many areas to competition. At the same time, Congress sought
to protect shippers that were dependent exclusively on the railroads for transportation of
their goods.

Under regulatory reform, the railroads were accorded substantial pricing freedoms.
They were allowed to raise their rates up to 6 percent per year from 1981 through 1984,
and then 4 percent per year to a maximum of 18 percent. The basis of the rates is a cost
recovery index that was initially set at 170 to 180 percent of variable costs. The index is
computed by the American Association of Railroads and is published by the ICC on a
quarterly basis.

Nearly two-thirds of all railroad rates have been freed from maximum rate regulation. However, the ICC does retain jurisdiction over maximum rates for traffic in locations where the railroad is the dominant carrier.

The complaint mechanism available to both shippers and the ICC is limited. While
shippers can protest rates, the burden of proof is on the shipper to show that the pricing is

inappropriate or discriminatory. The ICC can initiate complaints at the extreme high range of rate increase, but the burden of proof lies with the ICC. The Commission cannot suspend these rates during the investigation.

Congress also increased the ability of the railroads to compete with barge and motor transportation by allowing them to institute minimum rates according to their own discretion. The floor of the rates was to be the "going concern value" or recovery of variable costs.

The days of general rate increases in the railroad industry seem to be limited. They are basically limited to joint rate increases and general inflation "catch-up" raises. If the concept of general rate increases is eliminated by the ICC in 1984, the Commission may institute percentage increases instead. Carriers would, of course, be free at the time to accept or reject such increases.

Under the new legislation, the railroads are required to give only 20 days' notice for rate increases and 10 days' notice for decreases. An interesting provision deals with shipper complaints. If a shipper does manage to obtain a suspension of a rate on the basis that it will cause severe injury, the shipper is responsible for all undercharges plus interest if the rate is ultimately upheld.

While there are many other provisions in the legislation, several are particularly important to shippers. For the first time in the history of the railroad industry, carriers are permitted to function as contract carriers. The contracts are filed with the ICC, and the ability of other shippers to file complaints is severely curtailed. The contracts are enforceable by the courts rather than by the ICC.

The Staggers Act also contains an abandonment provision, which will prove extremely interesting to many shippers. Instead of dragging on for years, ICC decisions regarding unprotested abandonments will be made within 75 days. After an abandonment provision has been filed, protestors have a total of 120 days in which to lodge their complaints. The abandonment, if approved, will take place within 330 days of the decision. The legislation does make provision for state subsidization of the line or a buy-out by a private firm.

The act also facilitated ICC deliberations regarding the issue of mergers. Throughout the traditional regulatory era, the ICC had basically taken the view that mergers, especially of side-by-side lines, were anticompetitive. The ICC policy regarding end-to-end mergers was somewhat more liberal. However, both types required extensive hearings to debate not only the anticompetitive impact of such mergers, but also the impact upon the competitors themselves. Such hearings often consumed years of extensive regulatory review before final decisions were rendered. For example, the New York Central–Pennsylvania Railroad merger was originally proposed in March 1962, but was not given the regulatory go-ahead until 1968!

While the criteria for mergers have not changed substantially, the reform legislation does expedite the merger process. The ICC must reach a decision on a proposed merger within two years of the date the original proposal is filed.

Consequences of Regulatory Reform

Regulatory reform is a relatively new phenomenon, and it is difficult to note all the benefits and disadvantages that will occur under this new set of rules. Many of the claims of both proponents and critics of reform are hard to assess for two primary reasons.

First, relatively little time has elapsed since the advent of reform. Regulatory reform for the airline industry was enacted during the 1977–78 period, while reforms for trucking and railroads were passed in 1980.

The second difficulty encountered in assessing the impacts of reform stems from the economic conditions characterizing American industry during the early 1980s, when the economy was in its worst state since the Great Depression. It is ironic that the regulation of the trucking, intercity bus, and airline industries had been instituted during the Great Depression, when similar conditions prevailed.

While studies of regulatory reform have been conducted by government agencies and academics during both the recessionary and recovery periods, much of the data collected and the conclusions derived therefrom remain distorted because of these economic aberrations.

Carrier Strategies Under Regulatory Reform

The new regulatory environment has brought wide-ranging changes to many participants in the airline and air cargo industries. Overnight, the managements of such entities have switched their decision-making emphasis from the tactical to the strategic arena, from the level of service and scheduling to pricing and route planning.

At the Transportation Research Forum Conference in October 1979, and in a paper published in the *Transportation Journal*,[3] this author identified at least five criteria that would likely determine the survival of passenger airlines in the coming years. These included:

1. Strong cash position

2. Low debt/equity ratio

3. Low operating cost structure

4. Strategic marketing capability

5. Selective aggressiveness

The air freight side of the industry encountered problems similar to those afflicting passenger carriers. Many quickly adopted price discrimination strategies only to find that some of the rates set using such strategies were unremunerative. In other cases, carriers expanded so rapidly that their reliability of service deteriorated.

Air freight company strategies have differed widely in the period of regulatory reform. Some carriers, such as Tiger International, expanded rapidly, with particular attention paid to the major hub airports. With its acquisition of trucking firms, Tiger seemed to be moving towards the establishment of a multimodal transportation company. Unfortunately, Tiger International ran into severe problems with its expansion plans. Because of depressed economic conditions, traffic at the major hub airports never materialized. The multimodal concept experienced difficulties resulting from the additional costs encountered in the meshing of unionized work forces in newly acquired trucking subsidiaries, as well as in the air freight subsidiary, Flying Tiger, Inc.

Regulatory reform in the air cargo industry has also resulted in the blurring of organizational lines within the industry. Many air and surface freight forwarders have become operators of their own cargo aircraft.

Emery Worldwide, for example, has acquired a fleet of aircraft for domestic and international air cargo operations. United Parcel Service also has established a fleet of aircraft for air cargo purposes. Purolator, which has traditionally served as an intracity surface freight specialist, has started to develop an aircraft fleet to compete with Federal Express and United Parcel Service.[4]

The air freight industry has also used the pricing and service flexibility permitted under regulatory reform to emphasize the logistics concept in marketing its services. During the 1960s, many carriers marketed this concept but met resistance when they could not prove cost savings. The carriers now have access to quantitative techniques to demonstrate these cost savings. They also have launched training programs for their sales forces in order to ensure that customers will understand the logistical cost savings which result from usage of air freight.

American Airlines has launched a marketing effort to explain the role of air freight in logistical cost trade-offs. The program is targeted at the medium-size shipper. Such shippers, according to American Airlines, tend to have less knowledge about their costs than do large shippers. Hence, American's service assistance in analyzing overall logistical costs can prove valuable.

There is substantial information available regarding the preliminary stages of regulatory reform in the trucking industry. Under the 1980 MCA, the ICC must monitor the progress and the effects of regulatory reform on the trucking industry. The ICC publishes reports for public inspection regarding its findings.

According to the ICC, the 1980 Motor Carrier Act has created an opportunity for substantial new entry into the industry, as well as for the development of more cost-efficient practices. Since July 1, 1980 (the date the MCA was passed), the ICC has authorized 18,221 new trucking entities. The agency authorized 3,806 new entrants in the first six months of 1983.[5] At the same time, many corporations with private trucking fleets have used the new provisions of the act to engage in intercorporate hauling. Previously, such firms were forced to set up trucking fleets for each subsidiary they owned. As of December 1983, 960 companies, with approximately 10,580 subsidiaries, were engaged in such activities.[6]

While new entry and cost efficiencies have occurred under regulatory reform in the trucking industry, the reform legislation has created problems for many existing trucking operators. Such carriers have had to face the issues of asset redeployment, pricing, and marketing of services. These new management decisions have occurred at the same time that new carriers were discounting prices and traffic was falling because of the recent recession.

These carriers have developed a wide range of pricing and service options to compete with new and existing carriers. The first reaction of many established carriers, such as Roadway Express, Overnite Transport, and Trans Con Lines, was to slash rates drastically. Many carriers, however, have recently begun searching for other ways in which to serve customers without having to resort to price reductions.

Many carriers have started to develop strategies that emphasize intramodal coordination and various types of specialization. For example, two Michigan companies, Hoover Trucking and Parker Motor Freight, have developed pooling operations to improve efficiency and service. Hoover concentrates on pickup and delivery service, while Parker takes care of line-haul operations.[7]

Large existing carriers have carefully examined the alternative strategies that offer maximum protection against the rate-slashing tactics of new entrants. In many cases, they have concluded that less-than-truckload shipments offer growth opportunities because of the more substantial capital investment required (terminals) and the opportunities for economies of scale.[8] As a consequence, many large carriers have intensified efforts to develop their terminal networks.[9]

Trucking firms have also initiated changes in corporate strategy to deal with the new competitive environment. Consolidated Freightways is planning to acquire Air Express International, with the objective that the latter's international operations will complement Consolidated's domestic operations.[10] Ryder Truck Lines and Pacific Intermountain Express have merged in order to take advantage of single carrier service on a nationwide basis. TNT Pilot and Schuster Express have merged in order to extend the overall service area of the combined entity.[11]

Many large carriers, such as Burlington Northern, Carolina Freight Carriers Corporation, Yellow Freight System, and Preston Trucking Company, have formed holding companies. The aim of these holding companies is basically to improve the companies' returns on investment through acquisition or merger.[12]

Despite all of these efforts to compete effectively, the new environment has taken an economic toll within the trucking industry. According to the American Trucking Association, 232 ICC-regulated carriers ceased operations between mid-1980 and mid-April 1983. In addition, 68 ICC-regulated carriers are operating under Chapter 11. Many of these carriers have fallen prey to the twin problems of new competition and economic recession.

The railroad industry has received many benefits from regulatory reform. Changes in rate-making procedures have allowed the railroads to price their products more in relation to their identifiable costs. It has also facilitated pricing actions that increase the industry's ability to compete with other modes of transportation. The new pricing flexibilities are already reflected in the formulation of long- and short-term contracts with shippers and the new competition for items, such as agricultural products, that could be moved by other modes.

The administrative regulatory reform actions of the ICC and Congressional legislation have resulted in significant rate changes for intermodal services. For example, the ICC granted deregulation of rates to the carriers for trailer-on-a-flatcar (TOFC) and container-on-a-flatcar (COFC) traffic. TOPF and COFC stand for carriage of a tractor trailer or container placed on a flatcar. The railroads provide these services under several different plans, using either their own equipment or the equipment and services of a motor carrier or the shipper.

TOFC service transports trailers on the flatcar combining the efficiencies of railroad service with the flexibility of a motor carrier. The most popular TOFC plan involves the railroad providing the flatcar, trailer, and line-haul transportation, while the shipper arranges pickup and delivery.

COFC is popular for international movements, since export goods can be sealed in the container when leaving the production plant or warehouse. It is also used for "land bridge" traffic when a water carrier company substitutes land transport for ocean transportation.

Other benefits were provided by the new merger provisions of the reform legislation. There were 12 Class I railroads prior to deregulation. Mergers have reduced this number to six, creating the potential for significant marketing synergies.

These synergies have basically resulted from offering services to shippers over the full length of the system. Previously, these services were offered only by the initial carrier, and the shipper's products were often subject to the whims of a second railroad that had little concern for the originating carrier's promises.

The merger movement has spawned two other noticeable trends in the chessboard of railroad corporate strategy. Many analysts are betting that new merger partners are only waiting for full consolidation of their separate parts before embarking upon efforts to establish integrated transcontinental systems. If such predictions become reality, it would not be impossible to envision three transcontinental systems by 1990.[13]

The second trend in railroad corporate strategy is seen in efforts to form multimodal transportation companies or fully integrated physical distribution firms. Recent railroad holding company activities have included an expansion of existing trucking lines and acquisition of barge lines and warehouse operations.[14]

Shippers' Perspective of Regulatory Reform

Thus far, there has been one valid criticism of regulatory reform from the perspective of the shipper. The regulatory commissions and reform legislation passed by Congress have generally disregarded the investment in logistical systems that had been made by shippers prior to reform. Shippers had invested billions of dollars in plant locations and distribution systems based on the regulatory structure that had existed for transportation during the previous hundred years.

Regulatory reform has encouraged carriers to enter and exit various markets and to price their services on the basis of their *actual* costs. Such actions have changed the value of investments in logistical systems made by many shippers. Railroad and trucking regulatory reform, in particular, has affected the shipping patterns of thousands of shippers.

While many shippers have enjoyed substantial benefits from regulatory reform, they have expressed anxiety over future relationships with carriers. Among questions shippers are asking are the following:

1. Are the low trucking rates a permanent result of deregulation, or do they constitute merely a temporary by-product of new competition during a period of economic recession?

2. Are the new service and pricing options offered by railroads to be enjoyed only during the transitional period that has followed enactment of the Staggers Act? Will they disappear as soon as there have been a certain number of mergers resulting in railroads exerting monopoly powers?

Since "the jury is still out," the answers to these questions are unknown.

A gradual phase-in of regulatory reform would have provided time in which to address such questions. Shippers would have had a transitional period during which to reduce their investment in current plant and warehousing facilities and/or to contemplate new systems based on their anticipation of future transportation rates and services. Government agencies and academics would have had an adequate period during which to examine the issues in an unbiased fashion rather than being forced to accept them as faits accomplis.

Unfortunately, the railroad and trucking legislation contained no such provisions. The assumption that the quick introduction of competition into these industries would be beneficial to both carriers and shippers may have overlooked the circumstances of many shippers, especially those of a "captive" and smaller nature.

Shipper Strategies and Options

In order to understand the impacts of regulatory reform on shipper strategies, it is necessary to clarify the historical and changing functions of transportation administration and control, or traffic management, within an organization. This function is usually managed by an individual called the traffic manager or the director of transportation. In theory this individual has both administrative and research functions. In a company in which the distribution concept is utilized, some of these research functions are centralized in the staff of the manager in charge of the overall distribution system.

The administrative functions of the traffic manager often include the following:

- Freight classification

- Rate negotiation

- Equipment scheduling

- Documentation

- Tracing and expediting

- Auditing

- Claims

- Fleet management

The freight classification process had traditionally entailed assigning a classification to a product according to the nature of the product. The traffic manager and/or his staff would then obtain a rating for the product within the classification. The actual price of the freight movement was determined by the rating and the distance over which the product would be moved.

Since deregulation, however, the traffic manager has had to devote increasing amounts of time to rate negotiations with carriers. In the new regulatory environment, traffic management not only seeks to negotiate short-term rates with carriers for its own freight, but must also constantly monitor agreements being made between carriers and the company's competitors.

In essence, the primary function of the traffic manager in the rate area has changed from tariff interpretation and a preoccupation with regulatory affairs to the point where today he functions as a highly specialized purchasing agent for the distribution system.

The new regulatory environment has created exciting possibilities for the enterprising traffic manager. Today he is able to acquire the service standards he requires at negotiable prices. Service options include premium service, reduced service levels, and shipper loading and unloading. Price options include volume rates and introductory discounts, among a host of others. This new flexibility, however, increases the need for the traffic manager to recognize fully the demands of his company's distribution system and to purchase the precise standards of transportation services needed.

Traffic managers are coping with the complexity of this new environment by negotiating company-specific agreements with carriers. For example, Section 208 of the Staggers Rail Act officially allowed railroads and shippers to develop contracts covering rates and conditions of service. Varying in duration between a couple of months and several years, these contracts contain discount or fixed rates for minimum tonnage, as well as pickup and delivery, storage, car utilization, and mileage options. The Association of American Railroads predicts that eventually over one-third of all rail traffic will move under such agreements.

However, the nature of the rules governing rail contracts demonstrates the dilemma facing the traffic manager. The ICC approval process requires only the submission of a public tariff summary, together with a more detailed confidential version. The public tariff contains so little information as to be useless for gauging the competitive environment. While such vehicles offer opportunities for significant cost savings, the potential savings are often difficult to establish.

This new environment dictates that traffic managers understand the "search" process inherent in consumer and industrial buyer behavior. Besides reviewing rate and service proposals submitted by carriers, traffic managers have also recently started to solicit carrier proposals by advertising for carrier "bids" on proposed movements.

The traffic manager is also responsible for other functions that may result in cost savings. He is responsible for scheduling equipment and services with common carriers or with the firm's own trucking fleet. The scheduling responsibility includes trying to eliminate any type of special charges associated with pickup or unloading of freight. This effort usually includes the reduction of demurrage charges, which occur when rail cars or trucking rigs are detained for longer periods of time than are normally granted by carriers to shippers.

The traffic manager must also ensure the proper preparation of bills of lading and freight bills. Other functions include tracing and expediting, auditing of freight bills, and claims.

The auditing of freight bills is often performed by outside auditors, who audit the bills, arrange for refunds, and divide the refunds on a 50-50 basis with the company's traffic management department. If no overcharges are uncovered, the auditing firm does not charge for its services. This service often provides cost savings for a medium-size company that has inadequate manpower to conduct its own audits.

The traffic manager also has a research obligation. Basically, his research function involves two areas of concern. He must monitor the performance of carriers, as well as the trends in rates. Of primary interest is the degree of consistency in transportation services provided by carriers.

Various studies have indicated that traffic managers place greater emphasis on achieving consistency of delivery times to plants, warehouses, and customers than on small differences in rates. Inconsistency in transit services creates strains in the logistics pipeline. The costs of these inconsistencies may result in lost customers and, hence, render differences in transportation costs of little importance.

Another duty of the traffic manager is to conduct research into loss and damage claims. Certain carriers may, for example, display a record of damage to or loss of their clients' shipments. While such losses are covered by the carrier's liability insurance, the claims consume time, interrupt the logistics pipeline, and create ill-will among customers. A proper monitoring system often avoids such problems.

Research can also prove valuable in monitoring rate trends for shippers. The fundamental question for the traffic manager to ask himself is: Given our customer service objectives, is my company getting cheaper transportation rates than my competitors are getting?

Many traffic managers have sought to maximize the efficiency of their operations by computerizing carrier rates. While such rate data require constant updating because of frequent rate changes associated with regulatory reform, computerized rate systems for repetitive and routine transportation purchases seem to ensure that the firm gets the best rate for its transportation needs.

An additional area of responsibility for the traffic or transportation manger is private fleet management. In the days of economic regulation, the justification for a company's operating its own fleet was fairly easy to identify. Since common carrier rates were relatively stable, the traffic manager could calculate the fleet's overall cost and compare it with the cost that would be incurred using a common or contract carrier service. The private fleet could also be justified in terms of the higher quality of customer service that was possible.

Unfortunately, the great fluctuation in carrier rates since regulatory reform has complicated the traditional "make or buy" decision. Under budgetary pressures during the recent economic recession, many traffic managers have curtailed private fleet operations and are taking advantage of falling common and contract carriage trucking rates.

This latter strategy is somewhat suspect from a long-term perspective. Trucking rates have been depressed because of the new competitive environment and recent economic recession. Bankruptcy and limited bank credit have curtailed modernization and capital reequipment programs. As the economy has rebounded from the recession, rates have increased to reflect the limited supply of trucking services. Traffic management without long-term contracts at depressed rates will likely face increasing transportation costs.

Traffic management in a small company is often supervised by a manager with a limited staff and many other responsibilities. Such managers require alternatives to the traditional traffic management concept. Shippers' associations provide one such alternative worth considering.

Shippers' associations offer the small shipper an opportunity to obtain cheaper rates and better service. The purpose of the associations is to consolidate small shippers' goods into truckload, carload, or containerload shipments. Such shipments receive considerably lower rates than could be obtained by any one small shipper acting alone. The associations basically act as forwarders. Shippers' associations primarily consolidate outbound shipments, although some also perform inbound service. Many perform pickup and delivery, as well as operate terminals for consolidating the freight.

Since shippers' associations are non-profit organizations, any profits are redistributed to members at the end of specified periods. New members are charged entrance or initiation fees.

The small shipper is also flexing his muscles at the national level in an effort to enjoy some of the benefits that large shippers are receiving from regulatory reform. The National Small Shippers' Traffic Conference has recently gotten permission to form a shippers' council that is designed to give small shippers some combined leverage in acquiring better rates for themselves.[15]

Conclusions

This chapter has described the historical evolution of transportation regulation and its consequences, as well as the causes, nature, and impacts of regulatory reform. The recent changes in the transportation field have created great opportunities for shippers in terms of the cost savings that can be realized and in terms of their ability to purchase transportation services that are customized to meet their own special needs. In essence, more change has occurred in the carrier–shipper relationship in the past five years than occurred during the previous hundred years. In reality, the options available to the distribution management of a company are no longer precluded by a regulatory umbrella, but instead seem to be largely a function of the imagination, knowledge, and persuasive power of the distribution manager.

Notes

1. George C. Eads, "Railroad Diversification: Where Lies the Public Interest?" *Bell Journal of Economics and Management Science*, Autumn 1974, pp. 595–613.

2. Ibid.

3. Lawrence F. Cunningham and Wallace W. Wood, "Diversification in Major U.S. Airlines," *Transportation Journal*, Quarterly Journal of the American Society of Transportation and Logistics, Spring 1983.

4. Joan Feldman, "A Robust Year for Air Freight Lies Ahead," *Handling and Shipping Management*, January 1984, pp. 30–33.

5. Statement of Reese H. Taylor, Jr., Chairman, Interstate Commerce Commission, before the Senate Committee on Commerce, Science and Transportation, on implementation of the Motor Carrier Act of 1980, on September 21, 1983.

6. Ibid.

7. "Highlights of Activity in the Property Motor Carrier Industry," Staff Report No. 9, Office of Transportation Analysis, Interstate Commerce Commission, July 1983, p. 6.

8. Ibid., p. 7.

9. Ibid., p. 11.

10. Ibid., p. 8.

11. Ibid., p. 9.

12. Ibid., p. 10.

13. Perry A. Trunick, "Rail's Future Requires Oversight and Insight," *Handling and Shipping Management*, January 1984, pp. 26–29.

14. Ibid.

15. Dave Russ, "Shifting into High Gear," *Handling and Shipping Management*, January 1984, pp. 23–24.

Managing Transportation Productivity

JOHN KREITNER

Introduction

The purpose of this chapter is to help the reader plan and execute an improvement in the productivity of the expenditure for freight transportation.

Transportation—the most costly physical distribution (PD) function—seems to many the hardest function to manage. Yet much of the productivity improvement possible for all PD must come out of freight expense. How will this be done? First, by recognizing that this expense is very reactive to factors such as inventory position, customer service priorities, manufacturing schedules, and field stock location configurations. Then by adopting cost and productivity controls that will reveal to PD managers the impact of their options on transportation. Finally by adopting specifications for management of the transportation function.

This chapter is organized into two sections: (1) management of productivity of purchased and internally produced (private) transportation, and (2) evaluative criteria for an industrial traffic management operation.

Sizing Up Productivity Opportunities

Both the cost and benefit of pursuing improved productivity in transportation will vary greatly from business to business. When faced with setting up programs to improve or measure transportation productivity, one should consider the several factors shown in Table 21–1. In general, productivity efforts will be most rewarding for businesses and operations on the *left* end of the ranges shown. For businesses at the *right* end, cost/benefit expectations should be reviewed carefully before committing to programs as complex and expensive as those appropriate for those at the left.

Purchased versus Private Transportation

The productivity of the expenditure for freight transportation can be controlled in two ways, depending on whether the transportation is purchased from external carriers or produced within a business for its own use. When transportation is purchased, productivity of the buyer's expense dollar can be controlled by managing transportation *quantity*, *mix*, and *price*. The productivity of transportation produced by a business for itself can be controlled by managing *input factors* such as labor, vehicles, and fuel.

Purchased Transportation

Managing the productivity of purchased transportation—frequently the dominant element of total transportation—is an exercise not readily distinguishable from managing transportation cost (Figure 21–1).

There is a discoverable set of opportunities for improving transportation cost which can be identified by comparing a given transportation management operation with the attributes contained in the "Transportation Base Line" (see pages 532–539). To the extent that an actual operation's practices do not meet the base line's relevant attributes, opportunity to improve productivity may exist.

Measuring Productivity

Inputs and Outputs

When transportation is purchased from sources external to a business, the buyer's key input is money, and the key output is the movement of the buyer's materials to locations where they can be used or sold. The transportation buyer cannot do much to control the productivity of the factors used by the seller to produce the transportation (fuel, labor, vehicles), but he can control how he spends his dollars with the various suppliers that sell him transportation. Specifically, the buyer has some control over the following cost factors:

- *Quantity*: The ton-miles (i.e., weight × distance/2000) purchased from carriers during a period

- *Mix*: The distribution of these ton-miles to the variously priced methods of delivery

- *Price*: The freight rate paid a carrier for a particular method of delivery

If the buyer purchases less, gets along with minimum adequate mix, and negotiates prices downward, then the average dollar paid to the sellers will produce better results, i.e., will move more goods to a point of utility.

Table 21-1   A Transportation Productivity Opportunity Screen

Factor	Range	
	Left	*Right*
Output of business or operation	Standard products	Services
Transportation cost:	Over:	Under:
Relative to sales	2%	2%
Absolute	$1 million	$1 million
Site cost	$250 thousand	$250 thousand
Transportation terms of sale:		
Freight is	Absorbed	Passed on
Typical customer shipment size	100–5000 lbs.	Packages, full loads
Product shape	Constant	Variable
Products made	For stock	To order
Product destinations	Stable	Erratic
Transportation methods	Standard for line	Fitted to each order
Delivery lead time	Days	Hours, months
Field location rationale	Cost efficiency	Proximity, presence

Present State of Control

Because of the generally unsophisticated transportation cost reporting systems now in use, many managements must be content if annual transportation cost as a percentage of sales does not increase from year to year (the same statistic for shorter periods is frequently unreliable). A *few* reporting systems make rudimentary distinctions about *mix* by segmenting costs by transportation mode (rail, truck, air).

Even fewer systems segregate costs by city-pairs so that geographical segments can be inspected and compared. In general, prevailing systems are of limited use in controlling transportation quantity, mix, or price. Consequently, managements behave as if freight is uncontrollable, governed largely by external causes (customers, carriers, inflation, etc.). Managements often do have cost reduction projects in place, but results are usually measured by those responsible for the project and not confirmed by the financial reporting system. In a nutshell, effective transportation cost reporting—let alone productivity control—is an area of unexploited opportunity in the typical business.

Heads = Cost

Tails = Productivity

Figure 21-1   Manage the Cost of Purchased Transportation to Manage its Productivity

Improving Control

When buying transportation, the first consideration is *service*. Businesses aim to buy the minimum level of transportation service that will satisfy their customers and their other needs. With service determined, be it air freight or piggyback service, the next consideration is *price*. Managements want to pay the minimum price for the service selected.

There is not much obvious about the level of price (freight rate) for a given shipment, because it is stated usually as so much per hundredweight between the origin and destination with no mention of the intervening distance (Table 21–2). A price cannot be evaluated without relating it to some standard unit of transportation "work" that a carrier performs in return for the price. If there were a standard unit of work, managements could compare a carrier's price with other prices for the same service, and once identified, they could attempt to negotiate any high prices downward, or they might rethink the decision on service quality. Conclusion: the ratio of *price* to *work unit* is vital to the control process; however, it does require a standard measure of the quantity of transportation work purchased.

Quantifying Transportation Work

Frequently managements fail to recognize and exert control over the higher prices they pay for transportation because calculating transportation work is not a common capability of their information systems. Existing transportation statistics quantify transportation work by focusing on units of product or weight shipped. Neither units nor weight recognizes an essential element of transportation: distance. Just as manufacturing changes the form of goods to make them useful, transportation changes their location. To ignore distance is to pretend that all customers are permanently sited at some imaginary average location, a pretense especially invalid for a business dealing with a changing set of customer locations. Relatively few businesses even bother to segregate costs by high-volume origin-destination city-pairs to avoid the one-customer-location pretense, a valid approach when avenues of flow are limited in number and fairly stable.

Ton-Miles and Ton-Miles Per Dollar

The best single measure of transportation work is ton-miles (TM). These are readily calculable from the shipping weight and the distance taken from printed and computerized tables of standard distances between the origin and destination ZIP codes shown in freight bills. Obviously, the time to record TMs is when a freight bill is paid and the cost booked to a freight account. Then the cost reporting system can show the price paid for a unit of transportation work, i.e., transportation cost per ton-mile, or \$T/TM. Inverting this ratio gives the key productivity measurement, TM/\$T—or how many weight-distance units were achieved per dollar. (Readers concerned with shipping light, bulky goods that use up vehicle space capacity before weight capacity may consider substituting cube-miles for ton-miles; however, this will entail recording the dimensions of every piece shipped.)

Table 21-2 Specimen of a Transportation Price (Freight Rate) Published by The Middlewest Motor Freight Bureau on Behalf of its Member Carriers (Based on Tariff MWB 215-B)

Rates in Cents per 100 Pounds, Except as Otherwise Provided

Item	Commodity (See Item 500)	From (and points taking same rates as provided in Items 150 thru 250)	To	Rate (See Item 102)	Min. Wt. (In lbs)
18640 (Con-cluded)	ELECTRICAL EQUIPMENT GROUP, VIZ.: Motors, electric or Parts thereof, NOI. (18640)	Ft. Wayne...IN Tiffin......OH Tipp City...OH Tyler......TX	Tyler........TX Tyler........TX Little Rock...AR Ft. Wayne ...IN	380 383 277 380	30,000

"Ton-miles" are calculated by multiplying a weight in pounds by the miles separating origin and destination of a shipment, then dividing the result by 2000. Take, for example, a 5500 pound shipment from Schenectady to Dallas, which are 1625 miles apart:

$$5500 \times 1625/2000 = 4468 \text{ ton-miles}$$

Questions can arise about this straightforward process:

Q: Which weight on a freight bill is to be used?

A: The *actual* weight, not a greater "billed" weight that might have been shown for the purpose of getting a lower rate.

Q: Depending on transportation mode and route, several different distances might be experienced on shipments between the same two cities; which of these is to be used?

A: A "standard" mileage should be used for all modes and routes connecting a pair of cities, so that comparisons will be based upon a consistent approach to distance calculation.

Q: Where can standard mileages be obtained?

A: If trucking is the dominant transportation mode, it is best to obtain mileages from the *Household Goods Carriers' Bureau Mileage Guide*, a trucking industry standard of sorts.

Q: Are mileages between all pairs of points shown in the *Guide*?

A: A matrix of distances between 1100 "key points" can be used in connection with maps to construct a distance between any two points in most of the United States, Canada, and Mexico. However, it is suggested that just the matrix mileages between the key points best representing the actual origin and destinations will suffice for intercity standard mileages

Q: Can this matrix be obtained in computer file form?

A: Yes, files are available that can be accessed by origin and destination ZIP codes, meaning that if the ZIPs are known, the distance between them can be produced by computer.

Q: What about intracity distances for which no mileage may be shown?

A: Use a ruler and the distance scale on a local map to determine mileage to each local customer location just once; carry this information thereafter in the Order-Ship-Bill data base for display in documents (e.g., the bill of lading) that are present when TMs and transportation cost are recorded. Or adopt a standard trip length for shipments within a three-digit ZIP area.

Some distinctions must be observed in applying this cost/productivity control measure, distinctions concerning *mix* and *scale*. Considering mix first, TM/$T is a valid measure of productivity of each carrier's price, but businesses normally use a mixture of carriers and special services, depending upon product line, length of haul, lot size, and time requirements. Naturally, one would not expect the same TM/$T on shipments via truck and air freight. It follows that users of cost data cannot judge a period cost without knowing the *mix* of services it is for. Therefore, both TMs and $T must be placed in different reporting "buckets" according to class of service (see Figure 21–2).

Class of service refers to a method of shipping from which a unique service or cost level is expected. The most popular classes are:

Water (W)	Transportation via water, including charges for any related overland movement paid to a water carrier.
Carload (C)	A shipment subject to a carload rate and minimum quantity loaded in or on a railroad car.
Bulk (B)	A shipment that requires a tank or dry-bulk vehicle.
Piggyback (P)	Transportation at vehicle-load rates in trailers or trailer bodies on special rail cars. Rates are less for additional loads and more for door-to-door service. Subdividing this class may be desirable.
Truckload (T)	A shipment by motor carrier in a quantity sufficient for application of a truckload rate.
Stop-off (S)	Unlike the foregoing classes, which normally involve one consignee per shipment, stop-off refers to peddling consignments off an initially full truckload to two or more consignees along a fairly straight route. For each drop, the truckload rate to the farthest point plus a stopping charge of around $50 is assessed.
Less-than-truckload (L)	A shipment by motor carrier, freight forwarder, or shippers' association insufficient in quantity for the application of a truckload rate. A flat minimum charge or one of several rates that diminish with rising quantity is assessed.

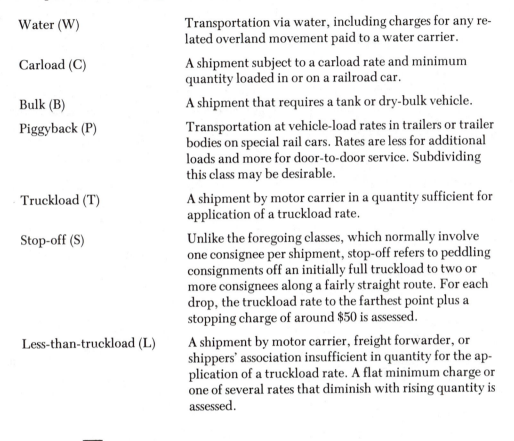

Distance (miles) that one ton can be shipped for $100

Figure 21-2   Transportation—Productivity of a Dollar Paid to an External Carrier

Air (A)   Transportation via air, including any charges for related surface movement paid to an air carrier.

The use of TMs to measure transportation productivity raises one additional difficulty: "phantom" changes in productivity due to changes in shipment scale. It has been noted by Wyckoff of Harvard that changes in scale (e.g., average shipment weight, average length of haul) affect carrier TM cost. Transportation buyers see this reflected in lower prices for heavier and more distant shipments.[1]

Information systems that employ TMs as a unit of transportation quantity should (and easily can) produce statistics on shipment scale, so that phantom changes in TM/$T will not be mistaken for real productivity changes.

In summary, the productivity of purchased transportation for a given class of service is measured best by the ratio TM/$T, i.e., the ton-miles produced by a dollar expenditure. Aggregate TM/$T must be interpreted in the light of distinctions of transportation quality (sometimes called "value of service") and scale. The most important of these distinctions are:

1. Transportation quality factors

   - What is moved
     - Handling characteristics
     - Care required, etc.
     - Expected level of loss, damage
   - Where moved
   - Attendant services
   - Speed
   - Reliability
   - Safety (physical)
   - Trade-off impact on other functions

2. Transportation scale factors

   - Ratio of partial to full loads
   - Average length of haul
   - Average weight of partial loads

Reporting Systems

Criteria

Several design criteria for a transportation productivity reporting system can be suggested.

1. Transportation productivity cannot be controlled without controlling transportation cost, so there should be an integrated reporting system that deals with both as one.

2. The finance function should be responsible for collecting data and issuing reports; this will increase the probability that the data will be collected reliably and pro-

cessed efficiently, that those measuring will be independent from those being measured, and that reports will be perceived as legitimate.

3. Report formats should be designed so as to reveal changes in period transportation cost, both absolute and relative to output volume.

4. Designs should contain features that explain changes in absolute and relative cost, i.e., diagnostics such as ton-miles, cost per ton-mile, class of service mix, geographic mix, product mix, average shipment size, etc.

5. The cost and burden of data collection routines should be acceptable.

6. A hierarchy of reports and their timing should lead to useful management behavior with respect to managing transportation cost and productivity.

A Model Transportation Budgeting and Reporting System

The system described below was designed in recognition that managing the productivity of purchased transportation should focus on mix and price. Mix is managed by keeping average shipment high and by avoiding premium-priced carriers. Price is managed by negotiating with carriers for lower rates. Getting low prices is the responsibility of the traffic managers; achieving a favorable mix is the responsibility of the entire business and is accomplished organizationally upstream from the shipping door, a reality that must be reflected in the design and distribution of transportation reports.

Budgets are developed, as shown in Table 21–3, by applying mix and price bogies to planned activity levels. It may be necessary to defer the first budget on this model until the associated new reporting system has revealed the present levels of quantity (volume), price and mix. With these data in hand, sales volume and transportation price change forecasts can be used to determine budgets for the ensuing period. The reporting system to be described next will provide the actual performance of each division, product line, operating location, channel of distribution, and marketing region for which a sub-budget is prepared. The system will also support budgeting for incoming transportation, broken down by division, receiving location, key feedstock, etc.

Table 21–3   Sample Transportation Budget

June, 19____

(Expected volume: 7 million ton-miles)

Class of Service	Planned Mix (%)	Ton-Miles (Volume × Mix %)	Planned Cost/TM	Budgeted Transp. Cost
Carload	.20	1,400,000	.07	$ 98,000
Piggyback	.15	1,050,000	.08	84,000
Truckload	.40	2,800,000	.09	252,000
Stop-off	.12	840,000	.11	92,400
LTL	.127	889,000	.40	355,600
Air	.003	21,000	4.00	84,000
Total		7,000,000		$966,000

Reporting actual performance against a budget that quantifies volume in ton-miles and focuses on mix and price will require that the freight bill payment system be upgraded. The system must produce new statistics and must separate activity in a new breakdown by responsibility center. Table 21–4 depicts the general structure of the reports required for a company having multiple divisions and locations. The strategy is to show each report reader the cost and activity levels that concern him, supplemented by several statistics that explain trends and suggest who might do what to improve those trends in future periods. The statistics presented in columns 1 through 12 are listed here:

1. Class of service percentage
   Reflects mix of high price, low price and penalty types of transit

2. Ton-miles (or cube-miles)
   Measure of period transportation "work"

3. Expense/Ton-mile
   Pure price of transportation

4. Freight expense
   Measure of period transportation expense

5. Number of shipments
   Transactions on shipment level

6. Number of lots
   Transactions on sub-shipment level

7. Weight shipped
   Measure of period volume

8. Average shipment weight
   Reflects whether releases are consolidated

9. Average lot weight
   Reflects release lot size trend

10. Pounds/cubic foot (optional)
    Measure of density

11. Expense/cwt
    Material unit costs of transportation

Table 21–4   Transportation Report Structure

Data Arrangements	Statistics 1 through 12											
Period	n	n	n	n	n	n	n	n	n	n	n	n
Division	n	n	n	n	n	n	n	n	n	n	n	n
Cost center (manufacturing, distribution)	n	n	n	n	n	n	n	n	n	n	n	n
Product or commodity	n	n	n	n	n	n	n	n	n	n	n	n
Operating location	n	n	n	n	n	n	n	n	n	n	n	n
Customer or supplier location	n	n	n	n	n	n	n	n	n	n	n	n
Stage of distribution	n	n	n	n.	n	n	n	n	n	n	n	n
Shipment size	n	n	n	n	n	n	n	n	n	n	n	n

12. Expense/cubic foot (optional)
    Material unit costs of transportation

The following list describes a set of ten data arrangements that constitute a uniform reporting package for a large company made up of many businesses involved with multiple operating locations, products, stages of distribution, stock location networks, and freight payment sites. Not every business needs every report: a one-product business does not need the report that presents statistics on each product line, so it is discarded or not produced. Monthly and year-to-date information is reported on inbound, outbound, and third-party shipments. Seven *cost* reports contain the statistics in the list above, revealing the cost level and nature of the period's activity for each of the various data arrangements. The cost reports are backed up by two *traffic* reports showing detail at the individual shipment level, to support the search for ways to improve cost levels. Finally, analysts are provided with a *shipment profile* report that enables them to hone in on the shipment sizes in the product and supply markets that should receive attention first.

Seven Cost Reports. Period and year-to-date transactions summarized by:

1. Division
   Manufacturing cost center (MCC)
   Distribution cost center (DCC)

2. Division
   DCC product line
   MCC commodity category

3. Division
   DCC shipping point (plant, distribution center, reforwarding point)

4. Division
   DCC shipping point
       Product
   MCC receiving point
       Commodity

5. Division
   DCC market territory
       Market area
       Shipping point

6. Division
   MCC receiving point
       Sourcing territory
       Sourcing area

7. Division
   DCC market territory
   MCC sourcing territory

Two Traffic Reports. Period individual transactions listed by:

8. Division
   DCC origin (plant, warehouse)

          Destination state or territory
          Destination area
          Fiscal week
          Date
     MCC destination (plant, warehouse)
          Origin state or territory
          Origin area
          Fiscal week
          Date

9. Site (for multi-divisional sites)
     DCC origin (plant, warehouse)
          Destination state or territory
          Destination area
          Fiscal week
          Date
     MCC destination (plant, division warehouse)
          Origin state or territory
          Origin area
          Fiscal week
          Date
          Division

One Shipment Profile Report. Period and year-to-date transactions summarized by:

10. Division

     MCC sourcing territory
          Weight group

     DCC market territory
          Weight group

Three years' experience with such a system indicates that it will cost around $25,000 to install (much less for a single-business company) and will add 25¢ to 35¢ per freight bill to the cost of operating a payment system that does not produce management information for control of transportation cost/productivity. For companies that prefer not to undertake the system development task, there are contractors that can provide a payment and reporting package at a lower start-up cost.

Difficulties with Transportation Cost Reporting

For goods that move through a multi-stage distribution system (e.g., through a field warehouse), the transportation cost formats suggested above make no provision for reporting a total (i.e., "landed" or "through") cost of transporting each shipment from factory to customer. Some readers may feel that this is a shortcoming that will prevent accurate matching of revenues with the costs incurred to obtain those revenues, but transportation is a function where cost-revenue matching for control purposes has its limitations.

It is true that controlling transportation cost against related sales revenue has great popular appeal in both transportation and financial management. Specifically, it is felt that the total transportation expense it takes to land product in the marketplace should be compared with the sales revenue derived from each sale; if the ratio of transportation to sales dollars ($T/$S) is small enough, management would be satisfied that cost was under control. Management might even settle for comparing $T/$S for a period aggregation of orders with a standard or at least with its historical counterpart. Unfortunately, great difficulty is encountered with this approach at levels of detail useful for deciding upon a specific course of action to restore an acceptable product-price transportation-cost relationship. Frequently, $T/$S is available for the entire business or a major product line for one year, but rarely is management informed of the true $T/$S for Product X during April on sales to Customer Y located at Z, which is what is needed to evaluate delivery cost performance. The familiar danger is one of drowning in a river averaging one foot deep. And the problem is easier to recognize than to deal with, because transportation cost flows have some idiosyncrasies that obstruct usefully segmented cost-revenue matching.

First, because of the esoteric nature of carrier price schedules, the transportation charges and adjustments that will be incurred are usually unknown when a shipment is dispatched and billed to a customer. Therefore, an accurately predicted transportation cost rarely gets captured by order-ship-bill systems, which eliminates the opportunity to report how much of each order's margin is lost to delivery expense.

Second, it is no easier to match freight to revenue at the period level than at the order level, because freight payment lags behind shipping transaction in two ways: (1) freight expenses are not known for three to four weeks subsequent to shipment, and (2) freight for part of the journey to the customer, i.e., to a field warehouse or breakbulk point, may be paid within a range of a year before to a few days after the date of the customer shipment. It is, therefore, usually unworkable to match total freight expenses to the associated customer billings on a (short) period basis.

In the case of certain very simple distribution systems (one factory, one product line, one delivery channel, etc.) it might be feasible to attempt cost-revenue matching by:

1. Focusing on customer consignments only, burdened with a fair allocation of expense incurred for a prior movement, e.g., to a stocking or breakbulk point. (A first-in, first-out—FIFO—strategy of recognizing inbound freight expense could help get around the problems encountered during inventory build-ups or depletions.)

2. Recognizing only those transactions on which freight had been paid, i.e., making no attempt to match period revenues reported for income determination with period freight payments, since the sets of transactions differ.

In businesses with more complex distribution systems, linking inbound (to distribution centers) and outbound transportation expenses at the level of the outbound shipment for the purpose of investigating $T/$S at the segment level cannot be accomplished without dealing with several complications:

Mix of sources	Combination outbound of stock and reforwarded shipments
Mix of products	
Mix of inbound modes, public and private	FIFO inbound burden on stock shipments
Mix of inbound shipment sizes	LIFO inbound burden on reforwardings

Perhaps it is beyond the scope of cost reporting systems to reveal a true landed cost of product at customer or even market city levels for comparison with revenue or with cost standards. This may be more properly a role for modeling, e.g., distribution simulation (Figure 21-3), wherein the complications listed above may be overcome by making simplifying assumptions about the inbound mixtures of conditions. In other words, one might use modeling to plan least-cost distribution flows to market segments and accounting at a higher level of detail (e.g., business or distribution center) to measure results.

Internally Produced Transportation

The previous subsection focused on improving and controlling the productivity of transportation dollars paid to external carriers. This section focuses on improving and controlling the productivity of inputs such as labor, vehicles, and fuel used by a business to produce transportation for its own use or for sale to another business.

The point was made that managing the productivity of *purchased* transportation boils down to managing quantity, mix, and price, since these factors determine the purchaser's cost. It was maintained that there is little that a purchaser can do directly about the producer's cost, since the purchaser doesn't manage the use of the producer's inputs. However, when a business goes into private trucking, it becomes a producer and thereby is afforded an opportunity to manage the productivity of the basic inputs. After the following discussion of management of fleet cost and productivity, several suggestions on how to improve fleet productivity will be offered.

Fleet Cost and Productivity Management

Management faces three interrelated issues involving the operating costs of proposed or existing private fleets:

1. Is operating its own fleet more attractive than buying the service from external (e.g., contract) carriers?

2. Once in operation, how will management remain informed about the current levels of the operating cost that were involved in the decision to operate a fleet?

3. Faced with increasing input prices and with a plethora of operating and equipment alternatives, including discontinuance, what are the appropriate productivity measurements for improving or preserving the initial cost level at which private trucking was entered?

These issues suggest that once the fleet is initiated on a sound financial basis, management needs *cost measurement* to know what costs are, and *productivity measurements* to do something about them. The two tasks should be accomplished by one system that employs consistent definitions of inputs (natural costs) and functional distinctions (e.g., local versus over-the-road). Otherwise, management will be trying to improve the cost of apples with productivity data on oranges. In the remainder of this section, an integrated set of cost and productivity measurements is described.

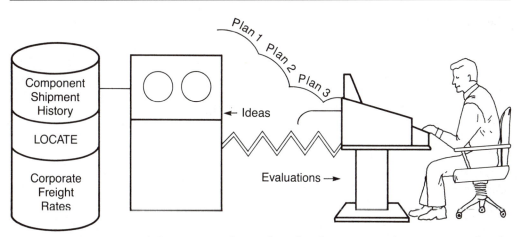

Figure 21-3 Evaluating Delivery Networks. Product distribution networks are systems of pathways from factories to customers consisting of finished goods warehouses, shipment reforwarding locations, and transportation lines. Many businesses have not adequately investigated their networks, even though large cost reductions can be obtained by changing the number, location, and served territories of a business's distribution points. Reason: evaluating one scenario can involve millions of freight calculations. Now, however, LOCATE, a distribution cost simulation in time-sharing mode, is available for medium large businesses. This analysis could produce a plan for reducing transportation cost 5 to 10 percent in some businesses.

Recommended Chart of Cost Accounts

Table 21-5 contains the structure of accounts preferred by the author for truck fleet cost reporting. As a condensation of the structure prescribed by the Interstate Commerce Commission (ICC) for large motor common carriers, its advantages are that (1) several of the user's unit costs can be compared with those published for public carriers, and (2) the ICC's extensive cost account definitions may be adopted for internal use.

Productivity Measurements

With an adequate chart of accounts and supporting definitions identified, how to measure productivity of key inputs can be addressed. Key inputs are the ones used intensively in the dominant activities (functions) making up the fleet operation. Table 21-6 indicates the relative importance of the dominant activities by showing the percentage of operating cost for contract carriers attributable during 1981 to the activities identified in the recommended chart of accounts presented in Table 21-5. (Of the various types of for-hire carriers reporting to the ICC, contract carriers may be the type most similar to private fleets with respect to costs and operations.)

Table 21-6 suggests that attempts to control overall fleet productivity must center on the linehaul activity. This is obviously true for private fleets that handle mostly full loads (thereby avoiding pickup, delivery, and platform expenses), that also lease vehicles at a price that includes maintenance. However, certain other private fleets incur pickup and delivery, platform, and maintenance expense amounting to in excess of 10 percent each of total operating cost; therefore, productivity measures will be suggested for those activities also, to be used when appropriate.

Table 21-5   Recommended Chart of Accounts

Natural Classification	(0) Total	(1) LH	(2) PUD	(4) Platform	(3,5-9) Other
		ICC Activity Group Numbers *			
		Productivity Measurement Nos.			
Employee Compensation		1,2	8,9	10,11	13
Base salaries, wages					
Overtime					
Benefits					
Contract Help		1,2	8,9	10,11	13
Total					
Vehicles					
Depreciation		5,6,7	6,7		
Rentals/leases		5,6,7	6,7		
Road taxes, licenses, registrations					
Insurance & Uninsured Losses:					
Public liability, property damage					
Fire, theft & collision					
Fuel		3,4	3		
Oil, lubricants, coolants					
Tires, tubes					
Vehicle maintenance		12	12		
Own labor					
Own material					
Purchased maintenance					
All other					
Total					
Other Expenses					
Cargo insurance & uninsured losses					
Travel & living					
Road tolls					
General supplies & expenses					
Total					
Support					
Facilities & equipment					
Communications, utilities, other					
Total					
Purchased Transportation					

*From Title 49, Part 1207 Code of Federal Regulations

LH = Linehaul
PUD = Pickup & Delivery

Returning to Table 21-5, the numbers 1 through 13 shown at the intersections of Natural Classification and Activities identify the measurements recommended for gauging period productivity. Measurements 1 to 13 are decoded in the left-hand column of Table 21-7. In general, an increase in the value of a numerator relative to its denominator means improvement in productivity that should affect the corresponding cost account. The right-hand column indicates how backup data on workers and vehicles might be segregated to facilitate improvement of a ratio.

Table 21-6   Contract Carrier Operating Costs by Major Activity (Function)*

Activity	Percentage Total Cost
Linehaul	84.6
Pickup/delivery	1.6
Platform	.4
Maintenance	2.4
Indirect, other	11.0
Total	100.0

*Findings based on 236 carriers.
SOURCE: *Trinc's Blue Book of the Trucking Industry* (1982 ed.), published annually by Trinc Transportation Consultants, Suite 4200, 475 L'Enfant Plaza, S.W., Washington, D.C. 20024.

Opportunity to improve a ratio can be assessed to some extent by considering the standard deviation (SD) of values that make up each simple productivity average. For example, for a fleet that averages five miles per gallon, the greater the standard deviation for values among tractors, the more optimistic management would be about replacing the bad performers and thereby improving average performance. In other words, variability may be taken to be an indicator of opportunity. And when the desire is to compare the level of variation between reporting periods or between fleets possessing quite different means, then the coefficients of variation (SD/mean) can serve as measures of variation relative to associated means. That is, coefficients of variation can be used to see how one fleet or period stacks up against another; the greater the value, the greater the potential for improvement.

The sources of information for the measurements presented in Table 21-7 are shown below.

Table 21-7   Proposed Measures of Private Trucking Productivity & Opportunity

Productivity Measures. Simple Average for Fleet	Opportunity Measures. Standard Deviation Based On
1. Miles per road driver hour worked	Driver ID
2. Ton-miles per road driver hour worked	Driver ID
3. Miles per gallon fuel	Vehicle ID
4. Ton-miles per gallon fuel	Vehicle ID
5. Ton-miles per driven vehicle	Vehicle ID
6. Miles per driven vehicle	Vehicle ID
7. Miles per trailer (calendar) day	Trailer ID
8. Customer stops per local driver hour	Driver ID
9. Weight handled per local driver hour	Driver ID
10. Shipments handled per platform employee hour	Work date
11. Weight handled per platform employee hour	Work date
12. Fleet miles per maintenance employee hour	Period
13. Fleet transactions per (other indirect) employee hour	Work date

Adapted from D. Daryl Wyckoff, "Issues of Productivity," distributed by the Regular Common Carrier Conference, 1616 P Street, Washington, D.C.; this is a series of reprints of articles that originally appeared in *Traffic World* between September 1972 and February 1973.

Measurement No.	Source of Information
1–7	"Miles" are those obtained from tractor odometers and trailer hubometers.
1,2,8–13	"Hours" are hours worked and paid for.
2,4,5,9,11	"Tons" and "weight" refer to the actual weight of shipments, equivalent to the bill of lading actual weight on a common carrier shipment.
2,4,5	"Ton-miles" are obtained by multiplying tons carried by the odometer distance the weight was carried.
3,4	"Gallons" are those consumed on a trip or during a time period begun with full tanks and completed with a "topping off" of the tanks.
7	Monthly or quarterly readings; days are calendar days.
9,11	Use the weight actually handled by the employees to which the measurement refers. If a local driver loaded and unloaded his vehicle, the weight counts twice. If the night shift loaded and he unloaded, "platform" and "local" each get credit once. If the night shift loaded and the customer unloaded, "local" receives no weight credit.
10–13	"Hours" refers to hours worked by the defined group engaged in the activity on a given date.
12	"Fleet miles" are the odometer miles accomplished in driven vehicles that are maintained in-house.
12	"Transactions" must be defined by each user and may be "loads dispatched" for one fleet and "customer bills" for another.

Dealing with "Phantom" Changes in Productivity

Productivity ratios can be expected to change in value from period to period when shipment characteristics change, *even if actual productivity does not*. To avoid being misled along these lines, a system should be designed so as to produce certain statistics about the shipments that moved during the measurement period under scrutiny. The statistics and the measurements to which they pertain are presented in Table 21–8.

Make or Buy Decisions

A second and very important use of these statistics is as input to purchased versus private transportation decisions; they enable the decision-maker to see how well the shipment profiles of his private carriage cost match the profiles of shipments moving in common carriage that might be taken over by the private fleet. A good match would suggest that present private costs could be extended to the new set of shipments.

Utilization and Performance

A. T. Kearney, Inc. researchers observed that to improve productivity a manager had to change methods, equipment, utilization, or performance. Several suggestions concerning

Table 21-8   Statistics Needed When Evaluating Fleet Productivity Reports

	Traffic Characteristics Affecting Productivity			
Productivity Measures	Average Shipment Weight	Average Stops Assigned	Average Load Weight	Average Length of Haul
Simple Average:				
1. Miles per road driver hour worked		X	X	X
2. Ton-miles per road driver hour worked		X	X	X
3. Miles per gallon fuel		X	X	X
4. Ton-miles per gallon fuel		X	X	X
5. Ton-miles per driven vehicle		X	X	X
6. Miles per driven vehicle		X		X
7. Miles per trailer day		X		X
8. Customer stops per local driver hour	X			X
9. Weight handled per local driver hour	X	X		
10. Shipments handled per platform employee hour	X			
11. Weight handled per platform employee hour	X			
12. Fleet miles per maintenance employee hour	X	X	X	X
13. Fleet transactions per (other indirect) employee hour	X			

Adapted from D. Daryl Wyckoff, "Issues of Productivity," distributed by the Regular Common Carrier Conference, 1616 P Street, Washington, D.C.; this is a series of reprints of articles that originally appeared in *Traffic World* between September 1972 and February 1973.

methods and equipment are offered after the following discussion of the concepts of utilization and performance.[2]

"Utilization" refers to how well the capacity for accomplishing work is matched to the work to be done. In private carriage, two capacities that should be watched for utilization are those related to personnel and freight vehicles: personnel should be kept busy on productive work and vehicles should be kept loaded and moving. While improvement will be reflected in the associated productivity measurement and on through to the cost account, it is wise to have direct measurement of utilization in order to be certain that this aspect is under control. The measurements of utilization could include:

- Personnel: Hours worked productively per hours available

- Vehicles: Ton-miles hauled per ton-mile capacity
  Loaded miles per total miles operated
  Hours operated per hours available

"Performance" seems to have two applications: It sometimes refers to how well the productivity performance matches a goal that has been set; other times, "performance" refers to how well job specifications are being adhered to. In both cases, there is a comparison of actual performance with some criterion. The forms of criteria include standards, budgets, norms, and goals. Depending on which is the most feasible, these criteria are arrived at by both historical data and engineered approaches such as time study, work sampling, regression, and predetermined time standards.

In private carriage, each productivity measurement should have a performance criterion against which it is compared in every evaluation period, be that a day or a year. In addition, compliance with key job requirements that affect productivity should be measured and compared with an objective. Three examples involve route mileage, backlogs, and maintenance:

- A driver who travels unnecessary miles can seem to be very productive when measured by ton-miles hauled, when in reality the performance was a cost disaster.

- A platform crew can seem very productive based on shipments handled per hour, when in reality the performance is a service disaster if large backlogs have been permitted to accumulate in order to obtain an even work flow.

- High productivity of maintenance labor might involve too many vehicle breakdowns.

The relevant measurements of job behavior could be:

- Route mileage: Miles driven per standard miles, or hours driven per standard hours

- Backlogs: Actual backlog compared to permissible backlog

- Vehicle
  maintenance: Road breakdowns per fleet mile

In summary, management of productivity involves control of actual performance against (1) productivity, (2) utilization, and (3) job behavior objectives.

Tips for Improving Fleet Productivity

Before the transportation base line is presented, the following "tips" for improving fleet productivity are offered; these tips, while potentially useful, were deemed either too specific or not applicable broadly enough to be included in the base line.

1. Change practices that affect productivity:
   - Use vehicles on second and third shifts
   - Change routes to reduce mileage and/or driving time; consider computerized route determination
   - Reduce empty mileage
   - Use relay driving to reduce layover expense
   - Have dispatching supervisors and industrial engineers accompany drivers occasionally, perhaps once per month per driver
   - Increase trailer capacity utilization (weight, cube)
   - See that loaders and dispatchers know all unloading requirements
   - Check on every vehicle that hasn't moved for a number of days

2. Limit allocation of fleet capacity to the most "profitable" trips, substituting purchased transport for the remainder. There are computer programs available that can generate management information useful for fleet profitability control.*

3. Relate compensation to work performed, e.g., miles driven, tons handled, etc.

4. Investigate equipment features affecting productivity:

   - Match of equipment specification to the hauling job
   - Block and fuel heaters
   - Sleepers for consistently overnight runs
   - Power tailgates, hand trucks, hoists, etc.
   - Tractor convenience and comfort options
   - Trailer capacity
   - Fuel saving devices:

     — Larger tanks
     — Temperature controlled fans
     — Synthetic lubricants
     — Radiator shutters
     — Tractor air shields
     — Smooth-side and radius-corner trailers
     — Radial tires
     — Lightweight components (aluminum, fiberglass)
     — Turbochargers
     — Economy engines, transmissions, and rear axles
     — Semi-automatic coupling devices

5. Improve management of vehicle maintenance:

   - Upgrade maintenance to prolong vehicle life
   - Record data useful for future equipment selection
   - Identify patterns of driver abuse
   - Identify patterns of vehicle component failure
   - Recap tires two, three, or four times, depending on casings
   - Limit the number of vehicle makes and types to simplify maintenance and reduce parts inventory
   - Use modern diagnostics to improve engine performance (e.g., dynamometers, oil analysis, tachographs)
   - Investigate new, longer-life engine oils and automatic lubricators
   - Let a road service supply spare tires for owned vehicles
   - Tighten tire inflation disciplines

---

*One such program is TRUXBUX, a General Electric management information system that uses variable cost and income data to identify particular intercity round trips as winners or losers in terms of fleet profitability. TRUXBUX then helps find the reason for trip unprofitability among causes such as revenue, fuel, equipment, and drivers. Administrative output such as financial summaries and allocation of fleet costs to clients can flow from the TRUXBUX data base. TRUXBUX is most relevant for managers whose fleet capacity can be re-allocated to improve savings on somewhat irregular trips.

6. Improve loading and unloading interfaces:

- Schedule pickups and deliveries to reduce driver waiting
- Study loading and unloading for mechanization possibilities (forklift trucks, conveyors, pallet-pullers, etc.)
- Consider palletizing and other forms of unit handling to reduce handling cost; balance against use of vehicle cube

Transportation Base Line Attributes

This final subsection presents the specification for a traffic management operation that (1) purchases transportation from external sources, and (2) operates its own fleet. In the General Electric Company, this specification is called the "Transportation Base Line." Since the base line is meant to be a description of a properly constituted and adequately resourced operation, divergence of one's own operation from base line attributes may represent opportunities to improve transportation performance and productivity.

A. *Carriers are selected that will charge the least for the required transportation services.*

Best Practice

- Modes and specific carriers are chosen either by personnel with traffic expertise or through their preparation of a "routing guide" from which others specify routings in bills of lading and purchase orders.

- Traffic personnel who develop routings possess up-to-date tariffs (carrier price books) or ponies (tariff abstracts) for use in selecting least-cost routings (modes, carriers) for typical (as to weight, product, geographic area) shipments.

- New carriers are screened for requisite operating authority, sufficient cargo insurance, financial stability, and reputation for competent performance.

- Routings include internal transportation operations that offer lower prices.

- Routing guides provide alternative routings for the service levels likely to

Impact of Weak Practice

- Routing by uninformed individuals results in higher cost and inferior delivery service.

- The price for the least-cost mode, carrier, and route cannot be determined without referring to the current tariffs; not knowing prices increases costs.

- Poor service and unsatisfied claims result from the use of unqualified carriers.

- Transportation costs are higher than necessary if internal transportation operations are not considered when routings are prepared.

- Users of the guides are unable to make cost-rational routing decisions; some

be needed; they also contain average cost per hundredweight, expected transit time, and liability coverage for each routing.

- Extensive routing guides are prepared by computer; a convenient routine exists for updating and distribution.

- Cost-significant vendor shipments to warehouses or customers are controlled by direct intervention in carrier selection or by issuance of "standing instructions."

- Purchases are concentrated with few enough carriers to maximize volume price discounts and loading efficiency while maintaining the beneficent effect of competition on carrier service.

shipments cost too much or receive inadequate service or insurance coverage.

- Unnecessary clerical expense is incurred and guides are not updated regularly.

- Shipments that do not touch a location where traffic expertise resides usually escape control.

- Higher cost, loading area congestion, or poor service can result.

B. *The shipping workload is organized and tendered to carriers so as to achieve the maximum transportation cost economies possible without degradation of customer services.*

Best Practice
- Multilevel shipment consolidation takes place:
  — Parts of a customer order
  — Orders for the same customer
  — Orders that became available on different days
  — Orders for different customers in a common area, if cost is reduced.

- When service requirements permit, each customer's orders are shipped on one bill of lading on a fixed day of the week; this date is displayed in all paperwork used in planning and routing shipments.

- Personnel actually ordering service from carriers know the date of delivery that will satisfy the customer, thus providing maximum lead time for arranging least-cost transportation.

- When terms of sale make the consignee or third party responsible for

Impact of Weak Practice
- Economies of scale in freight charges are missed, customers receive their goods in more frequent and smaller shipments than necessary, transit time may be extended, and the probability of physical damage is increased.

- Transportation costs are higher than necessary, shipping floor activities are more costly, and deliveries are less predictable.

- The least-cost transportation arrangements cannot be made without accurate knowledge of the customer service requirements. The result is higher than necessary transportation charges.

- Prepaying and billing freight to customers increases administrative ex-

freight, shipments are made "collect" with the fewest possible exceptions.

- Bill of lading terms (prepaid, collect, prepay and charge, etc.) are consistent with the product line freight policy.

pense and investment in working capital, due to the difference in collection cycles.

- Freight expenditures are made that have not been planned into the product price.

C.   Transportation prices (freight rates) can be reduced by negotiation with competing carriers.

Best Practice
- Reduced rates in the form of "commodity rates" or contractual prices have been secured for vehicle-load movements between each origin-destination pair that occurs weekly or oftener. Purchase of other services (less-than-truckload, air freight, etc.) is concentrated with competent carriers in return for discounts or like concessions.

- Rates enjoyed by competitors and by shippers of like commodities have been compared with rates being paid like carriers, within the last twelve months.

- Rates and service are negotiated on new products and flows prior to substantial movement from factories, warehouses, or breakbulk points to markets and job sites.

- The classification nomenclature (for rating purposes) being applied to every volume product has been reviewed for propriety; "released" and "actual value" criteria have been updated for inflation.

- Competitive quotations are obtained for significant purchases of service under contracts rather than on bills of lading at published tariff rates.

Impact of Weak Practice
- Failure to use volume leverage allows prices to remain unnecessarily high.

- Failure to recognize and deal with inequitably high rates keeps cost higher than necessary.

- A new movement may suffer high cost and poor service.

- Application of improper generic names or "values" to the goods actually shipped may increase transportation cost.

- Absence of competition among suppliers manifests itself in less favorable prices and services under contracts for local delivery, handling, etc.

D.   *The freight payment system gets validated bills paid on time and makes provision for correction of errors and generation of useful management information.*

Best Practice

- Freight bills are matched to payment records and internal documents (e.g., bills of lading) to determine that they are open obligations.

- Freight charges that exceed a cost-benefit cutting line are audited for errors in weight, rate, classification, and extension before payment; audit is completed in time for timely payment of bills.

- Primary audit and payment are done in-house or by contractors subject to written specifications.

- Freight bill processing cost does not exceed $1.50 per bill. ("Processing" includes validation, audit, charging to accounts, payment, and computerized generation of cost and traffic flow data.)

- Freight charges are paid from a "controlled disbursement" account not funded until checks clear.

- Initial audits of freight invoices are followed by one or more supplementary audits within one year.

- "Standard" weights used in bills of lading are checked for accuracy at least annually or when product or packaging design changes occur.

Impact of Weak Practice

- Payments not owed are made.

- Overcharges in the range of 0.5 to 1.5 percent of total freight are not detected.

- Control suffers when outsiders take over audit, payment, and reporting with programs designed for other clients.

- Administrative cost is too high.

- Investment in working capital is increased.

- Freight bill errors undetected previously are not discovered.

- Freight charges are calculated on erroneous "standard" weights.

E.   *Carrier loss and damage to shipments is fully reimbursed; prevention is pursued.*

Best Practice

- A continuous log of claims is maintained showing losses, recoveries, key dates, routings, apparent causes, etc.

Impact of Weak Practice

- There is insufficient control over claim status and recognition of patterns of causality as a means of reducing the incidence of loss.

- Loss, damage, and overcharge claims are not declined due to untimely filing or inadequate documentation.

- Avoidable losses are incurred.

- Both traffic and finance personnel participate in negotiated settlements for a reduced amount.

- Not using the traffic department's influence with the carrier and familiarity with similar cases results in unnecessary write-offs.

- The normal level of loss and damage is known for each major product line and mode of transportation.

- An abnormally high level of loss and damage is not recognized as such.

- Programs exist to reduce the incidence of claims that have recurring patterns.

- Financial losses and customer inconvenience resulting from transit loss or damage are not being reduced, and may even be increasing.

F.   A comprehensive management information system supports (1) control of productivity, cost, and service levels, and (2) provision of advisory services to interfacing functions.

Best Practice (for Control)
- Transportation cost and productivity performances are reported from one integrated system employing common definitions, periods, etc.

Impact of Weak Practice
- Separate systems cost more and produce conflicts that are troublesome to reconcile.

- Productivity of purchased transportation is controlled through monthly reporting of payments per ton-mile for each class of service (carload, truckload, less-than-truckload, premium, etc.) against price and mix bogies. Reasons for major changes are investigated.

- Profits are being eroded by the payment of higher than necessary prices and by over-use of premium-priced services.

- In project-oriented businesses, project transportation performance is reviewed and critiques of cost and service performance are distributed to relevant personnel.

- Without feedback on prior projects, transportation performance on future projects does not improve, and may even degrade.

- Premium and penalty transportation charges are either recovered from customers or vendors or are charged to internal responsibility centers; they are *not* buried in accounts containing routine freight.

- Absorption of air freight, vehicle detention or demurrage, etc. is greater than necessary.

- Transit time and other key aspects of carrier service quality are sampled, compared, and used in decision making on future routings.

- The number of requests for advisory services (tracing, rates, etc.) is recorded and reported; reports contain the mean and extreme times to satisfy such requests.

Best Practice (for Advisory Services)
- Traffic information of interest (tracings, transit times, routes, rates, expected rate increases, etc.) is furnished promptly upon request; written instructions for obtaining such information have been circulated.

- The transportation cost/productivity system provides statistics to functional managers on the impact of their policies and tactics (customer service levels, billing targets, finished goods inventory levels, etc.) on shipment size, service mix, etc.

- Without such information there is no adequate basis upon which to select future routings.

- Cost and performance are not under control.

Impact of Weak Practice
- Customer service and operational planning suffers.

- Transportation cost usually runs 50 percent of total physical distribution cost. Carrier selection, price negotiation, etc. are important, but the strongest influence on transportation cost is the set of policies and practicies within which the transportation operation functions. Without feedback on the effect of factors such as inventory position, customer service priorities, manufacturing schedules and field stock locations, the greatest opportunity to affect transportation productivity is lost.

G.   *Advanced analyses are in use to discover ways to reduce transportation expense consistent with other physical distribution objectives (customer service, inventory investment, etc.).*

Best Practice
- Freight bill data on carrier payments and shipment patterns that account for the bulk of transportation expense are reviewed at least annually; computer programs that organize data for analysis are in use.

- Freight expense is analyzed by seg-

Impact of Weak Practice
- Cost and service improvement opportunities are being missed.

- Major opportunities to be found "be-ment in an attempt to correct margin depletion problems associated with particular customers, projects, market channels, geographic areas, products, and shipment sizes.

- The number, location, and service areas of field locations (warehouses, breakbulk points) and alternative factory sources or products are investigated at least annually, using advanced techniques such as the LOCATE program (Figure 21–3).

- Shipment statistics (frequency, tonnage, geographic patterns, present costs) are reviewed with qualified carrier representatives, and their suggestions for reducing costs are solicited.

neath" the average cost/revenue ratio are being missed.

- Transportation cost may be 10 percent higher than for an acceptable alternative network.

- Carrier representatives make far fewer mutually beneficial cost and service proposals.

H.   The private trucking operation (if any) competes effectively with for-hire (public) carriers for shipments on which private trucking offers substantial savings and/or superior service.

Best Practice
- With the exception of the overall manager, personnel responsible for purchasing external transportation are not also responsible for operation of a private fleet within the same business.

- The specifications of vehicles in use match the operation to which each is assigned.

- A formal schedule exists for preventive maintenance of vehicles.

- A maintenance reporting system provides feedback to management on equipment and driver performance patterns.

- A vehicle replacement formula has been endorsed; related equipment plans and budgets have been issued.

Impact of Weak Practice
- Bias toward one's own fleet results in selection of transportation sources that may not offer the best cost-service mix.

- Inappropriate vehicles are making fleet operating cost too high.

- The operating performance of equipment is not assured and maintenance cost is excessive.

- Management cannot pinpoint problems and the causes associated with selecting, operating, and maintaining equipment.

- The timely and orderly replacement of old vehicles with new ones of the proper specification at the lowest price is not assured. Over-age vehicles can increase cost by 50 percent.

- A routing guide that describes the fleet's coverage, routes, and service standards has been issued to clients and fleet employees.

- Key aspects of customer service (transit time, claims ratio, etc.) are measured against standards.

- Fleet "savings" are audited by independent transportation price experts at least annually.

- A productivity measurement system monitors output from the use of key resources employed in private carriage (labor, equipment, and energy) against standards; productivity measurements are complemented by related utilization and performance measurements.

- Full use of the fleet's resources is not made by client components and fleet employees.

- Management is not correcting substandard performance.

- Inaccurate estimation of savings results in unwarranted expansion of fleet resources and may deprive the fleet's client of the lowest transportation cost.

- Fleet cost is too high and resources are underutilized.

Notes

1. D. Daryl Wyckoff, "Issues of Productivity," distributed by the Regular Common Carrier Conference, 1616 P Street, Washington, D.C. This is a series of reprints of articles that originally appeared in *Traffic World* between September 1972 and February 1973.
2. A. T. Kearney, Inc., "Measuring Productivity in Physical Distribution: A 40 Billion Dollar Goldmine" (Chicago: National Council of Physical Distribution Management, 1978), pp. 9–11.

Transportation Strategies for the Eighties

LEWIS M. SCHNEIDER, PAUL E. FULCHINO, *and* MICHAEL S. GALARDI

Introduction

There can be little question that our nation's transportation system is in the process of adapting to some of the most profound changes in its history. The rules of the game have been altered by legislative and administrative rulings. Almost overnight, years of accumulated learning and patterns of behavior have become obsolete.

The transportation industry has witnessed revolutions in the past, but these have been primarily technological—the dethroning of the steam locomotive by the diesel, or the victory of the container over the traditional breakbulk maritime system. The current revolution, however, is dramatically different because it concerns ideology—not technology. As a nation, we have consciously—or, as some critics would allege, unconsciously— chosen to place far greater reliance on competitive forces and the actions of the free market than on regulation. As a result, transportation managers now have the opportunity to gain competitive advantages for their companies rather than settle for parity under the historical regulatory umbrella.

This chapter is based on the following published material: *Transportation Strategies for the Eighties*, prepared by Temple, Barker & Sloane, Inc. for the National Council of Physical Distribution Management (Oak Brook, Illinois, 1982); Dr. Lewis M. Schneider, Paul E. Fulchino, and Michael S. Galardi, "Transportation Strategies for the Eighties," *1983–1984 Presidential Issue—Handling & Shipping Management* (Cleveland, Penton, 1983); and "Transportation Strategies for the Eighties," prepared by Dr. Lewis M. Schneider for the 25th Annual Meeting, Transportation Research Forum, November 2–5, 1983 (to be published by the Transportation Research Forum in its Proceedings—Twenty-Fourth Annual Meeting, Volume 24, Number 2, and also by the Transportation Research Board).

What have been and, perhaps more importantly, what are likely to be the impact deregulation on the organization and management of the transportation industry? 1 was the focus of a major study recently commissioned by the National Council of Physical Distribution Management (NCPDM).

In the fall of 1981, the NCPDM contracted with Temple, Barker & Sloane, Inc. (TBS) to undertake research with five specific objectives:

- To develop a framework for defining transportation strategy and describing its interrelationship with corporate and logistics strategies

- To identify and analyze key external factors that will affect transportation management in the 1980s

- To assess how the U.S. domestic transportation modes might respond to these factors

- To analyze the impacts of the changing external factors and modal responses on transportation and physical distribution management decisions

- To show how the information, data, and methodologies contained in the study could be effectively used by shippers and receivers to plan transportation strategies

Response to the NCPDM study, *Transportation Strategies for the Eighties*, has been gratifying. One of the leading transportation and physical distribution periodicals commented: "The report seems to us to be an exceptionally valuable document for shippers and carriers. The NCPDM has served the transportation industry well by its sponsorship of this research project."[1]

Are the key findings of the NCPDM study still valid? If so, what are the implications of these findings? Before undertaking this review, it would be useful to summarize the results of the first NCPDM task—the development of the overall conceptual framework for the analysis.

A Framework for Defining Transportation Strategy

Transportation management decisions are not made in a vacuum. External economic, political, and technological pressures affect carriers and shippers alike. In turn, carriers formulate their strategies, and the combined external pressures and carrier strategies affect shippers and receivers. Simultaneously, corporate and logistics internal strategies explicitly or implicitly establish the boundaries within which transportation decisions are made. Figure 22–1 is a graphic representation of these relationships.

Despite these pressures, transportation managers have a variety of opportunities to influence the performance of their companies. These strategic decision areas can be grouped into three major categories:

1. What transportation services are needed to fulfill the logistics mission? Included in this area are specific decisions concerning:

   - Which modes of transportation, or mix of modes, should be used?
   - How should individual carriers be selected?

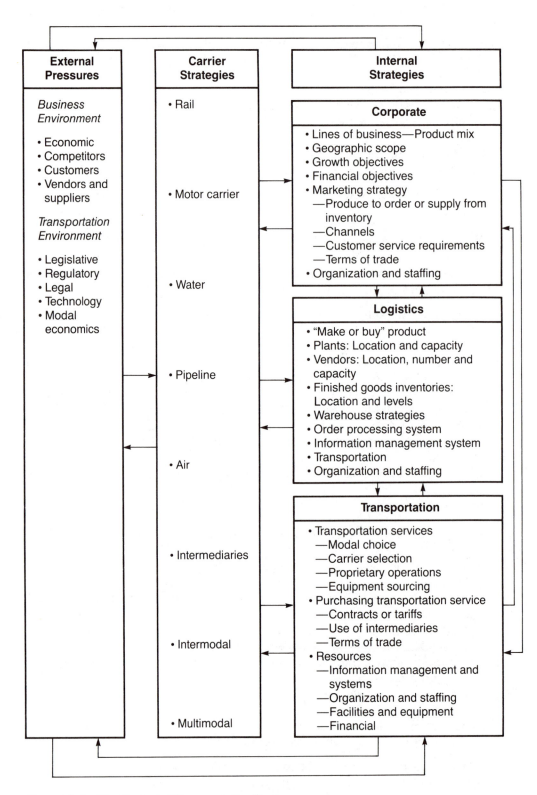

Figure 22-1 The Context of Transportation Strategy

- What is the appropriate role, if any, of proprietary trucking or rail operations?
- Should the firm provide its own equipment, and, if so, how should that equipment investment be financed (i.e., lease or purchase)?

2. How should the required purchased transportation services be obtained? The specific decisions include:

- To what extent should contracts be used in lieu of relying on carrier offerings under tariff terms and conditions?
- When and under what circumstances should intermediaries be used?
- Should the firm seek to control the purchase of transportation by changing its terms of trade?

3. What resources are needed to support the firm's transportation strategies? Resource decisions include:

- What information is required by transportation management, and how should data be collected and analyzed to provide that information?
- What human resources are required, and how should those resources be organized and deployed?
- How should technology be exploited? What level of investment should be made in facilities, transportation equipment, and materials handling and packaging systems?
- Ultimately, what financial resources, both capital and operating funds, must be devoted to the firm's transportation activities?

It is important to recognize that the arrows in Figure 22–1 are bidirectional. It is certainly true that shipper and receiver transportation strategies are constrained by external pressures, carrier strategies, and the firm's corporate and logistics strategies. Yet effective transportation managers also have the capability to influence their internal and external environments. The key is strategic planning, and, not surprisingly, this message is emphasized throughout the study.

Transportation Strategy Planning

The NCPDM study identified seven steps in the shipper transportation strategy planning process (Figure 22–2):

1. Audit current status and performance

2. Develop base case projections

3. Analyze external and internal trends to identify key strategic issues

4. Formulate and evaluate response options to the key strategic issues

5. Prepare a recommended strategic plan incorporating the most promising options

6. Obtain approval of the strategic plan

7. Implement the approved strategic plan and provide for feedback to the next strategic plan

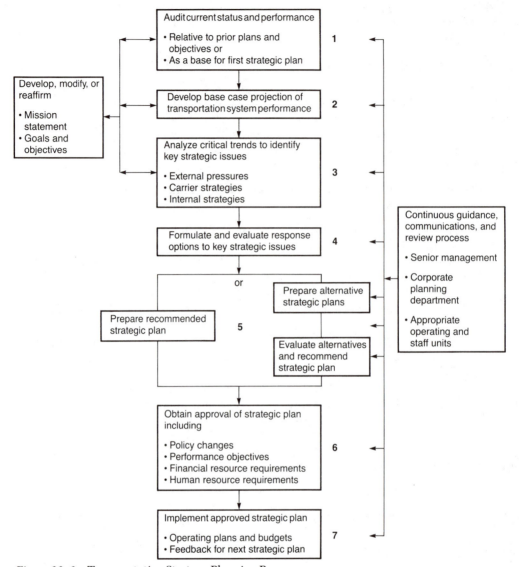

Figure 22-2   Transportation Strategy Planning Process

During the first three steps, transportation managers should develop, modify, or reaffirm a statement of mission, goals, and objectives. Throughout the process there should be continuous guidance, communications, and review by senior management, the corporate planning department, and appropriate operating and staff units.

Clearly, the assessment of internal and external trends (step 3) is central to the strategy planning process. The NCPDM study analyzed the most important external trends under four broad headings: macro-economic and modal cost trends, legal and regulatory developments, technology, and carrier strategies.

Assessment of the External Environment

Macro-economic and Modal Cost Trends

One important task of the NCPDM study was to systematically look at the long-term (1980–1985–1990) cost trends for the competing transportation modes. Costs for 14 modal/shipment categories were analyzed. Five scenarios were presented incorporating varying assumptions as to productivity, user fees, and fuel price increases. The most important findings were as follows:

- In the most likely (1980–1990) case, 9 of the 14 modal segments would experience cost increases greater than the producer price index (formerly the wholesale price index), signifying that the transportation industry might have difficulty coping with inflationary pressures.

- Productivity gains would be crucial. The high productivity scenario revealed 7 to 39 percent reductions in annual cost increases, as compared with the no-productivity-gain scenario.

- Despite technological differences, there would be relatively little difference in the annual cost-increase percentages in the highly competitive segments—rail carload, intermodal, general truck, and private truck.

The economic projections underlying the NCPDM study had been developed during the winter of 1981–82. More recent forecasts—published during the fall of 1983—show a different picture (Table 22–1):

- The growth rates in the producer and consumer price indices have been substantially reduced.

- The growth rate in labor compensation has been reduced by one-third. The growth rate in petroleum prices has been slashed from 11.3 percent to 2.3 percent per year between 1980 and 1985, but the growth rate between 1985 and 1990 has been more modestly reduced—from 10.6 percent to 10.2 percent per year. Petroleum prices will still increase at substantially faster rates than inflation during the latter half of the decade.

- Interest rates will be lower than originally forecast, but still somewhat higher than the reference year 1973.

These changes in the economic outlook, plus adjustments to the previous productivity estimates, yield a new set of modal cost projections for the 1980s (Table 22–2).

Excluding oil pipelines, the modal costs over the full decade are expected to grow at rates ranging from 4.6 percent to 6.7 percent per year versus the NCPDM study projections ranging from 7.5 percent to 9.8 percent per year. Ten of the 14 categories will increase faster than the producer price index. Bulk transportation costs will tend to increase at a higher rate than the producer price index (Table 22–3).

Table 22-1   Comparative Economic Outlook—NCPDM Study versus Fall 1983
Estimates

| | | Compound Growth Rates (%) | | | |
| | | 1980–1985 | | 1985–1990 | |
	Historic 1973–1980	NCPDM Study*	Fall 1983	NCPDM Study*	Fall 1983
Real GNP	3.1	2.7	2.2	2.9	3.1
FRB production index	2.9	4.2	2.1	3.9	3.9
Producer price index	9.1	8.6	5.0	8.6	5.9
Consumer price index	8.8	8.6	5.9	7.7	5.7
Compensation	9.2	9.8	6.7	9.9	6.9
Petroleum prices	24.9	11.3	2.3	10.6	10.2

Annual Rates (%)

	1973	1980	1985	1985	1990	1990
Prime Rate	8.0	15.3	11.9	11.3	9.8	9.7
AAA corporate bonds	7.4	11.9	11.4	10.8	9.9	9.5

*Forecasts reflect data provided by Data Resources, Inc., Chase Econometrics, and Wharton Econometric Forecasting Associates during the winter of 1981–1982.

Perhaps most important, a critical finding of the NCPDM study remains undisturbed: "There will be surprisingly few differences in the cost increases for highly competitive markets—for example, intermodal door to door versus general truckload and private truckload. The key differentiating elements within and between modes will be carrier strategy, for it will be the actions of carrier managements that generate productivity gains, exploit the potentials of the changed regulatory environment, and either meet or fail to meet the needs of shippers and receivers."

Legal and Regulatory Developments

The NCPDM study presented 57 planning assumptions for the 1980s, organized under the major modal headings, as well as summary impact statements for carriers, shippers, and receivers. To date, virtually all the key actions have been consistent with the trends projected in the research. For example:

- The Motor Carrier Rate Study Commission recommended the elimination of antitrust immunity for collective ratemaking on both single line and joint rates. The National Industrial Transportation League has endorsed a proposal to withdraw antitrust immunity for collective ratemaking on shipments under 1000 pounds.

- The ICC reportedly will approve existing motor carrier rate discount practices, thereby reinforcing a policy of promoting shipper-tailored rates and services.

- Trip leasing of private carrier drivers and equipment to for-hire carriers was approved by the Interstate Commerce Commission (ICC), as was the leasing of driv-

Table 22-2   Comparative Modal Cost Projections—NCPDM Study versus Fall 1983 Estimates (Percentage Comparison)

Modal Category	1985–1990		1980–1990	
	NCPDM Study*	Fall 1983	NCPDM Study*	Fall 1983
Motor carrier—LTL	+ 50	+ 31	+ 106	+ 57
Surface—Small parcel	+ 58	+ 36	+ 121	+ 68
Air—Small parcel	+ 54	+ 37	+ 135	+ 76
Air—Combination carrier	+ 52	+ 38	+ 132	+ 71
Air—All cargo	+ 50	+ 38	+ 135	+ 74
Intermodal (door-to-door)	+ 48	+ 31	+ 124	+ 69
For-hire truck	+ 47	+ 33	+ 128	+ 72
Private truck	+ 48	+ 33	+ 125	+ 71
Rail carload	+ 55	+ 37	+ 131	+ 77
Bulk truckload	+ 54	+ 36	+ 142	+ 82
Barge tow	+ 52	+ 36	+ 155	+ 91
Rail unit train	+ 57	+ 40	+ 141	+ 81
Large barge tow	+ 50	+ 36	+ 153	+ 89
Oil pipeline	+ 33	+ 23	+ 74	+ 40

*Forecasts reflect data provided by Data Resources, Inc., Chase Econometrics, and Wharton Econometric Forecasting Associates during the winter of 1981–1982.

ers and equipment from a single source. The ICC has also proposed elimination of the 30-day owner-operator minimum lease period.

- Congress liberalized uniform motor truck size and weight standards in exchange for increases in truck fuel, excise, and use taxes. Although debate currently rages over which parts of the national highway system "double-bottoms" can run, it seems reasonable to predict that motor carriers will be able to increase their productivity substantially because of the new legislation. The benefits, however, will not accrue equally to all types of carriers. In addition, the use tax will probably be modified to include a mileage factor.

- The "special circumstances" doctrine relating to the operations of railroad-owned motor carriers was eliminated. Railroad trucking subsidiaries are now free to compete in whatever markets they desire. The ICC has also proposed that the special circumstances doctrine as a criterion in motor carrier acquisitions be eliminated. The public interest and competitive tests would remain on a case-by-case approach.

- Although the ICC has required that certain additional information on railroad contract rates be made public, actual rates will still remain confidential, and it appears unlikely that many of the rates will be challenged. The railroads and shippers have responded by accelerating the pace of contract filings—increasing from a cumulative 768 as of December 1981 to 2573 as of October 1982 and to 9934 as of September 1, 1983.

- The NCPDM study considered railroad mergers to be one of the most important issues for shippers and receivers, for mergers will increase significantly the percentage of rail shipments moving in single line service. In the first 18 months after the study, the ICC approved the Union-Pacific–Missouri Pacific–Western Pacific mer-

Table 22–3   Modal Costs—Compound Growth Rates (Percent)

	Fall 1983 Update		
	1980–1985	*1985–1990*	*1980–1990*
Producer Price Index	5.0	5.9	5.4
Small Shipments			
Motor carrier—LTL	3.6	5.6	4.6
Surface—Small parcel	4.3	6.4	5.3
Air—Small parcel	5.1	6.5	5.8
Air—Comb. carrier	4.4	6.6	5.5
Air—All cargo	4.8	6.7	5.7
Volume Shipments			
Intermodal (door-to-door)	5.2	5.6	5.4
For-hire truck	5.3	5.9	5.6
Private truck	5.2	5.8	5.5
Rail carload	5.4	6.5	5.9
Bulk truckload	5.9	6.4	6.2
Barge tow	5.5	8.0	6.7
Mass Volume Shipments			
Rail unit train	5.2	6.9	6.1
Large barge tow	5.4	7.9	6.6
Oil pipeline	2.5	4.3	3.4

ger and eliminated the Detroit, Toledo & Ironton protective conditions from future consideration. More recently, the Santa Fe and Southern Pacific railroads announced their intention to merge, and the Santa Fe confirmed that it was studying a possible acquisition of Conrail. Thus the stage seems to be set for the emergence of three or possibly two national systems.

• Federal eminent domain legislation for coal slurry pipelines has not passed despite intensive lobbying.

To be sure, there have been some surprises. Most reflect a greater desire on the part of the ICC to hasten the pace of deregulation:

• The ICC voted to deregulate boxcar transportation and export coal traffic and broadened the railroad agricultural exemption. Only grain and soybeans remain major regulated agricultural commodities. Legal challenges to the export coal decision failed at the U.S. Court of Appeals level.

• The Reagan Administration will reportedly seek total deregulation of the trucking, barge, forwarder, and freight broker industries. Congress will probably be less enthusiastic, but the pace of deregulation may be somewhat greater than that envisioned in the NCPDM study.

• The Multi-Employer Pension Plan Amendments Act has not yet been modified, although proponents of such action are still optimistic. It still seems likely that there will be amendments to facilitate the restructuring that would ordinarily accompany deregulation in an industry.

Technology

The NCPDM study noted that a number of technological innovations introduced during the past 30 years—most notably the diesel, jet engines, the computer, and containerization—have revolutionized the transportation and distribution industries. During the 1980s, only one development of similar importance is expected—the rapid evolution of computerized information systems.

The advent of the computer has had a major impact on both shippers and carriers. To date, most computer applications have focused on transaction-oriented data-processing capabilities. As hardware and software costs have declined and micro personal computers have been introduced to the marketplace, a new set of computer applications—information systems—has emerged and will grow rapidly during the 1980s. In general, information systems convert raw data to usable information in a timely and efficient manner so management can improve the effectiveness of its decision making and its ability to plan and control operations.

Shipper Information Systems

The use of information systems by shippers has been most extensive in the areas of inventory control, order entry, and purchasing. During the 1980s, the application of information systems in these areas is expected to become more widespread. In addition, systems with increasing sophistication will be applied in the areas of rating, routing, and bills of lading. Also during the decade, shippers will increasingly use information systems to integrate their entire logics operations (warehousing, traffic, inventory control, purchasing, and marketing).

Carrier Information Systems

Carriers will increasingly use information systems that capitalize on the greater storage, computational capacity, and intercommunications capabilities of computers. Three areas of development that most directly affect the distribution community are shipment profitability systems, information interchange systems, and equipment control systems. These applications are not new. What is new is the effectiveness (measured in terms of physical capability, response time, and cost) with which they can now be applied.

Shipment profitability systems will have the greatest impact on shippers and receivers, because carriers have greater freedom to decide what markets they wish to serve. Shippers will use the same technology to estimate carrier costs and profitability as a part of the rate and service negotiating process.

Information interchange systems allow shippers to communicate directly with carriers and assist the carriers in billing, claims, and equipment planning and deployment. In turn, these systems can facilitate the loading and unloading scheduling of shippers and receivers. The more extensive use of these systems during the 1980s will lead to differentiated carrier services and improved productivity.

Equipment planning and control systems are not new, but again, advanced technology will facilitate the planning and control of expensive equipment. The payoffs in this area can be substantial.

Other Technological Developments

In addition to the development of carrier information systems, many other mode-specific technological innovations are expected to be introduced primarily to achieve increased fuel efficiency and greater equipment productivity.[2] Table 22–4 provides a useful reference point for evaluating modal fuel efficiency.

Carrier Strategies—NCPDM Findings

Chapter 5 of the NCPDM study addressed the important question of how the major modes of transportation are likely to respond to the changes in environment. The analysis began with the observation that transportation carriers, regardless of mode, face nine types of strategic decisions:

1. *Lines of Business.* What range of services should be offered?

- Traditional transportation—pickup and delivery, linehaul
- Distribution—warehousing, assembly and distribution, packaging, bulk storage inventory management, etc.
- Equipment leasing and maintenance
- Multimodal capability
- Intermodal capability
- Administrative services—billing, tracing, auditing, freight payment, etc.
- Door-to-door facilitation—freight forwarder, non-vessel operating common carriers (NVOCC), etc.

Table 22–4 Summary Estimates of Propulsion Energy Requirements (Btus per Ton-Mile of Cargo)

Mode	Range of Estimates	Typical Estimate	Estimate Adjusted for Energy Losses in Refining
Rail—Overall	550–690	630	660
TOFC	730–1,370	950	1,000
Unit Coal Train	220–410	350	370
Truck			
Average Intercity	1,400–2,530	2,000	2,100
Barge—Overall	250–500	400	420
Upstream	—	550	580
Downstream	—	210	220
Air			
All-cargo plane	23,310–28,630	25,000	26,250
Belly freight*	3,300–29,950	3,400	3,570
Oil pipeline	160–540	325	325
Coal slurry pipeline†	410–4,800	1,000	1,000

*The wide range of estimates results from the use of two different methods.

†The wide variation results from different degrees of comprehensiveness (pumping energy alone as against coal preparation and dewatering as well), and from the differences between engineering studies of large—as yet unbuilt—pipelines and the smaller-scale line now in operation.

SOURCE: *Energy Use in Freight Transportation*, Congressional Budget Office, 1982, p. 42.

2. *Scope*. Over what geographic territory should these services be supplied?

- Local
- Regional
- National
- International

3. *Control*. Should the company provide its services alone or jointly with others?

4. *Scale*. What size should the company be?

5. *Marketing*. What market strategy should be employed?

- Product planning, differentiation, and segmentation
- Provision of equipment
- Pricing
- Promotion
- Customer service and support
- Role of the field and headquarters marketing and sales organization

6. *Technology*. How should technology be exploited?

7. *Finance*. How should the company be financed?

8. *Labor*. What labor-relations strategy should be used?

9. *Organization and Staffing*. What organizational structure and personnel policies should the company adopt?

Inasmuch as the objective of the NCPDM study was to aid shippers and receivers in planning their transportation strategies for the 1980s, the research tended to focus on the first six strategic issues as they affect the external relationships between carriers and their customers. In addition, the book covered the strategies of noncarriers, such as leasing companies, as they relate to shipper-proprietary transportation programs.

Railroad Carrier Strategy

Mergers and the expansion of single line service will be the key element in railroad strategies. Continued end-to-end mergers will increase the percentage of single line service, tend to reduce the number of competitive routes, stimulate greater use of service contracts, and in general give the railroads the opportunity to meet the needs of their shippers with tailored services. As individual railroads gain complete origin-destination control over their products and services, the stage will be set for innovation in a free marketplace or, if unsuccessful, a return to regulation.

The evidence also suggests that the railroads will face tough modal competition, notwithstanding the benefits of the Staggers Rail Act. The modal cost projections demonstrate that productivity gains are critical if the railroads are to improve their costs relative to other modes. The larger railroads will expand their intermodal and multimodal activities to hold or increase traffic and to hedge against changes in the relative modal costs. It is less likely that they will broaden their lines of business into total distribution services. Exhibit 22–1 lists the key planning assumptions for the 1980s for this mode.

Exhibit 22–1   Railroad Carrier Strategy Planning Assumptions for the 1980s

Lines of business

- Will seek to provide rail, intermodal, and multimodal services, but will be less aggressive in offering total distribution services

- Will tend to supply less equipment, but will continue to provide labor, power, and right of way

- Will have significantly different linehaul, switching, pickup, and delivery strategies

- Will continue to handle a broad commodity mix

Scope, control, scale

- Will merge into three to five national railway systems by 1990

- Will sharply reduce competitive routes

- Will increase the percentage of single line service to the 75 to 85 percent range

Marketing, technology

- Will be more marketing-oriented with emphasis on market segmentation and commodity, industry, lane, and customer profitability

- Will offer both bundled and unbundled services

- Will reduce the number of marketing transactions through use of national accounts and intermediaries

- Will rely on contracts for one-third to one-half their traffic

- Will continue to price flexibly, particularly on seasonable and backhaul traffic, and seek to generate higher profits and return on investment

- Will seek a completely deregulated environment

- Will continue to have different technological strategies

- Will increase their information systems interfaces with major shippers

SOURCE: NCPWM, *Transportation Strategies for the Eighties*, p. 107.

Motor Carrier Strategy

The major impact of the Motor Carrier Act of 1980 will be in the structure and performance of the industry. There will be substantial shakeouts as the carriers restructure to meet the realities of the new competitive environment. Shippers will benefit through more favorable rates and improved service as they deal with fewer but broader companies. Whether the financial health of the industry will ever return to its previous levels is still open to question, but enough strong carriers should prevail to ensure good transportation service. The motor carrier planning assumptions for the 1980s are summarized in Exhibit 22–2.

Equipment Leasing Strategy

The major strategic issue for leasing companies in the 1980s will be lines of business. It is expected that they will continue to broaden their transportation and distribution services

Exhibit 22-2   Motor Carrier Strategy Planning Assumptions for the 1980s

Lines of business

- Trucking companies will tend to offer a broader range of services, but there will be few multimodal companies (such as Tiger International) or firms offering total distribution services on a multi-regional or national level.

- The distinctions will tend to disappear between general and special commodity carriers. The shift will be from clearly defined specialty carriers to a series of specialty services offered by the same carrier. For example, major household goods carriers might well generate a significant proportion of their revenue from stop-off less-than-truckload (LTL) traffic.

- General commodity carriers which formerly provided both truckload and LTL service will increasingly specialize in LTL traffic, because of diversions to private carriage and other truckload operators. Their remaining truckload operations will tend to be offered by non-union subsidiaries.

Scope, control, and scale

- The number of companies offering nationwide LTL service (more than 38 states) will hold steady or decline. Three to five firms will dominate.

- Interregional companies will tend to pull back from long-haul services and emphasize density and coverage. There will be a major shakeout as firms merge or cease operations.

- Regional carriers will tend to increase coverage within their territories, make selective expansions, and be acquired by holding companies such as Sun Carriers and ANR.

- The number of very large LTL companies (in excess of $100 million) might well decline, although the percentage of revenue accounted for by the largest companies will probably increase from approximately 50 percent (1980).

- Carriers will continue to emphasize single line service, but will increasingly utilize rail intermodal for substituted service or connections between regional operations.

- The general commodity truckload segment of the industry will remain highly fragmented, dominated by owner operators, relying on carriers and brokers to tender traffic.

Marketing

- Motor carriers
  - Will become more marketing-oriented with emphasis on commodity, industry, lane, and customer profitability.
  - Will enhance the role of national account marketing.
  - Will increasingly shift from tariffs to contracts.
  - Will simplify rates.
  - Will continue to offer substantial price discounts for volume tenders, but rates in general will firm and be more related to costs as the economy strengthens.
  - Will not generally adopt service performance rebates, but will include service standards in contracts.
  - Will selectively use intermodal service to penetrate new markets.

Technology

- General commodity carriers will rely primarily on suppliers for technological innovation.

Exhibit 22-2   *Cont.*

• Special commodity carriers will continue to innovate to meet particular needs.

Labor

• LTL carriers will continue to rely heavily on union labor.

• Truckload and special commodity carriers will rely more heavily on non-union labor.

SOURCE: NCPDM, *Transportation Strategies for the Eighties*, p. 107.

and that some major leasing companies will become the leaders in full-service intermodal and multimodal transportation. In addition, several of these companies will emerge among the largest motor carriers in the industry. Exhibit 22–3 summarizes the planning assumptions for the 1980s for leasing companies.

Barge Company Strategy

In many respects, the problems facing the barge industry mirror those of the truckload motor carriers. Each suffered financial reverses in the early 1980s. Each faces strong competition from proprietary fleets. Each experiences owner-operators who supply equip-

Exhibit 22-3   Equipment Leasing Strategy Planning Assumptions for the 1980s

Lines of business

• Leasing companies will broaden their business into a wider range of transportation and distribution services.

• Major leasing companies will emerge as some of the largest motor carrier, intermodal, and multimodal companies in transportation. These firms may offer both contract and common carriage.

• Smaller leasing firms will tend to specialize in types of equipment or modes.

Scope, control, and scale

• Large, national companies will continue to increase their share of the equipment leasing market.

• Some small leasing firms may merge or go bankrupt.

• National franchise networks will continue to play an important role in allowing small regional companies to compete.

Marketing, technology

• Firms will increase their segmentation of markets and add new services aimed at improving carrier and shipper productivity.

• Service-pricing packages will become more innovative.

• Full services will be emphasized where possible but as market segmentation increases the unbundling of services will increase.

• Companies will pursue diverse technology strategies with some looking to technological development for a competitive edge.

SOURCE: NCPDM, *Transportation Strategies for the Eighties*, p. 125.

ment to private shippers. Each relies on contracts, although depending on the commodity, individual barge operators tend to negotiate shorter- or longer-term agreements. Finally, each faces increased user charges, which may retard growth in the short run. Yet there are important differences primarily in lines of business and intermodal strategies. Exhibit 22–4 summarizes the barge company planning assumptions for the 1980s.

Air Freight Strategy

Strategic line-of-business issues will play a major role in the air freight industry and will result in continuing industry structural changes and innovative marketing strategies. It is also clear that the industry will continue to experience both intense intermodal and intramodal competition resulting in downward presssure on rates and increasing the need for company and market differentiation. Exhibit 22–5 summarizes the air freight industry planning assumptions for the 1980s.

Pipeline Carrier Strategy

The major pipeline issue confronting transportation and distribution managers is the future of slurry pipelines. The economics and environmental impacts have been subject to continuous debate for over a decade.

Exhibit 22–4   Inland Water Carrier Strategy Planning Assumptions for the 1980s

---

Lines of business

- Large bulk carrier companies will continue to engage in broader activities including terminals and shipyards, but will not diversify into overland collection and distribution.

- Large specialized carriers will tend to broaden their base; for example, liquid bulk will expand into dry bulk.

Scope, control, and scale

- The ten largest regulated companies may increase their share of capacity in the short run, but will continue to represent 15 to 20 percent of capacity in the long run.

- Carriers will continue to focus their activities on specific waterways.

- Proprietary fleets will increase their market share somewhat to approximately 20 percent and continue to exert major pressure on the marketplace.

- Intermodal service with railroads will not increase substantially, but railroads may purchase barge companies and account for a relatively small proportion of barge capacity.

Marketing

- Carriers might set prices in a completely deregulated market.

- Contracts will continue to reflect the different commodity patterns and practices.

- In general, barge operator margins will decline.

- Grain interests will be impacted most heavily by increased user charges.

SOURCE: NCPDM, *Transportation Strategies for the Eighties*, p. 130.

Exhibit 22–5   Air Freight Strategy Planning Assumptions for the 1980s

Lines of business

• Two types of firms will emerge: (1) multimodal firms offering a wide range of services for multiple types of freight, and (2) carriers specializing in a particular service or type of freight (e.g., small parcels).

• Major forwarders and intermediaries will increase operation of their own linehaul equipment with several operating as full-service cargo lines.

• Some combination carriers will operate dedicated freighters while others will carry only belly freight.

Scope, control, and scale

• There will be fewer combination carriers and plane-operating forwarders in the industry due to mergers and bankruptcies.

• Large carriers and forwarders will extend their territories through the use of intermodal service and by interlining with regional carriers.

• Combination carriers will pursue divergent strategies with some becoming aggressive in the direct marketing and pickup and delivery operations and others continuing to rely on intermediaries for this function.

Marketing, technology

• Emphasis will be increased on both market segmentation and customer-tailored rates and services to develop new markets.

• Pricing in new markets will reflect an "elastic demand" philosophy.

• Intramodal and intermodal competition will intensify, resulting in downward pressure on rate increases.

• Concern over rising fuel prices will temper increased use of intermodal containers.

• More sophisticated management information systems will be utilized to increase use of innovative marketing and rate programs.

SOURCE: NCPDM, *Transportation Strategies for the Eighties*, p. 140.

Advocates of the slurry pipeline claim that specific projects would save utility customers hundreds of millions, and even billions, of dollars over one or more decades. The railroads respond that the analyses are flawed, primarily because they compare uncertain slurry pipeline costs and rates with the maximum rates the railroads might charge in a deregulated environment rather than with the rates the railroads would actually charge.

The Slurry Transportation Association believes that more than 10,000 miles of lines would be constructed if Congress were to grant the right of eminent domain to slurry systems. But the prospects for federal legislaion appear dim, at least during the early 1980s.

Slurry pipeline developers face two possible strategies. The first is to press for federal action or state support along the proposed routes. The second is to assemble parcels without the eminent domain power, albeit at a higher cost. In all probability, at least a few new slurry pipelines will be constructed.

The most interesting strategy issue will be the response of the railroads. They can cut competitive rates (as they did with the Cadiz facility in 1963), develop their own systems, such as Southern Pacific's Black Mesa pipeline, or wait and see whether the anticipated economic advantages materialize. It would not be surprising if the railroads emerged as the major developers of pipelines should the next few slurry systems prove successful.

Carrier Strategies to Date

For the most part, carriers in each of the modes are responding to the environment of the 1980s as predicted in the NCPDM study. For example:

- The railroads are rationalizing their networks through abandonments and mergers, reducing the number of joint through routes, promoting intermodal service heavily, acquiring other modal carriers, improving their information systems and interfaces with customers, organizing to enhance their marketing effectiveness, expanding the use of contracts, and experimenting with different pricing tactics.

- The larger LTL motor carriers are capturing greater market share through restucturing, broadening services, expanding terminals, and aggressively competing in the marketplace.

- The regulated unionized motor carriers are withdrawing from the truckload business, which is now dominated by non-union owner-operators.

- Like the railroads, motor carriers are upgrading their information systems, including the use of electronic interchange.

- Truck leasing companies are increasingly capitalizing on their knowledge of equipment, maintenance, and private fleet operations to offer shippers a wide range of transportation and distribution services. The distinction between for-hire and private carriage is rapidly disappearing.

- More options are available to those shipping by air. For example, United Parcel Service has entered the air parcel express business to compete against Federal Express, Emery, Airborne, and the U.S. Postal Service.

- The inland water carriers have been adversely affected by the weak economy. Several carriers are exploring broadening their base through investments in terminals.

- Slurry pipelines are still seeking federal eminent domain rights.

In summary, shippers and receivers are now being pursued by aggressive, innovative carriers in a relatively free (as compared with the past 40 years) marketplace. How should they respond?

Implications for Shippers and Receivers

Transportation Strategies for the Eighties contained nine general guidelines for shippers and receivers, in addition to detailed promising strategies for different types of shipments. The nine guidelines are as follows:

1. Intensively manage the transportation function relying on strategic and operating plans, budgets, formal reviews, and effective organizational communications.

Companies such as Boise Cascade have incorporated the elements described in the NCPDM study into a formal corporate transportation strategic planning process.[3] Similarly, firms such as Warner Lambert have strengthened their corporate transportation function: ". . . because two-thirds of our distribution costs are in transportation, speaking to carriers with a single voice brings important payoffs in the new, deregulated environment."[4] On the other hand, other companies, perhaps in response to recessionary pressures, have reduced or even eliminated corporate transportation and distribution departments, and have transferred the responsibilities back to the operating divisions. At least one company, TRW, uses a transportation council to try to achieve the benefits of centralization within a decentralized operating philosophy.

2. Improve information planning and operating systems. At a minimum, generate freight flow information from the freight payment system. Without this information it is extremely difficult to negotiate effective agreements.

3. Use freight terms selectively to control or influence transportation decisions, consistent with marketing strategies. Many firms are finding that gaining control over inbound transportation offers excellent opportunities to reduce total transportation costs through better asset utilization and more negotiating leverage.

4. Review service requirements and ensure that premium transportation is used only when absolutely necessary. It is surprising how often inbound transportation is routed on premium next-day services when reliable second- or third-day delivery at substantially reduced costs would be satisfactory.

5. Consolidate shipments to build traffic volume. More options are available than ever, particularly with irregular route carriers.

6. Concentrate traffic with a limited number of carriers. Sears has reduced its carriers from over 4000 to less than 300. FMC has cut its roster of motor carriers by 30 percent. Spiegel Inc. is moving toward 6 to 12 carriers in place of 400. General Electric has combined traffic concentration with rate negotiations. Aided by a financial planning model, GE has been able to successfully link LTL discounts with a policy of increasing carrier market shares on specific traffic lanes.

7. Expand the use of contracts. Although most of the current contracts focus on rate reductions in return for volume commitments, the more innovative contracts remove the uncertainties of service variability, equipment supply, rate escalation, and the need to use the spot market.

8. Reassess the economic and service attributes of proprietary motor carrier operations. Although legislative and regulatory developments have given private carriage more flexibility, they have also made contract carriage a more effective competitor for shipments moving in proprietary fleets. If empty mileage is in excess of 10 to 20 percent, serious consideration should be given to shifting to for-hire transportation.

9. Develop or improve analytic and negotiating skills. In the regulatory world a premium was placed on the knowledge of tariffs and the ability to influence the regulatory process. In the deregulated world, the rewards accrue to those with strong negotiating and analytic skills.

Conclusions

Recent experience suggests that the findings of the NCPDM study will remain valid for the foreseeable future. The messages are simple, yet critical to management, as they look ahead to the remainder of the decade and beyond:

- The transportation environment has radically changed and will not revert to regulation.

- Intensive management can convert a traditional regulatory support function into an aggressive management function.

- Strategic planning will be the critical element to successful transportation management.

Notes

1. "Development of Transportation Strategy Plans," *Traffic World*, September 20, 1982, p. 7.
2. Particularly insightful articles providing forecasts of technological change in the transportation industry include Dr. V. C. Seguin, "Freight Transport Technology to the Year 2000—A Forecast Update," TRF Proceeding 1981 (Oxford, Ind.: Richard B. Cross, 1981); Jack Farrell, "Where We're Going," *Traffic Management*, January 1982, pp. 55–59; and Lisa Harrington, "New Transport Technology Overcomes Barriers to Efficiency," *Traffic Management*, May 1981. In addition, a 1982 Congressional Budget Office working paper, *Energy Use in Freight Transportation*, provides a useful reference point for evaluating fuel productivity. That comparison of modal fuel efficiency is presented in Table 22–4.
3. *1983–1984 Presidential Issue—Handling and Shipping Management*, p. 64.
4. "What Unifying Distribution Management Can Do," *Traffic Management* (September 1981), pp. 54–60.

Facilities

Warehouse Operations

KENNETH B. ACKERMAN *and* NORMAN E. LANDES

Distribution Facility Choices

When considering warehousing, every distribution manager goes through a series of "make or buy" decisions. For all practical purposes it is possible to manage a warehouse with internal staff. Therefore, the question about whether to seek outside management or whether to staff the operation internally is the classic purchasing problem. If the decision is to use an outside supplier, the next question is whether to select a public warehouse or a contract warehouse.

Factors affecting this make-or-buy decision include consideration of organizational influence and style, financial policy, labor relations, and cost trade-offs. It may well be that management has decided to provide distribution services with its own resources rather than buy them externally. Financial policy may also dictate whether a company owns real estate or uses short-term leasing arrangements as a result of its asset management policy. Personnel policy may also affect the decision, especially where union relationships are involved. Obviously, consideration of the total cost of the distribution facility is basic to the decision, once the other parameters are established. In some instances a mix of internally operated and supplied service is desired in order to maintain an economic balance and a check on each form of operation. Finally, the make-or-buy decision will also be affected by the overall business strategy of the corporation. Specifically, what activities does the corporation really want to engage in, and does that list include warehousing and distribution? In some company environments, warehousing and distribution may be selected as an area which should be pursued, partially to develop distribution management skills which may be needed for other areas of corporate activity, or perhaps to engage in warehouse real estate speculation.

In summary, the choice between managing distribution facilities internally or relying on an outside supplier is a decision which is based on corporate and management goals. It will be influenced by the organizational environment, by the financial strategy of the company, by attitudes toward labor relations and diversification, and ultimately by the strategic decision of what kinds of business the company should engage in.

Public versus Contract Warehousing

If the decision is to use an outside contractor, then the choice between public warehousing or contract warehousing must be made. Public warehousing is an arrangement in which charges are usually based on the unit or hundredweight of product handled, with no fixed charges other than the payment of a modest, minimum fee. Under a contract arrangement, the customer contracts with the warehouse operator for a specific period of time, frequently a number of years. Comparing the two services is not unlike the "risk sharing" approach taken in insurance. When the user signs a contract, he reduces the risk to the operator and in return receives a lower price. With a contract mode of operation, the buyer trades a measure of flexibility for a measure of cost control.

Basically, contract warehousing agreements will vary from one another in several areas.[1] Contract clauses will vary by the question of which party retains inventory responsibility (also referred to as bailment). Another variant is the question of how space is reserved—whether it is held under a lease, under a month-to-month rental contract, purchased by the unit, or not purchased at all. The same set of variables exists for handling and clerical services. Under some contract arrangements, the user may buy handling services without buying space because he would like the warehousing performed in a building that he already owns. Conversely, he may buy space without buying warehouse labor services, or without buying clerical services, because he wants his own people to provide one or both of these services. Ultimately, the choice between public or contract warehousing is based on a measurement of cost versus risk. As the cost of real estate escalates, or in a location with highly restrictive labor contracts, it may be difficult to find a public warehouse supplier who is willing or even able to absorb the risk of a fully public warehousing operation. There was a time when a typical airline could earn a profit when just over 50 percent of its seats were full, and there was also a time when many public warehouses passed the break-even point when occupancy rose above 50 percent. In both industries, the break-even point has moved considerably closer to 100 percent, and the risk of carrying empty seats or empty space must be compensated with proportionately higher rates for the services that are sold. Some airlines meet this problem with charter services. The warehousing equivalent is contract warehousing.

In either case, there are shades of public or contract warehousing agreement that may be developed to serve any particular need. Traditionally, the warehousing industry has held itself out to be extremely flexible in order to meet specific customer requirements.

Once the choice of operating style is made, the location decision follows.

Location

The question of where to put the distribution facility may be answered before or after the question of operating style is answered. Site selection is the most important decision made by most corporate planners. It involves a significant capital outlay if the facility is to be owned. Even if a structure is leased, it may represent a commitment in the form of a capitalized lease. Conceivably, a poor selection of location could spell the difference between success or failure in the overall distribution program.

This chapter will not attempt to duplicate the computer modeling decisions for facility location which are dealt with elsewhere in this handbook (see pages 390–395). Simulation techniques available today offer an input to site selection which was undreamed of a decade ago. Rather than repeating material covered elsewhere, we will discuss some of the qualitative inputs which should be considered as an added dimension to the computer model.

Customer Service Levels

A decision on site selection is likely to be influenced by corporate customer service policy. If a company intends to provide customer service that is superior to any other firm's service in the industry, the choice may be to select more cities than competitors in order to provide a higher standard of delivery service. In contrast, if corporate strategy is to provide the lowest cost product in the industry, the most sensible policy may be to serve the entire market from a distribution center located adjacent to the production plant.

A warehouse facility may serve as a consolidation center, a distribution point, or both. If it is to serve as a consolidation center, its location must be considered relative to accessibility of inbound materials and components.

Four New Factors

In the current environment, a site selection decision is likely to weigh heavily four factors which might not have been considered important only a short time ago. These are energy availability, environmental regulations, availability of capital, and quality of life.

Since the early 1970s both the cost and availability of energy have increased in importance. Changes in the trade-off costs between high-priced fuel and low-priced land may cause some site planners to choose a central city location rather than a rural location.

When capital becomes scarce or expensive, the availability of industrial revenue bond financing may dictate a site location that would not otherwise have been considered.

In weighing various locations, consideration must be given to production mix, customer mix, freight rates and freight allowances, and the production strategy of the corporation. Horizontally integrated firms will have different location requirements from vertically integrated firms. Location requirements will also differ depending on whether a firm's factories produce a single product or product family, or whether branch plants each produce a full product line.

The newest environmental change involves the deregulation of freight traffic. Published rates are rapidly becoming meaningless, and indeed freight rates may not be published within a few years. One possible effect of deregulation could be the emergence of a smaller number of larger and more highly automated distribution facilities. These large facilities might be used for product recall and recycling as well as for distribution of finished products.

In selecting a location, it is important to watch the *total* distribution cost and not just the facilities cost. That total cost must be compared to desired goals in customer service. Customer service goals must emphasize reliability, speed, or—if possible—both.

Additional considerations may be less tangible than those mentioned above. These may include the possibility of economies of scale if the facility is a large one. It is also important to determine whether the company is dealing with a rapid growth situation or a slow growth situation. Understanding future trends within the organization is required, if only to know whether site considerations plans should include plans for extensive expansion.

External Factors

Certain external factors, such as tax rates, the legislative and regulatory climate, and changes in freight transportation, must also be evaluated.

Choosing a distribution facility location is partly art and partly science. The computer model is the scientific part, but the human judgment involved in preparing and analyzing the results indicated by that model is still an art.

Why Measure Productivity?

Operational productivity must be a primary concern of all warehouse managers—those managing public, contract, or private warehouses. While buildings and equipment are generally similar from one location to another, people are not. People make the difference between mediocrity and excellence in warehouse operations. For maximum effectiveness, the warehouse staff must be motivated, scheduled, and controlled through an effective productivity management system.

Productivity improvement is important because it is the primary defense against spiraling inflation. With continued increases in wages, energy costs, and practically all other costs of operation, warehousing costs will necessarily increase unless there are productivity gains to offset these higher costs. Productivity measurement is a way to "keep score," and meaningful steps toward improvement cannot be taken unless measurements are expressed quantitatively.

Productivity in a warehouse also makes unique demands on the supervisor. A manager in the warehouse situation is faced with circumstances making direct supervision more difficult than in the more traditional manufacturing environment. Unlike the manufacturing counterpart, the warehouse supervisor typically cannot see subordinates. That is, with literally hundreds of stacks of merchandise located in many aisles, the supervisor cannot continuously keep all of the warehousemen in sight as they perform their tasks. This problem is compounded by the large areas covered by a warehouse, making it physically difficult for the supervisor to travel the long distances with any frequency. Therefore, in order to schedule and control the warehousemen, the supervisor must rely on a system of goals and standards to know when a particular task should be completed and a new task assigned.

Another important reason for measuring productivity is to manage the significant variance in demands placed on a distribution center. Unlike a manufacturer making thousands of the same item, the service demands placed on a warehouse vary from month to month, day to day, and even hour to hour. There are several reasons for these variations. First, while a manufacturing plant may produce only a few items, a typical distribution center will stock many line items covering the company's entire product line. Because not all customers are alike, order demands will vary, such as the differences between filling a less-than-truckload (LTL) order and a carload order. Customer service commitments also vary. Rush shipments, special marking or packaging, and customer pickups are just a few examples of varying demands. Finally, transportation carriers, both truck and rail, that serve the warehouse are subject to last minute changes due to equipment breakdowns, weather, etc.

What Is Productivity?

Productivity is the ratio of output to input, or the work performed at the warehouse divided by the resources used to produce that work. Productivity is the result of a three-factor equation combining efficiency, utilization, and performance (Figure 23–1).[2]

Efficiency relates to the methods, procedures, and equipment used to accomplish a warehouse task. For example, warehousemen might normally use electric powered pallet jacks to select orders, but when extremely busy, be forced to augment with push carts for the same task. These methods and equipment choices have different levels of efficiency.

Utilization is the proportion of capacity that a resource is used compared to what is available. If an individual is available for eight hours a day, but is inactive for the first two hours while awaiting clerical processing, then utilization would be 75 percent (six hours worked for eight hours available).

Performance is the ratio of standard hours earned to actual hours, or the ratio of actual output to standard output. For example, if the standard for unloading a 1000-case rail car is five hours, and the worker completed the task in four hours, then performance would be 125 percent. This can be calculated either as five standard hours divided by four actual hours, or as 250 cases per hour actual divided by 200 cases per hour standard.

Productivity Improvement

Management can improve productivity—the ratio of output to input—by affecting the three variables of efficiency, utilization, or performance (Figure 23–2). First, warehouse management must analyze and select the most efficient methods to be used to perform a given warehouse task. For example, an order selection line might be arranged according to product number sequence, or arranged according to the frequency of movement. Effi-

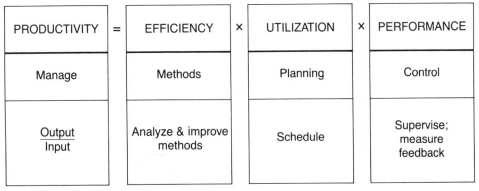

Figure 23-1   Productivity Equation

ciency is improved through the analysis, evaluation, and selection of methods. Many times, improved methods are not implemented because of limitations in capital investment and payback policies. Such capital investments usually relate to facilities and equipment, but capital improvement justification is not the only reason for methods analysis. Methods analysis can be used for storage layouts, order-picking methods, equipment selection, and other warehouse activities performed with modest regularity.

Productivity can also be increased through improved utilization, which requires planning and scheduling so that resources are made readily available and are properly allocated. A typical example might be the case of a receiving dock workload that requires ten forklift trucks during the morning and five during the afternoon, coupled with a shipping dock workload which requires five forklift trucks in the morning and ten in the afternoon. If each dock is assigned ten pieces of equipment at all times, the utilization would be 75 percent. However, if during the afternoon the five idle forklift trucks on the receiving dock could be shifted to the shipping dock, then the total forklift fleet of twenty could be reduced by five, yielding a 100 percent utilization factor. This same logic can be applied to warehouse labor, allowing management to improve utilization through planning and scheduling by shifting the available labor resources to the areas of the warehouse where resources are needed. Management should therefore negotiate as few job classification restrictions as practical in order to maximize flexibility of the work force.

Management can influence the performance of the work force—that is, comparison to standard—by maintaining proper motivation through effective supervision. The supervisor must have the ability to measure performance and provide appropriate feedback to the work force. The ability of the supervisor to do so will allow timely criticism or praise

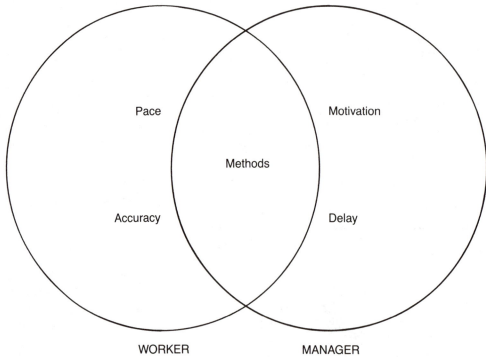

Figure 23-2   Labor and Management Influence Productivity

where appropriate. It should be noted that substandard performance is not proof that an employee was "goofing off," but might indicate that the wrong methods were used, the proper equipment was not available, or other factors outside the control of the worker affected performance.

Individual employees can also affect productivity in different ways. They should use the methods specified by management. However, if they have not had appropriate training, then improper methods may be in use which will adversely affect productivity. On the other hand, many productivity improvement ideas come from the persons actually doing the work. They may devise better methods, thereby improving efficiency and having a positive impact on productivity. Management's methods may not be the best methods.

Individual workers also control the accuracy of their output. A distribution center operation where individuals take pride in quality control and accuracy yields greater total productivity because it is easier to do it right the first time. Accuracy problems lower productivity because additional people are needed to check others' work and to reprocess earlier errors.

Finally, the individual worker controls the pace at which the job is performed. Employees can speed up or slow down for many reasons. Our working premise is that given the right tools, a reasonable work schedule, and supervisory feedback, warehouse workers will perform their assignments at a normal pace.

Motivation

Motivation is affected by management and translates into performance and utilization, both of which are improved when effective supervisors provide feedback, planning, and scheduling.

The average employee will work at a normal pace which results in output falling into a band defined as "normal performance" (Figure 23-3). There are periods during the day when output exceeds the normal range, but there are also times when work performance falls below the normal range, including times when no work is being performed. The work day shown in the figure has three significant areas. The first two areas are delays during which no work is being performed. The first occurred because management did not have work assignments or equipment available when the individual started work. The second delay was also caused by improper scheduling—the employee completed the work assignment but the supervisor had not planned ahead by having a subsequent job assignment ready. The final delay occurred near the end of the shift, and is related to Parkinson's Law[3]—work expands to fill the time available for its completion. In this case, the supervisor lacked control or failed to motivate the worker to meet the expected level of normal performance.

Productivity Management System

A closed loop productivity management system is the most desirable system to be implemented (Figure 23-4). The heart of the system is a planning and controlling function. Expected warehouse receipts, expected warehouse shipments, and any other work to be performed are input to the planning segment. Taking the available resources into account, the productivity management system develops a series of schedules that define the priori-

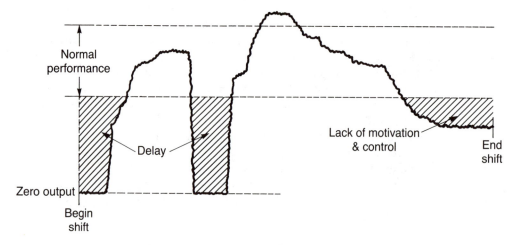

Figure 23-3   Daily Work Performance

ties for customer service, assign capital resources such as dock doors and equipment, and make the personnel work assignments. The warehouse supervisor uses these as a "road map" for the day's activities.

The actual work output and the resources used are input to the control and evaluation phase of the productivity management system which generates productivity reports that measure performance and utilization levels. The supervisor can use the performance reports to provide feedback to the individual warehouseman, while management and supervision can use the utilization reports as feedback on their effectiveness in scheduling resources. Finally, these reports become feedback into the planning segment of the productivity management system, where they can be of use in evaluating the efficiency of the warehouse operation.

Ways to Measure Productivity

The first step in measuring warehouse productivity is to categorize the functions being performed within the warehouse. The key tasks which can be independently measured and improved should be identified. While a rudimentary division would be receiving and shipping, more specific functions that can typically be identified for independent measure include truck receiving, rail receiving, put away, replenishment, order picking, packing, truck loading, rail loading and LTL loading.

It is not necessary to measure *every* activity within the warehouse because some tasks are so small and difficult to measure that the effort expended exceeds the benefit gained. Pareto's Law* applies: 80 percent of the warehouse effort goes into 20 percent of the activities. In most warehouse operations, measurement of receiving, order picking, and shipping will capture 80 percent of the effort expended.

Many managers seek an overall productivity measure encompassing the entire warehouse operation. Such measures have questionable value because so many diverse activi-

---

*Vilfredo Pareto, a 19th-century economist, observed that an 80–20 relationship describes many business activities, e.g., 80 percent of sales come from 20 percent of the customers.

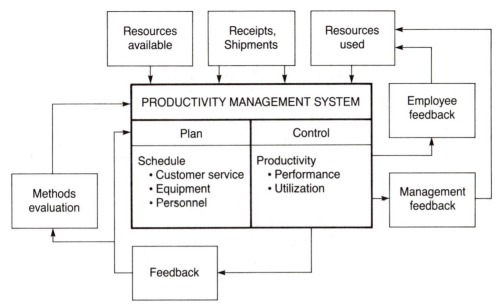

Figure 23-4   Closed-Loop Productivity Management System

ties are combined into one simplistic measure, such as pounds of throughput per man hour. These overall measures are something like the stock market's Dow-Jones Average. The Dow-Jones may provide an indication of overall market performance, but that performance is not indicative of the performance of a particular stock. Just as the price of General Motors stock may drop on a day when the Dow-Jones rises, order picking productivity may drop on a day when the total productivity indicator may increase. There are ways to improve these simplistic measures to make them more meaningful.

Characteristics of a Good Measure

A good measure and a good measurement system must be (1) valid, (2) accurate, (3)useful and complete, (4)cost-effective, and (5) timely.[4] Without these characteristics a measurement system can be abused by managers and supervisors alike, yielding false conclusions and bad decisions. Conversely, good measures will aid in making correct decisions. Good measures will be equitable both to those using the measures and to those being measured, and thus should not be a deterrent to positive labor relations.

The first characteristic, validity, deals with the question of whether output is related to input. Measurements must accurately reflect changes in the *real* productivity of the work force. If the warehouse task is to unload pallets of merchandise from a rail car, then the dollar value of the merchandise on each pallet is inconsequential in terms of productivity. Therefore, the measure should be stated in physical terms such as pallets unloaded per hour, and not in economic terms such as dollars unloaded per hour.

Accuracy relates to the level of detail being applied to the activity under study. This is the case of separating "apples and oranges" before measuring. For example, if a warehouse were required to order pick both pallet quantities and individual cases, but on separate bills of lading, then it would be more accurate to measure case picking separately from pallet load picking.

The third characteristic of a good measure encompasses usefulness and completeness. A complete measure includes all work performed, and does not fail to capture some element of what is being done. The usefulness of a measure can be gauged by its understandability. If the work force and supervisors cannot understand or relate to the measure, it has limited usefulness. The measure must provide information which is useful to planning, scheduling, or evaluation.

A cost-effective system is one in which the costs of developing and maintaining the measurement system are less than the benefits received. The size of the operation will often dictate whether automated measurement systems will be cost effective.

Timeliness is an important attribute. If the information cannot be gathered and reported in a timely fashion, then the measure will have limited use. Likewise, to provide feedback to supervisors and workers, measurements must be reported within reasonable time of when the work occurred. A daily productivity report which is a week late has little value.

Types of Measures

There are four basic types of productivity measures which are currently in use: (1) historical/goal setting, (2) time study, (3) predetermined times, and (4) regression-based.

Historical/Goal Setting

Historical standards are developed from records of past experience and take the form of an average single-variable output per labor hour. These standards are easily developed by recording the outputs and inputs each day, then calculating an average based on this sample. Historical averages can be gross in nature, such as throughput pounds per hour, or they can be broken into greater detail. An example would be the number of cases unloaded per hour for cased paper goods, floor loaded on a rail car, and received on the day shift. The most common input unit is labor hour, but even this requires evaluation. For example, if the input labor hours are taken from payroll records, they probably include non-working time such as breaks, vacations, sick leave, etc. The preferred measure would be based on net time actually devoted to performing the task under study.

Historical standards can be categorized in four ways. The first would be classified as *trend standards*. Over time, a relationship such as seasonality may develop which becomes the trend. A second form of historical standards is based on comparisons between either people or warehouse locations. Outputs of various individuals within a given warehouse might be compared, or various warehouse locations within the company. A third category would be "agreed-upon goals." In this case, a negotiated goal becomes the standard. Examples include agreements where supervisors commit themselves to improve productivity to a target level and similar goal setting involving the warehouse work force. Figure 23–5 illustrates these three forms.

The final form of historical standards is based on industry comparisons. These are similar to historical comparisons between company warehouses, but in this case become intercompany comparisons based upon industry commonality. A well known example of such industry comparisons is compiled by the National American Wholesale Grocers' Association (NAWGA). The results of these tabulations are then made available to partici-

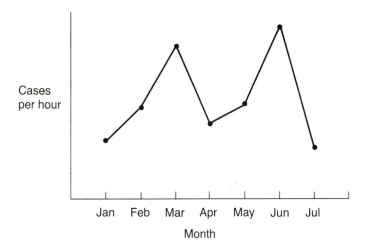

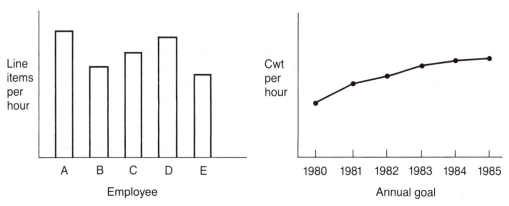

Figure 23-5   Historical Standards and Goals

pating members and others (Table 23-1). A 1980 article in *Modern Materials Handling* described NAWGA's reporting procedures:*

> These ratios are actual, average productivity figures from the wholesale grocers' industry as compiled by the National American Wholesale Grocers' Association (NAWGA). For several years, the association has tabulated productivity data from grocery distribution firms.
>
> NAWGA's approach to measuring productivity is complete and thorough, and can be used as a model by almost any firm or industry. Each year the member firms collect detailed data about their operation for a four-week period between July and September. The information represents 23 different productivity indices, covering every warehouse function. From the data, NAWGA computes overall warehouse productivity figures summarized here.

*Reprinted from "How to Measure Warehouse Productivity," *Modern Materials Handling*, **35**, No. 2B (February 22, 1980), pp. 54–59. Modern Materials Handling, Copyright 1980 by Cahners Publishing Company, Division of Reed Holdings, Inc.

You may not be able to apply all of their indices to your operation because the characteristics of their business—high volumes and large customer orders—may not be the same as yours. For example, NAWGA uses tons per hour and pieces selected per hour; you might measure cases received, stored, picked, or shipped per hour.

"Tons and pieces are two of the most valid and revealing indices for our industry," says NAWGA's president, Gerald E. Peck. "However, even they must be monitored carefully as output factors. The output value varies over time. For example, as the number of pieces per ton has increased, over the years, so has the number of individual handlings required. Also, delivering merchandise on a cart or pallet that moves directly to the display shelf in the store, gives it a greater value than the same merchandise delivered deadpiled. Similarly, cases with labels carrying computer-printed warehouse and retail store information have a greater value than the same cases without the labels.

"In looking at the figures compiled over the years, the indices of tons per manhour and pieces per manhour have remained fairly constant. Since the real value of the output has increased, we know our productivity has improved slightly, even with a constant ratio. But that's not good enough because during the same period the costs of labor, energy, and transportation have increased significantly."

The difficulty with historical standards is that they do not measure differences in what appear to be superficially similar tasks. Because the measures do not capture these differences, worker output can vary significantly from job to job, and scheduling using these standards is virtually impossible. Also, evaluation is limited in accuracy (Figure 23–6). That is, historical standards are not accurate in the short term, but become more accurate over the long term. Averaging is therefore of limited usefulness in improving productivity. However, historical standards are easy for the work force to understand. Data can be collected with reasonable ease, and can be reported in a timely fashion. A historical standards program can be low in both developmental and maintenance cost, particularly if automation is not involved.

Time Study

Work standards can be based on time studies which use the engineering approach of defining and documenting a task, and then taking time measurement observations of individuals performing those tasks. Unfortunately, this method generally has a bad connotation, particularly among labor unions, due to industrial engineering abuses in manufacturing environments years ago. The single most important requirement in useful time study methods is to have a qualified person performing the time study. The individual need not be a graduate engineer, but should have training in the observation and measurement of people at work. Because individuals work at different levels, it is necessary to rate each individual according to effort level, in order to create a "normal" time. Thus, an individual working at a slow pace might be rated .85 while an individual putting forth extra effort might be rated at 1.20.

Time study can produce standards which are valid and, though sometimes resented, generally understood. Since warehouse operations vary significantly (e.g. one order is different from another), averaging generally takes place. This introduces problems relating to accuracy. That is, the time study method will be very accurate when applied to the "average order," but may be inaccurate when applied to the majority of the orders which are not "average." Due to the qualifications and time needed to develop these standards, time study methods tend to be expensive, and little used.

Table 23-1 NAWGA Productivity Comparison (Small, Medium, and Large Warehouses)

What they measure	1976			1977			1978			1979		
	Small	Medium	Large	Small	Medium	Large	Small	Medium	Large	Small	Medium	Large
Tons per hour (total labor)	0.98	1.08	1.09	1.02	1.00	1.19	0.94	1.01	1.26	0.86	0.78	1.06
Pieces selected per hour	119	132	128	138	120	127	120	134	137	118	126	126
Stockturn rate (turns per year)	15.07	15.33	17.98	14.83	14.99	18.09	14.61	16.04	16.42	14.32	15.22	16.66
Payroll cost per case shipped	0.21	0.18	0.19	0.17	0.19	0.25	0.25	0.20	0.21	0.27	0.23	0.26
Payroll as percent of sales	1.6	1.6	1.7	1.4	1.6	2.1	1.6	1.6	1.8	1.8	1.8	2.0
Payroll cost per ton (in and out)	7.05	5.88	6.49	5.66	6.45	8.34	8.72	6.88	7.45	10.80	8.20	8.93

NOTE: Small—less than 100,000 sq ft; Medium—100,000 to 200,000 sq ft; Large—over 200,000 sq ft

SOURCE: Reprinted from "How to Measure Warehouse Productivity," *Modern Materials Handling*, 35, No. 2B (February 22, 1980), pp. 54–59. Modern Materials Handling, Copyright 1980 by Cahners Publishing Company, Division of Reed Holdings, Inc.

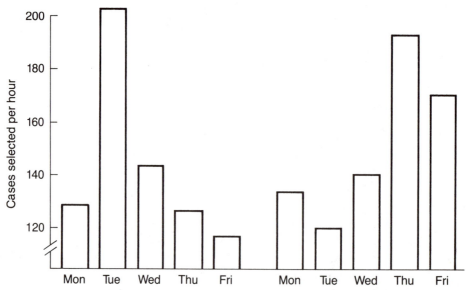

Figure 23-6   Variability in Historical Productivity. Because of order size and line item mix, significant variability can be noted in the actual cases picked per labor hour. With a historical average of 150 cases per hour, scheduling or evaluation is limited in that the historical average is accurate (± 5 %) on only two of the ten days shown.

Predetermined Times

An outgrowth of the engineered approach using time study resulted in predetermined engineered standards. These standards are printed time values which have been "predetermined." The time values are for small elements of warehouse tasks. Through careful detailing of a warehouse task, each of these elements can be identified and a time value assigned. The time values can then be summed together to give a time value for the entire task. This system provides a valid approach based on engineering principles.

The results of these engineered studies with elemental values are available from several sources. Most notably, the United States Department of Defense has published an eleven-volume set of such data covering diverse activities from material handling to forestry operations (Table 23-2). Likewise, industry groups, such as the American Warehousemen's Association, have funded studies and made the published predetermined times available to their members. Finally, many consulting organizations have in-house data which they apply for their clients. In addition to these sources of general purpose predetermined times, warehouse managers also have found occasion to use predetermined standards derived from equipment manufacturers' specification sheets and in-company time studies for specialized warehouse activities.

The greatest benefit of predetermined standards lies in the ability to evaluate various design and method alternatives before actually implementing such changes. Therefore, management can make economic justification decisions based on engineering disciplines. No other methods described herein allow this design parameter—the other methods discussed require the study of existing operations.

Predetermined time values rate very high in terms of accuracy and validity. Unfortunately, the complexity of these systems makes them more difficult for warehouse workers and supervisors to understand and accept. This complexity results in fairly high imple-

Table 23–2   Department of Defense Predetermined Time Standard

Operation: Obtain and Operate Manual Pallet Jack
Code: BEPJ
Description: This element includes all the time to secure, start, stop and return pallet jack. The element begins with securing the pallet jack, start, stop, run in empty, raise blades, run out loaded, position to drop, drop the blades and run out empty.

Element	*Source*	*TMU*
Get pallet jack	M22	50
Start pallet jack	M21	32
Stop pallet jack	M26	59
Run in empty	M28	118
Raise blades	M27	414
Run out loaded	M25	258
Start pallet jack—loaded	M21	32
Stop pallet jack—loaded	M26	59
Position to drop	M23	214
Drop blades (knob control)	M24	102
Run out empty	M29	180
Total normal time		1518

Source: Unites States Department of Defense, Washington, D.C.

mentation costs and ongoing maintenance costs. If the system is to be operated manually, it is many times simplified, using averages to improve timeliness. Introduction of such averaging adversely affects the accuracy of the system. Accuracy can be preserved and coupled with timely reporting through the use of a computer, but at significantly greater expense.

Regression Analysis

A relatively new approach, using a time-tested mathematical technique, has been successfully applied to warehouse operations. This technique involves multiple-variable regression analysis. The significant value of this technique lies in its ability to consider more than one variable as having an important impact on the time required to complete a warehouse task. This can be visualized (Figure 23–7) using a cube in which the vertical axis remains as the time required while the two horizontal axes represent two variables. For example, in loading LTL trailers, the two variables might be the number of bills of lading and the number of pallets. Though illustration of a fourth dimension is difficult, another variable to the previous example might be the number of cases to be loaded on the LTL shipments.

This method is applied by collecting performance times while recording data on what are considered to be important variables (e.g., cases, line items, etc.). These data must then be input to a multiple regression statistics program on a computer. Such programs are readily available from time-sharing services, as purchased software, and many times as a part of general purpose in-house computer libraries. The statistical program will consider each variable and its impact on the total time required, which can be translated into a mathematical formula assigning a weight to each of the variables:

Expected time = $AX_1 + BX_2 + \ldots +$ CONSTANT
Receiving   = 1.75 (number of pallets) + 2.80 (number of slipsheets) + 10

Order pick   = 2.83 (number of orders) + .30 (number of cases) +
3.45 (number of line items) + 4.5
Shipping   = 3.16 (number of bills of lading) + .0015 (weight) + 2.5

Though every variable may have an impact, many are insignificant and can thus be dropped from the final equation. The statistical program also provides a guide as to whether enough information has been collected to statistically allow use of the equation. Finally, this technique creates a range of performance which will be considered acceptable. That is, in addition to developing the time for a task, it also develops the band of performance that would normally be experienced. This is the only technique that provides such an indicator. An example of the output from such a program appears in Table 23-3.

Multi-variable regression analysis defines quantitatively what experienced workers and supervisors know qualitatively. There are several factors that determine whether a given warehouse task could be deemed easy or hard, resulting in less or more time being required. This technique accounts for those differences in tasks that heretofore could not be quantified. Therefore, although the mathematical technique is complex, the application is simple. This ease of application and resulting accurate information lead to understanding and acceptance by the warehouse work force and supervisors. The ease of application results in lower cost of operation. The installation cost, though greater than that for historical standards, is less than the other engineered approaches. Accuracy, validity, and timeliness are all attributes of this technique. Many applications of this technique are carried out on hand-held programmable calculators, making the information very portable for use throughout the warehouse.

Comparison of Measurement Types

Each of these measurement methods has advantages and disadvantages. In an extremely small warehouse environment (less than five workers), it may be uneconomical to install any but the simplest productivity measures—historical averages. Similarly, in a very large environment (over 100 workers), almost any system might be economically justified.

After economic considerations, these approaches can be compared from two additional viewpoints. First, the types of measures must be compared as to their effectiveness as a scheduling tool. Second, each approach should be compared as an evaluation tool. A summary (Figure 23-8) of these four methods shows that regression-based standards have some positive attributes that make them preferable for many applications. These standards work over wide ranges, in contrast to the other approaches which are adversely affected by the introduction of averaging.

Two important differences remain. Predetermined times allow for the creation and evaluation of alternate layouts, procedures, methods, etc. with the ability to evaluate such changes before implementation. Regression-based standards include a band of normal performance allowing management to make appropriate judgments concerning individual efforts. Depending on the situation, preferred applications can be found for each type.

Uses of Productivity Management Systems

Now that productivity has been defined—as a combination of efficiency, utilization, and performance—it is possible to use the productivity management system to improve pro-

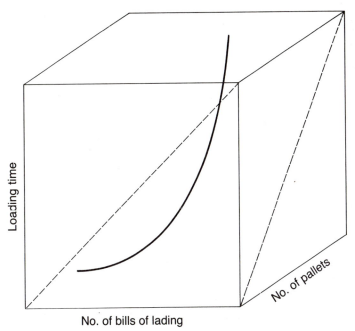

Loading time

No. of pallets

No. of bills of lading

Figure 23-7   Two-Variable Multiple Regression

ductivity. Efficiency—and thus productivity—can be improved by selecting those methods that maximize output for a given level of input, that is, "work smarter, not harder." The ability to evaluate alternate methods can have a significant impact on productivity gains. In order to evaluate alternate designs in advance, the availability of predetermined engineered standards is valuable. Without such tools, changes are based on "best guess" decision making. The difficulty with such decision making is that because of factors such as resistance to change, learning curve, etc., it really takes at least 90 days to evaluate whether or not a change has resulted in improvement.

Utilization is improved by increasing the time spent working and simultaneously minimizing non-productive time. This is achieved through work scheduling, which is the responsibility of management and serves as the key to productivity improvement. The "hurry up and wait" syndrome destroys productivity because it increases the fatigue level of the individual and results in zero output during idle waiting times.

A fair day's work at a normal pace results in acceptable performance. Performance must be monitored and reviewed, and corrective action should be taken in a timely fashion. Feedback on performance will be a positive boost to motivation because most people want to know how they measure against a fair and equitable goal.

Customer Service

The primary responsibility of each distribution center is to provide a satisfactory level of customer service for those being served by that warehouse. Warehousing provides a time utility, and so it is important to have what the customer wants at the time it is wanted. This can be achieved through effective scheduling of warehouse operations.

Table 23-3   Sample Computer Output—Three-Variable Multiple Regression

	ACCT	LINES	CASES	WEIGHT	EMP	TIME
1#	2	12	36	411	2	25
2#	2	10	25	767	4	13
3#	2	8	25	440	1	14
4#	2	6	28	449	2	13
5#	2	21	147	4570	1	71
6#	2	4	23	253	1	11
7#	2	10	25	317	2	14
8#	2	2	25	400	2	7
9#	2	2	75	1176	1	14
10#	2	7	154	2019	3	27
11#	2	7	25	796	2	11
12#	2	9	529	7040	2	78
13#	2	8	250	4331	3	39
14#	2	15	43	560	1	36
15#	2	4	26	295	3	12
16#	2	11	25	300	2	27

DEP. VARIABLE: TIME
IND. VARIABLES: LINES, CASES, WEIGHT
COLUMN FOR RESIDUALS:
COLUMN FOR COEFFICIENTS:

R-SQUARED = .954
F-VALUE (3, 12) = 83.59531
STD. ERROR OF ESTIMATE = 5.15140

INTERCEPT = 3.66547

VARIABLE	COEFFICIENT	T-VALUE
LINES	2.09095	6.08741
CASES	6.764020E-02	1.90112
WEIGHT	3.704011E-03	1.49404

Most distribution centers will at one time or another be stretched to or beyond capacity. A productivity management system will allow the warehouse operator to predict accurately the inputs needed, and then to arrange the warehouse activities to coincide with the priority of its customers. For example, receiving of noncritical items might be deferred so that selection and shipping of customers' orders can take place according to customer need. If customers' orders must be delayed, the productivity management system can identify the amount of the delay.

Personnel Assignments

In most warehouse operations, people are the most expensive asset. Matching people with work through effective scheduling will yield the greatest positive impact on productivity. The largest variable cost in warehousing is labor, and control of labor through scheduling results in lower overall distribution costs.

There are several reasons to schedule people effectively. For one thing, if too many people are scheduled into an activity or area of the warehouse, lower performance may result. The larger the crew, the more chance for congestion and time wasted in idle "chit-chat." On the other hand, it is impractical to assign one person to do everything related to a given operation or area of the warehouse. If more than one person is assigned to a task and if the output is dependent upon their interaction, then line balancing becomes crucial. That is, it is important that the components mesh together so that all parties are effectively utilized, and that no party is sitting idle. An example would be the offloading and storing of two rail cars of floor loaded merchandise. This task would not be completed in a timely fashion if only one warehouseman with a forklift truck were assigned to it. It might be possible to complete the task in a timely fashion if two warehousemen with two forklift trucks were each assigned to unload one of the boxcars. However, this would create significant underutilization of forklift equipment (while hand-stacking took place) which would be undesirable. Therefore, a crew of three might be assembled to perform this task, one forklift operator removing the loads to storage while the other two individuals are palletizing the floor loaded merchandise. If one boxcar is emptied by both laborers before beginning on the second, then lower productivity is likely to result. First, the two laborers will probably work at a slower pace, but one still faster than the pace with which the forklift operator can remove the palletized merchandise, resulting in idle time for both the laborers. However, if the laborers are individually assigned to each boxcar, they will work independent of peer pressure or interruptions from the other laborer. The forklift operator will be able to remove pallet loads alternating between one boxcar and the other, thus reducing and possibly eliminating idle time on the part of the laborers.

A second factor relating to personnel assignments is tied to Parkinson's Law—work will expand to fill the time available for its completion. In the absence of sufficient work for any given interval, there will be a tendency to work at a slower pace, thus extending the work time to fill the interval. A productivity management system will permit supervisors to assign work in interval quantities. In this way, the worker can reasonably complete assignments in the allotted time, yet not have excess time to waste. The warehouseman will have a goal, which can improve motivational levels. Likewise, the supervisor will

Types of Measures	Cost Effectiveness	Scheduling Effectiveness				Evaluation Effectiveness				Overall Effectiveness
		V	A	U	T	V	A	U	T	
Historical	Low	3	4	3	1	4	3	2	1	2.6 Fair
Time Study	High	2	3	4	3	3	3	4	3	3.1 Fair
Predetermined	High	1	1	2	3	1	1	3	4	2.0 Good
Multiple Regression	Middle	1	2	1	2	2	2	1	2	1.6 Good

V = Validity   U = Usefulness
A = Accuracy   T = Timeliness

Figure 23-8   Comparison of Measurement Types

know when a given assignment should be completed. In order to meet deadlines, the supervisor can vary the number of people assigned to a given activity area in order to match the manpower resources with the work output requirement and the time allotted.

Finally, productivity management systems can be useful in personnel assignments when a preferred match can be developed between individual and task. Individuals are more proficient in some tasks than in others, and the ability to match their strengths with the tasks at hand will enhance productivity.

Improved personnel scheduling will increase productivity by creating positive morale, reducing delays, encouraging a normal work pace, and properly matching individuals to assignments.

Other Asset Assignments/Utilization

In addition to the personnel resource, distribution centers also have other assets that impact on productivity. To begin with the physical structure, the warehouse layout is a compromise of storage and handling efficiencies. If inventory turnover is slow, then shortage efficiency is important. However, with a fast inventory turnover, handling efficiency is important, and can be predicted using the productivity management system. A change in layout may result in improved handling efficiency which can be anticipated by using predetermined engineered standards for evaluation prior to implementation. For example, a productivity management system can indicate improved order filling efficiency by altering a numerical sequence layout so that the largest volume line items are stored at floor level and closest to the beginning of the picking area.

The loading and unloading of merchandise at the distribution center is also a prime candidate for scheduling improvements. Though sufficient doors and maneuvering area may exist, it is wasteful to have all delivering carriers arrive at 8:00 in the morning and all LTL pickups made at 4:00 in the afternoon. The ability to load or unload a carrier efficiently at the dock door nearest to the merchandise location is enhanced through scheduling. Carriers will try to adhere to warehouse schedules if there is a benefit for them. Warehousemen who can provide the carrier with an appointment time and then process that carrier without delay will ultimately find that carriers appreciate such arrangements.

Material handling equipment, typically forklift trucks or order picking systems, are also assets whose utilization can be improved through scheduling. The quantity of equipment needed can be minimized if scheduling flexibility exists. As mentioned earlier in this chapter, the ability to shift equipment from department to department or the ability to extend the hours of receiving and shipping can have a significant impact on the number of pieces of equipment needed. Scheduling can also have an impact on preventive maintenance programs by making equipment available for maintenance without adversely impacting labor productivity.

Feedback

People want to know how they stand. A system creating work standards and supervisory reports, but lacking in feedback, will lead to low morale among the work force. Good supervisors use a productivity management system to provide feedback to subordinates.

This will create an atmosphere of positive morale where people want to know that they are contributing and carrying their fair share of the work. A good system allows the supervisor to provide positive or negative feedback as the situation warrants.

Incentives can also play a role in warehouse productivity. Some distribution centers have established direct incentive systems where productivity affects weekly pay. Other operations have productivity sharing systems where highly productive individuals receive time off with pay.

Inter-warehouse Comparisons

There are many reasons why warehouse operations should not be compared one to another. Such operations are not identical—there are differences in building facilities, layout, available equipment, order characteristics, and personnel. Because of these differences, management must be extremely careful in evaluating warehouses. A common approach is to look at the throughput tonnage per man hour and then rank warehouses accordingly. Though throughput tonnage per man hour may serve as a guide, conclusions should not be drawn on this information alone. A more accurate way to compare warehouses would be to establish individual standards for each warehouse, then compare each to its set of standards. These standards can be combined through regression analysis techniques to arrive at a weighted level of effectiveness, which can provide better insight into the comparison of warehouse locations.[5]

Productivity management is the cornerstone of effective warehouse operations. Variable demands can be met through effective scheduling of labor resources. Keeping people working at their normal pace and eliminating delay are two keys to improved productivity in a warehouse. This is achieved through an equitable and accurate measurement system which will improve planning and control of warehouse assets, including the most important asset, people.

Notes

1. See Roger W. Carlson, *What Is Contract Warehousing?* (Chicago: American Warehousemen's Association, 1979).
2. *Measuring Productivity in Physical Distribution* (Chicago: NCPDM, 1978), pp. 8–11.
3. C. Northcote Parkinson, *Parkinson's Law and Other Studies in Administration* (Boston: Houghton Mifflin Co., 1957), pp. 2–13.
4. See *Measuring Productivity*, pp. 11–13.
5. John F. Bohnsack and Brian P. Smith, "Establishing and Using a Productivity Measurement System," NCPDM Annual Conference Proceedings (Chicago: NCPDM, 1980), pp. 151–180.

CHAPTER 24

Distribution Facility Design and Construction

R. WILLIAM GARDNER

The design and construction of distribution facilities is a complex process, and a systematic approach which focuses on the components of the problem facilitates the analysis.

A systems approach suggests that material handling equipment should be an integral part of the design criterion. The most effective facility design is one which starts with the equipment and establishes the operating parameters of that equipment, using them as design constraints for the building. The building becomes secondary to the primary mission of creating a material handling system that will support the warehousing and distribution program.

Other chapters of this *Handbook* elaborate on systems differences; thus it is assumed that the user has established his basic system and is turning his attention to the design and construction of the shelter to "protect" the material handling system.

It is important that land considerations be reviewed because they impact the many building decisions. Overall building design criteria—including support facilities and the design parameters dictated by the material handling system—must also be evaluated. Finally, the various elements involved in constructing the facility must be reviewed in detail with reference to the various alternatives that may be available.

Equipment Planning

The characteristics of equipment that are relevant for building planning purposes can be categorized into three major types:

1. A fixed system—typified by a stacker crane installation which in its extreme becomes a rack supported building.

2. A semi-fixed system—typified by in-floor or fixed-path conveyer systems requiring strict building dimensions and construction detail. A building is designed *around* such a system but is not totally dependent upon the system as in the fixed system.

3. A flexible system—that typified by a forklift truck and storage rack system which requires modest space planning beyond column spacing and access point location. Such systems are typically put in place after construction is complete.

The nature of the system—fixed, semi-fixed or flexible—will determine the level of involvement in facility design that is required of materials handling engineers. The "sophistication" of the system will also affect the timetable for design and construction. In addition, some of the systems that are "more fixed" will require longer lead times for acquisition and installation which further constrains the many construction decisions. The purpose here is to point out the importance of considering equipment at a very early stage. Decisions regarding the appropriateness of that equipment are covered in Chapter 25.

Land

One of the early considerations in the design phase is the overall suitability of the parcel of land. All too often attempts are made to utilize a piece of ground that is less than satisfactory because it has greater "appeal" than an alternate site. The "appeal" relates to visibility, neighborhood, etc.

Size of the building site is an important initial consideration. Though long-term planning dictates a large plot of ground to allow for future expansion, economics normally will not support sizing for more than five years into the future. Obviously, if the need for more square footage is anticipated, the price of moving to an alternate location at a future date may be greater than the additional cost of ground. In some instances such decisions must be anticipated for ten or more years in advance. The cost of the land becomes a smaller proportion of the overall project cost as size and construction costs increase. This ratio should be determined—cost of ground to total cost of the completed facility—in order to calculate the cost impact of carrying additional ground.

Land coverage ratios are also important. Zoning requirements often dictate that no more than a certain percentage of the ground may be covered—normally on the order of 35 to 50 percent. A warehouse facility covering more than 50 percent of the ground is highly unusual. More typically, a 40 percent coverage ratio is used to satisfy the zoning requirements.

"Buildability" of ground is a term used to define the ease with which a structure can be put on the site. The term refers to terrain conditions and the degree of land preparation needed, as well as the number of site improvements still required. Site improvements include the entry point or "tap" for such various required utility services as:

1. Sanitary sewer

2. Electricity

3. Fuel gas

4. Domestic water

5. Fire protection water

6. Storm sewer connections

Access to major transportation right-of-way is extremely important. Many times a site that is otherwise ideally located will have poor access to rail or highway transportation. Access to the property itself is important, but so is access from the property to the community at large, including terminal facilities of major transportation companies.

The flood risk associated with a particular property should be evaluated very early. United States Geological Survey maps showing flood plains are available for all areas of the country, and will show the typical 50-year and 100-year flood plain lines. These documents should also be checked for unforeseen conditions that might make the property less desirable.

The tax structure for a particular locality can have a significant bearing on the specific piece of land chosen. A community's industrial base can favorably impact its tax structure and affect the attitude of neighbors. Specific millage rates and assessment ratios should be checked, as should current or potential assessments for additional services. The rating of the fire department—volunteer or full-time—and its typical response time, as well as available water pressures will affect potential fire protection. The fire insurance cost for any location should also be considered.

The purchase price for the ground itself is not the least of the considerations, but a "true total purchase price" cannot be determined unless each of the items described above is evaluated. A tract of ground that costs $10,000 per acre but requires $20,000 per acre in additional site improvements or costs associated with making the site "buildable" will be more expensive than one that costs $20,000 per acre on a fully developed basis. Know the total cost before making a commitment.

Building Design

The level of architectural and engineering services to be performed requires that management focus on the complexity of the design situation. Different levels of service can be obtained from architectural and engineering organizations, which may range in cost from 10 percent of the total design package for full services to a minimum service requirement, which can cost as little as 1.5 to 2 percent of the total construction price. Differences are primarily associated with the nature of the storage environment. In other words, a more complex building involving environmental control, specialized handling systems, and other complicating requirements demands higher levels of architectural and engineering services. On the other hand, if a speculative building is being considered, one where ultimate flexibility for multiple occupants is in order, and there is a minimum of complicated equipment or control, a lower level of service can be used. When pre-engineered metal buildings are employed, much of the design work can be a part of the building purchase agreement with the manufacturer or his representative. In any case, an initial evaluation of the complexity of the project is required to determine the level of services that will be appropriate prior to engaging architects and engineers.

Nature of Storage

The principal consideration in evaluating the nature of storage requirements is the basic product and the hazards attendant to storing and handling it. Most products have simple storage requirements and this consideration is of minimal difficulty. However, a growing number of products require special consideration. These include aerosol packages and other flammable products which have storage requirements specific to their fire hazard characteristics. Certain chemical products are toxic and must be handled in special ways to ensure that they do not contaminate neighboring storage. Odor problems associated with some products may create other storage hazards, particularly in view of requirements set by the Environmental Protection Agency (EPA) and the Occupational Safety and Health Administration (OSHA) that have greatly increased the number of considerations that must be taken into account prior to establishing the total storage environment. Products containing plastic also present storage problems and may require modifications in the sprinkler system design if product is to be stored efficiently. All of these items must be evaluated as they impact the storage situation.

Packaging for the product to be stored should also be considered. Packages that contain many voids demand lower stacking heights or the introduction of storage racks to allow multiple layer storage within a high ceiling area. Package size and construction—i.e., whether or not it has a cardboard carton or wooden crate which allows multiple layer stacking—are additional factors affecting storage.

Environmental considerations round out the list of storage considerations. Some products require temperature control, others humidity control, and some products require both. Significant differences in construction technique are required when sub-freezing temperatures are required for the storage. Facilities requiring temperatures below zero degrees centigrade (32 degrees Fahrenheit) *must* be designed and built specifically for that condition. Major expenses will be incurred—special flooring and insulated wall and ceiling sections will be required. When temperatures above freezing are required, the environmental constraints are less severe and less expensive construction can be utilized. Humidity control problems are primarily a function of heating and air conditioning equipment and do not require extensive construction detail changes.

Building Size

The size of the facility selected is primarily related to the job to be done. Many times a distribution facility is a portion, indeed, an extension of a manufacturing plant which may subsequently be used for manufacturing if the need arises. On many occasions, however, a facility is designed specifically for distribution and it is that facility that is of primary consideration here.

The most economical building from a construction standpoint is a square building. However, from an operating standpoint, it is seldom the most efficient. A rectangular building is generally the preferred choice, and the width to depth ratio is generally on the order of 2:1 to 4:1. Most distribution facilities are designed with the rail service on one side of the building and truck docks on the opposite side. Occasionally this pattern will be altered by having rail facilities in the center of the building and truck facilities on either side. Sometimes an L-shaped arrangement is used with the truck facilities perpendicular to the rail facilities. When speculative buildings are constructed, the nominal depth is on the order of 200 feet. This seems to work out best for people who are leasing warehouse space to many different users. Building width or length is generally determined by available land in situations like this. When a user-specific facility is designed, the width and depth can be tailored to the user's distribution requirements.

The building height that is most commonly found with today's construction is 24 feet at the eave. This permits a 20-foot stacking height with proper clearance under sprinklers and is within the technological capacity of most mobile equipment. Where specialized stacking equipment is utilized, heights of 35 feet are common. If highly automated stacker cranes are used, building heights can reach upwards of 60 feet. The limitations of equipment technology and fire insurance requirements are the primary constraints on building height.

Dock Facilities

A good rule of thumb for truck dock doors or access points with a normal distribution operation is one door per 10,000 square feet. A high velocity operation could require twice this number. Location is typically in a long wall and the truck dock area is generally adjacent to a trailer storage area. Adequate dock maneuvering area and turnaround space are also included in the construction plans for well-planned facilities. The through-the-wall or flush truck dock door is the most acceptable type. However, the interior dock space which is totally closed off from the outside is not uncommon in areas of extreme temperature or where security problems are significant. At the other extreme, outside dock ramps are occasionally found that use one or more access doors to a dock area which extends from the building. This exterior dock type is typically found in warmer climates. With adequate consideration for present over-the-road trailers and their dimensions, a 9-foot-wide by 10-foot-high door and a dock height of 48 inches seem to be the most appropriate dimensions. A truck berth that is 12 feet wide at this size door allows rapid turnaround if a dock area of at least 110 feet is available. The door used should have a vertical lift design to minimize the interference with movement around the dock area. A 9-foot width allows the entire truck entry to be contained within the door area even if the driver should misalign his unit.

A common dimension in speculative buildings is an 8-foot width, which does create unloading problems if a truck is off center since the truck opening is also 8 feet.* The 10-foot height is appropriate to provide total clearance of 14 feet from the truck pad to the door jamb, insuring that the typical 13.5-foot clearance limitation will be contained within the door opening. Extreme caution should be used to avoid depressed docks which can create drainage and—in colder climates—severe icing problems, with attendant truck movement problems. The typical dock facility is most efficient if the initial investment is made in a mechanical dock leveler, door shelter, and a dock light.

Railroad service to a distribution facility varies in importance with the nature of the product being distributed. While the use of piggyback service is increasing and makes the on-site availability of the railroad less critical, the growing energy problem and deregulation suggest that rail traffic may become increasingly important. Rail movement is more energy-efficient than truck movement, though slower service times have often forced shippers to favor more expensive truck shipments. Energy trade-offs may cause this to change. Deregulation is allowing more favorable rail rates, as well. The ideal site location is one that is served by more than one rail carrier. This situation is not common, but there are sites in many cities around the country that satisfy this requirement.

When on-site rail sidings are used, the railroad dock height from top of rail to top of floor on the adjacent loading platform should be 43 inches. Standard clearance between

---

*As this is written, changes have occurred in legislation which governs highway trailer dimensions. Width limits have been increased to 102″ and length limits to 48′. As a result, recommendations will be modified somewhat. For clarification on door and ramp dimensions and spacing (which is inconclusive but being refined), the reader is directed to publications by dock leveler manufacturers and the American Trucking Association (see p. 937).

the dock wall and the center line of the rail track is 8.5 feet. However, with special permission of the railroad company and the state public utility authority, a "close clearance" authorization can be obtained that reduces this dimension to as little as 5.75 feet. This close clearance is considered to be more desirable, because it reduces the gap between the rail car and the dock, allowing the use of shorter dock plates and permitting greater maneuverability into and out of rail cars.

Several arguments are offered concerning the appropriateness of inside or outside rail docks. On the one hand, the inside rail dock—or an outside rail dock with a continuous platform which has similar characteristics—allows any number of different length rail cars to be unloaded concurrently without regard to dimensions between the through-the-wall door openings. However, it is more common to find an outside rail track that is served by doors through the wall. The nominal dimension between doors on a center line basis is 68.5 feet where 60-foot-long rail cars are commonly received. One of the problems with this through-the-wall outside rail dock when a platform is not available is the limitation associated with concurrent handling of multiple length cars.

In building a rail track, one of the most important considerations is to provide proper drainage for the rail lead and the trackage. Poor drainage will contribute to a marginal road bed and frequent repairs as well as potential derailments, which are expensive. During the site selection process, careful consideration also should be given to the railroad carrier and the switching district constraints. A specific location may be a poor choice from a railroad standpoint because it is at the "end of the line" or does not have adequate storage track facilities nearby. Many potential problems can be avoided by arranging a meeting with the area operations management for the serving railroad to discuss the service that can be expected, the number of switches per day, and the time from the major yard serving the facility.

Elements of Construction

The following review of the major elements of construction for a distribution facility will focus on site preparation, foundations, floors, structural design, roof, walls, and other components of the basic building shell. In addition, the internal systems for the distribution facility will be discussed. These include the sprinkler system, the electrical system, the HVAC system (heating, ventilating, and air conditioning), and communications systems. Finally, consideration will be given to energy conservation, yard and dock areas, service areas, and outside storage areas.

Set-backs and Site Preparation

An early consideration in site preparation is that of zoning requirements for building set-back. In some municipalities truck docks cannot face the street. Often, a parking area or part of the truck maneuvering area can be used to satisfy the set-back requirement as long as there is no structure above the ground. Careful consideration must be given to this factor.

Once the set-back requirements are determined, the initial dimensions for the building can be established. Next, soil tests should be made to determine the nature of the foundations that will be required and to see if soil preparation will be needed in order to support the proposed building. Knowledge of soil conditions is extremely important in determining proper allowances for developing the floor and structural requirements. Load-bearing capacities for soils can range from 1000 pounds per square foot up to 6000 pounds per square foot and these capacities will govern the type of foundation that is appropriate.

Consideration should also be given to any height limitations that may be present in the building codes or zoning regulations for a particular piece of ground. Proximity to an airport is one of a number of factors that can create height limitations that affect building design, particularly where a stacker crane installation is anticipated.

With current EPA regulations becoming increasingly restrictive, the presence of a sanitary sewer system becomes important to the planning process. Though there are still areas of the country where a septic system is acceptable, the attendant requirements become expensive, almost to a point of dictating a small package sewer plant if sanitary sewers are not available.

Storm water drainage can be on the surface or piped. Typically, distribution of water by surface means will be less expensive than piping it underground, but local government regulations will affect this decision. When a distribution facility is constructed, much of the land that formerly "accepted" water and allowed it to percolate will be covered with buildings and paving, forcing the diversion of much of the water. Thus, an orderly drainage pattern becomes important to site development.

Foundation Design

After the soil has been evaluated for bearing characteristics, the foundation design can be developed. The depth below grade that is normally required for foundation walls is 36 inches. This will vary depending upon the climate, with deeper foundation walls required in colder climates (where the frost line is deeper). In the warmer climates of the southern states, 12 inches of foundation wall is often all that is required.

The foundation wall that is placed on the footing is typically concrete block or poured concrete. The excavation for this footing and foundation wall can be dug in a conventional manner with a backhoe or created with a trenching machine. The latter method is faster but not always acceptable to local building authorities. This foundation wall runs from below grade to the floor level, and, in some instances, is taken to a height of from 4 to 10 feet above the floor elevation. Many users prefer a solid wall (which is an extension of the foundation) to this height in the interests of appearance and security. Less durable wall forms are sometimes subject to greater ease of entry or damage from equipment operating near the wall.

With the concrete tilt wall construction method, it is not uncommon for the foundation wall and the above grade wall section to be one continuous concrete slab from the footing to the eave of the building.

Floor

One of the two most important components of the distribution facility is the floor; the roof is the other. The floor is basically a wearing surface or "table top" which must be of sufficient quality and smoothness to allow easy lateral movement and provide a platform for lifting and lowering if high rise systems are used.

The most important element of the floor can be the preparation of the sub-grade beneath the floor. Any fill material that is used to level the ground must be compacted properly, and a thorough inspection of that procedure should be undertaken to insure that it is done as specified.

Once the contractor turns from the preparation of the sub-grade to the point of creating the floor itself, there are several variables to consider. The typical floor is poured concrete with a usual thickness of 5 to 6 inches. It will contain reinforcing steel mesh, placed in the center of the floor section. The concrete is poured on a sub-grade of 4 to 12 inches of sand or medium size (three-quarter-inch) gravel. An alternative to the most popular poured concrete floor is the structural floor slab. This structural slab can be "key-locked" between one section and another or it can be poured with isolated steel dowels connecting adjacent sections. In the "key-locked" system a metal form that is put on the edge of the floor slab creates a mortise and tenon joint between sections.

Another type floor is the floating slab where sections are allowed to float free of each other. This would most likely be used where a solid sub-grade is available and there is little need to tie various sections together. In all cases, a floor must be placed in small enough sections or saw cut into small enough sections following the cure, to allow normal expansion and contraction with changes in temperature and humidity. Failure to do so will result in extensive cracking on a random rather than a controlled basis.

All floors eventually develop cracks. It is not necessarily a factor of poor construction, but the nature of a floor. Some firms, particularly in manufacturing, have chosen to use wood block floors to dampen vibration and noise. This type construction is seldom found in distribution facilities as it is more expensive and not necessarily a practical solution.

A proper surface treatment to the floor, regardless of how it may have been created, is an important final step. There are many curing and sealing compounds that will improve the wearing surface; the appropriate compound should be investigated with design personnel. Many consider the ultimate in finishing to be a polyurethane coating providing a "varnish-like" finish; however, such a surface can be slippery when wet or oil spotted. A more satisfactory floor finish for general service and wear is a penetrating sealant applied immediately after curing and before traffic or other dirt has an opportunity to accumulate. Another alternative is to put metal filings in the surface of the floor. These additives reduce abrasion, provide traction and allow for expansion and contraction, thereby making the surface more lasting.

Structural Design

The structural design system that is used for the building can be defined in its simplest form as the "roof support system." In other words, the whole purpose of a structural system is to support the roof and keep the contents of the building dry. The materials used for the structural system can be steel, concrete, or in some cases, wood. Steel is most commonly used in the structural design, with wood and concrete being chosen less frequently. Wood will be found most often in areas of the west where it is more readily available, or in older designs, particularly in complexes developed by the government during the 1930s and 1940s. Concrete structural systems are more expensive and are not seen frequently.

The most common steel structure is typified by a series of rigid frames developed with steel columns and rafters. Columns are either H or cylinder sections while the rafters are typically I-beam sections. These rigid frames are then joined together by a Z section purlin if the distance between frames is 30 feet or less, or by bar-joists (a lightweight structural joist constructed of two horizontal plates connected by diagonal bars) when the dimension exceeds 30 feet. Sometimes this rigid frame system is supported on its exterior perimeter by a load-bearing wall while other times it is supported by exterior steel columns. In the latter case the wall is a "curtain wall," one which does not transmit any load to the foundation.

The type of structural system selected depends on a number of factors, including the building size, the bay sizes desired, and the general building layout selected. A pre-engineered metal structure with "Z" purlins to connect the rigid frames can be developed at a reasonable cost with bay dimensions of 20 to 28 feet in one direction. The dimension for the perpendicular direction that seems to be most practical is 50 feet. In other words, a dimension of 20 to 28 feet in one direction by 50 feet in the other direction will prove to be an economical bay size from a construction standpoint with the purlin system.

When the short dimension exceeds 30 feet, the structural system quickly becomes one involving bar-joists rather than purlins. The most economical size with this method will be a bay size of approximately 40 feet square to one 50 feet square. Once interior dimensioning exceeds this range, construction costs for the structural members start escalating rapidly. The longer the clear span required in *both* directions, the more expensive the structural system due to loads on the structural system from the roof. This is particularly true of snow loads in the northern climates. By reducing dimensions to 20 to 28 feet in the short direction for bays, lighter weight steel sections can be used which will impact the costs favorably.

All of this is not to say that other bay sizes cannot be developed. Practically speaking, an infinite range of bay sizes can be developed if required for particular projects. However, practical cost limitations suggest that the range of bay dimensions described above will result in the most economical building design.

In recent years the rack supported building has come into its own. This is particularly the case where stacker crane systems are utilized and an entire distribution facility contains storage rack. In such cases, the storage rack can be used to support the roof system—in essence, the roof and walls are used to "envelop" the storage rack and stacker crane handling system. A typical installation is very much dependent upon a "true" floor which becomes an expensive portion of the system.

Roof

There are three basic types of roof systems that are found in widespread use today. The first two are closely related, and are applied on the top of a metal roof deck. These are the traditional bituminous roofing system, commonly referred to as a built-up roof system, and the monolithic system consisting of a closed-cell insulating material covered with an elastomeric membrane intended to provide a rubber-like weathering surface. These two systems are commonly applied over a wide variety of roof deck systems. Currently the steel roof deck with the built-up roof is the most common application. The third basic type of roof, commonly referred to as a "metal" roof, uses the metal deck as the wearing surface with insulating material applied to the underside.

The traditional built-up roof consists of metal decking, covered by a rigid insulation board three-quarter to one and a half inches thick, with three to five plies or layers of asphalt-impregnated roofing felt covered by a surface application of protective and reflective aggregates. This final coating is what creates the basic terminology of a "tar and gravel roof." This entire system weighs approximately 8 pounds per square foot and is a factor to be considered in the structural design of a building. In some instances, where roof pitch is adequate to shed the water fairly rapidly, roofing contractors will suggest that the owner omit the tar and gravel finishing surface to save weight and cost. There are mixed opinions as to whether or not this is an advisable practice.

The newer exotic roof systems made up of closed cell insulation and various elastomeric membranes or coatings are gaining increased acceptance. The costs of built-up roofs are rising rapidly with escalating labor rates and higher costs associated with all petroleum-based materials. The elastomeric systems require less labor, and offer lower weight and superior insulation values. However, elastomeric systems do not yet have a long history of successful performance, so a careful analysis and evaluation is recommended before that type is selected.

The metal roof is basically a metal deck with the insulation applied to the underside. This insulation typically consists of a 3-inch fiberglass bat with a vinyl film facing. With the metal roof design, it is important to have sufficient pitch to allow water to be rapidly shed by the roof. Modern metal roofs are usually joined by what is known as "standing-seam construction" which reduces the number of fasteners and consequently the number of opportunities for roof leaks. After all, the most important single factor in any roof selection is to have one that is maintenance free, meaning an absence of leaks! The desired end result is the most important consideration.

In the case of the built-up roof, maintenance is more expensive, and frequently involves annual patching and repair programs as well as a total re-covering every 15 to 20 years. However, because a built-up roof does not require the same rapid run-off and thus the pitch is lower, it is architecturally more appealing and its use more widespread.

Maintenance experience on the monolithic membrane system is sketchy to date, because of its limited application. Proponents suggest that the system is easily maintained, and that mechanical damage can be repaired quickly. Preventive maintenance is supposedly routine and nominal in cost based on current reports.

A metal roof can be practically trouble free; however, maintenance will require painting or coating every 15 to 20 years, and the required pitch results in more severe roof lines. Maintenance costs are generally low with the metal roof system.

Walls

Walls are basically of two general categories: load bearing or curtain. Load-bearing walls are typically constructed of pre-cast concrete panels or concrete block with structural columns (pilasters) at fairly frequent intervals. Other forms of masonry or factory-manufactured concrete structural shapes such as "standing Ts" are also used. These masonry wall sections are utilized to support some of the roof load, reducing the size of structural steel that is required in the overall design.

The curtain wall, one which does not bear any of the roof load for transmission to the foundation, can be of almost any material. It is often constructed of masonry either for the initial rise from the floor or occasionally for the entire wall height. Frequently a portion of the curtain wall is made of an insulated metal panel consisting of either two layers of metal with an insulation material sandwiched between, or a single exterior skin of metal with an insulation material affixed to the inside, without the second metal panel for the inside surface.

As energy codes dictate revisions to construction practice, one finds increasing requirements for insulation. It is not uncommon to have a masonry wall (either load bearing or curtain) which has to be insulated on the inside surface either by the use of furring strips and fiberglass batting, or with a hardboard insulation affixed directly to the surface.

Generally speaking, to obtain the same insulation value, economy will favor the insulated metal wall panel while architectural treatment favors the masonry exterior. Depending on the climate and the interior environmental requirements for heat and humidity, the wall section most frequently seen is some combination of both masonry and metal.

Fire Protection System

Distribution facilities almost always include a fire protection system as an integral component of the total building plan. Fire insurance underwriters should be involved in the design phase of the warehouse in order to plan properly for such a system. The nature of product to be stored and/or handled will determine the nature of the system and the associated insurance rate.

The hydraulically calculated sprinkler system is the most common fire protection found in distribution facilities. This system is designed to allow maximum stacking height of product by properly engineering the water flows to various sections of the building. Though such a system costs a modest additional amount, it can often result in significant storage gains by higher stacking of products, and thus can be a more economical solution to the unit cost design constraint.

Another important element of the fire protection system is the water supply to the building site. If publicly supplied water is either not available, or not available at high enough pressures to provide adequate supplies during an emergency, the fire insurance underwriter may require a reservoir system and/or a supplemental pump to increase supplies or pressures respectively.

In addition, underwriters will require that a local plant emergency organization be established and that certain supplemental fire-fighting equipment be available within the building. This will normally include hose drops for hoses smaller than those normally associated with fire hydrants and professional departments, as well as a series of extinguishers mounted in strategic locations. Where product characteristics or storage densities increase the hazard associated with storing the product, there will be requirements for placing intermediate sprinkler systems in storage racks.

In all cases, the best approach to designing a fire protection system that will be both economical and satisfactory is to work with the insurance underwriters at the early stages of the building design.

Two different kinds of systems can be developed for sprinkler control valves—a "wet system" that keeps water in the sprinkler pipes at all times and a "dry system" that uses air in the pipes, coupled with a system for exhausting that air to get the water into the pipes. The dry system is used where building heat is not sufficient to prevent the water from freezing in the pipes. The wet system is generally favored because it has a faster reaction time.

The value of an adequate fire protection system becomes obvious when one considers that insurance rates for a well-protected facility can be one-tenth what they would be for a building where no system is available.

Electrical System

The electrical system for a distribution facility is primarily associated with lighting, but also must take into consideration power for tools and equipment, with particular reference to electrically powered material handling equipment. Often data processing equipment will require a separate power line, but that is a relatively minor consideration. In reviewing the overall electrical system, careful attention should be given to the ability to use a three-phase power entry rather than single-phase power which is typically associated with lighting circuits. Three-phase power is less expensive from an operating standpoint and from a material standpoint since smaller gauge wire can be used.

Alternative lighting fixture systems may be selected based on preference. Mercury or sodium vapor types are newer and more expensive initially, but less expensive to operate. They are generally used for area lighting, and may be less satisfactory when directed light is needed. Sodium vapor lighting is currently considered the least expensive overall, but tends to change the appearance of colors. Fluorescent tubes mounted in industrial fixtures with reflective hoods are the most satisfactory lighting source according to most users. Systems should be designed for a minimum of 20 to 30 foot-candles in the aisles, while less lighting is required in the stacking areas away from the aisles. New developments in high-output fluorescent lighting are being promoted on the basis of lower energy costs with consistent illumination.

Three-phase power can be used for small hand tools that are wired for single-phase current by introducing a step-down transformer into the auxiliary outlet circuit. This is not expensive and is appropriate where single-phase powered hand tools are needed and three-phase current is the primary power available. Three-phase wiring is the choice where battery chargers (either rectifier or motor-generator type) are required, in order to recharge the power source for battery-powered forklift trucks and pallet trucks.

Sometimes lighting demands require a degree of flexibility. Additional (extra) circuits can be run in bays that will not receive lighting fixtures with the initial installation. Many times in a distribution facility, varying volumes of product and changing product mix will demand flexibility in aisle and lighting layouts. In order to provide this flexibility, fixtures can be wired with plug ends rather than directly into junction boxes, leaving "pigtails" attached to the plug ends. Lighting fixtures then can be easily moved to different locations. If additional outlet boxes (extra circuits) are also provided, a greater flexibility will exist when aisles are moved. At the time of initial construction, the additional runs of wiring and outlet boxes become a modest incremental investment.

A supplemental form of lighting which is most helpful and can be introduced at a modest cost is that of skylights. Two forms of skylight are available—those mounted in the roof and those that are sometimes referred to as "wall lights." The "wall light" is a strip of plastic panel at the top of a curtain wall which allows light to enter in a band under the eave of the building. This method of auxiliary illumination is very popular with the pre-engineered metal building trade and has been widely used with these structures. Obviously, it cannot be used with a load-bearing wall, but could conceivably be used with any curtain wall design.

Roof mounted skylights can be of the conventional plastic bubble type in a built-up roof or can be installed in a metal building roof as an insulated translucent panel. Historically, skylights in a built-up roof have been a source of roof leaks and have received "bad press" as a result. Present technology has solved most of those problems, and skylights in the roof, whether they be in the pre-engineered metal building roof or in a built-up roof on a conventional structure, should be a positive consideration in the design of a distribution facility.

Environmental Conditions

Heating, ventilating, and air conditioning equipment (HVAC) are used to create the "environmental" condition of the building. Obviously, heating is required in the winter, air changes are required, and special product requirements may necessitate separate temperature controls for cooling. Seldom is a distribution facility totally air conditioned for the comfort of the personnel.

Because of the constantly changing energy situation, an analysis of heating system needs should be made in consultation with mechanical engineers, who will be aware of the most acceptable fuel for heating in a local area. This can range from coal to oil to natural gas or propane, depending on the market. Traditionally, gas or oil fired forced air units have been used predominantly in distribution facilities. Forced air units provide a more uniform heat at an acceptable cost level when compared to other systems. Some firms have experimented with infrared panel systems and found them very expensive, not only from an operating standpoint but from an initial cost standpoint as well. As energy costs continue to escalate, radiant heating systems are being developed which, though expensive to install, promise to be more efficient and economical to operate. Temperature levels for a warehouse are typically 40 to 50 degrees at the personnel level in a structure. This will provide adequate heat for personnel movement, although temperature levels of 60 to 70 degrees are sometimes recommended, and some firms do provide such levels.

In most situations, a ventilation system that provides at least two air changes per hour within a facility is considered to be adequate. This is often accomplished at a very reasonable cost by using louvered fans in the end walls of a building. The resulting conditions provide a more productive environment for most personnel.

Though some firms choose to provide air conditioning in very warm climates, a typical distribution facility does not include that except in temperature-controlled rooms where perishable goods are stored. In these cases, depending on humidity and temperature requirements, supplemental facilities can be developed on the inside of the facility at nominal cost.

Energy

Serious consideration must be given to the energy codes required by state and local building authorities. Obviously, with this becoming an increasing problem, not enough can be said about taking proper precautions and the need for specialized assistance. This is a field unto itself, and requires constant updating with regard to insulation materials and energy sources. The most important thing here is to proceed with caution—insuring that a flexible posture is maintained and that alternate energy sources are available in case of need.

Communications Systems

Communications needs should be evaluated early in the design stage so that adequate preparation can be made for servicing the facility. With adequate notice the local telephone company can often prewire the facility with excess capacity, including anticipated data-processing interfaces as well as currently needed lines. Obviously voice communications offers choices to be made to rent equipment from the servicing public utility or to purchase equipment from one of the competitive systems. No recommendations are offered since this is currently changing quite rapidly.

Consideration should be given to the alternate long distance systems that are becoming available through private sources. They often reduce costs. Another consideration in the communications area is the use of teletype systems, electronic mail, or facsimile transmission, all of which are useful supplemental systems to the overall communications program. In this case, the ability to utilize these modes for short messages or to produce hard copy can be valuable.

Security

The degree of security necessary for the building depends primarily on its location and the product stored. Contemporary thinking suggests that guard services are outmoded and that electronic security surveillance is the best protection system. There are those who argue that there is no substitute for a guard on the premises, particularly a guard accompanied by a dog. The dog is a significant deterrent in spite of its vulnerability to "tampering."

In the area of electronic surveillance systems, there are many sonic and motion detectors as well as magnetic contact controls that can be connected by telephone lines to a central monitoring station.

An additional security consideration is the often overlooked need for exterior lighting. A well lighted building perimeter will many times be a significant deterrent to breaking and entering. Area fencing with controlled access through monitored gates is another form of security system that may warrant consideration, depending upon the nature of the product handled at the facility. In any case, adequate concern must be given to security, regardless of the form that is ultimately chosen.

Yard and Dock Areas

Dock facilities have already been discussed (see pages 588–589). In addition, the paved area required for trucking access should be given consideration. Actual depth of the truck maneuvering area (distance from curb to dock wall) should be two times the length of the largest highway tractor trailer combination that will be presenting itself for loading or unloading. This is a minimum depth; some operators favor additional paving to reduce parking time required. Consideration should also be given to making a clockwise backing maneuver to the dock itself, providing a turnaround area if counter-clockwise backing would be the normal entry to the property. Loading and unloading will be significantly slowed if these provisions prove to be inadequate.

An adequate paved area for employee parking is an element of construction that is often overlooked. Zoning requirements typically require "set-asides" for employee parking that are beyond the normal densities for distribution facilities. The overall appearance of the facility and its flexibility for alternate uses can be enhanced by the availability of adequate employee parking.

When the structure is completed, some consideration must be given to landscaping the site. Though not necessarily a "cost effective" improvement, landscaping and appearance can contribute to the value of the property over the long term. Some zoning ordinances require "green belts," and dictate a specified landscaping plan.

Outside Storage Areas

In some situations, consideration must be given to outside storage facilities. Certain products lend themselves to such storage, and adequate access and a proper foundation for such storage are primary considerations. A storage pad to support seldom-used material can be a useful addition to a major distribution facility. When inventory levels are unusually high this exterior space can be used to relieve the more critical inside environment. Often, outside areas are used for storing supplemental material such as pallets and dunnage, or surplus fixtures used for transporting material in rail cars or highway trailers. If adequate additional land can be purchased at the outset without creating a significant economic penalty, an outside storage area may be a worthwhile addition to the main facility.

Service Areas

Location of toilet facilities, lunchrooms, and locker rooms within a facility requires some attention from the planning staff. Depending upon the nature of the work, shower facilities may or may not also be necessary. The distance of such facilities from normal working areas can affect productivity rates. Often productivity can be improved by having two or three separate toilet facilities scattered throughout the building instead of one central facility. Building codes sometimes stipulate number and distance requirements for location of toilet facilities.

Maintenance facilities are a must in all but the smallest distribution operation. In smaller installations, it is sometimes possible to contract for maintenance of material handling equipment without maintaining on-site personnel. However such cases are decreasing in number as a result of the growing demands for greater efficiency and utilization of all equipment. As a result, the presence of a shop facility for maintenance of material handling equipment is increasingly important to the overall design package. Providing space for building maintenance personnel may also be desirable, though this can be more readily contracted from outside sources.

Wear and Tear Refinements

Some consideration should be given to protecting the building from the obvious buffeting it will take from equipment and delivery vehicles. The most common method is to place pipe columns at key spots likely to be subjected to pounding from equipment. These pipe columns can be located to protect overhead door tracks and jambs, electrical apparatus, and building corners. Some firms place such columns in front of steel storage rack corners in order to prevent major damage at aisle intersections.

Highway trucks can damage the building when backing in to a flush dock if adequate bumpering is not provided. If the recommended dock leveler is used, bumpering is an integral part of the leveler system and additional measures are seldom required. If they are installed at the time of initial construction, pipe columns filled with sand and capped with concrete will add little to the project cost, and can be helpful in preventing early maintenance expenditures.

Summary

The country as a whole and the distribution industry in particular are now in a state of flux. In addition to the normal transition of companies from "more outside space to less" and from more centralized distribution systems to decentralized systems, there is the growing problem of energy. This issue has already had a significant impact on the entire field of distribution, and this will continue to be the case for the foreseeable future. Availability of energy may well be more of a problem than cost. Alternative energy sources are now being developed, but these sources will not be likely to have practical application until 1990 or later. As a result, construction design is likely to undergo as many changes as distribution location theory. There are no necessarily "right" answers.

Careful consideration must be given to the land and the many mitigating circumstances to the land package. Local tradition will have a significant impact on building design. The complexity of the design package will dictate the level of architectural and engineering service that will be required. The nature of the storage problem, as well as the magnitude of the distribution requirement, will impact the development of access facilities, whether they be rail, truck, or both. This, in turn, will dictate many of the design constraints.

An orderly review of the elements of the design program from site preparation through foundations, floors, roofs, and ultimately exterior yard areas is mandatory. It is hoped that this chapter will serve as an outline—even a check list of sorts—for those whose job it is to specify distribution facilities. It is also hoped that the suggestions given here will prevent some of the pitfalls encountered in the past.

Materials Handling— A Common Denominator

E. Ralph Sims, Jr.

Viewpoint

In the final analysis the whole physical distribution process is a materials handling system. Its basic purpose is to move a product from its initial source to a user or consumer. The physical distribution system encompasses the movement of vegetables from the farm to the produce counter in the supermarket, the movement of coal from the mines to the stockpile at the power station, the movement of oil from the wellhead to the gas station, and the movement of health and beauty aids from the packaging line to the drug store. In all of these systems and markets, a product is moved many times. It also changes its shape and physical characteristics as it moves through the system. The unit of movement varies, the timing and rate of movement varies, and the need for storage and transportation varies as the product moves through the distribution system. When one looks at the distribution system from a materials handling engineering point of view, it is virtually impossible to characterize this complex business function in anything approaching a homogeneous technological pattern. Some products start as liquids and arrive at the destination as packages. Others start as bulk granular materials, are converted into packages, and then broken down into unit quantities for the final sale. Some products start as individual items and are assembled into sets for delivery to the customer. Hazardous and fragile products need special handling; other products may need security.

It is unfortunate that many executives view the materials handling function as an element of only one particular stage of the distribution system. They see it as a part of the distribution warehouse, truck terminal, public warehouse, or chain store receiving dock. But *materials handling equipment is the tooling of the distribution system. The movement of goods through the system is the physical manifestation of both marketing policy and cash flow.* The rate of movement, the safety of movement, and the manner of movement depend on the choice of tooling as applied to both the computerization of documentation and the handling of materials through the system. The "tooling" of the system must respond to the distribution policy. The materials handling system must not dominate, but it should physically define the distribution policy. Distribution policy must be based on optimum use of the opportunity offered by modern materials handling technology.

Materials Handling Categories

In order to discuss materials handling properly, it is essential to divide it into three general categories, (1) bulk handling, (2) volume package products, and (3) packaged products.

1. *Bulk handling* involves the movement of such items as coal, oil, grain, chemicals, granular plastics, and other flowable commodities which may or may not be packaged at some point in their distribution flow. For example, oil moves by pipeline during the early stages of its distribution but often is delivered to the customer in quart cans. The transitions during the process of distribution may be from the pipeline to a rail tank car or tank truck and by pipe into a customer's storage tank. Alternatively, it could also be put into a 55-gallon drum and then into one-quart cans. At each stage of the movement a different materials handling system must be applied; the characteristics or value of the product within the package have little or no effect on the choice of the system once it is confined in a safe package. Thus, the quart can of oil, in its carton or outside of its carton, has the same handling characteristics in the distribution system as a can of soup or a container of table salt, with the possible exception that oil is a flammable product. This transition from bulk to unit pack is inherent in the distribution system's materials handling structure.

2. *Volume package products* are those products which are generally moved in large unit loads. Examples of these would be strapped loads of plywood or wallboard, unit loads of two-by-fours, bundles of electrical conduit, large pieces of furniture such as sofas, farm supply items such as hog feeders and watering troughs, machinery, automobiles, and boats. These products generally move from the source or manufacturer all the way to the final retail distribution point or industrial user in the original unit load pattern. Farm products and building materials do break down into smaller delivery elements when they reach the distributor or retailer level but both of these product lines usually move from that point in user vehicles or in combination shipments from the retailer or wholesale supplier. The bulk unit has handling characteristics which differ from bulk products and from typical packaged goods, and the materials handling systems which support it must accommodate these characteristics.

3. *Packaged products* include almost all consumer goods, most industrial and office supply items, paints, packaged chemicals, food products, drug products, stationary, industrial supplies, spare parts, lubricants, instruments, and most of the items moved through a typical department store or grocery chain store. These are the items that most distribution managers deal with and that most of the modern distribution systems and materials handling systems have addressed. The technology of materials handling has generally focused on the handling of packages that fall within a size and weight pattern that is compatible with the 48-inch cube and the 4000-pound unit load or some element

thereof. Most forklift trucks and materials handling systems and almost all conveyor systems are designed to accommodate packages that fit within these dimensions. The modular relationship between the pallet, the intermodal container or highway vehicle, the rail car, and the conventional wheeled vehicle materials handling equipment has provided the basis for whatever standardization exists in materials handling systems. These dimensional parameters have tended to provide a self-imposed design limitation on most high volume products in order to permit their movement through the system which is generally configured around 24-inch conveyors, the 48- by 40-inch pallet, 4000-pound capacity forklift trucks, 96-inch-wide highway vans, and a 50-pound individual handling limit on manual operations. As a result, highly sophisticated modern materials handling systems generally deal effectively with packaged products that fall within these dimensional parameters. Distribution of items which are neither bulk (in the sense that they can be pumped or conveyor flowed) or packaged (in the sense that they fit within these dimensional parameters) find that modern technology has left their needs on the sidelines. There are a few developments in the heavy handling areas that deal with volume type merchandise. These are special engineering projects and are definitely not commonplace.

Order Picking

One of the major elements of the physical distribution system is the order-picking operation, which deals with individual pieces, packages, drums, bags, or cartons. Recent developments have made some automated order-picking capability available for individual consumer packaged material. These automatic picking machines are like industrial-style vending machines. They can deliver individual packages on a computer-controlled basis. Cartons, drums, and bags can be "picked" from automated storage systems by mechanical means under computer control. However, the conversion of order information into product movement at the individual piece part or package level in the distribution system generally remains a manual process.

Technology has improved the relationship between the order picker and the product. By delivering the order picker to the pick point on a machine under computer control and delivering information to the picker, the human content of the picking system has been greatly reduced. In other systems the product is delivered to the picker's work station by a computer-directed machine. The accuracy of the pick can be improved by computer display of picking instructions and a checking procedure. The product can be delivered from the pick site to the packing location mechanically. However, little has been accomplished to date to compete with the eye, hand, and brain combination of the human as the most versatile and efficient means of converting order selection information into product motion at the interface between the product storage point and the information source.

The State-of-the-Art

In examining the various levels of materials handling requirements it becomes apparent that the commercial characteristics of the operation and the physical characteristics of the product dominate the design of the materials handling system. The unit of sale, the character of the product, and the market cycles dominate the volume, product mix, and shape of the materials to be handled. In most systems the product mix is heterogeneous in its physical shapes, sizes, and quantities, and the flow is usually complex with a variety of routings, order patterns, and shipping methods. The solution to materials handling improvement must therefore lie in the homogenization of the materials handling system by application of common denominator handling modules. This will allow mechanization or automation to function in spite of the heterogeneous complexity of the distribution flow.

The first step in the development of this homogenization process was the invention of the pallet. Pallet handling can be automated, and the pallet does not "need to know" what product it is carrying or what the product is used for. The pallet serves as the common denominator of the handling system. Likewise, a tote box can homogenize loose picked products in a selection system and the carton can homogenize the handling system for almost any product which is packaged. As long as these common denominator handling elements have some similarity in their shape and size, high technology can be applied to a materials handling operation in the distribution system.

The larger segments or elements of the economy are based on the distribution of products that are to some degree homogenized by industry standards. For example, food packaging has fairly standard dimensional patterns because of the design of packaging machinery and standard can and bottle dimensions. Chemicals, oils, soft drinks, beer, cigarettes, canned goods, and almost all products that are manufactured and packaged in a highly automated production facility tend to have uniform rectilinear packaging when they reach the distribution system. The round aerosol can is placed in a rectilinear six pack within a rectilinear carton. The paint can becomes a part of the rectilinear carton and the steel drum has become a national standard. Thus, homogenization of products through standardized packaging and common denominator devices such as pallets and tote boxes has made the development of automated handling and storage systems feasible for complex distribution operations.

Another element of the state-of-the-art which started slowly but has not become a major factor in materials handling is the use of bar code identity systems. The capability to read optical font or bar codes at high speeds and the increasing application of the Universal Commercial Code and other bar code identity procedures on packages has made it possible to tie computer management to materials handling systems. Further, the use of mini- and microcomputers, programmable controllers, and a variety of sensing devices has made it technically possible to automate fully almost any warehousing and distribution facility. Progress is even being made toward the automated loading and unloading of highway vehicles and rail cars, although this is still a major challenge that has not been fully conquered.

In general, therefore, long-established standard materials handling devices have in recent years been upgraded through the use of computers to a sophisticated level of automation. In situations where the product shape or package is stable or can be stabilized by a common denominator interface, fully automated handling systems can be applied at every stage of the distribution flow. Fully automated warehouses are becoming commonplace. Such warehouses can handle all varieties of goods. They are highly capital intensive, labor limiting, computer dependent, and technologically sophisticated.

Materials Handling Equipment Applications

The scope of this *Handbook* does not allow a thorough analysis of materials handling equipment and its application. There are many handbooks and texts that address the equipment in detail. More importantly, the state-of-the-art in materials handling equipment is changing so rapidly that managers and planners should seek information about any particular piece of equipment from the supplier to assure that they are up to date with the state-of-the-art. But the analysis of the system and the definition of requirements are essential tasks for management to undertake. There are some basic rules for decision making and criteria for the selection of particular types of handling equipment. By its very nature the distribution warehouse often includes all classes of materials handling equipment and technology that apply to the miscellaneous product mix found in the physical distribution system. In summary, they may be described as:

1. *Storage furniture*, including pallet racks, shelving, pallets, self-supporting pallets or pallet frames, roll-through picking racks, and other stationary or sedentary devices for the storage and holding of merchandise.

2. *Storage systems*, including the storage/retrieval (AS/RS) machines that are designed for handling pallets and unit loads (Figure 25–1), mini-stackers that are designed to handle small parts in a tray-type system (Figure 25–2), carousel-type storage units, movable shelving or movable racks, overhead monorail type storage systems, and certain types of roll-through pallet storage operations. All of these devices require considerable engineering and careful analysis before they are installed and they are all based upon the concept of homogenization of the material through the use of a common denominator device such as a tote box or pallet.

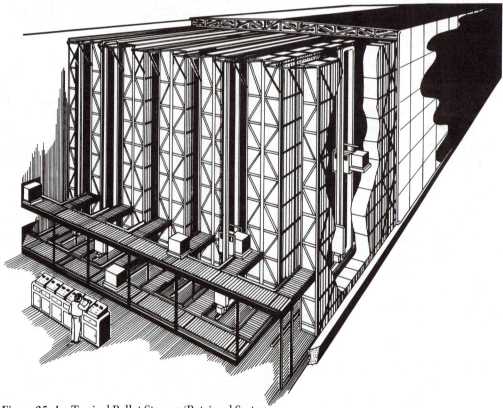

Figure 25-1   Typical Pallet Storage/Retrieval System

The Sims Consulting Group, Inc.

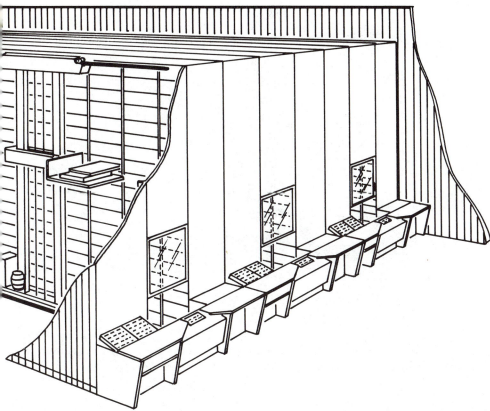

re 25-2   Typical Mini-storage/Retrieval System

ims Consulting Group, Inc.

3. *Manned wheeled vehicles*, including the conventional forklift truck (Figure 25–3), narrow-aisle forklift (Figure 25–4), turret-type forklift truck (Figure 25–5), order pick vehicle (Figure 25–6), pallet jack, warehouse cart, two-wheel hand trucks, and other equipment items which are designed to move products faster in larger sizes and weights than the human being is capable of doing alone.

4. *Conveyors*, including conventional, skate wheel, roller, and belt conveyor, overhead monorail, or power and free systems, tow-line systems, chain-type floor conveyors for pallets, and the conveyor systems that are used for live storage and roll-through operations.

5. *Lifts*, including conventional elevators, scissor and hydraulic lift tables, vertical conveyor systems, vehicle lifts, and pallet lifts for palletizing and depalletizing operations.

ien one thinks of modern warehouses the image often comes to mind of an automated h storage facility that handles pallet loads of merchandise into a storage/retrieval (AS/ machine under computer control and retrieves on computer demand. The mini-ker or mini-storage/retrieval machine fits into this same image. However, in distribu-1 warehouses there are a variety of sophistication levels that can produce highly onsive and economical operations. The high capital investment that automated ware-

Figure 25-3   Typical Counterbalance Forklift Truck

The Sims Consulting Group, Inc.

houses require makes them impractical for many firms—and frequently the decision to automate must be made on the basis of long-term return on investment.

Selection Criteria

Some of the criteria which must be applied to the selection of materials handling equipment are summarized here.

1. When random paths and random volumes are involved, manned or computer-controlled random path vehicular systems are usually most appropriate.

2. When the system involves constant path and/or constant flow, or high volume flow on an intermittent basis over a constant path, use of conveyors can often be justified.

3. When a conveyor must be manually loaded and unloaded in individual units, the use of a unit load system with either vehicular or conveyor transport is usually more appropriate.

4. Conveyor applications in warehouses are usually economical only when one end of the conveyor is a part of a manual operation that must be performed in any case (i.e., stacking cartons in a truck) and the other end is mechanically loaded, or when it is part of another operation which must be performed in any case (i.e., packing shipping cartons).

5. Unit load systems are usually more economical when both ends of a move require manual loading and unloading.

6. The pay-off on high-cube narrow-aisle forklift systems usually involves the cost of the land and building. The labor and performance factors in high-cube fork-

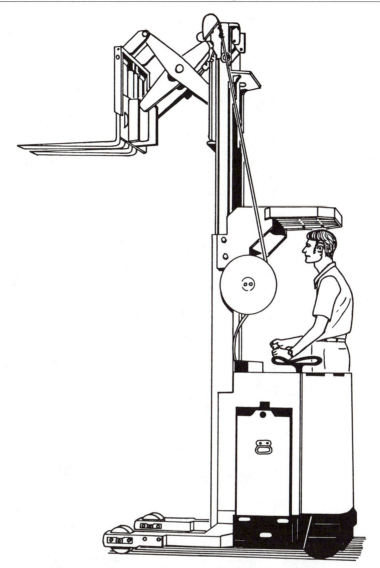

Figure 25-4   Typical Reach-Type Forklift Truck

The Sims Consulting Group, Inc.

lift operations are very little different from conventional forklift operations. Therefore, the return on investment is usually based upon a capital investment trade-off. In the case of rack supported buildings there may also be a tax advantage.

7. High-cube storage machines usually require a second handling between the storage system and the receiving or shipping docks since the high machines are not suitable for truck and rail loading or unloading in shipping and receiving operations.

8. Versatile narrow-aisle equipment which can both load vehicles and operate in narrow aisles is usually most effective for pallet operations in the distribution

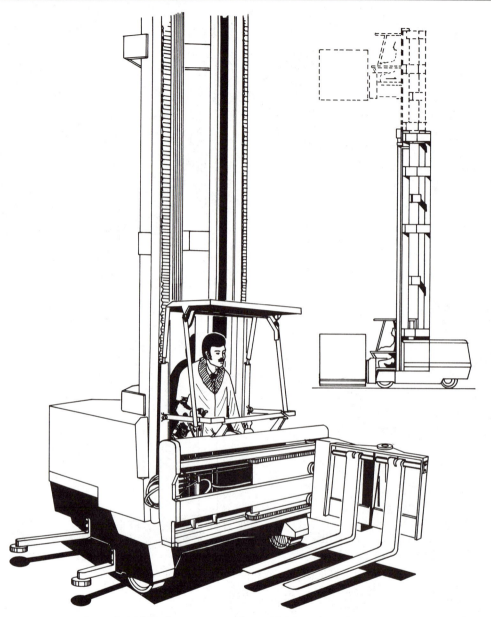

***Figure* 25-5**   Typical High-Cube Narrow-Aisle Forklift Truck/Order Picker
The Sims Consulting Group, Inc.

warehouse unless the system is automated. Used in combination with high order pickers this type of equipment can provide the best of narrow-aisle activities without the penalty of double handling.

9. Roll-through order-picking operations are generally effective only when the unit load or package is degraded from either a pallet load to a case or a case to an in-

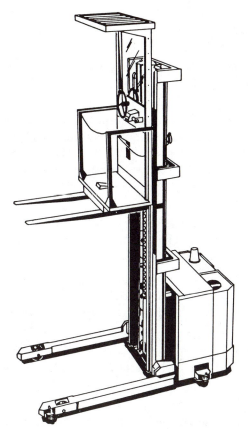

Figure 25-6   Typical Stockpicker Vehicle

The Sims Consulting Group, Inc.

dividual piece as the result of the pass-through. This is true because pass-through systems require double aisles and loading and unloading at both ends, and with the same unit of handling this saves nothing. If degradation is not accomplished, front loading of either pallet racks or shelving reduces aisle loss with no change in labor content if the restocking can be accomplished without interference with picking operations.

10. Order picking to a pallet or vehicle or other unit load device and the mechanical removal of that unit load to the packing station or shipping point should be combined with high order-picking equipment. This technique improves the ratio of picker selection time to travel time.

11. In general, pick and pack operations performed simultaneously are less efficient than separate picking and separate packing with checking. Pick and pack operations should only be used when the destination of the goods is in the control of the shipper or when the goods are of such low value that errors and/or shipping damage are not critical issues.

Quantifying the Analysis

In the analysis of materials handling operations, the selection rules described above can be applied through the following steps:

1. Define the transaction pattern and optimize the volume of goods movement per handling at each stage of the operation. An order and receipt profile study based on a sampling of documents can define the orders and receipts per day, the line items (SKUs) per order or receipt, the pieces or units per line item, and the number and types of outbound carrier vehicles in which the orders are shipped.

2. Define the storage profile in terms of cubic feet or pallets per inventory item (SKU), and optimize space and cube utilization through a combination of storage furniture, random storage layout, a locator system, and the application of high-cube storage techniques.

3. Use the computer and/or clerical system to preroute and schedule the order picking, put-away, and out-loading operations to minimize travel time; pregroup orders in vehicle or carrier batches prerouted to pick level locations and timed for work scheduling.

4. Optimize the use of the employees' eye-hand-brain capability by using equipment to minimize or speed up travel and the application of any automated handling systems.

As an example of the application of these steps, let us suppose we are planning for the distribution of health and beauty aids (HBA) in a drug or supermarket chain store warehouse. If there are 100 stores in the system and we make weekly deliveries, we might fill orders for 20 stores each day. If there are 4000 HBA items in the line and we experience a 50 percent hit rate with an average of 3 pieces per pick, the pick load is 6000 pieces for 20 stores each day. The store orders may average 600 items per week and the item order list will vary over the total list of 4000 items. The pick load will vary with season and product mix. Thus the transaction profile for this system might show an average of:

20 orders per day by truck

600 items per order

1800 pieces per order

The items per order would include:

150 case lot items

40 pallet lot items

300 inner pack items

110 each items

This profile would provide the basis for selecting a picking system. In this instance, radio-directed forklifts would probably pick the 40 pallet lot items, high order pickers could pick the 150 case lot items, and the balance might be picked from slope rack to tote boxes on conveyors. This is a marginal volume pattern for considering automation of part of the picking operation. Mechanization is appropriate here, but more volume might be needed to justify automation.

However, with 4000 items, a 50 percent hit rate, and 100 stores, the inventory profile would probably show about 20 percent (800 items) of the items in volume storage and about 60 percent with at least one pallet of backup inventory. In such a profile, consideration of automated pallet storage would be worthwhile. Also with 6 percent of the items picked in pallets lots (an average of 40 items per order) and most of the 2400 palletized items received on pallets, automated pallet storage begins to make some sense even if interfaced with forklift in-and-out movements. The 40 pallet-shipped items could then be computer picked in the automated storage system.

If we assume that every item that is normally picked in less than case lots (each) will be represented in the pick line, the cube analysis must develop the size and configuration of the shelving or slope racks for the complete inventory of the 40 to 60 percent of the items with no backup stocks and the modular (preferably pallet quantity) forward open stock capacity for all items in the pick line.

The pick locations and automated storage system's locations would be in the inventory or a separate warehouse computer. The pickers and AS/RS machines would be routed by sequencing the items, timing the work load, and minimizing travel time.

Measuring and Costing

The use of work measurement techniques in the analysis of handling operations is normal practice. In most instances, the use of work sampling or predetermined standard times is most practical in warehouse operations. *Materials handling costs are a function of the cube or physical volume of the material moved* and have no relationship to the value or function of the goods. Thus, the measurement of materials handling costs on the basis of a percentage of dollar sales or the measurement of storage costs on the basis of dollars of inventory is an invalid criterion. Handling costs should be defined in terms of cost per pallet, cost per tote box, or cost per cubic foot based upon distance traveled and time in storage. The only value factors that affect the cost of materials handling are the need for extra security or control and in storage, when it affects the cost of insurance.

Implementation

In general, the acquisition of materials handling equipment should be based upon the development of a complete system concept and equipment should be selected to fit the operating plan. An operating specification and system narrative should be prepared with supporting layouts, activity projections, and inventory support requirements. As a general rule, the system design should be based upon maximum predicted performance at 80 percent of system capacity to allow for breakdowns, surges, and a reasonable amount of unexpected growth. Competent engineering support should be given to the planning effort.

The plans, specifications, and operations narrative should be used as a part of the bid package offered to vendors when soliciting their proposals. In the case of sophisticated systems, it is desirable to pick a single vendor as the general contractor in order to assure the coordination of the system elements and proper function of the operation as a whole. Purchase of individual items from different vendors in a conventional system has a lower risk from poor coordination because of less interdependence among equipment types. As part of the equipment purchase process it is essential that the operating personnel be properly trained in the use and maintenance of the machinery. An adequate spare parts inventory must be included in the purchase and in the budget planning.

In summary, *the best handling is the least handling.* The fundamental rule of materials handling is to move the largest possible quantity as far as possible to the next point of use before breaking it down, and the fundamental principle of storage is to utilize air rights and cube to the optimum while maintaining a balance between labor and space efficiency.

A Look to the Future

When looking into the future in distribution warehousing and materials handling, one cannot help but feel that the development of automation and mechanization will continue to expand. The functional characteristics of high-cube warehousing, high narrow-aisle forklift trucks, conveyors, and system controls, and the application of information systems through computers to control distribution operations is approaching a high level of stability in terms of operating concepts and technological capability. The trends in the future will be toward more reliability, more simplicity of operation, and more sophistication of technology to make these concepts work better. The systems may increase their operating speeds, the storage systems may be built higher, and the distribution warehouses may be less labor-intensive.

One of the big gaps in the distribution system is the lack of a mechanized method for loading miscellaneous freight for delivery on highway vehicles. The hand selection of merchandise will probably still continue to be a necessity in most distribution systems. However, aside from these two elements, it is likely that almost everything else in the distribution warehouse can be mechanized. The main hurdle is management's continuing insistence on a short-term pay-off in the purchase of equipment with long-term advantages.

Inventory Management

Inventory and Physical Distribution Management

Lynn E. Gill (Subsections 1 *to* 8), George Isoma (Subsection 9), *and* Joel L. Sutherland (Subsection 10)

The following questions and statements are typical of those voiced by business managers faced with scheduling production, coordinating inventories in regional distribution centers, meeting customer service requirements, and managing the many other aspects of business impacted by inventories:

"Why are we always out of stock?"

"Our storage costs are too high!"

"How should we plan production for seasonal sales?"

"We have too many expensive production runs caused by poor inventory forecasting!"

"How often should we reorder?"

"We are losing business because our products are in the wrong places at the wrong times!"

"How can we schedule production when our sales are uncertain?"

"Freight costs are too high because of lack of sufficient inventories!"

They also typify the many conflicts of interest that often occur in the management of inventories.

The sales manager is most concerned about stock-outs that result in lost sales; the controller wants to minimize inventory investment. The traffic manager delays shipment of orders to allow effective consolidation, and the purchasing department buys in amounts that exceed current requirements in order to qualify for quantity discounts. It is hardly surprising that each manager is most concerned about costs that reflect on his own performance, even if minimizing those costs does not maximize the overall profit of the firm. These conflicts arise when there is no systematic approach to trading off, or balancing, inventory costs and service elements to best achieve the overall objectives of the firm. Figure 26–1 illustrates some of the conflicting pressures exerted on inventory levels.

1.   Inventory Decision Areas

Customer Service

In the final analysis, inventory is stocked so that good service can be provided to customers—by having the right products in proper quantities at the right places at the right times and in good condition, all at the most economical cost consistent with this service. The demand for good customer service and the need to provide it at an economical cost is the classic trade-off in physical distribution management.

Costs of providing customer service increase rapidly as customer service levels become greater. For example, if all orders were filled completely, without back orders, inventories in most firms would need to be exorbitantly large. Conversely, very low inventories would result in excessive out-of-stocks, back orders, and, consequently, lost sales. In this case, the basic trade-off is between the cost of providing good customer service and the cost of lost sales resulting from inadequate service.

As an example, consider a product that is ordered to be available at the beginning of the month to meet demand for the entire month. A typical distribution of sales demand is shown in Table 26–1, and the percentage of months each level of demand occurs is plotted as the familiar bell-shaped normal curve shown in Figure 26–2.

The cumulative demand distribution, showing the percentage of months in which demand is equal to or less than a given amount, is shown in Figure 26–3. This graph shows that if 4000 units are ordered monthly, all demand will be met 50 percent of the time, whereas if 5000 units are ordered monthly, all demand will be met 70 percent of the time.

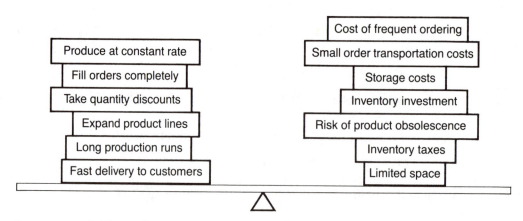

Figure 26-1   Conflicting Pressures on Inventory Levels

Table 26-1   Distribution of Demand over a Five-year Period

Demand per Month Between Range	Months Occurring (Frequency)	Percentage of Months Occurring	Cumulative Frequency*
0– 999	3	5	5
1000–1999	5	8	13
2000–2999	10	17	30
3000–3999	12	20	50
4000–4999	12	20	70
5000–5999	9	15	85
6000–6999	6	10	.95
7000 or greater	3	5	100
Totals	60	100	

*The percentage of months in which demand is less than or equal to top of range.

If 6000 units are ordered, 86 percent of demand will be met, and if 7000 units are ordered, demand will be met 95 percent of the time. Each increment of 1000 units ordered has resulted in 20 percent, 16 percent, and 9 percent greater order fill rate, respectively. Higher levels of customer service are obtained, therefore, at correspondingly higher inventory carrying costs, as less out-of-stock protection is provided by each greater level of inventory stocked.

Although a variety of other customer services are provided by the physical distribution system, it is primarily inventories that contribute to the ability to fill a high percentage of orders from stock (availability) and the ability to deliver the products to the customer quickly and consistently.

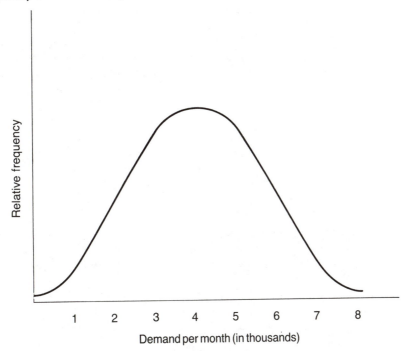

Figure 26-2   Normal Distribution of Demand

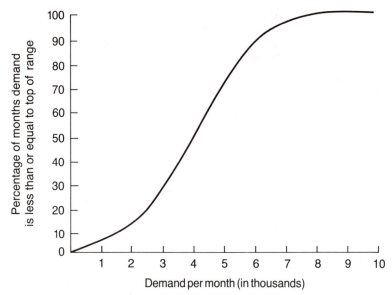

Figure 26-3   Cumulative Demand Distribution Illustrating Uncertain
Demand

A customer places an order with the expectation that it will be filled completely. It is always an inconvenience—and sometimes a disaster—when suppliers are out of stock and must ship partial orders or back-order shipments. Safety stock inventories ensure the availability of products to fill a high percentage of demand in the face of fluctuating demand patterns. In the examples cited above, safety stock is the amount ordered greater than that necessary to meet average demand (50 percent). The higher the percentage of complete orders filled, or the higher the percentage of total demand satisfied, the higher the levels of safety stock inventory needed to provide that service.

The ability to deliver products quickly and consistently often determines which supplier gets the order. A vendor who can provide consistent two-week delivery, when competing firms require four to six weeks, will be likely to be the preferred source. Quick and consistent delivery allows customers to reduce their own inventory levels because it reduces their risk of running out of stock.

One way to provide quick delivery is to maintain stocks of inventories in distribution centers close to customers' locations. Dividing inventories among multiple facilities, however, increases the total amount of inventory that must be carried.

A second way of providing for quick delivery is to produce for stock in anticipation of orders, instead of producing only after orders are received. Of course, this results in finished goods inventories that do not exist in produce-to-order systems. Although raw material inventories exist in produce-to-order systems, they are likely to be less than finished goods inventories in produce-to-stock systems because of the flexibility of making several finished goods from the same raw materials.

These examples demonstrate that increased service comes at the expense of increased inventory carrying costs. Figure 26-4 illustrates the general trade-off between customer service and inventory costs. As customer service (inventory) increases, the cost of lost sales due to inadequate service decreases. However, inventory carrying costs grow larger with those increasing service levels. The task of physical distribution managers, therefore, is to minimize the total of inventory carrying costs and cost of lost sales by providing levels of service which can be supported without excessive inventory carrying costs.

Inventory Costs

In most firms, inventory carrying costs are among the highest of all costs of doing business. Inventories of selected firms from a number of industries have been determined to represent from 30 to 70 percent of current assets, and up to 45 percent of total assets. And the costs of carrying this inventory are often substantially in excess of 25 percent per year of the value of the inventory. Inventory costs in many firms are about 30 to 40 percent of all logistics costs. Consequently, the typical distribution executive must devote a great deal of time to the control and management of inventory costs. (See pages 626–630 for an extensive discussion of how inventory carrying costs might be calculated.)

Many expenses are involved in holding inventory, the most obvious being storage costs—the rental or capital charge for warehouse space, heat, light, and so forth. Insurance and taxes on inventory, deterioration and obsolescence from holding products over extended periods of time, and capital costs must also be taken into account.

Capital costs require some explanation. When inventory is held, capital is tied up in the form of stored products. If money is tied up in plant equipment, that equipment is expected to return profits to its owners. Inventory, too, is created for the purpose of earning profits—an investment in inventory should return as much as any other capital investment.

When all of these costs are considered, many firms find that the annual cost of holding inventory is more than 25 percent of the value of the goods in storage. If the cost of a unit were $100, with an inventory carrying cost of 25 percent, it would cost $25 to hold one unit in stock for one year. It is not difficult to see why management should be interested in keeping inventories at the most economic levels consistent with the need to provide good customer service.

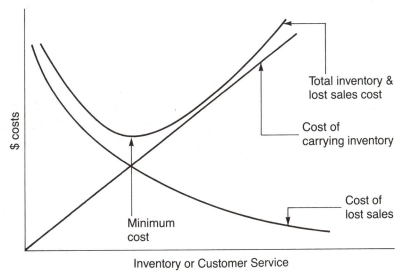

Figure 26-4   Trade-Off between Cost of Inventory and Costs of Lost Sales

Types of Inventory

In order to provide an adequate level of customer service in the face of fluctuating demand, it is necessary to carry inventory. Most firms will hold several types of inventory, including: (1) inventory to balance seasonal production or seasonal demand, (2) inventory that decouples production processes, (3) pipeline inventories, (4) inventory to allow purchase discounts, (5) inventory to support sales or to provide speedy delivery, (6) inventory to expand product lines, (7) inventory to allow economical manufacturing, (8) order cycle inventory, and (9) safety stocks.

Seasonal Balance

Apples tend to be harvested only once a year. Putting the entire apple crop on the market at one time would cause a tremendous oversupply and would result in low prices once a year and shortages for the remainder. Cold storage facilities permit the seasonal supply of apples to be matched more closely with year-round demand.

Similarly, many products such as bathing suits and toys have a seasonal demand. Of the several alternatives available to firms faced with seasonal demand patterns, one is to produce at a relatively steady rate throughout the year, building inventory stocks in anticipation of peak demands (Figure 26–5). Although this makes production efficient and thereby reduces production costs, this efficiency is offset by higher inventory carrying cost.

A second alternative is to vary production to schedule the peak period of production just before the time of peak demand. This approach requires changing the size of the work force, and the costs of hiring can be high—as are costs when trained employees have to be laid off. Also, plants sized to accommodate peak periods must run at less efficient, lower than capacity levels during much of the year. In actual practice, many firms combine these alternatives—varying capacity at different times of the year with multiple shift and overtime production as well as building inventories to meet seasonal peak demands.

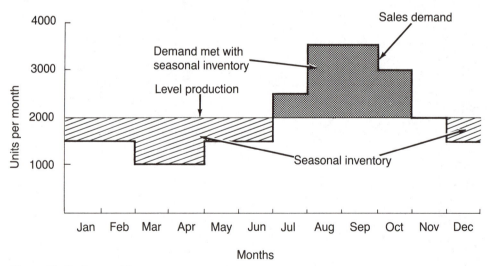

Figure 26-5   Seasonal Inventory

Decoupling

In most production systems, various processes are performed at different speeds. Inevitably, inventory accumulates between steps in these processes. It is also desirable to provide buffer stocks between processes, so that a breakdown occurring in one process will not result in shutting down the entire production line. Decoupling inventories are illustrated in Figure 26–6.

In-process inventories are necessary and normal for efficient production. Sometimes, though, unnecessary inventory results between production steps because workers often feel more comfortable and secure when they have a backlog of work. This "backlog syndrome" should be discouraged by keeping inventory at the level necessary to decouple production processes—but no more.

Pipeline Requirements

It is necessary to maintain a pipeline inventory of goods moving in transportation vehicles, and flowing through terminals and distribution centers. For example, it might take four days to ship products by truck to a distribution center, three days to handle the product there, and four more days to deliver the goods to the customer—a total of eleven days. If demand averages 1000 items per day, it would take 11,000 items to fill up the eleven-day pipeline before the first items could be sold. After that, an average of 1000 items would enter the pipeline daily and 1000 would leave it, resulting in a residual of 11,000 items in the pipeline at all times. Although pipeline inventories are often overlooked, they are definitely a cost item.

Of course, pipeline inventories can be reduced by shortening the length of the pipeline, substituting faster for slower transportation, or increasing distribution center throughput to squeeze inventory out of the pipeline. Such steps are often costly, however, and there is a trade-off between these costs and the cost of maintaining pipeline inventories.

Purchase Discounts

Many firms encourage large purchases by offering quantity discounts. This can result in buying more than is needed for current demands; in other words, the buyer accumulates an inventory. There is a trade-off between cost savings due to purchase discounts and the

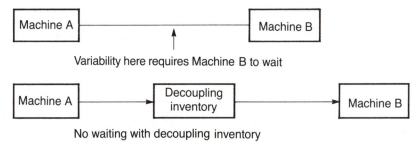

Figure 26-6   Decoupling Inventory

cost of carrying the additional stock. Only if savings from quantity discounts are greater than the cost of supporting the additional inventory are quantity discounts advantageous.

Sales and Delivery Support

When speedy delivery is a priority, some firms find it advantageous to place stocks close to customer demand locations. Then, when an order is received, it will be shipped a shorter distance. Increased sales obtained by placing inventory stocks close to customer demand naturally are offset by greater space and storage costs. Conversely, less inventory is required if stocks are located in one place rather than several, since the peaks and valleys of demand tend to cancel out one another. For example, if average demand is 100 tractors per month in each of two locations, a stockout would occur at one location if there were 80 units there and 120 in the other location. However, if the manufacturer held 200 units in one location to serve both markets, no stockout would result. Of course, the average shipping distances and related freight costs are greater when inventories are centralized.

Product Line Expansion

The tendency of modern marketing toward product proliferation has had a major impact. Additional inventory is required to support these expanded product lines. Profitability analysis for new products requires that additional inventory for the system be estimated. The cost of carrying additional inventory and other logistics costs incurred by the new product must be weighed against expected sales increases. In many cases, increased sales due to a new product may not be great enough to cover the additional logistics expenses.

Inventory to Allow Economical Manufacturing

In many manufacturing processes, several products are made on the same machines or production lines. One product is produced for a time, building up an inventory. Then, the machine or line is shut down for setup (change-over) of the machines to produce a second product. While the second product is being produced, the inventory of the first product is drawn down to meet sales demand. Figure 26–7 illustrates this production and inventory relationship.

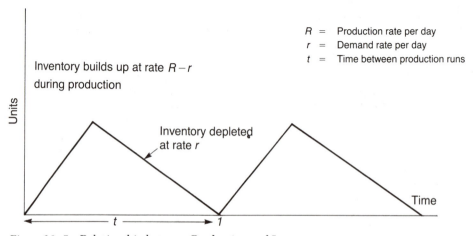

Figure 26-7   Relationship between Production and Inventory

Whenever a production process is shut down for change-over, costs are incurred. These costs include production lost while the machines are shut down, machine change-over costs, excessive scrap generated when production resumes, machine adjusting costs, lost production due to relearning by production personnel, and so forth.

To avoid repeated setup costs, production managers prefer long production runs. However, long runs result in the build-up of large inventory stocks. The trade-off in determining economic manufacturing lot sizes is to find the amount to be produced that minimizes the sum of inventory carrying costs and setup costs.

A second factor that allows economical manufacturing is an assured supply of raw materials for the production process. Production schedules are most often set on the basis of forecasts of demand for finished products. Supplies of raw materials sufficient to support production of these finished products, therefore, also derive from those same demand forecasts.

Once a production schedule has been established, a list or bill of raw materials required for production can be prepared. Orders should be placed according to the time needed to obtain the materials from vendors (vendor lead time), so that the materials will arrive at the appropriate times. This time phased method of ordering, based on deriving raw materials requirements from forecasts for finished products, is called *materials requirements planning* (MRP).

Order Cycle Stock

When orders are placed less frequently, more inventory is required. Figure 26–8 illustrates the effect of ordering frequency on average inventory. When 200 units are ordered every 30 days, an average inventory of 100 units results. When the time between orders (order interval) is reduced to 15 days, average inventory is also reduced, to 50 units. However, when orders are placed more frequently, the cost of ordering also increases. More order clerk time, paperwork, computer time to process orders, receiving inspections, and higher transportation costs because of smaller shipments can all result from more frequently placed orders.

Figure 26–9 illustrates the trade-off between ordering costs and inventory carrying costs. As the size of each order increases (and order frequency decreases), inventory carrying costs also increase. At the same time, the costs of ordering decrease since orders are

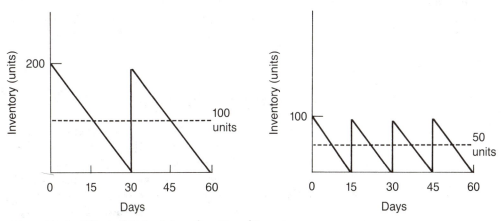

Figure 26-8   Effect of Order Interval on Size of Inventory

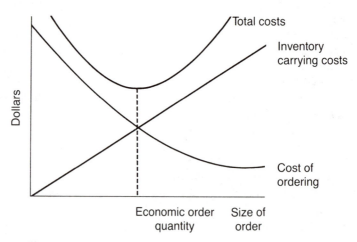

Figure 26-9   The Most Economic Order Quantity

placed less frequently. What is important, of course, is the *total* cost of placing orders— that is, the sum of inventory carrying costs and the cost of ordering. Amounts should be ordered that result in minimum total cost (the economic order quantity).

Safety Stocks

Ordering according to economic order quantity criteria minimizes the total of inventory and ordering costs. However, such ordering does not necessarily provide an adequate level of customer service. How much safety stock inventory should a firm provide to best serve its customers?

In Figure 26–10, 200 units are expected to last 30 days. If the rate of sales is greater than anticipated (as shown by the dotted line), 60 units of safety stock are needed to prevent a stockout.

Greater safety stocks naturally provide higher levels of customer service. But as higher levels are attained, more safety stock must be provided for relatively less gain in customer service, since greater demands occur less often. Costs of providing safety stocks must always be balanced off against the additional sales that will result from providing better customer service.

Forecasting demand as accurately as possible reduces the amount of safety stock inventory required, but even the best forecasts will include some error. To avoid lost sales in such situations, safety stock inventories must be provided.

2.   Determination of Costs Related to Inventory Decisions

In the subsections that follow, various types of inventory decisions will be discussed. Each of these decisions involves the trading off of the various applicable costs to determine the most economic inventory levels. Identifying all the pertinent costs and determining their levels is, therefore, a very important part of inventory management and control. Inventory decisions will only be as good as the cost data used in making those decisions.

It should be noted that inventory carrying costs are only one of the cost categories included in an integrated distribution, or logistics, system. Under the logistics system con-

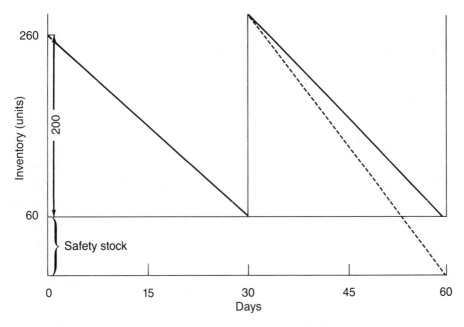

Figure 26-10   Provision of Safety Stock for Customer Service

cept, all costs must be considered in attempting to optimize overall system performance. According to the "total cost concept" of logistics, it is important not to unilaterally minimize one cost category, or even to minimize the total of two cost categories, without considering the impact on overall system costs. By doing so, costs in other parts of the system could be pushed up by a higher margin than those which are reduced. The object of overall logistics system design is to minimize the total of all logistics costs.

For example, the well-known economic order quantity (EOQ) formula determines the quantity to be ordered that minimizes the total of inventory carrying costs and order preparation costs. However, an order of that quantity could result in a less-than-truckload shipment, with correspondingly high freight costs, or it could mean that a lucrative quantity discount for purchasing a larger quantity is foregone. This results because the EOQ formula does not take into account transportation costs or quantity discounts, although attempts have sometimes been made to include those costs in revised EOQ calculations. Figure 27-15 in a later subsection illustrates the importance of including all costs in inventory analysis.

Some of the important cost categories having bearing on inventory decisions are: (1) inventory carrying costs, (2) order preparation costs, (3) production setup costs, (4) costs of quantity discounts foregone, (5) transportation costs, (6) costs related to multiple inventory locations, and (7) out-of-stock costs.

Inventory Carrying Costs

Inventory carrying costs are all of those costs that increase as inventories become larger, and shrink as inventories become smaller. In this regard, a long-range view should be taken; otherwise certain relevant costs will be ignored. For example, costs for private distribution center facilities are relatively fixed, and it is often easy to ignore those costs because "the space is available anyway and we can't do anything about it."

Obviously, an owned warehouse facility is not without cost, and there are costs involved in holding the space for inventories instead of making it available for alternative uses. Examples of alternative uses include sub-leasing warehouse buildings or sectioning off portions of distribution centers to rent on a month-to-month basis when inventories are cut back or during periods of business decline.

There are many costs of carrying inventories, and it is important not to overlook any relevant ones. Also, it is important to apply only the costs that are relevant to a particular situation. For example, when developing costs of carrying pipeline inventories (stocks moving in transportation equipment or through terminals) it is not logical to include costs of warehouse space. Warehouse space is related to inventories at rest, and pipeline inventories are inventories in motion. However, the cost of the capital tied up in inventory and risk factors such as damage costs are relevant for evaluating pipeline inventories.

Inventory carrying costs are generally expressed as a percentage of the average dollar inventory per year. The average dollar value of inventory can be determined from inventory records showing inventory status by week or by month, by simply adding up period-end inventory for all periods, and dividing by the number of periods (see Table 26–2). The carrying cost must then be related to the average dollar inventory. Carrying cost components are: (1) space costs, (2) inventory maintenance costs, (3) risk costs, and (4) capital costs.

Space Costs

Inventories at rest require storage space, either in public warehouses, or in privately owned or rented warehouses.

If a public warehouse is used to store inventories, space costs are easy to calculate. For example, assume that the storage rate in a public warehouse is $3 per pallet per month

Table 26–2 Month-end Inventories at Cost, Nonseasonal and Seasonal Patterns

	Month-end Inventory at Cost (Non-Seasonal)	Month-end Inventory at Cost (Seasonal)
January	$ 4,725,900	$ 3,071,700
February	4,555,350	2,733,300
March	4,670,550	2,568,600
April	4,788,900	2,394,450
May	4,828,950	2,897,550
June	4,736,700	3,552,300
July	4,694,400	3,755,250
August	4,802,850	4,562,550
September	4,856,850	5,584,950
October	4,647,600	4,415,400
November	4,714,650	3,771,450
December	4,677,750	3,274,200
Total	$56,700,450	$42,525,450
Average monthly inventory (Total divided by 12)	$ 4,725,038	$ 3,543,788

and the cost of the merchandise on a pallet is $450. Space cost expressed as percentage of average inventory cost per year is: $3 times 12 months equals $36 per pallet per year; divide this by $450 per pallet to equal a storage cost of 8 percent of product cost per year.

Determining the space costs in a private warehouse is somewhat more complicated. Costs of owning, or renting, and operating the building must first be calculated as a cost per square foot per year, and then related to the cost of inventory occupying the space. Space costs include: (1) building rental or opportunity cost, (2) property taxes on land and building, (3) liability and fire insurance (4) lights, heat, water, (5) maintenance and repairs, (6) security systems and installations, (7) depreciation representing wear and tear on the building, and (8) wages and fringe benefits for janitorial staff and watchmen. A proportional share of general administrative overhead (salaries and fringe benefits) should also be allocated on the basis of time involved in facility management.

The largest cost of space is the rental cost or opportunity cost of occupying an owned building. In today's business climate, many rental leases include frequent cost of living increases. If this is the case, current rental cost per square foot is the relevant cost to use.

If the firm has the good fortune of being locked into a long-term lease at a very low rental rate, the opportunity cost of occupying the building and not the actual rental cost is the appropriate cost to use. For example, if a building is being leased for 8¢ per square foot per month, and comparable neighboring buildings are renting for 20¢ per square foot, the firm occupying the building is foregoing an opportunity to earn rental income from subleasing the building. Therefore, the relevant cost of space occupied is 20 cents, not the actual 8 cents per square foot rental.

Similar logic applies to buildings that are owned. The relevant cost is the opportunity cost of occupying the building and foregoing rental profits. Appreciation in the value of the real estate has no bearing on space cost determination, since a building may be held as an investment and rented out in any case.

The following example illustrates the method used to calculate space costs and to relate them to inventory costs. A 100,000-square-foot distribution building is located in Southern California, and rented under a gross lease (owner is responsible for fire insurance and maintenance of roof and exterior walls).

Annual rental	$276,000
Property taxes	24,000
Liability insurance	2,500
Utilities	12,000
Security alarm	1,800
Janitorial	2,400
Maintenance and repairs	6,000
General and administration	3,200
Space cost per year	$327,900

The space cost per square foot per year is therefore $3.28.

Next, the cost per square foot of space must be related to the cost of the merchandise stored in inventory. The following analysis assumes that the building's size is appropriate for the inventory and that the building is being used efficiently. Also, it is assumed that the building is filled to effective capacity throughout the year, i.e., there are no seasonal periods when the building is partially empty. The first column of Table 26–2 shows a stable (nonseasonal) inventory, with an average inventory of $4,725,038.

Typically, 30 percent or more of a conventionally laid out distribution building is taken up with aisles, staging areas, offices, bathroom facilities, and so forth. Adjusting for 70 percent building utilization, the cost per square foot of usable space is $3.28 divided by 0.7, or $4.69 per square foot per year.

Next, honeycombing must be accounted for. Rarely is all of the usable space in a warehouse completely full. As pallets of products are withdrawn from storage, empty spaces result. These spaces often cannot be filled without blocking the products behind. A typical honeycombing factor is 70 percent utilization of usable space. To adjust for honey-combing, $4.69 is divided by 0.7; thus the cost of actual space under a stack of pallets is $6.70 per square foot per year. As a rule of thumb, the cost per square foot under the stack in a conventionally laid-out warehouse can be estimated by doubling the space cost per square foot (e.g., twice $3.28 is $6.56 per square foot).

Assuming the same value per pallet of $450, with 14 square feet of space required in which to store a pallet, and the ability to stack pallets three high, the following storage cost results: $6.70 per square foot per year times 14 square feet per pallet position equals $93.80 per pallet position per year. The value of three pallets equals $1350 and the storage cost is $93.80 divided by $1350, or 7 percent of product cost per year.

Using the second column of Table 26–2, which illustrates a seasonal inventory pattern, total space costs of $327,900 are divided by average inventory of $3,543,788. This results in a space cost of 9 percent of product cost per year.

Note that the space cost calculation is highly dependent on efficient utilization of the building. In the example, if seasonal patterns reduce building utilization to 75 percent, the product actually stored must bear an annual per square foot cost of $6.70 divided by 0.75, or $8.93 per square foot. For this reason, the storage cost rises to 9 percent of product cost per year.

Inventory Maintenance Costs

The major costs of maintaining inventories, those that grow and shrink as inventories expand and contract, are the costs of insurance and taxes on inventories. In addition, certain other costs such as taking physical inventories are relevant.

Insurance is usually carried by the owner of the goods to cover the full value of inventories against catastrophic loss from disasters such as fires, explosions, floods, sprinkler damage, and so forth. This insurance is provided by the goods' owner whether goods are stored in private or public warehouses since the public warehouseman's liability usually does not include the types of risks mentioned above. Insurance costs are relatively easy to determine, because paid insurance bills are available in accounting records. The insurance premium is directly variable with inventory valuation.

In certain states and local political jurisdictions, personal property taxes are assessed on inventories on hand as of a certain date. Local inventory taxes are usually quite small, and vary directly in proportion to inventory value.

Costs of performing "physical inventories" are affected by the size of the inventories on hand. The greater the inventory, the more boxes to count and the greater the employee time, tags, forms, and other materials required to take a physical inventory.

Inventory Risk Costs

There are certain risks that firms assume as inventories get larger. These include risks of obsolescence, damage, and pilferage. The cost of obsolescence is the cost of each unit that must be disposed of (written off) or marked down in value because it has become obsolete or has gone out of style. Generally, the faster inventory turns over (i.e., when inventories are small in relation to sales), the less are the risks of obsolescence. In some cases, however, the rates of obsolescence may be high because of overbuying on a particular item, not because inventory levels are high in general. In other cases, obsolete items are carried into later accounting periods to allow the write-offs to offset unusually high profits. For these reasons, estimating obsolescence costs requires careful analysis.

Similarly, some damage costs are related to the size of inventories. For example, handling damage can result from overcrowding, and slow inventory turnover can result in rusted parts or exceeded shelf-life pull dates. Other types of handling damage are related to throughput and would occur regardless of size of inventory. Those costs should not be included.

Pilferage or inventory shrinkage may be more closely related to security policy than to inventory levels. Nevertheless, the greater the stocks on hand, the greater the opportunity for pilferage. The relationship is difficult to quantify, but estimates can be made.

Capital Costs

Capital that is tied up in inventories could be used for some other productive purpose, such as investing it into new projects, putting it in an interest-bearing account, and so forth. When a budget request is made for a new machine or for a truck, a certain return of profits on the investment is generally required by management. Inventory, too, is carried for the purpose of earning profits, and an investment in inventory should return as much as any other capital investment.

Capital costs are the largest portion of inventory carrying costs in most firms. These capital costs will vary from firm to firm depending on financial policies or investment criteria.

Cost of capital should be based on the rate of return a company expects for its invested dollars, and on the risk involved. The estimated return should certainly be higher than the interest rate for bank borrowing; a firm would be unlikely to borrow at 18 percent if it didn't expect to make more than that. Only top financial management can properly assign the cost of capital figure for their firm, and the figure will change from time to time as conditions change.

The following factors affect the cost of capital assigned to the carrying of inventory:

1. *How much can the firm earn by putting its money into other projects?* The higher the return on investment of investment opportunities, the more valuable the money that could be made available by reducing inventories. If putting money into additional inventory means a firm must forego the opportunity to invest in a project earning 30 percent, then the capital tied up in inventory must be thought of as costing 30 percent.

2. *How much money does the firm have for investment in inventory and other projects?* When a firm has abundant cash beyond that needed to invest in available opportunities, the cost of capital is less than when funds are in short supply.

3. *How much does it cost to obtain additional funds?* If it becomes necessary to raise additional funds, what is the cost to the firm? This includes money borrowed from the bank, costs of floating and supporting a bond issue, or returns demanded by investors in order to justify stock issues. In the financial policies of some firms, a

weighted average of the cost of all the debt and equity instruments making up the capital structure is used to arrive at a weighted cost of capital. Evaluation of these factors will vary from firm to firm.

Handling Costs

Handling costs usually vary with warehouse throughput, not inventory levels. Normally, handling costs are not included in inventory carrying costs. For example, assume that the value of products moving through a warehouse during a month's time is $2 million, inventories are $1 million, and the cost of handling the products is $10,000. If throughput is doubled to $4 million while inventories remain the same (turnover doubles), handling costs would be expected to be $20,000, based on the greater volume of handling required. However, if inventory levels doubled to $2 million, the handling costs would still be expected to be $20,000, based on $4 million throughput.

It is possible that additional inventory in a warehouse could cause such congestion that handling costs would increase. In that case, the incremental handling cost due to crowding would be related to size of inventory, and should be included in inventory carrying costs.

Summary of inventory carrying costs

The following list shows the inventory carrying costs for the example firm.

Space costs	8.0 percent
Maintenance costs	
Product insurance	1.3
Taxes on insurance	0.3
Physical inventory costs	0.1
Risk costs	
Obsolescence	2.0
Damage	0.2
Pilferage	0.1
Capital costs	30.0
Total inventory carrying cost	42.5 percent

Based on the average inventory in Table 26–2 the cost of carrying inventory for the example firm is $4,725,038 times 0.425, or over $2 million per year.

Order Preparation Costs*

The less frequently orders are placed, the more inventory is required. When orders are placed less frequently, greater amounts must be ordered at each time. Figure 26–8 illustrates the effect of ordering frequency on average inventories. Inventories can be kept

*Reprinted by permission from *Wholesale Impact-Advanced Principles and Implementation Reference Manual.* ©1967 by International Business Machines Corporation, White Plains, New York.

very small by purchasing frequently; however, reductions in inventory carrying costs would be at least partially offset by the higher costs of more frequent ordering.

Order preparation costs are generally expressed as a fixed amount per order or line processed. The fixed amount per order is called *header cost*, and the cost of each individual line on an order that includes many items from one vendor is called *line cost*.

Each step of the ordering process involves costs: (1) checking inventory against reorder level, either manually or by computer, (2) purchase order paperwork, (3) selection of vendors and carriers, (4) preparation and processing of bills of lading, (5) order expediting, (6) receiving activities (inspecting, counting, etc.), (7) receipt document processing (posting, filing, etc.), (8) accounts payable activities, (9) costs of order paperwork, and (10) postage.

Most organizations are capable of absorbing a temporary increase in purchasing load with no increase in cost for personnel and facilities. The only increase in costs would be for stamps, forms, and similar materials. On the other hand, a significant and sustained increase in purchasing workload would require expansion of the work force. Additional costs would be incurred for personnel and probably for facilities. Therefore, identification of the variable costs of purchasing should be estimated by assuming a significant change in ordering rate (for example, 50 to 100 percent more orders.)

In Figure 26–11, 10,000 orders per year are currently placed, at a cost of $400,000. If 20,000 orders were to be placed, it is estimated that costs of $500,000 would be incurred. Although the same total volume of goods will be handled, the quantities of individual orders will be reduced.

Plotting these figures shows that in the range of 10,000 or 20,000 orders per year, fixed costs are estimated to be $300,000 by extending the line to the axis. Since 10,000 orders cost $400,000 and 20,000 orders cost $500,000, the incremental 10,000 orders cost a variable amount of $100,000 per year.

Therefore, the variable cost of one order is:

$$\frac{\$100,000 \text{ difference}}{10,000 \text{ orders}} = \$10 \text{ per order}$$

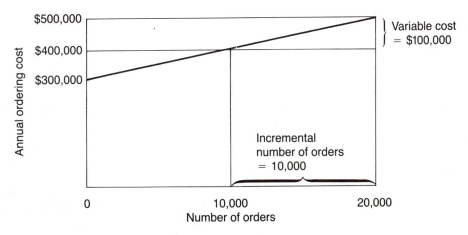

Figure 26-11   Ordering Cost Versus Number of Orders

While this approach is useful for estimating fixed and variable portions of total ordering costs, it is not the definitive identification of ordering costs required for inventory management. Ordering costs should be separated into two components:

Costs per header. This is the additional cost incurred each time another purchase order is processed.

Cost per line. This is the additional cost incurred each time another line item is added to a purchase order.

Why is it necessary to make this distinction between the two components? The line cost is always variable. The header cost, on the other hand, is a fixed cost for the items of some vendors and variable for others. This means that the purchasing cost for some items will be line plus header cost, and for others just line cost.

For example, consider a business that orders 200 items from one vendor. Some items will be ordered more frequently than others, of course, but assume that the total number of lines ordered per year is 2500. All items that need to be ordered on a given day will be accumulated and combined on one order.

With 2500 lines per year, it would be astounding if a single working day passed without the need to order one or more items. When ordering from this vendor, therefore, the header cost is fixed and should not be included when calculating the order cost for an item. The cost of ordering should be based on only cost per line.

If, on the other hand, orders placed with a vendor amount to only 20 lines per year, the header cost is definitely variable. It is unlikely that many lines will be accumulated on one order, and each order will incur a header cost. When ordering from this vendor, lot sizes must be calculated using a purchasing cost of header plus line cost.

The actual elements of purchasing cost will be found in several sections of the company. It will be helpful to construct a flow diagram of events generated by the ordering process. Next, each function should be examined, and appropriate personnel should be consulted to get their subjective estimates. Those functions that are not clear-cut should be observed. A typical chain of events is illustrated in Figure 26–12, which is intended as a representative example and not a model fitting all cases. The flow should include all activities; those that are variable must then be determined, as well as whether they are line or header costs.

Order Generation

A routine review of the status of each item should be done regularly to compare available stock to order point. This is the buyer's responsibility, but a computer can facilitate this task. In the short run, this comparison is a fixed cost of reviewing and does not vary with ordering strategy. However, as previously illustrated, if the number of orders were to increase significantly, more purchasing personnel or greater computer capacity might be required to make more frequent reviews. The variable cost per order for order generation can be estimated using the projection method.

When a signal to order is initiated by writing a line or entering data on a terminal, a line cost is incurred. In many cases the variability and classification (header or line) of clerical costs are fairly easy to determine; for example, if a full-time operator prepares 10,000 item orders per year, it seems likely that two operators would be required to prepare 20,000, and so forth.

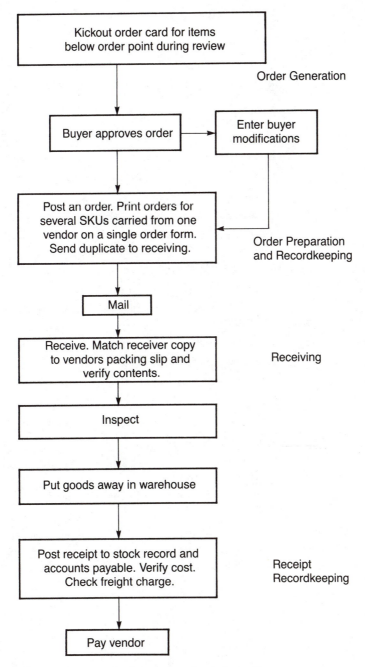

Order Generation

Order Preparation
and Recordkeeping

Receiving

Receipt
Recordkeeping

Figure 26-12   Typical Events in the Ordering Process

Buyer Activities

If the buyer approves computer-generated orders, the time spent will be divided between header and line cost. It will be helpful to prepare a form such as Form 26–1 for the buyers to complete. On the form illustrated, variable elements of header cost were considered to

Form 26-1   List of Typical Buyer Functions

Time	Percent	
_____	_____	1. Interview supplier representatives
_____	_____	2. Examine and determine the brands and number of items to be handled
_____	_____	3. Review order quantities
_____	_____	4. Approve and sign purchase orders
_____	_____	5. Make comparisons of price surveys
_____	_____	6. Approve cost corrections on receivers
_____	_____	7. Set up new items
_____	_____	8. Approve pickups and allowances to retailers
_____	_____	9. Hold conversations with retailers and company personnel
_____	_____	10. Issue bulletins to retail outlets
_____	_____	11. Prepare advertising layouts
_____	_____	12. Inform division and sales managers of merchandising programs
_____	_____	13. Visit customer outlets
_____	_____	14. Complete chargebacks to suppliers
_____	_____	15. Check and sort mail
_____	_____	16. Figure bids
_____	_____	17. Trace delayed shipments with suppliers
_____	_____	18. Check substitution lists
_____	_____	19. Perform other tasks (if pertinent to purchasing, please describe in detail)
=====	=====	Total (must equal 100 percent)

be items 4 and 17, while variable line costs were items 3, 6, and 14. The percentages are summed for each buyer, totaled for the department, and converted to annual variable costs. If the figures are available, it is possible to get a dollar figure for each buyer and then sum them.

Buyer	Header (%)	Line (%)
1	21	11
2	18	16
3	23	13
4	19	19
Total	81	59
Average	20.3	14.8

Annual salaries   = $19,600 × 4 buyers = $78,400
Annual variable header cost = 0.203 × $78,400 = $15,915
Annual variable line cost   = 0.148 × $78,400 = $11,603

If 10,000 purchase orders are issued annually, therefore, the contribution of the buyers to each header cost is $1.59 and to line cost is $1.16.

Posting Orders

The buyer-approved order card is brought back to post an on-order amount. This is a line cost. Purchase orders are prepared by computer, by typing, or some other means. Printing or typing of line items incurs a line cost. Printing of vendor name, address, and terms, as well as the cost of the form itself, is a header cost. Routing and filing a duplicate copy of the order pending receipt is a header cost. Postage and mailing are header costs.

Receiving

The cost of the first step in the receiving process—unloading goods off the carrier's vehicle onto the dock (if done by company employees)—can be difficult to estimate. The larger the total quantity on a single truck or rail car, the lower the cost per unit. These costs vary with size of order, and therefore are header costs. The cost to segregate or sort a mixed load would be a line cost.

The actual receiving operation begins with locating the appropriate receiving copy in the file of purchase orders—this is a header cost. The next step is making an item-by-item verification of the packing slip with the received merchandise (checking). To determine the line cost, it will be helpful to record the time required under varying conditions. Of interest is the time required to check shipments with a varying number of items. A plot of the results will often look like Figure 26–13. The time involved for the header is measured where the line intercepts the vertical axis and is four minutes in this case. The line cost is the slope of the line times the wage rate, calculated in the example as:

$$\frac{(8-4) \text{ minutes}}{10 \text{ lines}} \times \frac{\$15 \text{ per hour}}{60 \text{ minutes}} = \$0.10 \text{ per line}$$

The variability about the line is typically caused by the varying number of units per line item.

Inspecting

If the number of items inspected is a fixed quantity per order, it is a line cost because more orders will result in a greater number of items inspected. If, however, inspection is some fixed percentage of each receipt, the cost will be a header cost because the same total volume of goods will be inspected per year regardless of number of receipts.

Stocking

Here again it will probably be helpful to make some sample observations. Suppose one man puts away (i.e., leaves dock, finds locations, puts on shelves) 10,000 orders per year. Bearing in mind that total volume of goods handled will be unchanged, would it take two men to put away 20,000 orders? Perhaps not, depending on whether putting the goods on the shelf or finding the place to put them takes more time. There is a need to observe and measure the impact on handling time of a larger number of smaller orders. This is necessary because of the difficulty of judgmentally segregating the putting-on-shelf time from the seeking-location time.

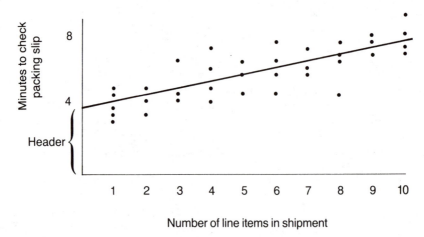

Figure 26-13   Time Required to Check Packing Slips with Various Numbers of Line Items

If a receiving supervisor isolates groups of approximately 100 pallets or cases, and it is possible to record the time elapsed between leaving the dock and returning to it, the plot may look like that shown in Figure 26–14. It shows that the absolute minimum time necessary to put away 100 cases of the same item is one hour; this is a fixed (header) cost. The contribution to line cost is:

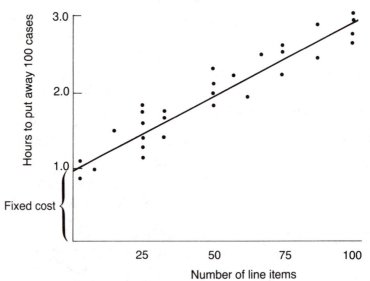

Figure 26-14   Time Required to Put Away 100 Cases of Varying Numbers of Items

Posting Receipts

Receipt recordkeeping is a clerical or data-processing function for which header and line costs can be more readily identified. Posting of receipts will incur a line cost in entering data and seeking the record (or manual posting). Verifying the vendor's charge for each item is a line cost. Any checking of freight charges that may be done will be a header cost.

Paying Vendor

Issuing a check to the vendor is neither a header nor a line cost if payment is made monthly. If, on the other hand, payment is made by invoice, a header cost is involved.

Production Setup Costs

Whenever production runs of a product are of long duration and the rate of production exceeds the demand rate, inventories of finished products build up. However, shorter production runs necessitate more frequent shutdowns of machines or production lines in order to prepare them for the production of alternate items. The costs of these production setups can include lost production during shutdown, wages paid to operators during shutdown, machine adjuster wages, scrap generated during start-up of the new process, reduced output during production shutdown and while operators are learning, additional inspection costs, additional production scheduling costs and expediting costs, and additional material handling costs.

An example will illustrate how setup costs may be determined. The firm chosen for the example produces polymers using a batch process which involves mixing of raw materials, heating, and extruding the finished product into various shapes and forms. The following production setup costs are incurred due to change-over from one product to another:

1. *Lost production*

   2 hours change-over time × 1000 pounds per hour × 50¢ per
   pound × 20 percent gross margin   = $200

2. *Wages paid to operator during shutdown*

   2 hours change-over time × $15 per hour   = $ 30

3. *Machine adjuster time*

   (2 hours change-over time + 1 hour machine adjustment time) × $20
   per hour   = $ 60

4. *Reduced efficiency during initial part of run*

   During the first hour of production, the machine adjuster shuts the
   machine down several times to make final adjustments. Production
   is reduced by 25 percent. 1000 pounds per hour × a 25 percent reduction in production × (1 hour − 1/3 hour production scrapped) × 50¢
   per pound × 20 percent gross margin   = $ 17

5. *Scrap*

   For 20 minutes traces of the first product are found in the second product, and this must be scrapped: 1/3 hour × 750 pounds per hour × 50¢ per pound   = $125

6. *Production scheduling costs*

   The production supervisor schedules 10 machines, and an average production run lasts one week, so currently 500 production changes per year are required. Six hours per week are required for scheduling production changes. With fringe benefits included, the production supervisor earns $20,000 per year, and therefore, the cost to schedule and follow up 500 changes is $3,000 per year or $6 per change. The production supervisor estimates that if 50 percent more changes were required, he would need an additional 2 hours per week to schedule the lots, at an additional cost of $1000 per year. From Figure 26–15 it can be seen that the fixed cost of scheduling production is $1000 per year, and the cost of scheduling an additional 250 changes is $1000. Result: variable cost per production change   = $ 4

7. *Total cost per change-over*   = $436

Cost of Quantity Discounts Foregone

Quantity discounts are offered by sellers for volume purchases. In effect, these are reductions in price offered to induce purchasers to buy in larger quantities. Quantity discounts may increase sales, and can reduce the costs of selling by encouraging fewer, larger or-

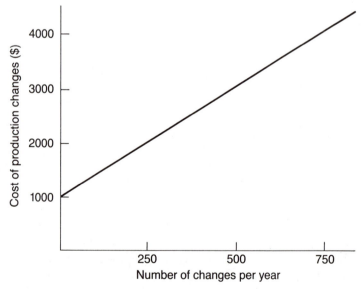

Figure 26-15 Estimating Production Scheduling Costs per Change-Over

Table 26-3   Quantity Discount Schedule and Discounts Foregone

Units Purchased	Price per Unit	Discount per Unit	Discount Foregone per Unit
0–99	$4.80	None	$0.90
100–199	4.60	$0.20	0.70
200–499	4.30	0.50	0.40
500 or more	3.90	0.90	None

ders. The seller also benefits from less paperwork and larger shipment sizes. Table 26–3 shows a typical quantity discount structure.

Whether or not quantity discounts should be taken depends upon the costs of carrying the larger inventory resulting from less frequent, larger orders. In order to compare value of quantity discounts to inventory costs resulting from larger purchases, it is useful to convert the quantity discount amounts into costs of quantity discounts foregone.

In Table 26–3, the lowest price of $3.90 can be obtained by purchasing in quantities of 500 or more. Compared to this alternative, if between 200 and 499 units are ordered at a cost per unit of $4.30, the discount of 40¢ per unit will be foregone. If between 100 and 199 units are ordered, 70¢ per unit discount will be foregone, and if orders are 99 or less, all of the potential discount of 90¢ will be foregone.

Transportation Costs

Transportation costs are linked to inventory in at least three ways: (1) freight rates vary with the amount ordered and shipped; (2) when slower modes of transportation are used, greater amounts of inventory will be in transit in the pipeline; and (3) the sum of inbound transportation costs to warehouses and outbound transportation from warehouses varies with the number of warehouses, and total inventory usually increases as more warehouses are added to the firm's logistics system.

Table 26–4 shows a typical freight rate structure for a product. In this example the cost is $5.77 per hundredweight (cwt) if a quantity of less than 2000 pounds is shipped. This is more than three times the $1.72 cost per cwt when a truckload amount is ordered. Ordering in smaller amounts reduces inventory levels, but it is usually at the penalty of greater per unit freight costs.

The lower transportation rates of slower modes of transportation must be balanced against pipeline inventory costs. For example, truckloads of a product move between Los

Table 26-4   Freight Rate Structure for Product

Weight Category	Cost Per Hundredweight (cwt)
0–1999	$5.77
2000–4999	4.38
5000–9999	3.89
10,000–truckload	3.11
Truckload (20,000 minimum)	1.72
Incentive (50,000 and over)	1.57

Angeles and Chicago at a rate of $8.98 per cwt in truckload quantities of 20,000 pounds or more, consisting of 200 units weighing 100 pounds each. Transit time is three and a half days. The same items can be shipped 400 units per load in boxcars at a rate of $3.52 per cwt and a transit time of seven days. The annual sales of 73,200 units require 366 truckload shipments or 183 boxcar shipments.

If products are shipped by truck (Figure 26–16), the first truckload is shipped on day one and arrives in Chicago three and a half days later at noon of day four. The second load of 200 units is shipped the morning of day two, arriving at noon on day five, and so forth. Once the system reaches steady-state, one truckload will arrive daily and three truckloads (600 units) will be in transit at any one time.

With the boxcar movement, the first shipment is made on the morning of day one and arrives in Chicago seven days later. The second is shipped on day three, the third on day five, and so forth. Three boxcar loads of 400 units each are in transit on most days, and four boxcar loads are in transit on days seven, nine, eleven, and so on, averaging 1257 units in the pipeline. This is more than double the pipeline inventory required by the truck movement. The lower transportation rate of slower modes of transportation must therefore be balanced against the costs of supporting a greater amount of inventory in the pipeline.

Generally speaking, greater amounts of inventory are required in multiple warehouse locations than if all inventory stocks were held in one location (Fig. 26–17). However, the transportation costs of shipping directly to customers from the factory might be very great. For a West Coast manufacturer serving a national market, shipping to East Coast customers directly from the factory would necessitate shipping less-than-truckload (LTL) amounts long distances. By establishing an East Coast warehouse, full truckloads or boxcar loads could be shipped inbound to the warehouse, and the freight cost from the warehouse to customers would be less because the small shipments would move shorter distances. Similarly, a second warehouse could be established in the South, a third in the Midwest, and so forth. As each warehouse is added, outbound transportation costs from the warehouse to customers would continue to fall because distances to customers from the warehouse would be reduced. At some point in the process of adding warehouses, however, the average amounts shipped from the factory to warehouses will fall below

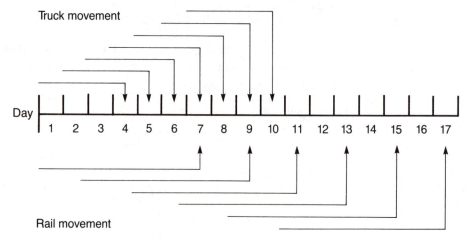

Figure 26-16   Pipeline Inventory

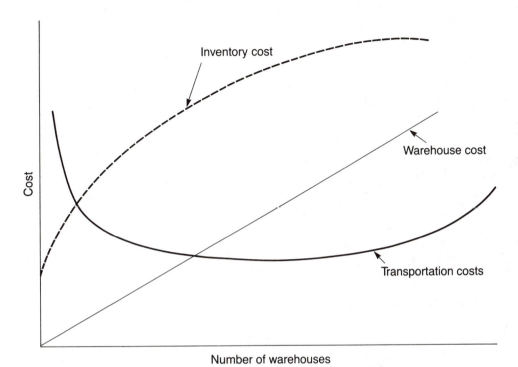

Figure 26-17   Relationship between Inventory Costs, Transportation Costs, and Number of Warehouses

truckload or carload amounts. At that point, the freight costs inbound to the warehouses will start to rise rapidly.

Out-of-Stock Costs

In order to consistently fill a high percentage of orders completely, without back orders, or to satisfy a large percentage of total demand for products, inventory above that needed to satisfy average requirements must be carried. As the percentage of orders or demand filled approaches 100 percent, the inventory required to provide that level of service becomes greater and greater (Figure 26–18). However, if customer service is inadequate a large number of orders will be back-ordered or shipped incomplete, and a percentage of demand will go unsatisfied. For this reason, the costs of being out-of-stock must also be evaluated in inventory decisions.

Two types of out-of-stock costs are back-order costs and costs of lost sales. Back-order costs result when the customer is willing to defer an order or part of an order until a later time. Costs of lost sales occur when customers cancel orders, or worse, shift their patronage to other suppliers that provide greater product availability.

Back orders may be calculated as the difference between orders booked and orders shipped during equivalent time periods. Order cancellations (lost sales) should be similarly accounted for. Sometimes cancelled orders are placed again, or back orders are later cancelled, which can make determination of order cancellation or back-order costs difficult to determine.

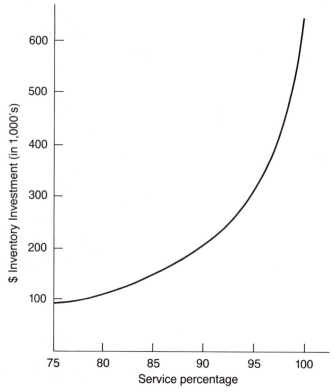

Figure 26-18 Inventory Investment Required for Various Service Levels

When an order is back-ordered for later shipment or part of an order is shipped and the balance back-ordered, the additional costs can include extra clerical time, order processing (computer time), additional paperwork, additional postage for split invoicing, and so forth. Additional freight costs result from shipping two or more smaller shipments instead of one larger shipment. In certain cases, shipment of the back-ordered portion of the order will have to be expedited, and will be more expensive. Similarly, additional handling and packaging costs are likely to occur. In some firms, out-of-stocks may necessitate rescheduling of production and changeover of machines or production lines to run emergency orders.

Order cancellations result in lost sales and the foregoing of profits that would result from these sales. When readily substitutable products are involved, sales are often lost to the alternatively available substitute product. Records of order cancellations can and should be kept in the order processing system.

Cost of lost sales due to reduction of customer good will, lost customers, or splitting of orders between vendors is more difficult to ascertain. The relationship between sales and customer service (product availability) is often determined by educated guess. However, in some cases special studies can be conducted to estimate costs of lost sales, or foregone profits from losing sales to competitors. For example, surveys of customers can be conducted to determine their probable purchase actions at different availability levels.[1]

In other cases, the effects of charging higher product costs for providing greater product availability may be determined. Some firms have experimented by offering different levels of product availability in various geographical areas, and measuring relative sales rates. This method entails some risk, because market share lost to competitors may be difficult to regain, even if customer service levels are later improved.

3.   Seasonal Inventory

Seasonal inventories must be carried because timing of supply does not always coincide with timing of demand. Many agricultural or fisheries products, for example, become available only at certain times of the year. When demand for these products is relatively constant during the year, inventories must be carried to adjust infrequent supply to accommodate steady demand.

Similarly, other products are demanded only at certain times of the year, or the rate of demand varies significantly during the various periods of the year. Examples of seasonal products are bedroom slippers—almost all of which are sold for Christmas gifts—toys, swimming suits, snowmobiles, and motorcycles.

Seasonal Supply

When a product has a seasonal supply pattern coupled with a relatively steady demand, it is often desirable to hold part of the supply off the market when first available, and release the product from inventory at a steady rate to meet demand. Most vegetables and fruits are canned and held "in the bright" for later labeling and sale. Similarly, products may be frozen or held in temperature-controlled areas, as is the practice for apples.

If the total supply of these products were released into the market at the time they became available, the price would plummet. In other periods, very little of the product would be available at any price. Figure 26–19, which shows a demand curve for cherries, illustrates the nature of this relationship. In the figure, 12 million pounds of cherries are harvested at one time. If all 12 million pounds were offered on the market when harvested, 2¢ per pound could be obtained. However, if the cherries were canned or frozen and released into the market at the rate of one million pounds each month, 20¢ per pound could be commanded. Of course, the additional value (time utility) added to the product by matching supply with demand must be weighed against the costs of processing and the inventory carrying costs for maintaining the seasonal inventories in storage.

Seasonal Demand

Aggregate planning and scheduling of production are of great importance in the control of production and inventory costs. Particularly when planning for seasonal demand, such as for toys, swimsuits, or motorcycles, aggregate planning is necessary to minimize the sum of production costs and inventory carrying costs.

Seasonal demand can be planned for in a variety of ways. If level production at factories is desired, seasonal inventories are used to absorb fluctuation in demand (see Figure 26–4). Therefore, economies of steady production must be weighed against the cost of carrying seasonal inventories which result from this policy.

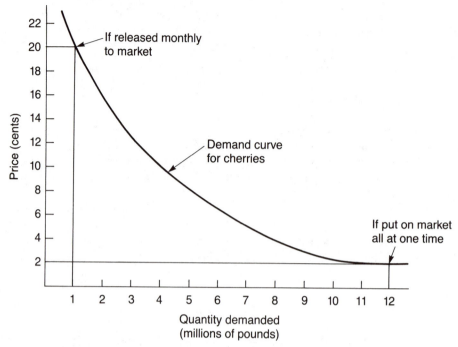

Figure 26-19   Comparison of Price for a Product with Seasonal Supply

Conversely, seasonal demand can be met by varying the rate of production at factories. Production rates are increased prior to peak sales periods, and are reduced prior to slow sales periods. This alternative tends to result in less inventory and reduced inventory carrying costs. Reductions in inventory costs, however, must be weighed against costs of varying the work force, hiring and laying off workers, varying the work rate by use of overtime and multiple shifts, and the additional scale of plant required to support peak production periods. Also, there may be opportunities to balance production between major markets with different seasonal characteristics, for example, the United States and Australia.

Table 26-5 shows forecasted sales for a manufacturer. Note that if two months are required to manufacture and ship a product to the point of sale, the sales forecast must be moved back two months to determine the production requirement. In the example, forecasted September sales of 1157 would need to be planned for production in July in order to allow production and distribution lead time. Table 26-6 adjusts the sales forecasts to allow production leadtime and lists three alternative production plans.

Figures 26-20, 26-21, and 26-22 illustrate a graphic technique used to develop the feasible alternate production plans to support forecasted sales.[2] The procedure is first to plot the curve for cumulative sales. The cumulative graph of units required to meet sales can then be used effectively to compare alternative ways of meeting requirements. The production plans are shown as lines drawn above the sales curve. Any production program that is feasible must fall entirely above the cumulative sales requirements curve.

The vertical distance between the cumulative production and cumulative requirement lines is the seasonal inventory accumulation for the production plan in question. It should be stressed that the graphic technique does not necessarily give the optimum pro-

Table 26-5 Sales Forecast

Month	Sales Forecast	Cumulative Sales
September	1,157	1,157
October	64,262	65,419
November	18,979	84,398
December	14,850	99,248
January	24,643	123,891
February	34,486	158,377
March	67,896	226,273
April	66,798	293,071
May	69,499	362,570
June	37,261	399,831
July	39,025	438,856
August	13,894	452,750

duction plan. It does allow evaluation of production and inventory costs for a number of alternative plans.

Steady (Level) Production Plan

Figure 26-20 shows a steady production plan which would tend to minimize production costs by building up inventory as a buffer against seasonality in sales. Table 26-7 shows the inventory status for the steady production plan. Total seasonal inventory carrying cost for the steady production plan is $4,708,046 per year. Average seasonal inventory investment is $15,693,485. Costs of carrying seasonal inventory will be greatest under this plan, but production is likely to be most economical. Safety stock inventories, of course, must be carried in addition to seasonal inventories.

Seasonal Production Plan

Figure 26-21 shows a feasible production plan with three rates of production at various times of the year (two capacity changes). This plan is the ultimate in reducing seasonal in-

Table 26-6 Alternative Production Plans

Production in Month	For Sale in Month	Level Production	Two Capacity Changes	One Capacity Change
July	September	40,300	23,334	34,000
August	October	40,300	23,334	34,000
September	November	40,300	23,334	34,000
October	December	40,300	23,334	45,000
November	January	40,300	23,334	45,000
December	February	40,300	23,334	45,000
January	March	40,300	68,334	45,000
February	April	40,300	68,334	45,000
March	May	40,300	68,334	45,000
April	June	40,300	38,334	34,000
May	July	40,300	38,334	34,000
June	August	40,300	38,334	34,000

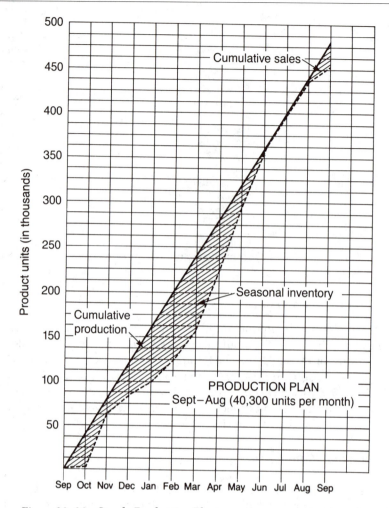

Figure 26-20   Steady Production Plan

ventory, with the exception of a perfectly variable production which is difficult to control.

Table 26–8 shows the inventory status under this alternative. Average investment in inventory to support sales is $4,275,425, inventory carrying cost is $1,282,628, and seasonal inventories are significantly lower than with the level production plan.

This plan, although it minimizes inventory, would likely be undesirable from a production standpoint. The plant would need to operate on a one-shift basis from July through December, with three shifts planned during January, February, and March, and two shifts during April, May and June. This would be the most expensive alternative from a production standpoint. Hiring and layoff costs would be great, and the plant size would have to allow peak period production.

One Production Capacity Change

Figure 26–22 shows a production plan with one capacity change. As delineated in Table 26–6, the plant would operate at 34,000 units capacity during the months of April

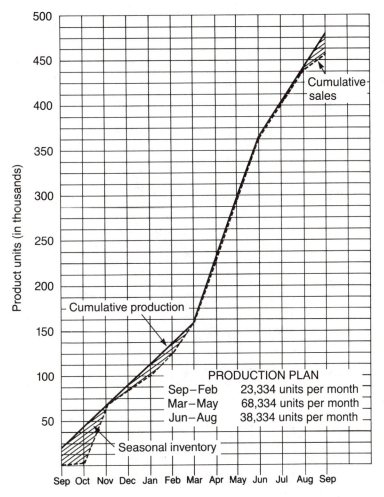

Figure 26-21   Seasonal Production Plan

through September and 45,000 units capacity from October through January, when labor is available for seasonal employment.

With one capacity change at the plant, average investment in seasonal inventory to support sales (Table 26-9) is $13,455,063, which is $2,238,000 less inventory than required with the level production plan. Inventory carrying costs are $4,036,519 or $671,527 less than with level production.

Costs of Production Capacity Changes

Three alternative production policies have been compared to determine the seasonal inventory resulting from each. The level production plan resulted in the greatest average seasonal inventory, and the production plan with two capacity changes resulted in the least. When one production capacity change was planned, the seasonal inventory was between the levels resulting from the other two plans. Which of the three plans should be selected? The answer depends upon the other cost factors involved.

Changes in the size of the work force affect the total costs of labor. When new work-

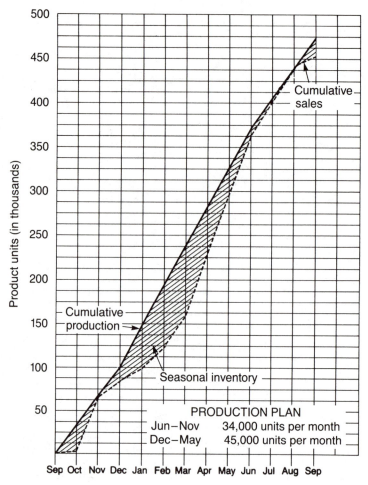

Figure 26-22 One Production Capacity Change

ers are hired, costs result from selection, training, and lower production effectiveness at the beginning of the learning curve. Reducing the work force by laying off workers may involve unemployment compensation and severance costs, costs of employee transfer and retraining, as well as intangible effects on public relations and the image of the firm.

Large changes in the size of the work force may mean adding or dropping an entire shift. When shifts are added, costs involved are possible second (swing) shift wage premiums as well as incremental supervision and other overhead costs. There may also be indirect costs related to revising production schedules.

If production fluctuations are absorbed through changes in the rate of production, overtime premium costs for increases and probably idle labor costs for decreases will also be incurred. When hours worked are reduced below normal levels, labor turnover and reduced production due to labor dissatisfaction are likely.

All of the costs related to varying production rates must be determined and compared to costs of carrying inventories in order to evaluate which production alternative is most economic. Table 26-10 illustrates the nature of the trade-offs between inventory costs and

Table 26-7 Inventory Cost with Steady Production

	Beginning Inventory	Availability from Production	Total Availability	Sales	Ending Inventory
September	—	40,300	40,300	1,157	39,143
October	39,143	40,300	79,443	64,262	15,181
November	15,181	40,300	55,481	18,979	36,502
December	36,502	40,300	76,802	14,850	61,952
January	61,952	40,300	102,252	24,643	77,609
February	77,609	40,300	117,909	34,486	83,423
March	83,423	40,300	123,723	67,896	55,827
April	55,829	40,300	96,129	66,798	29,331
May	29,331	40,300	69,631	69,499	132
June	132	40,300	40,432	37,261	3,171
July	3,171	40,300	43,471	39,025	4,445
August	4,445	40,300	44,746	13,894	30,852
Totals		483,600		452,750	437,568

Average inventory	36,464
Average inventory investment	$15,693,485
Inventory carrying cost (at 30%)	$4,708,046

Table 26-8 Inventory Cost with Two Capacity Changes

	Beginning Inventory	Availability from Production	Total Availability	Sales	Ending Inventory
September	20,000	23,334	43,334	1,157	42,177
October	42,177	23,334	65,511	64,262	1,249
November	1,249	23,334	24,583	18,979	5,604
December	5,604	23,334	28,938	14,850	14,088
January	14,088	23,334	37,422	24,643	12,779
February	12,779	23,334	36,113	34,486	1,627
March	1,627	68,334	69,961	67,896	2,065
April	2,065	68,334	70,399	66,798	3,601
May	3,601	68,334	71,935	69,499	2,436
June	2,436	38,334	40,770	37,261	3,509
July	3,509	38,334	41,843	39,025	2,818
August	2,818	38,334	41,152	13,894	27,258
Totals		460,008		452,750	119,211

Average inventory	9,934
Average inventory investment	$4,275,425
Total inventory carrying cost (at 30%)	$1,282,628

Table 26-9   Inventory Cost with One Capacity Change

	Beginning Inventory	Availability from Production	Total Availability	Sales	Ending Inventory
September	—	34,000	34,000	1,157	32,843
October	32,843	34,000	66,843	64,262	2,581
November	2,581	34,000	36,581	18,979	17,602
December	17,602	45,000	62,602	14,850	47,752
January	47,752	45,000	92,752	24,643	68,109
February	68,109	45,000	113,109	34,486	78,623
March	78,623	45,000	123,623	67,896	55,727
April	55,727	45,000	100,727	66,798	33,929
May	33,929	45,000	78,929	69,499	9,430
June	9,430	34,000	43,430	37,261	6,169
July	6,189	34,000	40,169	39,025	1,144
August	1,144	34,000	35,144	13,894	21,250
Totals		474,000		452,750	375,159

Average inventory   31,263
Average inventory investment $13,455,063
Total inventory carrying cost (at 30%) $4,036,519

costs related to varying production rates. In the example, when all costs are considered, the steady production alternative is most cost effective.

4.   Pipeline Inventory

In most logistics systems, at any given time considerable amounts of goods will be moving about in transportation vehicles or flowing through terminals or distribution centers. This type of inventory has been termed *pipeline inventory* and is inventory in motion, not sitting in a warehouse or in retail outlets.

For example, in the case of the Alaska Pipeline, which is thousands of miles long and four feet in diameter, millions of barrels of oil are required to fill the pipeline and those amounts continue to be in the pipeline at all times. Similarly, in a distribution channel or logistics system, the product "pipeline" must be filled before the first products are available at the end of the channel. Although pipeline inventories are often overlooked in ac-

Table 26-10   Inventory and Production Capacity Cost Comparison

	Steady Production Plan	Two Capacity Changes	One Capacity Change
Inventory carrying costs	$4,708,288	$1,282,711	$4,036,280
Second shift premium	—	2,072,540	2,733,000
Third shift premium	—	1,970,370	—
Hiring cost	—	168,000	27,000
Layoff cost	—	84,000	13,500
Totals	$4,708,288	$5,577,621	$6,849,780

counting for distribution system costs, they are definitely a cost item because of the investment in products that fill the pipeline.

Of course, pipeline inventories can be reduced by shortening the length of the pipeline, that is, substituting faster for slower transportation or increasing distribution center throughput to squeeze inventory out of the pipeline. In some cases, pipeline inventories can be decreased by making management information system changes. Types of pipeline inventories include: (1) in-transit inventories, (2) inventories to allow stock-mixing or freight consolidation, and (3) inventories resulting from replenishment lead times.

In-Transit Inventories

Figure 26–23 illustrates a production and inventory system. At all times in the system, inventory is in transit between facilities or moving through facilities. If demand equals 1000 units per day in the example, the following in-transit pipeline inventories would result:

	Days	Pipeline Inventory (Units)
In transit from raw material vendors	14	14,000
In process at factory	—	—
In transit to factory warehouse	2	2,000
Moving through factory warehouse	4	4,000
In transit to distributors' warehouses	7	7,000
Subtotal—Under control of firm	27	27,000
Moving through distributors' warehouses	2	2,000
In transit to retailers' warehouses	5	5,000
Moving through retailers' warehouses	2	2,000
In transit to retailers' stores	1	1,000
Moving through stores	2	2,000
Total	39	39,000

If the value of each unit in the pipeline is $10, the total investment in pipeline inventory for the channel system is $390,000. That is the amount needed to fill the pipeline before the first product can be sold. Note also that 39 days will elapse before the first product is available for sale. It is easy to see why trade financing in channels of distribution is required, and how lags in accounts receivables can cause working capital problems.

In the example, it is assumed that the firm purchases raw materials F.O.B. origin and sells finished products F.O.B. destination. In such cases, the firm has title to the products during the entire transit times, and the products are part of the firm's pipeline inventories.

Figure 26–24 illustrates an example in which analysis of in-transit pipeline inventories resulted in cost savings. A multinational electronics firm has both East and West Coast plants in the United States that ship parts to Singapore for assembly. The Singapore plant requires $200,000 worth of parts weekly from the East Coast plant. This plant minimized its transportation costs by shipping the parts by ocean around the Cape of Good Hope to Singapore. The average transit time was 12 weeks, that is, 12 weeks' worth of expensive inventories were constantly afloat in the holds of ships. With $200,000 in parts required in Singapore, $2,400,000 worth of parts were constantly in the transit pipeline.

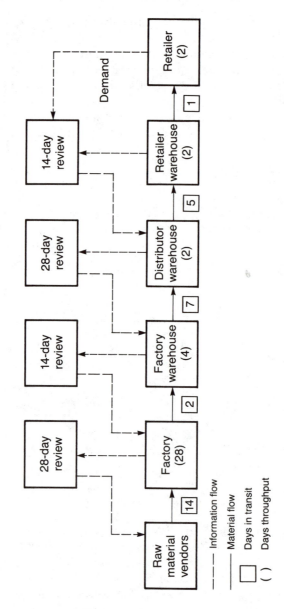

Figure 26-23 Production and Inventory System

Before: East Coast via Cape of Good Hope to Singapore

After: East Coast by truck to West Coast, by sea to Singapore

Figure 26-24   Effect of Transportation on Pipeline and Safety Stock Inventory

The method of transportation was changed to utilize motor carrier transport across the United States, and then by ocean transport to Singapore—slashing five weeks off transit time. However, this added $47,000 in truck transportation costs, since in the prior transportation method no truck transportation was required. It also added $11,000 to the ocean shipping costs, because of higher ocean tariffs in the Pacific trade.

Offsetting these higher transportation costs were reductions in pipeline inventory costs. Table 26–11 shows the reduction in pipeline inventory carrying costs due to the change. Inventory carrying cost was 20 percent, which includes capital costs, insurance, and deterioration costs, but not storage costs which are not applicable for in-transit inventories.

In addition, the revised transportation method reduced inventory in yet another way. As shown in Table 26–12, the transit time reliability of the new method of transportation was much greater. Previously, shipments could be as much as three weeks late, requiring the factory to stock three weeks' safety stock valued at $600,000 to assure continued production. The inventory cost savings resulting from reduced safety stock inventories was 25 percent, which includes storage costs.

Another significant savings resulted from a reduction in air transportation of emergency shipments from the West Coast plant to keep the Singapore plant running. Previously, frequent emergency fill-in orders had to be dispatched by air to prevent plant downtime. Table 26–13 shows the savings in air transportation costs, and summarizes the overall cost trade-offs. In this example, the cost savings were more than enough to offset added truck and ocean transportation costs. Pipeline inventory reductions resulted not

Table 26–11   Effect of Transportation Time on Pipeline Inventory Cost

	Before	*After*	*Change*
Transit time (average)	12 weeks	7 weeks	– 5 weeks
Range	9 to 15 weeks	6 to 8 weeks	– 3 to 7 weeks
Variability	± 3 weeks	± 1 week	± 2 weeks
Safety stock inventory	$600,000	$200,000	– $400,000
Inventory cost @ 25%	$150,000	$ 50,000	– $100,000

Table 26–12   Effect of Transportation Variability on Safety Stock Inventory Cost

	Before	After	Change
Ocean transportation	$ 33,000	$ 44,000	+ $ 11,000
Truck transportation	—	47,000	+ 47,000
Air transportation	104,000	10,000	− 94,000
Pipeline inventory cost	480,000	280,000	− 200,000
Safety stock inventory cost	150,000	50,000	− 100,000
Total cost	$767,000	$421,000	− $336,000
Annual savings	$336,000		

only directly from the shortening of the pipelines but indirectly from reduced safety stock inventories.

Inventories to Allow Stock-Mixing or Consolidation

In many logistics systems, products move through the system in various echelons of consolidation and breakbulk stages. The process of consolidation or stock-mixing allows economical transportation by building up larger loads that are more economical to ship. Rather than sending many small individual shipments from the origin to consignees in this same general distribution area, the small shipments are consolidated into one larger shipment for transportation. At the destination, the small individual shipments are broken out and shipped by local and short-haul carriers to the final consignees. In this way, the products move the longest distance as one large shipment with correspondingly low rates, and short distances as individual small shipments.

In order to make up consolidated shipments, it is often necessary to delay shipment of orders until a truckload or carload has been accumulated. To the degree that this delay occurs, a pocket of pipeline inventory has been created. The cost of carrying the pipeline inventory necessary to allow consolidation must be traded off against freight cost savings due to the consolidation.

For example, a manufacturer of automobile parts located in Tennessee sends, on average, 20 individual less-than-truckload (LTL) shipments to Southern California per week averaging 2000 pounds each, or 40,000 pounds total. The cost to ship the 20 individual LTL shipments is $7200 (400 cwt times $18 per cwt). However, the truckload rate on automobile parts is $8.50 per cwt, or $3400 for the truckload. A local Southern California warehouseman unloads (breaks out) the truckload for $300, and local and beyond freight charges from the warehouse to the customers are $2,400. The total cost of the 20 shipments using consolidation and breakout is therefore $6100, or a savings of $1100 compared to the nonconsolidated method of shipping.

Table 26–13   Cost Summary (Annual) Effect of Changed Transportation

	Before	After	Change
Transit time (average)	12 weeks	7 weeks	− 5 weeks
Pipeline inventory	$2,400,000	$1,400,000	− $1,000,000
Pipeline inventory cost @ 20%	$ 480,000	$ 280,000	− $ 200,000

Assume, however, that the value of the merchandise is $10 per pound, and that the cost to the firm of carrying inventory is 30 percent per year. The average inventory required to allow consolidation is one half of 40,000, or 20,000 pounds, as the inventory varies between zero and 40,000 pounds during each week. The cost of carrying this additional pipeline inventory is therefore $10 per pound times 20,000 pounds times 30 percent, divided by 52 to find the cost of carrying this amount of inventory for one week. This computes to a cost of $1154 per week for carrying the required pipeline inventory, which is greater than the freight savings due to consolidation.

Freight Cost of Individual Shipments		$7,200
Freight Cost of Consolidated Shipment	$3,400	
Warehouse breakout	300	
Local and beyond freight charges	2,400	6,100
Freight Saving Due to Consolidation		1,100
Inventory Cost Per Week		
20,000 lb. × $10/lb. × 0.30 ÷ 52		1,154
Gain (Loss) Due to Consolidation		($ 54)

Of course, in many cases the pipeline inventory carrying costs will be less than freight savings. It is important in any case to determine the trade-off between freight savings and additional pipeline inventory required to allow consolidation.

Inventories Resulting from Replenishment Lead Times

In-transit and in-process pipeline inventories are related to the physical limitations of moving materials through a manufacturing-distribution system. In addition to pipeline inventories related to physical time lags, there are also pipeline inventories caused by information time lags. Typical of these are inventories resulting from replenishment policies.

What is meant by replenishment time? This is the lead time required for the distribution system to replace a unit sold at one echelon in the distribution system. It includes the time required for information that an item has been sold to get to the next level of the distribution channel, processing of the order, packing and shipping the order, transportation of the order to the distribution point, and receiving it into inventory. For example, in Figure 26–24, the review time or frequency between reviews is 14 days at the factory warehouse. The factory warehouse reviews its inventory status every two weeks, determines what is needed, and transmits the order to the factory. The order is sent by mail, which on the average requires 3 days. The factory requires 11 days to process and prepare the order for shipment and 2 days are required for shipment of the merchandise to the factory warehouse. The replenishment time is therefore 30 days. With demand equal to 1000 units per day in the example, 30,000 units are required at the factory warehouse to meet demand during the lead time between when the replenishment order is placed and when the order is received.

Now, suppose that instead of reviewing stock every 14 days and mailing the order to the warehouse, a perpetual inventory is maintained and inventory status is transmitted daily from the factory warehouse to the factory. As shown in Table 26–14, 16 days are squeezed out of the replenishment lead time by streamlining the information flow. This results in a reduction in inventory carrying costs of $40,000. Of course, a perpetual inven-

Table 26-14   Effect on Inventory Due to Streamlining Information Flow

	Before		After		Difference	
	No. of Days	Inventory	No. of Days	Inventory	No. of Days	Inventory
Review interval	14	$140,000	1	$ 10,000	13	$130,000
Order transmittal	3	30,000	—	—	3	30,000
Factory processing	11	110,000	11	110,000		
Transit time	2	20,000	2	20,000		
Total	30	$300,000	14	$140,000	16	$160,000

$160,000 reduction × 0.25 carrying cost = $40,000

tory system and communication link are not without costs, and these costs must be traded off against the inventory savings to determine overall system advantage.

The warehouse replenishment lead time decision is an internal one, involving internal procedures only. It can be made by designing the procedures, programming the computer or processing software, and putting the communication link into operation. Inventories related to lead time that are not under direct control of management are more difficult to deal with.

Vendor lead times also have an effect on inventory levels. In Figure 26–23 the factory places orders with raw material vendors. One vendor requires 14 days from order receipt to process the order and prepare it for shipment. A second vendor requires only 10 days. The second vendor is preferable, as four days' less inventory will be needed at the factory to meet demand during the time between when an order is placed and when it is received into stock. Better service from shorter vendor lead times results in less inventory.

An additional factor relating to replenishment lead times is delivery reliability. For example, although the second vendor's order preparation time averages out to 10 days, lead time actually varies between 5 and 18 days. The other vendor averages 14 days, but order receipt from this vendor is very reliable. Which is preferable?

Generally, studies have shown that buyers prefer vendor reliability to faster delivery, if a choice must be made. That is because longer lead times can be built into the replenishment system, while uncertainty about vendor lead time results in having to carry greater safety stock inventories to buffer against stock-outs due to late deliveries. The effect of uncertain lead time on safety stock inventories is discussed below (see pages 667–668).

5.   Management Prerogative Inventory

It could be said that in the final analysis, virtually every management decision has an effect on inventory levels. For example, a marketing decision to introduce a new product creates new inventory in the logistics system. Too often, however, the costs of carrying inventory and other logistics costs are not considered when the decision is made. It is the responsibility of the logistics manager to provide inputs concerning cost impacts on the logistics system to other management personnel for use in assessing the costs and benefits of various management decisions.

The various management decisions tend to create "pockets" of inventory in the logistics system. Although there are many causes of inventory pockets, some of the most frequently observed are: (1) inventory to allow purchase discounts, (2) inventory to support sales or to provide speedy delivery, (3) inventory due to new products, (4) special deals and packaging, (5) discontinued items, (6) inventory to guard against strikes.

Inventory to Allow Purchase Discounts

Purchase or quantity discounts are offered by sellers as an inducement to purchase in larger volumes. They result in lower materials cost, but require the buyer to purchase in greater quantities. Should firms take advantage of purchase discounts? Not always! It depends on the cost of carrying the additional inventory.

In Table 26-15 the maximum purchase discount can be obtained by ordering 500 or more units. In addition to purchase discounts, there are further incentives for volume purchases: lower freight costs result from larger shipments, and lower ordering costs result from fewer orders. Of course, as orders become larger, so do the costs of carrying the resulting inventories. In this example it would be advantageous to take the full discount, but it is useful to know what costs (and whose budgets) are affected by the decision.

In the example, the lowest cost results when 500 units are purchased, and the full discount is taken. If only 50 units were ordered at a time, 90¢ per unit or $2,160 purchase discount would be foregone for the 2400 units purchased per year. The purchase discount, when combined with freight and ordering cost savings, is more than enough to compensate for the greater inventory carrying costs required.

If only inventory carrying costs and ordering costs were to be considered in making the purchase quantity decision, the economic order quantity (EOQ) formula could be used to calculate the order quantity (see page 663). Use of this formula would result in a decision to purchase 200 units, which is *not* the most economical quantity when purchase discounts and freight costs are included.

Note also that freight costs could be further reduced by ordering in quantities of 1000. In that case, however, the cost of carrying the larger inventory would outweigh the freight savings. It is important to consider the trade-offs between all relevant cost elements to determine the lowest overall cost.

In Table 26-16 a higher price and lower purchase discount structure are assumed, while all other cost elements remain the same. In this example, the most economic order quantity is 400 units. The cost of carrying additional inventory partially outweighs the benefits of the quantity discount. It is more economical to forego $480.00 of discounts in order to avoid $595.18 additional inventory carrying costs resulting from ordering 500 instead of 400 units.

This section has illustrated the importance of including all relevant cost elements in making logistics decisions. When attempting to minimize overall system costs, the individual costs of freight, quantity discounts foregone, and inventory carrying costs cannot be considered in isolation from each other. All cost elements must be traded-off to arrive at lowest total system costs.

Inventory to Support Sales or to Provide Speedy Delivery

The need to provide good customer service is central to logistics planning and management. Support of sales efforts in the marketplace and locating stocks of inventories close to

Table 26-15 Total Cost of Ordering Various Quantities

Quantity Ordered, Q	Quantity Discounts Foregone	Weight Per Shipment (pounds)	Annual Freight Cost	Cost Per Unit Plus Freight Per Unit	Average Inventory ½Q	Annual Inventory Carrying Cost	Orders Per Year	Annual Cost of Ordering	Total Annual Cost
50	$2,160.00	1,250	$6,924.00	$4.80 + $2.89	25	$ 48.06	48	$480	$9,612.06
100	1,680.00	2,500	5,256.00	4.60 + 2.19	50	84.88	24	240	7,260.00
200	960.00	5,000	4,668.00	4.30 + 1.95	100	156.25	12	120	5,904.25
400	960.00	20,000	2,064.00	4.30 + 0.86	200	258.00	6	60	3,342.00
500	—	25,000	2,064.00	3.90 + 0.86	250	297.50	4.8	48	2,409.50
1000	—	50,000	1,884.00	3.90 + 0.79	500	586.25	2.4	24	2,494.25

Demand — 2400 units per year

Cost per unit
- 0– 99 @ $4.80
- 100–199 @ 4.60
- 200–499 @ 4.30
- 500 + @ 3.90

Inventory carrying cost — 25% unit per year

Ordering cost — $10 per order

Weight per unit — 50 pounds per unit

Total weight shipped — 1200 cwt

Freight cost
- 0–1999 lbs. — $5.77 per cwt
- 2000–4999 — 4.38
- 5000–9999 — 3.89
- 10,000–TL — 3.11
- TL (20,000 min.) — 1.72
- Incentive rate (50,000 lbs.) — 1.57

Table 26–16 Purchase Discount and Inventory Carrying Cost Trade-off

Total Quantity Ordered	Cost Per Unit ($)	Quantity Discounts Foregone	Annual Freight Cost	Annual Inventory Carrying Costs	Annual Cost of Ordering	Total Annual Costs
50	$48.00	$1,080.00	$6,924.00	$ 318.06	$480.00	$8,802.06
100	47.90	840.00	5,256.00	626.13	240.00	6,962.13
200	47.75	480.00	1,668.00	1,242.50	120.00	6,510.50
400	47.75	480.00	2,068.00	2,430.50	60.00	5,024.50
500	47.55	0.00	2,164.00	3,025.68	48.00	5,137.63
1000	47.55	0.00	1,884.00	6,042.50	24.00	7,950.50

markets are valid factors in logistics system design. Planned inventory resulting from multiple facility decisions will be discussed below (see pages 688–702). However, opening of branch locations in some cases results in unanticipated pockets of inventory.

There are recognizable stages in the development of this problem.[3] Initially, a company might open branches in major markets in order to strengthen its competitive position. Its salesmen could then point to the company's presence locally as being advantageous to customers. The next step is to store inventories at branch locations and to fill unusual customer orders from branch stocks.

In time, the branches begin to regard their stocks not as reserves for making emergency shipments quickly, but as primary sources for making all shipments. Replenishment delays between the plant and the branches often prevent the hoped-for improvement in customer service from being realized. Thus, while branch inventories were originally intended to maintain a desirable level of customer service, they may not actually help very much. They do, however, duplicate factory safety stocks and create a pocket of inventory.

Many companies, particularly those whose competitive position is poor, look upon a full product line as essential to their well-being. These companies seek entree to potential customers by offering merchandise that is difficult to obtain through other channels. Trouble arises when production management, anxious to avoid the high costs of short runs, establishes minimums that often represent several years' supply. The result is an inventory pocket with its attendant carrying costs.

Production quality standards are often tightened at the insistence of a sales force that has been hearing more customer complaints than they consider tolerable. The company recognizes that its production costs would rise because of higher quality standards, and that its reject and rework losses would be higher. But another cost often goes unrecognized: closer tolerances and higher standards slow quality control procedures as queues of merchandise await inspection and testing. For example, with the factory working 2000 hours a year and turning out $10,000 of production per hour, an average delay of five hours results in $50,000 of additional inventory.

Modified products are often manufactured and stocked even though demand for them is low. The primary purpose is to prevent competitors from gaining a foothold. In any case, special items represent an inventory investment that is real and carrying costs that are inescapable. In one example, manufacturing costs for these products were $1 million annually. The company's production cycle, from the time raw materials were received to the time finished goods moved from plant to warehouse, was a reasonably short two weeks. If in a 50-week year the company were to meet its requirements by producing

25 equal lots, they would cost $40,000 each. A resultant plant inventory averaging close to $40,000 was buried in the financial reports of warehouse inventories.

Anticipating customers' needs can inflate the company's inventories. For example, in one firm, a few customers were favored by setting aside special reserves so that shipments could be made promptly on receipt of orders. This practice, originating with the sales force, can have serious consequences for companies that allow it to continue. Some companies have formalized their procedures for anticipating requirements by asking their customers to report inventories periodically. Others avoid the problem by entering into contracts that call for regular shipments at fixed dates.

New Products

A company's continued existence depends on its ability to offer for sale additions to its line of merchandise. But the introduction of a new product requires a marketing campaign, and as part of the concerted effort to launch a new product, it is generally necessary to build up sufficient stock to meet an initial flood of orders. Yet the size of this investment in inventory and the length of the holding period are seldom earmarked as a marketing responsibility in the financial reports.

Continuous expansion of product lines has been typical in most firms in recent years. This product proliferation imposes heavy burdens on the distribution system, particularly in inventory requirements. Assume that a single product is to be replaced with three new products, but with the same total sales volume. There is a characteristic relationship between inventory and sales, whereby the smaller the sales, the higher the inventory will be relative to sales. This relationship is explored in greater detail on page 689. In this example, selling three items in place of one would be expected to increase inventory by 60 percent.

Special Deals and Packaging

Promotional efforts, involving distinctive packaging for products in the regular line, require an inventory buildup prior to the opening of a sales campaign. The finished goods of a soap or cosmetics manufacturer can comprise promotional deals as high as 30 to 40 percent of the total.

Broken cases, odd lots, and other deviations from standard packaging can occur only if a marketing policy permits the sale of pieces in less than standard quantities. One company that occasionally permitted sales of individual bottles, leaving partial cases in stock, held $50,000 worth of open cases. In one extreme situation a total inventory of 23,000 feet of a single type of high priced cable was discovered to consist of only seven standard 1000-foot reels—the entire 16,000 feet of remaining stock consisted of assorted odd lengths that were not readily salable.

Discontinued Items

In many firms, items are removed from the product line each year because of technological progress, changing tastes, and innovations in design. Once a company decides to replace an item, it often stops producing it. Whatever is left in inventory is used to fill orders from customers who, out of habit or because of outdated information, order the old item instead of the new. For example, one firm waited two years before they disposed of discontinued items as obsolete merchandise. During the two years in limbo, those items had moved so slowly that there was an investment in them of $50,000 to $150,000 at all times.

Inventory to Guard against Strikes

In many industries, labor contract negotiations can affect inventory policy. For firms that require an assured supply of raw materials in order to continue operations, negotiation of labor contracts by their vendors is a matter of concern. Often, when an important contract will be coming up for negotiation, customers of the firm will build up a stockpile of goods in anticipation of a strike. Of course, this pocket of inventory is an insurance policy against shutdown. Nevertheless, an inventory carrying cost is incurred, which must be related to the underlying reason for that inventory.

Implications and Suggestions

Inventory pockets result from policies shaped by people outside the inventory management activity. Furthermore, these inventories are intractable from the standpoint of people responsible for inventory management. No matter how effectively they apply control techniques elsewhere, those techniques are simply not appropriate here.

As a result, people responsible for inventory control often feel thwarted by decisions not of their own making; and by being held responsible for the results of those decisions. Fortunately, however, there is a way to remove the frustrations caused by uncontrollable inventories—they must be separated from regular inventories in records and reports.

In financial reports, expenditures should be charged to those who bear the responsibility for incurring them. A common practice is to show the warehousing costs of regular stock as a departmental item under the control of a distribution executive. But since this person does not make the marketing decisions that create inventory pockets, he should not be held accountable for the costs incurred by those pockets. Rather, these costs should be charged to marketing or other operations. In budgeting, when inventory targets are established, there should be allocations for regular stocks and allowances for inventory pockets as well.

Allowances for inventory pockets are not to be thought of in terms of minimum and optimum levels. Some pockets vary over time in a way that makes the usual reorder procedures inappropriate. The job of controlling regular stocks can become unmanageable if inventory pockets get mixed in with regular stocks in such a way as to obscure the facts or distort the picture.

6. Order Cycle Inventory

Order cycle inventories result whenever a user purchases products in larger lots than are immediately needed. For example, in Figure 26–25, an amount (Q) is purchased and is then depleted during the time (t) between procurement orders. An average order cycle in-

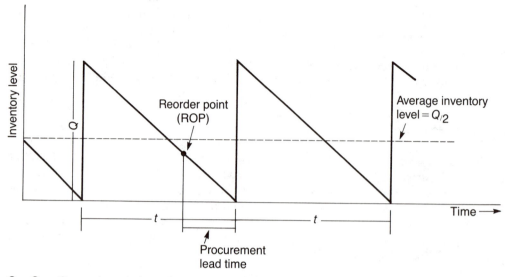

Q = Quantity purchased at one time
t = time between procurement orders

ventory of Q/2 thereby results. If, however, one half as much were purchased twice as frequently, the average order cycle inventory would immediately be cut in half (see Figure 26–8). Why, then, do firms not tend to order on a hand-to-mouth basis?

Firms recognize that it is costly to process frequent orders. Table 26–17 illustrates how costs vary for several alternative order quantities, and the cost are also plotted in Figure 26–26. In the example, total costs decline to a minimum when 200 units are purchased, and begin to increase again when greater quantities are purchased. The figures show that when order quantities are small, that is, when orders are placed frequently, ordering costs are greatest. Inventory carrying costs, of course, are lower because less inventory results from the frequent ordering. Conversely, when larger orders are placed less frequently, ordering costs are low but inventory carrying costs rise.

The formula by which the most economic order quantity (EOQ) can be calculated is

Table 26–17 Inventory Carrying Cost and Cost of Ordering for Various Order Sizes

Quantity Ordered	Average Inventory	Inventory Carrying Cost	Orders per Year	Cost of Ordering	Total Cost
50	25	$30	48	$480	$510
100	50	60	24	240	300
200	100	120	12	120	240
400	200	240	6	60	300
500	250	300	48	48	348

Demand	2400 units per year		Inventory carrying cost	25% per unit per year
Cost	$4.80 per unit		Ordering cost	$10 per order

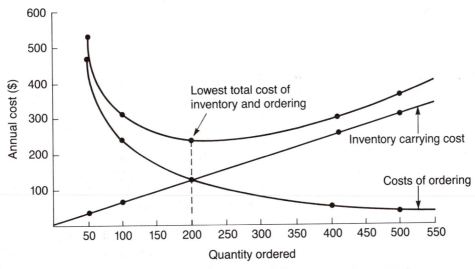

Figure 26-26   Trade-Off between Inventory-Carrying Costs and Costs of Ordering

$$EOQ = \sqrt{\frac{2DS}{IC}}$$

where
D = Annual sales in units	2400 units
S = Ordering costs	\$10 per order
I = Inventory carrying cost	25 % per unit cost per year
C = Unit cost	\$4.80 per unit

The formula determines the lowest total cost of inventory and ordering:

$$EOQ = \sqrt{\frac{2DS}{IC}} = \sqrt{\frac{2 \times 2400 \times 10}{0.25 \times 4.80}} = 200 \text{ units}$$

It is important to recognize that the only costs included in the EOQ formula are inventory carrying costs and costs of ordering. Important costs such as freight costs and quantity discounts are not included. In Table 26–5, the most economic order quantity was determined to be 500 units, not the 200 units determined by the EOQ formula. That is because in the example freight savings and quantity discounts received from purchasing larger amounts far outweighed either inventory carrying costs or cost of ordering. Along with the assumption that ordering costs and inventory costs are most important, the EOQ formula implies certain other conditions:

1. The most significant costs in the purchasing decisions are ordering costs and costs of maintaining cycle stock inventory.

2. The variable cost of an additional order is constant.

3. The variable cost of carrying an additional unit in inventory is constant.

4. The whole order quantity arrives at one time (no partial shipments).

5. Customer order size is small in relation to the order quantity developed by the EOQ formula.

6. Demand is known and constant.

7. The cost of an additional unit in a single purchase is constant; that is, there are no quantity discounts or freight savings.

8. The purchasing decisions made for one item are independent of the purchasing decisions for other items.

Of course, it would be an unusual firm that could satisfy all of these conditions. Rarely is demand known and constant, and in most firms joint purchasing of several items from each vendor is the rule instead of the exception. Nevertheless, the EOQ formula can be made operational in a manner that provides a useful guide to inventory management policy.

In order to do this, three questions must be answered: (1) What do we control? (2) When do we reorder? (3) How much do we order? In virtually every commercially available inventory management system and in those developed in-house, a type of economic order quantity calculation is contained, and these three questions are addressed.

What to Control—ABC Analysis

In the multiple item inventory that is typical in most firms, a decision must be made concerning which items will be controlled carefully and which less carefully. In this regard, ABC analysis is useful, in which fast moving "A" items, medium volume "B" items, and slow moving "C" items in an inventory are identified (Figure 26–27). In setting inventory policy, items in each of the categories can be given different treatment. In the example, A items accounting for 5 percent of items contributed 70 percent of sales, B items accounting for 10 percent of items added an additional 20 percent of sales, while 65 percent of C items contributed only 10 percent of sales. The last 20 percent of C items had no sales whatsoever! This statistical distribution, called the *lognormal distribution*, is almost always found in firms' inventories (the degree of concentration of sales among items will vary by firm, but the shape of the curve will be similar).

In inventory control, A items may be given very close control. For example, a daily or continuous review of inventory status might be appropriate for A items. B items might be reviewed less frequently, perhaps weekly, while the larger number of C items which contribute very little to total income receive the least attention.

Different customer service levels could be established for each of the categories. For example, an order fill rate of 98 percent might be set for A items, 90 percent for B items, and 85 percent for C items. This policy would result in an overall customer service level of:

Category	Percent of Sales	Customer Service Level (%)	Weighted Customer Service Level (%)
A	70	98	68.6
B	20	90	18.0
C	10	85	8.5
	100	Overall service level	95.1

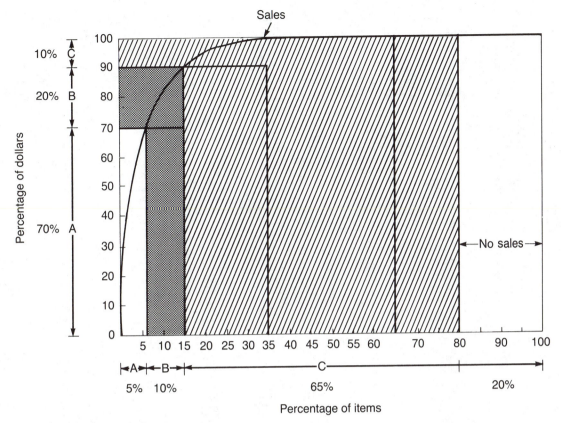

Figure 26-27 ABC Parts Classification

By focusing attention on the A items, greater emphasis is placed on the products that contribute the most to sales, while inventories may be kept lower for the B and C items categories.

Similarly, the amount of safety stock inventory in the distribution system will be less when lower volume items are stocked in as few locations as possible. For example, assume a national distribution system made up of 25 distribution centers. In this system, A items might be stocked in all 25 warehouses, B items in 5 regional warehouses and C items stocked only at the factory or in a single master warehouse. Obviously, transportation costs for B and C items will be greater with this scheme, but savings in safety stock inventories are usually more than enough to make such a *selective stocking* policy worthwhile. Selective stocking policies will be discussed later in this chapter.

Finally, it is possible to estimate beforehand the results expected from using a scientific inventory management system. The lognormal distribution has some interesting and useful statistical characteristics that allow such inventory estimates to be made. Various alternative policies can be tested, such as determining amounts of inventory expected with various levels of customer service. It might also be useful to analyze how the deletion of slow-moving items from the product line would affect inventory, or the impact that a 20 percent increase in sales might have on inventory.[4]

Categorizing items on an ABC basis is facilitated by preparation of a distribution-by-value report. Such a report is illustrated in Table 26–18. The distribution-by-value report is prepared by listing annual dollar sales for each item in descending sequence. In the example, some items are omitted from the sequence in order to fit the report onto one page. Various descriptive information can be included, such as product code, product nomenclature, unit cost, annual units sold, and so forth.

Distribution-by-value reports are particularly easy to prepare on computerized inventory systems. Items are sorted in the computer by annual dollar sales in descending sequence. After the items have been sorted, they are listed. As the line for each stock item is

Table 26–18   Distribution by Value Report

Rank Items	Part Number	Annual Dollar Sales	Cumulative Dollar Sales	One Month MAD	Cumulative Percent Items	Cumulative Percent Sales
1	K410	$126,773	$126,773	6,074	0.01	1.74
3	9999	74,130	285,602	10,780	0.02	3.92
5	410	44,800	397,075	4,030	0.03	5.45
8	2300	32,666	510,732	1,650	0.05	7.01
16	K820	22,838	730,034	5,038	0.10	10.02
35	2601	16,899	1,158,439	1,240	0.22	15.90
60	K53	13,009	1,467,356	1,168	0.39	20.14
90	5401	10,988	1,889,201	590	0.58	25.93
126	1101	9,388	2,191,561	592	0.82	30.08
168	K860	7,879	2,610,494	518	1.09	35.83
219	1302	6,538	2,936,895	505	1.42	40.31
279	3600	5,639	3,307,741	376	1.81	45.40
321	5601	5,017	3,567,115	158	2.08	48.96
351	K350	4,619	3,642,887	473	2.28	50.00
438	1603	3,823	4,047,249	246	2.84	55.55
543	540P	3,118	4,438,494	222	3.52	60.92
674	2305	2,496	4,837,759	128	4.37	65.91
839	920L	2,000	5,231,186	108	5.44	70.01
1000	K82T	1,635	5,508,045	179	6.48	75.60
1261	1304	1,186	5,784,905	76	8.18	79.40
1394	1806	1,017	5,908,764	53	9.04	81.10
1632	5304	831	6,127,337	113	10.58	84.10
1823	2600	693	6,312,395	38	11.82	86.64
2452	3501	463	6,570,312	30	15.90	90.18
2698	4200	357	6,775,043	25	17.49	92.99
2920	460P	300	6,787,428	25	18.93	93.16
3186	131M	250	6,906,187	12	20.66	94.79
3506	4304	207	6,953,544	22	22.73	95.44
4442	410G	116	7,130,588	9	28.80	97.87
5202	3500	78	7,150,989	5	33.73	98.15
5414	K542	71	7,176,762	5	35.11	98.50
5688	3402	60	7,193,246		36.88	98.73
6048	110G	50	7,198,345		39.22	98.80
6256	1308	45	7,208,546		40.56	98.94
6386	110P	42	7,210,732		41.41	98.97
6437	2306	41	7,212,917		41.74	99.00
6493	920K	40	7,249,346		42.10	99.50
7711	83J4	0.35	7,261,732		50.00	99.67
9253	172R	0.33	7,266,103		60.00	99.73
12318	4404	0.30	7,285,775		79.87	100.00
12970	X438	0	7,285,775		84.10	100.00
15422	999J	0	7,285,775		100.00	100.00

printed, the computer also prints two cumulative totals: (1) cumulative items and (2) cumulative sales. Each of these cumulative totals are also shown as percent of total items and percent of total sales.

How Much to Order and When to Order

Decisions about how much to order and when to reorder can be made in two ways. First, an amount equal to the EOQ can be ordered whenever the stock on hand falls to an amount (reorder point) sufficient to last during the lead time before the order is received from the supplier (Figure 26–28). The time between orders may, therefore, vary in this method.

In the second method, the interval between orders is always the same, but the quantity ordered may vary from review to review (Figure 26–29). An amount is ordered that is sufficient to satisfy demand until the next time that stock is ordered and received physically into inventory.

These two basic techniques to determine how much and when to buy are: (1) fixed order quantity, variable time (reorder point), and (2) fixed time, variable order quantity (periodic review).

Fixed Order Quantity, Variable Time (Reorder Point) System

In a fixed order quantity system, available stock is compared against a certain level of stock, called the reorder point (ROP), to see whether it is time to order an item. This comparison may be made every time there is an inventory transaction involving the item. When available stock is equal to or has fallen below the ROP, it is time to buy. When-

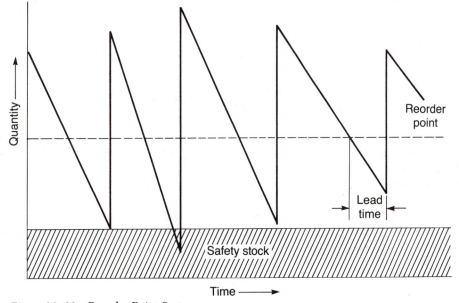

Figure 26-28   Reorder Point System

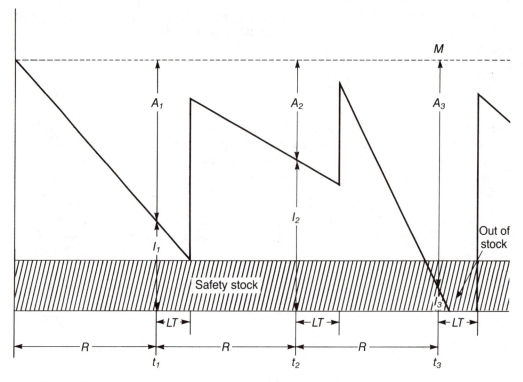

R = Review interval
t_n = Review points
M = Preset maximum inventory level
I = Inventory on hand at review
A = Amount ordered
LT = Lead time

Figure 26-29   Periodic Review System

ever the available stock falls below the ROP, a fixed order quantity is ordered. The order quantity is of course the economic order quantity (EOQ), calculated as shown on page 663.

Reorder point systems are sometimes referred to as "two-bin" systems. In some cases, stock equivalent to the reorder point is set aside in one bin, while regular stock is in a second bin. Orders are picked from the second bin, and when it is empty an order is placed. The bin containing an amount equal to ROP provides stock to last during the lead time before the order is received from the supplier.

Available stock is reviewed and compared with the reorder point to determine whether it is time to buy. Available stock is defined as stock on hand, plus stock already on order, less commitments against stock (such as customer back orders).

Available stock = stock on hand + stock on order − back orders.

If lead time is long (e.g., three months) and economic order quantity (Q) is equivalent to a shorter period of supply (e.g., one month), a new order would not be placed until stock on hand plus stock on order is less than the reorder point. That is because when lead times are long, several orders could be pending at any time.

For each item, the reorder point is that amount of stock which will just produce the level of customer service desired for the item. To properly determine this value, the following factors must be taken into account: (1) lead time, (2) forecast of usage per time unit, and (3) measure of forecast error.

Lead Time

Lead time starts when the decision to order is made and ends when the material is received and ready for use. It includes the time it takes the buying firm to process a purchase order and send it to the vendor, the vendor's order-processing time, time to pick and pack the order, transit time for shipment, as well as the time for receiving operations at the buyer's firm.

Inventory is, of course, depleted over time, as shown in Figure 26-25. Under ideal circumstances, it would be desirable to run out of an item just as a new shipment arrives. The result would be no lost sales and no excess inventory. To avoid lost sales, it is obviously necessary to place an order one lead time before running out. Setting of the reorder point simply consists of looking ahead one lead time to see when the present supply of goods will run out. Therefore,

$$\text{Reorder point} = \text{lead time in days} \times \text{usage per day}$$

Clearly, an accurate knowledge of the demand during the lead time is required. If 50 items are used each day, and lead time is two days, the reorder point is (2×50), or 100 units. Note that the longer the lead time, the higher the reorder point, Also, it is obvious that a vendor's lead time may vary from time to time. How to deal with uncertainty in vendor lead time is discussed on pp. 686–688.

Forecast of Usage per Time Unit

In discussing the effect of lead time on the reorder point, it has been assumed that the rate of usage is known. Normally, of course, one does not know, but has to forecast sales of an item during the lead time. Various techniques of forecasting item sales were discussed in Chapter 18. This forecast, to determine usage per day, will be used in determining the reorder point. The only trouble is that the forecast might be wrong.

Measure of Forecast Error

A forecast which is too low (exceeded by demand) can cause lost sales. Since *forecast errors* (the differences between forecasts and actual demand) would be expected to be normally distributed, forecasts will be too low about half the time and too high about half the time. However, a low forecast is of more concern since it can mean failure to meet customer demand. To allow for this, the reorder point might be increased, thus creating a buffer or safety stock to be dipped into when the forecast is too low (Figure 26–28). Adding this safety stock has the effect of increasing the average inventory, with an associated increase in inventory carrying cost:

$$\text{Average inventory} = \frac{Q}{2} + \text{safety stock}$$

This additional inventory may be considered a good investment up to some reasonable point, because of the sales that would otherwise be lost.

To understand better how this safety stock might work, consider the same demand situation, first without safety stock and then with it. With no safety stock, when sales are exactly equal to forecast, the inventory is reduced to zero just as the new shipment comes in, assuming that the forecast usage per time period was exactly right. If actual demand had been greater, sales would have been lost. In the second case, safety stock would have been used. Safety stock is protection against such an error in forecasting demand.

If the forecast were perfect, no safety stock would be necessary. Recognizing that the forecast cannot be 100 percent accurate, it is necessary to measure how wrong it is and let safety stock vary with forecast error. Thus the poorer the forecast, the larger the safety stock that must be provided.

Measuring forecast error to set safety stock levels is one of the most significant concepts of scientific inventory management. This is particularly true in distribution industries where safety stock typically forms the bulk of the inventory.

This section can be summarized by restating the reorder point formula:

Reorder point = lead time in days × forecast of usage per day + safety stock

where safety stock is based on a measure of forecast error.

When to Use Fixed Order Quantity Systems

Compared to periodic review (variable order quantity) systems, fixed order quantity systems require less safety stock inventory. That is because using the reorder point as an ordering trigger provides sufficient stock to meet demand during the lead time. In a periodic review system, safety stock must be carried to safeguard against stockout during the lead time *plus* the review interval.

The conditions under which fixed order quantity systems are preferable are:

1. Continuous review of inventory is possible; for example, when a computer perpetual inventory system is used.

2. Inventory consists of items of low unit value purchased infrequently in quantities that are large compared with usage rates.

3. Irregular purchase orders will not cause production or supply difficulties. For example, the item is a minor part of the supplier's total output or is a stock item.

4. Most items ordered are one-line orders; that is, items ordered from any one source are few in number and infrequently ordered. The likelihood of reordering several items on the same day is remote.

Fixed Time, Varying Quantity (Periodic Review) Models

In some firms, inventory is reviewed on a periodic basis. This system reduces the number of opportunities to buy per year, for example, to 52 for weekly review or to 12 for monthly review. Since the buyer does not know the inventory level of an item during the period between reviews (except in an emergency), he must allow for the usage which will take place between reviews. If he fails to do so, inventory could fall below lead time usage before the item is reviewed again, resulting in a stock-out.

An estimate or forecast is made of the number of units required to meet demand during a period that equals the review interval (R) plus the lead time (LT). For example, with a 30-day review interval between orders and a 15-day vendor lead time after an order is placed, the period for which there is a risk of stockout (replenishment cycle) is 45 days. Once a review time has passed, the stock level is not monitored until the next review. A stock-out could be the first warning that a shortage exists, and the stock-out situation would continue during the lead time after an order is placed until the products are received from the vendor (illustrated in the third cycle of Figure 26–29).

Once the demand forecast has been made, at the next review an order is placed that is sufficient to bring the total of inventory on hand (I) and on order (O) up to a preset maximum amount (M). That maximum amount is equal to the average units forecast to be required during one replenishment cycle ($R + LT$), plus safety stock. The amount ordered will therefore differ each time an order is placed.

The Review Interval (R)

The first step in developing a periodic reordering system of inventory control is to determine the appropriate review interval. This is accomplished by first calculating the economic order quantity (Q) using the formula given previously:

$$Q = \sqrt{\frac{2DS}{IC}}$$

Then, the number of orders per year (N) is deferred from the annual demand (D) divided by the economic order quantity (Q), or

$$N = \frac{D}{Q}$$

In the previous example, annual demand (D) was 2400 units and economic order quantity (Q) was calculated as 200 units. Therefore, the number of orders to be placed per year is

$$N = \frac{2400 \text{ units per year}}{200 \text{ units per order}} = 12 \text{ orders per year}$$

The review interval (R) is the number of time periods per year (e.g., 12 months, 52 weeks, 365 days) divided by the number of orders per year:

$$R = \frac{12 \text{ months per year}}{12 \text{ orders per year}} = 1 \text{ review per month}$$

Preset Inventory Level (M)

The next step is to determine the preset maximum (M) to which inventory on hand and on order must be increased by placing an order. An average of 200 units is forecast to be sold per month (30 days), or 6.67 units per day. With a 30-day review interval (R) plus a 15-day lead time (LT), it is estimated that 300 units are likely to be used during the 45-day replenishment cycle (R + LT).

$$\text{Usage during replenishment cycle} = 6.67 \text{ units per day } (30 + 15 \text{ days})$$
$$= 300 \text{ units}$$

To these an appropriate safety stock of 26 units must be added, so M is therefore 300 units required during the replenishment cycle plus 26 units of safety stock (i.e., M = 326 units). In the next subsection of this chapter, the calculation of the safety stock amount will be explained.

The Decision Rule

Now that the review interval (R) and the preset inventory level (M) have been determined, a decision rule for periodic ordering can be stated: At every review interval (R), review the inventory level and order an amount (A) sufficient to bring the inventory on hand (I) and on order (O) up to a preset amount (M). The amount to be ordered is therefore

$$A = M - I - O$$

and the preset amount (M) is, as was shown above,

$$M = (\text{demand in units per day})(R + LT) + \text{safety stock}$$

Assume that when the review is made, 151 units are in inventory and that no units are on order (because the 15-day lead time is less than the 30-day review interval). Therefore,

$$M = 6.67 \text{ units per day} \times (30 \text{ days} + 15 \text{ days}) + 26 \text{ units}$$
$$M = 326 \text{ units}$$
$$A = 326 \text{ units} - 151 \text{ units} - 0 \text{ units}$$
$$A = 175 \text{ units}$$

An amount (A) of 175 units should be ordered to bring the amount on hand (I) plus on order (O) up to the preset amount (M) of 326 units. The preset amount is sufficient to meet average demand during one review interval (R) plus one lead time (LT), plus safety stock to buffer against uncertainty.

When to Use Periodic Review

Periodic review inventory systems tend to result in greater amounts of safety stock than do reorder point systems. The period of time during which risk of stock-out could occur is not only the lead time, but also the review interval. In a reorder point system, safety stock must guard only against stock-outs during the lead time, so less safety stock is required.

Nevertheless, under the following circumstances, some firms may find it advantageous to use a periodic review system:

1. A manual book inventory system is used and it is convenient to review inventory stocks on a definite schedule. This might be done on a *cycle count* basis, in which a portion of stock is reviewed each day or week, perhaps on an ABC basis (reordering A items more often than B items, etc.). This also allows balancing of clerical workload.

2. A large number of items are to be jointly ordered from the same vendor sources.

3. Items ordered have a significant effect on the supplying plant's production output, and order predictability is desirable.

4. Significant transportation savings can sometimes result when several items are ordered at the same time.

Interaction between Items *

So far it has been assumed that an item is purchased without regard to the purchase of any other item—that is, decisions made for one item have no effect on whether other items are bought, and in what quantities.

As long as only one item is obtained from a particular vendor, this is a valid assumption. However, when more than one item is obtained from a vendor, the possible interaction among items obtained from the same source must be considered.

The key factors influenced by the interaction between items are (1) header cost, and (2) quantity discounts (or minimums) based on the total quantity ordered at any one time. The types of interaction that may occur, and their relationship to these two key factors, can be demonstrated by a series of examples. Assume that reviewing is performed weekly (52 opportunities to buy per year).

Example 1. Only one item is purchased from a vendor. Assume that the economic lot size will cause 10 orders per year. Each time the item is ordered, another purchase order must be placed. Header cost, therefore, varies directly with item order quantity and should be included in the economic order quantity formula. Meeting a vendor order minimum or earning a quantity discount must be based on the order quantity of this item alone; therefore vendor minimums and discount breakpoints should be considered as possible item order quantities in addition to the EOQ quantity.

Example 2. A second item of the same size is purchased from the same vendor. Now 20 purchase order lines are placed per year, 10 for each item. Although there is some chance that order quantities for the two items will fall together in any given review, most purchase orders will be one-line orders. As in the previous example, header cost should be included in the EOQ formula, and vendor minimum and discount breakpoints should be considered as possible item order quantities.

*Reprinted by permission from *Basic Principles of Wholesale Impact,* ©1967 by International Business Machines Corporation, New York. Based on material from pp. 15–21.

Example 3.   One hundred items are purchased from the same vendor. Total weekly demand for the vendor line is large relative to any vendor minimums or quantity discount breakpoints which may apply.

The EOQ formula, using line cost only, results in 20 orders per year per item, or 2000 line items per year per vendor. Each item is reviewed each week to see if it needs to be ordered. The decision to order an item is made without considering whether other items are to be ordered (that is, it is ordered independently). Since 2000 line items per year will be ordered from this vendor, management is virtually assured that a purchase order must be placed every week, regardless of the order quantity for any one item. Header cost is now fixed with respect to item lot size. The purchasing cost term in the EOQ formula, therefore, should include only line cost.

Reaching vendor minimums and discount breakpoints (if any) relates more to the total of the item order quantities ordered at any given week than to the size of any one item order quantity. Therefore, these minimums and discount breakpoints are not considered as possible item order quantities. Furthermore, since total weekly demand for the vendor line is large relative to any vendor minimums or quantity discounts that may apply, the total quantity ordered each week should normally exceed these minimums or breakpoints.

Example 4.   Assume the same circumstances as for Example 3, except that there is an attractive quantity discount offered if the total quantity ordered at one time exceeds a quantity that is large relative to total weekly demand for the vendor line. (For example, the discount is received for any order over 40,000 pounds, and total demand for the vendor line averages 10,000 pounds per week.)

If a purchase order is placed every week as in Example 3, few if any purchase orders would qualify for the quantity discount. There is now incentive to order the items "jointly"; that is, deliberately combine and control the ordering of all items in a vendor line in order to obtain the quantity discount. In this example, the average interval between orders would be four weeks. Note also that since the number of purchase orders per year is reduced from 52 to 13, there is a reduction in header cost.

These examples show that an ordering strategy that is right when ordering from one vendor can be quite wrong when ordering from another. An effective inventory management system must provide a selection of ordering strategies that will properly handle the different types of vendor ordering requirements normally encountered. Two basic types of vendor ordering strategies are: (1) independent ordering—which includes two substrategies, header-plus-line or line-only—and (2) joint ordering.

Independent Vendor Ordering Strategies

With an independent strategy, each item is reviewed periodically to see whether it needs to be ordered. The decision to order a given item is not influenced by decisions concerning other items purchased from the same vendor. When an item is to be ordered, a fixed order quantity is determined for each item, depending on which of two independent vendor substrategies is used.

1. *Header-plus-line.* This substrategy is based on the assumption that one-line purchase orders will predominate. The purchase cost used in the EOQ formula is equal to header cost plus line cost. In addition to the calculated economic order quantity, vendor minimum and vendor discount breakpoint quantities are consid-

ered as alternative item quantities. The most economic of these is selected as the item order quantity.

2. *Line-only.* This substrategy is based on the assumption that multiple-line purchase orders will predominate. The purchase cost used in the lot-size formula is equal to line cost only. Vendor minimum and vendor discount breakpoint quantities are not considered as possible item order quantities.

Joint Vendor Ordering Strategies

With a joint ordering strategy, items obtained from the same vendor are ordered together to obtain certain advantages, such as quantity discounts or lower freight rates. The frequency at which joint orders are placed is determined by the total order quantity objective, and is normally less than the number of review periods. For example, assume that the total order quantity objective is a rail carload of 50,000 pounds. If average total demand for the vendor is 10,000 pounds per review period, joint orders will be placed every fifth review period on the average. The quantity ordered for each item may vary from order cycle to order cycle. Item order quantities are controlled by allocation, which determines the order quantity of each item so as to:

- Proportion stock among the items in relation to their demand rates and service objectives

- Develop a total order quantity that is between specified limits

- Equalize the total of the item order quantities and the minimum vendor order quantity objectives (in many instances the former should not exceed some acceptable maximum vendor order quantity)

The operation of a joint ordering system will vary depending on the two forms of joint ordering.

1. *Reorder point system.* The interval between joint orders is allowed to vary. Every review period, the vendor line is analyzed to see whether the line needs to be ordered to maintain the desired service level. If the vendor line is to be ordered, the quantity of each item to be ordered is determined by allocation.

2. *Periodic review system.* The interval between joint orders is fixed. The vendor line is ordered only at the end of each fixed interval. It is not examined during intervening review periods. The quantity to be ordered for each item is determined by an allocation process that is roughly comparable to that for the variable-interval system, except that only upward allocation is allowed. That is, the order is not allowed to fall below that level calculated for the fixed interval and specified service, even though this may cause the total order quantity to exceed the specified upper limit.

The fixed-interval system should be used only when overriding scheduling considerations require it. For example, a vendor may accept an order only on the tenth day of each month. In all other respects, the variable-interval system is considered to be superior to the fixed-interval system.

The joint ordering process just described normally means that every item is ordered each time a joint order is placed. However, smaller items in a vendor line may have economic ordering frequencies which are considerably less than that with which joint orders are placed. For example, the economic order quantity formula may call for purchasing a particular item in a vendor line only once every six months, yet joint orders are placed with this vendor once every month on the average. To order this item every time a joint order is placed would increase the number of purchase order lines to an uneconomic level. This can be avoided by treating such items as "coordinated" items. Coordinated items in a vendor line can be purchased only when a joint order is placed. However, such items have fixed order quantities calculated by the lot-size formula. They may be ordered every second, third, or twentieth joint interval, depending on their economic lot size.

Selecting the Best Vendor Ordering Strategy

The choice between an independent or joint ordering strategy for a particular vendor line depends on the relative balance of a number of conflicting cost factors and operational requirements.

The factors favoring a joint ordering strategy include:

1. Economic quantity discounts (or more favorable freight rates) that would be missed with independent ordering can often be obtained.

2. Purchase order header costs are reduced through grouping many items on one order.

3. Positive control of the aggregate order quantity is provided to meet operating requirements. For example, assume that to qualify for a carload freight rate, a minimum of 40,000 pounds must be ordered, but the car will not hold more than 45,000 pounds. It is therefore necessary to develop an aggregate order quantity that falls within these limits. With an independent strategy, the total order quantity is normally the sum of an accidental combination of item order quantities and is likely to fall outside these limits. On the other hand, the allocation process used with a joint strategy provides a positive control of total order quantities to assure that they will be within the desired limits.

The disadvantages of joint ordering, as compared to independent ordering, are:

1. Safety stock is usually increased. Increasing the total order quantity to qualify for a quantity discount usually means placing a joint order less frequently than every review period. Yet any given item can be ordered only when a joint order is placed. This in turn requires more safety stock to produce a given level of service.

2. The control of a joint strategy is more complex than the control of an independent strategy and normally requires more computer processing time.

3. Individual item service is less subject to control in any given order cycle, even though the aggregate vendor service objective is under direct control, and the ser-

vice objective for each item should be met in the long run. The decision to place a joint order for a vendor line must be based on the aggregate stock status and service objectives for the entire line. In a particular review period, a single item may be at the point where it will fall below its service objective if it is not ordered, yet the other items in the vendor line have sufficient stock and do not need to be ordered. To place a joint order for the entire vendor line (for example, to order a carload) because of the single item would greatly inflate inventory above that required to produce the service desired for the vendor line. Therefore, the service for this item must suffer until the vendor line needs to be ordered. With an independent strategy, this item would be ordered when its individual service objective requires, a procedure that is attractive. However, the advantages of joint ordering (discounts, freight rates, header cost) would then be lost.

Summary

The questions of "how much to buy" and "when to buy" have been considered in this section. When only one item is purchased from a vendor and quantity discounts are not a factor, the quantity to buy is very simply determined by means of the economic order quantity formula. However, whenever more than one item is purchased from a vendor and quantity discounts become a factor, the matter becomes much more complex. The interaction among the various items in the vendor line must be considered. In addition to the individual item ordering frequency, consideration must be given to the ordering strategy for the entire vendor line.

7. Safety Stock Inventories

If it were possible to forecast accurately what the demand will be during the lead time before an order is received from the supplier, an inventory system could be operated with great certainty. No safety stock would be required in such a system. However, not only is the demand during lead time likely to deviate from what is forecasted, but the lead time itself is likely to vary. During the lead time, the order must be transmitted to the supplier and processed; the merchandise must then be picked, packed, shipped, received, and put into stock. The time needed to perform each of these activities is likely to vary. Because of these uncertainties, safety stocks must be carried to keep from reaching an excessive out-of-stock position.

Figure 26–30 illustrates that demand during lead time most often follows the normal distribution. That is, during most lead times demand will be close to average, and demands that are either very great or very low will occur less frequently. Lower than expected demand, of course, results in a building up of inventory, but not in poor customer service. Greater than average demand, however, results in stock-outs and a reduction in the service level, unless safety stock is carried.

Figure 26–31 illustrates the relationship between the amount of safety stock inventory carried and the number of stock-outs. As the number of stock-outs decreases, the amount of safety stock inventory required to prevent stock-outs increases rapidly. This is because very high demand peaks occur infrequently, and inventory carried to cover these high peaks is likely to be stored for a long time. For this reason, most firms plan to carry

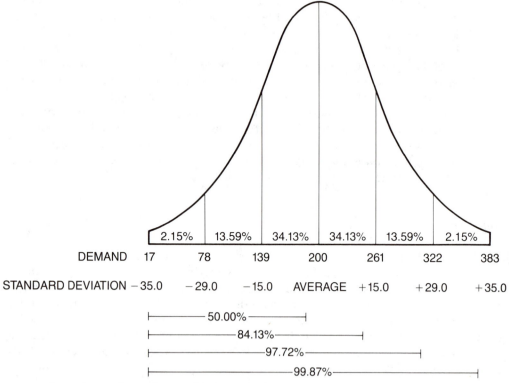

	2.15%	13.59%	34.13%	34.13%	13.59%	2.15%	
DEMAND	17	78	139	200	261	322	383
STANDARD DEVIATION	−35.0	−29.0	−15.0	AVERAGE	+15.0	+29.0	+35.0

├──────── 50.00% ────────┤

├──────────── 84.13% ────────────┤

├──────────────── 97.72% ────────────────┤

├──────────────────── 99.87% ────────────────────┤

Figure 26-30   Area Relationships under the Normal Curve—Standard Deviation

an amount of safety stock inventory which allows for a reasonable number of stock-outs to occur.

Service and Safety Stocks

Customer satisfaction is one of the most precious assets a business enterprise can have. The customer will tend to favor the supplier who most consistently provides a high percentage of the merchandise he has ordered. If a buyer can rely on his supplier he can safely operate with less inventory—a clear-cut saving for him.

While there are several ways of defining customer service, they all hinge on how effectively demand is met, and are most often expressed as a percentage figure. Customer service is often defined as the percentage of dollar demand that is filled from stock:

$$\text{Customer service \%} = \frac{\$ \text{ demand shipped}}{\$ \text{ demand ordered}} \times 100$$

Conversely,

$$\text{Out of stock \%} = 100 - \text{customer service \%}$$

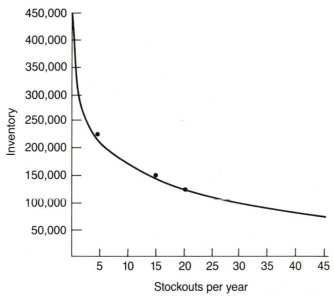

Figure 26-31   Relationship between Stock-Outs and Inventory

It is not economically justified in most cases to achieve 100 percent service because of the high levels of safety stock inventory it would require. Such a policy would be prohibitively expensive. Therefore, customer service policies are generally stated in terms of an acceptable percentage of demand that must be filled from stock. For example, it may be decided that in the long run (and on the average) 95 percent of demand will be filled from stock. This, of course, implies that the remaining 5 percent of the time the firm will be out of stock.

Effect of Forecast Error on Inventory

Figure 26–30 shows a normal distribution (bell-shaped) curve for demand data, which illustrates the relationships between average demand and standard deviation of demand. Standard deviation is a measure of how concentrated or dispersed data are around the average. For any data that are distributed normally, the percentage figures shown in the figure will hold.

Forecast error is the difference between a forecast and the demand that actually materializes. If the forecast were to be based on an average of past sales (200 units in Figure 26–30), demand during the lead time would be less than the forecast 50 percent of the time, and greater than the forecast 50 percent of the time. Thus, if the reorder point were set at the average usage, half the time there would still be stock on hand when the new order was received. Conversely, half the time there would have been a stock-out. Since most often it is not desirable to be out of stock that frequently, it is necessary to provide safety stock.

Figure 26–32 shows a distribution of forecast errors. Generally, forecast errors also approximate a normal distribution. In the example, when demand is 200, the forecast er-

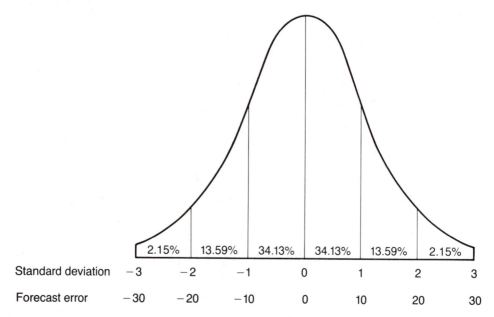

| 2.15% | 13.59% | 34.13% | 34.13% | 13.59% | 2.15% |

| Standard deviation | −3 | −2 | −1 | 0 | 1 | 2 | 3 |
| Forecast error | −30 | −20 | −10 | 0 | 10 | 20 | 30 |

Figure 26-32   Standard Deviation of Forecast Errors

ror is 0. Once the standard deviation of forecast error is calculated, the normal curve can be used to set safety stock for a particular probability of stock-out. Figure 26–32 shows that 34.13 percent of the forecast errors fall within one standard deviation above the average. In the example, the standard deviation of forecast error is 10. Thus, if 10 units are added to the reorder point, demand during lead time should be satisfied 84.13 percent of the time (50 percent + 34.13 percent). If two standard deviations are added to the average, protection is provided for 97.72 percent of demands. The resulting reorder point is $200 + (2 \times 10) = 220$. By adding three standard deviations of safety stock, protection is provided for 99.87 percent of demands. The reorder point in this case is $200 + (3 \times 10) = 230$.

It should be noted that this definition of servicing demand is based upon absence of stock-outs a certain percentage of the time. For example, if demand is satisfied 84.13 percent of the time, that implies that 15.87 percent of the time (100 percent minus 84.13 percent) demand will *not* be satisfied. If all demand is not satisfied, this definition of service says nothing about how large the stock-out might be—it could be 10 units or 1000 units. Later, a second definition of service based on percentage of total demand filled will be discussed.

Safety Stock Based on Standard Deviation

It is now possible to state the equation for calculating safety stock:

$$\text{Safety stock} = \text{standard deviation of forecast error} \times \text{safety factor}$$

The safety factor specifies the number of standard deviations required for a specific service level, and is determined from the normal curve.

The percentage relationships for the standard deviation always hold true regardless of the particular values for average demand and standard deviation. If forecasts are exceptionally good, the forecast errors will be very small. The safety stock can be correspondingly small, even when very high service is required.

In our example, average usage was 200, and the standard deviation of forecast error was 10. The reorder point would be only 230 to yield 99.87 percent service. On the other hand, if the forecast error is large, a large safety stock is needed. Thus, if average usage were 200, but standard deviation of forecast error were 61, the reorder point for 99.87 percent service would be 383 units. This suggests the following conclusions:

- A poor forecast creates a need for larger safety stocks. Accordingly, it is worth some effort to get good forecasts.

- A uniform level of service can be achieved only by taking the variability of the distribution into account.

Calculation of the Standard Deviation

Service levels and safety stocks can be effectively controlled through the use of standard deviation. The formula for calculating it is:

$$\text{Standard deviation} = \sqrt{\frac{\sum_{i=1}^{n}(X_i - \overline{X})^2}{n}}$$

where X_i represents demand, $\overline{X}$ represents average demand, and n is the number of periods.

From a computing point of view, calculating standard deviations is not appealing, because division and extraction of square roots are among a computer's slowest operations. Also, a complete history of forecasts and actual demands must be maintained in computer memory.

MAD—An Approximation of Standard Deviation

Fortunately, there is a good way of approximating standard deviation which requires substantially less computing time. For a normal distribution, it is just as accurate as standard deviation. This measure is called *mean absolute deviation* (MAD). With a normal distribution, the relationship between standard deviation and MAD is such that:

$$\text{Standard deviation} = 1.25 \times \text{MAD}$$

As with standard deviation, the normal distribution curve provides the method to find the safety factor related to MAD for a desired level of service. The normal curve areas for MAD are shown in Figure 26–33. Representative safety factors taken from the normal distribution to achieve a given level of service with MAD are listed in Table 26–19. Safety stock is calculated:

$$\text{Safety stock} = \text{MAD} \times \text{safety factor}$$

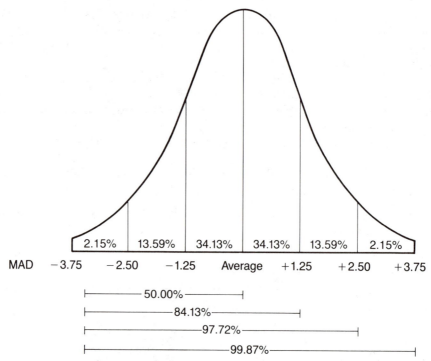

| 2.15% | 13.59% | 34.13% | 34.13% | 13.59% | 2.15% |

| MAD | −3.75 | −2.50 | −1.25 | Average | +1.25 | +2.50 | +3.75 |

50.00%

84.13%

97.72%

99.87%

Figure 26-33   Area Relationships under the Normal Curve—Mean Absolute Deviation (MAD)

As before, the safety factor simply specifies the number of MAD's required to be stocked to yield a specified level of service.

Calculation of Mean Absolute Deviation (MAD)

"Mean," of course, is just another term for average. "Deviation" is the difference between sales that actually occurred and what was forecasted to occur. "Absolute" means that the deviation is always considered to be positive, ignoring any minus signs. The formula is:

$$\text{Mean absolute deviation} = \frac{\sum_{i=1}^{n} \left| x_i - \overline{x} \right|}{n}$$

where x_i represents demand, $\overline{x}$ represents average demand (or forecast), and n is the number of periods.

The formula can be solved in two steps:

1. Calculate the deviation of each demand from the forecast without regard to sign

2. Divide the summed deviations by the number of deviations measured

Table 26–20 illustrates a calculation of MAD for both forecast errors and average demand. If demand were forecasted by using average demand, of course, a larger mean absolute deviation would occur.

Table 26-19   Safety Factors for Service Levels Using MAD (Service Based on Frequency of Stock-out)

Safety Factor	Percentage of Order with No Stock-out Cycles
0.00	50.00
0.32	60.00
0.66	70.00
0.84	75.00
1.00	78.81
1.06	80.00
1.25	84.13
1.30	85.00
1.61	90.00
2.00	94.52
2.06	95.00
2.50	97.72
2.58	98.00
2.92	99.00
3.00	99.18

Two Basic Definitions of Service

There are several ways of measuring the service provided by an inventory. However, the two most often used measures are:

1. *Frequency of stock-out per order cycle.* This is based on how frequently a stock-out will occur, but does not estimate the size of the stock-out. For example, with 98 percent service, there would be stock-outs 2 percent of the time. When a stock-out does occur it could be for one unit or a million units.

2. *Demand fill rate.* This is based on the percentage of demand routinely filled from stock. Although it need not be, demand is most often expressed in dollars. Thus, with 98 percent service, it is expected that of every \$100 of orders, \$98 will be filled from stock.

Frequency of Stock-out per Order Cycle

As has been discussed, safety stock can be based on a statistical measure of demand variability—the mean absolute deviation (MAD). To achieve a given level of service in the previous examples, a multiplier (the safety factor) was used, the value of which was taken from the normal curve. The safety factors listed in Table 26-19 are for service levels based on frequency of stock-out.

$$\text{Safety stock} = \text{MAD} \times \text{safety factor}$$

To illustrate, assume that a safety factor has been chosen to yield 98 percent service. From Table 26-19, the safety factor is 2.58. As calculated in Table 26-20, MAD is 61 when orders are based on average demand. Therefore,

$$\text{Safety stock} = 61 \times 2.58 = 157 \text{ units}$$

Table 26–20   Mean Absolute Deviation (MAD) Calculations

	Sales (X_i)	Absolute Deviation from Average Demand $(X_i - \overline{X})$	Forecast (F)	Absolute Deviation of Forecast Error $(X_i - F)$
January	134	| 66|	125	| 9|
February	140	| 60|	140	| 0|
March	153	| 47|	160	| 7|
April	193	| 7|	175	|18|
May	219	| 19|	200	|19|
June	258	| 58|	250	| 8|
July	271	| 71|	275	| 4|
August	304	|104|	300	| 4|
September	315	|115|	300	|15|
October	196	| 4|	175	|21|
November	134	| 66|	140	| 6|
December	83	|117|	75	| 8|
$n = 12$	$\Sigma X_i = 2400$	$\Sigma\|X_i\| = 734$		$\Sigma\|X_i - F\| = 119$

$$\overline{X} = \frac{\Sigma X_i}{n} = \frac{2400}{12} = 200$$

$$\text{MAD of average demand} = \frac{\sum_{i=1}^{n}|X_i - \overline{X}|}{n} = \frac{734}{12} = 61.0$$

$$\text{MAD of forecast errors} = \frac{\Sigma|X_i - F|}{n} = \frac{119}{12} = 10$$

If a forecast were made which recognized the seasonality of the product (Table 26–20), MAD would drop to 10 and the same 98 percent service level would be provided by

$$\text{Safety stock} = 10 \times 2.58 = 26 \text{ units}$$

After an item's stock level has reached the reorder point (and an order has been issued), the example indicates that all customer orders during the lead time will be filled 98 percent of the time. Two percent of the time it is expected that the item will run out before the new shipment arrives. There is no way of telling how large the shortage will be—whether it will be one unit or many.

In other words, there is an estimate of how frequently the item will run out, but no estimate of the quantity or size of unfilled orders. The expected frequency of stock-out is related to the frequency of orders to a vendor. That is, of every 100 orders placed for a particular item, it is probable that 98 of them will be received without a stock-out occurring. With weekly orders, there would be a stock-out two weeks out of 100, or about once a year.

Demand Fill Rate

Some firms prefer to satisfy a specified percentage of demand, which is quite a different measure of service than frequency of stock-out. To do so requires a different value of the safety factor for each item. It is possible to determine the appropriate value using Table 26–21 and the following formula:

$$\text{Service function} = \frac{\text{order quantity}}{\text{MAD during lead time}} (1 - \text{desired service level})$$

The service function has the physical meaning of the quantity of demand during an order cycle that is unfilled, expressed in units of MAD during lead time. For example, if order quantity is 100 units and desired service is 98 percent, the average amount of unfilled demand per order cycle should be two units. The safety factor required to produce the desired service level is determined from the service function by using Table 26–21.

The order quantity and MAD interact to affect the percentage of demand that is expected to be filled routinely. If order quantity is large in relation to forecast error, the order quantity alone will provide protection for some time after goods are received. This is illustrated in Figure 26–34, where item A has a larger order quantity, in terms of time supply, than Item B. Taking this into account will yield a lower safety factor for Item A than for Item B, while satisfying the same percentage of demand for both items. For example:

Item A

Order quantity: 600 (annual usage is 1200, so this represents a six-month supply)

MAD of forecast error during lead time: 75

Desired service: 95 percent

Service function: 600/75 (1 − 0.95) = 0.4

Table 26–21   Service Function for the Normal Distribution of Forecast Errors (Service Based on Demand Fill Rate)

Safety Factor	Service Function
0.0	.4998
0.2	.4062
0.4	.3252
0.6	.2561
0.8	.1985
1.0	.1510
1.2	.1131
1.4	.0829
1.6	.0600
1.8	.0425
2.0	.0294
2.2	.0199
2.4	.0134
2.6	.0088
2.8	.0056
3.0	.0035
3.2	.0023
3.4	.0015
3.6	.0009
3.8	.0005
4.0	.0004

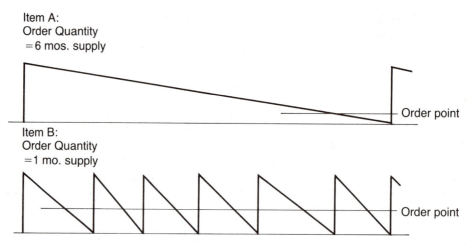

Figure 26-34   Exposure to Stockout of Items with Different Order Quantities

From Table 27–21, the safety factor for a service function of 0.4 is approximately equal to 0.2.

Item B

Order quantity: 100 (annual usage is 1200, so this represents a one-month supply)

MAD of forecast error during lead time: 75

Desired service: 95 percent

Service function: 100/75 (1 − 0.95) = 0.0625

From Table 26–21, the safety factor for a service function of 0.0625 is approximately equal to 1.6. Safety stock would therefore be eight times greater for Item B than for Item A (1.6 ÷ 0.2 = 8).

Note also that the safety factor for demand rate as a measure of service is lower than that when based on frequency of stock-out. In aiming to satisfy a given percentage of demand, it is not possible to know how frequently a stock-out will occur or how large any particular stock-out will be. What is specified is that over a period of time, some desired percentage of demand will be filled from goods on the shelf.

Uncertain Lead Time

Safety stock inventories discussed so far have been in response to uncertainty in demand and the resulting deviations between forecasted sales and actual sales (forecast errors). It has been assumed that lead times for stock replenishment are known and constant. However, it is unusual to find suppliers whose delivery is known exactly; some unreliability or uncertainty is to be expected. The components that make up lead time, such as order preparation and transmittal, order processing, order preparation, and shipping are all subject to variability. Therefore, uncertainty in lead time must be accounted for in inventory planning.

To determine demand during lead time distribution, the MAD of demand during lead time is given by:

$$\text{MAD}_{DLT} = \sqrt{t \cdot \text{MAD}_D^2 + \overline{X^2} \cdot \text{MAD}_{LT}^2}$$

where t = average lead time in periods
MAD_{DLT} = mean absolute deviation of demand during lead time
MAD_D = mean absolute deviation of the average demand distribution per time period (1 week)
$\overline{X}$ = average demand during one time period
MAD_{LT} = mean absolute deviation of the lead time period

If lead time is 2 weeks, MAD_D is 20 units, $\overline{X}$ is 100 per week, and MAD_{LT} is 0.5 weeks, then

$$\text{MAD}_{DLT} = \sqrt{2(20)^2 + 100^2(0.5^2)} = \sqrt{800 + 2500} = 57 \text{ units}$$

Safety stock for this example, if a 95 percent service level based on stock-outs is desired (Table 26–19), is:

Safety stock = MAD × safety stock factor = 57 × 2.06 = 117 units

The average demand during lead time is $t\overline{X}$, so that with 2 weeks lead time and average demand of 100 units per week, average demand during lead time is 200 units. With a known lead time and mean absolute deviation of demand of 20 units given for a one-week period, it is necessary to estimate the MAD of demand during the lead time. Through a process called *convoluting*, the MAD for the two-week lead time can be estimated from the known one-week MAD. Convoluting is accomplished by the formula:

$$\text{MAD}_N = \text{MAD}_D\sqrt{N}$$

where MAD_N = the mean absolute deviation for N periods
N = number of periods
MAD_D = original mean absolute deviation

If N is 2 weeks, and MAD_D is 20 units per week, then

$$\text{MAD}_N = 20\sqrt{2} = 28.3 \text{ units}$$

This is the expected MAD for a two-week lead time period. With a known (certain) lead time, safety stock required for a 98 percent service level based on stock-outs would therefore be:

Safety stock = 28.3 units × 2.06 = 58 units

In the same example, but with uncertain lead time, safety stock was 117 units. As shown in this example, vendor lead time unreliability tends to increase the amount of safety stock required in order to protect against stocking out because of late deliveries from vendors.

Summary

When goods are ordered, there is always uncertainty about customer demand rate during the interval prior to receipt. Decisions about when to order must allow for this uncertainty. If a decision to order is based on average usage, stock-outs can be anticipated during about half the replenishment cycles. Better service requires carrying safety stocks, which should be based on a measure of forecast error. Statistical concepts make it possible to find a safety factor that will yield a specified level of service. Two measures of service have been presented:

- *Frequency of stockout without regard to size of stock-out.* The safety factors are taken directly from the normal curve and are summarized in Table 26–19.

- *Size of stockout without regard to frequency of stock-out.* This measure of service aims at filling a given percentage of demand. The relationship between order quantity and forecast error is considered in setting the safety factor, through use of a formula and Table 26–21.

8.   Multiple Inventory Stocking Points

Two of the more important decisions in logistics system design are those related to how many warehouses should be established in the system and which inventory items should be stocked in each. A third decision is at what stage in the distribution process final changes should be made that differentiate products into unique stockkeeping units. Each of these decisions has to do with the spatial nature of inventories, that is, how inventories behave when divided into smaller lots or located in several stocking locations.

Some of the pioneering research in physical distribution examines the trade-offs between inventory and warehousing costs on the one hand, and transportation costs on the other. Over a relevant range, as more warehouses are included in a physical distribution network, inventory and warehousing are included in a physical distribution network, inventory and warehousing costs tend to increase, while transportation costs tend to decrease (Figure 26–18). Conversely, centralizing certain types of inventory into few locations may reduce inventory and warehousing costs so dramatically that premium cost transportation can be used to maintain or improve service levels. That was the conclusion of the 1956 study by Lewis, Culliton, and Steele,[5] considered by many to be a classic in physical distribution. The study is one of the first examples of the *total cost concept,* which holds that it is more important to minimize the sum of all relevant system costs than to minimize any of the costs independently.

John Magee and Wroe Alderson also recognized the benefits of holding inventories in fewer, larger lots. Magee explored the impact on inventories of proliferating product lines.[6] That is, when more versions of a product are offered (which tends to reduce the sales volume of each version), total inventory requirements are greater.

Alderson explored the timing of differentiation of goods, not only with respect to physical changes in the product but also in connection with the geographical dispersion of inventories. In stating the *Principle of Postponement,* he advocated postponement of changes in the form and identity of a product until the latest possible point in the marketing flow, and postponement of changes in the locations of inventories until the latest possible time.[7]

All of the results discussed above are based on what has come to be known as the *Square Root Law* of inventories. The law states that the total inventory is proportional to the square root of the number of divisions of the inventory into smaller lots, with more divisions requiring proportionately greater amounts of inventory.

Square Root Law of Inventories

In general, products that enjoy large sales require inventories that are proportionately smaller than products with small sales. Of course, in an absolute sense, inventories increase with sales, but they do so at a declining rate. That is because the variability of sales tends to be proportionately less for products with large versus small sales.

In Table 26–18, variability is shown for a typical product line, measured in terms of mean absolute deviation (MAD). The MADs for products in the inventory report from which the data are extracted are plotted on log paper in Figure 26–35. The figure shows that although there is a general correlation between sales variability (MAD) and sales, MAD tends to taper off for products with larger sales. In the figure, the relationship between MAD and sales is described by the formula:

$$MAD = \phi \, S^\gamma$$

where ϕ represents a constant of proportionality that usually lies between 0.2 and 0.6, and γ represents a power that is often close to 1.0.[8] As was discussed in a previous section, safety stock inventories result from demand variability. Therefore, products with larger sales and thus proportionately less demand variability will also require proportionately less inventory.

Based upon the relationship discussed above, if a product with sales of $10,000 per period were located in two warehouses that each averaged $5000 in sales each period, inventory required for the two stock locations would be expected to be greater than if all the stock were located in one warehouse. Intuitively, if demand during a period happened to by $6000 in one warehouse and $4000 in the other due to normal variability, the first warehouse would be out of stock while the second would have stock in excess of demand. If all the inventory were stored in one location, the over and under situation would balance out. In two locations, therefore, a greater amount of safety stock inventory is required to buffer against demand uncertainty.

Similarly, demand during shorter time periods exhibits more variability ("noise") than demand during longer periods. It is far easier to forecast annual demand for a product than daily demand, or even weekly or monthly demand. For each shorter period, the relative forecast error or demand variability will be greater.

Finally, if three versions of a product are offered instead of one, the total inventory required will be greater. For example, one Japanese motorcycle manufacturer offered several color choices for each motorcycle model, while a second manufacturer offered each model in only one color. The manufacturer that differentiated its product on a color basis needed to carry greater levels of safety stock inventory, because a customer who ordered blue often wasn't willing to accept red or green if blue was not in stock. The demand variability of the three stockkeeping units was proportionately greater than if only one color had been offered.

Following the same logic, if differentiation of a product can be deferred as long as possible in the distribution process, less inventory is required. For example, a red Toyota

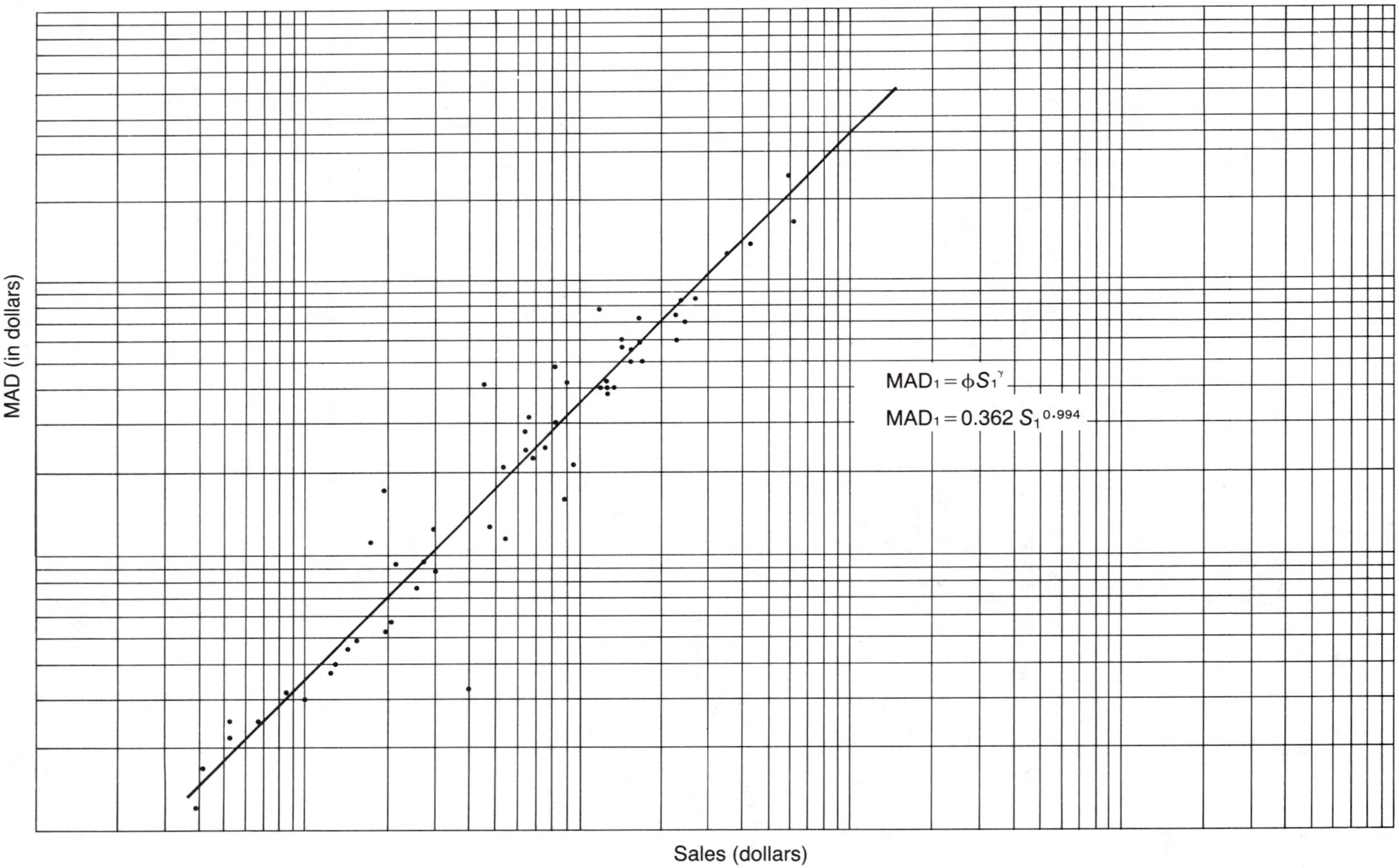

690

MAD (in dollars)

Sales (dollars)

$MAD_1 = \phi S_1^{\gamma}$

$MAD_1 = 0.362 \, S_1^{0.994}$

Figure 26-35 Correlation of MAD with Sal

can become either a red Toyota with air conditioning or one without air conditioning, if that accessory is installed at the port after the customer's specification is known. If the air conditioners were installed at the factory, a supply of automobiles both with and without them would need to be provided, and one could not be substituted for the other. Greater levels of inventory would therefore be required.

The square root law of inventories can be expressed as a formula:

$$I = \frac{I_n}{\sqrt{n}}$$

where I = inventory in one lot
I_n = inventory in n lots
n = number of lots or divisions

This formula determines the inventory that will result when stock is consolidated from n lots (warehouse locations, time periods, product versions etc.) into one lot. If inventory levels are controlled by some form of economic order quantity (EOQ) decision rule, the inventory referred to is the sum of cycle and safety stock inventories.[9] Otherwise, it is more accurate to apply the formula to safety stock inventories only. Safety stock inventory makes up the greater proportion of total inventory, in any case.

The formula may be stated alternatively as:

$$I_n = I\sqrt{n}$$

This version determines the inventory that will result if the inventory in one lot is divided into n sublots.

Finally, the expected demand variability (MAD) when demand for a longer time period is divided into n shorter time periods may be obtained from:

$$\text{MAD}_n = \text{MAD}_d\sqrt{n}$$

where MAD_n = the mean absolute deviation for n time periods
MAD_d = the mean absolute deviation for one time period
n = the number of time periods.

This formula for "convoluting" the probability distribution is repeated from the previous subsection on safety stock. Because safety stock inventory is determined from:

$$\text{Safety stock} = \text{MAD} \times \text{safety factor}$$

it can be seen that safety stock inventory for shorter time periods will also be proportional to the number of time periods.

Table 26–22 illustrates how inventories vary as inventory stocks are divided into a greater number of smaller lots. For example, if a product is stocked in four warehouses instead of one warehouse, inventory required would be $2 million instead of $1 million when the inventory is consolidated in one location. Conversely, a 50 percent reduction in inventory would result from consolidating inventories from four warehouses into one warehouse.

Table 26-22   Relation between Total Inventory and Number of Inventory Lots

Number of Inventory Lots	Dollar Value of Inventory $I\sqrt{n}$	Percentage Reduction in Inventory Due to Consolidation into Fewer Lots $[1 - (1/\sqrt{n})]$
1	$1,000,000	—
2	1,414,200	29.3
3	1,732,100	42.3
4	2,000,000	50.0
5	2,236,100	55.3
10	3,162,300	68.4
15	3,873,000	74.2
20	4,472,100	77.7

Similarly, if five versions of a product are offered instead of one, the amount of inventory required to support the greater variety would be $2,236,100—an increase of $1,236,000. Finally, if marking of a common part that could be stamped with three different part numbers were postponed until orders were received, a 42.3 percent inventory reduction could be effected.

Determining the Optimum Number of Warehouses

Establishing more than one warehouse in a logistics system will generally result in the need for greater amounts of inventory. Of course, if inventory costs were the only consideration, goods would be stocked only at the factories! But inventory costs are not the only factors that are considered in most warehouse location decisions.

In modern warehouse location models, the optimum number of warehouses and the locations of the warehouses are simultaneously determined.[10] Warehouse location models are discussed in detail in Chapter 15 of this handbook. In accordance with the total cost concept, all of the relevant costs, some of which are shown in Figure 26–36, must be considered in such warehouse location models.

Two of the more important costs included in warehouse location models (in addition to inventory costs) are transportation costs and customer service costs. As more warehouses are added to a logistics system, inventory costs tend to rise. However, over a relevant range, transportation costs will tend to decrease, and better customer service can also be provided. Better customer service results in a reduction in the costs of lost sales.

With warehouses acting as freight breakout or product mixing points, merchandise may be shipped to warehouses in more economical, larger, or consolidated shipments. Orders can then be assembled locally, and smaller shipments that are more expensive to ship will move shorter distances from warehouse to customer. This method is more economical than shipping many smaller shipments directly to customers from the factory or remote warehouses.

With stocks of goods located close to customers in markets, rapid delivery to customers is possible. Lost sales due to inadequate service will decline. Of course, as more and more warehouses are located in a logistics system, increased sales due to service improvements are outweighed by increased logistics costs. Also, with too many warehouses, transportation costs eventually begin to climb, because it becomes more difficult to ship to

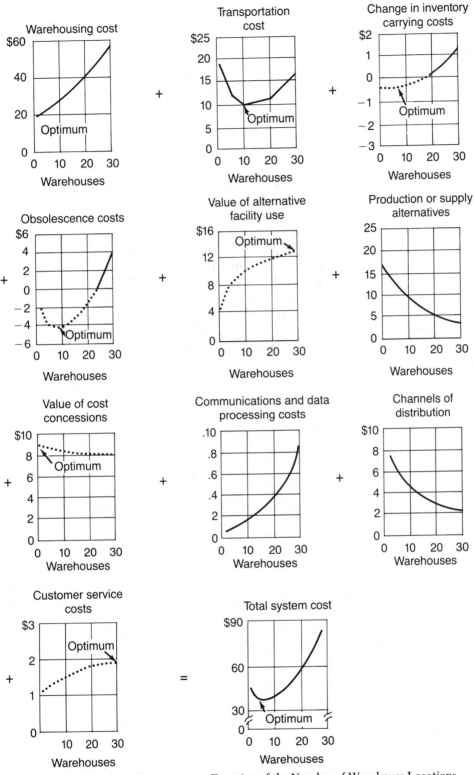

Figure 26-36 Ten Cost Categories as a Function of the Number of Warehouse Locations

SOURCE: Raymond LeKashman and John F. Stolle, "The Total Cost Approach to Distribution," *Business Horizons*, 8 (Winter 1965), p. 39.

multiple locations in full carload or truckload lots or to put together economic consolidations. Computerized warehouse location models trade off the costs of these and the other cost categories to determine the optimum number and location of warehouses.

Selective Stocking Decisions

Once the number and locations of warehouses have been determined, it is necessary to decide which items should be stocked in which warehouses. As discussed earlier, inventory can be reduced by centralizing certain types of inventory into fewer locations. As we have seen, products with a low volume of sales require a greater proportionate amount of inventory than products with greater sales. These "slow-moving" products are prime candidates to be centralized into a master warehouse or regional warehouses.

For example, using the ABC analysis (lognormal) concepts discussed previously (Figure 26–27), the A, B, and C items would typically not all be stocked in all warehouses. Assuming a network of 25 warehouses, the fast-moving A items might be stocked in all warehouses, the middle B items in five regional warehouses, and slow-moving C items stocked only in one master warehouse, or centralized at the factory. This pattern of allocating items to warehouses based on sales volume has come to be known as *selective stocking*. It is based on the fact that inventories for slower-moving items can be drastically reduced when those items are centralized from several to one or a few warehouses.

Of course, the trade-off concept in logistics is based on the fact that no cost reduction in the systems comes without its price. When one cost in a system is reduced, invariably another cost or costs in the system will increase. When inventories of slow-moving products are centralized, inventory costs are reduced. However, transportation costs for those items will increase because smaller quantities of these items will need to be shipped longer distances to customers from more remote warehouses. Unless a more rapid form of transportation is substituted, delivery times and customer service will suffer, often increasing lost sales. The trade-offs between all of the relevant costs must therefore be examined to develop the optimal, lowest cost, system.

An example will illustrate the nature of the analytical process in making selective stocking decisions. Table 26–23 is a sales and inventory comparison of the product line described in the distribution by value report shown in Table 26–18. In this product line, the slow-moving items constitute over 70 percent of all items. They account for only 2 percent of sales, but make up over 19 percent of inventories! Unfortunately, this sales and inventory distribution is very typical of many firms.

The relationship between sales, average inventory, and safety stock inventory is shown in Table 26–24.[11] In the study, all products were stocked in each of seven warehouses. The impact of centralizing the inventory of slow-moving items into one master warehouse can be expressed by the following formula:

$$SS_1 = \frac{SS_n}{\sqrt{n}}$$

where SS = safety stock for n locations
n = number of locations
SS_1 = safety stock for one location

If SS is \$1,906,014, and n is 7, then

Table 26-23   Sales and Inventory Comparison

	Item Rank	Percentage Items	Cumulative Sales	Cumulative Percentage Sales	Cumulative Inventory	Cumulative Percentage Inventory
Faster-moving items	5	0.03	$ 397,075	5.45	$ 65,494	0.89
	16	0.10	730,034	10.02	168,529	2.28
	35	0.23	1,158,439	15.90	273,619	3.71
	60	0.39	1,467,356	20.14	423,811	5.74
	90	0.58	1,889,201	25.93	519,596	7.04
	126	0.82	2,191,561	30.08	605,878	8.21
	168	1.09	2,630,165	36.10	818,810	11.09
	219	1.42	2,936,895	40.31	969,318	13.13
	279	1.81	3,307,741	45.40	1,170,275	15.85
	351	2.28	3,642,887	50.00	1,426,836	19.33
	520	3.37	4,328,478	59.41	1,983,765	26.87
	839	5.44	5,231,186	70.01	2,583,700	35.00
	1632	10.00	6,137,337	84.07	3,847,835	52.13
	2452	15.90	6,570,312	90.18	4,528,340	61.34
	4442	28.80	7,130,588	97.87	5,974,785	80.94
Slower-moving items	6493	42.10	7,249,346	99.00	6,382,854	86.47
	9253	60.00	7,273,243	99.83	7,308,491	99.00
	12318	79.87	7,285,775	100.00	7,352,416	99.60
	15422	100.00	7,285,775	100.00	7,381,999	100.00

	Percentage Items	Percentage Sales	Percentage Inventory
Faster-Moving Items	28.80	97.87	80.94
Slower-Moving Items	71.20	2.13	19.06
Total	100.00	100.00	100.00

Table 26–24   Relationship of Sales, Average Inventory, and Safety Stock Inventory

Category	Percentage Sales	SKUs	Average Inventory	Safety Stock
		1980 INVENTORY		
Faster-moving items	97	4,442	$5,974,785	$5,676,046
Slower-moving items	3	10,980	1,407,214	1,336,853
Totals	100	15,422	$7,381,999	$7,012,899
		1985 INVENTORY (ESTIMATE)		
Faster-moving items	97	6,600	$8,524,337	$8,098,120
Slower-moving items	3	15,400	2,006,331	1,906,014
Totals	100	22,000	$10,530,668	$10,004,134

$$SS_1 = \frac{\$1,906,014}{\sqrt{7}} = \$720,406$$

The consolidation of slow-moving inventory has reduced inventory from $1,906,014 to $720,406—a savings of $1,185,609.

To complete the analysis, it was necessary to analyze the impact on transportation costs and customer service of centralizing the inventories of slow-moving items into one warehouse. Table 26–25 contains comparative costs for shipping slow-moving parts from one master warehouse versus from the regional warehouses. If the same transportation methods were used, transportation costs would be expected to increase by $56,900. Delivery service would be decreased—customers would receive shipments within a three-to seven-day period instead of within three days. Because of the longer delivery time, the incremental costs of changing the shipping method to UPS Blue Label (air) service to maintain customer service delivery times were determined.

The inventory and transportation cost trade-offs relating to customer service, along with three alternative strategies, can be summarized as follows:

Inventory reduction due to master warehouse	$1,185,609
Inventory carrying cost	0.25
Reduction in cost of carrying inventory	$ 296,402
Increase in transportation cost	
(from 3 to 7 days' service, Table 26–25)	56,900
Net annual benefit of national (master) warehouse	$ 239,502
Less cost to provide 3-day service nationwide	74,896
Net annual cost savings with 3-day service	$ 164,606

Alternative Strategies

1. *Dealers absorb transportation costs.*
   Total reduction in inventory cost is savings to
   distributor: $ 296,402

Table 26-25 Comparative Costs for Shipping Slower Moving Parts from Master Versus Regional Warehouses

Shipping Point	Parts Sales in Dollars	Slow-Moving Parts (3%)	Weight in Pounds	Zone	No. of Outbound Shipments	Rate Per Shipment	Outbound Freight	Inbound Freight	Total Freight
NEW METHOD									
Slow-moving parts in one master warehouse at Los Angeles		$4,143,000	933,107	all	37,324	various	$209,536	$232,811	$442,347
OLD METHOD									
Slow-moving parts at regional warehouses									
Baltimore	$ 32,300,000	$ 969,000	218,243	4	8,730	2.90	$ 25,317	$ 63,727	$ 89,044
Atlanta	27,000,000	810,000	182,432	4	7,297	2.90	21,161	58,871	80,032
Lincoln	25,000,000	753,000	169,595	4	6,784	2.90	19,674	52,405	72,079
New Jersey	16,000,000	480,000	108,100	3	4,324	2.48	10,724	31,568	42,292
Los Angeles	14,400,000	432,000	97,297	5	3,892	3.68	14,323	24,276	38,599
Dallas	12,300,000	369,000	83,108	4	3,324	2.90	9,640	24,276	33,916
Seattle	11,000,000	330,000	74,324	5	2,973	3.68	10,941	18,544	29,485
Totals	$138,100,000	$4,143,000	933,107		37,324		$111,780	$273,667	$385,477

Increased transportation costs due to shipping from master warehouse (3- to 7-day service) $ 56,900

Incremental cost to provide 3-day UPS Blue Label Service to 31 eastern states   74,896

Total cost for 3-day service anywhere in country $131,796

2. *Distributor absorbs additional transportation
   cost for normal 3- to 7-day service.*
   Savings to distributor: $ 239,502
3. *Distributor absorbs transportation cost to pro-
   vide expedited (UPS Blue Label) service.*
   Savings to distributor: $ 164,606

Because in this example orders are shipped F.O.B. collect from the warehouses, all additional freight costs due to centralizing the inventory of slow-moving parts could feasibly be shifted to the dealers. In that case, the full reduction in inventory carrying costs would accrue to the distributor. However, this policy could very well result in lost sales, because the dealers' freight costs would be increased at the same time order delivery service for slow-moving parts would be decreased. Of course, dealers would also be faced with split deliveries of their orders, and A and B items shipped from the regional warehouses and C items shipped from the master warehouse.

In order to reduce the impact on the dealer, the distributor has the option of absorbing the additional surface transportation costs. In that case, the only impact on the dealer would be lengthier delivery times for slow-moving parts. Or, the distributor could absorb all of the transportation costs required to provide expedited service. In that case, the dealer would receive the same (or better) delivery service, and the distributor would still obtain a substantial cost reduction due to the magnitude of savings in inventory carrying costs.

The Principle of Postponement *

Postponement is the delay to the last possible moment of the final formulation or commitment of a product. Although the concept is simple, the full potential in industry of saving money through the practice of postponement has not been reached. What if, for example, you could make an inventory of 20,000 units replace a previous inventory of 100,000, simply by converting branded merchandise into products with no brand name? It's possible— and it's being done right now. Some of the questions a manager can ask to identify postponement opportunities are listed here:

1. Do we produce identical products under separate brands?

2. How is the final brand name applied?

3. Can the product be remotely assembled?

4. What is the cost saving in shipping the product in a knocked down (KD) condition?

5. What is the cost of remote assembly?

6. What are the quality control risks of remote assembly?

7. What are quality control risks of remote branding?

---

*This section is drawn from Kenneth B. Ackerman, "Postponement: A Dramatic Improvement in Logistics Efficiency," *Warehousing and Physical Distribution Productivity Report,* **14**, No. 12, (December 15, 1979).

8. What are customer service levels for the product?

9. Does our competition have a postponement strategy?

10. What is the cost advantage of bulk shipment of our product?

11. What is the cost of remote packaging of the product?

12. What is the quality control risk of remote packaging?

13. What is the cost of moving the product through each channel of distribution?

14. Can the product skip one or more of these channels?

Alderson was the first marketing expert to write about postponement. In 1950, he observed that the most general method which can be applied in promoting the efficiency of a marketing system is the postponement of differentiation for example, to postpone changes in form and identity to the latest point in the marketing flow or to postpone changes in inventory location to the latest possible time.[12] Minimization of the risk of speculation is achieved by delaying differentiation of the product to the time of purchase. Savings in transportation of goods are achieved because merchandise is moved in larger quantities, in bulk, or in relatively undifferentiated states.

Postponement was described by Alderson as the opposite of speculation. A speculative inventory is put into a distribution center whenever the cost of carrying that inventory is less than the profit derived from having that inventory readily available to stimulate purchases.

Types of Postponement

A typical product moves through four channels: from manufacturer to distributor to retailer to consumer. In practicing postponement, the manufacturer seeks ways to bypass or at least postpone the movement of the product through each of these channels. Movement through each involves costs of transactions as well as the costs of storage, transportation, and inventory carrying costs. The principle of postponement prescribes minimization of these costs by delaying or bypassing some of the stages between producer and consumer.

Postponement can take any of several forms:

1. Postponement of commitment

2. Postponement of passage of title

3. Postponement of branding or marking

4. Postponement of consumer packaging

5. Postponement of final assembly

6. Postponement of mixture or blending

POSTPONEMENT OF COMMITMENT

This is the delay of shipping of a product in order to reduce the risk of committing it incorrectly. One way to practice postponement is to use air freight, which enables some manufacturers to eliminate field inventories by keeping the entire stockpile at a factory distribution center located at the end of the assembly line. Using air freight, product is moved into the market at speeds that are competitive with speed of shipment from regional distribution centers. This enables the manufacturer to avoid the potential waste of committing the wrong product to the wrong distribution center, later having to cross-ship products to correct an imbalance of inventory.

The most efficient distribution point is always at the end of the assembly line, since inventory which is at the point of manufacture will never have to be backhauled because of an error in commitment. If air freight is fast enough to allow all inventory to be kept at the factory, a manufacturer may trade off the premium costs of air freight by eliminating inventory losses from errors in commitment, or obsolescence.

With some merchandise, postponement of commitment includes avoidance of certain distribution channels. For example, an appliance retailer may have floor samples of each major appliance located on the sales floor to show prospective customers. However, when the customer's inspection results in a sale, the actual appliance delivered to that customer is not the same one that is in the store—indeed, it may not even be in the same city until after the customer has bought it. By using premium transportation from strategically located distribution centers, the appliance distributor will avoid committing inventory to each retail store. In this case, postponement is particularly useful because of the cost of handling, storing, and carrying inventory of bulky and costly items such as major appliances. If the customer cannot take the item home in a shopping bag, why put the item in the store?

POSTPONEMENT OF TITLE PASSAGE

Sometimes delaying passage of title is described by the term "consignment." For example, a chain grocery retailer makes annual purchase commitments for canned vegetable items. His purchasing agreement calls for these items to be shipped to a public warehouse located at a point convenient to the retailer. However, the contract also specifies that warehousing charges will be paid by the manufacturer, and passage of title is postponed until the product is released from the warehouse.

Since the public warehouseman is an independent bailee, the manufacturer still has a measure of control over the inventory. However, the retailer has control over the inventory also, since it is located at a point convenient to him and he has the power to release it upon call. By delaying passage of title, the buyer reduces his cost of carrying inventory. Yet, by positioning stocks at a warehouse which is convenient to him, he has postponed passage of title without any sacrifice in customer service.

POSTPONEMENT OF BRANDING OR MARKING

A vegetable canner may produce canned peas for his own house brand, as well as for the private brands of several different chain retailers. To meet these several brand requirements, he puts up all of the canned peas "in bright" (cans which contain no labels). Typically, these cans are held at the factory warehouse until orders are received for one of the private labels. The product is run through a casing and labeling line after the order is received, so that the manufacturer avoids the risk of putting the wrong label on a product and subsequently having to relabel it. He also avoids the possibility of being out of stock on some labels while trading excess supplies of others.

This type of postponement can be further refined if the manufacturer ships goods in bright to market area distribution centers. By positioning bright cans and casing and labeling lines in distribution facilities which are close to the market, the canner can substantially improve customer service and still avoid the speculation of producing private label merchandise which may be slow to sell. Also, by postponing a commitment to perhaps many different private labels, one field inventory can do the work of many.

POSTPONEMENT OF CONSUMER PACKAGING

A pioneer in the manufacture of soft drinks, Coca-Cola, determined many years ago that its manufacturing strategy would be to produce a concentrated syrup which would be delivered to soda fountains or regional bottlers who would dilute it with carbonated water and deliver it in a package that was convenient and attractive for the consumer. Similarly, manufacturers of whiskey move the product across the ocean in bulk, then bottle it in the country in which it is to be sold. The risk of breakage and pilferage of glass bottles is eliminated, and a more favorable customs duty applies in some cases.

Another example involves an Italian toy manufacturer who produces a light density item. The item is shipped in bulk boxes to a warehouse at the port of entry. At that point, consumer packages purchased in the United States for the American market are also received, and the product is moved from bulk shipping container to the final consumer package. Not only are freight costs reduced, but the consumer package is more attractive because it has not been subjected to the potential wear and tear of long distance transportation. If the packaging were done in a foreign trade zone (FTZ), the import duty on the product might also be reduced.

POSTPONEMENT OF FINAL ASSEMBLY

Postponement of final assembly is an accepted strategy in the automobile industry. Regional assembly plants allow the auto maker to delay final assembly of most vehicles until customer orders are received. Common components such as engines, frames, or body parts can be produced and inventoried at lower cost and lower risk than completed vehicles. When the Oldsmobile division of General Motors uses the slogan "Can we build one for you?" it is expressing the idea that a maximum number of vehicles are built to fill a customer or dealer order. By doing this, Oldsmobile avoids the risk of overproducing certain models in a California plant and then having to transport these vehicles to Ohio.

POSTPONEMENT OF BLENDING

One widely recognized example of a delay of mixture or blending is the multi-grade gasoline pump developed by Sun Oil Company. Sunoco offers its customers the ability to blend five different combinations of higher and lower octane gasoline at the time the purchase is made.

Several paint manufacturers offer customers the ability to have paint colors custom mixed at the retail outlet. This is a variation of postponement of final assembly, but in this case it simply involves controlling the final mixture or blending of the product which is sold.

Increased Distribution Efficiency

What does postponement do for distribution efficiency? First, it enables one inventory to do the work of many. Where blending is postponed, a single stockkeeping unit is convertible to many others as the final brand is applied. For example, in one line of automotive batteries, the only difference between private labels is a decal which is applied to the top of the battery. By delaying the application of the decal and the final consumer package until the last moment, the number of line items in the warehouse is dramatically reduced.

Second, postponement can result in significant reduction of freight costs, which are usually the largest component of physical distribution costs. In the auto industry, undoubtedly much of the incentive for regional assembly plants was freight reduction—it is far cheaper to ship densely packed components than finished cars.

The delay of final branding or packaging also reduces the risk of obsolescence. Certain brands may decline in popularity, and that decline reduces the warehouse turnover and increases the risk that the product will become obsolete from a marketing standpoint.

The possibilities of postponement are limited only by the imagination of the distribution manager. Any product that has multiple private brands, a fragile consumer package, a bulky configuration in final assembly, or a very slight modification from one form to another is a candidate for postponement. Products which today are packed only at the factory and are frequently subject to breakage, obsolescence, or high freight costs may be shipped in an unbranded, unpackaged bulk state to a regional distribution and assembly center. There is no reason why application of the principle of postponement may not be far more widespread in the future than it is today.

Potential Challenges

While productivity advantages is practices of postponement are substantial, the challenges are equally so. The practicing of postponement to a warehouse level usually requires the warehouse operator to enter a whole new business: that of assembly or packaging. This creates additional risks in quality control. In the course of packaging, the product may be damaged or contaminated. It could even be mislabeled or put in the wrong package. As final assembly is transferred to several remote locations, quality control in the assembly may be compromised.

Ultimately, the widespread use of postponement could turn today's distribution centers into tomorrow's packaging and light assembly centers. However, the management and labor skills involved at the warehouse level will be far higher than those needed for merely receiving, storing, and reshipping.

9.   Material Requirements Planning

Material requirements planning (MRP) differs from conventional inventory systems in two fundamental ways. First, MRP is based on dependent or derived demand while conventional inventory methods are based on independent demand. Demand is considered independent when it is not related to the demand for some other item. Independent demand is the cumulative effect of numerous unrelated purchase decisions whose logic is only partially known, at best.

Dependent demand, on the other hand, depends on or is related to the known demand for one or more items. For example, a manufacturer of wooden pencils needs a dozen erasers for every dozen pencils made. Ten erasers are not enough, and fourteen have no advantage over a dozen. The demand for erasers depends on the demand for pencils; when you know how many pencils you are going to make, you know how many erasers you need.

The other difference between MRP and conventional systems relates to the timing of inventory purchases and production. With conventional inventory systems, orders for additional stock are triggered by depletion of existing inventory levels. The orders have no direct relationship with the production processes that will use that inventory.

MRP tries to match purchases and production directly. With conventional inventory systems, planned purchases and inventories are related more to past than to future production. The manufacturer of pencils, however, needs the erasers at the time of production. Production cannot proceed if the erasers have not yet arrived and there is no advantage in having the erasers in stock a week before they are needed.

Requirements for MRP

MRP does not function in isolation (Figure 26–37). Its use requires or assumes several things. Probably the most important requirement for MRP is a master production schedule that has been fixed far enough in advance to allow for proper planning. The master production schedule is a statement of how many end items are to be produced and when they are to be made. This schedule is often based on a special scheduling calendar with consecutively numbered weeks, which makes planning easier and less ambiguous. The schedule can remain tentative for a while, but at some point it must be fixed so that proper planning can take place and the appropriate purchases of materials can be made. This fixed time period is mostly a function of the purchasing lead times involved. It does little good to schedule the production of pencils one week hence if it takes two weeks to procure the necessary erasers.

Another requirement is that the master production schedule must be stated in terms of the raw materials and subassemblies required. This requires an accurate and unambiguous bill of materials which lists all of the assemblies, subassemblies, and components that make up the end product. The schedule must also reflect the actual stages of production and their relationship. Each inventory item must be identified with a unique code or designation, and even minor differences will require a unique part number.

Accurate and up-to-date inventory records are also required. This means that every inventory item under control must go into and out of stock, however brief the time in inventory may be. MRP also assumes that lead times for every inventory item are known and unvarying.

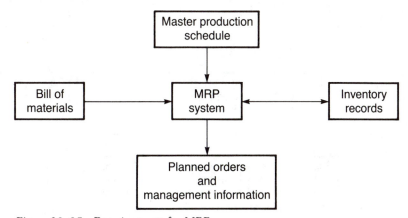

Figure 26-37   Requirements for MRP

The Logic of MRP

The following equation represents the underlying logic of MRP:

$$N = G - R - O$$

where N = net requirements
         G = gross requirements
         R = scheduled receipts
         O = inventory on hand

A positive value for net requirements represents a potential shortage that must be covered by an order for that item. This type of calculation must be performed for every controlled inventory item for every time period within the planning horizon.

An Example of MRP

To illustrate this concept, a small desk lamp will be used as an example. The bill of materials for this lamp is shown in Figure 26–38.

The master production schedule for this lamp is shown in Figure 26–39. In this example, production is scheduled six weeks in advance.

The term gross requirements refers to the demand at each part level. It does not refer to the total number of parts used in the end products. Using the desk lamp as an example, assume that 20,000 lamps are to be produced in a given week. Also assume that 1000 case assemblies are already in inventory. In this case, the gross requirement for switches is the

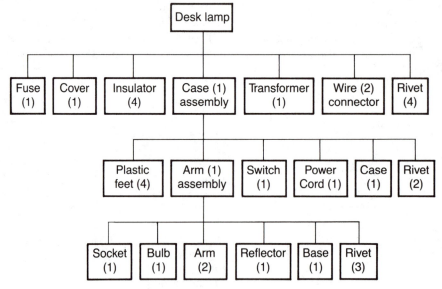

Figure 26-38   A Bill of Materials

Week	1	2	3	4	5	6
Production	20	15	20	25	10	20

Figure 26-39 Master Production Schedule (Thousands of Units)

19,000 switches needed to produce the 19,000 case assemblies required, not the 20,000 switches that will be in the 20,000 completed lamps.

To illustrate the calculation of net requirements, assume that 1000 case assemblies, 2000 arm assemblies, and 5000 rivets are currently in inventory. Further, assume that 50,000 rivets are already on order and scheduled to arrive in time for the planned production.

The gross requirement for case assemblies (Figure 26–40) is 20,000—the planned production for the net period. The gross requirement for rivets at this level is 80,000 because four rivets are required in the assembly of each completed lamp. This does not, however, represent the total gross requirement for rivets, because they appear in every level of production. To find the total gross requirement for rivets, the gross requirement has to be calculated for each level of production and then added.

The net requirement for case assemblies is 19,000. This is determined by subtracting the 1000 case assemblies already in stock from the gross requirement of 20,000. In the example, no scheduled receipts have been assumed. This net requirement represents the gross requirement for the next level of production.

The gross requirement for arm assemblies is 19,000 and for rivets it is 38,000. Because 2000 arm assemblies are in stock, the net requirement for arm assemblies is 17,000. Again, no arm assemblies have been assumed as scheduled receipts. These 17,000 assemblies represent the gross requirements for the final level of production. This generates an additional gross requirement for rivets of 51,000. The total gross requirement for rivets is 169,000, which yields a net requirement of 114,000 after subtracting the 5000 in stock and the 50,000 on order.

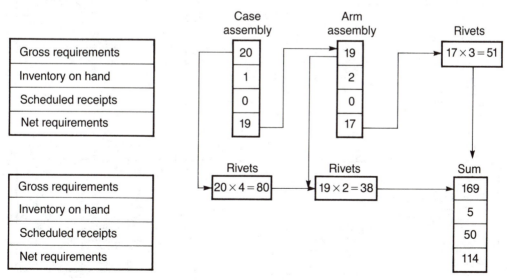

Figure 26-40 Net Requirement Calculations (Thousand of Units)

The previous calculations determined the magnitude of the net requirements from the master production schedule, but not the timing of these requirements. To do that, the lead time for the purchase or production of each inventory item is required. Assume that the lead time required for every item is one week, except for the case and arm assemblies which have a lead time of two weeks. Figure 26-41 shows how these lead times are accounted for. The 20,000 units of scheduled production are those shown in the master production schedule for the sixth week.

Figure 26-41 also illustrates the cumulative effect of lead time and multiple stages of production. Some of the rivets that will end up in lamps produced in the sixth week must be ordered as early as the first week. This is because it takes one week to receive the rivets after they are ordered, two weeks to make the arm assembly it is a part of, and two more weeks to make the case assembly that uses the arm assembly. Because the rivets appear in

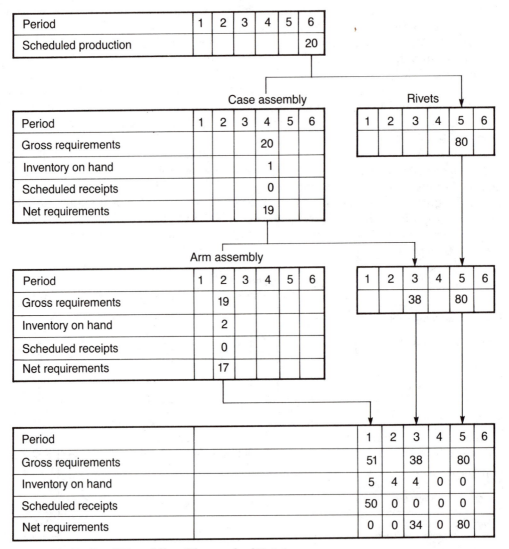

Figure 26-41   Lead Time Offset (Thousands of Units)

all three stages of production, the total requirement for rivets will appear in three different time periods. They cannot simply be added as was done in Figure 26–40, when timing was not considered. This cumulative effect of lead time has shortened our planning horizon substantially. Even though production is scheduled for a six-week period, we have only a single week of information relating to the components of the arm assembly. This is not a sufficient data base for long-term considerations such as capacity planning.

The basic output information of the MRP system is a schedule of planned orders over the planning horizon. Such a schedule is shown in Table 26–26 for a few selected items using the example master production schedule. The calculations in this table are based on a few additional assumptions. It was assumed that the production of case and arm assemblies is limited to a maximum of 20,000 units a week and that there are no penalties associated with producing fewer than this number. Further, it was assumed that rivets are ordered in lots of 400,000.

The planning horizon must be at least as long as the longest path through the bill of materials. If it is not, orders will not be placed soon enough and the MRP system will fail. It should be remembered that the bill of materials was designed to show the actual flow of production. In this example, every component of the arm assembly can be obtained with only one week's lead time. It takes two weeks more to make the arm assembly and an additional two weeks to make the case assembly. Since this plan starts one week in the fu-

Table 26–26   System Output

Period	1	2	3	4	5	6
Scheduled production	20	15	20	25	10	20
Planned orders—Case Assembly	20	25	10	20		
Planned orders—Rivets	100	80	60	40	80	
CASE ASSEMBLY						
Gross requirements	20	25	10	20		
Inventory on hand	5	5	0	0		
Scheduled receipts	20	20	0	0		
Net requirements	0	0	10	20		
Planned orders—Arm Assembly	10	20				
Planned orders—Rivets	50	20	40			
ARM ASSEMBLY						
Gross requirements	10	20				
Inventory on hand	0	0				
Scheduled receipts	10	20				
Net requirements	0	0				
Planned orders—Bulbs	20					
Planned orders—Rivets	60					
RIVETS						
Gross requirements	210	100	100	40	80	
Inventory on hand	10	200	100	0	0	
Scheduled receipts	400	0	0	0	0	
Net requirements	0	0	0	40	80	
Planned orders—Rivets			400			

ture, the planning horizon must be at least six weeks long in this example. The longest path need not be the path with the largest number of steps to be performed. In this example, if the lead time required for the purchase of transformers were six weeks instead of one week, it would create the longest path. The planning horizon would also have to be extended one week for a total of seven.

Safety Stock

No attempt was made in the previous examples to include safety stocks. They can, however, be incorporated by subtracting the desired level of safety stock from inventory on hand or adding that amount to the gross requirements. The primary purpose of safety stocks is to protect against unanticipated demand, but there is no unanticipated demand in the manufacturing environment discussed here. Safety stocks would be costly and serve no useful purpose in this instance.

There is a secondary purpose for carrying safety stock: to protect against uncertainty in supply. Minor supply problems can be handled without safety stock. Orders can be expedited, other sources of supply can be used or minor changes in the production schedule can be made.

If the uncertainty is significant or long-term, it may be better to carry safety stock. The amount of safety stock that is necessary is determined in the same way as it is for conventional inventory systems so these procedures will not be repeated here. Safety stocks are also required for those parts and assemblies made for service or repair usage. Even though these are exactly the same parts as used in the finished product, they are normally accounted for separately. Any uncertainties associated with the master production schedule are usually better handled with safety stocks of finished items. Again, these are not part of the MRP system.

Lot Size

Some very simple assumptions were made in the previous examples about lot size. Lot-for-lot ordering was assumed in most cases. The planned order quantity was simply the net requirement for each period. This is a very effective decision rule when purchasing very expensive items or when dealing with items that are seldom called for. It is also applicable to items that must be made continuously with specialized equipment. There are several disadvantages associated with this procedure, however. The procedure ignores important economic costs and the order quantity must be recomputed every time a change in plans is made.

Other methods used to determine the size of planned orders include arbitrary decision rules and several variants of conventional economic order quantity (EOQ) methods. Common arbitrary methods include ordering in truckload quantities or ordering the minimum quantity necessary to obtain a price discount. These are not totally inappropriate methods since they do consider some of the economic factors involved. They ignore inventory carrying costs and order or setup costs which are taken into account in conventional EOQ methods described elsewhere in this chapter. These methods attempt to minimize the sum of order costs and inventory carrying costs.

Variations of these methods try to make adjustments for discontinuous usage. The idea is to avoid receiving a large shipment at the beginning of a long period of low usage in anticipation of a large increase in demand at the end of the planning horizon. These procedures are quite involved and beyond the scope of this explanation. Standard computer algorithms, such as the Wagner-Whitin algorithm, are available. Lot size may also have to be adjusted for scrap allowance, space available for storage, financial constraints, processing requirements, and so forth.

Implementation

The problems of implementation must be considered at two levels. The first involves specific details of calculating procedures. The second involves the broader problems of switching from current inventory methods to MRP.

MRP systems require a basic unit of time to be selected for planning purposes. This time period is commonly one week. It is seldom less than one day or more than one month. At the end of this unit of time, all calculations are out of date. If we are planning on a weekly basis, for example, all calculations will be out of date at the end of every week.

Our plans for the week have become reality. However, things may not have gone as planned. Our production schedule has been extended another week so that we can utilize the new information available to us. We have to reevaluate and extend our plans.

Traditionally, all of our calculations are redone at the end of every planning period. Every product on the master production schedule must be exploded into component requirements. Every bill of material and inventory record must be examined and recomputed. This batch-processing run on the computer is called schedule regeneration. The longer our planning period, the more likely it is that our records are out-of-date and the longer it takes to become aware of deviations from our plans. If we reduce the length of the planning period, we increase calculation costs and output significantly.

The alternative is to examine only the differences caused by a change in plans or circumstances. This is called the "net change concept." Using this method of calculation, only those parts of the master production schedule, bill of materials, inventory records, and planned orders that are different will be examined. Timeliness is gained at the expense of efficiency.

When the decision has been made to abandon the conventional inventory methods now used in favor of MRP, what do you do? Do you set a date to change over and abandon the conventional methods completely at that point—quit "cold turkey"? Alternatives include the parallel approach and the pilot approach. The parallel approach involves the use of both methods for some period of time until the bugs have been worked out and the people involved have become familiar with MRP. With the pilot approach, a small part of the product line is selected and the MRP system is used on just that part for comparisons. The cold turkey approach will usually overwhelm and frustrate the people involved, while the parallel approach requires more time and resources than are usually available to do the job right. The pilot approach is therefore often the method recommended.

Using MRP

An MRP system requires action—a new action or a revision of a previously called-for action. If a new action is called for, the system must identify each separate item and specify the quantity to be ordered or manufactured. A release date and a due date must also be specified. A revision of a previous action can involve a change in quantity or due date or both. Increasing the order quantity or advancing the due date of the order will present the greatest problems and require more advanced planning. More rapid and more expensive communication and transportation may be required. Other suppliers may have to be located and overtime pay may have to be authorized.

An up-to-date MRP system does more than reduce production inventories. It can increase sales by allowing you to ship more promptly and reliably. The system can be programmed to provide an accounting of the uncommitted portion of the master production schedule. When a customer calls, you can quickly determine what you can promise in terms of quantity and date of availability. If you have customers who occasionally need rush orders, you may even want to build in some extra capacity just to meet emergency needs. If the emergency need does not arise, MRP will allow you to quickly convert the excess capacity to another use.

Planning and Control

If properly designed, an MRP system can also provide information useful for purposes other than inventory control. It can provide information to help plan and control open-order priorities and it can provide input for capacity planning.

The MRP system constantly reevaluates open-order due dates in an attempt to keep the order priorities valid. This is a simple mechanical problem of matching the due date with the date of need. Maintaining the integrity of priorities is more difficult. The master production schedule must not call for production that cannot be met for want of material, lead time, or capacity. The computer can be programmed to recognize some of these limits, but the inventory planner must look for some, too. Integrity is compromised when an item is not used in the quantities anticipated and there is still a large inventory when the next open-order due date approaches. Integrity is also compromised when a order for one component of an assembly is delayed beyond its due date while the due dates remain the same for the other components. If an order has been delayed beyond its due date, MRP allows the inventory planner to determine which parent items will be affected and how many resulting component orders will be affected. It will identify each affected order and determine exactly how it should be scheduled.

MRP also provides useful information to aid in capacity planning. Once the MRP system has generated period-by-period requirements, these requirements can be converted into the capacities required to produce these items. By comparing the projected load for each period with capacity, management will know if they have sufficient capacity to meet the master production schedule. If there is insufficient capacity in any period, the load report will indicate the duration of the shortage. If the shortage of capacity is only projected for a short time period, management can adopt temporary measures. Overtime and temporary transfers may allow them to increase capacity for a short period of time. If the load report indicates a continuing shortage of capacity, more permanent measures are indicated. New machines may have to be purchased or another shift added.

10.   Physical Inventory and Cycle Count Systems

In general, there are two ways to establish and maintain accurate inventory records. One is the *periodic (wall-to-wall) physical inventory*, where all stock is counted. The second is a *cycle count* system where selected items are counted on an ongoing basis (daily, weekly, monthly, etc.), with all items being counted at least once during the year. A proven cycle count system will be accepted by many accounting firms in lieu of the periodic physical inventory, saving costly shutdown time and expensive labor hours needed for the preplanning usually required for a periodic physical inventory.

The Periodic Physical Inventory

The most common method for counting inventory is the *periodic physical inventory*, or the wall-to-wall inventory, where all inventory items are counted and inventory records adjusted. In small companies, typically retail establishments, frequent physical inventories are taken to determine products and quantities still in stock. Larger companies, with established perpetual inventory control systems (either manual or computerized), need to count their inventory less frequently. An annual inventory is required by outside accountants to substantiate a corporation's inventory investment, and to attest that records are properly kept in an acceptable accounting method.

Before a physical inventory is taken, a comprehensive procedure should be written and agreed upon by both the management of the corporation and the outside accounting firm used by the corporation. Once this procedure is agreed upon, the physical inventory can be planned and conducted. The following basic planning steps can be followed.

1. Determine the inventory method to use

2. State in writing the procedure to be followed

3. Determine relevant inventory dates (paper work cut-off and shutdown), and notify company personnel, accounting firm, vendors, and customers

4. Assign inventory responsibilities

5. Conduct pre-inventory preparation

6. Determine supply and equipment needs

7. Train personnel

8. Count inventory

9. Verify count and correct any errors

10. Update the computer inventory records

11. Obtain an acceptance of inventory figure ("buy-off") from the auditors

12. Analyze and discuss all inventory problems encountered

13. Make corrections to inventory control procedures

14. Prepare and submit physical inventory report

Determining the Inventory Method to Use

Many factors have to be considered when determining the best method for taking physical inventory: how your inventory records are maintained (computer based or manually), the size and type of inventory to be counted, the method used for locating the stock, time and manpower restrictions, and auditing controls (to insure all stock is counted and counted accurately).

The two most determining factors are the inventory recordkeeping method and the auditing controls. If you have a computer-based inventory control system you can use either a preprinted computer listing or preprinted tags. Manual systems, using handwritten cards or tags, will not be discussed in this writing. The auditing can be done *in advance*, *during*, or *after* the inventory counting, or in some combination of these. The "advance" method is usually based on a predetermined number of inventory items (selected according to dollar value); the "during" method is based on a random sampling; and the "after" method is usually for items with dollar or quantity variances over a predetermined amount. The best method to use will be determined by the unique circumstances of each company.

There are as many inventory methods as there are companies. The method presented below uses a computer listing that offers:

1. Simplicity and speed in accurately updating computer-based inventory records. Since you only enter the exceptions to your inventory records you do not zero your computer inventory file. The input time is greatly reduced and the chance for error is reduced as well, because there are fewer inputs.

2. Better document control because each computer sheet contains about 30 items. Single inventory tags are more likely to be lost or misplaced.

Writing the Procedure to Be Followed

This procedure should be as comprehensive as possible. The purpose is to insure that all facets of the inventory are conducted according to a set schedule and that all necessary actions are taken. This procedure should outline the necessary actions from determining the inventory dates, through the actual inventory taking, to your final variance analysis and report to management. There are certain critical lead times when it comes to ordering supplies or renting additional equipment that must receive special attention. Ample time should be allowed to insure delivery ahead of the dates you will be requiring these items.

In many companies the annual inventory is taken at the same time each year, usually just before the end of the fiscal year. Because this is not generally one of the most popular company activities, personnel may sometimes "forget" the relevant dates and plan vacations during this time. These dates should be scheduled far enough in advance so that your accounting firm can dedicate auditing personnel. Your customers and vendors must be notified of the cut-off dates so that deliveries and shipments can be scheduled around this activity. It is possible to receive and ship during a physical inventory; because confusion and delays are likely to occur, this should be avoided if at all possible. A general outline for a physical inventory procedure should include:

A. Objective

B. Organization

C. Date of inventory

D. Operating cut-off needs

    1. Interplant movement
    2. Audit and clean-up guidelines
    3. Prepackaging instructions
    4. Special equipment locations

E. Pre-inventory planning

    1. Listing requirements
    2. Audit and clean-up guidelines
    3. Prepackaging instructions
    4. Special equipment locations
    5. Inventory listing and tag requirements

F. Inventory operating procedure

    1. Training
    2. Supervision guidelines
    3. Counting instructions
    4. Identifying and correcting stocking errors
    5. Auditing guidelines
    6. Inventory update steps
    7. Inventory pricing method

G. Inventory reconciliation

    1. Packing sheet suspense (orders filled but not shipped)
    2. Invoice suspense (invoices released but not paid)
    3. Work-in-process (reductions from stock not yet allocated)

H. Manpower requirements and sources

    1. Supervision
    2. Counters
    3. Auditors
    4. Coordinators
    5. Non-inventory personnel

I. Equipment requirements

    1. Communications equipment
    2. Recording devices
    3. Inventory listings and tags
    4. Check-sheets
    5. Count scales
    6. Step stools
    7. Clipboards
    8. Pencils
    9. Tape

J. Material movement procedure during inventory

    1. Logging requirements
    2. Order-processing method
    3. Paperwork control

    4. Auditing checks

    5. Invoicing steps

K. Advance inventory notification requirements

    1. Employee notification

    2. Vendor notification

    3. Customer notifications

L. Inventory guidelines (do's and don'ts)

Assigning Inventory Responsibilities

To prevent (or at least reduce) any confusion, all involved personnel should be advised of their responsibilities in this physical inventory. This includes forklift drivers, counters, control personnel, auditors, data processing, and so on. These people should be advised of the time schedule and be trained in their specific job functions far enough in advance so that they are comfortable with their assignment, but reasonably close enough to the physical inventory so they don't forget what they're supposed to do. In many companies there is not a sufficient number of personnel available to conduct a physical inventory in a "minimum" period of time. To fill this need many companies are coming into existence which will provide not only qualified counters, inside auditors, and supervision, but also assist you in developing the most appropriate physical inventory procedure for your company. Be sure you ask for, and check out, their references before deciding to use such a company. An unqualified service can end up doing more harm than good.

Conduct Pre-inventory Preparation

Examples of activities in this pre-inventory preparation include:

1. Insuring clear identification of locations and part numbers

2. Making sure that warehouse is orderly and neat

3. Identifying items that are *not* to be counted (i.e., some packing materials, miscellaneous items not in inventory records, receiving not yet input into the computer file, etc.)

4. Checking part numbers by location to ensure that all stock is located properly—to reduce the need for manual counts and the resulting time loss and confusion

5. Consolidating stock to reduce multiple locations

6. Arranging stock to facilitate easier counting (i.e., loose stock in front of bulk or packaged stock)

Determine Supply and Equipment Needs

As stated earlier, it is important that all supplies and equipment necessary for your physical inventory be ordered and delivered in time. Don't try to cut supply and equipment needs to the bare minimum—in most companies the emphasis is placed on reducing shutdown time, not on minimizing physical inventory costs. Running out of supplies (i.e., inventory tags, special forms) can bring your inventory to a screeching halt. Failure to order the right equipment (e.g., special rolling ladders, forklifts) can result in a waste of manpower and cause serious delays.

Don't forget your manpower needs. If you plan to use outside help, you may need to arrange for this months ahead of time.

Your checklist could include the following items:

1. Clipboards

2. Pencils

3. Marking pens

4. Masking tape

5. String, rope, or wire

6. Check sheets or control sheets

7. Step stools and/or carts

8. Count scales (for weight counting of small items)

9. Rolling stairs (8 to 10 feet high)

10. Additional forklifts

11. Warehouse floor plans and stock location reports

12. Extra tables and chairs

13. Additional beverages and food (cafeteria or catering truck should be notified in advance)

14. Scheduled release of computer reports

Train Personnel

Schedule inventory training dates, and provide advance notification to appropriate personnel. Conduct training with area supervision thoroughly, before having "working" personnel (counters, writers, auditors, etc.) instructed.

TRAINING SCHEDULE

Inventory supervisors should be instructed a minimum of a week prior to inventory, to allow them additional time to become familiar with their areas of responsibility and make necessary preparations. It is best to instruct working personnel as close to actual inventory as possible—perhaps on the night before or on the day of inventory—so that information will be fresh.

SUPERVISION TRAINING

Inventory training for supervisory personnel should cover the entire inventory program, including definitions of inventory areas (what parts to count or not to count), work assignments, and accountability. Accuracy should be stressed. Explanations and definitions of the various types of items to be inventoried, such as raw material, work-in-process, or finished goods, should be provided. Instructions should be prepared in detail on how listings (or tags) are to be prepared or used, collected, accounted for, and who they are to be given to.

SUBORDINATE TRAINING

Inventory training for working personnel would include how to count and keep records accurately, how to identify parts that have been inventoried, and how to handle merchandise without damaging it. They must also be warned that auditing discovery or repeated bad counts will result in dismissal of the persons responsible.

HANDOUT INSTRUCTIONS

An instruction sheet should be prepared and handed out to each person involved. This information sheet should illustrate and explain the method of taking inventory, reiterate certain key steps to follow, list assignments and accountability, and point out inventory "do and don't" guidelines.

INVENTORY "DO AND DON'T" ITEMS

Inventory guidelines can be presented as "do or don't" items. Information such as when and where lunch periods or breaks will be held, where smoking is permitted, the use of ladders in place of shelf climbing, and keeping inventory areas clean can be expressed in this manner. Specific "do and don't" items relating to inventory counting might include:

1. Do express count by the unit of measure assigned to the item being counted.

2. Don't count partial quantities of any items where the quantity would be less than an expressed unit of measure such as pounds, feet, and gallons.

3. Do individually count the contents of all opened packages.

4. Don't open sealed packages to count. Use the count marked on the outside.

5. Do approximate bulk item lengths such as hoses, wires, etc., where lengths are extensive and too costly to count.

6. Don't sight-count merchandise. Take out of containers to count.

7. Do put boxes or packages back in their original location after counting.

8. Don't disturb the rotation sequence of items counted that carry an assigned shelf life.

Add any "do and don't" items not shown above that fit the inventory being taken, and delete those that have no relationship. "Do and don't" items answer questions that might have been overlooked, and provide answers that can't be ignored. They help ensure a more accurate and meaningful inventory.

Count Inventory

This is the moment of truth. If your preparations have been good you should be able to move smoothly into this phase. If not, serious delays are a probable consequence.

You should have your count assignments made and counting packets ready to be issued. These counting packets should include all the items necessary to get the counters started. This typically includes:

1. Counting instructions

2. Warehouse plan with locations

3. Pencils

4. Inventory count sheet in location sequence (or tags)

5. Manual count sheet (for items not listed)

6. Stickers or labels for identifying counted items

7. Clipboards

An example of counting technique instructions and count sheet flow and control is provided in Exhibit 26–1. In general this flow is as follows:

1. Issue the inventory count sheet to an assigned counter or count team (counter plus writer).
   a. The count sheets list the stockkeeping units in location sequence.
   b. The count sheets are logically separated by section so that the work load can be evenly distributed. As each section is counted and verified, the computer files can be updated.
   c. A *manual count sheet* is logged out to each counter for items not shown on the computer count sheet.

2. When a count is made, the quantity is marked in the first count column of the count sheet and a round colored label is attached to the stock item to show that it has been counted.
   a. A manually counted item (not on the computer count sheet) is recorded on the *manual count sheet* and the same round label is placed on the counted item with a smaller round label (of lighter color) placed on top of the larger label. The page number of the manual count sheet is then marked on the smaller label for subsequent audit purposes.

3. As the assigned sections are completed, the count sheets are turned into the control desk for comparison to the *control sheet*.
   a. The *control sheet* page numbers are the same as the *count sheets*. Items are listed in the same sequence and spacing for easy comparison, and each part number listed is assigned the same *control number*. These control numbers are later used to update any counts different from those shown on the control sheet.

4. The count sheets are then separated into individual sheets and sorted into two groups:

   a. Count sheets which have one or more items requiring a recount
   b. Count sheets requiring no recounts (they either match control sheet quantities or are within the auditing allowance). These sheets can be processed immediately. Count sheets that have no variances can have all item counts updated by keying in the page number. Stock item counts can be updated by keying in the control number and then the quantity. The balance of the part numbers (those which exactly match the control sheet quantities) are updated by keying in the count sheet page number.

5. Count sheets that require second counts are sent out again, but with a different counter. If the second counts do not exactly match the first counts, the sheets are sent out for a third and final count by a supervisor or other authorized person (second and third counters must also sign the count sheet).

   a. When the count sheets for the second and third counts have been approved, they are keyed in as described in step 4.

6. A *missing page number report* can be run at any time to show pages not yet keyed in.

Verify Count and Correct Any Errors

After all pages have been input, an *inventory comparison report* is run showing quantity and dollar variances between the physical inventory count and the computer inventory record. All suspect variances or variances over a predetermined dollar or quantity amount are sent out for a recount. All locations for a "recount" part number must be counted.

Exhibit 26–1   Physical Inventory Counting Technique

1. Go to location assigned as indicated on count sheet.
   Important Points:
   • Count from merchandise (left to right and bottom to top) to count sheet. *Do not* count from count sheet to merchandise.
   • Merchandise may be located in more than one box or container. Make a total count and add quantities prior to entering total quantity. This will insure that all parts are counted.
   Procedure:
   • If part is on count sheet for that location, count items and record in the first count column and place a *blue* dot on the box or carton, making sure not to cover up the part number.
   • If part is not on count sheet for that location, count the merchandise and record (1) location, (2) part number, (3) quantity, and (4) page number of the inventory sheet on the manual count sheet.

   A manual count sheet will be given to you for *each* inventory control sheet. Place a blue dot on the box and a smaller yellow dot in the center of the dot. Write the number of the manual count sheet on the yellow dot.
2. When your counts are completed for each location, attach "manual count sheet" to "inventory location sheet" and return to the control desk for another set.
3. Be sure to sign your name at bottom of inventory sheet in the first count column.
4. Questions are encouraged. Please, no guessing. Know who your auditor is for your area.

PHYSICAL INVENTORY CONTROL SHEET

LOCATION	PART NUMBER	PRD GRP	DESCRIPTION	CONTROL NUMBER	1ST COUNT	2ND COUNT	3RD COUNT
4101E	M3276278	SV	BOLT PACK H . MHI	7470	*	*	*
4101E	MD276279	SV	BOLT PACK L . MHI	7471	*	*	*
4101E	W22ES3-U	PB	SPARK PLUG	7472	*	*	*
4101E	W22EX-UA	PC	SPARK PLUG	7473	*	*	*
4101E	W24FS-U	P3	SPARK PLUG	7474	*	*	*
4101E	090212-0050	DB	RACK	7475	*	*	*
4101E	090930-0190	0B	LEVER	7476	*	*	*
4101F	090012-0081	0B	NUT	7477	*	*	*
4101F	090052-0043	DB	SPRING	7478	*	*	*
4101F	090136-0120	0B	SPRING	7479	*	*	*
4101F	090260-0050	DB	PLATE	7480	*	*	*
4101F	090272-0111	DB	PACKING	7481	*	*	*
4101F	090841-0050	DB	STOPPER	7482	*	*	*
4101F	090915-0020	DB	CAPSULE	7483	*	*	*
4101F	091819-0174	DB	SPRING	7484	*	*	*

***********   **************************   ******************   ***************

COUNT TEAM 1   COUNT TEAM 2   COUNT TEAM 3

2

***   **   **   ***

Exhibit 26–1a   Count sheet issued to count team.

REPORT# PHI010
PAGE 530

PHYSICAL INVENTORY CONTROL SHEET

DATE PREPARED 11/22/
TIME PREPARED 14.05.57

LOCATION	PART NUMBER	PRD GRP	DESCRIPTION	CONTROL NUMBER	1ST COUNT	2ND COUNT	3RD COUNT
4101E	M3276278	SV	BOLT PACK H , MHI	7470	175		
4101E	M3276279	SV	BOLT PACK L , MHI	7471	8		
4101E	W22ES3-U	PB	SPARK PLUG	7472	84		
4101E	W22EX-UA	PC	SPARK PLUG	7473	1487		
4101E	W24FS-U	PB	SPARK PLUG	7474	11		
4101E	090212-0050	DB	RACK	7475	164		
4101E	090930-0190	DB	LEVER	7476	18		
4101F	090012-0081	DB	NUT	7477	136		
4101F	090052-0043	DB	SPRING	7478	119		
4101F	090136-0120	DB	SPRING	7479	172		
4101F	090260-0050	DB	PLATE	7480	23		
4101F	090272-0111	DB	PACKING	7481	1514		
4101F	090821-0050	DB	STOPPER	7482	68		
4101F	090915-0020	DB	CAPSULE	7483	301		
4101F	091819-0172	DB	SPRING	7484	200		

COUNT TEAM 1	COUNT TEAM 2	COUNT TEAM 3
2		

Exhibit 26–1b Items are counted and count sheet returned to control desk.

PHYSICAL INVENTORY CONTROL SHEET

DATE PREPARED 11/22/
TIME PREPARED 14.05.57

LOCATION	PART NUMBER	PRD GRP	DESCRIPTION	CONTROL NUMBER	1ST COUNT	2ND COUNT	3RD COUNT
4101E	M3276278	SV	BOLT PACK H , MHI	7470	175		175
4101E	M5276279	SV	BOLT PACK L , MHI	7471	8		
4101E	M22ESR-U	PB	SPARK PLUG	7472	84		
4101E	M22EX-UA	PC	SPARK PLUG	7473	1487		1487
4101E	M24FS-U	PB	SPARK PLUG	7474	11		
4101E	090212-0050	DB	RACK	7475	164		
4101E	090930-0190	DB	LEVER	7476	18		
4101F	090012-0081	DB	NUT	7477	136		136
4101F	090052-0043	DB	SPRING	7478	119		
4101F	090136-0120	DB	SPRING	7479	172		
4101F	090260-0050	DB	PLATE	7480	23		
4101F	090272-0111	DB	PACKING	7481	1514		
4101F	090821-0050	DB	STOPPER	7482	68		
4101F	090915-0020	DB	CAPSULE	7483	301		301
4101F	091819-0172	DB	SPRING	7484	200		200

COUNT TEAM 1   COUNT TEAM 2   COUNT TEAM 3

2

Exhibit 26-1c Control desk checks against control sheets, and then accepts and circles any counts that match or are within $25 and 25 items. Any items different, but acceptable, are recorded in third count column of count sheet.

REPORT# PHI02C
PAGE 580

PHYSICAL INVENTORY CONTROL SHEET

DATE PREPARED 11/22/
TIME PREPARED 14.17.13

ON-HAND	LOCATION	PART NUMBER	CONTROL NUMBER	COST
10 *11*	4101E	MB276278	7470	
10	4101E	N6276279	7471	
30	4101E	W22-SK-U	7472	
30 *26*	4101E	W22LX-JA	7473	
20	4101E	W24FS-U	7474	
2	4101E	090212-0050	7475	
1	4101E	090930-0190	7476	
27 *23*	4101F	090012-0061	7477	
25	4101F	090052-0043	7478	
120	4101F	090136-0120	7479	
21	4101F	090260-0050	7480	
16	4101F	090272-0111	7481	
30	4101F	090821-0050	7482	
16 *14*	4101F	090915-0920	7483	
20 *23*	4101F	091019-0172	7484	

Exhibit 26-1d Counts that do not match exactly but meet the $25/25-item criteria are also marked on the control sheet. NOTE: This step is necessary only if you wish to monitor how many first counts are accepted within the $25/25-item criteria.

DATE PREPARED 11/22/
TIME PREPARED 14.05.57

PHYSICAL INVENTORY CONTROL SHEET

LOCATION	PART NUMBER	PRD GRP	DESCRIPTION	CONTROL NUMBER	1ST COUNT	2ND COUNT	3RD COUNT
4101E	M3276278	SV	BOLT PACK H , MHI	7470	*	*	*
4101E	M0276279	SV	BOLT PACK L , MHI	7471	*	*	*
4101E	M22ESR-U	PB	SPARK PLUG	7472	*		*
4101E	M22EX-UA	PC	SPARK PLUG	7473	*	*	*
4101E	M24FS-U	PB	SPARK PLUG	7474	*	*	*
4101E	090212-0050	OB	RACK	7475	*	*	*
4101E	090930-0190	OB	LEVER	7476	*	*	*
4101F	090012-0081	OB	NUT	7477	*	*	*
4101F	090052-0043	OB	SPRING	7478	*	*	*
4101F	090136-0120	OB	SPRING	7479	*		*
4101F	090260-0050	OB	PLATE	7480	*	*	*
4101F	090272-0111	OB	PACKING	7481	*	*	*
4101F	090821-0050	OB	STOPPER	7482	*	*	*
4101F	090915-0020	OB	CAPSULE	7483	*	*	*
4101F	091819-0172	OB	SPRING	7484	*	*	*

COUNT TEAM 1	COUNT TEAM 2	COUNT TEAM 3
2	7	

Exhibit 26-1e First counts *not* accepted are sent back for second counts. The items requiring a second count are noted as shown.

723

Control Log
Computer Count Sheets
2nd Counts

Date _____

Page #	Team #	In	Page #	Team #	In	Page #	Team #	In	Page #	Team #	In
01			26			51			76		
02			27			52			77		
03			28			53			78		
04			29			54			79		
05			30			55			80		
06			31			56			81		
07			32			57			82		
08			33			58			83		
09			34			59			84		
10	7		35			60			85		
11			36			61			86		
12			37			62			87		
13			38			63			88		
14			39			64			89		
15			40			65			90		
16			41			66			91		
17			42			67			92		

Exhibit 26-1f   Counts are recorded on log when second count is sent out.

PHYSICAL INVENTORY CONTROL SHEET

DATE PREPARED 11/22/
TIME PREPARED 14.05.57

LOCATION	PART NUMBER	PRD GRP	DESCRIPTION	CONTROL NUMBER	1ST COUNT	2ND COUNT	3RD COUNT
4101E	M3276278	SV	BOLT PACK H . MHI	7470	*	*	*
4101E	M5276279	SV	BOLT PACK L . MHI	7471	*	*	*
4101E	W22ES3-U	PB	SPARK PLUG	7472	*	*86*	*
4101E	W22EX-UA	PC	SPARK PLUG	7473	*	*11*	*
4101F	W24FS-U	P3	SPARK PLUG	7474	*	*	*
4101E	090212-0050	0B	RACK	7475	*	*	*
4101E	090930-0190	0B	LEVER	7476	*	*	*
4101F	090012-0081	0B	NUT	7477	*	*	*
4101F	090052-0043	0B	SPRING	7478	*	*172*	*
4101F	090136-0120	0B	SPRING	7479	*	*	*
4101F	090260-0050	0B	PLATE	7480	*	*1513*	*
4101F	090272-0111	0B	PACKING	7481	*	*68*	*
4101F	090821-0050	0B	STOPPER	7482	*	*	*
4101F	090915-0020	0B	CAPSULE	7483	*	*	*
4101F	091819-0172	0B	SPRING	7484	*	*	*

************ ******************* ******************* ************ COUNT TEAM 3 **********
** ** ** ** ** ** ** ** ***

COUNT TEAM 1	COUNT TEAM 2
2	7

Exhibit 26-1g   Second counts are made and returned to control desk.

725

PHYSICAL INVENTORY CONTROL SHEET

DATE PREPARED 11/22/
TIME PREPARED 14.05.57

LOCATION	PART NUMBER	PRD GRP	DESCRIPTION	CONTROL NUMBER	1ST COUNT	2ND COUNT	3RD COUNT
4101E	M3276278	SV	BOLT PACK H . MHI	7470	(175)		175
4101E	M3276279	SV	BOLT PACK L . MHI	7471	(8)	86	85
4101E	W22ESR-U	PB	SPARK PLUG	7472	84		85
4101E	W22EX-UA	PC	SPARK PLUG	7473	(1487)		1487
4101E	W24FS-U	P3	SPARK PLUG	7474	11	(11)	11
4101E	090212-0050	DB	RACK	7475	(164)		
4101E	090930-0190	DB	LEVER	7476	(18)		
4101F	090012-0081	DB	NUT	7477	(136)		136
4101F	090052-0043	DB	SPRING	7478	(119)		
4101F	090136-0120	DB	SPRING	7479	172	(172)	172
4101F	090260-0050	DB	PLATE	7480	(23)		
4101F	090272-0111	DB	PACKING	7481	1514	1513	1514
4101F	090841-0050	DB	STOPPER	7482	68	(68)	68
4101F	090915-0020	DB	CAPSULE	7483	(301)		301
4101F	091819-0172	DB	SPRING	7484	(200)		200

COUNT TEAM 1   2

COUNT TEAM 2   7

COUNT TEAM 3

Exhibit 26-1h Second counts are recorded on original (first) count sheets. Accept and circle any second counts that match first counts, and record the accepted quantity in the third count column. Any counts not accepted are noted as shown in the third count column for final count.

726

PHYSICAL INVENTORY
Manual Count Sheet

Date __11/30__

LOCATION	PART NUMBER	DESCRIPTION	IN SYSTEM	NOT IN SYSTEM	ADDED TO SYSTEM	3rd COUNT	2nd COUNT	1st COUNT

Date _____

Control Log
Manual Count Sheets

Sheet #	Location	1st Count		2nd Count		To Inv. Control	To EDP
		Team #	Returned	Team #	Returned		
09	3A01-07	4	✓	7	✓		

Exhibit 26-1j   Manual count is sheet logged out.

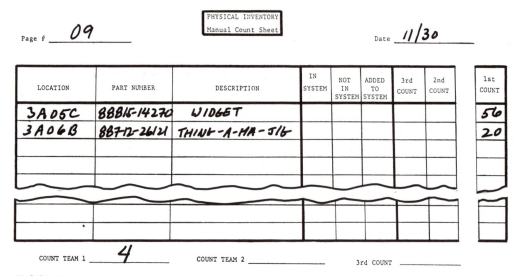

Page # ____09____   PHYSICAL INVENTORY / Manual Count Sheet   Date __11/30__

LOCATION	PART NUMBER	DESCRIPTION	IN SYSTEM	NOT IN SYSTEM	ADDED TO SYSTEM	3rd COUNT	2nd COUNT	1st COUNT
3A05C	BBB15-14270	WIDGET						56
3A06B	BB712-26121	THING-A-MA-JIG						20

COUNT TEAM 1 ____4____   COUNT TEAM 2 _____   3rd COUNT _____

Exhibit 26-1k   Manual count sheet is returned with any counts.

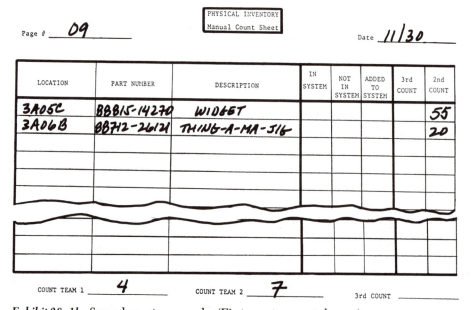

Page # ____09____   PHYSICAL INVENTORY / Manual Count Sheet   Date __11/30__

LOCATION	PART NUMBER	DESCRIPTION	IN SYSTEM	NOT IN SYSTEM	ADDED TO SYSTEM	3rd COUNT	2nd COUNT
3A05C	BBB15-14270	WIDGET					55
3A06B	BB712-26121	THING-A-MA-JIG					20

COUNT TEAM 1 ____4____   COUNT TEAM 2 ____7____   3rd COUNT _____

Exhibit 26-1l   Second counts are made. (First counts are *not* shown.)

Update the Computer Inventory Records

After all verifying counts are made, any physical inventory counts in error are corrected.

Obtain an Inventory "Buy-off" from the Auditors

Once you and your auditors are satisfied that your physical inventory is accurate (within the auditing guidelines), a final *inventory comparison report* is run.

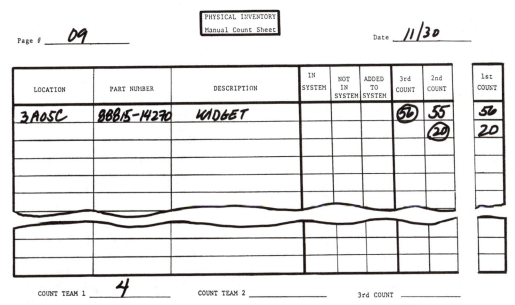

LOCATION	PART NUMBER	DESCRIPTION	IN SYSTEM	NOT IN SYSTEM	ADDED TO SYSTEM	3rd COUNT	2nd COUNT	1st COUNT
3A05C	88815-14270	WIDGET				(56)	55	56
							(20)	20

COUNT TEAM 1 ___4___   COUNT TEAM 2 _____   3rd COUNT _____

Exhibit 26-1m Any first and second counts not matching require a third and final count.

Analyze and Discuss Any Inventory Problems Encountered

This is one of the most important steps in a physical inventory. This is where you identify loopholes or problems in the system such as failure to record sales, keypunch errors (i.e., quantity, location, part number), picking and receiving errors, invoice errors, and shrinkage, just to name a few.

Make Corrections to Inventory Control Procedures

As a result of the post-inventory analysis, corrections and/or improvements to inventory control procedures can be made. It is a rare inventory system that doesn't need improvements or corrections; inventory control is a dynamic activity that is never the same from day to day, let alone from year to year.

Prepare and Submit the Physical Inventory Report

In most cases, the final inventory report is submitted to the company's controller, but this can vary depending on company structure. The controller usually has the final authority and responsibility for the inventory "buy-off." The controller must arrive at an adjusted book value for inventory as a result of this physical inventory. Your report should therefore list inventory variances, show a total ending quantity and dollar inventory, summarize your post-inventory analysis, and make recommendations for improvements.

The Cycle Count Inventory

The purpose of a cycle count system is to maintain a high level of inventory record accuracy on a timely basis. By counting your inventory on a more regular basis, identification and resolution of problems can be accomplished more effectively. A proven cycle count system can lead to the elimination of a periodic (wall-to-wall) physical inventory, thus reducing costly shutdown time. In addition, by assigning trained employees to regularly conduct your cycle count system, you can achieve a much more accurate count compared to using company personnel or outside labor on a temporary basis to conduct a periodic physical inventory.

As with the periodic phsyical inventory you must first decide on the inventory method to use and then write a comprehensive step-by-step procedure. However, the need to assign inventory responsibilities, conduct pre-inventory preparation, determine supply needs and equipment, and train personnel is no longer required since this is an ongoing operation with dedicated and trained personnel already assigned. The remaining steps required for the cycle count system are basically the same as for the periodic physical inventory, but not to the same degree.

There are two general ways to establish a cycle count system. One way is to count preselected part numbers at a given frequency, weighting each part number according to how long it takes to be counted, to insure a consistent monthly work load. It is important to make sure that each inventory item is counted at least once a year. The other way is to count *exception* items or *special situation items*. Many companies have found it best to combine these two methods to insure the most beneficial results. Only the first way will be considered here as a replacement for a periodic physical inventory since it insures that all items are counted at least once a year. An example of how this works is presented below:

Counting Preselected Part Numbers at Least Once a Year

1. An ABC analysis will tell you which items represent your highest dollar activity. From this you can determine the count frequency for each item.

Code	Items (%)	Dollars (%)	Count Frequency
A	5	65	Once a month
B	12	25	Once a quarter
C	83	10	Once a year

2. If you have 12,000 stockkeeping units (SKUs) then:

Code	Items (%)	×	SKUs	=	Items to Count Each Period	×	No. of Periods Per Year	Counts Per Year
A	5		12,000		600		12	7,200
B	12		12,000		1,440		4	5,760
C	83		12,000		9,960		1	9,960
	100				12,000			22,920

3. If experience shows that it takes an average of 0.2 hours to make first counts on each item, then:

Total Annual Counts	×	Time to Make One Count	=	Hours Per Year to Make All Counts	Hours Per Week (Use 50/yr) to Make Counts	Hours Per Day (use 5/wk) to Make Counts	Man-Days Required (Use 8/day)
22,920		0.2		4584	91.7	18.3	2.3*

*A simplified version is: 4584 hours ÷ 2000 Hrs/yr = 2.3

4. If you experience a 10 percent rejection rate of first counts, and it takes an average of 0.5 hours to recount and reconcile these items, then:

Counts Per Year	×	Time to Recount & Reconcile	=	Additional Hours Per Year to Make Recounts	Per Week (50 wks/yr)	Per Day (5 days/wk)	Man-Days Required (8 hrs/day)
22,920		0.5		11,460	·229.2	45.8	5.7

5. If 2.3 man-days (first counts) are added to 5.7 man-days (recounts and reconciliation), the total is 7.0. Therefore, it will require a combination of 7 full-time inventory analysts and counters to cycle count this inventory.

6. In order to insure an even workload thoughout the year you will need to apply a *load leveling factor* to each part number. If the annual number of counts is 22,290, it is necessary to count 22,920 ÷ 50 = 458 items per week, or 92 items per day. A simple weighting method is presented here. How you set up your own weighting system depends on the nature and complexity of your company's inventory.

Load Leveling (Weighting) Factors

Nature of Part	Weight
0 (case) stock on hand	0.5
Bagged or bundled	0.8
Small items—loose	1.0
Large items—loose	2.0

Weighting Factors Applied to ABC Coded Items

Code	Times Counted Per Year	Total No. of P/N's	Weight	No. of P/N's by Weight Factor	Counts Per Year	Total Counts Per Year
A	12	600	0.5	50	600	
			0.8	200	2,400	
			1.0	250	3,000	7,200
			2.0	100	1,200	
B	4	1,440	0.5	100	400	
			0.8	600	2,400	
			1.0	400	1,600	5,760
			2.0	340	1,360	
C	1	9,960	0.5	360	360	
			0.8	4,000	4,000	
			1.0	3,000	3,000	9,960
			2.0	2,600	2,600	
Total		12,000		12,000	22,920	22,920

Summary of Cycle Count System Results

Weight Factor Group	Counts per Year	Dividing by 250 Counting Days/Year	Max. Items Counted per Day
0.5	1,360	250	6
0.8	8,800	250	36
1.0	7,600	250	31
2.0	5,160	250	21
Total	22,920		94*

*Note that the previously stated goal was 92 items per day.

7. You will need the following types of counting materials:
   a. A basic *cycle count card* (first count) would list part number, description, count date, and location, and provide spaces for "counted by," "total quantity," and "unit of measure," plus a working area for calculations. This card would also have a sequential card number assigned for control purposes.

   b. A *recount card* would be the same as the cycle count card except for the card header—"Recount Card."

   c. An *adjustment card* would list part number, description, count date, recount quantity, and location, and provide spaces for "plus" and "minus" adjustments along with any additional information you would like to include (e.g. code number for error type, comments).

Counting Exceptions and Special Situation Items

A good way to familiarize yourself with the cycle count system is to first count exception and special situation items. By beginning with this easier but nevertheless effective cycle count method you can eliminate a number of bugs that would exist in the cycle count system previously described.

Some examples of exceptions or special situation items are presented below:

Exceptions	Special Situations
1. When on-hand balance is zero	1. At reorder
2. When on-hand balance is negative	2. At receipt
3. When receiving a claim for mis-packed, short-shipped, or over-shipped items	3. When consolidating stock
	4. When transferring stock
	5. When error is suspected
4. When stock is insufficient at picking location	6. At predetermined (low) inventory level

It should be noted that if you have a multiple location system, all locations for a given part number should be counted. This is true for the full cycle count system as well.

Notes

1. See, for example, Harvey N. Shycon and Christopher R. Sprague, "Put a Price Tag on Your Customer Servicing Levels," *Harvard Business Review*, 53, No. 4 (July–August 1975), pp. 71–78.

2. Elwood S. Buffa, "Aggregate Planning for Production," *Business Horizons* (Fall 1967), pp. 57–83.

3. Matthew C. Fox, "Hidden Investments in Marketing Decisions," *Journal of Marketing*, 32 (October 1968), pp. 9–12.

4. See, for example, Philip Schary and Keith Howard, "Logistics Strategy and Inventory Decisions," *International Journal of Physical Distribution* (October 1970), pp. 31–38.

5. Howard T. Lewis, James W. Culliton, and Jack D. Steele, *The Role of Air Freight in Physical Distribution* (Boston: Division of Research, Harvard University Graduate School of Business Administration, 1956).

6. John Magee, "The Logistics of Distribution," *Harvard Business Review* (July–August 1960), pp. 89–101.

7. Wroe Alderson, "Marketing Efficiency and the Principle of Postponement," *Cost and Profit Outlook*, III, 4 (September 1950).

8. For a discussion of how to determine ϕ and γ, see Philip Schary and Keith Howard, "Logistics Strategy," pp. 33–34.

9. D. H. Maister, "Centralization of Inventories and the Square Root Law," *International Journal of Physical Distribution*, 6, No. 3, pp. 124–134.

10. For a discussion of various types of warehouse location models, see Bruce J. McLaren and D. Clay Whybark, "A Comparison of Heuristic Approaches to Locating a Fixed Number of Facilities," *The Logistics and Transportation Review*, 11, No. 4 (1975), pp. 348–355.

11. The method for determining the amount of cycle stock and safety stock inventory making up total inventory may be found in Schary and Howard, "Logistics Strategy."

12. Wroe Alderson, "Marketing Efficiency."

13. For an application of this concept to production systems, see R. Scott Whiting, "Public Warehousing and the 'Just-in-Time' Production System," *Warehousing Review*, Distribution Executive Issue, 1982, pp. 2–10.

Packaging

CHAPTER 27

The Role of Packaging in Physical Distribution

Ralph M. Cox *and* Kenneth G. Van Tassel

Introduction

Packaging is a vast field that encompasses a wide range of materials, containers, closures, styles and configurations, graphics, equipment, and systems. For many consumer products, the costs of packaging can be *greater* than the cost of the products packaged. In many cases, too, the package itself is a major marketing and sales tool.

Packaging can generally be divided into two broad areas—consumer packaging and distribution packaging—although these areas do overlap. Consumer packaging is directly involved in and influences the sale of a consumer product at the point of purchase. In many cases consumer packaging involves sophisticated graphic design, and many packages are "custom" designed. Distribution packaging, on the other hand, affords protection to a product to insure safe arrival at the final destination and promotes effective handling, warehousing, and transportation throughout the distribution cycle. It does not normally involve a high degree of graphics design, and makes greater use of "standard" packages. In many cases the distribution package does not reach the ultimate consumer. Many distribution packages contain consumer packages.

Some examples of consumer packages include:

— Blister/card packages

— Pure-paks

— Plastic and glass bottles and jars

— Folding cartons

— Fiberboard boxes

— Paper sacks

— Plastic film bags and pouches

— Steel, plastic, aluminum, and composite cans

— Fiberboard and plastic trays

— Plastic nets

— Foil and paper containers, wrappers, and sleeves

— Plastic tubs

— Cartridges

— Egg cartons

— Plastic baskets

— Envelopes

Examples of distribution packages include:

— Corrugated fiberboard cases

— Multiwall paper, plastic, and textile shipping sacks

— Steel, plastic, and fiber drums

— Steel and wood kegs

— Steel and plastic pails

— Wood crates, boxes, and baskets

— Barrels

— Returnable and disposable pallets

— Returnable plastic tote boxes and trays

— Returnable wire baskets

It is the distribution packaging function that will be discussed in this chapter.

Conditions That Affect Packaging for Distribution

A wide variety of conditions and factors must be carefully considered before a judgment can be made as to the best package for distribution. These include the product, marketing requirements, the production or acquisition process, handling and warehousing, the transportation mode, governmental regulations, economics, and safety.

The Product

The first step in deciding on the best packaging for a product is usually to determine its physical characteristics. For rigid products these might include dimensions, surface finish, weight, or fragility; for bulk solids, characteristics might include bulk density or particle size; and for bulk liquids, specific gravity or viscosity. You might say, "Anyone knows that a liquid will have to be packed in a drum, pail, or can and a granular product *must* be packaged in a bag." This may not be so. A liquid can be packaged in a bag within a corrugated case and granular products can be packed in a fiber drum. Packaging should be approached in an open and creative, yet careful, manner.

The following questions might be asked in order to assess how the product affects the type of package selected.

— Does the product have a limited shelf life?

— Is the product hazardous, flammable, toxic, explosive or reactive?

— How valuable is the product?

— Is the product fragile? How fragile?

— Is the product light- or temperature-sensitive?

— Is the product likely to be affected adversely by the package?

— Is the product hydroscopic?

— Are the product's characteristics variable?

The value of the product often determines the packaging. For some low-cost products a low-cost container and the willingness to accept some product damage may be the most cost-effective solution. Surely you wouldn't package sand in a steel pail, nor would you package gold dust in a paper bag.

Marketing Requirements

We normally associate the marketing aspects of packaging with consumer packaging, but marketing requirements should also be considered in connection with distribution packaging.

First, what is the unit of sale? Certainly you wouldn't consider packaging two lawnmowers in a single container. Lawn mowers are not usually sold in pairs. A retailer purchases motor oil in "case" quantities, but how many cans should be in that case—6, 12, 24, 72, 144? What size should each can be? Should the primary distribution package contain an intermediate package that in turn contains the consumer package?

Second, what should the package say? Graphics are usually not as important in distribution packaging as they are in consumer packaging but the graphic design requirements must be determined. Who will see the package? More and more effort is being given to the use of art and color on everyday corrugated cases. Bleached papers are now being used as outer liners of paper shipping sacks to enhance their appearance. In some cases highly illustrated copy is being adhered to corrugated cases to give those containers a new look. Graphics can help sell an industrial product or leave a desirable company image throughout the distribution network.

Can the distribution package help sell the product in other ways? Special features can be incorporated in a distribution package to facilitate consumer usage. A tear tape might be provided on the top of a corrugated fiberboard shipper for easy opening. Special internal pour spouts can be provided on bulk liquid containers. Such special package features that will help sell a product are often overlooked in distribution package design.

The Production or Acquisition Process

Packaging may also be affected by the production process if the product is manufactured, or by the acquisition process if it is purchased from others. For example, if a product is produced in lots of 20, it may be awkward to package it in groups of 24. Or a product may not be produced uniformly—nothing may come off the production line for long periods of time, and then a large number may be released to be packed in a brief time.

If a product is marketed under a variety of labels, it might be appropriate to package the product with no label, store it, and apply the label only after an order has been received. What kind of package would be the easiest to handle in this fashion? If the product is purchased, how will it be packaged when it arrives? Will you be re-packaging it? Or will you be utilizing the packaging provided by the original manufacturer? Can the original manufacturer supply packaging to your specifications?

Handling and Warehousing

The design of the package and the make-up of the unit load directly affect the materials handling and storage equipment utilized in warehousing the product, and vice versa. In many cases, the direct cost impact in handling and storage can be measured according to the type of packaging and the size of the unit load selected. Will a pallet be used with the unit load or will slip sheets be used? If the pallet is to be conveyed, which way will the bottom boards be running? Will four-way entry be required? Can unit loads be stacked three high on the floor? Four or five high? Will any existing selective pallet racks be used? How smooth is the floor—will a columnar stacked load be stable? How rough is the handling?

Perhaps the roof height will allow three shorter unit loads but only two taller unit loads. How will this affect space requirements? If floor storage is to be used, how well does the unit load lay out with the building columns? Would a one- or two-inch difference in the unit load size allow an additional pallet between columns and save floor space? If a two-way pallet is planned, will the pallet have enough lateral strength for drive-in or drive-through pallet racks? How will the product be handled and stored at its ultimate destination?

Forklift trucks are usually taken for granted in the warehousing process. It is important, however, to plan their use carefully. For example, if two loads are to be stacked in a carrier, does the forklift truck have enough free lift? Can existing forklift trucks handle exceptionally big pallets when the load center is longer than the normal 24 inches? Will side shifters or an extra high-load backrest be required? Will extra forklift trips be required because the unit load could have held more product?

The Transportation Mode

How a product is to be shipped throughout the distribution system is of importance in determining the packaging. Often more than one mode of transportation is used, in which case the package should be designed or selected for the most severe situation. In many cases the type of transportation is dictated by distribution economics, above and beyond the economics of packaging.

We usually assume that both shipping and receiving points have rail access. If not, will extra handling be required? Quantities per shipment are normally higher for rail shipment and delivery time is longer. Truck shipments are not usually subjected to the impacts, vibration, and potential extra handling of rail shipments and, therefore, could result in different packaging requirements. Full truckload shipments could very well require less packaging than less-than-truckload (LTL) shipments. Packages may be handled over several freight docks in the LTL shipment mode.

How many times, and in what manner, will the product be handled throughout the transportation and distribution system? Is the product a made-to-order commodity that will be shipped directly to the customer without any intermediate handling or warehousing? If the product will be shipped to your own distribution center, should it be shipped to that center in bulk form for packaging when it arrives?

Governmental Regulations

There are regulations, governmental and carrier, that determine minimum container construction specifications for certain products and commodities. These regulations provide a basis for determining the package to use. Failure to comply with the proper regulation could mean a freight rate surcharge of up to 25 percent, the carrier's refusal to carry the freight, or the refusal of the carrier to pay damage claims.

Familiarity with these regulations is very important. Because they are constantly being revised and upgraded to meet changes in requirements and packaging techniques, it is virtually impossible to be current at all times on all the regulations, but it is important to know how to obtain the proper information when it is needed.

Economics

As noted above, economic considerations should play a part in the selection of the package in terms of comparative costs of packaging alternatives. The product's intrinsic value and the impact of additional or reduced costs in handling, warehousing, or transportation should be taken into account. Such cost comparisons can be valuable in assessing the impacts of packaging decisions.

The manner in which economic decisions are made varies widely from company to company. The economic comparisons between alternative packages under investigation, however, should (1) be over the long term, (2) make allowances for inflation, (3) include both capital investments (equipment generally) and operating expenses (labor, packaging materials, maintenance, etc.), (4) include depreciation for capital investments, (5) incorporate the time value of money through an accepted discounting technique, and (6) include the effects of income taxes. Costs for the package itself, and for the packaging line, handling, warehousing, transportation, and distribution must all be considered. Anticipated product volume growth or decline should also be taken into account. A present value, after tax figure for the *overall* cost of each alternative package would be revealing and should be used in the decision-making process.

Safety

The way in which a product's safety can be enhanced or reduced by its packaging is another consideration that can affect the handling, warehousing, transportation, and distribution cycles for all products.

Safety considerations are particularly important for those products for which the package remains an integral part of the product throughout its life. Commodities that are dispensed from a distribution package until it is empty are good examples. Particular attention should be given to how the product package will be used. Will the product be used a little at a time or will the entire contents be removed at one time? If it is necessary to reclose the package after it has been opened once, how will the original design of the package provide for this? Will the package be opened outdoors or indoors? Are any warning messages clear and appropriate?

Summary

It is easy to see that a wide variety of considerations must be undertaken in order to insure that the most appropriate package is selected. Careful thought about *all* of the stages through which the package will pass, from original manufacturer to its ultimate destination (and use or disposition there), will provide many useful parameters for the development of the best distribution package.

Packages and Containers

This section will not make the reader an expert in package selection or design. Its purpose is to acquaint the reader with the variety of distribution containers from which to choose. It may help in determining the basic range of containers or packages from which to proceed with further development. In many cases the product, the distribution mode, or the marketing methods will influence the type of package to be used for distribution. U.S. Department of Transportation regulations and carrier tariffs also play an important role in package selection.

Package sizing is an important factor in the total distribution effort.

- Properly sized packages should fit the selected distribution pallet for maximum cube utilization in the warehouse and in the carrier.

• The package should provide for an interlock between adjacent packages for good shipping stability and minimal transportation damage.

• A well-designed and correctly sized package should have good stacking properties.

As mentioned previously, it is difficult to define the line between distribution packaging and consumer packaging. The primary objective for distribution packages is to insure satisfactory performance throughout distribution cycle. It should be kept in mind, though, that in many cases the distribution package can also become a part of the purchase package, so that a well-designed package can enhance the sales effort at the marketplace.

The following pages will outline some of the basic types of distribution packages or containers. It should be noted that often it is necessary to obtain qualified help in developing actual container specifications. In most cases, suppliers can offer technical assistance to customers and potential customers as part of their sales efforts. Take advantage of these experts, use them, and you'll get better final results.

Packages for Dry Products

Corrugated Containers

Corrugated containers are widely used as distribution packages. They are usually manufactured to order. Industry standards have been established for corrugated board construction, but the case style, size, and strength are custom manufactured for each customer's exact needs. Corrugated cases are usually received "knocked down" and erected by the user. The manufacturers' joint is made by the case manufacturer normally, and the top and bottom closures made by the user.

Corrugated board is made of two layers of liner board (heavy kraft paper) with a corrugation medium in the middle. The burst strength of the final combination depends on the weight or strength of the liner board. Variations can also be obtained in the crushing or stacking strength by changing the number of flutes per inch in the corrugation medium. Wax coatings and water resistant adhesives can also be used to meet special requirements.

There are many types or styes of corrugated cases. The *regular slotted carton* (RSC) is probably the most common. It is a rectangular container with full width and length flaps on the top and bottom, all the same height. The two major flaps meet—but do not overlap—in the middle of the container. The two minor flaps are the same height, but meet in the middle only when the case is square.

Many different styles exist, including the *full overlay container* (FOL), *center special-slotted container* (CSSC), *half-slotted container* (HSC), and a wide variety of special die-cut containers.

Inner packaging can be used to provide product protection and enhance the total package performance. For example, fiber "egg crate" partitions are used to protect bottles from one another. Special slotted or scored sheets are used to improve the stacking strength of a container, particularly when the product is fragile or will not provide sufficient stacking strength on its own.

Corrugated containers are often used to hold other packages, i.e., consumer packages, such as canned goods, bottles, flexible packages, and the like. In this application they truly become distribution packages. In such instances corrugated cases are sometimes called "shippers." Empty containers to be filled are sometimes received inside an erected corrugated case, called a "re-shipper."

The corrugated container can also be used as the product package itself, as well as the distribution package. With a polyethylene liner it can be used, for example, as a container for dry bulk materials.

Solid Fiber Containers

Solid fiberboard should not be confused with folding carton materials. Solid fiberboard is a lamination of multiple layers of liner board. It does not contain the corrugation medium. Containers are fabricated from solid fiberboard in many of the same styles as corrugated containers, particularly regular slotted cases. The adhesives used in the laminating process are usually moisture resistant and the combined layers of board result in a very strong and rugged container. Military packaging often makes use of solid fiber containers because commodities must be stored for extended periods of time under severe conditions.

Because solid fiberboard cases are used relatively infrequently, the choice of suppliers is limited. Costs are higher than for comparable corrugated containers.

Wirebound Boxes

Wirebound boxes were developed in an effort to reduce the amount of lumber required for wooden boxes. Wooden cleats are used to provide the necessary rigidity, and sections of wooden panels are used to bridge the cleats. All the parts are held together with wire wrapping. The box can be knocked down for shipment to the user. Erection time is minimal and the resulting container is rugged and durable. Wirebound boxes are excellent for very heavy products and provide good protection.

Shipping Sacks and Bags

Shipping sacks or bags are flexible containers which provide a relatively low-cost distribution package. Like all other distribution packages there are many types of construction, materials, and closures. Some types of sacks lend themselves to very economical high-speed filling techniques. Bags are custom made for each individual application—style, size, and construction. Sizing of bags is largely an empirical process, although analytical techniques do exist.[1]

Multiwall Paper Sacks

In the United States, an abundance of trees has resulted in abundant kraft paper, and the paper bag is widely used. Early multiwall paper bags were open-mouth bags with a sewn top and bottom closure. These *sewn open-mouth* (SOM) bags can be either flat tubes (pillow type) or gusseted (side panels folded in). Filling of these bags is often slow and closure must be done with a sewing machine.

The *sewn valve bag* was developed to eliminate the need for the sewing operation but is not commonly used today. Such a bag has a valve or paper sleeve sewn into the top closure. The bag is filled through this sleeve, which is then tucked in to complete the closure.

Another development in the bag industry was the industrial version of the grocery bag. This multiwall paper bag is usually referred to as the *self-opening sack* (SOS). Sewn open-mouth filling and closing equipment can be used to fill this type of bag. The square bottom permits better palletizing then the SOM bag.

The type of bag most widely used today is the *stepped-end pasted valve bag* (SEPV), which has probably evolved out of all the previously mentioned bags. Both the top and bottom are folded and glued to form a square gusseted end when the bag is filled. The plies of paper on a stepped-end bag are cut and then glued in a stepped or overlapping manner, which provides a strong sift-proof end. A valve is glued into the top corner of the bag. This valve can be a tuck-in sleeve-type or the more popular self-closing internal sleeve valve. The self-closing sleeve is a paper or polyethylene tube that closes after filling as a result of internal product pressure. The pasted valve bag is as close to rectangular as a flexible package can be and can be stacked efficiently on a pallet. It can also be filled on high-speed packaging equipment, with manual bag placement or in conjunction with an automatic bag placer.

The most recent innovation in the bag industry is the *pinch-type* open-mouth multi-wall paper bag. This is an adaptation of the sewn gusseted bag. Instead of sewing the bottom, the paper plies are cut and folded over and glued. Hot melt adhesive is added to the top of the bag, which is heated, folded, and sealed after filling. Its shape approximates that of the pasted stepped-end valve bag when it is filled. Its major advantage is that it can provide a completely sealed package when it is filled and sealed.

The number of plies of paper, the strength of each ply, and the type of kraft paper can be varied according to the individual needs of the customer. Special plies of coated paper, polyethylene film or aluminum foil can also be incorporated in the bag to meet special requirements.

Like corrugated boxes, multiwall bags are made to order. The size, construction, and graphics are customized to the user's needs. All bag manufacturers provide technical assistance in developing specific bags to meet the needs of their customers.

Paper Balers

The kraft paper baler is sometimes used to unitize packages. A baler is a large square-bottom self-opening sack that is sized to accept a number of smaller bags. Consumer packages such as one-, two-, and five-pound bags of sugar, rice, or flour are usually consolidated in a baler. The total weight of the baler is usually 50 to 60 pounds maximum. Recently, shrink film bags have been used for the same purpose. Individual packages are grouped together, overwrapped with shrink film, and then subjected to heat, which produces a tight overwrap.

Plastic Film Bags

Polyethylene film is the major plastic material now being used in the construction of bags for distribution. The film is single ply and can be fabricated in many of the same styles as multiwall paper bags. Flat tube and gusseted open mouth bags are heat seal closed on the bottom and then heat sealed on the top after filling. The latest innovation in this field is a square-end valve-type bag; the ends are folded much like a stepped-end paper bag and glued with a special adhesive. Patches are glued over the top and bottom to provide additional strength. An internal self-closing valve—identical to that of the multiwall paper bag—is placed in the top corner. Higher bag costs have kept this bag from competing directly with the multiwall paper bag for general commodities.

There are some special materials used to make industrial bags. A woven polypropylene or high density material is used for square-end valve bags as well as sewn open-mouth bags where super strength is required. Slot-cast high-density polyethylene film has also been used for special applications.

Fiber Drums

A fiber drum is made from a multi-ply, laminated kraft paperboard cylinder with a fixed bottom and a lid. The bottom can be paperboard, wood, or metal and is usually attached to the cylinder sides with a crimped metal ring. The top is usually metal and attached with a metal locking ring. There are numerous standard capacity drums. The more popular sizes are made in different dimensional configurations, making it possible to nest one inside the other for economical empty drum shipments. Special laminations such as polyethylene coated sheets and aluminum foil liners can be used when extra protection is necessary. Sizes range from three-quarters of a gallon to 75 gallons in capacity. Sizes are specified in gallons even though the major usage is for dry solids.

There are several proprietary types of fiber containers that are closer to a rectangular shape and have an all-fiber top and bottom. These containers were developed to provide better cube utilization in warehousing and distribution.

Special Intermediate Bulk Containers

Large containers for bulk materials play a very important part in the distribution system. These containers require a pallet as part of the unit and must be moved by mechanical means.

The corrugated paperboard industry makes several styles of bulk containers for shipment of bulk solids, with capacities up to 2000 pounds. A good example is a 1000-pound corrugated container that is used extensively in the chemicals and plastics industries.

The wirebound box industry also makes a bulk container with an integrated pallet or skid as part of the box for shipment of very heavy materials such as castings.

Metal returnable containers are also used for shipping bulk solids. The metal container offers the advantage of outside storage with complete product protection. A disadvantage is the need to return the empty container.

Various types of laminated materials are used to fabricate large flexible bags that will hold 1000 to 2000 pounds of bulk materials. These bags can have a variety of features such as outlet sleeves at the bottom, and/or filling sleeves at the top. The filled container is either transported on a pallet or carried by several straps attached to the forks of a lift truck. These containers can be made one-way or disposable quality, or they can be strong enough to withstand multiple shipments.

Packages for Liquid Products

Metal Containers

For our purposes, metal cans will be considered consumer packaging rather than distribution packaging, although drawing a line between the two is difficult. Pails and small drums are usually considered distribution containers. Pails are made in sizes of 3 to 6.5 gallons. Generally they are of two types—open head and tight (closed) head. An open head pail can be made with a lever-type closing ring, a bolt-type closing ring, or a crimped closure. Pour spouts can also be incorporated into the removable lid. There are also a variety of spouts offered for the tight head pail. Different types of handles are also an option. The open head pail is primarily used for products that are too viscous to pour.

Steel kegs are larger than pails but smaller than drums and may also be either open head or tight head.

Steel drums are furnished in sizes ranging from 8 to 57 gallons. They are made with open head tops as well as tight (closed) heads. There are a wide variety of options in construction materials, such as the metal gauge of the sides, galvanized or stainless steel, and special coatings or liners. Steel drums can be constructed for one-way or returnable service. The most widely used steel drum is the DOT 17E, 55-gallon container. It can have either an 18 or 20 gauge body with an 18 gauge head and bottom.

Plastic containers are being used extensively as distribution containers, primarily for liquids. Most of the plastic containers for distribution are made from polyethylene. Pails are usually injection molded open head containers. Drums are usually of the tight head variety and are made by the rotational molding process. There are some options as to closures, but nowhere near the number of variations that are available in steel containers. Usually the designs, shapes, options, etc., are unique to each supplier. Plastic containers compete with metal containers where difficult-to-handle materials are involved, particularly when very exotic inner lining or coating materials are needed to protect the product.

Difficult to handle products can also be handled in a *combination* container—a blown polyethylene liner placed inside a steel drum. This combines the product protection feature offered by polyethylene containers with the strength of a steel drum. This same approach is sometimes taken with fiber drums. In both cases, an open head container is used as the overpack.

Liquid Intermediate Bulk Containers

There are few containers designed for intermediate bulk shipments of liquids. Several suppliers offer portable bins or tanks similar to those used for dry products. These are all returnable containers. A vulcanized rubber container that can be used for liquid shipments is available in a variety of sizes. Its advantage is that it can be rolled up when empty and requires much less space for the return cycle.

UNITIZATION

Unitizing of distribution packages is an important part of the distribution cycle. Palletization or unitization reduces damage to individual packages.

Unitizing of packages on pallets can be accomplished in several ways:

1. Package-to-package gluing

2. Strapping—metal or plastic

3. Stretch wrapping or shrink wrapping

A number of load-locking adhesives or solutions are available for gluing packages together to produce a solid unit load that can be transported efficiently but still depalletized easily at the point of consumption. The package or container must be sized and arranged so as to form an interlocking pattern in the unit load before this method can be used. Care must be taken in selecting the adhesive since it is desirable to use a material that has high shear properties and low tensile strength to prevent tearing when packages are depalletized.

Shrink films of polyethylene (PE) and polyvinyl chloride (PVC) are typically used to restrain packages on a pallet. A fabricated bag is placed over the unit load. As the bag is heated the film relaxes and then shrinks to form a tight load as it cools. This method provides a secure and watertight load. Its disadvantage is that the heat sources required to shrink the film are expensive and require a great deal of energy.

Stretch films of low density polyethylene (LDPE), linear low density polyethylene (LLDPE), polyethylene/ethyl vinyl acetate (PE-EVA), and polyvinyl chloride (PVC) are also used to restrain packages on a pallet.

Stretch films do not offer the degree of moisture protection obtained from shrink film, even when top caps are used, because the top is not totally wrapped in a single sheet of film, as is the case with the shrink film bag. Stretch film equipment requires less capital and is much more energy efficient. Stretch wrapping is less costly than shrink wrapping, but a number of factors should be taken into account before the choice between the two is made. Shrink wrapping may be more advantageous when all-weather protection is needed, when loads are irregularly shaped, and when full six-sided coverage is desired. Stretch wrapping is particularly advantageous with numerous load sizes, and when products are packaged in film bags.

The type of film to be utilized plays a major part in the success of any pallet over-wrapping operation. If the load is to be stored outside for an extended period, the use of an ultraviolet inhibitor in the film should be considered to prevent breakdown of the film. Although there are no standardized tests, Table 27–1 provides *general* guidelines to indicate the best film to use for a specific application.

It should be noted that certain properties are *very* important in some applications and of no value in others. Cling, for instance, is very important in conventional stretch wrapping applications, but of no particular benefit in "pass through" stretch wrapping. It should also be noted that properties of a basic film may be modified to enhance certain properties.

Steel or plastic strapping is used to secure materials and packages to pallets. Strapping is available in a variety of widths and thicknesses, depending on the strength required. Straps are placed around the unit load either horizontally, vertically, or both. The strapping is tightened with a tensioning tool and then sealed together. If the product being secured is fragile it may be necessary to provide corner protection to keep the strapping from damaging the package. Strapping performs very well for very heavy loads.

Packaging Equipment and Systems

Equipment and systems used in distribution packaging may vary widely. In addition to being of different size, configuration, and physical layout, they may be slow or fast, highly accurate or relatively inaccurate, heavily automated or very labor intensive, and may range in complexity from very simple to very sophisticated. In addition, even similar systems handling the same commodity and the same package may contain different functional components and may perform the operations in different sequences. For example,

Table 27-1   Comparative Properties of Commonly Used Stretch Films

	Polyethylene Film	*Linear Low-Density Polyethylene Film*	*Polyvinyl Chloride Film*	*Polyethylene- EVA Film*
Cling properties	Low cling	Low cling	*High cling*	Medium cling
Tear resistance	Low resistance	*Highest resistance*	Medium resistance	Medium resistance
Tensile strength	Low strength	*Highest strength*	Medium strength	Medium strength
Stress relaxation	*Low tendency to relax*	Medium tendency to relax	High tendency to relax	Medium tendency to relax
Temperature sensitivity	Medium sensitivity	Medium sensitivity	Most sensitive	*Least sensitive*
Optical properties	Medium transparency	Medium transparency	*Most transparent*	Least transparent
Toughness	Least tough	*Most tough*	Medium toughness	Medium toughness
Relative cost per pound	*Most economical*	Average cost	Most expensive	Average cost
Relative cost per finished load	Average cost	*Most economical*	Most expensive	Average cost

in one system containers might be labeled manually prior to filling using stencils and inked rollers, while in another system the same operations might be performed mechanically after the container has been filled.

After the distribution package itself has been selected, and assuming that all other marketing, warehousing, and physical distribution factors are equal, the final design of the packaging system is contingent on economics. A wide variety of alternatives exist, in most instances, ranging across the economic spectrum. The initial capital cost of a packaging system, together with its ongoing operating labor and maintenance costs, must be viewed in light of its packaging rate, expected uptime and downtime, anticipated packaging accuracy/product giveaway, and the anticipated spoilage of product and/or packaging materials. Subjective factors that might enter into the design of the packaging system include flexibility for handling other containers, the need for check weighing, future production requirements, appearance of the finished package (squareness of cases, appearance of finished loads, etc.), spare parts and local equipment service capabilities, interchangeability with other existing packaging equipment, and the like.

As in the preceding sections, we are concerned here with equipment and systems for distribution packaging—namely, with equipment and systems used for handling corrugated fiberboard boxes which might contain industrial products or consumer goods, and other packages used directly in transportation and distribution. The other packages we will be primarily concerned with include paper, plastic, and textile shipping sacks, steel and fiber drums, steel kegs, and steel and plastic pails, together with unitizing equipment for all of these distribution packages. As will be discussed further, generally speaking, packaging equipment and systems are presently more sophisticated in Europe than in the United States.

Case Handling Equipment

Corrugated fiberboard boxes, commonly called cases, easily qualify as the single most common distribution package. Cases are used as the primary distribution package for essentially all consumer goods as well as for a very wide variety of industrial products. The wide variety of case applications makes discussion of packaging equipment for case handling a complex matter. It is perhaps easiest to consider cases in three areas: (1) very large boxes used to distribute bulk chemicals, typically from a company in one of the chemical process industries to another company who will make use of the bulk chemicals in the manufacture of their own industrial or consumer products; (2) small and medium size cases (the great majority of all cases) used in the distribution of consumer goods from the manufacturer to the retailer and in the distribution of industrial products; (3) repacked cases used in the final distribution step for consumer goods between jobber's and retailer's distribution centers and retail stores and for industrial products between jobbers and distributors and industrial consumers.

Large Boxes

In the case of very large boxes, used for the distribution of bulk chemicals, a discussion of individual pieces of equipment as well as complete systems is in order. Typically, the boxes, ranging up to approximately 48 inches wide by 48 inches long by 60 inches high, might contain approximately 1000 to 2500 pounds of a single, dry, bulk product, in powder, flake, pellet, granular, or similar form. Commonly the distribution package consists of a single box on a pallet.

The major functions, exclusive of material handling, included in these bulk box packaging systems include the following:

Case make-up	Filling
Empty pallet dispensing	Vibrating for settlement
Empty case positioning on pallet	Sealing
Liner inflation	Unitizing

Generally speaking, these very large cases are almost always made up (assembled from knocked down blanks) on a manual basis. This is awkward and cumbersome, as well as inefficient; however, sufficient demand and justification has not existed in the past for the development of mechanized forming or erecting equipment for these cases.

The empty pallet dispensing function may involve simply manual handling of pallets near the filling point or, in higher rate operations, may involve an automatic pallet dispenser. An automatic pallet dispenser is a device into which stacks of empty pallets are placed by forklift truck, stored, and, when required, from which individual pallets are automatically dispensed. Most pallet dispensers in these types of systems hold a single stack of pallets, and usually have a capacity of from 10 to 20 pallets. Most also include a lifting mechanism for elevating the stack of pallets in order to allow the lowest pallet in the stack to be dispensed. An accessory that is relatively common for large box packaging systems involves the addition of gluing heads, usually for cold glue, to automatically dispense glue onto the top boards of the pallet to assist in securing the box to the pallet. Positioning the made-up empty box on the pallet is almost invariably done manually, although different accessories are used to make the job easier and to assure that the box is positioned squarely on the pallet.

The scale is the single most important component of a large box packaging system for bulk products, and may be either net weigh or gross weigh. Usually, as will be discussed later, the liner inflation, filling, and vibrating functions are incorporated into an automatic operation.

Net weigh (overhead) scales, which are in many cases very similar to open-mouth net weigh bagging scales, are commonly used for their high rate capability and the accuracy obtained. These net weigh scales are used in a two-stage, repetitive batch filling process wherein a weighing hopper is filled at high speed nearly to capacity and at slower speed up to capacity, dumped, and re-filled. A gate above the hopper controls the flow of bulk product into the weighing hopper. The bulk filling process establishes the speed and the dribble filling process establishes the accuracy. A wide variety of sophisticated electronic options now exist that permit automatic taring, automatic check weighing, and automatic trend sensing and compensating, for example. The weighing function can be a mechanical pivot and beam mechanism or an electronic load call.

When filling a 1000-pound box, such a scale might be used to process ten 100-pound weighments or, perhaps, four 250-pound weighments. The accuracy is dependent on the sum of the individual weighments. The hopper size is dependent on the product's bulk density. Depending to some extent on the flowability of the product and even more on the dexterity of the operator in moving empty boxes into the filling station and filled boxes out of the filling station, packaging rates in the range of 40,000 to 60,000 pounds per hour may be obtained.

Gross weigh (platform) scales are used more commonly in simple systems and less commonly in more sophisticated systems. The use of a gross weigh scale involves taring the empty pallet and empty box and utilizing either visually controlled or automatic cutoffs on the scale to control the flow of materials into the box. Automatic cutoffs may be photoelectric, fluidic, or magnetic.

Large boxes used for sensitive bulk products include an interior, plastic liner to contain the product inside the box. Liner inflation is usually required. Typically, the liner is manually placed in an empty box which has been made up and positioned on the pallet. At the filling station, the operator manually attaches the liner to a clamp which holds the liner during the filling process.

As mentioned previously, liner inflation, filling, and vibrating for settlement are commonly integrated into a single, automatic station. At the beginning of the filling cycle, liner inflation might be handled by a high-volume, low-pressure fan with filling being initiated automatically a few seconds later. Typically, as the filling progresses, vibrating of the product will be required in order to settle it and obtain the best utilization of the container volume. Vibrating assemblies usually lift the box and use air or electric vibrators to automatically vibrate the box as it is filled. The vibrating equipment utilized may vary in capacity and frequency, depending on the bulk flow characteristics of the product.

A wide variety of equipment exists for sealing large boxes. Usually, the liner is tied manually by the filling operator. In most instances, a cap is placed on the box, also manually. Sealing of the cap to the box and the box to the pallet may be accomplished in a variety of ways. Stapling of the cap to the box, perhaps using a mechanical lid press to hold the cap in position, may be done using either air-operated or electric, automatic or manually controlled stapling equipment.

Strapping, to accomplish the dual purpose of retaining the cap and securing the box to the pallet, may be done using a wide variety of manual, semi-automatic, and automatic equipment. Manual strapping equipment, of course, involves manually feeding the strap through the pallet (a difficult technique) with subsequent manual tightening and sealing of the strap. Semi-automatic equipment exists for feeding the strap around the load (as in pre-drape systems utilizing conveyors) and in feeding strap through the pallet with pallet void feeding equipment. Typically semi-automatic strapping involves manual tightening and sealing. Fully automatic strappers, complete with fully automatic pallet void strap feeding, tightening, and sealing are relatively common.

Most systems for packaging large boxes with bulk products link the packaging function with conveying equipment so as to form an integrated line. Stretch or shrink wrapping equipment, which can be used both for retaining caps and securing loads to pallets, will be discussed under unitizing equipment.

Small and Medium Size Cases

Packaging equipment for handling cases used for the primary distribution of consumer goods and industrial products is usually integrated into a packaging line involving other types of packaging equipment not under consideration here. For example, a beverage packaging line might include case forming equipment with which we are concerned, can filling and sealing equipment with which we are not concerned, and case packing, case sealing, and case palletizing equipment with which we are concerned. For this reason, individual pieces of equipment for handling this second type of case will be discussed as stand-alone entities. It is understood that these pieces of equipment usually serve as a component of an integrated system. The major types of distribution packaging equipment utilized for small and medium size cases are as follows:

Case forming and erecting equipment	Compression sections
Case packers	Wrap-around case packers
Case sealers	

Automatic case forming or case erecting equipment is commonly used in high-volume packaging lines, where manual case erection is impractical. Case erectors are manually loaded with knocked-down case blanks. These might be either top-loading or end-loading cases. Individual case blanks are automatically removed from the magazine and erected by the machine. Commonly, a case erector includes a bottom (glue) sealer and compression section for closing the bottom of the case. The erected case is then discharged from the machine with the top (or one end) flaps open. Automatic case erectors working in the 20 to 30 case per minute range are not uncommon. Note that automatic case erectors, handling only the cases themselves, are generally simpler and less expensive machines than case packers.

Automatic case packers, the most common type of case handling equipment, come in a wide variety of types of machines. The two main types are packers for top-opening cases and packers for end-opening cases, with a further breakdown for each type into single tier machines and multiple tier machines. Automatic case packers are not normally used in systems with independent automatic case erectors, because they typically incorporate the case erection function. Accordingly, the fundamental job of a case packer is to erect the case, receive a continuous stream of products to be packed, and pack these products into the cases. Case packers are normally used with automatic case sealers, as discussed below.

All case packers incorporate the layer forming function, involving equipment for arranging the product into the proper number of rows and segregating the in-feed stream(s) of rows into individual layers or tiers. Once the tier has been formed, it can be loaded into the case by a variety of means.

The simplest types of case packers pack a single tier of products into an end-loading case. These machines simply push the layer into the waiting erected case. The most complex case packers include multiple tier machines for end-loading and top-loading cases. Some of them can handle the insertion of internal corrugated product dividers.

Automatic case packers of all types are widely used for distribution packaging operations. Perhaps the most common types are those used in the food industry for canned goods. Depending on the size of the individual products to be packed, the individual product package, the number of packages per tier, and the number of tiers, operating rates may vary widely, but many can pack 20 to 30 cases per minute.

Automatic case sealers, which may be integrated with either automatic or manual case packing operations, are the simplest type of automatic case packaging equipment. Automatic case sealers receive the already packed case and seal (glue) either the top flaps only, the bottom flaps only (in a few instances), or both top and bottom flaps.

Compression sections, usually incorporating either rollers or conveyor belts, are utilized to hold the flaps in place long enough for the glue to set and may be either an integral part of the case sealer or an independent machine immediately down-stream. Case sealers may be considered in terms of the type of glue and the type of glue applicator utilized.

Automatic case sealers may utilize either "hot" or "cold" glue. "Hot" glue machines use solid glue and have an internal reservoir and control system for melting it and controlling its temperature. "Cold" glue systems utilize liquid glue at ambient temperatures. Different types of glue applicators are utilized, depending on the strength desired in the finished case for warehousing and transportation purposes. Applicators include single and multiple strip glue applicators as well as "area" type spray glue applicators. The automatic case sealer can be used to provide the proper amount of glue in precisely the desired area. Generally speaking, "cold" glue automatic case sealers are utilized for lower rate applications, up to, say, ten cases per minute. In the medium range, say from 10 to 20 cases per minute, both "cold" and "hot" glue automatic case sealers are utilized. Generally speaking, higher rate systems that handle more than 20 cases per minute are generally "hot" glue automatic case sealers.

A number of variations on the above three machines—automatic case erectors, automatic case packers, and automatic case sealers with compression sections—exist for semi-automatic applications. For example, an automatic bottom case sealer might be utilized in lieu of an automatic case erector, where the operator manually erects the case and places it on a mandrel, and the machine completes the bottom sealing operation. In the case packer area, manual effort might be utilized in forming the layer for subsequent insertion into the case by the packer. Likewise, semi-automatic case packers exist where the operator erects the case and loads it (while it is being held by the machine), with the only automatic machine function being that of sealing. Case sealers and compression sections are normally fully automatic.

All of the above case handling equipment, utilized in the distribution of consumer goods and industrial products, can generally handle regular slotted cases, the most common type of case. Automatic equipment also is utilized for packaging of products in wrap-around cases. Wrap-around cases are supplied to the user as pre-cut and scored (completely flat board) blanks, without a completed manufacturers' joint. Wrap-around case packers are usually fully integrated machines that incorporate the case erection, case packing, and case sealing functions into a single unit. Using blanks placed in a magazine, they receive products in a continuous stream, complete the case erecting, case packing, and case sealing function, and discharge a completed case. Major machine functions include row forming, segregation of layers, stacking of tiers if required, forming of the case directly around the products being packaged, sealing of the manufacturers' joint, sealing of the end flaps, compression, and discharge.

Wrap-around cases and automatic wrap-around case erector/packer/sealers are not very common but they do offer some distinct advantages in certain situations. Generally speaking, they result in a tighter finished package that is designed to utilize the products inside for structural support, instead of the sidewalls that are normally used for support in regular slotted cases. Wrap-around cases, therefore, generally lessen the susceptability to internal product damage during transportation and require less square footage of corrugated material per case. The exact corrugated board savings for a wrap-around case, as compared to a regular slotted case, depend on the case's specific length, width, and height dimensions, and the extent to which the case does or does not resemble a perfect cube. Operating rates up to approximately 35 cases per minute may be utilized, depending on the nature of the products being packaged (see Tables 27–2 through 27–5). Palletizing equipment and stretch and shrink wrapping equipment will be discussed under unitizing equipment (pages 766–769). Labeling and marking equipment will be discussed under miscellaneous equipment (pages 769–770).

Repacked Cases

The third type of case under consideration is commonly utilized but seldom mechanized. Repacked cases are used in the final distribution step for consumer goods and industrial products. These cases are available in a variety of sizes and are utilized on a daily basis for packaging different combinations of products ordered for shipment. Multi-product line distribution centers performing "broken" case order picking with repacking of different types of consumer goods for shipment to retail stores serve as a typical example.

Table 27–2 Typical Components of a Packaging System for Regular Slotted Cases

	Infeed	Discharge
Case erector (optional)	Knocked-down case blanks	Empty, erected cases
Empty product container unscrambler	Bulk empty containers	Oriented empty containers
Product filler	Oriented empty containers; bulk product	Open, filled product containers
Product capper	Bulk caps; open, filled product containers	Filled and capped product containers
Case packer	Knocked-down case blanks; glue; filled and capped containers	Open, packed cases
Case sealer and compression section	Open, packed cases; glue	Sealed cases
Case palletizer	Sealed cases; glue; empty pallets	Palletized cases

Table 27–3   Typical Components of a Packaging System for Re-shipper Slotted Cases

	Infeed	*Discharge*
Case depalletizer	Empty, palletized re-shippers	Empty, oriented re-shippers; empty pallets
Product filling equipment	Empty, oriented reshippers; bulk product	Open, filled product containers in re-shippers
Closing equipment	Bulk closures; open, filled product containers in re-shippers	Filled and closed product containers in re-shippers
Case sealer	Open, packed cases	Sealed cases
Case palletizer	Sealed cases; glue; empty pallets	Palletized cases

Case erection is generally done manually. Case packing is also usually done manually, although some equipment may be utilized for feeding cushioning materials into the packed case. Most of the equipment that would be of interest involves sealing of the case after the packing has been completed.

Many types of closures exist for these types of cases, depending generally on the product value, the weight of the case, and the nature of the transportation. Methods of closure include gluing, strapping, stapling, taping with paper tape or filament tape, tying, or simply closing the flaps in an interlocking manner. Major packaging equipment can be used in the first four of these operations. The many varieties of hand operated equipment and accessories that are available can improve productivity, but will not be discussed here.

Automatic case sealers utilizing both "cold" and "hot" glue have been discussed previously. These are not commonly used in this application, however, because of the wide variety of case sizes encountered and the possible incomplete filling of the re-packed case. If

Table 27–4   Typical Components of a Packaging System for Re-shipper Regular Slotted Cases with "Out-of-Case" Filling.

	Infeed	*Discharge*
Case depalletizer	Empty, palletized re-shippers	Empty, oriented re-shippers; empty pallets
Uncaser	Empty, oriented re-shippers	Empty, oriented product containers; empty cases
Product filler	Empty, oriented product containers; bulk product	Open, filled product containers
Product capper	Bulk caps; open, filled product containers	Filled and capped product containers
Case packer	Filled and capped product containers; empty cases	Open, packed cases
Case sealer and compression section	Open, packed cases; glue	Filled and sealed cases
Case palletizer	Sealed cases; glue; empty pallets	Palletized cases

Table 27–5   Typical Components of a Packaging System for Wrap-around Cases

	Infeed	*Discharge*
Can depalletizer	Bulk, empty cans (palletized)	Empty cans; empty pallets; slip sheets
Product canner	Empty cans; bulk product	Open, filled cans
Product seamer	Open, filled cans; bulk lids	Sealed cans
Wrap-around case erector/packer/sealer	Sealed cans; glue; knocked-down case blanks	Packed and sealed cases
Case palletizer	Sealed cases; glue; empty pallets	Palletized cases

all of the cases being repacked are of the same size, however, and if sufficient internal support is provided there is certainly no reason why an automatic case sealer and compression section could not be effectively used.

Other types of closing equipment, discussed below, are generally geared to accommodate random case sizes. They can be used at a number of different packing stations, with each station picking the case size to best accommodate the size of the order being shipped.

Case strappers utilizing plastic strap may be effective for sealing cases which might require subsequent reopening and resealing without damage to the case. These strappers may be either fully automatic or semi-automatic and include the strap feeding, tightening, and sealing functions. Case strappers are relatively new, compared to some other types of case handling equipment, and generally do not operate at very high rates. Case strappers utilizing steel strap might also be used for very heavy cases.

Stapling machines, including pedestal-mounted units and hand-held units, are usually manually controlled. In a typical operation a large pedestal stapler might be used to make the bottom flap closure, and a hand-held stapler used for the top flap closure after the case packing has been completed. Generally speaking, pedestal units are electrically operated and hand-held units are operated on compressed air. Obviously, staplers are designed for use on any size of case.

Automatic paper tapers include those dedicated to a particular case size as well as tapers designed to accommodate a range of case sizes. Tapers are fairly sophisticated machines involving devices to hold the top flaps in position while applying either top or top and bottom taped joints. The taped joints overlap the ends for a few inches and attach to, and close, both of the major case flaps. A floating taping head capable of automatically positioning itself to accommodate varying case heights is utilized on some machines.

As is the case with all these closures, the number, type, size and location for the top and the bottom case flaps may be varied to suit the distribution requirements.

Bag Packaging Equipment

Paper, textile, and plastic film shipping sacks of many types (all generally referred to as bags), are widely used for the distribution of bulk materials for industries and consumers. These bulk materials range from very fine powders to small aggregates, and may include almost any type of pellet, flake, granule, or other bulk material form. Bags are commonly used for chemicals and fertilizers, mineral-based rock products such as cement, specialty soils and other organic gardening materials, feeds and grains, food and food-related products. It is perhaps easiest to discuss bag packaging equipment by first discussing packing and sealing equipment for open-mouth, valve, and form, fill, and seal bags and then discussing related equipment and systems for all three types of bags.

Open-Mouth Bags

Open-mouth bags of all types—paper, textile, or film; gussetted or flat; sewn or pasted bottom—regardless of the number of plies or of the ply material, are generally filled (packed) on similar equipment. In virtually every case, the bag is placed underneath an open spout and the contents flow into the open bag.

The function of positioning the empty bag for filling is referred to as bag placing. This may be done manually, or mechanically by using an automatic bag placer. This machine retrieves an individual bag from a supply of empty bags held in a magazine, opens the bag, and places it directly on the bagging spout. Typically, the bag placer is electrically interlocked with the bag packer so that filling is automatically initiated as soon as the bag is in position. Automatic bag placers are commonly used with multiwall paper bags. Burlap and other textile bags, as well as film bags, cannot usually be handled utilizing automatic bag placing equipment.

Open-mouth bag packers fall into two general types—net weigh and gross weigh. Both are usually suspended from a support structure overhead, so that the bagging spout is readily accessible. In most cases, the bag is retained on the spout during filling by a manual or pneumatically operated bag clamping mechanism.

Net weigh bag packers, previously discussed for filling large cases with bulk products, are used for relatively expensive products that are free flowing. The bulk material flows from a feed system above the packer into the weigh hopper in a two-stage bulk and dribble flow technique. As soon as the weigh hopper is filled to, say, the 90 percent level, dribble flow continues to fill the hopper, allowing a high degree of accuracy. After the hopper has been filled, it dumps a single weighment directly into the bag. The filled bag is discharged and the weigh hopper is then refilled while the next empty bag is being positioned. Net weigh scales have a weigh hopper bearing on a scaling mechanism. They have historically been mechanical, but are now becoming almost exclusively electronic. As discussed previously, net weigh open-mouth bag packers may be outfitted with a wide variety of electronic options used to optimize the bagging rate and accuracy.

Belt-type heat sealers, used with pinch-type open-mouth paper bags, seal (glue) the top of the bag by passing the pre-glued bag through two parallel compression belts and a heat sealing station with the top in the folded (closed) position. The glue is heated and held in compression long enough for the seal to be made. The heat sealer may be hand fed or may be automatically fed with mechanisms which hold the top of the bag and fold it prior to leading the end into the entry of the heat sealer. Similar bond-type heat sealers may be utilized with film bags, which use no glue but rather heat the film and bond it to itself. Bags are usually conveyed on V-trough or flat belt conveyors with backboards through the heat sealing operation.

A net weigh open-mouth bag packer can be integrated with an automatic bag placer to yield a totally automatic open-mouth bag filling operation. These may also be integrated with automatic heat sealing equipment for a *totally automatic* bag packing and sealing system applicable to pinch-type open-mouth multiwall paper bags. This approach, although it requires a high capital investment and a sophisticated maintenance capability, yields the very lowest bag packaging costs per pound of product for open-mouth bags, particularly when several automatic arrangements can be maintained and monitored by a single group of operating personnel. Depending on the material being packed, the size of the bag, and the accuracy of the filling weight desired, automatic bag packing equipment may operate in the range of 20 to 24 bags per minute.

Gross weigh bag packers, for open-mouth bags of all types of paper, textile, and film, hold the bag on the bagging spout in the same manner as net weigh bag packers. However, the weigh hopper is eliminated and both the bag and the contents are weighed, because the bagging spout, from which the bag is suspended, is linked directly to a scaling mechanism. Product flows through the packer until the desired weight has been reached, at which time the flow is shut off.

Generally speaking, gross weigh open-mouth bag packers are used with less expensive products and, in some instances, with products that are not free flowing enough for the use of a self-dumping weigh hopper. The scaling system may be either mechanical or electronic. The operating rates usually depend to a great degree on the flowability of the product.

Sewing systems are used for bag closure in many instances, when contact between the product and the thread and/or holes is not detrimental to the distribution function. A sewing system includes a sewing head and a thread cutting mechanism, through which the bag passes in a vertical position, with the top of the bag being sewn. In the case of gusseted bags, the top must be reformed before the bag moves into the sewing head. As it leaves the sewing head, the thread is cut and the closure is complete.

For open-mouth bags—whether paper, textile, or film— a number of options exist as to type of bag and type of packing and sealing equipment. A great deal depends on the closure, which may be either bonded (film bags), glued (paper bags), or sewn (paper and textile bags). Positioning of the empty bag on the filling equipment may be mechanical (as in the case of paper bags) or manual (as in the case of film and textile bags). Packing of the bags may be either net weigh or gross weigh.

Products that might be packed in open-mouth multiwall paper bags include chemical products such as caustic soda, adipic acid, fertilizer, or pelletized polyethylene; food products such as flour or sugar; and food-related products such as dog food or charcoal. Typical products that might be packed in textile bags are caustic soda or rice that is packaged for export. Film bags might be used for pelletized polyethylene.

Valve Bags

Valve bags are used primarily in the distribution of bulk industrial products such as chemicals and rock products. As was mentioned earlier in this chapter, valve bags utilize an internal seal and require no external closure. The equipment required to package a valve bag is, therefore, limited to the filling equipment and the placing of the bag on the bagging spout.

Valve bag packers include gravity packers which may be either net weigh or gross weigh, air packers which are normally gross weigh, blow packers which are normally net weigh, and auger packers which are only gross weigh. Gravity packers are usually utilized for the most free flowing products, and air packers and blow packers for products that flow readily when fluidized. Auger packers are used for the hardest to handle products, including those that do not flow by gravity or fluidize well.

Placing of the bags may be either mechanical or manual for any of the four types of valve bag packers. All of the valve bag packers fill the bag in the vertical position, with the spout in the horizontal position, except for blow packers which may fill the bag in either the vertical or horizontal position, depending on the design of the particular machine.

In all instances, a spout is inserted into the valve of the valve bag, so that the product can flow directly into the bag. The spout is sized to fit the specific valve size of the bag being packed.

Empty bags may be placed manually on the filling spouts faster for valve bags than for open-mouth bags, primarily due to the fact that valve bag packers can be located in very close proximity to one another and due to the fact that the man can handle the valve bag with only one hand. When valve bag packers are placed in groups, usually of two to four packers, the operator can manually place the bags at rates of up to six bags per minute per spout, or an ultimate maximum of approximately 21 to 24 bags per minute.

Automatic valve bag placers may be utilized to reduce labor in the bag packaging operation, although they are only capable of rates up to 10 to 12 bags per minute.

Gravity valve bag packers are the simplest type of valve bag packer and, whether gross weigh or net weigh, simply consist of a horizontal spout through which product flows, when appropriate gates are opened. A *net weigh* gravity valve bag packer might simply consist of an open-mouth net weigh packer with an accessory spout located on the bottom. In the case of a *gross weigh* gravity valve bag packer, the bagging spout would be linked to a scaling mechanism in much the same way that the bagging spout in an open-mouth gross weigh bag packer is lined to a scaling mechanism. Except for difference of the spout, the operation of a net weigh or gross weigh valve bag packer would be the same as for an open-mouth gross weigh or net weigh bag packer.

Unlike gravity valve bag packers, air packers are normally floor-mounted, not suspended from overhead. In an air packer, a quantity of bulk product is introduced into a fluidizing chamber, which is then closed and pressurized with low pressure air. When the product has been fluidized, the discharge valve is opened and the fluidized product flows through the spout into the valve bag. When the proper weight has been reached, the infeed and discharge valves are reset and the process repeated. The bag on the spout is linked to a mechanical scaling mechanism. Air packers require the use of a low-pressure, high-volume blower and associated duct work. Powders are commonly filled on air packers and, because of the particle size and the air volume involved, a dust collection system is usually recommended. An air packer functions much like an air slide for handling bulk products.

Blow packers function in much the same manner as air packers, except that they utilize a net weigh scale to pre-weigh the proper amount of product for the bag. The scale dumps the required quantity of bulk product for a single bag into the pressurizing chamber, the chamber is pressurized, and product is blown into the bag. Unlike air packers, where the fluidized product essentially flows by gravity into the bag, the operation of the blow packer is more analogous to a dense-phase pneumatic conveying system which transfers the product into the bag without really depending on gravity. Blow packers are relatively recent developments and represent a response to the need for a net weigh fluidizing packer for chemical products.

Like air packers, auger packers are floor-mounted. They consist of a strong hopper from which a small screw-type auger conveys the product through the spout and into the bag. Auger packers operate at relatively slow rates, perhaps even as slow as two bags per minute per spout. As mentioned above, they are used for products that will not flow by gravity or may not be fluidized, but must be conveyed into the bag. The spout, as in the case of the gross weigh gravity packer and the air packer, is linked to a scaling mechanism which turns off the auger drive motor when the correct weight has been reached. Since auger packers usually handle products which do not flow well, a vibrating mechanism is usually added to vibrate the bag so as to increase product density. The design of the auger itself, including its taper and pitch, depends entirely on the product being handled and its flowability at the desired rate. Exotic auger designs are not uncommon. Abrasive products are not normally handled through auger packers because of the excessive wear the auger would suffer. The auger is usually reversed at the end of the filling cycle to clear the spout and eliminate product which might become trapped inside the valve. Open-mouth and valve bags are the predominant types utilized for distribution.

Form, Fill, and Seal Bags

Form, fill, and seal bags for *consumer packaging* of food products are quite common. Form, fill, and seal packers for *distribution packaging* of larger bags are relatively uncommon. Machines designed for packaging small consumer form, fill, and seal bags have been adapted for handling larger distribution packages, up to perhaps 25 pounds. These machines work from a roll of flat film stock, form the film into a continuous tube, and heat the vertical joint. In a single operation, a bottom seal is made together with the top seal of the previous bag and the two bags are cut, allowing the first one to discharge from the machine. After the bottom seal has been made, the net-weighed product is introduced into the continuous tube, then the bag indexes down and the top seal is made. These machines are not commonly used for distribution packaging, although they do exist.

In this area, European bag packaging equipment manufacturers are significantly more advanced than American manufacturers. Film is a more plentiful distribution packaging material in Europe and, as a result, form, fill, and seal machines for 50-pound or 25-kilogram bags have been developed and used successfully for many years. The European machines work from a large roll of continuous, tubular film stock. The machines measure the tubular stock for the length of the particular bag being manufactured, then make a bottom heat seal and cut the bags apart, leaving an open top for the next bag. The resulting open-mouth film bag is then automatically placed and filled utilizing an open-mouth net weigh scale. Subsequently, the bags are sealed automatically with a band-type heat sealer and any excess material is trimmed from above the heat seal, forming a finished bag. These types of machine are just beginning to be introduced into the United States and represent a large capital investment. Operating rates in the range of 20 bags per minute, assuming that the product is free flowing, can be achieved.

Related Equipment and Systems

Most bag packaging operations integrate the filling and sealing equipment, together with placing equipment, if utilized, into a system that includes a few other types of bag packaging equipment which are essentially the same regardless of the type of bag being filled.

Strictly speaking, after the bag has been placed, filled, and sealed, the packaging operation has been finished and packages may simply be manually palletized and loaded. In most systems, however, the next step is to orient the bag into proper position for conveying to a palletizing operation that may be located some distance away. One or more of the functions of check weighing, metal detecting, bag rejecting and bag flattening may be incorporated into the conveying system leading toward the palletizing function.

A check weigher is simply an in-line belt conveyor on which a single bag is handled for a few seconds so that it can be weighed while in motion and a determination made as to whether it is within the accepted weight range. If the bag is out of tolerance, the check weigher will determine if it weighs too much or too little and a variety of results may be directed, as discussed below. The check weigher consists of a short belt conveyor mounted directly on a high speed electronic scale with appropriate electrical controls.

The bag also might be conveyed through a metal detector in order to determine whether or not stray metal has inadvertently been packed in the bag with the product. A metal detector is an electronic device that creates a magnetic field in which no metal objects are located and through which the bag is conveyed. If there is metal in the bag, it is sensed by the metal detector and appropriate action can be taken. The amount of metal that may be detected in a bag depends on what type of metal it is, the configuration of the metal, the size of the opening through which the bag passes, and the sensitivity and adjustment of the metal detector.

Both check weighers and metal detectors may have electrical controls that can serve a variety of functions. A defective bag might simply be noted and counted, a warning light might be flashed, an alarm might be sounded, the line might be stopped, or, in the most sophisticated systems, a bag reject mechanism might be activated to remove the defective bag from the line.

Particularly in the case of check weighers, the frequency with which bags of different weights are found is usually noted and accounted for. Most check weighers have five weight ranges, including over heavy, over light, within tolerance, under light, and under heavy. Data retrieved from the check weigher may be used to adjust the scaling mechanisms in the bag packing equipment. In more sophisticated systems, automatic feedback control may be used to adjust the bag packer on an on-line, automatic basis.

Bag reject mechanisms are simply conveying devices used to remove the bag from the line. These can take many forms, including tilting belt units, in which the bag is conveyed onto a slick belt conveyor, which simply tilts and causes the bag to slide off the conveyor before the conveyor returns to its original in-line position. Jump-chain or belt-type bag reject units have narrow chains or belts located between powered rollers. The bag is conveyed on the rollers and, when the bag is in the proper position, the belts or chains are raised between the rollers to convey the bag at right angles from the line. The belts or chains then lower to their original position before the next bag arrives. Flipping-finger-type units operate in much the same way, utilizing steel fingers located between powered rollers to lift the bag up off of the rollers and slide it off of the main line.

The rates achieved by automatic bag check weighers and metal detectors depend primarily on the bag length and the speed limitations of the conveying equipment. The bag must be retained on the scale long enough for it to be weighed or for the metal to be sensed by the metal detectors. The rates depend on the amount of time required to remove one bag from the line prior to the arrival of the next bag. Jump-chain or belt-type bag reject units are usually the fastest. Bag check weighing and metal detecting at rates in the range of 20 to 24 bags a minute are possible. Bag rejecting is possible at rates of around ten to twelve bags per minute.

Bag flatteners are devices that remove air from the filled bag. This makes it possible to load more product into the railroad car or truck, and serves as the first step in shaping the bag for good palletizing. Bag flatteners consist of one conveyor that transports the bag and a separate overhead boom-mounted conveyor that compresses the bag between the two conveyors. The compression action may use a single boom or may be articulated with the boom divided into a number of segments, each of which functions independently. The compression action may be simply through gravity, using the weight of the boom conveyor and/or weights, or may be pneumatically or hydraulically created and controlled. The conveying surface used in the bag flattener depends on the type of bag and the product packed in the bag. Bag flatteners were originally designed around spring belt-type conveyors, but more recently have been constructed primarily of conventional belt conveyors. The length of the bag flattener is dependent on the construction of the bag, the amount of entrapped air, and the amount of pressure being applied to the bag as it is conveyed. Inasmuch as bag flatteners hold the bag securely, the flattener may be oriented so as to convey the bag horizontally, inclined at an angle, or vertically.

Labeling of bags with separate paper labels is not common and, even when performed, is only possible on a manual basis. Stenciling, of dates and blending or packaging lot numbers, is most commonly done mechanically while the bag is held in position on the packer. After the bag has left the packer, mechanical stenciling is difficult. Under *some* circumstances, mechanical stenciling may be performed satisfactorily using a rotary coder or an ink jet painter while the bag is being conveyed through a bag flattener.

The packaging machinery in a bag packaging system is usually linked together with belt or gravity skate-wheel conveyors to form an integrated system. Roller conveyors are not usually satisfactory for conveying bags. Palletizing equipment and stretch and shrink wrapping equipment will be discussed under unitizing equipment (pages 766–769).

Drum Packaging Equipment

Fiber drums with removable lids and steel drums, including both tight-head and full open-head types, are utilized primarily for the industrial distribution of chemical products, including lubricating oils, industrial chemicals, solvents, paints, food, and food related products. Although drums come in a wide variety of sizes and types of construction, it is perhaps easiest to consider two main types—drums filled with dry products and drums filled with liquid products. Drums are usually filled in the upright position on conveyors. The packaging equipment for the drums—including the filling, sealing, and palletizing equipment—may constitute a small portion of a larger conveyor system that may be as much as a few thousand feet in length. Large conveyor systems usually lead from the empty container unloading area through a series of banks of conveyors that store empty drums, with individual conveyors leading to the packaging area and from the packaging area to filled drum accumulation conveyors, and subsequently to palletizing equipment.

Dry Products

Although drums for dry products may be filled individually or several at a time on pallets, the equipment and the functions involved in filling drums with dry products are very similar to those used to fill dry, bulk products into large boxes (see pages 750–752). Both systems may be either net weigh or gross weigh and may incorporate liner inflation and vibrating for settlement. Except that the drum is cylindrical and the box is rectangular, the equipment used, including the net weigh scales, gross weigh scales, liner inflating equipment, and vibrating equipment, is essentially identical. Smaller weighments for net weigh scales might be expected, particularly for small fiber drums, and depending on the product and the size of the drum, vibrating might not be required. Of course, a liner may not be involved at all.

Drums are commonly filled with dry, dust-laden products for which dust control is more of a problem than normal for products typically associated with large boxes. Often a dust cover, which is essentially a vented flat plate, is utilized between the overhead scale or product chute and the drum itself in order to control dust. One or more drums is conveyed into the filling station. The dust cover, connected to the filling spout by a flexible connections, is lowered onto the drum(s) and the filling takes place with the drum(s) covered. The venting system might be a nozzle in the dust cover with a flexible connection leading to a dust collection system.

Sealing of the drum is a manual operation, and can be done at the filling station or after the drum is conveyed to an adjacent sealing station.

Liquid Products

Drum filling equipment stations for dry products are generally custom engineered stations consisting of equipment from several vendors. In contrast, fillers for drums of liquid products are purchased as complete units. Virtually all drum fillers for liquid products consist of a platform type scale, i.e., a gross weigh scale, together with an overhead mechanical nozzle for inserting the liquid into the drum, either under pressure or using gravity. The selection of the filler for a specific application, then, must take into account (1) the characteristics of the product and the required filling rate, and (2) which functions of the process can be handled by semi-automatic and automatic features and which functions will need to be handled manually. Filling and sealing of liquid products into (typically) tight-head steel drums include the following functions:

Removal of the bung plug

Drum interior inspection, if required

Top stenciling or labeling, if required

Side stenciling or labeling, if required

Conveying onto the filler

Taring of the scale (to eliminate the weight of the empty drum)

Addition of an anti-foam agent (rarely utilized)

Orientation of the bung hole underneath the filling nozzle

Introduction of the filling nozzle

Initiation of bulk fluid flow

Slow retraction of the filling nozzle while filling, with the nozzle remaining below the fluid level in the drum at all times (if required)

Cessation of bulk fluid flow and initiation of dribble fluid flow

Cessation of dribble fluid flow, upon reaching proper weight

Retraction of the nozzle

Control of drip

Replacement of the bung plug

Discharge from the drum filler

Tightening of the bung plug

Application and crimping of the bung seal

Application and crimping of the vent seal (if required)

Accuracy in drum filling is particularly important because most products distributed in drums are filled by weight but sold by volume. For this reason, most drum filling machines incorporate a bulk (high rate) flow cycle for filling the drum nearly full and a dribble (slow rate) cycle for topping off the drum to the desired weight. This bulk-dribble flow process functions in the same manner as for dry bulk net weigh scales. Automatic taring of the drum is usually justified in an effort to achieve greater accuracy.

Historically the scale portion of the drum filler has been mechanical, but these have been replaced by electronic scales, which allow greater flexibility for the control of the filling function. Scale cutoff mechanisms (such as photoelectric, magnetic, or fluidic controls) which sensed the dial needle on mechanical scales are no longer required.

The nature of the product, the filling rate required, and the product pressure are important considerations when choosing the type of filling machine to be utilized. These parameters particularly affect the choice of nozzle design, whether the unit is to be a "top" or "bottom" filling machine, and the number of filling stages to be utilized. Top fill machines can usually be used for products that have virtually no tendency to foam and/or that can be filled at relatively low product pressures. A top fill drum filler has a short (three- to six-inch) nozzle which is inserted only a few inches into the top of the drum. A top fill drum filler would use two stages, a bulk flow stage and a dribble flow stage. Products which are more prone to foaming and/or are to be filled at higher pressures usually use a bottom fill machine which uses a nozzle mounted on the end of a lance that is slightly longer than the height of the drum. The lance lowers to the bottom of the drum and then, as filling proceeds, rises slowly, always staying beneath the product level in the drum. Most bottom drum fillers are two-stage fillers, with bulk and dribble flow. For products with excessive tendency to foam, a three-stage bottom filler might be utilized. The three stages include (1) a dribble (slow rate) cycle to provide a small head of product in the bottom of the drum, so that the normal bulk (high rate) cycle will be beneath the surface, (2) the normal bulk cycle, and (3) another dribble cycle to achieve an accurate weight.

Drum fillers represent another area where European technology is more advanced in terms of machine automation than American technology. Fully automatic European drum fillers, incorporating essentially all the functions listed above, have been developed. In the United States, attempts have been made to develop a totally automatic drum filler; however, none exists at the present time. There are a few U.S. manufactured "automatic" drum filling machines that include most, but not all, of the above functions.

In the United States, bung removal is usually manual. Once the drum has been introduced onto the filler, however, equipment is available for automatically rotating the drum and locating the bung hole so that is may be aligned properly underneath the filling nozzle or lance. For hazardous products, this allows the filler to be completely enclosed. Automatic taring of the empty drum is now quite common. Initiation of the filling cycle is usually done by means of a push button, with the control of the flow stages, the insertion and retraction of the lance, and cutoff at the proper weight usually being fully automatic. The bung plug is usually manually re-inserted and loosely tightened by hand, before the filled drum is conveyed from the filler to an adjacent sealing station.

Sealing can be performed while the drum is still on the filler, but it is more often performed at an adjacent station while the next drum is being filled, so as to obtain the best production rate. Two fillers are commonly arranged facing one another, so that a single operator can operate both machines at one time. The number of operators necessary to perform both the filling and sealing operations efficiently depends to a great extent on the fluid flow time for the product in the drum.

A typical sealing station includes a bin containing bung seals and vent seals and a tool stand that holds manually or air operated sealing tools. Assuming that the vent plug is already in the drum, then a maximum of three tools is required: a wrench for tightening the bung plug, a crimper for attaching the vent seal, and a crimper for attaching the bung seal. Well-designed stations support air operated tools from tool balancers located above the drum so they can be used quickly and efficiently.

Once the sealing has been completed, the drum is usually ready to be conveyed to the full drum conveyor accumulation lines (where production from several fillers may be accumulated, segregated by product), and then conveyed to the palletizing operation. Check weighing on an adjacent or in-line platform scale could be performed; however, it is not commonly done.

Depending directly on the fluid flow time and the dexterity of the operator, drum packaging rates are usually in the range of one drum every 1 to 1½ minutes for one filling machine.

Palletizing equipment will be discussed under unitizing equipment (pages 766–769). Labeling and marking equipment will be discussed under miscellaneous equipment (pages 769–770).

Keg and Pail Packaging Equipment

Kegs and pails, whether steel or plastic, tight-head or full open-head, are filled with dry products and liquid products using similar or identical equipment to that used for drums. In addition, several other types of equipment are utilized.

In the case of full open-head steel kegs and pails, when lug type lids are used, a special 360-degree crimper must be utilized for sealing the lid. These crimpers consist of mechanical linkages, operating from a single drive shaft, which bend all of the lugs into their closed position. These crimpers may be manually operated, using two handles, or may be air operated.

Unlike drum fillers, where the communication between the scale and the fluid control valve is usually electrical, keg and pail filling equipment may utilize a mechanical connection to turn off the valve. Tight-head or open-head kegs and pails may utilize fillers that have the weighing mechanism mechanically linked directly to a mechanically operated control valve, so that when the desired weight is reached, a counterweight is overcome and the valve is closed. These are, of course, gross weigh fillers, but the counterweight may be adjusted to compensate approximately for the empty container weight.

These fillers may handle from one to four kegs or pails at a time. Again depending on the fluid flow time and the dexterity of the operator, the cycle time for *all* the containers on the filling machine is usually in the range of 45 seconds to one minute.

Another entirely different type of filler exists for tight-head pails. These are not weight fillers, but volume fillers, similar to those used for liquid filling of containers in consumer packaging. Utilizing a head tank of product open to atmospheric pressure, a nozzle is lowered into the bung hole, compressing a spring and opening an internal valve within the nozzle. Fluid flows through the level of the valve within the nozzle and then flow ceases automatically. As the nozzle is retracted from the container, the spring extends to close the valve once again. The accuracy of this type of filler, which fills up to six pails at a time to a specific dimensional level within the container, depends on the cross-sectional area within the container at the valve point. This type of filler would be more accurate on a percentage basis for a container with a neck than for a pail of uniform cross-section. The accuracies obtained, however, are usually satisfactory for all but the most expensive products.

Another difference between drums and kegs and pails would be the types of closures utilized. Bungs and bung seals are utilized on almost all tight-head drums; in the case of kegs and pails, several proprietary closures exist which incorporate internal spouts and similar features.

Palletizing equipment will be discussed below. Labeling and marking equipment will be discussed under miscellaneous equipment (see pages 769–770).

Unitizing Equipment

The handling of large, unitized, unit loads in order to minimize the number of trips required is an accepted materials handling technique for improving productivity. Unitizing for packaging includes both the equipment to form the unit load and equipment for the application of additional packaging materials to maintain the unit load securely throughout the distribution cycle to its ultimate destination.

In order for distribution packaging to be most effective in finished product storage and transportation, the overall unit load size and the sizes of the individual distribution packages must be carefully selected to minimize lost space. Normally, this means utilizing the full width of the trailer, rail car or container except for the necessary loading and unloading clearance, utilizing the full length with an even number of unit loads and utilizing the full height or the maximum height as dictated by materials handling, storage, or weight limit considerations.

Assuming that the overall unit load size has already been selected to maximize cube utilization within the carrier's equipment, the next step is to determine the best distribution package size to effectively utilize the cube of the unit load. This involves determining the overall size of the distribution package itself, along with the pattern on each layer within the unit load and the number of layers within the unit load. This determination is simple for most drums, kegs, and pails, but may be more involved for cases and bags.

Assuming that the desired unit load has been selected to be 48 inches by 40 inches by 60 inches, not including the pallet, and assuming that the size (unit weight or volume) of the case or bag has been dictated by marketing considerations, there will still be a three-dimensional flexibility for configuring the distribution package to maximize the utilization of the unit load cube and provide a stable, secure load that will protect the product adequately through warehousing and distribution.

Corrugated cases can present problems because of the concern with uneven weight distribution and crushing within the unit load. The case must be constructed not only to handle the products contained within, but also to handle the weight of products within the unit load bearing on lower layers. Normally, cases are designed, in addition, to handle the extra weight from additional unit loads stacked directly in the lower one (as in warehouse floor storage), under given humidity conditions. Most of a case's crushing strength is derived from its sidewalls, and this must be a major consideration in selecting the pallet pattern. Because the individual cases are usually stable (rectangular, with flat sides) in and of themselves, both interlocking patterns and columnar patterns can be utilized, although interlocking patterns are much more common.

Bags present a different kind of problem. First, the individual bags may not be nearly as stable as cases, depending on the construction of the bag and the volume of the contents. Second, since there are usually fewer bags in an individual layer, much less freedom exists in terms of the number of units placed on a layer and the number of ways in which they may be arranged. Accordingly, the choices of pallet pattern and number of layers are usually more limited if the entire volume of the unit load is to be used while at the same time providing stability. Drums, kegs, and pails present even fewer options, although the principles to be followed remain the same.

Machine palletizing, as opposed to manual palletizing, may be either semi-automatic or fully automatic. A fully automatic palletizer includes the following functions:

Dispensing of a single pallet

Dispensing of a slip sheet (if required)

Control of the infeed flow of packages so as to form a single layer

Layer squaring on all sides

Placement of the single layer on the pallet

Gluing of bottom layer to pallet (if required)

Layer compression (for bag palletizers only)

Formation of successive layers and placement on the pallet

Gluing of individual layers to one another (if required)

Discharge of the completed, palletized load

Fully automatic palletizers perform all of the required functions automatically, with operating labor required only for the addition of empty pallets or slip sheets, and the handling of completed loads. Semi-automatic palletizers usually utilize manual assistance for forming the individual products into layers, but allow the machine to perform all of the other functions. The layer-forming function requires the most dexterity and generally requires manual assistance, particularly on lower-speed lines.

A number of options exist for palletizers that may be of interest to the purchaser. Several types of mechanisms can be used to convey and position the package onto its layer (usually different types are made by different manufacturers). There are also a number of main power systems for lifting and lowering the pallet load (electric, electric/hydraulic, etc.), and specific control options to produce different pallet patterns, different numbers of layers, and so on.

In addition to the automatic and semi-automatic strapping equipment previously discussed, and manually applied steel, plastic or fabric straps, the predominant methods used to provide stability and protection for the palletized loads are gluing and stretch and shrink film overwrapping.

Gluing is used both between the packages and the pallet and between layers of individual packages to provide stability and minimize damage in handling and transit. Glue may be applied automatically, as in the case of a palletizer, and may also be applied automatically as the package moves along a conveyor toward a manual palletizing station. Glue may be applied manually, but automatic application is preferred so as to assure the proper quantity and distribution of the glue on the packages.

In the last ten years, full pallet overwrapping has become widespread. Overwrapping provides many of the advantages of gluing as well as well as some additional ones. It provides additional protection for the product from rain, snow, dust, and dirt. It also protects against abrasion from the side walls of the carrier during transit and serves as a deterrent to pilferage.

Shrink film overwrapping of a full pallet load involves placing a film bag over the entire load and then heating the bag to shrink it tightly around all sides and the top of the load. A wide variety of equipment exists for performing these two functions.

Most shrink films bags are preformed individual bags that are placed manually over the load. This is a moderately difficult task, even for two men, and usually some equipment is involved to assist the men. The equipment required depends on the exact size and shape of the load and, particularly, its height. Such equipment can include stationary and movable platforms, hydraulic scissor lifts, and conveyors. Automatic bag placers exist that automatically dispense the proper amount of film from tubular stock, make a heat seal to close the top of the bag, cut the bag from the film stock and automatically place the bag over the load. These sophisticated machines are capable of relatively high rates, in the range of 50 pallet loads per hour.

Equipment for heating the load can use *convection*, which heats the air surrounding the film and transfers the heat energy from the air to the film, or *infrared*, which utilizes electromagnetic waves to heat the film directly without heating the surrounding air. Several different types of equipment can be used to provide the heat, depending primarily on the required production rate. The most automated include high production ovens or tunnels which may be fully automatic or may require an operator to open and close doors and place the pallet in the oven and remove it. Ovens and tunnels may be either infrared or convection, the latter using either natural gas or electricity. Ovens and tunnels are insulated and are designed to retain as much heat as possible, thereby minimizing the use of energy.

Other types of equipment used to heat the film and shrink it to the pallet load include rings, where the loads remains in a stationary position and a four-sided ring is lowered from the top of the load to the bottom, heating the film as it goes. Rings usually use infrared elements and can shrink about 40 loads per hour. Shrink bells are hood-shaped enclosures which are lowered over the entire load. Once the load is contained completely inside the bell, it is heated and then the bell is raised and the load is removed. The lowest degree of automation for heating involves a hand-held gun to provide a convection heat source.

Full pallet stretch overwrapping has been developed since the introduction of shrink wrapping in order to provide most of the benefits, more flexibility, and reduced costs. Stretch wrapping equipment includes full web equipment and spiral wrapping equipment.

In full web wrapping there are basically two methods of introducing film to the load. Most full web systems utilize a rotating turntable assembly and a single film spool, with the film wrapped tightly around the load as the turntable revolves. A second method is to apply the full web in a "pass-through" system that utilizes a conveyor and two film spools instead of a turntable. As the load is conveyed through a film wall held by two vertical spools, it is surrounded by the film. After the load has been conveyed past the spools, a pair of sealing jaws tighten and seal the film at the back of the load. The sealed film from the two spools is then cut, releasing the finished load and providing a new wall of film, ready for the next load. Rotating turntable-type full web systems require an operator for attaching the film to the load at the outset. Full web "pass-through" systems are usually fully automatic.

Spiral wrapping equipment always involves both rotation of some element in the system and vertical movement on the part of a single film spool, so as to spiral the film around the load from top to bottom. Most equipment for spiral wrapping uses a turntable on which the pallet load rotates while the film spool moves vertically.

Spiral wrapping equipment can range from the very simple systems which depend on an operator to control all machine functions, attach the film to the load at the outset, and cut off the film at the completion of the wrapping, to fully automatic systems that perform all of the wrapping functions. In simpler systems the load is moved to and from the stretch wrapper by other materials handling equipment, typically a forklift, while in fully automatic stretch wrapping systems the load is conveyed onto a turntable, the wrapping is performed, and then the load is conveyed away.

In all stretch wrapping applications the tension of the film can be controlled. In the case of spiral wrapping applications, the number of wraps and their position on the load can also be controlled. This allows for the placement of the greatest amount of film where it will be needed and lesser amounts of film where less protection is desired.

Miscellaneous Equipment

Marking Equipment

Several types of equipment are used to mark the outside surfaces of distribution packages with appropriate information for identification and delivery. The type of equipment to be utilized depends on the number of individual packages to be marked with the *same* information, the finish of the package (painted steel, plastic, corrugated, kraft paper, etc.), the amount of information, and the rate at which the information must applied. In the simplest applications the operator simply uses a hand-held marker to write down the appropriate information. Permanent stencils with large letters are often used for information that is repetitive and must be applied to many packages. These stencils commonly include the manufacturer's designating symbol together with specific written information. Stencils are almost always prepared on stencil cutting machines that allow the operator to control the specific information being placed on the stencil and its spacing. Compound stencils which include certain "permanent" information and other "temporary" information are commonly used. In this case the permanent stencil is used with a separate temporary stencil, including information which varies from time to time, attached to it. A good example of this occurs in the case where permanent information includes the manufacturer's symbol and the product designation and the temporary information includes a date and/

or lot number. Information is usually applied through the stencil onto the package using self-inking rollers or, less commonly, spray paint. Small, temporary stencils, prepared on a typewriter or printer, may be used for a few impressions when each contains the same information. These are used for shipments where the same information will not be repeated over a long term, as when a few packages are sent to a specific customer. They may be prepared in conjunction with order write-up, placed on a self-inking pad, and then stamped onto the container. These stencils are normally used with corrugated or natural kraft surfaces.

Silk screening of distribution information onto containers is relatively rare. It provides similar information to that normally handled by large stencils, and provides a higher quality result in terms of appearance. Essentially flat surfaces are required.

Rotary coders use a small drum onto which letters are placed to spell out the desired information and an internal pad for inking the letters. Rotary coders range from small hand-held models usually containing a single line of information to conveyor-mounted rotary coders with drums large enough to contain several lines of information. The larger rotary coders are activated by the movement of the package on the conveyor. The coder is spring-loaded to provide an even pressure against the side of the package and, as the package moves past, the information is transferred onto it.

The newest development in equipment for marking distribution packages is a printer that utilizes ink jets to transfer ink from the printer to the package without any physical contact. These units have only been available for the past few years and further development is expected. They can be used to print large dot-matrix characters when the same information is applied to each package. Some units include microprocessors which allow the information to be reprogrammed through a keyboard for different packaging runs. The printing on the packages is of high quality, and under certain circumstances it can be applied to non-rigid surfaces such as multiwall bags that are not fully packed.

Labeling

Labeling equipment for distribution packaging includes machines for preparing labels and machines for applying the finished labels to the packages. Machines for preparing labels vary from simple models with manually positioned movable type, that are hand-cranked to move labels through the machines, all the way to microprocessor-based label-making machines on which the operator enters the required information through a keyboard and the labels are printed automatically. Some of these machines retain the required information in memory so that it can simply be recalled by the operator and printed again without further data entry. Automatic label application machines may be used for applying pressure sensitive labels to many types of distribution packages. There may be limitations in the packaging rate, the size of the pressure sensitive label, or the nature of the package surface to which the label is to be applied. Small labels that are applied at slow packaging rates onto rigid, flat surfaces can almost always be handled by automatic machines. Very large labels sometimes cannot be handled by automatic label application machines under any circumstances. Curved surfaces can be accommodated by automatic label application machines under certain circumstances. Such machines utilize a roll of pressure sensitive labels attached to a backing material and automatically remove the label from the roll and place it on the package, providing sufficient pressure on the label to insure proper adhesion to the package.

Regulations

The regulations that apply to packaging are wide-ranging in content and are controlled by a number of different federal and state authorities. In limiting our discussion to regulations which apply primarily to distribution packaging, as opposed to consumer packaging, we run a risk of presenting an incomplete picture. In cases where the distribution packaging may be used throughout the life of the product, the package designer should consult sources on consumer packaging regulations. In any event, the regulations discussed here represent only the tip of a very large iceberg.

All packaging regulations fall into one of two main groups—adulteration (of less concern to us here) and weights and measures and public safety. For our purposes, however, the regulations will be grouped by their controlling authority. In most instances we are concerned with both package construction and labeling and marking.

Federal Trade Commission (FTC)

The FTC is concerned with deception and with practices that allow unfair competition. In terms of package construction, the FTC considers a package deceptive if it contains an excessive headspace or a false bottom. The labeling and marking provisions of the Fair Packaging and Labeling Act of 1966 come under the jurisdiction of the FTC, but only if not controlled by another federal agency. In the area of distribution packaging, the FTC is concerned with labeling or marking that might be misleading.

Weights and Measures

The Model State Weights and Measures Law is concerned with accuracy in statements of package contents. A copy of the law can be obtained from the following:

National Conference on Weights and Measures
National Bureau of Standards
Washington, DC 20204

Interstate Commerce Commission (ICC) and Department of Transportation (DOT)

The original purpose of the ICC was to serve as a federal authority with control over economic matters in transportation. The ICC has since become involved with the specifications of certain containers. In 1967 the DOT was created and now handles those responsibilities relating to distribution packaging previously handled by the ICC. The two primary functions of the DOT relating to distribution packaging are (1) approval of tariffs issued by various carriers (primarily relating to package construction) and (2) promulgation of guidelines relating to the safe transportation of hazardous materials. The primary carrier tariffs approved under the authority of the DOT are summarized below.

Rail

The Uniform Freight Classification Ratings, Rules, and Regulations cover the *minimum* construction requirements for packages to be transported by rail. These requirements, which are too voluminous to be reproduced here, are quite explicit as to minimum specifications and are broken down by type of commodity in great detail. It should be noted that the minimum construction specified may be inappropriate in some instances and that it is the responsibility of the package designer to recognize such situations and develop an adequate package.

Rule 41 of the Uniform Freight Classification is perhaps the most commonly used, as it covers the requirements for corrugated cases. Rule 40 covers the requirements for other containers, including drums and bags. A copy of the tariff (currently #ICC UFC 6000-A) can be obtained from the following:

> Mr. G. F. Earl, Tariff Publishing Officer
> Uniform Freight Classification Committee
> 222 South Riverside Plaza, Suite 1106
> Chicago, IL 60606

Truck

The National Motor Freight Classification Classes and Rules cover the *minimum* construction requirements for packages to be transported by truck. Like the rail tariffs, these tariffs are voluminous, and are explicit as to minimum specifications, broken down by type of commodity. Again, the minimum construction specified may be inadequate in some instances.

Rules 222 and 200 in the National Motor Freight Classification are generally analogous to Rules 41 and 40, respectively, in the Uniform Freight Classification. A copy of the tariff (currently #ICC NMF 100-H) can be obtained from the following:

> Mr. James C. Harkins, Issuing Officer
> National Motor Freight Classification Board
> c/o American Trucking Association
> 1616 P Street, N.W.
> Washington, DC 20036

The tariffs relating to rail and truck transportation are of primary interest to packaging personnel.

Air

Packaging requirements vary depending on whether the shipment is being made on a passenger plane or on a cargo plane. The tariff relating to packaging requirements for *domestic* air transportation is available from the following:

> Airline Tariff Publishers, Inc.
> 1825 K Street, N.W.
> Washington, DC 20006

The tariff relating to packaging for *international* air transportation is available from the following:

International Air Transport Association
2000 Peel Street
Montreal, Quebec, Canada H3A 2R4

Hazardous Materials

As noted above, the DOT is also responsible for the establishment of standards for packaging for hazardous materials, including radioactive, corrosive, and flammable products, poisons, and explosives. Much of the DOT emphasis is on the proper labeling of hazardous materials, particularly through diamond shaped, color coded warning labels. Although certain *minimum* requirements for packaging hazardous materials are published by the carrier organizations noted above, it is particularly incumbent on the package designer to determine all the properties of the hazardous materials and develop an adequate package accordingly.

Requirements for the labeling and marking of hazardous materials and the construction of containers for hazardous materials are contained in the Federal Hazardous Substances Act and are available under Title 49, Code of Federal Regulations, Subtitle B, Subchapter C, Part 178. These requirements are also in the Hazardous Materials Tariff (currently #ICC ATA-111-F) published by the American Trucking Association and the Hazardous Materials Regulation (currently #BOE-6000-B) published by the American Association of Railroads, Washington, DC. The Hazardous Materials Tariff is available from the American Trucking Association at the address noted above. The Hazardous Material Regulation is available from the following:

Mr. Thomas Phemister, Issuing Officer
American Association of Railroads
1920 L Street, N.W.
Washington, DC 20036

Food and Drug Administration (FDA)

In the packaging area, the FDA is not concerned with the construction of containers, as such, but is concerned with the identification of packaging materials that are considered safe when used in contact with food substances.

Note

1. Robert H. Perry and Cecil H. Chilton, *Chemical Engineer's Handbook*, 5th ed. (New York: McGraw-Hill, 1973), Section 7.

International Distribution

The International Dimension of Physical Distribution Management

PAUL S. BENDER

Importance of International Logistics

During the 1970s, international logistics became an increasingly important activity in American businesses. The economic situation that is currently developing in the world is very likely to lead to an even more important role for international logistics in the 1980s, and beyond.

The main reasons for the increasing importance of international logistics are summarized below.

The Growth of International Trade

During the 1970s, American imports and exports grew dramatically, as shown in Table 28-1. This trend is very likely to continue in the future because of (1) our diminishing self-sufficiency, (2) the growth of foreign competition, and (3) a sharpening of comparative advantage.

Diminishing Self-sufficiency

In the last few years, the American economy has become dependent on substantial imports of raw materials and energy. For the first time in our history, we cannot depend exclusively on our own resources to support the growth of our economy. Basic raw materials such as chromium and cobalt are supplied almost entirely by imports; our needs for oil are increasingly filled by imports from abroad.

Table 28-1   U.S. Exports and Imports

Year	Exports	Imports	Balance
1965	26,461	21,510	4,951
66	29,310	25,493	3,817
67	30,666	25,866	4,800
68	33,626	32,991	635
69	36,414	35,807	607
1970	42,469	39,866	2,603
71	43,319	45,579	− 2,260
72	49,381	55,797	− 6,416
73	71,410	70,499	911
74	98,306	103,649	− 5,343
1975	107,088	98,041	9,047
76	114,745	124,051	− 9,306
77	120,816	151,689	− 30,873
78	142,054	175,813	− 33,759
79	182,055	211,524	− 29,469
80	221,974	248,709	− 26,735

NOTE: Dollar figures in millions of current dollars, excluding Department of Defense shipments.
SOURCE: Economic Report of the President (1981).

Under these conditions, it has become essential for the United States to undertake a major effort to increase exports, in order to pay for our imports. This is reflected in increasing government interest in export activities, to help equilibrate our balance of trade.

Increasing Foreign Competition

Competition from other industrialized countries as well as some developing countries has had significant impact on U.S. patterns of production, imports, and exports.

The West European and Japanese industrial recovery and expansion have led their industries to seek world-wide markets to gain efficiencies due to economies of scale and to achieve balance of trade. In addition, some less industrialized countries such as Brazil, Mexico, South Korea, Taiwan, and Singapore have become important exporters in specific industries such as textiles, apparel, and electronics. As a consequence, American companies must continuously improve their costs to remain competitive in markets where a decade or two ago they had little or no competition.

Furthermore, since U.S. exports to developing countries already exceed those to Europe and Japan combined, and this trend points to an increasing gap, the dispersion of demand in international markets is increasing. Under these conditions, an efficient logistic operation to support export markets has become of primary importance as a tool to keep export prices competitive while providing acceptable profit margins.

From the import point of view, the United States is faced with a situation in which many imported products are replacing domestic production. Foreign manufacturers can sell many products such as apparel and electronics at prices competitive with those of domestic products. Because of this, many American companies are finding it more profitable to import certain products or components, or to move their manufacturing operations overseas. In such instances, logistic costs become a major component of the total cost equation.

The main conclusion to be drawn from the points made above is that as the United States increases its total volume of international trade, the logistics capability needed to support import and export operations effectively will become a critical ingredient of our economic success, and thus will present great business opportunities.

Sharpening of Comparative Advantage

The principle of comparative advantage states that even if one of two regions is in absolute terms more efficient in the production of every type of goods than is the other, if each region specializes in the products in which it has a comparative advantage—that is, those products it produces most efficiently—trade will be mutually profitable for both regions. The principle of comparative advantage can be applied to any number of regions by induction. Its workings have been demonstrated in the United States in the last few decades.

We have seen how certain American industries have gained predominance in the world. These include food, aerospace, high technology equipment such as computers and scientific instruments, and a wide variety of services. On the other hand, certain American industries have lost their position. These include television sets, low-priced microelectronics, textiles, apparel, shoes, and fuels.

In spite of short-term diversions from this trend occasioned by sporadic protectionistic measures, in the long run the trend towards increasing specialization along the lines dictated by comparative advantage can be expected to continue. As a consequence, most U.S. companies can be expected to be increasingly involved in import and export operations, to maximize their profits.

In this regard, there is an important trend toward increasing use of barter in international trade, the reason being the increasing monetary instability of a growing number of countries. This circumstance makes it desirable to barter goods rather than to sell them for future payment—even in hard currencies.

According to the U.S. Department of Commerce, between 20 and 30 percent of world trade in 1983 was subject to some form of barter, including buybacks, offsets, or counterpurchases. Their projections indicate that the proportion of barter will increase to about 50 percent by 2000.

From a logistics point of view, this means that sellers may have to arrange for the distribution of their products, as well as for those resulting from barter transactions, on a bilateral or multilateral basis.

Simplification of International Trading Practices

One of the main reasons why many American companies have traditionally refrained from exporting their products has been the complexity of international trading practices, and especially the documentation needed for exports. This situation has shown steady improvement in the last few years because of the efforts of many international, foreign, and U.S. organizations. As procedures and documentation become simpler, we can expect increasing encouragement for U.S. companies to look into, or intensify their export operations. A similar trend, of course, can be expected in regard to imports, as well as off-shore production. The consequence of these expected trends will be a further increase in the importance of international logistics in the overall context of company operations.

ıg Integration Between Domestic and International Logistic Systems

ds described above have blurred the traditional line separating domestic and international logistics, thus emphasizing the increasing importance of international logistics. A growing number of companies are finding that there are many good reasons for integrating the two areas.

Taking Advantage of Local Conditions

Many companies marketing in the United States have realized that there are substantial advantages in purchasing or manufacturing abroad the products they distribute domestically. To accomplish this profitably, they must involve themselves directly in the procurement, manufacturing, transportation, and warehousing operations needed to keep a steady supply flowing into their markets at competitive prices. This approach becomes essential when operating minimum inventory systems, such as just-in-time. It is important for those companies to consider the possible advantages offered by various overseas locations. Those may include:

- Availability of low-interest loans

- Availability of special skills

- Availability of raw materials and energy

- Lower labor costs

- Lower taxes

- Free trade zones, where items may be assembled, finished, or repacked for export, without paying duties

Meeting Local Regulations

Companies exporting their U.S. made products overseas often must comply with regulations demanding that a minimum of local components be present in their products. To meet such regulations at maximum profit, it becomes necessary to plan and operate the total logistic system—including U.S. and foreign operations—as a single system, to ensure the best overall trade-offs between all cost elements involved.

In complying with such regulations, companies often find it most efficient to specialize local operations in the production of certain components or sub-assemblies that are later used not only as local components to meet legal requirements but also as exports to other plants. This approach specializes certain production operations and thus provides additional savings due to learning-curve effects.

Optimizing the Total Logistic System

An increasing number of companies are taking a global view of their businesses and are developing world-wide corporate strategies. This approach welds together world markets, financial conditions, manufacturing, and logistic resources, to maximize total profit.

The increasing appeal of this global approach derives from the advantages describe the points above, plus the effect of other conditions that prevail:

- The increasing similarity of products demanded throughout the world, brought about by continuously improving communications and transportation systems. This trend makes it increasingly feasible to export products even when they were originally conceived for one particular market only.

- The increasing scarcity of traditional raw materials, that forces businesses to procure them wherever they are available.

- The need to expand production volumes to maintain economies of scale, that makes it attractive to concentrate production in fewer, larger plants, to supply larger markets.

- The availability of increasingly efficient means for data transmission and processing, that makes it possible to consolidate world-wide order processing, for example, making possible world-wide control of inventories and better utilization of central computers.

- The deep disparities in governmental regulations affecting such areas as environmental controls, labor contracts, and depreciation schedules, for example.

- The need to meet competition world-wide in order to hold on to established markets, even in the United States.

- The significant differences in major cost elements such as labor, taxes, facilities, and customs duties, that offer increasing opportunities to alert businesspeople.

The Significant Export Potential in the United States

As an increasing number of American companies become aware of the profit potential they are missing because of lack of exports, there should be an important increase in the volume of U.S. exports. Recent statistics published by the U.S. Department of Commerce show the dimension of this potential. There are 4 million companies in the United States; of these 300,000 are manufacturing companies capable of producing goods for export. However, only 24,000 manufacturing companies, or 8 percent, have export operations. Of the 24,000 manufacturing companies that export, 200 companies account for 80 percent of all U.S. exports.

As the United States increasingly becomes an international trading nation, the logistics capability needed to support import and export operations effectively will become a critical ingredient in our economic success, and will thus afford substantial means for improving productivity and profits.

Similarities Between Domestic and International Logistics

There are many aspects in the design and management of international logistic systems where approaches and techniques are similar, or identical, to those used in domestic logistic systems. The most important similarities are in three areas: the techniques used to design the logistic network, the analysis of trade-offs, and most logistic management techniques. Let us examine these areas in some detail.

The Logistic Network

A typical world-wide logistic network is shown in Figure 28-1. The first conclusion that can be drawn from the diagram is that the number of levels involved in the system is substantially higher than in a domestic system. Typically, a large domestic system has four or five levels: suppliers, plants, distribution centers, warehouses, and demands. The system illustrated in Figure 28-1 has 12 levels.

The second conclusion that can be drawn is that there are many flows that by-pass certain levels. This is seldom the case in domestic networks. A third conclusion is that there are many more nodes in the network representing suppliers, existing and potential locations, and demand areas than would be used in a domestic network.

In addition to those readily apparent conclusions one other condition is important to consider. It is the degree of choice open among facilities, suppliers, and demands. Generally speaking, domestic networks tend to be much more constrained than international ones, thus providing fewer options for the solution of any given problem. From these conclusions it is clear that the logistic network structure is conceptually identical in domestic and international networks, and that their differences are related to size and complexity.

The techniques outlined in Chapter 9 for logistic system design apply equally to domestic or international systems. One point worth emphasizing in this regard is that because of the extensive number of facilities and levels encountered in international networks, it is even more important to use optimization techniques to find the best network configuration. Otherwise, the penalties associated with non-optimal solutions arrived at by heuristic means can be very high. By the same token, it is also exceedingly important in designing an international logistic network to tie together the logistic strategy with the marketing, production, and financial strategies. Otherwise the result is likely to be an impractical logistic strategy.

Another important consideration in the analysis of international networks relates to problems similar in nature to those found in domestic networks in the assessment of desirable locations to consider as options. For example, in a domestic network, potential warehouse sites must not only be favorably situated with regard to customers but must also have good access to transportation systems, have low taxes, and so on. Similar conditions prevail in the international area with the addition of some unique problems, including the following:

- *Port selection:* The selection of loading and unloading ports is of major importance in the design of an efficient logistic network. This is best accomplished by modeling the alternative ports on both sides as trans-shipment nodes in a logistic network. Then, given the surface transportation costs to and from the ports, and the ocean or air rates between them, the optimum number and location of ports can be calculated as part of the optimal configuration.

- *Free trade zones:* These are zones existing in many countries, including the United States, where production and warehousing can be performed on imported materi-

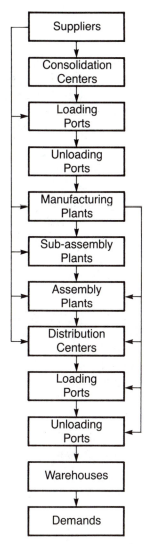

Figure 28-1 Typical World-wide Logistic Network

als so that the finished products are exported without paying customs duties. Free trade zones are of special interest in the design of international logistic systems because they can serve simultaneously as breakbulk and consolidation points, as well as processing points with relatively low costs.

- *Customs:* All products crossing international borders are liable to be taxed according to prevailing customs laws and regulations. Thus, customs duties and clearance times can become major cost elements in an international logistic network, very often affecting plant or warehouse location decisions.

Trade-offs

Since the techniques for designing international logistic networks are the same as those used for domestic networks, it follows that the goal must be to identify the optimal trade-offs between service requirements and their associated costs, and between different cost elements. The elements of cost and service considered in an international system, however, will receive different emphasis than those in a domestic system. Let us briefly review these concepts.

Cost/Service Trade-offs

The system design concepts outlined in Chapter 9 apply directly in the case of international logistics analysis. The service measures defined there covering response time, order completeness, shipping accuracy, and shipment condition apply equally, with the following changes in emphasis:

RESPONSE TIMES

Sales and costs are less sensitive to changes in response times, because generally these are considerably longer than in the case of domestic systems; thus, customers are used to planning their inventory levels and order lead times to compensate for the longer and usually less reliable response times found in international operations. International response times are generally longer and less reliable because

- The distances involved are much longer.

- A substantial fraction of international freight moves by ocean, at a lower speed and with less frequency than land transportation.

- Additional documentation and arrangements that are usually required, such as letters of credit and consular invoices, may take considerable time to complete.

ORDER COMPLETENESS

This is usually the most stringent service requirement in any logistic system, domestic or international. In the case of international systems it becomes even more important because of the response times involved, and the additional costs of processing and shipping back orders.

SHIPPING ACCURACY

This requirement is also much more stringent in an international system than in a domestic one, because of the response time and penalty costs associated with compensating any errors.

SHIPMENT CONDITION

This service requirement is very often taken for granted in domestic shipments because of short lead times and minimal need for re-handling. However, it is a major consideration in international systems not only because of the time and costs needed to replace damaged merchandise, but also because of the significant packaging costs that must be incurred in the first place.

Cost/Cost Trade-offs

The system design concepts outlined in Chapter 9 also apply directly in the analysis of international logistics. The costs elements involved in domestic systems—including purchasing, production, warehousing, information processing, inventorying, and transportation—are all of major importance in international systems; in addition, other cost elements are significant in international logistics: in-transit inventories, packaging, insurance, and customs duties; these sometimes exceed some of the cost elements considered major in domestic systems. Thus, cost/cost trade-off analysis has many more options, and is therefore more complex than in domestic systems, although the techniques of analysis are similar.

Management Techniques

The techniques needed to manage an international logistic system are similar to those prescribed for domestic systems. There are some differences of emphasis between domestic and international logistic management systems, and also the relative importance or usefulness of the various techniques available differs from country to country, depending on local conditions, regulations, and data availability.

In some areas such as fleet management, facilities management, and order entry, there are no significant differences other than the economics of automation of such management systems. In other areas, such as forecasting, inventory management, and production planning, there are additional considerations worth mentioning.

Forecasting

The technical approach to forecasting, including statistical, econometric, and marketing techniques, is the same for any system, domestic or international. However, in many countries there are significant problems in developing data, simply because there are no up-to-date, complete, reliable statistics for economic indicators, or industry figures, such as those published by the U.S. Department of Commerce, the Conference Board, and trade associations such as the National Retail Merchants Association and the American Paper Institute, among others. This can present serious problems when trying to build econometric models, for example. Similar problems may be encountered in attempts to develop marketing data or simple sales statistics in countries with hyperinflation, or in countries where real income per capita is varying rapidly.

Inventory Management

International inventory management systems are conceptually similar to domestic systems. However, there are certain conditions that usually complicate the problem:

- International systems usually have more inventory points at more levels between suppliers and customers; thus multilevel inventory systems are more complex and more common than in domestic systems.

- In-transit inventories can be substantially higher than for a domestic operation with similar products and similar sales volume. This results from the larger number of locations and levels involved, and longer transportation times.

Production Management

The basic approach to the design and operation of these systems is similar for domestic and international logistic systems. However, international systems are more complex because they must cope with additional conditions such as:

- Wider variety of labor costs, taxes, depreciation schedules, etc. in different countries, which affect the decision of where to produce at a given time.

- Special conditions, such as minimum local content, and minimum volumes that must be exported.

These conditions are constantly changing; therefore, it is necessary to review the structure of an international logistic system more frequently than a domestic system.

Differences Between Domestic and International Logistics

The discussion of similarities between domestic and international logistics showed that the concepts related to trade-off analysis, logistic network design, and logistic management systems are similar in both cases; however, we could see that there are many important additional considerations in each case that must be accounted for, to make the analysis of international systems meaningful.

In this section, we will review several aspects of international logistics that share some similarities with the domestic situation, but are basically different.

Marketing Considerations

The most important marketing considerations affecting the design and operation of an international logistic system are terms of sale and marketing channels.

Terms of Sale

Although international terms of sale are similar to domestic terms, their definitions are more extensive. The following check list contains the usual definitions.

1. *Ex (point of origin).*
   Domestic selling price at factory, warehouse, mine, etc., less export discounts, if any.

2. *F.O.B. car.*
   Ex (point of origin) price plus cost of:

   Export packing and marking
   Cartage to railroad station

Loading on rail carrier

Rail freight, if the point specified is other than the beginning station of the rail journey.

3. *F.A.S. vessel.*

F.O.B. car price at point of loading, plus charges for:

Switching, if any
Unloading
Lighterage, if any
Wharfage
Handling and trucking
Checking (quality, quantity, etc.), if any
Transit duties, if any
Forwarder's commission
Clean dock receipt

4. *F.O.B. vessel.*

F.A.S. price, plus costs of:

Loading on board vessel
Heavy lift, if any
Clean ship's receipt or clean on-board bill of lading (depending on country)

5. *C. & F.*

F.O.B. vessel price, plus costs of:

Ocean freight
Export license
Export duties and taxes

6. *C.I.F.*

C. & F. price, plus cost of:

Marine insurance on F.P.A. (free of particular average) basis

7. *Ex dock.*

C.I.F. price, plus costs of:

Consular invoice
Certificate of origin
Lighterage (if the vessel cannot be wharfed)
Unloading
Import licenses
Import tariffs and taxes
Customs clearance
Additional marine and war risk coverage

Marketing Channels

An international logistic system must usually support a variety of marketing channels, in different countires. In the design and operation of international logistic systems it is of primary importance to identify the different marketing channels that must be supported in different countries, and their respective service requirements. The most common types of marketing channels in international business are described here.

EXPORTING THROUGH A U.S.-BASED ORGANIZATION

If an organization is based in the United States, exporting can be of two types:

Indirect: using American export distributors, or shipping to overseas wholesalers or distributors.

Direct: shipping directly to buyers or consignees overseas.

ESTABLISHING AN OVERSEAS MARKETING ORGANIZATION

This approach can take several forms:

Manufacturers representatives, also known as commission agents. Their functions include prospecting for sales, and order-taking. Since these agents act only as go-betweens, they have no responsibility for after-sales service or technical support.

Independent distributors, who normally maintain their own inventories, thus accepting direct liability. In some cases, the exporter may supply inventories on consignment, in which case those inventories must be controlled as part of the total exporting company inventory.

Branches or sales offices, to act as company import-export agents overseas. Usually this type of channel is set up to provide warehousing services, and sometimes labeling and packaging support.

Assembly plants, to use U.S.-made components to be assembled locally, generally using some local components.

Manufacturing plants, to produce complete products locally.

ESTABLISHING COOPERATION AGREEMENTS OVERSEAS

There are several possible types of cooperation agreements. They include:

Joint ventures with an American or foreign company to start a new, jointly owned company, or to merge existing assets.

License arrangements with other companies to let them use patents, processes, or trademarks, in exchange for royalties.

Financial Considerations

A number of financial considerations can have a direct influence in the design and operation of international logistic systems. These considerations affect costs or lead times. From a logistic point of view, the most important of these are foreign financial incentives, U.S. government assistance, methods of payment, and currency rate of exchange.

Foreign Financial Incentives

Examples of such incentives include interest subsidies for loans, investment subsidies, subsidies for creating new jobs, and special tax breaks. These incentives are of great importance to American companies because they make available additional long-term capital, and have a direct impact on many elements of logistic costs, such as depreciation of facilities and equipment, labor, and the like. Financial incentives vary significantly not only from country to country, but also from region to region, and from city to city, in any given country.

U.S. Government Assistance

In addition to the financial incentives mentioned above, many companies can qualify for and take advantage of export assistance programs available in the United States. From an international logistics point of view, there are several arrangements of major interest.

DOMESTIC INTERNATIONAL SALES CORPORATION (DISC)

DISCs were created under the Revenue Act of 1971 as a new category of corporate entity added to the Internal Revenue Code. Their purpose is to promote exports of American goods. The basic qualifications required to form a DISC are:

- It must be a U.S. corporation.
- It must have one stock class, and minimum capital of $2500.
- At least 95 percent of its income must be derived from exports.
- At least 95 percent of its assets must be used for export purposes.

The main advantages of a DISC are that it is allowed a 50 percent tax deferral on export profits, and that marketing studies, promotion expenses, and shipping costs are qualified export promotion expenses if incurred by a DISC unrelated to the supplier. Because of the legal requirement to operate a DISC as an independent corporation, many aspects of logistics operations must be kept separate, including accounting, inventory management, transportation, and warehousing operations.

As of March 1984, we find that because of pressure from officials at the General Agreement of Tariffs and Trade (GATT), the U.S. government has committed itself to finding alternatives to DISC acceptable to GATT.

Several proposals currently before the U.S. Congress contain DISC replacement formulas. The most important of these is the Foreign Sales Corporation (FSC), which will affect all U.S. exports if it becomes law.

EXPORT IMPORT BANK (EXIMBANK)

The Eximbank is a U.S. government agency that provides financial support for international trade transactions. Exports of goods or services sold on deferred payment terms may be financed privately, but it is common for exporters to take advantage of financing offered by the Eximbank, in conjunction with insurance on payment terms provided by the Foreign Credit Insurance Association (FCIA), which is an association of private insurance companies.

OVERSEAS PRIVATE INVESTMENT CORPORATION (OPIC)

In many overseas markets, U.S. exporters may find that the only means of gaining a profitable market share is to invest in local production and logistic facilities. Such investments are subject to risks such as war, revolution, and confiscation. U.S. companies can protect themselves from such risks by insuring their investments through OPIC.

Working with the Eximbank, the FCIA, and OPIC means additional documentation and controls, but it can open many profitable avenues for U.S. companies to increase exports or manufacturing and distribution operations overseas, while substantially minimizing risks.

Methods of Payment

International logistic systems must handle a wider variety of methods of payment than domestic systems. In domestic systems, the common method of handling payments is the open account method, in which customers order against pre-established credit, and are billed upon shipment. This method is also commonly used in international transactions but several other methods of payment are popular and must be provided by the management system, including letters of credit and drafts.

LETTERS OF CREDIT

These are documents issued by foreign banks on behalf of their clients, to assure the U.S. seller of payment for goods or services exported. Letters of credit can be of three types:

- *Irrevocable*, opened by a foreign bank or by a U.S. bank at the request of a foreign correspondent, in favor of the exporter.

- *Confirmed irrevocable*, opened by a foreign bank and confirmed (guaranteed) by a U.S. bank, in favor of the exporter.

- *Revocable*, a pro-forma document used as guideline for the preparation of an irrevocable or confirmed irrevocable letter of credit.

The first two types of letters of credit cannot be cancelled without the consent of the exporter. In order to collect the payments specified in the letter of credit, the exporter is required to present specific shipping documents to demonstrate that goods or services have been delivered as promised.

DRAFTS

These are of two types:

- *Sight drafts*, whereby a foreign buyer defers payment until the representative of the U.S. exporter presents a draft to him, normally when the goods arrive at the country of destination. The buyer does not have title to the goods until the draft has been paid.

- *Time drafts*, whereby the foreign buyer gets title to the goods upon acceptance of the draft, but may defer payments, normally for 30, 60, or 90 days.

Shipment Insurance

In addition to the credit and investment insurance mechanisms discussed above, a major financial consideration in international logistic systems is that of shipment insurance, which in international shipments can make a heavy contribution to logistic costs.

Of special importance in cost trade-off analysis is the fact that the insurance premium for a given shipment can vary substantially depending on the transportation mode to be used. As a rule of thumb, the slower the transportation mode, the higher the insurance premium. Since transportation rates tend to vary in the opposite direction, insurance costs are a major consideration in the selection of transportation modes.

Currency Rate of Exchange

Variations in the rate of exchange of the dollar against foreign currencies represent a difference of major importance in international logistics just as they do in any other facet of international operations. The design and operation of an international logistic system is based on a set of units of measure. Thus, as the rates of exchange vary, so do the local costs associated with different local currencies; these include transportation, warehousing, inventorying, information processing, and other costs elements.

When variations in rates of exchange become substantial in magnitude, and significantly different between countries, it is usually necessary to re-evaluate the structure of the logistic system, to ensure that it is adjusted to keep it close to its optimal performance. By the same token, management reports must provide explicit identification of variations in costs due to variations in currency rates of exchange, as opposed to variations in performance.

Transportation Services

International transportation costs generally represent a much higher fraction of merchandise value than is the case in domestic transportation. The main reasons are the longer distances involved and the need to use intermodal transportation systems, with the consequent rehandling.

Intermodal transportation systems provide through freight service—from shipper to consignee—in a single unit, with a single bill of lading, a single insurance policy, and under uniform regulations and liability for all transportation modes used. The enormous growth of intermodal transportation has been made possible by the growth of containerization, mostly among the industrial countries of the world. This has brought about several important types of services, including:

1. *Landbridge*, a service in which foreign cargo crosses a country en route to another country. For example, European cargo en route to Japan may be shipped by

ocean to the U.S. East Coast, then moved by rail to the U.S. West Coast, and from there shipped by ocean to Japan.

2. *Minibridge*, a special case of landbridge, where foreign cargo originates or terminates at a point within the United States.

3. *Microbridge*, a relatively new service being provided by ports on the U.S. West Coast. In contrast with minibridge, this service provides door-to-door rather than port-to-port transportation. The big advantage of microbridge is that it provides a combined rate including rail and ocean transportation in a single tariff that is lower than the sum of the separate rates.

To place in perspective the relative importance and the trends of the different transportation modes used throughout the world, it is extremely difficult to assemble complete and accurate data. However, based on rather complete tonnage figures published by the United Nations, and assuming average shipment sizes and average distances, we can grossly estimate the data in Table 28–2 as indications of relative orders of magnitude.

From these figures we can see that more than half of the freight transported moves by ocean, and that volume transported by ocean is about three times larger than that transported by either rail or motor. Rail and motor volumes are roughly equal, and air freight volume accounts for a negligible fraction of total freight volume transported.

The average annual growth rates are also important because they indicate that freight volumes transported by ocean have grown faster than those transported by rail or motor. Furthermore, even if the rates of growth are maintained in the next decade or two, air freight would still be a negligible part of total freight transported. Actually, given the prices and supply conditions of fuel, and the relative efficiencies of the different modes, it is likely that in the next few years ocean and rail transportation may grow faster than in the past, and that truck and especially air transportation may grow more slowly. Let us now examine some of the characteristics of each mode of transportation.

Ocean Transportation

This mode has been used for several thousand years, in contrast to the other modes, which have been in existence for only 100 years or so. This explains the significant differences that exist between ocean operations and rail, truck, and air operations. It also explains why ocean transportation comes closest to a uniform mode of operation throughout the world, as opposed to the other modes that have been traditionally regulated on a national basis.

Table 28–2 Estimated Annual Freight Volumes Transported World-wide (In Ton Miles $\times 10^9$)

Mode	1965	1970	1976	Annual Growth Rate (1965 to 1976)
Air	3	7	12	13.5
Rail	2600	3100	3800	3.5
Motor	2400	3100	4300	5.5
Ocean	6300	9800	12600	6.5

There are three types of ocean transportation services:

- *Liner service*, provided by regular navigation lines on the basis of published schedules, as common carriers.

- *Charter service*, provided by so-called "tramp" vessels on a nonscheduled basis, as contract carriers.

- *Private carriers*, operating as part of a company's logistic system.

These services are available with a wide variety of vessels, such as:

- *Bulk vessels*: Examples include oil tankers, liquid natural gas (LNG) tankers, and ore-bulk-oil (OBO) ships.

- *Container vessels*: Accommodate containerized cargo loaded and unloaded by port gantries.

- *Lighter Aboard Ship (LASH)*: Vessels that carry their own gantries, to load and unload "lighters" which are floating containers. This type of ship provides very fast loading and unloading, thus reducing turnaround time and port expenses.

- *Roll-on/Roll-off (RO/RO)*: Vessels designed to carry trucks, tractor trailers, and other self-powered vehicles, that are "rolled onto" the ship at the port of loading, and "rolled off" at the port of unloading. Their advantages are similar to those of LASH ships.

- *Special vessels*: Examples include refrigerated ships.

With regard to tariffs and rates, ocean transportation is very different from the other modes. Rates for liner service are almost exclusively based on the *conference system*. Liners serving the same routes group themselves in unincorporated organizations called shipping conferences. These organizations establish and publish common rates, rules, and conditions for the common routes served by all their regular members. Conferences normally cover rates in one direction only, to a given area. Thus, many liners belong to a number of shipping conferences, covering different directions and areas.

Membership in a conference is voluntary. U.S. legislation provides all carriers with the right to join any conference upon application. However, a minority of carriers do not belong to conferences and offer different rates, rules, and conditions for shipment. The basic purpose of shipping conferences is to control competition by fixing common rates, allocating cargo among the members, and fighting competition from non-members. However, as a consequence of this type of arrangement, all shippers using conference members are assured of equal rates and treatment.

Ocean rates also differ form those in other modes in that no commodity classification has been adopted. Furthermore, rate structures are not uniform. Thus, different shipments of similar commodities may move at different rates on the same routes; in addition, the rate structure for a given commodity moving between two ports may be different from that for the same commodity moving between the same ports, but in the opposite direction.

The most common ocean rate structures are based on a cost per long ton (2,240 pounds), per short ton (2,000 pounds), or per measurement ton (40 cubic feet). The rate structure is selected on the basis of maximum revenue to the carrier. Ocean rates can be applied on the basis of class rates, or commodity rates, as in other modes. However, there are a number of additional rates that can be added, such as "heavy lift" rates, "extra length" rates, "ad valorem" rates which are added when the shipment value declared is in excess of bill of lading liability limits, and so on.

In addition to the ocean rate, a shipper usually must pay wharfage or terminal charges, to cover handling, transfer to or from the vessel, demurrage, storage, and the like. Another set of charges are port or dockage charges that are applied to a vessel. These include pilotage, towage, dockage, stevedoring, and others.

The complexity of the rates, rules, and conditions that govern ocean transportation makes it advisable for inexperienced users to engage the services of a freight forwarder, to take care of all details. Ocean transportation not only accounts for the bulk of freight moved in the world, but it is also important in every single region of the world. These facts are illustrated by the statistics in Table 28–3.

From the table we can see that the bulk of the tonnages handled are in Asia, Europe, and North America. This is mainly a consequence of differences in levels of industrialization, but it is also explained by the fact that those three areas have more—and better—ports than the rest of the world as a result of geographic characteristics; this is illustrated in Table 28–4, where we can see that Asia has the longest coastline in the world, and Europe and North America have the largest coastlines per square mile of surface.

Rail Transportation

The importance of railroads varies significantly throughout the world. This fact is best illustrated by the statistics in Table 28–5. We can see that 38 percent of the total rail track in the world is in North America—the United States alone accounts for 30 percent. Europe accounts for another 25 percent by itself—32 percent when the U.S.S.R. is added. Thus the industrialized nations of the world account for 70 percent of the world's rail track.

Looking at the track density available, we can see that it also varies from a maximum of .60 miles of track per square mile of territory in Belgium, to .01 in Brazil, China, U.S.S.R., and Australia, and even less in most nations of Africa and many in South America and Asia.

With the exception of the United States, in all nations the railroad systems are owned or controlled by the state and are usually run as a public service rather than as a profit-making enterprise. For this reason, rates do not necessarily reflect costs. Usually rates are not published as they are in the United States, but are negotiable.

Although the ton miles transported by rail have increased more slowly than those transported by motor carriers, the increasing costs of fuel, advances in railroad technology, and the growing use of containerization may work in favor of the railroads in the future. Railroads play a vital role in containerized intermodal transportation in North America and Europe. One of the most important developments in international rail transportation, both in the United States and Europe, is the emergence of special container trains, and of door-to-door service, interlining with other modes. In the rest of the world containerization of cargo has made minor inroads, or is nonexistent: many countries lack the means to handle containerized cargo.

Table 28–3   International Sea-Borne Shipping   (In Millions of Metric Tons)

Region	1965	1970	1976	*Annual Growth Rate (%) 1965–1976*
		Goods Loaded		
World	**1675**	**2576**	**3352**	**6.5**
Africa	192	377	394	6.8
America, N.	322	425	476	3.6
America, S.	263	305	297	1.1
Asia	529	882	1410	9.3
Europe	258	377	461	5.4
Oceania	32	103	179	16.9
U.S.S.R.	79	107	135	5.0
		Goods Unloaded		
World	**1673**	**2531**	**3233**	**6.2**
Africa	69	90	110	4.3
America, N.	378	471	679	5.5
America, S.	41	57	102	8.6
Asia	342	649	911	9.3
Europe	793	1208	1348	4.9
Oceania	37	42	42	1.2
U.S.S.R.	13	14	41	11.0
	Total Goods Loaded and Unloaded			
World	**3348**	**5107**	**6585**	**6.4**
Africa	261	467	504	6.2
America, N.	700	896	1155	4.7
America, S.	304	362	399	2.5
Asia	871	1531	2321	9.3
Europe	1051	1585	1809	5.1
Oceania	69	145	221	11.2
U.S.S.R.	92	121	176	6.1

Source: *World Statistics in Brief* (3d Edition), United Nations, 1978.

Since U.S. transportation is covered in detail in Section 8 of this *Handbook*, we will outline here some of the major characteristics of railroad freight service in Europe, which is the other region of major importance for this mode. A number of special container trains now cover most of Europe, such as:

- *Sea-freightliner*, connecting Harwich in the United Kingdom and Rotterdam in the Netherlands.

- *TEZ*, a shuttle connecting Amsterdam, Rotterdam, Antwerp, and Zeebrugge, as well as the Sea-freightliner.

- *Wupper*, connecting Rotterdam to the Ruhr region and southern Germany, as well as the United Kingdom through the Sea-freightliner.

- *Milan*, connecting Rotterdam and Milan through Germany and France.

Table 28-4   Coastline per Unit of Surface

Region	Coastline Miles	Surface ($\times 10^3$ Sq. Mi.)	Miles per 10^3 Sq. Mi.
Africa	19,000	11,663	1.63
America, N.	37,000	9,420	3.93
America, S.	16,000	6,875	2.33
Asia	39,000	17,170	2.27
Europe	24,000	4,055	5.92
Oceania	12,200	3,286	3.71

NOTE: The surface of the U.S.S.R. has been split between Europe and Asia along the Urals.

SOURCE: *Encyclopaedia Britannica*, 15th Edition (1974).

- *Trans-Siberian Landbridge*, connecting Vladivostok with Moscow. This service accounted in 1978 for 10 percent of the tonnage moving between the Far East and Europe.

Intermodal transfers of containers are much more prevalent in Europe than in the United States. This is due in great part to the coordination efforts of the Transport Combine de Marchandises (TCM) organization sponsored by the United Nations. All international rail transportation in Europe is regulated by a convention known as CIM defining the relations between shippers, carriers, and consignees. Furthermore, rail transport of dangerous cargo is governed by the RID regulations.

Another major service available in Europe by Eurail is a European Car Pool that offers standard pallets with the empty cars, to be exchanged by palletized cars.

Motor Transportation

The statistics in Table 28-6 show a breakdown of paved roads by major regions of the world. We can see that the situation in motor transportation is similar to that of rail transportation: the bulk of the paved roads available in the world is in North America (43 percent of world total) and Europe, including the U.S.S.R. (38 percent of world total).

Motor transportation in the United States is described in some detail in Chapters 20 and 21 of this *Handbook*. From the international logistics point of view, it is important in the context of trade with Canada and Mexico. In Western Europe, the motor industry has much less regulation than in the United States. Most motor carriers are small, private businesses: often an owner driver. For this reason, rates are negotiable with each carrier; furthermore carrier liability is usually much more limited than in the United States. In the socialist countries, all transportation is run by the state. In the rest of the world, most road transport is done on a contract carriage basis with individual operators or small companies. Because of lack of regulation and consequent lack of shipper protection, private road transport is extremely popular in Europe, Africa, Asia, and South America.

A convention of major importance in international motor transport is the Transports Internationales Routiers (TIR) convention, which was established by the U.N. Economic Commission for Europe. Its purpose is to make it possible for merchandise transported in sealed trucks, trailers, or containers to travel across one or more national borders without customs examination of goods or payment of duties. To accomplish this, a "TIR Carnet" is used as the basic documentation, showing that prior approval has been received by vehicles or containers, after fulfilling the requirements established by the convention.

Table 28–5 Characteristics of Railroad Systems

Region	Track Length (Mi.)	Track Density (Mi. per Sq. Mi.)	Freight (Ton Mi. × 10⁶)
Africa	**69,000**	. . .	**73,400**
S. Africa	19,600	.04	39,200
Other	49,400	. . .	34,200
America, N.	**437,100**	. . .	**924,700**
Canada	64,500	.02	130,600
Mexico	15,000	.02	15,700
U.S.A.	344,400	.10	777,100
Other	13,200	. . .	1,300
America, S.	**66,000**	. . .	**30,000**
Argentina	28,800	.03	9,100
Brazil	19,900	.01	17,300
Other	17,300	. . .	3,600
Asia	**178,600**	. . .	**354,900**
China	37,000	.01	206,000
India	62,100	.05	82,100
Japan	30,000	.21	42,800
Other	49,500	. . .	24,000
Europe	**291,500**	. . .	**378,600**
Belgium	7,100	.60	5,400
Czechoslovakia	15,000	.30	41,800
France	48,800	.23	45,700
Germany, E.	18,200	.44	28,400
Germany, W.	45,100	.47	50,400
Italy	18,200	.16	13,000
Poland	16,500	.14	68,000
Romania	11,200	.12	32,900
Spain	12,100	.06	6,200
Sweden	12,300	.07	11,800
United Kingdom	31,600	.33	15,100
Other	55,400	. . .	59,900
U.S.S.R.	**84,000**	.01	**1,803,500**
Oceania	**35,500**	. . .	**18,600**
Australia	32,500	.01	16,400
Other	3,000	. . .	2,200
World Total	**1,161,700**	. . .	**3,583,700**

Source: 1975 figures from various sources. Breakdown based on countries with more than 10,000 miles of track, except Belgium.

Although the TIR convention started among the European nations, it was later on extended beyond Europe to facilitate intermodal transportation with other countries. Thus, the parties to the TIR convention include the following European nations: Austria, Belgium, Bulgaria, Switzerland, Czechoslovakia, East Germany, West Germany, Denmark, Spain, France, Great Britain, Greece, Hungary, Italy, Ireland, Luxembourg, Liechtenstein, Norway, Netherlands, Portugal, Poland, Romania, Sweden, Finland, Turkey, and Yugoslavia. In addition, the following extra-European nations have joined the convention: Iran, Israel, Argentina, United States, Australia, Brazil, Canada, India, and Japan.

Another important international convention affecting motor transportation is the Contrat de Transport International de Marchandises par Route (CMR). This convention

Table 28-6   World Paved Roads, 1971   (Only countries with over 10,000 miles of paved roads are included)

Region	Miles	Region	Miles
Africa	**126,000**	**Europe**	**1,321,400**
Algeria	26,300	Austria	13,200
Morocco	11,200	Belgium	46,600
S. Africa	31,300	Czechoslovakia	30,000*
Other	57,200	Denmark	31,200
America, N.	**1,821,800**	Finland	14,400
Canada	110,400	France	402,600
Mexico	26,900	Greece	10,000
U.S.A.	1,658,400	Hungary	17,200
Other	26,100	Ireland	46,200
America, S.	**84,200**	Italy	159,100
Argentina	20,800	Netherlands	57,300
Brazil	32,900	Poland	55,700
Venezuela	11,600	Portugal	18,800
Other	18,900	Romania	15,000*
Asia	**441,300**	Spain	58,900
China	100,000*	Sweden	16,900
India	119,700	Switzerland	37,200
Indonesia	10,900	United Kingdom	70,000*
Japan	94,500	W. Germany	198,800
Pakistan	10,600†	Yugoslavia	11,200
Sri Lanka	12,100	Other	11,100
Turkey	13,000	**U.S.S.R.**	**300,200†**
Other	80,500	**Oceania**	**131,600**
		Australia	104,200
		New Zealand	26,000
		Other	1,400
		World Total	**4,226,500**

*Estimated.

†1969.

SOURCES: *Encyclopaedia Britannica*, 15th edition (1974), plus estimates from various sources.

governs contractual conditions for the international transportation of goods by road. One other international convention governing motor transportation is ADR, which affects the road transport of dangerous goods.

Air Transportation

Although air freight represents a minor portion of the ton miles transported in the world, it is the fastest growing mode of transportation, and its impact has been dramatic in specific industries such as computers, micro-electronics, fashion apparel, flowers, and gourmet foods. In many instances, the availability of scheduled air cargo has made it possible to create entirely new markets. Air cargo has proven a distinct bonus for products that exhibit one or more of the following characteristics:

- High value

- Fashion

- Extreme seasonality

- Perishability

- Unpredictable demand

Furthermore, this mode has proven very popular in the developing countries, for two major reasons. First, it is easier to build a few airports than to build a road of track network. Second, practically every country in the world has set up its own airline as a matter of prestige; thus the equipment and base personnel have been available to facilitate the development of air cargo. The relative importance of air cargo in different regions can be illustrated by the statistics in Table 28-7.

We can see that North America accounts for 49 percent of the ton miles of cargo flown in the world, and that Europe—including the U.S.S.R—accounts for 35 percent of the total. However, we can see that there are a number of countries in Africa, South America, Asia, and Oceania that have relatively important volumes of air freight.

In contrast with the other modes of transportation, air rates and fares are regulated and published by international organizations. The International Civil Aviation Organization (ICAO), created in 1947, is part of the United Nations. It is devoted to the development of regulations concerning the facilitation of air transport, and safety matters. Its membership includes 86 countries. Members of ICAO are eligible to associate themselves with the International Air Transport Association (IATA), which regulates air rates and fares among members. IATA includes three Traffic Conferences covering the Western Hemisphere; Europe, Africa, and the Middle East; and Asia and Australia. Actions taken by any conference relative to fares must be ratified by the member governments. In the United States this is done through the Civil Aeronautics Board (CAB).

In evaluating the potential for air cargo, it is essential to consider not just the transportation rates, but all the cost elements involved in moving cargo from door to door. The reason is that although air fares are substantially higher than those of other modes, air transport may allow significant savings in packaging costs, insurance, and inventory carrying costs. Further, in a large number of countries, it is much simpler and faster to pass merchandise through airport customs than through customs at other types of terminals.

Barge Transportation

In selected locations around the world, barge transportation plays a significant role. The most important barge operations are summarized in Table 28-8.

The most important rivers supporting barge operations are the Mississippi in the United States, and the Rhine in Europe. Barge traffic along the Mississippi River extends from the Canadian border to the Gulf of Mexico. The Rhine River starts near Basel, Switzerland, flows along the French border into the Ruhr region of Germany, and from there flows to Rotterdam, thus connecting the industrial heart of Western Europe.

Distribution and Consolidation Services

In an international logistic system, the distribution and consolidation of freight is frequently accompanied by other activities such as re-packing, or production-related activities such as finishing or labeling. In the United States and Canada it is easy to find warehousing facilities at competitive prices at or near almost any city. Many European cities also have those facilities. However, in most of the rest of the world such facilities are available mainly at seaports, and sometimes at airports.

Table 28–7   World Distribution of Air Cargo   (Only countries with more than 10 million ton miles are included)

Region	1000 Ton Miles	Region	1000 Ton Miles
Africa	**238,500**	**Europe**	**2,324,200**
Egypt	11,300	*Belgium*	127,700
Ethiopia	10,400	*Denmark*	43,400
Morocco	48,900	*Finland*	18,000†
S. Africa	50,400†‡	*France*	381,100†
Zaire	10,200	*Germany, E.*	18,300
Other	107,300	*Germany, W.*	393,000†
America, N.	**5,344,500**	*Greece*	24,700†
Canada	357,700†	*Ireland*	39,700
Cuba	12,400	*Italy*	221,800†
Mexico	29,000	*Netherlands*	263,000†
U.S.A.	4,917,800	*Norway*	44,000
Other	27,600	*Poland*	11,800
America, S.	**474,000**	*Portugal*	22,200
Argentina	200,500	*Romania*	24,000
Brazil	129,900†	*Spain*	104,600†
Chile	29,200	*Sweden*	66,900
Colombia	44,000†	*Switzerland*	118,500
Peru	16,100	*United Kingdom*	370,600†
Venezuela	42,400	*Other*	30,900
Other	11,900	**U.S.S.R.**	**1,420,000**
Asia	**812,300**	**Oceania**	**199,100**
China	70,000*	*Australia*	162,700
India	86,300†	*New Zealand*	25,200
Indonesia	11,300	*Papua and New*	
Israel	72,100	*Guinea*	10,000
Japan	272,000	*Other*	1,200
Korea, N.	10,000*	**World Total**	**10,812,600**
Korea, S.	14,600		
Kuwait	10,300†		
Lebanon	99,200§		
Pakistan	49,000		
Philippines	15,800		
Taiwan	49,000†		
Other	52,700		

*Estimate; See source note below.

†1971.

‡South African Airways only.

§Excluding scheduled domestic services.

SOURCE: 1971 figures published by *Encyclopaedia Britannica*, 15th edition (1974), plus various estimates indicated by asterisk (*).

In an international logistic flow cargo may flow through several types of warehousing facilities. The main ones are:

TRANSIT SHEDS

These are usually enclosed facilities at the piers; their main function is the temporary storage of in-transit cargo that may have to be transferred between a ship or plane, and a rail or motor carrier.

Table 28–8   Major Barge Cargo Movements in the World

Area	10^6 Ton Miles Transported
U.S.A.	307,000
Argentina	19,300
Brazil	10,000
Chile	5,600
China	51,000
Japan	74,500
West Germany	32,700

SOURCE: *Encyclopaedia Britannica*, 15th Edition (1974).

IN-TRANSIT STORAGE

Provided by the railroads, and located at airports and seaports, these facilities allow the shipper to negotiate through rates for the cargo, and still perform some operations on it before embarcation, such as packing, crating, or labeling. This arrangement saves the cost of shipping the crating materials from the point of origin, as well as the space for such operations.

HOLD-ON-DOCK STORAGE

When cargo has been delivered to a dock for shipment, the carrier provides on-dock storage, usually at no charge until the next scheduled sailing. Most shippers and forwarders take advantage of this circumstance to obtain temporary free storage at the docks. Hold-on-dock storage is a practice frequently used to consolidate goods at the port, at no additional charge.

PUBLIC WAREHOUSING

The facilities mentioned above may not suffice to protect the cargo when shipments are delayed for extended periods. This may occur when documentation is delayed or lost, export licenses revoked, and so on. In such cases, practically all ports offer public warehousing facilities available to all shippers.

SHARED WAREHOUSING

In many countries it is common to find several shippers—who are often competitors—sharing a facility contracted in common. This helps everybody's logistic system and lowers costs.

BONDED WAREHOUSING

Operated under customs supervision, these facilities are defined as buildings, or parts of buildings, and other enclosures, so designated by the Secretary of the Treasury, for the purpose of storing imported merchandise entered for warehousing, or taken possession of by the collector of customs, or under seizure, or for the manufacture of merchandise in hand, or for the re-packing, sorting, or cleaning of imported merchandise. This definition ⁱlies in the United States; however, similar conditions exist in practically all other na-ⁱs. There are many types of bonded warehouses, such as:

- *Public stores*, where the facilities are owned by the government

- *Private bonded warehouses*, which can be used to store merchandise only by the owner of the facility

- *Public bonded warehouses*, which can be used by different companies but only to store imported merchandise

- *Special bonded warehouses*, which can be of the types described above, but for some specific purpose, such as grain storage

Transportation in and out of bonded warehouses is only allowed to bonded carriers, licensed by customs authorities. All bonded warehouses are managed by a storekeeper appointed by customs authorities.

FOREIGN TRADE ZONES (FTZ)

Goods being imported can be warehoused at FTZs (usually known outside of the United States as *free trade zones*) without paying duties until they are interned. Goods for re-exporting do not pay any duties at all, as long as they do not leave the FTZ except to be shipped overseas. FTZs were created in 1934 by the Foreign Trade Zones Act. Since then, 91 FTZs have been created in the United States, and 10 more are waiting for approval, as of February 1984. Current and proposed FTZs are listed in Table 28–9.

In the United States, foreign trade zones differ from bonded warehouses in two major respects: First, bonded goods can be stored in bonded warehouses for a maximum of three years. If the goods are re-exported during that time no duties are paid; otherwise, duties must be paid after three years (or sooner if goods are interned before three years).

Second, bonded warehouses can only be used to store goods and to handle them within strict limitations. For example, goods cannot be processed, manufactured, or exhibited while at a bonded warehouse. No such limitations exist in FTZs.

Similar regulations exist in other countries for the operation of bonded warehouses and free trade zones.

Governmental Regulations

The number, complexity, and scope of governmental regulations that must be adhered to in international business far exceed those present in domestic operations. Thus, a thorough knowledge of governmental regulations affecting the flow of goods is essential to effectively design and manage an international logistic system. Because of the variety of regulations and their legal implications it is beyond our scope to cover them in any detail. However, some basic considerations are worth outlining, with regard to U.S. as well as foreign governmental regulations.

U.S. Governmental Regulations

All exports to foreign countries, except Canada, are subject to controls and require special export licenses for most products. Most export licenses are processed by the U.S. Depart-

Table 28–9   U.S. Foreign Trade Zones as of February 1984

State	No.	Location	State	No.	Location
Alabama	83	Huntsville	New York	23	Buffalo
	82	Mobile		54	Clinton County
	*	Birmingham		1	New York City
Arizona	60	Nogales		34	Niagara County
	75	Phoenix		90	Onondaga
	48	Tucson		37	Orange County
Arkansas	14	Little Rock		52	Suffolk County
California	50	Long Beach	North Carolina	57	Mecklenburg
	56	Oakland			County
	3	San Francisco		67	Morehead City
	18	San Jose		93	Raleigh/Durham
	*	City of Industry		66	Wilmington
Connecticut	76	Bridgeport	North Dakota	*	Grand Forks
	71	Windsor Locks	Ohio	46	Cincinnati
Delaware	*	Wilmington		40	Cleveland
Florida	64	Jacksonville		8	Toledo
	32	Miami		*	Clinton County
	42	Orlando		*	Dayton
	65	Panama City	Oklahoma	53	Rogers County
	25	Port Everglades		*	Oklahoma City
	79	Tampa	Oregon	45	Portland
Georgia	26	Shenandoah	Pennsylvania	35	Philadelphia
	*	Chatham County		33	Pittsburgh
Hawaii	9	Honolulu		24	Pittston
Illinois	22	Chicago	Puerto Rico	7	Mayaguez
	31	Granite City		61	San Juan
Indiana	72	Indianapolis	Rhode Island	*	Providence
Kansas	17	Kansas City	South Carolina	21	Dorchester
Kentucky	47	Campbell County			County
	29	Louisville		38	Spartanburg
Louisiana	2	New Orleans			County
	87	Port of Lake Charles	Tennessee	77	Memphis
Maine	58	Bangor		78	Nashville
Maryland	74	Baltimore	Texas	62	Brownsville
	73	Baltimore Int'l Airport		39	Dallas/Ft. Worth
	63	Prince Georges County		97	Del Rio
Massachusetts	27	Boston		96	Eagle Pass
	28	New Bedford		68	El Paso
Michigan	43	Battle Creek		36	Galveston
	70	Detroit		84	Harris County
	16	Sault Ste. Marie		94	Laredo
Minnesota	51	Duluth		12	McAllen
Missouri	15	Kansas City		95	Rio Grande City
	*	St. Louis County		80	San Antonio
Mississippi	92	Harrison County	Utah	30	Salt Lake City
Montana	88	Great Falls	Vermont	55	Burlington
Nebraska	59	Lincoln		91	Newport
	19	Omaha	Virginia	20	Suffolk
Nevada	89	Clark County/Las Vegas	Washington	85	Everett
New Hamp-				5	Seattle
shire	81	Portsmouth		86	Tacoma
New Jersey	44	Morris County	Wisconsin	41	Milwaukee
	49	Newark/Elizabeth			

NOTE: Some locations have more than one zone number.

*Denotes locations that have applied for FTZ status, but have not obtained approval as of February 1984.

ment of Commerce, although some special types of products require licenses issued by other governmental agencies. For example, all products that may have military uses must obtain export licenses from the Department of State. Such products include not only ammunition and other similar items, but may include certain types of computers, for example.

For the more general types of commodities, licensed by the Department of Commerce, there are two types of export licenses:

- *General licenses* allow a company to export specific commodities to specified destinations, within various other limitations described in the license, without having to apply for a license document for every shipment.

- *Validated licenses* allow a company to export a specific shipment, and are issued after formal application has been submitted by the shipper. They are needed to export strategic goods to any country except Canada. Furthermore, there are certain countries to which no exports of any kind are allowed.

Foreign Governmental Regulations

Practically all countries exercise some form of control over imports. These controls can be of many different types, such as import quotas for certain goods coming from certain countries, foreign exchange limitations, and import permits, among others. Certain types of goods are especially susceptible to controls. Examples are pharmaceutical products, foods and beverages, plants, animals, and hazardous materials.

In addition, most countries have special requirements relative to the labeling and marking of packages and containers. For example, in some countries labels and markings must be in the local language exclusively; in other countries only the metric system is acceptable in labels and documents.

In addition to the types of regulations just mentioned, practically all countries apply customs duties on imports. These vary from country to country, and depend on the type of commodity, its value, and its origin.

Packaging

Packaging costs are important in any system, domestic or international. However, in international shipments, the cost and functions of packaging become relatively more important than in a domestic system. The main reasons for this difference are:

- International shipments are typically re-handled more times, and must travel for longer periods of times than domestic shipments; thus they are more susceptible to damage and theft, and require more protective packaging.

- International shipments may have to travel through many different weather zones that vary significantly in temperature and humidity. Protective packaging must be provided to cope with such requirements.

- There are many other packaging requirements that are different from the U.S. norm. For example, some less-developed countries demand that all cargo exported to them be packaged in wooden crates; the reason is that such crates are an important source of lumber for construction purposes.

A major consideration in international packaging is the need to use metric units for packages, containers, and documentation. Since the United States is the only major country in the world that does not use the SI (Système Internationale) or metric system, these requirements may create additional work for some U.S. companies; most countries accept dual labeling, but practically no countries accept labeling in the English system alone. It is important to note that progress towards metrication is being made by many U.S. industries. Some industries, such as pharmaceuticals, converted to the metric system many years ago; others, including the automotive, industrial chemicals, wine, and computer industries, are now in the process of doing so.

As of March 1984, the International Standards Organization (ISO) is considering the adoption by the end of the year of five standard pallet sizes.

The proposed sizes in millimeters and their approximate equivalents in inches are:

1,200 mm × 1,000 mm (47.27 in × 39.37 in)

800 mm × 1,200 mm (31.50 in × 47.24 in)

1,135 mm × 1,135 mm (44.68 in × 44.68 in)

1,220 mm × 1,015 mm (48.00 in × 40.00 in)

1,100 mm × 1,100 mm (43.30 in × 43.30 in)

According to the definitions set forth by the ISO, containers are regarded as articles of transport *equipment*—not as vehicles or conventional packaging—having an internal volume of at least one cubic meter (35.3 cubic feet). Since containerization was developed in the United States, and even today the bulk of containers in use belong to American companies, the ISO has established standards that generally follow American container dimensions, expressed in the metric system.

Documentation

The many kinds of documentation that are a necessary part of engaging in international trade, have traditionally discouraged many companies from expanding into this area. In the last decade, however, great strides have been made to simplify documentation. These changes will be discussed below.

First, let us identify the major types of documents involved in export and import shipments.

Export Documents

The most important export documents are:

1. *Bill of Lading*: constitutes both a receipt for cargo accepted by the carrier, and also a contract for transportation between the carrier and the shipper. The bill of lading may be used as an instrument of ownership; it can be bought, sold, or

traded while the goods are in transit. For it to be negotiable in this form, it must be a so-called negotiable order bill of lading. Bills of lading can be classified according to the type of carrier: ocean or air bills of lading, waybills for railroads, and pro-forma bills of lading for trucking.

Other types of bills of lading are defined as follows: a *clean bill of lading* is issued when a shipment is received in good condition; it is not issued when shortages or damages are claimed. An *on board bill of lading* certifies that the cargo has been placed aboard a given vessel and is required by the shipper to obtain payment from a bank.

2. *Dock receipt*: used to transfer responsibility for cargo between the domestic and international carriers involved. The dock receipt is issued at the terminal where physical transfer takes place.

3. *Delivery instructions*: provide the inland carrier with detailed instructions about the arrangements made by the shipper or forwarder to deliver the cargo to a given pier, gate, or carrier.

4. *Consular invoice*: required by some countries to identify and control goods shipped to them. It is prepared on special forms available from each consulate.

5. *Commercial invoice*: a common invoice sent by the seller to the buyer. It is usually used by customs authorities to assess duties.

6. *Certificate of origin*: a document used to prove to the importing country the country of origin of the goods being exported. It is commonly issued by a recognized chamber of commerce.

7. *Insurance certificate*: provides assurance to the consignee that insurance has been obtained covering loss or damage for in transit cargo.

8. *Transmittal letter*: a list of details of a shipment and also a record of the documentation that is transmitted, together with instructions for disposition of the documents and other special instructions.

9. *Export declaration*: required by the United States Department of Commerce to control exports, in compliance with export licensing, and to provide export statistics.

10. *Letter of Credit* (see page 790).

Import Documents

The most important import documents are:

1. *Customs entries*: documents needed for goods entering the United States. There are four types of customs entries:

   - *Consumption entry*, required for bringing goods into the United States. This document contains information about the origin of the cargo, a description of the merchandise, and the estimated duties applicable to the commodity imported; estimated duties are to be paid when the entry is filed.
   - *Immediate delivery entry*, used to expedite the clearance of cargo. It allows 10 days for payment of estimated duty and for processing of the consumption entry.

Furthermore, it allows delivery of the goods before payment of estimated duties and allows subsequent filing of the consumption entry and duty.

- *Immediate transportation entry*, allows cargo to be transferred from the pier to any point inland by a bonded carrier without payment of customs duties or finalization of the entry at the arrival port.
- *Transportation and exportation entry*, allows goods coming from or going to a third country to enter the United States for the purpose of trans-shipment.

2. *Carrier certificate and release order*: used to advise customs of the details of the shipment. Through this document, the carrier certifies that the company or individual named in the certificate is the owner or consignee of the cargo.

3. *Delivery order*: issued by the consignee or his customs broker to the ocean carrier, authorizing the release of the cargo to the inland carrier. It includes the necessary information for the pier delivery clerk to determine whether the cargo can be transferred to the inland carrier.

4. *Arrival notice*: sent by the carrier to inform the "notify" party of the estimated arrival date of the vessel; it identifies shipment details, and shows expiration date of free time.

5. *Freight release or freight bill receipt*: provides evidence that freight charges for the cargo have been paid. It can be used at the pier to obtain release of the cargo.

6. *Special customs invoice*: required by United States Customs when the value of the cargo exceeds $500. Normally prepared by the foreign exporter, it is used by customs to determine the value of the shipment.

Drawback and its Documentation

A drawback is a refund of duties paid on imported materials used in the manufacture of products which are subsequently exported from the United States. The purpose of drawback is to encourage manufacturing operations in the United States by reducing the cost of imported raw materials by the amount of duty paid on them. This enables domestic manufacturers to compete more effectively in foreign markets.

The drawback principle is recognized and practiced by many countries throughout the world, and is an important consideration in international logistics. It is important to understand all its details, to use it to maximum benefit. For example, not only does it provide a refund of duties paid on imported material directly used in a product, it also allows a refund if domestic material of the same kind and quality is substituted for the imported materials in the production of the exported product. In addition, imported goods that do not conform to sample or specification are entitled to drawback if they are re-exported under the supervision of United States Customs. Drawback is considered a privilege, not a right, and requires compliance with customs laws (19 United States Commerce, Section 1313) and regulations (19 CFR22).

The following documents are needed to obtain a drawback:

1. *Application for a rate of drawback*: initiates the procedure needed to obtain the drawback. This document is sent in triplicate to United States Customs, and describes the manufactured article, the duty paid, materials used, probable date of first exportation, and similar information.

2. *Import entry or certificate of delivery of imported merchandise*: transfers drawback rights to the party designated in it. It is needed when the claimant or manufacturer is not the importer of record.

3. *Notice of exportation of articles with benefits of drawback*: contains a description of the articles exported, the exporter, and related information.

4. *Certificate of manufacture and delivery*: certifies the content of the goods manufactured and delivered for export.

5. *Drawback entry for exported articles*: used where a certificate of manufacture is needed.

6. *Drawback entry and certificate of manufacture for exported articles*: used where a combined entry and an abstract from manufacturing record as certificate will suffice.

International Documents Simplification

During the 1970s the United States and other major industrial countries took major steps to simplify international trade documentation in order to facilitate the flow of goods throughout the world. This effort was prompted by the complexity and cost that was involved in preparing the necessary forms to support international logistics operations. By the early 1970s the situation had reached a point where common international shipments might involve up to 28 different parties, originating more than 120 different documents to move the cargo. Documentation costs amounted to as much as 10 percent of the dollar value of the trade itself: enough to eliminate a substantial part of the profits.

Under those conditions, many industrialized countries established organizations devoted to the simplification of international documentation and the standardization of electronic data interchange protocols. Countries that have maintained such efforts include the United States, Canada, United Kingdom, France, Sweden, Norway, Finland, Belgium, Holland, the U.S.S.R., Czechoslovakia, and Japan.

In North America this work has been done principally by the National Committee on International Trade Documentation (NCITD) based in New York, by the Office of Facilitation of the United States Department of Transportation, and by the Canadian Organization for the Simplification of Trade Procedures (COSTPRO), based in Ottawa. The documentation standards developed and adopted by NCITD and COSTPRO are virtually identical; thus, the movement of goods between the United States and Canada is being greatly simplified.

Similar work, conducted by the United Nations Economic Commission for Europe (ECE) in Geneva, has resulted in the coordination of the efforts of more than 50 countries and 40 international organizations. The United Nations also assists in the implementation of trade facilitation programs throughout the developing countries through its other Economic Commissions: ECA in Africa, ECLA in Latin America, and ESCAP in the Far East.

As a result of the work outlined above, international documentation has been simplified to a few standard forms. Currently, those forms are based on the United States Standard Master for International Trade, developed by NCITD, and the ECE Layout Key.

Automated Data Interchange

Another area in which major improvements have been made in the last decade or so is that of electronic data interchange (EDI) for transportation. Work in EDI has been going on since the late 1960s in most industrialized countries of the world. In the United States, this work has been done mainly by the Transportation Data Coordinating Committee (TDCC) based in Washington, D.C. TDCC has developed an extensive set of standards for EDI that has been adopted by many major corporations as the basis for their transportation management information systems. Since COSTPRO in Canada has adopted EDI standards that are virtually identical to those proposed by TDCC, these have become in fact the EDI standards for North America. These standards cover both domestic and international transportation. As a matter of fact, one of their salient features is that no distinction is necessary between domestic and international shipments.

Considerable work in this area has also been done overseas. The ECE has adopted TCI standards developed by a committee headed by SITPRO in the United Kingdom, to support European EDI applications. Similar work has been taking place in Japan, and many other countries.

The advent of EDI standards and document standardization has made it practical to develop systems that can simplify dramatically the documentation work needed in international logistics. These systems are becoming a major incentive in the expansion of international trade. Some of the most noteworthy examples of such systems are:

Cargo Data Interchange System (CARDIS)

The CARDIS system is being developed under the direction of NCITD to support the requirements of companies involved in international trade. The basic functions that will be provided by CARDIS can be summarized as follows:

1. *Shipment file maintenance*, containing all the data needed to move a shipment under one bill of lading. This function includes routing of messages to and from the repository of the file.

2. *Electronic links*, between all the parties involved in the pickup, transportation, clearance, and delivery of a shipment.

3. *Documentation*, with the capability of producing specified international trade documents, including:
   Ocean bill of lading
   Export delivery instructions
   Export delivery permit and dock receipt
   Insurance certificate
   Import delivery receipt
   Import arrival notice

4. *Tracing*, providing shipment status data, and shipment file updating. This function will allow on-line inquiry on status until the shipment arrives at its destination.

5. *Statistical and summary reports*, generated as a by-product of the data processing function.

6. *Company and government interfaces*, including all information exchanges needed in relation to a shipment; within a company, between companies involved, and between companies and governmental authorities.

7. *Facilities research*, providing users with an automated source of information on trade and transportation facilities, documentation requirements of foreign countries, and lists of companies and services.

The use of CARDIS will provide American companies involved in international trade with a number of important advantages, including:

• Reduced warehousing and handling costs due to faster availability of data necessary to move cargo.

• Reduced clerical costs due to automation of documentation and reduction of penalties associated with clerical errors.

• More efficient shipping methods due to availability of research information.

• Savings in capital costs due to shortening of the credit cycle.

PORT INFORMATION AND CUSTOMS CLEARANCE PROGRAMS

During the 1970s a number of seaports and airports began installing port information and customs clearance systems to automate the processing of cargo documentation. The first system of this type started operation in August 1971 at London Airport. Known as the London Airport Cargo EDP Scheme (LACES), it provided four major related functions:

1. Maintain an inventory file of all incoming shipments.

2. Validate and process entry information, including calculation of customs duty and purchase tax, and selection of goods or documents for examination.

3. Prepare agent's debit schedules with customs.

4. Provide statistical information.

Systems similar to LACES have been implemented in many other facilities throughout the world, including the SOFIA system at the Paris Airport, and other systems at seaports such as Hamburg, Marseilles, and Seattle. Automated systems to process customs documentation have been implemented in many countries already. United States Customs is developing an automated system that is scheduled to be operational in the 1980s. The combined effect of the continuing efforts to simplify documentation, standardize electronic data interchange, and provide automated data processing and communications systems will have an increasing impact in the facilitation of international trade. These efforts will also shape the environment in which international logistics will operate in the future.

Communications

Communication facilities are the nervous system of any management process. In the United States they are taken for granted because of their availability, variety, efficiency, and low cost. This is not the case in most of the rest of the world: only Canada, New Zealand, Sweden, and Switzerland have communication systems comparable to those found in the United States. This is illustrated by the statistics presented in Table 28–10.

We have chosen the number of telephones in operation as the basic measure of communications facilities because they are an excellent indicator of the availability of voice-grade circuits. Since most information transmittal takes place over telephone lines, this is a direct measure of the extent of communications facilities in any region. The number of persons per telephone, on the other hand, gives a good idea of the availability of means of communications. Our experience has been that in places where the number of persons per telephone exceeds about 10, the quality of communications systems for business purposes is poor. A number under about 5 generally indicates acceptable conditions.

Communications systems that are readily available, reliable, and reasonably priced are quite essential for the managing of any international logistic system because of the need to move information faster than the goods it describes. Thus, in the design of an international logistic network, it is essential to evaluate the communications facilities available at potential facility locations.

Organizational Considerations

Large multinational companies typically have about a third of their personnel working outside their home countries. This applies not only to U.S. multinationals but also to European and Japanese companies. For this reason, it is important for such companies to develop human resources policies on a world-wide basis. For companies based primarily in one country this issue may be less important; however, the moment they engage in international operations—even of an import or export nature only—most considerations that concern multinationals become of concern to local companies. When dealing with human resources problems on an international basis, the following elements must be considered.

Languages

One of the most common mistakes made by companies that operate overseas is to send personnel who are technically qualified, but lack a working knowledge of the local language. If personnel who are sent abroad are to perform their jobs successfully they must possess a good basic knowledge of the languages used in the areas where they will be working.

Cultural Differences

In planning and implementing an international operation it is extremely important to pay attention to the cultural differences that exist among the countries in which a company operates. These differences can take a wide variety of forms, and may create serious problems for the unaware. A few examples can be used to illustrate this point:

- In many countries a person's authority derives from his family ties or tribal links, rather than from his position in an organization.

- Expatriate managers who show a lack of interest in the local way of life may generate very negative reactions from local people, not only towards them but also toward their companies.

Table 28–10   World-wide Distribution of Telephones (1971)   (Countries shown have fewer than 30 persons per telephone and more than 100,000 telephones, or have more than 1,000,000 telephones.)

Region	No. of Telephone Receivers (in thousands)	No. of Persons Per Receiver
Africa	3,300	. . .
S. Africa	1,600	14.0
Other	1,700	. . .
America, N.	132,400	. . .
Canada	9,800	2.2
Cuba	300	30.0
Mexico	1,500	33.0
U.S.A.	120,200	1.7
Other	600	. . .
America, S.	6,100	. . .
Argentina	1,700	13.0
Uruguay	200	13.0
Brazil	2,000	47.0
Chile	400	24.0
Colombia	1,000	22.0
Venezuela	400	26.0
Other	400	. . .
Asia	32,800	. . .
India	1,200	431.0
Israel	500	5.8
Japan	26,200	4.0
Lebanon	200	15.0
Singapore	200	13.0
Other	4,500	. . .
Europe	80,700	. . .
Austria	1,400	5.2
Belgium	2,000	4.8
Bulgaria	500	18.0

- A manager who consults his subordinates may be viewed in some areas as a weak or ignorant person.

- Attitudes towards bribes, conflicts of interest, taxes, and the like can be substantially different from those usually found in the United States.

- In some countries, status and titles motivate people much more than money; in other countries the reverse is true.

- Education and cultural environment may determine the most effective forms of communication in a company. For example, in the United States verbal communications are much more prevalent than written communications. The opposite is true in many European countries.

- Imported technology and methods must be adapted to local conditions to succeed. Otherwise, they are usually ignored or can be targets of sabotage.

Table 28–10   *(Continued)*

Region	No. of Telephone Receivers (in thousands)	No. of Persons Per Receiver
Czechoslovakia	2,000	7.2
Denmark	1,700	2.9
Finland	1,200	3.9
France	8,800	5.8
Germany, E.	2,100	8.2
Germany, W.	13,800	4.3
Greece	1,000	8.4
Hungary	700	15.0*
Ireland	300	9.6
Italy	9,400	5.8
Luxembourg	100	3.0
Netherlands	3,400	3.8
Norway	1,100	3.4
Poland	1,900	17.0
Portugal	700	12.0
Spain	4,600	7.3
Sweden	4,500	1.8
Switzerland	3,000	2.1
United Kingdom	15,000	3.7
Yugoslavia	700	28.0
Other	800	. . .
U.S.S.R.	**11,000**	**22.0**
Oceania	**5,300**	. . .
Australia	3,900	3.2
New Zealand	1,300	2.2
Other	100	. . .
World Total	**294,000**	. . .

*1970.

Source: *Encyclopaedia Britannica*, 15th edition (1974).

Labor Relations

Although such practices as collective bargaining and unionization have been established in most countries, there are many important differences that must be considered. One example is job security: in most countries outside the United States it is almost impossible to terminate people. Thus, careful planning and selection are even more important than they are in the United States.

Another important difference in labor relations is the German practice of *Mitbestimmung* whereby union representatives are members of corporate boards of directors. In those positions, they participate both in making company policy, and in negotiating on behalf of the employees. This type of practice is becoming accepted in other countries. Many other examples could be cited; the important point to remember when organizing foreign operations is that careful observation of all major local practices is essential.

Government Relations

Because of the increasing role of governments, not only in regulating but often in directing the economies of many countries, it is essential to assess their known policies and guidelines in relation to one's company's goals. A company's operations must be established in such a way that its objectives tie in with and support the local government's policies in such areas as job creation, investment regulation, technological transfer, location of facilities, product content, local ownership, and local management.

Climate

The effects of different climate conditions are seldom taken into account in planning for overseas operations. As a consequence, personnel performance may be considerably different than anticipated. Significantly different temperature and humidity levels can prevent U.S. personnel assigned overseas from performing at their usual levels of efficiency. Climate can also affect the performance of local personnel, not only on the job, but also on training programs. For these reasons, important considerations in an international operations planning are the scheduling of appropriate working hours, and the degree of flexibility required.

Organizational Structure

Although centralization of logistic management is appealing from a management point of view, highly centralized logistic organizations seldom work effectively in practice. The main reasons for this are the differences in cultural characteristics, governmental regulations, and labor policies mentioned above, and the need to maintain personal contacts with carriers, customers, and other groups.

When a logistic system operates in many areas of the world, the best type of organization is usually one in which the planning and control functions are centralized, and the operations functions are decentralized. When a logistic system has international scope but is concentrated in imports and exports from one area to the rest of the world, a centralized organization can work effectively. When a few major geographic areas originate substantial traffic within themselves in addition to external traffic, a decentralized operation will often be more effective.

Distribution Organization

Organizing for Effective Distribution Management

JAMES L. HESKETT

Whenever two or more people combine efforts to achieve a single goal, organization is required. It represents the identification and assignment of responsibilities and reporting relationships in order to make the effort of any group more effective and efficient.

There are only a few useful generalizations that can be made about organization for logistics. Among them are the following: However they are assigned, logistics functions and responsibilities are endemic to any organization, whether recognized or not. There is no one right answer to the so-called organizational problem. And there are as many organizational schemes for logistics as there are organizations.

Given that as background, however, we can benefit from a review of responsibilities for logistics activities to be organized, basic organization principles and alternatives in use in large companies today, basic factors influencing the structure of organization for logistics, and the process of formalizing or restructing an organization.

The Scope of Logistics Activities to be Organized

Certain logistics functions must be managed in any organization, regardless of how or where in the organization this is done. Some functions are formally recognized, appearing on the ever-present but often misleading organization charts that at least provide a kind of road map to an organization. Some never appear on an organization chart and must be recognized and managed by less formal means.

Logistics encompasses groupings of activities often associated with materials management (or the management of physical supply of raw materials and components) and physical distribution (typically involving the distribution of finished goods). Formal responsibilities encompassed by the term logistics are shown in Figure 29–1. They often are found on organization charts and are clearly assigned to one or more members of an organization.

As suggested in Figure 29–1, organization for effective logistics management may be complicated by the fact that logistics activities are grouped around flows of material and information. Materials and information flow through the organization in such a way that a decision concerning them is bound to affect the operations of two or more of the major functions shown in the boxes at the top of Figure 29–1. The organizational arrangement chosen must, therefore, allow for a great amount of coordination without crippling the decision-making process for logistics matters.

Less formal, but nonetheless important, logistics-related responsibilities often never appear on organization charts. Several are shown circled in Figure 29–2. They too are of interest to several major functional groups within an organization, as suggested by the maze of lines connecting functions with the responsibilities circled in the figure. The task of coordinating such matters often is assigned to committees, task forces, or integrators, about whom we will say more later.

The important thing is to insure that appropriate levels of attention and coordination for all of these activities are encouraged by the form of organization adopted, not necessarily that they all be grouped under one manager in the organization.

Basic Organization Principles

Over the years, practice has suggested the value of a relatively small number of principles in the development of any organization. While it is rarely possible or desirable to adhere strictly to all of them in any given situation, it is useful to keep them in mind. A relatively few such principles and terms provide us with all the shorthand notation we will need for this discussion.

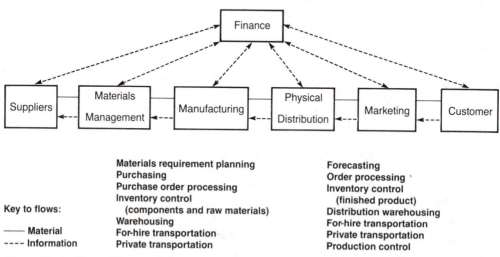

Figure 29–1   Formal Responsibilities (Often Appearing on Organization Charts) Associated with Materials Management and Physical Distribution

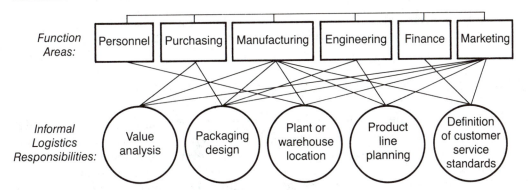

Figure 29-2   Informal Logistics Responsibilities (Often Omitted from Organization Charts) and Functional Areas Taking a Strong Interest in Them

Unity of Command

The principle of unity of command is used to emphasize the need for no more than one superior with direct authority (often shown with a solid line on an organization chart) over a subordinate. This "one boss per subordinate" rule often allows for so-called functional supervision (shown by a dotted line on the organization chart), generally intended to provide expert support to a subordinate without injecting a second boss into the relationship.

Span of Control

Span of control refers to the number of subordinates a manager can supervise. Naturally, limits have to be placed on span of control in an effectively managed organization. While these limits are sometimes stated in such terms as "no more than five to seven subordinates per manager," in fact they are determined by the type of people and tasks being supervised and the manner in which supervision is carried out. If there were no limits on span of control, all subordinates would report to the chief executive officer, a situation found only in the smallest organizations.

Responsibility and Authority

The terms responsibility and authority are two that are used and misused often in discussions of organization. We'll use responsibility to mean the results for which a manager is held accountable, whether measured in quantitative or non-quantitative ways. Authority, the delegated right to command action from a subordinate, is one way in which a manager discharges responsibility.

Theorists have long debated whether a manager's authority should be commensurate with his or her responsibility. As a matter of fact, authority without commensurate responsibility or accountability can lead to arbitrary, uncontrollable actions. But the reverse, responsibility without commensurate authority, is a fact of life for many corporate logistics managers today. It means they must seek alternatives to direct authority as a means of discharging their responsibilities and meeting their goals.

Line and Staff

Two other terms, line and staff, referring to types of responsibility and authority, will crop up repeatedly in our discussions. We'll use the term line to refer to those types of relationships in which the superior has direct authority over a subordinate and is responsible for using that action-oriented authority for getting things done. Staff relationships, by contrast, are often advisory or coordinative in nature. Little direct authority can be applied, although as person in a staff position may well be held responsible for achieving results by means of the advice or coordinative support provided to managers with line authority responsibility.

Centralization and Functional Organization

These terms refer to the relative levels in an organization to which responsibility, particularly for profits, is assigned. Top management in a centralized organization typically reserves the responsibility for itself. In order to carry out the responsibility, often it is necessary in a centralized organization for all important decisions to be made or coordinated at the top, requiring that information flows be directed to and from the highest levels.

A centralized organization often is structured along functional lines, with senior executives in charge of finance, marketing, manufacturing, and other major functions reporting directly to a chief executive officer responsible for coordinating major functional decisions.

Decentralization and Business-Oriented Organization

Responsibilities, particularly for profit, are delegated to lower ranks of management in a decentralized organization. Profit responsibility often is centered in so-called strategic business units, each with control over operating functions such as marketing, manufacturing, and logistics. Such organizations include in their ranks senior managers responsible for major staff or advisory functions, and the financial activities of raising funds and allocating them to the strategic business units.

Factors Influencing the Importance and Nature of Distribution in the Organization

The most important factors influencing the importance and nature of distribution in an organization are the importance of logistics in relation to total costs of doing business; the need to manage trade-offs between important logistics cost categories of transportation, inventory holding, and lost sales (customer service); the complexity of the logistics network; the need for flexibility in management; the nature of the overall corporate strategy; and the capacities of people available to manage.

Importance of Logistics Costs

Logistics costs of transportation, inventory holding, and lost sales may range from 2 percent of total costs in a firm manufacturing high technology equipment and components to 40 percent in a firm producing basic raw materials or agricultural products. Studies have shown some correlation between the level of the most senior logistics executive in an organization and the importance of logistics in a firm's total cost structure. However, the number of deviations from this relationship suggests that other factors may be even more important determinants of the importance of the function. And it is quite certain that these other factors are more important than cost levels in determining the nature of responsibilities assigned to the most senior logistics manager. Foremost among them is the need to manage trade-offs between important logistics cost categories.

Need to Manage Trade-Offs Between Important Logistics Cost Categories

Logistics cost trade-offs influence greatly the complexity and nature of the manager's task. Consider three case examples.

A producer of high technology components used in the manufacture of computers sells to a limited number of original equipment manufacturers (OEMs). Because of its high value, the product incurs high inventory holding costs. Failure to meet delivery schedules results in severe strains on customer relations and potentially high costs of lost sales. Transportation costs, in relation to total costs are, however, so low that even if air freight services are utilized consistently the costs are relatively insignificant. In this business, logistics costs not only are relatively low but the nature of cost trade-offs suggests that high cost transportation nearly always is preferable to build-ups in inventory or lost sales. While the scheduling of production may be important, the logistics task is carried out by a shipping manager with relatively little authority, opportunity to exercise judgement, or standing in the organization.

In a second firm which mines and ships coal, logistics costs may be 40 percent of the total cost of doing business. Here, however, the cost of transportation far outweighs inventory holding or customer service costs. The cost of carrying inventory is so low in relation to transportation costs that stockpiles of coal are established both at the shipping point and at customer locations, reducing the cost of a delayed shipment or delivery. The most important objective is to do whatever is necessary to ship in the lowest-cost quantity by the lowest-cost method of transportation. In this firm, a vice president of transportation reporting to the president manages the important transportation function. However, the nature of the task involves so few trade-offs between transportation and other costs that this high-ranking manager oversees a department immersed in coal tariffs and is not considered a serious candidate for general management because of his or her specialization.

In contrast to these two examples, a manufacturer of grocery products distributes a line of processed and packaged foods. In total, logistics costs may represent 15 percent of the cost of doing business for this firm. Costs of transportation are substantial, the costs of holding inventory on a per-pound basis are high, and failure to meet customer orders may result in substantial sales lost through the substitution for the manufacturer's brands of those of a competitor. The necessity of coordinating transportation and inventory decisions with those involving customer service requires that all three of these responsibilities be vested in one position, a manager of physical distribution responsible for managing trade-offs among three important cost areas. While this position may not report to the chief executive officer, it involves complexities sufficient to qualify it as a good training ground for general management.

Complexity of the Logistics Network

The logistics management task requires the servicing of a network of suppliers and customers, few of whom may be selected by the logistics manager. Service may be provided through varying numbers of collection points, plants, mixing points, and distribution warehouses. The addition of each "node" increases the network's complexity as well as the opportunity for error in analysis or management of the network and loss of control over logistics costs. Sooner or later, lack of control may lead to the focus of attention on the logistics function, thus encouraging management to highlight the function in the organization.

Goals for the logistics function in a firm may shift from time to time from cost minimization to a maximization of customer service. Often these shifts reflect the desires of management to achieve the highest profits in the long run, and the perceptions of various senior managers as to the most effective ways of achieving high profits under varying conditions. In industries typified by wide cyclical swings in the relation of supply and demand, such as paper manufacturing, the emphasis may change relatively rapidly from that of providing a high level of customer service during periods of excess supply to that of minimizing costs during periods of excess customer demand. Where this occurs, it is important to maintain a direct line of communication between those managers setting corporate strategy and those managing logistics operations. This may suggest the desirability of a direct reporting relationship to top management for the senior logistics manager.

Nature of the Corporate Strategy

Factors such as the number of businesses or divisions represented in a company's operating portfolio, the extent to which each is run as a profit center, and the degree to which distribution or logistics is regarded as a profit center influence the location and nature of the logistics function. All are elements reflecting corporate strategy. They determine whether a corporate staff advising divisions on logistics matters is necessary. They determine the extent to which logistics management is carried out in the divisions or business units. And they influence the extent to which common logistics facilities, such as private transportation fleets and warehouses, are used jointly by two or more businesses or divisions and how the logistics services are paid for or the costs divided.

Where logistics acts as a profit center, typically business units or divisions are charged a prorated portion of the costs, or better yet, a market rate less a discount for the transportation, warehousing, or other service provided. The performance of the function is judged on the extent to which its costs are kept in line with revenues.

Capacities of People Available to Manage

The textbook approach to organization suggests that the structure (or organization) should reflect a company's strategy and should follow from it. As a practical matter, management capability often is the most limiting constraint on a business. A lack of capacity or talent in the logistics management of a company may require that it adopt a strategy that minimizes the complexity of the logistics management task, delegate responsibility for logistics tasks to managers responsible primarily for other functions, or otherwise reduce the impact that any one logistics manager or department may have on the performance of the company. Conversely, the presence of a strong logistics function may induce general management to develop a strategy based in large part on its logistics capability, for example, for moving goods between two points or for establishing and closing distribution sites on short notice.

Organizational Alternatives for Distribution

Two areas of logistics management have developed in recent years. They have come to be known most commonly as materials management and physical distribution management. The former is a term applied to the management of flows of material inbound to the firm, and until relatively recently was confined largely to firms whose businesses were oriented to some degree around inbound material flows, firms such as those involved in aircraft manufacture and defense industries. More recently, with the growing emphasis on maintenance of relations with sources of supply in industries experiencing shortages as well as the increasing use of techniques for facilitating manufacturing control such as materials requirements planning, materials management as an organizational concept has spread to an increasing number of firms and industries.

Physical distribution management, the management of outbound materials flows and attendant flows of information, has been found most commonly as an organizational concept among firms experiencing much greater complexity in their distribution-oriented as opposed to supply-oriented activities. Thus, manufacturers of grocery products, pharmaceuticals, and other types of packaged goods have been major proponents of coordinated management for physical distribution activities such as finished goods storage, inventory control, transportation, order processing, and customer service.

A Comprehensive Logistics Organization

In theory, a firm with materials and physical distribution management activities thoroughly coordinated through the vehicle of a logistics organization would look much like that diagrammed in Figure 29–3. This type of firm is organized along functional lines, with logistics occupying a role comparable to finance, manufacturing, and marketing, among others. Based on our earlier discussion, the organization in the figure reflects a highly centralized management, with decisions made mostly by top management.

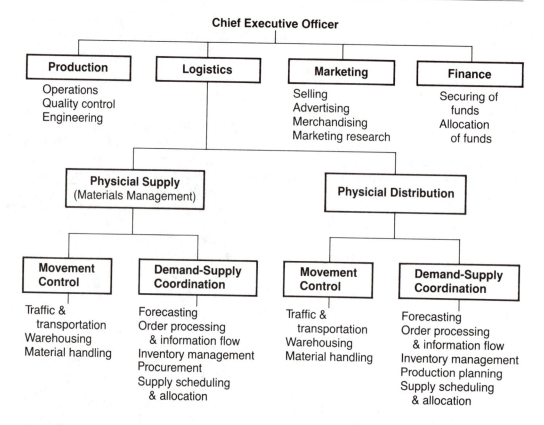

Figure 29-3   A Comprehensive, Highly Centralized Logistics Organization

SOURCE: Adapted from James L. Heskett, Nicholas A. Glaskowsky, Jr., and Robert M. Ivie, *Business Logistics*, 2d ed., (New York: Ronald Press, 1973), p. 27.

Benefits of such an organization are that it facilitates the management of activities common to both supply and distribution activities of transportation, warehousing, and inventory control. It insures visibility for logistics in management, particularly in the strategic planning process typically reserved for top management. And it establishes the logistics function on a "neutral" ground among three other functions—finance, manufacturing, and marketing—often at odds with one another concerning inventories, scheduling, costs, and customer service levels.

Firms with comprehensive logistics organizations are hard to find in American industry. As desirable as they might be, particularly for single-business firms with a limited amount of senior management talent, other forces and influences may override those of logistics to force various types of organizational compromises involving a division of responsibility for logistics activities among several major functions of the firm.

Centralization versus Decentralization

Logistics activities can be managed from corporate headquarters in the centralized firm or from the plant, sales office, or business units in a decentralized firm.

Basic advantages of centralized management are a more effective use of warehouse and private transport facilities, coordination of the purchase of transportation and other services, and central control over inventories supporting two or more business units.

In a decentralized approach to logistics management, two or more divisions or business units might boast such groups, as shown in Figure 29–4. Here, responsibility for profits is relegated to the divisional or business level, with corporate staff responsible only for advice on such matters as personnel, labor relations, legal, and the acquisition of financing and allocation of funds to divisions (finance).

Benefits of this type of organization are that it may complement a corporate strategy encompassing distinctly different types of business units with little need for coordination or common facilities. It relegates profit responsibility to lower levels of the organization, facilitating the preparation of talent capable of assuming general management responsibilities. And it makes available to all divisions or business units a common pool of experts housed in various corporate staff departments. According to a survey of 138 members of the National Council of Physical Distribution Management conducted by the Logistics Research Group at The Ohio State University in 1980, the largest proportions of organizations surveyed, 38 percent, combined divisional (decentralized) and centralized approaches, with only 20 percent organized along divisional lines and 26 percent on a purely centralized basis. Similarly, 81 percent of senior logistics managers responding to the same survey reported that they were responsible for both line and staff activities, with only 8 percent reporting responsibility only for staff activities and the remaining 11 percent reporting responsibility solely of a line nature. As in most aspects of business, it is hard to find the pure examples of logistics organizational alternatives that exist so often in theory. Given the complexity of the logistics function, this should be no surprise.

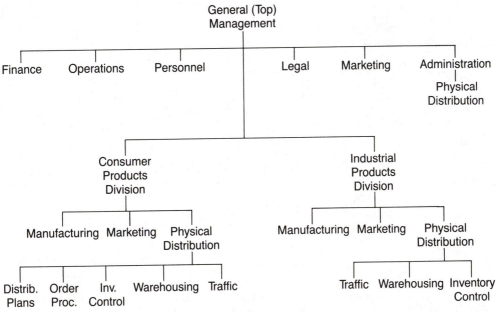

Figure 29-4 Organization for Logistics (Physical Distribution) Management in a Decentalized Firm

Line versus Staff in Logistics

Line, operating, or action responsibilities within the logistics function typically are concerned with the management of transportation, warehousing, order processing, or procurement activities. Depending on the degree of decentralization, they may be managed at either the divisional or corporate level.

Staff or advisory responsibilities most commonly are concerned with traffic management (particularly the negotiation and administration of rate matters and mode and carrier selection) and system design, including inventory control and materials or physical distribution on a shorter-term basis. Whether such staff activities are positioned at the corporate or divisional level in an organization varies with the size of the organization and the extent to which two or more divisions can utilize the same staff support.

The organization of a large manufacturing firm suggesting the presence of line and staff logistics groups at both the corporate and divisional levels is shown in Figure 29–5.

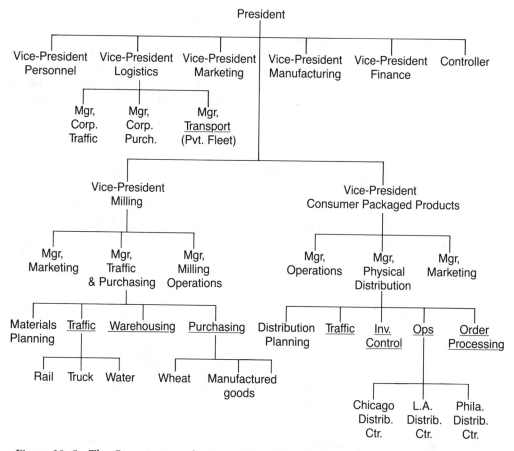

Figure 29-5 The Organization of a Large Firm Manufacturing Packaged Grocery Products. Line and staff logistics responsibilities are assigned at both corporate and division levels. (Line management responsibilities or logistics are underlined.)

Scope and Positioning of Responsibility

Results of a major survey of senior materials and physical distribution managers that suggests varying divisions of responsibilities for logistics-oriented activities are shown in Table 29–1. Since such surveys are often directed at the most visible and progressive companies, we might assume that respondents represented the "state-of-the-art" in the span of control over various functions in these organizations at the times they were taken. Nevertheless, they suggest an extensive sharing of responsibility for logistics-oriented activities among marketing, manufacturing, and finance managers as well as materials or physical distribution managers.

Reporting relationships for those holding primary responsibility for logistics activities vary greatly as well. For example, where physical distribution is viewed as a supporting activity in a marketing-oriented firm, its management often is responsible to senior marketing management. Similarly, materials management may be established in support of, and responsible to, manufacturing management. Organizations in which logistics is viewed primarily as the arbitrator between conflicting needs of marketing, manufacturing, and finance often assign the management of such activities to a non-functional reporting relationship, often to general management. This is reflected in the results of one recent organization survey shown in Chapter 30, Figures 30–1 to 30–3.

Table 29–1 Extent to Which Action Authority for Logistic Activities Resides with Senior Logistics Manager

Activity	Percentage of Companies with Action Authority	Percentage of Companies Reporting Increase in Authority	Percentage of Companies Predicting Increase in Authority
Administration	92	40	27
Transportation & traffic (raw materials)	61	46	48
Transportation & traffic (finished goods)	92	42	31
Interplant transfers	67	32	30
Raw material storage	29	30	26
Raw material inventory control	20	32	31
Finished products storage (plant)	40	36	35
Finished products storage (remote)	60	39	28
Finished products inventory control	45	40	31
Shipping container design	18	42	33
Packing for shipment	37	43	26
Customer order processing	51	47	30
Internal order processing	47	45	32
Customer credit	8	11	7
Package design	11	37	35
Purchasing	23	21	21
Production planning	27	44	28

Source: Adapted from D. H. Maister, "Organising for Physical Distribution," *International Journal of Physical Distribution & Materials Management*, 8, No. 3 (1977), pp. 147–179, at p. 172.

Matrix Organizations

In recent years matrix organizations have been formed to foster coordination among managers organized on some combination of functional, geographic, product, or customer bases. For example, product managers with responsibility for the profitability of designated product groupings might have to marshall resources for the proper distribution of their products from physical distribution, advertising, and sales departments with either profit or cost responsibility. The abilities to coordinate and manage conflict are highly prized in a matrix organization.

One such matrix organization proposed solely for logistics activities in an aluminum manufacturing firm is shown in Figure 29–6. In this firm, the flows of raw materials such as coal and bauxite were thought to be so important that product managers with responsibility for the procurement and associated logistical activities for each raw material were appointed to bring together the resources of the traffic, transportation, and functionally oriented departments on behalf of their particular commodity.

Matrix organization concepts will continue to grow in popularity as ways of fostering coordination and management dialogue in complex organizations.

The Multinational Firm—A Special Case

Contrasting organizational alternatives have risen among the growing number of firms engaged in multinational or global business activities.

Some firms with important costs associated with product flows, such as the aluminum producer shown in Figure 29–6, have organized on a product basis with strong emphasis on the central planning and management of such flows across national boundaries. In such firms, a central logistics function with high visibility and broad responsibility is quite common.

Other firms facing highly differentiated marketing and manufacturing tasks among nations or regions have tended to organize along such lines with separate, self-contained organizations for the "French" or "German" subsidiary. Area organizations predominate, for example, in companies facing strongly national consumer markets and restricted opportunities for importing, requiring local manufacture as well. Thus, the aluminum manufacturer utilizing a product-oriented organization with a strong central logistics function for the management of its raw material production was found to have an area organization for the fabrication and sale of consumer products manufactured from the basic aluminum. In the latter case, each area supported its own logistics function in the manner that a firm confining its activities to any one country might.

Staffing the Logistics Function

Successful staffing of the logistics functions requires job definition, an inventorying of available people and skills, and a matching of people with jobs. Given the nature of the logistics management task, it may be important that those selected for senior responsibilities possess strong integrative abilities.

Product Line Managers

Fabricated products	Other raw materials	Electrolite materials & chemicals	Ingot	Smelter materials	Alloys	Carbon materials	Special aluminas	Bauxite & alumina	Funtional Group (Managers)
									Raw materials
									Capital goods
									Consulting
									Quality control
									Market survey
									Expediting
									Planning and research
									Inventory control
									Rail
									Truck
									Ship
									Port
									Navigation charts
									Chartering bulk space
									Claims and marine insurance
									Leasing and purch. of ships
									Monitoring performance
									Scheduling
									Freight forwarding
									Terminal management
									Marine management
									Rail and truck management
									Accounting
									Insurance and Treasury
									Office management
									Systems
									RIMS

Figure 29-6   Proposed Matrix Organization for Logistics Management in a Large, Integrated, Multinational Aluminum Manufacturing Firm

Source: Adapted from Christine R. Hekman, Alcan Aluminum (B), Harvard Business School case 9–281–034 with permission.

Job Definition

Perhaps the most important and mutually detested job in organizing any function is that of job definition. That may account for the fact that few job descriptions prove helpful or are ever referred to after they are prepared. There are ways of simplifying the task and making its product more usable.

Basic elements of the job description include the title, reporting relationship, scope of responsibility, and measures of performance associated with the job. Titles and reporting relationships depend on factors cited earlier.

The scope of responsibility will reflect the size and complexity of various tasks to be performed. It can be described very simply, eliminating flowery, useless language. Each task can be designated by an action verb and an object noun. For example, a transportation manager may be responsible for hiring and firing owner-operators, scheduling loads, allocating equipment, or establishing internal private transport transfer prices.

Measures of performance are an integral part of the job description. Bases on which performance is to be measured as well as specific goals to be achieved on each may be agreed on by supervisor and subordinate, thus obtaining the commitment of the latter.

Inventorying People and Skills

In assessing available skills for logistics management within an organization, it is important to look beyond current managers of logistics activities. In fact, the desirability of a broad background resulting from experience in several functional areas of the firm is suggested by information shown in Table 29-2. This suggests that an important qualification for senior logistics management is multi-functional experience so important to the successful coordination of logistics material and information flows across functions.

Other skills thought to be useful for logistics management, based on responses of managers themselves, are shown in Chapter 30, Table 30-9. While no one person may possess all of them, such a list suggests the complement of skills that might be sought for the organization as a whole.

Table 29-2   Functional Backgrounds of 49 Senior Logistics Managers

Area	Percentage Indicating Area in Background
Accounting	29
Marketing	33
Sales	15
Production	63
Finance	10
Labor relations	4
Personnel	13
Engineering	6
Other	60
Total	233*

*Because managers could indicate one or more areas, this suggests that the mean number of areas in each manager's background was about 2.3.

SOURCE: Adapted from D. H. Maister, "Organising for Physical Distribution," *International Journal of Physical Distribution & Materials Management*, 8, No. 3 (1977), pp. 147–179, at p. 171.

Matching People and Jobs

Management by the book contends that people should be matched to jobs and not the reverse. Organizational life, however, often dictates an interactive process of job definition, inventorying of skills, and some adjustment of jobs and titles to fit the realities of available personnel. Only where major gaps or duplication in abilities exist may people have to be hired or relocated, respectively, to meet the needs of the job.

The Logistics Manager as Integrator

In many organizations logistics is a coordinative function. Its successful performance requires the cooperation of marketing, manufacturing, and finance. Its stock in trade is the trade-off of one type of cost for another. The logistics manager often must serve as referee and adjudicator among other functional managers, providing objectivity to the decision-making process. And at times this role must be performed without direct authority over those whose efforts are to be coordinated. This has come to be known as the role of an integrator, and it pervades much of logistics management today.

Research suggests the qualities that integrators possess, qualities that might well describe many successful logistics managers today.

One study* concludes that:

1. Integrators need to be seen as contributing to important decisions on the basis of their competence and knowledge, rather than on their positional authority.

2. Integrators must have balanced orientations (as, for example, between production and sales, short-range and long-range thinking, etc.) and behavior patterns (as, for example, between people-oriented and task-oriented jobs).

3. Integrators need to feel that they are being rewarded for their total product responsibility, not solely on the basis of their performance as individuals.

4. Integrators must have a capacity for resolving interdepartmental conflicts and disputes.

Trends in Organization for Logistics

Logistics management in the future will reflect trends in management in general. At least in American firms, it will become more multinational in its orientation. It will concentrate less on the development of new techniques of analysis and more on the utilization of developing technology for computing and communicating information. It will place more emphasis on the ability to interpret and act on data rather than generate it.

As a growing number of senior managers count logistics responsibilities among those from which they graduated to their current jobs, the logistics function should be inte-

---

*Reprinted by permission of the *Harvard Business Review*. Excerpt from "New Management Job: The Integrator" by Paul R. Lawrence and Jay W. Lorsch (November–December 1967). Copyright © 1967 by the President and Fellows of Harvard College; all rights reserved.

grated more effectively into the strategic planning of the business. It will, to an increasing extent, become a training ground for general managers.

This may all have to be accomplished without significant further change in the reporting relationships or scope of responsibility for logistics managers, given longitudinal data in Table 29–3 that suggest significant changes in recent years on these dimensions of logistics management.

Summary

Organization is essential to the performance of work and the accomplishment of goals. Because an organization is a reflection of both a business strategy and the job it suggests, as well as available people and skills, no two organizations do or should look alike. It is important, however, that logistics tasks inherent to any business organization reflect the complexity and importance of the function as well as the need to integrate logistics into a business strategy.

Whether oriented around materials or physical distribution activities, logistics involves the management of flows of material and information across more traditional functions. Thus, coordination is a byword for logistics management, whether it is achieved by the assignment of line responsibility for some or all logistics activities to one manager or by

Table 29–3   Comparison of Span of Control for Senior Logistics Managers in 12 Companies Known to Have "Progressive" Logistics Management Organizations

Activity	Number (and %) of Firms Reporting Action Responsibility			
	1960	(%)	1974	(%)
Administration	12	(100)	11	(92)
Transportation & traffic (raw materials)	9	(75)	7	(58)
Transportation & traffic (finished goods)	11	(92)	10	(83)
Interplant transfers	1	(8)	8	(67)
Raw material storage	1	(8)	4	(33)
Raw material inventory control	1	(8)	2	(17)
Finished products storage (plant)	5	(42)	7	(58)
Finished products storage (remote)	11	(92)	10	(83)
Finished products inventory control	7	(58)	9	(75)
Shipping container design	2	(17)	1	(8)
Packing for shipment	2	(17)	4	(33)
Customer order processing	9	(75)	8	(67)
Internal order processing	8	(67)	8	(67)
Customer credit	1	(8)	3	(25)
Package design	1	(8)	0	(0)
Purchasing	0	(0)	0	(0)
Production planning	1	(8)	3	(25)
Number of firms	12	(100)	12	(100)

Based on a follow-up survey by D. H. Maister reported in his article, "Organising for Physical Distribution," *International Journal of Physical Distribution & Materials Management*, 8, No. 3 (1977), pp. 147–179, at p. 173, of firms originally surveyed 14 years earlier.

the assignment of an integrator with many responsibilities but little authority to accomplish the task.

The most important factors influencing the value and nature of the logistics function in an organization are the importance of logistics in relation to total costs of doing business; the need to manage trade-offs between major logistics cost categories of transportation, inventory holding, and lost sales (customer service); the complexity of the logistics network; the need for flexibility in management; the nature of the overall corporate strategy; and the capacities of people available to manage.

These factors account for the wide array of organizational alternatives found for logistics in American industry today. Few organizations have comprehensive line authority for both materials and physical distribution management. The most commonly found arrangement combines centralized responsibility for the line management, for example, of private transportation and staff support for traffic, inventory, and facility planning with decentralized or divisionalized line responsibility for warehousing, inventory management, order processing, and traffic. The growth of matrix organizational arrangements has enhanced opportunities for coordination so important to effective logistics management.

As organizations grow more complex and the forces leading to the differentiation of tasks increase, integrators capable of coordinating actions of managers with potentially conflicting interests will become more important. Those sought out for logistics management will be evaluated to an increasing degree on their integrative skills. And, logistics management, because of its inherent nature, should become an important source of such capability to the extent it is required for more effective general management of the firm.

Note

1. Paul R. Lawrence and Jay W. Lorsch, "New Management Job: The Integrator," *Harvard Business Review* (November–December 1967), pp. 142–151, at p. 146.

Distribution Personnel

Career Patterns in Distribution: Profile 1983

BERNARD J. LA LONDE *and* DAVID E. LLOYD

Introduction

In each of the past twelve years, the Logistics Research Group at The Ohio State University has conducted a survey of the career patterns of distribution executives in U.S. firms. Originally this study sought to answer basic questions on the background, training, work experience and demographic characteristics of those executives. However, in recent years the survey has been expanded in scope to include trend analysis of the attitudes and opinions of distribution executives as well.

Specifically, the 1983 survey sought to find answers to the following basic questions:

1. How is the distribution function organized?

2. What are the primary responsibilities for the distribution executive?

3. Who is the distribution executive?—A demographic profile

4. How does the distribution executive perceive the future?

Methodology

The data utilized in this study were obtained from a detailed four-page questionnaire mailed to 567 members of the National Council of Physical Distribution Management

The authors wish to acknowledge the financial support of the Logistics Research Fund of The Ohio State University which funded this research project.

(NCPDM) during the summer of 1983. A concerted effort was made to achieve a sample balanced on both an industry and a geographic basis. In cases where two or more NCPDM members were listed within the same company, the survey was sent to the executive with the higher perceived position. The 171 questionnaires which were returned represented a response rate of 31.2 percent.

The questionnaires were coded, key punched, and analyzed using the computer facilities of The Ohio State University. Tabulation of the results involved utilizing standard two-variable cross-tabulations and summary statistics; the results are summarized here.

Every effort was made to classify accurately the open-ended survey responses and to interpret multiple job title classifications meaningfully. The responses to the 1983 survey indicated that a multitude of descriptive distribution job titles still exists for key distribution executives. However, because the primary objective of this research has been to provide trend analysis of broad classifications, the authors believed it best that the analysis of the data continue to utilize the three broad managerial classifications of *manager*, *director*, and *vice-president*.

The reader will note that in the discussion and tables, comparisons are made with survey findings from earlier years. Caution should be exercised in generalizing or interpreting the results of year-to-year comparisons since the returned questionnaires are anonymous and there is no way, given the research design, to ensure that the respondents are identical on a year-to-year basis.

Findings

Summary statistics of the 1983 study may be found in the tables and figures that accompany this chapter. The findings are organized around the basic questions noted earlier.

How Is the Distribution Function Organized?

During the past six years there has been some evidence of stability in primary organizational format of the distribution function (see Tables 30–1 and 30–2, and Figures 30–1, 30–2, and 30–3). That is, approximately 80 percent of the respondents reported both line and staff responsibility. On the specific positioning of the distribution function, 40 percent of the respondents reported a combined centralized and divisional organization. Of the remaining respondents, approximately 20 percent reported a divisional organization, 21 percent a centralized organization, and 18 percent a separate distribution division. The results show an apparent stabilization of the divisional form at the 20 percent level while the separate distribution division form of organization is increasing.

This conclusion is reinforced by the reporting relationships depicted in Figures 30–1 through 30–3. During the past several years there have been some shifts in the evolving patterns of organizational relationships. Specific shifts are difficult to identify, but the findings seem to suggest that the distribution function is being linked with pre-production

Table 30–1   Organizational Responsibility

Line and staff	76.0%
Staff	7.6%
Line	16.4%

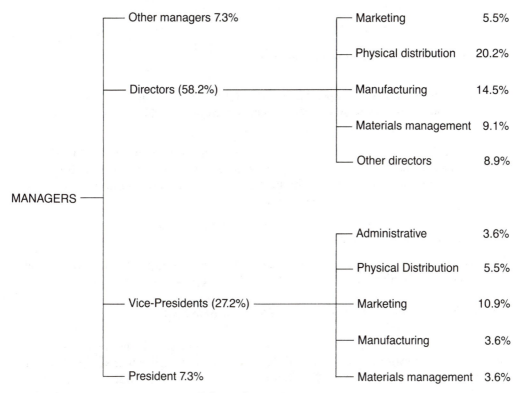

Figure 30-1   Managers—Reporting Relationships

activities (i.e., purchasing, production planning, etc.), and a new form of total material flow organizational format is emerging. Evidence for this trend is also supported by a tendency for those executives reporting to a functional vice-president to report to an operations function. Additionally, there may be a trend developing where the distribution logistics executive reports directly to the president.

What Are the Primary Responsibilities of the Distribution Executive?

Figures 30–4 through 30–6 and Table 30–3 respond to this question. The primary trends in specific responsibilities of the distribution executives have indicated a gradual shift from a narrow traffic and warehousing responsibility to a broader range of responsibility both within and outside the distribution area.

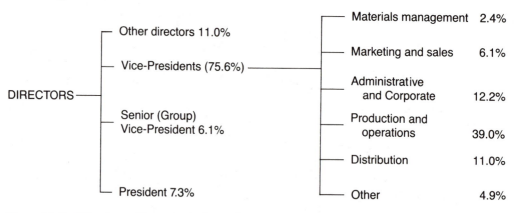

Figure 30-2   Directors—Reporting Relationships

- Distribution executives spend approximately 30 percent of their time outside the distribution function. About 60 percent of that outside time is spent in interacting with the marketing and production areas.

- Since deregulation, distribution executives are spending more time on traffic management. Managers continue to spend approximately 30 percent of their total time in the transportation and warehousing areas, whereas directors and vice-presidents spend 25 and 30 percent respectively.

- The amount of time spent at all levels in "general administration" has gradually risen over the past five years.

- Distribution executives at all levels now are spending approximately 20 percent of their non-distribution time interacting with data processing functions.

Who Is the Distribution Executive?—A Demographic Profile

The age distribution of physical distribution (PD) executives (Table 30–4) showed the same general patterns of recent years although the average age is increasing. The dominant age category for managers is 30–39; for directors it is 40–49, and for vice-presidents it is 50–59.

The educational profile of the distribution executive saw only some random sample variations from the previous year (Tables 30–5 and 30–6). Emphasis is still on the college educated executive: 96 percent of the 1983 respondents had at least some college and 91 percent had a college degree or more. Approximately half of the PD executives reported postgraduate work, with 36 percent reporting a master's degree or higher. Likewise, as indicated by Table 30–6, business administration and engineering and science background continued to dominate the undergraduate preparations of the executives in distribution capacities.

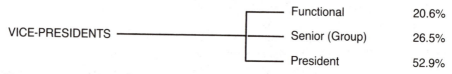

Figure 30-3   Vice-Presidents—Reporting Relationships

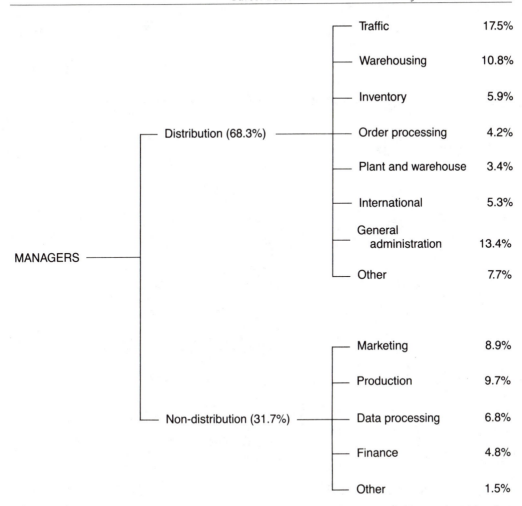

Figure 30-4 Time Expenditures on Distribution and Related Non-Distribution Activities for Managers—1983

Tables 30–7 and 30–8 show average compensation levels for 1983 and increases in compensation levels for the 1983 period. Although the average increase in compensation was 10 percent, not all positions participated equally. While average salary levels increased for managers and vice-presidents, the average salary level for directors was slightly lower than in 1982. For the first time, 3 percent of the executives surveyed reported reductions in compensation levels for 1983. While this reflects the current economic conditions existing in some industries, the general trend is still upward.

How Does the Distribution Executive Perceive the Future?

This year as in past years the respondents were asked, "If you were offered an opportunity to return to school in the near future for three months and could take a custom-designed curriculum, what kinds of things would you study?" For the first time since 1973, the financial area was not the dominant area (see Table 30–9). The trend noted in 1982 has been realized and the data processing, simulation, and modeling area has become the

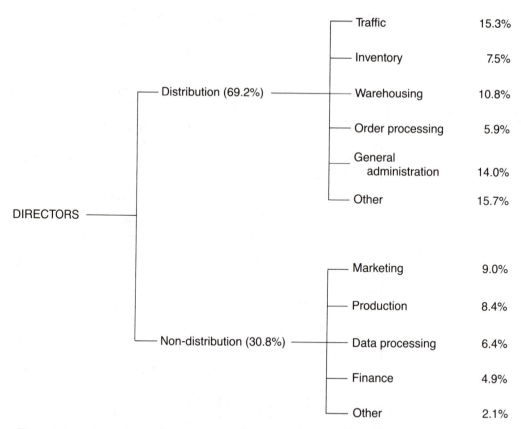

Figure 30-5   Time Expenditures on Distribution and Related Non-Distribution Activities for Directors—1983

dominant preference for both first and second choice. The financial area continues to be important and upward trends are noted in both general management and marketing areas.

The respondents were asked to "Identify the major factors which will influence the growth and development of the corporate distribution function during the next decade." Their summary responses are presented in Table 30–10. In the 1983 survey a number of significant changes occurred in the pattern of responses.

- The respondents continued to rank their ability to identify and control distribution cost as a key variable in the future of the distribution function. Note also the growing importance of customer service.

- The pattern of response indicates a global view of the distribution process. While external factors (e.g., deregulation and the economy) continue to be important environmental factors, the distribution executive appears to see the need to focus on internal factors (e.g., distribution costs, customer service, information systems, and management emphasis).

- The respondents continued to be concerned about the application of management information systems (MIS) concepts and data processing technology to the logistics function.

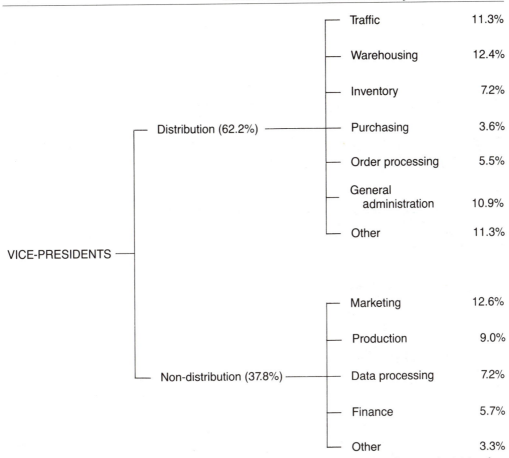

Figure 30-6   Time Expenditures on Distribution and Related Non-Distribution Activities for Vice-Presidents—1983

The respondents were also asked to share their attitudes concerning a number of logistical statements (Table 30–11). The findings include:

- 89 percent of the respondents noted that distribution is a more important corporate function than it was five years ago.

Table 30-3   Percentage of Distribution Executives with Full International Distribution Responsibility

Year	Percentage
1974	9.5
1975	16.0
1976	22.1
1977	19.0
1978	23.0
1979	27.7
1980	30.5
1981	30.8
1982	30.0
1983	27.5

Table 30-4   Age Distribution—1983

| | Title | | |
Age	Manager (%)	Director (%)	Vice-President (%)
Under 30	0.0	0.0	0.0
30–39	42.6	22.0	8.8
40–49	37.0	42.7	38.2
50–59	20.4	28.0	47.1
60 and over	0.0	7.3	5.9
Total	100	100	100

Table 30-5   Educational Background of PD Executives—1983

Level	Percentage
High school graduate	4.1
College, non-degree	5.4
College graduate	41.4
Graduate school, non-degree	13.6
Master's degree	35.5

Table 30-6   Undergraduate Degree Majors of PD Executives—1983

Area	Percentage
Business administration	33.1
Engineering and sciences	19.9
Transportation	9.9
Liberal arts	14.6
Industrial engineering/management	9.9
Economics	7.9
Other	4.7
Total	100

Table 30-7   Average Compensation of PD Executives (in Dollars)—1983

	Manager	Director	Vice-President
Top quarter	67,920	79,800	125,500
Second quarter	53,600	61,600	91,100
Third quarter	41,900	52,500	73,300
Lowest quarter	33,900	40,400	53,100
Average	49,300	58,500	85,600

- 92 percent of the respondents agreed that more specific goals had been developed for the distribution function in their firms over the past five years.

- 90 percent of the respondents agreed that the computer is the key to better productivity in their firms.

Table 30–8   Changes in Base Compensation—1982–1983

Percent Change	Percentage
– 10–0	2.7
0–5	9.4
6–10	57.7
11–15	19.5
Over 15	10.7
Average	10.0

Table 30–9   Educational Needs Reported by PD Executives—1983

	Percentage of Respondents	
Study Area	First Choice	Second Choice
Data processing, simulation, models	32.7	24.6
Finance	24.7	17.5
General management	19.3	9.9
Marketing	8.8	13.5
Legal environment	2.3	1.8
Other	6.5	18.1
None	4.7	14.6

Table 30–10   Distribution Executives on Future Trends—Results of Opinion Survey

Question: What are the major factors that will influence the growth and development of the corporate distribution function during the next decade?

	Percentage of Respondents	
Factor	Most Important	Second Most Important
Identification and control of distribution costs	22.8	9.8
Impact of deregulation	12.3	11.0
The economy	14.2	13.5
Customer service	14.2	23.2
Utilization of computer-based information systems	14.8	15.5
Increased management knowledge and involvement	6.2	9.0

- 89 percent of the respondents agreed that the planning process has assumed more importance in the distribution function in their firms during the past five years.

- 84 percent of the respondents agreed that deregulation will lower costs of transportation.

Study Implications

Since the study has been conducted annually for the past twelve years, it might be appropriate to identify the primary changes that have occurred in the distribution function dur-

Table 30-11 General Attitudes of PD Executives about Distribution—Results of Opinion Survey

Statement	Percentage of Respondents					
	Strongly Agree	Agree	No Opinion	Disagree	Strongly Disagree	Total
Distribution is considered a more important function in our firm than it was five years ago.	47	42	5	5	1	100
In the past five years we have developed more specific goals and standards for the operation of our distribution system.	44	48	3	3	2	100
Better use of the computer is the key to improved distribution productivity in our firm.	49	41	4	6	0	100
The distribution planning process has assumed more importance in our firm in the operation of the distribution function during the past five years.	47	42	5	5	1	100
In the 1980s, more firms will use inventory carrying costing for distribution decision making.	29	65	2	4	0	100
Deregulation is having a significant impact on the distribution of goods in our firm.	29	41	6	19	5	100
In the 1980s, most firms will maintain higher customer service levels for key accounts than for other customers.	20	64	6	10	0	100
Deregulation of the transportation system will lower costs of transportation.	36	48	1	12	3	100
Given the current and forecasted economic climate, we will use more public warehousing to meet any expanded storage needs in the period 1983–87.	9	49	11	26	5	100
Given the current and forecasted economic climate, we will use more private carriage capability in the period 1983–87.	8	24	13	43	12	100
In the face of sharply increased costs, customer service levels will be lowered by most business firms in the 1980s.	3	28	4	51	14	100
Deregulation will improve service levels in the U.S. transportation system.	14	45	11	25	5	100

ing that period. Again, caution should be exercised in interpreting these trends because of the unique character of the distribution function in many firms and year-to-year shifts in the sample base.

Positioning of the PD Function

Over the past ten years positioning of the distribution function has been shifted from a staff function to a line function or combination staff and line function. Moreover, the number of respondents at the director and vice-president levels has more than doubled since the early 1970s. This reflects an upward repositioning of the chief distribution executive of the firm.

Primary Responsibility of the Distribution Executive

Perhaps the most significant changes over the past decade have occurred in the primary areas of responsibility of the distribution executive. In the early 1970s the typical distribution executive was largely concerned with a narrow range of activity—usually transportation and warehousing. By the early 1980s the PD function had been broadened to include activities ranging from forecasting to order processing.

A corollary to the broadening of the PD function has been a shift in "outer directed" focus of the distribution executive. That is, the distribution executive of the 1980s is spending a significantly larger share of the day interacting with the marketing, production, finance, and data processing functions than his counterpart in the early 1970s.

Future Directions

For the past three years there has been evidence of a growing interest on the part of distribution executives in a more "management science" oriented approach to management. This interest surfaces in a number of different ways. For the first time, finance was not identified as the most important learning need. First place in both the primary and secondary categories went to the general area of data processing, simulation, and models. Consistent with this learning need priority, the utilization of computer-based information systems was identified as an important factor that will shape the growth and development of the corporate distribution function during the next decade. This interest has undoubtedly been present in parts of the corporate distribution function prior to this time, but these findings suggest strong acceptance by the chief distribution executive and distribution policy maker for the firm.

There is continued evidence that some organizational changes first noted in the 1980 survey are continuing. At this point the evidence is inconclusive but seems to suggest that an increasing number of firms are attempting to integrate the material flow process. That is, the organization and coordination of raw material, work-in-process, and finished goods are being more closely integrated. The evidence suggesting this trend comes from the titles of the respondents, their functional responsibilities, and their reporting relationships.

During the first ten years of the survey the common complaint by many managers was that senior corporate management "did not understand or appreciate" the corporate role of the PD function. The clear suggestion was that PD managers were trying to make changes that were beneficial to the company but change was hampered by a lack of understanding of the part of senior managers. The survey evidence indicates that the direction of change has reversed in many respondent firms. Change has started to come from the "top down" rather than the "bottom up." If indeed this finding is confirmed, it means that pressure for change will come from senior management and that the speed of change in the distribution and logistics function will increase.

CHAPTER 31

The Educational Needs of Physical Distribution Managers

Dᴀᴠɪᴅ P. Hᴇʀʀᴏɴ

Physical distribution management (PDM) may be defined as the process and functions involved in moving goods from raw materials through manufacturing and delivery to the ultimate consumer. It includes, but is not limited to, such functions as procurement, inbound transportation, production scheduling, order entry, warehousing, materials handling, transportation, and customer service.

There are a number of characteristics of PDM that cause additional education in this profession to be a continuing need.

1. The physical distribution manager requires a broad range of knowledge, not only in physical distribution itself but in the marketing and manufacturing operations that are almost always closely intertwined with distribution. There is insufficient course time for the PD manager to acquire all of this knowledge during his formal schooling.

2. There are relatively few courses in PDM available in colleges and universities. Particularly at the undergraduate level, courses in physical distribution are offered as electives as part of the business or engineering management curriculum.

3. The rate of technical progress in PDM is rapid. Techniques of mathematical programming, probability and statistics, decision analysis, and strategic planning, often carried out with the assistance of computers, are becoming essential tools of the PD manager. In many cases, PD managers have had no exposure to these techniques during their formal education.

4. New topical knowledge in the areas of government regulation, hazardous materials shipping, environmental impacts, and conservation of energy is being required of the PD manager at a seemingly accelerating rate.

5. Surveys have shown that many persons enter PDM after training and professional careers in some other field. In many cases these persons have not had the opportunities to acquire the techniques and knowledge needed for PDM; hence they need to obtain this essential information.

For these reasons, it is important to determine how well the existing opportunities for PD education are meeting the needs of managers in this field, and what further steps might be taken by professional management associations such as the National Council of Physical Distribution Management (NCPDM), by universities and colleges, and by professional training organizations.

Skills Required in Physical Distribution Management

The PD manager requires three types of skills: the technical skills for understanding and managing the various PD functions, skills required for interfacing distribution with other organizational functions, and skills required for interacting with other entities such as the public and the government.

Functional Skills

The functional skills required by the distribution manager will depend greatly on his specific environment. The following is a representative listing of such skills:

- *Procurement and inbound transportation.* Vendor selection; determination of most economic purchase quantity, considering discounts, procurement costs, inbound transportation costs, requirements in Material Requirements Planning (MRP) situations, and inventory carrying costs; annual purchase contracts; integration of incoming and outbound transportation.

- *Production scheduling.* Determination of master schedule, lot size planning, line scheduling, sequencing, in-process inventories, material management, geographical location of production facilities.

- *Order entry.* Communications network, equipment, operating procedures.

- *Warehousing and inventory management.* Size and location of warehouses, products handled, reorder points and reorder quantities, transportation modal mix, material handling.

- *Customer service.* Speed and reliability of response to customer orders, handling complaints, trade-offs of distribution system cost and effectiveness.

Managerial Skills

Physical distribution is labor intensive. Hence the PD manager must learn how to manage people, including supervision, motivation, and organization. In addition, he must know how to successfully plan the strategic and tactical aspects of his work, and how to measure both physically and financially the results of his operation, compare these results with goals or standards, and strive for improvements in productivity.

Interfacing Skills

Surveys have indicated that the PD manager spends considerable time interfacing with manufacturing and marketing managers. Hence he must have sufficient understanding of these functions so as to successfully integrate his operations with the manufacturing and marketing functions of the organization. In addition, he will be a part of the budgeting and financial control activities carried out for all functional operations, as well as a participant in labor negotiations.

Increased interfacing with the public and with government regulators is common in all corporate management, and the PD management position is no exception. Because of the labor intensiveness of distribution, the PD manager must possess the skills for dealing with these external groups.

It is apparent that the required skills as summarized here cannot all be obtained from formal courses, either in universities or on-the-job. Many of these skills come only from actual experience, from coaching by superiors, or from exchanging information with other PD managers. Also, many PD managers find that professional reading is indispensable as a continuing educational device, as will be further discussed in the next section.

Present Methods for Meeting Skills Requirements

In 1979, the National Council of Physical Distribution Management commissioned SRI International, a consulting organization, to undertake an extensive survey of the continuing educational needs in PDM.[1] Approximately 5000 NCPDM members, former members, and non-members were sent surveys, and over 700 valid replies were received. In addition, telephone and personal interviews with key PDM practitioners, educators, and editors were conducted to obtain more detailed information on important aspects of PDM education.

A major section of the survey was devoted to determining how PD managers presently attempt to meet the need for PDM skills. While there was some variation in the relative importance ascribed to present educational means by managers at various organizational levels, the reading of professional articles and attendance at the NCPDM national meeting ranked substantially higher than other means, as shown in Table 31-1. This table lists the frequency of Number 1 rankings of the present methods of meeting educational needs, as obtained from the mail survey.

An earlier survey by Davis and Marien[2] showed that the typical NCPDM member spent approximately 100 hours per year of his own time and 100 hours per year of company time on his continuing professional development. All in all, it is evident that the PD manager is willing to spend considerable time and effort in furthering his professional education.

Most Useful Subject Areas for Continuing PDM Education

Respondents to the mail survey were asked to indicate the subject areas they felt most important for their continuing PD education, and the format in which they felt each subject could most usefully be presented. Five subject areas—transportation, financial control, quantitative analysis techniques, inventory management, and computer systems—re-

Table 31-1   Frequency of No. 1 Rankings of Current Educational Methods

Reading professional articles	237
Attending NCPDM national meeting	140
Attending other national meetings	98
Attending trade association meetings	91
Attending NCPDM Roundtables	76
Continuing college education	66
Attending university-sponsored seminars	52
Attending company in-house courses	52
Attending non-NCPDM seminars	41
Attending professional education courses	37
Attending NCPDM seminars	14

ceived the greatest number of responses. A listing of the educational subjects mentioned most frequently, together with the preferred format for receiving further education in each subject, is shown in Table 31–2.

Several comments may be appropriate regarding the results shown in the table. Transportation represents the largest single expense area in physical distribution for most companies, so that its importance to PD managers would be expected. The other four subjects are concerned with quantitative aspects of PDM and emphasize the increasing concern of PD managers with the measurement and control of the physical distribution function.

Respondents who marked a subject as important also thought the probability was quite high that they could avail themselves of opportunities for taking that subject. For the five top subject areas tabulated in Table 31–2, from 30 to 50 percent of the respondents who indicated interest in these subjects believed there was at least 95 percent probability that they would take such courses if offered.

Role of Universities in PDM Education

Universities play an important part in education for PDM. Available university training is of four types:

- Regular courses in physical distribution and related subjects in the undergraduate and graduate curricula[3]

- Specialized training courses, such as preparation for the ICC practitioner examinations

- Short courses for individuals interested in broadening their PDM skills

- Seminars on PDM, often jointly sponsored by the university and an outside organization

As noted earlier, however, few universities grant degrees in physical distribution management. Instead, PDM courses are offered as electives in the business administration or engineering divisions. It has often been difficult to persuade the deans of such divisions that there is a growing need for courses in PDM because of escalating energy costs in product transportation and the high cost of money tied up in industrial inventories. We can hope that this situation will change.

Graduate and undergraduate training is undoubtedly one of the most effective means of education in PDM. Also, as shown in Table 31–2, university seminars are the preferred format for obtaining postgraduate education in a number of PDM subject areas.

Role of Professional Organizations in PDM Education

Respondents to the SRI survey made a large number of suggestions as to how professional organizations such as NCPDM could both improve their current activities and undertake additional activities for meeting the continuing educational needs in PDM. These suggestions may be classified in five subject areas:

Clearing House for Educational Information

Improvements are needed in the information available to distribution practitioners with respect to educational opportunities and PDM information at all levels. Suggestions were made that organizations such as NCPDM could:

- Prepare (perhaps as a joint effort by several professional organizations) a catalog of continuing educational opportunities at all levels.

- Prepare a comprehensive source bibliography of key articles on PDM subjects that have been published in the past ten years, and append a summary of further research needs on these subjects.

Sponsor of Technical Projects

NCPDM has achieved an outstanding reputation through its sponsorship of technical projects, such as the studies on customer service, inventory costing, accounting in PDM, and productivity improvement. Respondents recommended that this activity be continued. Specific suggestions were (1) updating the Schiff study on PDM accounting and control, (2) sponsoring the preparation of case histories of successful productivity improvements in physical distribution, and (3) studying how companies balance customer service levels and distribution costs.

Table 31–2   Frequency of No. 1 Rankings of Desired Subjects for Further PDM Education

Subject Area	Frequency	Preferred Format
Transportation	137	National professional meeting
Financial control	125	University seminar
Quantitative analysis techniques	86	University seminar
Inventory management	85	Professional educational organization
Computer systems	78	Company in-house training program
Warehousing	62	National professional meeting
Marketing	54	University seminar

Publisher of Technical Information

Currently there are several deficiencies in the form and type of technical information available in PDM. Professional organizations such as the NCPDM could perform an invaluable role in filling these gaps.

- In the key area of PD productivity, an NCPDM-sponsored study noted the following needs for additional technical material: (1) a standard operating procedures manual to guide the establishment of productivity measurement programs, (2) technical information on key impediments to increased productivity, and (3) a reporting system for productivity measurement. Professional organizations could actively promote work to prepare such material.[4]

- Professional organizations could explore the preparation of a home study course in PDM, or possibly prepare an outline for a survey course on PD for use in colleges and universities.

- Professional organizations could continue the placement of outstanding articles and speeches on PDM in key business publications.

Improvements in Professional Meetings

Professional meetings in PDM, such as the NCPDM national meetings, are generally of very high quality, but certain improvements have been suggested.

- Aim specific sessions of national meetings at selected segments of the membership.
- Expand the use of joint industry-educator speaking teams.
- Limit the amount of "selling" that consultants are permitted in their presentations.
- Increase the effort to obtain greater educator participation in NCPDM.

Cooperative Efforts Among Professional Groups in PDM

A number of professional organizations sponsor activities in the subject areas of PDM, but these are often undertaken with little knowledge of or coordination with similar activities by other organizations. Greater cooperation would both improve the quality and eliminate some of the overlapping of these activities. While formal ties between such professional organizations appear to be difficult to achieve, an annual meeting of the educational chairmen of these organizations to discuss planned activities of mutual interest should be highly beneficial.

It is also desirable for professional organizations in PDM to broaden their contacts with management and government groups to emphasize the importance of PDM in increasing national productivity and improving the standard of living.

Role of On-the-Job Training in PDM

On-the-job training is a main thrust of career development in PDM.[5] Many companies work out individual development programs for each employee, often consisting of a combination of job rotation, in-house seminars, and reimbursed outside courses. Because of the rapidly changing technology and environment in PDM activities, maintaining professional competence by managers and their staff members is virtually an endless frontier.

Conclusion

There is a substantial perceived need by PD practitioners for further education, as well as broad agreement on the principal subject areas in which such education is important. The NCPDM, universities, and professional education organizations, together with publications dealing with PD topics, have an important role to play in meeting this need. The steadily expanding opportunities for further education in PDM indicate that such organizations are aware of the need and are responding to it. These organizations can benefit both themselves and PDM practitioners by closer cooperation and coordination of their activities.

Notes

1. SRI International, *Educational Needs in Physical Distribution Management* (Chicago: NCPDM, 1979).
2. H. W. Davis and E. J. Marien, "Career Development in Distribution," *Handling and Shipping*, **17**, No. 8 (August 1977), pp. 47–52.
3. E. J. Marien, *College and University Courses in Physical Distribution Management* (Chicago: NCPDM, 1978).
4. A. T. Kearney, Inc., *Measuring Productivity in Physical Distribution* (Chicago: NCPDM, 1978).
5. F. J. Quinn, "Training: Important Today—Essential to the Future," *Traffic Management*, **16**, No. 11 (November 1977), No. 11.

CHAPTER 32

Labor Relations

William W. Allport

The specialized field of law that is the topic of this chapter is generically known as labor relations, but this term is a misnomer. A more appropriate label would be "applied psychology." The key to success in any business enterprise is proper motivation of its employees. Proper motivation is achieved through a prescription involving a mixture of 10 percent law, 30 percent common sense, and 60 percent psychology! Too often, labor unions are viewed as direct and formidable roadblocks in the path to achieving acceptable levels of motivation. This chapter is intended to assist you in the sometimes complex task of motivating your employees. It will also include a discussion of methods to employ in dealing with collective bargaining agents on a day-to-day basis. The chapter is divided into four areas:

1. How to operate under an existing collective bargaining agreement

2. How to prepare for contract negotiations

3. How to avoid EEOC and NLRB problems

4. What to do when faced with a slowdown, walkout, picketing, or work stoppage

How to Operate Under an Existing Collective Bargaining Agreement

If your employees have organized a union and have designated a collective bargaining agent, your ability to operate your business will, to some extent, be limited by the terms and conditions of your collective bargaining agreement. There are various philosophies with respect to operating within the framework of a collective bargaining agreement. Many entrepreneurs view a collective bargaining agreement as a limiting device which specifically defines both permissible and prohibited conduct. Those who share this view believe that if you are considering the institution of a new work process and your contract does not specifically provide for such an eventuality, you will be prohibited from instituting such a program.

You should not accept this interpretation. If a contemplated action is not specifically prohibited by your collective bargaining agreement, then you are in fact free to engage in such conduct. With the proper presentation, significant changes can be effected in your method of operation, notwithstanding the existence of a collective bargaining agreement.

Understanding Your Contract

If your employees are represented by a union, it is extremely important that you read each and every word of your collective bargaining agreement. This is true regardless of what level of management you may represent. It can be very helpful to prepare a table of contents and a topic outline of your collective bargaining agreement. These should be stapled to the collective bargaining agreement. It is also useful to index your collective bargaining agreement so that the items contained in your table of contents can be found easily by using a tab system. A thorough familiarity with your contract will enable you to handle problems in an authoritative manner as they arise instead of putting them in limbo until the contract is researched. Further, a sound knowledge of your contract will eliminate the common practice of relying on the union agent to interpret and apply the terms of the contract. No matter how fair your agent is or how impartial he appears to be, his bias will slip into every interpretation—this is human nature.

It is a good idea to review your contract at least once a month. You can never become too familiar with your collective bargaining agreement. If you accept the premise that you can do anything that is not specifically prohibited in your contract, you will obviously want to know exactly what items *are* prohibited by your collective bargaining agreement. After learning the "don'ts," you will be surprised at the vast area of flexibility left open to you.

Many managers have absolutely no conception of the contents of their collective bargaining agreements. This is often the case with companies that have become signatories to voluminous "industry" or "master" contracts. They accept the contract as a necessary evil and resign themselves to a "ho-hum" existence wherein they are unable to compete with their industrial opposition. It is difficult to operate a business profitably without knowing the explicit terms and conditions of your collective bargaining agreement.

Managers of operations that are large enough to justify the retention of labor professionals to handle labor relations matters should not divorce themselves from this area. They should make sure that they are as familiar with the collective bargaining agreement as their professional staffs. The cost of labor is generally the largest single expense item in American business, and one that cannot be ignored. You should feel free to offer your ideas concerning new innovations, work rule changes, or new methods of productivity to your labor staff. Encourage open communication between your other functional managers and your labor department.

Familiarizing Customers with Your Contract

Almost as important as your own understanding of your labor contract is the assurance that your customers are equally cognizant of your contractual obligations. In the transportation and warehousing industry, labor is one of the chief costs in computing rates for your customers. Thus, contract provisions relating to wages, hours, and working conditions can have a direct bearing on the fee that will ultimately be charged to your customer.

If the customer or user of distribution services is to understand properly the rate formulation process, it is important that he be aware of the current trends and settlements in collective bargaining. Those offering distribution services must never assume that the customer is aware of the current wage rates and benefit packages that affect distribution. Often he is too busy with his own functional area of the business to be more than peripherally concerned with yours.

Users of the firm's distribution division or of outside distribution services will be less likely to balk at rate changes if they are aware that the increase is predicated upon a rational basis. Thus, you should continually educate your customers or users in the realities of the collective bargaining relationship, including industry patterns, so that they will understand and appreciate the need for changes. Do not wait until after you have agreed to an increase. This is a preventative step which should be done well in advance of any anticipated increase in labor costs.

While it is important to keep the user fully informed of your collective bargaining process, it is equally important for your mutual benefit to insure that he does not become directly involved in the bargaining relationship between you and your union. The user of distribution services should be completely divorced from any direct relationship with your employees and/or your union representative. Public warehousemen and transportation companies especially should never allow customers or their representatives to be present at meetings they may have with their bargaining representatives. Such intervention could result in a co-employer determination being made by the National Labor Relations Board. A co-employer determination would make the customer liable on the collective bargaining agreement as if he were a signator.

Maintaining a Good Relationship with the Union Representative

One of the most important facets of collective bargaining is the relationship that you maintain with your union representative or business agent. Your union representative can be your best friend or best enemy depending on how he is treated. This relationship should never be social—rather it should be maintained strictly on a business plane. Your union representative should be treated with the same respect afforded others with whom you transact business. An arm's-length relationship that reflects mutual respect will reap far greater benefits than will an overly social or overtly antagonistic atmosphere.

Your union representative should always be kept fully informed of all pertinent matters affecting your employees. Quite simply, this means you should not spring any surprises upon him that will affect the members of the bargaining unit. Surprises will put him in a bad light with respect to the members of the bargaining unit which he represents. It is important to remember that your union business agent is a political being who must be reelected in order to retain his job.

Management, recognizing the political reality of the business agent's survival, can aid the agent by keeping him informed as to relevant company happenings. In order to successfully stand for reelection, the agent must present an acceptable track record. Agents who are kept informed of the possibility of new business prospects, cutbacks, layoffs, and so on, can better represent their members since *they* will know what is "in the wind" and will not find themselves in the embarrassing position of being told of major occurrences by their members *after* the event has occurred. Managers who adhere to the philosophy of keeping the union agent in the dark are creating future problems for themselves.

It is wise to deal with your business agent at arm's length, but with a good measure of respect. Be sure to include him and use his good offices for selling new ideas and concepts to your employees. Working around him or directly attacking him will only result in a situation where your union relationship evolves into a small-scale industrial war. Such an antagonistic relationship will prove costly in terms of both profit and employee morale. Never underestimate the abilities of your agent. Agents have survived reelection campaigns and deal with the largest corporations in America, often without much formal education; they are unique and competent individuals—respect them and work with them.

Therefore when considering any change of operation or the institution of productivity goals, it is imperative that your business agent be included from the earliest planning stages in the formulation of such a plan. If the agent is fully aware of the need for the program and understands that jobs will not be jeopardized by its institution, it is very possible that program can be instituted and accepted by your employees. Knowing and appreciating the political framework within which your union business agent operates is vitally important if you are to prosper in your operation.

The old "blood and guts" approach to labor relations on your part will generally result in the exact same approach being taken toward your operation by the union. If your employees have designated a bargaining agent, you and your employees' representative are, in a sense, partners in your operation. By no means does the presence of a union signal the kiss of death as far as productivity and profitability goals are concerned. Productivity plans can be instituted if they are presented properly to your union business agent and to your employees.

Gifts or contributions to your business agent or other union officers are illegal. The Labor Management Relations Act specifically prohibits various types of donations made by employers to unions. Generally speaking, any type of contribution or gift to your union is, per se, unlawful. Social entertaining should be kept to a minimum. Ideally, entertaining should be limited to picking up a lunch tab if business was discussed.

You should never become involved in the political framework of your employees' union. If an insurgent faction of the union were to take over control of the union, and the regime that you supported were ousted, your operation would be the target of much "retribution" by the new governing party. For the same reason it is unwise to develop any personal relationship with your business agent apart from purely business dealings. Such an involvement could make *you* a target of political retribution if that agent were replaced, and would place your operation in a precarious position. Accept the fact that your agent will not be in office forever and plan your strategy accordingly.

Instituting Work Rules and Operating Changes

In today's economic climate, most businesses are looking towards productivity and incentive arrangements as necessities in order to compete successfully. In order to institute operating changes or work rules which will result in incentive-type programs, it is extremely important that you include both your business agent and individual employees in the early planning sessions. Many employers develop incentive plans in total secrecy and then "spring" them on their employees using carnival barkers' selling techniques. The employees' natural reaction is one of bewilderment and concern for their job security. This can lead to wildcat strikes, slowdowns, and, before you know it, industrial war. Developing and introducing a productivity plan in this manner is sheer folly, and your chances of success are minimal.

When it becomes apparent you can no longer compete unless your company's level of productivity increases, meet with your business agent and several employee representatives. Be fully prepared to explain your financial plight in detail, using visual aids, charts, and graphs, if appropriate. Offer several alternative incentive plans to your employees. Be sure other cost-cutting devices are also being instituted elsewhere in the company so that your union members do not feel they are the only ones being affected. Then let your employees decide upon the type of plan they want.

This approach works. Incentive plans instituted in this manner have been accepted by employees. In fact, most employees refuse to go back to an hourly compensation scheme after they have tried incentive systems. Before such changes can be instituted, you must educate your union representative and your employees as to the need for the work rule or operational change. Your justification for instituting incentive programs will generally be based on a desire to remain in business. If your operation is noncompetitive and you are forced out of business, your employees will lose their jobs. You must present this information in a convincing manner. If you do, you will probably encounter little opposition.

To a young employee, the loss of a job may not appear to be too great a hardship. However, if "long timers" (those with five or more years of seniority), were to lose their jobs because of a shutdown, they would have to begin all over again with respect to accumulating seniority, vacation benefits, and the like. Therefore, job retention will be quite important to those employees. However, you should never lie or deliberately distort your company's financial picture. If you "shade" this picture, your employees are bound to learn of the misrepresentation. Once they do, your credibility will be destroyed, and the next time you really need help from your employees, your pleas for cooperation will fall on deaf ears.

No incentive program should result solely in a savings to management. The program should be constructed so that the employees themselves will also benefit. Further, it should be but one part of an overall cost-cutting program affecting every aspect of your business. The overall program should affect white collar and non-union employees as well as union employees. If the union people feel they are the only ones being affected by the program, you can expect little sympathy from them.

Before instituting any type of incentive system you should consult a highly qualified and reputable firm that is experienced in establishing such programs. Most major accounting firms in the country have departments experienced in this type of work. Ask the prospective firm to supply you with the names of corporations that have utilized their services. Then, get in touch with those customers to discuss at length the pros and cons of the systems that they instituted. If possible, check their relative profits and losses both before and after the incentive programs were instituted. Determine the most appropriate incentive system for your operation and request that the consulting firm supply you with a detailed presentation of their plan before you sign a contract. If the retention of a management consulting firm is not feasible, you can check with your trade association. Usually, such associations are familiar with programs that have been tried by companies similar to yours.

Any incentive program must be a two-way street. Initially, most employees will mistakenly assume that an incentive program is designed to cut their wages and may lead to lost jobs. This erroneous view can be dispelled by educating people as to the experiences of other companies that have instituted productivity programs. When your employees are shown that jobs are not lost and that they can make more money with an incentive program, these fears usually evaporate.

One of the worst steps you can take in setting up a productivity improvement program is to send a time study expert into your operation unannounced to your employees. The rumors about closing the facility, eliminating people, and the like will spread like wildfire. Before you are able to contain the rumors and explain to your employees the reasons for the study, your plant could experience wildcat strikes, slowdowns, and other types of concerted activity. Your hopes of instituting an incentive program will evaporate. Thus, an immediate and detailed presentation of the total program is essential.

The manner in which a productivity or incentive program is presented to employees is also crucial. If you can present the program in such a manner that your employees are positive and receptive to the program, your chances of successfully operating under the program are far better. As stated previously, your employees should be involved as early as possible in the planning process. Do not bypass your bargaining agent! Your agent should be informed initially of your plans and the reason for the plans. His reaction will generally be that if your employees are receptive to the program, he will not stand in your way. If he is not receptive to the plan, you should suggest that the proposal be submitted to the employees—i.e., the democratic answer. If he continues to refuse, then firmly inform him that you are going to proceed and his proper course of action is to file a grievance if he still has concerns about the plan.

Once the agent agrees to present the plan to the employees, be prepared to act quickly. Rumors will be rampant after your meeting with the business agent. The rumors must not be given time to solidify into unreasoned opposition. Therefore, within 48 hours you should be prepared to make a presentation to your employees. This meeting will be the most crucial part of instituting the program. It should be given all of the planning and preparation of a full-blown presentation to your best customer. The meeting should be held during working hours; coffee and donuts or other refreshments should be provided, and visual aids should be used.

Begin the meeting by explaining your true financial picture. Show the relative market position of your customers and your competitors. Then, identify the areas in which you can economize. Next, present the program, including all devices to be employed to make the company more competitive. Make it very clear to your employees that they are just one facet of the overall program. Solicit questions and promote "openness" throughout the meeting. Then, lay out a timetable as to when each facet of the program will begin.

If you sense your employees are vehemently opposed to the program, then sell it on the basis that it will be a temporary measure, and as soon as your market position improves, the program will be ended. Or, as an alternative, set a definite date for reevaluation of the program, i.e., a year or 18 months. Remain flexible. Experience indicates that once the program set in motion and employees see their take-home pay increase as a function of their input, the program will sell itself. The crucial task, then, is to get the program going, even if it is only accepted on a temporary basis. Your chances are excellent that the employees will refuse to give it up when the time for expiration or reevaluation occurs.

After instituting the program, be sure to work closely with employees on refining the program. Efforts directed at making the program run as smoothly as possible should be expended daily when the program is initially set in place. After the program is instituted, it should remain flexible. If problems are encountered, refine the program. No one program is a universal panacea for every industrial situation. Productivity programs must be adjusted constantly so that they remain workable. As the program continues and employees and supervisory staff become accustomed to performing under it, less frequent attention will be required.

Handling Grievances

Most individuals involved in industrial relations agree that the single most important part of the collective bargaining process is contract negotiations. However, most employers fail to realize that a company usually gives away more by losing grievances than it surrenders at the bargaining table. Many unions have a philosophy that if they are unsuccessful in securing a particular item at the bargaining table, then they will attempt to achieve it through the grievance procedure. If a union fails to secure a specific demand during contract negotiations, you can bank on the fact that within the next two to three months, you will receive a grievance addressing the same issue. If the grievance is not handled properly, you will have lost the ground you so valiantly fought to defend only a few months earlier. Handling grievances is an extremely important matter, and the following guidelines should help you manage this process.

Philosophy

The grievance process plays an extremely important part in the area of industrial psychology. Through grievances, employees are able to express their dissatisfaction with a particular aspect of the company's operation. It is a good avenue of "release" for normal frustrations which build in every employer-employee relationship. One of the main reasons unions were initially formed in the 1920s and 1930s was because employees believed they had no voice in the affairs of their companies. Modern surveys reaffirm the desire of American workers to have an effective voice in the management of the company. The grievance procedure is a vital part of the process in which employees can make their position known to management.

Oftentimes, businessmen will proudly point to the fact that they have not had a grievance filed against their company in a given number of years. In fact this can be a sign that something is drastically wrong with their business. It may indicate that they have "given away the ranch" without knowing it. A reasonable number of grievances is an indication that a healthy relationship exists between management and its employees. If the grievances are properly handled, they can be mutually beneficial to management and employees.

Legally, the right of an employee to file grievances is guaranteed to him under the National Labor Relations Act (NLRA) and, also, under his collective bargaining agreement. Thus, efforts directed at thwarting an employee from filing a grievance or refusing to process a grievance with due diligence should be avoided. Such activity will generally result in a charge being filed against your company with the National Labor Relations Board (NLRB). Employees should not feel intimidated in filing grievances. Your supervisors should realize that grievances are a fact of industrial life and treat them as such.

Your supervisors and managers should not take grievances personally. Do your best to discourage vendettas that attempt to "even the score" with an employee who exercises his grievance privileges. Such retribution is per se a violation of the NLRA and may result in a sizeable back pay award being levied by the NLRB against your company. The cost of a legal defense against these charges will also be substantial. Therefore, in terms of dollars and cents, attempts to tamper with the grievance process are something no American business can afford.

Trained Supervisors

Most grievances, before they are reduced to writing, will be presented directly to a supervisor in the form of an employee complaint. Your supervisors should be encouraged to recognize minor difficulties as they arise and redress them on the spot if possible. In no circumstance should a supervisor delay in handling a grievance. A problem that is given time to ferment becomes more difficult to resolve. Once "battle lines" are drawn, it is not easy to arrive peaceably at an amicable solution. The worst possible situation that can result is to allow grievances to accumulate to the point that they cannot be handled properly. In such cases wildcat strikes or other concerted actions, such as slowdowns, sickouts, and the like, may result.

This does not suggest that management should capitulate on grievances. Each grievance should be considered on its own merits. Its effect on the company's short- and long-range goals should be considered. If the employee is right, the issue should be resolved promptly. However, if the employee is wrong, do not be afraid to contest the matter. Grievances are extremely important, and unions can gain as much through grievance processing as they can at the bargaining table. Therefore, you should have an alert and qualified staff of supervisors who can recognize major grievances. Once a major grievance is identified, your entire management team, if necessary, should join force to resolve the matter satisfactorily.

A Myriad of Grievances

A few companies may find themselves in the unenviable position of being "grieved to death" by their employees. The number of grievances might suddenly increase from four to five a month to 25 or more during the same time period. This should be an immediate indication that something is drastically wrong with the labor relations program. Do not cast full blame on your union employees, although they will undoubtedly be partially at fault for the deteriorating conditions. A situation of this nature is usually attributable to a breakdown in communication.

Such breakdowns are generally due to errors in judgment on the part of both management and employees. Initially, the problem should be reviewed with supervisors. If a satisfactory course of action cannot be agreed upon, you should immediately interject yourself into the collective bargaining process. Call your business agent, explain the problem to him, and suggest a joint meeting. Include representatives of the union, management, and members of the work force. The meeting should prove to be enlightening to you *and* your business agent. You will discover areas in your operation that need attention. The union will learn about the realities of your operation and the reasons for the policies which are causing them concern. After the problem areas have been identified, don't spend a great deal of time rehashing who is "at fault" or who should take the blame for the existence of the problem areas. As quickly as possible after the areas are identified, solicit suggestions for solutions. When people are challenged to find solutions to existing problems, their thinking is shifted to more productive lines. This may help them appreciate the reasons underlying the existence of troublesome policies.

The chief operating officer should rarely become involved in any direct problem-solving ventures with employees, except in cases of full-blown crisis. Employees should not be allowed to sidestep their supervisors unless the situation has deteriorated to the point that the latter are no longer able to direct the work force. In those situations, immediate action is imperative. Delay will only make the problem worse.

Handling Arbitrations

Arbitrators versus Joint Committees

Most collective bargaining agreements outline one or two alternative procedures in the event that the normal process is unsuccessful. If a grievance cannot be resolved "in house," it will either be referred to an independent arbitrator or to a joint committee composed of union and company representatives. Varying results have been obtained from either course. However, when the pluses and minuses of each system are considered, the independent arbitrator is recommended. Independent arbitrators supplied by such services as the American Arbitration Association (AAA) and the Federal Mediation and Conciliation Service (FMCS) are competent individuals, well versed in the collective bargaining process. They are generally professors, lawyers, or labor relations experts who are genuinely interested in finding an amicable solution. If you are concerned about possible local bias, either service can provide a list of "out-of-town" arbitrators. In this manner, impartiality can virtually be insured.

It is true that an arbitrator will generally cost more than a committee (a per diem charge is generally $250 to $300). Most collective bargaining agreements specify that the company and the union will divide the charges. A positive aspect of the higher cost is the regressive impact it has on the number of grievances that are submitted. Because both the company and the union are cost conscious, both will want to explore every possible avenue of settlement before incurring the expense of an arbitrator. There does not seem to be the same impetus for settlement present in the joint committee process, where the costs are usually minimal.

The committee approach may also result in your competitors' deciding your grievances. In many situations winning a grievance may net your company a competitive advantage vis à vis your competition. If, however, your competitors comprise the grievance panel which will hear your dispute, you can be fairly certain that your competitors will not be overjoyed at the prospect of your company's gaining a competitive advantage. Thus, in close situations they may be prone to let the economics of the situation influence their otherwise impartial judgment. If a panel member is of a mind to take advantage of a toss-up situation—the joint panel committee system might be fertile ground for allowing such a situation to occur. It should be noted, however, the independent arbitrators are by no means infallible. They, too, make mistakes, but you are apt to receive a more impartial opinion from an arbitrator.

A final argument in favor of independent arbitrators has to do with the long-term effects of proposed solutions. Usually, joint committee decisions will result in the establishment of "area standards" which will be applied to all employers who bring their cases to the committee. Committees tend to believe that the standards they have established have universal application. Thus you may find yourself subjected to a contract interpretation that is foreign to the realities of your operation. You will not encounter these "across-the-board applications" in decisions rendered by independent arbitrators, who tailor the decisions to each specific operation. You will not be saddled with practices that were born out of the mistakes of your competitors. Also, there is less risk that antiquated procedures will creep into your operation.

Use of Legal Counsel

Although arbitrations were initially set up to avoid the formalistic procedures of the courtroom and eliminate the rules of evidence, over the past decade most arbitrations have evolved into a "quasi-courtroom" type of proceeding. If the union intends to present its case through a lawyer, you should also retain an attorney to present your case. Laymen are generally not equipped to present cases in the manner in which attorneys have been trained. However, if the union decides to present its case through a business agent, then you, too, may desire to present your case using in-house talent.

Presentation

The keys in presenting a grievance are *organization* and *preparation*. First, determine if the grievance was presented in a timely manner and according to contract procedure. Often contracts will specify that a grievance must be presented to the employer within a certain number of days following the occurrence. If the union fails to file the grievance within the specified time period, you should refuse to hear the grievance because it is untimely. Never address the *merits* of a grievance until a decision is rendered on its timeliness. If you win a grievance on a procedural issue such as timeliness, (1) you will win the grievance without having to address the merits, and (2) the union will not be able to file stale grievances that arise outside the time period specified in the contract. Always insist that the union conform to the presentation procedures contained in your contract. Exceptions can result in chaos.

If a grievance is timely and has been filed according to procedures contained in your contract, the second step is to identify the issues. Put them in writing. Then determine what sections of the contract have been breached. If the activity described in the grievance is not regulated by contract, deny the grievance on that basis. A duty that has been delineated in the contract must be breached before a grievance can arise: no duty—no breach—no grievance.

After you have identified the issues and have found the applicable sections of the contract which allegedly have been breached, you are ready to begin your research. First, interview all persons who were involved in the situation which gave rise to the grievance. Identify the issues as you see them and solicit their positions. Be sure to note times, dates, locations, and the names of other witnesses. Delve into the existence of past practice which may vary or supplement the terms of your contract. Study records of past grievances to determine if any have a bearing on your case. After all of this information has been summarized in writing, prepare your case.

First, compose a brief statement of the case. Provide sufficient background to impart to the arbitrator a working knowledge of your operation. Your operation should be explained in some detail. Be sure to identify contract sections that are applicable to the controversy. Second, define the issue in plain and concise terms. Third, identify the union's position, and fourth, identify the company's position. Finally, identify the arguments that support your position.

The organization of this statement is extremely important. Identify and separately number each argument. Eliminate extraneous material from each argument. Once you have prepared a written working document, you are ready to present your case. Copies of the document should be neatly typed and bound and presented to the arbitrator and the union on the day of the arbitration.

Prepare and use visual aids if the case lends itself to such a presentation. If statistics are to be used, prepare a chart showing the data. If you have a case that involves many dates, draw up a time line to clarify the chronology of the various occurrences. If you believe a plant tour would be appropriate, by all means conduct such a tour. Make your presentation as simple as possible. If your case is presented in a confusing manner, the arbitrator may miss your most crucial arguments. Be sure to supply the arbitrator with copies of the visual aids you use so that he will have them available when he writes his decision. You may also use photographs if a plant visit is not feasible.

One useful device in handling grievances is a grievance notebook. The pages of this notebook should be indexed according to the sections of your contract. As you encounter and resolve grievances and arbitrations, outline them on the appropriate pages of the notebook. In this manner, you will not only be able to keep a fairly accurate record of past practice, but you will also be able to identify quickly what areas of the contract are giving you the most problems and, thus, need the most attention during the next round of contract negotiations.

How to Prepare for Contract Negotiations

Long-Range Preparations for Renewing an Existing Contract

Perhaps the most common misconception about contract negotiations is the belief that a company is restricted to negotiating its contract during the period commencing 60 to 90 days prior to its expiration and continuing until a new contract is signed. Your collective bargaining agreement is subject to negotiation or renegotiation at any time you are so disposed. Of course, during the pendency of a contract, you must convince your collective bargaining agent that reopening the contract for negotiation is necessary.

If, during the period of the contract, one term becomes particularly troublesome to you and results in a situation of grave financial concern, you should contact your union representative immediately. Explain to him the problems you are experiencing. Request that the agent include employee representatives at the meeting. In this manner, troublesome provisions can often be suspended or completely eliminated. The name of the game in negotiations is ingenuity and creativity. You are limited only by the constraints of your own imagination in negotiating and operating under a collective bargaining agreement. The fact that you have not tried something in the past should not stop you from trying it in the future. Never hesitate to try new methods or means of negotiating your contract. Always look at the "downside" as compared to the "upside" risks of a particular bargaining item. After weighing them, your course of action should be fairly clear. If not, ask your labor counsel for his reactions.

Timing of Negotiation

You should begin negotiating your new contract the day after you have signed your existing contract. The worst mistake you can make is to wait until 60 to 90 days prior to the expiration of your existing contract. If you wait until the eleventh hour, you will have little room within which to negotiate. If your company is in the habit of waiting until the union presents you with its demands before you plan your strategy and identify your own demands, your labor relations policy is in sore need of immediate revision.

As soon as your current contract is agreed to, you should start to establish goals to be obtained during the next round of contract negotiations. This will give you a three-year period (assuming that is the term of your contract) within which to accomplish these goals. Make sure these goals are realistic. List every item that you would like to obtain through collective bargaining when your current contract expires in three years. First, identify those goals that you think you can reasonably achieve during the next round of negotiations. Second, identify the goals that may only be partially achieved at the next round of negotiations. Finally, identify those goals that you think you have no chance of obtaining at the next round of negotiations but that may be achieved in the longer term if you keep working at them in the future.

Review all of these goals with your operating staff and assign staff members to be responsible for specific goals. The smaller your staff, of course, the more limited your options will be. In formulating your goals, be realistic. "Pie-in-the-sky" dreams will never be realized, and you should not waste your staff's time and talent in meaningless endeavors.

A coordinated and centrally planned effort is crucial. Staff members should not be allowed to approach the business agent to demand immediate capitulation on specific goals. The agent will be overwhelmed and those efforts will be counterproductive. Instead, a sophisticated plan should be worked out, identifying which goals will be highlighted during each contract year. In this manner, you will not wear out your welcome with your union representative.

Each individual involved in this planning process should be expected to make a monthly progress report about what is being done to ensure that the company will attain the goal he has been assigned. These individuals should immediately commence the task of securing their assigned goals. This can be done in many ways. Initially, a low-key approach is best. Encourage your staff to identify the problems to your employees and then *solicit the employees' suggestions* for resolution. This can be done at the time a problem arises or during "bull sessions" at coffee breaks or in the cafeteria. There are unlimited opportunities to discuss anything with your employees if you really put your mind to it. You will be amazed at how often your employees will volunteer the solution you are seeking.

What you are doing is educating your work force in the operational realities of your enterprise. By continually highlighting operational inefficiencies and by making your employees a part of the solution to these difficulties, you will reap long-term benefits. If you diligently follow the course outlined, your employees and the business agent will appreciate the reasons for proposed changes during the next round of negotiations. Instead of being surprised by a particular demand, the employees will expect it. And not only will they expect it, but in many situations, they will already have provided the solution. With very little urging, you will receive the concession which you seek.

Obviously you will not be successful in realizing every goal you identify. But you will be eminently more successful in making real bargaining gains by utilizing the long-range educational process. If you are unsuccessful in obtaining a specific goal, keep working at it for the next round of negotiations. For those goals that you have identified as being attainable over the life of two or three contracts, continue to sell your employees on the reason for the concession.

Members of the business community often look with bewilderment to the substantial collective bargaining packages currently enjoyed by some trade unions. They cannot fathom how any employer could have been so near-sighted as to grant such concessions. The answer is simple. The unions secured these lucrative packages by obtaining several small concessions during each series of contract negotiations. Each concession may have been distasteful to the employer, but was calculated not to be so offensive as to result in the employer risking a strike rather than agreeing to it. During the next round of negotiations, a little more would be demanded in the same area. Over a 15- or 20-year period, these small concessions obviously add up.

If you are able to establish and implement a long-range collective bargaining goal-planning program, the same methods can be turned to work in your favor. Remember—collective bargaining should be a two-way street. If a union wants a concession from management, it must be willing to give something for that concession. Too often, employers blindly wait for the union's demands and then simply respond to those demands. No one who wants to remain competitive in today's marketplace can afford to maintain such a bargaining posture. Planning, goal setting, and follow-through are the keystones of successful bargaining. With two exceptions, every item in your collective bargaining agreement is negotiable. The two exceptions are the seniority and the union shop clauses.

Clipping

After a contract has been signed, it is important to clip regularly articles from newspapers, news periodicals, business magazines, and other sources that indicate wage and fringe settlements in your industry and in related industries. These settlements are often forgotten at the bargaining table. However, if you have details of these settlements readily available in "black and white," such information can go a long way towards tempering the demands of your union. They can also serve as an excellent resource when you formulate and identify worthwhile collective bargaining goals.

Whenever you see a new idea in a magazine, or think of something that would be appropriate for collective bargaining, jot it down in a notebook. Then, months or even years later when you are preparing your formal demands, you will have a wealth of material from which to draw. Too often, "great ideas" are forgotten with the passage of time, articles and the like are misplaced, and the benefits of incorporating these ideas into the bargaining process are lost. Be sure relevant articles are clipped and saved, and that your "flashes of genius" are put into writing.

Credibility

Your credibility is your most important asset in collective bargaining. You must neither lie nor distort the truth during contract negotiations. A misrepresentation will invariably be discovered. When it is, two things will happen. First, you will never be trusted again. Second, the union will fight fire with fire and also engage in distortions.

Maintaining your credibility with your employees is crucially important from a business standpoint. Most labor lawyers have been faced with the unpleasant task of attempting to bail out a company that has been virtually consumed with labor difficulties. One element that is generally present in each case is a strong mutual distrust between management and the union. The minute distrust enters the picture, communication ceases. When communication ceases, industrial strife results. Nothing is so important that it justifies the use of deception in collective bargaining.

The most successful companies in America enjoy relationships with their unions that are based on mutual trust. That trust is founded upon the credibility of the respective parties. Obviously, mistakes will occur in any relationship. However, as long as each party makes every effort to maintain credibility, the relationship with the union will be mutually beneficial.

Bargaining Teams

Most companies designate one individual to be responsible for collective bargaining. Depending upon the size of the bargaining unit in question, one individual may or may not be able to perform all the tasks attendant to negotiating the agreement. Where the agreement covers a substantial number of employees and involves a sufficient sum of money, it is often wise to appoint a bargaining committee to assist the designated individual at the bargaining table. Generally, the committee should consist of at least one representative from each of the following disciplines: (1) production, (2) finance, (3) law, and (4) labor relations. Other individuals can be added depending upon the peculiarities of your particular operation. One person should be appointed to be the committee's exclusive spokesman during negotiations.

A representative from each discipline on the bargaining committee will greatly enhance your company's position at the bargaining table. Such a "cross referencing" of disciplines will result in a realistic evaluation of what your company needs through bargaining and, also, what it can afford to give. Too often, bargaining is split into monetary and nonmonetary items. Such a differentiation is absurd. Every item at the table is a monetary item. Not every item will involve the direct outlay of cold cash, but all of them will have a direct effect on your bottom line. It is always proper strategy to delay agreement on the wage and fringe package until all other items have been agreed to. Once wages and fringes are agreed to, the union has little incentive to agree to further concessions.

One member of the committee should be entrusted with the important task of notetaking. This person will be responsible for keeping records of those sections of the contract or those proposals that are agreed to. He should note the date the agreement occurs and also make sure that the union representative signs that particular page. Waiting until the last minute to put the "agreement" in writing will result in utter chaos. Participants will have differing opinions about what was agreed to. Memories will fail even the most mentally astute members. The maintenance of an agreement notebook is a good way to eliminate subsequent confusion.

A vehicle for the resolution of disputes which might arise between members of the management committee should be established well in advance of the commencement of negotiations. Differences will naturally arise among committee members. The successful resolution of these differences will insure the existence of a cohesive unit. In most companies the chief executive office is the final arbiter. One suggestion to the individual entrusted with this function—do your best to encourage committee members to reach agreement without your input. Also, reserve your decision-making prerogative for only the most major areas of disagreement.

The bargaining committee should begin its work at least one year prior to the expiration of the current contract. Its final priority should be to review the bargaining goals which were established two years previously. These goals, along with any additions the committee deems appropriate, should be compiled into a document representing the formalized demands of the company. The existence of the negotiating committee should in no manner stifle the effort expended by those individuals who were charged with goal achievement. These individuals should continue their efforts.

The next step is to establish a bargaining calendar with the union. Take the initiative. Take charge of the negotiations. Contact your union representative well prior to the contract expiration date and set a date for the exchange of proposals. At the first meeting, set up at least three future dates for contract negotiations. Allow yourself plenty of time to negotiate the contract. Do not wedge yourself into a one- or two-week time frame and expect smooth negotiations. The more time you allow yourself, the more likely a rational and well-reasoned agreement will result. At all costs, avoid marathon bargaining sessions. In these sessions, the person with the greatest stamina is usually the most successful negotiator. Economic necessity—not physical stamina—should be the deciding factor in contract negotiations.

Identifying Strike Issues

As quickly as possible, the negotiating team should cost out such items as anticipated wage packages, holidays, pensions, health and welfare, sick time, funeral leaves, and all other areas in which the union is likely to make demands. As stated previously, there is no need to wait until the union presents its demands to begin the "cost" process. Any experienced negotiator should be able to estimate quite accurately the union's probable package well prior to receiving the union's formal demands.

When the costing-out process is completed, the bargaining team should identify the specific provisions of the settlement package that would be realistic to management. The next step is to drop back substantially from that model package and prepare *your* economic demands. Most companies make only non-economic demands at the bargaining table and then react to the union wage demands.

After the negotiating committee has arrived at a realistic settlement package, it must identify items over which management would be willing to risk a strike. These items must be sufficiently important to justify the cost that would be sustained during a strike. Your financial people should prepare figures that indicate what a strike will cost your company. Financial people generally can estimate within pennies what a one-day, two-day, three-day, etc., strike will cost your company. Such figures are invaluable when deciding which issues will be worth taking a strike over.

The specifics of weathering a strike are dealt with later on in this chapter. However, one important note concerning strikes should be made here. Twenty or thirty years ago, your employees were better able to mount a sustained strike effort than they are now. Over the years contract settlements have resulted in levels of affluence that blue collar employees did not enjoy previously. It is not unusual for a production line worker to own a vacation cottage, camper, or boat. However, concomitant with these luxuries are the ever-present payment books. With most American workers stretched to the limit financially, it is now much more difficult for them to endure a sustained strike. Furthermore, the vast majority of states still do not offer unemployment benefits to voluntary economic strikers. This, coupled with dwindling strike funds due to declining union memberships, gives the employer a significant advantage over his counterparts of twenty years ago.

This does not mean that you should engage in automatic bargaining to the point of impasse and then settle in for a long strike, hoping that the threat of bank foreclosures will eventually drive your employees back to work. A long strike is damaging to both sides and should be avoided. There are times, however, when in order to remain competitive, you must resist to the point of a strike on a certain issue. In such situations, the economics of affluence play in your favor to a greater extent than they did twenty years ago.

Use of Mediation Services

In general, the use of mediation services should be avoided. Well-orchestrated and planned negotiations should obviate the necessity of involving a third party in your industrial relations affairs. However, mediation services such as the Federal Mediation and Conciliation Service (FMCS) can be a very useful tool when both parties are at an impasse, and neither will contact the other because to do so might be interpreted as a sign of weakness. In such cases, one or both parties may contact the FMCS. The FMCS will "order" the parties to resume negotiations and offer its services to aid in dispute resolution. Thus either or both parties can save face by returning to the bargaining table under the pretense of being ordered to do so by a service of the federal government.

If you have never utilized the services of the FMCS, you should familiarize yourself with them. There is no charge for the service, and often your case will be assigned a mediator skilled in your industry who can indeed facilitate settlement of your dispute. It is important to note that a mediator cannot force you to agree to anything. He can reason, cajole, and use every known art of persuasion to facilitate a settlement, but he cannot force anyone to agree to anything. Consider the use of the FMCS if your negotiations break down, and you feel the injection of a new party with a fresh perspective is in order. Otherwise, deal head to head with your union without the intervention of a third party.

Engaging in Negotiations for a Contract Covering a Newly Established Operation

Various provisions of the National Labor Relations Act (NLRA) specifically govern new operations. In such cases the NLRA prohibits an employer from entering into a collective bargaining agreement with a union until a majority of his newly hired employees have indicated that they seek union representation. Existing contracts should be reviewed to be sure that a new operation is not an automatic accretion to an existing unit. An automatic accretion occurs where the jurisdictional clause of one of your existing collective bargaining agreements is sufficiently broad to encompass the new operation. In such a situation, your union will demand immediate recognition at your new facility. If this occurs, contact a labor lawyer immediately, as accretion questions are complex and can be very costly if not properly handled.

One mistake most employers make when establishing a new operation is the payment of substandard wages because there is no union contract that specifies the rate. The lure of a greater profit margin can seem overwhelming, but such practices are the best invitation you can give to a union organizer. The organizer's trump card in any campaign is money. He always promises your employees that they will receive the "going rate" immediately upon signing a contract. If the employees are already being compensated at the going rate and receive full company benefits, there is little incentive to join a union. In fact, the employees will be dollars behind when they begin paying dues and initiation fees with after-tax dollars.

Thus, in setting up a new operation, determine the going rate for the geographic area. Pay that rate or come substantially close. Offer full company benefits to your employees and, most importantly, set up a grievance procedure whereby a neutral party (i.e., an *outside* arbitrator) makes the final decisions. If you do these things, you will be able to operate on a non-union basis. If you pay substandard rates, the next man you meet will be your union organizer.

New operations are also fertile ground for the incentive and productivity programs that have been discussed previously. As soon as you decide to investigate the possibility of opening a new operation or expanding an existing operation, your labor people should be involved. They can discover the wage rate in the area. More important, they can devise a mutually beneficial productivity plan. This plan should establish realistic production quotas—the attainment of which will result in a well-compensated work force. If greater productivity means you are able to pay a better hourly wage than others in your geographic area, you will probably be besieged with employment applicants, and you will be less likely to be the target of union organizational efforts.

Increasingly there seems to be a desire on the part of employees not to be represented by a union in a new operation. Thus, when you commence a new operation, you should not immediately proceed to a union for contract negotiations. First, check with your industrial relations staff or your lawyer to make sure that none of your existing contracts can be stretched to cover your new operation. If they do not, then you have no choice, under law, but to commence the operation on a non-union basis.

After your operation is underway, you must wait for your employees to designate a collective bargaining representative to represent them in negotiations. The scope of this chapter does not permit a discussion of the specific number of authorization cards which a collective bargaining agent must have, your right to an election, and the entire area of union representation. Your labor counsel should be consulted on these matters so that you will be aware of your rights with respect to your employees' right to organize or not to organize.

Optimal Strategic Tactics at the Bargaining Table

The importance of doing your homework over the entire period of your contract has already been discussed at length. Goal setting and regular efforts expended towards attaining those goals are crucial. If this is done properly, your bargaining agent and your employees will not be surprised by any of your demands at the bargaining table. Not only will they be aware of the demands, but they will have been totally apprised as to the reasons for the demands. They may even be ready with answers to the problems. If your bargaining agent does not react with surprise to the demands that you place on the table, you should congratulate yourself for an excellent job of education. This system does not guarantee you will receive every concession—but you will do infinitely better than if you drop cold demands on the table and pray your employees will be overcome with benevolence!

Your List of Demands

A comprehensive list of your company's demands should be presented to your bargaining representative at the first negotiation session. After receiving the demands, your bargaining agent may do one of two things. He may either address himself directly to the demands of the company and begin negotiating on that basis, or he will counter with a list of union demands and will attempt to ignore the demands that you have made. You must insist that the agent consider your requests. It is your responsibility to insure that your demands remain on the table and that attention is given to them. Too often, a company will prepare a well-reasoned list of demands, present them to the union, and that is the last anyone ever sees of them.

Also, before any concessions are given to the union, make sure that something will be received from the union in return. It is not uncommon for the collective bargaining process to be viewed as a one-way street with the union demanding and receiving all the concessions. This concept must be eliminated in favor of a two-way street. If concessions are given to the union, concessions should be received in return.

Bargaining should not be a giveaway show. Never give away something for nothing. If you are going to grant a wage increase, shorter hours, or additional vacation time, it should only be done in the context of what you receive in return. In many areas, this will be a new form of bargaining to the union. Therefore, your initial venture into this area may be met by strong resistance from the union. Do not be intimidated—be resolute. Secure what you came for, or at least get a part of what you want, and get the rest later. Your agent will become accustomed to your new bargaining posture in time.

The Customer

Be sure your customer is kept up to date as to the status of your bargaining negotiations. He should know your realistic view of success or failure. Be sure to inform him of the possibility of a strike. In the warehousing industry it is often possible for a customer to insulate himself against a strike if he has enough lead time to take the necessary steps to ensure the continued distribution of his product. If something you are after is important enough to risk a strike, you should inform your customer as early as possible prior to the expiration of your contract that the possibility of a strike is very real. Then, you should help him to insulate his operation from the effects of your strike.

If a customer indicates that you will lose his business if there is a strike, obviously your alternatives are limited. Be sure the customer realizes that by taking such a position, he has tied your hands at the bargaining table and as a consequence that his rate will increase by an inflated amount. Usually, with proper customer education and proper planning for the eventuality of a strike, you will be able to take a strike in support of your position at the bargaining table.

Positive Posture

Always remain in charge of the talks. Never simply react to union demands. Present a positive program at the bargaining table, and control the tenor of the negotiations wherever possible. If you merely react to union demands and do not begin setting goals for your operation and attempt to attain those goals, you will forever be in a position of watching your competitors succeed. Do not be overwhelmed—one step at a time will get you to your destination. You cannot expect to get it all at once—take it back as you gave it—a little at a time. *Never* meet at the union hall—meet either at your company's offices or on neutral ground.

Pros and Cons of Multi-Employer Bargaining

Many employers are enamored of the concept of multi-employer bargaining. They point to such pluses as strength in number, unified front, trained negotiators, financial resources, grievance procedures, educational services, and all the other attributes normally associated with the typical multi-employer bargaining associations. Many companies have achieved great success through multi-employer bargaining. However, individual head-to-head bargaining with a union will more often result in a better contract for your specific operation than one reached through multi-employer bargaining.

One disadvantage of multi-employer bargaining is that the master contract which results from these negotiations may contain many provisions that in no way relate to your operation. If you subsequently decide to alter or change your operation, these provisions may in fact prohibit such restructuring. Also, a master contract generally results in employees receiving the same rate of pay across the country regardless of the economic realities of a specific geographic area. Thus in some areas of the country a signator to a master contract may not be able to compete against non-signators. Head-to-head contracts will more accurately reflect the going rate in a specific geographic area.

Another frequent criticism of multi-employer bargaining is that if you are not a "big" company, your voice will have little impact when the collective bargaining demands are formulated. Often, in multi-employer associations, the large business entities will be the ones with "significant" input respecting what will and will not be included in the collective bargaining demands. Even when the demands of the smaller operations are included initially, they are often bargained away, and the demands of the larger operations become the primary subject of bargaining.

The pluses in bargaining associations center on their ability to supply information concerning matters related to the collective bargaining process to their members. Most associations publish a periodic newsletter which can be very informative. Some also engage in lobbying activities which, in varying degrees, can result in real gains to the industry. Many bargaining groups also have established grievance procedures and machinery which are available to their members.

Each bargaining association should be reviewed on its own merits. Ask yourself whether the association has been able to negotiate a better contract than you can. Determine if your voice will be heard and to what extent the unique aspects of your operation will receive special attention. Too often a company will join a multi-employer association with the secret desire of letting the association do its labor work. In most industries, however, the cost of labor represents over 50 percent of the cost of operation, and no company can afford to ignore what is perhaps its single most important cost item. A great deal of money can be saved through proper negotiation, and the individual entrepreneur knows the realities of his operation better than anyone who is not involved with it on a day-to-day basis. A bargaining association can be very useful in many ways, but the responsibility for negotiating your collective bargaining agreement should remain in-house and be within the exclusive province of your company and its union.

How to Avoid EEOC and NLRB Problems

The Civil Rights Act of 1964 established the Equal Employment Opportunity Commission (EEOC). The EEOC is charged by Congress with the duty of enforcing the provisions of Title VII of that law. Essentially, the EEOC must insure that no person or corporation discriminates against any individual on the basis of sex, age, race, color, creed, religion, national origin, or physical handicap. Other laws protect veterans and ensure equal pay for equal work. Many states have adopted laws that supplement the federal laws. These state laws are enforced by state civil rights agencies. Even municipalities have adopted civil rights legislation to afford a city the right to enforce various civil rights laws or fair employment practices acts.

In essence, all of the municipal, state, and federal civil rights agencies were established to accomplish the same function—that of insuring that discrimination does not occur within the framework of employment. In some states, a person who claims to be a victim of unlawful discrimination by a company will be able to bring charges against that company before three civil rights agencies: (1) the city, (2) the state, and (3) the federal EEOC. Usually the lowest agency (the city) will conduct a complete investigation of the merits of the charge. If it determines that there is no cause to believe a discriminatory event occurred, the next administrative level (the state) will review the determination of the city agency. The state agency may either rubber stamp the city's determination or make its own investigation. The same is true with the federal EEOC.

Thus every disgruntled employee or employment applicant has more than one "bite at the apple" when attempting to secure redress against a company. These administrative headaches, when coupled with similar charges that can also be filed with the NLRB or Bureau of Unemployment Compensation, and a full-blown arbitration, make dismissing a nonproductive employee, in many instances, a very difficult and costly task.

Avoiding Charges of Discrimination

The easiest way to avoid a charge of discrimination is by applying work rules across the board. "Favorite" employees cannot be given special treatment. The rules must be applied evenly, and disciplinary actions must be documented in writing. It is always tempting to treat those employees who are "loyal" or whom you "like the best" on a different plane from those who create employment problems. An ability to divorce yourself from these purely human characteristics and treat all employees on the same basis would be in your best interest in relation to the EEOC laws. However, even those employers in the vanguard of affirmative action efforts often find themselves in the situation of being charged with employment discrimination.

You can win such charges by proving that a rule in question is reasonable and that other employees have been treated in a similar manner. If you have singled out a problem employee for special disciplinary treatment, the civil rights agencies may quickly label such special treatment as a discriminatory act. The burden will then shift to you as the employer to show why the special treatment was justified—an uphill battle at best.

Persons who file charges alleging discrimination generally do so for four reasons:

1. *Strikes and Labor Difficulties*: When you are experiencing strikes or labor problems, strikers may file discrimination actions against you in order to compound your miseries and bring greater pressure to bear against you. This is a cheap tactic but one that is being used with increased regularity. Such charges are devoid of merit and are filed only for purposes of administrative harassment.

2. *Opportunism*: A small percentage of persons will take advantage of any system, and some try to take advantage of the civil rights laws. These people will move from one employer to another filing charges alleging employment discrimination. They are hopeful that the employers will opt for a fast settlement rather than endure a full and complete investigation by the civil rights agency which has jurisdiction over the matter. In such

cases it is best to prepare a full and complete defense against each spurious charge, and not to settle anything until the entire matter has been presented in court, if necessary.

3. *Severance Pay*: When members of a protected category are discharged or otherwise disciplined, some may file charges against their former employer with every conceivable agency in the hope that the employer will offer a quasi "severance payment" rather than opting for a full investigation and the risk of a discrimination finding. Fortunately, some governmental agencies are becoming aware of such tactics. Such persons may also reap some psychological satisfaction from the aggravation they feel they will cause their employer by filing such charges against him. In any event, the number of charges being filed against American companies is increasing yearly. None should be taken lightly. Do not forego the cost of hiring a qualified labor lawyer to defend these charges should they be brought against your company. To entrust the defense of the matters to your staff functions would be a false economy.

4. *Charges That Truly Possess Merit*: If after your initial investigation of a charge it is your belief that you (or one of your employees) have committed a discriminatory act, contesting the matter would be foolish. You would only prolong the matter and aggravate your damages. In a case where you are clearly wrong, I would suggest exploring an immediate settlement of the charge. Bad cases never get better—only worse. The EEOC has instituted what they call a "no-fault" system of settlement. In this system the parties are brought together very quickly after a charge is filed. At the hearing, the EEOC will attempt to settle the manner on whatever terms the parties can agree. In such a scenario, you may be able to reach an extremely amicable settlement.

Contesting Spurious Charges

If you are confronted with a charge which after full investigation you believe does not possess merit, you should definitely contest it. Many employers view charges of employment discrimination as forms of coercion. An employer will generally go through the following thought process: "If I settle the charge now, it will cost $1000 in back pay. However, if I contest the charge, it will cost $4000 in attorney's fees. I can make the settlement now and save $3000." This simple dollar-and-cents approach to discrimination actions may seem economically sound in the short run. However, it could cause more problems than you have bargained for in the long run. Word of the "easy" settlement Mr. X was able to secure against your company will spread like wildfire throughout your employment ranks. The lure of "fast money" will be ever-present in the minds of opportunistic employees who do not mind milking the system. On the other hand, if you are successful in contesting a "bad" charge, the myth of "easy money" will be eradicated and other spurious charges will be discouraged.

Under no circumstances should employees be coerced with respect to their lawful rights granted by the various federal, state, and municipal statutes. However, a spurious charge filed by an opportunist in the hope of obtaining a fast settlement should be contested with all possible vigor by management.

Work Force Composition

One concrete factor that all civil rights agencies look at in investigating charges of employment discrimination is the composition of the work force. If your work force has no minority members or contains a disproportionate number of minority members, agencies will tend to believe that your hiring practices are discriminatory. Thus, if a minority applicant is denied work when work is available, the civil rights agency may presume your guilt based on your work force statistics alone. This situation can be prevented easily by hiring at least the appropriate percentage of minority workers.

In hiring minority workers, you must first determine what your locality's statistical metropolitan survey analysis (SMSA) reveals about the percentages of minority populations in your geographic area. Once you have determined the percentage of minority composition in your area, you should take the necessary actions to ensure that the your work force reflects that percentage. If your company has a 2-percent minority composition in a city where the minority composition of the total population is 50 percent, it is obvious that your hiring practices have resulted in a racially unbalanced work force. If your work force composition varies drastically from your SMSA, you should engage in immediate affirmative efforts to recruit minority applicants.

In simplistic terms, if you recruit and maintain a properly balanced employee complement and engage in realistic policies where to the greatest extent all employees are treated in a similar manner, your chances of avoiding a charge of discrimination are very much in your favor. Usually, companies that invite discrimination charges employ very few minority members and generally engage in discriminatory conduct—whether it be deliberate or unintentional.

Handling Discrimination Charges

The *first* thing you should do when you receive a discrimination charge is consult competent labor counsel. Do not entrust the defense of such a complicated matter to your supervisory staff. You will be encountering a very sophisticated government investigator whose purpose is to investigate the charge completely and exhaustively and make a determination as to whether or not your company engaged in discriminatory conduct. A number of procedural safeguards are available to you in such investigations, but without the aid of competent labor counsel, you will probably never be aware of those safeguards and, obviously, will not be able to take advantage of them.

In any investigation, you are permitted to present each and every piece of evidence that you believe will prove absence of discriminatory motives. Often government investigators are interested only in finding the existence of what may appear to be a discriminatory act—i.e., a prima-facie case of discrimination. Generally, if a company can present the proper explanation, a presumptively discriminatory act may prove to be totally neutral and, in fact, not discriminatory at all. Thus you need someone who can properly present your evidence to your own best advantage. These charges can be extremely costly—cases have been settled well into the millions of dollars. Thus the first and only thing to do when you receive a discrimination charge is to contact counsel immediately. These charges are too risky to handle otherwise.

Affirmative Action Programs

If you are a government contractor or subcontractor, you may be required to adopt an affirmative action program and assure that it is being properly implemented. As we are all aware, it is very difficult not to be a government contractor or subcontractor. If your company has signed an Executive Order 11246 request from one of your customers, make sure you are in compliance with its dictates. Executive Order 11246 requires all government contractors and subcontractors sign a certification to the effect that they do not maintain segregated facilities and that they further engage in affirmative action efforts where required. Failure to satisfy the conditions of the certification can result in your company losing your government contracts.

Regardless of the size of your operation, you should designate an affirmative action coordinator and provide sufficient staffing to ensure that your company is in compliance with the myriad federal, state, and local laws relating to affirmative action and civil rights compliance. Too often, companies simply assign these duties to an already overworked supervisor with no training in the area. Obviously, little effective attention will be devoted to complying with the various civil rights laws and orders. If this is the case in your company, you should take immediate steps to change it. If your operation is too small to justify a full-time staff or coordinator, then entrust these functions to a person who is directly involved in the personnel function. Send this individual to seminars designed to educate the EEO coordinators—there are a number of good privately conducted seminars on this subject. If you don't know where to find such a training seminar, a local college, university, or bar association can probably provide you with information about competent programs.

An individual who has been appropriately trained to serve in this capacity should also possess sufficient "clout" to bring about those changes that are necessary to place your company in compliance with the affirmative action regulations. The EEO coordinator, in order to do an effective job, will need time to devote full attention to the EEO function.

The National Labor Relations Act—An Overview

The National Labor Relations Act (NLRA) was passed by Congress to insure that all employees have the right to organize unions and bargain collectively if they so desire. The NLRA also gives an employee the right to refrain from joining unions and bargaining collectively. The role of the employer as envisioned by the Congress is one of complete neutrality. He may neither aid nor hinder his employees in the exercise of their rights guaranteed under the NLRA. To put it simply, an employer must treat all employes alike, whether they are members of a union or not. An employer may not discriminate against an employee because who wants to join a union or to bargain collectively. At the same time, an employer may not discriminate against employees who do not wish to join a union unless, of course, that employer is involved with a union security agreement. The most common type of unfair labor practice charge is that which alleges that an employer refused to hire or discharged or otherwise disciplined an employee who engaged in what is commonly known as "union activity"—i.e., filing grievances, attempting to organize a union, protesting conditions not in conformity with the collective bargaining agreement, or engaging in lawful economic or unfair labor practice strikes.

A phenomenon that has appeared in recent years is an apparent decline in union membership. Concomitant with this decline in membership is a corresponding increase in the number of decertification petitions being filed by employees with the NLRB. A decertification petition is a simple statement to the NLRB that a certain number of employees no longer desire union representation. Upon receipt of this petition, the NLRB can order a decertification vote whereby the union can be voted out by a majority of the employees. In such situations, the employer *must* remain totally neutral. In reality, your employees will generally approach you directly if they become disenchanted with their bargaining representative. In such an event, your only advice should be to tell them to proceed to the NLRB, which will handle the entire matter for them. You must neither favor nor oppose the decertification effort. If you do engage in unlawful conduct, you may unwittingly void your employees' request for an election. If you are confronted with a decertification petition, contact labor counsel immediately.

Charges of Unfair Labor Practice

If you receive a charge alleging discrimination from the NLRB, immediately contact competent labor counsel. Once again, there are procedural safeguards available to you that will be lost if you have not retained competent counsel. Further, it is very important that your case be presented in the best light possible and that all information pertinent to the charge be assembled and presented to the investigator. Labor lawyers are experts in this area and can prepare a case that will do the most towards having the charges brought against you dismissed. It is extremely important that counsel be retained as quickly as possible. The NLRB investigators operate within rigid time deadlines, and will be contacting you within a day or two after the copy of the charge is received. Once again, these are not matters which should be entrusted to your supervisors or even yourself—regardless of how sophisticated you may be in the area of labor relations. The complexities of these laws make it imperative for you to retain counsel for your own protection.

Filing an Unfair Labor Practice Charge

Many employers do not realized that the National Labor Relations Act is a two-way street. Often, employers simply react to charges that are filed against them by their union or by individual union members. However, there is an entire section of the law which relates to improper union conduct. It delineates, in no uncertain terms, what a union can and cannot do. One area of the law, which few employers realize is available to them, is the area of bad faith bargaining.

If a union comes to a bargaining table, presents a contract, and adopts a "take-it-or-leave-it" attitude, the union has engaged in bad faith bargaining. This can often be the case when unions are eager to sell "master" contracts. If a union representative informs you that you must sign a master contract and refuses to engage in bargaining concerning that contract, he has probably committed an unfair labor practice. With the proper evidence, the NLRB will order the union to abandon its "take-it-or-leave-it" attitude and engage in meaningful bargaining. A union's refusal to accede to the NLRB's order is unlawful.

If your union should come to the bargaining table with a "take-it-or-leave-it" attitude and throw a predetermined contract at you, you should remember that remedies are available to you under the NLRA. However, if you have followed some of the bargaining ideas discussed elsewhere in this chapter, you are much less likely to be faced with this eventuality. Also, if you should become involved in a fairly complicated labor relations situation, it might be wise to review the facts with counsel to see if there has been a violation of the National Labor Relations Act. If so, certain illegal and questionable conduct can be curtailed immediately.

Secondary Boycotts

A secondary boycott occurs when a union places economic pressure (usually picketing) upon a "neutral" business entity for the purpose of bringing pressure to bear on a "primary" employer who is directly engaged in a dispute with that union. Assume that you operate a warehouse known as "Y Corp." Assume also that you are engaged in contract negotiations with your union. Finally, assume that your warehouse holds certain goods for a very large corporation—"X Company." In order to being pressure to bear on Y Corp., the union sets up a picket line at X Company's manufacturing facility, located 100 miles away from your warehouse. The union's reasoning is that X Company does business with you and, thus, is as "guilty" as you are for the conditions which are present at your warehouse.

This is a a classic type of secondary boycott situation. X Company is obviously a "neutral" employer that has no dispute with your union. However, your union has established the boycott in the hope that X's president (your valued customer) will pressure you into settling your dispute so that the union will cease disrupting his business operations. If such a situation should occur, your labor counsel should immediately proceed to the National Labor Relations Board for relief. If the NLRB finds that a secondary boycott exists, it will take the case to federal court to obtain an injunction barring the unlawful action.

Never ask or allow a customer to perform work during a strike that would normally be performed by your striking bargaining unit. In a situation where another business entity performs "struck work," that business, too, can be picketed since it has become what is known as an "ally." An ally is a company that performs work which normally would be performed by the bargaining unit but for the strike. Therefore, before you farm out work during a strike, be sure you first check with legal counsel.

What to do When Faced with a Slowdown, Walkout, Picketing, or Work Stoppage

In the transportation industry, slowdowns, walkouts, picketing, and similar actions can become a way of life. Fortunately, over the years, most work disruptions have been eliminated through proper labor relations practices, no-strike clauses, and damage actions for unlawful strikes. However, even the cleanest operation may experience a strike or other form of work disruption. It is important to remember that being confronted with a strike does not mean, by any stretch of the imagination, that your labor relations posture is wrong. Strikes are at times a natural part of the industrial world.

Enduring a strike is not as difficult as many expect. People fear the threat of strikes because they have been preconditioned to relate strike activity with violence. Violence can occur during a strike. Tempers can wear thin. Caution should be used. However, a strike is not the end of the world, and you can operate during a strike if certain precautions are taken. Following the suggestions outlined below should enable you to handle a strike with a minimum degree of upset.

Before the Strike Occurs

1. *Gather information on the union*: Prepare a list of the names and home addresses of your union's officers and business agents and note the correct legal name and address of

the union itself. This will be utilized if a picketing injunction or other court action is necessary.

2. *Gather information on employees*: Prepare a list of your employees and their current home addresses. This, too, will be necessary in case a picketing injunction or other court action is necessary.

3. *Line up legal counsel*: Decide who will be your local counsel, and contact him well before the anticipated strike date to inform him that injunctive work may be necessary in the event of mass picketing or violence.

4. *Make security preparations*: Contact a reputable security company and put them on notice that you may be requiring the services of one, two, or more security officers for 24-hour-a-day duty in the event of a strike.

5. *Contact customers*: Be sure to contact your customers and, either over lunch or at formal business meetings, explain to them the possibilities of a strike and determine what their specific problems might be, if a strike occurs. Discuss these problems in detail and work out operating problems in advance of the strike rather than attempting to handle this problem on the day the walkout occurs.

6. *Contact police*: Call your local police department and get the name of an officer who is in charge of the labor unit or, in smaller localities, an officer who will be in charge of any specific problems which may occur at your locality. Be sure to contact this officer directly to explain your operation to him and assure him of your full cooperation.

7. *Prepare to take photographs*: Have a camera, telephoto lens, fresh film, and flashbulbs on hand at your facility so that you can take pictures of mass picketing or incidents of violence. Also, locate a rapid photo processing company and inform them that you may need one-hour service during the strike. This is necessary so that pictures you take can be developed immediately. You can then have them ready for court proceedings, should such an eventuality occur.

8. *Establish safe storage facilities*: If you plan to halt operations during a strike, be sure to locate a garage or suitable parking facility where your rolling equipment can be stored safely. Be sure equipment is unloaded and that windshields, radiators, and gas tanks are protected against possible acts of violence.

9. *Find alternate drivers*: Maintain lists of qualified drivers who can be made available on short notice and who are willing to drive during a strike. Make sure that they possess valid chauffeurs' licenses.

10. *Provide additional security*: If you do plan to operate during a strike, be sure that additional security personnel are hired to protect employees who cross the picket line. The logistics of the security measures should be worked out well in advance of any shipment that may be made during a strike.

11. *Inform employees of company policy*: Advise all non-union employees that they will be expected to work during the strike; however, if they are physically stopped from crossing a picket line (other than by the usual shouting and jeers of the pickets), they should not attempt to enter the premises.

12. *Prepare a "benefits" letter*: Employees who will be on strike should be advised of their status during the strike and of the possible forfeiture of their rights under your various benefit plans. If during a strike an employee loses all benefits, he should be notified of this fact so that he can take the necessary steps to pay for these benefits himself.

13. *Prepare a strike incident report form*: Form 32–1 shows a sample strike incident report form which you should have on hand during the strike. Be sure that any incident that takes place is recorded *in writing immediately* after the incident occurs. Waiting two hours or until the next day to record the incident will stale your memory and much-

needed information concerning the incident will be lost. Be sure to completely fill these out immediately after an incident takes place.

14. *Avoid a lockout*: If you shut down your operation in anticipation of a strike and do not report to work on the day of the strike, the union may contend that what you have done is "lock out" your employees. If it is determined that a "lockout" has occurred, your striking employees may be entitled to unemployment compensation benefits. Thus, you should be very careful not to turn an economic strike into a lockout situation. When the contract expires, be sure that your operation is manned as it normally would be (with the obvious exception of the striking workers), that all doors are open, and that anyone desiring to report to work can so report. Oftentimes, the union will send what is known as a "fish" to report to work. If the "fish" discovers that the doors are locked, the union will contend that a lockout is in effect.

15. *Hold advance meetings*: Meet with all of your supervisors and persons who will be working during the strike well in advance of the strike itself. Determine who will cross the picket lines and who will perform the various functions outlined here. Also, set up a telephone chain of command to facilitate communication in the evening or early morning hours while your supervisors are still at home. Be sure that all supervisors have each others' home phone numbers beforehand. They should also have the telephone number of the police officer you have contacted and the home and office numbers of your legal counsel.

The First Day of the Strike

1. *Arrive early*: In the event that you have advance notice that a strike will take place, be sure to arrive at your facility well before your normal starting time, because very few pickets will be likely to be there at that time. Also, you will have sufficient extra time to talk with your customers prior to the start of the normal work day. You will also be on the scene to witness any incidents of violence or mass picketing as your supervisory employees report for work. Do not lock yourself away in your office. Position yourself so that you have a clear view of the picket line.

2. *When crossing a picket line*:

   a. Do not become argumentative or attempt to justify the company position to the pickets. This is a waste of time and can also become very dangerous.

   b. Keep calm, cool, and collected and realize that your function in crossing the picket line is that of an observer. Observe such things as:

   > Number of pickets
   > Names of pickets
   > Number of picket signs and what they say
   > What time of day the incident occurred
   > Location of the pickets on the company property
   > Any actual stoppages being engaged in by the pickets
   > Presence of union business agents—names and capacity
   > Incidents of mass picketing

3. *Listen*: One of your most important functions in crossing a picket line and during the strike is to listen to the pickets should they wish to talk to you. Generally, by simply listening and not attempting to justify the company's position, you will learn a great deal about the picketing and about the union strategy. Remember, the men who are on the

Form 32–1   Strike Incident Report Form

Date of Incident	Time	a.m. p.m.	Location

Reported by: Prepared by:

What happened? _____

_____

_____

Striker, Union Representatives, and Others Involved (Identify by name):	Witnesses	Address	Phone No.

Note: Please be specific as to identity or description of persons involved. If vulgar, threatening, or profane language was used, quote it as accurately as possible. Automobile license numbers are particularly important. Describe injuries or property damage. Photographs made with telephoto lenses are very helpful. Tape recordings of the oral description made while details of the incident are fresh in mind are invaluable in the event of litigation or arbitration.

This report should be prepared by the person who has been involved in, or has observed, any strike activity that may be unlawful or contrary to Company rules.

picket line are not being paid and are anxious avoid a lengthy strike. Therefore, whenever possible during a strike, listen and be sure to record what you hear.

4. *Maintain a strike log*: Every day during the strike, and especially on the first few days when illegal activity and mass picketing generally occur, it is crucial that a strike log be maintained. One management individual should be given the responsibility of maintaining the log. In the log, you should record the information listed in item 2, above, as well as all rumors which you hear. This is not an easy task; it takes a great deal of time. However, it will be of crucial importance should legal action concerning picketing or breach-of-contract subsequently become necessary. *Do not fail to keep a strike log!* In addition to the strike log be sure to maintain a Strike Incident Report Form relative to any incidents of violence and/or property damage. (See Form 32–1.)

5. *Take photographs*: You should definitely take pictures throughout the strike of all the picketing activities that take place. If any incidents of violence occur, attempt to photograph the damage to property and vehicles and, if possible of course, photograph the violence itself. Your chances of catching the pickets in an act of violent activity are virtually nil. However, record the results of the violence—broken windows, ice-picked radiators, etc.—and have this film developed as quickly as possible. Be sure to assign the task of taking the pictures and maintaining the camera and film supplies to one of your supervisors.

6. *Inform your attorney of incidents of mass picketing*: If you decide to operate during the strike and if pickets prevent you from operating, contact your attorney immediately and inform him of the facts.

After the First Day

1. *Welfare and unemployment compensation*: If the strike proceeds beyond two or three days, inform your local welfare department and also your unemployment compensation bureau of the names and addresses of the strikers so that they will not receive welfare and unemployment benefits. Do not mail these lists! Take them to the offices in person, deliver them to the individual in charge, and explain to the individual the exact nature of your request. Be sure that you note the individual's name and the date and time that you informed him that these individuals are on strike. In most states, strikers are not entitled to unemployment compensation and welfare benefits.

2. *Legal action*:

    a. *Mass picketing*: If you want to operate, but strikers are engaged in mass picketing and are blocking shipping, receiving, or employees' access, it would be advisable to obtain immediately what is known as an "ingress-egress picketing injunction" in your local courts. Contact your attorney and meet with him about securing such an injunction.

    b. *Secondary boycotts*: In the event that employees of a customer are picketing your premises or "stranger" pickets are interrupting your operation, contact your attorney immediately and relate the facts to him. In such a situation, it is possible to proceed to the National Labor Relations Board for a secondary boycott determination, which will result in injunctive relief being sought in the federal courts.

    c. *Damage action*: If you are faced with a wildcat strike (not a strike resulting from a contract expiration), it is possible to file a damage action in federal court against the union that represents your employees for breach of your collective bargaining agreement. Obviously, this should be reviewed with your local counsel before proceeding.

    d. *Back-to-work injunction*: If, during the term of a contract and in violation of a no-strike clause, any member or members of your bargaining unit engage in a wildcat strike, you may get a back-to-work injunction in federal court ordering the strikers to return to their jobs. This, too, should only be done with the aid of local counsel. Such relief is not available when your contract has expired and an economic strike is underway.

3. *Discipline and replacement of strikers*: A company may be permitted during a strike to discipline or replace its strikers depending on the type of strike that is in effect. Generally when an economic strike occurs, i.e., when a contract has expired and the strike is over the terms and conditions of a new contract, an employer may hire permanent replacements to perform the work of the striking employees. Temporary replacements may also be hired. Replacements should be hired only when you have determined that you must operate during the strike.

In the event that you do hire permanent replacements, various ramifications may result with respect to the reinstatement of strikers after the strike has concluded. Such action of replacing or disciplining strikers should only be taken after consulting with counsel. These options are available to you and can be utilized during a strike. However, depending on the type of strike you are faced with, your options vary, and therefore in order not to commit an unfair labor practice and expose yourself to money damages, you must contact legal counsel before taking such action.

4. *Keeping your customer informed*: It is crucially important to keep your customer informed as to the status of the strike. It is also a good policy to keep him informed about exactly what you are doing to protect his interests during the strike.

5. *Establishing a separate gate*: Your operation may be located on a customer's property. If you anticipate a strike it may be wise to establish a separate gate, that is, one that restricts access to your portion of the premises to your employees. Employees and contractors of your customer *are not* permitted to enter the premises through this gate. When a strike occurs, the union may only lawfully picket at your gate and thus cannot shut down your customer. If your operation is located on your customer's premises, it would be wise to review with your legal counsel and your customer the advisability of establishing a separate gate.

6. *Notices regarding benefits*: Notices should be sent to all benefit carriers after the strike has commenced containing the names and addresses of all the individuals who are engaged in the strike. The carriers should be informed that these individuals are not entitled to benefits if such is the case.

7. *Communications with employees*: Generally, during a strike a company will want to keep its employees informed as to the status of negotiations. Thus, you may want to prepare an accurate description of what has occurred during a negotiating session. These communications, of course, should be reviewed by the supervisor in charge of the operation and your legal counsel prior to issuance to insure that you are not committing an unfair labor practice.

8. *Unfair labor practice charges*: If your company should receive a charge from the National Labor Relations Board alleging that your company has committed unfair labor practices, *contact a lawyer immediately*. Refer government representatives to your attorney. Be sure that your counsel advises you of the possibilities of your company filing NLRB actions against the union should the union engage in unlawful activity.

After the Strike

After the strike is concluded and a new contract has been ratified, the union will want all employees to return to work immediately. At this point, your customers will also be very interested in having the employees return to work promptly. However, you must be certain that you will have sufficient work available for your employees when they return. Thus, a wholesale reinstatement of all employees who engaged in the strike on a specific date might not be in order. It might be more advantageous from an economic standpoint to "phase in" the employees.

A strike settlement agreement is extremely desirable to avoid the many problems which can be associated with the resolution of a strike. Your attorney should be consulted to assist in the preparation of this agreement. General items which are included in the strike settlement agreement are:

1. The disposition of discipline and discharge cases

2. Reinstatement of striking employees

3. The status of permanent replacements hired during the strike

4. The order of recall of strikers

5. The status of charges and countercharges in courts or before the NLRB

A strike settlement agreement is not limited to the above items. Additional items may be included in the agreement in order for the return to work to be as smooth as possible.

Conclusion

Strikes are one of the most difficult situations within which to operate. However, if you maintain a calm, cool, and collected manner and realize that is is going to be a difficult situation during which you will not be able to operate normally, the situation can be made a lot easier. Remember, strikes are a natural part of any labor-intensified industry and should be treated as such. Do not hesitate to contact your immediate supervisor and legal counsel whenever you are in doubt as to a specific course of action.

Trade and Professional Organizations of Interest to Physical Distribution Management Personnel

NOTE: The following list of associations, names, and addresses is distributed by the National Council of Physical Distribution Management. The most current list can be obtained by writing directly to the Executive Director, NCPDM, 2803 Butterfield Road, Oak Brook, IL 60521 (telephone: [312] 655-0985).

Air Transport Association of America
American Marketing Association
American Production & Inventory Control Society (APICS)
American Productivity Center
American Society of Traffic & Transportation
American Trucking Associations
American Warehouseman's Association
Association of American Railroads
Association of Consulting Management Engineers (ACME, Inc.)
Association of General Merchandise Chains
Association of Transportation Practitioners
Association of Professional Material Handling Consultants
Australian Physical Distribution Management Association (Sidney)
Australian Physical Distribution Management Association (Victoria)
Bundesvereinigung Logistik e.v.
Canadian Association of Physical Distribution Management (CAPDM)
Canadian Industrial Traffic League
Chinese Society of Economics of Supplies
Containerization & Intermodal Institute
Delta Nu Alpha
German Society of Logistics
Grocery Manufacturers of America
Institute of Management Consultants
Institute of Physical Distribution Management
International Customer Service Association
International Material Management Society
Japanese Council of Physical Distribution Management (JCPDM)

Material Handling Equipment Distributors Association
National American Wholesale Grocers' Association
National Association of Freight Transportation Consultants
National Association of Manufacturers
National Association of Purchasing Management
National Committee on International Trade Documentation
National Council for U.S.—China Trade
National Council of Physical Distribution Management
National Defense Transportation Association (NDTA)
National Food Distribution Association
National Industrial Traffic League
National Perishable Transportation Association
National Small Shipments Traffic Conference (NASSTRAC)
National Society of Professional Engineers (NSPE)
National Wholesale Druggists' Association
Operations Council—American Trucking Association (ATA)
Physical Distribution Rationalization Institute
Private Carrier Conference—ATA
Private Truck Council of America, Inc.
Sales & Marketing Council—ATA
Shippers National Freight Claim Council, Inc.
Society of Logistics Engineers
Society of Packaging and Handling Engineers
The Material Handling Institute
Transportation Brokers Conference of America, Inc. (TBCA)
Transportation Data Coordinating Committee (TDCC)
Transportation Research Forum
U.S. Chamber of Commerce
Warehousing Education & Research Council

ORGANIZATION: Air Transport Association of America (ATA)

TYPE: A trade association in which corporations hold membership.

NUMBER OF MEMBERS: 31

DUES: Corporate dues are on a sliding scale based on revenue ton miles.

PURPOSE/OBJECTIVE: The Air Transport of America (ATA) is the trade and service organization of the scheduled airlines of the United States. Through ATA member airlines, while competitive individually, pool their technical and operational knowledge to form a single integrated airline system serving thousands of communities.

CHIEF ELECTED OFFICER:
Paul R. Ignatius
President/Chief Executive Officer
Air Transport Association of America
1709 New York Avenue, NW
Washington, DC 20006
(202) 626-4000

CHIEF OPERATING OFFICER:
Same As Above.

ORGANIZATION: American Marketing Association

TYPE: A professional organization in which individuals hold membership.

NUMBER OF MEMBERS: 43,000

DUES: Executive $150.00
Professional   40.00
Associate   25.00
Student   15.00
Emeritus   10.00

PURPOSE/OBJECTIVE: The American Marketing Association is a professional society of individual members with an interest in the study, teaching or practice of marketing. Our principle roles are: first, to urge and assist the professional development of our members, and second, to advance the science and practice of the marketing discipline.

CHIEF ELECTED OFFICER:
Elvin J. Schofield
Senior Vice President—Marketing
National Bank of Commerce of San Antonio
P.O. Box 121
San Antonio, TX 78291
(512) 225-2511

CHIEF OPERATING OFFICER:
Wayne A. Lemburg, CAE
Executive Vice President
American Marketing Association
250 South Wacker Drive
Chicago, IL 60606
(312) 648-0536

REMARKS: An interest in marketing and the willingness to pay the dues.

ORGANIZATION: American Production & Inventory Control Society

TYPE: A professional organization in which individuals hold membership.

NUMBER OF MEMBERS: 52,000

DUES: $45.00 per person.

PURPOSE/OBJECTIVE: APICS' primary objectives are to develop professional efficiency in production and inventory management through study, research and application of scientific methods; to disseminate general and technical information on improved techniques and new developments; and to further develop the professional body of knowledge and through the organized resources of the profession thereby advance the general welfare of the industrial economy.

CHIEF ELECTED OFFICER:
Edward M. Blackman
Elpac Power Systems
3131 S. Standard Avenue
Santa Ana, CA 92705
(714) 979-4440

CHIEF OPERATING OFFICER:
Henry F. Sander CAE
Executive Director
American Production & Inventory Control Society
500 West Annandale Road
Falls Church, VA 22046
(703) 237-8344

ORGANIZATION: American Productivity Center (APC)

TYPE: Non-profit organization concerned with productivity.

NUMBER OF MEMBERS: N/A

DUES: Varies, depending on type of membership.

PURPOSE/OBJECTIVE: The goal of APC is to compile a body of information and techniques for productivity improvement and make them available whenever they are needed by business industry, labor and government.

CHIEF ELECTED OFFICER:
Dr. C. Jackson Grayson
Chairman of the Board/President
American Productivity Center
123 North Post Oak Lane
Houston, TX 77024
(713) 681-4020

CHIEF OPERATING OFFICER:
Same As Above.

ORGANIZATION: American Society of Traffic & Logistics

TYPE: A professional organization in which individuals hold membership.

NUMBER OF MEMBERS: 2,600

DUES: Certified $50.00
Founder   50.00
Sustaining   90.00
Educator   50.00
Associate   30.00

PURPOSE/OBJECTIVE: The objects and purposes of the Society are to establish, promote and maintain high standards of knowledge and professional training to formulate a code of ethics for the profession; to advance the professional interest of members of the organization; to serve as a source of information and guidance for the fields of traffic, transportation, logistics and physical distribution management, and to serve the industry as a whole by fostering professional accomplishments.

CHIEF ELECTED OFFICER:
Richard Haupt SM—President
DT & T
Ford Motor Company
One Park Blvd., Suite 200
Dearborn, MI 48126
(313) 322-3000

CHIEF OPERATING OFFICER:
Carter M. Harrison CM
Executive Director
American Society of Transportation and Logistics
P.O. Box 33095
Louisville, KY 40232
(502) 451-8150

REMARKS: Offers a five-part certification examination.

ORGANIZATION: American Trucking Association
TYPE: A trade association in which individuals hold membership.
NUMBER OF MEMBERS: N/A
DUES: Information confidential.
PURPOSE/OBJECTIVE: The American Trucking Associations, Inc. represents the regulated and private motor carrier industry of the United States.

CHIEF ELECTED OFFICER:
Ernest S. Cox
Chairman of the Board
American Trucking Associations
1616 P Street NW
Washington, DC 20036
(202) 797-5000

CHIEF OPERATING OFFICER:
Bennett C. Whitlock, Jr.
President
Same as above.

ORGANIZATION: American Warehouseman's Association
TYPE: A trade association in which corporations hold membership.
NUMBER OF MEMBERS: 425
DUES: Corporate dues are on a sliding scale based on square footage.
PURPOSE/OBJECTIVE: To promote the general interests of persons, firms and corporations engaged in the public merchandise warehousing industry, and to promote a high standard of business ethics therein; to collect and disseminate statistical and other information pertinent to the business of its members; to conduct research into ways and means of improving efficiency in the conduct of the business and its members; to advise its members of national legislation and regulations affecting them; and in general, to engage in all activities for the benefit of its members and the public at large that are permitted by law and that are properly within the scope of a trade association.

CHIEF ELECTED OFFICER:
H. Bruce Lederer, Chairman of the Board
President
Lederer Terminals, Inc.
16645 Granite Road
Cleveland, OH 44137
(216) 475-7400

CHIEF OPERATING OFFICER:
Jerry Leatham
President
American Warehouseman's Association
1165 North Clark Street
Chicago, IL 60610
(312) 787-3377

ORGANIZATION: Association of American Railroads
TYPE: A trade association of railroad companies.
NUMBER OF MEMBERS: 131 U.S. railroads;
73 associate members; Mexican and Canadian rail companies.
DUES: Dues are assessed on the basis of revenues.
PURPOSE/OBJECTIVE: The Association of American Railroads serves two major purposes for its members. It provides industry support on matters that require cooperative handling to better enable the railroad to operate as a national system, in the areas of operations, maintenance, safety, research, economics, finance, accounting, data systems, and public information. It also provides leadership for the industry, working with committees made up of representatives of member railroads on matters affecting the progress of the industry as a whole.

Members account for 94% of rail mileage and they haul approximately 98% of the nation's rail traffic. They employ 92% of the nation's rail workers.

CHIEF ELECTED OFFICER:
William H. Dempsey
President & Chief Executive Officer
Association of American Railroads
1920 L Street NW
Washington, DC 20036
(202) 835-9100

ORGANIZATION: Association of Consulting Management Firms (ACME)
TYPE: A trade association in which corporations hold membership.
NUMBER OF MEMBERS: 60
DUES: Corporate dues are on a sliding scale based on billings.
PURPOSE/OBJECTIVE: To contribute to the development and better understanding of the art and science, practice and role of management in the economic and social systems of the free world through competent counsel on management problems. To conduct research for the development and improvement of the practice of management, and disseminate the results of such research in the public interest.

CHIEF ELECTED OFFICER:
C. Ian Sym-Smith, (Chairman)
General Partner
The Hay Group
229 South 18th Street
Rittenhouse Square
Philadelphia, PA 19103
(215) 875-2300

CHIEF OPERATING OFFICER:
Joseph J. Brady
President
ACME, Inc.
The Association of Managment
   Consulting Firms
230 Park Avenue
New York, NY 10169
(212) 697-9693

ORGANIZATION: Association of General Merchandise Chains (AGMC)
TYPE: A full-service trade association.
NUMBER OF MEMBERS: 400 company members
DUES: For retail members, based on annual sales.
PURPOSE/OBJECTIVE: Representation of the nation's discount and variety general merchandise retail industry. AGMC's memberships include companies that operate more than 20,000 discount, variety, dollar, junior department, family center off-price, factory outlet, catalog showroom and other general merchandise stores. Members range widely in size and include many of the nation's largest retail chains.

AGMC maintains contact with the entire retail community through its lobbying efforts and state legislative reporting service. In addition, AGMC offers professional development conferences in the areas of Physical Distribution, Advertising/Merchandising, Finance and Information Systems, and Personal/Labor Relations.
CHIEF ELECTED OFFICER:
Charles Lytle (Chairman)
President & CEO
G. C. Murphy & Company
531 Fifth Avenue
McKeesports, PA 15132
(412) 675-2000
CHIEF OPERATING OFFICER:
Edward T. Borda
President
AGMC
1625 I Street NW Suite 1023
Washington, DC 20006
(202) 785-2060

ORGANIZATION: Association of Transportation
Practitioners
TYPE: A professional organization in which individuals hold membership.
NUMBER OF MEMBERS: 3,000
DUES: $60.00 per person per year.
PURPOSE/OBJECTIVE: To promote the proper administration of the Interstate Commerce Act and related Acts; to uphold the honor of practice before the Interstate Commerce Commission; to cooperate in fostering increased educational opportunities and maintaining high standards of professional conduct; and to encourage cordial intercourse among the practitioners.

CHIEF ELECTED OFFICER:
John K. Maser III, President
Donelan, Cleary, Wood & Maser, P.C.
914 Washington Building
15th Street & New York Ave. NW
Washington, DC 20005
(202) 783-1215
CHIEF OPERATING OFFICER:
Mrs. Norma L. Iser
Executive Director
Association of Transportation
   Practitioners
1116 ICC Building
Washington, DC 20423
(202) 783-9432

ORGANIZATION: Association of Professional Material Handling Consultants (APMHC)
TYPE: A professional organization in which individuals hold membership.
NUMBER OF MEMBERS: 35
DUES: $25.00 per person
PURPOSE/OBJECTIVE: APMHC is a professional society. It is composed of individual consultants in the material handling field. Those whose services are available to several clients are general members; those who are captive staff specialists working for one organization are associate members.
CHIEF ELECTED OFFICER:
W. Semco
President
Semco, Sweet & Mayers, Inc.
2834 Gilroy Street
Los Angeles, CA 90039
(213) 644-2147
CHIEF OPERATING OFFICER:
Robert B. Footlik
Secretary
Association of Professional Material
   Handling Consultants
1548 Tower Road
Winnetka, IL 60093
(312) 441-5920

ORGANIZATION: Australian Physical Distribution Management Association-Victorian Division
TYPE: Professional association, affiliated with the Australian Institute of Management, in which individuals hold membership.
NUMBER OF MEMBERS: 230
DUES: Membership of Australian Institute of Management at appropriate rate plus $30.00 per annum per person. Membership of A.I.M. can be corporate or individual; membership of A.P.D.M.A. is individual only. Special joining fees apply for non-A.I.M. members to encourage membership of both organizations.
PURPOSE/OBJECTIVE: A.P.D.M.A. is a non-profit organization of business people and academics interested in, and/or practicing in the field of logistics. It seeks to improve the standard of individual and corporate skills in the area of logistics management, by running training courses (by itself

or jointly with other organizations); by conducting regular meetings of members to listen to, examine, and discuss recent or important issues; by providing a network of mutually interested people with the objective of sharing ideas and concepts.

CHIEF ELECTED OFFICER:
Richard A. Beaurepaire, (Chairman)
Divisional Manager-Marketing & Sales
Cardboard Containers Manufacturing Co.
Pty. Ltd.,
81-87 Blair Street, Broadmeadows, 3047
MELBOURNE, AUSTRALIA
(03) 534-8181
CHIEF OPERATING OFFICER:
Miss Michelle Sebrie
Australian Institute of Management-Victoria
10 St. Leonards Ave. St. Kilda, 3182
MELBOURNE, AUSTRALIA
(03) 534-8181
REMARKS: National Conference organized on a revolving basis with A.P.D.M.A. (New South Wales Division). This will be held in Melbourne in February 1984. At this stage there is no national association, although strong personal links exist between the N.S.W. and Victorian Divisions. It is reasonable to expect that a national association will evolve in the next couple of years.

ORGANIZATION: Bundesveriningung Logistik e.v.
TYPE: An organization in which membership is extended on both an individual and/or corporate basis.
NUMBER OF MEMBERS: 300 individuals;
80 corporate
DUES: DM 80 per person per year.
DM 300, DM 600, DM 1,000 corporate dues.
PURPOSE/OBJECTIVE: To promote an awareness of logistics thinking in private enterprise (industry, commerce, transport and other service industries) through the systematic compilation of logistics problems and their solutions.
CHIEF ELECTED OFFICER:
Dr. Hanspeter Stabenau
Vorsitzender
Bundesvereinigung Logistik, e.v.
P.B. 10 63-04 MarkstraBe 2
D-2800 Bremen 1
GERMANY

ORGANIZATION: Canadian Association of Physical Distribution Management
TYPE: A professional organization in which individuals hold membership.
NUMBER OF MEMBERS: 300
DUES: $95.00 per person.
PURPOSE/OBJECTIVE: To operate exclusively, without profit, a commercial trade association for the development of all aspects of physical distribution management. To aid and provide, through the cooperation with other organizations, for the promotional advancement of physical distribution management and to promote the training and development of members of the corporation in physical distribution and related fields.

CHIEF ELECTED OFFICER:
Donald J. Allison
Physical Distribution Manager
Manville Canada, Inc.
295 The West Mall
Etobicoice, Ontario M9C 427
CHIEF OPERATING OFFICER:
Brian D. Wheeler
Executive Director
Canadian Association of Physical
    Distribution Management
One Yonge Street
Toronto, Ontario M5E 1J9

ORGANIZATION: Canadian Industrial Traffic League
TYPE: A trade association in which corporations hold membership.
NUMBER OF MEMBERS: 475 member companies represented by approximately 1,000 member representatives.
DUES: By number of employees.
PURPOSE/OBJECTIVE: To develop a thorough understanding of the transportation and distribution requirements of industry and to promote, conserve and protect commercial transportation interests.
CHIEF ELECTED OFFICER:
G. C. Ramm
William Neilson Ltd/Ltee
277 Gladstone Ave.
Toronto, Ontario M6J 3L9
CHIEF OPERATING OFFICER:
T. J. McTague
General Manager
Canadian Industrial Traffic League
2360 Dundas Street West #242
Toronto, Ontario M6P 4B2
(416) 534-1101
REMARKS: Canadian counterpart to the National Industrial Transportation League.

ORGANIZATION: Chinese Society of Economics of Supplies
TYPE: Government agency.
NUMBER OF MEMBERS: N/A
DUES: N/A
PURPOSE/OBJECTIVE: To coordinate the movement of equipment and materials throughout the Peoples Republic of China.
CHIEF ELECTED OFFICER:
Mr. Mei Luo, Director
Bureau for Science Technology & Education
State Bureau Equipment & Materials
25 North Street Yue Tan
Beijing
Peoples Republic of China
CHIEF OPERATING OFFICER:
Yu Xiaogu
Chairperson
Chinese Society of Economic of Supplies
25 North Street
Yue Tan, Beijing
Peoples Republic of China
890941-633

ORGANIZATION: Containerization & Intermodal Institute

TYPE: A trade association covering the intermodal transportation industry. Corporate and individual memberships available.

NUMBER OF MEMBERS: 400

DUES: Corporate: $250.00 annually (Includes 6 individuals) Individual: $50.00 annually.

PURPOSE/OBJECTIVE: The Institute is a trade association that brings together and serves the many people, companies and organizations who have a common interest and stake in the field of containerization, unitization and intermodal transportation.

CHIEF ELECTED OFFICER:

J. C. Jessen, Chairman
804 Fairthorn Drive
Kennett Square, PA 19348
(215) 444-5925

Vincent P. Staunton, President
VP-Sea Land Service
P.O. Box 900
Edison, NJ 08817
(201) 632-2263

CHIEF OPERATING OFFICER:

Norman M. Stone
Executive Director
299 Madison Ave.
New York, NY 10017
(212) 697-3120

REMARKS: Among other activities the Institute holds three major conferences each year in various locations, attended by top and middle management people from all types of transportation carriers, shippers, equipment manufacturers and lessors, and government agencies. Panel presentations on timely topics are followed by intensive discussions. Conferences are open to non-members as well as members.

ORGANIZATION: Delta Nu Alpha

TYPE: A professional organization in which individuals hold membership.

NUMBER OF MEMBERS: 9,000

DUES: $20.00 per person.

PURPOSE/OBJECTIVE: Transportation education.

CHIEF ELECTED OFFICER:

Mr. Ralph Percival, President
Mrazek Van & Storage
2045 Firethorn Drive
St. Louis, MO 63131
(305) 894-0384

CHIEF OPERATING OFFICER:

Charles T. Harper, Jr.
Administrator
Delta Nu Alpha Transportation Fraternity, Inc.
1040 Woodcock Road #201
Orlando, FL 32802
(305) 894-0284

REMARKS: Membership is open to anyone who is interested in transportation.

ORGANIZATION: German Society of Logistics

TYPE: An organization in which membership is extended on both an individual and/or corporate basis.

NUMBER OF MEMBERS: 320 Individuals
180 Corporations

DUES: DM 90m per person per year.
DM 960 corporate dues.

PURPOSE/OBJECTIVE: The purpose of the club is the promotion of scientific research and development in the field of logistics, under particular consideration of industry, commerce and services.

CHIEF ELECTED OFFICER:

Harry Laessig-President
Fordertechnik Hamburg Harry Laessig
Hamburg, Germany 2000

CHIEF OPERATING OFFICER:

Gunther Pawellek
Deutsche Gesellschaft fur Logistik e.v.
Postfash 500500
Dortmund, Germany 4600 (0231) 755-2051

REMARKS: Membership in this organization is drawn from individuals, corporations, institutions, authorities, and societies, as well as legally constituted federations, clubs, companies, and business enterprises that have a functional interest in logistics.

ORGANIZATION: Grocery Manufacturers of America (GMA)

TYPE: A trade association in which corporations hold membership.

NUMBER OF MEMBERS: 135 corporate members.

DUES: Corporate dues are on a sliding scale based on gross sales through retail grocery channels in the United States.

PURPOSE/OBJECTIVE: The Grocery Manufacturers of America, Inc. is a trade association of the leading manufacturers and processors of food and non-food products sold in retail grocery outlets throughout the United States. GMA's objective is to solve for member companies those problems for which GMA group action is more effective than action by member companies working individually or through other associations.

CHIEF ELECTED OFFICER:

Robert M. Schaeberle, (Chairman)
Chairman
Nabisco Brands, Inc.
Nabisco Brands Plaza
Parsippany, NJ 07054
(201) 898-7100

CHIEF OPERATING OFFICER:

George W. Koch
President & Chief Executive Officer
Grocery Manufacturers of America, Inc.
1010 Wisconsin Ave. NW
Washington, DC 20007
(202) 337-9400

REMARKS: The staff member responsible for distribution related program is:
C. Edward Ashdown
Vice President, Operation
Grocery Manufacturers of America

ORGANIZATION: Institute of Industrial Engineers (IIE)
TYPE: A professional organization in which individuals hold membership.
NUMBER OF MEMBERS: 40,000
DUES: $60.00 per person per year.
$12.50 per student per year.
PURPOSE/OBJECTIVE: The purpose of IIE are to advance the general welfare of mankind through the resources and creative abilities of the Industrial Engineering profession and to encourage and assist education and research in the art and science of Industrial Engineering.
CHIEF ELECTED OFFICER:
Dr. John A. White
President
Georgia Institute of Technology
School of Industry & Systems Engineering
Atlanta, GA 30332
(404) 894-2304
CHIEF OPERATING OFFICER:
David L. Belden, Ph.D., P.E.
Executive Director
Institute of Industrial Engineers
25 Technology Park Atlanta
Norcross, GA 30092
(404) 449-0460

ORGANIZATION: Institute of Management Consultants Inc. (IMC)
TYPE: Professional Society which certifies individual management consultants.
NUMBER OF MEMBERS: 1600/24 Chapters
DUES: $250 per year: regular members
$175 per year: associate members
PURPOSE/OBJECTIVE: The primary purpose of the Institute of Management Consultants is to assure the public that members possess the ethical standards and the professional competence and the independence required for membership and are, therefore, qualified to practice.
CHIEF ELECTED OFFICER:
Michael Shays CMC-President
Coopers & Lybrand
333 Market Street
San Francisco, CA 94105
(415) 957-3112
CHIEF OPERATING OFFICER:
John F. Hartshorne-Executive Director
Institute of Management Consultants, Inc.
19 West 44th Street
New York, NY 10036
(212) 921-2885

ORGANIZATION: Institute of Physical Distribution Management
TYPE: A professional organization which is supported by contributions from corporations and individual membership.
NUMBER OF MEMBERS: 3,000
DUES: Sliding scale based on size of company and annual individual subscriptions.
PURPOSE/OBJECTIVE: To promote the art and science of physical distribution management. To provide services to members, including library, information services, regional activities, career advice and educational facilities.
CHIEF ELECTED OFFICER:
Sir Robert Lawrence (Chairman)
Chairman
British Railways Property Board
274/280 Bishopsgate
London EC2M 4XQ
CHIEF OPERATING OFFICER:
Raymond C. Horsley
Chief Executive
Institute of Physical Distribution Management
Management House
Cottingham Road
Corby, Northants NN17 1TT
England

ORGANIZATION: International Customer Service Association
TYPE: A professional organization in which individuals hold membership.
NUMBER OF MEMBERS: 900
DUES: $35.00 per year.
PURPOSE/OBJECTIVE: The International Customer Service Association's primary objectives are sharing common problems and solutions, professional development and recognition of customer service as a discipline or management function, serving as a clearinghouse for technology and support material, training and employment.
CHIEF ELECTED OFFICER:
Neil Stone
Thomas Laguban & Associates, Inc.
16535 West Bluemound Road
Brookfield, WI 53005
(414) 784-8080
CHIEF OPERATING OFFICER:
Doug Doherty
Owens Corning Fiberglas
T-16 Fiberglas Tower
Toledo, OH 43659
(419) 248-8786

ORGANIZATION:
International Material Management Society
Airport One
Suite #103
3900 Capital City Blvd.
Lansing, MI 48906
(517) 321-6713
TYPE: A professional organization in which individuals hold membership.
NUMBER OF MEMBERS: 4,900
DUES: $50.00 international, $15.00 members (rebate chapter)
PURPOSE/OBJECTIVE: IMMS is a professional society dedicated to coordinating and promoting the advancement of the art and science, theory and practice of material management and material handling principles and techniques among its members. Its membership includes practitioners, engineers, and executives in a wide range of industry, sales, university educators, governmental and military engineer-

ing specialists. IMMS has 52 local chapters in the United States and Canada, and affiliates in England, France, Germany, Japan and South Africa.

CHIEF ELECTED OFFICER:
James J. Way
Section Manager of Material
Bell Canada
85 Signet Drive
Weston, Ontario
M9L 1S2
(416) 929-2829

ORGANIZATION: Materials Handling Equipment Distributors Association
TYPE: A trade association in which corporations hold membership.
NUMBER OF MEMBERS: 780
DUES: Corporate dues are on a sliding scale based on gross sales and commission for distributors. Flat fee for allied/associate members.
PURPOSE/OBJECTIVE: To educate distributors in the methods and practice necessary for them to become the most efficient medium through which materials handling equipment manufacturers distribute their products. To educate manufacturers and suppliers of the value of distributors in the distribution of material handling products. To educate customers in the true value and economy of buying material handling equipment from locally-owned professionally operated independent distributorships.
CHIEF ELECTED OFFICER:
Mr. Wilson A. Tayloe, President
W.A. Tayloe Company, Inc.
11351 Anaheim, P.O. Box 59226
Dallas, TX 75229
(214) 484-7260
CHIEF OPERATING OFFICER:
Daniel R. Reilly
Executive Vice President
Material Handling Equipment Distributors Association
201 Route 45
Vernon Hills, IL 60061
(312) 680-3500

ORGANIZATION: The Material Handling Institute, Inc. (MHI)
TYPE: A trade association in which corporations hold membership.
NUMBER OF MEMBERS: 327
DUES: Information confidential.
PURPOSE/OBJECTIVE: MHI was formed and incorporated in 1945 as a non-profit corporation. Exceptionally able material handling industry executives organized the Institute for the purpose of achieving goals common to the material handling industry that no one company could attain alone.
CHIEF ELECTED OFFICER:
A. L. Leffler, President
Director of Marketing
Duff-Norton, Co.
100 Pioneer Road
Charlotte, NC 28232
(704) 588-0510

CHIEF OPERATING OFFICER:
Philip Trimble
Managing Director
The Material Handling Institute, Inc.
1326 Freeport Road
Pittsburgh, PA 15238
(412) 782-1624

ORGANIZATION: National American Wholesale Grocers' Association
TYPE: A trade association in which corporations hold membership.
NUMBER OF MEMBERS: 370
DUES: Corporate dues are on a sliding scale based on sales.
PURPOSE/OBJECTIVE: The National American Wholesale Grocers' Association is the trade association responding to the needs of wholesale food, food service and specialty food distributors. It represents members with government agencies and serves as an educational center for information, experiences, and know-how in innovative techniques and new technology.
CHIEF ELECTED OFFICER:
Mike Wright, (Chairman of the Board)
Chairman
Super Value Stores, Inc.
P.O. Box 990
Minneapolis, MN 55440
(612) 828-4000
CHIEF OPERATING OFFICER:
Gerald E. Peck
President
National American Wholesale Grocers' Association
201 Park Washington Court
Falls Church, VA 22046
(703) 532-9400

ORGANIZATION: National Association of Freight Transportation Consultants
TYPE: A professional organization in which individuals or companies hold membership.
NUMBER OF MEMBERS: 80-100
DUES: $50.00 minimum to $125.00 maximum.
PURPOSE/OBJECTIVE: Non-profit association of consultants in freight transportation who perform all phases of such services for shipper clients, and in some cases motor carriers.
CHIEF ELECTED OFFICER:
Donna F. Behme, Executive Director
National Association of Freight Transportation
  Consultants
3436 Tanterra Circle
Brookeville, MD 20833
(301) 924-3614
CHIEF OPERATING OFFICER: Same as above.
REMARKS: Annual meetings held the third week of November every year in different locales as our membership resides in all of the United States.

ORGANIZATION: National Association of Manufacturers
TYPE: A trade association in which corporations hold membership.
NUMBER OF MEMBERS: 13,000
DUES: Corporate dues are on a sliding scale based on company net worth.
PURPOSE/OBJECTIVE: The prime objective of NAM is to maintain an economic and political climate that offers maximum personal freedom and opportunity to our citizens, and the best possible climate in which industry can serve the nation by creating jobs, individual security and higher living standards.
CHIEF ELECTED OFFICER:
James B. Henderson, (Executive VP)
Chairman of the Board
Shell Oil
1 Shell Plaza
Houston, TX 77001
(713) 241-6161
CHIEF OPERATING OFFICER:
Alexander B. Trowbridge
President
National Association of Manufacturers
1775 F Street NW
Washington, DC 20006
(202) 626-3700

ORGANIZATION: National Association of Purchasing Management, Inc.
TYPE: A membership organization dedicated to research and education in the field of purchasing and materials management.
NUMBER OF MEMBERS: 28,500
DUES: $60.00 per member as of March 1, 1984, plus local association dues.
PURPOSE/OBJECTIVE: The National Assocation of Purchasing Management is committed to providing national and international leadership in purchasing and materials management. Through its 159 affiliated associations and over 28,000 members, the Association provides opportunities for purchasing and materials management practitioners to expand their professional skill and knowledge, and works to foster a better understanding of purchasing and materials management concepts.
CHIEF ELECTED OFFICER:
Frank P. Alcock, C.P.M. (President)
Manager of Corporate Purchasing
U.S. Borax & Chemical Corp.
3075 Wilshire Blvd.
Los Angeles, CA 90010
(213) 381-5311
CHIEF OPERATING OFFICER:
Roland J. Baker, C.P.M. Executive Vice President
National Association of Purchasing Management
496 Kinderkamack Road
P.O. Box 418
Oradell, NJ 07649
(201) 967-8585

ORGANIZATION: National Council on International Trade Documentation
TYPE: A trade association in which corporations hold membership.
NUMBER OF MEMBERS: 250
DUES: Corporate dues are on a sliding scale.
PURPOSE/OBJECTIVE: The National Council on International Trade Documentation is a non-profit, privately-financed membership organization that conducts research and implements recommendations to simplify and standardize international trade documentation and related procedures, reduce government regulations and encourage the automation and electronic transmission of trade data. Working through individuals and companies, members and non-members, United States and other governmental departments and agencies, and many national and international committees and organizations it serves as the coordinator and representative of American business in solving international trade paperwork problems.
CHIEF ELECTED OFFICER:
George A. Snyder, (Chairman)
Vice President, General Manager Distribution
Eastman Kodak Company
343 State Street
Rochester, NY 14650
(716) 724-4000
CHIEF OPERATING OFFICER:
Howard J. Henke
Executive Director
National Council on International Trade Documentation
350 Broadway #1200
New York, NY 10013
(212) 925-1400

ORGANIZATION: National Council for U.S.-China Trade
TYPE: A trade association in which corporations hold membership.
NUMBER OF MEMBERS: 450
DUES: Vary
PURPOSE/OBJECTIVE: The National Council for U.S.-China Trade is the focal point for China trade activity in the United States. American companies involved in trade with the People's Republic of China (PRC) look to the National Council for representation, practical assistance, and up-to-date information in developing and continuing their relations with the People's Republic of China.
CHIEF ELECTED OFFICER:
Walter S. Surrey, Esq. (Chairman of the Board)
Partner
Surrey and Morse
1250 Eye Street, NW
Suite 1100
Washington, DC 20005
(202) 682-4000
CHIEF OPERATING OFFICER:
Christopher H. Phillips
President
National Council for U.S.-China Trade
1050 17th Street, NW
Washington, DC 20036
(202) 429-0340

ORGANIZATION: National Council of Physical Distribution Management (NCPDM)

TYPE: A professional organization in which individuals hold membership.

NUMBER OF MEMBERS: 4500

DUES: $100.00 per person per year.

PURPOSE/OBJECTIVE: NCPDM is a non-profit organization of business personnel who are interested in improving their distribution management skills. It works with private industry, various organizations and institutions to further the development of the physical distribution concept. It does this through a continuing program of formal activities and informal discussions designed to (a) develop the theory and understanding of the physical distribution process, (b) promote the art and science of managing physical distribution systems, and (c) foster professional dialogue and development in the field.

CHIEF ELECTED OFFICER:
Roger W. Kallock, (President)
Chairman
Cleveland Consulting Associates
23925 Commerce Park Road
Cleveland, OH 44122
(216) 831-0430

CHIEF OPERATING OFFICER:
George A. Gecowets
Vice President/Executive Director
National Council of Physical Distribution Management
2803 Butterfield Road Suite 380
Oak Brook, IL 60521
(312) 655-0985

REMARKS: Over 2,500 distribution executives from all over the world participate in NCPDM's 2½ day annual conference which is usually held in late-September or early-October of each year.

ORGANIZATION: National Defense Transportation Association (NDTA)

TYPE: A professional organization in which membership is extended on both an individual and/or corporate basis.

NUMBER OF MEMBERS: 9,000 individuals
110 corporations

DUES: $ 25.00 per person
$850.00 per corporation

PURPOSE/OBJECTIVE: NDTA sees itself as a link between government transportation needs and industry's capabilities. It is a kind of communications line that permits free flow of information between civilian transportation executives and government leaders. It is also a vast pool of transportation resources, manpower, talent and know-how. In order to place this talent collection at the disposal of government, the association has divided itself into working groups or "councils" comprised of industry men who offer advice and channel their talents into economic and technical problem areas currently afflicting government.

CHIEF ELECTED OFFICER:
Richard H. Hinchcliff, Chairman of the Board
National Defense Transportation Association
727 North Washington Street #200
Alexandria, VA 22314
(703) 836-3303

CHIEF OPERATING OFFICER:
Brig. Gen. Malcolm P. Hooker USAF (R)
President
National Defense Transportation Association
727 North Washington Street #200
Alexandria, VA 22314
(703) 836-3303

ORGANIZATION: National Food Distributors Association (NFDA)

TYPE: Not-for-profit trade association in which distributor companies hold active membership and supplier companies hold associate membership.

NUMBER OF MEMBERS: 550

DUES: Active: $205 base with $5 for each salesperson, driver/merchandiser. Associates pay either $400 or $500 based on annual scales.

PURPOSE/OBJECTIVE: NFDA is a non-profit trade association formed to promote the progress and development of the business of its members:

— To establish better relations with the retail and institution trade at all levels;

— To establish and maintain standards of excellence of product and service;

— To encourage the spirit of cooperation among members;

— To carry on or assist in research for the purpose of securing better solutions of the problems of the industry, and to aid in industry development.

CHIEF ELECTED OFFICER:
Earle Freedman, Chairman of the Board
Jacob Hamburger Company
5300 N. Channel Ave.
Portland, OR 97217
(503) 285-4531

CHIEF OPERATING OFFICER:
William W. Carpenter, Executive Vice President
NFDA
111 E. Wacker Drive
Chicago, IL 60601
(312) 644-6610

REMARKS: Serving the retail grocery and institutional food industries, there are two major trade shows and educational seminars each year. There is an informational newsletter for members, legal and insurance services, a Young Executives Forum, a Past Presidents Council, an Associate Member Manufacturers Council and several Board of Directors and Executive Committee meetings annually. Other committees such as Convention Planning, Education, Nominating, Public Relations, Membership, Finance and Industry Affairs, meet periodically.

ORGANIZATION: The National Industrial Transportation League

TYPE: A transportation trade association.

NUMBER OF MEMBERS: 1,600

DUES: Corporate dues are based on a sliding scale based on a company's net worth.

PURPOSE/OBJECTIVE: The League's purposes are: to promote adequate national and international transportation; to interchange ideas and information concerning traffic and transportation matters as permitted by law; to cooperate with the regulatory agencies, both federal and state, with the DOT, and other transportation companies, in developing a thorough understanding of legislation that will be helpful to commerce.

CHIEF ELECTED OFFICER:

Donald F. Kuster, (President)
General Manager, Traffic & Distribution
Continental Can Company, Inc.
711 Jorie Blvd.
Oak Brook, IL 60521
(312) 986-0333

CHIEF OPERATING OFFICER:

James E. Bartley
Executive Vice President
The National Industrial Transportation League
1090 Vermont Ave., NW Suite 410
Washington, DC 20005
(202) 842-3870

ORGANIZATION: National Small Shipments Traffic Conference (NASSTRAC)

TYPE: Similar to a trade association in that corporations are members. It is not based on product similarity or other basic factors, except for a common interest in small shipments. Action is based on saving money for members on LTL shipments.

NUMBER OF MEMBERS: 300

DUES: Corporate dues are on a sliding scale based on gross annual domestic sales.

PURPOSE/OBJECTIVE: NASSTRAC is a national association of shippers and receivers of LTL dedicated to the principle of preventing exploitation of small shipments and ensuring essential transportation services for small shipments, (less than 10,000 pounds or LTL) at fair and reasonable rates and charges. NASSTRAC has acted as a legal cooperative providing legal representation in significant rate cases: rulemaking proceedings with State regulatory agencies, the ICC, rate bureaus, and courts when necessary. However, with the change in regulatory applications, NASSTRAC has embarked upon an extensive educational program to help members adjust to the rapidly changing distribution environment and save money on LTL shipments. Plans are being implemented to provide discounted LTL services for members.

CHIEF ELECTED OFFICER:

Myron B. Smith, (President)
Director of Traffic
American Home Products Corporation
685 Third Avenue
New York, NY 10017
(212) 878-5000

CHIEF OPERATING OFFICER:

Joseph F. H. Cutrona
Executive Director
National Small Shipments Traffic Conference
1750 Pennsylvania Ave., NW #1116
Washington, DC 20006
(202) 393-5505

ORGANIZATION: National Society of Professional Engineers (NSPE)

TYPE: Professional engineering society composed of graduate engineers (and students) from all branches of engineering and areas of specialty.

NUMBER OF MEMBERS: 80,000

DUES: National dues-$50.00. Individual's dues include local chapter, state society and national society—total ranging from approximately $75.00 to $150.00.

PURPOSE/OBJECTIVE: Promote the role of engineering in society with emphasis on involvement in public policy; the establishment and maintenance of high standards of engineering practice; and promotion of the social, professional and economic interests of engineers. Major programs encompass ethics, licensing of engineers, government and public affairs, public relations, continuing professional development, career guidance and employment practices.

CHIEF ELECTED OFFICER:

Louis A. Bacon, P.E.
President (7/1983-7/1984)
Heery & Heery, Architects and Engineers, Inc.
880 West Peachtree Street, NW
Atlanta, GA 30367

Herbert C. Koogle, P.E.
President (7/1984-1985)
Koogle and Pouls Engineering, Inc.
8338A Comanche N.E.
Albuquerque, NM 87110
(505) 294-5051

CHIEF OPERATING OFFICER:

Donald G. Weinert, P.E.
Executive Director (NSPE)
2029 K Street N.W.
Washington, DC 20006
(202) 463-2300

ORGANIZATION: National Wholesales Druggists' Association (NWDA)

TYPE: A trade association in which corporations hold membership.

NUMBER OF MEMBERS: 700

DUES: Dues are based on annual sales through NWDA wholesalers for the most recent fiscal year.

PURPOSE/OBJECTIVE: NWDA is the trade association responding to the needs of wholesale distributors of healthcare products (pharmaceuticals, proprietaries, toiletries, and sundries), to learn, to act, to be informed and to have a voice in those deliberations which vitally affect them. It represents members with all government agencies where representation is necessary to the welfare of the distributor. It is an educational center for information, experiences and know-how in innovative techniques and new technology, imperative to future development.

CHIEF ELECTED OFFICER:

Elmer M. Fiery
Bergen Brunswig Corporation
Park 80 Plaza East
Saddle Brook, NJ 07662
(201) 845-0850

CHIEF OPERATING OFFICER:
William L. Ford
President
National Wholesale Druggists' Association
105 Oronoco Street
Alexandria, VA 22314
(703) 684-6400

ORGANIZATION: Netherlands Organization for Logistics Management
TYPE: An organization in which membership is extended on both an individual and/or corporate basis.
NUMBER OF MEMBERS: 60 individuals and 320 corporations.
DUES: N/A
PURPOSE/OBJECTIVE: The purpose of the Dutch Organization for Logistics Management (NEVEM) is to promote the knowledge and dissemination of information about integral product flow, or transportation.
CHIEF ELECTED OFFICER:
A. H. Schaafsma
Chairman
NEVEM: Dutch Organization for Logistics Management
Van Alkemadelaan 700
2597 AW The Hague
Holland
(070) 264341
CHIEF OPERATING OFFICER:
L.J. Goede
Executive Secretary
NEVEM: Dutch Organization for Logistics Management
Van Alkenadelaan 700
2597 AW The Hague
Holland
(070) 264341

ORGANIZATION: Physical Distribution Rationalization Institute
TYPE: A professional organization in which individuals hold membership.
NUMBER OF MEMBERS: 300
DUES: $200 per person.
PURPOSE/OBJECTIVE: The Physical Distribution Rationalization Institute is a non-profit organization of business personnel who are interested in improving their distribution management skills. It works in cooperation with private industry to further the development of this connection; it does this through the following activities: (1) training seminars (2) study team tours and (3) distribution of literature.
CHIEF ELECTED OFFICER:
Sojiro Kamiyama
Chairman
Physical Distribution Rationalization Institute
1-18-16 Taiheidai, Tsujido
Fujidawa, Kanagawa
Japan 251
(0466) 36-7185

ORGANIZATION: Private Carrier Conference-ATA
TYPE: A trade association in which corporations hold membership.
NUMBER OF MEMBERS: 3,500
DUES: Corporate dues are on a sliding scale based on the number of trucks operated.
PURPOSE/OBJECTIVE: To represent the nation's private motor truck operators before the ICC, DOT, the U.S. Congress and other governmental agencies having jurisdiction over administrative, legislative and safety regulation pertaining to their highway operations. Members of the Conference include types of businesses utilizing private truck operations such as food distribution, textiles, construction, mining, petroleum, iron and steel public utilities, etc.
CHIEF ELECTED OFFICER:
George R. French
Vice President
Atlantic Cement Company
P.O. Box 30
Stamford, CT 06904
(203) 327-3100
CHIEF OPERATING OFFICER:
John R. Rosenbaum, Managing Director
Private Carrier Conference-ATA
1616 P Street NW
Washington, DC 20036
(202) 797-5404

ORGANIZATION: Private Truck Council of America, Inc.
TYPE: A trade association in which corporations hold membership.
NUMBER OF MEMBERS: 1,600
DUES: Corporate dues are on a sliding scale based on number of vehicles operated at that location.
PURPOSE/OBJECTIVE: The only dependent national organization representing non-transportation companies which operate trucks in furtherance of primary businesses other than for-hire transportation.
CHIEF ELECTED OFFICER:
Don A. Wilson, (President)
Distribution Systems Manager, Dairy Group
The Southland Corporation
P.O. Box 719
Dallas, TX 75221
(214) 828-7011
CHIEF OPERATING OFFICER:
Richard D. Henderson
Executive Vice President
Private Truck Council of America, Inc.
2022 P Street, NW
Washington, DC 20036
(202) 785-4900

ORGANIZATION: Sales & Marketing Council-ATA
TYPE: A trade association in which corporations hold membership.
NUMBER OF MEMBERS: 700
DUES: Carrier member annual dues are based on revenue category.
PURPOSE/OBJECTIVE: The Sales & Marketing Council is the only professional organization that furnishes continuing education programs and statistical services needed by sales and marketing executives in the motor carrier industry.

CHIEF OPERATING OFFICER:
Nancy A. Burns, CAE
Executive Director
Sales & Marketing Council-ATA
American Trucking Associations
1616 P Street, NW
Washington, DC 20036
(202) 797-5249

ORGANIZATION: Shippers National Freight Claim Council, Inc.
TYPE: A trade association in which corporations hold membership.
NUMBER OF MEMBERS: 900
DUES: $250.00 regular membership
$200.00 multiple subscribers
$200.00 associate members
PURPOSE/OBJECTIVE: An educational institution developing the latest teaching tools and techniques on carrier liability and claims administration, through seminars and publications, the objective of which is to develop a greater degree of professionalism in claim management.
CHIEF ELECTED OFFICER:
James H. Putman, President
Abbott Labs
1400 Sheraton Road
Chicago, IL 60064
(312) 937-7119
CHIEF OPERATING OFFICER:
William J. Augello
Executive Director/General Counsel
Shippers National Freight Claim Council, Inc.
120 Main Street
Huntington, NY 11743
(516) 549-8984

ORGANIZATION: Society of Logistics Engineers
TYPE: A professional organization in which individuals hold membership.
NUMBER OF MEMBERS: 8,000
DUES: $40.00 per person.
PURPOSE/OBJECTIVE: The Society of Logistics Engineers is a non-profit, international organization of individuals devoted to scientific, educational and literary endeavors to enhance the art and science of logistics technology, education and management.
CHIEF ELECTED OFFICER:
John J. Politovich, (Project Logistician)
General Dynamics
Ponoma Division
P.O. Box 2507
Ponoma, CA 91766
(714) 620-7511 x 3270
CHIEF OPERATING OFFICER:
Robert R. Leonard
Executive Director
Society of Logistics Engineers
303 Williams Ave. #922
Huntsville, AL 35801
(205) 539-3800/3833
REMARKS: Membership is open to all individuals working, studying or interested in the career fields of logistics technology, management, education, product support and physical distribution.

ORGANIZATION: Society of Packaging ar Engineers
TYPE: A professional organization in which indiv or corporations hold membership.
NUMBER OF MEMBERS: 1,500-2,000
DUES: $50.00 per year professional
PURPOSE/OBJECTIVE: Professional development in packaging and handling engineers.
CHIEF ELECTED OFFICER:
William E. Loy
Reynolds Medal Company
1140 Hammond Drive
Suite 3150
Atlanta, GA 30328
(404) 491-0906
CHIEF OPERATING OFFICER:
William C. Pflaum
Executive Director
Society of Packaging and Handling Engineers
Reston International Center
Reston, VA 22091
(703) 620-9380

ORGANIZATION: Transportation Brokers Conference of America, Inc. (TBCA)
TYPE: A professional trade association representing ICC licensed transportation brokers.
NUMBER OF MEMBERS: 400
DUES: $250.00 per year.
PURPOSE/OBJECTIVE: To represent, educate, support, encourage and self-police the ICC licensed transportation brokerage industry, working to accomplish these goals with licensed brokers, governmental agencies and other interested groups.
CHIEF ELECTED OFFICER:
Richard Tobey, President
Intermodal Consolidating Service
P.O. Box 221
Gladstone, NJ 07934
(800) 526-3972
CHIEF OPERATING OFFICER:
Charles M. Naylor
Executive Director
T.B.C.A.
P.O. Box 209
Oak Forest, IL 60452
(312) 687-0222
REMARKS: The TBCA is only 5 years old, and had 60 members as recently as summer of 1981. Since then, the TBCA has experienced a 5%-7% growth rate per month. We have a Spring & Fall convention. Fall of 1982 saw 85 people at that convention. Our just completed convention saw 265 people! This growth is continuing.

ORGANIZATION: Transportation Data Coordinating Committee (TDCC)
TYPE: A trade association in which corporations hold membership.
NUMBER OF MEMBERS: N/A
DUES: Corporate dues are on a sliding scale based on gross revenues (annual)

PURPOSE/OBJECTIVE: TDCC is a non-profit, public interest organization designed to develop, foster and maintain a program of action to achieve coordination of standards for intercompany computer electronic data interchange of business transactions.

CHIEF ELECTED OFFICER:
Richard H. Steiner
Senior Vice President-Marketing
Emery World Wide
Old Danbury Road
Wilton, CT 06897
(203) 834-3227

CHIEF OPERATING OFFICER:
Edward A. Guilbert
President
Transportation Data Coordinating Committee (TDCC)
1101 17th Street, NW #606
Washington, DC 20036-4775
(202) 293-5514

ORGANIZATION: Transportation Research Forum
TYPE: A professional organization in which individuals hold membership.
NUMBER OF MEMBERS: 800
DUES: $50.00 per person.
PURPOSE/OBJECTIVE: The Transportation Research Forum is a unique organization of professionals in the field of transportation. Its purpose is to provide a common meeting ground for both those who use research—carrier managers, shippers, labor unions, legislators, and governmental policy makers and program managers at all levels—whether in government, industry, consulting firms or universities.

CHIEF ELECTED OFFICER:
Douglas J. McKelvey
Federal Highway Adm. HHP-11
400 7th Street SW
Washington, DC 20590
(202) 426-0600

CHIEF OPERATING OFFICER:
Grant C. Vietsch
Vice President
Transportation Research Forum
P.O. Box AA
Northfield, NJ 08225
(609) 645-1639

ORGANIZATION: U.S. Chamber of Commerce
TYPE: A federation composed of corporations and companies, associations and chambers of commerce.
NUMBER OF MEMBERS: 238,141 Companies
2,721 Chambers of Commerce
1,269 Associations
DUES: $125 minimum per member per year.
Dues schedule available upon request.
PURPOSE/OBJECTIVE: To advance human progress through a better economic, political, and social system based on individual freedom, incentive, opportunity and responsibility.

CHIEF ELECTED OFFICER:
Edwin D. Dodd
Chairman of the Board
Owen Illinois
1 Sea Gate
Toledo, OH 43666

CHIEF OPERATING OFFICER:
Dr. Richard Lesher
President
Chamber of Commerce of the U.S.
1615 H Street NW
Washington, DC 20062
(202) 463-5300

ORGANIZATION: Warehousing Education & Research Council
TYPE: A professional organization in which individuals hold membership.
NUMBER OF MEMBERS: 850
DUES: $100.00 per year.
PURPOSE/OBJECTIVE: The purpose of the Council is to provide education and to conduct research concerning the warehousing process, and to refine the art and science of managing warehouses. The Council will foster professionalism in warehouse management. It will operate exclusively without profit and in cooperation with other organizations and institutions.

CHIEF ELECTED OFFICER:
Paul M. Solomon, (President)
President
Paul-Jeffrey, Co., Inc.
P.O. Box 512
Liverpool, NY 13088
(315) 451-4500

CHIEF OPERATING OFFICER:
Burr W. Hupp
Executive Director
Warehousing Education & Research Council
4022 Countryview Drive
Sarasota, FL 33583
(813) 924-3544

Gerald J. Godbout
Director, Cargo Services
AIR TRANSPORT ASSOCIATION OF AMERICA
1709 New York Avenue NW
Washington, DC 20006
(202) 626-4129

Marie Powers
Editor
AIRCARGO WORLD
Official Airlines Guides
6255 Barfield Road
Atlanta, GA 30328
(404) 256-9800

David L. Belden
Executive Director
AMERICAN INSTITUTE OF
    INDUSTRIAL ENGINEERS
25 Technology Park/Atlanta
Norcross, GA 30092
(404) 449-0460

Henry F. Sander
Executive Director
AMERICAN PRODUCTION & INVENTORY
    CONTROL SOCIETY
500 West Annandale Road
Falls Church, VA 22046
(703) 237-8344

Kathleen C. Sutton
Director of Public Affairs
AMERICAN PRODUCTIVITY CENTER

123 North Post Oak Lane
Houston, TX 77024
(713) 681-4020

Julie Whitmore
Editor
AMERICAN SHIPPER
1232 Simpson
Evanston, IL 60201
(312) 475-5925

Carter M. Harrison
Executive Director
AMERICAN SOCIETY OF TRAFFIC
    AND TRANSPORTATION
P.O. Box 33095
Louisville, KY 40323
(502) 451-8150

J.R. Halladay
Managing Director
Industrial Relation Division
AMERICAN TRUCKING ASSOCIATION
1616 P Street NW
Washington, DC 20036
(202) 797-5217

Jerry Leatham
President
AMERICAN WAREHOUSEMAN'S
    ASSOCIATION
1165 N. Clark Street
Chicago, IL 60610
(312) 787-3377

Thomas A. Johnson
Editor-in-Chief
ARMY LOGISTICIAN MAGAZINE
ARMY LOGISTIC MATERIAL COMMAND
Fort Lee, VA 23801
(804) 734-4342

Cezar De Castro Sucupira
President
ASSOCIACAO BRASILEIRA DE
    ADMINISTRACAO DEMATERIAL
AV. Beira Mar 406/207
Rio De Janeiro, RJ—CEP
20.021
BRAZIL

Daniel L. Lang
Vice President—Information
ASSOCIATION OF AMERICAN RAILROADS
1920 L Street NW
Washington, DC 20036
(202) 835-9100

Joseph Brady
President
ASSOCIATION OF CONSULTING
    MANAGEMENT ENGINEERS
203 Park Avenue
New York, NY 10169
(212) 697-9693

Edward T. Borda
President
ASSOCIATION OF GENERAL MERCHANDISE
    CHAINS, INC.
1625 Eye Street NW
Washington, DC 20006
(202) 785-2060

Norma L. Iser
Executive Director
ASSOCIATION OF INTERSTATE COMMERCE
    COMMISSION PRACTITIONERS
1112 ICC Building
Washington, DC 20423
(202) 783-9432

Mrs. P. Thorpe
Executive Officer
AUSTRALIAN PHYSICAL DISTRIBUTION
    MANAGEMENT ASSOCIATION (Sidney)
GPO Box 4280
Sidney, 2001 299 7888
Australia

Rich Beaurepaire
Chairperson
AUSTRALIAN PHYSICAL DISTRIBUTION
    MANAGEMENT ASSOCIATION (Victoria)
Management House
10 St. Leonards Avenue
St. Kilda
Australia

Marion Buhagiar
Editor
BOARDROOM REPORTS
500 Fifth Avenue
New York, NY 10110
(212) 354-0005

Gordon McKibben
Business Editor
BOSTON GLOBE
Boston, MA 02107
(617) 929-2000

Lynn Kettleson
Financial Editor
BOSTON HERALD AMERICAN
1 Harold Square
Boston, MA 02106
(617) 426-3000

Pamela Gilbert
Managing Editor
BRANDON'S SHIPPER & FORWARDER
One World Trade Center #3169
New York, NY 10048
(212) 432-0750

Hanspeter Stabenau
BUNDESVEREININGUNG LOGISTIK
MarkstraBe, Postfach
10 63 04
D-2800, Bremen 1
(042) 132-4303

Reggi Ann Dubin
Transportation Editor
BUSINESS WEEK
1221 Avenue of the Americas
New York, NY 10020
(212) 997-1221

Brian Wheeler
Manager
CANADIAN ASSOCIATION OF PHYSICAL
    DISTRIBUTION MANAGEMENT
One Yonge Street #1400
Toronto, Ontario M5E 1J9
(416) 363-1880

T. J. McTague
General Manager
CANADIAN INDUSTRIAL TRAFFIC LEAGUE
2360 Dundas W #242
Toronto, Ontario M6P 4B2
(416) 534-1101

General Manager
CANADIAN INSTITUTE OF TRAFFIC
    & TRANSPORTATION
44 Victoria Street #515
Toronto, Ontario M5C 1Y2
(416) 363-5996

Lou Volpintesta
Editor
CANADIAN TRANSPORTATION &
    DISTRIBUTION MANAGEMENT
1450 Don Mills, Ontario M3B 2X7
(416) 445-6641

Dr. Richard L. Lesher
President
CHAMBER OF COMMERCE OF THE
    UNITED STATES OF AMERICA
1615 H Street NW
Washington, DC 20062
(202) 659-6000

Tony Campbell
Financial Editor
CHICAGO SUN-TIMES
401 N. Wabash Avenue
Chicago, IL 60611
(312) 321-3000

Terry Brown
Business Editor
CHICAGO TRIBUNE
435 N. Michigan Avenue
Chicago, IL 60611
(312) 222-3502

Yu Xiaogu
Chairperson
CHINESE SOCIETY OF ECONOMICS
    OF SUPPLIES
25 North Street
Yue Tan, Beijing
Peoples Republic of China
890941-633

Gerald S. Standley
Editor
COMMERCIAL CAR JOURNAL
Chilton Way
Radnor, PA
(215) 964-4513

Thomas Dulaney
Editor
COMPUTER SYSTEMS REPORT
P.O. Box 453
Exton, PA 19341
(215) 363-7156

Ron Clark
Editor
CONTAINER NEWS
6255 Barfield Road
Atlanta, GA 30328
(404) 256-9800

Norman M. Stone
Executive Director
CONTAINERIZATION INSTITUTE INC.
299 Madison Avenue #1000 F 10
New York, NY 10017
(212) 697-3120

Dan Miller
Editor
CRAIN'S CHICAGO BUSINESS
740 N. Rush Street
Chicago, IL 60611
(312) 649-5200

Richard Oliver
City Editor
DAILY NEWS
220 E. 42nd Street
New York, NY 10017
(212) 949-1234

Dr. J. G. Mattingly
Editor
DEFENSE TRANSPORTATION JOURNAL
College of Business & Management

University of Maryland
Tydings Fall College Park, MD 20742
(301) 454-5943

C. Harper
Administrator
DELTA NU ALPHA
1040 Woodstock Road
Orlando, FL 32803
(305) 894-0384

Thomas A. Foster
Editor-in-Chief
DISTRIBUTION
Chilton Way
Radnor, PA 19089
(215) 964-4388

Clem Norgello
Editor
DUN'S BUSINESS MONTH
875 Third Avenue
New York, NY 10022
(212) 605-9461

P.O. Roessel
Editor-in-Chief
EIGEN VERVOER
Uitgevermaatschappij C. Misset bv
Hanzestraat 1
7006 Doetinchem
Postbus 4, 7000 BA
The Netherlands

Mickey Hirten
Money Today Editor
EVENING SUN
501 North Calvert
Baltimore, MD 21278
(301) 332-6522

James W. Michaels
Editor
FORBES
60 Fifth Avenue
New York, NY 10011
(211) 620-2200

Ann Hengstenberg
Story Development
Editor
FORTUNE
Time Life Building
Rockefeller Center
New York, NY 10020
(212) 841-3709

Fuergen Hlubek
Executive Director
GERMAN SOCIETY OF LOGISTICS
Postfach 50-05-00
Dortmund, Germany 4600
(0231) 755-2779

Richard Mulville
Publisher
GROCERY DISTRIBUTION

307 N. Michigan Avenue
Chicago, IL 60601
(312) 263-1057

C. Edward Ashdown
Vice President
GROCERY MANUFACTURERS OF AMERICA
1010 Wisconsin Avenue NW
Washington, DC 20007
(202) 337-9400

Dick Cutshall
Editor
HANDLING & SHIPPING MANAGEMENT
1111 Chester Avenue
Cleveland, OH 44114
(216) 696-7000

John A. Roberts
Managing Editor
INDUSTRIAL MARKETING
740 Rush Street
Chicago, IL 60611
(312) 649-5200

Brian Moskal
INDUSTRY WEEK
Regional Editor
Two Illinois Center Building
Chicago, IL 60601
(312) 861-0880

John F. Hartshorne
Executive Director
INSTITUTE OF MANAGEMENT CONSULTING
19 West 44th Street
New York, NY 10036
(212) 921-2885

Raymond Horsley
Chief Executive
INSTITUTE OF PHYSICAL DISTRIBUTION
    MANAGEMENT
Management House
Cottingham Road
Corby, Northants NN17 1TT
England

Lynn E. Dunston
National Secretary
INTERNATIONAL CUSTOMER
    SERVICE ASSOCIATION
323 Franklin Building South
Suite 804, Department I-61
Chicago, IL 60606
(312) 585-0730

Martin Christopher
Editor
INTERNATIONAL JOURNAL OF PHYSICAL
    DISTRIBUTION & MATERIALS
    MANAGEMENT
198/200 Keighly Road
Bradford, West Yorkshire
England BD9 4JQ
(0274) 499 891

Minoru Oikawa
Director
JAPAN MANAGEMENT ASSOCIATION
JMA Building
3-1-22, Shiba Park
Minato-ku, Tokyo, 105
Japan
(434) 6211

Joji Arai
Manager
JAPAN PRODUCTIVITY CENTER
United States Office
1901 N. Fort Myer Drive #703
Arlington, VA 22209
(703) 243-5522

Yo Kusuda
Manager
JAPANESE COUNCIL OF PHYSICAL
    DISTRIBUTION MANAGEMENT
12-8, 5 Chome Ginza Chuou-Ku
Tokyo, Japan
(03) 543-3230

Art Eddy
Editor
JET CARGO NEWS
P.O. Box 10973
Houston, TX 77292
(713) 688-8811

Barbara J. Shilneck
Editor
JOURNAL OF ACCOUNTANCY
1211 Avenue of the Americas
New York, NY 10036
(212) 575-6200

Bernard J. LaLonde
Editor
JOURNAL OF BUSINESS LOGISTICS
Ohio State University
1775 College Road
Columbus, OH 43210
(614) 422-0331

Greg Storey
Editorial Writer
JOURNAL OF COMMERCE
110 Wall Street
New York, NY 10005
(212) 425-1616

Thomas E. Caruso
Editor
MARKETING NEWS
250 S. Wacker Drive #250
Chicago, IL 60606
(312) 993-9517

Leslie Hansen Harps
Vice President—Operations
MARKETING PUBLICATIONS
8701 Georgia Avenue #608
Silver Spring, MD 20910
(301) 585-0730

Bernard Knill
Editor
MATERIAL HANDLING ENGINEERING

1111 Chester Avenue
Cleveland, OH 44114
(216) 696-0300

Daniel R. Reilly
Executive Vice President
MATERIAL HANDLING EQUIPMENT
    DISTRIBUTORS ASSOCIATION
201 Route 45
Vernon Hills, IL 60061
(312) 680-3500

Jane B. Hirsch
Director of Communications
MATERIALS HANDLING INSTITUTE
1326 Freeport Road
Pittsburgh, PA 15238
(412) 782-1624

Miles J. Rowan
MODERN MATERIALS HANDLING
221 Columbus Avenue
Boston, MA 02116
(617) 536-7780

F. Stewart Mitchell
Editor
MODERN RAILROADS
2020 Oakton Street
Park Ridge, IL 60068
(312) 399-0202

Jessie Glasgow
Financial Editor
MORNING SUN
501 N. Calvert Street
Baltimore, MD 21202
(301) 332-6100

Marguerite Grimm
Editor
MOTOR FREIGHT CONTROLLER
1616 P Street NW
Washington, DC 20036
(202) 797-5000

Richard A. Brown
Director, Technical Services
NATIONAL AMERICAN WHOLESALE
    GROCERS' ASSOCIATION
201 Park Washington Court
Falls Church, VA 22046
(703) 532-9400

N. F. Behme
Executive Director
NATIONAL ASSOCIATION OF FREIGHT
    TRANSPORTATION CONSULTANTS
3436 Tanterra Circle
Brookeville, MD 20833
(301) 924-3614

Roland J. Baker, CPM
Executive Vice President
NATIONAL ASSOCIATION OF
    PURCHASING MANAGEMENT
496 Kinderkamack Road
P.O. Box 418
Oradell, NJ 07649
(201) 967-8585

Howard Henke
Executive Director
NATIONAL COMMITTEE ON INTERNATIONAL
    TRADE DOCUMENTATION
350 Broadway #1200
New York, NY 10013
(212) 925-1400

George A. Gecowets
Vice President/Executive Director
NATIONAL COUNCIL OF PHYSICAL
    DISTRIBUTION MANAGEMENT
2803 Butterfield Road #380
Oak Brook, IL 60521
(312) 655-0985

Brig. General Malcolm P. Hooker
USAF (R)
President
NATIONAL DEFENSE TRANSPORTATION
    ASSOCIATION
727 N. Washington Street #220
Alexandria, VA 22314
(703) 836-3303

Arthur H. Klawans
Vice President—Industry Affairs
NATIONAL FOOD DISTRIBUTION
    ASSOCIATION
111 E. Wacker Drive
Chicago, IL 60601
(312) 644-6610

James E. Bartley
Executive Vice President
NATIONAL INDUSTRIAL TRAFFIC LEAGUE
1090 Vermont Avenue NW #410
Washington, DC 20005
(202) 842-3870

Raymond Ziemba
Traffic Manager
NATIONAL PERISHABLE TRANSPORTATION
    ASSOCIATION
Continental Freezers of Illinois
4220 S. Kildare Boulevard
Chicago, IL 60632
(312) 523-4850

James F. Slabe
Publisher
NATIONAL PRODUCTIVITY REPORT
33 West 60th Street
New York, NY 10023
(212) 489-5911

Joseph F. H. Cutrona
Executive Director
NATIONAL SMALL SHIPMENTS
    TRAFFIC CONFERENCE
1750 Pennsylvania Avenue NW #1116
Washington, DC 20006
(202) 393-5505

John T. Kane
Editor
NATIONAL SOCIETY OF PROFESSIONAL
    ENGINEERS

2029 K Street NW
Washington, DC 20006
(202) 331-7072

Richard C. Cook
Director Operations & Research
NATIONAL WHOLESALE DRUGGISTS
105 Oronoco Street
Alexandria, VA 22313
(703) 684-6400

Robert Gray
Editor
NATIONS BUSINESS
1615 H Street NW
Washington, DC 20062
(202) 463-5650

L.G. Goede
Secretary
NETHERLANDS ASSOCIATION FOR
LOGISTICS MANAGEMENT
Van Alkemadelaan 700
1597 AW DEN HAAG
Netherlands

John Lee
Financial Editor
NEW YORK TIMES
229 W 43rd Street
New York, NY 10036
(212) 556-1234

David Postal
Financial Editor
NEWS AMERICAN
Lombard and South Streets
Baltimore, MD 21203
(301) 752-1212

Paul T. Domer
Executive Director
OPERATIONS COUNCIL—ATA
1616 P Street NW
Washington, DC 20036
(202) 797-5438

Robert J. Bowman
Editor
PACIFIC SHIPPER
1139 Howard Street
San Francisco, CA 94103
(415) 981-7171

John P. Eichorn
Publisher & Editor
PACIFIC SHIPPER
P.O. Box 2000
Napa, CA 94558
(707) 252-3266

Nicole Knowton
Managing Editor
PACIFIC TRAFFIC
310 Washington Street
Washington Square Plaza #101
Marina del Ray, CA 90292
(213) 822-3132

R. Bruce Holmgren
Editor
PACKAGE ENGINEERING
1350 East Touhy Avenue
Des Plaines, IL 60018
(312) 635-8800

Sojiro Kamiyana
Chairperson
PHYSICAL DISTRIBUTION
    RATIONALIZATION INSTITUTE
1-8-16 Taiheidai, Tsujido
Fujisawa, Kanagawa
Japan 251
0466-36-7185

Vincent L. O'Donnell
Managing Director
PRIVATE CARRIER CONFERENCE—ATA
1616 P Street NW
Washington, DC 20036
(202) 797-5404

Richard D. Henderson
Executive Vice President
PRIVATE TRUCKING COUNCIL OF AMERICA
1101 17th Street NW
Washington, DC 20036
(202) 785-4900

Carl Wesselmann
Editor
PROGRESSIVE RAILROADING
20 N. Wacker Drive
Chicago, IL 60606
(312) 782-9592

Gus Welty
Editor
RAILWAY AGE
29 E. Madison Street
Chicago, IL 60602
(312) 641-5815

Nancy Burns
Executive Director
SALES & MARKETING COUNCIL—ATA
1616 P Street NW
Washington, DC 20036
(202) 797-5249

William J. Augello
Executive Director/General Council
SHIPPERS NATIONAL FREIGHT CLAIM
    COUNCIL INC.
120 Main Street
Huntington, NY 11743
(516) 549-8984

John Goodrum
SOCIETY OF LOGISTICS ENGINEERS
Park Plaza #922, 303
Williams Avenue
Huntsville, AL 35801
(205) 539-3800/3833

William C. Pflaum
Executive Director
SOCIETY OF PACKAGING &
    HANDLING ENGINEERS

Reston International
Reston, VA 22091
(703) 620-9380

Anne Pearce
Publisher
THE OFFICIAL EXPORT GUIDE
545 Madison Avenue
New York, NY 10022
(212) 371-4100

Frank Quinn
Editor
TRAFFIC MANAGEMENT
221 Columbus Avenue
Boston, MA 02116
(617) 536-7780

J. Delton Pattie
Vice President—Editor
TRAFFIC WORLD
1435 G Street NW #815
Washington, DC 20005
(202) 626-4515

William L. Smith
Editor
TRANSPORT TOPICS
1616 P Street NW
Washington, DC 20036
(202) 797-5251

Charles M. Naylor
Executive Director
TRANSPORTATION BROKERS OF AMERICA
P.O. Box 209
Oak Forest, IL 60452
(312) 687-0222

E. A. Guilbert
President
TRANSPORTATION DATA COORDINATING
    COMMITTEE
1101 17th Street NW #606

Washington, DC 20036-4775
(202) 293-5514

John C. Spychalski
Editor
TRANSPORTATION JOURNAL
509 Business Administrative Building
University Park, PA 16802
(814) 865-2872

Grant C. Vietsch
Vice President
TRANSPORTATION RESEARCH FORUM
P.O. Box AA
Northfield, NJ 08225
(609) 645-1639

Transportation Editor
WALL STREET JOURNAL
22 Cortlandt Street
New York, NY 10007
(212) 285-5000

Burr W. Hupp
Executive Director
WAREHOUSING EDUCATION
    & RESEARCH COUNCIL
4022 Countryview Drive
Sarasota, FL 33583
(813) 924-3544

Warren Blanding
Publisher
WAREHOUSING & PHYSICAL DISTRIBUTION
    PRODUCTIVITY REPORT
8701 Georgia Avenue #608
Silver Spring, MD 20910
(301) 585-0730

Dr. Guenther Pawellek
Editor
ZEITSCHRIFT FUER LOGISTIK
Kuehlenberg 65
Iserlohn 7, Germany 5860
(02374) 74328

Depositor–Warehouseman Agreements
Including Recommended Agreements Forms

TABLE OF CONTENTS

I. THE BACKGROUND

Since 1926, when the U.S. Department of Commerce gave its approval to a set of Standard Contract Terms and Conditions, which had been approved by warehousemen, carriers, and shippers, and designed to appear on the reverse of both negotiable and non-negotiable warehouse receipts, those Terms and Conditions, with various amendments through the years, have, along with the warehouse receipt form, represented the basic understanding between warehousemen and their customers.

In 1964, and again in 1968, revisions of the Standard Contract Terms and Conditions were included in a standard "Contract and Rate Quotation" document promulgated by the American Warehousemen's Association. While, in the great majority of instances, these are acceptable to the parties concerned, it has become evident that there are a number of customers of the public warehousing industry who feel that the Contract and Rate Quotation does not adequately set forth all that should be included in their particular warehouseman-depositor understanding. As a consequence, a number of warehousing customers have drafted contracts or agreements, unilaterally, and have offered them to the warehousemen with whom they were doing business or with whom they were contemplating doing business. In some instances, these contracts were not objectionable, but many of them contained contradictory, confusing, and poorly drawn clauses. Most serious, however, was the proposed imposition upon a warehouseman of a greater responsibility of care than that which is set forth in Article 7 of the Uniform Commercial Code, law in 49 states, and in the Uniform Warehouse Receipts Act, law in Louisiana. The major consequences were a warehouseman to sign such an agreement, both to the warehouseman and his customer, would be that his acceptance of additional liability might void his warehouseman's legal liability insurance, which in most instances provides the only source of payment for a major loss that might result from the warehouseman's failure to exercise the reasonable care required by statute.

In 1972, the American Warehousemen's Association began study, legal research, and consultation with customers of the industry with the intent of developing a new warehousing agreement that would adequately represent the proper interest of both depositor and warehouseman in those instances in which the Standard Contract Terms and Conditions might not be suitable. The "Warehousing Agreement" included herein is the result. It is for the most part based upon a warehousing agreement currently being used by one of America's major manufacturing companies, supplemented with additional clauses dealing with rail demurrage, truck detention, handling of damage, and receipt of contaminated or otherwise hazardous products.

The "Warehousing Agreement" also recognizes that no generally drawn contract can cover every possible detail of the individual requirements of every warehousing customer and therefore includes provision for additional understandings which do not conflict with the basic legal responsibility of both parties under the contract.

Finally, there are contained in this brochure discussions of further understandings that have been accepted in practice, in varying degree, dealing with the averaging of overages and shortages, shrinkage allowance, and waiver of subrogation.

CONTRACT AND RATE QUOTATION

TO _____

PROPOSAL DATE _____

COMMODITY, PACK, TYPE OF CONTAINER	SIZE (LENGTH, WIDTH, HEIGHT, CUBE)	GROSS WEIGHT	STG. RATE PER MONTH OR FRACTION THEREOF	HANDLING IN & OUT RATE
			PER	PER

ROUTING INSTRUCTIONS: SHIPMENTS TO BE CONSIGNED TO _____

IN CARE OF THE _____   DESTINATION _____

DELIVERING CARRIER _____

BILL OF LADING AND MANIFEST OF CONTENTS ARE TO BE RECEIVED BY WAREHOUSE BEFORE ARRIVAL OF SHIPMENT.

STANDARD CONTRACT TERMS AND CONDITIONS FOR MERCHANDISE WAREHOUSEMEN
(APPROVED AND PROMULGATED BY THE AMERICAN WAREHOUSEMEN'S ASSOCIATION, OCTOBER 1968)

ACCEPTANCE — Sec. 1

(a) This contract and rate quotation including accessorial charges endorsed on or attached hereto must be accepted within 30 days from the proposal date by signature of depositor on the reverse side of the contract. In the absence of written acceptance, the act of tendering goods described herein for storage or other services by warehouseman within 30 days from the proposal date shall constitute such acceptance by depositor.

(b) In the event that goods tendered for storage or other services do not conform to the description contained herein, or conforming goods are tendered after 30 days from the proposal date without prior written acceptance by depositor as provided in paragraph (a) of this section, warehouseman may refuse to accept such goods. If warehouseman accepts such goods, depositor agrees to rates and charges as may be assigned and invoiced by warehouseman and to all terms of this contract.

(c) This contract may be cancelled by either party upon 30 days written notice and is cancelled if no storage or other services are performed under this contract for a period of 180 days.

SHIPPING — Sec. 2

Depositor agrees not to ship goods to warehouseman as the named consignee. If, in violation of this agreement, goods are shipped to warehouseman as named consignee, depositor agrees to notify carrier in writing prior to such shipment, with copy of such notice to the warehouseman, that warehouseman named as consignee is a warehouseman and has no beneficial title or interest in such property and depositor further agrees to indemnify and hold harmless warehouseman from any and all claims for unpaid transportation charges, including undercharges, demurrage, detention or charges of any nature, in connection with goods so shipped. Depositor further agrees that, if it fails to notify carrier as required by the next preceding sentence, warehouseman shall have the right to refuse such goods and shall not be liable or responsible for any loss, injury or damage of any nature to, or related to, such goods. Depositor agrees that all promises contained in this section will be binding on depositor's heirs, successors and assigns.

TENDER FOR STORAGE — Sec. 3

All goods for storage shall be delivered at the warehouse properly marked and packaged for handling. The depositor shall furnish at or prior to such delivery, a manifest showing marks, brands, or sizes to be kept and accounted for separately, and the class of storage and other services desired.

STORAGE PERIOD AND CHARGES — Sec. 4

(a) All charges for storage are per package or other agreed unit per month.

(b) Storage charges become applicable upon the date that warehouseman accepts care, custody and control of the goods, regardless of unloading date or date of issue of warehouse receipt.

(CONTINUED)

(c) Except as provided in paragraph (d) of this section, a full month's storage charge will apply on all goods received between the first and the 15th, inclusive, of a calendar month; one-half month's storage charge will apply on all goods received between the 16th and last day, inclusive, of a calendar month, and a full month's storage charge will apply to all goods in storage on the first day of the next and succeeding calendar months. All storage charges are due and payable on the first day of storage for the initial month and thereafter on the first day of the calendar month.

(d) When mutually agreed by the warehouseman and the depositor, a storage month shall extend from a date in one calendar month to, but not including, the same date of the next and all succeeding months. All storage charges are due and payable on the first day of the storage month.

TRANSFER, TERMINATION OF STORAGE, REMOVAL OF GOODS — Sec. 5

(a) Instructions to transfer goods on the books of the warehouseman are not effective until delivered to and accepted by warehouseman, and all charges up to the time transfer is made are chargeable to the depositor of record. If a transfer involves rehandling the goods, such will be subject to a charge. When goods in storage are transferred from one party to another through issuance of a new warehouse receipt, a new storage date is established on the date of transfer.

(b) The warehouseman reserves the right to move, at his expense, 14 days after notice is sent by certified or registered mail to the depositor of record or to the last known holder of the negotiable warehouse receipt, any goods in storage from the warehouse in which they may be stored to any other of his warehouses; but if such depositor or holder takes delivery of his goods in lieu of transfer, no storage charge shall be made for the current storage month. The warehouseman may, without notice, move goods within the warehouse in which they are stored.

(c) The warehouseman may, upon written notice to the depositor of record and any other person known by the warehouseman to claim an interest in the goods, require the removal of any goods by the end of the next succeeding storage month. Such notice shall be given to the last known place of business or abode of the person to be notified. If goods are not removed before the end of the next succeeding storage month, the warehouseman may sell them in accordance with applicable law.

(d) If warehouseman in good faith believes that the goods are about to deteriorate or decline in value to less than the amount of warehouseman's lien before the end of the next succeeding storage month, the warehouseman may specify in the notification any reasonable shorter time for removal of the goods and in case the goods are not removed, may sell them at public sale held one week after a single advertisement or posting as provided by law.

(e) If as a result of a quality or condition of the goods of which the warehouseman had no notice at the time of deposit the goods are a hazard to other property or to persons, the warehouseman may sell the goods at public or private sale without advertisement on reasonable notification to all persons known to claim an interest in the goods. If the warehouseman after a reasonable effort is unable to sell the goods he may dispose of them in any lawful manner and shall incur no liability by reason of such disposition. Pending such disposition, sale or return of the goods, the warehouseman may remove the goods from the warehouse and shall incur no liability by reason of such removal.

HANDLING — Sec. 6

(a) The handling charge covers the ordinary labor involved in receiving goods at warehouse door, placing goods in storage, and returning goods to warehouse door. Handling charges are due and payable on receipt of goods.

(b) Unless otherwise agreed, labor for unloading and loading goods will be subject to a charge. Additional expenses incurred by the warehouseman in receiving and handling damaged goods, and additional expense in unloading from or loading into cars or other vehicles not at warehouse door will be charged to the depositor.

(c) Labor and materials used in loading rail cars or other vehicles are chargeable to the depositor.

(d) When goods are ordered out in quantities less than in which received, the warehouseman may make an additional charge for each order or each item of an order.

(e) The warehouseman shall not be liable for demurrage, delays in unloading inbound cars, or delays in obtaining and loading cars for outbound shipment unless warehouseman has failed to exercise reasonable care.

DELIVERY REQUIREMENTS — Sec. 7

(a) No goods shall be delivered or transferred except upon receipt by the warehouseman of complete instructions properly signed by the depositor. However, when no negotiable receipt is outstanding, goods may be delivered upon instructions by telephone in accordance with a prior written authorization, but the warehouseman shall not be responsible for loss or error occasioned thereby.

(b) When a negotiable receipt has been issued no goods covered by that receipt shall be delivered, or transferred on the books of the warehouseman, unless the receipt, properly indorsed, is surrendered for cancellation, or for indorsement of partial delivery thereon. If a negotiable receipt is lost or destroyed, delivery of goods may be made only upon order of a court of competent jurisdiction and the posting of security approved by the court as provided by law.

(c) When goods are ordered out a reasonable time shall be given the warehouseman to carry out instructions, and if he is unable because of acts of God, war, public enemies, seizure under legal process, strikes, lockouts, riots and civil commotions, or any reason beyond the warehouseman's control, or because of loss or destruction of goods for which warehouseman is not liable, or because of any other excuse provided by law, the warehouseman shall not be liable for failure to carry out such instructions and goods remaining in storage will continue to be subject to regular storage charges.

EXTRA SERVICES (SPECIAL SERVICES) — Sec. 8

(a) Warehouse labor required for services other than ordinary handling and storage will be charged to the depositor.

(b) Special services requested by depositor including but not limited to compiling of special stock statements; reporting marked weights, serial numbers or other data from packages; physical check of goods; and handling transit billing will be subject to a charge.

(c) Dunnage, bracing, packing materials or other special supplies, may be provided for the depositor at a charge in addition to the warehouseman's cost.

(d) By prior arrangement, goods may be received or delivered during other than usual business hours, subject to a charge.

(e) Communication expense including postage, teletype, telegram, or telephone, will be charged to the depositor if such concern more than normal inventory reporting or if, at the request of the depositor, communications are made by other than regular United States Mail.

BONDED STORAGE — Sec. 9

(a) A charge in addition to regular rates will be made for merchandise in bond.

(b) Where a warehouse receipt covers goods in U. S. Customs bond, such receipt shall be void upon the termination of the storage period fixed by law.

MINIMUM CHARGES — Sec. 10

(a) A minimum handling charge per lot and a minimum storage charge per lot per month will be made. When a warehouse receipt covers more than one lot or when a lot is in assortment, a minimum charge per mark, brand, or variety will be made.

(b) A minimum monthly charge to one account for storage and/or handling will be made. This charge will apply also to each account when one customer has several accounts, each requiring separate records and billing.

LIABILITY AND LIMITATION OF DAMAGES — Sec. 11

(A) THE WAREHOUSEMAN SHALL NOT BE LIABLE FOR ANY LOSS OR INJURY TO GOODS STORED HOWEVER CAUSED UNLESS SUCH LOSS OR INJURY RESULTED FROM THE FAILURE BY THE WAREHOUSEMAN TO EXERCISE SUCH CARE IN REGARD TO THEM AS A REASONABLY CAREFUL MAN WOULD EXERCISE UNDER LIKE CIRCUMSTANCES AND WAREHOUSEMAN IS NOT LIABLE FOR DAMAGES WHICH COULD NOT HAVE BEEN AVOIDED BY THE EXERCISE OF SUCH CARE.

(B) GOODS ARE NOT INSURED BY WAREHOUSEMAN AGAINST LOSS OR INJURY HOWEVER CAUSED.

(C) THE DEPOSITOR DECLARES THAT DAMAGES ARE LIMITED TO_____, PROVIDED, HOWEVER, THAT SUCH LIABILITY MAY AT THE TIME OF ACCEPTANCE OF THIS CONTRACT AS PROVIDED IN SECTION 1 BE INCREASED ON PART OR ALL OF THE GOODS HEREUNDER IN WHICH EVENT A MONTHLY CHARGE OF_____WILL BE MADE IN ADDITION TO THE REGULAR MONTHLY STORAGE CHARGE.

NOTICE OF CLAIM AND FILING OF SUIT — Sec. 12

(a) Claims by the depositor and all other persons must be presented in writing to the warehouseman within a reasonable time, and in no event longer than either 60 days after delivery of the goods by the warehouseman or 60 days after depositor of record or the last known holder of a negotiable warehouse receipt is notified by the warehouseman that loss or injury to part or all of the goods has occurred, whichever time is shorter.

(b) No action may be maintained by the depositor or others against the warehouseman for loss or injury to the goods stored unless timely written claim has been given as provided in paragraph (a) of this section and unless such action is commenced either within nine months after date of delivery by warehouseman or within nine months after depositor of record or the last known holder of a negotiable warehouse receipt is notified that loss or injury to part or all of the goods has occurred, whichever time is shorter.

(c) When goods have not been delivered, notice may be given of known loss or injury to the goods by mailing of a registered or certified letter to the depositor of record or to the last known holder of a negotiable warehouse receipt. Time limitations for presentation of claim in writing and maintaining of action after notice begin on the date of mailing of such notice by warehouseman.

Additional Terms and Conditions Applicable to this Contract and Rate Quotation.

Nothing entered hereon shall be construed to extend the warehouseman's liability beyond the standard of care specified in Section 11 above.

THE ABOVE QUOTATION IS HEREBY ACCEPTED AND TERMS HEREIN AGREED TO

_____
                 DEPOSITOR

BY _____ DATE _____   BY _____

WAREHOUSING AGREEMENT

THIS AGREEMENT, Made and entered into this _____ day of _____ , 19____ , by and between _____
(Company, City, State)
hereinafter referred to as "DEPOSITOR," and _____
hereinafter referred to as "WAREHOUSEMAN."

WITNESSETH

WHEREAS, DEPOSITOR is desirous of obtaining and utilizing certain warehouse facilities and services in the _____ area; and

WHEREAS, WAREHOUSEMAN has certain warehousing facilities and services of the type and kind desired by DEPOSITOR located at _____ ; and

WHEREAS, WAREHOUSEMAN desires to make said facilities and services commercially available to DEPOSITOR subject to the terms and conditions herein specified;

NOW, THEREFORE, for and in consideration of the mutual agreements, covenants and promises herein contained, it is hereby mutually agreed, covenanted and promised as follows:

ARTICLE I. TERM OF AGREEMENT

The term of this Agreement shall commence on the date of its execution by the parties thereto and shall continue thereafter in full force and effect for a period of _____ and shall thereafter automatically renew on a month-to-month basis subject only to either party's right to terminate at any time by serving not less than thirty (30) days prior written notice to that effect upon the other party, said notice to be effective upon receipt. This Agreement shall be deemed cancelled if DEPOSITOR does not store goods with WAREHOUSEMAN for any period exceeding one hundred and eighty (180) days.

ARTICLE II. ACCEPTANCE OF GOODS, RATES AND CHARGES

During the term of this Agreement, and any extensions or renewals thereof, WAREHOUSEMAN agrees to provide for DEPOSITOR certain warehousing facilities and services described in this Agreement and the attached Schedules "A" and "B" which are made a part hereof, and to accept and keep in a neat and orderly condition such goods described in Schedule "A" as from time to time may be tendered by DEPOSITOR. WAREHOUSEMAN further agrees to furnish sufficient personnel, equipment, and other accessories necessary to perform efficiently and with safety the services herein described. Rates and charges for public warehousing services are set forth in Schedule "A" and for extra services and conditions in Schedule "B". For any services not specified in Schedule "A" or Schedule "B", DEPOSITOR shall pay to WAREHOUSEMAN such consideration and compensation as may mutually be agreed upon. Consideration for WAREHOUSEMAN'S performance of this Agreement shall be paid to WAREHOUSEMAN by DEPOSITOR within _____ days after receipt by DEPOSITOR of WAREHOUSEMAN'S statement.

ARTICLE III. SHIPPING

DEPOSITOR agrees not to ship goods to WAREHOUSEMAN as the named consignee. If, in violation of this Agreement, goods are shipped to WAREHOUSEMAN as named consignee, DEPOSITOR agrees to notify carrier in writing prior to such shipment, with a copy of such notice to WAREHOUSEMAN, that WAREHOUSEMAN named as consignee is a warehouseman under law and has no beneficial title or interest in such property. DEPOSITOR further agrees to indemnify and hold harmless WAREHOUSEMAN from any and all claims for unpaid transportation charges, including undercharges, demurrage, detention, or charges of any nature, in connection with goods so shipped.

ARTICLE IV. TENDER FOR STORAGE

All goods tendered for storage shall be delivered at the warehouse in a segregated manner, properly marked and packaged for handling. DEPOSITOR shall furnish or cause to be furnished at or prior to such delivery, a manifest showing the goods to be kept and accounted for separately, and the class or type of storage and other services desired.

ARTICLE V. STORAGE PERIOD AND CHARGES

(A) Storage charges become applicable upon the date that WAREHOUSEMAN accepts care, custody and control of the goods, regardless of unloading date or date of issue of warehouse receipt.

(B) Unless otherwise stated in Schedule "A" hereof, storage rates and charges shall be computed and are due and payable as follows:

   1. Goods received on or after the first (1st) day of the month up to and including the fifteenth (15th) day of the month shall be assessed the full monthly storage charge;

   2. Goods received after the fifteenth (15th) day of the month up to and including the last day of the month shall be assessed one-half (½) of the full monthly storage charge; and

   3. A full month's storage charge will apply to all goods in storage on the first day of the next and succeeding calendar months. All storage charges are due and payable on the first day of storage for the initial month and thereafter on the first day of the calendar month.

ARTICLE VI. TRANSFER, TERMINATION OF STORAGE, REMOVAL OF GOODS

(A) Instructions to transfer goods on the books of WAREHOUSEMAN shall not be effective until said instructions are delivered to and accepted by WAREHOUSEMAN, and all charges up to the time transfer is made shall be chargeable to DEPOSITOR. If a transfer involves the rehandling of goods, it will be subject to rates and charges shown in the attached Schedule "A" or Schedule "B" or as otherwise mutually agreed upon. When goods in storage are transferred from one party to another through issuance of a new warehouse receipt, a new storage date is established on the date of such transfer.

(B) WAREHOUSEMAN may, without notice, move goods within the warehouse in which they are stored; but shall not, except as provided in VI (C), move goods to another location without prior consent of DEPOSITOR.

(C) If, as a result of a quality or condition of the goods of which WAREHOUSEMAN had no notice at the time of deposit, the goods are a hazard to other property or to the warehouse or to persons, WAREHOUSEMAN shall immediately notify DEPOSITOR and DEPOSITOR shall thereupon claim its interest in the said goods and remove them from the warehouse. Pending such disposition, the WAREHOUSEMAN may remove the goods from the warehouse and shall incur no liability by reason of such removal.

ARTICLE VII. HANDLING

(A) Handling rates and charges as shown in the attached Schedules shall, unless otherwise agreed, cover the ordinary labor involved in receiving goods at warehouse door or dock, placing goods in storage, and returning goods to warehouse door or dock. Additional expenses incurred by the warehouseman in loading or unloading cars or vehicles shall be at rates shown in attached Schedules or as otherwise mutually agreed upon.

(B) WAREHOUSEMAN shall not be liable for demurrage, detention or delays in unloading inbound cars or vehicles, or detention or delays in obtaining and loading cars or vehicles for outbound shipment unless WAREHOUSEMAN has failed to exercise reasonable care and judgment as determined by industry practice.

(C) If detention occurs for which WAREHOUSEMAN is liable under Paragraph (B) of this Article, payment of such detention shall be made by DEPOSITOR to the carrier and WAREHOUSEMAN shall reimburse DEPOSITOR for such payment. WAREHOUSEMAN shall keep records concerning the detention of vehicles to assist DEPOSITOR in processing any objection to carrier's imposition of detention charges.

(D) DEPOSITOR shall be responsible for payment of all demurrage charges resulting from receipt by WAREHOUSEMAN of more than _____ carloads of DEPOSITOR'S goods received in any regular working day.

ARTICLE VIII. DELIVERY REQUIREMENTS

(A) No goods shall be delivered or transferred except upon receipt by WAREHOUSEMAN of complete instructions properly signed by DEPOSITOR. However, when no negotiable receipt is outstanding, goods may be delivered or transferred upon instructions received by telephone, TWX, Dataphone or other agreed upon method of communication, but WAREHOUSEMAN shall not be responsible for loss or error occasioned thereby except as caused by WAREHOUSEMAN'S negligence.

(B) When goods are ordered out, a reasonable time shall be given WAREHOUSEMAN to carry out instructions, and if he is unable to because of acts of God, war, public enemies, seizure under legal process, strikes, lockout, riots and civil commotions, or any other reason beyond WAREHOUSEMAN'S reasonable control, or because of loss or destruction of goods for which WAREHOUSEMAN is not liable, or because of any other excuse provided by law, WAREHOUSEMAN shall not be liable for failure to carry out such instructions provided, however, that goods remaining in storage will continue to be subject to regular storage charges as provided for herein.

ARTICLE IX. EXTRA AND SPECIAL SERVICES

(A) Warehouse labor required for services other than ordinary handling and storage must be authorized by DEPOSITOR in advance. Rates and charges will be provided for herein or as mutually agreed by the parties hereto.

(B) Special services requested by DEPOSITOR will be subject to such charges as are provided herein or as mutually agreed upon in advance.

(C) Dunnage, bracing, packing materials or other special supplies used in cars or vehicles are chargeable to DEPOSITOR and may be provided at a mutually agreed upon charge in addition to WAREHOUSEMAN'S cost.

(D) By prior arrangement, goods may be received or delivered during other than usual business hours, subject to a reasonable charge.

(E) Communication expense including postage, teletype, telegram or telephone will be charged to DEPOSITOR if such expense is the result of more than normal inventory reporting or if, at the request of DEPOSITOR, communications are made by other than regular First Class United States Mail.

ARTICLE X. BONDED STORAGE

(A) A charge in addition to regular rates will be made for merchandise in bond.

(B) Where a warehouse receipt covers goods in U.S. Customs bond, such receipt shall be void upon the termination of the storage period fixed by law.

ARTICLE XI. INBOUND SHIPMENTS

(A) WAREHOUSEMAN shall immediately notify DEPOSITOR of any known discrepancy on inbound shipments and shall protect DEPOSITOR'S interest by placing an appropriate notation on the delivering carrier's shipping document.

(B) WAREHOUSEMAN may refuse to accept any goods that, because of infestation, contamination or damage, might cause infestation, contamination or damage to WAREHOUSEMAN'S premises or to other goods in the custody of WAREHOUSEMAN and shall immediately notify DEPOSITOR of such refusal and shall have no liability for any demurrage, detention, transportation or other charges by virtue of such refusal.

(C) All notices required under paragraphs A or B of this Article shall be directed to the attention of _____

_____ .

ARTICLE XII. LIABILITY AND LIMITATION OF DAMAGES

(A) WAREHOUSEMAN shall be liable for loss of or injury to all goods while under his care, custody and control when caused by his failure to exercise such care in regard to them as a reasonably careful man would exercise under like circumstances. He shall not be liable for damages which could not have been avoided by the exercise of such care.

(B) In consideration of the rates herein, DEPOSITOR declares that said damages will be limited to _____

ARTICLE XIII. LEGAL LIABILITY INSURANCE

WAREHOUSEMAN shall maintain at its sole expense and at all times during the life of this Agreement a policy or policies of legal liability insurance covering any loss, destruction or damage for which WAREHOUSEMAN has assumed responsibility under the terms of Article XII. WAREHOUSEMAN further agrees to provide satisfactory evidence of such insurance upon request by DEPOSITOR.

ARTICLE XIV. NOTICE OF LOSS AND DAMAGE, CLAIM AND FILING OF SUIT

(A) WAREHOUSEMAN agrees to notify DEPOSITOR promptly of any loss or damage, howsoever caused, to goods stored or handled under the terms of this Agreement. All such notices shall be directed to the

attention of _____

_____

(B) Claims by DEPOSITOR must be presented in writing to WAREHOUSEMAN not longer than either sixty (60) days after delivery of the goods by WAREHOUSEMAN or sixty (60) days after DEPOSITOR is notified by WAREHOUSEMAN that loss or injury to part or all of the goods has occurred, whichever time is shorter.

(C) No action may be maintained by DEPOSITOR against WAREHOUSEMAN for loss or injury to the goods stored unless timely written claim has been given as provided in paragraph (B) of this Article and unless such action is commenced either within nine (9) months after the date of delivery by WAREHOUSEMAN or within nine (9) months after DEPOSITOR is notified that loss or injury to part or all of the goods has occurred, whichever time is shorter.

(D) When goods have not been delivered, notice may be given of known loss or injury to the goods by the mailing of a registered or certified letter to DEPOSITOR. All such notices shall be directed to the at-

tention of _____

_____

Time limitations for presentation of claim in writing and maintaining of action after notice begin on the date of receipt of such notice by DEPOSITOR.

ARTICLE XV. RECORDS

DEPOSITOR reserves the right upon reasonable request to enter WAREHOUSEMAN'S premises during normal working hours to examine and count all or any of the goods stored under the terms of this Agreement. WAREHOUSEMAN shall at all reasonable times permit DEPOSITOR to examine its books, records and accounts for the purpose of reconciling quantities and determining with WAREHOUSEMAN whether certain amounts are payable within the meaning of the Agreement.

ARTICLE XVI. INDEPENDENT CONTRACTOR

It is hereby agreed and understood that WAREHOUSEMAN is entering into this Agreement as an independent contractor and that all of WAREHOUSEMAN'S personnel engaged in work to be done under the terms of this Agreement are to be considered as employees of WAREHOUSEMAN and under no circumstances shall they be construed or considered to be employees of DEPOSITOR.

ARTICLE XVII. COMPLIANCE WITH LAWS, ORDINANCES, RULES AND REGULATIONS

(A) WAREHOUSEMAN shall comply with all laws, ordinances, rules and regulations of Federal, State, municipal and other governmental authorities and the like in connection with the safeguarding, receiving, storing and handling of goods.

(B) DEPOSITOR shall be responsible for advising WAREHOUSEMAN of all laws, ordinances, rules and regulations of Federal, State, municipal and other governmental authorities and the like relating specifically to the safeguarding, receiving, storing and handling of DEPOSITOR'S products.

ARTICLE XVIII. NOTIFICATION OF PRODUCT CHARACTERISTICS

DEPOSITOR shall notify WAREHOUSEMAN of the characteristics of any of DEPOSITOR'S products that may in any way be likely to cause damage to WAREHOUSEMAN'S premises or to other products that may be stored by WAREHOUSEMAN.

ARTICLE XIX. ASSIGNMENT

This Warehousing Agreement shall inure to the benefit of and be binding upon the successors and assigns of the parties hereto, provided neither party to this Agreement shall assign or sublet its interest or obligations herein, including but not limited to the assignment of any monies due and payable, without the prior written consent of the other party.

ARTICLE XX. APPLICABLE STATUTES

The parties understand and agree that the provisions of Article 7 of the Uniform Commercial Code as enacted by the State law governing this Warehousing Agreement shall apply to this Warehousing Agreement. (In the State of Louisiana the provisions of the Uniform Warehouse Receipts Act shall apply.)

ARTICLE XXI. ADDITIONAL TERMS AND CONDITIONS

(Nothing entered hereon shall be construed to extend WAREHOUSEMAN'S liability beyond the standard of care specified in Article XII (A) above.)

ARTICLE XXII.

This Agreement constitutes the entire understanding between DEPOSITOR and WAREHOUSEMAN, and no working arrangements, instructions, or operating manuals intended to facilitate the effective carrying out of this Agreement shall in any way affect the liabilities of either party as set forth herein.

IN WITNESS WHEREOF, the parties hereto have duly executed this Agreement in duplicate the day and year first above written.

WAREHOUSEMAN

By:_____

DEPOSITOR

By:_____

SCHEDULE A
STORAGE AND HANDLING RATES AND CHARGES

Attached to and made a part of Agreement dated the _____ day of

_____ , 19 _____ , by and between _____

_____and_____

DEPOSITOR

_____.

WAREHOUSEMAN

SCHEDULE B
ACCESSORIAL RATES AND CHARGES

Attached to and made a part of Agreement dated the _____ day of _____ , 19 _____ ,

by and between _____ and

DEPOSITOR

_____ .

WAREHOUSEMAN

ADDITIONAL CONTRACT CONDITIONS AND CONSIDERATIONS

AVERAGING OF OVERAGES AND SHORTAGES

The concept of warehousemen and depositors averaging routine "overs" and "shorts" has for many years been considered valid on an almost universal basis, but the manner in which overages and shortages are averaged ranges widely. At one extreme we find simple letter agreements stating, without further explanation, that "overages and shortages will be averaged out," leaving to the parties the resolving of how this will be done, presumably upon the basis of individual facts in a situation and in a manner that is equitable to both. Depending upon the good faith of both parties, this appears to have worked fairly well. Somewhere in the middle, there are written attempts to set forth the understanding in more detail. At the other extreme, although admittedly not frequently, there are letter agreements in which the depositor states to the warehouseman simply, "You will pay us for all shortages and we will pay you for all overages."

For a long time, even though the obvious intent of both parties is that neither will receive an unearned "windfall" at the expense of the other, one area of the overages and shortages situation has generally been ignored by most warehousemen and depositors, and this has to do with the definition of the word "shortage." It appears that the customary intent of warehousemen and depositors is that averaging arrangements handle the normal relatively minor (in relation to total volume) overages and shortages that may be expected in the normal course of business due to clerical error, faulty inventory count, over or under shipments on the part of either depositor or warehouseman, and the like. Few, if any, understandings regarding the averaging of overages and shortages, however, place any quantity, percentage, or dollar limitation on the averaging arrangements.

It is not contended that a warehouseman has either right or title to overages. It would be, however, improper and unwise for a warehouseman to assume responsibility for a "shortage" with no limitation on the amount and without regard to the question of whether or not he has exercised the reasonable care required by law. In fact, there is the serious probability that the warehouseman's so doing might be considered as assuming a liability that would negate his warehouseman's legal liability insurance.

While it is recognized that, in many instances, accounting procedures of both depositor and warehouseman cannot allow adjustment from one inventory period to another "ad infinitum," equitableness demands that provision should be made for adjustment from one period to the next in the case of obvious miscount or proven clerical error. There have been numerous situations, at least one of which involved several hundred thousand dollars, in which a shortage was indicated at the end of an inventory period. Subsequent investigations disclosed that the depositor had never shipped the supposedly "short" product, that the supposed shortage never existed, and actually resulted from a clerical error or (as in the case of the large item referred to) computer malfunction. Similar situations have existed as to overages. Obviously, these possibilities should be considered in any effort to set forth an understanding with respect to this subject.

It would appear to be best to clearly define in detail the circumstances under which overages and shortages will be averaged, the method of settlement, and the method and basis for determination of values involved, and the following is intended to accomplish that definition:

1. *Inventory Period.* The period for settling stock differences shall be _____ months, each period ending on the _____ (day) of _____ (month), or a date as near thereto as may be mutually agreed upon by Depositor and Warehouseman. Joint Depositor-Warehouseman physical inventories will be taken on those dates.

2. Additional physical inventories may be taken by Depositor's personnel at any time during normal working hours of Warehouseman, provided that such personnel must, for security and safety reasons, be accompanied by an employee of Warehouseman and, provided further, that Warehouseman shall be reimbursed on the hourly basis as set forth in Schedule "B" or as separately agreed, for time of Warehouseman's employee or employees so engaged.

3. If stock differences are found in any count, the Warehouseman will list gains as receipts, and losses as deductions, thus correcting the book record to agree with the actual stock on hand. These changes will be based upon counts agreed to and signed by Depositor's representative and Warehouseman's representative.

4. For purposes of determining the net balance on the Warehouseman's account, all debits and credits for the period shall be netted together without regard to commodity group.

5. If there be a net-money debit balance for the period covered, after netting across commodity lines, that amount shall be payable to Depositor by Warehouseman. Unless otherwise agreed, if there be a net-money credit on the account, the account shall be closed.

6. The dollar values used to establish the net-money balance shall be _____

_____

_____

_____

7. Carry-over of net debits or net credits from a settlement period to succeeding ones, or carry-back to preceding periods will not be made except under one or more of the following conditions:

   a. Proven miscount in physical inventory,

   b. Proven clerical error by either Depositor or Warehouseman,

   c. Located or recovered mis-shipment.

8. The maximum total payment by Warehouseman to Depositor for shortage in any one inventory period as defined in Paragraph 1, above, shall be $_____. Payment by Warehouseman for any greater net-money debit shall depend upon determination of whether, with respect to the shortage involved, Warehouseman has exercised the degree of care that a reasonably careful man would exercise under similar conditions (Article 7-204, Uniform Commercial Code).

SHRINKAGE ALLOWANCE

While not a universal practice, an increasing number of depositor-warehouseman understandings recognize that the nature, variety, and volume of products handled, and reduction in the quality of packaging that cause carton failure in handling and in the stack may result in a small percentage of loss in both the depositor's own facilities as well as those of the warehouseman. These understandings, permitting a "shrinkage allowance," result from two considerations.

The first is recognition that the clerical and administrative time involved in making adjustments can cost more than the loss involved. The second is acceptance of the "reasonably careful man" concept of care set forth in the Uniform Commercial Code, it being the assumption that the depositor in the operation of his own facilities is reasonably careful, that he suffers "shrinkage" of a certain percent, and that the reasonably careful warehouseman should not be asked to assume liability should he fail to do better than the depositor.

The following article meets the above described situation:

> In further consideration of the rates herein, and in keeping with the definitions of warehouseman's legal liability contained herein and in Article 7-204 of the Uniform Commercial Code, Depositor agrees to a shrinkage allowance of _____ % of the value of the goods stored for which, in the case of loss or damage to goods or mysterious disappearance, however caused, Warehouseman will not be liable.

WAIVER OF SUBROGATION

Most manufacturers, as a matter of sound business practice, carry "output insurance" on their goods (raw product through delivery of the finished product) wherever they may be—in their own facilities, in transportation, or in public warehousing. Practically all warehousemen carry warehouseman's legal liability insurance to cover losses which may result from their failure to exercise the reasonable care required by law. The goods in the hands of the warehousemen are, therefore, the object of double insurance. If there is a major loss, the depositor's output insurance covers, because payment is not dependent upon the circumstances involved. Since no insurance company likes to pay a loss, it is not uncommon for the depositor's insuror to gamble that a case of negligence can be made against the warehouseman, retain counsel on a contingent fee basis, and, (in the name of the depositor) sue the warehouseman. This is referred to as "subrogation." Subrogation is particulary appealing to the depositor's insurance company because the premium rates on output insurance do not include any reduction factor for subrogation and, if the courts find the warehouseman negligent, the warehouseman's insurance company pays for the loss, resulting in a boon to the depositor's insuror.

The "double" insurance and expenses of litigation constitute an additional cost of doing business that, while hidden in the warehouseman's insurance premiums, must be reflected in charges for his services. In recognition of this, some depositors have provided the warehouseman with a "waiver of subrogation" (which is permitted under manufacturers' output policies) which waiver prevents depositor's insuror from seeking recovery on a loss paid under the policy. The waiver does not include any dollar loss that is less than the deductible in the depositor's policy.

One known waiver of subrogation clause, reflecting the above considerations, is as follows:

> In further consideration of the rates herein, Depositor, for itself and its insurers, waives all claims against Warehouseman for loss and damage to goods, however caused, to the extent that such claims exceed $_____ or the amount of the deductible on insurance carried by Depositor applicable to loss and damage to such goods, whichever is less.

HAZARDOUS MATERIALS

Increased regulations and new laws designed to protect the public have placed new responsibilities upon warehousemen. The regulations of the U.S. Department of Transportation concerning the shipping requirements for hazardous substances are the most extensive. To conform with these regulations a warehouseman must be furnished with necessary instructions and information. For warehouse agreements which will cover such substances the following language may be helpful:

> When Depositor requests that Warehouseman ship goods of the Depositor which are considered hazardous materials under the regulations of the U.S. Department of Transportation, Depositor agrees to advise Warehouseman that such goods are hazardous under the regulations and to furnish Warehouseman with all the correct and necessary information and instructions to permit Warehouseman to prepare the shipment, and necessary shipping papers and certifications, to conform with the regulations, and Depositor appoints Warehouseman as its agent for the purpose of preparing the shipment and signing the certifications and shipping papers covering the shipment.

APPENDIX

Uniform Commercial Code, Article 7

**Warehouse Receipts, Bills of Lading
and Other Documents of Title**

PART I

GENERAL

Sec. 7-101. *Short Title*

This Article shall be known and may be cited as Uniform Commercial Code—Documents of Title.

Sec. 7-102. *Definitions and Index of Definitions.*

(1) In this Article, unless the context otherwise requires:

    (a) "Bailee" means the person who by a warehouse receipt, bill of lading, or other document of title acknowledges possession of goods and contracts to deliver them.

    (b) "Consignee" means the person named in a bill to whom or to whose order the bill promises delivery.

    (c) "Consignor" means the person named in a bill as the person from whom the goods have been received for shipment.

    (d) "Delivery order" means a written order to deliver goods directed to a warehouseman, carrier or other person who in the ordinary course of business issues warehouse receipts or bills of lading.

    (e) "Document" means document of titles as defined in the general definitions in Article 1 (Section 1-201).

    (f) "Goods" means all things which are treated as movable for the purposes of a contract of storage or transportation.

    (g) "Issuer" means a bailee who issues a document except that in relation to an unaccepted delivery order it means the person who orders the possessor of goods to deliver. Issuer includes any person for whom an agent or employee purports to act in issuing a document if the agent or employee has real or apparent authority to issue documents, notwithstanding that the issuer received no goods or that the goods were misdescribed or that in any other respect the agent or employee violated his instructions.

    (h) "Warehouseman" is a person engaged in the business of storing goods for hire.

(2) Other definitions applying to this Article or to specified Parts thereof, and the sections in which they appear are:

        "Duly negotiate." Section.7-501.

        "Person entitled under the document." Section 7-403(4).

(3) Definitions in other Articles applying to this Article and the sections in which they appear are:

        "Contract for sale." Section 2-106.

        "Overseas." Section 2-323.

        "Receipt" of goods. Section 2-103.

(4) In addition Article 1 contains general definitions and principles of construction and interpretation applicable throughout this Article.

Sec. 7-103. *Relation of Article to Treaty, Statute, Tariff, Classification or Regulation.*

To the extent that any treaty or statute of the United States, regulatory statute of this State or tariff, classification or regulation filed or issued pursuant thereto is applicable, the provisions of this Article are subject thereto.

Sec. 7-104. *Negotiable and Non-Negotiable Warehouse Receipt, Bill of Lading or Other Doument of Title.*

(1) A warehouse receipt, bill of lading or other document of title is negotiable

    (a) if by its terms the goods are to be delivered to bearer or to the order of a named person; or

    (b) where recognized in overseas trade, if it runs to a named person or assigns.

(2) Any other document is non-negotiable. A bill of lading in which it is stated that the goods are consigned to a named person is not made negotiable by a provision that the goods are to be delivered only against a written order signed by the same or another person.

Sec. 7-105. *Construction Against Negative Implication.*

The omission from either Part 2 or Part 3 of this Article of a provision corresponding to a provision made in the other Part does not imply that a corresponding rule of law is not applicable.

PART 2

WAREHOUSE RECEIPTS: SPECIAL PROVISIONS

Sec. 7-201. *Who May Issue a Warehouse Receipt; Storage Under Government Bond.*

(1) A warehouse receipt may be issued by any warehouseman.

(2) Where goods including distilled spirits and agricultural commodities are stored under a statute requiring a bond against withdrawal or a license for the issuance of receipts in the nature of warehouse receipts, a receipt issued for the goods has like effect as a warehouse receipt even though issued by a person who is the owner of the goods and is not a warehouseman.

Sec. 7-202. *Form of Warehouse Receipt; Essential Terms; Optional Terms.*

(1) A warehouse receipt need not be in any particular form.

(2) Unless a warehouse receipt embodies within its written or printed terms each of the following, the warehouseman is liable for damages caused by the omission to a person injured thereby:

(a) the location of the warehouse where the goods are stored;

(b) the date of issue of the receipt;

(c) the consecutive number of the receipt;

(d) a statement whether the goods received will be delivered to the bearer, to a specified person, or to a specified person or his order;

(e) the rate of storage and handling charges, except that where goods are stored under a field warehousing arrangement a statement of that fact is sufficient on a non-negotiable receipt;

(f) a description of the goods or of the packages containing them;

(g) the signature of the warehouseman, which may be made by his authorized agent;

(h) if the receipt is issued for goods of which the warehouseman is owner, either solely or jointly or in common with others, the fact of such ownership; and

(i) a statement of the amount of advances made and of liabilities incurred for which the warehouseman claims a lien or security interest (Section 7-209). If the precise amount of such advances made or of such liabilities incurred is, at the time of the issue of the receipt, unknown to the warehouseman or to his agent who issues it, a statement of the fact that advances have been made or liabilities incurred and the purpose thereof is sufficient.

(3) A warehouseman may insert in his receipt any other terms which are not contrary to the provisions of this Act and do not impair his obligation of delivery (Section 7-403) or his duty of care (Section 7-204). Any contrary provisions shall be ineffective.

Sec. 7-203. *Liability for Non-Receipt or Misdescription.*

A party to or purchaser for value in good faith of a document of title other than a bill of lading relying in either case upon the description therein of the goods may recover from the issuer damages caused by the non-receipt or misdescription of the goods, except to the extent that the document conspicuously indicates that the issuer does not know whether any part or all of the goods in fact were received or conform to the description, as where the description is in terms of marks or labels or kind, quantity or condition, or the receipt or description is qualified by "contents, condition and quality unknown," "said to contain" or the like, if such indication be true, or the party or purchaser otherwise has notice.

Sec. 7-204. *Duty of Care; Contractual Limitation of Warehouseman's Liability.*

(1) A warehouseman is liable for damages for loss of or injury to the goods caused by his failure to exercise such care in regard to them as a reasonably careful man would exercise under like circumstances but unless otherwise agreed he is not liable for damages which could not have been avoided by the exercise of such care.

(2) Damages may be limited by a term in the warehouse receipt or storage agreement limiting the amount of liability in case of loss or damage, and setting forth a specific liability per article or item, or value per unit of weight, beyond which the warehouseman shall not be liable; provided, however, that such liability may on written request of the bailor at the time of signing such storage agreement or within a reasonable time after

receipt of the warehouse receipt be increased on part or all of the goods thereunder, in which event increased rates may be charged based on such increased valuation, but that no such increase shall be permitted contrary to a lawful limitation of liability contained in the warehouseman's tariff, if any. No such limitation is effective with respect to the warehouseman's liability for conversion to his own use.

(3) Reasonable provisions as to the time and manner of presenting claims and instituting actions based on the bailment may be included in the warehouse receipt or tariff.

(4) This section does not impair or repeal . . .

NOTE: Insert in subsection (4) a reference to any statute which imposes a higher responsibility upon the warehouseman or invalidates contractual limitations which would be permissible under this Article.

Sec. 7-205. *Title Under Warehouse Receipt Defeated in Certain Cases.*

A buyer in the ordinary course of business of fungible goods sold and delivered by a warehouseman who is also in the business of buying and selling such goods takes free of any claim under a warehouse receipt even though it has been duly negotiated.

Sec. 7-206. *Termination of Storage at Warehouseman's Option.*

(1) A warehouseman may on notifying the person on whose account the goods are held and any other person known to claim an interest in the goods require payment of any charges and removal of the goods from the warehouse at the termination of the period of storage fixed by the document, or, if no period is fixed, within a stated period not less than thirty days after the notification. If the goods are not removed before the date specified in the notification, the warehouseman may sell them in accordance with the provisions of the section on enforcement of a warehouseman's lien (Section 7-210).

(2) If a warehouseman in good faith believes that the goods are about to deteriorate or decline in value to less than the amount of his lien within the time prescribed in subsection (1) for notification, advertisement and sale, the warehouseman may specify in the notification any reasonable shorter time for removal of the goods and in case the goods are not removed, may sell them at public sale held not less than one week after a single advertisement or posting.

(3) If as a result of a quality or condition of the goods of which the warehouseman had no notice at the time of deposit the goods are a hazard to other property or to the warehouse or to persons, the warehouseman may sell the goods at public or private sale without advertisement on reasonable notification to all persons known to claim an interest in the goods. If the warehouseman after a reasonable effort is unable to sell the goods he may dispose of them in any lawful manner and shall incur no liability by reason of such disposition.

(4) The warehouseman must deliver the goods to any person entitled to them under this Article upon due demand made at any time prior to sale or other disposition under this section.

(5) The warehouseman may satisfy his lien from the proceeds of any sale or disposition under this section but must hold the balance for delivery on the demand of any person to whom he would have been bound to deliver the goods.

Sec. 7-207. *Goods Must Be Kept Separate; Fungible Goods.*

(1) Unless the warehouse receipt otherwise provides, a warehouseman must keep separate the goods covered by each receipt so as to permit at all times identification and delivery of those goods except that different lots of fungible goods may be commingled.

(2) Fungible goods so commingled are owned in common by the persons entitled thereto and the warehouseman is severally liable to each owner for that owner's share. Where because of overissue a mass of fungible goods is insufficient to meet all the receipts which the warehouseman has issued against it, the persons entitled include all holders to whom overissued receipts have been duly negotiated.

Sec. 7-208. *Altered Warehouse Receipts.*

Where a blank in a negotiable warehouse receipt has been filled in without authority, a purchaser for value and without notice of the want of authority may treat the insertion as authorized. Any other unauthorized alteration leaves any receipt enforceable against the issuer according to its original tenor.

Sec. 7-209. *Lien of Warehouseman.*

(1) A warehouseman has a lien against the bailor on the goods covered by a warehouse receipt or on the proceeds thereof in his possession for charges for storage or transportation (including demurrage and terminal charges), insurance, labor, or charges present or future in relation to the goods, and for expenses necessary for preservation of the goods or reasonably incurred in their sale pursuant to law. If the person on whose account the goods are held is liable for like charges or expenses in relation to other goods whenever deposited

and it is stated in the receipt that a lien is claimed for charges and expenses in relation to other goods, the warehouseman also has a lien against him for such charges and expenses whether or not the other goods have been delivered by the warehouseman. But against a person to whom a negotiable warehouse receipt is duly negotiated a warehouseman's lien is limited to charges in an amount or at a rate specified on the receipt or if no charges are so specified then to a reasonable charge for storage of the goods covered by the receipt subsequent to the date of the receipt.

(2) The warehouseman may also reserve a security interest against the bailor for a maximum amount specified on the receipt for charges other than those specified in subsection (1), such as for money advanced and interest. Such a security interest is governed by the Article on Secured Transactions (Article 9).

(3) A warehouseman's lien for charges and expenses under subsection (1) or a security interest under subsection (2) is also effective against any person who so entrusted the bailor with possession of the goods that a pledge of them by him to a good faith purchaser for value would have been valid but is not effective against a person as to whom the document confers no right in the goods covered by it under Section 7-503.

(4) A warehouseman loses his lien on any goods which he voluntarily delivers or which he unjustifiably refuses to deliver.

Sec. 7-210. *Enforcement of Warehouseman's Lien.*

(1) Except as provided in subsection (2), a warehouseman's lien may be enforced by public or private sale of the goods in bloc or in parcels, at any time or place and on any terms which are commercially reasonable, after notifying all persons known to claim an interest in the goods. Such notification must include a statement of the amount due, the nature of the proposed sale and the time and place of any public sale. The fact that a better price could have been obtained by a sale at a different time or in a different method from that selected by the warehouseman is not of itself sufficient to establish that the sale was not made in a commercially reasonable manner. If the warehouseman either sells the goods in the usual manner in any recognized market therefor, or if he sells at the price current in such market at the time of his sale, or if he has otherwise sold in conformity with commercially reasonable practices among dealers in the type of goods sold, he has sold in a commercially reasonable manner. A sale of more goods than apparently necessary to be offered to insure satisfaction of the obligation is not commercially reasonable except in cases covered by the preceding sentence.

(2) A warehouseman's lien on goods other than goods stored by a merchant in the course of his business may be enforced only as follows:

    (a) All persons known to claim an interest in the goods must be notified.

    (b) The notification must be delivered in person or sent by registered letter to the last known address of any person to be notified.

    (c) The notification must include an itemized statement of the claim, a description of the goods subject to the lien, a demand for payment within a specified time not less than ten days after receipt of the notification, and a conspicuous statement that unless the claim is paid within that time the goods will be advertised for sale and sold by auction at a specified time and place.

    (d) The sale must conform to the terms of the notification.

    (e) The sale must be held at the nearest suitable place to that where the goods are held or stored.

    (f) After the expiration of the time given in the notification, an advertisement of the sale must be published once a week for two weeks consecutively in a newspaper of general circulation where the sale is to be held. The advertisement must include a description of the goods, the name of the person on whose account they are being held, and the time and place of the sale. The sale must take place at least fifteen days after the first publication. If there is no newspaper of general circulation where the sale is to be held, the advertisement must be posted at least ten days before the sale in not less than six conspicuous places in the neighborhood of the proposed sale.

(3) Before any sale pursuant to this section any person claiming a right in the goods may pay the amount necessary to satisfy the lien and the reasonable expenses incurred under this section. In that event the goods must not be sold, but must be retained by the warehouseman subject to the terms of the receipt of this Article.

(4) The warehouseman may buy at any public sale pursuant to this section.

(5) A purchaser in good faith of goods sold to enforce a warehouseman's lien takes the goods free of any rights of persons against whom the lien was valid, despite noncompliance by the warehouseman with the requirements of this section.

(6) The warehouseman may satisfy his lien from the proceeds of any sale pursuant to this section but must hold

the balance, if any, for delivery on demand to any person to whom he would have been bound to deliver the goods.

(7) The rights provided by this section shall be in addition to all other rights allowed by law to a creditor against his debtor.

(8) Where a lien is on goods stored by a merchant in the course of his business the lien may be enforced in accordance with either subsection (1) or (2).

(9) The warehouseman is liable for damages caused by failure to comply with the requirements for sale under this section and in case of willful violation is liable for conversion.

PART 3

BILLS OF LADING: SPECIAL PROVISIONS

(Omitted)

PART 4

WAREHOUSE RECEIPTS AND BILLS OF LADING: GENERAL OBLIGATIONS

Sec. 7-401. *Irregularities in Issue of Receipt or Bill or Conduct of Issuer.*

The obligations imposed by this Article on an issuer apply to a document of title regardless of the fact that

(a) the document may not comply with the requirements of this Article or of any other law or regulation regarding its issue, form or content; or

(b) the issuer may have violated laws regulating the conduct of his business; or

(c) the goods covered by the document were owned by the bailee at the time the document was issued; or

(d) the person issuing the document does not come within the definition of warehouseman if it purports to be a warehouse receipt.

Sec. 7-402. *Duplicate Receipt or Bill; Overissue.*

Neither a duplicate nor any other document of title purporting to cover goods already represented by an outstanding document of the same issuer confers any right in the goods, except as provided in the case of bills in a set, overissue of documents for fungible goods and substitutes for lost, stolen or destroyed documents. But the issuer is liable for damages caused by his overissue or failure to identify a duplicate document as such by conspicuous notation on its face.

Sec. 7-403. *Obligation of Warehouseman or Carrier to Deliver; Excuse.*

(1) The bailee must deliver the goods to a person entitled under the document who complies with subsections (2) and (3), unless and to the extent that the bailee establishes any of the following:

(a) delivery of the goods to a person whose receipt was rightful as against the claimant;

(b) damage to or delay, loss or destruction of the goods for which the bailee is not liable [but the burden of establishing negligence in such cases is on the person entitled under the document];

NOTE: The brackets in (1) (b) indicate that State enactments may differ on this point without serious damage to the principle of uniformity.

(c) previous sale or other disposition of the goods in lawful enforcement of a lien or on warehouseman's lawful termination of storage;

(d) the exercise by a seller of his right to stop delivery pursuant to the provisions of the Article on Sales (Section 2-705);

(e) a diversion, reconsignment or other disposition pursuant to the provisions of this Article (Section 7-303) or tariff regulating such right;

(f) release, satisfaction or any other fact affording a personal defense against the claimant;

(g) any other lawful excuse.

(2) A person claiming goods covered by a document of title must satisfy the bailee's lien where the bailee so requests or where the bailee is prohibited by law from delivering the goods until the charges are paid.

(3) Unless the person claiming is one against whom the document confers no right under Sec. 7-503 (1), he must surrender for cancellation or notation of partial deliveries any outstanding negotiable document covering the

goods, and the bailee must cancel the document or conspicuously note the partial delivery thereon or be liable to any person to whom the document is duly negotiated.

(4) "Person entitled under the document" means holder in the case of a negotiable document, or the person to whom delivery is to be made by the terms of or pursuant to written instructions under a non-negotiable document.

Sec. 7-404. *No Liability for Good Faith Delivery Pursuant to Receipt or Bill.*

A bailee who in good faith including observance of reasonable commercial standards has received goods and delivered or otherwise disposed of them according to the terms of the document of title or pursuant to this Article is not liable therefor. This rule applies even though the person from whom he received the goods had no authority to procure the document or to dispose of the goods and even though the person to whom he delivered the goods had no authority to receive them.

PART 5

WAREHOUSE RECEIPTS AND BILLS OF LADING: NEGOTIATION AND TRANSFER

Sec. 7-501. *Form of Negotiation and Requirements of "Due Negotiation."*

(1) A negotiable document of title running to the order of a named person is negotiated by his indorsement and delivery. After his indorsement in blank or to bearer any person can negotiate it by delivery alone.

(2) (a) A negotiable document of title is also negotiated by delivery alone when by its original terms it runs to bearer.

   (b) When a document running to the order of a named person is delivered to him the effect is the same as if the document had been negotiated.

(3) Negotiation of a negotiable document of title after it has been indorsed to a specified person requires indorsement by the special endorsee as well as delivery.

(4) A negotiable document of title is "duly negotiated" when it is negotiated in the manner stated in this section to a holder who purchases it in good faith without notice of any defense against or claim to it on the part of any person and for value, unless it is established that the negotiation is not in the regular course of business or financing or involves receiving the document in settlement or payment of a money obligation.

(5) Indorsement of a non-negotiable document neither makes it negotiable nor adds to the transferee's rights.

(6) The naming in a negotiable bill of a person to be notified of the arrival of the goods does not limit the negotiability of the bill nor constitute notice to a purchaser thereof of any interest of such person in the goods.

Sec. 7-502. *Rights Acquired by Due Negotiation.*

(1) Subject to the following section and to the provisions of Section 7-205 on fungible goods, a holder to whom a negotiable document of title has been duly negotiated acquires thereby:

   (a) title to the document;

   (b) title to the goods;

   (c) all rights accruing under the law of agency or estoppel, including rights to goods delivered to the bailee after the document was issued; and

   (d) the direct obligation of the issuer to hold or deliver the goods according to the terms of the document free of any defense or claim by him except those arising under the terms of the document or under this Article. In the case of a delivery order the bailee's obligation accrues only upon acceptance and the obligation acquired by the holder is that the issuer and any indorser will procure the acceptance of the bailee.

(2) Subject to the following section, title and rights so acquired are not defeated by any stoppage of the goods represented by the document or by surrender of such goods by the bailee, and are not impaired even though the negotiation or any prior negotiation constituted a breach of duty or even though any person has been deprived of possession of the document by misrepresentation, fraud, accident, mistake, duress, loss, theft or conversion, or even though a previous sale or other transfer of the goods or document has been made to a third person.

Sec. 7-503. *Document of Title to Goods Defeated in Certain Cases.*

(1) A document of title confers no right in goods against a person who before issuance of the document had a legal interest or a perfected security interest in them and who neither

(a) delivered or entrusted them or any document of title covering them to the bailor or his nominee with actual or apparent authority to ship, store or sell or with power to obtain delivery under this Article (Section 7-403) or with power of disposition under this Act (Sections 2-403 and 9-307) or other statute or rule of law; nor

(b) acquiesced in the procurement by the bailor or his nominee of any document of title.

(2) Title to goods based upon an unaccepted delivery order is subject to the rights of anyone to whom a negotiable warehouse receipt or bill of lading covering the goods has been duly negotiated. Such a title may be defeated under the next section to the same extent as the rights of the issuer or a transferee from the issuer.

(3) Title to goods based upon a bill of lading issued to a freight forwarder is subject to the rights of anyone to whom a bill issued by the freight forwarder is duly negotiated; but delivery by the carrier in accordance with Part 4 of this Article pursuant to its own bill of lading discharges the carrier's obligation to deliver.

Sec. 7-504. *Rights Acquired in the Absence of Due Negotiation; Effect of Diversion; Seller's Stoppage of Delivery.*

(1) A transferee of a document, whether negotiable or non-negotiable, to whom the document has been delivered but not duly negotiated, acquires the title and rights which his transferor had or had actual authority to convey.

(2) In the case of a non-negotiable document, until but not after the bailee receives notification of the transfer, the rights of the transferee may be defeated

(a) by those creditors of the transferor who could treat the sale as void under Section 2-402; or

(b) by a buyer from the transferor in ordinary course of business if the bailee has delivered the goods to the buyer or received notification of his rights; or

(c) as against the bailee by good faith dealings of the bailee with the transferor.

(3) A diversion or other change of shipping instructions by the consignor in a non-negotiable bill of lading which causes the bailee not to deliver to the consignee defeats the consignee's title to the goods if they have been delivered to a buyer in ordinary course of business and in any event defeats the consignee's rights against the bailee.

(4) Delivery pursuant to a non-negotiable document may be stopped by a seller under Section 2-705, and subject to the requirement of due notification there provided. A bailee honoring the seller's instructions is entitled to be indemnified by the seller against any resulting loss or expense.

Sec. 7-505. *Indorser Not a Guarantor for Other Parties*

The indorsement of a document of title issued by a bailee does not make the indorser liable for any default by the bailee or by previous indorsers.

Sec. 7-506. *Delivery Without Indorsement: Right to Compel Indorsement.*

The transferee of a negotiable document of title has a specifically enforceable right to have his transferor supply any necessary indorsement but the transfer becomes a negotiation only as of the time the indorsement is supplied.

Sec. 7-507. *Warranties on Negotiation or Transfer of Receipt or Bill.*

Where a person negotiates or transfers a document of title for value otherwise than as a mere intermediary under the next following section, then unless otherwise agreed he warrants to his immediate purchaser only in addition to any warranty made in selling the goods

(a) that the document is genuine; and

(b) that he has no knowledge of any fact which would impair its validity or worth; and

(c) that his negotiation or transfer is rightful and fully effective with respect to the title to the document and the goods it represents.

Sec. 7-508. *Warranties of Collecting Bank as to Documents.*

A collecting bank or other intermediary known to be entrusted with documents on behalf of another or with collection of a draft or other claim against delivery of documents warrants by such delivery of the documents only its own good faith and authority. This rule applies even though the intermediary has purchased or made advances against the claim or draft to be collected.

Sec. 7-509. *Receipt or Bill: When Adequate Compliance with Commercial Contract.*

The question whether a document is adequate to fulfill the obligations of a contract for sale or the conditions of a credit is governed by the Articles on Sales (Article 2) and on Letters of Credit (Article 5).

PART 6

WAREHOUSE RECEIPTS AND BILLS OF LADING: MISCELLANEOUS PROVISIONS

Sec. 7-601. *Lost and Missing Documents.*

(1) If a document has been lost, stolen or destroyed, a court may order delivery of the goods or issuance of a substitute document and the bailee may without liability to any person comply with such order. If the document was negotiable the claimant must post security approved by the court to indemnify any person who may suffer loss as a result of non-surrender of the document. If the document was not negotiable, such security may be required at the discretion of the court. The court may also in its discretion order payment of the bailee's reasonable costs and counsel fees.

(2) A bailee who without court order delivers goods to a person claiming under a missing negotiable document is liable to any person injured thereby, and if the delivery is not in good faith becomes liable for conversion. Delivery in good faith is not conversion if made in accordance with a filed classification or tariff or, where no classification or tariff is filed, if the claimant posts security with the bailee in an amount at least double the value of the goods at the time of posting to indemnify any person injured by the delivery who files a notice of claim within one year after the delivery.

Sec. 7-602. *Attachment of Goods Covered by a Negotiable Document.*

Except where the document was originally issued upon delivery of the goods by a person who had no power to dispose of them, no lien attaches by virtue of any judicial process to goods in the possession of a bailee for which a negotiable document of title is outstanding unless the document be first surrendered to the bailee or its negotiation enjoined, and the bailee shall not be compelled to deliver the goods pursuant to process until the document is surrendered to him or impounded by the court. One who purchases the document for value without notice of the process of injunction takes free of the lien imposed by judicial process.

Sec. 7-603. *Conflicting Claims; Interpleader.*

If more than one person claims title or possession of the goods, the bailee is excused from delivery until he has had a reasonable time to ascertain the validity of the adverse claims or to bring an action to compel all claimants to interplead and may compel such interpleader, either in defending an action for non-delivery of the goods, or by original action, whichever is appropriate.

CHAPTER 3: The Role of the Physical Distribution Manager

Constantin, James A.; Anderson, Ronald D.; and Jerman, Roger E. "Views of Physical Distribution Managers." *Business Horizons*, April 1977.

Farrell, Jack W. "Distribution Departments Gain Ground." *Traffic Management*, September 1981.

Kearney: Management Consultants, Inc. "Integrated Logistics Management—Emerging Top Management Focus for the 1980's." Executive Summary Report.

La Londe, Bernard J. "Career Patterns in Distribution." Proceedings of the Annual Meeting of the National Council of Physical Distribution Management (published annually).

_____, and Lambert, Douglas M. "A Comparative Profile of the United States and Canadian Distribution Managers." *International Journal of Physical Distribution*, 7, No. 5.

Lancioni, Richard A. "1980—The Decade of Challenge for the Distribution Manager." *Distribution*, December 1979.

Murray, Robert E. "Matrix Management and Distribution." *Presidential Issue—Handling and Shipping Management*, 1980–1981.

Quinn, Francis J. "Training: Important Today . . . Essential to the Future." *Traffic Management*, November 1977.

CHAPTER 4: A Look to the Future

Related Articles by Donald J. Bowersox (Subsection 4)

Logistical Management, 2d ed. New York: Macmillan, 1978.

"Physical Distribution Development, Current Status and Potential." *Journal of Marketing*, January 1979.

"Physical Distribution in Semi-Maturity." *Air Cargo*, January 1966.

"Physical Distribution—Past, Present and Future." *Transportation and Distribution Management*, January 1966.

"Some Unresolved Channel Research Opportunities and One Framework for Integration." In Harvey and Lush, eds.: *Marketing Channels: Domestic and International Perspectives*, University of Oklahoma, 1982.

"The Changing Missions of Physical Distribution." Proceedings of the National Council of Physical Distribution Management Annual Meeting, October 1976.

"The Logistics of the Last Quarter of the 20th Century." *Journal of Business Logistics*, 1, No. 1, 1979.

With M. Bixby Cooper, Douglas M. Lambert, and Donald A. Taylor. *Management in Marketing Channels*. New York: McGraw-Hill, 1980.

With Jay U. Sterling. "Multinational Logistics." *Journal of Business Logistics*, 3, No. 2, 1982.

CHAPTER 6: A Framework for Logistics Planning

CONTRIBUTOR'S NOTE: My original plan was to select ten from more than 125 in my personal planning library to include in this bibliography. The basic criterion for selection was their usefulness to me in my profession of learning, teaching, and writing and in my business. I had two other criteria in mind. I wanted some which were thorough in their *discussion* of concepts and yet were very useful in taking the reader through the steps in planning. Also I wanted to include some that were oriented to "how to do it," with adequate comment on concepts.

I am comfortable with the "ten" selected and very uncomfortable about not including all 27 pulled in the first go 'round. (If I could only keep one of my planning books, I would keep Anthony.) One note of caution: don't let the dates of publication upset you. All of these are current in their approaches. Almost any student of planning would consider most to be classics (whatever they are!).

Here are "ten" really good planning books.

Ackoff, Russell L. *A Concept of Corporate Planning*. New York: Wiley-Interscience, 1970, 158 pages.

Andrews, Kenneth R. *The Concept of Corporate Strategy*, revised ed. Homewood, Ill.: Dow Jones-Irwin, 1980, 245 pages.

Ansoff, H. Igor. *Corporate Strategy*. New York: McGraw-Hill, 1965, 241 pages.

Anthony, Robert N. *Planning and Control Systems: A Framework for Analysis*. Boston: Harvard University, 1965, 180 pages.

Attwood, Peter R. *Planning a Distribution System*. London: Gower Press, 1971, 220 pages.

Drucker, Peter F. *The Practice of Management*. New York: Harper and Row, 1954, 404 pages.

Ewing, David W. *The Practice of Planning*. New York: Harper and Row, 1968, 149 pages.

_____, ed. *Long-Range Planning for Management*, 3d ed. New York: Harper and Row, 1972, 464 pages.

Kastens, Merritt L. *Long-Range Planning for Your Business*. New York: Amacom, 1976, 160 pages.

Lorange, Peter, and Vancil, Richard F. *Strategic Planning Systems*. Englewood Cliffs, N.J.: Prentice-Hall, 1977, 364 pages.

Mockler, Robert J. *Business Planning and Policy Formulation*. New York: Merideth Corporation, 1972, 424 pages.

_____. *The Management Control Process*. New York: Merideth Corporation, 1972, 357 pages.

Steiner, George A. *Top Management Planning*. New York: Macmillan, 1969, **I, II, III**, 795 pages.

_____. *Strategic Planning*. New York: Free Press, 1979, 323 pages.

CHAPTER 7: Operational Planning

Distribution Planning

Attwood, P. R. *Planning a Distribution System*. London: Gower Press, 1971. (Chapter 2, Strategic Planning for Distribution, pp. 21–38; Chapter 8, Preparing Distribution Plans, pp. 125–153.)

Bowersox, D. J. *Logistical Management*. New York: Macmillan, 1974. (Part Four, Logistical System Administration. pp. 417–434).

Buijtenen, P. V. *Business Logistics*. The Hague, 1976. (Part III, Logistics Planning and Control, pp. 243–289).

Buxton, G. *Effective Marketing Logistics*. New York: Holmes and Meier, 1975.

Farrell, J. W. *Physical Distribution Case Studies*. Boston: Cahners Books, 1973.

Firth, Denham, Griffin, Heffernan. *Distribution Management Handbook*. Toronto: McGraw-Hill Ryerson, 1980. (Planning Improvements in Distribution, pp. 286–334.)

Martin, C., Walters, D., with John Gattorna. *Distribution Planning and Control, A Corporate Approach*. London: Gower Press, 1977. (Chapter 1, "Approaching the Planning and Control Problem"; Chapter 2, "Relating Corporate Planning to PDM"; Chapter 3, "Relating Marketing Planning to PDM"; Chapter 4, "Distribution Planning and Auditing: A System Approach"; Chapter 7 "Distribution Strategy, The Distribution Plan"; Chapter 8, "Some Examples of Physical Distribution, Planning and Control Applications".)

Corporate Planning

Ackoff, R. L. *A Concept of Corporate Planning*. New York: Wiley, 1970.

Bibeault, D. B. *Corporate Turnaround*. New York: McGraw-Hill, 1982.

Hodgetts, R. M. *Management: Theory, Process and Practice*. Philadelphia: W. B. Saunders, 1979.

Hussey, D. E. *Corporate Planning Theory and Practice*. New York: Pergamon, 1974.

Jones, D. C. *Business Planning and Forecasting*. New York–Toronto: Wiley, 1974.

Koontz, H., and O'Donnell, C. *Management—A System and Contingency Analysis of Managerial Functions*. New York: McGraw-Hill, 1976.

Petit, T. A. *Fundamentals of Management Coordination*. New York–Toronto: Wiley, 1975.

Reeser, C. *Management Functions and Modern Concepts*. Glenview, Ill.: Scott, Foresman, 1973.

Wild, R. *Concepts for Operations Management*. New York: Wiley, 1977.

CHAPTER 8: Contingency Planning for Distribution Managers

American Management Association. *Contingency Planning* (92019). New York: 1983.

Bittel, Lester R. *Encyclopedia of Professional Management*. New York: McGraw-Hill, 1978.

Blanding, Warren. *Blanding's Practical Physical Distribution*. Washington, D.C.: The Traffic Service Corporation, 1978.

"Contingency Planning: Prepared for the Worst," *Handling & Shipping Management Magazine*, October 1981, pp. 58–64.

Lancioni, Richard A. *Distribution*. Radnor, Pa.: The Chilton Company, 1979.

National Association of Wholesaler-Distributors. *Reducing Energy Costs in Wholesale Distribution*. Washington, D.C.: 1979.

O'Connor, Rochelle. *Planning Under Uncertainty: Multiple Scenarios and Contingency Planning*. New York: Conference Board, 1978.

Research Institute of America. *Coping with Energy Shortages and Higher Costs*. New York: RIA, 1977.

_____. *Disaster Guide for Management*. New York: RIA, 1979.

_____. *How to Survive the Squeeze of Other People's Strikes*. New York: RIA, 1979.

Steiner, George A. *Strategic Planning*. New York: Free Press, 1979.

Chapter 9: Logistics System Design

Bender, Paul S. *Resource Management: An Alternative View of the Management Process*. New York: Wiley, 1983.

_____. *Design and Operation of Customer Service Systems*. New York: American Management Associations, 1976.

_____. *Physical Resource Management: Beyond Physical Distribution and Logistics*. New York: Wiley, to be published in 1986.

Blanchard, Benjamin S. *Logistics Engineering and Management*. Englewood Cliffs, N.J.: Prentice-Hall, 1974.

Isard, Walter. *Location and Space Economy*. Cambridge, Mass.: M.I.T. Press, 1956.

Schwarz, L. B. *Multi-Level Production/Inventory Control Systems: Theory and Practice*. New York: North-Holland, 1981.

Söderman, Sten. *Industrial Location Planning*. Stockholm: Almqvist & Wiksell International, 1975.

Chapter 14: Management Guide to Productivity

A Management Guide to Productivity. Philadelphia: Yale Materials Handling Division, Yale and Towne, Inc., 1961.

Basics of Material Handling. Pittsburgh: The Material Handling Institute, Inc., 1973.

"Executive Report on Productivity." *Material Handling Engineering*, 34, No. 5, May 1979.

Gatts, R. R., Massey, R. G., and Robertson, J. C., *Energy Conservation and Program Guide for Industry and Commerce*, NBS Handbook 115, Catalog No. C13.11:115. Washington, D.C.: Superintendent of Documents, September 1974.

Grant, E. L., Ireson, W. G., and Levenworth, R. S. *Principles of Engineering Economics*, 6th ed. New York: Wiley, 1976.

"How to Save Energy in Material Handling." *Modern Materials Handling*, November 1978, p. 81.

Improving Productivity through Industry and Company Measurement, Series 2. Washington, D.C.: National Center for Productivity and Quality of Working Life, October 1976.

Kehlbeck, J. H. "Productivity—An International Contest." *Industrial Engineering*, January 1978, pp. 18–22.

Measuring Productivity in Physical Distribution: A 40 Billion Dollar Goldmine. Chicago, Ill.: NCPDM, 1978.

Mundel, M. E., ed. *Productivity: A Series from Industrial Engineering*. Norcross, Ga.: American Institute of Industrial Engineers, Inc., 1978.

"Productivity: A Crisis for Management." *Hardware Retailing*, October 1978, pp. 53–92.

Productivity Improvement for Profit Program. Norcross, Ga.: American Institute of Industrial Engineers, 1977.

Productivity in the Changing World of the 1980's, Final Report. Washington, D.C.: National Center for Productivity and Quality of Working Life, 1978.

"Productivity Lag Presses Buyers to Slash Costs." *Purchasing*, 24 January 1979, pp. 87–91.

Schillo, J. "Improving Productivity: A Matter of Measurement." *Material Handling Engineering*, 34, No. 5, May 1979, pp. 80–85.

Thuesen, H. G., Fabrycky, W. J., and Thuesen, G. J. *Engineering Economics*, 5th ed. Englewood Cliffs, N.J.: Prentice-Hall, 1977.

The Future of Productivity. Washington, D.C.: National Center for Productivity and Quality of Working Life, Winter 1977.

Tompkins, J. A., and White, J. A. *Facilities Planning*. New York: Wiley, 1984.

Warehousing and Physical Distribution Productivity Report, Marketing Publications, Inc., 14, No. 7, 15 July 1979.

Webb, R. E. "Material Handling and Energy Management", *Proceedings*, 1978 Fall Industrial Engineering Conference, Atlanta, Ga. Institute of Industrial Engineers, Inc., December 1978.

White, J. A. *Identifying the Material Handling Research Needs for Discrete Parts in the Automatic Factory: A Workshop Approach*. Atlanta: School of Industrial and Systems Engineering, Georgia Institute of Technology, May 1979.

White, J. A., Agee, M. H., and Case, K.E. *Principles of Engineering Economic Analysis*, 2d ed. New York: Wiley, 1984.

CHAPTER 18: Demand Forecasting

The following is a selected list of books and articles that provide supplementary information on sales forecasting.

Books

Abramowitz, Irving. *Production Management*. New York: Ronald Press, 1967. Portions of Chapter 18 have been developed from the ideas in this book.

American Management Association. *Practical Sales Forecasting*. New York: AMA, 1970.

Bean, L. H. *The Art of Forecasting*. New York: Random House, 1969.

Butler, W. F.; Kavish, R. A.; and Platt, R. B., eds. *Methods and Techniques of Business Forecasting*. Englewood Cliffs, N.J.: Prentice-Hall, 1974.

Chambers, J. C.; Mullick, S. K.; and Smith, D. D. *An Executive's Guide to Forecasting*. New York: Wiley, 1974.

Chisholm, R. K. *Forecasting Methods*. Homewood, Ill.: Richard D. Irwin, 1971.

Conference Board. *Forecasting Sales*. New York: Conference Board, 1964.

_____. *Sales Forecasting Practices: An Appraisal*. New York: Conference Board, 1970.

Hirsch, A. H., and Lovell, M. C. *Sales Anticipation and Inventory Behavior*. New York: Wiley, 1969.

Keay, F. *Marketing and Sales Forecasting*. Elmsford, N.Y.: Pergamon Press, 1972.

Lippett, V. G. *Statistical Sales Forecasting*. New York: Financial Executives Research Foundations, 1969.

Pearce, C. *Prediction Techniques for Marketing Planners: The Practical Application of Forecasting Methods to Business Problems*. New York: Wiley, 1971.

Silk, L. S., and Curley, M. L. *A Primer on Business Forecasting*. New York: Random House, 1970.

Articles

"After Many Years Comes a Matrix." *Sales Management*, 15 January 1970, pp. 54–55.

Ahl, D. H. "New Product Forecasting Using Consumer Panels." *Journal of Marketing Research*, May 1970, pp. 160–67.

"At Johnson & Johnson, the Sales Budget Gets the Best of Care." *Sales Management*, 19 May 1975, pp. 9–11.

Benz, W. "Marketing Forecasting: Planning for a Surprise-Free Tomorrow." *Sales Management*, 6 August 1973, pp. 24–25.

Courtney, H. M., and Brooks, F. V. "Cumulative Probabilistic Sales Forecasting." *Management Accounting*, May 1972, pp. 44–47.

Ezzati, A. "Forecasting Market Shares of Alternative Home-Heating Units by Markov Process Using Aggregate Time Series Data." *Management Science*, December 1974, pp. 462–73.

Geurts, M. D. "Documented Sales Data Improves Forecasting." *Journal of Systems Management*, August 1973, pp. 32–34.

_____, and Ibrahim, I. B. "Compares Box-Jenkins and Exponential Smoothing as Forecasting Techniques in Short-Term Models." *Journal of Marketing Research*, May 1975, pp. 182–88.

Hanan, M. "Today's Forecast: High Hopes and Little Chance of Clearing." *Sales Management*, 14 October 1974, pp. 36–38.

_____, and Amstutz, A. "Short-Term Strategy Planning: Now You Can Be Ready for Quicksand or Fire Storm." *Sales Management*, 10 June 1974, pp. 30–32.

"Honest Salesmen, Honestly." *Sales Management*, 11 November 1974, pp. 7ff.

"Input-Output Searches the Seventies." *Sales Management*, August 1968, pp. 27–29.

Jones, H. G. "Use of Forecasts in Target Setting." *Operations Research Quarterly*, December 1973, pp. 547–60.

Kierulff, H. E., Jr. "Best Estimate Forecasting—A Better Alternative." *California Management Review*, Fall 1972, pp. 79–85.

Kwon, I. "Marketing Executives Want More Help from the Computer." *Data Management*, April 1975, p. 18–20.

Leyshon, A. "Sales Forecast Is a Top Management Problem." *Director*, April 1973, pp. 93–96.

Lowe, E. S., and Shaw, R. W. "Accuracy of Short-Term Business Forecasting: An Analysis of a Firm's Sales Budgeting." *Journal of Industrial Economics*, July 1970, pp. 275–89.

Markwalder, A. S. "Vote for Profit Forecasting." *Management Accounting*, December 1974, pp. 23–25.

Neuwirth, P. D. "Computer Forecasting—No More Surprises." *Financial Executive*, October 1974, pp. 58–60ff.

Osborne, H. "Characteristics of Sales Forecasts Based on Gross National Product." *Financial Analysts Journal*, September 1970, pp. 39–46ff.

Parker, G. G. C., and Segura, E. L. "How to Get a Better Forecast." *Harvard Business Review*, March–April 1975, pp. 99–109.

Rakes, H. W. "Grass Roots Forecasting." *Management Accounting*, September 1974, pp. 38–40.

Ranard, E. D. "Use of Input/Output Concepts in Sales Forecasting." *Journal of Marketing*, February 1972, pp. 53–58.

Roshwalb, I. "Two Methods of Estimating Sales from a Sample of Retail Outlets." *Journal of Marketing Research*, August 1970, pp. 96–98.

Sandbulte, A. J. "Sales and Revenue Forecasting." *Management Accounting*, December 1969, pp. 17–23.

Staelin, R., and Turner, R. E. "Error in Judgmental Sales Forecasts: Theory and Results." *Journal of Marketing Research*, February 1973, pp. 10–16.

Stephenson, J. S., and Smith, H. "New Marketing Information System." *Management Accounting*, August 1974, pp. 11–14.

Taylor, T. "Throwing More Light on Hard-to-See Profit Sources." *Sales Management*, 19 May 1975, pp. 41–44.

"The Computer in Marketing: Rapping with the Digital Beast." *Sales Management*, 15 August 1971, pp. 48–49.

"The Computer in Marketing: 'Tis the Season to Forecast." *Sales Management*, 27 December 1971, pp. 31–33.

Vaughn, D. E. "Sales Forecasting." *Management Accounting*, March 1972, pp. 39–41.

CHAPTER 19: Managing the Purchasing Function

Aljian, George W., ed. *Purchasing Handbook*, 4th ed. New York: McGraw-Hill, 1982.

Bolton, R. A. *Systems Contracting*. New York: American Management Association, 1966.

Browning, John M., and Andrews, M. A. "Target Purchasing: The Price-Volume Distinction." *Journal of Purchasing and Materials Management*, Summer 1978.

Calero, H. H. *Winning the Negotiation*. New York: Hawthorne Books.

Calero, H. H., and Nierenberg, G. I. *How to Read a Person Like a Book*. New York: Hawthorne Books, 1971.

Carter, P. L., and Monczka, R. M. "MRO Inventory Pooling," *Journal of Purchasing and Materials Management*, Fall 1978, pp. 27–33.

Corey, E. R. *Procurement Management: Strategy, Organization and Decision-Making*. Boston: CBI Publishing, 1978.

Fearon, Harold. *Purchasing Research: Concept and Current Practice*. New York: AMACOM, A Division of American Management Association, 1976.

Karrass, Chester L. *Give and Take*. New York: Thomas Y. Crowell, 1974.

———. *The Negotiating Game*. New York: Thomas Y. Crowell, 1970.

Miles, L. D. *Techniques of Value Analysis and Engineering*, 2d ed. New York: McGraw-Hill, 1972.

Monczka, R. M., Carter, P. L., and Hoagland, J. H. *Purchasing Performance: Measurement and Control*. East Lansing, Mich.: Division of Research, Graduate School of Business Administration, Michigan State University, 1979.

———, and Fearon, H. F. "Coping with Material Shortages." *Journal of Purchasing and Materials Management*, May, 1974, pp. 4–19.

———. Unpublished research on purchasing organization.

National Association of Purchasing Management, Inc. *Guide to Purchasing*, 1–3. New York: NAPM, 1965, 1968, 1973.

CHAPTER 20: Transportation and Distribution Management

Coyle, John J., and Bardi, Edward J. *The Management of Business Logistics*. St. Paul, Minn.: West Publishing, 1980.

Fair, Marvin L., and Williams, Ernest W., Jr. *Transportation and Logistics*. Plano, Texas: Business Publications, Inc., 1981.

Meyer, John R. and others. *Airline Deregulation: The Early Experience*. Boston: Auburn House Publishing, 1981.

Wood, Donald F., and Johnson, James C. *Contemporary Transportation*. Tulsa: Petroleum Publishing Company, 1980.

CHAPTER 24: Distribution Facility Design and Construction

Books

Shoemaker, Morrell M., and McClurg, William M., eds. *The Building Estimators Reference Book*. Chicago: Frank R. Walker, 1977.

Civil Engineering Handbook. New York: McGraw-Hill (current edition).

Periodicals

Buildings. Stamats Communication, Inc., Cedar Rapids, Iowa.

Building Design and Construction. Cahners Publishing Company, Boston, Mass.

ENR. McGraw-Hill, Inc., New York, N.Y.

Professional Builder. Cahners Publishing Company, Boston, Mass.

Progressive Architecture. Reinhold Publishing, Division of Penton; Cleveland, Ohio.

Other Publications of Interest

American Trucking Associations, Inc., The Operations Council. "How Big Is a Truck—How Sharp Does It Turn." Washington, D.C.: ATA, Operations Council, 1974.

Rite-Hite Corporation, "Truck & Rail Dock Planning for the 1980's." Milwaukee, Wis.: Rite-Hite, 1980.

Sources of Technical Manuals

Asphalt Institute.

Factory Mutual System—Loss Prevention Data.

National Fire Protection Association.

Portland Cement Association.

City and state building codes for various municipalities where construction takes place.

In addition to the above items, sales literature and technical manuals are provided by major manufacturers of various component parts of the building. These include the structure itself (metal building manufacturers), roof components, and various other elements all the way from the smallest electrical fixtures to lighting, dock boards, and other parts.

CHAPTER 27: The Role of Packaging in Physical Distribution

Professional and Trade Organizations

Adhesive Manufacturers Association of America (AMAA)
111 E. Wacker Drive
Chicago, IL 60601

American Paper Institute (API)
260 Madison Avenue
New York, NY 10016

American Plywood Association (APA)
1119 A Street
Tacoma, WA 98401

American Society for Testing and Materials (ASTM)
1916 Race Street
Philadelphia, PA 19103

American Trucking Association, Inc. (ATA)
1616 P Street, N.W.
Washington, DC 20036

American Association of Railroads (AAR)
1920 L Street, N.W.
Washington, DC 20036

Canadian Corrugated Case Association (CCCA)
1 Yonge Street
Toronto, Ontario, Canada

European Federation of Manufacturers of Corrugated Board (FEFCO)
37 Rue d'Amsterdam
75008 Paris, France

Fibre Box Association (FBA)
5725 East River Road
Chicago, IL 60631

Forest Products Laboratory (FPL)
Forest Service, U.S. Dept. of Agriculture
P.O. Box 5130
Madison, WI 53705

International Corrugated Case Association (ICCA)
5725 N. East River Road
Chicago, IL 60631

International Organization for Standardization (ISO)
1, Rue de Varembe
1211 Geneva 20, Switzerland

Magazines for Industry (MI)
777 Third Ave.
New York, NY 10017

Marking Device Association (MDA)
708 Church St.
Evanston, IL 60201

Material Handling Institute (MHI)
1326 Freeport Road
Pittsburgh, PA 15238

National Institute of Packaging, Handling and Logistics Engineers (NIPHLE)
P.O. Box 2765
Arlington, VA 22202

National Safe Transit Association (NSTA)
6022 W. Touhy Ave.
Chicago, IL 60648

National Wooden Pallet and Container Association (NWPCA)
1619 Massachusetts Ave., N.W.
Washington, DC 20036

Naval Publications and Forms Center
5801 Tabor
Philadelphia, PA 19120
(Source for Copies of Federal and Military Specifications)

Packaging Education Foundation, Inc. (PEF)
2217 Beechmont Ave.
Cincinnati, OH 45230

Packaging Machinery Manufacturers Institute (PMMI)
2000 K St., N.W.
Washington, DC 20006

Paper Shipping Sack Manufacturers Association (PSSMA)
2 Overhill Road
Scarsdale, NY 10583

Society of Packaging and Handling Engineers (SPHE)
Reston International Center
Reston, VA 22091

Steel Shipping Container Institute, Inc. (SSCI)
2204 Morris Ave.
Union NJ 07083

Technical Association of the Pulp and Paper Industry (TAPPI)
1 Dunwoody Park
Atlanta, GA 30341

Textile Bag Manufacturers Association
P.O. Box 2145
Northbrook, IL 60062

The Gummed Industries Association, Inc.
380 North Broadway
Jericho, NY 11753

The Packaging Institute, U.S.A. (PI/USA)
342 Madison Ave.
New York, NY 10017

United Parcel Service (UPS)
51 Weaver St., Greenwich Office Park 5
Greenwich, CT 06830

Wirebound Box Manufacturers Association, Inc. (WBMA)
1211 W. 22nd Street
Oak Brook, IL 60521

Publications

"A Total Systems Approach to Corrugated Container Design." *Package Development*, May–June 1974.

Adhesive Manufacturers Association of America. "Packaging's Role in Physical Distribution", Management Bulletin No. 77. New York: AMAA, 1966.

———. *Recommended Practices*. Chicago: AMAA.

American Association of Railroads. *Tariff No. 32 (Hazardous Materials)*. Washington: Association of American Railroads.

American National Standards Institute. *Commercial Pails* (ANSI Standard Nos. MH 2.9, 2.10, 2.15, 2.16 and 2.17). New York: ANSI.

———. *Full Removable Head Drums* (ANSI Standard Nos. MH 2.2, 2.5, 2.8, 2.11, 2.12, 2.13 and 2.14). New York: ANSI.

———. *Pallet Definitions and Terminology* (ANSI Standard Number MH 1.1.2-1972). New York: ANSI.

———. *Pallet Sizes* (ANSI Standard Number MH 1.2.2-1975). New York: ANSI.

———. *Pictorial Markings for Handling of Goods* (ANSI Standard Number MH6.1). New York: ANSI.

———. *Procedures for Testing Pallets* (ANSI Standard Number MH 1.4.1-1977). New York: ANSI.

———. *Standard on Unit Load and Package Sizes* (ANSI Standard Number MH 10.1M-1980). New York: ANSI.

———. *Tight Head Drums.* (ANSI Standard Numbers MH 2.1, 2.3, 2.4, 2.6, and 2.7) New York: ANSI.

American Paper Institute. *Paper Recycling: The Art of the Possible, 1970–1985.* New York: Solid Waste Council of the Paper Industry.

———. *Solid Waste Management and the Paper Industry.* New York: Solid Waste Council of the Paper Industry.

American Plywood Association. *Plywood Design Manual—Coating* (#T210). Tacoma, Wash.: APA.

———. *Plywood Design Manual—Industrial and Agricultural Pallet Bins* (#Y205). Tacoma, Wash.: APA.

———. *Plywood Design Manual—Pallets* (#Z200). Tacoma, Wash.: APA.

———. *Plywood Pallet Specification Check List* (#E255). Tacoma, Wash.: APA.

———. *Specifications for Softwood Plywood Pallets* (#P380). Tacoma, Wash.: APA.

American Trucking Association. *Hazardous Materials Tariff No. 111-F.* Washington: ATA.

———. *National Motor Freight Classification No. 100-H.* Washington: ATA.

Amo, D. J. *Unit Load Forming and Stabilizing Techniques.* PI/USA Professional Seminar, 1978. New York: The Packaging Institute, U.S.A. (#P-7801).

Barail, Louis C. *Packaging Engineering.* New York: Reinhold, 1954.

Beauregard, R. *The Hazardous Material Transportation Act: Its Impact on, Compliance with and Exemption from the D.O.T. Packaging Regulations.* PI/USA Professional Seminar, 1976. New York: The Packaging Institute, U.S.A. (#P-7610).

Bettendorf, H. J. *A History of Paper Board and Paper Board Containers.* Chicago: Board Products Publishing Co.

Bolz, H. A., and Hagemann, G. E. *Materials Handling Handbook.* New York: Ronald Press, 1958.

Boyer, Paul M. "How to Cut a Package's Costs Without Hurting Its Performance." *Package Engineering*, June 1973.

Bradstock, W. E. *Update on Corrugated Forming and Sealing Machinery.* PI/USA Midwestern Regional Packaging Forum, 1977. New York: The Packaging Institute, U.S.A. (#F-7703).

British Standards Institution. *British Standard Glossary of Packaging Terms.* London: BSI, 1959.

Brody, Aaron L. "Systems Integration of Packaging." *Modern Packaging*, May 1958.

Brooks, Durward L. "Essentials of Export Packaging and Marking." *Transportation and Distribution Management*, June 1973.

Brown, Kenneth. *Package Design Engineering.* New York: Wiley, 1959.

Bryant, D. H. *Good Manufacturing Practices: Their Impact on the Selection and Use of Packaging Materials and Equipment.* PI/USA National Technical Seminar, PAC, 1976. New York: The Packaging Institute, U.S.A. (#T-7613).

Clark, T. M. *Performance Characteristics of Hot Melt Versus Wet Glue Application Systems.* PI/USA Eastern Regional Packaging Forum, 1976. New York: The Packaging Institute, U.S.A. (#F-7604).

DeBruyne, N. A., and Houghwick, R. *Adhesion and Adhesives.* Houston: Elsevier, 1951.

Delmonte, John. *Technology of Adhesives.* New York: Reinhold.

DiPalmenberg, S. M. *Avoiding Impact of Inflation by Using Shrink and Stretch Films.* International Packaging Week Assembly, 1978. New York: The Packaging Institute, U.S.A. (#IPW-7808).

Dixon, James M. "Taking a Long Step Toward Damage-Free Transportation." *Distribution Worldwide,* June 1972.

European Federation of Manufacturers of Corrugated Board. *International Fibreboard Case Code.* Paris: FEFCO.

Fibre Box Association. *Certification Manual: A Guide to Certificates and Other Markings for Fibreboard Boxes.* Chicago: FBA.

———. *Corru-Facts* (Bi-Monthly Brochures on Corrugated Box Usage). Chicago: FBA.

———. *Creative Corrugated Packaging.* Chicago: FBA.

———. *Fibre Box Handbook,* 17th ed. Chicago, Illinois: FBA.

———. *Recommended Practices.* Chicago: FBA.

———. *Voluntary Standards.* Chicago: FBA.

Friedman, W. F. *Packaging and Automated Warehousing: How Are They Connected?* PI/USA Midwestern Regional Packaging Forum, 1974. New York: The Packaging Institute, U.S.A. (#F-7408).

———. "The Need for a Broadened Focus in Package Design." *Package Development,* May–June 1975.

———. "The Role of Packaging in Physical Distribution." *Transportation and Distribution Management,* February 1968.

———. *What Really Is an Optimum Distribution Package?* PI/USA Professional Seminar, 1978. New York: The Packaging Institute, U.S.A. (#P-7802).

———. *Where Does Packaging Stop & Physical Distribution Begin.* International Packaging Week Assembly, 1975. New York: The Packaging Institute, U.S.A. (#IPW-7513).

———, and Kipnees, Jerome J. *Distribution Packaging.* Huntington, N.Y.: Robert E. Krieger, 1977.

———, and ———. *Industrial Packaging.* New York: Wiley, 1960.

Goldberg, Robert I. "The Packaging Systems Approach, Its Effect on Creative Development." *Package Development,* November–December 1975.

Gordon, G. A., and Wheeler, E. E. *The Properties of Cushioning Materials for Use in Packaging.* Surrey, England: The Printing, Packaging, and Allied Trades Research Association, 1961.

Griffin, Roger C., Jr., and Sacharow, Stanley. *Principles of Package Development.* Westport, Conn.: AVI Publishing, 1972.

Guins, Sergei G. "Pick Your Corrugated Board by Tests Instead of Guesses." *Package Engineering,* May 1973.

Hanlon, Joseph. *Handbook of Package Engineering.* New York: McGraw-Hill, 1971.

Hansen, J. I. *You and Your Contract Packager: Silent Partners.* PI/USA Professional Seminar, 1977. New York: The Packaging Institute, U.S.A. (#P-7722).

Harris, C. M., and Crede, C. E. *Shock and Vibration Handbook*, 3 Vols. New York: McGraw-Hill, 1961.

Henry, Alan D. "Eleven Ways to Reduce Packaging Costs." *Army Logistician*, January–February 1972.

Hillhouse, A. S. *How Packaging Designed for Efficient Distribution Is a Profit Source*. International Packaging Week Assembly, 1975. New York: The Packaging Institute, U.S.A. (#IPW-7517).

Hyden, S. *Quality Assurance Procedures in Contract Packaging*. PI/USA Professional Seminar, 1977. New York: The Packaging Institute, U.S.A. (#P-7723).

Ievans, U. *Update on Corrugated Container Manufacturer*. PI/USA Midwestern Regional Packaging Forum, 1977. New York: The Packaging Institute, U.S.A. (#F-7708).

Janson, B. G. *Multiwall Bags from an End Users' Viewpoint*. International Packaging Week Assembly, 1977. New York: The Packaging Institute, U.S.A. (#IPW-7715).

Kohke, J. *Metric Packaging for the United States*. International Packaging Week Assembly, 1978. New York: The Packaging Institute, U.S.A. (#IPW-7812).

Kufahl, M. M. *How to Demand Higher Standards of Capabilities in Performance in the Packaging Function*. International Packaging Week Assembly, 1976. New York: The Packaging Institute, U.S.A. (#IPW-7618).

Lako, W. R. *Quality Control of Corrugated*. International Packaging Week Assembly, 1979. New York: The Packaging Institute, U.S.A. (#IPW-7913).

Leask, Pat; Reid, Bob; and Cox, Ralph. "Bag Packaging Machinery." *Material Handling Engineering*, September 1980.

Leffler, Walter H. "Evaluating Existing Machinery Systems, Justifying the New," Part I and Part II. *Package Development*, November–December 1973.

Leonard, Edmund. *Introduction to the Economics of Packaging*. New York: Morgan Grampian, Inc.

Lesser, Lawrence M. "Protective Packaging: What Shippers are Doing." *Traffic Management*, April 1972.

Little, Arthur D. *Packaging in Perspective*. Cambridge, Mass.: Arthur D. Little.

Magazines for Industry. *International Container Directory* (Box Plants and Other Converters in all Countries except U.S. and Canada). New York: MI.

————. *Official Container Directory* (Box Plants and Other Converters in U.S. and Canada). New York: MI.

————. *The New Art of Corrugated Container Production, Parts I, II, and III*. New York: MI.

Material Handling Engineering. *Material Handling Engineering Handbook and Directory*. Cleveland: Industrial Publishing Co., published annually.

Material Handling Institute, Inc. "Automatic Identification Manufacturers . . . Present the Emerging Impact of Automatic Identification Systems on Material Handling." Pittsburgh: MHI.

McGuire, E. Patrick. *Packaging and Paper Converting Adhesives*. New York: Palmerton, 1963.

McHugh, M. *Contract Packaging of Chemical Products*. PI/USA Professional Seminar, 1977. New York: The Packaging Institute, U.S.A. (#P-7724).

McKinley, A. H. *Distribution Engineering: Packaging and Handling Together Solving Distribution Problems*. International Packaging Week Assembly, 1977. New York: The Packaging Institute, U.S.A. (#IPW-7722).

"Mechanized Case Packing: Now for Almost Everyone!" *Modern Materials Handling*, September 1973.

Modern Packaging. *Modern Packaging Encyclopedia.* New York: McGraw-Hill, published annually.

Morris, C. B. *Corrugated and Solid Fibre Boxes.* International Packaging Week Assembly, 1976. New York: The Packaging Institute, U.S.A. (#IPW-7629).

National Safe Transit Association. *Test Procedures.* Chicago: NSTC.

National Wooden Pallet and Container Association. *Handbook on Wooden Pallet Containers and Container Systems.* Washington, D.C.: NWPCA.

_____. *Handbook on Wooden Pallets and Palletization.* Washington, D.C.: NWPCA.

_____. *Specifications and Grades for Hardwood Warehouse Pallets.* Washington, D.C.: NWPCA.

_____. *Specifications and Grades for Warehouse Pallets of West Coast Woods.* Washington, D.C.: NWPCA.

_____. *Technical Leaflet on Expendable Pallets.* Washington, D.C.: NWPCA.

_____. *Technical Pamphlet on Care and Maintenance of Pallets.* Washington, D.C.: NWPCA.

Paine, F. A. *Packaging Materials and Containers.* London: Blackie and Sons, 1967.

Phillips, J. P. *Package Design Considerations for the Distribution System.* International Packaging Week Assembly, 1977. New York: The Packaging Institute, U.S.A. (#IPW-7927).

Packaging Institute, U.S.A., The. *Directory of Contract Packagers and Their Facilities*, 8th ed. New York: PI/USA, 1972.

_____. *Glossary of Packaging Terms.* New York: PI/USA.

_____. *Home Study Course in Packaging Materials and Technology.* New York: PI/USA.

_____. *Petroleum Packaging Notebook: Containers for the Petroleum Industry.* New York: PI/USA.

_____. *Petroleum Packaging Notebook.* New York: PI/USA.

_____. *Source Book for Closures.* New York: PI/USA.

_____. *Source Book for Fundamental Resins for Packaging Adhesion to Board Manual.* New York: PI/USA.

_____. *Technical Reports.* New York: PI/USA.

_____. *The Last Frontier for Cost Reduction: Physical Distribution Packaging.* New York: PI/USA.

_____. *Who's Who in Packaging.* Directory of P.I./U.S.A. Membership, People in Packaging and Guide to Professional Packaging Expertise. New York: PI/USA, published annually.

Packaging Machinery Manufacturers Institute. *Packaging/Converting Machinery Components Manual*, Training Course—Operation, Maintenance and Repair of Packaging and Converting Machinery. 5 Vol. Washington, D.C.: PMMI.

_____. *Packaging Machinery Directory*, Directory of Member Companies. Washington, D.C.: PMMI, published annually.

_____. *Recommended Practices.* Washington, D.C.: PMMI.

Promisel, R. *Slip Sheets Versus Pallets: The Decision-Making Process.* PI/USA Western Regional Packaging Forum, 1979. New York: The Packaging Institute, U.S.A. (#F-7914).

"Proper Pallet Maintenance Means Dollars for Users." *Materials Handling Engineering*, October 1970.

Raften, B. *Packaging Line Control Systems: Design and Implementation Criteria.* International Packaging Week Assembly, 1975. New York: The Packaging Institute, U.S.A. (#IPW-7534).

Sardo, William H., Jr. "Wooden Pallet Basics." *Plant Engineering*, 3 April 1980.

Schreiber, F. W. "How Package Development Can Work Most Effectively With Marketing." *Package Development*, March–April 1975.

Steel Shipping Container Institute. *A Buyers' Guide to Steel Drums.* Union, N.J.: SSCI.

_____. *A Buyers' Guide to Steel Pails.* Union, N.J.: SSCI.

_____. *Guide for Export Shippers of Hazardous Materials.* Union, N.J.: SSCI.

Stern, Walter. *The Package Engineering Handbook.* Chicago: Board Products Publishing Company, 1954.

Technical Association of the Pulp and Paper Industry. *Corrugate Container Test Procedures.* Atlanta: TAPPI.

"Thinking Steps in a Program to Standardize Shipping Containers." *Package Development*, July–August 1974.

Tiemann, R. L. *Computer Simulation of Packaging Line Layouts.* International Packaging Week Assembly, 1978. New York: The Packaging Institute, U.S.A. (#IPW-7835).

"Unit-Load Shrink-Wrapping Comes of Age." *Modern Materials Handling*, May 1973.

United Parcel Service. *Guide for Handling Hazardous Materials.* Greenwich, Conn.: UPS.

_____. *Packaging for the Small Parcel Environment.* Greenwich, Conn.: UPS.

U.S. Business and Defense Service Administration. *Sources of Information on Containers and Packaging.* Washington, D.C.: U.S. Government Printing Office, 1965.

_____. *Western Europe Standardizing Packaging Dimensions.* Washington, D.C.: U.S. Government Printing Office.

U.S. Department of Agriculture, Forest Service, Forest Products Laboratory. *List of Publications on Box and Crate Construction and Packaging Data*, 65-038. Washington: USDA, January 1966.

_____. *Wood Crate Design Manual.* Washington, D.C.: USDA.

Wallin, Walter B. "New-Operating Guidelines for Reducing Pallet Damage." *Modern Materials Handling*, March 1975.

Way, Howard E., Jr. *The Relation of Unit Load Size to Material Handling and Distribution.* PI/USA Midwestern Regional Packaging Forum, 1974. New York: The Packaging Institute, U.S.A. (#F-7435).

Weber, R. Frank. "Applying the Systems Approach to Packaging." *Modern Materials Handling*, August 1967.

Westvaco. *Multiwall Bag Workshop Manual.* New Orleans, La.: Westvaco Bag Division. Provided to workshop participants; updated annually.

Wheeler, R. C. *Effecting Cost Reductions on Packaging Line Operations.* International Packaging Week Assembly, 1977. New York: The Packaging Institute, U.S.A. (#IPW-7737).

Williams, Stewart E. "Recognizing, Analyzing and Solving Corrugated Box Problems." *Package Development*, September–October 1974.

Young, W. E. *Criteria for Selection of Machinery to Minimize Packing Costs.* International Packaging Week Assembly, 1978. New York: The Packaging Institute, U.S.A. (#IPW-7840).

Zando, P. A. *Packaging Hazardous Materials in Multiwall Bags.* International Packaging Week Assembly, 1977. New York: The Packaging Institute, U.S.A. (#IPW-7741).

CHAPTER 28: The International Dimension of Physical Distribution Management

The author of Chapter 28, Paul S. Bender, has also written about international distribution in his upcoming book, *Physical Resource Management: Beyond Physical Distribution and Logistics* (New York, Wiley, to be published in 1986).

For readers interested in further information, two sources of references are given here: useful contacts in the United States and publications containing regulatory and statistical data.

Contacts

The U.S. Government is an excellent source of information on international trade. Its major sources of information are:

(01) U.S. Department of Commerce
   Washington, DC 20230

(02) Superintendent of Documents
   Government Printing Office
   Washington, DC 20402

(03) National Technical Information Services (NTIS)
   5285 Port Royal Road
   Springfield, VA 22151

Other good sources of information are:

(04) Chamber of Commerce of the U.S.
   1615 H Street, N.W.
   Washington, DC 20006

(05) Sales Section
   United Nations
   New York, NY 10017

(06) European Economic Community
   245 East 47th Street
   New York, NY 10017

(07) Budd Publications
   80 Wall Street
   New York, NY 10005

(08) Dun & Bradstreet Publications
   P.O. Box 2088
   Grand Central Station
   New York, NY 10017

(09) Brandon
   One Broadway
   New York, NY 10004

(10) Export Import Bank of the U.S.
   811 Vermont Avenue
   Washington DC 20571

(11) Croner Publications Inc.
   211-03 Jamaica Avenue
   Queens Village, NY 11428

(12) Kelly's Directories
   220 East 42nd Street
   New York, NY 10017

(13) American Register of Exporters and Importers
   90 West Broadway
   New York, NY 10010

(14) National Association of Credit Management
   44 East 23rd Street
   New York, NY 10010

(15) Foreign Credit Insurance Association
Woodward Building, Suite 539
15th & H Streets, N.W.
Washington, DC 20005

(16) Overseas Private Investment Corporation
1129 20th Street
Washington, DC 20527

(17) Information Clearing House, Inc.
3 East 48th Street
New York, NY 10017

(18) Bottin International
5714 W. Pico Boulevard
Los Angeles, CA 90019

(19) National Committee on International
Trade Documentation (NCITD)
350 Broadway
New York, NY 10013

(20) Transportation Data Coordinating Committee (TDCC)
1101 17th Street, N.W.
Washington, DC 20036

(21) Business International Corporation
757 Third Avenue
New York, NY 10017

Additional sources of information on international trade include

Foreign embassies and consulates

Banks

Freight forwarders

U.S. Department of Commerce Field Offices (in more than 40 U.S. cities)

International common carriers

Publications

The following publications are a selection of introductory as well as detailed sources of information. Numbers in parentheses refer to the sources listed above.

The EMC—Your Export Department. Summary of Export Management Companies (EMCs), and their mode of operation. (01)

Summary of U.S. Export Control Regulations. Describes how to apply for licenses. (02)

Foreign Business Practice. Information on laws, regulations, practices overseas. (03)

Free Trade Zones and Related Facilities Abroad. Data on customs and privileged areas overseas. (02)

American Import and Export Bulletin. Monthly with articles on regulations, trade opportunities. (07)

Commodity Trade Statistics. Periodic, covering most of world trade statistics on a quarterly basis. (05)

Exporters Encyclopaedia. Procedures, laws, and regulations governing shipping to every country in the world, plus diverse information on international trade. (08)

Foreign Commerce Handbook. Bibliography of foreign trade functions of government and private agencies. (04)

Guide to Foreign Information Sources. Lists foreign embassies, consulates, trade organizations and services. (04)

DISC—A Handbook for Exporters. (02)

Kelly's Manufacturers and Merchants Directory. Annual directory of companies in the United States and overseas. (12)

Trade Directories of the World. Reference manual, updated monthly. (11)

American Register of Exporters and Importers. U.S. firms active in exporting and their products. (13)

Sources of Credit on Foreign Firms. (02)

Sources of Export Financing. (03)

Export Financing Counseling Service. A government supported service to exporters and financial institutions to help solve problems in financing exports. (10)

An Introduction to OPIC. (16)

World Trade Directory Reports. Covers specific companies abroad, including organization, method of operation, product lines, officers, capital, sales volume, reputation, etc. (01)

Foreign Production and Commercial Reports. Unclassified reports prepared by the U.S. Foreign Service on commodities, industries by SIC code, and country. (01)

Trade Contact Surveys. Designed to locate agents, distributors, or licensees abroad. (01)

Market Share Reports. Statistics on international trade. (03)

Foreign Economic Trends. Reviews of current business conditions, near term prospects, GNP, foreign trade, wage and price indices, etc. (02)

Country Market Surveys. Describes potential for U.S. products in individual countries. (02)

World Markets for U.S. Industry. Published for each of 30 major countries, detail market research information to help U.S. manufacturers of products with high export potential. (01)

How to Get the Most from Overseas Exhibitions. Describes facilities and services available to help U.S. companies exhibit at international trade fairs. (01)

Worldwide Exhibitions Schedule. Provides information about trade fairs in which the U.S. government sponsors U.S. participation. (01)

CHAPTER 31: The Educational Needs of Physical Distribution Managers

Dempsey, W., and Lancioni, R. A. "Logistics Education and Training." *Logistics Spectrum*, 13, No. 2, Summer 1979, pp. 29–34.

Foggin, J. H., and Langley, C. J., Jr. "College Curricula for Physical Distribution Management: An Analysis of Practitioners' Perceptions." In Grabner, J. R., Jr., ed., *Logistics Education for the 1980's*. Transportation and Logistics Research Fund, The Ohio State University, Columbus, Ohio, 1982.

Gecowets, G. A. "Distribution Management—The Anonymous Profession." *Handling and Shipping*, 18, No. 8, August 1977, pp. 53–57.

La Londe, B. J., and Brand, R. "Distribution Career Patterns 1982." *Distribution*, 81, No. 11, November 1982, pp. 67–73. (An annual survey.)

Marien, E. J. *College and University Courses in Physical Distribution Management*. Chicago: NCPDM, 1978.

Marien, E. J., and Davis, H. W. "Career Development in Distirbution." *Handling and Shipping*, 18, No. 8, August 1977, pp. 47–52.

Quinn, F. J. "Training: Important Today . . . Essential to the Future." *Traffic Management*, 16, No. 11, November 1977, pp. 60–67.

CHAPTER 32: Labor Relations

Texts

Aaron, Benjamin, et al. *Employment Relation and the Law*. Boston: Little, Brown, 1957. Paperback, 1962.

Blum, Albert A. *A History of the American Labor Movement*. AHA Pamphlets, No. 150. Washington, D.C.: American Historical Association, 1972.

Bok, Derek C., and Dunlop, John T. *Labor and the American Community*. Beaverton, Ore.: Touchstone, 1970.

Cox, Archibald. *Law and the National Labor Policy* Monograph Series, No. 5. Los Angeles: UCLA Institute of Industrial Relations, 1960.

Elkouri, Frank, and Elkouri, Edna A. *How Arbitration Works*, 3d ed. Washington, D.C.: Bureau of National Affairs, 1973.

Fairweather, Owen. *Practice and Procedure in Labor Arbitration*. Washington, D.C.: Bureau of National Affairs, 1973.

Gregory, Charles O. *Labor and the Law*, 2ed. New York: Norton, 1958. With supplement, 1961.

Labor Law Group Trust. *Labor Relations and the Law*, 3d ed. Edited by J. S. Williams et al. Boston: Little, Brown, 1965. With supplement, 1967.

McGuiness, Kenneth C. *How To Take a Case Before the National Labor Relations Board*, 4th ed. Washington, D.C.: Bureau of National Affairs, 1976.

McCullough, Frank, and Bornstein, Tim. *The National Labor Relations Board*. New York: Praeger, 1974.

Meltzer, Bernard D. *Labor Law: Cases, Materials, and Problems*, 2d ed. Boston: Little, Brown, 1977.

Millis, Harry A., and Brown, Emily C. *From the Wagner Act to Taft-Hartley*. Chicago: University of Chicago Press, 1950.

Updegraff, Clarence M. *Arbitration and Labor Relations*, 3d rev. ed. Washington, D.C.: Bureau of National Affairs, 1970.

Law Review Articles

Asher, L. "Secondary Boycott—Allied, Neutral and Single Employers." *Georgetown Law Journal*, **52** (1964), p. 406.

Baird, J. "Lockout Law: The Supreme Court and the NLRB." *George Washington Law Review*, **38** (1970), p. 396.

Cooper, R. "Boulwarism and the Duty to Bargain in Good Faith." *Rutgers Law Review*, **20** (1966), p. 653.

Cox, A. "Strikes, Picketing and the Constitution." *Vanderbilt Law Review*, **4** (1951), p. 574.

———. "Rights Under a Labor Agreement." *Harvard Law Review*, **69** (1956), p. 601.

———. "The Duty to Bargain in Good Faith." *Harvard Law Review*, **71** (1958), p. 1401.

Getman, J. "The Protection of Economic Pressure by Section 7 of the National Labor Relations Act." *University of Pennsylvania Law Review*, **115** (1967), p. 1195.

Goldberg, S. "The Labor Law Obligations of a Successor Employer." *Northwestern Law Review*, **63** (1969), p. 735.

Lesnick, H. "The Gravamen of the Secondary Boycott." *Columbia Law Review*, **62** (1962), p. 1363.

Martin, B. "The Rights of Economic Strikers to Reinstatement: A Search for Certainty." *Wisconsin Law Review*, **1970** (1970), p. 1062.

Platt, E. "The Duty to Bargain as Applied to Management Decisions." *Labor Law Journal*, **19** (1968), p. 143.

St. Antoine, T. "Secondary Boycotts and Hot Cargo: A Study in Balance of Power." *University of Detroit Law Journal*, **40** (1962), p. 189.

Schatzki, G. "Majority Rule, Exclusive Representation, and the Interests of Individual Workers: Should Exclusivity Be Abolished?" *University of Pennsylvania Law Review*, **123** (1975), p. 897.

Case Law

Amalgamated Association of Electric Railway Workers v. Lockridge, 403 U.S. 274; *reh. den.*, 404 U.S. 874 (1971).

Dinger v. Anchor Motor Freight, Inc. et al., 501 F. Supp. 64 (S.D. N.Y. 1980).

Fox v. Mitchell, 621 F.2d 498 (4th Cir. 1981).

Hines v. Anchor Motor Freight, Inc., 424 U.S. 554 (1976).

Humphrey v. Moore, 375 U.S. 335 (1964).

Industrial Personnel Corp. v. National Labor Relations Board, 657 F.2d 226 (8th Cir. 1981).

Palnau v. Detroit Edison, 301 F.2d 702 (6th Circ. 1962).

Republic Steel v. Maddox, 379 U.S. 650 (1965).

Spielmann v. Anchor Motor Freight, Inc. et al., 551 F. Supp. 817 (S.D. N.Y. 1982).

Vaca v. Sipes, 386 U.S. 171 (1967).

Weissman v. Anchor Motor Freight, Inc. et al., N.Y. Jury Verdict Rep. Vol. III, Issue 1-100 (S.D. N.Y. 1983).

Index